INTERMEDIATE ACCOUNTING

Liz Bentz
Box 352
Vernon, Ond 47282

812 - 346 - 2654

INTERMEDIATE ACCOUNTING

THIRD EDITION

WALTER B. MEIGS, Ph.D., C.P.A.
Professor of Accounting
University of Southern California

A. N. MOSICH, Ph.D., C.P.A.
Professor of Accounting and
Chairman, Department of Accounting
University of Southern California

CHARLES E. JOHNSON, Ph.D., C.P.A.
Late Professor of Accounting
University of Oregon

THOMAS F. KELLER, Ph.D., C.P.A.
Professor of Accounting
Duke University

McGRAW-HILL BOOK COMPANY

New York   St. Louis   San Francisco   Düsseldorf   Johannesburg
Kuala Lumpur   London   Mexico   Montreal   New Delhi   Panama
Paris   São Paulo   Singapore   Sydney   Tokyo   Toronto

INTERMEDIATE ACCOUNTING

5 6 7 8 9 0 KPKP 7 9 8 7 6 5

This book was set in Vega by York Graphic Services, Inc. The editors
were Jack R. Crutchfield, Michael Elia, and Edwin Hanson; the
designer was Pencils Portfolio, Inc.; and the production supervisor was
Joe Campanella.
Kingsport Press, Inc., was printer and binder.

Library of Congress Cataloging in Publication Data

Meigs, Walter B
    Intermediate accounting.

    1. Accounting. I. Title.
HF5635.M493 1974   657'.044   73-21560
ISBN 0-07-041380-0

Contents

Today's challenges to the accounting profession. Internal and external users of accounting information. General objectives of financial accounting and financial statements. The attest function and the CPA. Organizations and institutions affecting financial accounting. American Institute of Certified Public Accountants (AICPA). Accounting Principles Board. Accounting Research Studies. Financial Accounting Foundation. Financial Accounting Standards Board (FASB). Comparison of the FASB and the APB. American Accounting Association (AAA). Securities and Exchange Commission (SEC). Cost Accounting Standards Board. The income tax law. Qualitative objectives of financial accounting. Generally accepted accounting principles. Sources of generally accepted accounting principles. The business entity principle. The continuity or "going-concern" principle. The monetary principle. The time-period principle. The cost principle. The revenue principle. The matching principle. The objectivity principle. The consistency principle. Accounting changes. The disclosure principle. Materiality. Conservatism. Cash flows and income measurement. Cash basis of accounting. Accrual basis of accounting.

Recording financial transactions. Business papers. Electronic data processing. Double-entry system. The accounting period. The ledger: classification by type. The accounting cycle. The journals: books of original entry. Trial balance. Use of journals. Adjusting entries. Apportionment of recorded costs. Purchase debited to asset account. Purchase debited to expense account. Accrual of unrecorded revenue. Apportionment of recorded revenue. Liability account credited upon receipt of cash. Revenue account credited upon receipt of cash. Accrual of unrecorded expenses. Valuation of receivables. Closing procedures. Closing revenue and expense accounts. Closing inventory and related accounts. Closing the income summary account. Reversing entries. Adjusted entries which are not to be reversed. Adjusting entries which are commonly reversed. Working-paper techniques. Purpose of the work sheet. Illustration of work sheet for a merchandising firm. Working

Statement of financial position.   Statement of retained earnings.   Comparative statements.   Statement of stockholders' equity.

Planning cash activities.   The cash budget.   Estimated cash receipts and payments method.   Sales forecast.   Forecasting cash receipts.   Forecasting cash payments.   Cash budget illustrated.   Cash forecast as a planning aid.   Adjusted net income method of forecasting cash flow from operations.   Cash flow statement.   Additional information for year 2.   Working paper for cash flow statement.   Cash flow statement.   Alternative approach: Cash basis net income.   Uses of cash flow data.   Management of cash.   Internal control.   Controlling cash receipts and payments.   Imprest cash funds (petty cash).   Illustration of the use of a petty cash fund.   Change fund.   Reconciliation of bank balances.   Illustration.   Reconciliation of cash receipts and payments.   Cash overdraft.   Secondary cash resources.   Investment of idle cash.   Recording transactions in marketable securities.   Illustration.   Computation of interest on bonds owned.   Cost selection.   Price fluctuations and valuation of marketable securities.   Valuation at cost versus valuation at lower of cost or market.   Presentation of cash and marketable securities in the balance sheet.

Valuation of receivables.   Receivables from sale of goods and services.   Receivables from miscellaneous sources.   Customers' accounts.   Accounting system and internal control.   Recognition of trade receivables.   Valuation of customers' accounts.   Determining the amount due.   Trade discounts.   Cash (or sales) discounts.   Method A.   Method B.   Method C.   Credit card fees and other collection expenses.   Sales returns and allowances.   Freight allowances.   Sales and excise taxes.   Container deposits.   Time of collection and valuation of receivables.   Estimating probability of collection.   Estimate of uncollectibles based on sales.   Estimate of uncollectibles based on accounts receivable.   Estimated uncollectibles and income measurement.   Collection of accounts previously written off.   Direct charge-off method of recognizing uncollectibles.   Selling and assigning accounts receivable.   Sale of accounts receivable.   Assigning receivables.   Installment receivables.   Notes receivable.   Valuation of notes receivable.   Discounting notes receivable.   APB Opinion No. 21, "Interest on Receivables and Payables."   Notes received for cash.   Notes received in exchange for cash and other rights or privileges.   Determining an appropriate interest rate and present value of note.   Analysis of accounts receivable.   Presentation of receivables in the balance sheet.

allowance for write-down of inventory. Anticipation of price declines. Losses on purchase commitments. Appraisal of the lower-of-cost-or-market rule. Valuation of inventory at replacement cost (market). Valuation of inventory at net selling price. Scrap. Inventory valuation for long-term construction contracts. Accounting for long-term construction contract illustrated. Completed-contract method. Percentage-of-completion method. Income tax considerations. Disclosure and consistency.

Gross profit method. Determining the gross profit and cost of goods sold percentage. Gross profit stated as percentage of cost of goods sold. Applying the gross profit method to departments. Inventory estimation from incomplete records. The retail method. Uses of the retail method. Retail trade terminology. Application of the retail method—average cost basis. Application of the retail method—lower of average cost or market. Limitation of the assumption of average markups on the retail method. Retail method and lifo valuation. Retail method and fifo valuation. Changes in price levels and the retail lifo method. Comparison of the gross profit and retail methods. Estimating the cost of manufacturing inventories. Relative sales value method of allocating joint production costs. Inventories of supplies and short-term prepayments. Inventories and financial reporting standards. Accounting Research Study No. 13.

Classification of assets used in business. Basis of reporting in accounting records. Determining the cost of plant assets. What is included in the cost of plant assets? Capital versus revenue expenditures. Land. Buildings. Leaseholds and leasehold improvements. Machinery and equipment. Self-constructed assets. Interest during construction. Capitalization of interest by regulated companies. Profit on self-construction. How is cost of plant assets measured? Cash discounts. Deferred payment contracts. Lump-sum acquisitions. The escrow statement. Securities issued in exchange for assets. Assets acquired by gift. Investment tax credit. Cost after acquisition. Additions. Improvements, renewals, and replacements. The substitution procedure. A charge to the asset account. A charge to the accumulated depreciation account. Rearrangements and moving costs. Ordinary repairs and maintenance. Retirement and disposal of plant assets. Trade-ins and exchanges of plant assets. Involuntary conversions. Insurance on plant assets. Coinsurance clause in an insurance policy.

mon stock and preferred stock. Class A and B stock. Typical characteristics of preferred stock. Cumulative and noncumulative preferred
stock. Participating and nonparticipating preferred stock. Convertible
preferred stock. Callable preferred stock. Preferences in event of
liquidation. Preferred stock regarded as owners' equity. Par value and
no-par value stock. Stated capital. Accounting for capital stock transactions. Ledger accounts for contributed capital. Capital stock accounts. Accounts for paid-in capital in excess of par or stated value.
Journal entries for issuance of stock for cash. Discount on capital stock.
Assessments on capital stock. Issuance price and subsequent market
price of stock. Subscription to capital stock. Journal entries for stock
subscriptions. Defaults by subscribers to capital stock. Stockholders'
ledger and stock certificate book. Issuance of two types of securities as
a unit. Capital stock issued for property or services. Watered stock.
Secret reserves. Incorporation of a partnership. Establishing accounting
records for the new corporate entity. Tax aspects concerning incorporation of a partnership.

Warrants and stock rights. Rights granted to existing stockholders.
Rights issued in combination with bonds or preferred stock. Rights to
purchase convertible debentures. Stock option contracts. Impact of tax
regulations: Qualified stock options. Stock options which prove worthless. APB Opinion No. 25, "Accounting for Stock Issued to Employees."
Noncompensatory plans. Compensatory plans. Measuring compensation
for services. Illustration of stock option plan. Estimating the fair value
of stock options. The option period. Does current practice understate
compensation expense represented by stock options? Disclosure of stock
options. Convertible securities. Characteristics of convertible preferred
stock. Definitions applicable to convertible preferred stock. Conversion
of preferred stock into common. Conversion of bonds into common
stock. APB Opinions and convertible bonds. Protection against dilution
of conversion rights. Presentation of stockholders' equity in the balance
sheet. Pro forma financial statements.

Retained earnings. Distinguishing between paid-in capital and earned
capital. Classifying elements of corporate capital by source. Currently
accepted terms for the stockholders' equity section. Paid-in capital in
excess of par. Unrealized appreciation from revaluation of assets. The
retained earnings account. Dividends. Cash dividends. Property divi-

CHAPTER 17 TREASURY STOCK; BOOK VALUE AND EARNINGS PER SHARE

CHAPTER 18 BONDS PAYABLE

the cost and equity methods. Selecting the appropriate method. Accounting for investments in bonds. Computing the present value of a bond. Acquisition between interest dates. Illustration. Discount and premium on bond investments. Interest revenue. Methods of discount accumulation or premium amortization. Straight-line method. Effective interest method. Accounting for investments between interest dates. Illustration. Special problems in accounting for securities. Cost identification. Accounting for stock dividends and stock splits. Stock purchase warrants and stock rights. Accounting for stock warrants acquired by purchase. Accounting for stock rights. Illustration. Tax rules. Convertible securities. Valuation of investments at lower of cost or market. Other long-term investments. Investments in special-purpose funds. Accounting for funds. Cash surrender value of life insurance. Presentation in financial statements.

Accounting changes. Major types of accounting changes. Introducing accounting changes into financial statements. Change in accounting principle. Cumulative effect of change reported in current period. Change requiring restatement of prior years' financial statements. Change in accounting estimate. Correction of errors. Correction of an error in previously issued financial statements. Correction of error and corrected financial statements illustrated. Types of errors. Errors affecting only balance sheet accounts. Errors affecting only income statement accounts. Errors affecting both balance sheet and income statement accounts. Counterbalancing errors. Noncounterbalancing errors. Analyzing the effect of errors. Working-paper analysis of errors. Illustration. Statements from incomplete records. Balance sheet from incomplete records. Determining income from single-entry records. Preparation of income statement from incomplete records illustrated. Reconstructing gross sales. Reconstructing other revenue. Reconstructing cost of goods sold. Reconstructing operating expenses. Working paper for preparation of financial statements from incomplete records.

Objectives of statement of changes in financial position. Working capital. Analysis of changes in financial position: a simple illustration. Working paper for statement of changes in financial position. Statement of changes in financial position. Summary of procedures. Special problems. Measuring working capital provided by operations. Gain or loss on sale of securities. Uncollectible accounts. Analysis of changes in plant and equipment accounts. Exchange transactions: the all financial resources concept of funds. Purchase of a going business. Reclassification of noncurrent items into current category. Comprehensive illustration of statement of changes in financial position. Schedule of changes in working capital. Working paper for statement of changes in financial position. Analysis of transactions in the working paper. Statement of changes in financial position. Alternative form of statement showing revenue and expense detail. Reporting practices by corporations. Working-paper format using only changes in account balances.

Sources of financial information available to outsiders. Published reports. Securities and Exchange Commission (SEC). Credit and investment advisory services. Audit reports. What is financial analysis? Procedures of analysis. Ratios. Component percentages. Changes over time. Analytical objectives. Analysis of earnings performance. Net income and accounting practices. Trend in earnings. Return on investment. Interpreting return on investment. Trading on the equity. Earnings and dividends per share. Price-earnings ratio and dividend yield. Earnings and fixed charges. Times interest earned. Times preferred dividends earned. Analysis of financial strength. Ability to meet short-term obligations. Working capital position. Need for working capital. Inventory turnover. Receivables turnover. Length of operating cycle. Number of days' operations to cover working capital deficit. Interpreting the analysis of current position. Analysis of capital structure. Debt and equity ratios. Evaluating capital structure. Creditors' view. Stockholders' view. Capacity for additional investment and growth in earnings. Standards for comparison in analysis. Past record of the company. Comparison with competitors or industry as a whole. Comparison and independent statistical measures. Inflation and analysis of financial statements. Summary of ratios and other analytical measurements.

Financial statements restated for changes in the general price level. Needed: A stable unit of value. Historical costs versus current fair value. Effects of inflation on financial statements. Income or recovery of capital? Monetary items and general price-level gains and losses. Emergence of price-level accounting—summary of APB Statement No. 3. Illustration of price-level accounting. Data for illustration. Exhibit 1—Statement of income and retained earnings. Sales. Beginning inventories. Purchases. Ending inventories. Operating expenses (other than depreciation). Depreciation expense. General price-level loss. Income tax expense. Dividends paid. Exhibit 2—Computation of general price-level gain or loss. Exhibit 3—Comparative balance sheet. Monetary items. Inventories. Land. Equipment and accumulated depreciation. Capital stock and paid-in capital in excess of par. Retained earnings. Price-level information in practice. Fair-value accounting. Significance of changes in value. Relationship between price-level and fair-value accounting. Use of fair values in preparation of financial statements. The meaning of *value*. Arriving at fair (current) value. Capitalization of net cash inflows. Liquidation value. Replacement cost. Specific-price index replacement cost. Implementing fair-value accounting.

Preface

This third edition of *Intermediate Accounting* is the second volume in the three-volume Meigs and Johnson coordinated accounting series. This book is designed for use in an intermediate-level accounting course following the introductory course in accounting. The emphasis throughout is on accounting theory and concepts and an analysis of the special problems that arise in applying these underlying concepts to financial accounting. As in the first volume of the series, attention is focused on the use of accounting information as a basis for decisions by management, stockholders, creditors, and other users of financial statements and accounting reports.

This third edition is a major revision reflecting the rapid changes which have been occurring in the development and application of accounting concepts. Chapter 1 has been completely rewritten to place in perspective for the student the development of accounting theory and practice. Attention is given to the transition from the Accounting Principles Board to the Financial Accounting Standards Board and to the increased awareness on the part of accountants of the important role that financial reporting must play in the achievement of important economic and social goals. Chapter 1 also includes a discussion of the relationship between cash flows and the income-determining revenue and expense flows.

A brief and rapid review of basic data-collecting processes in Chapter 2 reinforces the student's understanding of fundamental recording, classifying, and summarizing procedures. This background leads naturally to a consideration, in Chapters 3 and 4, of the assumptions and basic principles on which the accountant's determination of periodic income and periodic reports of financial position are based. The discussion in these chapters (and throughout the remainder of the book) is not limited to a description of acceptable practices. We believe it is important at this stage in accounting education to encourage students to participate in a critical evaluation of accounting concepts and to make students aware of the conflicts and shortcomings that exist within the traditional structure of accounting theory. At the same time it is important to provide students with an analytical basis for making this evaluation, to help them see that most of the controversial areas of accounting ultimately center on underlying issues and questions to which there are no neat and simple answers. To this end, the critical evaluation of accounting concepts is correlated with all of the *Opinions* published by the Accounting Principles Board, with *APB Statements,* and with *Accounting Research Studies.*

The first four chapters of the book constitute an overview of the entire accounting process and are designed to provide a gradual transition from the introductory course in accounting to the more rigorous professional level of analysis in the following chapters.

Chapters 5 through 7 deal with the problems that arise in accounting for and controlling cash, marketable securities, receivables, and current liabilities. The common bond of valuation and control concepts applicable to these money-value items provides an underlying thread of continuity in this section.

In Chapters 8 through 13 attention is centered on the problems of accounting for and reporting on a firm's investment in productive resources: inventories, plant and equipment, and intangible assets. In this area the accountant faces some of the most vexing issues of valuation and cost allocation. In evaluating alternative methods of accounting for inventories and plant and equipment, the effect of changes in specific prices and general price levels is given particular attention.

Chapters 14 through 21 are concerned with the special accounting problems peculiar to corporate organizations. These problems focus largely on the stockholders' equity and long-term debt sections of the balance sheet, but their implications are often considerably broader. Such contemporary and controversial topics as stock options (Chapter 15), accounting for leases in financial statements and accounting for pension plans (Chapter 19), and income tax allocation (Chapter 20) are explored in depth. A major part of Chapter 17 consists of an entirely new presentation of earnings per share. Chapter 21, "Long-Term Investments in Corporate Securities," has been largely rewritten to emphasize the increased importance of the equity method in accounting for long-term investments in corporate securities.

Chapter 22 explains the new standards of disclosure required when corporations make significant accounting changes. It also deals with the effect of errors on financial statements and the process of constructing financial statements from incomplete records.

The new basic financial statement, Statement of Changes in Financial Position, is presented in Chapter 23 along with evaluation of the significance of cash and other fund flow information. Chapter 24 is devoted to the important issues that make the analysis of financial statements both a demanding and an interesting process. The final chapter (25) is a new one devoted to price-level and fair-value accounting in recognition of the increasing impact on financial reporting of changes in the purchasing power of the dollar and economic values of assets.

New features of this edition

Among the several entirely new features of this edition is the inclusion of a group of short exercises as part of the assignment material at the end of each chapter. Typically an exercise covers a specific important point or topic and does not require extensive computations. Many instructors will wish to use the exercises to supplement problem assignments, for class discussion, and for examination purposes.

A second new feature of this edition is a complete series of objective tests closely correlated with the text. The eight achievement tests each cover three or four chapters and are intended for use in a 50-minute class period. Two comprehensive examinations are provided covering the first and second halves of the book. The increased use of objective questions on recent Uniform CPA Examinations has provided an extensive source of this type of test material. The use of these tests should aid the student interested in preparing for the Accounting Theory and Accounting Practice sections of the Uniform CPA Examination, as well as providing comprehensive testing over all chapters in the book.

A third new feature is a *Study Guide* prepared by the authors and designed to help the student measure his progress by immediate feedback. The *Study Guide* contains for each chapter an outline of the most important points in the textbook plus a variety of objective questions and short exercises. Answers to the questions and exercises appear in the back of the *Study Guide* to help the student in a prompt self-evaluation of his understanding of each chapter.

Among other new features are the illustration of four sets of recent financial statements of leading corporations as an appendix of the book. Another appendix consists of a discussion of present and future value of cash flows and compound-interest tables provided for those instructors who wish to emphasize the present and future value concepts presented in numerous sections throughout the book. A summary of the recommendations of the Study Group on Objectives of Financial Statements (Trueblood Committee) is presented in a third appendix.

Still another new feature is the inclusion of two groups of problems, Group A and Group B. This arrangement allows each instructor to vary his problem assignments in different sections of the course, or from year to year. The problems in the two groups are of similar difficulty and require about the same solution time. Either the A Group or B Group of problems provides more than enough material for assignments throughout an offering of the course.

Questions, exercises, cases, and problems

An abundance of question and problem material is provided at the end of each chapter. This material is divided into four groups: questions, exercises, short cases for analysis and decision, and problems.

The questions are intended for use by the student as a self-testing and review device to measure his comprehension of key points in each chapter. Many of the questions are also of a provocative nature, which makes them suitable for written assignments and engenders lively class discussion. The exercises, a new feature of this edition, have already been described.

The short cases for analysis and decision are essentially problems that require analytical reasoning but involve little or no quantitative data. In this category of problem material the student is called upon to analyze business situations, to apply accounting principles, and to propose a course of action. He is not required, however, to prepare lengthy schedules or otherwise to manipulate accounting data on an extensive scale.

These short cases have all been class-tested and have proved their worth as a means of encouraging students to take clear-cut positions in the argument of controversial accounting issues. In all but the early chapters of the book, a number of the short cases for analysis have been adapted from CPA examination material. The cases (and selected questions) are especially recommended if the instructor wishes to develop in students skill in communicating accounting concepts and in weighing the merits of opposing arguments.

Problem material has been completely revised as well as rearranged into Group A and Group B problems. Many of the problems are new, and those carried over from the preceding edition have been thoroughly revised. Special attention has been given to the inclusion of an adequate number of shorter problems in each chapter. The problems range in difficulty from simple to complex. Most of the problems in the Accounting Theory and Accounting Practice sections of recent Uniform CPA Examinations which are appropriate to intermediate accounting are included, although many have been considerably modified. In addition, several problems have been designed especially to demonstrate the concepts presented in the theoretical discussion. Probably no more than a fourth of the total case and problem material would be used in a given course; consequently ample opportunity exists to vary problem assignments from year to year.

Aiding the student to achieve proficiency in handling professional-level problems

A feature of this third edition is the inclusion of a greater number of short problems closely correlated with the text material. No CPA problems are used in the early chapters of the book. The gradation of problems in difficulty is carefully tailored to aid the student in a smooth progression from introductory accounting to a professional level of achievement.

A checklist of key figures is provided for the longer and more difficult problems. This list is available in quantity to instructors who wish to distribute key figures to students. The purpose of the checklist is to aid students in verifying their problem solutions and in discovering their own errors.

Two sets of partially filled-in working papers are published separately from the textbook. One set is designed for Group A problems and one set for Group B problems. Partially filled-in working papers are thus provided for *all* problems. On these work sheets, the company names, problem numbers, numerous headings, and some preliminary data (such as trial balances) have been entered to save student time and to facilitate rapid review by the instructor. Abundant material is included in either set of problems for a comprehensive course, hence the acquisition of a single set of partially filled-in working papers will meet a student's needs for the course.

Contributions by others

The many instructors and students who used the earlier editions of this book have contributed immeasurably to the improvements in this edition. Their suggestions for modification of certain problems and expansion or contraction of certain sections of the text material have been most useful and constructive. Especially helpful was the advice received from Professors Herbert K. Bell, Boise State College; Robert Vanasse, California State University, Fullerton; Robert E. Hamilton, University of California, Berkeley; Carol Inberg, California State University, Hayward; William K. Harper, University of Southern California; Robert W. Hill, University of Southern California; Robert F. Meigs, California State University, San Diego; James W. Pratt, University of Houston; E. J. Larsen, University of Southern California; Bruce Samuelson, University of Southern California; Paul Grosch, Loyola University, Los Angeles; David O. Jenkins, Stanislaus State College; Leslie R. Loschen, University of Southern California; Thomas G. Secoy, Illinois State University; Lou Gilles, University of Arkansas; Mohamed Moustafa, California State University, Long Beach; and Clarence G. Avery, Florida Technological University.

Our special appreciation goes also to the following students at the University of Southern California: John Lacey, Carl Maier, Tim McClean, John Nelson, Chris Floryan, Mel Woods, and John Cooke.

We acknowledge with appreciation permission from the American Institute of Certified Public Accountants to quote from many of its pronouncements and to utilize materials adapted from the Uniform CPA Examinations.

Walter B. Meigs
A. N. Mosich

CHAPTER 1

The development of accounting theory and practice

Today's challenges to the accounting profession

Fair presentation of financial affairs is the essence of accounting theory and practice. With the increasing size and complexity of American business organizations and the increasing economic role of government, the responsibility placed on accountants for presenting fairly the results of business operations is greater today than ever before. If accountants are to meet this challenge fully, they must have a logical and consistent body of accounting theory to guide them. This theoretical structure must be realistic in terms of the economic environment and designed to meet the needs of the major users of accounting information.

Financial statements and other reports prepared by accountants are vital to the successful working of our society. Economists, investors, business executives, labor leaders, bankers, and government officials all rely upon these reports as fair and meaningful summaries of the multitude of financial transactions which comprise day-to-day economic history. In addition, these groups are making increasing use of accounting information as a basis for forecasting future economic trends. The accountant is being challenged to go beyond the timely reporting and interpretation of past events and to aid in the creation of useful forecasts of future operations. The accountant and the theoretical principles he uses, therefore, stand at the very center of our financial and economic activities.

Internal and external users of accounting information

The basic assumptions which underlie current accounting practice have evolved over the years in response to the needs of various users of financial reports. The users of accounting information may conveniently be divided into two broad groups: the *internal users* and the *external users.*

The internal users include all the management personnel of an organization who use accounting information either for planning and controlling current operations or for formulating long-range plans and making major decisions. The term *managerial accounting* relates to internal reporting; it includes the development of detailed current information helpful to all levels of management in decision making designed to achieve the organization's goals.

The external users of accounting information include stockholders, bondholders, potential investors, bankers and other creditors, financial analysts, economists, labor unions, and numerous government agencies. The field of *financial accounting* is directly related to external reporting, that is, providing investors and other outsiders with the information they need for decision making.

In this book we are primarily concerned with financial accounting, and we shall therefore concentrate upon the accounting principles and reporting standards that produce timely and informative financial statements. The increasing importance of financial accounting rests upon the premise that the public has a right to know whether large business organizations are functioning efficiently and in harmony with the broader goals of society.

General objectives of financial accounting and financial statements

The objectives of financial accounting and financial statements are derived from the needs of the external users of accounting information. Financial statements intended to serve all external users are often called *general-purpose financial statements.* Stating the objectives would be simpler if all external users had the same needs and interests, but of course they do not. For example, the banker considering the granting of a 90-day loan is primarily interested in the short-run debt-paying ability of the reporting entity, whereas the long-term investor in common stocks is more concerned with earning capacity and potential growth in earnings per share.

To aid the external users of accounting information in making informed economic decisions, financial statements should:

1 Provide reliable financial information about the company's economic resources and its obligations. This information is helpful in judging the ability of the business to survive and to grow in an ever-changing environment.

2 Provide reliable information on the profitability of the enterprise. Nearly everyone with an interest in the business (including employees) will benefit from its ability to operate successfully.

3 Provide financial information helpful in estimating the future earning potential of the enterprise. The **trend** of earnings is usually a better aid to prediction than the operating results of a single year.

4 Provide other needed information about changes in economic resources and obligations. Such information may include fund flows and transactions between the entity and its owners.

5 Provide other information relevant to the needs of the external user. For example, such disclosures might describe contingent liabilities or accounting policies concerning depreciation and inventory methods.[1]

A more concise statement of objectives is simply "to provide quantitative financial information about a business enterprise that is useful to statement users, particularly owners and creditors, in making economic decisions."[2]

We have emphasized that general-purpose financial statements serve a variety of users; consequently the interests of some users must necessarily be given greater emphasis than the interests of others. In present-day practice the interests of the potential investor or creditor are subordinated to those who have already committed resources to the company. This emphasis leads management to stress the use which has been made of the resources entrusted to it. A deep concern over reporting on management's role as custodian of resources may be one reason for the adherence to historical cost despite substantial changes in the general price level. This tradition may also explain, in part, the omission from the financial statements of social costs, which may be increasingly important to a society rapidly becoming more aware of the need for preserving the quality of its environment.

The attest function and the CPA

A conflict of interest may exist between a business preparing financial statements and some of the persons using those statements. For example, a company applying for a loan from a bank may tend to be overly optimistic in portraying its financial strength. Similarly, a corporation attempting to raise funds by selling its capital stock to the public has an incentive to exaggerate its earnings capacity. To protect the users of financial statements against a natural bias or outright misrepresentation, it is important to have an independent professional accountant, an auditor, examine the financial statements (and supporting evidence) prepared by the internal accounting staff of a company. The auditor then has a basis for expressing his professional opinion on the fairness of the financial statements. This **attest function** is the primary role of the **certified public accountant.** To attest to financial statements means to vouch for their fairness and validity, thus avoiding a "credibility gap."

[1] APB Statement No. 4, "Basic Concepts and Accounting Principles Underlying Financial Statements of Business Enterprises," AICPA (New York: 1970), par. 77–81.
[2] Ibid., par. 73.

Performance of the attest function requires the existence not only of an independent public accounting profession, but also of a body of generally accepted accounting principles to serve as guidelines for both the preparation and the audit of financial statements. Adherence to generally accepted accounting principles provides assurance that financial statements are reasonably comparable. If financial statements are comparable, then investors, bankers, and other outsiders are better able to judge the progress of a company from one year to the next and to form an opinion on the relative attractiveness of supplying resources to various companies.[3]

Because of the public interest in *audited financial statements,* each state recognizes public accountancy as a profession and issues the certificate of Certified Public Accountant to those who demonstrate through written examinations and the satisfaction of educational and experience requirements their competence to enter the public accounting profession.

Organizations and institutions affecting financial accounting

Certain professional organizations, governmental agencies, and legislative acts have been extremely influential in shaping the development of the existing body of accounting theory. Among the most important of these institutional forces have been the American Institute of Certified Public Accountants, the American Accounting Association, the Securities and Exchange Commission, and the Internal Revenue Code. Of course many other organizations have exerted significant influence on the development of accounting principles. Among these might be mentioned the New York Stock Exchange, the National Association of Accountants, the Financial Executives Institute, the Cost Accounting Standards Board, the Institute of Internal Auditors, the Federal Government Accountants Association, and the whole complex of federal, state, and local tax regulations.

Awareness of the roles of these institutional forces is helpful in gaining an understanding of current accounting practice. Efforts to improve existing principles of accounting will have a better chance of success if they are made with full recognition of the needs and special problems of the businessmen, financial analysts, investors, government agencies, and others who use accounting data in performing their respective functions.

American Institute of Certified Public Accountants (AICPA) The American Institute of Certified Public Accountants is the professional organization of the practicing certified public accountant. As a professional organization, the Institute has been vitally concerned with developing stand-

[3] This concept of the role of the CPA in the allocation of economic resources is adapted from Meigs, Larsen, & Meigs, *Principles of Auditing,* 5th ed., Richard D. Irwin, Inc. (Homewood, Ill.: 1973), pp. 2–4.

ards of practice, both ethical and professional, of its members. The AICPA has published *The Journal of Accountancy* monthly since 1905 as a forum for the practitioner. Beginning in the early 1930s the Institute, in concert with the newly created Securities and Exchange Commission, began to develop standards of financial reporting. During the 20 years from 1939 to 1959, the Institute published 51 *Accounting Research Bulletins* dealing with a wide variety of timely accounting problems.

Accounting Principles Board In 1959 the AICPA took the formal step of committing itself to a more comprehensive program of research into the problems of financial reporting. The Accounting Principles Board was formed with the responsibility of formulating accounting principles related to financial reporting based on underlying research. The charter creating the APB stated:

> The general purpose of the Institute in the field of financial accounting should be to advance the written expression of what constitutes generally accepted accounting principles, for the guidance of its members and of others. This means something more than a survey of existing practice. It means continuing effort to determine appropriate practice and to narrow the areas of difference and inconsistency in practice. In accomplishing this, reliance should be placed on persuasion rather than on compulsion. The Institute, however, can, and should, take definite steps to lead in the thinking on unsettled and controversial issues.

The APB issued two separate series of publications. The more influential series consisted of the *Opinions of the Accounting Principles Board,* 31 separate Opinions published between 1959 and 1973 dealing with current accounting problems. The format of the Opinions resembled the *Accounting Research Bulletins* published during the forties and fifties. Prior to 1964, pronouncements by the AICPA were not binding upon practicing CPAs but merely dependent upon their persuasiveness for acceptance. In October, 1964, however, the Institute began requiring that departures from *APB Opinions* be disclosed either in footnotes to financial statements or in the audit reports of members in their capacity as independent auditors. Stated bluntly, this pronouncement meant that a CPA could not give his approval to financial statements which deviated from *APB Opinions* unless he wanted to assume the considerable personal risk and burden of proof of defending the "unauthorized practices." Since few companies or auditors were anxious to assume in public the burden of defending financial statements which differed from *APB Opinions,* this action gave a new strength and authority to Opinions of the APB. In brief, *APB Opinions* achieved the status of constituting substantial authoritative support for generally accepted accounting principles.

A second series of APB publications consisted of *Statements,* which did not carry the official force of Opinions but which constituted recommendations which hopefully would lead the way in the development of improved accounting principles and practices. Especially important was

Statement No. 4, "Basic Concepts and Accounting Principles Underlying Financial Statements of Business Enterprises." *Statement No. 4* was intended to advance "the written expression of financial accounting principles for the purpose of increasing the usefulness of financial statements."[4] This statement provides a discussion of the nature of financial accounting, the environmental forces that influence it, the potential and limitations of financial statements in providing information, the objectives of financial accounting, and finally a description of present generally accepted accounting principles.[5]

Accounting Research Studies A series of *Accounting Research Studies,* published by the Director of Accounting Research of the AICPA, was begun in 1961 with the intent of providing the Accounting Principles Board with background material that would aid in establishing accounting principles. Prior to the termination of the APB in the middle of 1973, 15 of these studies were published. They have covered topics ranging from broad sets of tentative accounting principles to such specifics as accounting for pension plans, goodwill, and inventories. The most recent Studies have been transmitted to the Financial Accounting Standards Board, which replaced the APB in 1973.

Financial Accounting Foundation The Financial Accounting Foundation was created in 1972 with the principal purpose of appointing members of the Financial Accounting Standards Board and raising funds for its operation. The Foundation has nine trustees, of whom four must be CPAs engaged in the public practice of accounting. The other five trustees are chosen from the ranks of financial executives, financial analysts, and accounting educators, thus assuring a broader perspective than if the Foundation represented only the public accounting profession. To launch this new approach to establishing accounting principles, the leading national CPA firms pledged several million dollars to finance operation of the Foundation and of the Financial Accounting Standards Board for the first five years.

Financial Accounting Standards Board (FASB) The Financial Accounting Standards Board was established in 1972 for the purpose of developing and issuing standards of financial reporting for business organizations and other entities including institutions and not-for-profit organizations. This new independent body, in contrast to the former Accounting Principles Board, is limited to seven full-time, well-paid members, whereas the APB consisted of 21 part-time, unpaid individuals.

Lending support and counsel to the seven full-time members of the FASB is a larger Financial Accounting Standards Advisory Council. Among the 27 initial appointees to the Advisory Council in 1973 were

[4] *APB Statement No. 4,* par. 1.
[5] *Ibid.,* par. 2.

several financial executives from banks, stock exchanges, governmental agencies, and brokerage firms in addition to prominent accounting educators, lawyers, and certified public accountants.

Certified public accountants are not the only persons deeply concerned with financial reporting. Consequently, the articles of incorporation creating the Financial Accounting Standards Board require that only four members shall be CPAs drawn from public practice; the other three members must be highly qualified in the field of financial reporting but need not be certified public accountants. An individual appointed to the FASB must sever all economic connections with other organizations in order to avoid any suggestion of conflict of interest.

The FASB is authorized to issue Statements of Accounting Standards to guide persons and organizations in preparing financial statements. These same Statements of Accounting Standards will of course be utilized by CPAs in the audit of their clients' financial statements.

Briefly stated, the public accounting profession is now engaged in a strenuous effort to improve the quality of financial reporting through the creation of an independent rule-making body which includes representatives from outside the field of public accounting.

Although the Financial Accounting Standards Board was established on June 30, 1972, a full year was required for it to become operational. During this transition period, the Accounting Principles Board continued to function by completing a number of studies and publishing several additional Opinions. On July 1, 1973, the Financial Accounting Standards Board completed its organizational period and officially replaced the Accounting Principles Board. All the Opinions previously issued by the APB were continued in force by its successor, the Financial Accounting Standards Board.

Comparison of the FASB and the APB

Considerable time must pass before the accomplishments of the Financial Accounting Standards Board can be compared with those of the Accounting Principles Board. However, certain significant differences in the two bodies are immediately apparent.

The change from a large (21-member) group to a small full-time, well-paid board, including representatives drawn from outside the public accounting profession, indicates a greater commitment to the task with more diversity in the experience and interests of members and with more emphasis on independence of thought and action.

APB *Opinions* often disclosed a division of opinion among the members, and individual dissenting views were published as part of the Opinions. Pronouncements of the FASB do not set forth any dissenting opinions, although the views of individual members are preserved in the public record of the Board's proceedings.

Because the Accounting Principles Board consisted of part-time unpaid representatives, some critics felt that APB members may have been subject to pressures from clients and others. The FASB, being comprised of well-paid, full-time members who have severed all economic ties with other organizations, should be free from doubts as to conflicts of interest. The development of accounting standards should reflect the broader organizational structure of the FASB, with representatives having backgrounds in industry and government as well as in public accounting. The continuity of effort from a full-time board should also permit more effective direction of research programs.

The operating procedure followed by the FASB has been to appoint a number of task forces to study items placed on the Board's agenda. Among the first topics assigned for such study were the following:[6]

1 Accounting for foreign currency translation, which is concerned with how to report assets, liabilities, and results of operations of foreign subsidiaries and branches in dollars in the financial statements of United States parent companies.

2 Reporting by diversified companies, which involves the question of whether information about the various segments of diversified companies is necessary for fair presentation in financial reports.

3 Criteria for determining materiality. A definition of the standard of materiality and criteria for its application are considered necessary by the Board.

4 Accounting for leases by lessees and lessors. The Board recognizes the substantial diversity that exists in this area of accounting.

5 Accruing for future losses. This topic includes self-insurance reserves, catastrophy reserves and accruals against exposure of overseas operations to loss.

6 Accounting for such costs as research and development, start-up, and relocation. The announced objective is to narrow the differences in existing accounting practice and to provide guidance for appropriate accounting.

7 Broad qualitative standards for financial reporting.

Public hearings are held to permit discussion of the material gathered by the task forces and public exposure drafts made available of statements which the Board proposes to issue. Official statements issued by the FASB set forth the opinion of the Board as a whole, appropriate background information, and the effective date of the statement.

Despite these differences between the APB and the FASB, it is significant that both represent the private sector of the economy. To secure compliance with higher standards of financial reporting without the use of governmental authority is an objective inherent in the FASB as was true for its predecessor, the Accounting Principles Board.

American Accounting Association (AAA) The American Accounting Association, an organization of college professors and of practicing accountants, has had an important part to play in the development of accounting principles. The activities of this group have emphasized the development of a logical and theoretical basis of accounting rather than the application

---

[6] *Status Report,* Financial Accounting Standards Board (Stamford, Conn.: June, 1973).

of the theory to practical situations. The AAA encourages accounting research and continuous appraisal of accounting concepts through the quarterly publication of *The Accounting Review* and the work of its members in committees. Among the most influential publications of the American Accounting Association has been a series of statements concerning accounting theory. The most recent of the series, published in 1966, was entitled *A Statement of Basic Accounting Theory.* This publication took a normative approach to accounting; that is, it stressed "what should be" as opposed to "what was or what is."

Securities and Exchange Commission (SEC) The SEC, created by an act of Congress in 1934, has exerted tremendous influence on the development of financial reporting to the public. A corporation which intends to issue securities for sale to the public must file with the SEC financial statements which are satisfactory to the Commission. The primary concern of the SEC is *adequate disclosure* of all pertinent facts about the financial affairs of publicly held companies. The Commission has not so far participated directly in the development of accounting principles, but it has exerted great influence on public reporting through its continual review (and occasional rejection) of financial statements. It has endorsed the role planned for the Financial Accounting Standards Board. The SEC has a limited number of regulations (most of which have been developed jointly with the AICPA) which pertain to financial reporting of publicly held companies.

Cost Accounting Standards Board Although our interest in this book is focused on financial accounting rather than managerial or cost accounting, our listing of organizations which are contributing importantly to improved accounting practices must include the federal Cost Accounting Standards Board. The primary goal of the CASB is to issue standards that achieve more uniformity in accounting practices among companies holding government contracts and more consistency in the accounting treatment of various types of costs incurred by these contractors. Since almost every large industrial business holds government contracts, the issuance of standards by the Cost Accounting Standards Board will inevitably have a considerable impact upon financial statements as well as in the measurement of contract costs. The Board has already published its views on criteria for determining the materiality of transactions and decisions.

The Income Tax Law The enactment of the federal income tax law in 1913 and the subsequent amendments and legal interpretations comprising the present tax law have been perhaps the most important forces on the development of applied accounting procedures, as distinguished from accounting theory. As the rate of taxation has increased, every business manager has attempted to lessen the impact of the tax on his firm. The result has been the adoption of accounting procedures which purportedly conform to the basic principles of accounting and which minimize taxable income.

The Internal Revenue Code has developed with the interests of the government as its focal point, which means that Congress has been more concerned with public policy objectives than with the development of accounting theory. The acceptance of certain tax regulations as the basis for accounting has resulted in the adoption of procedures which have as their primary rationale the fact that they result in accelerating the recognition of expenses or postponing the recognition of revenue. In Chapter 20 we shall consider some of the reporting problems created by these differences, and throughout the book reference will be made to particular tax regulations and their specific impact on accounting practice. We must keep in mind, however, that this book is concerned with the principles and procedures of accounting, not of income taxation, and the issues of accounting will be evaluated in this light.

Qualitative objectives of financial accounting

For accounting information to be useful, it should possess several specific qualities or characteristics. Seven such qualities were suggested by the APB in *Statement No. 4.* These seven desired qualities are:[7]

1 *Relevance.* Relevance means that the information bears on the decisions for which it is used. The APB ranked relevance as the primary qualitative objective since information not bearing on the decisions to be made is useless. This emphasis upon relevance raises a question as to whether the balance sheet and income statement are relevant to the decisions that statement users must make. For example, would a profit forecast be more relevant to an investor in deciding on a purchase of common stock?

2 *Understandability.* If accounting information is to be useful to decision making, it must be presented in terms understandable to the user. However, the complex nature of many business transactions prevents reporting in an extremely simple manner. The user of financial statements must have some knowledge of accounting.

3 *Verifiability.* If accounting information is verifiable, substantially the same results would be reached by different accountants working independently and observing the same principles of measurement. Thus, the CPA conducting an independent audit of a company's financial statements can verify the overall fairness of the statements. He cannot, however, determine that the statements are "correct" or precisely accurate, because of the necessity of using judgment and estimates in the accounting process.

4 *Neutrality.* Since published financial statements are general-purpose statements designed to serve a variety of users, the information should be directed toward the common needs of all users rather than being tailored to the presumed desires of any specific group of users. Trying to make the information more helpful to a few users may injure other users with opposing interests and thus constitute biased reporting.

5 *Timeliness.* Since the basic reason for developing accounting information is to use it in making economic decisions, the information must be available when

[7] *APB Statement No. 4,* par. 87–106.

such decisions need to be made. The traditional annual report issued two or three months after the close of the fiscal year leaves much to be desired with respect to the factor of timeliness. Even though quarterly or monthly reports may involve greater reliance on estimates and some sacrifice in accuracy, this trade-off of precision in favor of timeliness is often necessary.

6 Comparability. Comparability of financial information refers to comparisons of successive financial statements for a single business and also to comparison of financial statements for different enterprises. In making these comparisons, we are looking for similarities and differences which will influence economic decisions. It is, therefore, essential that the similarities and differences appearing in the financial statements reflect basic conditions in the business or businesses and not merely differences in the accounting treatment of like transactions.

Consistency in the use of accounting methods is an important factor in achieving **comparability over time.** For example, financial statements would not be comparable in a business which switched its method of depreciation back and forth between the straight-line method and the declining-balance method or changed its method of inventory pricing between fifo and lifo. This does not mean that accounting methods once adopted should remain forever unchanged. Change for the better is urgently needed, and accounting standards and the methods of applying them inevitably change as accounting theory develops.

The issuance of a new standard adopted by the Financial Accounting Standards Board may necessitate a change in accounting practice. The effect of such a change should be disclosed in the period in which the change occurs.

In **APB Opinion No. 20,** dealing with "Accounting Changes," it was concluded that an accounting principle once adopted should not be changed unless there is evidence that an alternative principle would be preferable.[8] In other words, change without improvement is not desirable.

Achieving comparability between enterprises is more difficult than attaining comparability within a single enterprise. However, the increasing importance of public investment in corporate securities demands greater comparability of financial statements. How can the public make intelligent investment decisions on the basis of published financial statements if identical events in different companies are accounted for and reported in a variety of ways? Accountants have long been aware of the need to narrow the wide range of "acceptable alternative methods" of accounting for factual situations that are essentially alike. However, we cannot ignore basic differences in the circumstances under which different businesses operate. For example, a business engaged in long-term construction contracts need not time the recognition of revenue at the point of sale as does a retail store. Such basic differences in operating circumstances should be reflected by different accounting methods. The problem, then, is to identify the circumstances which require the use of a particular accounting method to achieve meaningful reporting, and to eliminate alternative practices under these circumstances. Until accounting research has made this accomplishment possible, we should recognize that financial statements of different companies are not fully comparable. Different enterprises do, at present, employ different but "acceptable" accounting methods which cause their financial statements to show differences not supported by basic differences in the enterprises or their transactions.

7 Completeness. Completeness means that all financial accounting information which meets the preceding six objectives should be reported. This concept has often been described as "full disclosure," but a better term is "adequate

---

[8]*APB Opinion No. 20,* "Accounting Changes," AICPA (New York: 1971), p. 391.

informative disclosure.'' Excessive detail and trivial items should not be permitted to clutter the financial statements. Furthermore, certain information should not be disclosed, because to do so would injure the business, its stockholders, creditors, and employees. For example, a business named as defendant in a large lawsuit should not disclose in its financial statements the maximum amount which management would be willing to pay to achieve an out-of-court settlement of the suit. Disclosure of this maximum dollar amount would ensure that the opposing party would refuse to accept any less favorable settlement.

Disclosure of some information can be made most efficiently in notes accompanying the financial statements. Such notes represent an integral part of the financial statements.

In summary, completeness of financial information calls for adequate informative disclosure in a manner that facilitates understanding and avoids misleading implications.

Generally accepted accounting principles

The term *generally accepted accounting principles* has long been used in the standard form of audit report and in accounting literature generally. This term is used by the CPA in his audit report to indicate whether the company being audited has prepared its financial statements in an acceptable manner, so that they may fairly be compared with the prior year's statements and with the financial statements of other companies.

Alternative terms for *accounting principles* include standards, postulates, assumptions, basic concepts, axioms, and conventions. The variety of terms employed indicates the many efforts that have been made to formulate a satisfactory framework of accounting theory. These efforts are still in process, and the goal of a concise and consistent statement of accounting principles has not yet been achieved. The principles of accounting are not rooted in the laws of nature as are the physical sciences. Therefore, *accounting principles or standards must be developed in relation to what we consider to be the most desirable objectives of financial reporting.* The most difficult task of all may be reaching agreement on the most important purposes of financial statements.

These difficulties in devising a satisfactory structure of accounting theory have not prevented great improvements in the quality of financial reporting in recent years. However, a need for further progress clearly exists.

Sources of generally accepted accounting principles

Although a body of generally accepted accounting principles has long been recognized by businessmen, courts, and governmental agencies, as well as by professional accountants, no complete official list of such accounting principles exists. The most authoritative source of generally accepted accounting principles in recent years has been the Opinions of the Accounting Principles Board. The *Accounting Research Bulletins,* as modified by *APB Opinions,* also continue to represent an important source. In the future, statements issued by the Financial Accounting Standards Board are expected to constitute the major source of additions to and changes in the body of accounting principles.

Another authoritative source of more detailed principles is found in pronouncements of the Securities and Exchange Commission which specify requirements for financial statements and reports submitted to that agency. Accounting textbooks represent another source of detailed accounting principles in areas not specifically covered by official AICPA pronouncements. Although no one textbook by itself establishes accounting principles, a consensus of opinion by numerous writers indicates the existence of detailed principles in addition to those set forth officially by the AICPA. The important influence on accounting theory of publications by the American Accounting Association has already been noted. In summary, we may say that the sources of generally accepted accounting principles include accounting literature as a whole, but that the official pronouncements of the APB and the FASB represent the most authoritative sources with the greatest impact upon current practice.

In the remainder of this chapter we shall discuss a number of important accounting principles or standards. These principles are broad in nature and represent concepts developed by the accounting profession in an effort to meet the needs of the users of financial statements. In later chapters we shall consider the more detailed application of these broad principles to specific issues, such as the valuation of inventories or the depreciation of plant and equipment.

The business entity principle

Since economic activity is carried on by various legal and economic entities, accounting results are summarized in terms of these entities. Accountants deal primarily with three general kinds of business entities: the individual proprietorship, the partnership, and the corporation. Regardless of the form of organization, however, the business is considered an entity and its affairs are distinguished from those of its owners. We see the effect of this principle when accounting income is measured as it accrues to the entity in the form of realized increases in net assets, not when it is distributed to owners. Similarly an obligation of the entity to owners is treated as a liability on the balance sheet, despite the fact that in a sense the owners owe a portion of the debt to themselves.

The accountant sometimes finds it useful to prepare financial statements for economic entities that do not coincide with legal entities. For example, *consolidated financial statements* are often prepared for an economic entity which includes several corporate entities operating under common control exercised through stock ownership. On the other hand, separate financial statements may be prepared for divisions of a single corporation, when such divisions are operated as distinct profit centers.

The continuity or "going-concern" principle

Briefly stated, the continuity principle means that the accountant assumes that the business entity will continue indefinitely. In deciding how to report various items on financial statements, the accountant is often faced with this issue: "Shall I assume that the business will continue to operate, or shall I assume that the business will be terminated in the near future?" Obviously the most probable situation for businesses in general is that they will continue to operate for an indefinite period of time, and this general assumption, commonly known as the *continuity* or *going-concern* principle, is one of the basic assumptions of accounting.

The primary significance of the going-concern principle is that it removes a "liquidation complex" from the accountant's view of business affairs. The possibility that certain productive assets could be liquidated only at a loss, or the fact that if a business ceased operations certain liabilities would mature immediately and require a payment in excess of their present value, is not allowed to become a basis for accounting for such items. In addition the assumption of continued existence provides the logical basis for recording probable future economic benefits as assets and probable future outlays as liabilities.

The continuity principle implies not permanence of existence but simply that the business will continue in existence long enough to carry out present plans and meet contractual commitments. This proposition affects the classification of assets and liabilities on the balance sheet. Since it is assumed that assets will be used and obligations paid in the normal course of operation, no attempt is made to classify assets and liabilities in terms of their ultimate disposition or legal priority in case of liquidation.

There are times when the going-concern principle gives way to evidence that a business entity has a limited life or intends to terminate operations. The accountant is sometimes called upon to prepare a position statement for a firm contemplating liquidation.

The monetary principle

The monetary principle means that accountants assume money to be a useful standard measuring unit for reporting the effect of business transactions. Money is thus the common denominator throughout the accounting process. Some of the information necessary to give a comprehensive picture of a business entity is difficult or impossible to quantify and express in money or other units of measurement. Examples are the competence, health, and morale of management and employees, and the effect of the operations of the entity upon the natural environment. If information is to be included in the body of financial statements, however, it must be expressed in monetary terms. If such measurement is not practicable, a possible alternative method of communication is to use explanatory notes which accompany the financial statements.

In the United States the monetary unit is the dollar. To meet the test of being a *useful standard measuring unit,* the dollar should ideally be of unchanging value. Prior to World War II the rate of price-level change in the United States was not considered to be great enough to cast any serious doubts on the usefulness of the dollar as a stable measuring unit. In more recent years, however, the continuing and relatively rapid inflation has made the monetary assumption one of the most controversial elements of generally accepted accounting principles.

If someone says, "Our football field was 100 yards long 20 years ago; it is 100 yards today; and if we were to build an improved one it would be 100 yards also," we assume, and rightly so, that the yardstick the speaker is using as a standard measuring unit has not changed during the 20-year period.

However, when it is said of an electric generating plant that: (*a*) it cost $4 million to build; (*b*) it would cost $6 million to reproduce today; and (*c*) it would cost $8 million to build an improved plant having similar capacity, we should consider whether the dollars in the (*b*) and (*c*) parts of that statement are the same size as the dollars in part (*a*). Similarly, when the accountant reports that revenue of $100 was realized from the sale of goods and services which cost $90 at varying times in the past, there is some point in asking whether the $100 of revenue is measured in dollars of the same size as the $90 of costs. But what do we mean by the "size" of a dollar?

By the size of a dollar we usually mean the quantity of "real" goods and services that this monetary unit will command. What kind of common denominator will enable us to measure the physical quantities of all the diverse goods and services that money will buy?

The statistical solution to this dilemma is the familiar *price index.* An index number is a somewhat imperfect device for measuring changes in the weighted-average price of a representative collection of goods and services between two points in time. That index numbers are imperfect is not the fault of statistical techniques but of the basic impossibility of the problem under consideration. The quality and nature of the goods and services available in a modern dynamic economy will simply not hold still long enough to give the statistician a standard of comparison. Despite all their shortcomings, price indices covering broad categories of goods and services are useful, if rough, tools for measuring changes in the value of money, that is, the size of the dollar.

Since a price index is expressed as a percentage, its reciprocal may be thought of as a measure of the change in the quantity of goods that a unit of money will buy. For example, if an index of prices in general rose from 100 to 125, this would indicate that the value of money (in terms of the quantity of goods and services that a dollar will command) had fallen from 100 to 80 (100 ÷ 1.25 = 80).

Whenever prices in general rise or fall by a significant amount, the value of money changes in the opposite direction, and the accountant's measuring unit—the dollar—changes in size. Note that changes in particular prices do not necessarily reflect changes in the value of money. Speaking very roughly, if the price of everything doubled overnight the *relative value of goods and services* would remain unchanged, but the *value of money* would be cut in half. On the other hand, if the prices of one-half of all goods and services in the economy rose 10% while the prices of the other half fell by 10%, the *relative value* of these goods and services would have changed, but the *value of money* would remain constant. The point is that an increase in the price of a particular good may reflect a change in its real value relative to all other goods and services in the economy, and not simply a change in the size of the monetary measuring unit.

The lack of stability of the dollar as a measuring unit has led many accounting educators to urge that price-level accounting replace the historical-cost basis or that a system of "fair-value accounting" be adopted. These proposals are considered in detail in Chapter 25.

In *Statement No. 3,* "Financial Statements Restated for General Price-Level Changes," the APB suggested that price-level-adjusted statements might be useful if presented as a supplement to conventional financial statements. Despite the grave concern over the extent of price-level changes, generally accepted accounting principles continue to require use of the stable-dollar assumption in financial statements.

The time-period principle

As indicated earlier in our discussion of timeliness as an objective of financial reporting, accounting measurements for arbitrary short time periods are less accurate than would be possible for the entire life span of an enterprise. However, the urgent need for frequent timely reports causes accountants to accept this mode of reporting despite its inevitable inaccuracies. To make accounting measurements for short time periods in the life of a business entity requires accruals and deferrals to achieve the necessary cutoffs.

Although accounting periods may be as short as one month or one quarter, the normal accounting period is one year, beginning on any given day and ending 12 months later. A *calendar* year accounting period ends on December 31; all other 12-month accounting periods are known as *fiscal* years. Business firms frequently adopt accounting periods that end when operations are at a low ebb in order to simplify year-end procedures and facilitate a better measurement of income and financial position. Such an accounting period is referred to as a *natural business year* because it conforms to the natural annual cycle of the enterprise.

The cost principle

The cost principle is a pervasive concept that affects a great many aspects of financial accounting. *Cost* (or more precisely *historical cost*) is assumed to be the proper basis of accounting for assets acquired, for services received, and for the interests of creditors and owners of a business entity. Completed transactions are the events to be recognized and made part of the accounting records under the cost principle. At the time of a transaction, the exchange price usually represents the fair market value of the goods or services exchanged, as evidenced by the agreement of an informed buyer and seller. With the passage of time, however, the economic value of an asset such as land or a building may change greatly, particularly in periods of inflation. However, the cost principle requires that historical cost, rather than a later "fair market value," continue to serve as the basis for values in the accounts and in the financial statements.

How should cost be measured when assets or services are acquired in non-cash transactions? For example, land and buildings may be acquired in exchange for a corporation's own shares of capital stock. Cost is then defined as the cash equivalent or fair value of the assets acquired, or the cash equivalent (fair value) of the capital stock issued, whichever is more clearly evident. If the capital stock is listed on a stock exchange and widely traded, the existing market price of the shares will be stronger, more objective evidence of the cost of the land and buildings being acquired than an appraisal of the property.

The cost principle applies to the measurement of liabilities as well as of assets. The dollar valuation assigned to a liability should be its cash equivalent. For example, if a business borrows $100,000 and signs a note promising to repay $106,000 a year later, the cash equivalent value of the liability is $100,000, and this is the net amount at which the liability should be shown in a balance sheet prepared immediately after obtaining the loan. Thus, the cost principle is consistently applied to all types of transactions.

The implications of the cost principle will be considered in more detail in our study of income determination in Chapter 3 and later chapters of this book.

The revenue principle

Revenue may be defined as the value of goods and services which a business entity transfers to its customers. Thus, revenue is the factor responsible for all increases in the net assets of a business, apart from investments by owners. For a given time period, revenue is equal to the inflow of cash and receivables from sales made during that period. For a single transaction, revenue is equal to the asset values received from the customer.

Any definition of revenue immediately raises questions as to timing— the concept of *realization* of revenue. At what point or points during the creation of marketable products or services should revenue be recognized? What is the critical event which indicates revenue has been realized and which justifies recording a change in net assets by replacing the cost of goods produced with a higher valuation representing their market value? Ideally, since each step in the process of producing and distributing goods is essential to earning revenue, the accounting recognition of revenue should be continuous rather than being linked to a single critical event. As a practical matter, however, objective evidence is needed to support the recognition of revenue. Thus, for most businesses, that evidence lies in an arm's-length transaction in which title to goods passes to the customer. The reasoning underlying this widespread practice of recognizing revenue at the point of sale will be evaluated at length in Chapter 3.

The matching principle

The matching principle means that after the revenue for an accounting period has been determined, the costs associated with that revenue must be deducted in order to measure net income. The term *matching* refers to the close relationship that exists between certain costs and the revenue recognized as a result of incurring those costs.

Expenditures for advertising attract customers and generate sales. The outlay for the advertising is one of the costs to be deducted from the revenue of the period. The recognition of uncollectible accounts expense illustrates the importance of the time period in the matching of costs and revenue. Uncollectible accounts expense is caused by selling goods on credit to customers who fail to pay their bills. To match this expense with the related revenue, the expense must be recorded and deducted in the year the sales are made, even though the receivables are not determined to be uncollectible until the following year. The use of estimates is necessary in this and in many other cases in order to carry out the matching principle. One of the most difficult examples is the necessity of estimating the relationship between research and development costs and the revenue attributable to such costs.

The objectivity principle

To the maximum degree possible, accounting should be based on objective evidence. Business documents showing the details of "arm's-length" completed transactions provide clear strong evidence that can be verified. To *verify* means to prove something to be true by examination of evidence or underlying facts. As explained in our earlier discussion of the objectives of financial accounting (page 10), if accounting information is verifiable, the same conclusion would be reached by different accountants working independently and following the same measurement standards.

Of course financial statements are not completely factual; estimates on such matters as the future useful life of depreciable assets and the salability of inventory are inherent in the accounting process. However, the objectivity principle calls for accountants to adhere as closely as possible to objective evidence. The alternative approach would be to establish accounting values through unrestricted use of appraisal reports, estimates of future events, and expressions of opinion. Such an approach to accounting would make it difficult or impossible for the CPA to perform an independent verification of financial statements and would probably lessen public confidence in financial reporting.

The consistency principle

Comparability of the annual financial statements of a business from one year to the next is essential if favorable and unfavorable trends in the business are to be identified. If the financial statements for the current year show higher earnings than for the preceding year, the user is entitled to assume that operations have been more profitable. If a change in accounting principles has occurred, however, the reported increase in earnings *could* have been caused solely by this accounting change, rather than by any improvement in the underlying business activity. Consistent application of accounting principles for a business entity from one period to the next is therefore needed so that the financial statements of successive years will be comparable.

An important part of the opinion issued by a certified public accountant in reporting on his audit of a company's financial statements deals with consistency. This part of the standard audit report is worded as follows:

> In our opinion the aforementioned financial statements present fairly the financial position of XYZ Company at December 31, 19___, and the results of its operations and the changes in its financial position for the year ended, in conformity with generally accepted accounting principles applied on a basis *consistent with that of the preceding year.*[9]

Accounting Changes Examples of accounting changes which can have a material effect on net income and other elements of financial statements are: (1) a change in the method of depreciation from straight-line to accelerated depreciation, and (2) a change in the valuation of inventory from the first-in, first-out (fifo) method to the last-in, first-out (lifo) method.

The consistency principle does not mean that a particular method of accounting once adopted can never be changed. Accounting principles and methods change in response to changes in the environment of accounting. When an accounting change is desirable, it should be made, *together with appropriate disclosure* of the change and its effect in dollar amounts on the reported income of the year in which the change is made.

APB Opinion No. 20, "Accounting Changes," stated that:

> The presumption that an entity should not change an accounting principle may be overcome only if the enterprise justifies the use of an alternative

---

[9] *Statement on Auditing Standards No. 1,* "Codification of Auditing Standards and Procedures," AICPA (New York: 1972), p. 81.

acceptable accounting principle on the basis that it is preferable. . . .

The nature of and justification for a change in accounting principle and its effect on income should be disclosed. . . . The justification for the change should explain why the newly adopted accounting principle is preferable.[10]

The disclosure principle

The disclosure principle requires that financial statements be complete in the sense of including all information necessary to a fair presentation. If the omission of certain information would cause the financial statements to be misleading, then disclosure of such information is essential.

Published accounting reports include not only the financial statements themselves but also the attached explanatory notes, which are considered to be an integral part of the statements. Disclosures made in the attached notes should *supplement* the information in the body of the statements, however, and never be used to correct improper presentation of information in the body of the financial statements.

Typical examples of information often disclosed in notes attached to financial statements include the following: a summary of significant accounting policies, descriptions of stock option plans and pension plans, status of litigation in which the company is a party, amount and nature of contingent liabilities and commitments, and the terms and status of proposed acquisitions of other companies. The first item listed above (a summary of significant accounting policies) is prescribed by *APB Opinion No. 22,* "Disclosure of Accounting Policies" as essential. Among the policies to be described in this particular note to financial statements are changes in accounting principles and justification therefor, depreciation methods, inventory pricing methods, accounting for research and development costs, and translation of foreign currencies.[11]

If the accounting principles used in audited financial statements represent departures from official positions set forth by the Accounting Principles Board or the Financial Accounting Standards Board, it is essential that the departures be disclosed either in notes attached to the statements or in the reports of the independent auditors.

The concept of disclosure applies not only to transactions and events that have occurred during the period covered by the financial statements, but also to material *subsequent events* that occur after the balance sheet date but before published financial statements are released. For example, the sale or destruction of a major segment of the business, a significant decline in the market price of raw materials, the institution or settlement of important legal proceedings are all events likely to have a substantial influence on the earnings and financial position of a company, and they should therefore be disclosed in financial statements.

The examples cited indicate that disclosure by notes to financial

---

[10] *APB Opinion No. 20,* p. 391.
[11] *APB Opinion No. 22,* "Disclosures of Accounting Policies," AICPA (New York: 1972), p. 436.

statements may be rather lengthy and involved. However, these notes, as well as the financial statements themselves, should be as concise as possible in order to keep financial reporting understandable and not excessively detailed. (Additional examples are shown in the published financial statements presented in Appendix B.)

Disclosure should *not* be made of events that are merely interesting, rather than essential to a fair presentation. Neither should there be disclosure of general risks or uncertainties which apply to most business entities, such as the threat of war, a business depression, or the probable appearance of new competitors.

Materiality

Materiality is an accounting concept closely related to the principle of adequate disclosure. Disclosure is necessary in financial statements only for *material* matters. The meaning of materiality in an accounting context is a state of relative importance. Items that are trifling in amount need not ordinarily be treated in strict accordance with accounting theory but rather should be handled in the most economical and convenient manner.

For example, most companies establish a minimum dollar amount in considering whether an expenditure should be recorded as a depreciable asset. In theory the cost of a new pencil sharpener or wastebasket should be capitalized and depreciated over its useful life. As a practical matter, however, the expense of making such allocations of cost would exceed the cost of the item and would represent an unjustifiably wasteful accounting policy. Even though more than one accounting period will benefit from the use of a pencil sharpener, the concept of materiality indicates that the cost of such an item should immediately be charged to expense. However, such exceptions to accounting standards should be carefully controlled by clearly stated written policies; otherwise, the argument that convenience should outweigh good accounting practices may be applied to more and larger transactions, with the end result of defeating the basic objectives of financial accounting.

That which is material for one business may not be for another. In a small company an uninsured loss, say $10,000, might be considered as material; in a large company it would not be a significant event. In deciding upon the materiality of an item in terms of financial statement disclosure, it is helpful to consider whether knowledge of the item would be likely to influence the decisions of persons using the financial statements as a basis for economic decisions.

Qualitative standards should be considered in judging the materiality of an item as well as its dollar amount. For example, a transaction between a company and its president is not at arm's length and suggests a possible *conflict of interests.* Disclosure of the transaction may therefore be appropriate, even though disclosure of a similar transaction between parties dealing at arm's length would not be warranted.

In this discussion of materiality, we have described it as an accounting *concept* rather than as an accounting *principle.* One reason for the distinction is that the concept of materiality tells us that we may under carefully designed policies disregard certain accounting principles in favor of expediency in the treatment of insignificant details.

Conservatism

Many decisions by the accountant in the areas of asset valuation and income determination involve the making of estimates and the exercise of judgment. In other words, many accounting determinations do not have a single "correct answer"; a choice must be made among alternative assumptions under conditions of uncertainty. The concept of conservatism holds that when reasonable support exists for alternative methods and for different measurements, the accountant should select the accounting option with the least favorable effect on net income and financial position in the current period.

Conservatism is usually regarded not as an accounting principle, but as a powerful influence stressing caution against the danger of overstating earnings or financial strength. However, many enterprises are definitely not in favor of conservative accounting policies. Companies trying to raise capital by selling capital stock to the public naturally try to project an image of superior management and rising profits. A business that reports higher earnings year after year gains the reputation of being a "growth company"; financial analysts refer to its capital stock as a "glamor issue"; and the market price of its stock often rises to a high multiple of earnings per share. Once such a reputation is established, a company finds it easier to raise more capital through the issuance of additional securities or through bank loans. Attracting able ambitious employees is also easier. Executive compensation tends to rise, both in salaries and through stock option and pension plans. All these pleasant consequences of a reputation for rising earnings give corporate management a powerful incentive to choose accounting methods that *maximize* current income.

On the other hand, small businesses that do not seek capital from the public and do not report their earnings to anyone other than income tax authorities have an incentive to choose accounting alternatives that hold income to the lowest level that can be justified.

All companies with capital stock widely held by the public must be audited each year by certified public accountants. Many small businesses are not audited at all. The professional auditing firm thus has many clients with reasons to choose accounting practices that tend to overstate rather than to understate net income. Certified public accountants have often been named as defendants in lawsuits by investors who claim that audited financial statements on which they relied in making investments actually overstated the net income and financial strength of the companies. Almost never is a CPA firm sued on the grounds that audited financial statements were too conservative and understated net earnings and stockholders' equity. Consequently, the CPA, although trying to be objective and impartial in his role as *independent* auditor, has reason to favor a conservative resolution of doubtful accounting issues. Conflicting views between the client company and the CPA firm on such matters have sometimes led to the replacement of the auditors with another CPA firm.

Ideally, accountants should make estimates and select accounting methods which neither overstate nor understate the current income and financial strength of a business. The concept of conservatism should not be distorted to the point of deliberate understatement. On the other hand, judicious use of conservatism in accounting may help to prevent the catastrophes which have befallen many investors and many employees when companies with excessively optimistic accounting policies suddenly reached the limit of credibility and collapsed.

Among the familiar examples of the influence of conservatism on accounting practices are the valuation of inventories at the lower of cost or market, the prompt write-off of assets when doubt arises as to their value, and the refusal to recognize appreciation in the value of assets until confirmed by a completed sales transaction.

A new business which adopts the conservative practice of valuing inventories at the lower of cost or market will probably have a more conservative income statement and balance sheet at the end of the first year, but not necessarily for the following year. Inventory written down below cost at the end of the first year of operations and sold in the second year will show a larger profit in the second year than if the write-down had not occurred.

Will the use of an accelerated depreciation method rather than straight-line depreciation cause the financial statements to be conservative over the entire life of a depreciable asset, or only in the early years of its use? (Accelerated depreciation methods require writing off most of the cost of an asset in the early portion of its useful life.) If we focus our attention on a single depreciable asset, such as a building, accelerated depreciation will result in large amounts of depreciation in the early years of the asset's life and correspondingly *small* amounts of depreciation expense in later years. Thus the conservative effects of the policy are reversed over a span of years. However, it is more realistic to consider the effect of accelerated depreciation on all the depreciable assets of a business and to assume that the business acquires some new plant assets each year. The conservative effect of the accelerated depreciation policy may continue indefinitely as long as the business continues to acquire new depreciable units.

In a growing enterprise which is adding new units of plant and equipment more rapidly than old, fully depreciated units are being retired, the use of an accelerated depreciation method may cause the financial statements to be increasingly conservative as long as the growth of plant and equipment continues.

Cash flows and income measurement

The accountant assumes that a business entity has continuous existence. Therefore, he records the prospect of future cash inflows as an increase in assets and as revenue whenever he has objective evidence of the amount of the future cash receipt. Cash inflows often occur before a business has performed its part of the bargained contract. In this latter case, an increase in assets is recorded but a liability is recognized instead of revenue. The liability indicates an obligation on the part of the enterprise to perform in accordance with the contract. When performance is completed, the revenue will be earned and recognized. We can readily see that cash inflows are closely related to revenue recognition; however, the assumptions lying behind the timing of revenue recognition do not always permit cash inflows and revenue to be recorded in the same accounting period.

Similarly, cash outflows are closely related to business expenses; however, the cash outflow and the expense may not be recorded in the same period. For example, businesses frequently acquire for cash in one period property which will be productive over several future periods, and property which is productive only during the current period is often acquired in exchange for a promise to pay cash in a future period.

Information about cash flows is important to the accountant in tracing realized revenue and expired costs as determinants of business income. The cash flows of one period are usually not sufficient for a meaningful determination of income for that period; however, selected cash flows of past, present, and future periods taken as a whole can be related to the process of income determination for a given accounting period.

Cash basis of accounting

Under the *cash basis of accounting,* revenue is recognized only when cash is received; expenses are recorded when they are paid in cash. The determination of income thus rests upon the *collection* of revenue and the *payment* of expenses, rather than upon the *earning* of *revenue* and the *incurring* of expenses. A business using the cash basis of accounting is not following the *matching principle* described earlier in this chapter. Consequently, financial statements prepared on the basis of cash receipts and cash payments do not present the financial position or operating results of a business in conformity with generally accepted accounting principles.

A strict cash basis of accounting is seldom found in practice, but a modified cash basis (really a mixed cash-accrual basis) is allowed for income tax purposes. Nearly all individual taxpayers prepare their returns on the modified cash basis. Also many physicians, law firms, other professional firms, and small service-type businesses rely on a modified cash basis of accounting. Taxpayers generally elect the cash basis of accounting because of its simplicity and because it tends to postpone the recognition of taxable income and the payment of income tax.

Under the version of cash basis accounting accepted for tax purposes, the taxpayer who buys property having a service life of more than one year cannot deduct the entire cost in the year of purchase. He must treat the cost as an asset to be depreciated over its useful life. Expenses such as rent or advertising paid in advance are also regarded as assets and are deductible only in the period to which they apply. Expenses paid *after* the year in which incurred are deductible only in the year paid. Revenue is reported for tax purposes in the year received. For this reason some individuals or firms may deliberately postpone making collections near the year-end.

In any business in which the purchase, production, or sale of merchandise is a significant factor, these transactions must be reported on an accrual basis. For example, when merchandise is sold on credit, the revenue must be recognized immediately. The cost of goods sold must reflect purchases on credit and inventories on hand whether paid for or not. In any merchandising business the revenue from sales, the cost of goods sold, and the gross profit on sales will be the same on either the accrual basis or the so-called cash basis acceptable for income tax purposes. Use of the cash basis of accounting is limited principally to service-type businesses, farms, professional firms, and individuals in situations not requiring financial statements prepared in conformity with generally accepted accounting principles.

Information concerning cash flows during any period is extremely valuable in judging the ability of the firm to pay its debts, to maintain regular dividend payments, to finance replacements of productive assets, and to expand the scope of the business operations. A measure of the net increase or decrease in cash during a given period is not very useful in evaluating a company's operating performance, however, because cash receipts and disbursements are not representative of the economic activities carried on in specific periods.

Accrual basis of accounting

The accrual basis of accounting is assumed throughout this book. Revenue is recognized when it is realized and expenses are recognized when incurred, without regard to the time of receipt or payment. The focus of accrual accounting is on the realization of revenue, the incurrence of costs, and the matching of revenue realized and the costs expired. Adopting the assumption that revenue is recognized when realization occurs and the corollary assumption that costs contributing to the earning of this revenue can be traced through the earning process requires the use of an accrual-deferral system of accounting.

The need for frequent and current appraisals of the past performance of the enterprise as the basis for decisions about the future by management and investors alike has forced the accountant to progress from cash basis to accrual accounting. The financial statements resulting from accrual accounting are less precise than cash flow statements but are at the same time more complex and more useful.

Under the accrual system, the accounts are adjusted periodically to make the data which have been recorded consistent with the basic assumptions of the system. The accountant reviews the accounts periodically, usually annually, to ascertain whether all revenue realized has been recognized in the accounts, whether the costs incurred in current and prior periods have been allocated properly, whether any revenue has been recognized that has not met the test of realization, and whether any costs have been incurred but not recorded. In reality, the accountant is adjusting the cash flows for leads and lags which have occurred during the period.

REVIEW QUESTIONS

1 Identify the institutional forces or organizations that have been primarily responsible for the development of present accounting principles and practices. What is the relationship between each of these forces or organizations and the practicing certified public accountant?

2 Are generally accepted accounting principles equally applicable to the fields of financial accounting and managerial accounting? Explain.

3 If the chief accounting officer of a large corporation has a CPA certificate and was formerly a successful member of a CPA firm, would there be any reason for the corporation to retain a CPA to perform an annual audit? Explain.

4 Distinguish between the **Statements of the Accounting Principles Board** and **APB Opinions.**

5 Some of the Opinions of the Accounting Principles Board included a statement of dissenting views of some members who voted against issuance of an Opinion. Are such dissenting views also likely to be found in standards issued by the Financial Accounting Standards Board? Explain.

6 Among the specific qualities or characteristics considered as desirable for financial statements are relevance and verifiability. Are these qualities as likely to be found in an earnings forecast as in a balance sheet? Explain.

7 Summarize briefly the size and composition of the Financial Accounting Standards Board, and state the approximate time of its organization.

8 "The monetary principle of accounting assumes that money is a useful standard measuring unit for reporting the effects of business transactions." State and explain briefly two major criticisms or limitations of this accounting principle.

9 What is meant by the continuity or going-concern principle of accounting? How does it affect the valuation of assets? When is the principle not applicable?

10 Identify the following as being governmental organizations or part of the private sector of the economy: Financial Accounting Standards Board, Cost Accounting Standards Board, Securities and Exchange Commission, New York Stock Exchange, American Accounting Association.

11 In any long-run review of the development of generally accepted accounting principles, consideration might be given to the contribution of the Financial Accounting Standards Board, the Accounting Principles Board, the Committee on Accounting Procedure, and the Securities and Exchange Commission. Identify the time period in which each has functioned.

12 Explain briefly the nature and purpose of the Financial Accounting Foundation.

13 One of the publications of the American Accounting Association entitled **A Statement of Basic Accounting Theory** stresses a normative approach to accounting. State briefly the meaning of a normative approach to accounting.

14 The Laser Corporation acquired land and buildings in exchange for 50,000 shares of its own $5 par value common stock. How should the cost principle of accounting be applied in recording this transaction?

15 What is meant by the accounting concept of materiality? What does this concept have to do with a transaction involving a possible "conflict of interests?"

16 Describe briefly the concept of conservatism. Is a "growth company" with its stock widely distributed among public investors and with a reputation for consistently rising earnings per share the kind of organization in which you would expect emphasis upon conservative accounting? Explain.

17 Distinguish briefly between the cash basis of accounting and the accrual basis of accounting. Will financial statements prepared under either method present fairly the financial position and operating results of a business in conformity with generally accepted accounting principles?

EXERCISES

Ex. 1-1 Select the best answer for each of the following multiple choice questions.

a Several organizations have been influential in the development of an accepted body of accounting principles or concepts, which are followed by most business organizations in order that their financial statements be generally accepted. Which of the following organizations has been most active in formulating this body of accounting principles?
(1) The Securities and Exchange Commission
(2) The American Institute of Certified Public Accountants
(3) The American Accounting Association
(4) The Internal Revenue Service

b The attest function as applied to financial statements means:
(1) The expression of an opinion on the financial statements by an independent firm of certified public accountants
(2) Filing of a letter with the Securities and Exchange Commission signed by officers of the company issuing the financial statements and accepting responsibility for the accuracy of the statements

(3) Compliance by a listed corporation with the regulations of the New York Stock Exchange

(4) Notarization of financial statements by a notary public licensed by the state in which the company is incorporated

c One of the qualitative objectives of financial accounting as suggested by the APB in *Statement No. 4* is relevance. The term *relevance* as applied to financial statements is illustrated by:

(1) Adherence to historical cost as the basis of accounting for assets

(2) The requirement that financial statements of publicly owned companies be audited by CPAs

(3) Valuation of inventories at the lower of cost or market

(4) Disclosure of current market value of investments in marketable securities

Ex. 1-2 The financial statements of Portland Company include the items shown below, along with the related notes accompanying the financial statements.

Cash (Note A). . . . . $ 96,500

Accounts receivable (Note B) 210,300

Note A: *The amount reported as cash includes four checking accounts, two petty cash funds, and one change fund.*

Note B: *Accounts receivable include the amount of $48,400, representing the selling price of merchandise shipped on a consignment basis and held for sale by consignees acting as our agents at December 31. It is anticipated that this merchandise will be sold within the near future and that none of it will have to be returned to stock.*

You are to discuss the appropriateness of Notes A and B to Portland Company's financial statements as a means of carrying out the disclosure principle of accounting and the objectives of general-purpose financial statements.

Ex. 1-3 The general-purpose financial statements of Lobo Corporation contain the following item and a related note to the financial statements.

Inventories (Note A) $285,600

Note A: *Inventories are valued at the lower of cost or market. Cost is determined on the first-in, first-out basis.*

Discuss the appropriateness of the note relating to inventories in relation to the accounting principle of disclosure.

Ex. 1-4 Identify each of the following phrases as being associated with (1) the cash basis of accounting or (2) the accrual basis of accounting:

a Revenues recognized at time of collection

b Individual income tax returns

c Business entity in which inventories are material

d Minimum amount of record keeping

e Generally accepted principles of accounting

f Postponement of recognition of revenue

g Flexibility in determining timing of expenses

h Emphasis upon consistency and time period in measurement of income

i Sophisticated accounting system

j Small service-type firm with accounting records limited to information required for income tax purposes

Ex. 1-5 Blue Springs Company, which follows the accrual basis of accounting, reported advertising expense for the current year of $83,460. Prepaid advertising at the end of the year amounted to $6,320, and cash payments for advertising during the year amounted to $87,580. There was no accrued advertising expense at either the beginning or end of the current year. What was the amount, if any, of prepaid advertising at the beginning of the current year? Show computations.

Ex. 1-6 The usual audit report by a CPA includes an opinion that the financial statements he has examined are presented in conformity with generally accepted accounting principles. In evaluating the acceptability of specific accounting principles used by the client being audited, the CPA must determine whether the principle has substantial authoritative support.

What sources might the CPA consult to determine whether an accounting principle has substantial authoritative support? Distinguish between primary and secondary sources.

SHORT CASES FOR ANALYSIS AND DECISION

Case 1-1 A financial newspaper carried an advertisement of a small manufacturing company being offered for sale by its owner. The advertisement emphasized the unusual profitability of the business. Assume that you were interested in purchasing a business of this type and you therefore contacted the owner, Jon Blackburn, who stated that the Blackburn Company in its first year of operation had produced a profit of $46,000. You inquired whether the accrual basis of accounting had been used in determining the $46,000 of net income and Blackburn replied as follows:

"We use a mixed cash-accrual basis of accounting just as so many other small concerns do. As you probably know, a strict cash basis is not satisfactory, but a modified or mixed cash-accrual basis is acceptable for income tax purposes and meets our other needs very well. For example, our purchases of merchandise are recorded only when cash payment is made. Our sales are recorded immediately, whether on a cash or credit basis. We do not guess about uncollectible accounts in advance, but we do not hesitate to write off any receivable that proves to be uncollectible. We took a complete physical inventory at year-end and recorded it on the books. We did not record any depreciation on equipment as all equipment was acquired by issuance of long-term notes. No entry will be made for these transactions until cash payments are required. We find this system gives us better results than a pure cash basis and requires less work than a full accrual basis."

Instructions Evaluate point by point the statement by Blackburn. Would you regard his system as conforming to the usual standards of a "modified cash basis" of accounting? Would the determination of net income of $46,000 during the first year be a valid measurement? Explain.

Case 1-2 Comparative balance sheets of Ironhill Mines for the years 1975 and 1965 are presented below and on page 30:

IRONHILL MINES
Comparative Balance Sheets

Assets	*1975*	*1965*
Cash	$ 870,000	$ 100,000
Accounts receivable	80,000	–0–
Inventories	200,000	–0–
Unmined iron ore (unamortized part)	800,000	1,600,000
Plant assets	400,000	400,000
Less: Accumulated depreciation	(200,000)	–0–
Total assets	$2,150,000	$2,100,000

Liabilities & Equities		*1975*	*1965*
Current liabilities		$ 50,000	$ –0–
Capital stock		2,100,000	2,100,000
Total liabilities & equities		$2,150,000	$2,100,000

The president informs you that he has adopted a policy of paying cash dividends in an amount equal to net income each year; in spite of this, there has been a continual increase in his cash balance, as is apparent on the above balance sheet.

Instructions Explain to the president why his cash balance has been increasing. Include in your explanation an analysis of the changes in individual balance sheet items during the 10-year interval between the two balance sheets.

Case 1-3 The board of directors of Instant Communications, Inc., is debating whether to adopt straight-line depreciation or an accelerated depreciation method. You are asked for an opinion as to whether the conservative effect of accelerated depreciation on income and financial position will be felt for only a few years or whether it will continue indefinitely to result in the reporting of lower earnings and a lower valuation of plant and equipment.

PROBLEMS

Group A

1A-1 McDuff Corporation was organized by George Mack and William Duffy for the purpose of operating a hardware store. Each invested $20,000 cash and each received 1,000 shares of $1 par value common stock. Mack also loaned $10,000 to the corporation and received a two-year, 6% promissory note. The corporation then issued 1,200 shares of its common stock in exchange for land and a building. The land alone was appraised at a fair market value of $10,000.

A stock of merchandise costing $15,000 was acquired on open account and a salesman was employed to begin work the following week at a weekly salary of $150. Office supplies and some used office equipment were acquired for $3,000 cash. The office supplies were valued at $400 and the used office equipment at $2,600.

Instructions
a What cost should be recorded for the land and building acquired in exchange for McDuff Corporation's stock? Explain the reasoning underlying your answer.
b Record the above transactions in general journal form.
c After two years of operation, McDuff Corporation had a strong current position but retained earnings amounted to only $7,000. Under these circumstances, would it be proper for the corporation to make payment of the two-year, $10,000 note payable to George Mack? Explain.

1A-2 In a discussion of the concept of conservatism as an influence on financial accounting, Douglas argued that conservatism was often used as a means of unjustifiably understating the income of the current period and the financial position. Barnaby defended conservatism on the ground that the accountant frequently had to make choices among alternative assumptions under conditions of uncertainty and that making such choices on a conservative basis would help avoid dangerous exaggeration of earnings, which could seriously injure both investors and certified public accountants.

Douglas and Barnaby considered the five following situations but were unable to reach agreement on the proper accounting treatment in any one of them.

(1) A company has expended $100,000 (which is 5% of its annual sales) for research in an effort to develop new commercial products. No specific products have emerged from this research as yet, but management believes that the research if continued will eventually lead to important new products. Furthermore, management believes that its existing products will lose their market appeal in a few years and that the company must have new products to survive.

Douglas favored including the $100,000 on the balance sheet as an intangible asset, Deferred Research and Development. Barnaby favored treating the $100,000 as expense of the current year.

(2) After occupying an old building on leased property for 17 years of a 20-year lease, the tenant company constructed a new frame building, because the old building was unsatisfactory and the owner refused to make repairs. Improvements on the land will revert to the owner at the end of the lease. There is a possibility, but no assurance, that the owner will agree to renew the lease.

Barnaby favors writing off the cost of the building as expense of the current period. Douglas favors capitalizing the cost of the building.

(3) The products sold by a manufacturer are warranted for a period of one year. Barnaby favors recording warranty expense and crediting a liability of estimated amount in the period of sale. Douglas favors recognizing warranty expense only as claims are presented which require repairs or replacement of products.

(4) The inventory contains a large quantity of an item for which demand has largely disappeared. Barnaby favors writing off the cost of this item. Douglas opposes this action on the grounds the item is not subject to deterioration and customer demand for it may revive.

(5) Credit terms are 30 days. Barnaby favors writing off a large receivable six months past due from a customer who went to Europe for an extended stay and cannot be located. Douglas is opposed, because the customer has been delinquent before and later paid in full.

Instructions For each of the above five situations, state your opinion on the proposed action and explain fully the reasoning underlying your position.

1A-3 Highly condensed balance sheet data at the end of the current year are presented below for three companies of similar size and nature of operations. All are in the same industry.

	Anthony Company	Bedford Company	Cranford Company
Cash	$ 10,000	$ 10,000	$ 10,000
Accounts receivable	50,000	50,000	50,000
Inventories (Note A)	100,000	110,000	115,000
Plant and equipment (net)	100,000	100,000	100,000
Total assets	$260,000	$270,000	$275,000
Accounts payable	$ 15,000	$ 15,000	$ 15,000
Other current liabilities	45,000	45,000	45,000
Capital stock	50,000	50,000	50,000
Retained earnings	150,000	160,000	165,000
Total liabilities & stockholders' equity	$260,000	$270,000	$275,000

Note A:

Anthony Company: Three years ago, Anthony Company changed its methods of pricing inventories from the cost basis to the lower-of-cost-or-market basis, which is now in use.

Bedford Company: Bedford Company prices its inventories at cost. Last year it used the first-in, first-out method of determining cost, but for the current year it used the last-in, first-out method.

Cranford Company: Cranford Company prices all its inventories at cost, but determines cost on the first-in, first-out method for one category of its inventories and the average-cost method for the remainder of its inventories.

The three companies had not been audited previously by independent public accountants, but this year all three companies have retained the same CPA to audit their financial statements for the current year. The president of each company is hopeful that the CPA's audit report for his company will indicate that the financial statements were prepared "in conformity with generally accepted accounting principles applied on a basis consistent with that of the preceding year."

During an informal meeting of the three presidents, Anthony expressed some fear that the differences in accounting for inventories by companies in the same industry might be regarded as a serious lack of consistency.

Instructions

a Do you believe that the accounting principle of consistency as applied to the valuation of inventories in these three companies would prevent the CPA from issuing audit reports giving his full approval to the financial statements of each company and using the language quoted in the problem? Assume that the audits indicated that all other aspects of the financial statements were satisfactory. Explain fully the reasoning underlying your answer.

b Would you expect the CPA to take a different position if the three companies were in three different industries? Explain.

1A-4 a Hudson Corporation issues notes payable frequently in borrowing from various sources. Some of the notes provide for payment of interest in advance; others do not. (For the purposes of this problem, you need not challenge the propriety of prepaid interest.) Hudson Company uses the accrual basis of accounting. Information relating to prepaid interest and to interest payable at two successive balance sheet dates appears below.

	Dec. 31, 1975	Dec. 31, 1976
Prepaid interest.	$ 800	$ 500
Interest payable.	1,000	1,400

Interest expense for the year on the accrual basis was $7,500.

Instructions Compute the amount of cash payments for interest during 1976.

b Hudson Corporation owns several properties which it rents to numerous tenants. Some tenants pay rent in advance; others do not. The following information relates to rent receivable and unearned rent revenue at two successive balance sheet dates.

	Dec. 31, 1975	Dec. 31, 1976
Rent receivable.	$4,500	$3,800
Unearned rent revenue	1,700	2,300

The amount of rent collected during 1976 was $25,500.

Instructions Using the accrual basis of accounting, compute the amount of rent revenue earned during the year 1976.

Group B

1B-1 James West and Robert Bar formed Westbar Corporation for the purpose of operating a charter fishing boat. Each contributed $18,000 cash, for which each received 2,000 shares of $1 par value common stock. The corporation also issued 800 shares of its common stock to acquire a used boat. William Mason, the former owner of the boat, had pledged it as collateral for a $15,000 bank loan and this $15,000 liability was assumed by Westbar Corporation in the agreement for acquisition of the boat.

    William Mason displayed records showing that the original cost of the boat when new had been $50,000 and that he had written off by straight-line depreciation a total of $30,000.

    Westbar Corporation acquired fishing equipment for $4,000 cash and supplies for $500 cash. A crew member was hired to begin work the following week at a weekly salary of $175.

Instructions
a What effect, if any, does the amount of recorded depreciation and the depreciation method used by William Mason have upon the depreciation program to be used for the boat by Westbar Corporation? State briefly the reasoning supporting your answer.
b What cost should be recorded for the boat acquired in exchange for 800 shares of Westbar Corporation stock? Explain fully.
c Record the above transactions in general journal form.

1B-2 White River Company is a successful enterprise and is expanding rapidly. On May 1 additional manufacturing facilities were acquired from the partnership of Lamb and King, which was terminating operations because of a dispute between the partners. The property had been advertised for sale at a price of $800,000. Lamb asserted that the land alone was worth that much and that the building was insured for $400,000, its cost of construction.

    White River Company acquired the property by issuing to the partnership 80,000 shares of its $5 par value capital stock and agreeing to assume full responsibility for a $100,000 mortgage payable on the property which was owed to a bank. Prior to the acquisition, White River Company hired a firm of industrial engineers to inspect and appraise the building. The report from this firm set forth a current value for the building of $460,000. The common stock of White River Company is listed on a stock exchange and was being actively traded on May 1 at a price of $8.50 a share.

    Shortly after acquiring the property, White River Company received a letter from a large national organization offering to buy the property for $900,000 cash.

Instructions
a At what dollar amount should this transaction be recorded by White River Company? State the dollar amounts applicable to land and to the building.
b Identify the accounting principle or principles involved and explain the reasoning underlying your answers to part ***(a)***.

1B-3 Limestone Corporation owns several office buildings and rents space to tenants. One of these office buildings was acquired at a cost of $800,000 and has been depreciated for five years on a straight-line basis. Salvage value is assumed to be zero. The carrying value, net of accumulated depreciation, will be $700,000 at the end of the current year.

At the time of acquiring the building, Limestone Corporation had borrowed $800,000 from Robert Smith, one of the founders of the company and presently a director and major stockholder. The note payable issued for the loan made no mention of interest but called for repayment of $1,000,000 five years from the date of the note. In a directors' meeting near the end of the current year, Smith stated that because of rising price levels, he considered the building to be worth more than it had cost. Smith offered to accept the office building in full settlement of the $1,000,000 promissory note which was about to mature.

During a discussion of the offer by the board of directors, the following opinions were expressed.

Director Adams: "If we give up this building in settlement of this $1,000,000 note payable, we would increase our earnings this year by $200,000, and we would have to correct our prior years' earnings by eliminating all depreciation on the building, because this transaction provides objective evidence that the building has not depreciated. My understanding of accounting principles is that the objectivity principle would require that our accounting treatment of the transaction utilize the objective evidence provided by Smith's offer."

Director Burns: "In my opinion we could accept the offer and not have to recognize any profit. The company would not be receiving cash, receivables, or any other asset so there is no gain involved. The revenue principle of accounting says you must have an inflow of cash or receivables in order to have revenue."

Director Crail: "The corporation received only $800,000 when it issued the note payable, and it has never paid or recorded any interest. Now we will give up an asset that cost $800,000 to discharge a recorded liability of the same amount, so this is a perfect example of the matching principle of accounting and no gain or loss is involved."

Instructions

a Evaluate the opinions expressed by each of the three directors in turn, giving special attention to the references made to an accounting principle. Use a separate paragraph or paragraphs for evaluation of each director's position and indicate what accounting principles are involved.

b Explain how the proposed transaction should be accounted for in your judgment. Indicate the accounting principle or principles you consider to be applicable. Include in your answer whether interest and depreciation should be recognized and the amount of the gain or loss, if any, which would result from acceptance of Smith's offer.

c In the financial statements prepared immediately after carrying out the exchange with Smith, would it be necessary to make any special disclosure of this transaction apart from the normal accounting for disposal of a building? Explain.

d Assuming that the corporation accepts Smith's offer, draft a journal entry to record the transaction. You should assume that depreciation has been recorded for the current year but that the books have not been closed. No interest expense has ever been recorded on the note payable. The entry made at the time of issuing the note payable consisted of a debit to Cash for $800,000, a debit to Discount on Notes Payable for $200,000, and a credit to Notes Payable for $1,000,000. **Suggestion:** The interest applicable to prior years may be debited to Correction of Prior Years' Income (Interest Expense).

1B-4 a Treetop Company, which uses the accrual basis of accounting, owns real estate which it rents to various tenants. The amounts of rent receivable and of unearned rent revenue at two successive balance sheet dates were as follows:

	Dec. 31, 1975	Dec. 31, 1976
Rent receivable	$17,100	$20,250
Unearned rent revenue	10,350	7,650

The amount of rent collected during 1976 was $114,750.

Instructions Compute the amount of rent revenue which should appear in the income statement for the year 1976, using the accrual basis of accounting.

b Treetop Company, which uses the accrual basis of accounting, borrows frequently from its bank and from private lenders by issuing notes payable. The amounts of prepaid interest and interest payable applicable to the various notes payable at two successive balance sheet dates are shown below:

	Dec. 31, 1975	Dec. 31, 1976
Prepaid interest	$1,750	$2,800
Interest payable	4,900	3,500

Interest expense for the year 1976 on the accrual basis was $26,250. For the purpose of this problem, the practice of recording interest as prepaid is to be treated as acceptable.

Instructions Compute the amount of cash payments for interest during 1976.

CHAPTER 2

The accounting process

Accounting has frequently been called the "language of business." This designation is applied to accounting because it is the method of communicating business information. Like other languages, it is undergoing continuous change in an attempt to discover better means of communicating.

The accounting process consists of three major parts: (1) the recording of transactions during the period, (2) the summarizing of information at the end of the period, and (3) the reporting and interpreting of the summary information.

During the accounting period the accountant records transactions as they occur, reflecting the situation as it exists at the time of the transaction. The recording phase of accounting is thus a continuing activity. At the end of each accounting period the accountant carries out the functions of summarizing and reporting. After a trial balance has been prepared to ensure that the double-entry system has maintained an equality of debits and credits, certain adjusting entries are necessary. Some adjustments must be made to the recorded data for changes that have occurred since the transactions were recorded. Other adjustments are needed for events which have not been recorded but which affect the financial position and operating results of the business. Examples of these unrecorded events are depreciation and other expiration of asset services and the accrual of expenses such as interest.

When the records have thus been made as complete, accurate, and up-to-date as possible, the accountant prepares financial statements reflecting financial position and the results of operations. An important measure of the success of the accounting process is the responsiveness of financial reporting to the needs of the users of accounting information.

RECORDING FINANCIAL TRANSACTIONS

If the accounting process is to provide the users of accounting information with reliable, timely reports, transactions during the period must be interpreted in conformity with generally accepted accounting principles and recorded promptly and accurately. A *transaction* is an event that causes a change in the assets, liabilities, or owners' equity of a business entity. Transactions may conveniently be classified into two broad groups: (1) external transactions, or those between the business and another entity, and (2) internal transactions, such as the expiration or transfer of costs within the organization. Examples of this second group include the depreciation of assets, the recognition of obsolescence in inventory, and the transfer of production costs from goods in process to finished goods.

Business papers

A business paper (sometimes called a form, source document, or voucher) is the first record prepared for a transaction. Such papers show the date, amount, and nature of the transaction, and the persons involved. Business papers support entries in the books of original entry; for example, sales invoices support entries in the sales journal. The original copy of a sales invoice is sent to the customer, who uses it as a basis for recording his purchase; a duplicate copy is retained by the seller as evidence of the sale. Some business papers never leave the organization as, for example, cash register tapes, receiving reports, time cards, journal vouchers, and minutes of directors' meetings.

Any verification of financial statements or accounting records is likely to include tests in which summary figures are traced back to the underlying business papers. The practice of identifying each type of business paper with serial numbers and accounting for all numbers in the series helps prevent the unknowing omission of a transaction because of a missing document. Proper design and use of business papers is an important element in the system of internal control, regardless of whether the business uses a simple manual accounting system or sophisticated electronic data processing equipment.

Electronic data processing

The increasing use of computers by business, government, and other organizations has greatly modified the methods of recording, summarizing, and classifying accounting information. The computer not only processes data with incredible speed and a high degree of accuracy, but also permits the classification and summarization of data in more forms and at lower cost than has been possible with the older methods.

The input data for the computer are often on punched cards or tapes, created as a by-product when preparing business papers. The computer output, also on cards or tapes, is read by printers that can produce reports and financial statements of traditional appearance.

In business concerns using sophisticated electronic data processing systems, the recording, classifying, and summarizing steps in creating accounting data may be blended into one. With an *on-line, real-time computer system,* the recording of a transaction causes instantaneous updating of all relevant files. You have probably encountered these on-line, real-time (OLRT) systems at airline ticket offices and in savings and loan associations. At any branch of a savings and loan association, a teller can update a customer's account immediately merely by recording his deposit or withdrawal on a computer terminal. It is not difficult to envision an electronic data processing system which daily produces a set of financial statements or special reports updated to include all transactions to date and also providing the current amounts of accruals for such elements as interest, depreciation, and labor costs.

Although the traditional forms of journals and ledgers are not essential to the electronic data processing of accounting information, the concepts implicit in these records are inherent in a computerized system. Furthermore, the output of the computers can be programmed to provide information in a form similar to traditional journals and ledgers.

Because our primary goal in this book is an understanding of accounting principles rather than expertise in accounting systems, we shall rely upon manual recording methods as the simplest and clearest means of illustrating the application of accounting principles to business transactions.

Double-entry system

The standard accounting model for accumulating data in a business entity consists of the *double-entry system* based on the fundamental accounting equation. As the name implies, the entry made for each transaction is composed of two parts: one or more debits and one or more credits. All accounting entries are made within the framework of the fundamental accounting equation (assets equal liabilities plus owners' equity). Each transaction must therefore be analyzed in terms of its effects on the elements of this equation. The advantages of the double-entry system include built-in controls which automatically call attention to many types of errors and offer assurance that once assets are recorded, they will not be forgotten or simply overlooked. Management's responsibility for the custody of resources entrusted to it is thus strengthened by the internal discipline of the double-entry system. The self-balancing nature of this accounting model facilitates the preparation of a complete integrated set of financial statements as frequently as desired.

The double-entry system is in practically universal use; it takes its name from the fact that equal debit and credit entries are made for every transaction. The terms *debit* and *credit* can be related to the equation $A = L + OE$ in the following way:

Asset accounts	= Liability + Owners' Equity accounts
Increases are recorded by debits	Increases are recorded by credits
Decreases are recorded by credits	Decreases are recorded by debits

Assets and liabilities are the two independent variables in the above equation; the dependent variable, owners' equity, is derived from the valuation assigned to assets and liabilities. One source of change in the owners' equity is the change in the *net assets* (assets minus liabilities) as a result of operations, measured by two classes of temporary accounts—revenue and expenses. Revenue accounts measure the inflow of assets resulting from producing and distributing goods and services to customers. Expense accounts measure the outflow of assets necessary to produce and distribute these goods and services. The net change in the assets as a result of these two flows is reflected in the owners' equity. Revenue and expense accounts are subject to the rules of debit and credit which were applied to the real or permanent accounts (assets, liabilities, and owners' equity). The application of the rules of debit and credit for revenue and expenses may be summarized as follows:

Expenses	Revenue
Increases in expenses are recorded by debits	Increases in revenue are recorded by credits
Decreases in expenses are recorded by credits	Decreases in revenue are recorded by debits

As the terms *debit* and *credit* are used in accounting, they have no meaning except as a directive for recording data in ledger accounts. Debit refers to the left side of the account and credit refers to the right side.

The accounting period

The normal accounting period is one year, beginning on any given day and ending 12 months later. A *calendar-year* accounting period ends on

December 31; all other 12-month accounting periods are known as *fiscal years.* Business firms frequently adopt accounting periods that end when operations are at a low ebb in order to simplify year-end procedures and facilitate a better measurement of income and financial position. Such an accounting period is referred to as a *natural business year* because it conforms to the natural annual cycle of the enterprise.

Statements issued for shorter periods, such as one quarter of the year or one month, are called *interim statements.* These interim reports on the operating results of listed corporations are needed to assist investors in reaching decisions to buy, hold, or sell securities. Traditionally, interim financial statements have not been audited by certified public account-ants. At present, however, there is a new awareness of the need for CPAs to review their clients' interim statements to assure consistency with the annual financial statements.[1]

The accounting cycle

The accounting cycle is a complete sequence of accounting procedures which are repeated in the same order during each accounting period. The cycle in a traditional manual system (and with modifications in an EDP system) includes:

1 Recording transactions in the books of original entry, the journals
2 Classifying data by posting from the journals to the ledger
3 Summarizing data from the ledger on a trial balance
4 Adjusting, correcting, and updating recorded data after due consideration of all pertinent facts
5 Summarizing adjusted data in the form of financial statements
6 Closing the books to summarize the activities of the period
7 Reversing certain adjusting entries to facilitate the recording process in sub-sequent periods

When these steps are completed, the cycle begins again for the next period.

The journals: books of original entry

The information shown on business papers is recorded in chronological order in the appropriate journals. Since a journal is organized chrono-logically by transaction, we may say that the unit of organization for a journal is the individual transaction. Although a very small business could conceivably record all transactions in a single journal, this approach is seldom used. When numerous transactions of the same nature occur (such as transactions involving the receipt of cash), a special journal can be designed as a more efficient means of entering and summarizing these

---

[1] For a discussion of the special measurement problems relating to interim financial state-ments, see *APB Opinion No. 28,* "Interim Financial Statements," AICPA (New York: 1973).

transactions possessing a common characteristic. Several types of special journals are illustrated later in this chapter.

The journalizing process requires analyzing transactions in terms of debits and credits to the accounts they affect: (1) assets, (2) liabilities, (3) owners' equity, (4) revenue, and (5) expenses. In this book our interest in journal entries lies in their usefulness as a clear, concise analytical device. To portray a business transaction in a journal entry, we must identify and classify each important element of the transaction. Such rigorous analysis demands a full understanding of a business event.

The ledger: classification by type

We have indicated how the information on business papers is analyzed and expressed in terms of debits and credits by entry in the journals. Next is the step of transferring this information to accounts in the ledger. This transfer process is called *posting,* which means that each debit and credit amount in the journals is listed in the appropriate account in the ledger.

A ledger consists of a number of accounts. Each account represents stored information about a particular kind of asset, liability, owners' equity, revenue, or expense. As previously indicated, the transaction is the unit of organization for the journal; similarly, the account is the unit of organization for the ledger. When computers are used, accounting information may be stored on magnetic tapes rather than on the loose-leaf pages of a traditional ledger. However, the printed form of ledger page is most convenient for our illustrations and analyses and is still used by many businesses. For our purposes ledger accounts are a conceptual device for discussion of accounting principles rather than specific examples of system design.

Ledger accounts are often classified as *nominal* (temporary) and *real* (permanent) accounts. The nominal accounts are closed at the end of the period by transferring their balances to other accounts. The real accounts are the balance sheet accounts which remain open and normally show a balance after the books are closed. During the accounting period, a balance sheet account or an income statement account may contain both real and nominal elements. In this situation, it is often referred to as a *mixed account.* For example, Unexpired Insurance may include both unexpired premiums and expired premiums before the end-of-period adjusting entries are made. When the time arrives for preparing financial statements, the nominal and real portions of a mixed account are separated by adjusting entries. Thus the nominal element in the Unexpired Insurance account would be transferred to Insurance Expense.

The account form shown at the top of page 42 is illustrative of a ledger account and the information found therein.

In many cases greater detail is desired for a particular account included

				Accounts Receivable				Account No. (7)
Date 19__		Explanation	Ref.	Amount	Date 19__		Explanation	Ref.	Amount
Jan.	1	Balance		12,682	Jan.	24		J70	150
	31		S50	42,460	Jan.	31		CR42	31,780
					Jan.	31	Balance		23,212
				55,142					55,142
Feb.	1	Balance		23,212					

in the general ledger, and a **subsidiary** ledger is set up to contain the details supporting the main or **controlling** account. For example, the controlling account, Accounts Receivable, is perfectly adequate for general purposes; however, in order to facilitate the preparation of monthly bills, it is desirable to have each customer's purchases and payments separately classified. In such situations a subsidiary or detailed ledger is established to provide the desired information. At all times, the total of the detailed ledger should agree with the controlling account in the general ledger.

In addition to the use of a controlling account and subsidiary ledger for accounts receivable, other common examples of this concept include:

A Vouchers Payable controlling account supported by a voucher register (illustrated later in this chapter)

A Plant and Equipment controlling account supported by a plant and equipment subsidiary ledger

A Capital Stock controlling account supported by a stockholders' ledger

Separate sudsidiary ledgers not only provide the detailed information needed for certain purposes, but also strengthen internal control by quickly bringing to light most kinds of errors in recording transactions.

Trial balance

At the end of each period a trial balance of the general ledger is prepared to determine that the mechanics of the recording and posting operations have been carried out accurately. The trial balance consists of a listing of all accounts and their balances; it provides evidence that an equality of debits and credits exists in the ledger. The account balances are then used as a basis for preparing the financial statements. The trial balance illustrated on page 43 summarizes the account balances in the general ledger of the Merchandise Mart.

Schedules of the subsidiary ledgers may also be prepared to prove that their balances agree with the balances in the related controlling accounts which are part of the general ledger. These schedules may also be used for other purposes; for example, a copy of the accounts receiv-

MERCHANDISE MART
Trial Balance
January 31, 19___

	Debit	Credit
Cash	$ 15,450	
Accounts receivable	23,212	
Allowance for uncollectible accounts		$ 850
Inventory	47,860	
Unexpired insurance	200	
Land	45,000	
Building	80,000	
Accumulated depreciation: building		10,000
Equipment	16,000	
Accumulated depreciation: equipment		4,000
Vouchers payable		12,000
Notes payable		10,000
Advances from customers		500
Capital stock: par value $10 per share		75,000
Paid-in capital in excess of par		75,000
Retained earnings		34,363
Net sales		45,627
Cost of goods sold	21,000	
Salaries	9,540	
Advertising expense	4,620	
Delivery expense	2,180	
Property taxes	1,220	
Interest expense	80	
Miscellaneous expense	978	
Totals	$267,340	$267,340

able schedule may be sent to the credit department for use in following up collections and as a basis for setting future credit policy.

MERCHANDISE MART
Schedule of Accounts Receivable
January 31, 19___

D. A. Adams	$ 1,500
R. O. Black	3,410
(not listed here to avoid unnecessary detail)	18,302
Balance of Accounts Receivable controlling account	$23,212

The number of accounts, type of statements, and other aspects of the accounting system should be geared to meet the individual requirements of a particular business; the preceding examples merely suggest the type of system employed in many small and medium-sized businesses.

Use of journals

A growing enterprise is usually compelled to modify its accounting system to handle efficiently the increasing volume of transactions. One purpose of the accounting system is to facilitate the summarization of a large volume of transactions into meaningful totals for various uses. The basic accounting problems for large and small businesses are quite similar; however, the procedures adopted for accumulating and distributing accounting data are frequently quite different. When there is a large volume of data, procedures must be developed which permit the data to be handled rapidly.

Every business, regardless of its size, has certain established routines which are basic to the collection of financial data. For example, source documents are used to initiate transactions or to report their occurrence. As the complexity of the business increases, methods such as the preparation of multicopies of these documents may be instituted; the use of various types of billing machines and mechanical registers may be begun; and in some cases preprinted and standard forms may be employed. In this way the time lag between the initiation of a transaction and its ultimate disposition can be shortened. Obviously, as the volume of similar transactions increases, the degree of automation possible in handling the data increases.

The great majority of financial transactions fall into one of four types, and for that reason most of the data can be handled by using four special multicolumn journals and a general journal. The primary transaction types and the associated journals are:

Type of transaction	Journal
Sales of merchandise on credit	Sales journal
Purchases of merchandise, supplies, etc., on credit	Voucher register (or purchases journal)
Receipts of cash	Cash receipts journal
Payments of cash	Cash payments journal (or check register)
Other transactions	General journal

A set of five journals, similar to those listed, can handle the transactions of many small businesses. The general journal is necessary, regardless of the special journals involved, to record unusual and nonrepetitive transactions and also to record adjusting and closing entries at the end of the period.

The following journal forms are presented merely as an illustration of one form for each journal. The columnar headings will obviously be dictated by the circumstances of each business.

Illustration The Merchandise Mart uses special multicolumn journals to facilitate the handling of the transactions involving sales, purchases, cash collections, and disbursements. Subsidiary ledgers are used for accounts receivable and accounts payable.

The procedure for recording sales requires that all credit sales be entered at the gross amount in the sales journal and all cash sales in the cash receipts journal. There is no need for a breakdown of sales by item or department and the accounts receivable ledger is posted from the sales journal. When the individual accounts are posted, a check mark is placed beside the amount in the journal. The total of the one money column is posted monthly as a debit to Accounts Receivable, account no. 7, and a credit to Sales, account no. 115. All credit sales are subject to terms 2/10, n/30.

		Sales Journal			(Page 50)
Date 19__		Customer	Inv. no.	Ref.	Amount
Jan.	2	D. A. Adams	1001	√	600
	3	R. O. Black	1002	√	850
	5	Dan Crane	1003	√	1,020
	28	A. R. Taylor	1025	√	690
	29	Jack Urbanks	1026	√	1,215
					42,460
					(7) (115)
					Dr, A/R
					Cr, Sales

All cash receipts are recorded in the cash receipts journal (see page 46) from a detailed list of checks received by mail, a statement by the internal auditor of daily cash sales and store collections, and a statement by the treasurer of other cash sources. If a credit customer takes the cash discount offered, it is recorded at the time cash is received. The customers' accounts are posted daily from the cash receipts journal. The sundry general ledger accounts are posted weekly from the Other Accounts columns, and the column totals are posted monthly except for the Other Accounts columns, for which totals are not posted (N/P). The

Cash Receipts Journal

Date 19__	Explanation	Debits Cash	Sales discounts	Other accounts Name	Ref.	Amount	Accounts receivable ✓	Amount	Credits Cash sales	Other accounts Name	Ref.	Amount
Jan. 2	1st Union Bank	10,000								Notes Payable	71	10,000
5	D. A. Adams	833	17				✓	850				
6	Cash sales	452							452			
8	Dan Crane	98	2	Notes Receivable	8	920	✓	1,020				
31	Cash sales	800							800			
		46,807	256			1,240		31,780	3,423			13,100
		(1)	(117)			N/P		(7)	(115)			N/P

Voucher Register

Date 19__	Payee	Explanation	Ck. no.	Vou. no.	Credit vouchers payable	Debits Purchases	Freight-in	Accrued payroll	Other accounts Account	Ref.	Amount
Jan. 2	Adams Supply Co.	Merchandise		1500	8,000	8,000					
2	Bross Trucking	Freight	1001	1501	50		50				
5	1st Union Bank	Pay note and interest	1002	1502	4,040				Notes Payable	71	4,000
									Interest Expense	170	40
31	Ace Co.	Merchandise		1598	900	900					
					44,920	31,680	980	8,220			4,040
					(70)	(104)	(105)	(72)			(N/P)

treasurer is furnished with a daily statement of receipts to facilitate cash planning.

The Merchandise Mart has found that control over cash disbursements is improved with the use of the voucher system. The voucher register is a subsidiary ledger record of vouchers payable, as well as the book of original entry for purchases. The system of internal control requires that all checks be supported by a voucher. At the time a voucher is paid, the check number is entered in the appropriate column of the voucher register. Any vouchers entered in the register without check numbers are unpaid and constitute the liability to vendors at that time. Note in the illustrative journal on page 46 that voucher no. 1500 has not been paid and that voucher no. 1501 was paid by check no. 1001. The totals of the special columns are posted monthly and the individual accounts in the Other Accounts columns are posted at least once a month. The total liability represented by unpaid vouchers may include certain vouchers from the preceding month.

In this system the check register is designed as the book of original entry for all cash disbursements. The requirement that all disbursements be supported by a voucher means that only one column is needed in the check register. The total of this one column is posted to the Vouchers Payable account as a debit and the Cash account as a credit. Recording the payment in the subsidiary record of vouchers payable, the voucher register, is done by simply entering the check number in the voucher register. The totals of the check register are posted monthly; however, the treasurer is notified daily of the total checks written.

Check Register (Page 60)

Date 19__		Payee	Vou. no.	Check no.	Amount
Jan.	5	Bross Trucking	1501	1001	50
	5	1st Union Bank	1502	1002	4,040
	31	Dart Brothers	1593	1090	570
					42,690
					(70) (1)
					Dr, V/P
					Cr, Cash

The general journal is used as the book of original entry for all transactions which do not involve accounts represented in the special journals and for adjusting, closing, and reversing entries. The vast majority of all transactions will normally be recorded in the special journals.

The posting instructions for the illustrated entries in the general journal are: Post the debits and credits to the accounts in the general ledger indicated by the account numbers in the ledger page column. Post the $150 credit to the accounts receivable subsidiary ledger to the credit of John Doe. The check mark indicates that the posting to the subsidiary ledger has been completed.

		General Journal			(Page 70)
Date 19__		Account titles and explanations	LP	Debit	Credit
June	30	Interest Expense	140	30	
		Accrued Interest Payable	72		30
		Interest accrued at end of fiscal year on $12,000,			
		6% note.			
	30	Allowance for Uncollectible Accounts	8	150	
		Accounts Receivable—John Doe	7/ √		150
		Write off John Doe account of $150, which is			
		uncollectible.			

ADJUSTING ENTRIES

Financial reporting on an annual, quarterly, or monthly basis requires the accountant to summarize the operations of the business for a specific time period. Transactions which were recorded during the period in balance sheet or income statement accounts may affect two or more accounting periods, and an end-of-period adjustment may therefore be needed. Some financial events not recognized on a day-to-day basis must be recorded at the end of the period to bring the accounts up to date. If one should choose to record depreciation daily or to accrue interest expense daily, no adjustment for depreciation or interest expense would be needed at the end of the accounting period except to correct errors.

Note that almost every adjusting entry affects both a balance sheet account and an income statement account. This characteristic of adjusting entries reflects their dual purpose of (1) proper valuation of assets and liabilities and (2) proper measurement of income.

In illustrating the wide variety of adjusting entries, it will be helpful to classify them into the following major groups:

Apportionment of recorded costs
Apportionment of recorded revenue
Accrual of unrecorded expenses
Accrual of unrecorded revenue
Valuation of receivables

Apportionment of recorded costs

Costs which will benefit more than one accounting period are frequently incurred. These costs must be apportioned between periods in a manner which approximates the usefulness derived from the goods and services in the production of revenue; this apportionment process is a necessary step in determining net income of each period.

The assignment of the periodic depreciation charge is an example of a cost apportionment adjusting entry, as shown below:

Depreciation Expense	*12,000*	
Accumulated Depreciation: Building		*12,000*
To record the expense of using the building for a year.		

The periodic depreciation expense is considered a cost of production or a period expense to be deducted from earned revenue, depending on the nature of the asset and the service performed. The Accumulated Depreciation account is deducted from the cost of the asset.

Cost apportionment is also involved in accounting for other prepayments. The adjusting entry will vary, however, depending on the accounting procedure followed in recording the original transaction.

To illustrate, assume that office supplies are acquired during the year at a cost of $5,000. At the end of the accounting period a physical inventory reveals that supplies on hand are worth $550. At the time the supplies were acquired, the $5,000 purchase may have been debited to (1) an asset account, or (2) an expense account. The required adjusting entry for each situation is as follows:

Purchase Debited to Asset Account   The adjusting entry required is to transfer the *expired* portion of the cost to an *expense* account.

	Office Supplies Inventory		*Office Supplies Expense*	
Dec. 31				
Balance	*5,000*			
Adjusting entry		*4,450*	*4,450*	

Purchase Debited to Expense Account   The adjusting entry required is to transfer the *unexpired* portion of the cost to an *asset* account as illustrated on page 50.

Under either original recording, the final result is the same. There is an asset valued at $550 and an expense of $4,450. In both cases the amount of the unexpired cost was determined; the adjusting entry is that

	Office Supplies Inventory		Office Supplies Expense	
Dec. 31				
Balance			5,000	
Adjusting entry	550			550

entry necessary to make the respective accounts agree with the information available to the accountant. Adjusting entries are based on recorded data in the relevant accounts and the additional information ascertained by the accountant.

Apportionment of recorded revenue

Occasionally a business will receive payment for goods and services before the goods are delivered or the service performed. A liability exists which will be satisfied when performance takes place. When cash is received, the original transaction may be recorded in either of two ways: (1) a liability account may be credited, or (2) a revenue account may be credited.

Assume that customers paid in $500,000 for magazine subscriptions during the current year; however, $75,000 represented payments for copies to be delivered in subsequent periods. The adjusting entries for each of the two methods of recording the cash receipt are:

Liability Account Credited upon Receipt of Cash The required adjusting entry to recognize the *earned* revenue for the period appears below:

	Unearned Subscriptions Revenue		Subscriptions Revenue	
Dec. 31				
Balance		500,000		
Adjusting entry	425,000			425,000

Revenue Account Credited upon Receipt of Cash The required adjusting entry is to transfer the *unearned* revenue to a liability account.

	Unearned Subscriptions Revenue		Subscriptions Revenue	
Dec. 31				
Balance				500,000
Adjusting entry		75,000	75,000	

Accrual of unrecorded expenses

The incurring of certain expenses is related to the passage of time. These expenses are usually not recorded until payment is required, unless the end of the accounting period comes before the required date of payment. Interest charges and salaries are typical of the expenses which accrue with the passage of time and which are recorded only when paid, except when the end of the accounting period occurs between the time the expense was incurred and the payment is due. In order to achieve a realistic measurement of the expenses of the period, an adjusting entry is necessary to record such an expense and the corresponding liability.

For example, interest of $18,000 on a $600,000 note payable is paid on March 1 and September 1 of each year. If the expenses and liabilities are to be properly reported at December 31, a year-end adjusting entry should be made as shown below:

Interest Expense *12,000*
    Accrued Interest Payable *12,000*
To record the interest owed on a 6%, $600,000 note for four months to Dec. 31.

Accrual of unrecorded revenue

Revenue which has been earned but not recorded must be recognized at the end of the accounting period. For example, revenue which is earned on assets leased to others or on interest-bearing loans is seldom recorded until the cash is received, except at the end of the accounting period. In order to measure properly the results of operations and to avoid shifting income between periods, revenue should be recognized in the period earned.

To illustrate, assume that rents totaling $625 which have been earned but not collected for the month of December have not been recorded. The following year-end adjusting entry is required for a complete reporting of revenue and assets.

Rent Receivable *625*
    Rent Revenue *625*
To record the rent earned during December.

The revenue is earned because the space has been available to the tenants in accordance with the terms of the lease. The receivable is a legitimate current asset based on the contract between the two parties.

Valuation of receivables

A policy of making sales on credit almost inevitably results in some receivables which prove wholly or partially uncollectible. To achieve a logical matching of revenue and related expenses, the estimated expense arising from sales on credit should be recognized in the period in which the sales occur. This estimate of probable expense from the granting of credit requires a year-end adjusting entry to revise the valuation originally assigned to accounts receivable. Once the estimate of the uncollectible accounts is established, the following adjusting entry is made:

Uncollectible Accounts Expense	*2,500*	
Allowance for Uncollectible Accounts		*2,500*
To record estimated uncollectible accounts expense.		

The Uncollectible Accounts Expense account is usually included as an operating expense on the income statement. Some accountants would prefer to deduct it from the revenue of the period to derive a measure of net sales, since no revenue will be realized if the receivables will not be collected. On the balance sheet the credit balance of the allowance account is deducted from accounts receivable to indicate the net collections expected.

CLOSING PROCEDURES

Closing revenue and expense accounts

Revenue and expense accounts are closed at the end of each accounting period by transferring the balances in each such account to a summary account, Income Summary. Revenue and expense accounts are merely extensions of the owners' equity account and are used to provide additional information about the business in each operating period. Once this information has been summarized, the accounts have served their purpose and the net increase or decrease in owners' equity is transferred to an owners' equity account. Thus the closing of the books keeps separate the accounting activities of each period.

If we assume that a Subscriptions Revenue account after adjustment has a credit balance of $425,000, the closing entry will be:

Subscriptions Revenue	*425,000*	
Income Summary		*425,000*
To close the Subscriptions Revenue account.		

The balance in the Subscriptions Revenue account is now zero. Temporarily, the Income Summary account will indicate a credit balance of $425,000. All other revenue accounts will be closed similarly.

To close an expense account, one must transfer its debit balance to the left side of the Income Summary account. The following journal entry to close a Salaries Expense account with a debit balance of $61,625 is illustrative of this phase of the closing process.

Income Summary.	61,625	
Salaries Expense		61,625
To close the Salaries Expense account.		

The expense account now has a zero balance, and the balance in the Income Summary account is reduced by the debit for salaries expense. All other expense accounts will be closed similarly. When there are a number of expense accounts, each one can be closed individually to the Income Summary account or all of them can be closed in one journal entry, with one debit to the Income Summary account and a separate credit for each expense account closed.

Closing inventory and related accounts

The entry to establish the cost of goods sold for the period and the ending inventory balance may be thought of as an adjusting entry; however, since there may be little need for a ledger account for cost of goods sold, the adjusting and closing entries are frequently combined. This procedure is accomplished by closing the beginning inventory account, purchases, and all related accounts to the Income Summary. The ending inventory is then established by debiting the Inventory account and crediting the Income Summary. The balance remaining in the Income Summary account is the cost of goods sold for the period. To illustrate, let us assume the following facts: January 1 inventory, $80,000; purchases, $275,000; freight-in, $40,000; purchase returns and allowances, $2,500; December 31 inventory, including applicable freight, $60,000. The journal entries required to close the accounts and to record the ending inventory are as shown at the top of page 54.

Purchase Returns and Allowances	2,500	
Income Summary	392,500	
Inventory, Jan. 1		80,000
Purchases		275,000
Freight-in		40,000

To close beginning inventory and cost of goods acquired for the period.

Inventory, Dec. 31	60,000	
Income Summary		60,000

To record the ending inventory.

The debit balance in the Income Summary account after these two entries is $332,500, the cost of goods sold for the period. Some accountants prefer to use a separate account, Cost of Goods Sold, to summarize the merchandising accounts before these costs are transferred to the Income Summary.

The entry for inventory and purchases data *reflecting cost of goods sold as a separate account* is:

Purchase Returns and Allowances	2,500	
Inventory, Dec. 31	60,000	
Cost of Goods Sold	332,500	
Inventory, Jan. 1		80,000
Purchases		275,000
Freight-in		40,000

To record cost of goods sold.

The entry required to close the Cost of Goods Sold account is illustrated below:

Income Summary	332,500	
Cost of Goods Sold		332,500

To close the Cost of Goods Sold account.

Closing the Income Summary account

At this point the balance of the Income Summary account indicates the income or loss of the business as a result of the operations of the period.

A credit balance in the Income Summary account indicates a profitable year and an increase in owners' equity. A debit balance indicates a loss from operations and a decrease in owners' equity: that is, the expenses of the period exceeded the revenue. The Income Summary account is closed by transferring its balance to Retained Earnings.

REVERSING ENTRIES

After the books have been adjusted and closed at the end of the year, reversing entries may be made bearing the date of the new accounting period. The purpose of the reversing entries is to simplify the recording of routine transactions by disposing of the accrued items (assets and liabilities), which were entered in balance sheet accounts through the adjusting entries. A reversing entry, as the name implies, is the exact reverse of an adjusting entry. It consists of the same accounts and dollar amounts as the adjusting entry, but the debits and credits are reversed and the date is the beginning of the new period.

For example, assume that X Company owes a long-term, 6% note payable for $200,000 and pays interest of $3,000 every three months. The last payment of the current year was made on October 31; the next interest payment is due on January 31. The company is on a calendar-year basis. Before the books are closed on December 31, an adjusting entry must be made debiting Interest Expense and crediting Accrued Interest Payable for $2,000, the amount of interest applicable to November and December. If no reversing entry is made, the next quarterly interest payment of $3,000 at January 31 will be recorded by debiting Accrued Interest Payable $2,000, debiting Interest Expense $1,000, and crediting Cash $3,000. However, assume that on January 1 the following reversing entry is made:

Jan. 1	Accrued Interest Payable	2,000	
	Interest Expense		2,000
	To reverse the interest accrual made Dec. 31.		

This reversing entry has eliminated the liability account Accrued Interest Payable and has caused the Interest Expense account to start off the new year with a $2,000 credit balance. Consequently, the cash payment of three months' interest at January 31 will not need to be apportioned. The January 31 entry will consist simply of a debit to Interest Expense for $3,000 and a credit to Cash for $3,000. In other words, the interest payment at January 31 (by reason of the reversing entry) can be recorded in exactly the same manner as the three other quarterly interest payments during the year. After the January 31 interest payment has been recorded, the Interest Expense account for the new year will contain a debit for $3,000 and a credit for $2,000 which produces the correct debit balance of $1,000 representing January interest expense.

An argument for reversing entries is apparent from this example. Clerical employees with little knowledge of accounting can be instructed to follow a standard procedure for recording all operating transactions of a given category. The reversing entries as well as the year-end adjusting entries are recorded in the general journal by an accountant who understands the issues involved.

Adjusting entries which are not to be reversed

Adjusting entries which allocate to expense the expired portion of a cost originally recorded as an asset should not be reversed. Examples are adjusting entries for depreciation and for the amortization of intangible assets. The adjusting entry to record uncollectible accounts expense and adjust the allowance for uncollectible accounts is another example of an adjusting entry which should not be reversed. In brief, reversing entries should not be made for adjusting entries which transfer expired costs from asset accounts to expense accounts. To reverse such adjusting entries would reinstate expired costs as assets, which is certainly not a defensible action.

Similar reasoning tells us that adjusting entries which transfer to revenue the earned portion of a receipt originally recorded as a liability should not be reversed. To reverse such an adjusting entry would reinstate a liability which no longer exists.

Adjusting entries which are commonly reversed

When adjusting entries are made **to accrue expenses** at the end of the accounting period, the making of reversing entries will often simplify the later transactions when the expenses are paid. The example of reversing the adjusting entry to accrue interest expense on a note payable has already been illustrated. Other adjusting entries to accrue expenses at year-end, for which reversing entries may be helpful, are the accrual of wages and salaries expense, and the accrual of water, light, heat, telephone, and similar expenses.

Another group of adjusting entries, for which reversing entries may be helpful, consists of adjustments **to accrue revenue** at year-end. A common example is interest earned on notes receivable and investments in bonds. The following example illustrates the effect of reversing entries for accrued revenue.

The interest revenue on notes receivable for the year represented by cash collections totals $500 and the uncollected interest accrued at year-end totals $75. The appropriate ledger accounts appear as follows after making the year-end adjustment and closing the accounts:

	Interest Revenue		Accrued Interest Receivable	
Dec. 31				
Balance		500		
Adjusting entry		75	75	
Closing entry	575			

If the reversing entry is made and subsequently cash of $125, representing interest collections, is received, the accounts will appear as follows:

	Interest Revenue		Accrued Interest Receivable	
Dec. 31				
Balance		500		
Adjusting entry		75	75	
Closing entry	575			
Jan. 1				
Reversing entry	75			75
Collection		125		

The $50 credit balance in the Interest Revenue account is the interest earned in the second year. If the reversing entry had not been made, this transaction would be recorded as follows:

Cash	125	
Interest Revenue		50
Accrued Interest Receivable		75

To record the collection of interest accrued at the end of the previous year and since.

If the year-end accrual had represented the accrued interest on several notes, the task of separating the accrual on each note would be a tedious and time-consuming job which could have been facilitated by the use of the reversing entry.

When advance payments (as for magazine subscriptions) are received from customers for services to be rendered, the debit to Cash may be offset by a credit either to a liability account (Unearned Subscriptions Revenue) or to a revenue account (Subscriptions Revenue). Assume that the entry to record the original transaction contains a credit to the liability account. Then, the year-end adjusting entry will transfer the earned portion from the liability account to a revenue account and no reversing entry should be made.

On the other hand, assume that the company's policy is to record subscriptions when received as credits to a revenue account. Then, the year-end adjustment will transfer the unearned portion to a liability account, and a reversing entry will be helpful. This latter situation in which revenue is credited in the original transaction is illustrated below.

	Unearned Subscriptions Revenue		Subscriptions Revenue	
Dec. 31				
Balance				500,000
Adjusting entry		75,000	75,000	
Closing entry			425,000	
Jan. 1				
Reversing entry	75,000			75,000

A parallel line of reasoning applies with respect to expenditures for such items as office supplies and insurance premiums. The cost may be debited to an asset account (such as Office Supplies Inventory or Unexpired Insurance). In this case, the year-end adjustment will transfer the expired portion to expense, and no reversing entry should be made.

On the other hand, assume that the payment is debited to an expense account (such as Office Supplies Expense or Insurance Expense) on the assumption that the benefits will probably be consumed during the year. If some portion of the amount recorded as expense has not been consumed by year-end, an adjusting entry is made to transfer the unexpired portion from the expense account to an asset account. A reversing entry will be helpful as illustrated below.

	Office Supplies Inventory		Office Supplies Expense	
Dec. 31				
Balance			5,000	
Adjusting entry	550			550
Closing entry				4,450
Jan. 1				
Reversing entry		550	550	

The ideas implicit in these illustrations may be summarized as follows: Reversing entries may be desirable for adjusting entries which:

1 Accrue expenses for which cash payments are to be made later
2 Accrue revenue earned for which cash collections are to be received later
3 Transfer the unearned portion of recorded revenue to a liability account
4 Transfer unexpired costs from expense accounts to asset accounts

WORKING-PAPER TECHNIQUES

Accountants have found the work sheet to be an invaluable aid in facilitating the year-end procedures and statement preparation. Working papers are especially useful in avoiding errors in the journal and ledger in more complex situations.

Purpose of the work sheet

A work sheet is a columnar sheet of paper designed to facilitate the organization and arrangement of the accounting data required at the end of the period. It is designed to minimize errors by automatically bringing to light many types of discrepancies which might otherwise be entered in the permanent accounting records. The accountant prepares the working paper as an informal record strictly for his own purposes. It does not replace any record or financial statement and is never presented as the end result of the accountant's work. The work sheet is a tool which permits the adjusting and closing entries and the financial statements to be prepared informally before any part of this work is formalized.

The work sheet may be thought of as a testing ground on which the ledger accounts are adjusted, balanced, and arranged in the general form of financial statements. The satisfactory completion of the work sheet provides considerable assurance that all the details of the year-end accounting procedures have been properly brought together. The finished work sheet then serves as the source or guide for the preparation of the formal financial statements and the adjusting and closing entries which are recorded in the journal and posted to the ledger.

Illustration of work sheet for a merchandising firm

A commonly used form of work sheet with appropriate headings for Village Store is illustrated on pages 62 and 63. The work-sheet heading should contain the name of the company, the title (work sheet), and the period covered. The body of this working paper contains six pairs of money columns, each pair consisting of a debit and credit column. The procedures required in the preparation of the work sheet are described below.

1 Enter the ledger account titles and balances on the work sheet, using the first two money columns—the Unadjusted Trial Balance. The accountant can often save time and effort by arranging the accounts in the order in which they will appear on the financial statements. Frequently several adjustments will affect a single account; consequently, several lines should be left blank following this account to facilitate listing the adjustments.

2 Enter the adjustments in the Adjustments columns. Adjusting entries should always be entered on the work sheet before they are journalized. One of the functions of the work sheet is to establish the correctness of the adjusting entries. The information used as the basis for the adjustments illustrated on the work sheet for Village Store is stated below.

(*a*) The marketable securities are government bonds on which accrued interest receivable amounts to $33 at December 31.

(*b*) The accounts receivable arising from sales of the current period which are expected to be uncollectible are estimated to be $\frac{1}{2}$ of 1% of gross sales.

(*c*) Accounts totaling $520 are considered to be uncollectible and the credit manager has authorized the write-off of these accounts.

(*d*) The Prepayments account is composed of (1) unexpired insurance at January 1 of $750, the unexpired portion of a three-year policy acquired at a cost of $900; (2) miscellaneous supplies inventory balance at January 1 of $600; and (3) prepaid rent at January 1 of $150. The miscellaneous supplies inventory at December 31 is found to be composed of items with a cost of $700. The building occupied by Village Store is leased from Roberts Rental Company for six more years at the same monthly rental of $400 per month; the rent for January of the next year has been paid.

(*e*) The furniture and fixtures are estimated to have a useful life of 10 years, with no salvage value at the end of that time.

(*f*) Accrued interest payable on the notes payable amounted to $40 at December 31.

(*g*) Salaries accrued since the last payday total $818 at December 31.

(*h*) The inventory on December 31 totals $28,900.

(*i*) Income taxes are estimated at $669.

After the adjustments (*a*) through (*g*) are entered on the work sheet, the Adjustments columns must be totaled to prove the equality of the debits and credits. Without this proof of arithmetical accuracy, errors are likely to be carried forward in the remaining work.

3 Determine the new account balances and enter these in the Adjusted Trial Balance columns. The purpose of this step is merely to prove the accuracy of the work of combining the adjustments and the original balances. The Adjusted Trial Balance columns are often omitted from the work sheet if adjustments are few.

4 Extend each balance from the adjusted trial balance or from the first four columns into the Income Statement, Retained Earnings, or Balance Sheet columns.

5 Enter the ending inventory in the Income Statement credit column and the Balance Sheet debit column. This procedure in effect deducts the ending inventory from the total goods available for sale to leave the costs comprising the cost of goods sold in the Income Statement columns.

6 Total the Income Statement columns. The balancing figure is the income or loss for the period before income taxes.

7 Compute the income taxes and related income tax liability at the applicable rates based on the income before taxes. Since the Adjustments columns have been balanced, this adjustment is entered in the Income Statement debit column as a revenue deduction and in the Balance Sheet credit column as a liability.

8 Balance the Income Statement columns with the income taxes included. The difference between the credit and debit columns in this illustration represents the earnings of the business entity. The balancing figure is entered in the debit column of the Income Statement to achieve equality and in the credit column of the retained earnings reconciliation. The income after taxes represents an increase in the stockholders' equity as a result of operations.

9 Balance the Retained Earnings columns and enter the difference in the debit column and in the credit column of the Balance Sheet. This adjusts the retained earnings balance for changes during the period.

10 Total the Balance Sheet columns. Considerable assurance of the arithmetical accuracy of the year-end procedures is provided if these two columns balance. The Balance Sheet columns prove the equation that assets are equal to the total of liabilities and stockholders' equity.

Although the work sheet proves the mathematical accuracy of what has been done, it does not prove that some important adjustments have not been omitted.

Working Papers and Year-end Procedures The accountant's working papers are the source of the formal adjusting entries. Once the entries are made on the work sheet, the accountant can easily record the identical information in the general journal and the ledger. The adjusting journal entries for Village Store are illustrated below and on page 64.

Adjusting Entries

(a)	Accrued Interest Receivable....................	33	
	Interest Revenue.......................		33
	To accrue interest on marketable securities owned.		
(b)	Uncollectible Accounts Expense	875	
	Allowance for Uncollectible Accounts		875
	To increase the allowance for uncollectible accounts by $\frac{1}{2}$ of 1% of gross sales.		
(c)	Allowance for Uncollectible Accounts	520	
	Accounts Receivable		520
	To write off uncollectible accounts.		
(d)	Prepayments	50	
	Insurance Expense	300	
	Rent Expense		250
	Miscellaneous Expenses		100
	To adjust prepayments to year-end balance.		
(e)	Depreciation Expense	600	
	Accumulated Depreciation................		600
	To record depreciation at 10% of cost.		
(f)	Interest Expense......................	40	
	Accrued Interest Payable		40
	To accrue interest expense on notes payable.		

VILLAGE STORE
Work Sheet
For the Year Ended December 31, 19___

	Unadjusted trial balance		Adjustments		Adjusted trial balance		Income statement		Retained earnings		Balance sheet	
	Debit	Credit	Debit	Credit	Debit	Credit	Debit	Credit	Debit	Credit	Debit	Credit
Cash	8,650				8,650						8,650	
Marketable securities	2,000				2,000						2,000	
Accounts receivable	15,700			(c) 520	15,180						15,180	
Allowance for uncollectible accounts		800	(c) 520	(b) 875		1,155						1,155
Inventory	28,000				28,000		28,000	28,900			28,900	
Prepayments	1,500		(d) 50		1,550						1,550	
Furniture and fixtures	6,000				6,000						6,000	
Accumulated depreciation		1,800		(e) 600		2,400						2,400
Accounts payable		10,000				10,000						10,000
Notes payable		4,000				4,000						4,000
Capital stock		40,000				40,000						40,000
Retained earnings, Jan. 1		3,170				3,170				3,170		
Dividends	1,500				1,500				1,500			
Sales		175,000				175,000		175,000				
Sales returns & allowances	2,500				2,500		2,500					
Sales discounts	3,150				3,150		3,150					
Purchases	128,000				128,000		128,000					
Purchase returns & allowances		3,000				3,000		3,000				

Account	Trial Balance Dr	Trial Balance Cr	Adjustments Dr	Adjustments Cr	Adjusted Trial Balance Dr	Adjusted Trial Balance Cr	Income Statement Dr	Income Statement Cr	Retained Earnings Dr	Retained Earnings Cr	Balance Sheet Dr	Balance Sheet Cr
Salaries expense	22,500		(g) 818		23,318		23,318					
Rent expense	5,050			(d) 250	4,800		4,800					
Advertising expense	9,000				9,000		9,000					
Janitorial services	1,500				1,500		1,500					
Miscellaneous expenses	2,000			(d) 100	1,900		1,900					
Interest expense	120		(f) 40		160		160					
Property taxes	600				600		600					
Accrued interest receivable			(a) 33		33						33	
Interest revenue				(a) 33		33		33				
Uncollectible accounts expense			(b) 875		875		875					
Insurance expense			(d) 300		300		300					
Depreciation expense			(e) 600		600		600					
Accrued interest payable				(f) 40		40						40
Accrued salaries payable				(g) 818		818						818
Totals	237,770	237,770	3,236	3,236	239,616	239,616	204,703	206,933				
Income before income taxes							2,230					
Totals							206,933	206,933				
Income before income taxes								2,230				
Income taxes							669					669
Net income							1,561			1,561	1,561	
Totals									1,500	3,231		
Retained earnings, Dec. 31									3,231			3,231
Totals									4,731	4,731	62,313	62,313

(g) Salaries Expense *818*
        Accrued Salaries Payable *818*
    To accrue unpaid salaries.

(h) Income Summary *153,000*
    Purchase Returns and Allowances *3,000*
        Purchases *128,000*
        Inventory, Jan. 1 . . . .   *28,000*
    To close beginning inventory and net purchases.

    Inventory, Dec. 31 . . . .   *28,900*
        Income Summary *28,900*
    To record the ending inventory balance.

(i) Income Taxes Expense *669*
    Income Taxes Payable *669*
    To record estimated tax liability.

The closing entries can also be made by using the data in the Income Statement columns. When working papers are prepared, the closing process is usually summarized in one compound entry, as shown in the entry below. Note that the inventory and cost of goods acquired have been closed in entry **(h)** above.

Closing Entries

Sales *175,000*
Interest Revenue *33*
    Sales Returns and Allowances *2,500*
    Sales Discounts *3,150*
    Salaries Expense *23,318*
    Rent Expense *4,800*
    Advertising Expense *9,000*
    Janitorial Services *1,500*
    Miscellaneous Expenses *1,900*
    Interest Expense *160*
    Property Taxes *600*
    Uncollectible Accounts Expense *875*
    Insurance Expense *300*
    Depreciation Expense *600*
    Income Taxes Expense *669*
    Income Summary *125,661*
To close revenue and expense accounts to Income Summary.

Income Summary *1,561*
    Retained Earnings *1,561*
To close net income to retained earnings.

Retained Earnings	1,500	
Dividends		1,500
To close Dividends account.		

Illustration for a manufacturing firm

The procedures for preparing working papers for a manufacturing firm are similar to those used for a merchandising firm. The addition of a pair of columns to summarize the manufacturing operation is the major difference. These columns merely allow for one more step in the classification of the data. The adjusted trial balance, which is an optional step, is omitted from this illustration.

The following data are the basis for the adjusting entries included in the work sheet for Cole Manufacturing Company on pages 68 and 69.

(a) Uncollectible accounts expense is estimated to be $3,000 for the current year.

(b) A three-year insurance policy was purchased 18 months ago at a cost of $1,800. The insurance expense should be divided between miscellaneous factory costs and general expense on an 80-20 basis.

(c) The wages accrued since the last pay period amount to direct labor $1,800 and indirect labor $950. The officers, office staff, and salesmen are paid monthly on the last day of the month.

(d) The bonds payable bear interest at the rate of 6%, with interest payable April 1 and October 1.

(e) Depreciation for the plant assets is computed using the straight-line method on the following basis:

Asset	Life, years,	Salvage	Cost allocation, %	
			Factory	General
Building	40	$ –0–	80	20
Machinery & equipment	10	–0–	100	–0–
Furniture & fixtures	20	2,000	10	90

(f) Research and development costs applicable to production during the year are estimated to total $8,000.

(g) The light bill for December has not been received as of December 31. Based on past experience, the cost applicable to December is estimated to be $1,450.

(h) An inventory of factory supplies on December 31 indicates that supplies costing $850 are on hand.

(*i*) Physical inventory counts and reasonable estimates indicate that the cost of inventories at December 31 is:

Finished goods	$41,500
Goods in process	26,350
Raw materials	12,650

(*j*) The income tax rate applicable to profits of Cole Manufacturing Company is assumed to be 50%.

Working Papers and Year-end Procedures The entries for closing the manufacturing accounts, for adjusting the inventory balances, for closing the revenue and expense accounts, and for closing the Dividends account are illustrated below for Cole Manufacturing Company.

Cost of Goods Manufactured	434,770	
Raw Materials, Dec. 31	12,650	
Goods in Process, Dec. 31	26,350	
Purchase Returns and Allowances	4,000	
Raw Materials, Jan. 1		8,000
Goods in Process, Jan. 1		21,000
Raw Material Purchases		125,000
Transportation-in		3,500
Direct Labor Costs		194,300
Indirect Labor Costs		73,550
Heat, Light, and Power		13,750
Miscellaneous Factory Costs		14,630
Depreciation: Building		3,000
Depreciation: Machinery and Equipment		13,000
Depreciation: Furniture and Fixtures		40
Research and Development Costs		8,000

To record the ending inventory of raw materials, goods in process, and cost of goods manufactured.

Finished Goods Inventory, Dec. 31	41,500	
Cost of Goods Sold	441,270	
Cost of Goods Manufactured		434,770
Finished Goods Inventory, Jan. 1		48,000

To record the finished goods inventory and the cost of goods sold.

Sales	633,600	
Cost of Goods Sold		441,270
Sales Returns and Allowances		3,600
Advertising		35,000
Sales Salaries		42,000
Delivery Expenses		8,000
Administrative Salaries		50,000
Office Salaries		20,000
Telephone and Telegraph		1,800
Miscellaneous General Expense		2,920
Interest Expense		4,500
Uncollectible Accounts Expense		3,000
Depreciation: Building		750
Depreciation: Furniture and Fixtures		360
Income Taxes Expense		10,200
Income Summary		10,200
To close revenue and expense accounts.		
Income Summary	10,200	
Retained Earnings		10,200
To close the net income into retained earnings.		
Retained Earnings	6,000	
Dividends		6,000
To close Dividends account.		

Statement of cost of goods manufactured

The cost of the goods completed during an accounting period is summarized in a statement of cost of goods manufactured. The information
for such a statement, illustrated on page 70 for the Cole Manufacturing
Company, is taken from the Manufacturing columns of the work sheet.

Using accounting data

The ultimate objective of accounting is the *use* of accounting information,
through analysis and interpretation as a basis for business decisions.
Information derived from accounting records serves management in
controlling current operations and in planning future operations. Published financial statements afford outsiders a means of analyzing and
interpreting past operations of businesses in which they have an interest.
These published financial statements have traditionally been for the most
part reports of past events. The past is often the key to the future,
however, and for this reason accounting information is highly valued by
decision makers both inside and outside the firm.

COLE MANUFACTURING COMPANY
Work Sheet
For the Year Ended December 31, 19___

	Unadjusted trial balance Debit	Credit	Adjustments Debit	Credit	Manufacturing Debit	Credit	Income statement Debit	Credit	Retained earnings Debit	Credit	Balance sheet Debit	Credit
Cash	32,000										32,000	
Accounts receivable	70,000										70,000	
Allowance for uncollectible accounts		1,200		(a) 3,000								4,200
Inventory, Jan. 1:												
Finished goods	48,000				48,000			41,500			41,500	
Goods in process	21,000				21,000	26,350					26,350	
Raw materials	8,000				8,000	12,650					12,650	
Unexpired insurance	1,500			(b) 600							900	
Land	40,000										40,000	
Buildings	150,000										150,000	
Accumulated depreciation: Bldgs.		45,000		(e) 3,750								48,750
Machinery and equipment	130,000										130,000	
Accumulated depreciation: M & E		52,000		(e)13,000								65,000
Furniture and fixtures	10,000										10,000	
Accumulated depreciation: F & F		3,000		(e) 400								3,400
Deferred research and development costs	40,000			(f) 8,000							32,000	
Accounts payable		41,300		(g) 1,450								42,750
Bonds payable		75,000										75,000
Capital stock		100,000										100,000
Paid-in capital in excess of par		100,000										100,000
Retained earnings, Jan. 1		88,875								88,875		
Dividends	6,000								6,000			
Sales		633,600						633,600				
Sales returns & allowances	3,600						3,600					
Raw material purchases	125,000				125,000							

Worksheet (partial)

Account	Trial Balance Dr	Trial Balance Cr	Adjustments Dr	Adjustments Cr	Cost of Goods Mfd Dr	Cost of Goods Mfd Cr	Income Statement Dr	Income Statement Cr	Retained Earnings Dr	Retained Earnings Cr	Balance Sheet Dr	Balance Sheet Cr
Purchase returns & allowances		4,000				4,000						
Transportation-in	3,500				3,500							
Direct labor costs	192,500		(c) 1,800		194,300							
Indirect labor costs	72,600		(c) 950		73,550							
Heat, light, and power	12,300		(g) 1,450		13,750							
Miscellaneous factory costs	15,000		(b) 480	(h) 850	14,630							
Advertising	35,000						35,000					
Sales salaries	42,000						42,000					
Delivery expense	8,000						8,000					
Administrative salaries	50,000						50,000					
Office salaries	20,000						20,000					
Telephone & telegraph	1,800						1,800					
Miscellaneous general expense	2,800		(b) 120				2,920					
Interest expense	3,375		(d) 1,125				4,500					
Uncollectible accounts expense			(a) 3,000				3,000					
Accrued wages payable				(c) 2,750								2,750
Accrued interest payable				(d) 1,125								1,125
Depreciation: Bldg., factory			(e) 3,000		3,000							
general			(e) 750				750					
Depreciation: M & E, factory			(e)13,000		13,000							
Depreciation: F & F, factory			(e) 40		40							
general			(e) 360				360					
Research & development costs			(f) 8,000		8,000							
Factory supplies on hand			(h) 850								850	
Totals	1,143,975	1,143,975	34,925	34,925	477,770	43,000						
Cost of goods manufactured						434,770	434,770					
Totals					477,770	477,770	654,700	675,100				
Income before income taxes							20,400					
Totals							675,100	675,100				
Income before income taxes								20,400				
Income taxes							10,200					
Net income							10,200			10,200		
Totals							20,400	20,400	6,000	99,075		
Retained earnings, Dec. 31									93,075			93,075
Totals									99,075	99,075	546,250	546,250

COLE MANUFACTURING COMPANY
Statement of Cost of Goods Manufactured
For Year Ended December 31, 19___

Goods in process inventory, Jan. 1, 19___		$ 21,000
Raw materials used:		
Raw materials inventory, Jan. 1, 19___	$ 8,000	
Raw materials purchases (net)	124,500	
Cost of raw materials available for use	$132,500	
Less: Raw materials inventory, Dec. 31, 19___	12,650	
Cost of raw materials used	$119,850	
Direct labor costs	194,300	
Factory overhead costs (see work sheet for details)	125,970	
Total manufacturing costs		440,120
Total cost of goods in process during the year		$461,120
Less: Goods in process inventory, Dec. 31, 19___		26,350
Cost of goods manufactured		$434,770

Forecasts of future operations

At the present time much effort is being expended by the public accounting profession and by the SEC to find a satisfactory basis for including
forecasts of future operations in audited financial statements. Virtually
every large business prepares forecasts of future operations as a means
of defining goals and measuring performance. The problem is how to
make such information available to the investing public yet avoid the
danger of misleading investors through erroneous forecasts.

Limitations of accounting data

The objective of this book is to examine the basic principles and their
effectiveness as the underlying assumptions of accounting, to explore
the rules and conventions, and to consider the possible uses of the data
once they are accumulated. One must be aware of the fact that accounting is justified only because the data so accumulated and presented are
useful. At the same time one must remember that the data are often
limited because many factors which are not subject to measurement in
terms of money have necessarily been omitted. Examples are the human
resources of an organization and the political and economic climate in
which the business exists. Furthermore, in recent years drastic changes
in the purchasing power of the dollar have made this monetary unit an
imperfect means of measurement.

REVIEW QUESTIONS

1 Describe the accounting cycle briefly and list the sequence of procedures.

2 State in a concise form the rules of debit and credit for the five basic types of accounts.

3 Describe briefly the function of the journals or books of original entry.

4 What is the function of the ledger?

5 Explain the advantage of using controlling accounts and subsidiary ledgers.

6 What is the purpose of the trial balance? Does it provide proof that there have been no errors in the recording, classifying, and summarizing of business transactions?

7 How are the temporary or nominal accounts (revenue and expense accounts) related to the equation $A = L + OE$?

8 What is the objective of utilizing special multicolumn journals as books of original entry?

9 With the advent of electronic computers, the cost of the equipment and the complexity of operations increased many times. What economies are available to the user to offset the added costs of converting to and using this type of equipment?

10 What are adjusting entries and why are they necessary?

11 Why is it necessary to prepare adjusting entries to change the value of the accounts receivable when the entries of these accounts are usually made only upon objective evidence of a negotiated sales and purchase agreement?

12 Prepare the adjusting entry indicated by the following data:
   a Accrued wages at June 30 total $3,000.
   b The estimate of uncollectible accounts is $2,000 and the allowance for uncollectible accounts has a zero balance.

13 What are closing entries? Why are they made? What accounts are closed?

14 You are given the following information about the merchandise accounts of ABC Co. and are asked to make the necessary entries to adjust the inventory balance and close the relevant accounts to cost of goods sold.

Inventory, Jan. 1 (ledger balance)	$ 44,000
Purchases	276,400
Purchase returns	1,200
Purchase discounts	3,800
Purchase allowances	500
Freight and transportation-in	4,800
Handling and storage costs	26,800
Inventory, Dec. 31 (physical count; value at net invoice cost plus freight, handling, and storage costs)	46,200

15 What are reversing entries and under what circumstances are they most commonly used?

16 Which of the following adjustments might be reversed? For each entry indicate your reasons for reversing or not reversing.

a Unearned Subscriptions 10,000

      Earned Subscriptions Revenue 10,000

b Office Supplies Inventory 5,000

      Office Supplies Expense 5,000

c Interest Expense 300

      Accrued Interest Payable 300

d Depreciation Expense 8,000

      Accumulated Depreciation 8,000

17 What is the purpose of the accountant's working papers and what benefits may be derived from using them?

EXERCISES

Ex. 2-1 All but one of the accounts of Hale Shoe Store, owned by J. D. Hale, appear in the following list of balances at December 31 of the current year.

Accounts receivable	$ 7,500
Accounts payable	11,000
Accrued liabilities	300
Accumulated depreciation (plant and equipment)	10,000
Cash	5,000
Inventory	14,000
Land	6,000
Notes payable	25,000
Plant and equipment	25,000
Short-term prepayments	500

On January 1 of the current year, Hale's equity in the business amounted to $15,000. During the current year he withdrew $5,200 in cash and made an additional investment of $3,000 in equipment which had previously been part of another business owned by Hale.

Compute the net income or net loss of Hale Shoe Store for the current year, and show in an orderly manner the data supporting your answer.

Ex. 2-2 The following events occurred during January, the first month of operations, at the Jade Paint Store.

(1) Sales on account totaled $13,000. Terms, 2/10, n/60.
(2) Cash sales amounted to $24,000.
(3) Purchases of merchandise (paint) totaled $50,000.
(4) Payments of $28,600 were made to creditors, in full settlement of purchase invoices totaling $29,000.
(5) Accounts receivable in the face amount of $10,000 were collected; one-half of these collections occurred within the 10-day discount period.

(6) Jade, the owner, withdrew merchandise for his personal use which had a cost of $1,000 and had been marked for sale at $1,300. He also withdrew $500 in cash during the month.

(7) Inventory on hand at the end of January was determined by physical count to consist of goods which cost $23,000.

(8) Other expenses for the month totaled $8,500.

Determine the net income or net loss of Jade Paint Store for the month of January. Show supporting computations in good form.

Ex. 2-3 The ledger accounts of Pollard Company include an asset account, Office Supplies, and an expense account, Office Supplies Expense. On September 1, Pollard Company carried out the transaction shown in the following journal entry:

Office Supplies Expense	600	
Cash		600

To record the purchase of office supplies.

As of December 31, office supplies with a cost of $500 were determined to be on hand.

a Give the adjusting entry required on December 31.

b What reversing entry would it be appropriate for Pollard Company to make as of January 1?

c Prepare the journal entry required if Pollard Company had debited a real (asset) account in recording the purchase of office supplies on September 1.

d If a real account had been debited in the transaction of September 1, what adjusting entry and what reversing entry (if any) would be appropriate at year-end?

Ex. 2-4 The accounting policies of Collins Publishing Company provide that subscriptions received from customers be credited to Subscriptions Revenue when received. Purchases of supplies are regularly debited to Supplies Expense at time of purchase.

The post-closing trial balance at December 31, 1975, follows:

	Debit	Credit
Cash	$ 4,900	
Accounts receivable	13,000	
Allowance for uncollectible accounts		$ 2,000
Supplies inventory	1,150	
Plant assets	125,000	
Accumulated depreciation		39,000
Accounts payable		6,500
Notes payable		15,000
Accrued interest payable		150
Accrued wages payable		975
Unearned subscriptions revenue		1,045
Dividends payable		5,000
Capital stock		60,000
Retained earnings		14,380
Total	$144,050	$144,050

Make all appropriate reversing entries as of January 1, 1976.

Ex. 2-5 The following data provide selected account balances of Mylan Company before and after the December 31 adjusting entries.

	Before adjustment	After adjustment
a Allowance for uncollectible accounts	$ 2,000 credit	$ 5,500 credit
b Accumulated depreciation	14,000 credit	16,000 credit
c Sales salaries	24,200 debit	24,650 debit
d Income taxes payable	3,700 credit	6,250 credit
e Interest revenue	6,500 credit	6,585 credit
f Royalty revenue	5,000 credit	5,800 credit

In general journal form, give the adjustments that were made for each account on December 31.

Ex. 2-6 Mitch Company's records provide the following information concerning certain account balances and changes in these account balances during the current year.
  a Accounts receivable: Jan. 1, balance, $15,000; Dec. 31, balance, $20,500; uncollectible accounts written off during the year, $2,500; accounts receivable collected during the year, $56,000.
  b Allowance for uncollectible accounts: Jan. 1, balance, $1,500; Dec. 31, balance, $2,200; adjustment entry increasing allowance at Dec. 31, $4,800.
  c Office supplies; Jan. 1, balance, $1,500; Dec. 31, balance, $1,350; office supplies expense for the year, $9,500.
  d Equipment: Jan. 1, balance, $20,500; Dec. 31, balance, $18,000; equipment costing $8,000 was sold during the year.
  e Accounts payable: Jan. 1, balance, $9,000; Dec. 31, balance, $11,500; purchases on account for the year, $48,000.
  f Interest revenue: Jan. 1, accrued, $325; Dec. 31, accrued, $475; earned for the year, $4,500.
  Transaction information is missing from each of the above. Prepare the entry to record the missing information for each account.

SHORT CASES FOR ANALYSIS AND DECISION

Case 2-1 After many years in military service, John Hayden retired on January 1, 1975, and used his savings to establish a business called Hayden Appliances. His first step was to sign a three-year lease on a store building at a monthly rental of $300 and to make the first monthly payment on January 1, 1975. Also on this date, Hayden purchased store equipment for $10,000 and inventory for $16,000. The store equipment was expected to have a useful life of 10 years with no salvage value. Hayden made no other investment of any kind in the business.

Both Mr. and Mrs. Hayden worked in the business; they had no employees. From time to time Hayden withdrew cash from the business to meet his personal needs. Since Mr. and Mrs. Hayden had no prior business experience, they chose to minimize record keeping. The only records maintained were a checkbook which was reconciled monthly with the bank statement, a file folder of unpaid purchase invoices, and a file folder of uncollected charge tickets for a few select customers.

At December 31, 1976, Hayden carried out the following procedures in an effort to see how the business stood after two years of operation.

(1) Took a physical inventory of the merchandise and priced the items, using invoice prices of recent purchases. This procedure indicated a total value for the inventory of $45,000.
(2) Reconciled the December 31 bank statement with the checkbook and found the cash balance to be $7,200.
(3) Added the unpaid purchase invoices in the file which showed a total liability to suppliers of $22,700.
(4) Added the uncollected charge tickets and found that the total amount receivable from customers was $4,200.
(5) Estimated that his withdrawals of cash from the business during the course of the two-year period had amounted to $16,000.

Instructions
a Prepare a balance sheet for Hayden Appliances (a single proprietorship) at December 31, 1976. (You are to ignore the subject of income taxes, including the fact that apparently no income tax return was prepared to reflect the first year of operations.)
b Explain to Hayden the advantages of a double-entry accounting system as compared with his present set of records. Could the same information be obtained from his present system as from a double-entry system?
c Tell Hayden what you can about the results of operation over the past two-year period.

Case 2-2 Frank Foster began his working career in the accounting department of Midtown Manufacturing Company. Although Foster had never taken a formal course of study in accounting, he gradually developed a thorough knowledge of Midtown's accounting policies and eventually he was promoted to the position of chief accountant.

While attending a regional meeting of accounting executives, Foster was puzzled by a statement made in a group discussion. The statement was: "Reversing entries are frequently very helpful in accounting for business transactions; however they are seldom, if ever, essential to the record-keeping function." Foster was concerned because reversing entries had regularly been used by Midtown Manufacturing Company and he had always considered them essential.

Instructions
a Explain why reversing entries are not essential but why they may be helpful. Your answer should include an explanation as to when reversing entries are appropriate and when they should not be used.
b Using the data below, demonstrate with journal entries how reversing entries may be used or ignored. It is company policy to debit Supplies Expense for all supplies purchased. The value of supplies on hand at December 31, 1974, was determined by count to be $800. The balance in the asset account, Inventory of Supplies, in the ledger was zero. The following adjusting entry was made:

Inventory of Supplies	*800*	
Supplies Expense		*800*

During the year 1975, supplies were purchased at a cost of $20,000 and debited to Supplies Expense. The inventory of supplies at December 31, 1975, was $700.

PROBLEMS

Group A

2A-1 During the current period the following transactions were completed by Anderson Corporation. The company uses a periodic inventory system.

(1) Sales on account totaled $18,800.

(2) Building and tract of land were acquired at a cost of $300,000. The value of the land was estimated at $90,000. One-fourth of the purchase price was paid in cash and an 8% mortgage payable was signed for the balance.

(3) Merchandise costing $24,000 was purchased, subject to a cash discount of 2% if paid within 10 days. (Record invoice at net amount.)

(4) Freight charges, related to merchandise acquisitions, of $105 were paid.

(5) Accounts receivable of $525 were written off. Anderson Corporation employs an allowance for uncollectible accounts and makes provision for uncollectible accounts at the end of each period.

(6) The invoice for the purchase in item (3) was paid within the discount period.

(7) Collections on customers' accounts totaled $15,600.

(8) Equipment which originally cost $14,500 and on which accumulated depreciation amounted to $10,400 was sold for $3,000 cash.

(9) A cash dividend of 28 cents per share on 100,000 shares was declared and paid.

(10) 22,000 shares of $10 par value common stock were sold for $18 per share.

(11) Defective merchandise, which was purchased on account for $1,800 (net amount), was returned for full credit.

(12) A customer's check for $125 received and deposited by Anderson Corporation was returned by the bank marked "not sufficient funds."

Instructions Record the above transactions in general journal form.

2A-2 Brandt, Inc., maintains subsidiary ledgers for accounts receivable and accounts payable to support the respective balances of the two controlling accounts in the general ledger. The following schedules summarize the two subsidiary ledgers at December 31.

Schedule of Accounts Receivable
December 31, 19___

Foster	$17,500
Goodman	(4,000)
Hodge	2,500
Simmons	5,000
Total	$21,000

( ) denotes credit balance

Schedule of Accounts Payable
December 31, 19___

Angel	$ 9,250
Ewing	1,470
Ferrell	3,530
Strong	(2,270)
Total	$11,980

( ) denotes debit balance

Brandt, Inc., offers its customers a cash discount of 2% on all sales for which payment is received within 10 days from the invoice date. Sales transactions are recorded at the gross amount of the invoices. On purchases of merchandise it is the company's policy to take advantage of all cash discounts by paying within the discount period. Because of this policy the company records all purchase invoices at the net amount. Any adjustments for discounts (either because sales discounts are taken by customers or because purchase discounts are lost through failure by Brandt, Inc., to pay promptly) are made at the time cash is received or disbursed.

In the preparation of financial statements, any customers' accounts which have credit balances are reclassified as liabilities, and any creditors' accounts which have debit balances are reclassified as assets. Although such accounts are reclassified in the preparation of a balance sheet, they are not removed from the subsidiary ledgers; thus a customer's account which acquires a credit balance continues to be part of the accounts receivable subsidiary ledger.

The following selected transactions occurred during January:

(1) Received a check from Simmons for $4,900 representing settlement in full of his account within the discount period.
(2) Purchases from Ewing totaled $13,000, terms 2/5, n/30. (Record at net amount.)
(3) Issued to Angel a check in the amount of $9,250.
(4) Made sales to Goodman of $30,000, terms 2/10, n/30.
(5) Cash received from Hodge, $3,900, including a $1,400 advance payment. Collection of the receivable existing at December 31 was after the discount period.
(6) Payment of $14,500 was made to Ewing in settlement of the account. The payment was made after expiration of the discount period. (Debit Purchase Discounts Lost.)
(7) Cash received from Foster, $14,700, in partial payment of his bill. The regular cash discount was allowed on the portion of the receivable collected, since cash was received within the discount period.
(8) Paid Ferrell $5,500, which represented payment of the balance due within the discount period and a $1,970 advance on a large order.
(9) Purchased merchandise from Angel, net amount $43,000.

Instructions
a Enter the December 31 balances in ledger accounts for both the general ledger and the subsidiary ledgers for accounts receivable and accounts payable. You need not maintain a ledger account for cash. Record each January transaction directly in both the general ledger and a subsidiary ledger. Since this problem does not include journals or monthly totals, each January transaction should be entered in a general ledger controlling account as well as in a subsidiary ledger account. (The three-column, running-balance form of account is recommended.)
b Prepare schedules of the subsidiary ledgers at January 31 and determine that the totals are in agreement with the controlling accounts.
c Determine whether any balances should be reclassified in accordance with the company's policy. If so, indicate which ones, and state how they should be presented in the balance sheet.

2A-3 Listed below are the account balances from the ledger of Milton Company at October 31, except for retained earnings, which is the October 1 balance. There are no assets or liabilities other than those listed. The Dividends account represents the amount declared and paid during October.

Accounts payable	$ 20,000
Accounts receivable	16,000
Accumulated depreciation	32,000

Capital stock: $10 par value	$110,000
Cash	21,000
Dividends	4,000
Inventory	32,000
Plant and equipment	110,000
Retained earnings, Oct. 1	16,000

Instructions

a Compute the net income of Milton Company for October by preparing a balance sheet at October 31 which includes details showing the beginning balance of retained earnings, increases and decreases, and the ending balance.

b What was the amount of total sales for October, assuming that the accounts receivable amounted to $18,000 on October 1 and that $80,000 was received in collections from customers and from cash sales during October? Show computations.

c Determine the cost of goods sold for October, assuming that inventory of October 1 was $29,000 and that October purchases of merchandise totaled $55,000. What was the total of all other expenses for the month? Show computations.

d Determine the total cash outlay for merchandise during October, assuming that the beginning balance of accounts payable was $19,000 and that October purchases of merchandise (all on credit) amounted to $55,000. Show computations.

2A-4 Oakes Corporation adjusts and closes its books at the end of each calendar year. The information presented below provides the basis for making the adjusting entries needed at December 31.

(1) On October 1 received $3,600 of rental revenue covering a one-year period beginning with the date of receipt. Credited a nominal account.

(2) A real account was debited on September 1, when Oakes Corporation paid a $2,700 premium for a three-year insurance policy effective on that date.

(3) Oakes Corporation borrowed $60,000 on March 1 by issuing a three-year, 8% mortgage note with interest payable quarterly. Interest payments were made on May 31, August 31, and November 30.

(4) Bonds in the face amount of $10,000 with an interest rate of 7% were acquired as an investment on April 1. Interest payment dates, April 1 and October 1.

(5) The building occupied by Oakes Corporation has a cost basis of $120,000. Estimated useful life is 40 years with no expected salvage value. Straight-line depreciation is used.

(6) An aging analysis of the accounts receivable at December 31 indicated $3,700 to be a reasonable estimate of probable uncollectible amounts. At this date the allowance for uncollectibles had a credit balance of $1,350.

(7) A nominal account was debited on July 1 when $1,200 was paid to the city for a business license which must be renewed annually on July 1.

Instructions

a Prepare year-end adjusting entries. Include in the explanation portion of each entry any calculations used in developing the amount of the adjustment.

b Draft the appropriate reversing entries.

2A-5 Newport Furniture operates a retail store and uses a fiscal year ending on October 31. The unadjusted trial balance at October 31, 19___, is shown on page 79.

	Debit	Credit
Cash	$ 7,700	
Accounts receivable	37,000	
Allowance for uncollectible accounts		$ 2,500
Inventory	57,500	
Unexpired insurance	8,400	
Plant and equipment	100,000	
Accumulated depreciation		26,000
Accounts payable		17,500
Notes payable		50,000
Capital stock		150,000
Retained earnings		19,700
Sales		400,000
Purchases	240,000	
Salaries expense	75,000	
Office expenses	31,400	
Insurance expense	8,000	
Heat, light, and power expense	10,600	
Selling expense	88,000	
Interest expense	2,100	
Total	$665,700	$665,700

Additional data
(1) Uncollectible accounts expense is estimated to be 0.5% of sales.
(2) At year-end, unexpired insurance is $900.
(3) Depreciation of plant and equipment is $8,000 for the year.
(4) Accrued salaries payable at October 31 total $1,450.
(5) Accrued interest on notes payable at October 31 is $400.
(6) Estimated electricity expense for October is $670.
(7) Income taxes for the year are estimated to be $25,000.

Instructions Prepare the necessary entries to adjust the accounts at October 31, 19____ .

2A-6 Cline, Inc., is a merchandising business using a periodic inventory system and maintaining its accounts on a calendar-year basis. The trial balance shown below was prepared from the general ledger at December 31, 1975, and no adjusting entries have been made as yet.

Reversing entries were made by Cline, Inc., on January 1, 1975, for the accrued interest payable and the accrued salaries and wages payable which had been recorded by adjusting entries a year earlier on December 31, 1974.

	Debit	Credit
Cash	$ 22,000	
Accounts receivable	40,000	
Inventory, Dec. 31, 1974	23,000	
Land	90,000	
Building	200,000	

Accumulated depreciation		$ 42,000
Equipment	$ 240,000	
Accumulated depreciation		59,500
Accounts payable		38,000
Accrued interest payable		–0–
Salaries and wages payable		–0–
Bonds payable, 6%		100,000
Capital stock		200,000
Retained earnings, Dec. 31, 1974		75,200
Sales		800,000
Purchases	479,500	
Salaries and wages expense	55,200	
Selling expenses	120,000	
General expenses	40,000	
Interest expense	5,000	
Total	$1,314,700	$1,314,700

Additional data
(1) The company has decided after an aging and analysis of accounts receivable to establish an allowance for uncollectible accounts of $3,000.
(2) The building is being depreciated on the straight-line basis; total useful life, 40 years, salvage value zero. Useful life for equipment is 15 years and estimated salvage value, $15,000.
(3) Interest is payable May 1 and November 1 on the bonds payable.
(4) Salaries and wages earned by employees but unpaid at December 31 amount to $6,000.
(5) The inventory at December 31, 1975, was determined by physical count to amount to $28,000.
(6) Income taxes are estimated to be 40% of income before income taxes.

Instructions
a Prepare a 12-column work sheet to adjust the accounts and classify the balances as to income statement, retained earnings, and balance sheet. (Include columns for an adjusted trial balance.)
b Use the work sheet as a source for preparation of closing entries in general journal form. (Adjusting entries are not to be prepared.)
c Prepare reversing entries dated January 1, 1976, with respect to the accrued salaries and wages payable and to the accrued interest payable for which adjustments were made at December 31, 1975.

2A-7 The following unadjusted trial balance was prepared from the ledger of Burns Manufacturing Company at December 31. The company used reversing entries on January 1 to reverse accrued wages and interest.

	Debit	Credit
Cash	$ 27,050	
Accounts receivable	80,000	
Allowance for uncollectible accounts		$ 5,000
Inventories, Jan. 1:		
Raw materials	12,000	

Goods in process	$ 56,000	
Finished goods	80,000	
Prepaid expenses	9,000	
Land	50,000	
Building	457,000	
Accumulated depreciation: building		$ 50,000
Machinery and equipment	400,000	
Accumulated depreciation: machinery and equipment		120,000
Accounts payable		70,000
Accrued wages payable		–0–
Accrued interest payable		–0–
Bonds payable, 6%		200,000
Capital stock: $10 par value		400,000
Paid-in capital in excess of par		170,000
Retained earnings		56,025
Sales—net		980,000
Raw materials purchases	310,000	
Direct labor	292,900	
Factory overhead costs	120,000	
Selling expenses	95,000	
General and administrative expenses	52,000	
Interest expense	10,075	
Total	$2,051,025	$2,051,025

Additional data

(1) The allowance for uncollectible accounts should be increased to make it equal to 12% of accounts receivable.

(2) Prepaid expenses are as follows (insurance considered as administrative expense):

	Jan. 1	Dec. 31
Unexpired insurance (two years remaining Jan. 1)	$3,600	$1,800
Factory supplies	5,400	7,000
Total	$9,000	$8,800

(3) Invoices for raw materials included in the ending inventory but not recorded total $12,000.

(4) The straight-line method of depreciation is used to allocate the cost of plant assets. Other relevant data are:

	Estimated life, years	Estimated salvage value	Percentage allocated to	
			Factory	Administration
Building	50	$7,000	70	30
Machinery & equipment	10	5%	80	20

(5) Interest payments to bondholders are made semiannually on May 1 and November 1 at the annual rate of 6%.

(6) The factory power bill for December $3,200, has not been recorded.

(7) Direct factory wages earned but not paid at December 31 total $1,800.

(8) The ending inventories at December 31 are: Raw materials, $18,000; goods in process, $53,000; and finished goods, $75,000.

(9) Income taxes are estimated to be 40% of income before income taxes.

Instructions

a Prepare a work sheet to adjust the accounts and classify the data as to manufacturing costs, income statement, retained earnings, and balance sheet. Do not include an adjusted trial balance.

b Prepare in general journal form the entry required to adjust the inventory accounts and to record the cost of goods sold. You need not close any accounts to Income Summary.

c Prepare reversing entries as of January 1 of the next year relating to the accrued wages payable and interest payable.

Group B

2B-1 Transactions of the current period for Long Corporation are given below. The periodic inventory system is in use.

(1) Sales on account totaled $67,500.

(2) The corporation acquired a building and tract of land at a total cost of $275,000. One-fifth of the purchase price was paid in cash and a 9% mortgage payable was signed for the balance. The building had an estimated value of $175,000.

(3) Purchased merchandise costing $32,000. The invoice price is subject to a 2% cash discount if paid within 10 days. Long Corporation records purchase invoices at the net amount.

(4) The corporation paid $850 for freight charges on merchandise purchased.

(5) Accounts receivable of $350 were written off as uncollectible. The corporation maintains an allowance for uncollectible accounts and makes provision for uncollectible accounts expense at the end of each period.

(6) The invoice for the purchase of merchandise in item (3) was paid within the discount period.

(7) Collections on customers' accounts amounted to $14,100.

(8) Cash of $4,000 was received from disposal of equipment. The original cost of the equipment was $20,000 and the accumulated depreciation $17,500.

(9) Declared and paid a cash dividend of 15 cents per share on 80,000 shares of capital stock.

(10) Returned defective merchandise to a supplier for full credit. The merchandise had been purchased on account for $750 (net).

(11) Long Corporation issued 15,000 shares of its $10 par value common stock and received cash of $12.50 per share.

(12) A customer's check for $250, received and deposited by Long Corporation, was returned by the bank marked "not sufficient funds."

Instructions   Record the above transactions in general journal form.

2B-2 Subsidiary ledgers and related controlling accounts for accounts receivable and accounts payable are maintained by Creel Company. The following schedules summarize the two subsidiary ledgers at December 31.

Schedule of Accounts Receivable
December 31, 1975

Pittman	$ 1,000
Spears	16,000
Tracey	(2,500)
Woods	3,500
Total	$18,000

( ) *denotes credit balance*

Schedule of Accounts Payable
December 31, 1975

Anthony	$ 294
Farthing	(1,070)
Lucas	8,050
Parr	2,330
Total	$ 9,604

( ) *denotes debit balance*

Creel Company offers credit terms of 2/10, n/30 to all its customers and records all sales at gross prices. Purchases of merchandise from suppliers are recorded at net prices because it is the company's policy to take all purchase discounts available.

In any transaction in which Creel Company fails to take advantage of a cash discount offered by a supplier, the entry to record payment of the supplier's invoice should include a debit to Purchase Discounts Lost.

Creel Company carries customers' credit balances as an offset against debit balances, and suppliers' debit balances as an offset against credit balances in the ledgers. These balances are reclassified for reporting purposes to reflect customers' credit balances as liabilities and suppliers' debit balances as assets.

Transactions for January 1976 are presented below:

(1) Received a check from Woods for $3,430 in full settlement of his account within the discount period.
(2) Purchases from Anthony totaled $11,224.49, terms 2/10, n/30. Record at net.
(3) Payments to Lucas of $8,050 within the discount period.
(4) Sales to Tracey of $28,000, terms 2/10, n/30.
(5) Cash received from Pittman $3,500, including a $2,500 advance payment.
(6) Payment of $11,300 to Anthony in settlement of the account payable. Because of an oversight, the payment was not made until after the discount period had lapsed on the December invoice. Also made new purchase from Anthony of $27,000, terms 2/10, n/30.
(7) Cash received from Spears $12,740 in partial payment of his bill. The discount was allowed on this portion of the bill, since cash was received within the discount period.
(8) Paid Parr $4,000, which represented payment of the balance due within the discount period and $1,670 advance on a larger order.

Instructions

a Enter the December 31 balances and the above transactions directly in the appropriate ledger accounts in **both** the general ledger and subsidiary ledgers for accounts receivable and accounts payable. You need not maintain a ledger account for cash. (Since this problem does not include journals or monthly totals, each transaction should be individually entered in a general ledger controlling account as well as in a subsidiary ledger account. The use of three-column, running-balance-account forms is recommended.)

b Prove the accuracy of the records by preparing schedules of the subsidiary ledgers at January 31 and by determining that the totals agree with the respective controlling accounts.

c Which accounts with customers and suppliers should be reclassified on financial statements prepared at January 31? Explain how such accounts should be presented in the balance sheet.

2B-3 The account balances listed below are taken from the ledger of the Wilcox Company at September 30, except for the balance of retained earnings, which is the September 1 balance. The Dividends account represents the amount declared and paid during September. There are no assets or liabilities other than those listed.

Cash	$ 24,000
Accounts receivable	18,000
Inventory	36,000
Plant and equipment	120,000
Accounts payable	21,600
Accumulated depreciation	36,000
Capital stock: par value $10	120,000
Retained earnings, Sept. 1	18,000
Dividends	3,600

Instructions

a Compute the net income of Wilcox Company for September by arranging the information provided in a balance sheet at September 30. Include in the balance sheet the details of retained earnings: beginning balance, increase during September, decrease during September, and ending balance.

b Assume that the account receivable balance was $12,000 on September 1 and that a total of $84,000 was collected from accounts receivable and from cash sales. Compute the total sales for September.

c Assume that the inventory at September 1 was $39,600 and that purchases of merchandise during September amounted to $60,000. Compute the cost of goods sold and also the total of all other expenses for the month.

d Assume that the balance of accounts payable at September 1 was $30,000 and that the only liabilities incurred during September were for purchases of merchandise as stated in **(c)** above. Determine the total cash outlay for merchandise during September.

2B-4 The information given below for Warren, Inc., provides a basis for making all necessary adjusting entries at December 31, the end of the company's fiscal year. You may assume that all transactions were properly recorded in accordance with the company's accounting policies.

(1) On June 1, the company borrowed $40,000 by issuing a 6% mortgage note which called for interest to be paid quarterly.

(2) The company owns a building with an estimated useful life of 25 years and no expected salvage value. Cost was $60,000. Straight-line depreciation is used.

(3) On October 1 the company paid $1,800 for three years of insurance coverage commencing on that date. A real account was debited.

(4) A nominal account was credited when $2,400 in rental revenue was received from a tenant on November 1. This amount represented one year's rent in advance.

(5) Bonds with total par value of $5,000 and an annual interest rate of 8% were purchased as an investment on May 1. Interest payment dates are April 1 and October 1.

(6) An annual city business license of $360 was paid on October 1 and recorded by debiting a nominal account.

(7) On December 31, after careful study of an aging schedule of accounts receivable, it was estimated that probable uncollectible amounts would total $4,500. The Allowance for Uncollectible Accounts had a credit balance of $1,850.

Instructions

a Prepare the necessary adjusting entries at December 31. Include in the explanation portion of each entry any calculations you performed in developing the adjusting entry.

b Prepare the appropriate reversing entries.

2B-5 Marina Supplies, Inc., is a retail business which maintains its accounts on a calendar-year basis. The unadjusted trial balance at December 31 appears below.

	Debit	Credit
Cash	$ 5,050	
Accounts receivable	40,000	
Allowance for uncollectible accounts		$ 5,000
Inventory	49,000	
Unexpired insurance	4,100	
Plant assets	90,000	
Accumulated depreciation		30,000
Accounts payable		18,150
Notes payable		30,000
Capital stock		125,000
Retained earnings		24,500
Sales		345,000
Purchases	228,000	
Salaries expense	57,000	
Office expense	21,700	
Insurance expense	2,000	
Utilities expense	7,400	
Selling expense	72,000	
Interest expense	1,400	
Total	$577,650	$577,650

Additional data
(1) Depreciation for the year, $5,000.
(2) No billings have yet been received for electricity and other utilities during December but the amount owed at December 31 is estimated to be $750.
(3) Salaries accrued at December 31 total $1,100.
(4) Unexpired insurance is $2,300 at December 31.
(5) It is the company's policy to make provision for uncollectible accounts as a percentage of sales. Experience has shown that a provision equal to 1% of sales is required.
(6) Accrued interest on notes payable is $600 at December 31.
(7) Estimated income taxes for the year are $21,000.

Instructions Prepare the necessary adjusting entries as of December 31.

2B-6 Wagner, Inc., maintains its accounts on the basis of a fiscal year ending October 31. The following unadjusted trial balance was prepared from the general ledger at October 31, 1975. Reversing entries had been made by Wagner, Inc., on November 1, 1974, the first day of the current fiscal year, for the accrued interest payable and the accrued salaries and wages payable which had been recorded by adjusting entries on October 31, 1974.

	Debit	Credit
Cash	$ 20,000	
Accounts receivable	32,000	
Inventory, Oct. 31, 1974	47,000	
Land	84,000	
Building	210,000	
Accumulated depreciation: building		$ 44,000
Equipment	252,000	
Accumulated depreciation: equipment		62,700
Accounts payable		45,000
Accrued interest payable		–0–
Salaries and wages payable		–0–
Bonds payable, 9%		100,000
Capital stock		200,000
Retained earnings, Nov. 1, 1974		88,800
Sales		820,000
Purchases	490,000	
Salaries and wages expense	56,500	
Selling expenses	122,500	
General expenses	41,000	
Interest expense	5,500	
Total	$1,360,500	$1,360,500

Additional data
(1) After a careful analysis of accounts receivable, a decision is made to establish an allowance for uncollectible accounts in the amount of $2,200.
(2) Estimated life of the building is 40 years; salvage value zero. Estimated life of the equipment is 20 years with salvage value of $12,000.

(3) Interest on the bonds payable is payable January 1 and July 1.
(4) Salaries and wages earned but unpaid on October 31 amount to $5,000.
(5) The inventory at October 31, 1975, cost $26,000.
(6) The income tax expense is estimated to be 40% of income before income taxes.

Instructions
a Prepare a 12-column work sheet to adjust the accounts and classify the balances as to income statement, retained earnings, and balance sheet. (Include a pair of columns for an adjusted trial balance.)
b Prepare closing entries in general journal form.
c Prepare reversing entries at November 1, 1975, relating to the accrued salaries and wages payable and to the interest payable.

2B-7 The following unadjusted trial balance was prepared from the ledger of Gage Manufacturing Co. at December 31. The company used reversing entries on January 1 to reverse accrued wages and interest payable.

	Debit	Credit
Cash	$ 20,000	
Accounts receivable	73,300	
Allowance for uncollectible accounts		$ 5,000
Inventories, Jan. 1:		
Raw materials	11,000	
Goods in process	52,000	
Finished goods	70,000	
Prepaid expenses	8,000	
Land	42,000	
Building	350,000	
Accumulated depreciation: building		51,375
Machinery and equipment	375,000	
Accumulated depreciation: machinery and equipment		100,000
Accounts payable		50,000
Accrued wages payable		–0–
Accrued interest payable		–0–
Bonds payable, 6%		200,000
Capital stock: $10 par value		440,000
Retained earnings		54,000
Sales—net		950,000
Raw materials purchases	305,000	
Direct labor	281,000	
Factory overhead costs	110,000	
Selling expenses	96,000	
General and administrative expenses	47,000	
Interest expense	10,075	
Total	$1,850,375	$1,850,375

Additional data
(1) Uncollectible accounts are estimated to total 10% of the Accounts Receivable balance.
(2) Prepaid expenses are as follows (insurance considered as administrative expense):

	Jan. 1	Dec. 31
Unexpired insurance	$3,500	$2,000
Factory supplies	5,100	6,000
Total	$8,600	$8,000

(3) Invoices for raw materials included in the ending inventory but not recorded total $13,000.
(4) The straight-line method of depreciation is used to allocate the cost of plant assets. Other relevant data are:

	Estimated life, years	Estimated salvage value	Percentage allocated to	
			Factory	Administration
Building	50	$7,000	70	30
Machinery & equipment	10	5%	80	20

(5) Interest payments to bondholders are made semiannually on May 1 and November 1 at the annual rate of 6%.
(6) The factory power bill of $4,000 for December has not been recorded.
(7) Direct factory wages earned but not paid at December 31 total $2,100.
(8) The ending inventories at December 31 are: Raw materials, $15,000; goods in process, $49,000; and finished goods, $65,000.
(9) Income taxes are estimated to be 40% of income before income taxes.

Instructions
a Prepare a 12-column work sheet to adjust the accounts and classify the data as to manufacturing costs, income statement, retained earnings, and balance sheet. Columns for an adjusted trial balance are not to be included.
b Prepare in general journal form the entry required to adjust the inventory accounts and to record the cost of goods sold. You are not required to make the entry to close the revenue, cost of goods sold, and expense accounts to the Income Summary account.
c Prepare reversing entries on January 1 of the next year relating to the accrued wages payable and interest payable.

CHAPTER 3

The income statement: a report on results of operations

INCOME MEASUREMENT

Arriving at an estimate of the periodic income of a business enterprise is perhaps the foremost objective of the accounting process. The word *estimate* is appropriate because income is one of the most elusive concepts in the business and economic world. The art of accounting will probably never progress to the point where periodic business income can be defined to everyone's satisfaction.

To illustrate the complexity of defining income, let us assume that newly organized Blue Hills Corporation buys a large tract of land for the purpose of developing a residential community within commuting distance of a large city. Purchase of the land required only a small down payment (and the assumption of a large mortgage), but even that small payment used up most of the corporation's cash. Some of the land is level, some rolling, and some extremely steep. A golf course, riding stables, tennis courts, and a lake are to be constructed, and a first step is to create colorful sales brochures showing how attractive the community will appear when completed. These improvements are to be financed with revenue from sale of lots, and, if possible, by borrowing.

Residential lots are immediately offered for sale to individuals at varying prices, but with a down payment of only 1% of the sales price. Assume that 100 lots are sold very quickly with an average down payment of $100 received, along with long-term sales contracts calling for monthly payments on the balance due. How much, if any, income should be recognized when the first lots are sold?

As indicated in Chapter 1, income is usually determined by measuring revenue and deducting the related costs. But how shall we measure either the revenue or the costs? Among the questions which arise are: What is the value of a long-term sales contract from a person making a small down payment on a vacant lot? How many of the 100 buyers will actually make the agreed monthly payments? What will be the costs of developing roads, sewers, the golf course, lake, and other recreational facilities which Blue Hills Corporation has promised to provide? How many lots will be sold, and at what prices and on what terms? How should the total estimated costs be allocated among the level lots, sloping lots, hillside lots, and "lakefront" lots?

Despite all the effort which has been devoted to developing uniform accounting standards, it is painfully clear that a wide range of answers could be given to the question of how much, if any, income is earned from the sale of the first 100 lots. We might even question whether a sale has really occurred, or whether Blue Hills Corporation is a "going concern" reasonably capable of carrying out its commitments and thus warranting application of the continuity principle.[1] Assuming that Blue Hills Corporation does carry the development project to a successful completion, the income can then be measured as the amount of revenue received from customers minus the costs of the land and the costs of developing and selling it. However, the objective of timeliness in financial reporting requires the making of decisions as to the income being earned long before the project is completed. This example of a land development company, although somewhat extreme, suggests some of the very real practical difficulties faced by accountants in measuring business income.

In this chapter we shall first consider the nature of business income and the basic assumptions made by the accountant in attempting to measure it. Then we shall turn to the problem of reporting on the income statement the results of our measurement efforts.

The meaning of periodic income

In a very general sense, the objective in measuring income is to determine by how much a business has become better off during some period of time, as a result of its operations. Business income might be described as the maximum amount of resources that could be distributed to the owners over a given period of time and leave the business as well off at the end of that period as it was at the beginning. The weasel words in this definition are in the phrase "as well off." Anyone who studies the

---

[1] *Accounting Series Release No. 95,* issued by the Securities and Exchange Commission, "Accounting for Real Estate Transactions Where Circumstances Indicate That Profits Were Not Earned at the Time the Transactions Were Recorded," indicates that the circumstances set forth above would make it inappropriate to recognize gross profit as realized at the time of the sale.

concept of income will soon discover that controversies over the meaning and measurement of periodic income center on the problem of determining what the position of a business is at any given time, whether its position has improved or worsened, and by how much.

Let us begin with a relatively simple problem in income determination. If we were asked to measure the lifetime income of a business at the time it was being liquidated, we could probably agree on the following computation:

Total proceeds received on liquidation of the business	$800,000
Add: Amounts withdrawn by owners during the life of the business . . .	300,000
Less: Amount of capital invested in the business by its owners	(600,000)
Lifetime income of the business	$500,000

If we ignore the time value of money and assume a stable price level, lifetime income of a business is comparatively easy to measure. The reason is that at the beginning and end of the life of any business, the value of its net assets can be established with reasonable accuracy. The original investment of the owners and the proceeds on liquidation are usually definite sums of money or their equivalent.

At any stage prior to final liquidation, however, the net assets of a business constitute a complex set of resources, whose collective value depends largely on future earning power. In theory the only direct way to determine how well off a business is at any point in time is to compute the net present value of all its future revenue and disbursements. This is sometimes called the process of *direct valuation.*[2] Estimates of future earning power are obviously subject to material error. Anyone who has observed the behavior of the market prices of corporate stocks is impressed with the fact that humans are not endowed with any notable ability to forecast accurately the future course of economic events.

The accountant readily admits an inability to determine at frequent time intervals the *direct value* of business net assets. For this he can hardly be criticized for undue caution or modesty; he is simply being realistic about his limitations. The role of an economic reporter is perhaps less glamorous than that of the economic forecaster, but it is no less useful. Thus in measuring how well off a business is at any time, in order to measure periodic income, accountants agree to reflect in their records only those changes in business position that can be substantiated by reasonably objective evidence.

[2]Using direct valuation to measure theoretical business income under assumed conditions of certainty about future events is discussed and illustrated in *Advanced Accounting,* the third volume in this series.

The meaning of objective evidence

Facts form a basis for most intelligent decisions and forecasts of the future. Most of what is contained in accounting records purports to be factual. Like everyone else, however, the accountant often has considerable difficulty in deciding what the facts are. The famous tale of the blind men and the elephant reminds us that not all persons agree even in reporting what they have experienced.[3]

Businesses are engaged in the continuing process of transforming one series of economic goods and services (inputs) into another essentially different series of goods and services (outputs), in the expectation that the aggregate output will command a higher price in the market than the cost of the input. In reporting periodic progress in this endeavor, the accountant seeks objective evidence to support the data he presents. But what is meant by objective evidence? The important element in the objectivity of any observation or interpretation is verifiability, the agreement of competent persons as to what has been observed or experienced. The term *objective evidence,* then, means evidence that is sufficiently clear cut that reasonable men will vary in their interpretation of it only within fairly narrow limits.

External Data Purchases of asset services, hiring and paying employees, sales of goods and services, borrowing funds, selling shares of stock—all are examples of market transactions between a business and outsiders. These economic events stem from express or implied contracts and usually represent an exchange between independent parties at an arm's-length or bargained price. In other words, there is external evidence to support an accounting record of what has taken place.

At times the evidence is somewhat hazy or ambiguous. For example, if a tract of land originally acquired as a site for plant construction is exchanged directly for a smaller site with a complete operating plant and equipment, no explicit market price is established, and the accountant is forced to look for evidence of an implicit price at which to record the transaction. He tries to obtain independent evidence of the value of the operating plant and equipment or the current market value of the vacant land given in exchange. Such independent evidence is needed in order to estimate the bargained price that would have been established had the plant and equipment been acquired and the vacant land sold for cash. A similar problem arises in the "basket purchase" situation, where two or more different assets are acquired at a combination price. The problem is to divide the total price among the assets received, and the accountant

---

[3]For those whose memory of childhood fables is fuzzy: The man who felt the elephant's trunk reported that an elephant is like a snake; the man who felt a leg reported a great similarity between an elephant and a tree; and the man who touched the side observed that elephants were much like walls.

must seek independent evidence to support his allocation. Despite these troublesome cases, arriving at a reasonable and acceptable basis for recording most transactions between the business and outsiders causes relatively little difficulty.

Internal Data The second type of economic event in business leaves a much less distinct trail of evidence; consequently, it creates a far more troublesome set of problems for the accountant. The amount spent for materials, labor, and productive services can be objectively measured. The continuous process of transforming these inputs into more valuable outputs, however, is an internal, not an external, affair. In tracing the effect of this productive process and portraying it in terms of dollars, the accountant does not have the objective evidence of market transactions with outsiders as a basis for his recorded valuations.

The flow of costs

Ideally all costs should be associated with some physical product or output. In a very simple situation, where the entire resources of a business are devoted to the production and sale of a single product, this assumption might be reasonable. All costs incurred could be accumulated as inventory costs until the sale of the product provided objective evidence of gain or loss.

Even in this single-product case, however, it is apparent that some costs are more directly related to production than others. The costs of raw materials, direct labor, and some kinds of variable factory overhead, for example, can be traced to physical production because the relationship between effort and accomplishment is relatively clear. At the other extreme, such costs as sales salaries, advertising expenditures, and administrative overhead are productive, but the relationship between effort and accomplishment is far more nebulous. A sales visit today may result in a sale two years hence. The installation of a new cost accounting system may provide better control over operations and produce benefits to the business for years to come. In either case it is virtually impossible to trace these efforts to physical product with any degree of precision. When we shift this problem to the more realistic setting of a business producing not one but many different products or services, the difficulty of cost assignment increases immensely, and one can easily see that tracing costs is more an art than a science.

Confronted with this sort of vague evidence, the accountant finds it necessary to adopt a series of reasonable, but somewhat arbitrary, assumptions. It is hardly surprising that opinions as to what is "reasonable" in any given case will differ. The fact that alternative accounting procedures, each of which may produce significantly different results, may be "generally accepted" stems directly from these differences of opinion.

Product and Period Costs   In measuring business income certain costs, called *product costs,* are traced to physical output and are accumulated in inventory accounts until evidence of gain or loss is available. For example, the costs of direct labor and raw material used in fabricating a product can be directly identified with the cost of producing a unit of inventory.

Other costs, called *period costs,* are considered an expense of the time period in which they occur. These costs, as for example, advertising and other selling expenses, are usually not related to the flow of production and are charged against revenue immediately on the ground that the benefits expire in the same period as the expenditures are made. As pointed out in *APB Statement No. 4,* "Enterprises never acquire expenses per se; they always acquire assets. Costs may be charged to expenses in the period goods or services are acquired . . . if they only benefit the period in which they are acquired. . . ."[4]

Making a theoretical distinction between product costs and period costs may be easier than the practical application of the concept. To illustrate this problem, consider the cost of merchandise purchased by a trading concern. There are certain costs directly related to the acquisition of a given quantity of merchandise, such as the price paid to vendors and the cost of transportation-in. There are other not-so-direct costs of buying, handling, storage, and display. The salary of a purchasing agent may be one of these borderline cases. Decisions on the treatment of some costs as product costs or as period costs are likely to differ between companies and may often be resolved on the grounds of convenience. If such controversial expenditures are material in amount, different practices may lead to significantly different income figures.

In addition to the question of product versus period costs, another issue arises when identical goods in stock have been acquired in different lots and at different prices. As these goods are sold, decisions must be made as to which of the different unit acquisition costs are to be assigned to the particular units sold. The decision to assume a first-in, first-out, a last-in, first-out, or a weighted-average flow of acquisition costs is somewhat arbitrary, but important, since different assumptions may produce materially different periodic income figures.

The Cost of Asset Services   Certain asset services, such as buildings, equipment, or patents, are acquired in an aggregate quantity some time in advance of their use. In buying manufacturing equipment, for example, a business acquires a bundle of productive services. Some portion of the total services will be withdrawn from the bundle and used in manufacturing during the current period; other portions will not be withdrawn for several years. The accountant is faced with the problem of deter-

---

[4]*APB Statement No. 4,* "Basic Concepts and Accounting Principles Underlying Financial Statements of Business Enterprises," AICPA (New York: 1970), par. 184.

mining whether the cost of expired machine services is a period or a product cost. In addition, he is confronted with two even more perplexing questions: (1) How much of the total bundle of lifetime services has been used during the current period? (2) What is the cost of these used services? In the case of raw materials or merchandise, there is at least a physical flow of goods to indicate the changes that are taking place. Productive assets such as machinery, on the other hand, exhibit little or no change in their physical characteristics as they yield useful services.

The services of some productive assets expire as a function of time. If a three-year premium is paid on an insurance policy, for example, the service acquired is three years of freedom from a given amount of risk. It seems reasonable to assume that one-third of the cost of acquiring this service is used up in each of the years involved.

Suppose, however, that the asset in question is an apartment building. The services acquired are a given amount of building space which can be rented to tenants. The value of the right to occupy a new building, however, is greater than that of an older building. It follows that the rental revenue during the early life of the building will tend to be higher than during its later years, and thus the value of the services yielded by the building will be higher in early years than in later. These facts should be considered in establishing a cost flow assumption. Objective evidence of the value of services year by year, however, is difficult to obtain. Furthermore, the service life of the building is indefinite. The accountant knows objectively only that the investment in future building services has been X dollars, that the owner may dispose of the building at some future time, and that if he does not, the building will eventually be worthless and must be torn down. The accountant also knows that the business must recover the cost of expired building services out of revenues in order to be as well off in monetary terms at the end of any period as at the time the original investment was made. In the face of these imponderables, it is likely that any solution adopted will prove to be erroneous to some degree. It is not surprising that the measurement of depreciation has always been a controversial area of accounting.

In subsequent chapters we shall consider these issues in greater detail, and examine some of the assumptions and techniques that accountants employ in dealing with internal cost data. Our purpose at this stage is to make the point that measuring costs is something far short of a precise operation. The cost factor in income determination is, at best, an intelligent estimate of the prices paid for resources used up in business operations during any accounting period.

Revenue recognition (realization)

Realization of revenue refers to the timing of its recognition in the accounts. A practical working rule is needed to signal that an increase in net assets has resulted from the activities of a business entity. Discussion of the revenue principle in Chapter 1 stressed that each step in producing and distributing goods and services is essential to earning revenue. Ideally, the accounting recognition of revenue should be continuous rather than occurring at a single critical point in the activities of the business.

If the plans of a business are carried out, it is clear that at some time in the productive process (in fact continuously) there is an increase in the monetary value of the resources controlled by the business entity. Since continuous direct valuation is a practical impossibility, an alternative procedure must be found to measure this increase as objectively as possible in order to reflect periodic income. The basis assumption adopted as a means of dealing with this problem is called the *realization concept.*

When a business acquires asset services in exchange for money (or promises to pay money), the accountant assumes an even exchange of values; that is, that no gain or loss occurs at the time of purchase. An arm's-length exchange price is viewed as the best objective evidence of value at the time of acquisition, and a subjective judgment that the buyer has obtained something for nothing or has received the worst of the bargain is not sufficient to overcome such evidence. In tracing the flow of costs internally, the assumption of an even exchange continues to control accounting procedures. For example, in allocating raw material, direct labor, and factory overhead costs to inventories, the allocation is limited to the actual cost incurred, and the fact that there may be an increase in value beyond the costs added is ignored.

Somewhere along the line, however, objective evidence that the value of the output is greater (or possibly less) than the cost of the inputs must arise. When such evidence becomes conclusive, the accountant stops dealing solely in costs. The value of the output is measured and revenue emerges on the accounting scene. *The realization concept is the set of rules adopted by accountants in deciding when a change in the value of output should be recognized in the accounting records.*

When is revenue realized?

The two primary criteria for recording in the accounts that revenue has been realized are:

1 Sufficient objective evidence exists as to the market value of the output. Usually such evidence is provided by an arm's-length sales transaction.

2 The earnings process (in essence the creation of marketable goods and services) must be substantially complete. This means that all necessary costs have been incurred or can be reasonably estimated.

Revenue Recognized at Time of Sale In applying these criteria to various practical situations, the most widely accepted evidence of realization is the sale of goods. There is little question about the quality of evidence: a completed transaction with outsiders which transfers possession of, and usually title to, the product in return for money or the promise to pay money at some future date. One may question, however, why the accountant chooses so *late* a stage in the productive process to measure revenue and thus income. The answer comes in two parts: (1) At any point prior to the sale, the expected sales price of nonstandard products and the ability to sell them at a given price are such uncertain factors that they do not, in the minds of most businessmen, constitute good enough evidence to justify an upward revaluation of the product. (2) For most businesses, actually selling goods and services is the most important element in the earning process. Until a sale is made the future stream of revenue is in this sense "unearned." It is axiomatic among businessmen that it is easier to make a good product than to develop adequate customer acceptance and sell the product in quantity.

The wide use of the sale as evidence of realization attests to the general acceptance of these arguments. It should not be assumed, however, that *sale* and *realization* are synonymous. Under certain circumstances, accountants are willing to record realized revenue at the three other stages in the productive process discussed below.

Revenue Recognized during Production   In some businesses the product consists of a small number of major projects which require considerable time to complete. Major construction projects such as dams or large ships are examples. For such projects, production is the major element of the earning process; the final sale is assured by a binding contract subject only to satisfactory performance by the producer. To recognize revenue only at the point of final sale, under these conditions, would result in a highly distorted picture of income for various accounting periods. Therefore, as progress on the project is made, portions of the construction are revalued and a percentage of the ultimate contract price is recorded as realized revenue. This procedure is discussed in Chapter 9.

Revenue Recognized when Production Is Complete   When a business deals in standard goods that are sold on an organized market at prices that can be objectively determined at any time, there is a basis for valuing output as soon as it is produced. An ideal example of such a product is gold, which must be sold to the government at a fixed price. Farm products and a wide variety of commodities sold in standard grades on organized markets also meet all the conditions requisite to the use of this test of realization. In these cases it is possible to value inventories at selling prices less any marketing costs not yet incurred (sometimes called "net realizable value"), thus recognizing income as soon as production is completed.

Revenue Recognized when Cash Is Received   The two procedures just discussed move the point of realization forward to an earlier stage in the production process, that is, prior to the point of sale. Another possibility is that the recognition of revenue should be delayed beyond the point of sale until additional evidence corroborates the significance of the sales transaction. Under some conditions a transaction that purports to be a sale may be lacking in substance and therefore constitute inadequate evidence of realization. An example is found in a land sale contract in which the purchaser makes only a nominal down payment, has no established credit status, and is free to cancel the agreement at any time without any penalty other than the loss of the payments he has made. In many states the seller has no legal right to take any action on such defaulted agreements other than to repossess the property sold. However, as the number of cash payments by a given customer under a sales agreement of this type accumulates, the evidence of an authentic sale and valid receivable is increased.

An extreme application of this test of realization is the so-called cash basis of accounting. In its most unrefined state, the cash basis procedure calls for recognizing revenue only when cash is received, and recognizing expenses at the time cash is paid out. However, the term "cash basis" is also used loosely to describe a variety of practices which fall short of accrual accounting in varying degrees. For federal income tax purposes, for example, a cash basis determination of business income is allowed only when receivables and inventories are not material factors. Tax rules provide that plant assets and other expense prepayments must be recorded as assets and amortized over their service lives.

Another practical application of the view that realization coincides with the receipt of cash is a procedure known as the "installment sales" method. As the name suggests, this procedure is applied when the sales contract calls for payment in periodic installments. The installment sales method delays the recognition of revenue (and thus income) until collections from customers are actually received.

Cash basis and installment sales methods are widely used in the computation of taxable income, because their use makes it possible for a business to defer the payment of income taxes. However, the acceptability of these methods for income tax purposes is not in itself any reason for their use in financial statements.[5] The income tax rules are based on the belief by government that it must collect income taxes when the taxpayer has in hand the cash arising from a business transaction, rather than upon any rational analysis of the timing of revenue recognition.

Pressures for speeding up the recognition of revenue

Many companies, in an effort to enhance their ability to attract capital from investors and bankers, are impelled to treat revenue as realized at the earliest possible moment. In the franchising field, using restaurants, convenience food outlets, and motels as familiar examples, the franchis-

---

[5] In December 1966 the Accounting Principles Board of the AICPA stated that "the installment method of recognizing revenue is not acceptable" unless circumstances are such that there is no reasonable basis for estimating the collectibility of installment receivables (*APB Opinion No. 10,* p. 149).

ing firms have often recognized large profits at the time of signing contracts. The contracts typically called for the franchisor to guide the franchisee in locating a site, training a work staff, and commencing operations. In return, the franchisor received notes receivable but no cash. The collectibility of the notes was dependent upon the success of the proposed new business and upon a rather indefinite commitment by the franchising company to render future advisory services.

The rapidly rising earnings reported by franchising firms as they granted new franchises was often attributable to recognizing these dubious notes receivable as assets worth their face value. In part the abuse of the realization concept was mitigated by issuance of **APB Opinion No. 21,** which required that notes receivable be valued not at their face value but at their fair market value or (if that were not determinable) at a discounted amount computed by using an imputed interest rate consistent with the credit status of the issuer of the note.[6]

Although the discounting of receivables to their present value reduces the opportunities for the so-called "front ending" of profits on long-term agreements, it does not provide a direct answer to the question of when revenue should be recognized on the types of contracts described above. Because of the current widespread use of innovative financing arrangements, the accountant faces a more difficult problem than ever before in determining when a "sale" is a genuine sales transaction.

Matching costs and revenue

The interrelation of the cost and realization assumptions is often described as a process of "matching costs and revenue." This phrase is not particularly helpful, however, because it implies that costs and revenue fit together somehow like pieces of a jigsaw puzzle. In reality, accountants associate costs with output and then determine the value of output at the point of realization. Any costs treated as period costs are simply related to whatever output has been valued during that accounting period.

A simple illustration will make this point clear. A department store sells a dress for $60 to a charge customer. Look behind this transaction and you will find that the "product" sold in this case is a great deal more than a dress. The business has sold some portion of the service potential of the building in which the sale took place. It has also sold the services of an expert dress buyer who studied fashion trends and made one or more trips to the designers' showrooms. Freight, insurance, storage, handling, pricing, and accounting services have also been sold, as well as advertising and the services of a salesclerk. Our list is not complete, but let us assume that the cost of acquiring the dress and all services necessary to put that dress where our hypothetical customer would buy

[6]*APB Opinion No. 21,* "Interest on Receivables and Payables," AICPA (New York: 1971), par. 12–13.

amount to $45. In exchange for this the customer gives the store a contractual promise worth $60. An ideal accounting for this transaction would show that the store had invested $45 in an asset (the "product" sold to this customer) and that this asset had been revalued from $45 to $60 (and retitled accounts receivable) at the time of sale, when evidence of value became available.

This way of looking at the process of matching costs and revenue sheds considerable light on the nature of the accountant's problem of measuring income. It will aid us in judging the merits of alternative accounting procedures which might be employed and which can obviously only approximate the ideal.

Using money as a unit of measurement

We have seen how the cost and realization assumptions affect the accounting measurement of income. Now let us look briefly at an accounting assumption that is equally fundamental—the assumption that money is a useful **standard measuring unit** for reporting the effect of business transactions.

Assume that a company invests $80 in Year 1 to produce a machine which is expected to sell for $120. The cost of producing the identical machine has risen to $130 in Year 2, and because demand is strong the company is able to sell its machine for $180 in that year. Between Year 1 and Year 2, prices in general throughout the economy have risen 10%. On these facts the income from this transaction might be computed in three different ways:

Method 1. Ordinary Accounting Mixed-Dollar Income

Revenue realized in Year 2.	$180
Actual costs incurred in Year 1	80
Monetary income.	$100

Method 2. Mixed-Dollar Income with Price Gain Isolated

Revenue realized in Year 2.	$180
Replacement cost at the date of sale	130
Operating margin.	$ 50
Add: Price gain (the difference between current replacement cost of $130	
and actual cost of $80)	50
Monetary income.	$100

Method 3. Income Measured in Constant Dollars

Revenue in current (Year 2) dollars $180

Cost of production, expressed in dollars of current (Year 2) purchasing
  power ($80 × 110%) 88

Net income measured in dollars of equal value . . . . $ 92

Accounting income (method 1) reflects the entire difference between dollars of revenue and dollars of cost, without regard to differences in their size. Under method 2 the effect of changes in *specific* prices is isolated, and the fact that one-half of monetary income is due to a price gain is revealed. Both these methods, however, use money as the unit of measurement.

In method 3 the unit of measurement has been changed to dollars of constant value. Both costs and revenue are expressed in Year 2 dollars. Net income in Year 2 dollars is only $92, since the firm must recover 88 Year 2 dollars in order to be as well off as it was when it invested 80 Year 1 dollars in producing the machine.

During and immediately following periods when prices in general are changing, a clear understanding of the limitations of the dollar measuring unit is invaluable in interpreting financial statements. Despite the attention given to this problem, however, and the widespread criticism of the accountant for using a variable measuring unit, no serious move toward measuring business income in other than mixed-dollar terms is yet in evidence. This topic is considered more fully in Chapter 25.

INCOME REPORTING: THE INCOME STATEMENT

We have seen that the problem of measuring income is formidable. Also important, but fortunately less imposing, is the related problem of presenting income measurement information in statement form. A good income statement is something more than an itemized list of revenue and expenses. The accountant should give some thought to such issues as the system of classification, the amount of detail that is useful, the order of presentation, the relation between the elements of net income, and the titles used to describe the items appearing on an income statement.

To management a report of net income for the enterprise may not be as significant as statements showing income by products, departments, or divisions of responsibility. Managers are obviously interested in detailed accounting and statistical data that throw light on the contribution of the various segments of a business to its overall efficiency and success. Such information might also be of great interest to outsiders, but because management is unwilling to reveal operating details to competitors, the information appearing in published income statements is usually highly condensed. More detailed income statements are often submitted to credit grantors and other persons having a special interest in a firm's affairs.

Earnings per Common Share Since the issuance of *APB Opinion No. 15* in 1969, the reporting of earnings per common share has been a required disclosure in the income statement.[7] The disclosure often includes (1) net income before extraordinary items, (2) extraordinary items (net of applicable income tax), and (3) net income per share representing the total of the two preceding per-share amounts. In some cases, of course, there will be no extraordinary items, and net income per share will be the only figure to express the results of operations on a per-share basis. A detailed discussion of earnings per share appears in Chapter 17. Examples of the reporting of per-share data also appear in the published financial statements comprising Appendix B at the back of this book.

Single-step versus multiple-step income statements

The choice between the multiple-step and single-step form of income statement is an unsettled question in income reporting. In the multiple-step form (illustrated on page 103) various intermediate balances, such as gross profit on sales, operating income, and income before income taxes, are computed and labeled on the statement. The single-step approach (illustrated on page 104) is to group all revenue in one category, all expenses in another, and derive a single resultant net income figure.

Those who favor the multiple-step form argue that there are a number of significant subtotals on the road to net income. The *gross profit on sales* figure indicates the average markup on product sold which is available to cover selling and administrative expenses. The distinction between operating and financial revenue and expenses permits the showing of *operating income* as a measure of operating results. The figure *income before income taxes* reflects pre-tax earnings and emphasizes the special nature of the income tax levy.

Proponents of the alternative single-step approach maintain that net income emerges as the overall amount by which a firm is better off after taking into account all revenue and all expenses incurred in producing that revenue. They object to the implication of the multiple-step form that there is a priority of cost recovery; that is, that cost of goods sold is recovered first, then operating expenses, then financial expenses. The multiple-step form also implies relationships that do not exist. For example, showing interest revenue as a special form of income implies that interest is realized without cost; yet some administrative expenses of a business are usually incurred in producing interest revenue. Also mis-

[7] *APB Opinion No. 15,* "Earnings per Share," AICPA (New York: 1969).

SAMPLE CORPORATION
Income Statement
For the Year Ended December 31, 19____
(multiple-step form)

Sales revenues:			
Gross sales			$935,000
Less: Sales returns and allowances		$ 16,200	
Sales discounts		13,400	29,600
Net sales			$905,400
Cost of goods sold:			
Beginning inventory		$ 89,000	
Purchases	$545,500		
Transportation-in	63,300		
Delivered cost of purchases	$608,800		
Less: Purchase returns and allowances . . .	(18,300)		
Purchase discounts	(12,100)	578,400	
Goods available for sale		$667,400	
Less: Ending inventory		68,000	
Cost of goods sold			599,400
Gross profit on sales			$306,000
Operating expenses:			
Selling expenses:			
Sales force expense	$ 63,000		
Advertising and promotion expense	44,000		
Product delivery expense	9,000		
Building occupancy expense	12,000		
Other selling expenses	4,000	$132,000	
General and administrative expenses:			
Administrative salaries	$ 48,000		
State and local property taxes	10,400		
Depreciation of office equipment	4,000		
Other administrative expenses	18,600	81,000	
Total operating expenses			213,000
Operating income			$ 93,000
Other revenue:			
Interest	$ 4,500		
Dividends	10,000	$ 14,500	
Other expenses:			
Interest expense		2,500	12,000
Income before income taxes			$105,000
Federal and state income taxes			55,000
Net income			$ 50,000
Earnings per share of common stock			$1.25

SAMPLE CORPORATION
Income Statement
For the Year Ended December 31, 19___
(single-step form)

Revenue:

Net sales	$905,400
Interest	4,500
Dividends	10,000
Total revenue	$919,900

Expenses of operation:

Wages, salaries, and employee benefits	$116,000	
Merchandise and supplies	603,900	
Payments for services	72,800	
Depreciation of office building and equipment	9,300	
State and local property taxes	10,400	
Interest expense	2,500	
Federal and state income taxes	55,000	
Total expenses		869,900
Net income		$ 50,000
Earnings per share of common stock		$1.25

leading is the common practice, in multiple-step statements, of offsetting "other income" and "other expenses" to arrive at a net figure (often unlabeled). Nonoperating expenses or losses are seldom related to nonoperating revenue or gains.

Most published income statements appear in single-step form; this may be caused in part by the more concise format of the single-step statement. The sequence of listing expenses and the amount of detail shown vary considerably, as will be apparent from inspection of the published financial statements in Appendix B at the back of this book.

The multiple-step income statement is more likely to be found in more detailed financial statements prepared for the use of management, bankers, or other creditors.

Classification of revenue

For most companies the major source of revenue is the production and sale of goods and services. Examples of secondary sources are dividends, royalties, interest, rents, and gains on the disposal of assets. One objective in reporting revenue on an income statement is to disclose the major sources of revenue and to separate primary from ancillary sources. Some companies, for example, report revenue from defense contracts separately from revenue from civilian sources, which enables the reader to form some opinion of future prospects in the light of projected governmental defense expenditures. Railroads commonly report revenue from freight separately from passenger revenue; electric utilities report commercial sales separately from residential revenue. Industrial companies have been less prone to disclose this kind of information in public statements, but there is little question that it would be useful.

Revenue offsets should be clearly distinguished from expenses and deducted from gross revenue in the income statement. Such items as sales discounts and sales returns do not represent expenses, but rather revenue that is never in fact realized.

Classification of expenses

Expenses are classified in income statements to help the reader grasp important operating cost relationships. Classification may be according to the nature of the expense elements, business functions, areas of responsibility, or any other useful basis.

Natural Classification   In many published reports, expenses are reported in single-step form, classified according to the nature of the expense elements. The single-step income statement on page 104 illustrates this basis of classification, in which expenses are grouped in categories that reflect the kinds of resources used during the period.

Functional Classification   The multiple-step income statement on page 103 illustrates a classification of expenses into three broad categories on a functional basis:

Expense	Function
Cost of goods sold	Manufacturing or purchasing products
Selling expenses	Promotion and sales effort
General and administrative expenses	Overall administration of the business

For internal reports, the usefulness of the functional classification system is improved by identifying many more than three functions. For example, material handling, production scheduling, assembly, packing, and crating are manufacturing subfunctions. Similarly, advertising, sales supervision, and delivery are subfunctions within the selling expense category. Allocating expenses within functional categories is not always easy; many expenses fall on the borderline; others are common to two or more functions and can be allocated only on rather arbitrary bases. A consistent allocation procedure followed period by period, however, will usually produce results that are comparable for a given firm and serve the purpose of measuring the cost of performing various operating functions.

Expenses versus Losses In theory losses are nonproductive expenditures or asset expirations that have no observable relation to either current or future revenue. Thus the cost of mistakes, waste, and unusual casualties or calamities over which there can be no control may be distinguished from ordinary operating expenses on the grounds that the former are nonproductive. This distinction, while difficult to draw in many practical situations, can be quite useful for managerial purposes. The distinction between productive and nonproductive outlays, for example, forms in part the basis for a system of cost allocation known as *standard costs* and the basis for interpreting the differences between actual and standard costs. For external reporting, minimum standards of disclosure require that material and unusual losses be disclosed in the income statements.

Cost offsets or savings

Cost offsets or savings should be distinguished from revenue. Revenue arises from realized increases in the value of assets. Cost offsets are expenditures that a business is able to avoid. For example, suppose that a machine can be purchased for $1,000 in cash or $1,200 on a time-payment basis. If the buyer chooses to pay $1,200, he has acquired two distinct types of asset services—the machine for $1,000 and the privilege of deferring payment for $200. If the buyer chooses to pay cash, the $200 is not a revenue but a cost saving, and the machine still costs $1,000. Similarly, cash discounts on purchases are cost savings that should not be confused with revenue.

Offsetting revenue and costs

When business assets are sold, the price received (revenue) and the book value of the asset (cost) are offset and only the net gain or loss is shown on the income statement. Since the sale of such assets is not a part of ordinary operations, the net result is the significant figure.

In some cases revenue is reported as a cost reduction. For example, revenue realized through the sale of scrap or by-products is often recorded as a reduction of the cost of the main product. Because the main product and by-products usually emerge jointly from a single raw material (and joint cost allocation is an insoluble problem), this procedure has merit. If carried to extremes, however, offsetting revenue against costs would detract from the significance of the gross revenue figure.

Extraordinary gains and losses and prior period adjustments

A troublesome problem in reporting periodic income is the proper treatment of extraordinary gains and losses and of prior period adjustments.

General agreement exists that these items, if material in amount, should be clearly disclosed on financial statements. They should be distinguished from the ordinary and current operating revenue and expenses of the period. The issue that has provoked controversy is whether such disclosure is better accomplished by moving these items off the income statement and treating them as direct credits or charges to retained earnings, or by including them on the income statement and reporting them as specifically labeled elements of the net income of the current period.

The practice of including extraordinary items on the income statement and thus making them an element of net income for the current period is called the **all-inclusive concept** of income reporting. The opposing approach, called the **current operating performance concept,** held that extraordinary items should be charged or credited directly to retained earnings rather than being permitted to distort net income of the current period. The controversy between supporters of these opposing views virtually ended with the issuance of **APB Opinion No. 9,** which, in essence, required use of the all-inclusive concept in reporting net income.

APB Opinion No. 9 and APB Opinion No. 30

In 1966 the Accounting Principles Board of the AICPA issued an opinion that net income should reflect all items of gain or loss recognized during the period with the sole exception of prior period adjustments, which it specifically defined.[8] **Opinion No. 9** stated that extraordinary items should be segregated from the results of normal operations and shown separately on the income statement, together with a full disclosure of the nature and amounts of such gains or losses. In single-period statements, prior period adjustments should be reflected as adjustments (net of income tax effect) of the opening balance of retained earnings.

APB Opinion No. 30, issued in 1973, narrowed drastically the definition of extraordinary items previously stated in APB No. 9. To qualify as an extraordinary item under the stringent requirements of **APB Opinion No. 30,** an event must be of **unusual nature and not expected to recur in the forseeable future.** Examples cited as meeting these two criteria were ". . . a major casualty (such as an earthquake), an expropriation, or a prohibition under a newly enacted law. . . ."[9] Emphasis was placed on the point that extraordinary events occur infrequently, but that infrequency of occurrence of a particular event does not in itself warrant treatment as an extraordinary item.

A clear understanding of extraordinary items may be aided by pointing out certain transactions or events which do not qualify as extraordinary items and which should be included in current operations without separate disclosure on the income statement. **Not** included in the category

---

[8] *APB Opinion No. 9,* "Reporting the Results of Operations," AICPA (New York: 1966).
[9] *APB Opinion No. 30,* "Reporting the Results of Operations," AICPA (New York: 1973), p. 566.

of extraordinary items are gains or losses on disposal of a segment of a business, write-downs of receivables, inventories, development costs, or adjustments of accrued contract prices. Neither is the effect of fluctuations in the rates of foreign exchange to be considered as extraordinary. These latter items are considered of a character typical of the customary activities of the entity.

Current criticism of extraordinary items

The existing criteria for extraordinary items are probably not sufficiently clear to produce consistent uniform application in different companies. If the interpretation of what constitutes an extraordinary item varies widely among companies and from year to year, the placing of emphasis upon earnings before extraordinary items may not be helpful to investors.

Moreover, it is apparent from a review of published financial statements that extraordinary items represent losses far more often than gains. Critics suggest that some companies have abused the concept of reporting extraordinary items. It may be possible to report rising earnings for several years by accumulating questionable balances in asset accounts. Then, in a single year, all dubious assets may be written off as an extraordinary loss. In that year, earnings after extraordinary items will drop sharply, but the stage has thereby been set for showing good earnings in the following years. It is also argued that if a company is going to issue a single annual report with decreased earnings, damage to the market price of its stock will not be much worse in case of a large one-time earnings decline than for a small one.

Perhaps the overall quality and comparability of financial statements would be improved if the category of extraordinary items were discontinued and all revenue, expenses, gains, and losses were utilized before presenting an amount representing net income.

Prior period adjustments

In contrast to extraordinary items, *prior period adjustments* are excluded from the determination of net income for the current period and are reported in the statement of retained earnings. Prior period adjustments are defined as:

> those material adjustments which (a) can be specifically identified with and directly related to the business activities of particular prior periods, and (b) are not attributable to economic events occurring subsequent to the date of the financial statements for the prior period, and (c) depend primarily on determinations by persons other than management and (d) were not susceptible to reasonable estimation prior to such determination. Such adjustments are rare in modern financial accounting.[10]

Examples of these rare events which are to be classified as prior period

---

[10] *APB Opinion No. 9, op. cit.,* par. 23.

adjustments and reported in the statement of retained earnings are:

1 Material nonrecurring adjustments or settlements of income taxes

2 Adjustments resulting from renegotiation of government contracts or of utility rate processes

3 Settlements of significant amounts from litigation or other claims

To define more sharply the limited types of events which classify as prior period adjustments, it is helpful to emphasize that prior period adjustments do *not* include the normal recurring corrections and adjustments which inevitably result from the use of estimates in the accounting process. Changes in the estimated remaining lives of plant and equipment affect the amounts of depreciation, but these changes are considered prospective in nature, hence not prior period adjustments. Relatively immaterial adjustments of the provisions for liabilities, including income taxes, which were made in prior periods are considered as recurring items to be included in reporting the results of operations for the current period. Other uncertainties such as those relating to the collectibility of receivables, the ultimate recovery of deferred costs, and the realizability of inventories do *not* qualify to be treated as prior period adjustments. In these matters, economic events of the current period enter into the elimination of the previously existing uncertainty and thus make the adjustments elements in determining net income for the current period.

The discussion of prior period adjustments in *APB Opinion No. 9* did not make as clear as needed the treatment of accounting changes and of outright material accounting errors in prior periods. These topics have been considered in *APB Opinion No. 20,* "Accounting Changes,"[11] which is analyzed at length in Chapter 22. A brief consideration of accounting changes at this point, however, will be useful in this discussion of the income statement.

Accounting changes

A type of accounting change closely related to the preceding discussion is the correction of accounting errors. These errors might include arithmetical mistakes, the misuse or omissions of information, mistakes in the application of accounting principles or procedures, and failure to interpret properly the accounting aspects of a major transaction.

If the error is discovered in the period in which it occurs and before financial statements are issued, correction can be made without difficulty. If the error is material and is not discovered until a subsequent period, *APB Opinion No. 20* states that *the correction should be made as a prior period adjustment.*[12] Any asset or liability accounts affected would be restated to corrected amounts as of the beginning of the current period; the effect

---

[11]*APB Opinion No. 20,* "Accounting Changes," AICPA (New York: 1971).
[12]*Ibid.,* par. 36, pp. 398–399.

of the error on the earnings of prior periods would be shown in the statement of retained earnings as an adjustment of the beginning balance of retained earnings for the current year.

When correction of an error is made as a prior period adjustment, the issuance of comparative financial statements for the current and preceding year will require restatement of the prior year's statements to reflect the information which has become available.

Another type of accounting change is a *change in estimates* such as the revision of an original estimate of an 8-year life for aircraft to a 12-year life. The new estimate affects only the current and future years' financial statements; no correcting entries are necessary. The undepreciated cost of the aircraft at the date of the change in estimated useful life will be allocated among the estimated remaining years of useful life.

The adoption of a generally accepted accounting principle different from the one used previously is exemplified by a change from lifo to fifo in the valuation of inventory, from accelerated depreciation to straight-line depreciation, or from capitalizing research and development costs to charging them to expense as incurred. Such changes require the restatement of assets and liabilities as of the beginning of the current period to the amounts that would have existed if the newly adopted principle had been used in prior years. The related debit or credit reflecting the cumulative effect of the change on earnings of prior years is reported in the current year's income statement between any extraordinary items and the figure for net income. The method of reporting the cumulative effect of the change is the same as for extraordinary items.

Income tax allocation

Income taxes on corporate income constitute a major expense of doing business. *Taxable income* is a legal concept; it is related to accounting income but there are significant differences. As a result a corporation's taxable income for the year may differ substantially from its accounting income before income taxes, as reported in the income statement. Accountants have attempted to deal with this problem by *income tax allocation,* which is the subject matter of Chapter 20. At this point only the general nature of income tax allocation will be considered, with attention focused on the method of presenting clearly on the income statement the tax effect of extraordinary gains and losses.

Tax allocation is most conveniently considered as falling into two major types: (1) *interperiod tax allocation,* and (2) *intraperiod tax allocation.*

Interperiod tax allocation means that income tax expense should be allocated between years because certain revenue or certain expenses appear on the income statement either before or after they are included on the income tax return. By means of interperiod tax allocation, the income tax expense on the income statement is based on earnings as shown on the income statement rather than at the amount of income tax payable for the year as shown on the corporation's tax return. In brief, income taxes are allocated between periods as are other expenses.

Intraperiod tax allocation is the process of allocating income tax expense to income from operations, to extraordinary items, and to any prior period adjustments on the retained earnings statement. Such allocation is a required practice, as indicated by the following statement in *APB Opinion No. 11:*

> The income tax expense attributable to income before extraordinary items is computed by determining the income tax expense related to revenue and expense transactions entering into the determination of such income, without giving effect to the tax consequences of the items excluded from the determination of income before extraordinary items. The income tax expense attributable to other items is determined by the tax consequences of transactions involving these items.[13]

Income taxes, extraordinary items, and prior period adjustments

Extraordinary gains and losses should be reported *net of taxes* in the income statement. Prior period adjustments should be reported *net of taxes* in the statement of retained earnings. Consequently, the amount of income taxes deducted from operating income is the amount of taxes that would be owed if there were no extraordinary gains and losses and no prior period adjustments. Thus, on the financial statements, income tax accompanies the item that gave rise to the tax. The income tax on an extraordinary gain is netted against the gain; the tax reduction caused by an extraordinary loss is offset against the loss. At present corporations are subject to a lower rate of income tax on the first $25,000 of net income than on income above that amount. To achieve simplicity in illustrations (and recognizing that income tax rates may change at any time), we shall, whenever convenient, assume a rate of 40% in illustrating the above practices.

Illustration of extraordinary gain, net of tax   Assume that Model Corporation, a company with 100,000 shares of capital stock, has operating income of $500,000 taxable at 40%, and an extraordinary gain of $300,000 taxable at 30%. The total income tax is $290,000 ($200,000 + $90,000), and a partial income statement would be prepared as illustrated on page 112.

If intraperiod tax allocation had not been used in this illustration, the income before extraordinary item would have been shown at a distorted figure of $210,000 and the extraordinary gain at $300,000. The data on earnings per share would also have been distorted.

Illustration of extraordinary loss, net of tax   As a parallel example, assume that instead of an extraordinary gain, Model Corporation had a fully deductible fire loss of $300,000. Operating income, as before, was $500,000, taxable at 40%. The total income tax would be $80,000,

---

[13] *APB Opinion No. 11,* "Accounting for Income Taxes," AICPA (New York: 1967), par. 52.

MODEL CORPORATION
Partial Income Statement
For Current Year

Income before income taxes and extraordinary item		$500,000
Income taxes (actual taxes are $290,000, of which $90,000 is applicable to extraordinary gain)		200,000
Income before extraordinary item		$300,000
Extraordinary gain	$300,000	
Less: Applicable income tax	90,000	210,000
Net income		$510,000
Per share of capital stock:		
Income before extraordinary item		$3.00
Extraordinary gain		2.10
Net income		$5.10

($200,000 − $120,000). A partial income statement would show this situation as follows:

MODEL CORPORATION
Partial Income Statement
For Current Year

Income before income taxes and extraordinary item		$500,000
Income taxes (actual taxes are $80,000 as a result of the tax reduction from the extraordinary loss)		200,000
Income before extraordinary item		$300,000
Extraordinary loss from fire	$300,000	
Less: Applicable income tax reduction	120,000	180,000
Net income		$120,000
Per share of capital stock:		
Income before extraordinary item		$3.00
Extraordinary loss		(1.80)
Net income		$1.20

If tax allocation procedures had not been followed, the income statement would have shown income before extraordinary item at the distorted amount of $420,000 less an extraordinary loss of $300,000, and per-share data would have been quite misleading.

Illustration of prior period adjustment, net of tax Assume that Model Corporation, as the result of court settlement of litigation begun in a prior year, received a taxable payment of $400,000. As in the preceding example, operating income was $500,000, taxable at 40%, and there was a fully deductible fire loss of $300,000. The total income tax is $240,000, ($200,000 − $120,000 + $160,000). The balance of retained earnings at the beginning of the year was $600,000; dividends during the year were $100,000. A partial income statement and a statement of retained earnings follow:

MODEL CORPORATION
Partial Income Statement
For Current Year

Income before income taxes and extraordinary item		$500,000
Income taxes (actual taxes are $240,000, reflecting $160,000 applicable to a prior period adjustment, and a tax reduction of $120,000 resulting from an extraordinary loss)		200,000
Income before extraordinary item.		$300,000
Extraordinary loss from fire	$300,000	
Less: Applicable income tax reduction	120,000	180,000
Net income		$120,000
Per share of capital stock:		
Income before extraordinary item		$3.00
Extraordinary loss		(1.80)
Net income		$1.20

MODEL CORPORATION
Statement of Retained Earnings
For Current Year

Retained earnings, beginning of year:		
As originally reported.		$600,000
Add: Prior period adjustment—damages received from settlement of litigation	$400,000	
Less: Applicable income tax	160,000	240,000
Retained earnings at beginning of year as restated		$840,000
Net income for year		120,000
Subtotal		$960,000
Cash dividends paid ($1 per share)		100,000
Retained earnings, end of year		$860,000

In this illustration, if intraperiod tax allocation had not been used, the total income tax expense of $240,000 would have been deducted from the $500,000 of income before taxes and extraordinary items. This would have resulted in numerous distorted amounts, including the income before extraordinary items, the extraordinary loss, the net income, data on earnings per share, and the restated beginning balance of retained earnings.

Statement of retained earnings

Changing concepts of financial reporting in recent years, as described earlier in this chapter, have firmly established the all-inclusive income statement, thus tending to shorten and simplify the statement of retained earnings. Also significant has been the trend away from the use of reserves, or appropriations of retained earnings. Consequently, the typical statement of retained earnings today merely lists the beginning balance of retained earnings, shows the net income for the year as an addition, the dividends as a deduction, and concludes with the ending balance of retained earnings. The information on dividends customarily shows the cash dividends per share as well as the total amount declared during the year. Reporting dividends per share provides useful information to the stockholder in computing the yield on an investment.

The basic format may be amended by the restatement of the beginning balance to show the effect of any prior period adjustment, as was done in the illustrated statement on page 113.

As with other financial statements, the statement of retained earnings is often presented in comparative form showing data for two years. This comparative form of retained earnings statement is used in all four of the sets of published financial statements in Appendix B.

Combined statement of income and retained earnings

In an effort to put all relevant information relating to the change in stockholders' equity during the year in one place, some companies combine the income statement with the statement of retained earnings. Such a presentation has the advantage of displaying in one statement both the prior period adjustments and extraordinary gains and losses, thus reducing the possibility that any of these items will be overlooked. One minor objection to this form of reporting is that the net income figure inevitably appears in the middle, rather than as the final figure in the statement.

A combined statement of income and retained earnings showing comparative data for two years is presented below for Texas Gulf, Inc. Note in this illustration that the per-share data appears at the end of the combined statement. An alternative approach, when there are no extraordinary items, is to show the earnings per share parenthetically on the line for net income.

Texas Gulf, Inc. and Consolidated Subsidiaries
Consolidated Statements of Income and Retained Earnings

	Year ended December 31 1972	Year ended December 31 1971
Gross Sales	$316,048,000	$271,324,000
Less outside zinc and lead smelting and refining charges	45,506,000	53,625,000
	270,542,000	217,699,000
Royalties, Interest and Other Income	2,876,000	3,250,000
	273,418,000	220,949,000
Costs and Expenses		
Operating, delivery and other related costs and expenses	188,922,000	148,004,000
Exploration	6,229,000	11,641,000
Selling, general and administrative	13,323,000	12,981,000
Interest	12,032,000	8,847,000
Income taxes	22,350,000	14,250,000
	242,856,000	195,723,000
Income Before Extraordinary Charge	30,562,000	25,226,000
Extraordinary Charge relating to abandonment of mining equipment due to change from underground to solution mining, net of applicable income tax of $3,227,000	—	(4,675,000)
Net Income	30,562,000	20,551,000
Retained Earnings at January 1	371,122,000	368,803,000
	401,684,000	389,354,000
Cash Dividends	18,238,000	18,232,000
Retained Earnings at December 31	$383,446,000	$371,122,000
Per Share of Capital Stock		
Income before extraordinary charge	$1.01	$ .83
Extraordinary charge, net of tax	—	($ .15)
Net Income	$1.01	$ .68
Dividends	$ .60	$ .60
Average Number of Shares Outstanding	30,395,912	30,386,007

REVIEW QUESTIONS

1 Ten accountants, if asked to measure the lifetime income of a business and to assume no change in the purchasing power of the dollar, would probably agree within narrow limits on this long-run income measurement. The same ten accountants might vary over a wide range in their measurement of periodic income for the same business. Why?

2 A committee of the American Accounting Association published, in 1966, a study entitled *A Statement of Basic Accounting Theory.* One of the basic standards recommended as a criterion to be used in evaluating accounting information was *verifiability.* Explain how you would expect this standard to be related to the accountant's search for objective evidence.

3 What is the distinction between product and period costs? Give an example of each type of cost. Give an example of a cost that might be either a period or a product cost, depending on the nature of the expenditure.

4 What is the accounting concept of *realization* and how does it affect the measurement of periodic income? What are two primary criteria used in determining when revenue has been realized?

5 Describe three stages in the earning process, other than the point of sale, at which revenue might be recognized. Give an example of a situation in which each of these three tests of realization might be appropriate.

6 The owner of an appliance store has just sold a refrigerator to a customer for $350. An employee recorded cost of goods sold of $240 relating to this sale. What elements are probably included in this cost figure? What elements of cost are probably omitted from the $240?

7 Would you expect a newly organized corporation engaged in the restaurant franchising field, having limited capital and attempting to secure capital from public investors and bankers, to favor accounting policies that would speed up the recognition of revenue or delay it? Explain.

8 Distinguish between a *functional* and a *natural* classification of expenses. What are the advantages of a functional classification for managerial purposes?

9 Distinguish between *expenses* and *losses,* and between *revenue* and *cost offsets.*

10 For many years a difference of opinion among accountants caused considerable debate in accounting literature between the advocates of the *all-inclusive income concept* and the *current operating performance income concept.* What was meant by these terms and how was the controversy affected by the issuance of *APB Opinion No. 9,* "Reporting the Results of Operations"?

11 Explain the principal differences between the *single-step* and the *multiple-step* forms of income statement. Should earnings per share data be shown with either or both these forms of income statement?

12 What are the criteria that a business transaction or event must meet in order to qualify as a *prior period adjustment?* Give an example of such a transaction or event.

13 The accounting process requires the making of estimates of many types, as, for example, the collectibility of receivables and the extent of future benefits to be derived from research and development costs. With the passage of time, information becomes available which makes clear the nature and extent of error in past estimates. Generally speaking, should the adjustments to revise these estimates be presented on the income statement as extraordinary items? Explain.

14 Explain briefly the meaning of *intraperiod tax allocation* and *interperiod tax allocation.*

15 If a corporation's income statement includes both extraordinary gains and extraordinary losses, how many earnings per share figures should be shown on the income statement? Explain.

EXERCISES

Ex. 3-1 The Cole Company declared and paid cash dividends of $10,000 during 1975. The company's records show that changes in account balances occurred as follows during 1975:

	Increase	Decrease
Cash	$30,000	
Accounts receivable		$1,000
Merchandise inventory	15,000	
Equipment (net)	18,000	
Building (net)	30,000	
Accounts payable		7,000
Notes payable	50,000	
Capital stock	30,000	
Paid-in capital in excess of par	10,000	

Assuming that there were no transactions affecting retained earnings except the cash dividend, calculate the net income for 1975.

Ex. 3-2 Hughes, Inc., had general expenses of 10% of sales and 20% of cost of goods sold. Selling expenses are an amount equal to 20% of sales. The beginning merchandise inventory was $100,000 and purchases amounted to 55% of sales. Income before taxes was $80,000. Assume an income tax rate of 40%. Prepare an income statement in good form for the year ended December 31, 19____. (Give supporting computations.) **Suggestion:** (1) Compute the cost of goods sold as a percentage of sales by using the information given relating general expenses to cost of goods sold **and** to sales; (2) prepare an income statement in percentages, including all items from sales to income before taxes, with sales representing 100%; (3) prepare an income statement in dollars, using the dollar amounts given and deriving the other dollar amounts from the percentage relationship.

Ex. 3-3 For the following list of events and transactions, you are to state for each one whether or not there is immediate realization of revenue or gain. Indicate briefly the reason supporting your conclusion.

a Tavis, a Midwestern farmer, has harvested 20,000 bushels of grain for which a government-guaranteed price exists. Tavis is holding the grain in hope of rising prices and is following closely the daily grain price quotations in Chicago newspapers.

b Sale for cash of a $200 gift certificate, which may be exchanged by the holder for merchandise in a subsequent period.

c Land purchased for $45,000 in 1970 has a current appraised value of $65,000.

d After receiving bids of $205,000 and $206,000 from independent contractors for construction of a new factory building, the X Company constructed the building itself for its own use at a cost of $190,000.

e Securities with a market value of $17,650 are received from a customer in settlement of an account receivable for $16,600 which was more than a year past due.

f Merchandise with a cost of $480 is sold under a 24-month installment contract for a 10% down payment of $60. Title to the merchandise remains with the seller until all installment payments have been collected.

g Land held for investment is planted in lettuce. If the crop is harvested successfully and demand remains strong, cash receipts are expected to exceed expenses by $20,000. The crop growth is halfway to maturity at this time.

h Rendered services to a customer and received from him a check drawn on a small out-of-state bank.

Ex. 3-4 Select the best answer for each of the following multiple choice questions:

a Conventionally accountants measure income:
(1) By applying a value-added concept
(2) By using a transactions approach
(3) As a change in the value of owners' equity
(4) As a change in the purchasing power of owners' equity

b When financial statements for a single year are being presented (without comparative statements), a prior period adjustment recognized in the current year ordinarily would:
(1) Be shown as an adjustment of the beginning balance of retained earnings
(2) Affect net income before extraordinary items of the current year
(3) Be shown as an extraordinary item on the current year's income statement
(4) Be included in an all-inclusive income statement

c The accounting concept of matching is best demonstrated by:
(1) Not recognizing any expense unless some revenue is realized
(2) Associating effort (cost) with accomplishment (revenue)
(3) Recognizing prepaid rent received as revenue
(4) Establishing a Reserve for Possible Future Market Decline in Inventory account

d The occurrence which most likely would have no effect on 1975 net income (assuming that all involved are material) is the:
(1) Sale in 1975 of an office building contributed by a stockholder in 1960
(2) Collection in 1975 of a receivable from a customer whose account was written off in 1973
(3) Settlement based on litigation in 1975 of previously unrecognized damages from a serious accident that occurred in 1973
(4) Worthlessness determined in 1975 of securities purchased on a speculative basis in 1971

Ex. 3-5 Given below are account balances for the Staple Corporation.

Beginning inventory	$ 89,000		Selling expenses	$132,000
Ending inventory	68,000		Administrative expenses	81,000
Sales	935,000		Interest earned	4,500
Purchases	545,500		Dividends earned	10,000
Sales discounts	13,400		Interest expense	2,500
Purchase discounts	12,100		Income taxes	55,000
Sales returns	16,200		Retained earnings, beginning	200,000
Purchase returns	18,300		Retained earnings, ending	220,000
Transportation-in	63,300			

From the foregoing information, compute the following:
a Total net revenue
b Total expenses
c Net income
d Dividends declared during the year

SHORT CASES FOR ANALYSIS AND DECISION

Case 3-1 The financial statements of Prospect Publishing Company are presented to the board of directors for review upon completion of the annual audit. One of the directors asks why the income statement is based on the assumption that an equal proportion of the revenue is earned with the publication of every issue of the company's magazine. He feels that the "crucial event" in the process of earning revenue in the magazine business is the cash sale of the subscription. He says that he does not understand why—other than for the smoothing of income—most of the revenue cannot be "realized" in the period of sale.

Instructions

a List three accepted methods for recognizing revenue in the accounts and explain when the methods are appropriate. Do not limit your listing to the methods for the recognition of revenue in magazine publishing.

b Discuss the propriety of timing the recognition of revenue in the Prospect Publishing Company's accounts with:

(1) The cash sale of the magazine subscription
(2) The publication of the magazine every month
(3) Both events, by recognizing a portion of the revenue with the cash sale of the magazine subscription and a portion of the revenue with the publication of the magazine every month

Case 3-2 The combined statement of income and retained earnings shown below was prepared by an employee of Melody Corporation. The company is in a retail business and makes most of its sales on credit. Accounts receivable are aged at the end of the period and the allowance for uncollectible accounts is adjusted to the level required to value receivables at their estimated collectible amount.

MELODY CORPORATION
Statement of Income and Retained Earnings
Years Ended December 31, 1975, and December 31, 1974

	1975	1974
Revenues:		
Gross sales including sales taxes	$876,900	$782,500
Less returns, allowances, and cash discounts	18,800	16,200
Net sales	$858,100	$766,300
Dividends, interest, and purchases discounts	30,250	18,300
Recoveries of accounts written off in prior years	11,800	3,000
Total revenues	$900,150	$787,600
Costs and expenses:		
Cost of goods sold, including sales taxes	$415,900	$332,200
Salaries and related payroll expenses	60,500	62,100
Rent	19,100	19,100
Freight-in and freight-out	3,400	2,900
Uncollectible accounts expense	24,000	26,000
Total costs and expenses	$522,900	$442,300
Income before extraordinary items	$377,250	$345,300
Extraordinary items:		
Loss on discontinued styles (Note 1)	$ 24,000	$ 4,800

Loss on sale of marketable securities (Note 2)	52,050	
Loss on sale of warehouse (Note 3)	86,350	
Retroactive settlement of federal income taxes for 1974 and 1973 (Note 4)	31,600	
Total extraordinary items	$194,000	$ 4,800
Net income	$183,250	$340,500
Retained earnings at beginning of year	312,700	163,100
Total	$495,950	$503,600
Less: Federal income taxes	$120,000	$170,000
Cash dividends on common stock	21,900	20,900
Total	$141,900	$190,900
Retained earnings at end of year	$354,050	$312,700
Net income per share of common stock	$1.83	$3,41

Notes to the Statement of Income and Retained Earnings:

(1) New styles and rapidly changing customer preferences resulted in a $24,000 loss on the disposal of discontinued styles and related accessories.

(2) The corporation sold an investment in marketable securities at a loss of $52,050, with no income tax effect.

(3) The corporation sold one of its warehouses at an $86,350 loss.

(4) The corporation was charged $31,600 retroactively for additional income taxes resulting from a settlement in 1975 of this amount. $14,000 was applicable to 1974 and the balance was applicable to 1973.

Instructions Identify and discuss the weaknesses in classification and disclosure in the single-step statement of income and retained earnings above. Your discussion should explain why you consider these treatments to be weaknesses and what you consider to be the proper treatment of items. Do not discuss form and terminology, and do not prepare a revised statement.

Case 3-3 The Glenview Advertising Agency handles advertising for clients under contracts which provide that the agency shall develop advertising copy and layouts and place ads in various media, charging clients a commission of 18% of the media cost as its fee. The agency makes advance billings to its clients of estimated media cost plus its 18% commission. Later adjustments of these advance billings are usually minor. Often both the billings and receipt of cash from these billings occur before the period in which the advertising actually appears in the media.

In devising a system for measuring income, the agency considered the following possible points at which revenue and costs might be recognized and income measured: (1) At the time of the advanced billing; (2) when payment is received from clients; (3) in the month in which the advertising appears in the media; (4) when the bill for advertising is received from the media.

The agency chose (1) as the point at which it would recognize income, on the grounds that it has a contract with clients for specified advertising and thus income is earned when billed. At the time of billing, the agency establishes accounts receivable with clients and records the estimated liability to the media and its commission earnings. At this time the agency also estimates its expenses and establishes a liability for the estimated expense related to the client's billing. Adjusting entries are made to establish actual cost and revenue amounts when billings are received from media, when actual expenses are finally determined, and when final statements are sent to clients.

Instructions Discuss each of the four points at which the Glenview Advertising Agency might recognize income, and state your opinion as to the proper basis for accounting for income in this case. If you disagree with the method followed by the company, explain the basis for your disagreement and why you support an alternative occasion for income recognition.

Case 3-4 On May 8, 1974, Folley Corporation signed a contract with Morton Associates under which Morton agreed to (1) construct an office building on land owned by Folley, (2) accept responsibility for procuring financing for the project and finding tenants, and (3) manage the property for 50 years. The annual profit from the project, after debt service, was to be divided equally between Folley Corporation and Morton Associates. Morton was to accept its share of future profits as full payment for its services in construction, obtaining finances and tenants, and management of the project.

By April 30, 1975, the project was nearly completed and tenants had signed leases to occupy 90% of the available space at annual rentals aggregating $2,600,000. It is estimated that, after operating expenses and debt service, the annual profit will amount to $850,000. The management of Morton Associates believed that the economic benefit derived from the contract with Folley should be reflected on its financial statements for the fiscal year ended April 30, 1975, and directed that revenue be accrued in an amount equal to the commercial value of the services Morton had rendered during the year, that this amount be carried in contracts receivable, and that all related expenditures be charged against the revenue.

Instructions
a Explain the main difference between the economic concept of business income as reflected by Morton's management and the measurement of income under generally accepted accounting principles.
b Discuss the factors to be considered in determining when revenue has been realized for the purpose of accounting measurement of periodic income.
c Is the belief of Morton's management in accord with generally accepted accounting principles for the measurement of revenue and expense for the year ended April 30, 1975? Support your opinion by discussing the application to this case of the factors to be considered for asset measurement and revenue and expense recognition.

PROBLEMS

Group A

3A-1 The following information was compiled from the accounting records of the Del Mar Company as a basis for preparation of an income statement for the current year:

Beginning inventory	*$101,380*
Ending inventory	*86,215*
Purchase returns & allowances	*7,015*
Common stock ($10 par)	*100,000*
Sales	*896,730*
Sales returns & allowances	*13,560*
Depreciation on buildings and equipment (75% selling; 25% administrative)	*42,400*
Dividends declared	*18,000*
Rental revenue	*14,890*
Interest on notes payable	*8,480*
Transportation-in on merchandise	*39,690*
Purchase of merchandise	*398,560*

Selling expenses:

Salaries and wages	*48,650*
Purchased services	*25,780*
Materials and supplies	*12,640*

Administrative expenses:

Salaries and wages	*137,930*
Purchased services	*42,530*
Materials and supplies	*9,270*
Income taxes	*59,010*

Instructions
a Prepare a multiple-step income statement for the current year. Include earnings per share.
b Prepare a single-step income statement for the current year, using a natural classification of expenses. Include earnings per share.
c Explain which form you prefer, giving reasons for your answer.

3A-2 Foster Corporation's capital structure consists solely of common stock, of which 200,000 shares are authorized and 50,000 shares are outstanding. At December 31, an analysis of the accounts and discussions with company officials revealed the following information:

Sales	*$1,320,000*
Sales discounts	*22,600*
Purchase discounts	*17,800*
Purchases	*752,400*
Earthquake loss	*76,000*
Selling expense	*142,000*
General and administrative expense	*140,000*
Dividend revenue	*10,800*
Cash dividends declared	*75,000*
Interest expense	*17,000*
Inventory, Jan. 1, 1975	*152,000*
Inventory, Dec. 31, 1975	*125,000*
Retained earnings, Jan. 1, 1975	*390,000*

The amount of income taxes applicable to ordinary income for 1975 was $123,800, but the tax effect of the loss from the earthquake amounted to $38,000, leaving income tax expense for the year of $85,800.

Instructions Prepare a combined statement of income and retained earnings for the year ended December 31, 1975. Use the single-step form.

3A-3 In 1970 Ruth Hill began a small business by investing $28,800 in cash and other property (land and a building) worth $72,000. In 1972 the business became a partnership with the admission of James Harvey as a partner. Harvey made a cash investment in the business of $88,000. At the end of 1975, the balance sheet of the business appeared as follows:

Cash	$ 20,960	Current liabilities	$ 34,528
Accounts receivable (net) . .	46,256	Mortgage payable	80,000
Inventories	51,360	R. Hill, capital	293,648
Plant & equipment (net) . . .	393,600	J. Harvey, capital	104,000
	$512,176		$512,176

At this point, the partners disagreed over business policies and decided to liquidate the business. Inventories were sold for $40,000 and plant and equipment for $440,000. Of the receivables, $19,200 were collected; $25,600 of receivables were sold to a financing firm (without recourse) for $20,000; and $1,456 were written off as uncollectible. All debts were paid, including $320 of interest on the mortgage not accrued at the date of the above balance sheet. During the life of the business (1970 through 1975), Ruth Hill had withdrawn $267,200 from the business and Harvey had withdrawn $47,792.

Instructions
a Compute the lifetime net income of the business on the basis of the above information. Since a single proprietorship and a partnership are not taxable entities, you are to disregard income taxes.
b Discuss any areas of uncertainty in your determination of lifetime net income in this case.

3A-4 The information listed below was available for the Berman Corporation at December 31, 1975.

Extraordinary gain	$ 96,000
Sales	868,500
Income taxes applicable to extraordinary gain	33,600
Income tax refund for prior year after settlement of litigation in current year	64,000
Dividends declared on common stock	50,000
Purchases	696,000
Purchase discounts	10,000
Inventory, Jan. 1, 1975	73,000
Income taxes applicable to ordinary income	40,000
Selling expenses	50,000
General and administrative expenses	48,000
Inventory, Dec. 31, 1975	76,000
Sales returns and allowances	12,500
Interest revenue	5,000

The balance in the Retained Earnings account on January 1, 1975, was $466,000. There are 100,000 shares of common stock outstanding.

Instructions
a Prepare a multiple-step income statement, including per-share data.
b Prepare a statement of retained earnings.

3A-5 At the beginning of the current year, John Howard, owner and operator of a large farm, had no inventories on hand. During the current year, he produced 8,000 bushels of soybeans, 10,000 bushels of barley, and 16,000 bushels of rye. During the year Howard sold one-half of each of his crops at the following prices:

soybeans $4.50 per bushel, barley $3.25 per bushel, rye $2 per bushel. Howard follows the daily price quotations of these commodities very closely, and at the end of the year he noted that the market price per bushel for each of these commodities was as follows: soybeans $5 per bushel, barley $3.50 per bushel, and rye $2.20 per bushel.

The total expenses incurred in operating the farm during the year were $48,550, including depreciation of buildings and equipment. Howard estimates that his cost of selling and delivering these crops is 40 cents per bushel. The selling and delivering expenses applicable to the portion of the crops sold during the year are included in the total operating expenses given above.

Instructions

a Prepare an income statement for Howard for the current year. Explain the concept of realization employed in your measurement of income and, in particular, the basis you used in assigning a valuation to the commodities on hand at the end of the period.

b In measuring income during the current year, what consideration did you give to the possibility that the market value of these three commodities might change between the end of the current year and the time Howard finally sold them?

c What is the essential difference between the problem of measuring income for Howard, and measuring income for a manufacturer of farm machinery?

Group B

3B-1 Los Robles Company is a merchandising corporation with $10 par common stock, of which 16,000 shares are outstanding. In addition to its merchandising activities, the company obtains rental revenue of $23,824 a year for a part of its building leased to another company.

The following information is available concerning the merchandising activities for the current year:

Ending inventory (a decrease of $24,264 during the year)	$ 137,944
Purchases of merchandise (of which $11,224 was returned)	637,696
Transportation-in	63,504
Sales (of which $21,696 were returned by customers)	1,434,768
Selling expenses (salaries & wages, $77,840; purchased services, $41,248; supplies, $20,224)	139,312
Administrative expenses (salaries & wages, $220,688; purchased services, $68,048; supplies, $14,832)	303,568
Depreciation on buildings and equipment (75% selling and 25% administrative)	67,840

In addition to these operating revenue and expenses, Los Robles Company incurred interest expense of $13,568 on notes payable and declared dividends of $28,800. The provision for income taxes was $94,416.

Instructions

a Prepare a single-step income statement for the current year, classifying expenses on a natural rather than a functional basis. Include data on earnings per share.

b Prepare a multiple-step income statement for the current year. Include earnings per share.

c Discuss the relative merits of the two forms of income statement.

3B-2 The following data were taken from the ledger of the Wilson Company at the end of 1975. Income taxes for the current year applicable to ordinary income are $25,200. Income taxes applicable to the extraordinary gain are $7,500. Income tax credit applicable to the extraordinary loss is $16,000. Wilson Company has 50,000 shares of common stock issued and outstanding.

Cost of goods sold.	$ 650,000
Depreciation expense	20,000
Cash dividends declared	12,000
Extraordinary gain	25,000
Insurance expense.	7,000
Sales	1,000,000
Extraordinary loss	40,000
Salaries.	175,000
Retained earnings, Jan. 1, 1975.	65,000
Other operating expenses	85,300

Instructions
a Prepare a combined statement of income and retained earnings. Use the single-step form.
b Provide earnings per common share information.

3B-3 Marvin Rogers began a small business in 1970, investing $18,000 in cash and property (land and building) worth $45,000. In 1973, the business became a partnership with the admission of Lee Davis as a partner. Davis invested $55,000 cash in the business at the time of his admission. By the end of 1975, the balance sheet of the business appeared as follows:

Cash	$ 13,100	Current liabilities	$ 21,580
Receivables (net).	28,910	Mortgage payable	50,000
Inventories	32,100	Rogers, capital	183,530
Plant & equipment (net) . . .	246,000	Davis, capital	65,000
	$320,110		$320,110

At this date the partners disagreed over business policy and decided to liquidate the business shortly. Inventories were sold for $25,000 and plant and equipment for $275,000. Of the receivables, $12,000 were collected; $16,000 were sold to a financing firm (without recourse) for $12,500; and $910 were written off as uncollectible. All debts were paid, including $200 of interest on the mortgage not accrued at the time of the above statement. During the life of the business, Rogers had withdrawn $167,000 and Davis had withdrawn $39,870 from the business.

Instructions
a Compute the lifetime net income of this business on the basis of the above information. Income taxes are to be ignored, since a partnership is not a taxable entity.
b Explain whether there are any areas of uncertainty in your determination of lifetime net income in this situation.

3B-4 The following information regarding Robertson Corporation was available at December 31, 1975:

Common stock outstanding	50,000 shares
Retained earnings balance, Jan. 1, 1975	$100,000
Inventory, Jan. 1, 1975	77,000
Extraordinary gain	25,000
Purchases	730,000
Sales	912,000
Dividend revenue	10,000
Inventory, Dec. 31, 1975	72,000
Selling expenses	61,200
Sales returns and allowances	13,000
Purchase discounts	12,000
Dividends declared on common stock	50,000
Income taxes applicable to extraordinary gain	8,750
Income taxes applicable to ordinary income	34,800
General and administrative expenses	46,500
Collection of damages from settlement of litigation begun in prior year	60,000
Income taxes applicable to damages collected	24,000

Instructions

a Prepare a **single-step** income statement. (A number of accounts balances should be combined to obtain summary amounts to appear in the single-step format for the income statement.) Include per-share data.

b Prepare a statement of retained earnings.

3B-5 A temporary employee of Carlton Manufacturing Corporation prepared the following income statement for the year ended December 31, 1975.

CARLTON MANUFACTURING CORPORATION
Income Statement
For the Year Ended December 31, 1975

Sales	$300,000	
Royalty revenue	4,800	
Purchase discounts	1,000	
Purchase returns & allowances	500	
Interest revenue	400	
Increase in inventories of finished goods, materials, and factory		
supplies	1,350	$308,050
Administrative expenses	$ 15,000	
Depreciation on manufacturing plant	8,000	
Transportation-in	1,650	
Sales returns	2,000	
Sales discounts	1,800	
Selling expenses	21,500	
Various factory costs	209,000	258,950
Income before income taxes		$ 49,100
Income taxes		19,640
Net income		$ 29,460

In discussions with officials of the company, you are informed that company policy calls for completion of all goods in process each December; consequently, there was no inventory of goods in process at either the beginning or end of 1975. Management also provides you with the following additional information:

Inventory of raw materials, Dec. 31, 1975	$ 8,500
Inventory of factory supplies, Dec. 31, 1975	2,200
Inventory of finished goods, Dec. 31, 1975	10,000
Purchases of factory supplies during 1975	1,850
Factory supplies used during 1975	1,300
Purchases of raw materials during 1975	72,000
Raw materials used during 1975 (after deducting purchase discounts; cost of	
transportation-in included)	74,000
Direct labor	57,750
Indirect labor	8,900
Other factory overhead costs	68,500

There are 10,000 shares of common stock issued and outstanding.

Instructions
a Prepare a statement of cost of goods manufactured (see illustration, page 70) and label it Exhibit A. Use supporting schedules to compute:
(1) Beginning inventory of raw materials
(2) A reconciliation of "Various factory costs—$209,000" as shown in the problem with the supplementary data provided
(3) Computation of beginning inventory of finished goods
b Prepare a corrected income statement in multiple-step form. Show earnings per share.

CHAPTER 4

The balance sheet: a report on financial position

A balance sheet presents the financial position of an economic entity. The financial position of a business at a given date comprises the assets, liabilities, and owners' equity, and the relationship among them. An integral part of the balance sheet (or statement of financial position) consists of notes to the financial statements, which disclose contingencies, commitments, and other financial matters relevant to the business.

A balance sheet provides an historical summary of the following elements, as defined in *APB Statement No. 4:*[1]

1 *Assets*—economic resources of an enterprise that are recognized and measured in conformity with generally accepted accounting principles. Assets also include certain deferred charges that are not resources but that are recognized and measured in conformity with generally accepted accounting principles.[2]

2 *Liabilities*—economic obligations of an enterprise that are recognized and measured in conformity with generally accepted accounting principles. Liabilities also include certain deferred credits that are not obligations but that are recognized and measured in conformity with generally accepted accounting principles.

3 *Owners' equity*—the interest of owners in an enterprise, which is the excess of an enterprise's assets over its liabilities.

---

[1] *APB Statement No. 4,* "Basic Concepts and Accounting Principles Underlying Financial Statements of Business Enterprises," AICPA (New York: 1970), par. 132.

[2] An example of "deferred charges that are not resources" is deferred charges from income tax allocation. Deferred credits from income tax allocation are a prominent example of "deferred credits that are not obligations." Both these items are discussed in Chapter 20.

The balance sheet is basically an historical report, because it shows the cumulative effect of past completed transactions. It is often described as a detailed expression of the fundamental accounting equation:

Assets = Liabilities + Owners' Equity

The theoretical concept of an asset may readily be related to our discussion in Chapter 3 of revenue and expenses shown in the income statement. Assets are costs that have **not** been applied to past revenue; they represent **expected future economic benefits.** However, the rights to assets have been acquired by the entity as a result of past transactions. If no future economic benefit can reasonably be expected from a cost incurred by a business, then it follows that the cost in question does not qualify as an asset and should not be included in the balance sheet.

Liabilities also result from past transactions; they are obligations which require settlement in the future, either by conveying assets or by performing services.

Implicit in these concepts of the nature of assets and liabilities is the meaning of owners' equity as the residual interest in the assets of a business entity.[3]

SIGNIFICANCE OF THE BALANCE SHEET

At one time the balance sheet[4] was considered the primary end product of accounting. However, experience pounded home the economic lesson that earning power is the prime determinant of business worth, and users of financial information gradually became aware of the serious limitations of balance sheets. Today the balance sheet is considered secondary in importance to the income statement for most businesses.

It does not follow, however, that balance sheets are of little importance. Balance sheets, particularly when presented in comparative form covering several points in time, provide a great deal of information to creditors, stockholders, management, prospective investors, and the public. The short-run solvency of an enterprise, commitments that must be met in the future, the relative interest of creditors and equity investors, favorable or unfavorable trends in a company's financial condition year by year—

[3] These definitions are based on those proposed by Robert T. Sprouse and Maurice Moonitz in "A Tentative Set of Broad Accounting Principles for Business Enterprises," *Accounting Research Study No. 3,* AICPA (New York: 1962), p. 8.
[4] The term *balance sheet,* though widely used, is not a very descriptive bit of terminology. Various alternatives, such as *statement of financial condition, statement of financial position,* or simply *position statement,* have been proposed, with considerable merit.

useful information about all these factors is contained in balance sheets for those who know how to read and interpret them. Periodic statements of financial position thus add considerable candlepower to the light shed on business affairs by periodic income statements.

Limitations of the balance sheet

In an ideal balance sheet the list of assets and liabilities would be all-inclusive and each would be reported at its present economic value. As a result the residual equity (assets minus liabilities) would reflect the true net worth of the business entity, that is, the value of the owners' interest. The major limitation of the balance sheet lies in the accountant's inability to measure the value of the entire collection of net resources comprising the business entity. The true worth of any group of productive net assets is the present value of the stream of future receipts which the organization is capable of producing for its owners. If we could measure net worth in this sense, the balance sheet would be the most useful compilation of information that could be obtained about any business. The function of stock markets would be drastically changed, because the book value of the stockholders' equity reported on the balance sheet would accurately reflect the value of the shares, and investors would be foolish to pay a higher price for them.

The inability of accountants (or anyone else) to foresee future economic events accurately forces us to prepare balance sheets on a different basis. It is necessary to use indirect methods of valuation to express some kinds of assets and liabilities on the balance sheet. Furthermore, we are unable to identify and provide a valuation for many factors that have a material bearing on the condition of a business at any given time. The quality, morale, and character of management and company personnel, the market position of a firm and the reputation of its products, the growth potential implicit in the nature and diversity of its operations—all these are subjective and intangible factors of great importance in evaluating the financial position of a business entity at any given point in time. None is reported directly in the dollar and cents framework of the accounting process that leads to a balance sheet.

Most managerial and investment decisions are based on estimates of future events. Both the balance sheet and the income statement are historical records, useful largely because they give perspective to estimates about the future; the really relevant data lie in the pages of history not yet written.

Some critics, in discussing the merits of various accounting concepts and procedures, take the position that because the balance sheet does not reflect "fair value" it does not matter what figures appear in it. There is a serious defect in such thinking. To imply that *meaningful* income statements can be prepared as an adjunct to *meaningless* balance sheets shows a failure to understand the relation between these two statements.

Balance sheets are vital links in the chain of periodic income statements, and a chain is no stronger than its weakest links. A consistently applied and meaningful set of assumptions governing the valuations appearing on the balance sheet is a prerequisite of consistent and meaningful income data. If the balance sheet is to be simply a residual dumping ground for any amounts not reflected in income determination, it cannot serve usefully even its limited function.

Accounting principles underlying the balance sheet

A number of important basic principles of accounting impinge on the data appearing in balance sheets. Since all the principles discussed in the preceding chapters are relevant, we shall concentrate here only on their balance sheet implications.

The Valuation Principle   Realization, which is a key factor in income measurement, also forms the basis for distinguishing methods of valuation used in reporting assets.

A general class of assets, called *monetary assets* is usually carried on the balance sheet at figures closely approximating present value. Examples are cash, certificates of deposit, investments in bonds, and receivables; all these represent available purchasing power. *APB Opinion No. 21* stressed that notes receivable and notes payable which are non-interest-bearing or which carry an unreasonably low rate of interest are not to be valued at face amount, but at their present value. *Present value* may be determined by discounting all future payments on a note by using an imputed rate of interest reflecting prevailing market rates of interest. This requirement for discounting receivables and payables to their present value applies principally to notes and is not applicable to receivables and payables arising from transactions with customers or suppliers which are due within one year or less.[5]

Another broad category of assets, which might be termed *productive resources,* is reported at *cost,* that is, the original amount spent in acquiring the asset services that remain in potential at any given time. Inventories and prepayments are examples of short-term productive resources that will be realized (that is, contribute to revenue) at an early date. Buildings, equipment, patents, and investments in affiliated companies are examples of long-term commitments of funds that will be realized over a number of accounting periods.

Until realization occurs, productive resources are measured and reported on the balance sheet on the basis of past or present exchange prices; after realization, valuations of quick assets generally approximate current value. These valuation assumptions govern the accounting for enterprise assets.

[5] *APB Opinion No. 21,* "Interest on Receivables and Payables," AICPA (New York: 1971), par. 1–3.

Since a liability is an obligation to convey assets or perform services, the appropriate valuation of liabilities on the balance sheet is in terms of the cash (or cash equivalent) necessary to discharge the obligation at the balance sheet date. If payment is to be made later, liabilities should be measured at the present discounted value (determined by using a yield or market interest rate) of the future payments necessary to discharge the obligation.[6] In the double-entry system of accounting, the present value of a debt at the time it is incurred determines the cash proceeds of the borrowing or the cost of the asset received in exchange for the contractual promise to make future payments. As the maturity of a debt approaches, its present value may increase or decrease and this change is a part of the computation of the interest cost of carrying the debt. This problem is considered in greater detail in Chapter 18.

The measurement of assets and liabilities on the balance sheet is closely related to the measurement of income on the income statement. Since revenue arises as the result of increases in assets or decreases in liabilities, and expenses result from increases in liabilities and decreases in assets, the problem of valuing assets and liabilities is inevitably linked to the problem of measuring income.

The Continuity or Going-Concern Principle The valuations used in a balance sheet and the classification of items into current and noncurrent groups are based on the continuity or going-concern principle previously discussed in Chapter 1. This principle, as specifically applied to the balance sheet, means an assumption that the business will continue operations long enough for assets to be used or sold according to plan. The going-concern principle is applicable to all cases except when specific evidence, such as inability to meet the demands of creditors, indicates that the assumption of continued operations is unreasonable.

The Monetary Principle The monetary principle was described in Chapter 1 as an assumption that the dollar is a useful standard measuring unit, and implications of this principle on income determination were discussed in Chapter 3. The principle is reflected on the balance sheet by valuations expressed in dollars of different time periods, that is, dollars having different real values (if there have been changes in the general price level).

If the monetary assumption were changed and balance sheets were expressed in "current dollars," the two categories most affected would be productive assets and the ownership equity. As we have noted, monetary assets and current liabilities are stated at approximately their

---

[6]The concept of present value as applied to liabilities has been expressed as follows: "If the creditor will not or cannot accept cash now in discharge of the liability, the appropriate amount is that sum which, if invested now (e.g., in a sinking fund), will provide the sums needed at maturity, even though in fact no explicit sinking fund or other investment device is actually used." *Accounting Research Study No. 3,* p. 39.

current values and are thus automatically expressed in current dollars. The accounting valuation of productive assets, however, is a mixture of historical costs. Similarly, paid-in capital and retained earnings in the ownership equity section of the balance sheet are expressed in dollars of past periods.

To illustrate this point, consider the case of Inflation Company which has operated for a period of 10 years, during which the general price level has risen steadily. Shown below is a balance sheet (in highly condensed and somewhat unorthodox form) for this company, expressed in both "mixed" dollars and "current" dollars. Compare the figures in the two columns.

INFLATION COMPANY
Balance Sheet
As of End of Current Year

	"Mixed" dollars (monetary assumption)	"Current" dollars (revised assumption)
Assets		
Monetary assets (cash, investments in debt securities, and receivables)	$200,000	$200,000
Productive resources (inventories, land, plant and equipment, and intangibles)	400,000	700,000
Total assets	$600,000	$900,000
Liabilities & Stockholders' Equity		
Liabilities (both short- and long-term)	$300,000	$300,000
Stockholders' equity:		
Capital stock	$200,000	$400,000
Retained earnings	100,000	60,000
Unrealized general price level gain	–0–	140,000
Total stockholders' equity . . .	300,000	600,000
Total liabilities & stockholders' equity	$600,000	$900,000

Note the upward revision of productive assets and stockholders' equity when expressed in current dollars. The decline in retained earnings when expressed in current dollars (from $100,000 to $60,000) is due to the fact that the cost of goods sold and depreciation on plant equipment and intangibles would be higher when expressed in current dollars during a period of inflation. The "unrealized general price level gain" ($140,000) is more complex. It results from the fact that productive resources were financed in part by debt. Creditors are entitled to a repayment of only a fixed number of dollars. Thus when unused productive resources are stated in terms of an increased number of current dollars, the company has gained at the expense of its creditors. Bear in mind that this illustration does not use current market prices, but historical costs adjusted for the change in the general price level.

Financial reporting in terms of constant dollars has been tried in a few countries where extreme price inflation followed as an aftermath of the two world wars. In the United States experiments with supplementary current-dollar statements have attracted considerable attention, but it appears unlikely that the monetary assumption will be abandoned in primary accounting statements, barring a greater change in the value of the dollar than we have thus far experienced. The detailed procedures for converting mixed-dollar accounting data to current dollars are discussed in Chapter 25.

Other Accounting Principles and Concepts   The *disclosure principle* and the closely related *concept of materiality,* which were discussed in Chapter 1, are especially applicable to the balance sheet. Adequate disclosure does not require the listing of precise dollar amounts. In the published financial statements of most large companies, all amounts are rounded off to the nearest thousand dollars. The extremely large companies go a step further and place the heading "amounts in thousands" at the top of the balance sheet and other financial statements. For example, if Sears, Roebuck and Co. has a ledger balance for accounts receivable of $4,291,827,329.71 and a related allowance for uncollectible accounts of $30,000,000.00, the balance sheet would show among the current assets "Receivables . . . . $4,261,827." In reading these figures, one must bear in mind that five digits have been omitted. Supplementary information concerning credit operations, including the provision for uncollectible accounts, would appear in notes to the financial statements.

In order that the balance sheet may provide a fair presentation of the financial position of a business, it is usually necessary to go considerably further than listing and classifying ledger account balances. Additional vital information, such as the existence of contingent liabilities and contingent assets, a summary of accounting policies, changes in accounting principles, and the occurrence of important events subsequent to the date of the balance sheet are most conveniently reported in notes to the financial statements.

FORM AND PRESENTATION OF THE BALANCE SHEET

The accounting objectives in presenting information in a balance sheet are clarity and disclosure of significant facts within the framework of the basic assumptions of accounting. Balance sheet classification, terminology, and the general form of presentation should be studied with these objectives in mind.

Balance sheet classification

The classifications, group headings, and number of items on a balance sheet will vary considerably depending on the size of the company, the nature of its operations, and whether the financial statements are intended for wide distribution or for the use of a few owners and creditors. As an example of the diversity encountered in published financial statements, public utility companies usually place plant assets at the top of the balance sheet followed by current assets. They may also use such distinctive group headings as "Assets and Other Debits," along with "Liabilities and Other Credits."

As a generalization subject to many exceptions, the following classification of balance sheet items is suggested as representative. However, alternative groupings will be used at times in this and following chapters to reflect acceptable alternatives.

Assets:
  Current assets
  Investments (held for control or not readily marketable)
  Property, plant, and equipment
  Intangible assets
  Other assets (including deferred charges)
Liabilities:
  Current liabilities
  Long-term liabilities (including deferred credits)
Stockholders' equity:
  Capital stock
  Paid-in capital in excess of par
  Retained earnings

The above classification reflects only the three elements of the fundamental accounting equation, and in the opinion of the authors, is theoretically supportable. In practice, it is not unusual to find a fourth category placed between liabilities and stockholders' equity (often with the caption "Reserves" or "Deferred Credits"), to include such items as deferred income taxes, unamortized investment tax credits, reserves for overhaul of leased equipment, and minority interest in subsidiaries. The possibilities for elimination of this separate category are discussed later in this chapter and in Chapter 16.

Working capital

The working capital of a business is defined as the excess of current assets over current liabilities. This figure has always been of considerable interest to credit grantors as an easily interpreted measure of the short-run solvency of a concern—the ability to finance current operations and to meet obligations as they fall due. The amount of current assets and of current liabilities, and the relation between them, are widely quoted in financial circles and are often incorporated in contractual arrangements between a company and outsiders. It is therefore of some importance that there be a generally accepted and consistent basis for determining which items are included and which are excluded from the current asset and current liability categories.

A new basic financial statement, entitled Statement of Changes in Financial Position, became a requirement for reporting on the financing and investing activities of a business with the issuance of **APB Opinion No. 19** in 1971.[7] This statement, which superseded the older and optional Statement of Source and Application of Funds, is discussed in detail in Chapter 23.

Current Assets   As a practical matter, the rough-and-ready difference between a current asset and a noncurrent asset is readily grasped. The border between these two categories, however, is hazy, and defining an exact boundary is not an easy task.

Five general types of assets are usually included in the current asset classification:

1 *Cash:* money in any form—cash awaiting deposit, balances on deposit in checking accounts, established expendable cash funds.
2 *Secondary cash resources:* various investments that are readily marketable. Any such funds with availability for current use restricted by contract or other formal arrangement are excluded.
3 *Short-term receivables:* open accounts receivable and notes receivable with short-term maturities.
4 *Inventories:* raw materials, supplies, goods in process, finished goods. This category includes items held for sale in the ordinary course of operations, items in process of production for sale, and items that will be currently consumed in production of goods or services that will be available for sale.
5 *Short-term prepayments:* the cost of various services, such as insurance, taxes, rent, that have been paid for in advance of use in operations. Short-term prepayments are sometimes referred to as prepaid expenses.

There is little question or difficulty about including cash, secondary cash resources, and ordinary receivables in the current asset category. As might be expected, the troublesome area is the distinction between short- and long-term investments in productive goods and services.

The test usually applied in distinguishing current from noncurrent

---

[7]*APB Opinion No. 19,* "Reporting Changes in Financial Position," AICPA (New York: 1971).

productive assets is whether the investment in these assets will be realized within the operating cycle of a business, or one year, whichever is the longer period of time.

The term *operating cycle* refers to the circulation of items within the current asset category. In a typical business, cash is invested in materials, supplies, labor, and various overhead services, and these costs are traced through and attached to inventories. Inventories are eventually realized by conversion into trade receivables, and receivables are in turn collected and become once more available in the form of cash. The average lapse of time between the investment in materials and services and the final conversion back to cash is the length of the operating cycle of a business. In most cases this is a matter of days or months; in some industries, where processing time is extensive, the cycle may extend beyond one year. Thus the conventional time test for current assets is realization within one year or one operating cycle, whichever is longer.

There are some theoretical flaws in the application of the time test. In a realistic sense all asset services that will be used in producing revenue during the immediately succeeding operating cycle or accounting period will be realized and converted into liquid resources. Some portion of the investment in plant asset services will be realized in the same sense as will be the investment in raw materials. It may be argued, for example, that standing timber that will be manufactured into plywood in the next operating cycle has as good a claim to inclusion among current assets as the stock of glue that will bind the layers of wood. Thus the attempt to distinguish between assets that are consumed in definite physical installments and assets that yield services gradually through use has some logical stumbling blocks in its way. These conceptual niceties are largely ignored in reporting current assets on the balance sheet.

In any system of classification, there will be troublesome items that do not fit nicely into designated niches. For example, if money has been borrowed for the express purpose of constructing plant, it may be argued that its inclusion in working capital is misleading. The common practice of buying insurance for three- or five-year periods raises questions about the logical consistency of including the full amount of unexpired insurance as a current asset.

In resolving these difficulties, the accountant finds himself at odds in varying degrees with a neat, logical statement of the characteristics that distinguish a current asset. He may explain his trouble as an inevitable conflict between theory and practice, but the result is that the practical distinction between current and noncurrent assets is based more on a rule of thumb than on a precise definition.

Current Liabilities The distinction between current and noncurrent liabilities is less troublesome than its counterpart on the asset side of the balance sheet. Current liabilities may be defined as "obligations whose liquidation is reasonably expected to require the use of existing resources properly classifiable as current assets or the creation of other current liabilities."[8]

Three main classes of liabilities fall within this definition:

1 Obligations for goods and services which have entered the operating cycle. These include trade payables and accrued liabilities such as wages, commissions, taxes, etc.

2 Other debt that may be expected to require payment within the operating cycle or one year. This includes short-term notes and the currently maturing portion of long-term obligations.

3 Collections received in advance of the delivery of goods or the performance of services. These advances are often described as "deferred revenues," but it is the obligation to furnish the goods or services or to refund the payment that puts them in the liability category.

Some liabilities that will be paid shortly after the balance sheet date are nonetheless excluded from the current liability category because of the requirement that a current liability must involve the use of current assets for its extinction. Examples are: (1) obligations due at an early date that will be retired by issuing new long-term debt securities, for example, bonds that will be refunded; (2) debts that will be paid from fund accumulations reported as noncurrent assets, for example, a life insurance policy loan that will be liquidated by cancellation against cash surrender value or by deduction from the proceeds of the policy at maturity.

Noncurrent Assets The definition of current assets automatically determines by exclusion the assets that should be reported as noncurrent. There are at least three identifiable types of noncurrent assets:

1 Long-term or restricted funds, investments, and receivables. A variety of long-term commitments of funds do not qualify as secondary cash resources. Investments in the stock of subsidiaries made for the purpose of control would be included in this category. Also included are noncurrent receivables (such as long-term advances to affiliated companies), the **cash surrender value of life insurance,** and funds established for such purposes as the payment of pensions, retirement of capital stock, or repayment of long-term debt.

   Assets being held for sale but not includable in inventory are listed in this group. Raw land held for speculative purposes is an example. Another is plant and equipment items which have been retired from operating use and are being held for sale. A future plant site not presently in use is another example of an asset properly included in this category of noncurrent assets.

2 Long-term tangible resources used in the operation of the business. The distinguishing characteristics of assets of this type are that they are tangible (have physical substance) and are held for productive use in business operations. All kinds of business sites, natural resources subject to depletion, business structures, equipment, machines, tools, and leasehold improvements are included. Long-term prepayments for the use of physical assets, such as leaseholds, easements, or rights of way, may also be included in this category, though some accountants group these in the next class.

3 Long-term intangible resources. Long-term rights and privileges of an intangi-

[8] *Accounting Research and Terminology Bulletins, Final Edition,* AICPA (New York: 1961), p. 21.

ble nature may be of greater importance to a business than its tangible assets. Examples of such assets are patents, goodwill, trademarks, copyrights, organization costs, relocation costs, and the know-how resulting from research and development expenditures. Under current accounting standards, however, these items are recognized as assets only when an expenditure has been made to acquire an intangible right.

A special category of assets labeled "long-term prepayments," "deferred charges," or "other assets" is sometimes found on balance sheets. These classifications may be useful in special cases, but it is difficult to think of a noncurrent asset that will not fit into one of the three categories just described.

Noncurrent Liabilities A noncurrent liability is an obligation that will not require the use of current assets within the next year or operating cycle, whichever is longer. There is some question whether there is any useful basis for subclassification within this category. In general practice a distinction is sometimes drawn between the following two classes:

1 *Long-term debt based on security issues or related contractual arrangements.* Included in this category would be notes, bonds, and mortgages. The distinguishing characteristic is that there is a borrowing transaction supported by a contractual obligation to pay principal and interest.

2 *Other long-term obligations.* As the word "other" implies, this includes all long-term liabilities that do not fit into the previous category. An amount received in advance on a long-term commitment to furnish goods or services would be an example. Any portion of such advances that will be earned during the current period should be reported as a current liability. Other examples are long-term advances from affiliated companies, amounts payable under pension plan agreements, deferred revenue, deferred income taxes, and minority interests in subsidiary companies.

Contingent Liabilities Liabilities that *may* come into existence as a result of transactions or activities that *have not yet been finalized* are not reported in dollar amounts on the balance sheet. Not only is the evidence with respect to such obligations too vague to be called objective, but the events necessary to bring the liabilities into existence have not yet been completed.

On the other hand, if, as a result of contracts or activities undertaken, there are possible liabilities whose existence is merely conditional upon the happening of some future event, these obligations, known as *contingent liabilities,* should be disclosed. The disclosure is usually made by means of a note to the financial statements. The obligation to reimburse a bank in case of default by the maker of a discounted note receivable, pending lawsuits that may result in an obligation to pay damages or other costs, taxes and other charges that are being contested, possible renegotiation refunds on government contracts—all are examples of contingent liabilities.

Management would be imprudent to provide dollar estimates on anticipated renegotiation refunds, or unfavorable results from pending lawsuits, since such disclosure might be considered an admission of the merits of the opposing case. If the item is material, however, disclosure in general terms is essential.

A common error is the failure to distinguish between contingent liabilities and obligations that exist but are not definite either as to amount, due date, or both. These latter may be called **estimated liabilities.** There are varying degrees of uncertainty about liabilities; some may be estimated with a high degree of accuracy; others may be subject to no more than an informed guess. The amount of income tax liability or the amount of payments due employees under pension plans are examples of estimated liabilities which can usually be established with reasonable precision on the basis of tentative tax returns or actuarial data. On the other hand, the cost to a company of making good its product guarantees is an existing obligation that can be estimated only within a fairly wide range of probability. When liabilities exist, the accountant should make the best possible determination of their present value and include them on the balance sheet, even though the amounts are uncertain.

Contingent Assets Assets, as well as liabilities, may be contingent. A contingent asset is a property right whose existence is conditional on the happening of some future event. It is usually not appropriate to recognize contingent assets in the accounting records, because to do so would violate the concept of realization. There is a lack of objective evidence and the earnings process has not been substantially completed. However, the disclosure of the existence of contingencies which may result in material gains or assets is useful. An example of such disclosure in a recent annual report read as follows: ". . . the Company had a tax loss carry-forward of $8,400,000 which can be deducted from future taxable earnings. . . ."

Contra Asset and Liability Accounts The valuation of some asset and liability accounts is commonly reported in two amounts as a convenient means of disclosing more information about these items than would be afforded by a net valuation. For example, the net amount of accounts receivable is sometimes reported as the difference between the gross amount due from customers and an allowance for accounts estimated to be uncollectible. Similarly bond discount may be separately shown as a deduction from the maturity value of the liability. The general criterion for determining whether to display a balance sheet item in one amount or two is the degree of usefulness of the added information. The amount of estimated uncollectibles may provide the reader with information about the expected bad debt experience on current accounts; showing the amount of cumulative depreciation on plant and equipment separately from original cost may give some information about the relative age of the plant or the company's depreciation policy. The disclosure may be made as a separate valuation account in the balance sheet, or by a parenthetical notation of the amount that has been deducted in arriving at a net valuation.

Offsetting Assets and Liabilities The use of contra or valuation accounts should be carefully distinguished from an actual *offsetting* of asset and liability accounts. When valuation accounts are used, the amount deducted from an asset is not a liability, and the amount deducted from a liability is not an asset; the deductions represent modifications of the gross valuation of assets and liabilities.

Offsetting assets and liabilities is improper because it implies an irrevocable association between the two that seldom exists. For example, if a company informally accumulates a special fund to meet a debt when it matures, the intention may be revoked before the money is actually devoted to that purpose. The cash fund should be reported as an asset and the debt as a liability until payment is actually made.

There is a sound basis for the rule against offsetting assets and liabilities. A limited amount of offsetting in a few cases would probably not cause a material distortion in financial statements, but there is no obvious place to draw the line. The issue is disclosure in a manner that is not misleading, and there is little doubt that offsetting in general is likely to result in misleading information.

One recognized exception to the rule against offsetting occurs when a company purchases securities acceptable for the payment of taxes in circumstances such that the purchase is an advance payment of taxes otherwise due in the near future. This may occur as an accommodation to a governmental unit which issues securities specifically designated as acceptable for the payment of taxes.[9]

Ownership equity

The ownership equity in a business is the residual interest in assets, after liabilities have been deducted. The amount appearing in the owners' equity section of a balance sheet is thus directly dependent upon the valuations attached to assets and liabilities. When owners invest in a business, it is the asset valuation that determines the amount added to ownership equity. When operating results are summarized, the increase in net assets determines the amount of net income added to the owners' equity. This point is worth noting, because accountants are sometimes tempted to reverse this process and assume that if a figure (for example, the par value of stock) is associated with an element of ownership, there must be an asset to match.

Because of differences in the nature of the owners' equity in incorporated and nonincorporated businesses, there are variations in the balance sheet presentation of ownership equity for these two types of business organization.

[9] *APB Opinion No. 10*, "Omnibus Opinion—1966" AICPA (New York: 1966), p. 147.

Single Owner or Partnership Organizations The ownership equity in a proprietorship or partnership is usually reported on the balance sheet as a single amount for each owner. There is no reason why the amount of capital invested by each owner should not be shown separately from his reinvested earnings, but because there is no legal restriction on the amounts proprietors or partners may withdraw from a business, such information is less significant than in the case of corporations.

The ownership rights of a partner are typically more complex than those of a corporate stockholder. Contractual arrangements among partners governing salaries, interest on capital, share of residual profits and losses, and investment and withdrawals make it important that the relative rights of each partner are accurately determined and fully reported on the balance sheet. A statement showing the change in each partner's equity for the current period may accompany or appear on the partnership balance sheet, as shown for the A B Partnership below.

A B PARTNERSHIP
Statement of Partners' Capitals
For the Current Year

	Partner A	Partner B	Total
Ownership equity, Jan. 1	$25,000	$34,000	$59,000
Add: Net income for the year	12,600	18,200	30,800
Less: Withdrawals	(15,000)	(10,000)	(25,000)
Ownership equity, Dec. 31	$22,600	$42,200	$64,800

Corporations The presentation of stockholders' equity on a corporate balance sheet is strongly influenced by legal considerations. As a result there are a number of classifications (particularly within the "invested capital" section) that have no particular accounting significance. Below is an outline of the main elements of corporate ownership equity:

1 *Invested capital*
   a Stated capital. The amount contributed for or assigned to shares of stock outstanding to the extent of their par or stated value is known legally as the stated capital of a corporation. This amount usually appears under the heading **capital stock.** For each class of stock, the amount of par or stated value per share; the number of shares issued, outstanding, and held in the treasury; and any dividend or liquidating preference should be disclosed.
   b Additional capital. This category includes all amounts contributed for or assigned to shares in excess of par or stated value. The terms **paid-in capital in excess of par,** and **paid-in capital in excess of stated value** are used throughout this book. Another alternative term used in a considerable number of published financial statements is **additional paid-in capital.** The annual editions of **Accounting Trends & Techniques,** a survey of accounting

practices followed in 600 stockholders' reports, published by the AICPA, show a continuing trend away from the term **surplus** either standing alone or in such combinations as **capital surplus** or **paid-in surplus.** Use of the term **surplus** has long been discouraged by the AICPA. The word is generally unsuitable in a stockholders' equity section of a balance sheet because its popular meaning—something over and above what is necessary—gives it a misleading connotation.

Capital in excess of par or stated value may include both positive and negative amounts. If a corporation receives less than par or stated value for its stock, the contra-capital account Discount on Capital Stock belongs in this section of the balance sheet. Positive items include any amount in excess of par or stated value arising from the sale of unissued stock, the sale of treasury stock at more than cost, donations of assets to the corporation, or transfers from retained earnings through stock dividends by authorization of the board of directors.

2 *Increase in stockholders' equity through the retention of net income*
  a *Retained earnings.* Net income on past periods that has been retained in the business and is legally available as a basis for dividends falls in this category. The term **retained earnings** is used far more widely than any other to describe this element of stockholders' equity. Alternative terms including the word "earnings" are **earnings retained for use in the business, retained earnings invested in the business,** and **earnings retained for growth.** The term **earned surplus,** although still used by a few companies, is gradually becoming obsolete.
  b *Appropriated retained earnings.* A corporate board of directors may sometimes wish to indicate that a portion of a company's retained earnings has been appropriated. A formal segregation of retained earnings is an indirect means of disclosing that future dividend payments are restricted to some degree, either because of legal or contractual agreements or by management intent. The use of appropriations of retained earnings as a means of disclosure is gradually disappearing; other more effective means of indicating the restriction of retained earnings are available, principally the use of notes to the financial statements.
3 *Unrealized appreciation from revaluation of assets*
Under unusual circumstances a company may report unrealized appreciation in the value of its assets on the balance sheet to disclose a serious discrepancy between book value and current value. This procedure is an **exception** to the basic accounting assumption that only realized increases in asset values are recognized in the accounts. The offsetting increase in ownership equity should therefore be separately shown and clearly designated as an unrealized element of the owners' equity if unrealized appreciation is to be recorded. This item is sometimes captioned **appraisal capital.**

Use of the term "reserve"

In the past the term **reserve** has been used by accountants in a number of different and somewhat misleading ways. A reserve, in nonaccounting usage, is usually thought of as something held for a specific purpose, often for emergencies. This popular connotation leads to misinterpretation when the word "reserve" is included in the title of an asset valuation or estimated liability account. Therefore, the trend in modern accounting terminology is to avoid the use of the word "reserve," as can be seen in the following examples:

Obsolete Terminology	*Modern Terminology*
Asset valuation accounts	
Reserve for bad debts	*Allowance for uncollectible accounts*
Reserve for depreciation	*Accumulated depreciation*
Estimated liabilities	
Reserve for income taxes	*Income taxes payable*
Reserve for guarantees	*Obligation under guarantees*

The term *reserve,* when used to describe an appropriation of retained earnings, is considered acceptable, although its use continues to decline. Such titles as Reserve for Plant Expansion are more likely to be misunderstood than Retained Earnings Appropriated for Plant Expansion. If used at all, the term reserve should appear only in the stockholders' equity section of the balance sheet. Since its principal purpose is to indicate a restriction of retained earnings, the nature of the restriction can be set forth more clearly in a parenthetical comment or in a note to the financial statements than by dividing up the retained earnings.

Standards of disclosure

The accountant should apply the adequate disclosure test as a basis for resolving a number of questions that arise in the preparation of balance sheets.

Account Titles In providing titles for general ledger accounts, considerable leeway is permissible, in deference to convenience and economy of space. The persons involved in the record keeping presumably understand the nature of the item and thus short titles are a matter of convenience. In preparing financial statements, however, the user of the information must be kept in mind, and a clearly worded description of each item is clearly desirable. Thus the title Accounts Receivable may be converted to Amounts Due from Customers on the balance sheet, and Intangibles may be expanded to Amounts Spent in Obtaining and Developing Patents and Trademarks, less Cumulative Amortization. It is true that brevity is a virtue even in statement presentation; but in the choice between brevity and clarity, the latter should control. Of course, a great many ledger accounts may be combined into a single financial statement item, such as Plant and Equipment.

Basis of Valuation Informed readers of balance sheets are presumed to be familiar with the general assumption governing the accounting valuation of assets and liabilities. Variations in accounting procedures in applying this assumption, however, often produce balance sheet figures whose significance is difficult to interpret unless the procedure used is disclosed. The choice of "fifo" or "lifo" cost in inventory valuation, for example, results in materially different asset figures. An acceptable standard of disclosure requires that the basis of valuation be indicated in the caption of all balance sheet items, unless it is obvious (as in the case of cash, for example).

Notes (Footnotes) to the Financial Statements Disclosures which used to be called "Footnotes to the balance sheet" are now generally referred to as "Notes to the financial statements." The change in terminology reflects the greatly increased use of these explanatory comments as a means of disclosing material facts not presented in the body of the financial statements. Often a note may be applicable to both the balance sheet and the income statement, and the list of notes in its entirety may occupy several pages. As explained in Chapter 1 (page 20), a note summarizing significant accounting policies is prescribed as essential by *APB Opinion No. 22,* "Disclosure of Accounting Policies." For such matters as stock option plans, pension plans, lease agreements, and acquisitions, the only reasonable way to provide an adequate explanation is by using notes to the financial statements.

Supporting Schedules If the detail involved in a full picture of a section of the balance sheet interferes with a concise presentation, it may be desirable to summarize the item on the balance sheet and show the detail in a supporting schedule. For example, inventories might be reported as one figure and the detailed amounts of raw materials, goods in process, goods on consignment, and finished goods put in a supporting schedule attached to the balance sheet. Companies having a large number of debt issues outstanding find it convenient to show long-term debt as a single amount and include supporting schedules in which the details are furnished. For the reader who wants only "highlight" information, the balance sheet thus gives this in a concise and easily digestible manner. The analyst who desires more detailed information will find it in the supporting schedules.

Form of the balance sheet

Fairly standard ways of presenting balance sheet information have been developed in accounting, but there is no one stereotyped form. The objectives are clarity and adequate disclosure of all pertinent and material facts; there are various ways of meeting these objectives, and experimentation should be encouraged. For example, in published balance sheets it is useful to make the major headings as descriptive as possible. Assets may be headed "The Company Owns," liabilities may be displayed under the heading "The Company Owes," and stockholders' equity may be captioned "Sources from Which Capital Was Obtained."

The arrangement of the major elements of the balance sheet may also be varied. We shall illustrate the basic feature of three general forms of presentation; within the framework of these three patterns a number of variations are possible.

Account Form A model balance sheet for a hypothetical company in the traditional balancing form appears on pages 148 and 149. The distinguishing characteristic of this form is that all assets are listed on the left-hand side and liabilities and stockholders' equity are "balanced" against them on the right-hand side. The illustrative balance sheet, includes typical accounts in each classification and follows modern standards of disclosure and terminology. The appropriate degree of condensation in financial statements depends on the nature of the audience. A statement prepared for stockholders will be more condensed than one prepared for operating officials. Notes to the balance sheet are purposely omitted from this illustration, since numerous illustrations of explanatory notes are presented at the end of this chapter and also in Appendix B.

Report Form of Balance Sheet The report form of balance sheet differs from the account form only in that the liability and stockholders' equity sections are listed below rather than to the right of the asset section. Both forms are widely used. For an example of the report form, see the Eastman Kodak balance sheet in Appendix B.

Statement of Financial Position The great majority of published financial statements use the account form or report form of balance sheet, both of which express the equation *Assets = Liabilities + Stockholders' Equity.* A few companies, however, prefer to use a format which emphasizes working capital; this usually carries the title Statement of Financial Position. This is a *vertical* format in which current assets are listed and totaled; then current liabilities are listed next and the total deducted from the total of current assets to derive an amount for working capital. Other assets are then added and other liabilities deducted, leaving a residual amount as the stockholders' equity. This general type of format is illustrated in Appendix B in the financial statements of Indiana Telephone Corporation. The vertical format, which may be summarized by the equation, *Working Capital + Other Assets − Other Liabilities = Stockholders' Equity,* has been declining in popularity in recent years. At present, less than 5% of the 600 large companies studied in the annual edition of *Accounting Trends & Techniques* use this format, and the other 95% use the account form or report form of balance sheet.

Statement of retained earnings

A statement explaining the changes in retained earnings during the current period is an integral part of the balance sheet, regardless of the form of presentation employed. If the items involved are few, an explanatory schedule may appear on the face of the balance sheet itself. As noted in the previous chapter, the statement of retained earnings may be combined with the income statement. A statement of retained earnings in comparative form for two years, appears below.

HYPOTHETICAL CORPORATION
Statement of Retained Earnings
For the Years Ended December 31, 19___ and 19___

	Current year	Prior year
Balance at beginning of year	$1,840,000	$1,569,000
Net income	1,057,000	928,000
Subtotal	$2,897,000	$2,497,000
Dividends declared:		
On preferred stock	(57,000)	(57,000)
On common stock	(800,000)	(600,000)
Balance at end of year	$2,040,000	$1,840,000

Comparative statements

To keep the preceding illustration of different balance sheet formats simple and concise, the balance sheets showed data for only one point in time. The inclusion of comparative figures is highly desirable and is fully illustrated in the five sets of financial statements in Appendix B. Many companies publish 10- or 15-year summaries which bring out quite clearly important trends affecting the business and thus aid the reader in judging long-run performance.

Statement of stockholders' equity

As previously explained, a statement of retained earnings explains the changes which have occurred in retained earnings. However, changes calling for explanation may also occur in the other elements of stockholders' equity, that is, in capital stock and additional paid-in capital. Consequently, an increasing number of companies prepare *statements of stockholders' equity* which explain the changes in capital stock and

HYPOTHETICAL CORPORATION
Balance Sheet
December 31, Current Year

Assets

Current assets:

Cash			$ 485,000
Marketable securities (at cost, market value $220,000)			210,000
Notes receivable and accrued interest			125,000
Amounts due from customers		$862,000	
Less: Allowance for uncollectible accounts		50,000	812,000
Inventories (at lower of average cost or market)			580,000
Short-term prepayments			60,000
Total current assets			$ 2,272,000

Investments:

In stock of affiliated companies, not consolidated (at equity)	1,200,000

Plant and equipment:

	Original cost	Accumulated depreciation or depletion	Book value	
Land	$ 500,000	$ -0-	$ 500,000	
Buildings	10,950,000	4,800,000	6,150,000	
Equipment	8,430,000	2,720,000	5,710,000	
Natural resources	2,860,000	1,192,000	1,668,000	
Totals	$22,740,000	$8,712,000		14,028,000

Intangibles:

Organization costs	$100,000	
Cost of developing patents (net of $160,000 amortization)	280,000	
Long-term prepayments	90,000	
Total intangibles		470,000

Total assets	$17,970,000

additional paid-in capital, along with the changes in retained earnings. Typical of such statements is one for Continental Air Lines, Inc., illustrated on page 150. Following the statement are the Notes to Financial Statements and the **opinion** or **audit report** of the firm of certified public accountants which performed the annual audit.

Liabilities & Stockholders' Equity

Current liabilities:

Long-term debt: amounts due within one year	$ 100,000
Accounts payable to trade creditors	420,000
Accrued liabilities	130,000
Income taxes payable	400,000
Dividends payable	125,000
Advances by customers	20,000
Retirement benefits payable within one year	40,000
Total current liabilities	$ 1,235,000

Long-term liabilities:

7% debenture bonds, due Jan. 5, 19___	$1,000,000	
Less: Unamortized discount	30,000	
Subtotal	$ 970,000	
Less: Amount due within one year (shown as current)	100,000	
Due in future years	$ 870,000	
Employees' retirement benefits payable in future years	230,000	
Total long-term liabilities		1,100,000
Total liabilities		$ 2,335,000

Stockholders' equity:

6% cumulative preferred stock, $100 par value (callable at $105 per share, authorized 10,000 shares, outstanding 9,500 shares) . .		$ 950,000
Common stock, no par, stated value $5 (authorized 1,000,000 shares; outstanding 800,000 shares)		4,000,000
Paid-in capital in excess of par or stated value:		
On preferred stock	$ 95,000	
On common stock	8,550,000	8,645,000
Total paid-in capital		$13,595,000
Retained earnings		2,040,000
Total stockholders' equity		$15,635,000
Total liabilities & stockholders' equity		$17,970,000

Continental Air Lines, Inc.

Statements of Stockholders' Equity

Years ended December 31, 1972 and 1971

	1972	1971
Common stock (notes 2 and 4):		
Amount at beginning of year	$ 5,778,939	$ 5,777,035
Par value of shares issued under stock option plans—177,548 shares in 1972;		
3,809 shares in 1971	88,774	1,904
Par value of 1,250,000 shares issued in connection with		
common stock offering	625,000	—
Amount at end of year	$ 6,492,713	$ 5,778,939
Capital in excess of par value:		
Amount at beginning of year	$ 40,040,631	$ 39,999,990
Excess of option price over par value of common stock issued under		
stock option plans	1,968,208	40,641
Excess of proceeds from the sale of common stock over par value,		
net of expenses of $1,639,834	24,766,416	—
Reduction in income taxes resulting from tax benefit of exercise of nonqualified		
stock options and early disposition of stock obtained under qualified		
stock option plan	734,361	—
Amount at end of year	$ 67,509,616	$ 40,040,631
Retained earnings (note 2):		
Amount at beginning of year	$ 60,296,928	$ 51,885,891
Net earnings	9,187,480	8,411,037
Amount at end of year	$ 69,484,408	$ 60,296,928

Notes to Financial Statements

December 31, 1972 and 1971

1 Summary of Significant Accounting Policies
The following is a summary of significant accounting policies of the Company used in preparing and presenting the accompanying financial statements. Reference should also be made to notes (4) and (6) for information regarding other significant accounting policies of the Company.

(a) Investments in Subsidiaries and Affiliates:
On January 1, 1972, the Company changed its method of accounting for investments in subsidiaries and twenty to fifty percent owned companies from the cost basis to the equity basis in accordance with Accounting Principles Board Opinion No. 18. Financial statements prior to January 1, 1972 have not been retroactively restated, since the effect of the change had no material effect upon the Company's total carrying value of its investments or upon the Company's net earnings of prior periods.

(b) Spare Parts and Supplies:
Inventories of flight equipment expendable parts and materials, and supplies are priced at average cost. A reserve for obsolescence is provided for flight equipment expendable parts to allocate the costs of the assets, less estimated residual value, over the useful lives of the related aircraft and engines and is included in depreciation and amortization in the accompanying statements of earnings.

(c) Capitalized Interest Costs:
Interest costs relating to advance payments on flight equipment orders are capitalized as part of the cost of the flight equipment.

(d) Property and Equipment:
Flight equipment and other property are carried at cost. Major additions, betterments and renewals are capitalized. Maintenance and repairs are charged to earnings, or, in the case of major flight equipment overhaul, to the reserve provided by charges to income on an hours-flown basis.

Depreciation and amortization for book purposes is computed on the straight-line basis over the estimated useful lives of the related assets which, for aircraft and related flight equipment, is 12 to 14 years and for other property and equipment, two to ten years.

At the time assets are retired or otherwise disposed of, the cost and accumulated depreciation and amortization are removed from the respective accounts and the balance, net of proceeds, is recorded as a gain or loss.

(e) Preoperating Costs:
Direct costs necessary to place new aircraft into service, principally training costs, are deferred and amortized over the period for which benefits will be derived, in most cases, three years.

REVIEW QUESTIONS

1 What are three major limitations of the balance sheet as a source of information useful to management and investors?

2 In describing the accounting valuation assumptions, assets may be classified into two groups: monetary assets and productive resources. What is the relation between the method of valuation applied to these two classes of assets and the measurement of revenue and expenses?

2 Long-term Debt

Long-term debt less portion due within one year is unsecured
except as noted and is summarized as follows:

	1972	1971
Notes payable to bank, 5% to 6½%, payable $4,196,428 quarterly	$ 9,732,143	$ 24,517,858
Note payable to bank, ½ of 1% over prime rate, payable in varying quarterly instalments to 1978	83,492,500	43,333,333
Notes payable to institutional lenders 5¼% to 10½%, payable $2,328,681 semiannually to 1991	74,219,159	76,535,520
Notes payable, other, 1% above prime rate, payable in varying monthly and quarterly instalments to 1977	8,569,965	—
Flight equipment purchase agreements, interest at 1% over prime rate, payable in monthly instalments, with final maturity in 1972	—	26,117,170
Notes payable, 5% to 7½%, subordinated, payable in quarterly instalments to 1978 . .	24,031,530	21,430,487
Subordinated notes, 1% over prime rate, payable upon delivery of equipment	9,832,500	23,125,000
Notes payable, subordinated, 125% of prime to a prime rate of 8%, thereafter 2% over prime rate. Payable $550,000 quarterly	18,700,000	—
Convertible subordinated notes, to institutional lenders, 8%, payable $505,750 semiannually, 1982 to maturity in 1991. Convertible into common stock at $12.25 per share, on which basis 971,429 shares of common stock were reserved at December 31, 1972	11,900,000	11,900,000
Other notes and purchase agreements payable in instalments to 1974, secured by other property and equipment amounting to $7,963,015	—	2,380,617
Convertible subordinated debentures, 3½%, due May 1, 1992. Convertible into common stock at $35.10 per share, on which basis 997,151 shares of common stock were reserved at December 31, 1972	35,000,000	35,000,000
	$275,477,797	$264,339,985

Under the most restrictive of the provisions of the long-term
debt agreements relating to the payment of dividends, other
than in stock of the Company, retained earnings were restricted
to the extent of $48,969,809 as of December 31, 1972.

The aggregate amounts of principal maturities of the debt outstanding at December 31, 1972 for the five subsequent years
are as follows: 1973, $46,237,479; 1974, $44,507,378; 1975,
$38,295,813; 1976, $35,459,970; and 1977, $24,849,123.

3 Income Taxes

The amount of income taxes charged to earnings in 1972 and 1971
(including $864,000 charged to the extraordinary item in 1971)
is comprised of:

	1972	1971
Taxes deferred, net	$ 8,325,275	$ 6,039,420
Amortization of investment tax credits utilized	(452,000)	(360,000)
Taxes currently payable	282,000	—
	$ 8,155,275	$ 5,679,420

Deferred taxes result principally from timing differences between
financial and tax reporting with respect to depreciation practices.
Investment tax credits utilized on tax returns are being amortized over periods approximating the useful lives of the related
assets. Investment tax credits not utilized on tax returns
amounted to $30,957,000 at December 31, 1972, and expire as
follows: $276,900 in 1974; $4,204,700 in 1977; $9,511,000 in 1978;
$9,438,900 in 1979; and $7,525,500 in 1980.

4 Stock Options to Officers and Key Employees

Certain information with respect to the Company's qualified
stock option plan follows:

	Options granted	Shares available for grant	Total shares reserved for stock option plans	Price per share
Balance at January 1, 1971 . .	697,212	73,837	771,049	$ 4.40-35.00
Options granted —1971	128,000	(128,000)	—	13.12-18.25
Options exercised —1971	(3,809)	—	(3,809)	4.40-11.19
Expired and canceled options—1971 . .	(111,846)	111,846	—	11.19-29.21
Balance at December 31, 1971.	709,557	57,683	767,240	4.40-35.00
Additional shares reserved by Board of Directors .	—	402,567	402,567	—
Options granted —1972	139,500	(139,500)	—	20.87-25.62
Options exercised —1972	(52,548)	—	(52,548)	4.40-21.19
Expired and canceled options —1972	(188,585)	188,585	—	13.12-35.00
Balance at December 31, 1972	607,924	509,335	1,117,259	8.12-25.63

Option prices are 100% of market price on the date granted. The
outstanding options expire five years from the date granted and
are exercisable in three equal amounts commencing one year
after date of grant. Options exercisable as of December 31, 1972
and 1971 were 375,429 and 498,567, respectively.

In addition, 50,000 shares and 75,000 shares of the Company's
common stock were issued upon the exercise of a nonqualified

3 Buzzell Company issued $100 million of 8% bonds, receiving proceeds of $98 million. The bonds are callable at any time at 103. An argument has arisen over the proper valuation of these bonds on the company's balance sheet. One official supports $98 million; another argues for maturity value, $100 million; a third argues that $103 million is the proper figure since the bonds may be called at any time. What basic accounting principle should govern the decision? Which position would you support, and why?

4 A partnership earned $25,000, divided equally between two partners. Each stock option at prices of $12.00 and $8.00 per share, respectively, in 1972.

At the time the options are exercised the Company records the issuance of the stock, and the excess of the option price over the par value of the common stock issued is credited to the account "Capital in Excess of Par Value." No charges are reflected in income with respect to the issuance of stock under the stock option agreements because no material compensation is involved.

5 Commitments and Contingent Liabilities

The Company was committed at December 31, 1972 to acquire additional aircraft, spare engines and other property at a total cost of approximately $316,000,000, of which approximately $52,000,000 has been paid to manufacturers and contractors to be applied on the commitments.

The Company has guaranteed certain obligations of its subsidiaries in the amount of $15,090,742.

The Company occupies various ground facilities and office space under leases expiring at various dates through the year 2010. Aggregate rentals under such leases are expected to approximate $5,300,000 annually in 1973 through 1977.

On December 31, 1972, various legal actions were pending against the City of Los Angeles and various actions and cross-actions were pending against the Company and other airlines, alleging excessive aircraft noise in the vicinity of Los Angeles International Airport. Counsel to the Company in these actions, which counsel also represents most of the other airlines, is of the opinion that the airlines have substantial defenses to the imposition of any liability.

The Company is also a defendant, together with numerous other airlines, in various legal actions relating to claims for refunds of certain passenger fares and charges for in-flight services. The Company believes these actions will not result in any material liability to the Company.

6 Pension Plans and Incentive Compensation Plan

The Company has pension plans for substantially all of its employees. Pension costs to the Company for 1972 and 1971 were approximately $8,373,000 and $6,562,000, respectively. Unfunded past service costs (which aggregated approximately $5,753,032 at the date of the latest actuarial report) are being funded over thirty years beginning January 1, 1960. Vested benefits are fully funded.

The Company has an Incentive Compensation Plan for officers and certain other key employees. The maximum amount which may be paid or accrued under the Plan with respect to any year is 10% of that year's pretax earnings, as defined in the Plan, after deducting from such earnings an amount equal to 10% of stockholders' equity, as defined in the Plan. Amounts awarded under the Plan for the years ended December 31, 1972 and 1971 were $468,000 and $366,000, respectively.

7 Mutual Aid Payments

As a participant in the airlines' Mutual Aid Agreement, the Company made payments aggregating $1,140,292 in 1972 and $261,817 in 1971 to certain air carriers struck during various periods in 1972 and 1971, which amounts have been deducted from miscellaneous operating revenue.

8 Earnings per Share

Earnings per common share has been computed using the weighted average number of shares outstanding during each year. Shares used in the computation of earnings per common share, assuming full dilution, are determined on the following basis:

	1972	1971
Weighted average number of shares outstanding	12,230,768	11,556,849
Effect of assumed exercise of stock options	176,584	210,058
Shares issuable upon assumed conversion of:		
Convert. subordinated debentures	997,151[1]	— [2]
Convert. subordinated notes	971,429[1]	971,429[1]
	14,375,932	12,738,336

[1]In calculating earnings per common share assuming full dilution, net earnings have been increased $1,132,040 in 1972 and $480,760 in 1971 for interest less applicable income taxes.

[2]The convertible subordinated debentures were not included in the determination of fully diluted earnings for 1971 because the effect would be antidilutive.

PEAT, MARWICK, MITCHELL & CO.
CERTIFIED PUBLIC ACCOUNTANTS
555 SOUTH FLOWER STREET
LOS ANGELES, CALIF. 90071

The Board of Directors
Continental Air Lines, Inc.:

We have examined the balance sheets of Continental Air Lines, Inc. as of December 31, 1972 and 1971 and the related statements of earnings, stockholders' equity and changes in financial position for the respective years then ended. Our examination was made in accordance with generally accepted auditing standards, and accordingly included such tests of the accounting records and such other auditing procedures as we considered necessary in the circumstances.

In our opinion, the aforementioned financial statements present fairly the financial position of Continental Air Lines, Inc. at December 31, 1972 and 1971 and the results of its operations, changes in stockholders' equity, and changes in its financial position for the respective years then ended, in conformity with generally accepted accounting principles applied on a consistent basis.

January 29, 1973

Peat, Marwick, Mitchell & Co.

---

partner will pay income taxes of $3,600 on his share of the partnership income. One partner argues that a liability of $7,200 should appear on the partnership balance sheet, since both partners plan to withdraw from the partnership an amount sufficient to pay their income taxes. What accounting principle is at issue? What is your position, and why?

5 As a supplement to its regularly published balance sheet, a company prepared a comparative balance sheet expressed in current dollars. On the supplementary statement the amount of liabilities was the same as on the historical-dollar balance sheet. One company officer commented, "We know that the general price level has been rising in recent years. Why should our liabilities be the same on these two statements?'' Explain.

6 Smith is a member of the American Institute of Certified Public Accountants. In auditing the records of X Corporation, Smith found that the company followed an accounting principle with which he agrees but which has not been accepted by the Accounting Principles Board or the Financial Accounting Standards Board. Assuming that the difference in treatment has a material effect on the statements of the company, what are the alternatives facing Smith in preparing his audit opinion on the statements of X Corporation?

7 What is the distinction between a **contingent** and an **estimated** liability? Give an example of each.

8 How is the definition of a **current liability** related to the definition of a **current asset?**

9 What is the basis for the rule against offsetting assets and liabilities?

10 In practice, the term **reserve** has been used to describe: a contra-asset account, an estimated liability, and an appropriation of retained earnings. Why are these uses of the term reserve in account titles objectionable? In which of the three uses is the term least misleading?

11 The financial statements prepared by a corporation include several items which taken together represent the excess of assets over liabilities. What are these items and what is the term used to describe them as a group?

12 Nelson Corporation issues its note payable at 8% interest to obtain a bank loan, but concurrently it issues a three-year note payable to a supplier at an annual interest rate of only 3%. Should both the notes payable be recorded at their face values? Explain.

13 Could the current liability section of a balance sheet properly include an obligation for which no specific creditor could be named and no cash payment was required? Explain.

14 In the published financial statements of a large corporation, would you expect to find a summary of the significant accounting policies followed by the company? Explain.

15 Explain the term **operating cycle** and its significance in the classification of balance sheet items as current or noncurrent.

16 Indicate circumstances under which liabilities falling due within a month or two after the date of the balance sheet should be excluded from the current liability classification.

EXERCISES

Ex. 4-1 The balance sheet of Mirror Company contains the following group headings:

A Current assets	F Current liabilities
B Investments and restricted funds	G Long-term liabilities
C Property, plant, and equipment	H Deferred credits
D Intangible assets	I Invested capital
E Other assets (including deferred charges)	J Retained earnings

For each of the following items, indicate the preferable balance sheet classification by listing the appropriate letter from the listing on page 153.

1 Accrued interest on bonds payable
2 Premium on preferred stock
3 Mortgage payable (outstanding for 19½ years; due in six months)
4 Raw land held for speculation
5 Payroll bank account
6 Patents
7 Discount on bonds payable
8 Unexpired insurance
9 Cost of moving home office (including employees) from New York to California
10 Leasehold improvements
11 Allowance for uncollectible accounts
12 Cash surrender value of life insurance policies
13 Premium on bonds payable
14 Accumulated depreciation
15 Paid-in capital in excess of par
16 Short-term prepayments
17 Machinery retired from use and held for sale
18 Accrued payroll
19 Sears Roebuck & Co. common stock (100 shares owned 10 years)
20 Advance payments by customers

Ex. 4-2 Assume that you are a CPA auditing Northeast Corporation, which has just issued a large, long-term note payable. Terms of the borrowing agreement require that, during the life of the loan, Northeast Corporation shall not declare any cash dividends which would: (a) cause its retained earnings to fall below the $5 million level prevailing at the date of the loan; (b) cause the working capital to fall below $2 million; or (c) cause the current ratio to fall below 1.6.

Under these circumstances, would you insist as a condition for issuing your audit report that the board of directors create an appropriation of retained earnings of $5 million? Would you insist upon any disclosure other than the maturity date, amount, and interest rate of the note payable? Explain.

Ex. 4-3 From the following balances, compute (a) the amount of working capital and (b) the book value per share of stock:

Investment in affiliated companies	$100,000
Cash surrender value of life insurance policies owned	10,000
Organization costs	5,000
Interest receivable	2,000
Other current assets	198,000
Other current liabilities	60,000
Reserve for contingencies	50,000
Retained earnings—unappropriated	150,000
Common stock, $10 par	500,000
Additional paid-in capital	200,000
Deferred income taxes payable	40,000
Construction in progress (for customers)	50,000
Cash in bond sinking fund	80,000
Bonuses payable (in form of common stock)	20,000
Product warranties outstanding	6,000

Ex. 4-4 Prepare a skeleton balance sheet for Company X in account form, showing only major classifications (approximately ten topics or group headings).

Ex. 4-5 You have been asked to assist the chief accountant of the Vermont Corporation in the preparation of a balance sheet. The outline presented below represents the various classifications suggested by the chief accountant for the balance sheet; classification O has been added for items to be excluded from the balance sheet. (You are not asked to approve or disapprove the various classifications set forth below.)

A Current assets
B Investments
C Plant and equipment
D Intangibles
E Other assets, including deferred charges
F Miscellaneous debits
G Current liabilities
H Long-term liabilities, including deferred credits
I Reserves and other miscellaneous credits
J Preferred stock
K Common stock
L Additional paid-in capital
M Retained earnings
N Appraisal capital
O Items excluded from the balance sheet

The twenty-five accounts listed below are to be classified according to the preferred classification group from the preceding list.

1 Dividend payable (on Vermont Corporation's preferred stock)
2 Plant construction in progress
3 Factory building (retired from use and held for sale)
4 Premium on bonds payable
5 Land (held for possible future building site)
6 Merchandise inventory (held by Vermont Corporation on consignment)
7 Stock dividend to be distributed, stated at par (in common stock to common stockholders)
8 Office supplies inventory
9 Sinking fund cash (First National Bank, Trustee)
10 Reserve for retirement of preferred stock
11 Installment sales accounts receivable (average collection period 18 months)
12 Premium on preferred stock
13 Advances to officers (indefinite repayment date, non-interest-bearing)
14 Unredeemed merchandise coupons issued to customers
15 Discount on bonds payable
16 Inventory of small tools
17 Contingent liability on notes receivable discounted
18 Liability for loss on merchandise purchase commitments
19 Allowance to reduce inventory to market
20 Matured capital stock subscriptions (called by the board of directors and considered collectible)
21 Common stock subscribed (Vermont Corporation's stock)
22 Sinking fund
23 Securities held as collateral for loan to officer
24 Bank overdraft (Other checking accounts of the company with the same bank have large debit balances.)
25 Contracts payable, retained percentage

Using the letters representing the various balance sheet classifications, identify each of the 25 items according to the preferred balance sheet presentation. If an account is an offsetting or valuation account, mark an *X* before the letter. For example, "Allowance for Uncollectible Accounts" would be "X–A."

SHORT CASES FOR ANALYSIS AND DECISION

Case 4-1 Michael Rogers, a consulting engineer, developed and patented a device for measuring temperatures encountered in space travel. He offered to sell the patent rights to Telespace Company. An agreement was signed under which Telespace Company acquired the patent rights and gave Rogers in exchange $500,000 in cash and a note for $500,000. The note provided for payment only in shares of the common stock of Telespace Company, at the rate of 4,000 shares of the company's $25 par value common stock per year for each of the next five years.

The accountant for Telespace Company included $100,000 among the current liabilities labeled Note Payable in Stock, and $400,000 among the long-term liabilities similarly labeled. He attached a footnote to the financial statements explaining the terms of the agreement with Rogers.

The president of the company, who was about to present the company's financial statements to a bank in support of a loan application, objected to this treatment, contending that the company's liabilities were overstated. The accountant replied that liabilities were obligations to convey something of value and that the company's common stock had value.

Instructions

a Discuss the appropriate balance sheet treatment of the note, giving reasons for your conclusions.

b Suppose that under the terms of the note, Rogers had the option of accepting each year $100,000 in cash or 4,000 shares of common. Would this change your answer? Why?

Case 4-2 Ross Jensen owns a resort located on an excellent fishing lake. His busy season begins May 15 and extends through mid-fall. During the winter he engaged a contractor to build a boathouse and boat dock for a total price of $25,000. The contract called for completion by May 15, because the resort was completely reserved for the week of May 15 to 22, the opening week of the fishing season. Because the completion date was so important to Jensen, he specified in the contract that if the construction was not completed by May 15 the price would be adjusted downward by a penalty of $100 per day, until completed.

The construction was not completed until June 9, at which time Jensen paid the contract price of $22,500, deducting $100 for each of the 25 days of delay. Jensen is convinced that he lost goodwill because his facilities were inadequate and that several of his clients reduced their stay because the facilities were still under construction.

In his balance sheet prepared at September 30, the end of his fiscal year, Jensen included the boathouse and dock as assets valued at $25,000. Included in his revenue was an item "Penalty payments received in lieu of lost revenue, $2,500."

The auditor who examined Jensen's report objected to this treatment and insisted that the facilities be recorded at their actual cost, $22,500. Jensen stated that he could not understand the logic of this position. "Accounting principles are out of tune with reality," he complained. "What if the contract had been 250 days late and the boathouse and dock had cost me nothing; would you record on my balance sheet that I had no asset? I lost at least $100 per day in revenue because of the construction delay."

Instructions At what amount should these facilities be reported in the balance sheet at September 30? (You may ignore any question of depreciation from June 9 to September 30.) Explain your position in terms of accounting principles.

Case 4-3 Blair Company at December 31 of the current year showed on its balance sheet current assets of $1,457,000 and current liabilities of $678,000, including a cash dividend of $110,000 declared by the board of directors near the end of the year. The bond indenture relating to an issue of Blair Company bonds provides that "the company shall maintain current assets in an amount at least twice as large as its current liabilities. If at any time the amount of current assets falls below this amount, no dividends shall be paid on common stock until the company's working capital position meets the above-stated standard (after taking into account the dividend)."

Early in January the company received a letter from the trustee for the bond-holders asking for detailed information about several items on its year-end financial statement. Subsequently the trustee wrote to the president of Blair Company stating that the dividend declared late in December violated the bond indenture. Excerpts from the trustee's letter are cited below:

Included among your current assets is prepaid insurance of $20,480. According to information furnished by your accountant, $8,420 of these premiums apply to insurance coverage for the year following your balance sheet; the remainder of the premiums are for insurance coverage two or more years after the balance sheet date. Thus $12,060 of the prepaid insurance should not be classified as a current asset since these costs will be charged against revenue earned in subsequent years.

Included in your inventories is $54,000 of spare parts and supplies used in maintaining your manufacturing equipment. These spare parts will ultimately be converted into long-term assets, and therefore it is improper to classify them as a part of current assets.

Among the long-term liabilities on the balance sheet are notes payable of $120,000. These notes were given to finance cutting rights to certain standing timber. The notes are secured by an assignment of the proceeds to be received from the sale of the logs to a manufacturing subsidiary and will be paid from the proceeds of these sales. The notes mature at the rate of $20,000 each month, beginning six months after the balance sheet date, and are therefore properly classified as a current liability.

According to our analysis, your current assets are overstated in the amount of $66,060 and your current liabilities are understated by $120,000. If these corrections were made, current assets would be less than twice as large as current liabilities. The dividend declaration on common stock is therefore in violation of the bond indenture. You should rescind this dividend declaration immediately.

Instructions   The president of Blair Company has referred this letter to you for your advice. Write a memorandum to the president commenting on the points in the trustee's letter, and stating your recommendation on the question of rescinding the dividend declaration.

PROBLEMS

Group A

4A-1 The following memorandum contains information concerning the financial position of Yamato Air Freight at December 31 of the current year.

Our properties and equipment *presently in use* consist of aircraft and other flight equipment acquired at a cost of $8,700,000, on which we have recognized depreciation to date of $1,351,200. In addition, we have one other aircraft which has been withdrawn from use and is being held for sale. The book value of this airplane is $750,000 and we are currently negotiating for its sale at a price of $600,000. The negotiations for this sale will soon be completed.

The extensive training program required to make our flight crews familiar with the new aircraft placed in service during the last two years cost $1,800,000, of which all but $582,000 has been amortized. The balance will be written off over the next 12 months.

We have cash in checking accounts amounting to $945,600 and certificates of deposit for $621,600 which bear interest at rates from 6 to 9%. The general ledger controlling account for accounts receivable shows a debit balance of

$960,000, but this total includes a credit balance of $120,000 from a customer who made an advance payment. The allowance for uncollectible accounts amounts to $44,400. Our inventories are carried at average cost and amount to $91,200. Prepaid expenses of several types aggregate $42,000. The cash surrender value of life insurance policies, naming the company as beneficiary, amounts to $147,600.

Among our liabilities are $3,000,000 in 8% long-term notes payable, of which $300,000 falls due within the coming year. Accounts payable total $2,520,000, accrued liabilities $100,000, and income taxes $585,200.

We have 10 million shares of $1 par value capital stock authorized, of which 720,000 shares are outstanding. They were issued at a price of $4 per share. Our earnings which we have reinvested in the business represent a total of $2,209,200.

Instructions Use the above information to prepare a balance sheet in report form. Use two money columns, with rulings as necessary under subtotals. Notes to accompany the balance sheet are not required.

4A-2 Presented below is an alphabetical list of account balances taken from the ledger of Washburn Corporation at December 31 of the current year.

Accounts payable	$ 878,900
Accounts receivable	816,000
Accumulated depreciation: Buildings and equipment	1,104,000
Allowance for uncollectible accounts	10,400
Buildings and equipment (at cost)	4,951,800
Cash	124,600
Cash surrender value of life insurance	115,000
Claim for insurance recovery*	150,000
Common stock, $50 par	2,500,000
Dividends declared, preferred stock	45,500
Dividends declared, common stock	43,500
Inventories (fifo cost)	1,146,000
Income summary (credit balance)	176,300
Income taxes payable	92,600
Marketable securities (market value $192,000)	175,000
Preferred stock, 7%, $100 par	650,000
Paid-in capital in excess of par: common stock	295,000
Premium on serial notes	96,700
Deferred research and development costs	462,400
Retained earnings, Jan. 1	?
6% notes payable	2,000,000
Unamortized note issue costs	34,900
Unearned rental revenue	24,000

*Settlement in this amount has been agreed upon by the insurance company.

Instructions On the basis of the above data, prepare in a form suitable for publication a balance sheet and a statement of retained earnings.

4A-3 A highly condensed balance sheet of Olympic Company at the end of the current year is shown below:

OLYMPIC COMPANY

Balance Sheet

End of Current Year

Cash	$ 87,000	Current liabilities	$132,000
Receivables	138,000	Long-term debt	350,000
Inventories	78,000	Capital stock	225,000
Plant and equipment (net)	650,000	Retained earnings	246,000
	$953,000		$953,000

During a discussion by the board of directors concerning the above balance sheet, one of the directors raised a question as to what effect inflation had on the financial position of the company. He pointed out that the general price level had doubled since the organization and original sale of the company's capital stock and that there had been a substantial increase in prices after the company had acquired much of its plant and equipment.

The president expressed the opinion that an answer to this question would require some study, and he therefore asked the controller of the company to restate the company's balance sheet on the basis of current dollars as of the end of the year, using a general price index to measure the change in the value of money. After considerable analysis, the controller has determined that the book value of the plant and equipment, stated in terms of its equivalent in current dollars, would be $910,000 and that the equivalent of $90,000 in current dollars had been invested in inventories. Realized retained earnings stated in current dollars were computed by the controller to be $172,000.

Instructions

a Using the information compiled by the controller, restate the balance sheet data of the Olympic Company in terms of current dollars. Prepare a comparative balance sheet showing both mixed-dollar and current-dollar amounts.

b Write a report to the board of directors explaining the significance of the supplementary data expressed in current dollars, which appear in your comparative statement.

4A-4 Baylor Company is seeking a short-term loan to enable it to meet heavy payments to suppliers arising from a seasonal buildup of inventories. The company is also in need of cash to pay an impending installment on its serial bonds payable. Norman Taylor, the loan officer of the Western National Bank, is reviewing the loan application from Baylor Company. Included in the file is the balance sheet on page 160 prepared by the company at the close of the calendar year just ended.

After some study of this balance sheet, Taylor decided to ask Baylor Company to have an audit by a CPA firm. During the course of the audit, the CPA firm discovered the following additional information:

(1) Cash includes demand deposits of $65,000, cash change funds of $800, and an IOU signed by the company president for $18,900. (The IOU was collected three days later.)

(2) The balance of receivables is composed of the following items:

BAYLOR COMPANY
Balance Sheet
December 31, 19___

Assets		Equities	
Cash	$ 84,700	Accounts payable	$ 181,500
Receivables	194,300	Accrued expenses	23,800
Inventories	276,200	Reserve for income taxes	50,000
Land, buildings, and property	940,000	Bonds payable	450,000
Marketable securities	88,600	Reserve for depreciation	420,000
Prepaid expenses	18,400	Reserve for bad debts	1,800
Notes receivable	43,000	Reserve for guarantees	10,900
Patents	75,000	Capital stock, common	225,000
Bond discount	12,000	Capital stock, preferred	206,000
Organization costs	35,000	Earned surplus	198,200
Total assets	$1,767,200	Total equities	$1,767,200

Balances in trade customers' accounts	$231,500
Advances to employees for expenses, to be covered by expense account reports	12,800
Claim for insurance recovery	35,000
Less: Customers' deposits on goods not yet manufactured	(85,000)
	$194,300

(3) It is estimated that approximately $4,700 of the customers' accounts will prove uncollectible.

(4) The original cost of land owned by the company was $40,000, of buildings $750,800, of equipment $299,200. The building account has been reduced by $150,000, representing 6% mortgage notes due in 10 years on which interest of $750 is accrued but unrecorded at December 31. Accumulated depreciation on buildings is $240,000, on equipment $180,000.

(5) Marketable securities consist of the following:

		Cost	Market value
United States Treasury bonds		$20,000	$20,800
Second mortgage on building of Jay Company, a supplier		66,390	?
Accrued interest:			
Treasury bonds	$ 250		
Mortgage	1,960	2,210	2,210
		$88,600	

(6) Inventories consist of the following, at average cost:

Raw materials	$107,380
Goods in process	17,530
Finished goods	151,290
	$276,200

(7) Notes receivable are short-term and were acquired in connection with sales;

unrecorded accrued interest at December 31 is $870. It is estimated that $2,400 of the notes may prove uncollectible.

(8) Last year the company sold $500,000 of 6% serial bonds, due in annual installments, to a major stockholder. Of the total, $50,000, plus unrecorded accrued interest of $13,500, is due five days after the balance sheet date. The bond discount applies to these serial bonds and has been correctly amortized during the year.

(9) The reserve for guarantees represents the estimated amount of the company's obligation to service its products for a period of six months following sale.

(10) Common stock represents 15,000 shares of $10 par value stock originally sold at $15 per share; 2,000 shares of 7%, $100 par value preferred stock callable at 102 were originally sold at $103 per share.

(11) The company is the defendant in a lawsuit with the potential for a loss to the company in excess of its insurance coverage. Legal counsel for the company are of the opinion that the outcome of the litigation will probably not have a material effect on the company's financial position.

Instructions Prepare in good form with modern terminology a revised balance sheet for Baylor Company, utilizing the information made available by the audit. Use a separate supporting schedule to show your computation of the revised ending balance of retained earnings. Make adequate disclosure, by means of a note attached to the balance sheet, of the status of litigation against the company.

Group B

4B-1 The following information (listed in random order) is available for Wildcat Company at December 31 of the current year.

Income taxes payable	$ 57,100
Cash surrender value of life insurance	12,300
Accounts receivable (net of credit balances of $10,000 arising from advance payments by customers)	80,000
Allowance for uncollectible accounts	3,700
Cash on hand	800
Cash in Second National Bank	52,000
Cash in First National Bank	26,000
Short-term prepayments	3,500
Retained earnings	208,900
Current installment of long-term debt	25,000
7% long-term note payable (including current installment of $25,000)	250,000
Accounts payable	210,000
Inventories, at fifo cost	332,600
Marketable securities (at cost, market value, $68,700)	51,800
Buildings and equipment	400,000
Accumulated depreciation	112,600
Paid-in capital in excess of par	155,200
Organization costs	26,500
Capital stock	60,000
Long-term advance to affiliated company	50,000
Patents	22,000

Detailed information concerning the capital stock issue is deliberately omitted to minimize the details involved.

Instructions Use the information given to prepare a balance sheet in report form. Use two money columns with rulings as necessary under subtotals. Notes accompanying the balance sheet are not required.

4B-2 On January 1 of the current year, Don Lee and Fred Day organized a partnership known as the Westside Computer Service. Lee, who had been in business for himself, contributed data processing equipment having a fair market value of $29,000. This equipment had originally cost him $38,000 and had been depreciated by $14,000 on his records. Day contributed $30,000 in cash and a set of unusual data-compiling forms which he had developed and which the partners agreed were worth $5,000. The two partners agreed to share profits equally.

The firm immediately acquired a small computer for $250,000, paying $25,000 down and signing a 6% note for the balance, promising payments of $45,000 per year plus interest. The first payment on this contract is due shortly after the end of the current year.

During the first year the firm collected $99,500 in cash for computer rentals and had receivables of $14,800 at the end of the year. Day borrowed $2,000 from the firm on October 1 to meet some emergency medical bills. He has agreed to pay this back at the rate of $100 per month, starting six months from the date of the loan, with interest at 4% on the unpaid balance of the loan. The interest rate is to be regarded as reasonable.

The firm paid rent on a building and other operating expenses totaling $36,250. Lee withdrew $500 per month from the business, while Day withdrew $600 per month. As of December 31, one month's rent ($650) on the building had been paid in advance. The partners agreed to depreciate the new computer at the rate of 10% per year, and the used equipment at the rate of 20%, using the straight-line method. The systems forms developed by Day were to be amortized over a four-year period.

The firm had unpaid bills for operating expenses of $6,470 at December 31.

Instructions
a Prepare a balance sheet for Westside Computer Service at December 31 of the current year; also prepare a separate statement of partners' capitals.
b Prepare three separate supporting schedules to explain the computation of amounts in the balance sheet and statement of partners' capitals, as follows: (1) a schedule of cash receipts and payments concluding with the December 31 balance of cash; (2) a schedule showing the computation of depreciation on the computer and related equipment; and (3) a schedule listing revenue and expenses and concluding with the net income of the partnership. References to the first two of these supporting schedules should appear in the balance sheet on the lines for cash and for accumulated depreciation. Reference to the schedule of revenue and expenses should appear on the line for net income in the statement of partners' capitals.

4B-3 The controller of Westport Company must prepare at June 30, the close of the company's current fiscal year, a statement of working capital. This report must be filed with the Midtown Bank, the trustee of the company's bond issue. The purpose of this required reporting procedure is to demonstrate that the company's working capital exceeds $1 million, the amount Westport Company agreed to maintain under the terms of the bond indenture. The bond indenture defines **working capital** as the excess of current assets over current liabilities. The statement at the top of page 163, based on information taken from the accounts at June 30, was prepared by an assistant.

Current assets:

Cash		$ 244,000
Notes and securities		480,000
Receivables		542,500
Inventories and prepayments		562,300
Total		$1,828,800

Current liabilities:

Notes and accounts payable	$391,300	
Payroll taxes and pension liabilities	495,000	
Reserve for contingencies	100,000	
Total		986,300
Working capital		$ 842,500

The controller, after some investigation, has made the following notes on the items included in the above statement:

Notes and securities. Includes $280,000 of notes receivable, of which $100,000 has been discounted at the bank. Also, $250,000 face value of United States Treasury notes (current market value $238,700) purchased for $216,000, on which $8,500 of interest has accrued since the last interest date. Westport holds $84,000 in five-year notes receivable from a subsidiary company, on which $5,200 of interest is accrued at June 30.

Receivables. A single controlling account is used for receivables. The balance of the account, $542,500, includes trade receivables of $394,040, a current receivable from a subsidiary company of $40,000, advances to employees of $28,460, and an installment note of $80,000 received in payment for the sale of a warehouse, due in four installments of $20,000 per year; accrued interest on this note at June 30 was $4,800. Certain customers have credit balances in their accounts, totaling $35,000, because they have made advances prior to the shipment of goods ordered. Of the trade receivables, $12,000 are worthless and should be written off; it is estimated that $20,000 of the remainder will prove uncollectible.

Inventories and prepayments. The inventory of merchandise on June 30 on a lifo cost basis amounted to $320,750; its current replacement cost is estimated to be $475,000. Included in the $562,300 balance shown in the above statement is $98,000 of equipment that is rented to customers and $19,750 of merchandise on order for delivery during the next six months, the full cost of which is included in accounts payable. Also included in this balance are short-term prepayments of $94,800 and $29,000 representing a defalcation loss, of which $25,000 is expected to be recovered from the insurance company.

Current liabilities. Current accounts payable amount to $241,300, and the company owes $150,000 on a 90-day note to the bank, on which unrecorded interest of $900 has accrued. Amounts withheld from employees for various payroll taxes amount to $70,000; the company's required contribution to such taxes of $28,700 has not been recorded. A provision for employee pensions amounts to $425,000, of which $53,400 will be paid within the coming fiscal year. The reserve for contingencies was set up to provide for possible claims that may arise from renegotiation of profits on a government subcontract.

Instructions On the basis of this information, prepare in good form a statement of working capital of Westport Company at June 30. List current assets in detail, followed by a detailed list of current liabilities. Provide supporting schedules as needed to show how specific items are computed. Is the company complying with the terms of the bond indenture as to the maintenance of working capital?

4B-4 The financial position of Rainbird Company at the end of the current year is indicated by the highly condensed balance sheet prepared by the company's accountant:

Current assets	$ 960,000	Current liabilities	$ 450,000
Noncurrent assets	7,640,000	Long-term liabilities	2,500,000
		Paid-in capital	4,800,000
		Retained earnings	850,000
	$8,600,000		$8,600,000

Below are listed a series of comments, taken from an auditor's notes, describing certain components of the above balance sheet. Some of these comments indicate that the accountant has handled certain items improperly.

(1) Included in the long-term liabilities is an installment payable of $250,000 due within one year from the date of the balance sheet.

(2) A $125,000 dividend to be distributed in common stock of the company appears among the current liabilities.

(3) Included in the amount of current liabilities is a $42,000 contingent liability.

(4) Included among noncurrent assets is $87,000 in cash surrender value of life insurance on officers of the company. Included among the current liabilities is a $60,000 loan made against this cash surrender value. The company intends to renew this borrowing at the maturity date.

(5) Discount on long-term debt of $161,500 is included among the noncurrent assets.

(6) Included in long-term liabilities is an $800,000 appropriation of retained earnings for retirement of preferred stock.

(7) The corporation purchased some of its own common stock for $400,000, its par value. This amount is included among the noncurrent assets.

(8) Rent received in advance in the amount of $74,800 is included in retained earnings.

(9) A cash dividend of $80,000 declared prior to the end of the year, but not payable until after the end of the current year, is included in current liabilities.

(10) A fully depreciated asset was sold for $28,000 and the proceeds were credited to the Plant and Equipment account.

(11) Deposits of $38,000 made with suppliers in advance of the delivery of ordered goods have been netted against the accounts payable controlling account.

(12) An investment in 18% of the stock of an affiliated company, at a cost of $750,000, is included among current assets.

(13) Research and development costs incurred in developing a new product that will shortly go on sale appear among the noncurrent assets at cost, $325,000. The new product is expected to be a successful revenue-producing item for five years or more.

Instructions

a List the dollar amounts of each of the six categories of the company's balance sheet on the first line of a six-column working paper. On separate lines below show the effect of any necessary corrections to the accountant's figures as a result of the information contained in the auditor's notes. Show as an end result the corrected balance sheet data as of the end of the current year. If the information contained in any of the auditor's notes does not indicate an erroneous treatment, explain why no adjustment is necessary in each case.

b Would your interpretation of the company's financial position be substantially changed as a result of the revised data? Explain.

CHAPTER 5

Cash, cash flows, and secondary cash resources

Cash is a medium of exchange which a bank will accept for deposit and immediate credit to the depositor's account. Cash includes currency and coin, personal checks, bank drafts, money orders, and cashiers' checks, as well as money on deposit with banks. Items which are usually under the control of the cashier and are sometimes confused with cash include postage stamps, postdated checks, and IOU's. Postage should be classified as a short-term prepayment; postdated checks and IOU's should be classified as receivables.

Deposits with a trustee, for example, a bond sinking fund which is not under the control of management, should not be included in cash. As another example, American Airlines recently had more than $100 million in cash deposits with manufacturers for purchase of flight equipment. Such deposits do not qualify as current assets since they are not available for payment of current liabilities.

Certificates of deposit are properly classified as short-term investments rather than as cash because they are not available for immediate withdrawal. Strictly speaking, savings deposits also may not be withdrawn without prior notice to the bank, but banks very seldom enforce this requirement. Consequently, savings deposits are usually considered as a part of the cash balance. Petty cash funds and change funds are minor elements of cash under the control of management even though these funds are usually intended to be used for very specific purposes. The limitations placed on the use of these funds do not remove them from the category of cash but simply aid in the overall control of the cash resources.

In summary, the criteria generally used in defining cash are that the item be a medium of exchange, be immediately available for the payment of current debts, and be free from any contractual restriction which would prevent management from using it to meet any and all obligations.

PLANNING CASH ACTIVITIES

The administration of cash is of major importance in any business because cash is the means of commanding goods and services. In addition, careful scrutiny of cash transactions is required because this asset may be readily misappropriated.

The administration of cash generally is centered around two areas: cash budgeting and accounting control. The responsibility of management with respect to cash is (1) to ensure that there is sufficient cash to carry on the operations, (2) to invest any idle cash which is not distributed to the owners, and (3) to prevent loss of cash due to theft or misappropriation. Cash budgeting is necessary for the proper planning of future operations and to assure that cash is available when needed but that cash balances are not excessive. Accounting safeguards are necessary to provide a basis for the planning function, and in addition to assure that the cash is used for proper business purposes and not wasted, misused, or stolen. Management is responsible for controlling and protecting all assets of a business. Special problems exist in controlling cash, however, because money is universally attractive and can be easily misappropriated.

The cash budget

The cash budget is a forecast of cash transactions for a stated time period. It is a statement of estimated cash receipts and payments. The cash budget is neither a pro forma operating statement nor a forecast of financial results. Rather it is a prediction of the cash flow through the enterprise based on analysis of past operations and study of future requirements of the business. This forecast is necessary to enable management to plan the financial affairs of the business, an area of decision making equally as important as the planning of production operations and sales activities.

The time covered by a cash budget is largely determined by the pattern of operations. A company which demonstrates an erratic sales pattern presents special problems for the forecaster, and a very short-range forecast may be all that is feasible and useful. On the other hand, a useful cash forecast can be made for several months in the future for a company which demonstrates a regular pattern of sales. Normally cash budgets are prepared for each month of the budget period; however, if large inflows or outflows of cash occur at particular times during a month, the interval may be changed to reflect these special situations. The manager needs information about the extremes of the cash position; these extreme points do not always occur at the end of the month.

There are two types of cash budgets: (1) the **short-term** or **operating budget,** which usually encompasses a year or a shorter time period, and (2) the **long-term budget,** which usually covers several years. The short-term budget is used in planning daily operations and serves as the basis for planning required borrowing or the investment of temporarily idle cash. The long-term budget involves much less detail and is used primarily in planning for plant acquisitions, debt repayment, new borrowing, and dividend policy.

Estimated cash receipts and payments method

A key step in the preparation of the cash budget is the forecast of expected cash receipts and payments. These estimates are presented in a form indicating (1) the source, amount, and expected date of the estimated receipts and (2) the purpose, amount, and expected date of estimated payments. For companies operating with minimum cash balances or experiencing wide swings in cash requirements, the estimated time of each receipt and payment is often critical. A predicted cash surplus on December 31, for example, offers little consolation to a manager who discovers on July 31 that there is not sufficient cash to meet the payroll that day.

Sales Forecast   The sales forecast is the basis for planning operations, which in turn are basic to estimating cash requirements. In addition, sales are the major source of cash receipts. A detailed analysis of economic indices and regional and national economic trends, as well as the individual problems of the business entity, is often an essential preliminary step to successful sales forecasting.

The process of forecasting sales may begin with consideration of the probable course of economic events for the next several years. From this rather general concept, the data which relate to the near term are used to predict trends for a few months to a year. The situation of the industry is related to these predictions to obtain information about the probable future course of the industry. An analysis of past relationships between the enterprise and the industry is made to derive the forecast for the enterprise. The forecast must take into consideration monthly and seasonal variations.

Forecasting Cash Receipts   The primary source of cash for a business is the sale of its product or service. There is, however, a lag between sales and the collection of cash caused by the traditional practice of buying and selling on credit. The time lag is generally highly predictable for a given business if credit terms, types of customers, and anticipated economic conditions are reviewed. Once the sales pattern is forecast, a reasonable estimate of cash collections can be made.

Miscellaneous sources of cash are often dependent on other activities not closely related to sales. Interest and dividends from investments, for example, may depend upon the operation of other companies which bear little or no relation to the sales volume of the investing company. Other sources of cash, such as sales of scrap and nonessential assets, may not be predictable. Cash records of prior years are helpful in providing estimates of the importance and nature of these miscellaneous sources.

Forecasting Cash Payments Cash payments are also largely dependent on sales volume; however, other factors, such as credit terms, also influence the timing of these outlays. Payments for merchandise, materials, and salaries and wages involve major expenditures which may be governed by the sales forecast. On the other hand, lease payments, repayment of debt contracts, debt service costs, and salaries of certain management personnel are frequently determined by contract and seldom reflect year-to-year fluctuations in sales volume.

There are of course other disbursements which are determined partially by contract and partially on the basis of sales volume, for example, commissions and bonuses paid to employees, utilities, and, to some extent, hourly wage costs. Management may have much more discretion over other outlays, such as dividend payments, acquisition of plant and equipment, research, advertising, and plant maintenance; such outlays may be referred to as *discretionary expenditures.*

Cash Budget Illustrated The summary of expected cash flows can be prepared in the degree of detail desired. Generally speaking, a detailed cash budget is the best aid in planning efficient use of cash. The cash budget shown on page 169 is one type which might be used. Most of the figures included in the budget would normally be ascertained by careful analysis of past and expected future activities; for the purposes of this illustration, however, we have assumed these amounts.

We must remember that much of the cash movement listed in this budget was planned months in advance. In the same manner, much of the cash flow for future months has been planned; consequently, the use of any balance indicated as being available for discretionary purposes may have already been earmarked for specific purposes.

Cash forecast as a planning aid

Before management can decide what disposition to make of a monthly excess of receipts over payments or how to obtain the necessary cash if planned payments exceed receipts, it must know how long the excess or shortage is likely to exist. Although the forecast of cash movement is tentative, it does provide an outline for planning the use of cash.

A series of monthly forecasts, similar to the January forecast for Urban

URBAN HARDWARE COMPANY
Cash Budget for January, 1975

Cash on hand, Jan. 1, 1975		$ 75,000
Receipts:		
Cash sales and trade receivables		122,900
From miscellaneous sources		16,000
Total cash available		$213,900
Payments:		
Merchandise and supplies	$62,600	
Salaries and wages	21,250	
Amounts withheld from employees.	6,250	
Other miscellaneous payments	16,250	
Equipment.	18,130	
Repayment of bank loan, including interest	15,000	
Total payments		139,480
Estimated cash balance, Jan. 31, 1975		$ 74,420
Cash balance desired for normal operations (approximate).		30,000
Cash available for discretionary purposes, Jan. 31, 1975		$ 44,420

Hardware Company, provides a basis for establishing the existence of a potential cash deficiency or surplus. On the basis of this type of analysis, the amount of idle cash and the length of time this cash is likely to remain idle can be estimated. Similarly, the amount which must be borrowed can be estimated and the term of the borrowing can be determined in advance of the time when the cash is required.

Adjusted net income method of forecasting cash flow from operations

The adjusted net income method of cash forecasting, an alternative to the estimated receipts and payments method, is based on pro forma (estimated) income statements which are adjusted to reflect cash flows from operations. This method is used primarily by companies which have demonstrated a stable pattern of operations and which are seldom faced with large periodic cash requirements. Since the forecast is usually in terms of aggregate cash flows rather than in terms of components, as in the estimated receipts and payments method, this method is not an effective control technique for many companies.

CASH FLOW STATEMENT

In preparing a forecast of cash position, useful information may be obtained from an analysis of cash receipts and payments for the most recent fiscal period. A summary of *actual* cash transactions for a month or a year is referred to as a *cash flow statement.* Such a statement is a useful analytical tool for management and other users of financial statements because it provides answers to questions such as the following: How much cash was generated by recurring operations last period? What use was made of cash receipts? How much cash was received from nonrecurring sources? Why is the company short of cash? Can the current level of cash dividend payments be maintained? The preparation of a cash flow statement from a highly condensed set of financial statements is illustrated here for the Port Supply Company, using the financial statements (prepared on the accrual basis of accounting) and the additional information for Year 2 shown below:

PORT SUPPLY COMPANY
Comparative Balance Sheet
December 31

Assets	Year 2	Year 1	Net change Debit (Credit)
Cash	$ 24,900	$ 14,000	$ 10,900
Accounts receivable (net)	33,000	27,000	6,000
Inventories.	30,000	40,000	(10,000)
Short-term prepayments	1,600	1,000	600
Equipment	130,000	100,000	30,000
Less: Accumulated depreciation	(19,500)	(12,000)	(7,500)
Total assets	$200,000	$170,000	$ 30,000

Liabilities & Stockholders' Equity	Year 2	Year 1	Net change Debit (Credit)
Accounts payable	$ 15,500	$ 23,400	$ 7,900
Interest payable.	1,500	–	(1,500)
Income taxes payable	7,000	6,600	(400)
Long-term notes payable	20,000	–	(20,000)
Capital stock, $10 par value	100,000	100,000	
Retained earnings	56,000	40,000	(16,000)
Total liabilities & stockholders' equity	$200,000	$170,000	$(30,000)

Additional information for Year 2

1 Equipment costing $30,000 was acquired for $18,000 cash and a long-term note payable for $12,000.

2 The company borrowed $8,000 from a private investor by signing a note due in Year 5.

3 Cash dividends of $5,000 were paid at the end of the year.

PORT SUPPLY COMPANY
Income Statement
For the Year Ended December 31, Year 2

Sales (net)		$107,000
Cost of goods sold:		
Beginning inventories	$40,000	
Purchases (net)	50,000	
Cost of goods available for sale	$90,000	
Less: Ending inventories	30,000	
Cost of goods sold		60,000
Gross profit on sales		$ 47,000
Expenses:		
Operating expenses (excluding depreciation)	$10,000	
Depreciation expense	7,500	
Interest expense	1,500	19,000
Income before income taxes		$ 28,000
Income taxes		7,000
Net income		$ 21,000
Earnings per share		$ 2.10

Working Paper for Cash Flow Statement An illustrative cash flow working paper for Port Supply Company for Year 2 appears on page 173. The balances in asset, liability, and stockholders' equity accounts at the end of the Year 1 are entered in the first column of the working paper and balances in these accounts at the end of Year 2 are entered in the last column. The transactions for Year 2 are then summarized in the next two columns with the objective of reconciling beginning account balances for Year 2 with the ending balances. In doing this we identify those transactions involving cash and list the sources and uses of cash in the lower section of the working paper. Each account should be inspected after the analysis of transactions is completed to make sure that the ending balance in the account is equal to the beginning balance adjusted for the effect of the transactions. Brief explanations of the working paper transactions for Year 2 follow:

(1) The first step in determining the net cash provided by operations is to record the net income of $21,000 under cash receipts and as a credit to the Retained Earnings account. This figure will be adjusted in transactions (2) through (8) for non-cash items (such as depreciation) and for changes in inventories, accrued liabilities, accounts receivable, short-term prepayments, and accounts payable. As a result of these adjustments, the net income will be converted to a *cash basis.*

(2) The decrease of $10,000 in inventories is recorded as an additional source of cash generated from operations (a debit) and as a credit to the beginning inventory. A decrease in inventories indicates that purchases of merchandise in Year 2 were less than the cost of goods sold. When the decrease of $7,900 in accounts payable is taken into account (transaction 8), the cost of goods sold will be converted to a cash basis.

(3) Depreciation is a non-cash expense and is recorded in the working paper as an addition to net income and a credit to the Accumulated Depreciation account.

(4) The increase of $1,500 in interest payable is equal to the interest expense shown in the income statement. This indicates that no cash was paid for interest in Year 2. The working paper entry recognized this by adding $1,500 to net income and recording $1,500 as interest payable.

(5) Income tax expense for Year 2 was $7,000 and this amount is shown in the Income Taxes Payable account at the end of Year 2. The income taxes payable at December 31, Year 1, were paid in Year 2. In order to convert the income tax expense to a cash basis, the $400 increase in the Income Taxes Payable account is added to net income.

(6) The increase of $6,000 in accounts receivable indicates that sales for Year 2 exceeded the cash collections from customers by this amount. A debit to accounts receivable and a credit to net income on the working paper are needed in the process of converting net income to a cash basis.

(7) Short-term prepayments increased from $1,000 to $1,600 during Year 2, thus more cash was spent for short-term prepayments than was recognized as expense. The increase of $600 in the short-term prepayments balance is shown as a reduction (credit) in net income in arriving at the cash flow from operations.

(8) The decrease in accounts payable during Year 2 indicates that the amount paid to merchandise creditors exceeded the purchases of merchandise. Accounts Payable are reduced by a debit entry of $7,900 and net income is reduced by $7,900. At this point, the cash effect of transactions (1) through (8) is summarized to show that the net cash provided from operations was $25,900. This amount may also be obtained by converting the income statement to a cash basis of accounting as illustrated on page 175.

(9) In Year 2, the company borrowed cash of $8,000 by issuing a long-term note; this is recorded in the working paper as a cash receipt and as a credit to Long-term Notes Payable.

(10) Equipment costing $30,000 was purchased in Year 2 by paying $18,000 in cash and issuing a long-term note payable for $12,000. This is recorded in the working paper as a debit to the Equipment account, $30,000, a credit to Long-term Notes Payable, $12,000, and a credit to cash payments for purchase of equipment, $18,000.

(11) Cash dividends of $5,000 are recorded in the working paper as a reduction in retained earnings and a cash payment to stockholders.

(X) After transactions (1) through (11) are recorded, the account

	Account balances, end of Year 1	Analysis of transactions for Year 2		Account balances, end of Year 2
		Debit	Credit	
Debits				
Cash	14,000	(X) 10,900		24,900
Accounts receivable	27,000	(6) 6,000		33,000
Inventories	40,000		(2) 10,000	30,000
Short-term prepayments	1,000	(7) 600		1,600
Equipment	100,000	(10) 30,000		130,000
Totals	182,000			219,500
Credits				
Accumulated depreciation	12,000		(3) 7,500	19,500
Accounts payable	23,400	(8) 7,900		15,500
Interest payable	—		(4) 1,500	1,500
Income taxes payable	6,600		(5) 400	7,000
Long-term notes payable	—		(9) 8,000 (10) 12,000	20,000
Capital stock, $10 par value	100,000			100,000
Retained earnings	40,000	(11) 5,000	(1) 21,000	56,000
Totals	182,000	60,400	60,400	219,500
Cash receipts:				
Operations, net income		(1) 21,000		
Add: Decrease in inventories		(2) 10,000		
Depreciation expense		(3) 7,500		
Increase in interest payable		(4) 1,500		
Increase in income taxes payable		(5) 400		From operations, $25,900
Less: Increase in accounts receivable			(6) 6,000	
Increase in short-term prepayments			(7) 600	
Decrease in accounts payable			(8) 7,900	
Borrowing on long-term notes		(9) 8,000		
Cash payments:				
Purchase of equipment			(10) 18,000	
Dividends			(11) 5,000	
Total cash receipts and payments		48,400	37,500	
Increase in cash during Year 2			(X) 10,900	
		48,400	48,400	

balances at the end of Year 2 may be determined and compared with the balance sheet at December 31, Year 2 (see page 170) to make certain that the amounts are in agreement. Before this step can be completed, however, the debit and credit items in the cash receipts and cash payments section of the working paper are added in order to determine the net increase in cash. The increase in cash of $10,900 is recognized in working paper entry (X) as a debit to the Cash account in order to complete the "Account Balances, End of Year 2" column and to reconcile the difference between cash receipts and cash payments.

Cash flow statement

A cash flow statement prepared from the working paper is shown below:

PORT SUPPLY COMPANY

Cash Flow Statement

For Year Ended December 31, Year 2

Cash receipts:		
Operations		$25,900
Borrowing on long-term notes		8,000
Total cash receipts.		$33,900
Cash payments:		
Purchase of equipment.	$18,000	
Dividends	5,000	
Total cash payments.		23,000
Increase in cash during the year		$10,900

Because the detail for cash receipts from operations is shown in the working paper, it is not repeated in the cash flow statement illustrated above.

Alternative approach: Cash basis net income

Instead of showing a single figure for cash provided by operations in the cash flow statement, the income statement may be converted from the accrual basis to a cash basis in order to show cash receipts from operations and cash payments for expenses. Receipts from customers, payments to merchandise creditors, and payments for specific expenses are thus shown with other sources and uses of cash in the cash flow statement. This approach is illustrated on page 175 for the Port Supply Company:

PORT SUPPLY COMPANY
Conversion of Income Statement from Accrual to Cash Basis
For Year Ended December 31, Year 2

	Income statement (accrual basis)	Add (deduct)	Cash basis
Sales	$107,000		
Less: Increase in accounts receivable . .		$ (6,000)	$101,000
Cost of goods sold.	60,000		
Add: Decrease in accounts payable . .		7,900	
Less: Decrease in inventories		(10,000)	57,900
Gross profit on sales	$ 47,000		$ 43,100
Expenses:			
Operating expenses (excluding			
depreciation).	$ 10,000		
Add: Increase in short-term			
prepayments		600	$ 10,600
Depreciation expense.	7,500	(7,500)	–0–
Interest expense	1,500	(1,500)	–0–
Income taxes	7,000		
Less: Increase in income taxes			
payable		(400)	6,600
Total expenses	$ 26,000		$ 17,200
Net income—accrual basis.	$ 21,000		
Net income—cash basis (cash flow			
from operations)			$ 25,900

PORT SUPPLY COMPANY
Cash Flow Statement
For Year Ended December 31, Year 2

Cash receipts:

Collections on accounts receivable		$101,000
Borrowing on long-term notes		8,000
Total cash receipts.		$109,000

Cash payments:

Merchandise creditors	$57,900	
Operating expenses.	10,600	
Income taxes	6,600	
Purchase of equipment.	18,000	
Dividends	5,000	
Total cash payments.		98,100
Increase in cash during the year		$ 10,900

Uses of cash flow data

Reference to cash flow information for a fiscal period can be justified primarily on the grounds that it provides useful predictive information for decision makers. Management and outside users of financial statements are concerned with the ability of a business to meet its obligations and remain solvent. Cash flow is viewed by many businessmen as a barometer of financial health.

A cash flow statement, however, should not be viewed as a substitute for the income statement. A cash flow statement reports the sources and uses of cash; the income statement reports the efforts and accomplishments (expenses and revenue) in providing goods and services to customers. Cash flow from operations is no more than the net increase in cash as a result of business operations; it is not a summary of revenue realized and expenses incurred. The profitability of a business is measured by comparing expired costs with realized revenue, not by computing income on a cash basis.

Reference has often been made by financial analysts to "cash flow per share," determined by adding back depreciation and amortization charges to net income and dividing the result (income before non-cash expenses) by the number of shares of common stock outstanding. The Accounting Principles Board consistently discouraged computations of this sort. In *APB Opinion No. 19,* for example, it suggested that:

> Terms referring to "cash" should not be used to describe amounts provided from operations unless all non-cash items have been appropriately adjusted. The adjusted amount should be described accurately, in conformity with the nature of the adjustments, e.g., "Cash provided from operations for the period." . . . The Board strongly recommends that isolated statistics of working capital or cash provided from operations, especially per-share amounts, not be presented in annual reports to stockholders. If any per-share data relating to flow of working capital or cash are presented, they should as a minimum include amounts for inflow from operations, inflow from other sources, and total outflow, and each per-share amount should be clearly identified with the corresponding total amount shown in the Statement.[1]

The Securities and Exchange Commission has similarly discouraged the inclusion of cash flow per share in registration statements filed with the Commission and in annual reports to shareholders. The Commission states that presentation of cash flow per share statistics "appear designed to decrease the credibility of conventional statements as a measure of business activity."[2] The Commission considers the reporting of cash flow per share (whether based on the amount of cash generated from operations or the amount of net income before depreciation and

---

[1] *APB Opinion No. 19,* "Reporting Changes in Financial Position," AICPA (New York: 1971), pp. 377–378.

[2] *Accounting Series Release No. 142,* "Reporting Cash Flow and Other Related Data," Securities and Exchange Commission (Washington, D.C.: 1973).

amortization) to be both misleading and irrelevant. Accordingly, it urges that per-share data other than that relating to net income, net assets, and dividends should be avoided in reporting financial results. Briefly, the position of the Commission may be summarized as follows:

> If accounting net income computed in conformity with generally accepted accounting principles is not an accurate reflection of economic performance for a company or an industry, it is not an appropriate solution to have each company independently decide what the best measure of its performance should be and present that figure to its shareholders as Truth. This would result in many different concepts and numbers which could not be used meaningfully by investors to compare different candidates for their investment dollars.
>
> Where the measurement of economic performance is an industry-wide problem, representatives of the industry and the accounting profession should present the problem and suggested solutions to the Financial Accounting Standards Board which is the body charged with responsibility for researching and defining principles to financial measurement.[3]

MANAGEMENT OF CASH

Internal control

The purpose of a system of internal control is to assure that assets which belong to the enterprise are received when tendered, are protected while in the custody of the business, and are used only for business purposes. The system of internal control consists of all measures employed by a business for the purposes of (1) safeguarding its resources against waste, fraud, and inefficiency; (2) promoting accuracy and reliability in accounting and operating data; (3) encouraging and measuring compliance with company policy; and (4) judging the efficiency of operations in all divisions of the business.[4] Internal controls are not designed primarily to detect errors but rather to reduce the opportunity for errors or dishonesty to occur.

Implicit in all systems of internal control is the concept that no one person should handle all phases of a given transaction from beginning to end. For example, if one person were permitted to order merchandise, receive it, write a check in payment, and record the transaction in the accounts, there would be no protection against either fraud or accidental errors. In larger organizations separate and independent departments are established for such functions as purchasing, receiving, selling, finance, and accounting, which assures that no one department handles all phases of a transaction.

---

[3] *Ibid.*

[4] This definition of internal control was adapted from Walter B. Meigs, E. John Larsen, and Robert F. Meigs, *Principles of Auditing,* 5th ed., Richard D. Irwin, Inc. (Homewood, Ill.: 1973), p. 124.

In many cases the system of internal control is improved by physical safeguards. Business machines help to improve the efficiency and accuracy of the record-keeping function. Cash registers, safes, and prenumbered business forms are very helpful in safeguarding cash and establishing responsibility for it. The system, regardless of the plan, must be supervised with care if it is to function effectively.

If an attempt is made to design a foolproof system, it should be remembered that management's primary responsibility is profitable operation of the business. The cost of the system of internal control must be balanced against the benefit to be derived in preventing errors and losses. When the cost of adding an additional safeguard cannot be justified in terms of its contribution to the overall performance, the risk of errors and losses may be accepted with full knowledge of the circumstances.

Controlling cash receipts and payments

The objective sought in the control of cash receipts is to ensure that all cash due to the business is collected and recorded without loss. The system of controlling cash payments should be designed to ensure that no unauthorized disbursements are made. Control is accomplished by division of responsibility so as to achieve independent verification of cash transactions without duplication of effort. Cash is safeguarded by depositing it in banks and through the use of special cash funds.

Imprest cash funds (petty cash)

The term *imprest cash* refers to a fund of fixed amount used for making small expenditures that are most conveniently paid in cash. The imprest fund is restored to its original amount at frequent intervals by writing a check on the general bank account payable to Petty Cash. The replenishment check is equal in amount to the expenditures made from the fund. Imprest cash funds placed in the custody of responsible employees thus serve to maintain control over cash without involved procedures for small disbursements.

The size of the fund should be sufficient to meet the normal need for small cash payments for a period of two or three weeks. As each cash payment is made, a voucher or receipt is placed in the fund in lieu of the cash removed. These vouchers are reviewed and canceled when the fund is replenished.

Illustration of the Use of a Petty Cash Fund On December 1, Luis Corporation established a petty cash fund of $250 for the purpose of paying certain bills. On December 21, the cashier requested reimbursement for bills paid during the intervening period. The following itemized list of disbursements was presented on December 21 for reimbursement and on December 31 in connection with the year-end audit:

Composition of Petty Cash Fund

	Dec. 21	Dec. 31
Cash in fund	$ 9	$150
Office supplies expense.	175	77
Miscellaneous sales expenses.	65	25
Cash over and short	1	(2)
Total	$250	$250

The petty cash fund should also be replenished at the end of the accounting period so that the expenses paid from the fund will be recorded in the proper period and the year-end cash balance will be accurately stated. The entries required to account for the petty cash fund for the month of December are as follows:

Dec. 1	Petty Cash Fund	250	
	Cash		250
	To record the establishment of a petty cash fund.		
Dec. 21	Office Supplies Expense	175	
	Miscellaneous Sales Expenses	65	
	Cash Over and Short	1	
	Cash		241
	To reimburse the petty cash fund and to record expenses incurred.		
Dec. 31	Office Supplies Expense	77	
	Miscellaneous Sales Expenses	25	
	Cash Over and Short		2
	Cash		100
	To record the expenses incurred since December 21 and to reimburse the petty cash fund.		

If for any reason the petty cash fund is not replenished at the year-end, it is still desirable that the expenses be recorded before the books are closed. In this situation the December 31 entry illustrated above would be changed in only one respect: the credit of $100 would be to Petty Cash Fund rather than to Cash. The effect on the year-end financial statements is the same as if the fund had actually been replenished.

Change fund

A change fund is an imprest fund used to facilitate the collection of money from customers. The amount of the change fund is deducted from the total cash on hand at the close of business each day to determine the daily collections. The cash should be counted and checked against the cash register tape daily as a step in the internal control system. In general, change and petty cash funds are combined with cash on hand and in the bank for balance sheet purposes.

Reconciliation of bank balances

The cash balance indicated on the monthly bank statement will seldom agree with the cash balance indicated by the depositor's ledger account for cash. These two balances do not agree even though they purport to measure the same quantity, because there is a lag between the time that transactions are recognized by the two parties, the bank and the depositor. For example, the depositor will credit the ledger account, Cash, when he writes a check in payment of a bill. The bank will not reduce the depositor's account until the check is presented for payment by the creditor. Another common difference between the two balances results when the deposit of cash receipts is made after the bank closes its records for the month. Both of these differences are self-correcting over time; the outstanding checks will be presented for payment and the deposit will be entered by the bank within a few days.

There are also time lags in transactions initiated by the bank. For example, a company is generally not notified of the bank's charges for servicing the account or for collecting a note receivable until the monthly bank statement is received.

In addition to items which involve merely a lag in the recording process, there are occasionally errors made by the company or by the bank. The process of reconciling the balances forces a careful review of all transactions involving cash and provides a means of proving the accuracy of the company's records. The value of this review stems from the fact that two independent agents have recorded the same transactions and that their records are being compared. When differences arise they must be explained. Those differences which are self-correcting require no further consideration. Corrections must be made, however, for omissions or other errors in recording transactions in the ledger. Errors made by the bank should be called to its attention for correction.

Two forms of bank reconciliation are in common usage: (1) both the bank balance and the ledger balance are reconciled to a correct balance, and (2) the bank balance is reconciled to the ledger balance (or the ledger balance to the bank balance). The first form is generally preferred by accountants and is illustrated on page 181.

Illustration The Cash in Bank ledger account for Baldwin and Company shows a debit balance of $10,592.66 on December 31. The bank statement indicates a balance on deposit of $12,019.02 on December 31. Receipts of December 31 in the amount of $1,144.60 were left in the night depository on December 31 but were not included on the bank statement. The December bank statement included a debit memorandum for $13.50 for service charges for November. A credit memorandum included with the statement indicated that a note receivable in the amount of $2,000, left with the bank for collection, had been collected and credited to the Baldwin and Company account by the bank for $2,030, including interest of $30. Comparison of the paid checks with the check stubs indicated that check no. 821 for $463.90 on December 15, for the purchase of office equipment, had been erroneously entered in the cash payments journal as $436.90. In addition, it was learned that the following checks, all written in December, had not been paid by the bank:

No. 811	$421.96
No. 814	93.00
No. 823	116.50

Also included with the bank statement was a check for $50 from W. Davis, a customer of Baldwin and Company. This check was marked NSF (not sufficient funds).

A reconciliation of both balances to a correct cash balance is given below:

BALDWIN AND COMPANY
Bank Reconciliation
December 31, 19__

Balance per bank statement		$12,019.02
Add: Deposit in transit.		1,144.60
		$13,163.62
Less: Outstanding checks nos. 811, 814, and 823		631.46
Correct cash balance		$12,532.16
Balance per ledger.		$10,592.66
Add: Proceeds of note collected by bank (*includes interest of $30*).		2,030.00
		$12,622.66
Less: Bank service charges for November	$13.50	
NSF check of W. Davis	50.00	
Error in recording check no. 821	27.00	90.50
Correct cash balance		$12,532.16

The bank reconciliation serves three functions: (1) to arrive at the correct cash balance to be reported in the balance sheet, (2) to uncover errors made in recording cash transactions, either by the bank or the company's personnel, and (3) to provide information necessary to bring the accounting records up to date. The journal entry required to adjust the accounts for errors and omissions is taken from the lower section of the bank reconciliation. All the items appearing on the reconciliation as additions to or deductions from the "balance per ledger" must be reflected in the entry. The journal entry required to adjust the books of Baldwin and Company follows:

Cash	1,939.50	
Office Equipment	27.00	
Accounts Receivable: W. Davis	50.00	
Miscellaneous Expense	13.50	
Interest Revenue		30.00
Notes Receivable		2,000.00
To adjust Cash to correct balance as shown on December bank reconciliation.		

The balance per the ledger, $10,592.66, plus the debit of $1,939.50 in the journal entry, equal the correct cash balance of $12,532.16.[5] If there had been arithmetic errors in balancing the Cash account, these would be corrected and the balance per ledger on the reconciliation would also be changed. Errors of this type are seldom found in bank reconciliation procedures if a trial balance of the general ledger has been properly prepared prior to the time the reconciliation is prepared.

The deposit in transit and the outstanding checks will be processed by the bank in the regular course of business during January.

Reconciliation of cash receipts and payments

Cash balances per the bank statement and the company's ledger are reconciled in order to establish the accuracy of the cash records. A full reconciliation of cash receipts and payments may also be made in establishing the accuracy of the cash balance and the effectiveness of controls over cash. An example of this form of reconciliation for Baldwin and Company is found in Case 5-2 on page 195.

Cash overdraft

The issuance of checks in excess of the balance on deposit will create an overdraft in the bank account. Banks often (but not always) refuse

---

[5] As a general rule, the entry resulting from a bank reconciliation is the only example of an adjusting or correcting entry which involves the Cash account.

to pay a check which exceeds the amount of the depositor's account. Such refusal of course prevents an overdraft from occurring. In the rare situation in which a company maintains only one bank account and that account is overdrawn at the balance sheet date, the overdraft should be shown as a current liability. However, if a company has other bank accounts with larger positive balances, it is reasonable to present the net balance of cash as a current asset. This treatment is based on the reasoning that the users of the financial statements are interested primarily in a company's total cash position rather than the status of individual bank accounts.

In rare instances, the accountant will encounter a situation in which checks are written (and recorded) in excess of the amount on deposit, but the checks are not mailed to the payees. In preparing financial statements, the credit balance in the Cash account should be eliminated by an entry debiting Cash and crediting Accounts Payable by the amount of the checks written but not released.

SECONDARY CASH RESOURCES

Investment of idle cash

To achieve efficient use of all resources, management frequently turns unproductive cash balances into productive resources through investment in marketable securities. In some cases we find that corporations follow a policy of holding, more or less continuously, securities which can be converted into cash whenever the circumstances demand.

Marketable securities (usually short-term notes or bonds and occasionally common stocks) held by a business for the purpose of earning a return on cash resources are characterized by their salability at a readily determinable market price. Stocks and bonds which are not widely held or frequently traded usually do not meet the marketability test; consequently, securities of this latter type are not considered in this discussion.

Investments in securities of other companies purchased as a means of exercising control over the operations of such companies are of a quite different character and should not be considered as temporary investments. If the holding is for the purpose of exercising control, the effective operation of the enterprise may be hampered by the liquidation of the investment. Investments of this nature are discussed in Chapter 21.

In summary, marketable securities which are classified on the balance sheet as current assets must be readily salable and should not be held for purposes of bolstering business relations with the issuing corporation. On the other hand, there is no requirement that the securities be held for a limited time only or that management express its intent as to the duration of the holding. The objectives of investments in marketable securities are therefore twofold: (1) to maximize the return on capital and (2) to minimize the risk of loss from price fluctuation.

When excess cash is available for short periods, the investment media typically used are *certificates of deposit, commercial paper,* and *bonds* (both government and corporate) with near-term maturities (in order to minimize price fluctuations). *Commercial paper* is the term used in the money market for short-term unsecured promissory notes issued by corporations and sold to investors, generally other companies. Longer-term bonds and common stocks, although occasionally used as a medium for investing idle cash, do not meet the objective of limited price fluctuation. Long-term bond prices fluctuate with changes in the level of interest rates, as do prices of bonds with short-term maturities; the degree of fluctuation is greater, however, the longer the time to maturity. Stocks, on the other hand, are subject to wide and erratic price movements because of changes in investor sentiment, corporate earnings, and other factors which are difficult to predict.

Recording transactions in marketable securities

At acquisition, marketable securities are recorded at cost, the price of the security in the market plus any cost incident to the acquisition, such as broker's fees and transfer taxes. Bonds acquired between interest dates are traded on the basis of the market price plus the interest accrued since the most recent interest payment. The accrued interest is a separate asset which is purchased simultaneously with the bond. The cost of these two assets should be separated to achieve a clear picture of the results of the security transaction.

Illustration On January 31, 1975, Smith & Co. placed an order with a broker to buy 100, $1,000, 6% South Atlantic Railroad bonds which mature on November 30, 1978, with interest dates May 31 and November 30. The bonds were purchased on the same day at 103, plus accrued interest of $1,000 for two months. The brokerage commission on the transaction was $500. The total cost of the bonds and the total cash outlay are computed as follows:

Market price of bonds ($1,030 × 100)	$103,000
Add: Brokerage commission	500
Total cost of bonds	$103,500
Add: Accrued interest for two months on $100,000, at 6% per year	1,000
Total cash outlay	$104,500

The journal entry required to record the purchase is as follows:

Marketable Securities (South Atlantic Railroad bonds)	103,500	
Accrued Interest Receivable	1,000	
Cash		104,500
To record purchase of 100 bonds at 103 plus accrued interest of $1,000 and brokerage commission of $500.		

On April 30, the South Atlantic Railroad Bonds are sold at the market price of 104¾ plus accrued interest for five months. The cash received upon sale of the securities, assuming the brokerage commission to be $500, is computed as follows:

Market price of securities ($1,047.50 × 100)	$104,750
Less: Brokerage commission	500
Proceeds on sale of bonds	$104,250
Add: Accrued interest for five months on $100,000, at 6% per year . . .	2,500
Total cash received	$106,750

The following journal entry is required on April 30 to record the sale of the bonds and to recognize the interest earned:

Cash 106,750	
Marketable Securities (South Atlantic	
Railroad bonds)	103,500
Accrued Interest Receivable	1,000
Interest Revenue	1,500
Gain on the Sale of Marketable Securities	750
To record sale of South Atlantic Railroad bonds at 104¾, less brokerage commission of $500, plus accrued interest of $2,500.	

The gain of $750 realized on the sale of the South Atlantic Railroad bonds is the result of a change in the market price of the bonds, which may have occurred for any number of reasons. The two most likely causes of such a gain are (1) a decline in the level of interest rates, or (2) a more favorable appraisal of this particular bond issue. If the level of interest rates had risen since January 31, 1975, these bonds probably would have been sold at a loss. The $1,000 of accrued interest on the bonds acquired on January 31 might at that time have been recorded as a debit to the

Interest Revenue account. This procedure would require that the $2,500 of accrued interest received on April 30 be credited to the Interest Revenue account. The net effect would be to show $1,500 as interest earned during the three months the bonds were owned.

In accounting for temporary investments in bonds, it is usually unnecessary to amortize premiums or to accumulate discounts. Bonds purchased as temporary investments generally have near-term maturities; consequently, any premium or discount is likely to be negligible. The holding period by the investor is also likely to be very short, which means that any change in market price is usually attributable to the two causes mentioned above rather than to the approach of the maturity date. In theory the amortization of premium or the accumulation of discount is always proper, but as a practical matter such amortization or accumulation would add little to the accuracy of income measurement on temporary investments in bonds.

Computation of Interest on Bonds Owned   Accrued interest on notes and bonds issued by business firms is generally computed on the basis of a 360-day year.[6] Any full month expired, whether it has 31 days, 30 days, or only 28 days, would be viewed as one-twelfth of a year. Additional interest is determined on the basis of the number of days elapsed. For example, interest from April 25 to August 10 would be computed for three months (May, June, and July) and 15 days (5 days in April and 10 days in August), or 105/360 of a year.

Interest on U.S. government obligations is computed on the basis of a 365-day year; thus the *exact number of days* for the interest computation period must be determined. Interest on a U.S. Treasury bond from April 25 to August 10, for example, would be 107/365 of a full year's interest.

Cost Selection   The cost of securities sold is not always as definite as in the preceding illustration. If there are several purchases of the same security at different dates and prices, and it is then decided to sell a portion of the holdings, some procedure of cost selection must be employed. Among the methods commonly used are specific identification, first-in, first-out, and average cost. For income tax purposes only specific identification and first-in, first-out are acceptable.

Stock and bond certificates generally have serial numbers which make it easy to identify the cost of specific acquisitions. By using the specific identification method, management may influence the recorded gain or

---

[6] Not long ago, Chairman Wright Patman of the House Banking Committee accused banks of manipulating the calendar to collect about $150 million of extra interest a year. According to Mr. Patman, "The banks are charging interest over the full 365 days (in a year) but are giving the customer the use of the money for only 360 days. In short, on a 12-month loan, the borrower pays five days of extra interest, and over a five-year period he will pay almost a full extra month's interest." As a result of widening criticism, some banks now compute interest on the basis of a 365-day year.

loss by deliberately selecting the certificates to be sold from a high-cost lot or a low-cost lot. As an example, assume that Black Company buys 100 bonds of American Telephone at a total cost of $96,000 and a few months later buys another 100 bonds at a cost of $99,000. A month later Black Company decides to sell 100 American Telephone bonds. The market value is then $98,000. The sale will show a profit of $2,000 or a loss of $1,000, depending on whether Black Company elects to deliver bonds from the first or the second purchase.

Price fluctuations and valuation of marketable securities

Since marketable securities are in a sense an extension of the cash account, the current market prices of these securities are important both to management and to other readers of the financial statements. These securities are secondary cash resources which can be converted into cash when the need arises.

Normally an asset is recorded at cost and this cost is associated with the revenue which arises from the use of the asset. If the asset loses its value without producing revenue, the cost is written off as a loss. The concept of *realization* usually allows recognition of increases in the value of an asset only when it is sold. Whether realization should be limited to the point of sale for marketable securities is a question worth considering. By definition, marketable securities are readily salable at a quoted market price. This same characteristic is not usually found in the inventory or plant assets. This basic difference between these types of assets suggests that the test of realization should not control the valuation of marketable securities.

The consistent use of market prices in setting a valuation on marketable securities at the end of any accounting period has some advantages: (1) The income statement will show the results of decisions to hold or sell such securities period by period. For example, if the market price rises in one period and falls in the next, the gain from holding securities in the first period and the loss sustained by failure to sell at the higher price will be revealed. (2) Valuation at market eliminates the anomaly of carrying otherwise identical and interchangeable securities at different amounts because they were acquired at different prices. (3) The market value is more meaningful to the creditor, who studies the current section of a balance sheet in order to judge the debt-paying ability of the company.

The following example illustrates the issues that arise when market value is used as the basis for valuation. At the close of business on December 31, Dixon Foundry had an inventory of marketable securities which cost $148,000 and which had a market value of $151,500. The question at issue is whether on December 31 there has been a gain of $3,500. If we follow the test of realization, no gain would be recognized until the securities are sold. If valuation at market is accepted, the following journal entry would be recorded:

Marketable Securities	3,500	
Gain in Market Value of Securities		3,500
To record appreciation of marketable securities.		

Thus the gain is recognized in the period in which the price changed rather than in the period in which securities are sold.

Subsequently, on March 28, the securities are sold for $149,800. Has there been a gain or a loss on the sale of securities? If traditional realization rules were followed, the gain in market price was not recognized earlier; since a sale has now taken place, a gain of $1,800 should be recorded. If the securities were valued at market on December 31, the entry to record the sale would show a loss of $1,700 sustained since the end of the preceding year.

The question which must be answered is, "What event in the life of the enterprise gives rise to the recognition of gains and losses from holding marketable securities in lieu of cash?" The traditional answer has been "Sale of the securities," but the logic of this answer is questionable.

Valuation at cost versus valuation at lower of cost or market

Most companies publishing financial statements today show marketable securities in their balance sheets at cost but also disclose market values parenthetically.[7] Only a few companies apply the lower-of-cost-or-market rule to investments in marketable securities.[8] For many years the AICPA has held the position that:

> In the case of marketable securities where market value is less than cost by a substantial amount and it is evident that the decline in market value is not due to a mere temporary condition, the amount to be included as a current asset should not exceed the market value. . . . It is important that the amounts at which current assets are stated be supplemented by information which reveals for temporary investments, their market value at the balance-sheet date. . . .[9]

[7] There are notable exceptions to the general approach. Insurance companies, securities brokers and dealers, mutual funds, and others used special methods based on market value to account for investments in securities. For example, Bear, Stearns & Co. (a stock brokerage firm) recently reported marketable securities at market value of $42,879,231. In contrast, the Trust Company of Georgia (a bank) reported common stock owned in Coca-Cola Co. at a cost of $110,000 and presented the market value of $149,324,000 in a footnote.

[8] The 1972 edition of *Accounting Trends & Techniques* published by the AICPA shows that 377 of the 600 companies sampled reported marketable securities in their balance sheets; 244 of them used cost, 11 used lower of cost or market, only 4 used market value (although 247 companies referred to market value parenthetically), and 76 did not disclose the basis of valuation used.

[9] *Accounting Research and Terminology Bulletins, Final Edition,* AICPA (New York: 1961), chap. 3A, p. 23.

In the early 1970s, the Accounting Principles Board attempted to issue an opinion which would have required the reporting of marketable securities at market value. Much difficulty was encountered in finding a satisfactory method for reporting unrealized gains and losses on marketable securities and as a result the issuance of a formal opinion was postponed indefinitely. In the opinion of the authors, the current market value of investments in marketable securities is the most relevant valuation because it is most likely to aid users in making the types of decisions for which they use financial statements. The APB in *Statement No. 4,* issued in 1970, identified relevance as the primary qualitative objective of financial accounting.[10] It seems reasonable to anticipate that accountants will eventually find a satisfactory method of applying current market value to the various aspects of accounting for marketable securities.

Presentation of cash and marketable securities in the balance sheet

Cash is the most liquid asset which a business possesses, in the sense that it is most easily converted into other assets and services. This characteristic justifies its position as the first item in the current asset section of the balance sheet. There is seldom any reason to be concerned about the valuation of cash. There are few sources of possible loss except for theft, which cannot be anticipated. Loss due to bank failure has all but disappeared in recent years with the institution of the Federal Deposit Insurance Corporation. This agency of the United States government insures accounts with banks which are covered under provisions of its charter. Cash is, therefore, reported on the balance sheet at the value which represents its exchange value.

Banks often require that borrowers maintain *compensating balances* of cash on deposit as a condition for borrowing money. The net effect of such arrangements is to increase the effective interest rate on loans because the full amount of the loan is not available to the borrower. Compensating balance agreements with banks should be disclosed in financial statements in order to give more information about the effective cost of borrowing and the relationship of business entities and banks.

An investment in marketable securities ranks next to cash in liquidity and should be listed in the current asset section of the balance sheet immediately after cash. Marketable securities represent highly liquid assets, regardless of how long they have been held or how soon they may be sold. Whether marketable securities are reported at cost or at the lower of cost or market, disclosure of the current market value is desirable. A number of large corporations present "Cash and marketable securities" as a single item in their published balance sheets.

The AICPA has expressed the opinion that government securities specifically designated as acceptable in payment of taxes may be offset

---

[10] *Statements of the Accounting Principles Board, No. 4,* "Basic Concepts and Accounting Principles Underlying Financial Statements of Business Enterprises," AICPA (New York: 1970), p. 36.

against the liability for taxes. This exceptional procedure may not be extended to other assets or liabilities. **APB Opinion No. 10** described this **rule of offset** as follows:

1. It is a general principle of accounting that the offsetting of assets and liabilities in the balance sheet is improper except where a right of setoff exists. Accordingly, the offset of cash or other assets against the tax liability or other amounts owing to governmental bodies is not acceptable except in the circumstances described in paragraph 3 below.
2. Most securities now issued by governments are not by their terms designed specifically for the payment of taxes and, accordingly, should not be deducted from taxes payable on the balance sheet.
3. The only exception to this general principle occurs when it is clear that a purchase of securities (acceptable for the payment of taxes) is in substance an advance payment of taxes that will be payable in the relatively near future, so that . . . the purchase is tantamount to the prepayment of taxes. This occurs at times, for example, as an accommodation to a local government and in some instances when governments issue securities that are specifically designated as acceptable for the payment of taxes of those governments.[11]

Two examples of the way corporations report cash and marketable securities in the balance sheet follow:

Hilton Hotels Corporation:
Current assets:

Cash, including certificates of deposit of $7,132,000	$16,335,000
Marketable securities, at cost which approximates market	19,450,000

Carnation Company:
Current assets:

Cash	$18,784,362
Short-term commercial obligations, at cost (approximately market)	42,890,361
Other marketable securities, at cost (quoted market value $13,950,000).	5,453,744

REVIEW QUESTIONS

1 What are the normal components of **cash?**

2 How would you classify the following items on a balance sheet?
 a Travel advances to employees
 b Cash deposited with a trustee for the repayment of bonds
 c Undeposited cash representing receipts of the prior day
 d Customer's check returned by the bank marked NSF
 e A nonreturnable deposit with a real estate broker to pay for an option on a tract of land

---

[11] *APB Opinion No. 10*, "Omnibus Opinion—1966," AICPA (New York: 1966), p. 147.

f Deposit in foreign banks where exchangeability is limited

g United States Treasury bills temporarily held until cash is needed to make payments on building under construction

h A petty cash fund composed of the following:

Coin and currency	$110
Vouchers:	
Selling expenses	61
General expenses	29

3 What is **management's responsibility** with respect to cash? What techniques are used to aid in carrying out this responsibility?

4 What is a **cash budget?** What are its uses?

5 Why is the **sales forecast** crucial to cash budgeting?

6 What is the meaning of the term **discretionary expenditures?**

7 What useful information might management find in a **cash flow statement** for a fiscal year just ended? Would such a statement be helpful to outsiders?

8 Briefly outline the procedure for converting net income from the **accrual** to the **cash basis.**

9 Is **cash flow per share** a better measure of operating results than net income per share?

10 What is a system of **internal control?** Why is internal control over cash and marketable securities particularly important?

11 Tucker Corporation has developed a reasonably effective system of internal control over cash transactions; however, the controller has decided he needs a petty cash fund to expedite the payment of small bills. The controller cannot decide whether he will use the regular cashier or the typist who has a desk near the cashier's window. Which would you recommend and why?

12 Kay Company has a change fund of $100. The cash sales tickets for May 25 total $2,049.60 and cash in the cash register, verified by count, totals $2,151.25. Prepare the journal entry necessary to record the day's sales.

13 Why are adjusting entries usually not made to reflect outstanding checks as liabilities and deposits in transit as cash on hand?

14 Why is management concerned with investing cash, which is only temporarily in excess of actual requirements, in marketable securities? What can be done to eliminate or minimize the risk of loss from temporary fluctuations in the market price of securities?

15 Why might the **cost principle** be violated in reporting and accounting for marketable securities held as temporary investments?

EXERCISES

Ex. 5-1 The following information is available for Errox, Incorporated:

	Balances end of April	Estimated for May
Accounts receivable:		
March sales (20% of total).	$ 40,000	
April sales (50% of total).	120,000	
Accounts payable (2% discount is available)	30,000	
Sales:		
Cash		$ 50,000
On credit		250,000
Purchases:		
Cash		10,000
On account (subject to 2% discount)		150,000

Sales on account are collected as follows: 50% in month of sale; 30% in month following sale; 15% in second month following sale; 5% of accounts receivable are generally not collected. Two-thirds of purchases on account are paid within the discount period in month goods are purchased and the balance is paid within the discount period in the following month.

Prepare schedules determining (a) collections from customers and (b) payments for merchandise purchases for the month of May.

Ex. 5-2 From the following data, compute the net cash flow from operations during the past year:

	Dec. 31	Jan. 1
Accounts receivable	$20,200	$15,200
Accounts payable	15,000	24,000
Accrued liabilities	3,600	1,600
Accumulated depreciation (no retirements during the		
year).	32,000	26,000
Inventories.	30,000	27,500
Miscellaneous short-term prepayments	2,200	3,000
Net income (accrual basis).	25,000	

Ex. 5-3 Lilly Wang Corporation reported net income of $40,000 and paid dividends of $15,000 in Year 2. Comparative balance sheets at the end of Year 2 and Year 1 follow:

Assets	Year 2	Year 1
Cash	$ 82,500	$ 12,500
Accounts receivable	67,500	37,500
Inventories.	80,000	100,000
Equipment (net)	340,000	300,000
Total assets	$570,000	$450,000

Liabilities & Stockholders' Equity

Accounts payable	$ 20,000	$ 25,000
Bonds payable	100,000	100,000
Capital stock, no par	250,000	150,000
Retained earnings	200,000	175,000
Total liabilities & stockholders' equity	$570,000	$450,000

Equipment was purchased for $75,000 and additional capital stock was sold to the public.

Prepare a cash flow statement for Year 2 which will explain the increase of $70,000 in the cash account. Compute the cash flow from operations in a separate supporting schedule.

Ex. 5-4 The petty cash fund balance for Cord Electronics is $100. During March $15.00 was spent on entertainment, $18.10 was spent on office supplies expense, $26.50 was spent on postage expense, $20.00 was spent for merchandise, $14.40 was spent on miscellaneous items, and $6.00 remained on hand. What entry would be made to replenish the petty cash fund at the end of the month?

Ex. 5-5 From the following data, **(a)** compute the cash balance on the books before adjustments are recorded and **(b)** give any entries required to bring the books up to date:

Balance per bank statement	$17,560
Checks outstanding	7,050
Receipts recorded not yet deposited	1,710
Bank service charges not recorded on books	20
Note collected by bank not recorded in books of company (includes interest of $40)	4,040

Ex. 5-6 The following bank reconciliation was prepared for Kemp Company at September 30, 19___:

Balance per bank		$23,398
Add:		
Deposit in transit	$ 690	
Check incorrectly charged by bank	150	
Bank service charges	10	
NSF check received from a customer	80	930
		$24,328
Less:		
Proceeds of bank loan	$4,000	
Outstanding checks	2,640	
Error in recording check in payment of invoice	18	6,658
Balance per ledger		$17,670

Prepare the journal entry necessary to adjust the ledger balance to the correct cash balance. Interest on the bank loan is payable at maturity and all payments on invoices are debited to Accounts Payable.

Ex. 5-7 Prepare journal entries to record the following transactions relating to marketable securities:

June 11 Purchased $50,000 par value 7½% bonds issued by Reed Company. Total purchase price was $52,175, which included accrued interest of $625 from Apr. 11.

Oct. 11 Received semiannual interest on Reed Company bonds, $1,875.

Dec. 11 Sold $20,000 par value Reed Company bonds for total consideration of $20,250, which included accrued interest of $250 from Oct. 11.

Dec. 31 Recorded accrued interest for 80 days on remaining Reed Company bonds.

SHORT CASES FOR ANALYSIS AND DECISION

Case 5-1 The accountant for Television Productions, Inc., prepared the following condensed cash flow statement for Year 1:

TELEVISION PRODUCTIONS, INC.

Cash Flow Statement

For Year 1

Cash receipts:		
Operations		$ 80,000
Sale of stock		250,000
Sale of surplus equipment		30,000
		$360,000
Cash payments:		
Retirement of notes payable	$150,000	
Dividends	25,000	
Additions to plant and equipment	135,000	310,000
Increase in cash during Year 1		$ 50,000

Sales in Year 1 were $2,000,000 and net income was $100,000. Sales for Year 2 are expected to increase by 10%, resulting in a net income of $180,000. The owner is interested in the cash flow for the coming year and suggested that "since our sales will go up by 10%, our cash flow from operations should be approximately $88,000 for Year 2." The accountant, however, estimated cash flow from operations at $144,000 because "our net income will be 80% higher; therefore, our cash flow should be that much higher."

Instructions

a Evaluate the estimates for Year 2 of cash flow from operations made by the owner and by the accountant. How would you prepare a cash flow statement for the coming year?

b How is it possible for net income to increase by 80% in Year 2 when sales are expected to increase by only 10%?

Case 5-2 The accountant for Baldwin and Company (see pages 181–182 in text) prepared the following "proof of cash" for December, 19___.

BALDWIN AND COMPANY

***Reconciliation of Cash Receipts and Payments for December
and Cash Balance at December 31, 19___***

	Balance, Nov. 30	Receipts	Payments	Balance, Dec. 31
Balances per bank statement . .	$6,947.26	$24,581.42	$19,509.66	$12,019.02
Deposit in transit:				
Nov. 30	1,055.52	(1,055.52)		
Dec. 31		1,144.60		1,144.60
Outstanding checks:				
Nov. 30	(681.42)		(681.42)	
Dec. 31			631.46	(631.46)
Adjust for NSF check		(50.00)	(50.00)	
Correct balances	$7,321.36	$24,620.50	$19,409.70	$12,532.16
Balances per ledger	$7,321.36	$22,640.50	$19,369.20	$10,592.66
Bank service charges			13.50	(13.50)
Proceeds of note collected		2,030.00		2,030.00
Record NSF check		(50.00)		(50.00)
Error in recording check no. 821			27.00	(27.00)
Correct balances	$7,321.36	$24,620.50	$19,409.70	$12,532.16

The owner objected to the form and suggested that the accountant "prepare a bank reconciliation statement in simpler form." The accountant explained to the owner that "the last column of his statement is a bank reconciliation and that his form is more useful to management."

Instructions
a Do you think that the "proof of cash" form of bank reconciliation as prepared by the accountant for Baldwin and Company is more useful to management?
b Briefly explain the accountant's treatment of the various additions and deductions in the Receipts and Payments columns of his reconciliation.

Case 5-3 Cos Cob Imports Company is projecting an increased level of operations for the coming year, which will require an additional investment in inventory and accounts receivable. The minimum cash balance required is $50,000. After a detailed review of the prospects for the coming year, the following forecast of monthly cash balances is prepared (brackets indicate projected cash deficit):

January.	$110,000	July.	$395,000
February	50,000	August	450,000
March.	(100,000)	September	80,000
April.	(230,000)	October	(250,000)
May	(150,000)	November	(290,000)
June	150,000	December.	(50,000)

Investment decisions are made and loans are negotiated on the fifteenth of each month in an amount equal to the projected cash surplus or deficiency for the month. Changes in the investment or loan position are made in multiples of $5,000.

Assume that excess cash can be invested in short-term government bonds bearing 5% interest and that borrowed funds cost $7\frac{1}{2}\%$.

Instructions

a Prepare a schedule of the net cost (interest expense less interest revenue on temporary investments) of short-term borrowing to finance the operations for the year ended December 31. Carry computations to nearest dollar.

b If Cos Cob Imports Company is to avoid short-term borrowing, how much long-term or permanent capital must be raised? Would you recommend that the company attempt to raise the capital or follow a policy of short-term borrowing? Why?

Case 5-4 The management of Great Basin Coal Company foresees a period of three to five years of reduced operations. During this period the management does not expect to replace any plant assets. Management presents the board of directors with a plan (1) to maintain the current ratio of dividends to net income at 60%, and (2) to invest all cash which accumulates in excess of normal operating needs in a diversified list of high-quality common stocks. Management also proposes that the stocks be carried on the balance sheet at current market value at the date of the statement. Any change in market value from date of purchase or the most recent evaluation for statement purposes is to be reflected in the current report of earnings.

Instructions

a What are the advantages of accounting for and reporting this investment holding in this manner?

b What objections might be made to this method of reporting the investment?

c Should this investment be reported as a current or a long-term asset? Why?

PROBLEMS

Group A

5A-1 The bank reconciliation for Ginny Jacobs Corporation at the end of November included deposits in transit of $2,400 and outstanding checks of $3,000. The following additional information is available at December 31:

	Per accounting records	Per bank statement
Deposits during December	$24,600	$21,175
Payments during December	27,800	29,000
Collection of note by bank, including $25		
interest revenue not recorded on the books		2,025
Bank service charges		20
Cash balance at Dec. 31	10,200	8,180

Instructions

a From the foregoing information, prepare a bank reconciliation arriving at corrected balances at the end of December.

b Prepare a compound journal entry to bring the books up to date.

5A-2 On February 1, Korn-Ferry Company has $90,000 of cash in excess of its imme-
diate needs. The management decides to invest this cash, and any other cash
which appears to be temporarily in excess of current needs, in short-term U.S.
government obligations. The following transactions occur during the following
fiscal year.

Feb. 1   Purchased for $87,934, including accrued interest of $334, U.S.
Treasury 4% bonds, due in six years, maturity value $100,000 with
interest payable June 30 and December 31. Debit Accrued Interest
Receivable for $334.

June 1   Sold for $45,634, including accrued interest of $834, one-half of the
U.S. Treasury 4% bonds acquired February 1.

June 30   Received interest on U.S. Treasury 4% bonds, $1,000.

Aug. 1   Purchased 40 U.S. Treasury 6% $1,000 bonds, interest payable April
1 and October 1, at 102 plus accrued interest of $800 and a commission
of $125. These bonds mature three years after the next interest date.

Oct. 1   Received interest on U.S. Treasury 6% bonds, $1,200.

Dec. 15   Sold for $42,917, including accrued interest of $917, the remainder
of the U.S. Treasury 4% bonds acquired February 1.

Jan. 16   Purchased $100,000 par value U.S. Treasury 7% notes for a net price
of $107,250. Interest is paid on these notes on January 16 and July
16.

Jan. 31   Adjust the accounts to reflect interest accrued to the end of the fiscal
year. The management decided that the premium on bonds and notes
purchased will not be amortized. Interest on U.S. Treasury obligations
is computed based on the exact number of days elapsed, using a
365-day year. Compute interest on each issue to the nearest dollar.

Instructions
a Record the above transactions in general journal entry form.
b The market quote for the 6% bonds and the 7% notes at the close on January
31 was 102½ and 108, respectively. Prepare a partial balance sheet showing
all the data for marketable securities. Assume that marketable securities are
reported at cost and that market value is shown parenthetically.

5A-3 Comparative financial data as of the close of Years 1 and 2 for the William Keast
Company are shown below:

	As of Dec. 31	
Debits	**Year 2**	**Year 1**
Cash	$ 39,220	$ 15,800
Receivables (net)	20,400	24,000
Inventories	27,600	36,800
Prepaid expenses	4,180	4,400
Land	19,000	19,000
Buildings	276,000	250,000
Equipment	381,600	360,000
Patents	32,000	40,000
Total debits	$800,000	$750,000
Credits		
Accumulated depreciation: buildings	$ 90,000	$ 80,000
Accumulated depreciation: equipment	238,000	220,000
Accounts payable	36,000	30,000

Accrued liabilities	$ 20,000	$ 10,000
Long-term debt	60,000	90,000
Common stock ($25 par)	210,000	200,000
Capital in excess of par	55,000	40,000
Retained earnings	91,000	80,000
Total credits	$800,000	$750,000

During Year 2 the board of directors of the company ordered that $25,000 be transferred from retained earnings to reflect a 5% stock dividend. In addition, cash dividends of $6,000 were paid. There were no sales or retirements of buildings and equipment during the year, and no new expenditures were made for patents. Net income for Year 2 was $42,000.

Instructions
a Prepare a working paper for a cash flow statement similar to the one illustrated on page 173.
b Prepare a cash flow statement from the working paper in part *(a)*.

5A-4 The following data pertaining to the cash transactions and bank account of Street Corporation for September are available to you:

(1)	Cash balance per ledger	$13,102.70
(2)	Cash balance per bank statement	29,090.80
(3)	Bank charges for previous month's service	7.20
(4)	Debit memo for checkbook delivered by the bank; the charge was not recorded by Street Corporation	5.00
(5)	Deposit of Sept. 30 not recorded by bank until Oct. 1	3,870.00
(6)	Outstanding checks	18,128.30
(7)	Proceeds of a bank loan not recorded in ledger (interest payable at maturity)	2,970.00
(8)	Proceeds from customer's note, principal amount $800, collected by the bank; collection fee of $3 charged by the bank	810.00
(9)	Check no. 1086 to a supplier had been entered in the accounts as $1,879.10; it was deducted from the bank statement in the correct amount of	1,789.10
(10)	A stolen check lacking an authorized signature had been deducted from the account by the bank in error	867.50
(11)	A customer's check was returned by the bank marked NSF, indicating that the customer's balance was not adequate to cover the check; no entry has been made to record the returned check	1,260.50

Instructions
a Prepare a reconciliation of the cash balances to the correct cash balance at September 30.
b Prepare the journal entry required to adjust the ledger balance at September 30 to the correct balance.

5A-5 The Lord Company needs $72,500 on April 1, 1975, to pay off a loan, including interest. Sales to customers are made at 2/10, n/30. Experience indicates that

30% of the customers pay within 10 days in the month the sale is made, 30% of the customers pay in the month the sale is made, but after the discount period, 25% of the customers pay (without discount) in the first month following the sale and 10% pay in the second month following the sale. The remaining accounts (5%) are written off as uncollectible.

Liabilities for purchase of merchandise are paid one month after they are incurred, except for those on which discount is offered, which are paid in the month incurred. A discount of 3% is available on 60% of the purchases. The following information is available for your consideration:

Sales:		Purchases:	
November 1974	$ 95,000	November 1974	$85,000
December 1974	110,000	December 1974	75,000
January 1975.	100,000	January 1975	45,000
February 1975	80,000	February 1975.	60,000
March 1975.	75,000	March 1975	70,000

Additional information
(1) The cash balance on January 1, 1975, is $25,000.
(2) Operating expenses per month which must be paid in cash amount to $10,000 plus 5% of sales.
(3) Surplus equipment will be sold for $2,200 cash in February.
(4) Cash dividends of $20,000 will be paid in March.
(5) The company generally likes to have a minimum cash balance of $30,000 on hand.

Instructions
a Prepare a monthly cash budget for the first three months of 1975, showing the cash balance at the beginning and the end of each month. You may prepare a single statement using three columns, one each for January, February, and March. Prepare supporting schedules showing collections from customers and payments on merchandise purchases.
b How much will the company probably have to borrow on April 1, 1975, in order to be able to repay the bank loan and have $30,000 of cash on hand?

5A-6 The following financial data are presented to you by the management of Kevin Romano Company:

KEVIN ROMANO COMPANY
Balance Sheets

Assets	End of Year 5	End of Year 4
Cash on hand and in banks	$ 78,200	$ 12,200
Marketable securities	60,000	–0–
Accounts receivable (net)	65,000	80,000
Prepaid expenses	1,200	2,000
Inventories.	42,000	50,000
Investment in real estate	–0–	30,000
Equipment	350,000	300,000
Less: Accumulated depreciation	(78,000)	(50,000)
Total assets	$518,400	$424,200

Liabilities & Stockholders' Equity

Accounts payable	$ 34,400	$ 30,000
Income taxes payable	35,100	21,200
Other miscellaneous liabilities	3,800	3,000
Unearned fees	4,200	6,000
Capital stock, $5 par value	250,000	230,000
Premium on capital stock	90,000	60,000
Retained earnings	100,900	74,000
Total liabilities & stockholders' equity	$518,400	$424,200

KEVIN ROMANO COMPANY
Income Statement
For Year 5

Sales and fees for services	$350,000
Cost of goods and services	200,000
Gross profit on sales and services	$150,000
Operating expenses	80,000
Income from operations	$ 70,000
Income taxes	27,100
Income before extraordinary item	$ 42,900
Extraordinary item—gain on disposal of real estate (net of taxes)	24,000
Net income	$ 66,900

Per share of capital stock:

Income before extraordinary item	$1.72
Extraordinary gain	.96
Net income	$2.68

Additional information for Year 5

(1) Real estate was sold for $62,000 at a gain of $32,000 before income taxes. The sale was recorded as follows:

Cash	62,000	
Investment in Real Estate		30,000
Income Taxes Payable		8,000
Gain on Disposal of Real Estate		24,000

(2) Capital stock was issued in exchange for new equipment early in Year 5. No equipment items were retired during the year.
(3) Dividends of $30,000 were paid to stockholders.
(4) An additional tax assessment for Year 2, $10,000, was charged directly to retained earnings as a prior period adjustment.

Instructions

a Convert the income statement (through income before extraordinary item) for Year 5 from the accrual basis to the cash basis. Use the form illustrated on page 175.
b Using the cash flow from operations determined in (*a*), prepare a cash flow statement for Year 5.

Group B

5B-1 The bank statement for Brandt Corporation showed a balance of $50,491.20 on December 31, 1975. In comparing the bank balance with the book balance, the corporation's accountant discovered the following:
(1) Checks amounting to $13,450.00 had not cleared the bank.
(2) A check was recorded on the books for $357.20; the correct amount on the check was $375.20.
(3) A customer's check for $528.50 was returned marked NSF. No entry has been made on the accounting records to record this bad check.
(4) A deposit of $8,975.50 had not been recorded by the bank.
(5) The charge for printing checks was $4.25.

Instructions
a What is the balance per books before any of the foregoing corrections and adjustments are made?
b Prepare a bank reconciliation which shows the correct cash balance and prepare a compound journal entry to bring the books up to date.

5B-2 On September 30, 1975, the marketable securities owned by Schattke Corporation are shown below:

	Cost
6% U.S. Treasury notes, $100,000 par value	$ 98,000
1,500 shares of $7 preferred stock of Hemesphire Telephone Company, $100 par value	156,000
Total	$254,000

Accrued interest receivable on the U.S. Treasury notes on this date was $2,000. This amount has been recorded in the Accrued Interest Receivable account. Transactions relating to marketable securities during the three months ended December 31, 1975, are listed below:

Oct. 15   Purchased $40,000 par value 7½% bonds of General Corporation at a price of 104, plus commissions of $200 and accrued interest of $375 from September 1. Record interest acquired in the Accrued Interest Receivable account.

Oct. 30   Received quarterly dividend on Hemesphire Telephone Company $7 preferred stock.

Nov. 10   Sold entire holdings of Hemesphire Telephone Company $7 preferred stock for $153,800 net of commissions.

Dec. 1   Received semiannual interest on the 6% U.S. Treasury notes, $3,000.

Dec. 31   Sold $30,000 par value, 6% U.S. Treasury notes at 101 net of commissions, plus accrued interest of $150 for one month.

Instructions
a Record the transactions in general journal form, including the adjusting entry to accrue interest on bonds owned at December 31, 1975. Do not amortize premium or accumulate discount on bonds owned. Compute accrued interest on the U.S. Treasury notes on the basis of a 360-day year.
b Assuming that the market value of the bonds owned is $105,200, show three alternative ways that marketable securities might be presented on the balance sheet at December 31, 1975.

5B-3 The adjusted trial balances of the Brice Company at the close of two recent years were as follows:

BRICE COMPANY

Adjusted Trial Balance

December 31

(in thousands of dollars)

Debits	Year 2	Year 1
Cash	$ 630	$ 440
Receivables (net).............................	830	700
Inventories...................................	750	500
Supplies and unexpired insurance	210	250
Land	95	95
Buildings.....................................	1,050	915
Equipment	460	340
Cost of goods sold............................	1,600	1,500
Operating expenses	600	580
Income taxes	180	90
Dividends (cash)	75	40
Interest expense	20	25
	$6,500	$5,475

Credits

Credits	Year 2	Year 1
Accumulated depreciation: buildings...........	$ 380	$ 340
Accumulated depreciation: equipment...........	200	170
Accounts payable (merchandise creditors)	590	690
Income taxes payable..........................	80	50
Accrued liabilities	300	160
Bonds payable, 5%	400	500
Capital stock, par $20........................	1,100	800
Capital in excess of par	340	100
Retained earnings (beginning of each year) ...	430	365
Sales (net)...................................	2,680	2,300
	$6,500	$5,475

Bonds payable were retired at par in Year 2. No disposal of plant assets took place in Year 2.

Instructions (All figures in your solution may be stated in thousands of dollars.)
a Prepare a comparative income statement for each year and determine the ending balances in retained earnings.
b Convert the income statement for Year 2 to the cash basis. Use the form illustrated on page 175.
c Prepare a cash flow statement for Year 2. Use the amount determined in **b** as cash flow from operations. Other cash receipts and payments can be obtained by analyzing the changes during Year 2 in the following accounts: Buildings, Equipment, Bonds Payable, Capital Stock, Capital in Excess of Par, and Retained Earnings.

5B-4 Local Lumber Company received the bank statement for the month of September shown below:

LOCAL LUMBER COMPANY
In account with BANK OF COMMERCE
Logan, Utah

Checks			Deposits	Date	Balance
				Sept. 1	3,658.75
31.15	35.48	130.00	72.80	Sept. 2	3,534.92
60.00			361.00	Sept. 5	3,835.92
70.00	515.00		280.00	Sept. 7	3,530.92
90.00				Sept. 8	3,440.92
13.30	62.50		510.00	Sept. 9	3,875.12
28.00			205.60	Sept. 12	4,052.72
650.00			180.14	Sept. 14	3,582.86
			345.00	Sept. 16	3,927.86
85.00			427.50	Sept. 19	4,270.36
24.10	125.06			Sept. 20	4,121.20
40.00	65.00		90.00	Sept. 21	4,106.20
162.40			360.00	Sept. 23	4,303.80
15.00			625.00	Sept. 26	4,913.80
355.00	270.00	225.00	130.25	Sept. 28	4,194.05
155.00	25.00	5.00S	280.50	Sept. 30	4,289.55

The entries in the cash journals for the month of September are shown on page 204.

The cash balance in the ledger as of August 31 agreed with the balance per bank statement. The bank service charge for September was $5.00.

Instructions
a Prepare a bank reconciliation statement as of September 30.
b Prepare the necessary journal entry to adjust the Cash account as of September 30.

5B-5 The Harned Corporation is a wholesaler whose fiscal year ends on December 31. As the company's CPA, you have been requested early in January, 1975, to assist in the preparation of a cash forecast. The Company had a cash balance of $111,500 on December 31, 1974. The following information is available regarding the company's operations:
(1) Management believes the 1974 sales pattern is a reasonable estimate of 1975 sales. Sales in 1974 were as follows:

January	$360,000	July	$350,000
February	420,000	August	550,000
March	600,000	September	500,000
April	540,000	October	400,000
May	480,000	November	600,000
June	400,000	December	800,000

Problem 5B-4 concluded

Cash Receipts Journal				Cash Payments Journal			
Date			Cash (debit)	Date		Check no.	Cash (credit)
Sept	1		72.80	Sept	1	65	130.00
	3		361.00		1	66	90.00
	6		280.00		1	67	35.48
	8		510.00		2	68	31.15
	10		205.60		4	69	60.00
	13		180.14		4	70	70.00
	15		345.00		5	71	515.00
	17	•	427.50		9	72	62.50
	20		90.00		10	73	13.30
	22		360.00		10	74	28.00
	24		625.00		13	75	650.00
	27		130.25		19	76	125.06
	29		280.50		19	77	40.00
	30		315.25		19	78	85.00
			4,183.04		20	79	24.10
					21	80	38.60
					22	81	65.00
					22	82	162.40
					23	83	150.00
					26	84	15.00
					28	85	270.00
					28	86	105.20
					28	87	225.00
					28	88	355.00
					30	89	25.00
					30	90	45.00
					30	91	155.00
							3,570.79

Problem 5B-5 (continued)

(2) The accounts receivable at December 31 total $380,000; all uncollectible accounts originating prior to November have been written off. Sales collections are generally made as follows:

During month of sale	60%
In first subsequent month	30%
In second subsequent month	9%
Uncollectible	1%

(3) Accounts payable for purchases at December 31, 1974, amounted to $345,000. Purchases are estimated as follows: January, $342,000; February, $288,000; March, $300,500. All purchases are paid for on the tenth of the following month.

(4) Recurring fixed expenses, in addition to those listed in (5) and (6) below, amount to $120,000 per month, including depreciation of $20,000. Variable

expenses amount to 10% of sales. Payment for expenses are made as follows:

	During month incurred	In following month
Fixed expenses	55%	45%
Variable expenses	70%	30%

(5) Annual property taxes amount to $50,000 and are paid in equal installments on December 31 and March 31. The property taxes are in addition to the expenses in item (4) above.

(6) During the winter unusual advertising costs will be incurred which will require cash payments of $10,000 in February and $15,000 in March. The advertising costs are in addition to the expenses in item (4) above.

(7) It is anticipated that cash dividends of $20,000 will be paid each quarter on the fifteenth day of the third month of the quarter.

(8) Equipment replacements are estimated to average $3,000 per month for 1975.

(9) On March 15, 1975, a payment of $10,000 is scheduled to be made to the Internal Revenue Service representing the balance due on 1974 taxes.

(10) At December 31, 1974, the company had a bank loan with an unpaid balance of $280,000. The loan requires a principal payment of $20,000 on the last day of each month plus interest at $\frac{1}{2}$% per month on the unpaid balance at the first of the month. The unpaid balance of $240,000 is due on March 31, 1975.

Instructions Prepare a cash forecast by months for the first three months of 1975 for the Harned Corporation. The forecast should show the amount of cash on hand (or deficiency of cash) at the end of each month. All computations and supporting schedules should be presented in good form.

5B-6 The comparative trial balances on page 206 were furnished to you by the Inberg Corporation.

The following information was also available:

(1) All purchases and sales were on account and all dividends were paid in cash.

(2) Equipment with an original cost of $15,000 was sold for $7,000.

(3) Selling and general expenses includes the following:

Expired insurance	$ 2,000
Building depreciation	3,750
Equipment depreciation.	19,250
Uncollectible accounts expense.	4,000
Interest expense	18,000

(4) A six-month note payable for $50,000 was issued toward the purchase of new equipment.

(5) The long-term note payable requires the payment of $20,000 per year, plus interest, until paid.

(6) Treasury stock was sold for $1,000 more than its cost. The excess was credited to Paid-in Capital in Excess of Par Value.

Instructions

a Prepare a schedule as illustrated on page 175 converting the income statement to a cash basis. Do not show the following accounts on your schedule: Loss on Disposal of Equipment, Capital Gains Tax, and Gain on Disposal of Investment in Land.

b Prepare a cash flow statement without using a complete working paper. Show the amount determined in (*a*) as "cash flow from operations" and give supporting computations for all other receipts and payments included in the cash flow statement.

INBERG CORPORATION
Comparative Trial Balances
At Beginning and End of Fiscal Year Ended October 31, 1975

	Oct. 31, 1975	Increase	Decrease	Nov. 1, 1974
Cash	$ 316,000	$186,000		$130,000
Accounts receivable	148,000	48,000		100,000
Inventories	291,000		$ 9,000	300,000
Unexpired insurance.	2,500	500		2,000
Long-term investment in land				
(at cost).	10,000		30,000	40,000
Land and building	195,000			195,000
Equipment	215,000	125,000		90,000
Discount on bonds payable	8,500		500	9,000
Treasury stock (at cost).	9,000		5,000	14,000
Cost of goods sold	539,000			
Selling and general expenses . . .	230,000			
Income tax expense	32,000			
Loss on disposal of equipment . .	1,000			
Capital gains tax	3,000			
Total debits	$2,000,000			$880,000
Allowance for doubtful accounts .	$ 8,000	3,000		$ 5,000
Accumulated depreciation:				
building	26,250	3,750		22,500
Accumulated depreciation:				
equipment	39,750	12,250		27,500
Accounts payable	55,000		5,000	60,000
Notes payable—current	70,000	50,000		20,000
Accrued expenses payable	18,000	3,000		15,000
Income taxes payable	35,000	25,000		10,000
Uneārned revenue	1,000		8,000	9,000
Notes payable—long-term.	40,000		20,000	60,000
Bonds payable—long-term	250,000			250,000
Common stock, $2 par value . . .	300,000	100,000		200,000
Paid-in capital in excess of				
par value	120,000	111,000		9,000
Retained earnings	184,000		8,000	192,000
Sales and other revenues	841,000			
Gain on disposal of investment				
in land.	12,000			
Total credits	$2,000,000			$880,000

6

Receivables

The term *receivables* includes a variety of claims that will generally result in the future inflow of cash. Receivables come into existence as a result of transactions such as sale of goods or services, loans made, subscriptions obtained from investors for stocks or bonds, claims for tax refunds, claims for damages to property, and amounts due from leasing properties to others.

Receivables from customers frequently represent a substantial part of a company's liquid resources. As a result, the accounting procedures for receivables and the maintenance of adequate controls over credit granting and collections assume major significance. Poor screening of credit applicants and slow collection of accounts can result in large write-offs and require the investment of additional capital to finance sales. Sound management of credit terms and collections are important elements in achieving profitable operating results.

Valuation of receivables

An essential characteristic of a receivable is that the amount of money to be received and the due date can be reasonably estimated. The accountant is thus faced with a relatively certain future inflow of cash, and his problem is to determine the value of this inflow.

A number of factors must be considered in valuing prospective cash inflow. One factor is the probability that a receivable will actually be collected. For any single receivable, the probability of collection might be difficult to establish; for a large group of receivables, however, the probability of collection outweighs the probability of noncollection, and a reasonably accurate estimate of uncollectible accounts is usually possible.

A second factor to be considered in valuing receivables is the length of time until collection. A sum of money due at some future time is not worth as much as the same sum due immediately. The longer the time to maturity, the greater the discrepancy between the *maturity value* and the *present value* of a receivable. When the time to maturity is long, many receivable contracts call for the payment of interest to compensate for the time value of money, and the present value of such a contract may correspond to its maturity value. The present value of any non-interest-bearing receivable is less than the amount that will be received at the due date. If the lapse of time to maturity is short, this difference is usually ignored. An ordinary 30-day unsecured account, for example, is almost always recorded at its face amount. The discrepancy between present value and amount due should always be considered, however, since there are times when this discrepancy is significant.

Receivables from sale of goods and services

The most common receivables are those that result from revenue-producing activities, such as the sale of goods and services. The unsecured *open account,* or *trade account,* is the most important of these. Contractual arrangements governing open accounts are typically informal and are supported by such documents as sales orders, specifications, invoices, and bills of lading. Most open accounts are not interest bearing. In the retail trade, however, the addition of an interest or service charge to revolving charge accounts or installment receivables is a common practice. Manufacturers and wholesalers use cash discounts as a form of interest charge if payment is made after the discount period.

Trade receivables are also represented by various commercial credit instruments such as promissory notes, time bills of exchange, and conditional sales contracts. Such contracts have a stronger legal status than open accounts, and because the terms are clearly specified in writing, the holder finds it somewhat easier to borrow against them.

When a customer asks for an extension of time on an open account, he is often asked to sign a note so that the holder can discount the note and receive cash immediately. Most notes and commercial credit instruments bear interest because they involve credit for longer periods of time. Amounts due from employees and owners of a business may be included among trade receivables, if they result from sales of goods and services and are subject to the usual credit terms.

Receivables from miscellaneous sources

Some receivables result from transactions not directly related to the sale of goods and services. For example, a short-term advance to an affiliated company, to a subcontractor, or to a customer, is in essence a lending transaction made in anticipation of future benefits. A claim against an insurance company and a claim based on a legal suit for damages are other examples of miscellaneous receivables. Prospective refunds of amounts previously paid, such as a claim for refund of income taxes paid, represent receivables whenever the outcome of the claim is reasonably certain. Sale of stocks and bonds to subscribers and sales of plant and equipment items also represent sources of miscellaneous receivables. Any type of receivable which is quite material in amount should be listed separately in the balance sheet. If collection of miscellaneous receivables is expected within one year, they are reported as current, otherwise they should be reported as Other Assets or as Investments.

Accruals of interest, dividends, rent, and royalties are revenue-related current receivables that represent a prospective inflow of cash. Rent and interest receivable accrue as a function of time. Dividends are usually not recognized as a receivable until the date of declaration or the ex-dividend date. Royalties usually accrue as a function of the manufacture or sale of a product or the extraction of natural resources.

Occasionally a receivable arises out of a debit balance in accounts payable when, for one reason or another, overpayment has been made to a creditor. If the buyer expects a cash refund the amount involved is clearly a receivable. The rule against offsetting assets and liabilities requires that any sizable debit balance be treated as a receivable rather than an offset against other accounts payable. Similarly, a large credit balance in a customer's account should be reported as a current liability. An advance payment on a purchase contract is properly reported as a prepayment for goods rather than as a receivable.

Receivables arising from certain types of leasing transactions are discussed in Chapter 19.

CUSTOMERS' ACCOUNTS

A large portion of retail trade in the United States involves credit in some form; at the wholesale and manufacturing level almost all business is transacted on a credit basis. Terms on ordinary open accounts range from the 10 days typically allowed in taking cash discounts to as long as six months or a year in a few cases.

Accounting System and Internal Control Companies having a large volume of credit transactions usually adapt their recording procedures to the use of accounting machines or computers. A relatively simple machine system will enable the operator to record the credit sale, post to the control account, and post to subsidiary ledger accounts in a single operation. Modern electronic data-processing equipment makes possible a system that is highly automated. All information pertaining to a credit sale may be recorded on cards, tapes, or memory drums. The computer prepares a sales journal, posts to the control and customers' ledger accounts, prepares monthly statements, and issues a list of receivables at required intervals.

A procedure known as *cycle billing* eases the receivable systems problem of large department stores and public utilities where accounts with 100,000 or more customers may be found. Accounts receivable subsidiary ledgers are divided into a number of groups on the basis of geographical location, type of customer, or alphabetically, with each group having its own subcontrol account. The customers in each subcontrol group are then billed at different times during the month. This procedure has the advantage of spreading the work of preparing customer statements more evenly through the month and assuring a more uniform cash flow from operations.

It is possible to reduce detailed record keeping by eliminating subsidiary receivable ledgers altogether. Invoices for credit sales are first sorted by subcontrol groups and the total amount is entered directly in the control account. The individual invoices are then filed according to customer. At the end of the month or cycle billing period, the amount due from each customer is summarized on a statement, the duplicate copy of which becomes the subsidiary ledger record for that customer. Invoices are reproduced (to provide a record for the company) and are then mailed to each customer along with the statement of his account. At the billing date, customers' statements can be reconciled with the amount shown by the appropriate subcontrol account to disclose any discrepancies.

Effective internal control over the sale of goods and cash collections is an integral part of the system for handling trade accounts receivable. The responsibility for recording sales and collections in customers' accounts should not be assigned to individuals who handle cash receipts or who prepare bank deposit slips and bank reconciliations. Without such controls a dishonest employee could abstract cash collections from customers and conceal his theft by recording the collection as a debit to Sales Returns and Allowances. A similar fraudulent action consists of writing off the receivable against the Allowance for Uncollectible Accounts.

Recognition of trade receivables

Two important questions faced by accountants in recording trade receivables are:

1 At what point in the stream of business activities between a company and its customers does a trade account receivable warrant recognition in the accounts as a valid asset?

2 How should the amount of trade accounts receivable be measured so that this asset and also the related revenue and uncollectible accounts expense will be properly stated?

Trade accounts receivable are generally recorded on the books when the sale is made and title to the goods has passed. Receivables for services should be recognized only as services are performed. Receivables should not be recorded when a customer's order is received, or when goods are produced. Shipments on consignment are not sales since title to the goods does not pass until sales agents (consignees) actually sell the consigned goods. Receivables should be recognized for work completed on long-term construction contracts or on cost-plus-fixed-fee contracts.[1]

When it has been ascertained that revenue has been earned and recognition of the claim against customers is warranted, the question of measuring the amount of the receivable (and the revenue) still remains. For example, assume that a parcel of land is sold by a land developer for $5,000. The buyer can pay $5,000 in cash or pay $1,000 down and $1,100 at the end of each year for five years. If the sale is made on the deferred payment plan, should the receivable be reported at $4,000 ($5,000 cash price less the $1,000 down payment) or at $5,500, the face amount of the five remaining payments of $1,100 each? Is the revenue realized in the current year $5,000, $6,500, or some other amount? One of the objectives of this chapter is to explore these and similar questions.

Valuation of customers' accounts

The valuation assigned to accounts receivable is directly linked with the amount of revenue ultimately realized. There is no way of measuring revenue independently of the value of the claims against customers or others resulting from revenue transactions.

The problem of valuation of accounts receivable centers on three issues: (1) the amount due, (2) the time of collection, and (3) the estimate of the probability that the receivable will be collected. A number of problems in these three areas are discussed in the following sections.

Determining the amount due

Trade Discounts In some industries it is customary to bill customers a gross price subject to one or more trade discounts. The gross price is

[1] Accounting problems relating to consignment sales are covered in *Advanced Accounting* of this series; procedures relating to long-term construction contracts are covered in Chapter 9 of this text.

usually the suggested price for resale and the trade discount represents the difference between gross or list price and the price to the buyer before cash discounts. The use of a fixed list price and varying trade discounts enables the seller to change his prices, or to grant special discounts to large buyers, without reprinting catalogs or price lists. For accounting purposes these discounts should be recognized for what they are: a convenient means of pricing. The amount that a given customer will pay is the net price after trade discount, and this is the amount at which the receivable and the related revenue should be recorded.

Cash (or Sales) Discounts Cash discounts are widely used to establish a *cash* price when payment is received shortly after the delivery of the goods, as distinct from a higher *time payment* price. For example, if an invoice for $10,000 provides for terms of 2/10, n/30, the customer is faced with two alternatives. He may pay $9,800 within 10 days or he may wait the full 30 days and pay $10,000. The differential of $200 represents an effective interest rate of 36.7% for the use of the $9,800 for the extra 20-day period, and thus offers a strong incentive for payment within the 10-day period.[2]

A theoretical valuation of receivables subject to cash discounts should allow for the probability that discounts will be taken. In the case cited above, for example, if the probability is high that the customer will take the discount, the receivable is ultimately worth only $9,800; if it is expected that he will pay the face amount, it will be worth $10,000.

In dealing with a large number of receivables, past experience is usually a good guide in estimating customer reaction to proffered discounts. In view of the generous saving inherent in the cash price, the assumption that most customers will take the discount is reasonably justified.

Three alternative methods by which the seller may account for cash discounts are briefly described below:

Method A Accounts Receivable and Sales are recorded at gross, and discounts taken by customers are reported as debits to Sales Discounts. No entry is made at the end of the period to anticipate discounts that will probably be taken on outstanding accounts receivable. This method is simple and is widely used.

Method B Same procedure as in method A, except that an adjusting entry is also made at the end of the accounting period to accrue discounts that will probably be taken on outstanding accounts receivable. Sales Discounts is debited and Allowance for Sales Discounts is credited for the potential discounts on accounts receivable at the end of the period. The Allowance for Sales Discounts is deducted from Accounts Receivable as a step in valuing receivables at their estimated cash realizable value.

[2] Since there are eighteen 20-day periods in one year, the annualized rate earned can be computed as follows: ($200 × 18) ÷ $9,800, or 36.7%.

Method C Accounts Receivable are recorded at gross, Sales are recorded net of estimated discounts and the Allowance for Sales Discounts is credited at the time of sale and is debited as discounts are taken or as discounts expire. In the latter case, Sales Discounts Not Taken would be credited and reported in the income statement as a special revenue item.

Using method A, accounts receivable and net income will be overstated by the amount of estimated sales discounts not accrued. The overstatements inherent in method A do not exist in methods B and C. Both methods B and C yield identical results and are consistent with the objective of reporting accounts receivable and revenue at *net realizable amounts* in the financial statements. It should be pointed out, however, that the anticipation of sales discounts is not allowed for income tax purposes. Perhaps for this reason, the anticipation of discounts is not often encountered in practice.

Credit Card Fees and Other Collection Expenses The fees charged to businesses by credit card companies on sales made to customers using credit cards represent a combination of cash discount, uncollectible accounts expense, collection fees, and bookkeeping expenses. Credit card fees generally range from 3 to 7% of sales price. Since there is no uncertainty whether the fees will be charged, the sound accounting procedure would be to accrue fees as soon as sales to credit card customers are recognized. Receivables from the credit card company are recorded net, an expense account is debited for the amount of the credit card fees, and the Sales account is credited by an amount equal to the retail price of goods or services sold. A less satisfactory procedure would be to record both the receivable and sales net of the credit card fees. This procedure is objectionable because it does not record a cost of doing business and may materially distort income statement statistics.

Valuation of receivables, other than those arising from credit card customers, should also take into account expected collection expenses. Sears, Roebuck and Co., for example, deducts an "Allowance for Collection Expense and Losses on Customer Accounts" from the receivables, and Fingerhut Corporation recently reported its receivables as follows:

Accounts receivable:

Customers' installment accounts, substantially all of which are due within one year	$58,216,135
Other	926,889
	$59,143,024
Less allowance for returns, losses in collection, and collection expenses	13,563,641
	$45,579,383

This example also illustrates the magnitude of the valuation account for certain types of businesses. (Fingerhut Corporation is a mail-order merchandiser of consumer products.)

Sales Returns and Allowances   The value assigned to accounts receivable should also recognize the probability that some customers will return goods that are unsatisfactory or will make other claims requiring reduction in the amount due. Potential sales returns and allowances reduce the amount that will ultimately be collected from customers and thus reduce the realizable value of accounts receivable. If the amounts are material and can be objectively estimated, periodic income measurement will be improved by an adjustment for estimated returns and allowances.

To illustrate, assume that experience shows that sales returns will average 5% of accounts receivable as of the end of any period and that an average of 60% of the original selling price is ultimately realized from the returned goods, after allowing for the cost of restoring the goods to salable condition. If gross receivables at the end of the period amount to $100,000, the appropriate adjusting entry would be as shown below:

Inventory—Anticipated Sales Returns (realizable value)	3,000	
Sales Returns (contra Sales).	2,000	
Allowance for Sales Returns (contra A/R)		5,000
To record anticipated sales returns, net of the estimated realizable		
value of returned goods.		

The effect of this entry is to reduce current assets and net sales by $2,000—the difference between the original sale price and the estimated realizable value of anticipated sales returns.

This adjusting entry could be reversed on the first day of the new period; then, as sales returns are made by customers, the normal entry of debiting Sales Returns and Allowances and crediting Accounts Receivable can be made.

The anticipation of sales returns (as in the case previously discussed of anticipating sales discounts) is not permissible for income tax purposes and is not widely used in practice.

Freight Allowances   Occasionally goods are sold on terms "F.O.B. destination" with the understanding that the customer will pay the transportation charges and then deduct that amount from his remittance. In such instances, accounts receivable should be valued at the net amount to be collected. The easiest way to deal with this problem is to record the sale net of the transportation charge. If it is difficult or inconvenient to estimate the actual freight charges that will be incurred, it may be preferable to record the receivable at the gross amount and to set up an estimated allowance for freight. This allowance account is deducted from accounts receivable and the offsetting debit to Freight Paid by Customers, may be deducted from sales or reported as a selling expense.

Sales and Excise Taxes Many governmental units impose sales and excise taxes on particular products or on the sales transaction itself. Usually the seller is responsible for the remittance of these taxes to the government; in some cases he receives some compensation for acting as a tax collector. In theory a manufacturer's excise tax imposed on the manufacture of a product is a part of the cost of production, while an excise tax on the sale of the product is imposed upon the buyer of the goods and collected by the seller. In practice this distinction is at times difficult to apply.

If sales and excise taxes are collected as separately disclosed additions to the selling price, they should not be confused with revenue but should be credited to a liability account. Whether this is done at the time of each sale or as an adjustment at the end of the period is a matter of accounting convenience.[3] It is generally preferable to record the tax liability at the time of sale. For example, if a day's sales amount to $8,000 and are subject to a 5% sales tax, the sales tax payable will be $400, and the entry to record sales would be:

Accounts Receivable (or Cash)	8,400	
Sales Tax Payable		400
Sales		8,000
To record sales and sales tax liability.		

Container Deposits Customers may be charged for deposits on containers, with the understanding that the deposit will be refunded when the container is returned. If the container deposit is collected in cash, the only problem is the correct accounting for the refund obligation. When the container is returned, the liability will be canceled by the refund of the deposit. If the container is not returned, the liability no longer exists and the difference between the amount of the deposit and the cost of the containers not returned represents a gain or loss which should be com-

[3]Companies account for sales and excise taxes in a variety of ways: Some do not report such taxes either in sales or in expenses; others include such taxes in gross sales then deduct them in arriving at net sales; still other companies report sales and excise taxes either as part of cost of sales or as operating expenses. The amounts of excise taxes can be staggering: The American Distilling Co., for example, recently reported gross sales of $145 million less excise taxes of $110 million, leaving net sales of only $35 million; Philip Morris, Incorporated, reported operating revenues of $1.5 billion and federal and foreign excise taxes of $519 million, which were included under cost of sales.

bined with the account reporting the depreciation on containers. When no time limit is set for the return, an estimate should be made of the number of containers that will not be returned, and adjustments should be made periodically on the basis of the company's experience.

In some cases, the container fee is charged to customers' accounts. This creates an uncertainty with respect to the amount that will actually be collected. Until the uncertainty is resolved, accounts receivable should show as a separate item the amount charged to the customer for containers, and a liability should be established for the refund obligation.

Time of collection and valuation of receivables

Mention has previously been made of the need to consider the length of the collection period and the need to assign a present value to receivables. The procedure is particularly significant when the collection period is long and interest is not charged to customers. For example, if a receivable of $2,120 is expected to be collected one year hence and money is worth 6%, the receivable and sales should be recorded at $2,000 ($2,120 ÷ 1.06) and interest revenue of $120 should be recognized during the period the receivable is outstanding. The APB position on receivables and payables is discussed in another section of this chapter.

Estimating probability of collection

Thus far we have considered the problem of determining the amount due and the time of collection under the terms of a credit sale. A third major valuation problem is to evaluate the probability that customers will be willing and able to pay their accounts. Since businessmen do not make credit sales unless ultimate collection is reasonably assured, the probability of loss with respect to any given sale is presumably low. Even the best efforts of a capable credit department, however, cannot eliminate all uncollectible accounts. Furthermore, the managerial objective is not to minimize this expense but to maximize net income. Too stringent a credit policy may cause loss of sales which more than offsets the reduction in the uncollectible accounts expense.

Receivables that will never be collected have a zero present value, and the corresponding revenue will not be realized. The accountant's objective in attempting to anticipate uncollectible accounts, therefore, is to prevent an overstatement of assets and revenue in the period in which sales are made.

In the balance sheet, the estimate of uncollectible accounts is carried as a credit balance in a valuation account titled Allowance for Uncollectible Accounts or Allowance for Doubtful Accounts. A separate valuation account is used because it is not known which specific accounts will prove uncollectible, and the Accounts Receivable control account should agree with the subsidiary ledger detail. The allowance account is deducted from gross receivables to arrive at the net realizable value of the claims against customers. Under no circumstances should the Allowance for Uncollectible Accounts, or any asset valuation account, be shown among liabilities or elsewhere on the credit side of the balance sheet.[4]

The uncollectible accounts expense can be classified several ways on the income statement. Logically, uncollectible accounts expense should be classified as an offset against gross sales, on the grounds that it represents revenue that will not be collected. In practice, uncollectibles appear more often among operating expenses than as an offset against sales. Finally, some consider uncollectibles expense as a financial management item and report it as "other expense." Since each of these reporting practices produces the same net income, the issue is a minor one.

Two kinds of evidence are used in making estimates of uncollectibles: (1) the average relationship between sales and uncollectibles in past years and (2) an analysis of the quality and age of receivables at the end of an accounting period.

Estimate of Uncollectibles Based on Sales The average percentage of credit sales that have not been collected in past periods is a logical basis for estimating the portion of current credit sales that will prove uncollectible. This approach, often referred to as the *income statement approach,* is simple to apply and makes possible an estimate of future uncollectibles as soon as credit sales are recorded. It results in a logical matching of costs and revenue, and is especially appropriate in preparing interim statements. For example, if sales for the first quarter of the current year are $250,000 and uncollectible accounts expense is estimated at 1% of sales, the following entry would be required:

Uncollectible Accounts Expense	*2,500*	
Allowance for Uncollectible Accounts		*2,500*
To record estimated uncollectible accounts expense at 1% of		
sales for first quarter of year.		

If the ratio of cash sales to credit sales is relatively constant, estimating uncollectible accounts expense as a percentage of *total sales* may produce reasonably accurate results. Strictly speaking, however, the estimate of uncollectibles should be based on *credit sales* only. The estimate may be further refined by analyzing the experience for different classes of customers or in different geographical locations, if the necessary information is available.

[4]*APB Opinion No. 12,* "Omnibus Opinion—1967" AICPA (New York: 1967), p. 188.

Applying the appropriate percentage to the credit sales for any period provides an estimate of the sales of that period that will not be collected. The degree of error in the estimate cannot be determined until the record of collection experience is in. It is useful, therefore, to make periodic tests to determine the adequacy of the provision for uncollectibles in the light of changing business conditions.

Estimate of Uncollectibles Based on Accounts Receivable. A good way to test the adequacy of the allowance for uncollectible accounts and to recognize the current charge against revenue is to make an analysis of accounts by age group and probability of collection. This procedure is known as the *balance sheet approach* of measuring uncollectible accounts expense. Generally a strong correlation exists between the length of time an account is past due and its collectibility. A schedule classifying the balances of all accounts receivable according to whether the amount is not yet due, or past due by varying lengths of time, is known as an *aging of accounts receivable.*

The number of different age classes to be used depends on company experience and the terms of sale. An estimate of the average collection experience for each age class provides a basis for estimating the portion of outstanding accounts receivable that may be uncollectible.

The following summary of an accounts receivable aging is illustrative:

X COMPANY
Aging of Accounts Receivable
June 30, 19___

Classification by due date	Balances in each category (summarized from analysis of individual accounts)	Expected uncollectibles, %	Estimated uncollectibles
Not yet due	$2,400,000 (75.0%)	1	$24,000
Under 30 days past due	416,000 (13.0%)	3	12,480
30–60 days past due	208,000 (6.5%)	5	10,400
61–120 days past due	96,000 (3.0%)	10	9,600
121–180 days past due	48,000 (1.5%)	30	14,400
Over 180 days past due.	32,000 (1.0%)	Individual analysis	25,000
Totals	$3,200,000 (100.0%)		$95,880

If an aging of receivables is used as a basis for estimating uncollectible accounts expense, the current provision will be an amount sufficient to bring the Allowance for Uncollectible Accounts up to the amount indicated by the aging analysis. For example, if the balance in the Allowance for Uncollectible Accounts for X Company at June 30 is $40,000, the analysis above calls for the following entry to bring the allowance account to the required $95,880:

Uncollectible Accounts Expense	55,880	
Allowance for Uncollectible Accounts		55,880
To adjust allowance to required balance of $95,880.		

A simpler method sometimes followed is to increase the allowance to a given percentage of receivables or to increase the allowance by a given percentage of receivables. These latter procedures are not recommended; the results they produce are only rough approximations.

In the process of aging the accounts receivable, management should evaluate current financial statements of major customers in order to assess more fully the probability of collection. The credit department in many companies is assigned responsibility for a continuing analysis of the financial statements of customers and prospective customers so that it may prevent credit sales to customers who represent excessive risk of nonpayment.

Estimated uncollectibles and income measurement

It is most unlikely that estimated uncollectibles will agree with actual write-offs applicable to each year's revenue. So long as there is a reasonably close correlation between the annual estimate and actual experience, minor discrepancies year by year may be ignored.

A major adjustment to reduce or increase the Allowance for Uncollectible Accounts may involve receivables originating in prior periods. Such adjustments should be made to uncollectible accounts expense for the current period or listed separately in *computing income before extraordinary items;* they should not be treated as prior period adjustments, as extraordinary items, or as changes in *accounting principle* (discussed in greater detail in Chapter 22).

In *APB Opinion No. 9,* the Accounting Principles Board stated:

> Certain gains or losses (or provision for losses), regardless of size, do not constitute extraordinary items (or prior period adjustments) because they are of a character typical of the customary business activities of the entity. Examples include (a) write-downs of receivables, inventories and research and development costs. . . . The effects of items of this nature should be reflected in the determination of income before extraordinary items. If such effects are material, disclosure is recommended.[5]

[5] *APB Opinion No. 9,* "Reporting the Results of Operations," AICPA (New York: 1966), p. 115.

A major adjustment to the allowance for uncollectible accounts or a revision of the method used to compute uncollectibles is viewed as a *change in accounting estimate* in *APB Opinion No. 20,* which states:

> Future events and their effects cannot be perceived with certainty; estimating, therefore, requires the exercise of judgment. Thus accounting estimates change as new events occur, as more experience is acquired, or as additional information is obtained.[6]
> The Board concludes that the effect of a change in accounting estimate should be accounted for in (a) the period of change if the change affects that period only or (b) the period of change and future periods if the change affects both. A change in an estimate should not be accounted for by restating amounts reported in financial statements of prior periods or by reporting pro forma amounts for prior periods.[7]

The effect of a change in the accounting estimate on income before extraordinary items, net income, and earnings per share of the current period should be disclosed *if material* in amount. Estimates made each period in the ordinary course of accounting for uncollectible accounts need not be disclosed.

In preparing income tax returns, a change in estimates may be treated differently from the method used for financial reporting purposes. Income tax regulations presently provide that an excessive or inadequate balance in the allowance account may be corrected by adjusting the rate used in estimating uncollectible accounts expense in subsequent years—in effect, overstating or understating taxable income in future years until the allowance is brought into line.

Collection of accounts previously written off

When the decision is made to charge off an uncollectible account, the charge against the Allowance account and credit to Accounts Receivable has no effect on either the book value of accounts receivable or on the net income of the period in which the write-off occurs. If an account that has been written off is later collected, a common procedure is to debit Accounts Receivable and credit Allowance for Uncollectible Accounts. This reverses the entry, erroneously made, and the collection is then recorded in the usual manner. This method has the advantage of providing in the customer's account a complete record of credit experience with him.

Direct charge-off method of recognizing uncollectibles

Some businesses may elect to recognize uncollectible accounts only as they become worthless. While this practice gives the appearance of being more objective, it overstates the net realizable value of receivables and

---

[6]*APB Opinion No. 20,* "Accounting Changes," AICPA (New York: 1971), p. 388.
[7]*Ibid.,* p. 397. See Chapter 22 for a more complete discussion of changes in accounting estimate.

does not properly match the uncollectibles with the revenue from which they originate, as required by the accrual concept of accounting. Under this procedure, for example, an account representing a sale in Year 1 may be recognized as an expense in Year 2, and accounts originating in Year 2 may be charged off against revenue of Year 3 or Year 4. In applying this method, subjective judgment is still required in determining when an account becomes worthless. The direct charge-off method is therefore likely to be less objective than it appears at first glance. Uncollectible accounts under this method are written off by a charge to Uncollectible Accounts Expense and a credit to Accounts Receivable. Collection of an account written off in a previous period is credited to Uncollectible Accounts Recovered; recovery of an account written off earlier in the current period is recorded as a credit to Uncollectible Accounts Expense, thus eliminating the expense which was prematurely recorded.

Either the allowance or the direct charge-off method can be used for income tax purposes, but the method adopted must be consistently followed. The allowance method is generally more advantageous for income tax purposes since deductible expenses are anticipated and income taxes are not paid on revenue which may never be collected.

Selling and assigning accounts receivable

In the normal operating cycle of a business, cash needed for current operations is provided through the collection of accounts receivable. It is possible to accelerate this process by selling receivables or by borrowing money and pledging accounts receivable as collateral. In some industries such procedures are quite common; in other industries this may be done only in times of financial stress.

Sale of Accounts Receivable The purpose of selling accounts receivable is to shift the risk of credit, the effort of collection, and the waiting period in granting credit to the buyer, for a fee. Accounts receivable are usually sold *without recourse.* As a result, the discount on the sale may be quite high, depending on the quality of the receivables. The discount (financing expense) on sale of accounts receivable should be included in the determination of income before extraordinary items.

Persons or financial concerns making a business of buying receivables are known as *factors,* and the process of selling receivables is often called *factoring.* A factor may buy receivables outright, with or without recourse, or he may extend credit to a company needing money and take the collections on accounts receivable in repayment.[8] Customers are generally notified and directed to make payment directly to the factor.

[8]"With recourse" means that the factor is protected by the seller against loss; "without recourse" means that the factor assumes full risk of failure to collect the accounts purchased.

Factoring arrangements vary widely. If the factor advances money with the expectation of obtaining accounts receivable from the borrower, interest is charged on the amount advanced plus a commission of from 1 to 3% of the net amount of receivables purchased, depending upon the size of the transaction, the terms of the sale, and the credit standing of the customers involved. Often it is agreed that the selling company will withdraw cash only as needed and will pay interest only on cash withdrawals made.

Factoring transactions raise no special accounting problems for the seller. Accounts receivable are converted into cash and the factor's commission and interest are recorded as expenses. The factor may hold back from 5 to 10% of the agreed amount as a margin of protection against sales returns and allowances. This amount should appear in the accounts as a receivable from the factor unless experience indicates that the probability of receiving it is small, in which case an allowance for sales returns and allowances should be established.

Assigning Receivables Instead of selling receivables, management may prefer to borrow money using accounts receivable as collateral. This may involve an informal pledge of accounts receivable under an agreement that the proceeds from their collection will be used to retire the loan. Alternatively, receivables may be *assigned* under a more formal arrangement whereby the business (*assignor*) pledges the receivable to the lender (*assignee*) and executes a note. Assignment gives the lender the same right to bring action to collect the receivables that the assignor possesses. The assignor assumes its own credit risk and collection effort, and promises to make good any accounts that cannot be collected. The customer is usually not notified of the assignment and makes payments directly to the assignor; he may, however, be instructed to make payments to the assignee. The assignor has some equity in the receivables, since the financing company usually advances less than 100% of the face amount of receivables assigned.

The primary accounting problem raised by assignment of receivables is to measure the company's equity in the assigned accounts and its liability to the assignee. Assigned accounts should be transferred to a separate account, Assigned Accounts Receivable, and a liability to the assignee should be established. As collections are received, assigned receivables will be reduced and the liability to the assignee will be correspondingly reduced as cash is remitted by the assignor. Commissions and interest charges will be included in the remittance and will be recorded as expenses.

To illustrate, assume that on January 2, Year 1, the Adams Company assigns accounts receivable of $50,000 to the Finance Corp. and receives $45,000, less a financing charge of 2% on the advance. Interest of 1% of the unpaid balance of the loan is to be paid monthly. The journal entries that are required on the Adams Company books to record the assignment and subsequent transactions are shown on page 223.

Transaction	Entry on Adams Company books

Jan. 2. Assigned accounts receivable of $50,000. Finance Corp. remitted 90% of account balances, less 2% financing charge.	Assigned Accounts Receivable 50,000
	   Accounts Receivable . . 50,000
	Cash 44,100
	Financing Expense 900
	   Notes Payable to
	     Finance Corp. 45,000

Jan. 31. Collected $30,150 on assigned accounts. Paid this amount to Finance Corp., including interest at 1% per month on unpaid balance of loan, $45,000.	Cash 30,150
	   Assigned Accounts
	    Receivable 30,150
	Notes Payable to Finance Corp. 29,700
	Financing Expense 450
	   Cash 30,150

Feb. 28. Collected $17,000 on assigned accounts. Paid balance owed to Finance Corp., plus interest at 1% per month on unpaid balance, $15,300.	Cash 17,000
	   Assigned Accounts
	    Receivable 17,000
	Notes Payable to Finance Corp. 15,300
	Financing Expense 153
	   Cash 15,453

Transferred balance of assigned accounts to Accounts Receivable.	Accounts Receivable 2,850
	   Assigned Accounts
	    Receivable 2,850

The assignor's interest in assigned receivables may be shown by deducting the obligation to the assignee from the amount of the assigned receivables. Offsetting the liability against the asset is appropriate in this case because collections on assigned accounts are contractually earmarked to liquidate the loan. This treatment is illustrated below for the Adams Company at January 31, Year 1:

Current assets:
Accounts receivable $200,000
Assigned accounts receivable $19,850
Less: Notes payable to Finance Corp. 15,300
Equity in assigned accounts receivable 4,550
   Total receivables $204,550

Full disclosure should be made of accounts receivable pledged, assigned, or sold, including any related contingent liabilities.

Installment receivables

Many individuals and businesses find it convenient to buy certain items on the installment plan. The installment contract, in essence a note providing for payment over a period of time, is a widely used credit instrument. Some companies selling on an installment basis have adequate financial resources to carry their own contracts and thus earn interest in addition to other service charges included in the contract. Many companies, however, sell or discount their installment contracts receivable with finance companies.

Installment receivables from sale of goods or services in the ordinary course of business, including those not falling due for more than one year from the balance sheet date, are included in current assets. In valuing installment receivables, unearned interest and service charges included in the contract are excluded both from installment receivables and from sales. For example, Harris-Intertype Corporation recently reported its receivables as follows:

Trade accounts and notes receivable:

Accounts receivable	$ 74,030,052
Installment notes, including $31,000,000 due after one year . . .	52,592,454
	$126,622,506
Less: Deferred interest income ($8,050,000) and allowances for	
collection losses	9,887,994
Total trade accounts and notes receivable	$116,734,512

Interest and service charges should be recognized as revenue only as earned and should be separately disclosed. Deferred income tax liabilities related to installment receivables are also reported as current. For example, in a recent annual report, Sears, Roebuck and Co. included "Deferred Income Tax Credits—Net" of $690 million under current liabilities. Accounting for installment sales is covered in *Advanced Accounting* of this series.

NOTES RECEIVABLE

The term *notes receivable* is used in accounting to designate several types of credit instruments. The distinguishing characteristic common to all is that they are written contractual agreements containing an unconditional promise to pay a certain sum of money under terms clearly specified in the contract. Most credit instruments used as a basis for business transactions are *negotiable,* which means in essence that a *holder in due course* is free of certain equity defenses that might otherwise be available to prior parties. Negotiability is a valuable characteristic which makes the instrument freely transferable and thus enhances the ability of the holder to sell it, discount it, or borrow against it.

Notes receivable are often used when the goods sold have a high unit or aggregate value and the buyer wants to extend payment beyond the normal 30- to 90-day period of trade credit. In the banking and commercial credit field, notes are the typical form of credit instrument used to support lending transactions. Notes receivable may also result from sale of plant and equipment items or a variety of other business transactions, including the investment of idle cash.

Valuation of notes receivable

As in the case of accounts receivable, the proper valuation of notes and similar credit instruments is their fair market value (present value) at the time of acquisition. The accountant can value notes because he generally has, in the terms of the note, sufficient and clear evidence of the rights inherent in it. Except for questions of collectibility, there is little uncertainty with respect to the amount that will be received and the date on which it will be received.

Notes, like trade accounts, may prove to be uncollectible. If a company uses notes as a regular credit medium and has a large volume outstanding at any given time, the amounts of probable bad notes may be estimated, and an allowance for uncollectible notes established using procedures similar to those discussed for accounts receivable.

Strictly speaking, there is no such thing as a non-interest-bearing note; there are only notes that contain a stated provision for interest and notes that do not. The time value of money is present in any case since the present value of a promise to pay money at some future date is not as great as the amount to be paid at maturity. The so-called non-interest-bearing note has a present value smaller than its face or maturity value by an amount equivalent to an interest charge. On the other hand, if a note bears a fair rate of interest, its *face value* and *present value* are the same at the date of issuance.

This point may be illustrated by an example. Suppose that two notes are received in connection with the sale of goods. In settlement of the first sale, Customer A gives a one-year, 6% note, having a face value of $24,000. In settlement of the second sale, Customer B gives a one-year note having a maturity value of $25,440 with no interest provision specified in the note. If the accountant looks only at face values, he might be tempted to record these notes as follows:

Customer A			Customer B		
Notes Receivable.	24,000		Notes Receivable.	25,440	
Sales		24,000	Sales		25,440

A careful examination of the evidence indicates that the two contracts are identical, assuming that 6% is a reasonable rate of interest. Both customers have promised to pay $25,440 at the end of one year, and both notes have a present value of $24,000 ($25,440 ÷ 1.06). A logical method of accounting would be to record both notes at $24,000 and to record interest of $1,440 as it is earned. Thus, the note received from Customer B may be recorded in the same way as the note from Customer A, or by using a Discount on Notes Receivable account as illustrated below:

Notes Receivable.	25,440	
Discount on Notes Receivable.		1,440
Sales		24,000

The discount on notes receivable is transferred periodically to Interest Revenue and the balance in the discount account should be reported as a deduction from Notes Receivable in the balance sheet.

In practice, non-interest-bearing, short-term notes received from customers are recorded at the outset at their face amount (maturity value). The foregoing analysis shows that this procedure overstates assets and fails to recognize interest revenue. Although *APB Opinion No. 21* requires that notes be recorded at present value, the provisions of this Opinion do not apply to receivables arising from transactions with customers in the normal course of business which are due within one year. When the amount of the unearned implicit interest is substantial, this treatment may result in a significant overstatement of assets, stockholders' equity, and net income.

Discounting notes receivable

Negotiable notes receivable may be sold or discounted. The term *sale* is appropriate when a note is endorsed to a bank or finance company on a *nonrecourse* basis; that is, in the event the maker of the note defaults, the bank or finance company has no recourse against the company selling the note. The term *discounted* applies when a company borrows against notes receivable and endorses them on a *recourse* basis, which means that the borrowing company must pay the note if the original maker does not.

The *proceeds* received when a note is discounted are computed by deducting from the maturity value of the note the amount of interest or discount charged by the bank or other financing source. Banks sometimes compute the discount on the *maturity value* of the note rather than on the proceeds or amount borrowed, which in effect gives the bank a higher effective rate of interest than the quoted discount rate.

To illustrate these points and the accounting involved, assume that Lynn Company wishes to discount two notes receivable arising from the sale of merchandise. Both notes have a face amount of $100,000 and are due in one year. Note C carries no provision for interest; Note D is to be paid with interest at 6%. The bank also charges a 6% discount rate.

If we assume that the notes are discounted immediately upon receipt, the proceeds would be determined as follows:

	Note C	Note D
Face amount of note	$100,000	$100,000
Interest to maturity	-0-	6,000
Maturity value	$100,000	$106,000
Bank discount (6% of maturity value for one year)	6,000	6,360
Proceeds	$ 94,000	$ 99,640
Present value @ 6% (maturity value ÷ 1.06)	94,340	100,000
Difference between proceeds and present value	$ 340	$ 360

The difference between the proceeds and the present value of each note on a 6% basis represents additional interest charged by the bank due to the fact that the 6% discount is computed on maturity value rather than on the amount actually borrowed (proceeds). The additional interest should be recognized as expense over the remaining life of each note.

If Lynn Company records the notes at present value, the entries to record the discounting of these notes would be as shown below:[9]

	Note C			Note D	
At time of sale:					
Notes Receivable	94,340		Notes Receivable	100,000	
Sales		94,340	Sales		100,000
At time notes are discounted:					
Cash	94,000		Cash	99,640	
Interest Expense	340		Interest Expense	360	
Notes Receivable		94,340	Notes Receivable		100,000

[9] An alternative approach is to view the proceeds received from the bank as the "true" present value of the notes. This interpretation would call for the recording of the two notes and related sales at $94,000 and $99,640, respectively, thus eliminating the need to recognize interest expense when the notes are discounted.

An alternative procedure for recording the discounting of notes receivable includes a credit to Notes Receivable Discounted (a contra-asset account) rather than a credit to Notes Receivable. If a Notes Receivable Discounted account is used, it should be deducted from Notes Receivable in the current asset section of the balance sheet, thus disclosing the contingent liability to the bank. However, it should be pointed out that the full contingent liability on Note C is $100,000 (not $94,340) and on Note D it is $106,000 (not $100,000).

When a Notes Receivable Discounted account is used, the amount credited thereto must be transferred to Notes Receivable when the contingency is ended by either the payment or dishonor of the note. Since most discounted notes are paid at the maturity date, the more efficient procedure is to credit the Notes Receivable account at the time the note is discounted and thus avoid the need for a subsequent entry. The contingent liability created by the discounting of notes receivable may be maintained on a memorandum basis, and disclosure of the contingency may be made on the balance sheet by a footnote.

If Lynn Company had held these notes for some time before discounting them, interest earned prior to the time the notes were discounted should be recorded. The discounting of the notes would then be recorded in the manner previously illustrated.

If the discounted notes are dishonored, Lynn Company would be required to pay the bank. The amount that would be due in such an event, however, is not the present value at the time the note was received but rather the maturity value of the note plus any protest fees.

Notice of the dishonor of a discounted note must be given promptly; therefore, the borrower may assume that payment has been made if no notice is received within a few days after maturity date. If notes are dishonored, the total amount paid to the bank should be debited to Accounts Receivable or Dishonored Notes Receivable. Subsequent collection would be recorded as a credit to this account; failure to collect would require that the receivable from the maker of the note be charged off to Allowance for Uncollectible Accounts.

A company discounting notes receivable is contingently liable if the maker of the note fails to pay at maturity. The contingent liability can be disclosed on the balance sheet as follows: (1) footnote, (2) parenthetical note, (3) in a separate contingent liability section, or (4) by using a Notes Receivable Discounted account and deducting it from Notes Receivable. Disclosure by means of a footnote is by far the most common practice. A more detailed discussion of contingent liabilities is included in Chapter 7.

APB Opinion No. 21, "Interest on Receivables and Payables"

Opinion No. 21 issued by the Accounting Principles Board, is applicable if the face amount of a receivable (especially a note) does not reasonably represent the present value of the consideration given in exchange. This situation may arise if no interest is explicitly stated or if the stated rate of interest is not appropriate. Recording the receivable at an amount in excess of the fair present value, for example, overstates the sales price and gross profit recorded by the seller and understates the interest earned in subsequent periods.

As a highly simplified example, assume that A buys a tract of land for $6,000 cash and immediately sells it to B for $10,000 with payment consisting solely of a 10-year, non-interest-bearing note for $10,000. It would be absurd for B to record this transaction as producing a $4,000 gain, because the non-interest-bearing, 10-year note has a present value far less than its $10,000 face amount.

APB Opinion No. 21 applies to secured and unsecured notes, debentures, bonds, mortgage notes, equipment obligations, and some accounts receivable and payable. It is not intended to apply to "receivables and payables arising from transactions with customers or suppliers in the normal course of business which are due in customary trade terms not exceeding approximately one year."[10] A brief summary of *APB Opinion No. 21* as it relates to receivables follows.

Notes Received for Cash Interest on a cash loan is generally equal to the excess of the amount the borrower agrees to repay over the amount of cash he receives. The stated interest rate may differ from the prevailing rate for similar notes and the proceeds may differ from the face amount of the note. These differences indicate that the present value of the note at the time of issuance differs from the face amount. The difference between the face value and the proceeds is recorded as premium or discount to be amortized over the life of the note. Alternatively, the note may be recorded at its present value (face value plus any premium or less any discount).

Notes Received in Exchange for Cash and Other Rights or Privileges Instead of issuing a note solely for cash, the parties may agree to exchange other rights or privileges (stated or unstated). These rights and privileges should be given accounting recognition by taking into account any implicit discount or premium on the note. For example, assume that on December 31, Year 1, the Cashrich Corporation lends $108,000 to a supplier payable in one year, without interest, even though the going rate of interest for this type of loan is 8%. The parties agree that all the Cashrich Corporation's lumber needs in Year 2 will be met at a favorable price by the supplier. This loan should be recorded on December 31 of Year 1 as follows:

---

[10] *APB Opinion No. 21*, "Interest on Receivables and Payables," AICPA (New York: 1971), p. 418.

Notes Receivable.	100,000	
Property Rights in Contract with Supplier.	8,000	
Cash		108,000

To record non-interest-bearing loan to supplier.
Present value of note, $108,000 \div 1.08 = \$100,000$.

The account Property Rights in Contract with Supplier would be classified as a current asset because it is similar to an advance on merchandise purchases. In this example we assumed that the note received by Cashrich Corporation was non-interest-bearing; if the note stipulated an unreasonably low rate of interest, the present value of the note would be less than $108,000 but more than $100,000, thus reducing the amount recorded in the Property Rights in Contract with Supplier account.

When payment is received on the note at December 31 of Year 2, the following entry would be required:

Cash	108,000	
Purchases	8,000	
Notes Receivable.		100,000
Property Rights in Contract with Supplier.		8,000
Interest Revenue		8,000

To record proceeds and implicit interest earned on note receivable and to recognize value assigned to the contract with supplier as an additional cost of lumber purchased.

The foregoing procedure properly recognizes interest revenue in Year 2, $8,000 ($100,000 × 8%) and the full cost of purchases through the recognition of the implicit interest on the note receivable as an additional cost of lumber purchased from the supplier.

When notes are received in exchange for assets or services, and interest is either not stated or is unreasonably low, the notes and the sales price should be recorded at the fair value of the assets or services or at the market value of the note, whichever is the more clearly determinable. In the absence of exchange prices for the assets or services or evidence of the market value of the note, the present value of a note should be determined. This determination should be made at the time the note is acquired; any subsequent changes in interest rates should be ignored.[11]

---

[11] Ibid., pp. 421–422.

Determining an Appropriate Interest Rate and Present Value of Note The appropriate interest rate for finding the present value of a note receivable depends on factors such as the credit standing of the issuer, terms of the note, the quality of collateral offered by the issuer, and the general level of interest rates. The interest rate selected for this purpose should approximate the rate at which the debtor could obtain similar financing from other sources. Therefore, the interest rate selected would represent an arm's-length negotiated rate for the borrower and the lender.

To illustrate the computation of the present value of a note, assume that on January 1, Year 1, Computer Software Associates sends a $39,930 invoice for services to the Poor Corporation. The Poor Corporation protests the amount of the invoice and asks that it be allowed to pay it in three annual installments of $13,310, starting in one year. Computer Software Associates agrees to this arrangement and receives three non-interest-bearing notes for $13,310 each. How should these notes be recorded on the records of Computer Software Associates if an interest rate of 10% is considered appropriate? It is first necessary to compute the present value of the notes as follows:

Present value of notes at beginning of Year 1	Payments to be received		
	End of Year 1	End of Year 2	End of Year 3
	$13,310	$13,310	$13,310
$12,100 ← ($13,310 ÷ 1.10)			
11,000 ← ($12,100 ÷ 1.10) — $12,100 ← ($13,310 ÷ 1.10)			
10,000 ← ($11,000 ÷ 1.10) — $11,000 ← ($12,100 ÷ 1.10) — $12,100 ← ($13,310 ÷ 1.10)			
$33,100 Present value of ordinary annuity of three payments of $13,310 discounted at 10%			

By reference to Table 4 in Appendix A, the present value of the three notes may be determined by a shorter method as follows:

Amount of annual receipts (notes)	$13,310
Multiply by present value of ordinary annuity of $1 at 10% interest . . .	2.4869
Present value of three annual receipts of $13,310 at 10% interest. . . .	$33,101*

Difference of $1.00 is due to rounding off of values in present value of ordinary annuity tables.

The entries to record the receipt of the notes on January 1, Year 1, and the three annual collections from the Poor Corporation are illustrated below. We have assumed that no prior entry was made to record the receivable from the Poor Corporation and that a Discount on Notes Receivable account is not used.

January 1, Year 1:

Notes Receivable.	33,100	
Revenue		33,100

Receipt of non-interest-bearing note for $39,930 payable in three annual installments. The note is recorded at its **present value** based on an interest rate of 10% per year.

End of Year 1:

Cash	13,310	
Notes Receivable.		10,000
Interest Revenue		3,310

To record collection of first note. Interest for first year: $33,100 × 10% = $3,310.

End of Year 2:

Cash	13,310	
Notes Receivable.		11,000
Interest Revenue		2,310

To record collection of second note. Interest for second year: ($33,100 − $10,000) × 10% = $2,310.

End of Year 3:

Cash	13,310	
Notes Receivable.		12,100
Interest Revenue		1,210

To record collection of third note. Interest for third year: ($33,100 − $10,000 − $11,000) × 10% = $1,210.

As an alternative, it would be possible to record the notes at face value, $39,930, and credit Discount on Notes Receivable for $6,830, representing the total interest occurring on the notes over the three-year period. Discount on Notes Receivable would be debited and Interest Revenue credited as interest is earned ($3,310 in Year 1; $2,310 in Year 2; and $1,210 in Year 3).

See Appendix A for a more complete discussion of present-value concepts.

Analysis of accounts receivable

Accounts receivable are an important factor in analyzing financial liquidity and projecting cash flows. Changes in the length of the average collection period or the number of days' sales in receivables, for example, should be carefully watched and action initiated to correct unfavorable trends. A discussion of analytical techniques for receivables appears in Chapter 24.

Presentation of receivables in the balance sheet

Within the current asset section of the balance sheet the amounts of the following classes of receivables should be separately reported: (1) notes and other receivables based on written negotiable contracts, (2) ordinary trade receivables, (3) installment accounts receivables, and (4) other current claims. Negotiable notes and contracts have a special status because of the ease with which they can be converted into cash through discounting. Statement analysts may be interested in the percentage relationship between trade receivables and credit sales as an indication of a company's collection experience.

Receivables that have been pledged should be identified, and any receivables that will not be collected within the next year or operating cycle should be excluded from the current asset category. A credit balance in an individual account receivable, if material, should be shown as a current liability.

Receivables from officers, employees, and stockholders are generally classified as noncurrent unless current collection is definitely assured.

The balance sheet presentation of various kinds of receivables and related accounts is illustrated below:

Included in Current Assets

Receivables:
Trade notes receivable (net of notes discounted of $50,000 and
 unearned discounts of $5,000) . . . . $ 205,000
Trade accounts receivable (net of allowances for uncollectible
 accounts and sales discounts of $32,500) 620,000
Installment receivables (net of unearned interest and service
 charges) 400,000
Current amount due from affiliated company, interest at 7% 45,000
Miscellaneous (including $2,000 debit balance in accounts payable) 10,000
 Total receivables $1,280,000

Included in Other Assets

Receivable from sale of equipment (*due with interest at 8% in 3 years*)	$ 150,000
Notes due from officers and employees (*due with interest at 6% in installments over 10 years*)	85,000
Dishonored notes receivable (*net of allowance of $6,000 for estimated uncollectibility*)	12,000

Included in Current Liabilities

Container deposits by customers	$ 17,500
Accounts receivable with credit balances	2,250

REVIEW QUESTIONS

1 Briefly discuss the significance of accounts receivable in analyzing the financial position of a business unit.

2 What is meant by *valuation of receivables?* If accountants generally require that assets be recorded "at cost," why are accounts receivable not recorded at the cost of the merchandise sold?

3 What is the distinction between *trade receivables* and *miscellaneous receivables?* Give two examples of each.

4 At what point should trade receivables be recorded? Are shipments to consignees or sales agents recorded as receivables?

5 Describe a *cycle billing system* and state its advantages.

6 Describe how the following items affect the valuation of receivables: *trade discounts, sales discounts, returns and allowances, freight allowances, sales and excise taxes,* and *container deposits.*

7 Briefly describe three methods of accounting for cash (sales) discounts.

8 Some accountants classify Uncollectible Accounts Expense as an *operating expense* while others classify it as a *contra-revenue* account. Discuss the reasoning behind these alternative positions. What objection do you have to the account title "Loss from Bad Debts"?

9 What is an *aging of accounts receivable?* Describe how such an analysis may be used in estimating uncollectible accounts expense and in analyzing the quality of accounts receivable.

10 According to *APB Opinion No. 20,* how should a change in estimating uncollectible accounts expense and a major increase or decrease in the allowance for doubtful accounts be reported in the income statement?

11 Briefly discuss the logic of basing the estimate of possible uncollectibles on (*a*) total sales, (*b*) credit sales, and (*c*) a fixed percentage of receivables at the end of the period.

12 Discuss the accounting procedures necessary to record recoveries of accounts previously written off (*a*) if an allowance for uncollectibles is used, or (*b*) if the direct charge-off method is used.

13 Explain the distinction between *factoring* and *assigning* accounts receivable.

14 City Equipment Company sells certain merchandise having a list price of $10,500 on an installment plan covering 24 months. Payments of $500 are to be made by the customer each month. Interest of $1,300 and service charges of $200 are added to the listed sales price in arriving at total installment receivables. The company records the sale by a debit to Installment Contracts Receivable and a credit to Sales for $12,000. Evaluate this procedure.

15 What error is introduced into the accounting records when a non-interest-bearing note receivable due in one year is recorded at face value? Explain.

16 Describe various ways that the contingent liability relating to notes receivable discounted can be presented on the balance sheet.

EXERCISES

Ex. 6-1 Streetman Company acquired merchandise having a cost of $4,000. The merchandise was offered for sale by Streetman Company at a list price of $6,500, before a trade discount of 20% and a cash discount of 2% if the invoice is paid within 10 days. Streetman Company billed customers net of the trade discount, and recorded accounts receivable and sales at the invoice price.

Prepare journal entries to record (*a*) the sale and the cost of the goods sold, and (*b*) the collection of the account within 10 days, assuming that the company uses a perpetual inventory system.

Ex. 6-2 The Waco Corporation started in business in Year 1 and has outstanding accounts receivable of $300,000 at the end of the year. In arriving at the valuation of receivables at the end of the year, management wishes to take into account the following:

Estimated uncollectible accounts . . expense of current period	$5,200
Estimated collection costs	1,800
Estimated price adjustments and other allowances on outstanding receivables (no	
returns are anticipated)	3,000
Estimated cash (sales) discounts	3,600

a Prepare a compound adjusting entry to recognize management's estimate of the net realizable value of accounts receivable at the end of Year 1. No accounts were written off in Year 1.
b Show how accounts receivable should be reported in the balance sheet at the end of Year 1.

Ex. 6-3 From the following information, compute the uncollectible accounts expense for Year 1: Beginning balance in Accounts Receivable was $80,000; beginning balance in Allowance for Uncollectible Accounts was $5,000; ending balance in Accounts Receivable is $100,000, of which 4% is estimated to be uncollectible. During the year, $6,248 of accounts receivable were written off as uncollectible.

Ex. 6-4 Your accounts receivable clerk, to whom you pay a salary of $450 per month, has just purchased a new Cadillac. You decide to test the accuracy of the accounts receivable balance of $29,000 as shown in the ledger.

The following information is available for your first year in business: Collections from customers, $125,000; payments for merchandise purchases, $130,000; ending inventory, $40,000; and ending accounts payable to merchandise suppliers, $30,000. All goods purchased were marked to sell at 40% above cost (sales price equals 140% of cost).

Compute an estimate of the ending balance of accounts receivable from customers that should appear in the ledger and any apparent shortages.

Ex. 6-5 The following accounts appear in the ledger of the Holmes Company at the end of 1975:

Sales	Accounts Receivable	Allowance for Uncollectible Accounts
$1,200,000	$500,000	$4,000—debit balance

Prepare an entry to recognize uncollectible accounts expense for each independent assumption below:

a The Allowance for Uncollectible Accounts is increased to a balance of $16,000, thus requiring an additional debit to Uncollectible Accounts Expense of $20,000.

b The company recognizes 3% of sales as uncollectible accounts expense.

c By aging the accounts, $24,250 of accounts receivable is considered uncollectible.

Ex. 6-6 On March 1, 1975, the Henke Company assigned accounts receivable of $60,000 to General Acceptance Co. and received $54,000 less a 2% financing charge. Interest is charged at the rate of 1% per month of the unpaid balance. The Henke Company made collections on the assigned accounts and remitted the proceeds at the end of each month to General Acceptance Co. Collections in March were $30,000.

Prepare journal entries to record the transactions for March relating to the assignment of accounts receivable.

Ex. 6-7 You are auditing the accounts of the Wendy Corporation at the end of its fiscal year. Your review of accounts receivable and discussions with the client disclose that the following items are included in the accounts receivable (both control and subsidiary ledgers):

Customers' accounts with credit balances, $1,850

Receivables from officers, $12,500

Advances to employees, $2,200

Accounts that are definitely uncollectible, $2,444

Prepare a correcting journal entry to reclassify items which are not trade accounts receivable and to write off uncollectible accounts.

Ex. 6-8 According to **APB Opinion No. 21,** how would you record a low-interest, one-year loan for $250,000 by Company A to a supplier who agrees to sell raw materials to Company A at a favorable fixed price during the period of the loan?

Explain the approach used in recording this transaction. Prepare an entry on Company A's books to record the loan, assuming that the present value of the note is $225,000.

Ex. 6-9 The Sullivan Corporation sells an old machine having a cost of $20,000 and a book value of $2,000 for $9,000, payable $1,014 down and $2,662 at the end of each of the next three years. No interest is mentioned in the agreement, although 10% would be a fair rate for this type of transaction.

Compute the present value of the $7,986 to be received over the next three years and record the sale of the machine as recommended in *Opinion No. 21.*

SHORT CASES FOR ANALYSIS AND DECISION

Case 6-1 During the audit of accounts receivable of the Martinelli Corporation, the president asks why the current year's expense for uncollectible accounts is charged merely because some accounts may become uncollectible next year. He then said that he had read that financial statements should be based upon verifiable, objective evidence, and that it seemed to him to be much more objective to wait until individual accounts receivable were actually determined to be uncollectible before charging them to expense.

Instructions
a Discuss the theoretical justification of the allowance method as contrasted with the direct write-off method of accounting for uncollectible accounts.
b Describe the following two methods of estimating uncollectible accounts. Include a discussion of how well each accomplishes the objectives of the allowance method of accounting for uncollectible accounts.
(1) The percentage of sales method
(2) The aging method
c Of what merit is the president's contention that the allowance method lacks the objectivity of the direct write-off method? Discuss in terms of accounting's measurement function.

Case 6-2 As a result of earthquake losses, the Sandison Company, one of the oldest and largest customers of Cosmetics Distributors, Inc., suddenly and unexpectedly became bankrupt. Approximately 30% of the total sales of Cosmetics Distributors, Inc., have been made to the Sandison Company during each of the past several years.

The amount due from Sandison Company—none of which is collectible—equals 25% of total accounts receivable, an amount which is considerably in excess of what was determined to be an adequate allowance for uncollectible accounts at the close of the preceding year.

Instructions How should Cosmetics Distributors, Inc., record the write-off of the Sandison Company receivable, if it is using the allowance method of accounting for uncollectible accounts? Justify your suggested treatment.

Case 6-3 The annual report for Year 10 of National Systems Corporation, which operates a group of correspondence and resident schools, includes the following relating to contracts receivable and sales:

Under current assets:	
Contracts receivable, less allowance for doubtful accounts of $3,228,180	
(Note 2)	$ 6,599,399
Under current liabilities:	
Estimated costs to service contracts	$ 264,281
Unearned tuition income (Note 2)	1,074,226
In income statement:	
Sales, net of discounts and allowances of $2,076,911	$14,350,698
Provision for doubtful contracts	3,863,800

Note 2—Contracts receivable:

Students in home study courses enter into contracts which contain various payment plans, generally for a term of one to three years. Similarly, home study courses are generally completed over a term of one to three years. Income on home study courses and estimated cost to service the contracts are recorded when the contract is received.

Many of the contracts receivable are due from resident students (Atlantic School, Inc.) and represent advance registrations for classes which will begin subsequent to December 31, Year 10. Tuition income on these contracts and a portion of tuition applicable to the class in progress at December 31, Year 10, net of an allowance for cancellations, has been deferred and will be credited to income as earned over the period of attendance.

It is estimated that gross contracts receivable of approximately $1,900,000 at December 31, Year 10 were not expected to be realized within one year. It is not practical, however, for the Company to separately state the long-term portion of contracts receivable in the accompanying consolidated balance sheet due to the difficulty in determining the allowance for doubtful contracts relating to the long-term contracts receivable.

Instructions Briefly evaluate the accounting practices of National Systems Corporation. Your answer should refer to such accounting concepts as revenue realization, matching of costs and revenue, conservatism, objectivity, and classification of contracts receivable as current based on the length of the operating cycle.

Case 6-4 You have been requested by Acme Restaurants, Inc., a national hotel restaurateur, to evaluate certain accounting treatments proposed by Acme's treasurer regarding a contract for Acme to operate the restaurant of the new Rocklin Hotel for 30 years. A condition necessary for securing the contract was that Acme would aid in financing the new hotel by loaning Rocklin $300,000 in addition to paying a normal rental for the facilities. It is estimated that the operations will yield pre-tax profits of $150,000 annually to Acme.

The $300,000 loan will be for 30 years with no payment unless the contract is canceled by Rocklin. Interest is to accrue at 4% per year compounded annually for the first 20 years, and no interest is to accrue during the last 10 years. After 20 years, Acme will cancel 10% of the principal and accrued interest each year. If Rocklin should cancel the contract, the uncanceled principal and interest would become payable immediately.

Acme's treasurer has proposed accounting for the transaction over the contract life as a loan receivable with interest accruing at 4% per year for the first 20 years and the unpaid principal plus accrued interest being charged off at 10% per year over the last 10 years. The treasurer's reasoning is that this accounting treatment will be in accordance with the terms of the legal documents and with the accounting treatment that Rocklin plans to employ. Also, the interest income for each of the first 20 years would enhance earnings during an anticipated growth period and the income tax effect for the first 20 years will be offset in the last 10 years of the contract.

Because the amounts involved will be material, Acme requested your opinion to avoid any statement presentation problems at the end of the year.

Instructions

a Does the treasurer's proposed accounting for the contract constitute proper presentation on the financial statements? Support your conclusions by discussing the effects of the proposed treatment on (1) the income statement and (2) the balance sheet. State any alternatives you believe might be preferable.

b What disclosure, if any, would you include in Acme's financial statements in regard to the agreement with Rocklin?

PROBLEMS

Group A

6A-1 The accountant for Jenkins Company was hired at the beginning of the current year. At the end of the year, before making any adjusting entries, he prepares a trial balance which includes the following items:

	Debit	Credit
Accounts receivable	$80,000	
Notes receivable (received in exchange for accounts receivable)	10,000	
Allowance for uncollectible accounts	2,360	
Sales		$610,000
Sales returns and allowances	2,950	
Sales discounts.	5,180	

Instructions Prepare the appropriate adjusting entry to provide for estimated uncollectible accounts under each of the following independent assumptions. Explain the basis for each entry:

a Company experience indicates that 80% of all sales are credit sales and that on the average 2% of gross credit sales prove uncollectible.

b An analysis of the aging of accounts receivable indicates that potential uncollectibles at the end of the year amount to $5,000.

c Company policy is to maintain an allowance for uncollectible accounts equal to 4% of outstanding trade receivables, including notes received from customers.

d The allowance for uncollectible accounts is increased by 1% of gross sales, and an allowance for sales discounts of $1,000 on outstanding accounts receivable is to be established.

6A-2 The following information for Cove Marine Supply Company appears in the balance sheet at December 31, Year 1:

Notes receivable		$15,000	
Less: Notes receivable discounted		9,000	$ 6,000
Accrued interest receivable on Allison note			200
Accounts receivable		$70,000	
Less: Allowance for uncollectible accounts.	$2,800		
Allowance for sales discounts	1,000	3,800	66,200

The notes receivable consist of the following:

Six-month 8% note from James Allison dated July 31, Year 1	$6,000
60-day 6% note from Ed Barnes dated Nov. 15, Year 1. This note was discounted	
at Western Bank on Nov. 30, Year 1	9,000

A summary of transactions relating to notes and accounts receivable during January of Year 2 are as follows:

Jan. 11 Received a 90-day, 6% note from a customer, Peter Campo, in exchange for an account receivable of $1,800.

Jan. 13   Collected from Jane Reeves an account receivable written off in Year 1, $217.

Jan. 15   Notice was received from Western Bank that Ed Barnes paid the $9,000 note due Jan. 14.

Jan. 20   Uncollectible accounts of $1,200 from several customers were written off.

Jan. 30   Received payment on Allison note, including interest of $240.

Jan. 31   Sales on account for the month, $172,150.

Jan. 31   Collections on accounts receivable, excluding Reeves account:
   From balance outstanding on December 31, Year 1, after sales discounts of $750, $60,000.
   From current month's sales, after sales discounts of $1,350, $92,000.
   Debit Sales Discounts for all discounts allowed.

Jan. 31   Recorded accrued interest on note from Peter Campo for 20 days.

Jan. 31   Aging of accounts receivable shows that $3,500 is required in the Allowance for Uncollectible Accounts and $1,400 is required in the Allowance for Sales Discounts.

Instructions

a Record the transactions and other information given for the month of January in journal entry form. The company does not reverse any adjusting entries.

b Show how the information relating to notes and accounts receivable should appear in the balance sheet at January 31, Year 2.

6A-3 The Allowance for Uncollectible Accounts of the Ramsdell Company for the year 1975 is shown below:

Allowance for Uncollectible Accounts

Mar. 31	Write-off, 1973 accounts	3,600	Jan. 1	Balance	13,000
June 30	Write-off, 1974 accounts	4,100	Mar. 31	Provision	3,650
Sept. 30	Write-off, 1974 accounts	6,900	June 30	Provision	3,700
Dec. 31	Write-off, 1975 accounts	13,400	Sept. 30	Provision	4,100
			Dec. 31	Provision	5,500

The company sells on 30-day credit and has followed a practice of charging Uncollectible Accounts Expense in an amount equal to 2% of sales. The accountant regularly prepares quarterly income statements and makes adjusting entries at the end of each quarter in order to state accurately the quarterly net income figure. At the end of 1975, the accountant suggests that an aging be made of accounts receivable to test the adequacy of the Allowance for Uncollectible Accounts. The aging of receivables at December 31, 1975, follows:

Current accounts, outstanding 30 days or less	$160,000
31–60 days old	45,200
61–120 days old	30,000
121 days–6 months old	11,000
Over 6 months old	12,800
Balance in control account at Dec. 31, 1975	$259,000

After discussion with the sales manager of the company, the accountant estimated that the following percentages represented a reasonable estimate of the uncollectible accounts in each category: current accounts, 3%; 31 to 60 days old, 5%; 61 to 120 days old, 10%; 121 days to 6 months old, 20%; over 6 months old, 50%.

Instructions

a On the basis of this information, test the adequacy of the balance in the company's Allowance for Uncollectible Accounts at December 31, 1975.

b Prepare any necessary adjusting journal entry that should be made as a result of your analysis. Books have not been closed for the current year. You should adjust the Uncollectible Accounts Expense for 1975 for any required increase or decrease in the Allowance for Uncollectible Accounts because the balance at January 1 was a reasonably close estimate of the write-offs applicable to 1973 and 1974 accounts.

6A-4 Double Knit Corporation finances some of its current operations by assigning accounts receivable to a finance company. On July 1 of the current year, it assigned under guarantee accounts receivable amounting to $200,000, the finance company advancing 80% of the accounts assigned, less a commission charge of 2% of the total accounts assigned. Customers are instructed to make payment directly to the finance company. Collections in excess of the loan and finance charges will be remitted to Double Knit Corporation. At this time, the accountant for the Double Knit Corporation transfers any balance in Assigned Accounts Receivable to the regular Accounts Receivable account.

The status of assigned accounts receivable at the end of July and August follows:

July 31 Double Knit Corporation received a statement that the finance company had collected $120,000 of the assigned accounts receivable and had made an additional charge for interest of 1% of assigned accounts outstanding at July 31, this charge to be deducted from the first remittance by the finance company to Double Knit Corporation.

August 31 Double Knit Corporation received a second statement from the finance company, together with a check for the amount due. The statement indicated that the finance company had collected an additional $44,000 and had made an additional charge for interest of 1% of assigned accounts outstanding at August 31.

Instructions

a Prepare the journal entries necessary to record the above transactions on the books of the Double Knit Corporation.

b Show how the information regarding assigned receivables should be presented in the balance sheet (1) at July 31 and (2) at August 31.

6A-5 Harold Arnett operates a small furniture manufacturing business in Michigan. Although sales have been growing rapidly, he has not been able to earn a consistently satisfactory net income because of price competition, losses as a result of excessive inventories, inability to collect on several large accounts, and ineffective controls over manufacturing costs. He likes to pay his bills promptly, but his customers do not. As a result, he is short of cash and cannot start production of a new line of dining room furniture.

In an effort to obtain seasonal financing, he requests a working capital statement from his accountant with instructions to "make it look good." The accountant prepared the following statement for Arnett, Inc., at April 8, 1975:

Current assets:

Cash	$ 2,800
Accounts receivable (*net of $12,000 received from customers as deposits on*	
special orders. No allowance for uncollectibles is used.)	66,000
Merchandise inventory—*at actual cost*	49,150

Receivable from U.S. Treasury for tax refund filed (net of income taxes payable of $4,000 due Apr. 15)		$ 2,800
Receivable from subsidiary company—no due date		34,000
Miscellaneous (all current)		8,250
Total current assets		$163,000
Less: Current liabilities:		
Accounts payable	$34,300	
Accrued wages.	5,000	
Notes and miscellaneous, including property taxes of $1,800 due on Apr. 10, 1975	15,000	54,300
Working capital (current ratio 3 to 1)		$108,700

Arnett presents this statement to three bankers, hoping to obtain a loan of $40,000 for one year. Each turns him down, giving reasons as follows:

Banker A: "We do not extend credit on the basis of partial balance sheets and without an income statement. We also like to see a cash forecast for the coming year. Incidentally, you should hire a certified public accountant who understands generally accepted accounting principles."

Banker B: "You have an exceptionally good working capital position and do not need a loan. Besides, we are fully loaned up at the present time."

Banker C: "Since you do not need the money immediately, I would suggest that you take the following action before we make a final decision on your loan request:

(1) Make a stronger effort to collect your receivables, write off the worthless accounts, and provide an allowance for additional uncollectibles.

(2) Cut production until inventories are reduced, auction some slow-moving items to raise cash, and postpone payments on payables as long as possible.

(3) Obtain the services of an accountant who can help you reduce costs, improve inventory controls, and reduce credit losses.

Instructions

a Briefly evaluate the position taken by each of the bankers.

b Assuming that $6,000 of the accounts are definitely uncollectible, that an allowance of 5% of the remaining receivables is considered adequate, and that the replacement value of inventories is approximately $42,000, prepare a revised summary of working capital for Arnett, Inc., at April 8, 1975.

6A-6 Don Garner, owner of a merchandising firm, has not prepared financial statements for three years, since December 31, Year 1. Garner used the accrual method of accounting and reported income on a calendar-year basis prior to Year 2. During the past three years (Years 2, 3, and 4), Garner has maintained cash records and has entered sales on account in an accounts receivable ledger; however, no general ledger postings have been made.

The balances at the beginning and end of the three-year period accumulated as a result of your examination are presented on page 243.

No accounts receivable have been written off during the three-year period. Garner estimates that the rate of gross profit remains relatively constant from year to year.

Instructions

a Prepare a schedule showing the gross profit on sales for Years 2, 3, and 4. First compute cost of goods sold as a percentage of sales for the three-year period.

b Prepare the adjusting entry necessary to write off uncollectible accounts and

	Dec. 31	
	Year 4	Year 1
Aging of accounts receivable:		
Less than 1 year old	$14,000	$7,700
1–2 years old	1,900	600
2–3 years old	1,400	
Over 3 years old (all uncollectible)	1,100	
	$18,400	$8,300
Inventories	$ 9,400	$5,800
Accounts payable: merchandise purchases	$ 6,500	$4,308

Other information compiled from the records follows:

	Year 4	Year 3	Year 2
Cash received on account, relating to:			
Current year's collections	$104,500	$80,900	$74,400
Accounts of the prior year	8,400	7,500	6,700
Accounts of two years prior	1,000	200	300
Total	$113,900	$88,600	$81,400
Accounts to be written off in addition to the $1,100			
which are over 3 years old	$ 500	$ 820	$ 1,250
Of receivables remaining at end of Year 4, estimated			
uncollectible percentage	10%	50%	80%
Cash sales	$ 15,600	$13,200	$ 8,400
Payments for merchandise purchases	$ 86,900	$70,600	$62,500

then set up an adequate allowance for estimated uncollectibles at the end of Year 4. Debit current year's expense account for the full amount required to establish the allowance for uncollectible accounts.

c Garner wishes to know what percentage of credit sales would be reasonable as an estimate of yearly uncollectible accounts expense in the future, based on the experience of the past three years. Support your recommendation with an orderly schedule.

Group B

6B-1 The following information is taken from the trial balance for the Rock & Roll Music Shop at June 30, the end of its fiscal year:

	Debit	Credit
Notes receivable from customers	$ 20,000	
Accounts receivable	100,000	
Allowance for uncollectible accounts and notes	2,200	

Allowance for sales discounts		$ 1,100
Sales—cash		50,000
Sales—on account		230,000
Sales returns	$2,500	
Sales discounts	3,000	

Accounts written off during the year were charged to the Allowance for Uncollectible Accounts; merchandise returned by customers was recorded in the Sales Returns account; and cash discounts allowed to customers were recorded in the Sales Discounts account.

Instructions

a Prepare an adjusting entry (in compound form) to adjust the Allowance for Uncollectible Accounts and Notes and the Allowance for Sales Discounts under each of the following independent assumptions:

(1) Uncollectible accounts expense for the year is estimated at 2% of sales on account; an allowance for sales discounts is maintained at $1\frac{1}{2}$% of accounts receivable outstanding at the end of the fiscal year.

(2) Aging of accounts and notes receivable indicates that the following balances are required at the end of the fiscal year:

Allowance for uncollectible accounts and notes	$4,250
Allowance for sales discounts	1,920

b Assuming that the Allowance for Uncollectible Accounts and Notes is adjusted to a credit balance of $4,250 and the Allowance for Sales Discounts is increased to $1,920, show how sales and receivables will appear in the financial statements at June 30. Uncollectible accounts expense is reported as an operating expense in the income statement.

6B-2 In auditing the records of the Bray Company for 1975, you discover the following information:

(1) On April 30, 1975, the company received a non-interest-bearing note for $10,900 maturing in one year, as payment for a consulting fee. The fee was originally established at $10,300 but, because the client was short of cash, the company agreed to accept the note. The note was recorded at $10,900 by a debit to Notes Receivable and a credit to Fees Earned. A discount account representing unearned interest is used by the company.

(2) The company sold a piece of real estate on December 31, 1975, for $10,000 in cash and a non-interest-bearing note of $30,000 due in three years. The land had a cost basis of $15,100 and Gain on Sale of Land was credited for $24,900. You ascertain the present value of the note to be approximately $23,100.

(3) A note receivable of $4,000 on which interest receivable of $120 had been recorded was discounted at a bank at a rate of interest higher than the rate on the note. Proceeds of $4,074 were credited to Notes Receivable. The company uses a Notes Receivable Discounted account.

(4) The company has recognized uncollectible accounts expense only as specific receivables were deemed to be worthless. You ascertain that an allowance of $6,200 is required at the end of 1975.

(5) Interest accrued on investment in bonds amounts to $2,025.

(6) Accounts receivable in the amount of $1,810 are considered worthless and an additional provision of $2,100 for possible uncollectible accounts is required at December 31, 1975.

Instructions Prepare an adjusting or correcting entry for each item (1) through (6) above. The accounts are still open for 1975.

6B-3 In 1973, the Pinto Corporation adopted a policy of providing for uncollectible accounts at the rate of 2% of credit sales. A record of the company's experience for the past three years follows:

	1975	1974	1973
Credit sales	$425,000	$380,000	$320,000
Cash collected on credit sales:			
1973			$211,580
1974		$318,420	85,000
1975	$310,000	50,000	14,000
Accounts written off as uncollectible:			
1973			500
1974		5,180	6,800
1975	900	6,400	2,120
		$380,000	$320,000
Balance in accounts receivable at Dec. 31, 1975 .	114,100		
	$425,000		

The company's accountant made no entries or adjustments affecting receivables other than those necessary to record sales, collections from customers, the annual provision for uncollectible accounts, and the write-offs of individual accounts against the allowance account.

The Pinto Corporation engaged you at the end of 1975 to make an examination of its records for the purpose of supporting a loan application. You have the above information available as a basis for determining the adequacy of the allowance for uncollectible accounts. You decide to adjust the allowance to conform to the actual experience relating to uncollectible accounts expense during 1973 and 1974.

Instructions

a Set up ledger accounts for Accounts Receivable, Allowance for Uncollectible Accounts, and Uncollectible Accounts Expense and post all entries as the company's accountant made them.

b Prepare in journal entry form, and post to these accounts, any adjusting entries you deem necessary as of the end of 1975, assuming that the books have not yet been closed. Explain briefly the reasons for your adjustments and the basis for your determination of the proper allowance for uncollectible accounts at December 31, 1975. The company follows a policy of recording corrections of prior years' uncollectible accounts expense in the current year's uncollectible accounts expense.

6B-4 Textile Factors, Inc., was incorporated in December 1974. The capital stock of the company consists of 100,000 shares of $10 par value each, all of which was paid in at par. The company was organized for the purpose of factoring (purchasing) accounts receivable.

Textile Factors, Inc., charges a commission to its clients of 5% of all receivables factored and assumes all credit risks. Besides the commission, an additional 10% of gross receivables is withheld on all purchases and is credited to the Liability to Clients account. This account is used for merchandise returns, etc., made by customers of the clients for which a credit memo would be due. Payments are made to its clients by Textile Factors, Inc., at the end of each month to adjust the Liability to Clients account so that it equals 10% of the uncollected receivables as of the end of the month.

Based on the collection experience of other factoring companies in this area, officials of Textile Factors, Inc., decided to make monthly provisions to Allowance for Uncollectible Accounts based on 1% of all receivables purchased during the month.

The company also decided to recognize commission revenue on only the factored receivables which have been collected; however, for accounting simplicity all commissions are originally credited to Commissions Revenue and an adjustment is made to Unearned Commissions Revenue at the end of each quarter, based on 5% of accounts receivables then outstanding.

Operations of the company during the first quarter of 1975 resulted in the following:

Accounts receivable factored: January	*$400,000*
February	*500,000*
March	*800,000*

Collections on the above accounts receivable totaled $950,000.

General and administrative expenses paid during the period were as follows:

Salaries	*$7,500*
Office rent	*1,500*
Advertising	*800*
Equipment rent	*1,600*
Miscellaneous	*1,450*

On January 31, 1975, a six-month 6% bank loan was obtained for $200,000, with interest payable at maturity.

For the first three months of the year, the company rented all its office furniture and equipment; however, on March 31, 1975, it purchased various office furniture and equipment at a cost of $10,200. This purchase was not recorded in the financial records.

Instructions
a Prepare a work sheet to summarize the activities of the company for the quarter ended March 31, 1975. (Disregard all withholding taxes and the company's liability for FICA and federal income taxes.)
b Prepare a balance sheet for the company at March 31, 1975.

6B-5 John Wells started in business on January 4, 1973, and reported net income of $22,000 in 1973, $35,000 in 1974, and $32,000 in 1975. The books for the year ending December 31, 1975, are closed.

Wells did not use accrual accounting for some items. It was agreed that adjustments should be made in the accounts to report the assets, liabilities, and owner's equity on the accrual method of accounting.

Accounts receivable at the end of each year consisted of the following:

	1973	*1974*	*1975*
Relating to sales made in:			
1973	*$20,000*	*$ 6,000*	*$ 3,000*
1974		*24,000*	*7,500*
1975			*35,000*

Uncollectible accounts expense was recorded when accounts were deemed uncollectible. It was agreed that an allowance for uncollectible accounts should be established at the end of 1975 and should be recognized as follows: Current accounts, 2%; accounts relating to sales of 1974, 5%; accounts relating to sales of 1973, 20%. Uncollectible accounts expense previously recorded and years of sale were:

Uncollectible accounts expense recorded		Uncollectible accounts expense recorded for sales made in		
Year	Amount	1973	1974	1975
1973	$1,500	$1,500		
1974	2,000	1,400	$ 600	
1975	5,500	500	2,000	$3,000
Totals	$9,000	$3,400	$2,600	$3,000

Salaries and insurance were recorded as expense when paid. The amounts of accrued salaries and unexpired insurance at the end of each year were:

	Dec. 31		
	1973	1974	1975
Accrued salaries	$ 800	$ 1,050	$ 1,420
Salaries paid in cash	20,000	25,000	26,500
Unexpired insurance.	600	800	950
Insurance premiums paid.	2,500	2,000	2,200

Instructions
a Determine the required balance in the Allowance for Uncollectible Accounts at December 31, 1975.
b Compute net income for 1975, using the accrual method of accounting. First prepare schedules computing each of the following expenses for 1975, using the accrual method of accounting:
(1) Uncollectible accounts expense
(2) Salaries expense
(3) Insurance expense
c Prepare the compound journal entry required to restate the accounts to a full accrual basis at December 31, 1975. Close the net adjustment to net income for the three-year period to the John Wells, Capital account.

6B-6 You are examining Anton Corporation's financial statement for the year ended December 31, 1975. Your analysis of the 1975 entries in the Notes Receivable account is presented below:

Date 1975	Analysis of transactions	Notes Receivable Debit	Credit
Jan. 1	Balance	$118,000	
Feb. 28	Received 6%, $25,000 note due Oct. 28, 1975, from Daley, whose account was past due. (Memorandum entry only.)		

Feb. 28	Discounted Daley note at 6%			$ 24,960
Mar. 29	Received non-interest-bearing demand note from Edge, the corporation's treasurer, for a loan	$ 6,200		
Aug. 30	Received principal and interest due from Allen and, in accordance with agreement, two principal payments in advance			34,200
Sept. 4	Paid protest fee on note dishonored by Charnes		5	
Nov. 1	Received check dated Feb. 1, 1976 in settlement of Bailey note. The check was included in cash on hand on Dec. 31, 1975.			8,120
Nov. 3	Paid protest fee and maturity value of Daley note to bank. Note discounted Feb. 28, 1975, was dishonored		26,031	
Dec. 27	Accepted fixtures with a market value of $24,000 in full settlement from Daley			24,000
Dec. 31	Received check dated Jan. 3, 1976, from Edge in payment of Mar. 29, 1975, note. (The check was included in petty cash until Jan. 2, 1976, when it was returned to Edge in exchange for a new demand note for the same amount.)			6,200
Dec. 31	Received principal and interest on Charnes note			42,437
Dec. 31	Accrued interest on Allen note for six months		1,200	
	Totals		$151,436	$139,917

The following additional information is available:
(1) Balances at January 1, 1975, were a debit of $1,400 in the Accrued Interest Receivable account and a credit of $400 relating to Bailey's note in the Unearned Interest Revenue account. The $118,000 debit balance in the Notes Receivable Account consisted of the following three notes:

 a Allen note dated Aug. 31, 1971, payable in annual installments plus accrued interest at 6% each Aug. 31. . . . . $70,000

 b Bailey note discounted to Anton at 6% on Nov. 1, 1974, due Nov. 1, 1975 8,000

 c Charnes note for $40,000 plus 6% interest, dated Dec. 31, 1974, due on Sept. 1, 1975 40,000

(2) No entries were made during 1975 to the Accrued Interest Receivable account or the Unearned Interest Revenue account, and only one entry for a credit of $1,200 on December 31 appeared in the Interest Revenue account.
(3) All notes were from trade customers unless otherwise indicated.
(4) Debits and credits offsetting related credit and debit entries to Notes Receivable were correctly recorded unless the facts indicate otherwise.

Instructions Prepare a working paper to adjust or correct each entry and to properly reclassify it, if necessary. Enter your adjustments in the proper columns to correspond with the date of each entry and use a Notes Receivable Discounted account when notes are discounted. Do not combine related entries for different dates. Your completed working paper will provide the basis for one compound journal entry to correct all entries to Notes Receivable and related accounts for 1975. Use the following headings for your working paper:

Date 1975	Analysis of transactions	Notes Receivable		Adjustment or reclassification required				
				Notes Receivable	Accounts Receivable	Interest Revenue	Other accounts	
		Debit	Credit	Debit (Credit)	Debit (Credit)	Debit (Credit)	Account title	Debit (Credit)

CHAPTER 7

Current liabilities

A *liability* is an obligation, based on a past transaction, to convey assets or perform services in the future. Liabilities are recorded when obligations are incurred, and are measured at the amounts to be paid or at the present value of these amounts.[1] The distinction between current and long-term liabilities is important in evaluating the financial position of a business and in forecasting its ability to meet maturing commitments. This chapter deals with the problems of accounting for current liabilities; long-term liabilities are discussed in Chapters 18 to 20.

The distinction between current and long-term liabilities

Traditionally, one year marked the accounting boundary between current and long-term liabilities. The maturity-within-a-year rule was simple and easy to follow, but arbitrary. When strictly applied it sometimes caused a misleading financial picture, particularly when the operating cycle of a business exceeded one year.

The modern convention is that current liabilities include: (1) all obligations for which payment will require the use of existing current assets or the creation of other current liabilities, and (2) all other obligations that will probably be paid from current assets within one year. The definition of current liabilities is logically correlated with the definition of current

---

[1] These guidelines for recording and measuring liabilities are taken from *Statement of the Accounting Principles Board, No. 4,* AICPA (New York: 1970), p. 73.

assets. Thus current liabilities include obligations for items which have entered into the operating cycle, such as payables to suppliers and employees, collections received in advance of the delivery of goods or performance of services, and accruals for rentals, taxes, etc. Obligations incurred outside of the operating cycle and payable more than one year hence are considered long-term liabilities.

The importance of current liabilities

Short-term credit is an important source of financing for most businesses. In part, its use is involuntary; current obligations such as accounts payable and other accrued liabilities regularly arise from business operations. An important element, however, results from a conscious decision by management to obtain credit from suppliers and to borrow from banks and others to meet cash needs during periods of expanding or peak activity.

Financial analysts keep a close watch on the amount of current liabilities, the relationship of current assets to current liabilities, and the relationship between cash balances and current liabilities. These relationships are considered by many analysts to be important indicators of financial stability and *solvency* (ability to pay debts as they mature).

The omission or understatement of a current liability is accompanied by an understatement of assets, an overstatement of long-term liabilities, or an overstatement of stockholders' equity resulting from an overstatement of net income. An error in distinguishing between short- and long-term liabilities has a direct effect on the amount of working capital. A complete record of current obligations and their due dates is essential in preparing cash budgets and forecasts of financing requirements. Accurately measuring and reporting current liabilities in the accounting records and financial statements of a business is thus an important step in the accounting process.

Valuation of current liabilities

A logical measure of any liability at the time it is incurred is the *present value* of the required future outlay of money.[2] In practice, however, current liabilities are usually carried in accounting records at face value. The difference between the present value of a current liability and the amount that will ultimately be paid at maturity is usually not large because of the

---

[2] The present value of a liability is the sum of expected future payments discounted to the present date at an appropriate rate of interest. *APB Opinion No. 21* states that presentation of liabilities at their discounted present value is not required for "payables arising from transactions with customers or suppliers in the normal course of business which are due in customary trade terms not exceeding approximately one year." The Opinion is also not intended to apply to estimates of warranty obligations assumed in connection with sales of property, goods, or services.

short time period involved. Thus the slight overstatement of liabilities that results from recording current obligations at maturity value may often be excused as a compromise of accuracy in favor of convenience.

When is a prospective future outlay a liability?

Every going business faces the prospect of a wide variety of future cash outlays in order to continue in operation. It must, for example, buy materials, pay wages, pay for services, replace equipment, and pay taxes. We might take an extreme view and consider the present value of all these future outlays as the total debt of the company at any given time. This would correspond to the concept of assets as the present value of all future cash inflows. These theoretical extremes, however, are beyond the accountant's powers of measurement; as a practical matter, we need a basis for establishing some practical limits on the liability concept.

A logical starting point is to say that the amounts of all legally enforceable debts should appear as liabilities on financial statements. But what about legal obligations that are highly uncertain in amount? Since accounting liabilities must be measured, the ability to determine valuation with reasonable accuracy is important. Then we must consider whether a strict legal test excludes any obligations to convey assets that are significant in an economic sense. The process of determining periodic income may require that a valuation be placed on future outlays that result from past transactions, because the cost incurred should be deducted from revenue.

These two elements, *measurability* and *relation to past events,* lead us to conclude that liabilities should be defined to include all future outlays that result from transactions or events of the past (not the future) and that can be estimated (measured) with reasonable accuracy. As we shall see in later sections of this chapter and in the chapters dealing with long-term liabilities, there are some legal obligations so uncertain in amount that they cannot be measured, and there are future outlays relating to past events and transactions that should be recognized as liabilities even though they are not legal obligations.

Because we are dealing with a *future* payment, the element of uncertainty plays an important role in the problem of accounting for current liabilities. To emphasize the importance of the degree of uncertainty, we shall discuss some of the specific problems relating to current liabilities under the following headings: (1) definitely determinable liabilities, (2) liabilities dependent on operating results, (3) estimated liabilities, and (4) contingent liabilities.

DEFINITELY DETERMINABLE LIABILITIES

Liabilities in this category are the result of contracts or the operation of legal statutes such that the amount of the obligation and its due date are known with reasonable certainty. The accounting problem is to ascertain that the obligation exists and to record it properly in the accounting records.

Trade accounts and notes payable

The accounting procedures for recording and controlling the payments for the purchase of goods and services are usually systematized so that the existence, amount, and due date of such liabilities are readily determinable. The accountant should give particular attention to transactions occurring near the end of one accounting period and at the beginning of the next period to see that the record of goods and services received is consistent with that of the liability. For example, if goods are received near the end of the period but an invoice has not arrived, the goods may have been counted as part of the ending inventory but the recording of the liability may have been overlooked.

As in the valuation of accounts receivable, cash discounts applicable to accounts payable should be anticipated and recognized by a debit to Allowance for Purchase Discounts and a credit to Purchase Discounts. The Allowance for Purchase Discounts should be deducted from Accounts Payable on the balance sheet. As an alternative, Accounts Payable may be recorded net of purchase discounts and only Purchase Discounts Lost recorded in the accounts.

Loan obligations

In this category are included short-term notes (including *commercial paper*[3]) issued as evidence of borrowing transactions, and any portion of long-term indebtedness that matures currently. If long-term debt currently maturing will be retired from sinking funds, from the proceeds of new long-term indebtedness, or through conversion into stock, current funds are not required and the debt should be reported as noncurrent, accompanied by a note disclosing the plan for its liquidation.

No special problems arise in connection with the issuance of short-term notes payable bearing the prevailing rate of interest. Cash or Accounts Payable is debited and Notes Payable is credited at the time the notes are issued. If notes payable bear an unrealistically low interest rate or are non-interest-bearing, the notes should be recorded at no more than present value in order to recognize the actual cost of borrowing or any other obligations implicit in the borrowing contract.

To illustrate, refer to the situation on page 229 in which a supplier borrows $108,000 on December 31, Year 1, from the Cashrich Corporation at no interest when the going rate of interest is 8%. The supplier

---

[3] Commercial paper (as defined in Chapter 5) is the term used in the money market for short-term unsecured promissory notes issued by corporations and sold to investors, generally other companies.

agrees to repay the note on December 31, Year 2, and to sell lumber to the Cashrich Corporation for one year at a favorable price. The borrowing by the supplier on December 31 of Year 1 may be recorded as follows, assuming that a Discount on Notes Payable account is not used:

Cash	108,000	
Notes Payable		100,000
Contractual Obligation to Customer		8,000

To record non-interest-bearing note issued to customer. Present value of note, $108,000 \div 1.08 = \$100,000$.

The account Contractual Obligation to Customer would be classified as a current liability because it represents a legal obligation to sell lumber at a favorable price. This account represents, in effect, an advance from the customer (Cashrich Corporation). The customer paid $8,000 for the privilege of buying lumber at prices below the prevailing market price and the supplier received $108,000 in exchange for two promises: (1) to repay $100,000 plus interest at 8% one year hence and (2) to supply the customer's lumber needs at $8,000 below the prices charged to other customers. When the supplier makes payment on the note at December 31 of Year 2, the following entry would be required:

Notes Payable	100,000	
Contractual Obligation to Customer	8,000	
Interest Expense	8,000	
Cash		108,000
Sales		8,000

To record payment on non-interest-bearing note, the implicit interest expense on the note, and to recognize obligation assigned to the contract with customer as additional revenue.

The procedure illustrated above recognizes interest expense for Year 2, $8,000 ($100,000 $\times$ 8%) and the full implicit value of sales made pursuant to the borrowing contract with the customer.

Dividends payable

Cash dividends are declared by action of the board of directors. At the date of declaration, the corporation incurs a legal obligation to pay the amount of the dividend at the specified time, and stockholders gain creditor status to the extent of the declared amount. Since the time between declaration and payment is short, dividends payable in cash are always a current liability. Accumulated but undeclared dividends on preferred stock are normally disclosed by footnote, but there is no legal obligation to pay dividends on preferred stock until they are declared. Undistributed *stock dividends* should not be included among current liabilities, because no cash outlay will be required; the account Stock Dividends to Be Distributed should be classified as part of the stock-holders' equity.

Advances from customers

When a customer makes payment in advance of performance by the seller, a liability is created. The selling company is obligated to perform by delivery of goods or services, or to refund the advance if it fails to perform. Generally, the cost of performance will not be as great as the advance, since there is an element of unrealized profit in the price charged. The profit element emerges only with performance by the selling company; prior to this time the selling company is essentially a trustee of the funds received from customers. As performance is made under the terms of the agreement, the amount of the liability diminishes and should be transferred to a revenue account. The costs of performance are recorded as expenses and income (or loss) emerges.

Advances from customers which are expected to be realized as revenue within a year or within the company's operating cycle should be classified as current liabilities. Examples include deposits on sales orders received, magazine subscriptions received in advance, and billings in excess of costs incurred on long-term construction contracts. Advances from customers which are not expected to be realized as revenue within one year or the operating cycle should be classified as noncurrent liabilities. It is possible to argue that certain short-term unearned revenues, such as rentals and interest received in advance, should be classified as noncurrent liabilities because the realization of such revenues is not expected to require current expenditures. Although this position has some merit, it has not been widely accepted, because the amounts involved are generally immaterial and because it may be difficult to estimate the expenditures to be incurred in the process of realizing short-term unearned revenue items.

Deposits received from customers for containers will be refunded when the containers are returned (usually within a short period); therefore, such deposits should be classified among current liabilities.

Accrued liabilities

The term *accrued liabilities* (sometimes improperly referred to as *accrued expenses*) is used to designate obligations that come into existence as the result of past contractual commitments or as the result of tax legislation such as income, property, and sales tax laws. Because of their materiality, tax liabilities should be listed separately among the current liabilities. Most other accruals may be combined under one heading, or, as in the case of accrued interest, combined with the liability to which they relate. The problems involved in determining some types of accrued liabilities require special mention.

Liabilities relating to payrolls

Because employees are usually paid after the services have been performed, an obligation for unpaid salaries or wages may exist as of a given date. The employer is by law a tax collector for the federal and state governments with respect to employees' old age, survivor and disability insurance tax, a hospitalization insurance tax, and income taxes withheld from employees' salaries. By agreement with employees, an employer may also withhold from salaries and wages amounts for such items as union dues, state disability insurance, group life insurance, pension plans, and for purchase of savings bonds.

The accountant should be familiar with the general terms of payroll tax legislation, which are reviewed briefly below.

Social Security Taxes (FICA) The Federal Insurance Contributions Act provides for old age and survivors' benefits for qualified employees and members of their families, while hospitalization insurance (Medicare) provides for certain medical costs for those over sixty-five years of age. These payroll taxes are often referred to as *social security taxes* and are levied against both the employer and the employee at the same rate, based on the employee's gross earnings. Both the rates and base earnings have been increased many times in recent years and are scheduled to change in the future.[4] For purposes of discussion and problems in this chapter, we shall assume that a rate of 5% applies for both the employer and employee on earnings up to $9,000.

FICA taxes apply to employers of one or more persons, with certain exceptions. The amount of both the employer's and employee's FICA tax must be remitted monthly (or more frequently if the amounts withheld are large) by the employer to an authorized depositary, unless the combined amount of old-age benefit taxes and withheld income taxes is less than $200. If the cumulative liability does not reach $200 until the third month of the quarter, payment is not required until the quarterly return is filed. A tax return showing employee earnings and tax withheld must be filed quarterly by the employer with the Director of Internal Revenue.

---

[4]For example, the actual FICA tax rate in 1972 was 5.2% on earnings up to $9,000; for 1973 the tax was 5.85% on earnings up to $10,800; and for 1974, the tax was 5.85% on earnings up to $13,200.

Federal Unemployment Insurance Tax   The Federal Unemployment Tax Act (FUTA) provides for a system of unemployment insurance established in cooperation between state and federal governments. Employers of one or more persons, with certain exceptions similar to those under FICA legislation, are subject to the federal tax. Recently, the tax has been levied on the first $4,200 of compensation paid to each employee during the calendar year. The federal tax is levied only on employers at a rate of 3.2% (as of 1974). However, a credit against the federal tax up to 2.7% of taxable salaries and wages is allowed for contributions which an employer is required to make to a state plan for unemployment compensation. Thus when an employer is subject to a tax of 2.7% or more under state unemployment legislation, the tax due the federal government is only 0.5% of taxable salaries and wages. The return for each calendar year is due annually on or before January 31 of the succeeding year. Employers must make quarterly deposits when these taxes are in excess of $100.

State Unemployment Insurance Tax   The provisions of the various state laws governing unemployment compensation differ from the federal law, and differ among various states. Most state laws tax only employers, but a few apply taxes to employees as well. Provisions with respect to the classes of employers that are exempt, the number of employees that are required before an employer is subject to the tax, the rate of tax applicable, and the limit of taxable salaries and wages to which the tax applies are different in various states.

An important feature of all the state unemployment compensation laws is the *merit rating* provision, under which a reduction in the tax rate levied by the state is granted to employers whose unemployment experience is better than a specified standard. Thus, although the state law may provide for a normal unemployment tax rate of 2.7% or higher, employers whose employee turnover rate is low may be entitled to a lower state tax rate. In order to make this type of incentive toward stable employment effective, the federal law provides that an employer who pays less than 2.7% to any state under a merit rating system is still entitled to the full 2.7% credit against the federal tax.

Income Tax Withholding   Employers of one or more persons are required to withhold from an employee's earnings an amount approximating the federal income tax due on those earnings. A number of cities and states which levy income taxes also require that income taxes be withheld from employees' earnings. An employer is required to withhold income taxes only if the legal relationship of employer and employee exists; this excludes payments to persons who perform services as independent contractors. Certain other limited classes of wage payments are exempt from withholding.

The amount of income tax withheld is determined by formula or may be read from tables prepared by the government; it varies according to the length of the pay period, the amount of taxable earnings, and the marital status and number of dependents of the employee. The employer makes payment of income taxes withheld and FICA taxes at regular intervals, as described in the discussion of FICA taxes.

Vacation Pay Paid vacations are today a standard element of the employment contract of most employees. The right to a vacation with pay usually depends upon the length of employment; the length of vacation often increases after an employee has completed a given number of years of service.

When does the liability for vacation pay come into existence for accounting purposes? Does it arise only when an employee has met all the conditions, or does it accrue through the employment period? From the standpoint of cost determination, it seems clear that an employee who earns $200 per week and is entitled to a two-week vacation is paid $10,400 for 50 weeks of actual productive services, or $208 per week. This reasoning suggests that vacation pay accrues at the rate of $8 per week during the 50 productive weeks prior to the vacation.

Whether a definite legal liability exists depends on the terms of the employment contract. If the paid vacation is contingent upon the employee remaining in service until his vacation period, the legal obligation does not arise until this condition has been met. However, an economic obligation exists that meets all the tests of a determinable liability, since a company may estimate its total liability for vacation pay on the basis of its employee turnover experience. Generally, the probability is high that a future outlay for vacation pay will be made and recognition of a liability is warranted.

Recording Payroll Liabilities The volume of clerical work and computation that goes into the preparation of a payroll would astound the average employee. It is not surprising that the earliest applications of electronic data-processing equipment were in the payroll accounting area. Fortunately we are here concerned primarily with summary payroll data.

The liability aspect of the problem of accounting for payroll centers on the amounts due employees, the liabilities associated with withholdings from employees' earnings, and the employer's share of payroll taxes and fringe benefits. There is also a cost side to the problem. The total costs incurred for employee services, including gross earnings, payroll taxes, and other fringe benefit costs, must be allocated to functions or departments to provide useful cost information for management.

To illustrate the kinds of data necessary to record a payroll, we have assumed some payroll data for a manufacturing company for the month of August. Because this is the eighth month of the year, some employees will have received salaries or wages in excess of the limits subject to payroll taxes, so that the amount subject to payroll tax will be less than the total amount earned. We have also assumed that the company is entitled to a merit rate of 2% on state unemployment taxes.

A summary of the salaries and wages subject to payroll taxes is presented below:

Classification of expense	Salaries and wages earned	Earnings subject to payroll taxes		
		FICA taxes, 5%	Federal unemployment tax, 0.5%	State unemployment tax, 2%
Direct labor	$ 41,000	$40,000	$30,000	$35,000
Indirect labor	27,000	24,000	20,000	23,000
Sales salaries	18,000	14,000	10,000	12,000
Administrative salaries .	14,000	2,000	–0–	–0–
Total	$100,000	$80,000	$60,000	$70,000

The employer's total payroll costs, including fringe benefits, are summarized below:

Payroll costs	Total	Direct labor	Indirect labor	Sales salaries	Administrative salaries
Salaries and wages earned	$100,000	$41,000	$27,000	$18,000	$14,000
FICA taxes	4,000	2,000	1,200	700	100
Federal unemployment taxes	300	150	100	50	–0–
State unemployment taxes	1,400	700	460	240	–0–
Vacation pay accrued . . .	4,800	1,600	1,200	1,100	900
Total payroll costs	$110,500	$45,450	$29,960	$20,090	$15,000

The amounts withheld from employees' wages are as follows:

Total salaries and wages		$100,000
Withholdings:		
FICA taxes	$ 4,000	
Income tax withheld	14,000	
Hospital insurance premiums (private plans)	1,500	19,500
Employees' net take-home pay		$ 80,500

Assuming that payroll taxes are combined with gross earnings for accounting purposes, the following summary entry would be prepared to record the payroll for the month of August:

Direct Labor.	45,450	
Factory Overhead—Indirect Labor	29,960	
Selling Expense—Salaries	20,090	
Administrative Expense—Salaries	15,000	
FICA Taxes Payable		8,000
Liability for Income Tax Withheld		14,000
Hospital Insurance Premiums Payable		1,500
Federal Unemployment Taxes Payable.		300
State Unemployment Taxes Payable		1,400
Vacation Pay Payable		4,800
Accrued Payroll.		80,500
To record payroll for the month of August.		

Payroll taxes on employers become a legal liability when salaries and wages are paid, rather than at the time the services by employees are rendered. For example, if salaries and wages accrued at year-end amount to $1,500, payroll taxes would not be levied on these earnings until next year. As a practical matter, many businesses do not accrue payroll taxes at the end of the calendar year because the legal liability does not accrue until the following year when the wages are paid. Although this practice does not follow the accrual concept of accounting, it may be viewed as acceptable if consistently followed or if the amounts are not material.

Property taxes

Property taxes, based on the assessed value of real and personal property, usually represent the primary source of revenue for local governmental units. From the viewpoint of the business owning property, they are a part of the cost of the services of such property. Legally such taxes arise as of a particular date, usually on the so-called *lien date,* the day established by law on which the taxes become a lien against the property. When property is sold or transferred, the lien date determines whether the buyer or the seller is legally liable for payment of the tax.

The accounting issues relating to property taxes are: (1) When should the liability for property taxes be recorded? (2) To which period does the corresponding tax expense relate? The legal liability for property taxes arises on the lien date, and there is thus a clear basis for recognizing the liability at this time. Some accountants argue, however, that the liability accrues throughout the tax year. Since property taxes are expenses associated with the right to use property during the fiscal year of the taxing authority, it seems reasonable to charge the tax expense against revenue during this time period.

The following illustration will help to clarify the issues. Assume that a company has property subject to property taxes by city and county governmental units. The fiscal year of the city and county runs from July 1 to June 30. Property taxes of $36,000 were assessed against the company on January 1, covering the fiscal year starting on the following July 1. The lien date is July 1 and taxes are payable in two installments of $18,000 each on December 10 and on April 10.

On page 262, the accounting for property taxes for the period from July 1 to December 31 is illustrated under two alternative methods. Using method A, the property tax liability is recorded on the lien date (July 1) and the deferred property taxes (an asset) are amortized monthly throughout the following 12-month period; using method B, property taxes are accrued monthly during the fiscal year of the taxing authority.

Under method A, deferred property taxes of $18,000 will appear as a current asset in the December 31 balance sheet, and this amount will be amortized at the rate of $3,000 per month during the first six months of the next calendar year; under method B, neither a prepayment nor a liability is reported in the balance sheet at December 31. Since the liability comes into existence on the lien date (July 1), method A provides a more complete record of the company's financial position and is preferred by the authors. The AICPA, however, has taken the position that "monthly accrual on the taxpayer's books during the fiscal period of the taxing authority for which the taxes are levied"[5] is generally the most acceptable method.

LIABILITIES DEPENDENT ON OPERATING RESULTS

The amount of certain obligations cannot be measured until operating results are known. These include income taxes, bonuses, profit-sharing distributions, royalties, and contributions to employee retirement plans. There is no particular accounting problem in determining such liabilities at the end of a fiscal year, when the operating results are in. For *interim* (monthly or quarterly) financial statements, however, difficulties may arise in estimating some of these obligations in advance of the final determination of annual net income.

Income taxes

The most familiar example of a liability whose amount is dependent upon operating results is income taxes payable. Individual proprietors and

[5] *Accounting Research and Terminology Bulletins—Final Edition,* AICPA (New York: 1961), pp. 83–84.

Explanation	Method A		Method B	
July 1. Liability for property taxes of $36,000 comes into existence on July 1, the lien date.	Deferred Property Taxes . . . . . Property Taxes Payable .	36,000 36,000	No entry	
At the end of July, August, September, October, and November. To record monthly property taxes expense, $3,000.	Property Taxes Expense . . . . . Deferred Property Taxes	3,000 3,000	Property Taxes Expense . . . . . Property Taxes Payable .	3,000 3,000
Dec. 10. Payment of first installment of property tax bill, $18,000.	Property Taxes Payable . . . . . . Cash	18,000 18,000	Property Taxes Payable . . . . . . Deferred Property Taxes . . . . . Cash	15,000 3,000 18,000
Dec. 31. To record monthly property taxes expense.	Property Taxes Expense . . . . . Deferred Property Taxes	3,000 3,000	Property Taxes Expense . . . . . Deferred Property Taxes	3,000 3,000

members of a partnership are subject to personal income taxes on their share of the profits of the business entity. Business units organized as proprietorships or partnerships are not taxable entities, and income tax liabilities do not appear on their balance sheets.

Corporations, estates, and trusts are separate taxable entities in the eyes of the law and are subject to income taxes. Income tax liabilities therefore will appear in the balance sheets of such organizations. In most cases, corporations are required to make payments in advance of the estimated income tax liability. If payments of the estimated tax are not made when due, there is a penalty of 6% of the underpayment. The remaining tax not covered by the estimated payments is payable on March 15 of the year following the taxable calendar year. Calendar-year corporations may, however, elect to pay the remaining tax in two equal installments (on March 15 and June 15).[6]

The estimated tax payments can be recorded in a Prepaid Income Taxes account or as debits to Income Taxes Payable if the accrued tax liability had been previously recorded on the books. A credit balance in Income Taxes Payable would be reported as a current liability. If U.S. government securities are held which can be used to pay income taxes and are clearly intended to be used to pay income taxes, they may be deducted from the estimated tax liability in the balance sheet. Most securities now issued by governments are not designed specifically for the payment of taxes and therefore should not be deducted from taxes payable.

Income taxes on interim statements

When monthly or quarterly financial statements are prepared, an estimate of accrued income tax liability must be made before the actual tax liability for the year is known. If income taxes were assessed at a flat rate, it would be a relatively simple matter to compute the tax on the income to date. However, the progressive feature of the corporate income tax raises the question whether the income to date should be annualized and the proportionate income tax accrued for the period to date, or whether the first amount of income earned should be taxed at the lower rate. A reasonable solution is to make the "best estimate of the effective tax rate expected to be applicable for the full fiscal year."[7] A less satisfactory solution is to follow the *marginal principle* and accrue the tax applicable to each additional dollar of income.

A similar question arises in businesses having a seasonal income pattern. For example, high income experienced early in the year may be offset by losses during the latter part of the year. If we follow the marginal

---

[6] These rules were applicable in 1973; changes in tax rates as well as rules regarding estimated tax payments are frequently made.
[7] *APB Opinion No. 28,* "Interim Financial Reporting," AICPA (New York: 1973), pp. 527–528.

principle, the income tax liability (in terms of the actual amount that will ultimately be paid) will be overstated during the early part of the year and must be adjusted downward during the latter part of the year when losses are sustained.

Interperiod Allocation of Income Taxes A more serious problem in accounting for income tax obligations arises because of differences between *taxable* income and *accounting* income. As a result of such differences and high income tax rates, the amount of income tax liability incurred by a corporation in any given year may differ materially from the amount of income tax expense reported in the income statement. Many companies report Prepaid Income Taxes as an asset or Deferred Income Taxes Payable as a liability. These accounts may be current or noncurrent, depending on the reasons for the differences between taxable income and income reported in the income statement. Because the issues are complex, an extensive coverage of this topic is presented in Chapter 20.

Bonus and profit-sharing plans

Contractual agreements covering rents, royalties, or employee compensation sometimes call for conditional payments in an amount dependent upon revenue or income earned during the period. We shall use the term *bonus* to describe conditional payments of this type.

Conditional expenses based on revenue cause little difficulty. For example, if a rental contract calls for a fixed rent of $100 per month and 1% of all sales over $100,000 per year, the fixed rental obligation accrues at the rate of $100 per month and when sales reach $100,000 each additional dollar of sales creates an additional rent obligation.

Some bonus plans provide for a bonus based on income. The plans are generally drawn so that the income figure to be used in determining the bonus is clearly defined. The bonus, for example, may be based on: (1) income before income taxes and the bonus, (2) income after the bonus but before income taxes, or (3) *net* income after both the bonus and income taxes.

To illustrate the calculations involved, assume that a company has an incentive compensation plan under which a branch manager receives 20% of all income over $20,000 earned by his branch. Income for a given branch amounted to $80,000 before either the bonus or income taxes. Assume for purposes of illustration that income taxes are 40% of income. The bonus under each of the three plans is computed as follows:

1 Contract provides that bonus shall be computed on income in excess of $20,000 but before deducting income taxes and the bonus:

Bonus = .2($80,000 − $20,000) = **$12,000**

2 Contract provides that the bonus shall be computed on income in excess of $20,000 after deducting the bonus but before income taxes have been deducted:

$B = $ **Bonus**

$B = $ **.2($80,000 − $20,000 − B)**
$B = $ **$16,000 − $4,000 − .2B**
1.2B = $12,000
$B = $ **$10,000**

The computation of the bonus can be proved by taking 20% of the amount by which income after the bonus exceeds $20,000. Thus, 20% of $50,000 ($80,000 − $10,000 − $20,000) equals the bonus of $10,000.

3 Contract provides that the bonus shall be computed on *net* income in excess of $20,000 after deducting both the bonus and income taxes:

Let $B = $ **Bonus**

and $T = $ **Income taxes**
Then $B = $ **.2($80,000 − $20,000 − T − B)**
and $T = $ **.4($80,000 − B)**

Substituting for T in the first equation, we can compute B (bonus) as follows:

$B = $ **.2[$60,000 − .4($80,000 − B) − B]**

$B = $ **$12,000 − $6,400 + .08B − .2B**

1.12B = $5,600

$B = $ **$5,000**

The computation of the bonus can be proved by taking 20% of the amount by which the net income after the bonus of $5,000 and income taxes of $30,000 (40% of $75,000) exceeds $20,000. Thus, 20% of $25,000 ($80,000 − $5,000 − $30,000 − $20,000) equals the bonus of $5,000.

The entry to record the bonus under plan 3 is:

Bonus Expense	*5,000*	
Bonus Payable		*5,000*
To record liability for bonus to branch manager.		

Bonus Expense would be included as an operating expense in the income statement and Bonus Payable as a current liability in the balance sheet. The Securities and Exchange Commission requires disclosure (description and expense) of bonus and profit-sharing plans which "are not available to all employees on a pro-rata basis."[8]

[8] *Regulation S-X*, Rule 3-16(j), Securities and Exchange Commission (Washington, D.C.).

ESTIMATED LIABILITIES

The term *estimated liabilities* is used to describe obligations which definitely exist but which are uncertain as to the amount and the due date. The primary accounting problem is to obtain objective evidence on which to base a reasonable estimate of the amount of the liability at any given time.

Estimated liabilities may be current or long-term. Some examples of estimated current liabilities are described in the following sections; estimated long-term liabilities, such as obligations under pension plans and leases, are covered in Chapter 19.

Coupons and trading stamps

In an effort to promote the sales of certain products, a company may issue coupons exchangeable for prizes in cash or merchandise. In such cases the company incurs an estimated liability equal to the cost of the prizes which are expected to be claimed by customers.

The estimated liability for prizes to be distributed should be based on the company's past and anticipated experience with redemptions of coupons. For example, assume that in Year 1 a company issues coupons which may be redeemed for prizes costing $2,500 if all the coupons are presented for redemption. If past experience indicates that only 80% of the coupons issued will be presented for redemption, the actual estimated liability would be $2,000 (80% of $2,500, the maximum cost of prizes that may actually be claimed by customers).

The purchase of prizes to be given, such as reproductions of famous paintings, toys, and kitchen utensils, is recorded as follows:

Inventory (Prize Merchandise)	2,800	
Cash (or Accounts Payable)		2,800
To record purchase of merchandise to be offered to customers as prizes.		

Generally, the cost of the coupons is immaterial in amount and would not be accounted for separately; if the cost of coupons is material, the cost may also be recorded in an appropriate inventory account. Assuming that customers present coupons during Year 1 in exchange for prizes costing $1,500, the following entry would be made:

Promotional Expense	1,500	
Inventory (Prize Merchandise)		1,500
To record redemption of coupons by customers.		

At the end of Year 1, an adjusting entry is required to recognize the promotional expense and the estimated liability relating to the coupons outstanding. In our example, the total cost of prizes expected to be claimed by customers was estimated at $2,000, and $1,500 of this amount has been redeemed during the year. Thus, an estimated liability of $500 exists at the end of Year 1. This estimated liability for coupons expected to be redeemed in Year 2 (or later) is recorded below:

Promotional Expense	500	
Estimated Liability for Coupons Outstanding		500
To record estimated liability for coupons outstanding at the end of Year 1.		

At the end of Year 1, the inventory of prize merchandise is $1,300 ($2,800 − $1,500). This inventory should be listed among the current assets in the balance sheet. The liability for coupons outstanding, $500, should be included among current liabilities. The promotional expense for the year, $2,000, is classified as a selling expense in the income statement.

A slightly different situation exists when a retailer gives his customers *trading stamps* (Blue Chip Stamps, Green Stamps, etc.) to be redeemed by another company engaged in the sale and redemption of trading stamps. The retailer pays a fixed price for the trading stamps which are recorded in an Inventory of Trading Stamps account. When stamps are issued to customers, an operating expense account is debited and the Inventory of Trading Stamps account is credited. The obligation to redeem the stamps is assumed by the trading stamp company.

The trading stamp company records the sale of stamps in a revenue account and recognizes an estimated liability for the cost of merchandise and related service costs to be incurred when stamps are redeemed. For example, the balance sheets of two trading stamp companies included the following among current liabilities:

Blue Chip Stamps:	
Liability for unredeemed trading stamps	$ 86,189,000
The Sperry and Hutchinson Company:	
Liability for stamp redemptions	$228,373,000

The estimated liability for Blue Chip Stamps was based on the assumption that 97.5% of all stamps issued would be redeemed and included $74,587,000 for the cost of merchandise and $11,602,000 for estimated redemption service expenses. The estimated liability for the

Sperry and Hutchinson Company was based on the assumption that 95% of stamps sold would be redeemed and consisted of $179,508,000 for the cost of merchandise and $48,865,000 for estimated redemption service expenses.

Liabilities from sale of gift certificates and service contracts

Some companies issue tickets, tokens, or gift certificates which are promises to perform services or to furnish goods at some later date. The measure of the liability is equal to the amount advanced by customers. As redemptions are made, the liability account is debited and a revenue account is credited. Examples of this type of transaction are meal tickets issued by restaurants, coupons issued by garages and gasoline stations, tickets and tokens issued by transportation companies, gift certificates issued by retail stores. Because such advances are in small individual amounts and relatively numerous, it is almost certain that some will never be presented for redemption. Estimating the amount of forfeited claims is fairly simple when there is an agreement that the obligation lapses after a stated time. When the offer is of indefinite duration, it is necessary to estimate the claims that will not be redeemed along with redeemed claims, and to transfer this amount from the liability account to a revenue account.

Companies selling or servicing major household appliances often sell a service contract to customers under which they agree to service the appliance for a specified period of time. In this case, the price of the service contract constitutes deferred revenue, which is earned by performance over the period of the contract. To illustrate, assume that a service agency sells television service contracts for $50, agreeing to service a customer's set for one year. If 1,000 such service contracts are sold, the entry would be:

```
Cash (or Accounts Receivable) . . . . . . . . . . . . . . . . . . . .   50,000
        Deferred Service Contract Revenue  . . . . . . . . . . . .            50,000
To record sale of 1,000 service contracts.
```

During the ensuing 12-month period, the service contract obligation will be converted into realized revenue by performance, and the actual cost of servicing the television sets should be charged to expense. On the basis of experience, it is often feasible to establish a pattern of probable service calls as a guide in recognizing revenue. For example, if the bulk of the service calls tend to be made in the first part of the guarantee year, a policy of crediting revenue with, say, 30% of the contract price in the first month, 20% in the second, and 5% in each subsequent month might be reasonable. The entries below are illustrative of this procedure for the first month:

Deferred Service Contract Revenue *15,000*
    Service Contract Revenue *15,000*
To record 30% of deferred service contract revenue as earned during first month.

Service Contract Expense *12,250*
    Parts Inventory *4,000*
    Accrued Payroll, etc. *8,250*
To record expenses incurred under service contracts.

Liabilities under guarantees and warranties

Estimating the liability that arises in connection with various kinds of guarantees and warranties often poses a difficult problem. Guarantees to replace or repair a product if it proves unsatisfactory within some specified time period are made by most companies. The Admiral Corporation, for example, included "Product and Service Warranties" of $7,872,314 among its current liabilities. Such liabilities arise at the time of sale, and may be recorded in the accounts either at the time a sale is made or at the end of the accounting period.

The following entries would be made if the liability is recorded at the time of sale:

Guarantee and Warranty Expense . . . . *xx*
    Estimated Liability under Guarantees and Warranties . . . .   *xx*
To record estimated liabilities under guarantees and warranties.

Estimated Liability under Guarantees and Warranties . . . . *xx*
    Cash (or Accounts Payable, Accrued Payroll, Inventory of Parts,
    etc.) . . . .   *xx*
To record costs of servicing customer claims.

The balance in the liability account at the end of the accounting period should be carefully reviewed and adjusted if necessary to make sure it reflects a reasonable measure of potential customer claims on outstanding guarantees and warranties.

An acceptable alternative would be to make no entry in the estimated liability account at the time of sale; Guarantee and Warranty Expense would be debited as actual costs are incurred in servicing customer claims and at the end of the period to recognize outstanding potential claims.

Income tax regulations allow the deduction of guarantee expense only when the cost has been incurred. Some companies follow the tax law and fail to record the guarantee liability in their accounting records, thus overstating net income and understating liabilities. When estimated liabilities under guarantees and warranties are significant, neither the tax rules nor the uncertainty of the amount of expense to be incurred are valid excuses for a failure to include the expected expenses and related liabilities in financial statements.

Operating "reserves" as current liabilities

Some companies charge an expense account and credit a "reserve" account for hypothetical expenses such as repairs or maintenance not actually performed, and for assumption of uninsured risks. Also, estimated disbursements for deferred compensation, restoration of leased properties, termination of store operations, and plant relocation costs are sometimes included in the liability section.

The recording of these estimated costs is presumably an effort to implement accrual accounting by recognizing an expense or loss when an obligation to incur a cost in the future can be identified with reasonable certainty. When such costs are incurred, they are charged to the *operating reserve* (liability) account.

The accountant should evaluate carefully the nature and probability of payment attached to such items and determine whether they represent current liabilities, long-term liabilities, appropriations of retained earnings, asset valuation accounts, or simply a means of relieving future periods of some expenses and losses which should correctly be reported in the income statements of such future periods. There is some evidence that so-called "operating reserves" have at times been used by management as income-smoothing devices. Some of these "reserves" are discussed in greater detail in Chapter 16 and elsewhere in this text.

CONTINGENT LIABILITIES

Contingent liabilities were defined in Chapter 4 as potential obligations the existence of which is conditional upon the happening of some future event. Note the distinction between *contingent liabilities* and *estimated liabilities:* the latter are liabilities which definitely exist but which may be uncertain as to amount or due date. Some examples of contingent liabilities are discussed in the following paragraphs.

Obligations arising from endorsements

A contingent liability may arise from discounting notes receivable with recourse, from assigning accounts receivable with recourse, and from accommodation endorsements added to the obligations of other parties such as a customer, employee, or affiliated enterprise. In such cases little question exists as to the amount of the obligation or its due date. The central issue is whether the person primarily liable will pay the liability. If the probability is strong that the original debtor will make payment, the chance of the endorser being required to pay is correspondingly low. The liability of the endorser is therefore contingent rather than definite.

Lawsuits pending

If a company is the defendant in a lawsuit calling for the payment of damages, a contingent liability exists. The outcome of such litigation can seldom be predicted with any assurance. The decision of the court may release the company of any obligation or it may establish an enforceable claim against it. However, the possibility of an appeal to a higher court still may exist. Another very possible outcome is an out-of-court compromise settlement between the parties, thus ending the litigation.

Even though the evidence available at the balance sheet date does not seem to favor the defendant company, it is hardly reasonable to expect the defendant to publish in its financial statements a dollar estimate of the probable outcome. Such publicity could influence unfavorably the chances of an out-of-court settlement or encourage the opposing party to intensify its efforts. As a generalization, then, we may say that contingent liabilities from pending litigation should be adequately disclosed by footnotes or other means. This disclosure will seldom, if ever, reach the point of estimating the dollar amount of a future settlement. To do so would weaken the company's position in the dispute.

Additional income taxes

The Internal Revenue Service may disagree with the treatment of items in the computation of taxable income and (within the period of the statute of limitations) may assess additional taxes. Because this contingency is well recognized and understood, no specific disclosure is required prior to the time that an actual assessment has been made. Except in cases of fraud or failure to file a return, the statute of limitations on federal income tax deficiencies is three years; thus at any given time it is only the income tax of the last three years that may be in doubt as to matters involving an interpretation of the law. A footnote reference is frequently attached to financial statements indicating that tax returns have been examined and final determination of tax made for certain years.

Additional income tax assessments applicable to earlier years are *prior period adjustments* and should be excluded from the determination of current year's net income; they are entered in the accounting records by a debit to Retained Earnings and a credit to Income Taxes Payable.

Reporting contingent liabilities in the balance sheet

The objective in reporting contingent liabilities is to disclose the nature of the contingency and, if possible, an indication of the amount involved. Adequate disclosure may be accomplished in a number of ways: (1) by a parenthetical comment included in the heading of an item on the financial statement, (2) by a footnote to the financial statement, (3) by showing the item among the liabilities but not extending the amount to be included in the liability total, or (4) by an appropriation of retained earnings authorized by the board of directors. Disclosure by footnote is probably the most satisfactory procedure and is almost universally used. An example of such disclosure by General Motors Corporation is shown below:

Contingent Liabilities:
There are various claims and pending actions against the Corporation and its consolidated subsidiaries in respect of taxes, product liability, alleged patent infringements, warranties, alleged air pollution, and other matters arising out of the conduct of the business of the Corporation. Certain of these actions purport to be class actions, seeking damages in very large amounts. The amounts of the Corporation's liability on these claims and actions at December 31, 19__ were not determinable but, in the opinion of the management, the ultimate liability resulting will not materially affect the consolidated financial position or results of operations of the Corporation and its consolidated subsidiaries.

Future liabilities and commitments

Most businesses are continuously planning activities for some time in the future. In many instances, commitments may be made that will result in substantial liabilities in the near future. At any balance sheet date, a company ordinarily will have made certain commitments that are of a recurring nature and normal in amount; these do not require any special disclosure. When unusual commitments that are large in amount have been made, however, a disclosure of their nature and amount should be made. Examples are commitments for an unusually large purchase of materials, a major expansion of plant, acquisitions of natural resources, additional payments to be made contingent on earnings of an acquired business, or unusually large commitments for advertising or research activities.

The accounting problems relating to estimated losses on major purchase commitments are discussed in Chapter 9. Such losses generally involve the recognition of estimated current liabilities.

Current liabilities in the balance sheet

Two questions of presentation arise in connection with current liabilities: (1) the order in which they are to be listed and (2) the extent of the detail necessary in disclosing different types of liabilities.

Current liabilities can be reported in the *order of maturity* or according to amount (largest to smallest). It is difficult to satisfy both objectives, and the usual compromise is to rank them in order of size unless differences in maturity are significant. However, bank overdrafts and notes maturing immediately after the balance sheet date are usually listed first in deference to their priority of maturity.

The matter of detail will depend to some extent on the purpose for which the balance sheet is prepared. In statements prepared in support of a loan negotiation or for the use of the treasurer in forecasting financial requirements, a listing of current obligations in greater detail is desirable. For financial reporting purposes, the classification illustrated in the following example is recommended:

Current liabilities:	
Notes payable to banks	$100,000
Notes payable to trade creditors	50,000
Accounts payable to trade creditors	425,200
Current maturities of long-term debt (including bonds, mortgages, and equipment contracts payable)	150,500
Income taxes payable (net of estimated payments and Treasury bills which will be used to pay income taxes)	112,500
Other accrued liabilities (payroll, interest, royalties, guarantees, property taxes, etc.)	29,000
Dividends payable	25,000
Miscellaneous current liabilities (advances from customers, credit balances in customers' accounts, etc.)	21,800
Total current liabilities	$914,000

If the due date of any liability can be extended, the details should be clearly disclosed. Any liability which will be liquidated by issuance of capital stock should be reported under stockholders' equity.

REVIEW QUESTIONS

1 Liabilities are sometimes referred to as "equities of outsiders in the assets of a business." Do you agree with this description of liabilities?

2 Distinguish between a **liability** and a **commitment.** Should the currently maturing installment of a deferred compensation agreement which is to be liquidated by issuance of stock be reported as a liability on the balance sheet? Explain.

3 What is the basis for distinguishing between a **current** and a **long-term liability?**

4 Distinguish the following: **definitely determinable liability, liability dependent upon operating results, estimated liability, contingent liability.** Give an example of each.

5 When should deferred revenues (or unearned revenues) be reported as current liabilities? When should deferred revenues be reported as noncurrent?

6 What are the usual liabilities that arise in connection with payroll transactions?

7 When should the liability for property taxes be recognized in the accounting records? Over what period should property taxes be charged to expense? Explain.

8 Where would the liability for current year's income taxes appear on the balance sheet of a partnership?

9 A company secures certain patent rights in return for an agreement to pay royalties equal to "10% of the company's net income." What difficulties may arise in interpreting this contract?

10 Briefly describe the accounting for promotional plans involving coupons and prizes, product guarantees, and the sale of service contracts.

11 The Larson Co. does not carry workmen's compensation insurance but it does have its own plan. Should estimated obligations to employees under this plan be reported as a liability? Are potential losses on "self-insurance" plans properly reported as liabilities? Why?

12 Included among the current liabilities of American Beef Packers, Inc., is an item described as "Excess of Checks Outstanding over Balance in Bank Account, $506,041." The current liabilities of Liggett & Myers, Incorporated, include "Estimated Costs Relating to Closing of Richmond Plant, $3,430,041." Briefly explain the nature of these two liabilities.

13 Explain how each of the following items would be measured and reported in financial statements:
a Bank overdraft
b Customers' accounts having credit balances
c Service guarantee on products sold
d Bonds maturing in three months, to be paid from a sinking fund
e Dividend payable in common stock of the issuing corporation
f Dividends in arrears on preferred stock
g Balance in account Allowance for Purchase Discounts
h Interest on notes payable, deducted from the face of the note in determining the net proceeds
i Estimated payments to workers under a three-year union contract
j Potential payments to stockholders of an acquired company based on future profits of the acquired company.

14 Describe four ways in which a contingent liability may be disclosed in financial statements.

15 Under what circumstances should commitments for future expenditures be disclosed in financial statements? How should this disclosure be made?

16 List some general guidelines in reporting current liabilities in the balance sheet.

EXERCISES

Ex. 7-1 At December 31, 1975, Yukon Salvage Company issued a two-year non-interest-bearing note with a face value of $11,664 for some scrap metal. The transaction was recorded as follows:

Purchases	*11,664*	
Notes Payable.		*11,664*

Prepare a correcting entry on December 31, 1975, assuming that a fair rate of interest is 8% per year and that books for 1975 are still open.

Ex. 7-2 The following information is taken from the records of the Townhouse Villa for the first three months of its operations:

Month	Total salaries and wages	Income tax withheld	FICA withheld	Remitted to Internal Revenue Service
January.	$ 2,600	$ 290	$130	$ –0–
February	3,400	360	170	550*
March.	4,000	410	200	700†
Totals	$10,000	$1,060	$500	$1,250

*Income and FICA taxes withheld from employees' salaries and wages in January and employer's FICA taxes for January.
†Income and FICA taxes withheld in February and employer's FICA taxes for February.

Entries to record the payroll for January and February, including taxes on the employer (FICA, 5%; state unemployment tax, 2.7%; and federal employment tax, 0.5%) were properly recorded. Remittances to the Internal Revenue Service were debited to the respective liability accounts.
a Prepare a compound journal entry to record the payroll for March. Record all payroll taxes on the employer in Payroll Taxes Expense account.
b Prepare the entry at the end of April to record payment of the amounts due for income tax withheld, FICA taxes, and state unemployment taxes for the first quarter of the year.

Ex. 7-3 Charles Nagy has a contract with Nils Corporation in which he is to receive a bonus of 20% of any net income over $97,500. Income before the bonus and income taxes for the year is $250,000. Taxes are 50% of taxable income.
Compute the amount of the bonus, assuming that it is computed on the net income in excess of $97,500 after deducting both the bonus and income taxes.

Ex. 7-4 Discount Gas, Inc., offers a coupon with each full gallon of gasoline sold. A customer who turns in 100 coupons is given a choice of prizes consisting of a football, a basketball, or a baseball glove. These prizes cost the company $2.50

each. The Promotional Expense account is debited as redemptions are made during the year and also at the end of the year when an estimate of outstanding coupons which will be redeemed is made. The following summary transactions occurred in Year 1:

a Purchased for cash 800 coupon books, each containing 1,000 coupons, for a total cost of $800. Debit Inventory of Coupons.

b Issued 500,000 coupons to customers.

c Purchased for cash 2,200 pieces of prize merchandise (footballs, basketballs, and baseball gloves).

d Issued 1,500 prizes to customers.

e Of the coupons issued, it is estimated that another 120,000 will be redeemed.

Prepare journal entries to record these transactions.

Ex. 7-5 East Equipment Company sells a machine early in the year for $1,200 along with a one-year warranty. Maintenance on each machine during the warranty period averages $100.

Give entries to record the sale of the machine and the subsequent expenditure of $88 to service the machine during the guarantee period, assuming that Guarantee Expense account is debited at the time of sale. (The sale is recorded at $1,200.)

SHORT CASES FOR ANALYSIS AND DECISION

Case 7-1 Rosen Company has a bank loan which is due within three months of the balance sheet date. The loan has been in existence for five years, although it is of short maturity, and it is the intent of both the company and the bank to renew the loan indefinitely. The loan is secured by the cash surrender value of a life insurance policy.

The company over a period of years has been offering to officers and employees the right to buy $6\frac{1}{2}\%$ bonds, which will be redeemed at the holder's request at any time after two years from the date of issue. In the past, certain bonuses have been paid to employees by issuing these bonds. All the bonds presently outstanding have or will have an issued status for two years within one year of balance sheet date. During the past 10 years, bonds redeemed amounted to less than 10% of bonds outstanding, and informal evidence indicates that no employee-bondholders intend to redeem their bonds within the coming year.

Instructions State how you would classify the cash surrender value of life insurance, the bank loan, and the bonds payable on the balance sheet of the Rosen Company at the end of the current year. Give reasons for your answer.

Case 7-2 At the end of the current year, the balance sheet of the Rawlings Corporation, a medium-sized firm, did not include among the current liabilities the following items (all of which are material in amount):

(1) Notes payable to a group of stockholders, the notes to become due and payable on demand of at least eight of the group of twelve stockholders

(2) A note due three months after balance sheet date, in settlement of which the holder accepted 1,000 shares of preferred stock 15 days after balance sheet date

(3) Rent collected one year in advance

(4) Bonds payable maturing in 60 days

Instructions Assuming that in each case the exclusion from current liabilities was based on logical reasoning, state the arguments in support of the statement presentation used by this company. If your answer involves assumptions as to facts not given in the question, state your assumptions.

Case 7-3 Bonito Trading Stamps, Inc., was formed early this year to sell trading stamps throughout the country to retailers who distribute the stamps gratuitously to their customers. Books for accumulating the stamps and catalogs illustrating the merchandise for which the stamps may be exchanged are given free to retailers for distribution to stamp recipients. Centers with inventories of merchandise have been established for redemption of the stamps. Retailers may not return unused stamps.

The following schedule expresses Bonito's expectations as to percentages of a normal month's activity which will be attained. For this purpose, a "normal month's activity" is defined as the level of operations expected when expansion of activities ceases or tapers off to a stable rate. The company expects that this level will be attained in the third year and that sales of stamps will average $2,000,000 per month throughout the third year.

Month	Actual stamp sales, %	Merchandise purchases, %	Stamp redemptions, %
6th	30	40	10
12th	60	60	45
18th	80	80	70
24th	90	90	80
30th	100	100	95

Bonito Trading Stamps, Inc., plans to adopt an annual closing date at the end of each 12 months of operations.
a Discuss the accounting alternatives that should be considered by Bonito Trading Stamps, Inc., for the recognition of its revenue and related expenses.
b For each accounting alternative discussed in (*a*) above, give balance sheet accounts that should be used and indicate how each should be classified.

Case 7-4 The Staubus Company has a fiscal year ending on March 31. The controller is in the process of preparing the monthly statement of financial position as of October 31 of the current year and requests your advice in determining an estimate of the federal income tax liability as of that date.

Taxable income for the six months ended September 30 is reported to be approximately $100,000; applicable tax rates are 20% on the first $25,000 and 50% on all taxable income over $25,000. Management is not at all certain as to the earnings to be anticipated for the remaining six months of its fiscal year. The sales manager believes the same rate of earnings can be maintained as has been earned in the six months ended on September 30. The controller is not so optimistic; he suggests that a loss may occur if needed materials (currently unavailable because of a strike at a supplier's plant) are not obtained soon. The president recalls that only $30,000 was earned in the six months between September 30 and March 31 last year; he believes the company's performance during the current six-month period will be comparable.

It is particularly important that a good estimate of the income tax liability be made as of September 30 this year because the president has arranged to sell part of his stock in the company at 150% of book value as of that date.

Instructions Prepare a brief memorandum for submission to the controller discussing the problems involved in determining the proper accrual of federal income taxes on September 30 of the current year. Describe briefly the methods by which such an accrual could be computed and indicate the method you would consider preferable in the circumstances, giving reasons for your choice. Do not make, or describe in detail, the actual computations.

PROBLEMS

Group A

7A-1 Listed below are selected transactions for the Roark Company relating to current liabilities during the current fiscal year:

Jan. 10   Purchased merchandise for $20,000. A 2% discount is offered by suppliers. The Roark Company records purchases and accounts payable net of discounts.

Jan. 19   Paid $14,700 on invoice of January 10. The invoice was billed to Roark Company for $15,000.

Jan. 31   Paid balance of January 10 invoice, $5,000, after the discount period.

Apr. 1   Issued one-year note to supplier in settlement of invoice for $10,000 dated March 31. The invoice was recorded net of 2% purchase discount or $9,800. The face value of the note was $10,584, including interest at 8% on $9,800 for one year. The note was recorded at face value.

Apr. 30   Wages for April were $6,000 before the following withholdings:

Income taxes	$880
FICA, 5%.	300
Union dues	125

The company records payroll taxes at the end of each month in a Payroll Taxes account. All wages for April are subject to 2.7% state unemployment taxes and 0.5% federal unemployment taxes.

May 20   The company declared dividends as follows:

Cash	$12,500
Stock	10%

The dividends are scheduled for distribution to stockholders on June 25. There are 100,000 shares of $5 par value capital stock outstanding; the current market value of the stock is $40 per share. Debit Retained Earnings for total value of dividends.

June 25   Paid the cash dividend and distributed the stock dividend declared on May 20.

Dec. 31   The company sells service contracts on its products and credits Deferred Service Contract Revenue when payments from customers are received. For the current year, $3,500 of the service contract revenue is considered realized.

Dec. 31   Recognized interest expense for the current year on the note issued to supplier on April 1.

Instructions Prepare journal entries to record the transactions listed above.

7A-2 Mortimer Company operates in a state which levies a 10% tax on corporate net income, after federal income taxes. The state tax for any year is an allowable deduction in computing the federal tax for that year. Federal income tax rates are 40% on all taxable income. During the current year, the corporation had $500,000 of income subject to both state and federal income taxes, before deduction for either state or federal taxes.

Instructions
a Compute the company's liability for both federal and state income taxes for the current year, and prepare a schedule proving that the computed amounts are consistent. (Round all amounts to the nearest dollar.)
b Prepare journal entries to record the income tax liabilities for the current year, and compute net income after income taxes.

7A-3 Apple Products Corporation sells carbonated apple juice in six-packs, cases, and through vending machines. In order to promote the drink among teen-agers and others who might otherwise be indifferent to the product, the company inaugurated in 1975 a promotional plan called "Drink-N-Win." For every 10 bottle caps and 10 cents turned in, customers receive an attractive ball-point pen and become eligible for a grand prize of $100 in cash, one of which is awarded for every 15,000 caps turned in. The company estimates that only 30% of bottle caps reaching the hands of customers will be presented for redemption. A summary of transactions for 1975 follows:

(1) Sold 3,000,000 bottles of apple juice for $1,282,200 cash.
(2) Purchased 45,000 ball-point pens for $27,900. Debit Inventory (Prize Merchandise).
(3) Expenses paid in cash and directly attributable to the promotional plan, $5,600.
(4) A total of 37,500 ball-point pens were distributed as prizes to customers and an appropriate number of grand prizes were awarded.

At the end of each year, the company recognizes a liability equal to the estimated cost of potential prizes outstanding. The 10 cents received for each pen is considered sufficient to cover the direct expenses of handling each request; therefore, neither the estimated direct expenses nor the potential remittances from customers are accrued at the end of the year.

Instructions

a Prepare journal entries, with appropriate explanations, to record the transactions relating to the promotional plan for the year 1975. Expenses of the promotional plan are recorded in a Promotional Expense account.

b Compute the balances in all accounts relating to the promotional plan and explain how each would be reported in the balance sheet and income statement of Apple Products Corporation as of December 31, 1975.

7A-4 Described below are selected transactions of Lamden Company during the current year:

(1) The Lamden Company is obligated under a rental contract calling for the payment of monthly rent of $400 in advance, plus an additional rent (payable by the 10th day of the following month) equal to 8% of the net income earned by its branch store, after both total rent and a 40% provision for income taxes have been deducted. Net operating income of the branch store during January (before rent and income taxes) was $12,000. Compute rent expense to the nearest dollar and debit Rent Expense for both the rent advance on January 1 and the accrual of rent on January 31.

(2) The company issues gift certificates in denominations of $5, $10, and $25. These certificates are redeemable in merchandise having an average gross profit of 25% of selling price. During March, the company sold $24,000 of gift certificates and redeemed certificates having a sales value of $20,800. It is estimated that 5% of the certificates issued will never be redeemed. The company uses a periodic inventory system and thus does not compute the cost of goods sold until the end of the fiscal year. The sales of gift certificates are recorded in an Estimated Liability for Gift Certificates Outstanding account.

(3) Sales during June totaled $204,080, of which $175,000 were on open account. The company operates in a state where there is a 3% sales tax. Included in the sales amount are sales taxes collected from customers on all items except food, which is exempt from sales tax. Food sales amounted to 32% of total sales before the sales tax was added.

(4) The payroll for November was $480,000, of which $80,000 represented amounts paid over $9,000, and $130,000 represented amounts paid over $4,200 to certain employees. Income tax withheld totaled $60,000, and FICA tax withholdings were at the rate of 5% (on wages up to $9,000 per year). The company is subject to a state unemployment tax rate of 2.7% and a federal unemployment tax rate of 0.5% (on wages up to $4,200 per year).

Payroll taxes on the employer are recorded in separate expense accounts. The accrued payroll and related payroll tax liabilities are recorded in the same entry.

Instructions
a Prepare all necessary journal entries to record the transactions described above. An entry to record the accrual of income taxes for January should be made in part (1).
b Prepare a list of all current liability accounts involved in your journal entries in (a).

7A-5 Presented below is a descriptive summary of financial position of Rio Grande Cotton Corporation, as of December 31, 1975:

Cash—includes an overdraft of $1,250 with Central Bank, a receivable from
  employees of $300, and checks from customers of $3,500 dated January
  10, 1976, which have been recorded as collections . . . . $ 34,300
Customers—includes notes of $20,000 (accrued interest of $800 has not been
  recorded), open accounts of $77,500 (including an uncollectible account
  of $1,200 which should be written off), and an allowance for uncol-
  lectibles of $1,300. Aging of accounts indicates that an allowance of
  $4,200 is required on December 31, 1975. Customers' notes of $10,000
  due in 90 days have been discounted at the bank   96,200
Merchandise—includes worthless goods carried at $6,800, and goods held
  on consignment, $5,000, owned by P. F. Company.   60,000
Prepayments—includes tools of $2,000, cash surrender value of life insur-
  ance of $3,100, and long-term utility deposits of $1,000   12,500
Fixtures—net of $34,500 of accumulated depreciation   97,000
Total assets $300,000
Current liabilities, recorded in a single account which includes the following:
  Note—due in three annual installments; interest at 7½% since
    Sept. 1, 1975, has not been accrued $45,000
  Accounts payable   40,000
  Payable to P. F. Company for consigned goods.   5,000
  Estimated liability for coupons outstanding . . . .   1,500 $ 91,500
  (The company has been sued for damages of $20,000 but does
    not anticipate that any liability will result.)
Capital—100,000 shares of no-par stock issued for $120,000, less 1,000 shares
  of treasury stock reacquired for $2,800, and retained earnings of $91,300   208,500
Total liabilities & stockholders' equity $300,000

Instructions Prepare a revised balance sheet in good form, including notes. Ignore the income tax effect of any corrections to previously reported net income. The use of work papers to determine correct account balances is recommended. Use the following form:

Accounts	Unadjusted balances		Adjustments and corrections		Corrected balances	
	Debit	Credit	Debit	Credit	Debit	Credit

7A-6 In January 1975 you were examining the financial statements of McGill Manufacturing Company for the year ended December 31, 1974. The company filed the necessary payroll tax returns for the first three quarters of 1974 and had prepared pencil drafts of the returns to be filed by January 31, 1975. The company has not made timely deposits of federal unemployment taxes as required by law.

The following information is taken from the general ledger, filed copies and the pencil draft of payroll tax returns, and other sources:

Information from general ledger:

Account	Balance Dec. 31, 1974	Composition of balance
Wages (various expense accounts)	$121,800	12 monthly entries from payroll summaries.
Payroll Taxes Expense . . .	7,650	FICA (5% of $100,000) $5,000; state unemployment tax (2.7% of $61,000) $1,647; federal unemployment tax (.5% of $100,000) $500; amounts withheld from employees for FICA tax in October and November and paid to depositary $503.
Liability for Income Tax Withheld	2,280	December income tax, $1,530; October through December FICA, $750.
Employer's Payroll Taxes Payable	990	December FICA, $247; October through December state unemployment tax, $243; 1974 federal unemployment tax, $500.

	Totals for year	First three quarters (duplicate copies of returns)	Last quarter (pencil draft)
Gross wages	$121,800	$95,870	$25,930
Wages taxable for FICA	100,000	85,000	15,000
FICA tax	10,000	8,500	1,500
Income tax withheld	15,740	11,490	4,250
Wages taxable for state unemployment tax	61,000	52,000	9,000

Total state unemployment tax— employer only	$1,647	$1,404	$243

Total federal unemployment tax—
  employer only (pencil draft of return
  for full year), $100,000 × .5% . . .
	500		

Information from other sources:
(1) In October 1974 six laborers were hired to tear down an old warehouse building located on the site where a new warehouse would soon be constructed. The laborers' 1974 wages totaling $1,000 were charged to the Building account. Payroll taxes were not withheld from employees.
(2) Included in a 1974 Wages Expense account is one month's salary of $1,400 paid to an employee representing retroactive vacation pay for 1973.
(3) A gross factory payroll of $1,200 through December 31, 1974, and the related FICA taxes (employer and employee) were accrued on the general ledger at year-end for a portion of the week ending January 4, 1975. Each of the employees included in this payroll earned between $5,000 and $6,000 as a McGill Manufacturing Company employee in 1974.
(4) In December 1974, an independent contractor was paid a fee of $2,000 for making repairs to machinery usually made by company employees and the amount was charged to Wages Expense. No payroll taxes were withheld.

Instructions
a Prepare a schedule presenting the computation of total taxable wages to be reported on the 1974 payroll tax returns for FICA and for state unemployment taxes.
b Prepare a schedule presenting the computation of the amounts (to the nearest dollar) which should be paid with each of the year-end payroll tax returns to be filed in January 1975 for (1) FICA taxes and income tax withheld, (2) state unemployment tax, and (3) federal unemployment tax. Assume that wages subject to federal unemployment tax are the same as wages taxable for state unemployment tax.
c Prepare a schedule to reconcile the differences between the amounts which should be paid with payroll tax returns to be filed in January 1975 (as computed for b) and the balances shown at December 31, 1974, in the related general ledger liability accounts.

Group B

7B-1 Account balances and other data relating to liabilities, obligations, and commitments of the Dudley Curry Corporation at December 31, 1975, are as follows:

Accounts payable	$ 82,100
Notes payable.	40,000
Discount on notes payable	1,800
Accounts receivable, excluding $20,000 which have been sold to a factor on a "recourse" basis	110,000
Bonds payable, $100,000 due at June 30 of each year	800,000
Retained earnings appropriated for general contingencies	25,000
Accrued payroll.	2,750
Payroll taxes payable	620
Liability for income tax withheld	1,150

Property taxes payable	$ 600
Allowance for purchase discounts	1,200
Stock dividends to be distributed (at par)	10,000
Income taxes payable	17,100
Deferred income taxes payable (resulting from use of accelerated depreciation method for income tax purposes)	110,000
Estimated liability for coupons outstanding	7,500
Unearned service contract revenue (contracts are for one year)	4,000
Loans from officers (renewed annually)	50,000

The company signed a contract on October 10, 1975, to purchase merchandise in 1976 at a fixed price of $100,000. This merchandise has a market value in excess of $115,000 on December 31, 1975.

Instructions Prepare the current liability section of the balance sheet at December 31, 1975, and list any contingent liabilities or commitments which should be disclosed on this date.

7B-2 The general manager of Auto Accessories, Inc., wants to ask for a bonus based on income of the current period, which he estimates will be approximately $330,000 before the bonus and before federal and state income taxes.

Instructions If the bonus rate is established at 10% and total income taxes amount to 50% of taxable income, compute the estimated amount of the bonus to the general manager under each of the following assumptions. (Round all answers to nearest dollar.)
a Bonus is based on income before both income taxes and the bonus.
b Bonus is based on income after the bonus but before income taxes.
c Bonus is based on income after both income taxes and the bonus.

7B-3 Selected transactions completed by the Walter Hanson Company during the current year are described below:
(1) On February 26, the company had an opportunity to obtain for $24,000 a special stock of merchandise being closed out by a manufacturer. The company purchased the merchandise on February 28 and paid for it on March 1 by borrowing $24,000 from the Nishi Bank, signing a note for $25,500 due on March 1 of next year. Assume that the company uses a periodic inventory system and that it records notes payable at face value.
(2) On July 1, property taxes on the company's retail stores for the ensuing 12-month period became a lien against the property. The company treasurer estimated that property taxes for the year in the amount of $6,600 would be paid on November 1. (Do not record the payment of the tax on November 1 because the actual amount of the tax is not yet known.)
(3) On August 10, the company purchased $20,000 of merchandise from Y Company, terms 2/10, n/30; and $8,000 of merchandise from Z Company, terms 1/10, n/e.o.m. The company uses a periodic inventory system and records accounts payable net of cash discounts offered. The invoice from Y Company was paid on August 18, but the invoice from Z Company was not paid until August 30 and the cash discount was lost.
(4) On December 1, the sales department launched a special one-month promotion of one of the company's products. Included in each product package sold during December was a coupon which, if sent back to the company with $1 enclosed, entitled the customer to receive a toy. The sales manager estimated that 50% of the customers would accept the offer, which would cost the company 80 cents for each toy claimed plus 30 cents in packaging

and shipping costs. The company purchased 50,000 toys for cash. During December, 100,000 of the products were sold for $3 each (debit Cash), and 30,000 coupons were presented for redemption. You should credit the Packaging and Shipping Expense account for 30 cents for each coupon redeemed because actual costs incurred in packaging and shipping were recorded in this account. At December 31, on the basis of experience to date, it was estimated that only 15,000 additional coupons will be presented by customers before the offer expires. Toys which will not be distributed as prizes can be sold for 45 cents each and the inventory of prize merchandise is written down accordingly by a charge to a Promotional Expense account.

Instructions
a Prepare journal entries to record the transactions described above.
b Assume that no entries have been made other than the entries to record the above transactions as they occurred. Prepare any necessary adjusting entries on December 31 relating to each of the four transactions.
c Prepare a list of accounts used in (a) and (b) and indicate the financial statement classification, that is, current asset, current liability, cost of goods sold, operating expense, etc., for each account.

7B-4 Oro Rico Mine started mining in the current year on certain land leased from Betts Land Company. The Oro Rico Mine had previously paid minimum royalties of $36,000 during a three-year period prior to the current year. The royalty provisions in the lease are as follows:
(1) Minimum annual royalty is $12,000, with a minimum of $3,000 payable quarterly. Unearned minimum royalties may be recovered in any subsequent period from earned royalties in excess of minimum royalties.
(2) Earned royalty shall be 10 cents per ton shipped from the mine plus a per ton amount equal to 2% of the amount that the market value of the ore at the mine exceeds $4 per ton.
Operations in the current year are summarized below:

Quarter	Tons shipped	Market value at destination, per ton	Freight from mine to destination, per ton
1st	None		
2d	150,000	$11.50	$3.50
3d	300,000	12.50	3.50
4th	None		

Instructions
a Compute the amount of royalty to be paid to Betts Land Company for the current year and the amount of unearned minimum royalty at the end of the current year.
b How should the unearned minimum royalty paid be reported on the balance sheet of Oro Rico Mine at the end of the year?

7B-5 Electronics Co. requests that you make an estimate of the company's product warranty obligation as of the end of the first six months of the current year.
   The company manufactures television tubes and sells them under a six-month guarantee to replace defective tubes without charge. At the beginning of the year, the company reported a Liability for Product Warranty of $495,000. By June 30, this account had been reduced to $84,500 by charges for the net cost of defective tubes returned which had been sold in the previous year. The net cost of replacing defective tubes sold in the current year (January to May) was recorded in Product Warranty Expense.

The company began the current year expecting tube returns to equal 8% of the dollar volume of sales for the year. However, as a result of the introduction of new models during the year, this estimated percentage of returns was increased to 10% as of May 1. It is assumed that no tubes sold during a given month are returned in that month. Each tube is stamped with a date at the time of sale so that the warranty may be properly administered. The following table indicates the likely pattern of sales returns during the six-month period of the warranty, starting with the month following the sale of the tubes.

Month following sale	Percentage of total returns expected
First	20
Second	30
Third	20
Fourth–sixth (10% each month)	30

Gross sales of tubes for the first six months of the year were:

January	$3,600,000	April	$2,850,000
February	3,300,000	May	2,000,000
March	4,100,000	June	1,960,000

The company's warranty also covers the payment of shipping cost on defective tubes returned and on new tubes sent out as replacement. This shipping cost averages approximately 10% of the sales price of the tubes returned. The manufacturing cost of the tubes is roughly 80% of the sales price, and the salvage value of returned tubes averages 15% of their sales price. Returned tubes on hand at the beginning of the year were thus valued in inventory at 15% of their original sales price.

Instructions Prepare a schedule in support of your estimate of the company's liability under its product warranty at June 30. Prepare also the necessary adjusting journal entry. (Income tax considerations may be ignored.)

7B-6 The partnership of Vanasse and Corman was formed on January 2, Year 1. Early in Year 2, you are called in to help Corman determine the proper figures for Salary Expense and Payroll Taxes accounts at December 31, Year 1. The partnership has three employees and each is paid a salary of $800 per month. At the end of **each month,** Corman prepares the following payroll summary and journal entry to record the payroll:

Name of employee	Salary expense	Income tax withheld	FICA taxes withheld, 5%	Employees' take-home pay
Joseph Allen	$ 800	$ 85	$ 40	$ 675
Janice Bales	800	110	40	650
Clayton Cameron	800	80	40	680
Totals	$2,400	$275	$120	$2,005

Salary Expense	2,005	
Cash		2,005
To record monthly payroll.		

On the fifteenth day of each month of Year 1, except January and the months following the end of each calendar quarter (April, July, and October), Corman paid the taxes withheld and FICA taxes due (both employer's and employees' portions) for the preceding month. He recorded these payments eight times (first two months of each quarter) during Year 1 as follows:

Salary Expense	515	
Cash		515

Remittance of taxes to Internal Revenue Service ($275 + $120 + $120).

At the end of each of the first three quarters of Year 1, the following entry was made when the quarterly tax returns were filed in April, July, and October:

Payroll Taxes	515	
Cash		515

To record quarterly tax remittance, determined as follows:

Withheld, $275 for 3 months	$ 825
FICA taxes, $120 per month for 3 months	360
Employees' portion of FICA taxes, $120 per month for 3 months	360
Total to be remitted	$1,545
Less: Payments made earlier ($515 × 2)	1,030
Balance due for each quarter.	$ 515

The first $9,000 of salary paid to an employee is subject to FICA taxes. However, Corman continued to withhold 5% for FICA taxes on **all** salaries paid during Year 1.

State unemployment taxes are levied at a merit-rating rate of 2% on salaries up to $4,200. Corman computed the amount due at the end of the first quarter of Year 1 at $144 and at the end of the second quarter at $108; he recorded both these payments as debits to Payroll Taxes and credits to Cash. Federal unemployment taxes are computed at the end of the year at 0.5% on salaries up to $4,200. The balances in Salary Expense and Payroll Taxes at the end of Year 1, before adjustments, are $28,180 and $1,797, respectively.

Instructions
a Prepare an entry to record federal unemployment taxes for Year 1.
b Prepare a compound entry to correct all accounts for Year 1 relating to the payroll. Record any unpaid FICA taxes and income tax withheld in a Payable to Internal Revenue Service account. (**Note:** Keep in mind that you have already recorded the federal unemployment tax in **a**.)
c List the balances relating to the payroll as they should appear in the balance sheet at December 31, Year 1.

CHAPTER 8

Inventory: cost, cost flow assumptions, and control

Inventories consist of goods held for sale to customers, partly completed goods in production, and materials and supplies to be used in production. Inventory is acquired and sold continuously in a merchandising business; or acquired, placed in production, converted into a finished product, and sold in a manufacturing business. The sale of merchandise or finished products is the primary source of revenue for most business enterprises.

Some of the more important accounting issues relating to inventories are discussed in this and the two chapters that follow. Inventory valuation and guidelines for inventory management are presented in this chapter; special valuation procedures are described in Chapter 9; and special techniques for estimating inventories are considered in Chapter 10.

Retail versus manufacturing

In a retail or merchandising operation, inventories consist principally of products purchased for resale in their existing form. A retail business may also have an inventory of supplies such as wrapping paper, cartons, and stationery. A manufacturing business, on the other hand, has several types of inventories: raw materials, goods in process, finished goods, and factory supplies.

Raw materials are basic commodities, acquired from others or obtained directly from natural resources, which will be physically incorporated in the production of other goods and which can be traced directly to the end product of the production process. *Factory supplies* are similar to raw materials, but their relation to the end product is indirect. In the manufacture of shirts, for example, the bolts of cloth are inventoried as raw materials, whereas the cleaning materials and the oil to lubricate the machines are classified as factory supplies.

Goods in process (or work in process) is the title given to the inventory of partially completed product. The goods in process inventory includes the cost of raw materials, direct labor, and factory overhead which can be associated with the units that are in process but not complete and ready for sale.

Finished goods are items which are complete and ready for sale. The cost of finished goods is composed of the same elements as those found in goods in process, the difference being that *all* necessary production costs have been incurred in connection with the completed product.

Inventory procedures

Two methods are employed by accountants to ascertain the inventory quantities on hand: (1) the periodic system and (2) the perpetual system. In most enterprises both systems are employed simultaneously for various parts of the inventory.

The *periodic system* relies on a periodic physical count of the goods on hand as the basis for control, management decisions, and financial reporting. Although this procedure may give very accurate results at a given time, there is no continuing record of the inventory. The planning and control of inventory quantities cannot be completely effective without continuous information about inventory quantities.

The *perpetual system* requires a continuous record of all receipts and withdrawals of each item of inventory. This procedure can be time-consuming, but it provides a better basis for control than can be obtained under the periodic procedure. In most perpetual systems a physical count of the goods on hand is required periodically as a check on the accuracy of the perpetual system. Any discrepancies discovered must be corrected. Usually the perpetual record is adjusted to reflect the physical count. The choice between the periodic and perpetual systems of determining inventory quantities is usually made on the basis of importance of the *control function,* of which there are two facets: (1) protection of the inventory and (2) assurance of desired inventory levels.

The perpetual inventory record is generally kept in terms of quantities only. The process of recording the transactions under a perpetual system is often no different from that used under the periodic system. Although frequently the perpetual system is associated with the requirement that each sale or issue be recorded by journal entry at the time of the sale or issue, this is not an essential procedure. The primary purpose of the perpetual system is to aid the control and planning of the inventory; it is not to determine the daily net income of the enterprise.

Inventory valuation and income measurement

The valuation of inventories has important effects on both the balance sheet and the income statement. The investment in inventory is frequently a significant part of a firm's total assets, and its valuation has a direct effect on the determination of the cost of goods sold, an important factor in the determination of net income.

The significance of the inventory valuation and the interrelationship of the balance sheet and the income statement are illustrated in the schedule below:

Cost of Goods Sold during January	
Beginning inventory	$ 20,000
Add: Purchases (or cost of goods manufactured) for January	80,000
Total cost of goods available for sale	$100,000
Less: Ending inventory	15,000
Cost of goods sold during January	$ 85,000

In the illustration the cost of goods available for sale is $100,000, composed of the beginning inventory and the costs incurred during January. The cost of goods available for sale is allocated into two parts: (1) the inventory on hand which will be economically useful in future periods, $15,000, and (2) the cost of goods which have been sold during the current period, $85,000. In this example the cost of goods sold is assumed to be the difference between the total cost of goods available for sale and the cost of those goods considered useful for future periods. Any failure to determine accurately either the cost of goods available for sale or the ending inventory can have a significant effect on financial statements. For example, if the cost of goods available for sale had been incorrectly determined, the cost of goods sold would also be erroneous, causing net income to be misstated, even though the ending inventory was valued correctly.

COST AND QUANTITY ACCUMULATION

When the accountant is accumulating the cost of goods available for sale during a particular time period, he must frequently make decisions as to whether certain goods become the property of the company in the current or the succeeding period. If acquisitions of goods are not recorded in the period in which they become the property of the buyer, the result will be errors in the financial statements.

Three common types of timing errors in recording inventory acquisitions may occur. The errors and their effect on financial statements are:

1 The purchase is recorded properly but the goods are not included in the ending inventory. The result is to understate the assets and net income.

2 The purchase is not recorded but the goods are included in the ending inventory. The result is to state the assets properly but to understate the current liabilities and to overstate net income.

3 The purchase is not recorded and the goods are not included in the ending inventory. Net income in this case is unaffected since purchases and ending inventory are understated by the same amount. The current assets and the current liabilities are both understated and the current ratio is overstated.

The first two errors are most likely to occur when the periodic inventory procedure is used. The third type may occur under either procedure, but it is more likely when the perpetual procedure is employed.

In many cases timing errors will be automatically corrected in the following period; however, the fact that the errors may be self-correcting does not remove the need for correct presentation of financial position and results of operations for each period.

 ### Goods in transit

Orders for goods which have not been filled by the seller present little difficulty for the accountant. Those orders which have been filled by the seller but not received by the buyer are the crucial ones. The problem which must be resolved in these cases is to determine whether the goods held by the common carrier are the property of the buyer or of the seller. The passage of title from the seller to the buyer marks the time when the legal responsibility for the goods changes from one party to the other. The accountant relies upon the passage-of-title test when transactions have not been completed by the end of the accounting period.

Purchase contracts usually specify which party is responsible for the goods and the exact location when the responsibility changes. This point is usually indicated by the letters *"F.O.B.,"* meaning *"free on board,"* followed by the designation of a particular location, for example, "F.O.B. St. Louis." This means that title is held by the seller until the goods are delivered to a common carrier in St. Louis who will act as an agent for the buyer.[1]

The following example illustrates this concept:

The Kansas City Shirt Shop orders 200 shirts from the New York Shirt Co. to be shipped "F.O.B. New York City" the bill to be paid within 10

---

[1] Other important F.O.B. designations are "F.O.B. point of destination" and "F.O.B. point of shipment," meaning that title passes at buyer's plant and at seller's plant, respectively.

days after shipment. When the New York Shirt Co. delivers the goods in New York to the carrier who is acting as an agent of Kansas City Shirt Shop, the title to the goods passes to the buyer. At this time Kansas City Shirt Shop should make an entry debiting Purchases and crediting Accounts Payable. Of course the freight charges in this case must be paid by Kansas City Shirt Shop; however, this liability does not arise until the agent has delivered the goods in Kansas City.

Suppose at the same time Kansas City Shirt Shop also orders 1,000 shirts from the Stay-neat Collar Co. in Chicago, delivered "F.O.B. Kansas City." In this case the shirts are the goods of Stay-neat Collar Co. until they are delivered in Kansas City. The Kansas City Shirt Shop does not recognize the asset or the liability until the goods are actually received; in this case there is no identified and separate transportation cost to the buyer.

Goods on consignment   *account for them*

Goods may be transferred by one party to another without the typical sale and purchase agreement. The party receiving the goods, the **consignee,** agrees to accept the goods without any liability, beyond that of providing reasonable protection from loss or damage, until the goods are sold to a third party. At this time the consignee must remit to the shipper, the **consignor,** the sales price less a selling commission and expenses incurred in connection with the sale. The consignor has, therefore, retained title to the goods until the time of sale to the third party and the consignee, acting only as an agent, has never taken title to the goods. If the goods are not sold by the consignee they must be returned to the consignor. Therefore, until the goods are sold by the consignee, they remain the property of the consignor and must be included as a part of his inventory at cost, including the handling and shipping costs involved in the transfer to the consignee. The consignee does not own the consigned goods and, therefore, should not include them as a part of his inventory. Problems that arise in recording consignments are discussed in **Advanced Accounting** of this series.

Conditional and installment sales

When goods are sold on conditional or installment contracts, the seller usually retains legal title to the goods until full payment has been received; however, the prevailing practice is to exclude such goods from inventory of the seller. The expectation is that customers will make full payment in the ordinary course of business; therefore strict adherence to the "passing-of-title" rule is not considered a realistic approach to recording the transaction.

Inventoriable costs

The two most important functions in accounting for inventories are (1) to determine the quantity of goods to be included in inventory and (2) to determine the proper cost of the inventory on hand. The first function involves the *taking of inventory,* the second a *valuation of inventory.*

After the quantity of goods on hand has been determined, the starting point in the valuation process is to ascertain the inventoriable cost elements of merchandise purchased or products manufactured. For inventory items purchased from outsiders, the net invoice cost is generally considered as the inventoriable cost. *Net invoice cost* is the invoice price of the item less any cash (purchase) discount *available* to the buyer. Cash discounts should not be included as part of inventory cost, regardless of whether the buyer takes advantage of the discount or fails to do so.

In theory, the indirect costs of ordering, freight-in, handling, and storing merchandise should be added to the net invoice cost to determine the total cost of goods acquired. However, the work involved in allocating these costs to inventory often is greater than the benefits to be derived from increased accuracy of inventory valuation. Furthermore, the allocation of some indirect costs to goods acquired may be highly subjective.

If a given cost will contribute to the production of revenue at a future date, this cost should be inventoried and associated with the goods acquired. *Economic usefulness* is, therefore, the first test in ascertaining the desirability of allocating costs to inventory; *significance and controllability* of cost is the second test. If the cost is not significant, there is little reason to be concerned with allocation; if it is not controllable in terms of volume of purchases or production, then it is a fixed cost and probably has little relation to the goods acquired or produced. In developing information for internal use, a policy of *direct costing* may be helpful. Direct costing is a system whereby all fixed factory overhead costs are excluded from manufacturing inventories and thus treated as period costs. It is not a generally accepted accounting principle and is not used in financial reporting to outsiders.

When costs are incurred which are necessary to the acquisition or production of goods but which do not meet both prerequisites of allocation, the costs are usually not included in inventories. Instead the cost will be considered a period cost to be deducted from revenue of the current period. The foregoing discussion is summarized in a diagram on page 293.

Although the assignment to inventory of all costs incurred in readying goods for sale is desirable, unrealistic allocations of indirect costs should be avoided to prevent conveying a false implication of certainty and precision in the measurement of inventory costs.

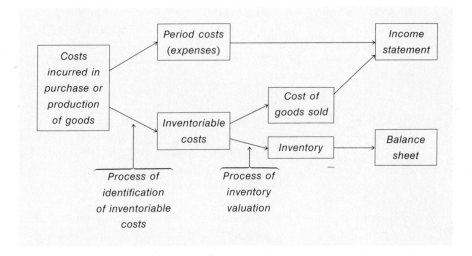

Merchandise Inventories All costs incurred in ordering, securing, handling, and storing merchandise are as much a part of the total cost of the merchandise as the net invoice cost itself. Consider a simplified example: You want to buy a set of golf clubs. The pro shop in your home town has priced the clubs you want at $150. A mail-order house 500 miles away has the same clubs priced at $135. If you fail to consider all the costs, you would purchase the clubs from the mail-order house. If you remember, however, that freight and packing cost must be paid, you might find it cheaper to purchase the clubs at your own pro shop in spite of the fact that the advertised price is higher. A factor which might also be important is the time period during which you would not have the use of the clubs if they were ordered. After considering the relative total costs, as well as the subjective factors, a decision is made.

Every businessman must make many similar decisions; without a realistic measure of total cost his decisions are quite likely to be ineffective. If an individual consumer makes an erroneous decision, it may not be very important; in a competitive situation, however, a bad decision by a business manager can be financially disastrous.

The following example involving the Kansas City Shirt Shop purchase of merchandise illustrates some of the circumstances relating to the cost of goods acquired.

Assume that the invoice from New York Shirt Co. indicates the price of the 200 shirts to be $5 each, with terms 2/10, n/30. This means that Kansas City Shirt Shop must pay New York Shirt Co. $980 within 10 days of the date of the invoice or pay $1,000 within 30 days after the date of the invoice. The net invoice cost is therefore $980. If payment is not made within 10 days, the $20 discount lost should be treated as a financing expense *of the period* rather than as a cost of acquiring inventory.

The cost of deciding to order these particular shirts, the actual cost of ordering them, the transportation cost, and the handling and storage cost incurred after receipt of the shirts, are all costs which might be added to the net invoice cost. Let us consider the cost of deciding to order these shirts in terms of the two tests cited earlier. Nelson is charged with managing the entire operation of Kansas City Shirt Shop. He is responsible for buying merchandise, hiring employees, advertising the goods, and conducting day-to-day operations. That part of Nelson's salary which he earned while deciding to order these particular shirts is certainly economically useful in terms of earning future revenue. In the absence of the decision no shirts would have been ordered. The first test (economic usefulness) is satisfied. That part of his salary earned in making this decision is probably not a significant part of the cost of the goods, however. In addition the cost is not controllable in relation to the volume of items purchased. The second test (significance and controllability) is not satisfied; therefore, the salary cost probably should not be considered a part of the cost of the shirts purchased. When the expense of cost allocation exceeds the benefit to be derived from the information developed, precise cost measurement becomes impracticable.

Manufactured Inventories   In many ways the problems of measuring inventory costs are the same in a manufacturing concern as they are in a retail establishment. This is particularly true of raw materials and other purchased inventoriable items. The major difference is found in measuring the cost of finished goods and goods in process. Tracing the movement of goods and costs through the production process is often difficult, but if done with reasonable care, the resulting information is useful to both management and outsiders.

Three classes of inventory are usually found in a manufacturing business: (1) raw materials and factory supplies, (2) products not completed, and (3) products completed and ready for sale. The cost of these inventories emerges as a part of the general process of measuring the cost of the resources that flow through the manufacturing process and of tracing these costs to specific quantities of finished and partially finished product. A typical manufacturing concern incurs three broad categories of cost: raw materials, direct labor, and factory overhead. These three basic ingredients are combined into finished products through a manufacturing process such as that diagramed below:

Raw materials
Direct labor $\Big\}$ ⟶ goods in process ⟶ finished goods
Factory overhead *

*Heat, light, power; indirect labor; rent or depreciation; insurance; supplies; special tools, etc.

In this operation costs are traced to processes and products and accumulated to derive the total cost of production. Each cost is incurred with the idea that an economically useful product will result. There are basically two systems of accumulating product costs for a manufacturing enterprise: (1) by job order and (2) by operation or process.

The *job order cost system* is used when the enterprise is manufacturing several distinct products in limited volume. For example, the job order system would be used for a construction firm or a specialty product firm. Each product or group of products is distinct in some way and the production costs are identified with the specific job. *Job order cost sheets* are used to accumulate the cost of material, direct labor, and factory overhead incurred on each job. Costs entered in job order cost sheets make up the goods in process inventory until the jobs are completed. The cost of completed jobs is a part of the finished goods inventory until the title to the product passes to a buyer.

The *process cost system* is used when large numbers of similar units are produced on an assembly-line type of operation. The production process is typically divided into *cost centers* or departments, based on logical divisions for the assignment of responsibility. Raw material, direct labor, and factory overhead costs are then accumulated by cost center and the goods in process inventory is the sum of all costs incurred on the uncompleted units in the various centers. The finished goods inventory is composed of a portion of all costs incurred through the entire manufacturing operation. The computation of goods in process and finished goods inventories when a process cost system is used is illustrated in Chapter 10.

Standard costs are estimates of what costs should be and are used extensively by companies engaged in manufacturing. Standard costs may be incorporated in either the job order or process cost system. The basic purpose of standard costs is to aid in measuring the efficiency of an operation, but standard costs are also sometimes used for inventory valuation. The very factors that make standard costs a good control mechanism serve to reduce their usefulness as an inventory pricing device. To be a good control device, standards should represent what costs *ought to be,* not what they *are* or *have been.* When standard costs are used for inventory pricing, the accountant should ascertain that the standard costs are a reasonable approximation of costs actually incurred in producing the goods on hand.

COST FLOW ASSUMPTIONS

The term *cost flow* refers to the inflow of costs when goods are purchased or manufactured and the outflow of costs when goods are sold. The cost remaining in inventory is the difference between the inflow and outflow of costs. During a given time period such as a year or a month, identical goods may be purchased or manufactured at different costs. The accountant then faces the problem of determining which costs apply to items in inventory and which to items that have been sold.

In adopting a cost flow assumption, the accountant must consider its effect not only on inventory valuation but on periodic net income. These problems must be considered simultaneously since the valuation assigned to inventory has a direct effect on the net income of both the current and the following period. The *assumed flow of costs* to be used in assigning costs to inventory and to goods sold need not conform to the physical flow of goods through the business. *Cost flow assumptions relate to the flow of costs rather than to the physical flow of goods because our chief goal is a realistic measurement of periodic income.* The question of which physical units of identical goods were sold and which remain in inventory is not of any particular inportance in the accounting problem of income determination.

The several widely used methods of inventory valuation are all based on the *cost principle;* no matter which method is selected the inventory is considered to be stated at "cost." In selecting an inventory valuation method (or cost flow assumption), we are matching costs with revenue, and the ideal choice is the method that most clearly reflects periodic net income. The principal methods of inventory valuation in wide use at the present time are:

1 First-in, first-out method (fifo)
2 Last-in, first-out method (lifo)
3 Weighted-average method
4 Specific identification method

A recent survey of 600 corporate annual reports indicated that fifo was used by 333 companies; average cost was used by 220 companies; lifo was used by 144 companies; and 125 companies applied a variety of other methods to the valuation of inventories. Only 15 companies apparently used the specific identification method. Obviously, some companies used more than one method.[2]

First-in, first-out method

The first-in, first-out procedure assumes a procession of cost through the business based on the proposition that the oldest goods are sold before newer stock is sold. This assumption about cost flow has much to recommend it. It conforms to reality; management usually finds it desirable to keep the oldest items in the inventory moving out to customers in order to keep a fresh stock on hand. The method is systematic and easy to apply; it adheres to the cost principle; and the cost assigned to inventory is likely to be in close harmony with the current prices being paid for inventory replacements.

[2] *Accounting Trends & Techniques,* 26th ed., AICPA (New York: 1972), p. 76.

To understand the technical application of the fifo method, assume the following data for a given item in the inventory of West Company:

	WEST COMPANY		
	Record of Acquisitions during January		
Jan. 1	Inventory on hand	200 units @ $ 7	$ 1,400
Jan. 8	Purchase	1,100 units @ $ 8	8,800
Jan. 25	Purchase	300 units @ $ 9	2,700
Jan. 30	Purchase	400 units @ $10	4,000
	Total	2,000	$16,900

A physical inventory taken on January 31 shows 700 units on hand. The inventory could be composed of any combination of 700 units on hand at the beginning of the period or purchased during the period. If we follow the fifo procedure, however, we assume that the inventory is composed of the items which have been acquired most recently. The calculation of the inventory cost at January 31 based on fifo assumption is illustrated below:

Inventory: First-in, First-out Method		
Jan. 30 (last purchase)	400 units @ $10	$4,000
Jan. 25 (next to last purchase)	300 units @ $ 9	2,700
Total	700	$6,700

The cost of goods sold is therefore $10,200 (total goods available $16,900 less ending inventory $6,700). The cost of goods sold for the period has been charged with the earliest costs incurred for the goods. The fifo method will give the same result whether the accounting period is one month or one year, or whether the periodic or perpetual inventory system is used. Each withdrawal of goods is from the oldest stock. For example, if the perpetual inventory system is used and the cost of units sold is determined on a daily basis, the cost of goods sold is computed as shown at the top of page 298. The cost of the inventory on the fifo basis using a perpetual inventory system, therefore, is also $6,700 ($16,900 goods available for sale less $10,200 cost of goods sold).

Last-in, first-out method

The lifo method of inventory valuation is based on the cost flow assumption that current acquisition costs are incurred to make possible current

Cost of Goods Sold: First-in, First-out Method

Jan. 6	100 issued @ $7	$ 700
Jan. 9	200 issued $\begin{cases} 100 @ \$7 \\ 100 @ \$8 \end{cases}$	1,500
Jan. 15	400 issued @ $8	3,200
Jan. 27	600 issued @ $8	4,800
Total	1,300	$10,200

sales, while maintaining an adequate inventory of goods on hand. Under this view the latest costs are most closely associated with current revenue, and thus the matching principle of income determination is carried out. On the balance sheet, however, inventory under the lifo method tends to be valued at the original cost of accumulating a minimum level of inventory.

The following record of acquisitions and sales of a given item in the inventory of West Company are the same as those used for the fifo illustration:

WEST COMPANY
Record of Acquisitions and Sales during January

Acquisitions					Sales	
Date		Units	Price	Total	Date	Units sold
Jan. 1	Inventory	200	$ 7	$ 1,400	Jan. 6	100
Jan. 8	Purchase	1,100	8	8,800	Jan. 9	200
Jan. 25	Purchase	300	9	2,700	Jan. 15	400
Jan. 30	Purchase	400	10	4,000	Jan. 27	600
	Total	2,000		$16,900	Total	1,300

The cost assigned to the ending inventory using lifo depends on whether the periodic or perpetual inventory method is used.

Based on the cost information presented above, the cost of the 700 units on hand at January 31 is computed at the top of page 299 under the periodic inventory system.

We should note that the lifo inventory at January 31 is composed of layers, the base stock of 200 units plus the layer of 500 units added during January. Should sales exceed purchases in any subsequent period, the cost of units comprising the most recently added layer or layers would be removed from inventory and added to cost of goods sold. The cost

Inventory: Last-in, First-out Method (Periodic System)

Jan. 1 (beginning inventory)	200 units @ $7	$1,400
Jan. 8 (first purchase)	500 units @ $8	4,000
Total	700	$5,400

of the original layer would not be reduced until all subsequently added layers had been assigned to cost of goods sold. The cost of goods sold for January is $11,500 ($16,900 cost of goods available for sale less $5,400 cost of inventory at January 31) and is comprised of the most recent costs incurred for the purchase of merchandise.

Unlike the first-in, first-out method, the last-in, first-out method will not produce the same result if the perpetual inventory system is used. When a perpetual inventory system is used, each withdrawal must come from the most recent purchase; however, this may mean that under certain conditions items will be withdrawn from the beginning inventory or early purchases when the time period is very short. If we assume the same record of acquisitions and withdrawals as occurred under the fifo procedure repeated above, the costs applicable to the goods sold using a perpetual system would be $10,600, computed as follows:

Cost of Goods Sold: Last-in, First-out Method (Perpetual System)

Jan. 6	100 issued @ $7	$ 700
Jan. 9	200 issued @ $8	1,600
Jan. 15	400 issued @ $8	3,200
Jan. 27	600 issued { 300 @ $9	2,700
	{ 300 @ $8	2,400
Total	1,300	$10,600

The ending inventory amounts to $6,300 ($16,900 − $10,600) and consists of the following:

Inventory: Last-in, First-out Method (Perpetual System)

Jan. 1	100 units @ $ 7	$ 700
Jan. 8	200 units @ $ 8	1,600
Jan. 30	400 units @ $10	4,000
Total	700	$6,300

Thus it becomes apparent that the results of the lifo method of valuing the inventory under the perpetual inventory system may vary rather widely, depending on the timing of the withdrawals.

Unit-lifo Method The practical problems of determining inventory cost using the lifo procedure are occasionally overwhelming, especially without the aid of a computer. In situations where there are large numbers of similar items and numerous transactions, the weighted-average unit cost of the items purchased during the period is considered the cost for purposes of calculating *additions* to inventory for the period. Such a procedure eliminates the need for identifying the cost of particular units. This adaptation is used in conjunction with a periodic inventory system and is called the *unit-lifo method.* Using the data presented on page 298 for the West Company, we can compute the lifo inventory at January 31 as follows:

Inventory: Unit-lifo Method

Beginning inventory	200 units @ $7.00	$1,400
Layer added in January.	500 units @ $8.61*	4,305
Total	700	$5,705

* Calculation of weighted-average unit cost for units acquired in January:

Cost of purchases $15,500
Total units purchased in January 1,800
Weighted-average unit cost of purchases: $15,500 ÷ 1,800 . . . . $ 8.61

The unit-lifo method would be applied only when there is an increase in the inventory during the period. The layer added in January would retain its identity in subsequent months as long as the inventory consists of 700 units of more. If the inventory decreased to 400 units in February, however, the inventory would consist of 200 units at $7 and 200 units at $8.61.

A special procedure for estimating inventories when identification with specific acquisitions is not possible is known as the *dollar-value lifo* method. It is illustrated later in this chapter.

Base Stock Method The *base stock method* is similar to lifo but because it is not acceptable for income tax purposes and has little theoretical support, it is seldom used in practice. This method assumes a continuous existence of a minimum stock of goods and inventory is considered to be a permanent asset. Any excess over the base stock is considered a temporary accretion and is priced at current replacement cost; any shortage or deficiency in the base stock is considered to be temporary and is charged against revenue at the current replacement cost.

The base stock method differs from lifo in that it uses **current replacement cost** as an element in pricing inventory; on the other hand, lifo relies exclusively on actual costs.

Weighted-average method

The weighted-average method of valuing inventory is based on the assumption that all the goods are commingled and that no particular batch of goods is retained in the inventory. The inventory is thus priced on the basis of average prices paid for the goods, weighted according to the quantity purchased at each price. Using the information for the West Company, the ending inventory and cost of goods sold would be determined under the weighted-average method as follows:

Inventory and Cost of Goods Sold: Weighted-average Method

Cost of goods available for sale.	$16,900
Total units available for sale	2,000
Unit price = cost ÷ number of units ($16,900 ÷ 2,000)	$ 8.45
Inventory valuation: 700 × $8.45	$ 5,915
Cost of goods sold ($16,900 − $5,915)	$10,985

This method produces a result, both for inventory valuation and income determination, which lies between the results achieved under fifo and those achieved under lifo. The assumption on which the method is based may be attacked on the theory that few businesses withdraw goods from stock completely at random. The method will not produce an inventory value consistent with the current cost of the items in the inventory; by its very nature it will lag behind the market prices. During a period of rising prices the inventory cost will tend to be below market price and during a period of falling prices it will tend to be above market price.

If a perpetual inventory system is used, the weighted-average method will give the result of a **moving weighted average.** Under a perpetual system, a new weighted-average unit cost is computed after each purchase and for this reason is known as the moving weighted average. Issues are priced at the latest weighted-average unit cost. Using the information for the West Company, this effect is demonstrated on page 302.

Specific identification method

At first thought one might argue that each item of inventory should be identified with its cost and that the sum of these amounts should constitute the inventory value. While such a technique might be possible for a concern handling a small number of items, for example, an automobile

Inventory: Moving Weighted Average (Perpetual System)

	Units	Amount
Jan. 1 inventory	200 @ $7.00	$1,400
Less: Jan. 6 issue	(100) @ $7.00	(700)
Balance, Jan. 6.	100 @ $7.00	$ 700
Jan. 8 purchase	1,100 @ $8.00	8,800
Balance, Jan. 8 (new unit cost computed)	1,200 @ $7.92	$9,500*
Less: Jan. 9 issue	(200) @ $7.92	(1,584)
Balance, Jan. 9.	1,000 @ $7.92	$7,916*
Less: Jan. 15 issue	(400) @ $7.92	(3,168)
Balance, Jan. 15	600 @ $7.92	$4,748*
Jan. 25 purchase.	300 @ $9.00	2,700
Balance, Jan. 25 (new unit cost computed)	900 @ $8.28	$7,448*
Less: Jan. 27 issue	(600) @ $8.28	(4,968)
Balance, Jan. 27	300 @ $8.28	$2,480*
Jan. 30 purchase.	400 @ $10.00	4,000
Balance, Jan. 31 (inventory at new unit cost)	700 @ $9.26	$6,480*

* Slight discrepancy due to rounding of average cost to nearest cent.

retailer, it becomes completely inoperable in a complex manufacturing concern when the identity of the individual item is lost. Practical considerations thus make specific identification inappropriate in most cases.

Even when specific identification is a feasible means of valuation, it may be undesirable from a theoretical point of view. The method opens the door to profit manipulation when there are like items acquired at varying prices. By choosing to sell the item which was acquired at a specific cost the management can cause material fluctuations in profits. For example, assume that the Atlas Grain Company acquires 1 million bushels of wheat in four equal lots of 250,000 bushels each, at costs of $2.50, $3, $3.50, and $4 per bushel. Atlas receives an order to sell 250,000 bushels at $3.75 per bushel. If the management is accounting for inventory in accordance with specific identification, then it can determine the profit reported for the period by selecting that batch of wheat which will produce the desired objective. The results of the transaction could range from a profit of $312,500, if the $2.50 wheat were sold, to a loss of $62,500 if the $4 wheat were disposed of. If an assumption regarding the flow of goods were adopted, for example, the first goods purchased are the first ones sold, the effect of such arbitrary decisions on reported profits would be removed.

The total profit or loss derived from the sale of the 1 million bushels of wheat will be the same, ignoring tax effects, regardless of the order in which the batches are sold. The important consideration here is the periodic report of income and financial position, which may be changed as a result of varying assumptions regarding the flow of goods through the business. Consequently, a systematic inventory flow assumption is desirable in the interests of objective financial reporting.

Summary of inventory valuation methods

The inventory valuation and cost of goods sold for the West Company as determined in the preceding illustrations are summarized below. Results using the specific identification method are not shown because we did not identify the composition of the units in inventory by date of purchase.

Inventory and Cost of Goods Sold: Various Cost Flow Assumptions

Cost flow assumption	Goods available for sale	Inventory	Cost of goods sold
First-in, first-out method	$16,900	$6,700	$10,200
Last-in, first-out method:			
Periodic inventory system . . .	16,900	5,400	11,500
Perpetual inventory system . .	16,900	6,300	10,600
Unit lifo	16,900	5,705	11,195
Weighted-average (periodic system)	16,900	5,915	10,985
Moving-weighted-average (perpetual system)	16,900	6,480	10,420

In the West Company example, the costs assigned to inventory range from a high of $6,700 using the fifo method to a low of $5,400 when the lifo method is used in conjunction with the periodic inventory system. The disparity in inventory valuation under the various cost flow assumptions depends on the trend and volatility of prices paid for new acquisitions and, of course, the length of time the lifo system has been in use. For example, the replacement cost of inventory for some companies which adopted lifo over 30 years ago may be more than four times the inventory value reported in the balance sheet.

Lifo versus fifo

Although both lifo and fifo are accepted methods of cost selection for the determination of inventory balances, they may lead to significant differences in the financial statements. Since neither method achieves an entirely satisfactory reporting of both the inventory and cost of goods sold when prices are changing, the accountant has attempted to rank the financial statements in terms of relative importance. The controversy has, thus, centered around the relative importance of the working capital position and net income.

Effect on Working Capital   As illustrated earlier, the fifo method has the effect of assigning the most recently incurred cost to the valuation of the inventory, whereas the lifo assumption assigns the first costs incurred as the inventoriable costs. During periods of stable prices, the choice of methods has no effect on inventory valuation. During periods of changing price levels, inventory valued on the fifo basis will more closely approximate the current value of the stock; the cost of items valued on the lifo basis will vary from the current price. The magnitude and direction of the variation depend on the degree and direction of the price change. The lifo method produces a seriously distorted inventory valuation when it is used over a long period during which the price level moves steadily in one direction or when the price level is changing very rapidly in one direction.

The understatement of inventory resulting from the use of the lifo method is objectionable because of the effect on working capital, current ratio, inventory turnover rate, and other measures of short-run financial stability. The problem is rather serious when no indication is included in the financial statements of the degree of understatement. The advocates of lifo minimize the importance of this understatement by their insistence that the income statement is more important. A more accurate report of income may justify a less meaningful balance sheet.

Effect on Net Income   The AICPA has emphasized the importance of inventory valuation in the measurement of net income:

> A major objective of accounting for inventories is the proper determination of income through the process of matching appropriate costs against revenues.

> Cost for inventory purposes may be determined under any one of several assumptions as to the flow of cost factors (such as, first-in, first-out, average, and last-in, first-out); the major objective in selecting a method should be to choose the one which, under the circumstances, most clearly reflects periodic income.[3]

The question that remains unanswered at this point is, what is periodic income? The proponents of the lifo method argue that realized revenue should be matched with the cost of acquiring goods at or near the time the revenue is realized. They contend that during periods of rising prices, for example, two types of profits, holding profits (or holding gains) and operating profits (or trading profits), are likely to be included in the determination of income unless diligence is exercised to avoid the inclusion of holding profits. *Holding profits* arise as a result of holding inventory

---

[3] *Accounting Research and Terminology Bulletins—Final Edition,* AICPA (New York: 1961), chap. 4, pp. 28 and 29.

during periods of rising prices and *operating profits* are the result of selling a product at a price above current cost. Since the lifo method matches the most recently incurred costs with realized revenue, it excludes holding profits from income determination.

Proponents of lifo favor the excluding of holding profits from income, on the premise that inventory which is sold must be replaced and that income is not earned unless the revenue realized exceeds the cost of replacing the item sold. Fifo proponents agree that there may be two types of profits, holding and operating, but they consider both to be an element of periodic income realized at the time of sale. They argue that the proponents of lifo confuse two separate concepts, income determination and utilization of cash. Further they state that if the proponents of lifo are truly interested in measuring *real,* as opposed to *monetary,* income, they should extend their proposal to use replacement cost to all assets. The cost of goods sold should not be the most recently incurred costs but rather those costs which will be incurred to replace the items which have been sold. This method has been referred to as the *next-in, first-out (nifo)* method of inventory valuation. At the present time it is not acceptable because it is considered a departure from the cost principle.

The measurement of *real income* poses another problem when the general price level in the economy is rising. To illustrate, assume that an item was purchased for $100 when the general price-level index stood at 120 and sold for $150 when the general price-level index stood at 132 and when the replacement cost of the item on the open market was $124. The apparent profit of $50 ($150 − $100) on the sale of the item may be allocated between the (1) general price-level adjustment, (2) holding gain, and (3) operating profit as follows:

General price-level adjustment: ($100 × 132/120) − $100 (original cost) . . . $10
Holding gain: $124 (replacement cost) − $100 (original cost) − $10 (general price-level adjustment)   14
Operating profit: $150 (selling price) − $124 (replacement cost)   26
  Total difference between selling price and original cost ($150 − $100) . . . $50

The holding gain of $14 is the increase accruing as a result of *owning* the item while the *specific* price (replacement cost) of the item was rising. The holding gain does not include the $10 increase in price of the item caused by inflation. Finally, the operating profit is the real economic reward to the seller for distributing the unit to his customers.

Managerial Implications   The proponents of lifo argue that the method is an invaluable aid to management since it excludes "holding profits" in the determination of income. Although management is concerned with holding profits, external factors which are unrelated to managerial competence are often a significant factor in creating holding profits. Moreover, holding profits are invested in inventory, which means that disposable income is approximated more closely by the use of lifo or some similar inventory valuation procedure.

Fifo advocates agree that management may need further information about replacement cost of the inventory and its effect on profits; however, they maintain that this information can be compiled without distorting the current position and the amount of net income (including holding gains) reported in financial statements. Moreover, they argue that if the holding profits derived from inventory are excluded, then similar profits derived from other investments should be eliminated. If in fact management decisions regarding dividend declaration, wage negotiations, and prices are based on the concept of disposable income, then a more extensive modification of the determination of income is needed than that achieved by lifo.

Income Tax Implications Despite the theoretical arguments built up in support of lifo as an inventory valuation procedure, the dominant reason for its popularity appears to be the income tax benefits that result from the use of this method. During periods of rising prices, taxable income and income taxes are reduced through the use of lifo. If prices later fall to the level at the time lifo was adopted, this reduction is simply a deferral of the tax. If prices continue to rise the reduction will be permanent. In either case the lifo user gains, since a postponement of taxes has economic value. The federal income tax law requires that lifo be used for financial reporting if it is adopted for income tax purposes.

The income tax benefits of lifo are not guaranteed. If prices fall below levels at the time lifo is adopted, or if the quantity of inventory is reduced below the amount on hand at the inception of lifo, it is conceivable that the lifo method could produce a tax disadvantage. Before adopting lifo solely for tax reasons, therefore, management should consider such factors as the expected course of prices, future tax rates, inventory fluctuations, the company's net income pattern, and the existence of provisions in the tax law (such as operating loss carry-forwards) which tend to even out the tax burden over periods of income and loss.

Dollar-value lifo

The *dollar-value lifo* method is another procedure designed to facilitate the calculation of inventory cost using the lifo technique. The inventory can be priced at current cost, which eliminates the need for identification of the cost of the units comprising the inventory. The current cost of the inventory is then restated, by means of a specific price index, to the cost prevailing when lifo was adopted. The ending inventory in terms of base-year dollars is compared with the beginning inventory also priced at base-year dollars to determine the physical change in the inventory on hand. Increases or decreases are then assigned costs prevailing at the end of the period in which the items were acquired.

The essence of the dollar-value method can be observed in the following simplified example. If the beginning inventory cost $10,000 and the ending inventory cost $11,000, there has been an apparent increase in the number of units on hand of 10%. If the unit cost of the goods is unchanged, there is a real increase in the quantity of 10%; if there were originally 1,000 units, there are 1,100 units now. On the other hand, if the unit cost of goods has increased by 10%, there has been no increase in the number of units on hand despite the 10% increase in dollar amount of inventory. If the quantity of goods on hand is unchanged, the lifo inventory valuation should not be increased or decreased.

In valuing lifo inventory by the dollar-value method, the accountant is attempting to ascertain first the *actual* increase or decrease in the physical inventory and then to assign an appropriate cost to the increase or decrease. Since the original inventory is the basis from which changes occur, the inventory must be translated to costs of the base period.

Any increase in the inventory quantity should be valued at costs prevailing during the current year. In practice the index of costs as of the *end of the current year* is often used to value the added layer. Although the use of the year-end cost index implies the use of the fifo method, practical limitations of computing several indices during a given year have led to acceptance of the year-end cost index for this purpose. A decrease in the inventory is deducted from the most recent addition to the inventory at the costs prevailing in the year when the layer was added.

The following data concerning ending inventories and the specific cost index for this commodity at the end of each year are used to illustrate the application of the dollar-value lifo method for Years 1 through 4, as shown on page 309.

Year ended	Inventory at end-of-year costs	Cost index at end of year
Dec. 31, Year 1	$36,000	100
Dec. 31, Year 2	57,500	125
Dec. 31, Year 3	60,000	150
Dec. 31, Year 4	65,800	140

For Year 2, the ending inventory valuation of $57,500 is converted to a valuation of $46,000 at base-year costs by dividing the year-end cost of $57,500 by the cost index prevailing at the end of the year, 125%, expressed as a percentage of the index of the base period, December 31, Year 1. The increase in the inventory is then determined by subtracting the beginning inventory from the ending inventory, both measured in terms of the base period's costs. In Year 2 there was an increase of $10,000 ($46,000 — $36,000 beginning inventory). The increment is then converted to year-end costs by multiplying this figure, stated in base-year costs, by the cost index at the end of the year expressed as a percentage of the base year's cost index ($10,000 × 1.25 = $12,500). The ending inventory at dollar-value lifo cost is thus $48,500, the beginning inventory of $36,000 plus the current year's increment of $12,500.

The procedure for handling a decrease in the inventory quantity is illustrated by reference to the information for Year 3, which indicates a decrease in the inventory of $6,000 ($46,000 — $40,000) when the beginning and ending inventory values (stated at base-year costs) are compared. This decrease in the lifo inventory should be considered a reduction in the most recent addition to the inventory. In this case the most recent addition was $10,000 (in terms of base-year costs), which took place in Year 2. The reduction of $6,000 from the $10,000 layer leaves only $4,000 of the Year 2 increase in inventory at the end of Year 3. This $4,000 is then converted to the cost level at the end of Year 2, when this layer was acquired. Thus the ending inventory at the end of Year 3 consists of the base-year layer of $36,000 plus the remaining portion of the layer added in Year 2, $5,000 ($4,000 × 1.25), or a total of $41,000. An alternative computation would be to subtract the decrease in inventory in Year 3, $7,500 ($6,000 × 1.25), from the inventory figure at the beginning of Year 3, $48,500, to arrive at the Year 3 inventory of $41,000 ($48,500 — $7,500).

In Year 4, the inventory of $47,000 ($65,800 ÷ 1.40) at base-year costs shows an increase of $7,000 ($47,000 — $40,000) during the year (in terms of base-year costs). This increase is multiplied by 1.40 to convert it to the year-end cost of $9,800. The increase in terms of year-end cost is then added to the beginning inventory in arriving at the Year 4 dollar-value inventory of $50,800 ($41,000 + $9,800).

The key feature of the dollar-value lifo method is the conversion of both beginning and ending inventory to a common base. The difference between the two converted inventory figures indicates the increase or decrease in the quantity of goods on hand expressed in terms of a common base dollar measure. The lifo layers must then be valued according to the costs prevailing when they were added.[4]

Cost Index Specific cost indices such as the index for nonferrous metals or for department store prices are often used in making inventory cost adjustments to arrive at dollar-value lifo data.

---

[4]For an excellent illustration of dollar-value inventory computation, see A. Jay Hirsch, "Dollar-Value and Retail LIFO: A Diagrammatic Approach," *The Accounting Review* (October 1969), vol. 44, pp. 840–842.

Dollar-value Lifo Method
Years 1 through 4

Year	Inventory at end-of-year costs	÷	Deflator (cost index at year-end)	=	Inventory at base-year costs	Determination of inventory layers	Dollar-value inventory at year-end
1 (base year)	$36,000	÷	1.00	=	$36,000	$36,000 × 1.00	$36,000
2	$57,500	÷	1.25	=	$46,000	$36,000 × 1.00 = $36,000 10,000 × 1.25 = $12,500 $46,000	$48,500
3	$60,000	÷	1.50	=	$40,000	$36,000 × 1.00 = $36,000 4,000 × 1.25 = $ 5,000 $40,000	$41,000
4	$65,800	÷	1.40	=	$47,000	$36,000 × 1.00 = $36,000 4,000 × 1.25 = $ 5,000 7,000 × 1.40 = $ 9,800 $47,000	$50,800

In the absence of an appropriate index, the accountant can take a *sample* of the inventory and value this sample at both current year's costs and at the base period's costs. The total cost in terms of the current year's prices is then divided by the total cost in terms of the base period's prices. The index so determined is used to value the entire inventory. In calculating this cost index, discontinued and new products deserve special consideration. The best approach is to eliminate these items from the general calculation. They in turn must be valued separately, and in many cases the only feasible way is to refer to particular invoice costs.

The cost index for a sample of inventory items can be computed as follows:

| | | Unit costs | | Total costs | |
Item	Inventory quantity	End of current period	Base period	End of current period	Base period
A	150	$40.00	$36.00	$6,000	$5,400
B	60	15.00	13.00	900	780
C	200	4.00	4.10	800	820
				$7,700	$7,000

Cost index: $7,700 ÷ $7,000 = 110%

This computation indicates that prices paid for the items in inventory have risen on the average by 10%.

INCREASING PROFITS THROUGH EFFECTIVE INVENTORY MANAGEMENT

Control over inventory is one of the more important functions of management in many enterprises. The quantity of goods on hand must be minimized to reduce the cost of carrying the inventory, which may be as high as 30% per year, yet the quantity carried should be adequate to allow for normal uninterrupted service to customers. In many cases the losses caused by an inefficient inventory policy are many times greater than the fraud losses that management makes a very diligent effort to control. The importance of the control function is directly related to the dollar value of the asset or expenditure to be controlled, and inventories are among the most valuable assets of many companies.

One of the basic tools of inventory control is continuous records of quantities purchased, sold, and on hand. The record for the current period is necessary to control the quantity of the item on hand, and the historical perpetual inventory record can be used as a basis for statistical studies designed to provide better control over the inventory in the future. Complete records provide much of the basic data for implementing inventory control.[5]

Goals of inventory management

In order to develop an effective system of control, management must first define goals or objectives. Probably the most important goal is that the inventory should be **where** it is to be used **when** it is needed. In addition, this objective should be accomplished at the minimum cost. Many conflicts must be resolved in implementing a plan to achieve this desired goal. For example, a large stock of goods may be required to assure that items are at the proper place when they are needed, but such an inventory may be inconsistent with minimization of cost. On the other hand, what is the cost of not having the goods at the time and place demanded by a customer? How is the cost of a lost sale or a lost customer to be measured? If one is to attempt to minimize cost, he must know the cost of an inventory shortage as well as the cost of carrying an excessive stock of goods.

The costs of carrying an additional stock of goods need to be compared to the gains derived from having no shortages. The costs of carrying an inventory of goods include the following:

Storage costs include the cost of the space itself, that is, depreciation of and interest on the investment in storage facilities.

Handling and protection costs involve the cost of physically moving the inventory, insurance, storeroom clerks, and watchmen.

Taxes involve the property taxes levied on asset values by local and state governments.

Interest is the cost of the capital committed to the inventory.

Risk entails the loss that may occur from damage, obsolescence, or price fluctuation.

If these costs of carrying a "protective" inventory are less than the gains to be derived therefrom, then the cost is justified; if the cost is greater than the gain, a loss results from the inefficient inventory management.

The cost of failing to fill a customer's order is more difficult to measure than is the cost of carrying excessive inventory. Such costs are, however, important to the decision-making process. Some of the costs of an inventory shortage are:

Lost sales. The customer buys the item from a competitor because he has it readily available. This may represent the loss of one particular sale or the loss of a customer more or less permanently.

---

[5] For an extended discussion of inventory control techniques, see Raymond A. Hoffman and Henry Gunders, *Inventories: Control, Costing, and Effect upon Income and Taxes,* 2d ed., The Ronald Press Company (New York: 1970).

Excess cost of rush orders. This cost is calculable to a certain extent; however, the dissatisfaction of the customer is not.

Work stoppages. These result in nonproductive time, layoffs, and overtime costs to make up for lost production.

A policy of "no inventory shortages" is seldom feasible, since most businesses are faced with uncertainties of demand for the product by the customers and uncertainties of supply by the vendors. Because of the highly unpredictable nature of the variables, statistical procedures using average expectations may often be applied to the events surrounding the inventory position to provide a basis for minimizing both the quantity of inventory and shortages which may result.

Planning quantities

Planning is the essence of inventory control. This means that the sales or usage for a period, as well as the time interval required to restock the inventory, must be estimated. The average sales for a day, or other meaningful time period, can be derived from past records and adjusted for current trends. The average time lag between the order date and the date of receipt of the goods can be obtained through an analysis of past activities. The average time lag may be decreased by more efficient ordering and receiving procedures. Once the operations have been reviewed and the statistics arrayed, there are two guides which should be established for each item in the inventory: (1) a reorder point and (2) an optimum order size. These concepts are generally included in managerial and cost accounting courses; therefore, only a brief description of them is given here.

The *reorder point* is the minimum level which the inventory can reach before a replenishing quantity is ordered. This point should be set in such a way that normal operations can continue until the ordered items are received.

The *optimum order size* is that which yields the lowest cost per unit for the items ordered. Many variables must be considered. Some costs are minimized by placing many small orders; others are minimized by placing a few large orders.

Turnover rate and control of inventory

The *inventory turnover rate* is a useful device in inventory management. This ratio of the cost of goods sold divided by the cost of the average inventory on hand is important in considering the relationship of inventory to the volume of business. The turnover rate gives clues regarding the adequacy of the inventory and the flow of goods through the enterprise. In general, the inventory balance at the end of the year is not representative of the average quantity on hand during the period. Consequently, a turnover rate computed on the basis of year-end inventories is often higher than it would be if more realistic inventory figures were used. For this reason the turnover rate is often computed using both year-end and quarterly inventory balances.

In the following illustration, we can observe a significant difference in the two rates of inventory turnover. The quarterly balances usually provide for a more realistic estimate of the average stock of goods held during the year and for that reason the turnover of 9.2 times per year is probably more indicative of the true situation.

	Inventory on hand	Year-end balances	Quarterly balances
Inventory balances:			
Jan. 1	$1,000	$ 1,000	$ 1,000
Mar. 31	2,000		2,000
June 30	1,500		1,500
Sept. 30	1,700		1,700
Dec. 31	850	850	850
Totals		$ 1,850	$ 7,050
Divided by number of balances		2	5
Average inventory balance		$ 925	$ 1,410
Cost of goods sold during year		$13,000	$13,000
Divided by average inventory balance . .		$ 925	$ 1,410
Turnover rate per year		14.1 times	9.2 times
Working days in a year		245	245
Divided by turnover rate		14.1	9.2
Number of working days' sales in average inventory		17.4 days	26.7 days

Although the turnover rate is an important statistic in inventory control, it is not the only consideration. A very high turnover rate might well indicate that the inventory is not adequate for the volume of sales. In such a situation there may be many costly delays in delivery and production caused by the inadequacy of the stock of goods. Also, a deceptively high turnover rate may result when inventories are valued on a lifo basis. In order to compute a meaningful turnover rate, both the goods sold and the average inventory should be priced at or near current prices.

Internal control over inventory

In addition to the methods of preventing and detecting inventory losses discussed thus far, some more obvious forms of loss exist. Always present is the possibility of theft, and errors in payment, shipment, and receipt of the inventory. These sources of loss can best be controlled by a systematic assignment of specific responsibility to individuals in the organization. For example, the responsibility for ordering, receiving, verifying, and paying for the inventory, as well as for custodial services, issuing goods, and maintaining records can be divided among several employees. *Internal control* over inventories embraces all methods of preventing and detecting waste or loss of inventories.

The system of internal control should be designed to ensure that the proper kind and quantity of goods are received at the right time and at the best price available. The system should also ensure that the goods are stored to provide protection from loss due to damage, obsolescence, and theft. The system should provide for the prompt payment of all invoices to permit full utilization of available cash discounts; however, no payment should be permitted until there is sufficient evidence that the goods ordered were received in good condition and that the amount of the invoice is correct. Finally, the system of internal control should ensure that there is no waste or fraud in the use and sale of the inventory, that is, that goods are withdrawn from stock only upon proper authorization and that all goods that are sold are properly billed as to item and amount.

The system of internal control is generally implemented by making an individual accountable for the items of inventory which he receives. Additions to the quantity for which an individual is accountable can be determined by reference to purchase invoices and receiving reports; reductions can be substantiated by properly completed requisitions for items to be issued. Generally, a perpetual inventory record is maintained and verified periodically by a physical count of the goods on hand. In some cases, statistical sampling techniques may be used to estimate the quantity of certain types of inventories.

REVIEW QUESTIONS

1 What features distinguish inventory costs from other costs which should be allocated into deferred and expired portions?

2 There are two methods of maintaining inventory records: (1) *periodic system* and (2) *perpetual system.* What are the basic differences and under what circumstances should each be used?

3 Why is the valuation of inventories critical to financial reporting? What criteria should the accountant use in deciding between alternative methods of valuation?

4 At the end of the period, the following purchase invoices dated December 27 are on hand but the goods have not been received. How would you handle each in the determination of the ending inventory?

a Invoice amount $12,670; terms, 2/10, n/30; "F.O.B. shipping point."
b Invoice amount $14,860; terms, 1/5, n/30; "F.O.B. destination."

5 Indicate the effects on the financial statements for the current and succeeding years of each of the following types of errors in accounting for the inventory. Merely indicate the direction of error—overstatement, understatement, or no effect.

a An invoice for goods shipped "F.O.B. shipping point" has been received but no entry has been made to record the purchase. The items have not been received and are not included in the ending inventory.

b An invoice for goods shipped but not received has been recorded properly to indicate that the goods legally belong to the buyer but the items have not been included in the ending inventory.

c Goods which have been received but the purchase of which has not been recorded in the accounts are included in the ending inventory.

d The ending inventory does not include goods shipped on consignment. The transfer of these goods has been recorded as a sale by the consignor even though they remain in the consignee's inventory at the end of both the current year and the succeeding year.

6 What costs should be included in the cost of inventories? What objectives are considered when one is deciding what costs are going to be added to inventory?

7 Midtown Faucet Company is licensed to manufacture and sell a certain product under a patent owned by Alan Bella. A royalty of 10 cents is payable to Bella for each unit sold. For costing purposes, Midtown Faucet Company treats royalty payments as a selling expense and does not accrue a royalty liability on the unsold faucets in inventory. The property tax assessor claims that 10 cents should be treated as a production cost and included in the valuation of inventory of faucets. Do you agree with the tax assessor?

8 The identification of the cost of *specific units sold* has been supported by some accountants as the ideal method of achieving a proper matching of cost and revenue. What objections may be raised to the use of this method as a practical means of valuing the inventory?

9 Differentiate between the *weighted-average* method and the *moving-weighted-average* method of determining cost of inventory.

10 Harris tells you that he is considering changing from the fifo to the lifo method of inventory valuation and that he would like your advice on the matter. He admits that his primary objective is to reduce his tax bill, and his friends at the country club tell him this is a good way to do it. What factors would you want to consider in advising Harris?

11 In the application of the *dollar-value lifo* method of valuing the inventory, it is considered necessary to convert both the beginning and ending inventory figures to base-year prices. Why? Why would a conversion of end-of-year prices to beginning-year prices not serve equally as well?

12 What are two goals of inventory management?

13 List some of the types of cost of carrying a stock of goods in inventory.

14 Define the following terms as they apply to inventory control: (*a*) *reorder point,* (*b*) *optimum order size.*

15 How is the *inventory turnover rate* used in planning inventory quantities?

EXERCISES

Ex. 8-1 Indicate the proper classification in the balance sheet for each of the following items:

Items	Inventory	Plant & equipment	Other (explain)
a Unexpired insurance			
b Freight-in on unsold goods			
c Goods held on consignment from others			
d Goods sold, delivered, but not yet billed			
e Small tools			
f Containers used to ship goods. .			
g Goods held for price appreciation (not for resale to customers) . . .			
h Factory supplies.			

Ex. 8-2 The following information relates to commodity A for January:

Inventory, Jan. 1	100 units @ $5
Purchases, January	500 units @ $6
Inventory, Jan. 31.	200 units

a What cost should be assigned to the ending inventory, assuming the use of the first-in, first-out cost flow method?
b What is the cost of goods sold for January, assuming the use of the last-in, first-out cost flow method?

Ex. 8-3 Given below is the inventory activity for product Z for the month of April:

Date	Transaction	Units	Cost	Total	Units sold
Apr. 1	Inventory.	1,200	$8.00	$ 9,600	
4	Purchase	800	8.25	6,600	
7	Sale.				600
10	Purchase	400	8.10	3,240	
13	Sale.				1,000
16	Purchase	700	7.90	5,530	
19	Sale.				900
22	Purchase	300	7.90	2,370	
25	Purchase	600	7.80	4,680	
28	Sale.				500
	Totals	4,000		$32,020	3,000

Assuming that a periodic inventory system is used, compute the inventory cost under each of the following cost flow assumptions:

a First-in, first-out
b Last-in, first-out
c Weighted-average

Ex. 8-4 Melcher Company is a wholesaler dealing in a single commodity. Inventory at December 31, Year 1, totaled $240,000. Quantities on hand were 800,000 and 1,000,000 on December 31, Year 1 and Year 2, respectively.
    Following are purchases made during Year 2:

	Quantity	Cost
January.	600,000	$210,000
April.	500,000	200,000
September.	1,000,000	246,000
November	400,000	160,000

    Prepare a schedule computing the cost of the inventory at December 31, Year 2, using the weighted-average method.

Ex. 8-5 Resthaven Company sells beds. The perpetual inventory was stated as $19,600 on the books at December 31, 1974. At the close of the year a new approach for compiling inventory was used and apparently a satisfactory cutoff for preparation of financial statements was not made. Some events that occurred are as follows:

(1) Beds shipped to a customer January 2, 1975, costing $2,000 were included in inventory at December 31, 1974. The sale was recorded in 1975.
(2) Beds costing $9,000 received December 30, 1974, were recorded as received on January 2, 1975.
(3) Beds received costing $1,900 were recorded twice in the perpetual inventory records.
(4) Beds shipped December 28, 1974, the date of shipping advice, which cost $7,000, were not recorded as delivered until January 1975. The beds were included in the ending inventory.
(5) Beds on hand which cost $2,300 were not recorded on the books in 1974.

    Prepare a schedule showing the correct inventory at December 31, 1974.

Ex. 8-6 Data Recall Corporation uses the dollar-value lifo method of pricing inventory. The inventory valued at end-of-year prices and the cost index are given below for the period 1973–1975:

Year	Inventory at year-end costs	Cost index at end of year
1973	$ 80,000	100
1974	90,000	125
1975	127,400	130

    Prepare a schedule showing the calculation of the ending inventory at dollar-value lifo cost for 1974 and 1975.

Ex. 8-7 A company acquired goods for $4,000 when the general price-level index was 110. These goods were sold for $7,500 when the replacement cost of the goods was $5,400 and the general price-level index stood at 121. The "gain" of $3,500 on the sale of the goods may be attributed to three factors: change in the general price level, holding profit, and trading profit (margin to seller for distributing the goods to customers). Compute the portion of the total "gain" caused by each of the three factors.

Ex. 8-8 Inventories for the Arnold Company for Year 5 are listed below:

Jan. 1	$ 50,000
Mar. 31	70,000
June 30	80,000
Sept. 30	100,000
Dec. 31	40,000

The cost of goods sold for Year 5 was $680,000. There are 245 working days in a year.

Compute the inventory turnover rate for Year 5 and the number of working days' sales in average inventory (computed by using quarterly inventories).

SHORT CASES FOR ANALYSIS AND DECISION

Case 8-1 Idaho Manufacturing Company purchased 10,000 pounds of raw material at an invoice cost of $50,000 with terms 3/5, 2/10, net 30. The freight cost applicable to this shipment was $4,500. The total cost of handling and storing raw materials was $50,000 a year, and the quantity handled each year was about 500,000 pounds. This $50,000 handling and storage cost was not controllable; that is, it was fixed in amount and did not vary in relation to variations in the quantity of raw material in storage. The quantity of raw material on hand fluctuated widely during the year. Idaho Manufacturing Company is debating whether this $50,000 should be treated as an expense or included in inventory.

Instructions
a Under what circumstances should handling and storage costs be included in inventory? Do these circumstances prevail in the case of raw material at the Idaho Manufacturing Company?
b Determine the cost per pound of this purchase of raw material.
c Would the cost per pound be different if the company did not pay the invoice within the first 15 days? What would the cost per pound be if the invoice were paid between the fifth and tenth day? State the accounting principle underlying your answers.

Case 8-2 The Wallace Company anticipates a price decline for its major raw material immediately after the first of the year. It is expected that the price of this material which is now $5 a pound, will drop by 10% to $4.50 per pound. The company uses the lifo method of valuing its inventory. At present the company has on hand its normal year-end stock of 100,000 pounds, priced at an average of $2 per pound. The company expects to sell 75,000 pounds of this stock before the end of the year. The purchasing agent argues that the company should place an order for delivery immediately after the first of the year at the new lower prices. The controller argues that they should place an order for immediate delivery of 75,000 pounds of the material even though it will cost 50 cents a pound more.

Instructions Who is right, the purchasing agent or the controller? Support your opinion with reasons. Answers to the following questions might help to develop your arguments.
(1) What, if any, is the difference in income before income taxes for the current year?

(2) Assuming a tax rate of 50%, what, if any, is the difference in net income after income taxes for the current year?

(3) What, if any, will be the difference in income before income taxes for the coming year, assuming an inventory at the end of the coming year of 100,000 pounds?

(4) What, if any, is the difference in the cash required for the two alternatives?

Case 8-3 Rodney Fears, a partner in the law firm of Mears, Sears, and Fears, wants to withdraw from the partnership effective on April 1, 1975. Because the partnership keeps books on a cash basis, no recognition is given to accounts receivable and work (legal action suits) in process in the preparation of financial statements for the partnership. The partnership agreement includes the following provision relative to the withdrawal of a partner:

"A partner terminating his association with the firm shall be entitled to an immediate cash payment equal to his capital account increased by (1) his share of uncollected accounts receivable and (2) his equity in work in process. No diminution in the withdrawing partner's capital will be made for outstanding liabilities."

The senior partner computed the value of work in process at March 31, 1975, as follows:

Direct reimbursable costs (travel, outside experts, etc.) chargeable to clients	$ 4,000
Salaries paid to staff attorneys working on cases (excluding time of any of the partners)	29,500
Total	$33,500

Fears objected to this procedure on grounds that it does not include the value of partners' time spent on work in process and the amount "represents a bare minimum value" of the work in process. He feels that the billable value of the work performed for clients to date amounts to at least $100,000 and that this amount represents the fair value of the work in process.

An accountant who was asked to arbitrate the dispute suggested that the senior partner's figure of $33,500 should be increased by $10,000, representing "general office overhead" applicable to the work in process. He feels that partners' time should not be treated as an inventoriable cost because partners' salaries are not a cost of doing business for the partnership form of organization.

Instructions Briefly evaluate each of the three approaches to the valuation of work in process and recommend the procedure you consider equitable in this circumstance.

Case 8-4 Marcus & Company buys the total stock of merchandise which its buyer estimates will be needed for an entire quarter although delivery is very prompt and the manufacturer fills orders quickly. When questioned about this, Marcus, the owner-manager, states that such a plan requires less effort and is cheaper. No quantity discounts are available; one person does all ordering and does not appear to be overworked. Marcus has been considering expansion but finds he is short of cash. There are frequent complaints because stock is incomplete in some respects. Price reductions at the end of the season are large, primarily because large quantities of particular items are on hand and many items are dirty and shopworn. One-third of total area of the premises is stock-room area.

Instructions Appraise the inventory policy of Marcus & Company. How might the operation be improved? What costs under the present policy might be reduced by a revised plan? What added costs might be incurred if the revision you suggest is adopted?

PROBLEMS

Group A

8A-1 The Slauson Corporation uses the first-in, first-out method of arriving at the cost of its inventory at the end of the fiscal year. The physical inventory at the end of the current year is summarized below:

Item no.	Unit cost*	Inventory count (units)	Freight applicable to inventory
10A	$ 2	2,000	$305
11B	5	3,000	225
15C	6	1,500	370
19D	10	800	320

*Before discount.

The company regularly takes a 2% discount on all purchases (excluding freight) and allocates an appropriate portion of freight charges to the ending inventory.

Additional information available at the end of the current year is presented below:

Beginning inventory	$ 33,500
Purchases (net of returns)	182,100
Purchase discounts	3,600
Freight charges on purchases	6,500
Sales (net of returns)	240,500
Sales discounts	3,100

Instructions
a Determine the appropriate valuation for the ending inventory.
b Prepare a partial income statement through gross profit on sales.
c What is the inventory turnover rate for the current year?

8A-2 The Crabill Corporation sells a single product which has been steadily going up in price in recent months. The inventory at January 1, and the purchases and sales for the current year are presented below:

	Number of units	Unit cost	Average sale price
Jan. 1, Inventory	8,000	$4.00	
Jan. 10, Purchase	3,000	4.50	
Jan. 21, Purchase	5,000	5.00	
Jan. 1–31, Sales for month	10,000		$ 7.00
Feb. 5, Purchase	4,000	6.00	
Feb. 18, Purchase	6,000	7.00	
Feb. 1–28, Sales for month	9,000		9.00
Mar. 5, Purchase	5,000	7.50	
Mar. 22, Purchase	10,000	8.00	
Mar. 1–31, Sales for month	13,000		11.00

The company does not use a perpetual inventory system. Inventories are valued at the end of each month.

Instructions

a Compute the amount of inventory on hand at the end of each of the first three months of the current year using (1) the first-in, first-out cost flow assumption and (2) the last-in, first-out cost flow assumption.

b Prepare a comparative statement summarizing the gross profit on sales for each month, assuming that inventories are valued using (1) the first-in, first-out method and (2) using the last-in, first-out method. Use the following format:

	(1) FIFO			(2) LIFO		
	January	February	March	January	February	March
Sales						

8A-3 You are auditing the records of Finci Manufacturing Company for the year ended December 31, 1975. To reduce the workload at year-end, the company took its annual physical inventory under your observation on November 30, 1975. The company's Inventory account, which includes raw material and goods in process, is on a perpetual basis and the first-in, first-out method of pricing is used. There is no finished goods inventory. The company's physical inventory revealed that the book inventory of $80,200 was understated by $5,000. To avoid distorting the interim financial statements, the company decided not to adjust the book inventory until year-end, except for obsolete inventory items.

Your audit revealed the following information regarding the inventory at November 30:

(1) Pricing tests showed that the physical inventory was overpriced by $3,100.
(2) Footing and extension errors resulted in a $600 understatement of the physical inventory.
(3) Direct labor cost included in the physical inventory amounted to $12,000. Factory overhead was included at the rate of 200% of direct labor cost. You determined that the direct labor cost was correct and that the factory overhead rate was proper.
(4) The physical inventory included obsolete materials recorded at $800. During December these obsolete materials were removed from the Inventory account by a debit to Cost of Goods Sold.

Your audit also disclosed the following information regarding the inventory at December 31:

(1) Total debits to certain accounts during December are listed below:

Purchases of raw materials	$ 42,000
Direct labor	24,000
Factory overhead (actual)	49,250
Cost of goods sold	142,300

(2) The cost of goods sold for December included direct labor of $30,000.

Instructions

a Compute the correct amount of the physical inventory at November 30, 1975.

b Compute the estimated amount of the inventory at December 31, 1975. Start your schedule with the correct physical inventory at November 30, 1975, as computed in (*a*). Do not adjust inventory for the underapplied factory overhead.

8A-4 The perpetual inventory records of Gardenia Sales Company indicate that the purchases, sales, and inventory quantities for product H-5 for the month of March are as follows:

	Purchases		Sales (units)
	Units	Unit costs	
Mar. 1 Inventory	800	$ 8	
6			500
10	700	9	
18			800
22	1,000	10	
30			400

Instructions

a Calculate the cost of the ending inventory and the cost of goods sold for March, assuming that the **perpetual inventory system** is used, using each of the following methods for inventory valuation. The following columnar headings are suggested: Date, Transaction, Units, Unit Cost, Inventory Balance.
(1) First-in, first-out
(2) Last-in, first-out
(3) Moving-average

b Assuming that a **periodic inventory system** is used, compute the inventory cost and cost of goods sold, using each of the following methods:
(1) First-in, first-out
(2) Last-in, first-out
(3) Weighted-average

c Where differences occur between **(a)** and **(b)**, explain why they exist. Under what conditions would you recommend the perpetual system? The periodic system?

8A-5 Listed below are selected account balances taken from the trial balance at December 31, 1975, for Metal Art, Inc., doing business in Chicago:

	Debits	Credits
Accounts receivable	$115,000	
Inventory (perpetual basis)	100,000	
Accounts payable		$ 80,000
Sales		280,000
Cost of goods sold.	185,000	

In preparing financial statements for the year ended December 31, 1975, you discover the following items relating to inventory, sales, and purchases:
(1) Goods costing $4,000 are included in the inventory, but the purchase was not recorded. The goods were shipped by the supplier "F.O.B. destination." The invoice has been received but the goods have not.
(2) Goods in transit costing $3,000 are excluded from the inventory, although the shipment was made "F.O.B. shipping point." The purchase was not recorded.

(3) Goods costing $5,500 are not included in the inventory although the sale for $8,000 and the cost of this sale were recorded. The goods were segregated in the warehouse for shipment pursuant to a purchase order from the customer who wants the goods shipped late in January.

(4) Goods having a cost of $1,500 were shipped on consignment and are excluded from the inventory. The shipment was not recorded as a sale, although the Cost of Goods Sold account was charged for $1,500.

(5) Goods costing $12,000 were sold for $18,000 and are included in the inventory. The sale was recorded and shipped "F.O.B. shipping point." No entry was made to the Cost of Goods Sold account.

(6) Goods costing $2,000 are not included in the inventory. These goods were sold for $3,000 but the sale was not recorded. The goods are set aside for delivery but title does not pass until the goods are delivered to the customer. The cost of these goods was transferred to the Cost of Goods Sold account.

(7) Goods in transit costing $2,800 are not included in the inventory, and the purchase was not recorded. The goods were shipped by the supplier "F.O.B. shipping point," thus title is held by Metal Art, Inc.

(8) Goods costing $4,800 are included in the inventory. The goods were rejected by Metal Art, Inc., because of poor quality and will be returned to the supplier. The goods were recorded as a purchase.

Instructions Prepare a schedule showing any required restatement of account balances. Give a brief explanation for each item (1) through (8) listed above. Use the following column headings:

Explanation	Accounts receivable	Inventory	Accounts payable	Sales	Cost of goods sold
Account balances per trial balance	$115,000	$100,000	$80,000	$280,000	$185,000

8A-6 On June 30, 1973, the end of the fiscal year, the New Orleans Corporation decides to adopt the dollar-value lifo method of pricing the ending inventory. The data on inventories valued at end-of-year prices and a cost index for the succeeding four years are provided as follows:

Date, as of June 30	Inventory at end-of-year costs	Cost index at end of year
1973 (base year)	$ 75,000	100
1974	100,000	125
1975	140,000	140
1976	110,400	115
1977	78,000	120

Instructions
a Prepare a schedule showing the calculation of the ending inventory at lifo cost for the four years, 1974–1977.
b Explain how the dollar-value method will facilitate the valuation of the inventory in terms of lifo cost.

Group B

8B-1 Lance Turino, the owner of Turino's Hardware, brings you the following information relative to the purchases of a given item he carries in his store for the first year of operations. Items are listed in the order received.

Voucher no.	Terms	Units	Freight charges	Invoice and freight charges
017	Net 30 days	100	$60	$ 7,560
121	1/5, n/30	75	50	5,650
175	1/10, n/30	50	35	4,035
280	3/5, 2/10, n/30	125	40	10,040
333	2/10, n/30	100	42	7,842

The handling and storage costs, to be allocated on a unit basis, applicable to these purchases are estimated to be $720. The ending inventory is composed of 125 units verified by a physical count. Turino informs you that there are other costs involved in obtaining these goods, but that he knows of no way to determine the amount of such costs. The purchase discount on voucher no. 121 was allowed to lapse; all other discounts were taken.

Instructions Compute the ending inventory and cost of goods sold during the period using the first-in, first-out method of inventory valuation. Lapsed discounts are excluded from cost of goods sold and inventory.

8B-2 The Swinger Shop began operations on January 1 with 150 units of item X at a cost of $1,410. The following data pertaining to purchase of item X were taken from the records at the end of the first year's operations:

Lot no.	Number of units	Cost
1	24	$ 240
2	84	924
3	126	1,242
4	96	864
5	120	1,440
	450	$4,710

A physical inventory on December 31 reveals that 200 units of item X remain in stock.

Instructions Based on the data provided, compute **(a)** the inventory cost at December 31 and **(b)** the cost of goods sold during the year, using each of the following methods of cost assignment:
(1) Lifo
(2) Fifo
(3) Weighted-average

8B-3 In the process of determining the ending inventory at June 30, 1975, for the

Rowan Corporation, you are presented with the following summary relating to material Y and finished part Z.

	Material Y (units)	Finished part Z (units)
Inventory summary:		
(1) Units on hand in warehouse per physical count. Cost is $4 per unit for material Y and $20.40 for finished part Z . . .	5,500	4,000
(2) Units in receiving department, to be refused because of poor quality. Invoice cost is $4.20 per unit	1,000	
(3) Units stored in parking lot considered worthless. Cost of these units is $21 per unit		100
(4) Units in receiving department; no invoice has been received. Price on purchase order is $4.10 per unit.	500	
(5) Units not received for which invoice marked "F.O.B. shipping point" has been received. Total cost in invoice, including freight, is $851	200	
(6) Units shipped on June 29, 1975; invoice marked "F.O.B. shipping point" has been mailed to customer. Total cost of these units is $6,330.		300
(7) Units completed in factory not yet transferred to warehouse. Cost is $21.50 per unit.		150
(8) Units in shipping department; invoice marked "F.O.B. shipping point" has been mailed to customer. Cost of these units is $20 per unit		50
(9) Units in shipping department; invoice has not been mailed to customer. Cost of these units is $20.30 per unit		80
(10) Units in hands of consignees having a total cost of $2,448		120

Instructions Prepare a schedule similar to the summary above showing the cost of the various items comprising the ending inventory of material Y and finished part Z. Place amounts (in dollars) in the two columns at the right. Give the reason for including or excluding each item.

8B-4 During the first two years of operations, the Reginald Corporation buys widgets as follows:

	First year				Second year		
Lot no.	Number of widgets	Unit price	Total cost	Lot no.	Number of widgets	Unit price	Total cost
1	6,500	$4.00	$26,000	1	6,000	$3.25	$19,500
2	2,000	3.75	7,500	2	3,000	3.50	10,500
3	6,000	3.50	21,000	3	2,000	3.50	7,000
4	2,500	3.50	8,750	4	2,500	3.75	9,375
5	4,000	3.00	12,000	5	8,000	4.00	32,000
	21,000		$75,250		21,500		$78,375

The replacement cost of these widgets at the end of the first year is $3.15 and at the end of the second year $4.20. There are 8,000 widgets on hand at the end of the first year and 10,000 on hand at the end of the second year.

Instructions
a Compute the inventory cost and the cost of goods sold for each period (1) under the fifo method and (2) under the lifo method.
b If 400 widgets had been stolen during the second year and you wanted to separate the theft loss from the cost of goods sold, how would you determine the amount of the loss?

8B-5 South Bay Company reported income before income taxes as follows:

1973	$150,000
1974	130,000
1975	140,000
Total	$420,000

An analysis of the inventories indicated the following:
(1) Inventory at December 31, 1972, was correct.
(2) Merchandise, costing $690, was received in 1973 and included in the ending inventory at the end of 1973; however, the entry to record the purchase was made in January 1974, when the invoice was received.
(3) The 1973 ending inventory includes 1,000 units of Item Z, which cost $7.30 per unit, erroneously priced at $3.70 per unit.
(4) Merchandise which cost $500 and which sold at $700 was shipped to a customer "F.O.B. shipping point" on December 31, 1974, and was not included in the 1974 ending inventory; however, the sale was not recorded until January 5, 1975.
(5) Merchandise costing $2,000, shipped "F.O.B. shipping point," was recorded as a purchase in 1974 when the invoice was received; however, it was not included in the ending inventory since it was not received until January 6, 1975.
(6) Merchandise costing $2,750 was sold for $4,000 and billed on December 31, 1974. This sale was recorded on December 31, 1974, but the merchandise was included in the ending inventory because it had not been separated from regular stock and was not shipped until January 15, 1975.
(7) The inventory at December 31, 1975, was correct.

Instructions
a Calculate the corrected income before income taxes for each of the three years and the total for the three years.
b Give the entries required at the end of each year to correct the income before income taxes for that year, assuming that transactions of the succeeding year have not occurred and that those of the prior year are corrected.
c Give the entry required during 1975 to correct the income before income taxes for 1975, assuming that the entries in (*b*) were not made. Any correction to income of 1974 should be made to "Restatement of Income for 1974." Ignore income taxes.

8B-6 Willie's Department Store decided in December 1973, to adopt the dollar-value lifo method for calculating the ending inventory for 1974, and each year thereafter. Willie feels that the published price indices are too general for his use; therefore, he intends to compute an index of price changes by sampling his stock of goods. The inventory at December 31, 1973, was $50,000 and this is considered the base year for purposes of applying the dollar-value technique.

The following data have been accumulated as the basis for inventory valuation:

Inventory quantities (sample items)				Inventory prices (end of year)				
Item	1974	1975	1976	Item	1973	1974	1975	1976
M	40	80	40	M	$10.00	$12.00	$13.00	$13.00
N	80	100	102	N	12.00	13.75	14.40	15.00
O	30	40	43	O	8.00	9.00	10.00	10.00
P	100	120	100	P	14.00	14.50	16.00	17.30
				Total inventory cost at end-of-year prices	$50,000	$66,000	$78,000	$67,500

Instructions
a Calculate the index of inventory costs for Willie's Department Store.
b Compute the dollar-value lifo inventory for 1974, 1975, and 1976.

CHAPTER 9

Inventory: special valuation methods

Absorption of inventory cost prior to sale

Pricing an inventory, as explained in Chapter 8, includes tabulating the number of units, determining the unit cost, and computing the total cost. We must now consider another possibility: that of a decrease in the value of inventory prior to its sale. If some items of inventory are used for display or demonstration, a part of the cost of these units should be absorbed prior to their sale. Whenever an asset contributes to the production of revenue and a part of the usefulness of the asset is consumed in so doing, a proportionate part of the cost should be charged against the revenue produced.

For example, an automobile dealer uses a new car to demonstrate his inventory to customers; by this action he hopes to sell more cars. Eventually the demonstrator will be sold at a reduced price because a part of the total usefulness of the product has been consumed. During each month the car is used as a demonstrator, a part of the cost should be charged to an operating expense account; the credit may be made directly to the inventory account or to an inventory valuation account.

Another illustration is that of the High Fashion Dress Shop. The proprietor wants his store to have a reputation as *the* fashion shop in his area. To accomplish his objective he knows that he must stock the extreme styles and he must stock them in sufficient volume to satisfy a substantial part of his clientele. In many cases he will buy more dresses than he expects to sell in order to maintain his reputation. To obtain a proper measure of income and to value his inventory properly, a part of the cost of the excess supply of dresses will have to be charged against revenue prior to the disposition of these dresses. Again the problem is one of ascertaining the amount of the cost that should be charged off. In both illustrations the loss of economic value is believed to have contributed to the production of revenue. In both cases the selling price of the article in question will have to be reduced. The expired costs in both cases may be added to the cost of goods sold or they may be segregated as a special expense or as a part of advertising and promotion expense.

Obsolescence and deterioration of inventory

In other situations part of the cost of inventory must be charged against revenue even though no benefit has accrued to the business. Inventory items frequently become unsalable at regular prices because of obsolescence, damage, or deterioration. If items which are to become a part of a manufactured article are damaged or spoiled in the ordinary production process, the loss need not be segregated but may become a part of the cost of the completed product. This procedure is acceptable provided the damage or loss is expected as a part of the normal operation of the plant. On the other hand, unusual loss or damage should not be included in the cost of goods manufactured. Losses of the kind described above are often difficult to distinguish from deterioration of assets through their contribution to the production of revenue. Consider the case of Atlantic City Sport Shop; the end of the season for swimsuits has arrived and a large stock of swimsuits remains. These suits have become somewhat obsolete. The manager might store the suits until next season or reduce the price and try to sell them now.

The questions which need to be answered are: How much of the economic value of the suits has expired, and should this expired cost be considered as an expense of producing revenue or as a loss? Undoubtedly some of the remaining suits were necessary to provide satisfactory service to the customers. On the other hand, a part of the inventory may be attributable to inefficient purchasing. For the best control of the business, the manager would like to be able to measure these two quantities; however, precise measurement is probably not possible.

Damaged or obsolete goods are frequently valued at *net realizable value,* estimated selling price less direct costs of completion and disposal. A more severe standard is to write the asset down to cash replacement cost—the price that the present owner would pay for the goods in their present condition if he were considering buying the goods for resale. In many cases an arbitrary percentage of the cost is written off; this is difficult to defend but in some cases no more objective basis is available. Finally, when there is doubt about the existence of any net realizable value, the cost of the items should be reduced to scrap value, or to zero in the absence of scrap value.

Price fluctuation and inventory valuation

The effect of price fluctuation on inventory valuation, although in many ways quite similar to physical change, deserves special consideration. If the prices of regularly stocked goods change subsequent to the date of acquisition, what accounting treatment is required? Has there been a change in the economic value of the items composing the inventory? If so, when should the gain or loss be recognized? Price changes which result in loss of economic usefulness of the inventory should be recognized as a deduction from revenue in the period in which the economic loss arises. Since the cost of the inventory is determined by negotiation between the buyer and supplier based on the expectation by the buyer of earning a normal profit upon resale, a significant decline in the selling price of the inventory may be just cause for recognizing a reduction in the carrying value of the inventory. When the accountant is attempting to value the inventory, he is in search of some measure of this reduction. The inventory value which is most appropriate in such situations is *replacement cost* (or a "derived market" value), that is, the value which will allow the business to recover the adjusted cost of the inventory and earn a normal gross profit.

At present, generally accepted accounting principles hold that gains attributable to price increases should not be recognized until the goods are sold. However, losses resulting from a decline in the prices of the inventoriable goods should be recognized in the period in which the price decline occurs. The basis for this rule, *the lower of cost or market,* can be found in the doctrine of conservatism which has guided accounting policy for a long time.

Lower of cost or market

The lower-of-cost-or-market rule requires that the accountant price the inventory at the lower of these two values: cost price or market price. The benefits attributed to this method of inventory valuation are (1) the loss, if any, is identified with the period in which it occurred, and (2) goods are valued at an amount that measures the expected contribution to revenue of future periods. The following statement supports this practice:

> A departure from the cost basis of pricing the inventory is required when the utility of the goods is no longer as great as its cost. Where there is evidence that the utility of goods, in their disposal in the ordinary course of business, will be less than cost, whether due to physical deterioration, obsolescence, changes in price levels, or other causes, the difference should be recognized as a loss of the current period. This is generally accomplished by stating such goods at a lower level commonly designated as *market*.[1]

The lower-of-cost-or-market rule provides a practical means of measuring the loss to be recognized and accounted for in the current period.

[1] *Accounting Research and Terminology Bulletins—Final Edition,* AICPA (New York: 1961), chap. 4, p. 30.

The measurement of utility is almost impossible and the adoption of the lower-of-cost-or-market price is a practical means of approximating the decline in utility.

The Meaning of "Market" What is meant by "market" in the expression "lower of cost or market"? Is it the price the item will bring when it is sold, or is it the price that would be paid to purchase the item? Current practice requires the use of the purchase price, that is, *replacement cost,* with certain limitations. Replacement cost is a broader term than purchase price since it can be held to include incidental acquisition costs, such as freight, handling, and storage. Replacement cost can also be applied to manufactured inventories with reference to the prevailing prices for raw materials, direct labor, and factory overhead. In cases where replacement cost is not reasonably determinable or exceeds the amount expected to be realized by the sale of the goods, the *net realizable value* should be used in place of replacement cost. The net realizable value is determined by subtracting from the expected sales price all prospective costs of conditioning and marketing the item. The AICPA, however, established the following limits (*ceiling* and *floor*) on market.

> As used in the phrase *lower of cost or market* the term *market* means current replacement cost (by purchase or by reproduction, as the case may be) except that:
>
> *1.* Market should not exceed the net realizable value (i.e., estimated selling price in the ordinary course of business less reasonably predictable costs of completion and disposal); and
>
> *2.* Market should not be less than net realizable value reduced by an allowance for an approximately normal profit margin.[2]

The AICPA allows a range for market value: The ceiling is selling price less estimated cost of completion and selling expenses; the floor is selling price less completion cost, selling expenses, and a normal gross profit. Replacement cost is used as market if it falls within this range; however, the ceiling figure is used for market when replacement cost is above the ceiling, and the floor figure is used for market when replacement cost is below the floor. This general rule is diagrammed at the top of page 332 for a unit costing $20, a ceiling limit on market value of $18, and a floor limit on market value of $15.

Once the adjusted figure for market has been determined, *the final step is to compare the cost of the inventory item with the adjusted market* in arriving at a lower-of-cost-or-market valuation. In each of the three assumptions at the top of page 332, the adjusted market is less than cost and would represent the valuation assigned to inventory.

Illustration of Selection of "Market" and "Lower of Cost or Market" The following example will illustrate the usual interpretation of the lower-of-cost-or-market rule with particular reference to the determination of

[2] *Ibid.,* p. 31.

if MV < cost
then figure out

if cost 13 – what
selling

Cost 13 $20	Different assumptions as to market value	Ceiling and floor limits on market value	Adjusted market in applying lower-of-cost-or-market rule
	a $19 (use ceiling because it is below market)————————↘		
		$18 (ceiling)————→**a** $18	
	b $17 (use market because it is between ceiling and floor)————→	————————————→**b** $17	
		$15 (floor)————→**c** $15	
	c $14 (use floor because it is above market)————————————┘		

market. The relevant inventory value is indicated for each case by a double line. Completion and selling expenses are estimated to be $6 in each case and the normal gross profit margin is 25% of the selling price.

	Inventory items				
	A	**B**	**C**	**D**	**E**
Selling price.	$20	$20	$28	$36	$40
Cost (determined by specific identification, fifo, average, etc.)	16	15	20	25	18
Selling price less $6 completion and selling expenses **(ceiling)**	14	14	22	30	34
Sales price less completion and selling expenses and normal gross profit margin of 25% of selling price **(floor)**	9	9	15	21	24
Market (replacement cost) at inventory date .	15	16	17	20	15

Explanation

Item A Market is less than cost but greater than the net realizable value, the ceiling; since market cannot exceed the ceiling, the inventory value is $14.

Item B Market is greater than cost but cost is greater than net realizable value, the ceiling; since market cannot exceed the ceiling, the inventory value is $14.

Item C Market is less than cost and within the ceiling-floor limit ($22 to $15); therefore, market of $17 is the inventory value.

Item D Market is less than cost and also below the floor; therefore, the floor of $21 is considered market.

Item E Cost is used although it is higher than market, because the floor figure ($24) is considered market and is higher than cost. In this case the normal gross profit margin will be earned when the unit is sold and therefore no loss should be recognized.

Meaning of "Market" for Income Tax Purposes The federal income tax regulations state that: "Under ordinary circumstances and for normal goods in an inventory, market means the current bid price prevailing at the date of the inventory for the particular merchandise in the volume in which usually purchased by the taxpayer." [3]

The "volume usually purchased" restriction in the income tax regulations is relevant when prices vary depending on the quantity purchased. There is another important difference between the tax and accounting rule; the AICPA uses the term replacement cost, whereas the taxing authority permits a lower cost by specifically referring to the "bid price," which excludes the incidental costs of purchasing.

It should also be pointed out that current income tax rules do not permit the use of the lower-of-cost-or-market rule when *cost* is determined by the last-in, first-out method.

Application of Lower of Cost or Market The lower-of-cost-or-market rule can be applied to (1) each individual item in the inventory, (2) major groups or classifications within the inventory, or (3) the inventory as a whole. Regardless of which of the three methods is adopted, each item in the inventory should be priced at cost and at market as a first step in the valuation process. It should be noted that the item-by-item method produces the lowest inventory value and that the application of the lower-of-cost-or-market rule to the inventory as a whole produces the highest valuation. The illustration on page 334 demonstrates the variation in lower-of-cost-or-market figures that will result from these three methods.

In valuing manufacturing inventories, the accountant must adjust goods in process and finished goods for any declines in raw material prices as well as for declines in direct labor and factory overhead costs.

Subsequent valuation problems

The question of subsequent treatment of inventory valued in accordance with the lower-of-cost-or-market rule is an interesting one. Suppose that at the end of the next accounting period 50 of the reels included in the water-sports category of the inventory illustrated on page 334 are still on hand and that the market price per reel has risen from $10 to $11. In accordance with the lower-of-cost-or-market rule, is the value of the 50 reels $600, $550, or $500? Generally, accountants have held that, once an inventory has been written down, this lower value *is considered cost for future periods.* Therefore, in the application of the item-by-item method

[3] Regulations, Sec. 39.22 (e) 4.

Determination of Inventory Value Using Lower of Cost or Market
Applying the Three Methods

Inventory item	Quantities	Unit cost	Market	Extensions Cost	Extensions Market	Item by item	Inventory sections	Inventory as a whole
Golf bags	15	$ 15	$ 14	$ 225	$ 210	$ 210		
Golf clubs	20 sets	200	210	4,000	4,200	4,000		
Golf carts	10	10	8	100	80	80		
Total golf category .				$ 4,325	$ 4,490		$ 4,325	
Footballs	75	$ 5	$ 4	$ 375	$ 300	300		
Helmets	50	15	13	750	650	650		
Shoulder pads	40	10	10	400	400	400		
Total football .... category				$ 1,525	$ 1,350		1,350	
Rods	100	$ 8	$ 9	$ 800	$ 900	800		
Reels	100	12	10	1,200	1,000	1,000		
Boats	10	300	315	3,000	3,150	3,000		
Total water-sport category				$ 5,000	$ 5,050		5,000	
Total all categories..				$10,850	$10,890			$10,850
Inventory value						$10,440	$10,675	$10,850

the value is $500; however, for the other two methods the reel inventory has not been written down and would be included in the category totals under cost at $600 and market at $550.

Comparison of cost with cost or market

The effect of the lower-of-cost-or-market procedure is to reduce income in the year of inventory write-down. In the following year, expired costs are less than if the inventory had not been reduced, because the beginning inventory is included as a part of the cost of goods sold. This fact is illustrated in the example on page 335. Data are for the London Marina Company for the first three years of operation.

In this simplified example, the gross profit on sales figure fluctuates with the pattern of sales when the inventories are valued at cost. When the lower-of-cost-or-market rule is adopted, there is little correlation between the fluctuations in sales and gross profit. The *total* gross profit for the first two years is the same ($107,000) under both methods because the inventory is priced at cost at the end of the second year under both methods. However, there is a shift of gross profit between the years.

	Year 3	Year 2	Year 1
Sales	$200,000	$150,000	$175,000
Purchases	150,000	100,000	180,000
Inventory, at cost.	70,000	62,000	60,000
Inventory, at market	55,000	68,000	50,000

LONDON MARINA COMPANY
Partial Income Statements
For the First Three Years of Operation
(inventory at cost)

	Year 3	Year 2	Year 1
Sales	$200,000	$150,000	$175,000
Beginning inventory	$ 62,000	$ 60,000	$ -0-
Purchases	150,000	100,000	180,000
Cost of goods available for sale.	$212,000	$160,000	$180,000
Less: Ending inventory, at cost	70,000	62,000	60,000
Cost of goods sold.	$142,000	$ 98,000	$120,000
Gross profit on sales	$ 58,000	$ 52,000	$ 55,000

LONDON MARINA COMPANY
Partial Income Statements
For the First Three Years of Operation
(inventory at lower of cost or market)

	Year 3	Year 2	Year 1
Sales	$200,000	$150,000	$175,000
Beginning inventory	$ 62,000	$ 50,000	$ -0-
Purchases	150,000	100,000	180,000
Cost of goods available for sale.	$212,000	$150,000	$180,000
Less: Ending inventory, at lower of cost or			
market.	55,000	62,000	50,000
Cost of goods sold.	$157,000	$ 88,000	$130,000
Gross profit on sales	$ 43,000	$ 62,000	$ 45,000

Valuation allowance for write-down of inventory

When inventories are written down below cost, the reduction may be
credited to an inventory valuation account. This procedure accomplishes
the objective of a write-down while permitting the original cost of the

inventory to be reported. The use of the valuation account is especially beneficial to a business using perpetual inventory records in terms of dollar cost since it eliminates the necessity of adjusting the detailed inventory records to a lower-of-cost-or-market basis.

The journal entry to record the reduction of inventory from a cost of $100,000 to a market valuation of $92,000 is illustrated below for the LCM Company:

Cost of Goods Sold	8,000	
Allowance for Inventory Price Decline		8,000
To record the reduction of value in the inventory caused by declining prices.		

In the balance sheet the inventory is listed at cost but reduced to market by deduction of the valuation account as follows:

Current assets:		
Inventory, at cost	$100,000	
Less: Allowance for inventory price decline	8,000	$92,000

In the income statement, the inventory may be shown in the cost of goods sold section at the net carrying value of $92,000, as shown below:

LCM COMPANY
Partial Income Statement—First Year

Sales		$400,000
Cost of goods sold:		
Beginning inventory, at cost.	$ 90,000	
Purchases.	325,000	
Cost of goods available for sale	$415,000	
Less: Ending inventory, at lower of cost or market. . . .	92,000	
Cost of goods sold.		323,000
Gross profit on sales		$ 77,000

If the write-down in inventory is quite material, it may be shown separately in the income statement. Such a write-down should be included in arriving at income from operations; under no circumstances should the write-down be reported as an extraordinary loss.

The inventory valuation allowance is not needed after the goods in question are sold. Therefore, at the time the cost of the beginning inventory is transferred to Income Summary (or to the Cost of Goods Sold account), the allowance account should also be closed, thus reducing the cost of the beginning inventory to market price. For example, the following journal entry would be made by the LCM Company at the end of the second year to close the beginning inventory, assuming that the periodic inventory procedure is used:

Income Summary.	92,000	
Allowance for Inventory Price Decline	8,000	
Beginning Inventory, at cost		100,000
To close beginning inventory to Income Summary.		

If the market value of the inventory at the end of the second year is below cost, an allowance for inventory price decline should again be established. Assuming, however, that inventory at the end of the second year had a cost of $82,000 and a market value of $84,000, the gross profit on sales for the second year would be shown as follows:

LCM COMPANY
Partial Income Statement—Second Year

Sales		$440,000
Cost of goods sold:		
Beginning inventory, at lower of cost or market	$ 92,000	
Purchases.	350,000	
Cost of goods available for sale	$442,000	
Less: Ending inventory, at cost (market $84,000)	82,000	
Cost of goods sold.		360,000
Gross profit on sales		$ 80,000

Failure to recognize the write-down in inventory to market in the first year would have resulted in a gross profit on sales of $85,000 ($77,000 + $8,000) and in the second year $72,000 ($80,000 − $8,000). Under no circumstances should the inventory valuation account be transferred to a revenue account. The write-down of inventories at the end of one period reduces the cost of goods sold in subsequent periods, but it does not add one dollar of revenue in subsequent periods.

Anticipation of price declines

The lower-of-cost-or-market rule is applicable to price declines which have actually occurred, not to possible future price declines. If management wishes to make formal provision in the accounts to indicate that future price declines are highly probable, this can be done by appropriating a portion of the retained earnings. This is not a common practice.

The AICPA has made the following distinction between inventory losses which can be measured by objective evidence and those which are measured by mere conjecture as to *possible* future losses:

> It has been argued with respect to inventories that losses which will have to be taken in periods of receding price levels have their origins in periods of rising prices, and that therefore reserves to provide for future price declines should be created in periods of rising prices by charges against the operations of those periods. Reserves of this kind involve assumptions as to what future price levels will be, what inventory quantities will be on hand if and when a major price decline takes place, and finally whether loss to the business will be measured by the amount of the decline in prices. The bases for such assumptions are so uncertain that any conclusions drawn from them would generally seem to be speculative guesses rather than informed judgments.[4]

An appropriation of retained earnings established in anticipation of future declines in inventory prices cannot be used to absorb inventory losses if and when they occur. To do so would cause a misstatement of net income. Any actual losses which arise from price declines should enter in the determination of net income.[5] The topic of appropriations of retained earnings is considered more fully in Chapter 16.

Losses on purchase commitments

Occasionally a business will enter into a contract to purchase goods from a supplier over a future period at a stated price per unit. It is assumed in this discussion that the contract is *not subject to cancellation* regardless of changes in market price. Such agreements are generally entered into in an effort to assure delivery of the items at the time desired. If the current price of the item falls below the price set in the agreement, the lower-of-cost-or-market rule should be applied to the commitment and the loss recognized promptly. The AICPA sums up the situation as follows: "Accrued net losses on firm purchase commitments for goods for inventory, measured in the same way as are inventory losses, should, if material, be recognized in the accounts and the amounts thereof separately disclosed in the income statement."[6]

The committee also concluded that if no loss is sustained because of the price decline, then the decline need not be recognized in the ac-

---

[4]*Accounting Research and Terminology Bulletins—Final Edition, op. cit.,* chap. 6, p. 42.
[5]*APB Opinion No. 9,* "Reporting the Results of Operations," AICPA (New York: 1966), p. 116.
[6]*Accounting Research and Terminology Bulletins—Final Edition, op. cit.,* chap. 4, p. 34.

counts. "The utility of such commitments is not impaired, and hence there is no loss, when the amounts to be realized from the disposition of future inventory items are adequately protected by firm sales contracts or when there are other circumstances which reasonably assure continuing sales without price decline."[7]

The loss should be recognized in the accounting period during which the price decline occurred. The value of the goods to be purchased under the commitment has been reduced just as though these units were currently included in the inventory. The entries required to record the loss and the subsequent purchase under a firm agreement to purchase goods at a fixed price of $100,000 are as follows:

Year of price decline:

Loss on Purchase Commitments Due to Price Decline	15,000	
Liability Arising from Purchase Commitments		15,000

To record loss due to decline in market price of goods ordered.

Year of purchase:

Inventory (or Purchases)	85,000	
Liability Arising from Purchase Commitments	15,000	
Accounts Payable		100,000

To record purchase of goods under contract on which a loss due to price decline was recognized in an earlier period.

The liability created by the entry in the year of loss may be regarded as the amount which the buyer would be required to pay the seller if he should decide to cancel the contract. When the goods are purchased, the liability created by the market decline is transferred to a liability of a different type—a regular account payable. If the expectation is that the purchase will be made during the regular operating cycle of the business, the liability arising from the purchase commitment should be listed as a current liability.

If contracts to purchase goods at a fixed price are subject to cancellation, no liability should be recognized for a decline in the market price of the goods.

As in the case of inventory on hand, *increases* in market prices of goods covered by purchase commitments are not recognized at the time of the increase because the increase had not yet been realized. Therefore, the recognition of a gain resulting from a favorable purchase commitment

[7] *Ibid.,* p. 35.

is delayed until the goods are sold. The gain resulting from the price increase is included in gross profit on sales in the period the goods are sold.

Appraisal of the lower-of-cost-or-market rule

The lower-of-cost-or-market rule originated in an era of emphasis on balance sheet conservatism. It exemplifies an old accounting axiom: "Anticipate no profit and provide for all possible losses." In following this axiom the accountant assumes that purchase prices and selling prices move in the same direction. Therefore if the price of purchased goods declines, the selling price of the product will decline also. By reducing the inventory to market, the income for the current period is reduced; however, presumably the business is enabled to earn a *normal* profit in the next period. On the other hand, if the price of the purchased commodity rises, accounting principles do not permit the value of the inventory to be increased. Such action would result in the *anticipation* of income before an arm's-length transaction took place.

In Chapter 8 the principle was stated that the inventory should include no elements of cost which are not related to the production of future revenue. Earlier in this chapter the treatment of damaged and obsolete goods was discussed in accordance with the principle of valuing assets at cost less an amount which measures any deterioration in usefulness. Now the argument has been presented that a decline in prices casts a shadow over a part of the inventory cost. Doubt is raised about the adequacy of the revenue in future periods to provide a margin of gross profit over the full cost of goods sold. The accountant has thus been led to the conclusion that the goods have lost a part of their value and that the unrecoverable cost should be written off.

One should not dismiss such an argument lightly; unrecoverable costs are hardly valid assets. On the other hand, every price decline does not necessarily mean that the cost of goods on hand will not be recovered. The price system is not so sensitive that it transmits related price movements instantaneously and uniformly throughout the economic system. Consider the following three possibilities with these questions in mind: Has a loss been suffered? If so, in what amount?

1 Selling prices for product A have declined substantially while the cost of replacing the inventory on hand is unchanged. Should a part of the inventory cost be written off? If the decline in selling prices is not sufficient to remove the entire margin of income, a write-down is hardly appropriate. On the other hand, if the decline in selling prices has been so severe as to make it impossible for the business to recover its inventory cost plus the cost of bringing the product to market, a loss has accrued. The loss is measured by the amount of cost that will not be recovered as a result of the decline in selling prices.

2 The cost of replacing the inventory has fallen significantly and the selling price for the product remains substantially unchanged. The lower-of-cost-or-market rule requires the reduction of inventory to market. Certainly no loss has ac-

crued. Instead, the gross profit margin has been temporarily increased. No manager would expect this situation to persist for long periods of time; however, there is no basis for recognizing a loss in the value of inventory.

3 Replacement costs have fallen and there has also been a corresponding decline in selling prices. Has a loss accrued? If the selling price has fallen to a point below the cost of the inventory plus the estimated direct costs of marketing the goods, a loss should be recognized.

The indiscriminate application of the lower-of-cost-or-market rule should never be allowed to replace sound judgment in the valuation of inventories. There are cases where cost absorption prior to physical disposition is justified; however, a careful appraisal of the particular circumstances is necessary before the amount of the loss can be determined. Using the concept of a *normal profit* in the determination of market entails the difficulty of establishing objectively what constitutes a normal profit.

Even if accountants could objectively determine what a normal profit should be, an unexpected rise in selling prices following a reduction in inventory to market would produce a profit greater than *normal.* A more reasonable objective for the lower-of-cost-or-market rule would be to price the goods at cost unless cost is impaired as a useful measure of the future value of the inventory because of severe price declines. The amount of the impairment is the loss which would result if the current selling price continued until the existing inventory was marketed in an orderly manner. The accountant should not compromise his standards by overstating expenses in the current year in order to assure that next year's income will be higher. Such manipulation would destroy the basis for the reliance which third parties place on financial statements.

Valuation of inventory at replacement cost (market)

The valuation of inventories at replacement cost has been advocated by accountants who believe that the current asset section of the balance sheet should reflect current values. The cost methods of inventory pricing frequently understate the value of the inventory, particularly during periods of rising prices. The significance of replacement cost as a measure of inventory value varies considerably depending on the type of inventory involved. In the retail market the selling prices of staple commodities, such as sugar, wool, cotton, etc., tend to follow cost prices closely. In such situations replacement cost of the inventory is quite important to the manager and often to outside parties also. In other cases where the selling prices have little relation to the cost of the inventory, replacement cost is much less valuable for decision-making purposes.

Replacement cost valuation of inventories has not been widely adopted. Perhaps the closest practical approach is the fifo method. Unless prices are rising quite rapidly, the fifo method of pricing presents the inventories on the balance sheet at or near current value without departing from the cost basis. The real need for disclosure of replacement costs arises when the lifo method is used in pricing the inventory.

The theoretical objection to the use of replacement cost as a method of inventory valuation is implicit in the arguments previously presented. Some of the advantages of inventory valuation at replacement cost can be achieved by the use of parenthetical notes in the balance sheet disclosing current replacement cost of inventories. In a research study, Moonitz and Sprouse argued for the adoption of replacement cost as a means of pricing inventory whether it is above or below cost. They based their argument on the AICPA position that: "As a general guide utility is indicated primarily by the current cost of replacement of the goods as they would be obtained by purchase or reproduction." They proposed that "if current replacement cost is objective, definite, verifiable and more useful when it is lower than acquisition cost, it also possesses those attributes when it is greater."[8]

The consistent use of replacement cost as a basis of valuing inventories would require some broadening of the realization test as presently applied. Under current accounting standards, revenue emerges at the time inventories are sold and converted into receivables, as indicated in the following diagram:

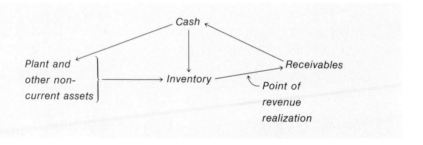

If replacement costs were adopted as the basis of inventory and plant asset valuation, gains and losses represented by the difference between cost and replacement cost would be recognized and included in income prior to the sale of finished products. The information resulting from such a procedure would be quite useful in periods when prices were changing significantly. The real issue is whether replacement costs can be determined with sufficient accuracy and objectivity to provide a reliable basis for financial reporting. At present, however, valuation of inventories at a replacement cost **higher** than actual cost cannot be considered a generally accepted accounting principle.

Some method of converting all cost dollars to a common measuring unit is another approach to the problem of changing prices; however,

---

[8] Robert T. Sprouse and Maurice Moonitz, "A Tentative Set of Broad Accounting Principles for Business Enterprises," *Accounting Research Study No. 3,* AICPA (New York: 1962), p. 31.

the elusiveness of the base unit, the purchasing power of the dollar, has thwarted most attempts in this direction. This subject is considered in Chapter 25.

Valuation of inventory at net selling price

The valuation of the inventory at *net selling price* (sales price less direct selling expense) has some appeal, especially when one considers that in reality value is added as the goods are brought to market. In a retail shop, for example, goods are more valuable than they were at the wholesaler's warehouse; value has been added by the process of bringing the goods nearer the ultimate market. In a manufacturing concern, as raw materials, direct labor, and factory overhead costs are blended together, a product emerges which is normally more valuable than the sum of the three cost factors. This method of inventory valuation, however, has not been widely adopted for two reasons: (1) lack of objectivity in determining the net selling price in many cases; and (2) the fact that the sales price has not been realized in terms of cash or claims to cash.

The valuation of inventory at net selling price is appropriate in some types of business. For example, the gold-mining industry might well use the price of gold established by the federal government as a basis of inventory valuation. The Treasury stands ready to buy all gold mined at a fixed price per ounce; therefore, when production is complete, income has been realized to the extent of selling price less the costs to deliver. The sale is an anticlimax. In other businesses where selling price is established by a firm contract, the sale follows production as a matter of course, and completed production might logically be valued at net selling price.

The use of net selling price in valuing inventories in effect moves the income realization point back one step in the earning process. As costs are incurred during the process of bringing an item to market, income is earned in the most fundamental sense. Each activity necessary to advance the goods closer to the customer and ultimately to close the transaction adds an element of income—the increase in sales price over the added cost. Therefore, if there are costs still to be incurred, there is still an element of income to be earned. The valuation of inventories at net selling prices means that an element of income is accrued before it is fully realized.

Scrap

The question of waste or spoiled material which has no residual value has been discussed earlier in the chapter; there are occasions, however, when scrap materials can be sold or used in the manufacture of other products. In such cases the inventory of these materials should be assigned a value.

Generally if scrap is to be sold it is priced at net realizable value, on the theory that this salvage price is a reduction in the effective cost of the main product. When scrap is to be used in the manufacture of another product, its value is based on an allocation of the cost of the basic material between the primary use and the scrap.

The major approaches to the allocation of cost to scrap are:

1 On the basis of volume. If 10% of the material is scrap, then 10% of the cost of the material should be assigned to the scrap.

2 On the basis of relative values. Assume that the basic material has a market value of $5 a pound and the scrap $1 a pound, and there are 5 pounds of scrap in 100 pounds of material purchased. For each 100 pounds purchased at a cost of $500, the relative values are $475 for the 95 pounds of good material and $5 for the 5 pounds that become scrap. Total value is $480, and the cost attributable to the scrap is $\frac{5}{480}$ of $500, the cost of the 100 pounds of material purchased.

3 On the basis of the net realizable value. If the scrap has a net realizable value of $5, then $5 is deducted from the cost of the main product and assigned to scrap.

In many cases the accountant will neglect the allocation of any part of the cost to the scrap, on the theory that the cost allocated is so insignificant that no useful purpose is served. The method selected should be applied consistently.

INVENTORY VALUATION FOR LONG-TERM little CONSTRUCTION CONTRACTS

Contracts for construction of ships, bridges, dams, and similar projects often require several years to complete. Such contracts present special problems of inventory valuation and profit recognition. For a business engaged in long-term contracts, two approaches to inventory valuation and profit recognition are available:

1 The completed-contract method
2 The percentage-of-completion method

Under the **completed-contract** method, inventory of construction in progress is valued at cost; no profit is recognized on the contract until the contract is completed and the work accepted by the customer. There may be some years in which no contracts are completed; consequently, in those years the company would have neither revenue nor profit on contracts. In fact, a loss would be reported to the extent of selling, general, administrative, and other expenses not chargeable to the inventories. In the years in which a long-term contract is finally completed, the entire profit created through several years of production would be recognized, even though only a small part of the work was performed in the final year of the contract.

To avoid such misleading reporting, many companies engaged in long-term contracts employ the *percentage-of-completion* method of accounting. This method (also known as the *production basis* of profit recognition) calls for accruing the profit over the life of the contract in accordance with the progress achieved each year. If the work performed in a given year is estimated to represent 10% of total performance under the contract, then 10% of the total estimated profit is considered earned. This accrual of profit is accomplished by increasing the carrying value of the inventory of construction in progress.

Accounting for long-term construction contract illustrated

A bridge is to be constructed by the Regal Construction Company beginning in Year 1 at a contract price of $900,000 with estimated construction costs totaling $750,000. The bridge is expected to be completed in Year 3. The construction costs incurred, cost estimates, and other pertinent data are presented below in summary form for each of the three years:

	Year 1	Year 2	Year 3
Construction costs incurred	$125,000	$495,000	$145,000
Estimated cost to complete the contract .	625,000	155,000	–0–
Amounts billed to customers.	110,000	565,000	225,000
Collections from customers on billings . .	90,000	520,000	265,000
Operating expenses incurred	15,000	30,000	22,500

Completed-contract Method Using the completed-contract method, the journal entries to record the transactions relating to the construction of the bridge are shown on page 346 for the Regal Construction Company.

Direct costs incurred on the contract are accumulated in the Construction in Progress account and amounts billed to the customer are recorded in the Partial Billings on Contract account. These account titles may vary. When the project is completed and approved by the customer, the costs applicable to the project are transferred to an expense account (Construction Costs Applicable to Revenue Realized) and partial billings relating to the project are transferred to Construction Revenue Realized.

The only closing entries required at the end of the first two years would be to close the Operating Expenses account, since no gross profit would have been recognized in these years. In cases where operating expenses can be identified with particular projects, inclusion of these expenses in the cost of the construction would be desirable. When a contract is expected to result in a loss, the loss should be recognized as soon as it is determinable by a debit to Loss on Long-term Contract and a credit

REGAL CONSTRUCTION COMPANY
Journal Entries—Completed-contract Method

Accounts and explanations of transactions	Year 1 Debit	Year 1 Credit	Year 2 Debit	Year 2 Credit	Year 3 Debit	Year 3 Credit
Operating Expenses .	15,000		30,000		22,500	
Construction in Progress	125,000		495,000		145,000	
Materials, Cash, etc.		140,000		525,000		167,500
To record operating expenses and construction costs.						
Accounts Receivable	110,000		565,000		225,000	
Partial Billings on Contract		110,000		565,000		225,000
To record billings on contract.						
Cash	90,000		520,000		265,000	
Accounts Receivable . .		90,000		520,000		265,000
To record collections from customer.						
Partial Billings on Contract					900,000	
Construction Costs Applicable to Revenue Realized					765,000	
Construction Revenue Realized. . . .						900,000
Construction in Progress . . .						765,000
To record contract revenue realized and applicable construction costs upon final approval of project by customer.						

to Construction in Progress. The credit to Construction in Progress eliminates from the inventory account the excess of the estimated cost of the contract over the total contract revenue.

In Year 3, balances in the Operating Expense account, the Construction Costs Applicable to Revenue Realized account, and the Construction Revenue Realized account would be closed to the Income Summary account. The income statement for Year 3 for the Regal Construction Company would show the following:

Construction revenue realized	$900,000
Less: Construction costs applicable to revenue realized	765,000
Gross profit on long-term construction contract	$135,000
Operating expenses	22,500
Operating income	$112,500

The balance sheet for the Regal Construction Company would include the following amounts when the completed-contract method is used:

	End of Year 1	End of Year 2	End of Year 3
Current assets:			
Accounts receivable	$20,000	$65,000	$25,000
Inventories:			
Construction in progress	$125,000		
Less: Partial billings on contract	110,000		
Costs of uncompleted contract in excess of related billings.	$15,000		
Current liabilities:			
Partial billings on contract		$675,000	
Less: Construction in progress		620,000	
Billings on uncompleted contract in excess of related costs . . .		$55,000	

Under the completed-contract method, the amount billed to customers may exceed the amount of construction costs incurred; therefore, when the Partial Billings on Contract account balance is deducted from the Construction in Progress account balance, a credit balance results. The AICPA offers the following guidelines in reporting such a balance in the balance sheet:

> When the completed-contract method is used, an excess of accumulated costs over related billings should be shown in the balance sheet as a current asset, and an excess of accumulated billings over related costs should be shown among the liabilities, in most cases as a current liability. If costs exceed billings on some contracts, and billings exceed costs on others, the contracts should ordinarily be segregated so that the figures on the asset side include only those contracts on which costs exceed billings, and those on the liability side include only those on which billings exceed costs. It is suggested that the asset item be described as "costs of uncompleted contracts in excess of related billings" rather than as "inventory" or "work in process," and that the item on the liability side be described as "billings on uncompleted contracts in excess of related costs."[9]

In our illustration of the bridge construction contract, the $15,000 excess of construction costs over partial billings on contracts at the end of Year 1 appears as a current asset on the balance sheet; at the end of Year 2, however, the $55,000 excess of partial billings on contracts over construction costs to date is included under current liabilities. These accounts are considered current because they arise in the normal operating cycle of a construction business. The balance in Accounts Receivable at the end of Year 1, $20,000, is composed of billings of $110,000 less collections to date of $90,000; at the end of Year 2, the balance in Accounts Receivable is $65,000, consisting of cumulative billings to date of $675,000 less total collections to date of $610,000; and at the end of Year 3, only $25,000 ($900,000 − $875,000) remains to be collected from the customer.

Percentage-of-completion Method The percentage of completion represented by each year's work may be based on (1) *engineering estimates* of the work performed to date relative to the total work required under the contract or (2) the *relationship between the cost incurred to date and the total estimated cost to complete the contract.* The percentage of completion determined by either of these two methods is applied to the contract price to determine the amount of revenue and gross profit earned to date.

In choosing between these two methods of establishing the percentage of completion, it is well to recognize that performance under some contracts will require that a substantial part of the material to be used for the entire contract be ordered before any actual construction takes place. These costs incurred for material can constitute a large part of the total costs of the contract, although little or no actual progress has been made

[9]*Accounting Research and Terminology Bulletins—Final Edition, ARB No. 45,* AICPA (New York: 1961), p. 6.

toward the completion of the project. When these conditions exist, a percentage of completion based on engineering and architectural estimates may be superior to that based on relative costs for purposes of recognizing realized contract revenue and gross profit. The AICPA has suggested that during the early stages of a contract, costs of items such as materials and subcontracts should be excluded from the total cost incurred in calculating the percentage of completion.[10] Mere acquisition of materials or making a deposit with a subcontractor does not give rise to the realization of revenue.

The AICPA has sanctioned the percentage-of-completion method under certain circumstances as follows:

> It is . . . a generally accepted accounting procedure to accrue revenues under certain types of contracts and thereby recognize profits, on the basis of partial performance, when the circumstances are such that total profit can be estimated with reasonable accuracy and ultimate realization is reasonably assured. Particularly when the performance of a contract requires a substantial period of time from inception to completion, there is ample precedent for pro-rata recognition of profit as the work progresses, if the total profit and the ratio of the performance to date to the complete performance can be computed reasonably and collection is reasonably assured.[11]

If the Regal Construction Company determines the percentage of completion on the basis of cost incurred to date as a fraction of the total estimated cost to be incurred on the contract, the journal entries for the three-year period would be as shown on page 350. The calculation of the gross profit earned on the basis of costs incurred related to total estimated costs is illustrated on page 351.

At the end of the second year, the estimate of the gross profit expected for the entire contract changed because the contract price was fixed while the **estimates of the cost** necessary to complete the contract changed. The percentage of completion in Years 1 and 2 was determined by relating the actual cost incurred to date to the total estimated cost to be incurred. This percentage was applied to the total estimated gross profit on the contract to determine the gross profit earned to date. The gross profit for the particular year was then determined by subtracting that gross profit which had been previously recognized from the gross profit earned to date.

Although the percentage-of-completion method allows for the recognition of gross profit as the work progresses, this same calculation may in some cases indicate that a loss is probable. In the event that a loss can be foreseen, **ARB No. 45** requires that "in most circumstances provision should be made for the loss on the entire contract. If there is a close relationship between profitable and unprofitable contracts, . . . the group may be treated as a unit in determining the necessity for a provision for

---

[10] *Ibid.,* p. 4.

[11] *Accounting Research and Terminology Bulletins—Final Edition,* AICPA (New York: 1961), chap. 11A, p. 95.

REGAL CONSTRUCTION COMPANY
Journal Entries—Percentage-of-completion Method

Accounts and explanations of transactions	Year 1 Debit	Year 1 Credit	Year 2 Debit	Year 2 Credit	Year 3 Debit	Year 3 Credit
Operating Expenses .	15,000		30,000		22,500	
Construction in Progress	125,000		495,000		145,000	
Materials, Cash, etc.		140,000		525,000		167,500
To record operating expenses and construction costs.						
Accounts Receivable	110,000		565,000		225,000	
Partial Billings on Contract. .		110,000		565,000		225,000
To record billings on contract.						
Cash	90,000		520,000		265,000	
Accounts Receivable		90,000		520,000		265,000
To record collections from customer.						
Construction in Progress	25,000		75,000		35,000	
Gross Profit on Long-term Contract		25,000		75,000		35,000
To recognize the gross profit earned, estimated on the basis of cost incurred to total estimated cost. (Calculation of gross profit earned appears on p. 351).						
Partial Billings on Contract					900,000	
Construction in Progress . . .						900,000
To record approval of project by customer.						

Calculation of Gross Profit Earned
Years 1, 2, and 3

Year 1 Actual construction cost incurred in Year 1 . . . . . $125,000

Estimated remaining cost to complete the contract   625,000

Total estimated cost of completing the contract . $750,000

Gross profit earned in Year 1:

Contract price, $900,000 × ($125,000/

$750,000) $150,000

Less: Actual construction cost incurred in

Year 1 . . . .   (125,000)

Gross profit earned in Year 1   . . . . $25,000

Year 2 Actual construction cost incurred to date

($125,000 + $495,000) $620,000

Estimated remaining cost to complete the contract   155,000

Total estimated cost of completing the contract . $775,000

Gross profit earned in Year 2:

Contract price, $900,000 × ($620,000/

$775,000) $720,000

Less: Actual construction cost incurred to date .   (620,000)

Gross profit earned to date $100,000

Less: Gross profit recognized in Year 1 . . . . . .   (25,000)

Gross profit earned in Year 2   . . . . $75,000

Year 3 Contract price $900,000

Less: Actual construction cost incurred in complet-

ing the contract . . . .   (765,000)

Actual total gross profit earned on contract $135,000

Less: Gross profit recognized in Years 1 and 2

($25,000 + $75,000) . . . .   (100,000)

Remaining gross profit earned in Year 3   . . . . $35,000

loss."[12] The loss would be recorded by a debit to Loss on Long-term Contracts and a credit to Construction in Progress. Thus, both the completed-contract and the percentage-of-completion methods of accounting for a given long-term contract produce identical results when it appears that a loss will be incurred on a given contract.

Although it would be possible to show only the **gross profit realized** each year in the income statement, the generally accepted practice is to show the full construction revenue realized and the construction costs appli-

[12] *Accounting Research and Terminology Bulletins—Final Edition, ARB No. 45, op. cit.,* p. 5.

cable to the revenue realized. This is illustrated for the Regal Construction Company below:

	Year 1	Year 2	Year 3
Construction revenue realized	$150,000	$570,000	$180,000
Less: Construction costs applicable to			
revenue realized	125,000	495,000	145,000
Gross profit realized on long-term con-			
struction contract	$ 25,000	$ 75,000	$ 35,000

The balance sheet for the Regal Construction Company would include the following amounts when the percentage-of-completion method is used:

	End of Year 1	End of Year 2	End of Year 3
Current assets:			
Accounts receiv-			
able	$20,000	$65,000	$25,000
Inventories:			
Construction			
in progress .	$150,000	$720,000	
Less: Partial			
billings on			
contract . . .	110,000	675,000	
Costs and			
profit on un-			
completed			
contract in			
excess of			
related bill-			
ings	$40,000	$45,000	

When the percentage-of-completion method of accounting is used, Construction in Progress is shown in the balance sheet as part of inventories (the same as under the completed-contract method). The inventory is valued at the cumulative construction cost incurred, plus the gross profit earned to date, less partial billings on the contract to date. The $150,000 balance in the Construction in Progress account at the end of Year 1 consists of construction costs of $125,000 plus the $25,000 gross profit earned in Year 1. At the end of Year 2, the balance of $720,000 in the Construction in Progress account consists of construction costs of $620,000 incurred in Years 1 and 2 plus $100,000 of gross profit earned in Years 1 and 2.

Income tax considerations

The income tax laws permit the use of either the completed-contract method (all gross profit recognized in year of completion) or the percentage-of-completion method (gross profit accrued as performance progresses). For tax purposes, expenses of the contractor which are not directly related to the project under construction are expenses of the year in which they were incurred. And, finally, the contractor is required to use one of the two methods consistently. A change in the method of valuing the construction in progress for tax purposes requires the approval of the Internal Revenue Service. If the percentage-of-completion method is used for financial reporting purposes and the completed-contract method for income tax purposes, deferred income taxes should be recorded to give effect to the timing difference in income recognition. This problem is considered in Chapter 20.

Disclosure and consistency

The fact that under varying conditions inventories may be valued at cost, the lower of cost or market, net selling price, replacement cost, or net realizable value has placed a tremendous burden on management and independent accountants. In view of the impact which inventory valuation has on the working capital position and the measurement of net income, the method used for pricing the inventory should always be disclosed. The method adopted should be used consistently; without the consistent application of one of the methods of pricing the inventory, the value of comparative financial statements would be diminished.

The desirability of applying accounting techniques consistently should not preclude a change in method. When a change in the application of accounting techniques is desirable to provide more complete or meaningful information, the change should be made. If such a change has a material effect on the financial statements, the effect should be disclosed. The reporting problems in connection with an accounting change for inventories are discussed in greater detail in Chapter 22.

REVIEW QUESTIONS

1 Under what conditions may a portion of the inventory cost be written off prior to the actual disposal of the items comprising the inventory?

2 Define the term **market** as used in the inventory valuation procedure usually referred to as the lower-of-cost-or-market rule.

3 What are the arguments against the use of the lower-of-cost-or-market method of valuing inventories?

4 Is there any difference, insofar as inventory valuation is concerned, between an item having a cost of $50 which regularly sells for $75 but which has been so physically damaged that it can be sold for no more than $55 and the same item when there is no physical damage but the cost of replacing the item has declined to $30?

5 Under what conditions, if any, is it permissible to recognize anticipated price declines in the accounts?

6 Under what conditions, if any, should losses arising out of price declines involving future purchase commitments be recognized in the accounts?

7 There are two accepted procedures for accounting for operations involving long-term construction contracts. What are the two methods? What criteria are used in choosing between the methods? How can you justify a departure from the accepted practice of recognizing revenue only at the time of sale?

8 When a business adopts the percentage-of-completion method of accounting for long-term contracts, there are two generally used methods of estimating the portion completed. What are these two methods and under what circumstances might each be used?

9 During the early stages of a construction project, some material costs and subcontract costs are not included in the total cost incurred when computing the percentage of completion. Why are these costs not included?

10 Under the percentage-of-completion method of accounting for long-term contracts, anticipated gross profits are recognized as the construction progresses but anticipated losses are recognized as soon as they can be reasonably ascertained. Why does this seeming inconsistency exist?

11 In view of the variety of procedures available for valuing the inventory and the diverse solutions that are produced by the various methods, how can the user of financial statements be assured that comparability exists between statements of the same company over a period of years?

EXERCISES

Ex. 9-1 Given below are three different sets of assumptions relating to an item in inventory:

	Case 1	Case 2	Case 3
Actual cost	$12,400	$20,000	$28,000
Selling price	$30,000	$30,000	$30,000
Cost to complete and ship to customers	$ 4,000	$ 4,000	$ 4,000
Normal gross profit on selling price	25%	25%	10%
Replacement cost	$14,000	$18,000	$26,500
Inventory value at lower of cost or market	$_____	$_____	$_____

Ex. 9-2 You are given the following facts about four items included in the inventory oɪ the Macao Corporation:

	Item			
	W	X	Y	Z
Actual cost	$50	$62	$29	$46
Replacement cost	52	48	25	40
Sales price less selling and completion expense.	53	59	23	42
Sales price less selling and completion expense and less				
normal profit	47	51	20	38

Indicate which figure would be used in pricing the ending inventory in accordance with the AICPA rule.

Ex. 9-3 The inventory for the General Hardware Company consists of two major groups listed below:

	Quantities	Unit cost	Replacement cost
Group A:			
Item XP	80	$ 6	$ 5
Item XQ	40	8	9
Item XR	30	10	8
Group B:			
Item YS	100	$ 4	$ 3
Item YT	150	9	8
Item YU	300	12	14

Prepare a schedule similar to the one illustrated on page 334, computing inventory value using the lower-of-cost-or-market method applied on (1) each item, (2) separate inventory groups, and (3) the inventory as a whole.

Ex. 9-4 The John-Sohn Company reports its inventory on the basis of lower of cost or market by using a valuation account to reduce cost to a lower market. Inventories at the end of the current year are as follows:

	Cost	Market
Inventories.	$200,000	$165,000

Prepare the entry to recognize the write-down of inventory to market and show how inventories should be reported in the balance sheet at the end of the current year.

Ex. 9-5 In October of the current year the Long Company agreed to purchase 7,500 tons of material next year at the fixed price of $100 per ton. The contract is not subject to cancellation. At the end of the current year the replacement cost of the material stands at $88 per ton.

Prepare the journal entry to recognize the loss on the purchase commitment at the end of the current year.

Ex. 9-6 Stanislaus Construction Co. began operations in 1975. By year-end, the first project was finished and a second project was underway, as follows:

	Project no. 1	*Project no. 2*
Cost incurred in 1975	$ 80,000	$ 85,000
Portion of estimated total cost.	100%	50%
Total contract price	$100,000	$200,000
Billings on contract during the year	$100,000	$ 95,000
Collections from customers during the year	$ 92,000	$ 75,000

Prepare journal entries for 1975 (excluding closing entries) to record the transactions relating to the two projects if (1) the completed-contract method of accounting for long-term contracts is used, and (2) the percentage-of-completion method of accounting for long-term contracts is used.

Ex. 9-7 Refer to Ex. 9-6. Show how the account balances relating to long-term construction contracts will appear in the balance sheet of the Stanislaus Construction Co. at the end of 1975 if (1) the completed-contract method of accounting is used, and (2) the percentage-of-completion method of accounting is used.

Ex. 9-8 Dale Company is in the construction business. A long-term contract was entered into in 1973. The contract price was $700,000 and the company expected to earn a gross profit of $80,000 on the contract. Following are data on experience to date:

Year ended *Dec. 31*	*Cumulative* *costs incurred*	*Estimated cost to* *complete contract*
1973	$ 49,600	$570,400
1974	172,800	467,200
1975	378,000	252,000

Prepare a schedule computing the gross profit earned in 1973, 1974, and 1975 by Dale Company under the percentage-of-completion method based on costs incurred to date and estimated cost to complete the contract.

SHORT CASES FOR ANALYSIS AND DECISION

Case 9-1 The Valdez Manufacturing Corp. had followed the practice of pricing the year-end inventory at the lower of fifo cost or market for many years. During this period prices had tended to move in a rather general upward trend. For the past three years the general trend of price movement has been very erratic and the management has become concerned with the effect on reported income of the lower-of-cost-or-market inventory valuation. You have been requested to analyze the situation and make a recommendation to management supported by calculations and accounting logic. The beginning inventory on January 1, 1973, was valued at both cost and market at $60,000; the remaining data are given on page 357.

	1975	1974	1973
Sales	$425,000	$325,000	$375,000
Net purchases	300,000	225,000	260,000
Year-end inventory:			
At cost	75,000	70,000	60,000
At market	55,000	82,000	45,000

Instructions
a Prepare partial income statements for each of the three years using (1) cost and (2) lower of cost or market in the determination of cost of goods sold.
b Draft a report to management explaining the effect of their present procedure on reported profits. Assuming that this pattern of fluctuating profits is expected to continue, which method would you recommend? Why?

Case 9-2 At December 31, 1975, the May Company has outstanding purchase commitments for purchase of 100,000 gallons, at $2 per gallon, of a raw material to be used in their manufacturing process. The company prices its raw material inventory at the lower of cost or market.

Instructions
a Assuming that the market price as of December 31, 1975, is $2.05, how would this matter be treated in the financial statements? Explain fully.
b Assuming that the market price as of December 31, 1975, is $1.70 instead of $2.05, how would you treat this situation in the statements? Give your reasoning.
c Give the entry in January 1976, when the 100,000-gallon shipment is received, assuming that the situation given in (b) above existed at December 31, 1975. Give an explanation of your treatment.

Case 9-3 The Loo Company has three contracts in progress at December 31, the data for which are presented below:

Contract no.	Contract price	Total estimated cost	Cost incurred to date (all in current year)	Billings to date	Collections to date
1	$ 750,000	$ 600,000	$400,000	$450,000	$405,000
2	1,000,000	1,050,000	525,000	400,000	380,000
3	900,000	675,000	202,500	225,000	202,500

Instructions
a Prepare partial financial statements for Loo Company reporting the details of the above contracts using (1) completed-contract method and (2) percentage-of-completion method, using estimated total cost and actual cost incurred to determine the degree of completion to date. Show total revenue and applicable costs in the partial income statement.
b What are the essential differences between the two sets of financial statements?
c Which set of statements do you think presents the more meaningful data about the long-term contracts of Loo Company?

Case 9-4 The following statement of financial position was prepared by employees of your client, Flintstone Construction Company:

FLINTSTONE CONSTRUCTION COMPANY
Statement of Financial Position
October 31, 1975

Current assets:

Cash	$ 182,200	
Accounts receivable (less allowance of $15,000 for uncollectible accounts).	220,700	
Materials, supplies, labor, and overhead charged to construction contracts	2,026,000	
Materials and supplies not charged to construction contracts	288,000	
Deposits made to secure performance of contracts	360,000	$3,076,900

Less current liabilities:

Accounts payable to subcontractors.	$ 141,100	
Payable for materials and supplies.	65,300	
Accrued payroll	8,260	
Accrued interest on mortgage note	12,000	
Estimated income taxes payable	66,000	292,660
Net working capital.		$2,784,240

Property, plant and equipment (at cost):

	Cost	Depreciation	Value	
Land and buildings	$ 983,300	$ 310,000	$ 673,300	
Machinery and equipment . . .	1,135,700	568,700	567,000	
	$2,119,000	$ 878,700		1,240,300

Deferred charges:

Prepaid taxes and other expenses	$ 11,700	
Points charged by lender on mortgage note	10,800	22,500
Total net working capital and noncurrent assets		$4,047,040

Less deferred liabilities:

Mortgage note payable.	$ 300,000	
Unearned revenue on construction in progress	1,898,000	2,198,000
Total net assets.		$1,849,040

Stockholders' equity:

6% preferred stock at par value	$ 400,000	
Common stock, at par value, 80,000 shares issued and outstanding	800,000	
Paid-in capital in excess of par value of common stock .	210,000	
Retained earnings	439,040	
Total stockholders' equity		$1,849,040

You discover that management is unable to develop dependable estimates of costs to complete contracts in progress. The average completion period for the company's jobs is 18 months. The company's method of journalizing contract transactions is summarized in the following pro forma entries:

(1) *Materials, Supplies, Labor, and Overhead Charged to Construction*
   Contracts . . . . *xx*
           Cash, Various Other Assets, Payables, Accumulated Depreciation,
           etc. . . . . *xx*
   To record actual cost incurred on contracts.

(2) *Materials, Supplies, Labor, and Overhead Charged to Construction*
   Contracts . . . . *xx*
           Unearned Revenue on Construction in Progress . . . . *xx*
   To record estimated profit on construction in progress to be de-
   ferred.

(3) *Accounts Receivable* . . . . *xx*
           Unearned Revenue on Construction in Progress . . . . *xx*
   To charge customers for costs incurred to date. [Most contracts
   provide that customers shall be billed for costs as incurred at the
   end of each month and that while jobs are in progress 95% of amounts
   billed shall be remitted within 15 days of billing. Upon job comple-
   tion the remainder of the contract price is billed and recorded in an
   entry (5 below) in which the gross profit realized on the job is also
   recognized.]

(4) *Cash* . . . . *xx*
           Accounts Receivable . . . . *xx*
   To record collections from customers.

(5) *Accounts Receivable* . . . . *xx*
   Unearned Revenue on Construction in Progress . . . . *xx*
           Gross Profit Realized on Completed Contracts . . . . *xx*
           Materials, Supplies, Labor, and Overhead Charged to Construction
           Contracts . . . . *xx*
   To record completion of certain contracts.

Instructions

a Identify the weaknesses in the statement of financial position prepared for Flintstone Construction Company.

b For each item identified in part (*a*), indicate the preferred treatment and explain why the treatment is preferable.

PROBLEMS

Group A

9A-1 The following data were taken from the inventory records of Neighborhood Supply Company at December 31 of the current year:

Department	Item no.	Quantity (units)	Cost per unit	Market per unit
Hardware	1104	40	$24.00	$25.00
	1105	50	12.10	11.70
	1107	10	8.00	9.60
Power tools	2140	60	4.00	3.00
	2142	14	14.00	13.00
	2143	8	36.00	37.00
Toys	3201	70	2.40	2.00
	3202	80	4.90	4.50
	3204	110	1.20	1.30

Instructions

a Price the inventory using the lower-of-cost-or-market method applied to: (1) each individual item in the inventory, (2) major groups within the inventory, and (3) the inventory as a whole.

b Which value would you recommend for inclusion in the financial statements? Why is the value you choose preferred to the other two?

9A-2 Oil Products Company manufactures and sells four products, the inventories of which are priced at the lower of cost or market. The company considers a gross profit margin of 30% of sales to be normal for all four products.

The following information was compiled as of December 31:

Product	Units	Original cost	Cost to replace	Estimated cost to dispose	Expected selling price
75A-1	100	$35.00	$42.00	$15.00	$ 80.00
75B-2	50	47.50	45.00	20.50	95.00
75C-3	120	17.50	18.00	4.00	21.00
75D-4	60	45.00	46.00	26.00	100.00

Instructions

a Why are expected selling prices important in the application of the lower-of-cost-or-market rule?

b Prepare a schedule containing unit values (including "floor" and "ceiling") for determining the lower of cost or market on an individual product basis. Underscore for each product the unit value for the purpose of inventory valuation resulting from the application of the lower-of-cost-or-market rule. The last column of the schedule should contain the extension for each product and the total valuation of inventory.

c What effects, if any, do the expected selling prices have on the valuation of the four products by the lower-of-cost-or-market rule?

9A-3 The trial balance on page 361 for Concrete-Rex, Inc., has been adjusted for all items except ending inventory and income taxes:

CONCRETE-REX, INC.
Trial Balance
December 31,1975

Cash	$ 16,000	
Accounts receivable	40,000	
Inventory (at cost), at Dec. 31, 1974	52,000	
Short-term prepayments	2,000	
Buildings	100,000	
Accumulated depreciation: buildings		$ 30,500
Equipment	125,000	
Accumulated depreciation: equipment		75,000
Accounts payable		35,000
Mortgage payable ($12,000 due in 1976)		40,000
Capital stock, no par value, 10,000 shares outstanding		50,000
Retained earnings, Dec. 31, 1974		61,500
Dividends	15,000	
Sales		305,000
Sales returns and allowances	10,000	
Sales discounts	5,000	
Purchases, including freight charges	180,000	
Purchase discounts		3,500
Selling expenses	25,000	
General expenses	30,500	
Totals	$600,500	$600,500

Additional information:
(1) Inventory at the end of 1975 consists of the following:

	Cost	Replacement cost (net of freight and cash discount)
Inventory (cost includes freight charges but has not been reduced for 2% cash discount)	$65,000	$55,000

The controller for the company wants to recognize the decline in the market value of the inventory by setting up an Allowance for Inventory Price Decline; the write-down is included in the cost of goods sold in the income statement. The cost of the inventory should be reduced for purchase discounts which are normally taken by Concrete-Rex, Inc. You also ascertain that the cost of ending inventory includes $2,700 of worthless goods and $2,300 of freight charges. Freight applicable to the worthless goods amounts to $40.

(2) Income taxes on corporate income are as follows:

On first $25,000 of taxable income	22%
On taxable income over $25,000	48%

Instructions

a Determine the adjusted cost of the inventory at December 31, 1975, and prepare an entry to record the estimated loss in value of the inventory caused by declining prices.

b Prepare an income statement for the year ended December 31, 1975. The write-down of inventory to market should be included in the cost of goods sold.

c Prepare a balance sheet at December 31, 1975.

9A-4 The Vaquero Construction Company signed a contract with the Lincoln School District to build a school building for a contract price of $2,500,000. The contract provides for progress billings to be made when the building is 25, 50, and 75% complete. The final 25%, plus 10% withheld from each of the three earlier billings, is to be paid upon final inspection and acceptance by the school board. The original estimate by the contractor of the cost to complete the contract was $2,250,000, exclusive of general administrative expenses.

The construction record for the project was as follows:

Date	Cumulative cost incurred to date	Estimated cost to complete	General administrative expenses for the year
Dec. 31, 1973	$ 675,000	$1,575,000	$50,000
Dec. 31, 1974	1,870,000	330,000	52,000
Sept. 1, 1975	2,225,000	–0–	53,500

Vaquero Construction Company keeps its books on a calendar-year basis. The general administrative expenses cannot be reasonably allocated to various jobs. Billings were made on December 20, 1973, July 20, 1974, January 15, 1975, and August 15, 1975.

The construction was inspected periodically and installment payments representing 90% of the amount billed were received on January 5, 1974, August 14, 1974, and February 26, 1975. The building was completed and finally approved and accepted by the school board on September 5, 1975. The final payment on the contract was received on September 10.

Instructions   Present the applicable portions of the balance sheet and income statement for each of the three years for (**a**) the completed-contract method and (**b**) the percentage-of-completion method.

9A-5 Trueblood Contractors, Inc., undertakes long-term large-scale construction projects and began operations on October 15, 1974, with contract no. 1, its only job during 1974. A trial balance of the company's general ledger at December 31, 1975, follows:

TRUEBLOOD CONTRACTORS, INC.

Trial Balance

December 31, 1975

Cash	$ 68,090	
Accounts receivable	136,480	
Construction in progress	421,320	
Plant and equipment.	35,500	
Accumulated depreciation		$ 8,000

Accounts payable		$ 70,820
Deferred income taxes		1,908
Partial billings on contracts		459,400
Capital stock, $5 par value.		139,000
Retained earnings		2,862
Selling and administrative expenses	$ 20,600	
Totals	$681,990	$681,990

The following information is available:
(1) The company has the approval to determine income on the completed-contract basis for income tax purposes and on the percentage-of-completion basis for financial reporting.
(2) At December 31, 1975, there were three jobs in progress, the contract prices of which had been computed as follows:

	Contract no. 1	Contract no. 2	Contract no. 3
Labor and material costs	$169,000	$34,500	$265,700
Indirect costs	30,000	5,500	48,000
Total costs	$199,000	$40,000	$313,700
Add: Gross profit in contract.	40,000	3,000	30,300
Total contract price	$239,000	$43,000	$344,000

During the year, billings are credited to Partial Billings on Contracts; at year-end this account is charged for the amount of revenue to be recognized as realized in the current year, which is credited to a Realized Contract Revenue account. Construction costs applicable to realized contract revenue are transferred from Construction in Progress to a Cost of Realized Contract Revenue account.
(3) All job costs are charged to Construction in Progress. Cost estimates are carefully derived by engineers and architects and are considered reliable. Data on costs to December 31, 1975, follow:

Contract no.	Original estimate	Incurred to date		
		Total	Labor & materials	Indirect
1	$199,000	$115,420	$ 92,620	$22,800
2	40,000	32,000	26,950	5,050
3	313,700	313,700	265,700	48,000
Totals	$552,700	$461,120	$385,270	$75,850

(4) At December 31, 1974, accumulated costs on contract no. 1 were $39,800; no costs had accumulated on contract no. 2 and contract no. 3. All work on contract no. 3 was completed on December 30, 1975.
(5) Assume that the income tax rate is 40%.

Instructions

a Prepare a schedule computing the percentage of completion of contracts at December 31, 1975.

b Prepare a schedule computing the amounts of revenue, related costs, and gross profit to be recognized in 1975 from contracts in progress at December 31, 1975.

c Prepare a schedule computing estimated income taxes and the income tax liability at December 31, 1975.

d Give the adjusting journal entries that are necessary at December 31, 1975, to recognize revenue realized to date, cost of recognized revenue, and income taxes.

Group B

9B-1 You are employed by Joe's Bargain Counter as an accountant. Joe presents you with the following information about several items included in the year-end inventory and asks you to indicate the proper unit price in accordance with the lower-of-cost-or-market rule. He tells you that he knows of the AICPA rule as to ceiling and floor but he does not understand the use of the two terms **replacement cost** and **net realizable value,** which seem to be used interchangeably.

Item	Original cost	Expected selling price	Replacement cost (market)
1	$ 2.00	$ 2.40	$ 1.75
2	5.00	7.50	5.25
3	2.15	3.00	2.00
4	6.82	6.50	6.00
5	1.05	1.20	1.00
6	14.60	18.00	15.00
7	3.80	4.20	3.75
8	4.50	5.00	3.20
9	6.00	9.00	6.50
10	8.80	10.00	8.00

Assume that selling expense is 10% and normal profit is 25% of selling price.

Instructions Indicate the unit value which should be used to price each of the items in the inventory in accordance with the lower-of-cost-or-market rule and explain each selection so that Joe can understand the application of the AICPA rule.

9B-2 **Part A** The inventory of the Paulson Manufacturing Company includes custom-made pollution control equipment which was assembled for the Valley Paper Mills, Inc. Because of financial difficulties, Valley filed for bankruptcy before the equipment was delivered. Provisions of the agreement between Paulson and Valley provided that Paulson may keep the deposit of $4,000, representing 25% of the total price, if Valley is unable to take delivery of the equipment. At the end of the current year Paulson reached an agreement with another customer to sell the equipment early in the following year for $9,500 after making certain changes which are estimated to cost $850. Paulson generally earns a 20% gross profit (on contract price) on the manufacture of custom equipment.

The actual costs of assembling the pollution control equipment and the estimated cost of duplicating the equipment at the end of the current year follow:

	Actual costs	Costs to duplicate
Parts and materials	$ 6,000	$ 6,500
Direct labor	4,000	4,800
Factory overhead.	3,000	3,200
Total	$13,000	$14,500

Instructions Determine the "ceiling" and "floor" limits on replacement cost. What is the value that should be assigned at the end of the current year to the pollution control equipment on a lower-of-cost-or-market basis?

Part B In the manufacture of Product Y, Paulson Manufacturing Company uses a raw material which costs $2 per pound. Scrap material resulting from shaping and trimming the raw material has a market price of 50 cents per pound and no costs are incurred in selling the scrap. During the current year, 10,000 pounds of the raw material were placed in production and 500 pounds of scrap were accumulated in inventory.

Instructions Compute the cost to be assigned to the scrap (1) on the basis of weight (volume), (2) on the basis of relative value of the raw material and scrap, and (3) on the basis of net realizable value of the scrap.

9B-3 You are engaged in the annual audit of the Sargent Company, a manufacturer of oil-field equipment and parts. At May 31, the end of the company's fiscal year, the finished goods inventory is on the books at $950,600. The company values its year-end inventory at the lower of cost or market, with market defined as net realizable value. For Sargent Company net realizable value means the "ceiling" or estimated net selling price less selling expenses, which are estimated to be 15% of the net selling price. In order to make this valuation, you decide to test the inventory using a representative sample. You select items representing a total cost of $256,425 for your test. Included in the sample group were four parts which have value relationships comparable to part no. 250. The relevant data for these parts are listed below:

Part no.	Per inventory of May 31		Most recent cost to produce	Latest net selling price
	Units	Unit cost		
250	6	$4,425	$4,154	$3,904.41
475	2	3,180		
625	3	7,250		
830	1	5,435		

On all other items included in your test, you determined that the inventory was stated in excess of net realizable value by $31,132.75.

In addition, there are two items, not included in the above test, in the May 31 inventory which require special consideration.

(1) One draw works listed at $65,000. This draw works was manufactured at a

cost of $140,000 and was written down to $65,000 at the end of the preceding year. The company expects to sell it for $96,000, and you have examined correspondence which tends to support this.
(2) One slush pump priced at a cost of $40,000. This is the first pump of this type produced by the company. The company expects to sell it for $38,000 less a 25% discount.

Instructions Assuming that your test is representative and valid, and taking into account the two special items above, compute the amount of write-down necessary to state the May 31 inventory at net realizable value. Make the necessary adjusting entry to record the write-down. (Use an Allowance for Inventory Price Decline account.) Present a partial balance sheet to illustrate how the inventory might be reported.

9B-4 Timely Construction, Inc., has contracted to build a section of a freeway system at a contract price of $45 million. Costs are estimated to total $40 million. The annual data with respect to this contract are as follows:

Year	Costs incurred	Estimated cost to complete	Billings	Collections
1	$ 9,720,000	$30,780,000	$ 9,000,000	$ 8,550,000
2	26,160,000	10,120,000	24,750,000	22,275,000
3	9,220,000	–0–	11,250,000	14,175,000

Instructions
a Record the summarized data in general journal form for (1) the completed-contract method and (2) the percentage-of-completion method. Do not prepare closing entries.
b Prepare a partial balance sheet for the (1) completed-contract method and (2) the percentage-of-completion method. Also prepare a summary of gross profit or loss on the contract for each year.

9B-5 The Davre Construction Company commenced doing business in January 1975. Construction activities for the year 1975 are summarized below.

Project	Total contract price	Contract costs to Dec. 31, 1975	Estimated additional costs to complete contracts	Cash collections to Dec. 31, 1975	Billings to Dec. 31, 1975
100	$ 310,000	$187,500	$ 12,500	$155,000	$155,000
101	415,000	195,000	255,000	210,000	249,000
102	350,000	320,000	–0–	300,000	350,000
103	300,000	16,500	183,500	–0–	4,000
	$1,375,000	$719,000	$451,000	$665,000	$758,000

The company is your client. The president has asked you to compute the amounts of revenue for the year ended December 31, 1975, that would be reported under the completed-contract method and the percentage-of-completion method of accounting for long-term contracts.

The following information is available:
(1) All contracts are with different customers.
(2) Any work remaining to be done on the contracts is expected to be completed in 1976.
(3) The company's accounts have been maintained on the completed-contract method.

Instructions
a Prepare a schedule computing the amount of gross profit by project for the year ended December 31, 1975, that would be reported under
  (1) The completed-contract method
  (2) The percentage-of-completion method
b Prepare a schedule under the completed-contract method computing the amounts that would appear in the company's balance sheet at December 31, 1975, for
  (1) Costs in excess of billings
  (2) Billings in excess of costs
c Prepare a schedule under the percentage-of-completion method that would appear in the company's balance sheet at December 31, 1975, for
  (1) Costs and estimated gross profit earned in excess of billings
  (2) Billings in excess of costs and estimated gross profit earned

CHAPTER 10

Inventory: other estimating techniques

In previous chapters we have considered the determination of inventory value through physical count and application of unit prices. In selecting these unit prices we have considered alternative methods of measuring cost as well as valuation at the lower of cost or market. The use of estimates is often an important factor in establishing inventory valuations, as we have noted in cases such as long-term contracts, and in the use of price indices for dollar-value lifo. In this chapter we are concerned with estimates of inventory either to establish or to verify the amount of inventory. This discussion is divided into three sections: (1) the gross profit method, (2) the retail method, and (3) the use of equivalent full units of output in estimating inventories for a manufacturing business.

GROSS PROFIT METHOD

The gross profit method is useful for several purposes: (1) to control and verify the validity of inventory cost; (2) to estimate interim inventory valuations between physical counts; and (3) to estimate the inventory value when necessary information normally used is lost or unavailable for any reason. The procedure involved is one of reducing sales to a cost basis; that is, cost of goods sold is estimated. The estimated cost of goods sold is then subtracted from the cost of total goods available for sale to arrive at the estimated inventory cost. We should point out that some department stores are able to determine cost of goods sold directly by attaching punched price tags to goods. When the goods are sold the tags are processed by computer to arrive at the total cost of goods sold.

Determining the gross profit and cost of goods sold percentage

The crucial factor in applying the gross profit method is the development of an accurate and realistic measure of the gross profit percentage. Frequently the best available measure is an average of the gross profit percentages for recent years, adjusted for any changes which are known to have taken place in the current year. The cost of goods sold percentage is determined by subtracting the gross profit percentage from 100%.

To illustrate the computation of ending inventory using the gross profit method, assume the following data for the Marina Sea Store:

Beginning inventory, at cost	$ 40,000
Net purchases	200,000
Net sales	225,000
Average rate of gross profit on net sales for past three years	30%

Assuming that the average rate of gross profit for the current period remained at 30%, the inventory cost at the end of the period would be estimated as follows:

Beginning inventory, at cost		$ 40,000
Net purchases		200,000
Goods available for sale		$240,000
Less approximate cost of goods sold:		
Net sales	$225,000	
Cost of goods percentage (100% − 30%)	.70	157,500
Approximate ending inventory		$ 82,500

The ending inventory computed by the gross profit method will be consistent with the usual method of pricing inventory. This follows from the fact that the gross profit percentage is based on historical records which have reflected the particular method of valuing the inventory. If the inventory is usually valued at lifo, the estimated inventory will approximate lifo cost; therefore, if the gross profit method is used as a basis for recovering an insured loss, the lifo inventory should, for insurance purposes, be priced at prevailing prices at the time of the loss.

Gross profit stated as percentage of cost of goods sold

The cost of goods sold percentage is obtained by subtracting the gross profit percentage, when stated as a percentage of net sales, from 100%. Frequently, the gross profit percentage is stated as a percentage of cost of goods sold. In such a situation the gross profit or cost of goods sold percentage must be converted to a percentage of net sales. The conversion is not difficult. One need only remember the relationship of net sales, cost of goods sold, and gross profit.

Assume the following data for Durham Golf Shop:

Beginning inventory, at cost	$ 25,000
Net purchases	150,000
Net sales	160,000
Gross profit percentage for the past two years as a percentage of cost of goods sold	25%

To convert this 25% of cost of goods sold to a comparable figure as a percentage of net sales, the following equation is helpful:

Net sales − cost of goods sold = gross profit on net sales

In the illustration, cost of goods sold = 100%, and gross profit on net sales = 25% of cost of goods sold. Therefore, net sales = 125% of cost of goods sold.

Net sales − cost of goods sold = gross profit on net sales

Let x = cost of goods sold

then

$$\$160,000 - x = .25x$$
$$\$160,000 = 1.25x$$
$$x = \frac{\$160,000}{1.25}$$
$$x = \$128,000$$
$$\$160,000 - \$128,000 = \$32,000$$
$$\frac{\$32,000}{\$160,000} = 20\%$$

Gross profit on net sales = 20% of net sales
Cost of goods sold percentage = 80% of net sales

The approximate inventory cost for the Durham Golf Shop can then be computed by the gross profit method as follows:

Beginning inventory, at cost		$ 25,000
Net purchases		150,000
Cost of goods available for sale.		$175,000
Less: Approximate cost of goods sold:		
Net sales	$160,000	
Cost of goods sold percentage	× .80	128,000
Approximate ending inventory		$ 47,000

Applying the gross profit method to departments

If there are several classes of goods which have a different markup percentage, the gross profit method yields accurate results only if the inventory for each class is computed individually. The use of a combined cost of goods sold percentage would require the unlikely assumption that the various classes of inventory are sold in the same relative proportions each year. To illustrate this point, assume that the gross profit percentage has averaged 50% for Department A and 30% for Department B. Thus the cost of goods sold percentage is 50% for Department A and 70% for Department B; the combined cost of goods sold percentage has averaged 65%. The cost of the ending inventory may be estimated as follows:

Estimate of Cost of Departmental and Combined Inventories
For the Current Year—Gross Profit Method

	Dept. A	Dept. B	Combined
Beginning inventory, at cost	$ 20,000	$ 40,000	$ 60,000
Net purchases	90,000	95,000	185,000
Cost of goods available for sale.	$110,000	$135,000	$245,000
Less: Approximate cost of goods sold:			
Net sales	$150,000	$150,000	$300,000
Average cost of goods sold percentage,			
prior years	50%	70%	65%
Approximate cost of goods sold	$ 75,000	$105,000	$195,000
Approximate ending inventory	$ 35,000	$ 30,000	$ 50,000

Using the combined cost of goods sold percentage (based on prior years' experience) produces an inventory estimate of $50,000, although the sum of the departmental inventories is estimated at $65,000

($35,000 + $30,000). The source of the error is clear when we note that the cost of goods sold percentage for the current period, determined by combining the departmental results, is not 65 but 60%, because a higher-than-usual proportion of total sales *this year* was made in Department A. The actual combined cost of goods sold percentage for the current year is determined below:

Total sales ($150,000 + $150,000) $300,000

Total estimated cost of goods sold ($75,000 + $105,000) $180,000

Combined cost of goods sold percentage for current year ($180,000
÷ $300,000) 60%

Inventory estimation from incomplete records

In the event that both inventory and records are destroyed by fire, the inventory value can be estimated by the use of the gross profit method. The gross profit percentage is established by referring to prior years' financial statements, which are presumably available. The beginning inventory for the current year is the ending inventory of the preceding year. Net purchases may be estimated by examining copies of the canceled checks retained by the bank and through correspondence with suppliers. Sales may be computed by reference to cash deposits and by estimation of the uncollected receivables by direct correspondence with customers.

THE RETAIL METHOD

The retail method is used primarily as a means of valuing the inventory of a retail business when there is an observable pattern between cost and sales price. Under periodic inventory procedures, the cost of the ending inventory is subtracted from the total cost of goods available to arrive at the cost of goods sold. Under the retail method, a record is kept of the sales value of goods available for sale, and the sales for the period are deducted from this total to produce an estimated ending inventory at selling price. The inventory valued at selling price is then reduced to approximate cost by applying the average ratio of cost to selling price.

Uses of the retail method

The uses of the retail method of estimating the cost of inventory are:

1 To verify the reasonableness of the inventory value at the end of the period. By using a different set of data from that used in pricing the inventory, the accountant can establish that the value assigned is reasonable.

2 To estimate the inventory at intervals between physical counts. In this way the retail method aids in the control function without requiring the detailed work of counting the items on hand.

3 To permit the valuation of an inventory when selling prices are the only accessible data. The use of this method allows the store to mark only the selling price on the merchandise and eliminates the need for referring to purchase invoices.

The retail method is illustrated in the following simplified example for the Eastern Company:

EASTERN COMPANY
Retail Method of Estimating Cost of Inventory
Current Year

	Cost	Retail
Beginning inventory	$ 45,000	$ 60,000
Net purchases	150,000	200,000
Goods available for sale	$195,000	$260,000
Cost to retail percentage ($195,000 ÷ $260,000) = 75%		
Less: Sales and normal shrinkage (cost = $210,000 × .75)	157,500	210,000
Ending inventory, at retail		$ 50,000
Ending inventory at estimated cost ($50,000 × .75) . . .	$ 37,500	

Although the retail method permits the calculation of inventory without a physical count of the items on hand, the accountant should insist that a physical inventory be taken periodically. Otherwise, "shrinkage" due to shoplifting, breakage, and other causes might go undetected and might result in an increasingly overstated inventory.

Normal shrinkage in the inventory is frequently estimated on the basis of the goods which were available for sale. The method which has received the most support in practice is to develop a percentage from the experience of past years, such as 1% of retail price of goods available for sale. This percentage is then used to determine the estimated shrinkage, which is deducted, along with sales, from goods available for sale at retail prices, to arrive at the estimated inventory at retail.[1] The cost of normal shrinkage should be included in the cost of goods sold; the cost of abnormal shrinkage (theft, unusual spoilage, etc.) should be reported separately in the income statement.

In the retail method the cost of the inventory is established by using an average cost ratio. The reliability of this procedure rests on one of two assumptions: (1) that there is a uniform relation between selling price and cost for all merchandise; or (2) that if the markup of various items

---

[1] When sales are made to employees or selected customers at a special discount price, such discounts should be added to sales in arriving at the estimated inventory at retail.

sold by the firm differs, the distribution of items in the inventory is roughly the same as the "mix" in the total goods available for sale. Because one of these assumptions is not likely to be valid for the business as a whole, the accuracy of the retail method is usually improved by applying it to individual departments of the business, and adding the resulting departmental inventories to arrive at the estimate of total ending inventory.

Retail trade terminology

The following terms, commonly used in retail business, should be understood by the accountant employing the retail method of estimating inventory.

Original sales price The price at which goods are originally offered for sale to the customer.

Markup The initial margin between retail and cost. It is variously referred to as **gross margin** or **mark-on.**

Additional markup An increase above the original sales price.

Markup cancellation A reduction in the selling price after there has been an additional markup. The reduction does not reduce the selling price below the original sales price. Additional markups less markup cancellations may be referred to as **net markups.**

Markdown A reduction in selling price below the original sales price.

Markdown cancellation An increase in the selling price, following a markdown, which does not raise the new selling price above the original selling price. Markdowns less markdown cancellations may be referred to as **net markdowns.**

To understand these terms, assume that an item which costs $20 is priced to sell at $30. The **markup** is $10, 50% of cost or $33\frac{1}{3}$% of the selling price. Generally, markups are expressed as a percentage of the selling price. In response to the great demand for the product, an **additional markup** of $3 is added, so that the selling price is raised to $33. As the demand decreases, the price is lowered to $31, a **markup cancellation** of $2. Subsequently, in order to dispose of the entire stock of the item, the price of the goods is reduced to $25, a markup cancellation of $1 and a **markdown** of $5. Finally management concludes that the remaining goods can be sold at a price of $28. A **markdown cancellation** of $3 is then made to increase the price from $25 to $28.

Application of the retail method—average cost basis

A clear understanding of the meaning of each term defined above is important in applying the retail method to arrive at a reasonably accurate estimate of inventory cost. The classification of net markdowns in the computation of the cost to retail percentage, for example, can have a significant effect on the estimated cost of inventory.

The following data for the Western Company are used to illustrate the treatment of net markups and net markdowns in the application of the retail method:

	Cost	Retail
Beginning inventory, Year 1	$16,000	$ 27,000
Net purchases during Year 1	75,000	110,000
Additional markups		5,000
Markup cancellations		(2,000)
Markdowns		(10,875)
Markdown cancellations		875
Net sales during Year 1		(90,000)
Ending inventory at retail		$ 40,000

The ending inventory at average cost, using the retail inventory method, is determined as follows:

WESTERN COMPANY
Estimate of Ending Inventory Using Retail Method—Average Cost Basis
Year 1

	Cost	Retail
Beginning inventory	$16,000	$ 27,000
Net purchases	75,000	110,000
Additional markups, less markup cancellations ($5,000 − $2,000)		3,000
Less: Markdowns, net of markdown cancellations ($10,875 − $875)		(10,000)
Goods available for sale	$91,000	$130,000
Cost to retail percentage ($91,000 ÷ $130,000) = 70%		
Deduct: Net sales (cost = $90,000 × .70)	63,000	90,000
Ending inventory at retail		$ 40,000
Ending inventory at estimated average cost ($40,000 × .70)	$28,000	

The cost to retail percentage is determined after adding net markups and deducting net markdowns to the goods available for sale at retail. This procedure results in valuation of the ending inventory at *average cost.* The estimated cost of the ending inventory, $28,000, would be accurate only if the goods on hand consist of a representative sample of all goods available for sale during Year 1. For example, if the ending inventory does not include any of the goods on hand at the beginning of the year, the cost of retail percentage should be computed without using the beginning inventory figures. Similarly, if all goods on which the net markups and markdowns were made have been sold, both the net markups and the net markdowns should be excluded from the computation of the cost to retail percentage. Under such circumstances, however, the net markups and markdowns still would be used to arrive at the amount of the ending inventory at retail.

Application of the retail method—lower of average cost or market

The retail inventory method can be adopted to produce inventory valuations approximating the lower of cost or market when there have been changes in the costs and selling prices of goods during the period. The crucial factor in the calculation of estimated cost of ending inventory by the retail method is the treatment of net markups and net markdowns in the cost to retail percentage. The inclusion of net markups and the exclusion of net markdowns in the computation of the cost to retail percentage produce an inventory valued at the *lower of average cost or market*. This is sometimes called the *conventional retail method* and is illustrated for the Western Company below:

WESTERN COMPANY
Estimate of Ending Inventory Using Retail Method—
Lower of Average Cost or Market
Year 1

	Cost	Retail
Beginning inventory	$16,000	$ 27,000
Net purchases	75,000	110,000
Additional markups, less markup cancellations ($5,000		
— $2,000)		3,000
Goods available for sale	$91,000	$140,000
Cost to retail percentage ($91,000 ÷ $140,000) = 65%		
Deduct:		
Net sales		(90,000)
Markdowns, less markdown cancellations ($10,875		
— $875)		(10,000)
Ending inventory at retail		$ 40,000
Ending inventory at lower of average cost or market		
($40,000 × .65)	$26,000	

Cost of goods sold ($91,000 — $26,000) = $65,000

Net markups and net markdowns change the relationship between the selling price and the cost of goods available for sale, and accordingly affect the dollar value of the ending inventory and the cost of goods sold computed by the retail method.

Thus in the schedule above, the cost to retail percentage is 65% and the ending inventory at estimated cost is $26,000. When both the net markups and net markdowns were used in the computation of the cost to retail percentage, the percentage was 70% and the ending inventory at estimated cost was $28,000. The inclusion of net markups in computing the cost to retail ratio assumes that the additional markups apply proportionately to items sold and to items on hand at the end of the period; however, net markdowns are assumed to apply only to the goods sold. Since the selling price of goods to which the markdowns apply is less than the original sales price, the net markdowns as well as sales must be deducted from goods available for sale at retail in order to determine the inventory at retail price. If these assumptions are correct, then the exclusion of net markdowns in the computation of the cost to retail percentage will value the ending inventory at original cost.

In many cases, however, the net markdowns do not apply solely to goods sold; instead, they apply to both goods sold and those in the ending inventory. In such cases the exclusion of net markdowns from the computation of the cost to retail percentage does not produce an inventory value in terms of actual cost but rather an inventory value below cost. Consequently, the assertion has been made that the inventory amount determined by the latter approach is the lower of cost or market.

As stated previously, the retail method is based on an assumption that the ending inventory is composed of the same mix of items as the total batch of goods from which sales were made. If there are markdowns for special promotions, then this assumption implicit in the retail method may not be valid. Some markdowns may apply to goods available for sale and to goods in ending inventory in equal proportions, but others may apply only to goods which have been sold. In essence we are saying that there are really two lines of merchandise, "special sale" items and regular items, on which the markup is different. These two different lines may not be held in equal proportions in the goods available and in the ending inventory. Attempts to handle the two items in one calculation are likely to prove inadequate as a means of deriving realistic inventory cost figures. This problem is discussed in more detail below.

Limitation of the assumption of average markups on the retail method

The retail method produces an inventory figure based on the assumption that the cost to retail percentage calculated for the goods available for sale also applies to the goods on hand at the end of the period. In other words the ending inventory is assumed to consist of a cross section of all goods handled during the period. If the markup on different types of goods varies, the use of the retail method on a storewide basis implies that the items making up the ending inventory are held in the same relative proportions as they were in the accumulation of all goods available for sale. Such an assumption is seldom justified and for this reason one calculation is seldom adequate for determining the inventory of a diversified store.

The calculation of separate departmental retail inventories is often necessary, and in some special cases a separate calculation should be made for goods purchased for promotional purposes. The promotional goods frequently have a lower markup than the regular goods carried in the department; consequently, the inclusion of the promotional goods in the computation of the cost to retail percentage will produce a distorted inventory value. In estimating the ending inventory when promotional goods have been purchased during the period, the promotional goods are usually treated as though they were held in a separate department.

The following example for the Best-Buy Store, which operates two departments with a substantial difference in markups, illustrates the desirability of separate calculations. If Department Y is considered to be composed entirely of promotional goods, we can also observe the desirability of separate calculations under these circumstances. The separate departmental cost to retail percentages yield an inventory cost of $17,400 ($15,000 + $2,400), whereas the calculation treating both de-

BEST-BUY STORE

Departmental and Combined Inventories Using Retail Method

	Department X		Department Y		Combined	
	Cost	Retail	Cost	Retail	Cost	Retail
Beginning inventory	$ 12,000	$ 20,000	$ 3,200	$ 4,000	$ 15,200	$ 24,000
Purchases . . .	90,000	150,000	72,000	90,000	162,000	240,000
Goods available for sale	$102,000	$170,000	$75,200	$94,000	$177,200	$264,000
Cost to retail percentage . .	60%		80%		67.12%	
Less: Net sales		145,000		91,000		236,000
Ending inventory at retail .		$ 25,000		$ 3,000		$ 28,000
Ending inventory at average cost	$ 15,000		$ 2,400		$ 18,794	

partments as one produces an estimated inventory cost of $18,794. The reason for the variation can be traced to the fact that the goods sold by the two departments were not proportional to the goods available for sale. In this case a greater proportion of the items with a lower gross profit percentage were sold; therefore, the actual inventory is less than is indicated by the combined cost to retail percentage.

If the gross profit percentage varies over time, the inventory should be calculated more frequently because of the effect of averaging on the cost to retail percentage.

The following new illustration, which assumes a change in the gross profit percentage from 30% on items purchased during January to approximately 25% on items purchased during February, will illustrate the effect on the inventory if it is estimated at the end of each month instead of being estimated only at the end of February.

	January		February		Two months, end of February	
	Cost	Retail	Cost	Retail	Cost	Retail
Beginning inventory	$21,000	$ 30,000	$24,500	$ 35,000	$ 21,000	$ 30,000
Purchases	49,000	70,000	48,800	65,000	97,800	135,000
Goods available for sale	$70,000	$100,000	$73,300	$100,000	$118,800	$165,000
Cost to retail percentage . . .	70%		73.3%		72%	
Less: Net sales .		65,000		80,000		145,000
Ending inventory at retail . .		$ 35,000		$ 20,000		$ 20,000
Ending inventory at average cost	$24,500		$14,660		$ 14,400	

A lower cost to retail percentage is obtained at the end of February by averaging the purchases of January and February together. Thus the ending inventory is estimated at $14,400 using a combined cost to retail percentage, compared to $14,660 if monthly inventories are computed. If there is a change in the markup percentage during an accounting period, the inventory should be estimated at the time of the change. Adherence to an annual estimate, like adherence to a storewide estimate, may cause the inventory to be valued incorrectly.

Retail method and lifo valuation

In the preceding discussion two variations of the retail method have been illustrated which produce an inventory valuation at **average cost** or at the **lower of average cost or market.** If the last-in, first-out method is used to estimate the cost of inventory, the retail method must be modified. The retail method can be adapted to approximate lifo cost by the calculation of separate cost to retail percentages for the beginning inventory and for the purchases during the period under consideration.

Since lifo is a cost (not lower-of-cost-or-market) method, both net markups and net markdowns must be included in the calculations of the cost to retail percentage for current purchases, in accordance with the discussion on pages 374 to 376.

The modification of the retail method necessary to value inventory at lifo cost is illustrated below for the General Dry Goods Company. For purposes of this illustration, assume that the selling prices have remained unchanged and that all additional markups and markdowns apply only to the goods purchased during Year 1. We have also assumed that the cost to retail percentage has increased since the beginning inventory was acquired at lower costs.

GENERAL DRY GOODS COMPANY

Retail Method Used to Calculate Lifo Cost Inventory

Year 1

	Cost	Retail
Beginning inventory (cost to retail percentage = 60%). . .	$24,000	$ 40,000
Net purchases	74,200	100,000
Additional markups, less markup cancellations ($10,000 − $2,000).		8,000
Less: Markdowns, net of markdown cancellations ($5,000 − $3,000).		(2,000)
Goods available for sale, at retail		$146,000
Less: Net sales		96,000
Ending inventory, at retail		$ 50,000

Percentage relationship between cost and retail price of goods purchased, including net markups and net markdowns ($74,200 ÷ $106,000*) = 70%

Ending inventory, at lifo cost:

$40,000 × .60 (beginning inventory layer)		$24,000
10,000 × .70 (layer added in Year 1)		7,000
$50,000 (ending inventory, at retail)		
Ending inventory, at estimated lifo cost (retail method)		$31,000

*$100,000 + $8,000 − $2,000 = $106,000.

The inventory is composed of the cost of the beginning inventory plus the cost of the layer which was added during Year 1. In the event that the inventory decreases in Year 2, the decrease would be taken from the layer added in Year 1, $7,000, and then from the layer on hand at the beginning of Year 1. For example, if the ending inventory for the General Dry Goods Company totaled $45,000 at retail at the end of Year 2, the inventory at lifo cost would be computed as follows:

Ending inventory at lifo cost—Year 2:

$40,000 × .60 (inventory layer at beginning of Year 1)	$24,000
$5,000 × .70 (one-half of layer added in Year 1)	3,500
Ending inventory, at estimated lifo cost (retail method)	$27,500

The computation of the cost to retail percentage for the current year's purchases is required *only when an increase in inventory at retail price occurs during the current year.* The percentage is computed for the sole purpose of pricing the incremental layer in inventory. On the other hand, if a decrease in inventory takes place, the ending inventory will consist of a fraction of the beginning inventory cost. For example, if the ending inventory at retail for the General Dry Goods Company at the end of Year 2 amounted to only $30,000, the lifo cost of this inventory would be determined as follows:

$$\$24,000 \times \frac{\$30,000}{\$40,000} = \$18,000$$

Retail method and fifo valuation

Observe that a *fifo* cost inventory can be calculated based on the data used in determining the lifo cost. For example, the cost of the inventory at the end of Year 1 for the General Dry Goods Company under the first-in, first-out assumption is $35,000 ($50,000 × .70). If the cost to retail percentage for Year 2 is assumed to be 72% and the inventory at retail amounted to $45,000, the inventory at *fifo* cost would be $32,400 ($45,000 × .72).

Changes in price levels and the retail lifo method

Let us now remove the simplifying assumption of the stability of selling prices. In reality, retail prices do change from period to period and this is particularly significant to the retailer who prices his inventory at lifo cost and who uses the retail method to approximate this cost. The procedure employed under these circumstances is similar to that used in the calculation of dollar-value lifo discussed in Chapter 8. The ending inventory at retail must be converted to beginning-year prices to ascertain the real increment in the inventory. An appropriate index of price changes must be found to use in making the conversion from end-of-year prices to beginning-of-year prices. There are several indices published regularly by various governmental agencies which might be used. The portion of the *Consumers Price Index* concerned with changes in prices of consumer nondurables would probably be most appropriate for department stores.

The procedure for estimating the lifo cost of the ending inventory, using the retail method and assuming fluctuating selling prices, is illustrated below. The sales price index at the beginning of the period, *when lifo was adopted,* is assumed to be 100 and the index at the end of the period is assumed to be 110, an increase of 10%.[2] In order not to complicate the example, we have assumed that there were no net markups or net markdowns during the period.

Application of the Retail Method
during Period of Fluctuating Selling Prices

	Cost	Retail
Beginning inventory (date lifo was adopted)	$18,000	$ 30,000
Purchases during the period (cost to retail percentage = 65%)	65,000	100,000
Goods available for sale during the period, at retail		$130,000
Less: Net sales during the period.		75,000
Inventory at end of period, at retail.		$ 55,000
Computation of inventory increase at end-of-period selling price:		
Inventory at end of period, at retail		$ 55,000
Less: Beginning inventory, at end-of-period selling price ($30,000 × 1.10)		33,000
Inventory increase, at end-of-period selling price		$ 22,000[3]

[2] When the base-year index is other than 100, the percentage increase is determined by dividing the index at the end of the current year by the base-year index and subtracting 100. For example, if the base-year index is 125 and the index at the end of the current year is 150, the increase would be 20% [(150/125) − 100].

[3] Alternative computation:

Inventory at beginning-of-period selling price ($55,000 ÷ 1.10)	$50,000
Less: Beginning inventory at selling price.	30,000
Inventory increase, at beginning-of-period selling price	$20,000
Inventory increase at end-of-period selling price, $20,000 × 1.10	$22,000

The inventory at the end of the period, at a selling price of $55,000, can now be valued at lifo cost as follows:

	Lifo cost	Selling price
Beginning inventory layer:		
At base-period prices.	$18,000	$30,000
Add: Increase due to increase in selling price ($30,000 × 1.10 − $30,000)		3,000
Increase in inventory, at end-of-period price ($55,000 − $33,000).		22,000
Increase in inventory, at cost ($22,000 × 65%)	14,300	
Ending inventory	$32,300[4]	$55,000

Comparison of the gross profit and retail methods

Both the gross profit and retail methods of estimating inventory rely heavily on the determination of a realistic cost to retail percentage. The gross profit method is based on past average relationships between selling price and cost. It is not particularly useful as a means of estimating ending inventory to determine income, because it rests on the assumption that the gross profit realized (and hence the cost of goods percentage) in this period is the same as in past years. It is used primarily as an independent test of the reasonableness of an inventory value established by other methods, and as a means of estimating inventories when it is impossible or uneconomical to take a physical inventory.

The retail method, on the other hand, requires elaborate records of the selling price of goods at the time of acquisition and of subsequent net markups and net markdowns in order to establish an accurate cost to selling price ratio. It is often an integral part of a complex system of inventory control used by large merchandising firms. Furthermore, inventories on hand are priced at retail rather than cost, and the retail method is used to produce an estimate of the ending inventory figure for income measurement purposes.

[4]Failure to recognize the increase in the price level would have resulted in an ending inventory cost of $34,250 as determined below:

	Lifo cost	Selling price
Beginning inventory layer.	$18,000	$30,000
Incremental layer [lifo cost = ($55,000 − $30,000) × 65%].	16,250	25,000
Ending inventory	$34,250	$55,000

don't worry

ESTIMATING THE COST OF MANUFACTURING INVENTORIES

The allocation of production costs (materials, direct labor, and factory overhead) between completed goods and unfinished goods is frequently a difficult task even when cost records are available. When a *job order cost system* is used, the cost of the goods in process and the goods finished is taken from *job order cost sheets.* When a *process cost system* is used, the cost of producing a complete unit of product is usually determined from departmental *cost of production reports.*

As stated in Chapter 8, a process cost system is used only when identical units are produced. The objective is to assign the total production costs incurred during a period in each department to the units produced in each department during the period. A special problem arises, however, when goods in process inventories are on hand at the beginning and at the end of the accounting period. In such cases, an estimate of

IDENTICAL MANUFACTURING COMPANY
Production Data for Year 10

	Degree of completion, %	Production costs	Source of information
Goods in process, Jan. 1:			
600 units at cost of			
$6,810			Accounting records:
Materials.	80		Observation and
Direct labor and factory			knowledge of
overhead (conversion			production process
costs)	60		
Cost and production data,			
Jan. 1–Dec. 31:			
Cost of materials		$ 59,520	Production records
Direct labor		49,200	Payroll records
Factory overhead (vari-			
able and fixed)		73,800	Accounting records
Total production costs		$182,520	
Units completed during the			Production records
period, 10,000			and physical count
Goods in process, Dec. 31:			
800 units			Observation and
Materials.	50		knowledge of
Direct labor and factory			production process
overhead (conversion			
costs)	25		

the productive effort in terms of physical units (equivalent full units) produced during the period should be made in order to compute the production cost per unit for the period. Once the production cost per unit is determined, costs can be assigned to the goods in process inventory, the finished goods inventory, and the cost of goods sold. This procedure will be illustrated using the information for the Identical Manufacturing Company on page 384.

Note that the Identical Manufacturing Company incurred total production costs of $182,520 and completed 10,000 units during Year 10. The cost per unit of production for Year 10, however, was *not* $18.252 ($182,520 ÷ 10,000) as might appear at first glance. Assuming a first-in, first-out flow of goods through the production process, 600 of the units completed during the period were started in production in Year 9. The remaining 9,400 units completed were begun and finished in Year 10. There were 800 units started during Year 10 which were not completed. What then is the number of equivalent full units produced during Year 10? There is not one answer, but rather two, as illustrated below:

IDENTICAL MANUFACTURING COMPANY
Computation of Equivalent Full Units Produced during Year 10

	Equivalent full units	
	Materials	*Direct labor and factory overhead*
Goods in process, Jan. 1:		
600 units 80% complete as to materials; 20% of the materials required to complete the goods were added during Year 10 (600 units × 20%)	120	
60% complete as to direct labor and factory overhead; 40% of the direct labor and factory overhead required to complete the goods were added during Year 10 (600 units × 40%)		240
Units completed totaled 10,000; however, only 9,400 were started and completed during Year 10; 600 were started in Year 9	9,400	9,400
Goods in process, Dec. 31:		
800 units 50% complete as to materials (800 units × 50%)	400	
800 units 25% complete as to direct labor and factory overhead (800 units × 25%)		200
Equivalent full units produced during Year 10 . . .	9,920	9,840

The cost of producing one complete unit during the year is computed as follows:

IDENTICAL MANUFACTURING COMPANY
Computation of Unit Cost for Year 10

	Production costs	÷	Equivalent full units	=	Unit cost
Materials	$ 59,520	÷	9,920	=	$ 6.00
Direct labor and factory overhead ($49,200 + $73,800)	123,000	÷	9,840	=	12.50
Total production costs	$182,520				$18.50

Inventory costs at the end of the year and the cost of goods sold are tabulated below. We have assumed that there was no beginning inventory of finished goods and that the ending inventory of finished goods consists of 2,000 units which were started and completed during Year 10.

IDENTICAL MANUFACTURING COMPANY
Determination of Inventories and Cost of Goods Sold for Year 10

Cost of finished goods inventory, 2,000 units × $18.50		$ 37,000
Cost of goods in process inventory, determined as follows:		
Materials: 800 units × 50% complete × $6.00.	$ 2,400	
Direct labor and factory overhead:		
800 units × 25% complete × $12.50	2,500	$ 4,900
Cost of goods sold during the year, determined as follows:		
Goods in process Jan. 1 (600 units).	$ 6,810	
Production costs (10,200 additional units placed in production)	182,520	
Total cost of goods in process during the year, 10,800 units	$189,330	
Less: Goods in process inventory, Dec. 31, 800 units (see above).	4,900	
Total cost of goods completed, 10,000 units	$184,430	
Less: Finished goods inventory, Dec. 31, 2,000 units (see above)	37,000	
Cost of goods sold, 8,000 units		$147,430

The assumptions made in connection with the foregoing illustration were:

1 Each unit produced is identical with every other unit produced.

2 No significant changes have occurred in the cost of production throughout the year.

3 The first-in, first-out procedure has been assumed for the flow of goods through the production operation and also for the sales of the finished product.

4 There was no beginning inventory of finished goods.

In cases where these assumptions do not conform with the facts, the accountant must change his method of analysis to fit the situation he faces.

Relative sales value method of allocating joint production costs

Accountants frequently encounter situations in which production costs in a given manufacturing process relate to two or more distinctly different products. The allocation of these *joint costs* is necessary to determine the unit cost of each product and is frequently made on the basis of the relative sales value of the *joint products.*

To illustrate the allocation of joint costs using the *relative sales value method,* assume that the cost of producing 5,000 gallons of three chemicals in the same production department for a given month amounts to $15,000. Production figures and selling prices per gallon for the three joint products are:

Product	Gallons	Selling price per gallon	Sales value	Cost of each chemical
Chemical X	3,000	$4	$12,000	$?
Chemical Y	1,500	6	9,000	?
Chemical Z	500	8	4,000	?
Totals	5,000		$25,000	$15,000

Because of inability to identify the joint cost of $15,000 with a specific chemical, the **total sales value** of the chemicals is used in the calculation of the cost per gallon and the total cost of each chemical. By dividing the total joint cost by the total sales value of the three chemicals, the cost percentage is determined to be 60% ($15,000 ÷ $25,000). The cost percentage is then applied to the selling price per gallon to determine the estimated cost per gallon as follows:

Product	Gallons	Selling price per gallon	Cost percentage	Cost per gallon	Total cost*
Chemical X ..	3,000	$4	.60	$2.40	$ 7,200
Chemical Y ..	1,500	6	.60	3.60	5,400
Chemical Z ..	500	8	.60	4.80	2,400
Totals	5,000				$15,000

* The allocation can also be made as follows:
Chemical X, $12,000/$25,000 × $15,000 = $7,200
Chemical Y, $9,000/$25,000 × $15,000 = $5,400
Chemical Z, $4,000/$25,000 × $15,000 = $2,400

Assuming that 100 gallons of each grade of chemical are on hand at the end of a period, the inventory valuation would be:

Chemical X, 100 gallons @ $2.40 .... $ 240
Chemical Y, 100 gallons @ $3.60 360
Chemical Z, 100 gallons @ $4.80 480
    Cost of ending inventory $1,080

Although the relative sales value approach is arbitrary, it is a practical way of solving a difficult cost allocation problem. Its use gives satisfactory results only if the joint products are assumed to yield the same rate of gross profit. If the rate of gross profit is assumed to vary for the different joint products or if varying amounts of additional costs are necessary to prepare the products for sale, the allocation of joint costs should be revised to allow for these differences.

Inventories of supplies and short-term prepayments

In addition to inventories of merchandise, finished goods, raw materials, and finished parts, a business enterprise may also have several types of supplies on hand. These include, for example, office supplies, promotional materials, shipping supplies, and factory supplies. The problems of determining cost and valuation of supplies are similar to those for inventories discussed earlier in Chapter 8. Supplies are purchased for use in the business and any quantities remaining on hand at the end of the period should be included among current assets. A business which finds that important amounts of supplies must be carried in stock should plan for acquisition and should control supplies on hand in the same manner as inventory of finished goods or raw materials.

The term *prepaid expenses* is widely used to describe unexpired costs which are expected to be consumed within a relatively short period of time. However, this term is somewhat of a misnomer and should be replaced by a more descriptive title such as *short-term prepayments.* A prepaid expense is a cost incurred to acquire an economically useful good or service that has not yet been consumed in the revenue-earning process. Strictly speaking, both depreciable plant assets and inventories fall within this definition. Plant assets are classified separately because their services are performed over relatively long time periods; inventories require separate designation because of their materiality and importance. There is a general presumption that a substantial portion of any good or service treated as a short-term prepayment will be consumed within one year or within the company's operating cycle; this is the reason for including these items among the current assets in the balance sheet.

Inventories and financial reporting standards

The objectives of reporting inventories on the balance sheet are to reveal the type, the relative liquidity, and the basis of valuation of the inventories. The accountant in reporting the investment in inventories, as in reporting other assets, is concerned with disclosing all significant information; he is particularly concerned that the investment in inventories has been determined on a basis consistent with that of preceding years. If a change is made in the method of calculating inventory cost, it should be explained fully as to its effect on the current year's statements and the corresponding effect for the prior year (or years). The accounting problems of reporting a change in the inventory valuation method are illustrated in Chapter 22 in the section dealing with "Accounting Changes."

When an inventory allowance is used as a means of valuing the inventory at the lower of cost or market, this allowance should be subtracted from the inventory cost.

Financial reporting standards require that the various categories of inventories be indicated under the general caption "Inventories" and that the basis of valuation and the method of tracing costs be noted. The replacement cost of the inventory also should be disclosed, but this is seldom done in practice. Most companies report inventories in highly condensed form. An example from an annual report of Mobil Oil Corporation follows:

Inventories:*

Crude oil and products.............................	$767,297,000
Materials and supplies	91,133,000

*Inventories are valued at cost, which was lower than their aggregate market value. Substantially all domestic inventories of crude oil and petroleum products—representing about 33% of Mobil's worldwide inventories—are valued under the last-in, first-out method. Other inventories are valued generally at average cost.

Goods on order and advance payments to suppliers should not be considered a part of the inventory unless title to the goods has passed to the buyer in accordance with the legal tests prescribed earlier. Inventories which have been pledged as collateral for loans should be included in the inventory section rather than being offset against the loans secured by the inventory. Unusual purchase commitments can be disclosed in footnotes relating to inventories.

Accounting Research Study No. 13

Because of the importance of inventories in measuring net income and in presenting the financial position of business enterprises, the Accounting Principles Board commissioned a research study on this topic. The study was published in 1973 as *Accounting Research Study No. 13*, "The Accounting Basis of Inventories." A brief summary of the findings and conclusions of this study follows:[5]

1 Significant differences exist in practice in (*a*) the composition of product costs and in the allocation of costs to units of production, (*b*) the cost flow assumptions used in compiling the cost of year-end inventories and cost of products sold, and (*c*) implementation of the concept of lower of cost or market.

2 The specific identification of costs and, if that is not practicable, the fifo cost flow assumption represent approaches to inventory cost determination which are sound in principle.

3 Enterprises using any cost flow assumption other than specific identification or fifo should be required to disclose (*a*) the effect on net income for the period and on the balance sheet inventory amounts of the method used as compared with fifo and (*b*) related tax effects.

4 The "net realizable value" rather than "market" should be the basis for measuring and recognizing potential losses in utility value of inventory items.

REVIEW QUESTIONS

1 List three uses that may be made of the *gross profit method.*

2 (*a*) Distinguish between gross profit as a percentage of sales and as a percentage of cost of goods sold. (*b*) Convert the following gross profit percentages based on sales to gross profit percentages based on cost of goods sold: 16⅔%, 25%, and 50%. (*c*) Convert the following gross profit percentages based on cost of goods sold to gross profit percentages based on sales: 25%, 50%, and 150%.

3 Explain the possible limitations of using an average cost of goods sold percentage for prior years to estimate the inventory under the gross profit method.

4 For what purposes may the *retail method* of inventory valuation be used?

---

[5] Horace G. Barden, *Accounting Research Study No. 13*, "The Accounting Basis of Inventories," AICPA (New York: 1973), pp. 10–14.

5 Distinguish between (*a*) *markup* and *additional markup*, (*b*) *markup cancellation* and *markdown*, (*c*) *markdown cancellation* and *additional markup*.

6 Briefly describe the computation of the cost to retail percentage when inventory is determined at average cost using the retail inventory method.

7 Briefly describe the computation of the cost to retail percentage when inventory is to be determined at the lower of average cost or market in applying the retail inventory method.

8 What is the basic assumption as to the composition of the ending inventory when the retail inventory method is applied on the basis of average cost or on the basis of the lower of average cost or market?

9 Describe the application of the retail inventory method when cost is determined on a last-in, first-out basis.

10 Describe the special procedure to be followed in estimating inventory in the *retail lifo* basis after retail prices have increased.

11 Briefly define the following terms: *job order cost system, process cost system,* and *equivalent full units.*

12 Explain how the cost of producing a unit of identical products is determined when a process cost system is used.

13 If two or more *joint products* are produced in a given department, how would the total production cost incurred in the department be allocated to the various joint products?

14 What objections can you give to the use of the term *prepaid expenses?* Can you offer a better alternative?

15 What objectives is the accountant seeking to achieve in reporting inventories in the balance sheet?

EXERCISES

Ex. 10-1 Dein Company uses the gross profit method for estimating monthly inventory balances. During recent months gross profit has averaged 30% of net sales. The following data for January are obtained from the ledger:

Beginning inventory	$ 25,550
Purchases	120,000
Purchase returns	5,000
Freight-in	6,000
Gross sales	175,000
Sales returns and allowances	10,000

Estimate the cost of the ending inventory for January, using the gross profit method.

Ex. 10-2 Herbert Bell computed the cost of his inventory at July 20, 1975, at $20,500. His fiscal year ends on June 30; therefore you find it necessary to establish an inventory figure as of June 30, 1975. You find that during the period July 1–20 sales were $70,500; sales returns, $1,800; goods purchased and placed in stock, $61,000; goods returned to vendors, $1,200; freight-in, $600.

Calculate the inventory at June 30, 1975, assuming that goods are sold at 25% above cost.

Ex. 10-3 Determine the gross purchases for Year 5 from the information given below:

Purchase returns	$22,500
Freight-in	33,750
Selling expenses	75,000
Ending inventory	80,000

Gross profit is 20% of net sales and the beginning inventory is equal to 10% of net sales. Cost of goods sold is equal to 600% of selling expenses.

Ex. 10-4 The following information is taken from the records of the Reliable Hardware Company for the current year:

	At cost	At retail
Inventory, Jan. 1	$ 25,000	$ 46,200
Purchases	120,000	191,800
Net additional markups		12,000
Sales		190,000
Net markdowns		3,800

You are to assume that all additional markups and markdowns apply to purchases of the current year, and that it is appropriate to treat the entire inventory as a single department with no markdowns having occurred during the prior year.

Compute the ending inventory at lower of average cost or market using the retail method.

Ex. 10-5 Using the information given in Ex. 10-4 for the Reliable Hardware Company, compute the ending inventory using the retail lifo method.

Ex. 10-6 Assuming that sales for the Reliable Hardware Company in the current year were $209,240 instead of $190,000, and that all other facts are identical to those given in Ex. 10-4, compute the ending inventory using the retail lifo method.

Ex. 10-7 During the current year the index of selling prices for merchandise handled by the Stever Company increased from 90 to 108. From the information below, compute the ending inventory at estimated lifo cost, taking into account the increase in selling prices:

	Cost	Selling price	Cost–selling price ratio
Beginning inventory (date lifo was adopted) .	$ 40,000	$ 50,000	80%
Purchases during the year	150,000	200,000	75%
Goods available for sale	$190,000	$250,000	
Less: Net sales during the year		178,000	
Inventory at end of year, at selling price . . .		$ 72,000	

Ex. 10-8 The data below relate to the inventories of the Streeter Mfg. Company for the month of March:

	March 1	March 31
Goods in process inventory		
(units)	800 (30% completed)	1,200 (80% completed)
Finished goods inventory		
(units)	12,000	11,000

Compute equivalent full units completed in March, assuming that 40,000 units were sold during the month.

Ex. 10-9 Materials are placed in production at the beginning of processing and cost $4.10 per unit. Direct labor and factory overhead costs in January amount to $12,276. There were 400 units 40% completed as to direct labor and factory overhead on January 1, and 800 units 80% completed as to direct labor and factory overhead on January 31. During January, 5,100 units were completed. What is the cost to be assigned to the goods in process inventory at January 31?

Ex. 10-10 Ridge Company buys and sells land. On January 1, 1975, a tract of land was bought for $100,000. Costs of leveling the land were $25,000. The lots were subdivided as follows:

    25 Class A lots to sell for $4,000 each
    30 Class B lots to sell for $3,000 each
    10 Class C lots to sell for $1,000 each

On December 31, 1975, the unsold lots consisted of 15 Class A lots, 6 Class B lots, and 3 Class C lots.

Prepare a schedule computing the cost of unsold lots at December 31, 1975. Total cost is allocated to the lots on the basis of relative sales value.

SHORT CASES FOR ANALYSIS AND DECISION

Case 10-1 The Rhode Company has used the gross profit method for estimating the investment in inventory and as a check on the physical count at the end of each year. The company has two lines of merchandise which have produced gross profit margins of 25 and 35%, respectively, on selling price over the past several years. The gross profit margin for the business as a whole has averaged 30% of sales. The operating data for the current year are as follows:

	Economy line	Quality line	Total
Sales	$100,000	$200,000	$300,000
Beginning inventory	10,000	25,000	35,000
Purchases	80,000	130,000	210,000
Gross profit margins	25%	35%	30%

A physical count of the merchandise reveals inventory to be $40,000, but the estimate using the gross profit method indicates ending inventory should be $35,000. The manager is of the opinion that the discrepancy is too great to accept without explanation. A test sample is selected and reveals that the gross profit margins on the two lines are unchanged at 25 and 35%.

Instructions
a Show how the manager computed the ending inventory using the gross profit method.
b Compute the ending inventory using the gross profit method in the manner in which you think it should be used in this situation.
c Explain to the manager why the difference exists between the physical count and his estimate of the inventory value.

Case 10-2 Beran & Company has been using the lifo method of valuing inventory. Walter Beran, the owner, is interested in the possibility of using the retail method to estimate his investment in inventory periodically, but he is not familiar with all the implications of this method and questions whether the retail method would be applicable to his situation.

You obtain the following data for the current year:

	Units	Cost	Retail
Beginning inventory	1,000	$ 6,000	$12,000
Purchases	5,000	40,000	60,000
Net additional markups			6,000
Net markdowns			3,000
Sales	4,500		56,250

Instructions
a Using the retail method, compute the ending inventory at (1) lifo average cost and (2) lower of average cost or market, assuming that additional markups and markdowns apply proportionately to beginning inventory and purchases.
b Compute the inventory at lifo cost using units and unit costs.
c Explain the principles of the retail method to Beran.
d Why is it desirable to know to which goods additional markups and markdowns apply?

Case 10-3 Inglewood Department Store uses the conventional retail method as a means of controlling the investment in inventory at its branch stores. Monthly the central accounting office summarizes the recorded activity at each branch and estimates the ending inventory. The estimate is then compared with a normal inventory investment based on expected volume. Store managers are asked to explain deviations of 5% or more from the expected normal inventory. The following data have been accumulated for the Compton Branch:

	Cost	Retail
Net sales		$630,000
Beginning inventory	$150,000	222,000
Net purchases	560,000	823,000
Net additional markups		20,000
Net markdowns		10,000
Estimated shrinkage		5,000

Instructions
a The normal inventory of the Compton Branch should be $200,000 at cost.

Compute the amount of the ending inventory at retail and at cost, and indicate the nature of the inquiry to be made of the store manager.
b What effect, if any, would the following events have on the effectiveness of the retail method as a control device?
(1) A widely fluctuating shrinkage factor
(2) A shift in the volume of goods handled at various markups
(3) The additional markups related to goods which are entirely sold out by year-end
(4) Markdowns included as markup cancellations
(5) Additional markups included as markdown cancellations

PROBLEMS

Group A

10A-1 The Nebraska Trading Outpost lost all its inventory by fire on January 1, 1975. No inventories had been taken on December 31, 1974. The following data are available for the three preceding years:

	1974	1973	1972
Inventory, Jan. 1	$200,000	$168,000	$161,600
Purchases	720,000	656,000	644,000
Purchase returns	40,000	32,000	36,000
Sales	812,000	788,000	724,000
Sales returns	12,000	8,000	12,000
Operating expenses	240,000	221,000	198,000
Accounts receivable	60,000	50,000	55,000
Accounts payable	40,000	35,000	28,000

Instructions Assuming that the cost of goods sold percentage in 1974 was two percentage points below the weighted-average cost of goods sold percentage for 1972 and 1973, compute the estimated cost of inventory destroyed by fire.

10A-2 Data concerning the operations of the men's sportswear department of Maxwell Clothiers are presented below:

	Cost	Retail
Beginning inventory	$ 45,000	$ 80,000
Purchases	215,600	385,000
Freight-in.	10,400	
Purchase returns	4,200	7,000
Additional markups		10,000
Markup cancellations		8,000
Markdowns		8,000
Markdown cancellations		1,600
Gross sales		386,100
Sales returns		6,700
Estimated shrinkage from theft and spoilage		2,000

Instructions Compute the ending inventory at sales price and at the lower of average cost or market for Maxwell Clothiers by the retail method. Calculations should be presented in good form.

10A-3 On January 1, the Ross Company installed the retail method of accounting for its merchandise inventory.

When you undertook the preparation of Ross' financial statements at June 30, the following data were available:

	Cost	Selling price
Inventory, Jan. 1	$25,400	$ 40,000
Markdowns		10,500
Additional markups		19,500
Markdown cancellations		6,500
Markup cancellations		4,500
Purchases	86,200	111,800
Sales		122,000
Purchase returns and allowances	1,500	1,800
Sales returns and allowances		6,000

Instructions

a Prepare a schedule to compute the Ross Company's June 30 inventory under the retail method of accounting for inventories. The inventory is to be valued at cost, using the lifo method. Assume that additional markups and markdowns apply to purchases.

b Without prejudice to your solution to part **(a)**, assume that you computed the June 30 inventory to be $44,100 at retail and the ratio of cost to retail to be 75%. The general price level has increased from 100 at January 1 to 105 at June 30. Round off figures to nearest dollar and percent. Prepare a schedule and compute the June 30 inventory at the June 30 price level, using the dollar-value lifo method. (Refer to Chapter 8 for illustration of the dollar-value lifo method.)

10A-4 On April 15, 1975, a fire damaged the office and warehouse of Home of Carpets, Inc. The only accounting record saved was the general ledger, from which the following trial balance was prepared:

HOME OF CARPETS, INC.

Trial Balance

March 31, 1975

	Debit	Credit
Cash	$ 20,800	
Accounts receivable	27,000	
Inventory, Dec. 31, 1974	50,000	
Land	24,000	
Building and equipment	120,000	
Allowance for depreciation		$ 27,200

Other assets	$ 3,600	
Accounts payable		$ 23,700
Other expense accruals.		7,200
Capital stock, $2.50 par value		100,000
Retained earnings		47,700
Sales		104,200
Purchases	42,000	
Other expenses.	22,600	
Totals	$310,000	$310,000

The following information has been gathered:
(1) The fiscal year of the corporation ends on December 31.
(2) An examination of the April bank statement and canceled checks revealed that checks written during the period April 1 to 15 totaled $11,600: $5,700 paid to accounts payable as of March 31, $2,000 for April purchases, and $3,900 paid for other expenses. Deposits during the same period amounted to $10,650, which consisted of receipts on account from customers, with the exception of a $450 refund from a vendor for goods returned in April.
(3) Correspondence with suppliers revealed unrecorded obligations at April 15 of $3,500 for April purchases, including $1,300 for shipments in transit on that date.
(4) Customers acknowledged indebtedness of $26,400 at April 15. It was also estimated that customers owed another $5,000 which will never be acknowledged or recovered. Of the acknowledged indebtedness, $600 will probably be uncollectible. All sales were on account.
(5) Assume that the weighted-average gross profit percentage for the past two years was in effect during the current year. The company's audited financial statements disclosed the following:

	Year ended	
	Dec. 31, 1974	**Dec. 31, 1973**
Net sales.	$400,000	$300,000
Net purchases	226,000	174,000
Beginning inventory	45,000	35,000
Ending inventory	50,000	45,000

(6) Inventory with a cost of $5,750 was salvaged and sold for $2,500. The balance of the inventory was a total loss.

Instructions Prepare a schedule computing the amount of the inventory fire loss. The supporting schedule of the computation of the cost of goods sold percentage should be in good form.

10A-5 You are examining the financial statements of the Lansing Company, a retail enterprise, for the year ended December 31, 1975. The client's accounting department presented you with an analysis of the Short-term Prepayments account balance of $31,400 at December 31, 1975, as shown below:

Unexpired insurance:		
Fire	$ 750	
Liability	4,900	
Utility deposits	2,000	

Loan to officer	$ 500
Purchase of postage meter machine, one-half of invoice price.	400
Discount on bonds payable	3,000
Advertising of store opening	9,600
Amount due for overpayment on purchase of furniture and fixtures.	675
Unsalable inventory—entered on June 30, 1975	8,300
Contributions from employees to employee welfare fund	(275)
Book value of obsolete machinery held for resale.	550
Funds delivered to Skyhigh Stores with purchase offer	1,000
Total	$31,400

Additional information available for your analysis:

(1) Insurance policy data:

	Period covered	Premium
Fire	Dec. 31, 1974 to Dec. 31, 1976	$1,000
Liability	June 30, 1975 to June 30, 1976	9,500

(2) The postage meter machine was delivered in November 1975 and the balance due was paid in January 1976. Unused postage of $700 in the machine at December 31, 1975, was recorded as Postage Expense at time of purchase.

(3) Discount on bonds payable represents the unamortized portion applicable to bonds maturing in 1976.

(4) The $9,600 paid and recorded for advertising was for the cost of an advertisement to be run in a monthly magazine for six months, beginning in December 1975. You examined an invoice received from the advertising agency and extracted the following description: "Advertising services rendered for store opened in November 1975. . . . $6,900." You ascertain that this transaction was not correctly recorded and that $2,700 is to be received as a refund from the agency.

(5) Lansing Company has contracted to purchase Skyhigh Stores and has been required to accompany its offer with a check for $1,000 to be held in escrow as an indication of good faith. An examination of canceled checks revealed the check had not been returned from the bank through January 31, 1976.

Instructions Assuming that you have examined acceptable underlying audit evidence, prepare the required adjusting and correcting journal entries to properly state the accounting records at December 31, 1975.

10A-6 The Salvage Manufacturing Company produces one item on an assembly line. A summary of the production and sales activity for one year is given below:

	Units	Amount
Raw materials inventory, Jan. 1		$ 65,000
Goods in process inventory, Jan. 1, 60% complete	2,000	34,500
Finished goods inventory, Jan. 1	5,000	150,600
Raw materials purchases		292,500
Direct labor costs		216,125
Factory overhead costs, control		158,775
Selling, general, and administrative expenses		85,000

Sales	20,280	$825,000
Income taxes expense		58,500
Raw materials inventory, Dec. 31		81,250
Goods in process inventory, Dec. 31, 65% complete	2,500	?
Finished goods inventory, Dec. 31	6,000	?

Instructions

a Calculate the cost per unit of the goods manufactured during the year, assuming an orderly flow of goods through production on a fifo basis. First determine the number of equivalent full units produced.

b Prepare a combined schedule of the cost of goods manufactured and cost of goods sold.

c Prepare an income statement for the year, assuming a fifo inventory procedure for finished goods.

Group B

10B-1 Miami Beach Fashions prepares quarterly financial statements. The inventories at the retail stores are estimated by the gross profit method since the relationship of selling prices and costs remains relatively stable during the year. The ending inventory is always determined by a physical count of the goods on hand at December 31. The following data for the first three quarters of the fiscal year ending December 31 have been taken from the accounting records.

	March 31	June 30	Sept. 30
Purchases	$695,000	$735,000	$665,000
Freight-in	9,500	9,100	8,210
Purchase allowances	500	2,400	4,630
Sales	993,600	963,000	848,500
Sales returns	13,000	20,000	8,000
Sales discounts	600	3,000	500
Selling and administrative expenses	102,000	103,000	94,400

The physical inventory at December 31 of the previous year was $105,000.

Instructions Assuming that the gross profit rate for the prior fiscal year was 25% of net sales and that this rate is expected to prevail throughout the current year, prepare quarterly income statements for the first three quarters. Assume income taxes are 40% of income before income taxes.

10B-2 The Greenwich Department Store has two basic categories of merchandise: (1) the prestige line, which carries an average margin of 35% of selling price, and (2) the regular line, which carries an average margin of 25% of selling price. The margin for the store as a whole has averaged 29% of selling price for the past three years. The manager has become concerned because he has discovered by sampling the cost prices of merchandise included in the inventory that the inventory is priced above cost. He gives you the following information and asks for an explanation:

	Prestige line	Regular line
Beginning inventory:		
Cost	$ 19,500	$ 90,000
Selling price	30,000	120,000
Purchases:		
Cost	195,000	900,000
Selling price	300,000	1,200,000
Sales	255,000	1,275,000

Instructions
a Compute the inventory for each department and the store as a whole in accordance with the lower-of-average-cost-or-market retail method.
b Explain the variation which results in the ending inventory.

10B-3 Marin County Department Store converted from the conventional retail method to the retail lifo method on January 1 and is now considering converting to the dollar-value lifo inventory method. Management requested during your examination of the financial statements for the year ended December 31, Year 3, that you furnish a summary showing certain computations of inventory costs for the past three years.
  Available information follows:
(1) The inventory at January 1, Year 1, had a retail value of $45,000 and a cost of $27,500, determined on the lower-of-cost-or-market retail method.
(2) Transactions during Year 1 were as follows:

	Cost	Retail
Gross purchases	$282,000	$490,000
Purchase returns	6,500	10,000
Purchase discounts	5,000	
Gross sales		492,000
Sales returns		5,000
Employee discounts granted (add to gross sales)		3,000
Freight inward	26,500	
Net markups		25,000
Net markdowns		10,000

(3) The retail value of the December 31, Year 2, inventory was $56,100; the cost to retail percentage for Year 2 under the retail lifo method was 62%; and the regional price index was 102% of the January 1, Year 2, price level.
(4) The retail value of the December 31, Year 3, inventory was $48,300; the cost to retail percentage for Year 3 under the retail lifo method was 61%; and the regional price index was 105% of the January 1, Year 2, price level.

Instructions
a Prepare a schedule showing the computation of the cost of inventory on hand at December 31, Year 1, using the retail inventory method applied on the lower-of-cost-or-market basis.
b Prepare a schedule showing the computation of the cost of inventory on hand at the store on December 31, Year 1 using the retail lifo method. Marin County Department Store does not consider beginning inventories in computing its

lifo cost to retail percentage. Assume that the retail value of the December 31, Year 1, inventory was $50,000.

c Without prejudice to your solution to part **(b)**, assume that you computed the December 31, Year 1 inventory (retail value $50,000) under the retail lifo method at a cost of $28,000. Prepare a schedule showing the computations of the cost of the store's Year 2 and Year 3 year-end inventories under the dollar-value lifo method. (Refer to Chapter 8 for a description of the dollar-value lifo method of estimating inventories.)

10B-4 The Chemex Corporation is a small manufacturing company producing a highly flammable fluid. On March 31, 1975, the company had a fire which completely destroyed the factory building and the inventory of goods in process; some of the equipment was saved.

After the fire a physical inventory was taken. The raw materials were valued at $30,000, the finished goods at $60,000.

The inventories on January 1, 1975, consisted of:

Raw materials.	$ 12,500
Goods in process	60,500
Finished goods	75,000
Total	$148,000

A review of the accounts showed that the sales and gross profit on sales for the last three years were:

	Sales	Gross profit on sales
1972	$300,000	$ 98,700
1973	330,000	120,500
1974	250,000	88,800

The sales for the first three months of 1975 were $160,000. Raw material purchases were $60,000, transportation-in on purchases was $5,000, and direct labor for the three months was $50,000. For the past two years factory overhead has been 60% of direct labor.

Instructions Compute the cost of inventory of goods in process lost, using the weighted-average gross profit for the preceding three years. Include calculations as a part of your answer.

10B-5 You have been requested to assist the accountant for Summit Builders, Inc., to prepare financial statements at the end of Year 1. Your job relates specifically to the Construction Projects in Progress account which is analyzed below:

Construction projects in progress, consisting of the following costs:

Raw land.	$ 40,000
Improvements—clearing.	30,000
Improvements—grading and streets	280,000
Construction contract	344,000
Miscellàneous costs (taxes, insurance, etc., all applicable to house construction)	30,000
Total in Construction Projects in Progress account	$724,000

Additional information

(1) The company constructed 40 houses during Year 1, its first year in business. Clearing, grading, and street work were performed by the company. Construction of the houses was completed by October 31. During November and December, 25 houses were sold as follows:

1 @ $15,000	$ 15,000
13 @ $17,500	227,500
5 @ $19,000	95,000
6 @ $20,000	120,000
Total balance in Sales account	$457,500

(2) The remaining 15 houses are expected to be sold at the following selling prices:

3 @ $15,000	$ 45,000
7 @ $17,500	122,500
5 @ $19,000	95,000
Total sales value of unsold houses	$262,500

(3) Charges amounting to $6,500 (grading and streets, $5,000, and miscellaneous costs, $1,500) included in the Construction Projects in Progress account are applicable to the two months after completion of construction.

(4) Additional costs, unpaid and not recorded at December 31, were:

Balance due on construction contract	$12,000
Liability insurance for period ending Oct. 31	3,500
Interest on notes payable for November and December	3,200

(5) It was learned that the wood flumes installed as street sewers must be replaced with steel pipe at an estimated cost of $19,000.

(6) Land purchased was plotted into 200 lots, of which 70 were subsequently improved by the company (with grading and streets). Approximately one-half of the land was cleared, and houses were erected on 40 of the 70 improved lots. The costs associated with the land and the construction of houses were considered to be proportional to the sales prices on the houses.

Instructions

a Prepare orderly schedules to determine:
  (1) Land cost on which improvements were made
  (2) Cost of houses and improved lots
  (3) Cost allocated to houses sold and to the inventory of unsold houses, using the relative sales value method to allocate costs
b Prepare all adjusting entries to bring the accounts up to date at December 31, Year 1. Include an entry to record the cost of houses sold.
c Determine the balance in the Construction Projects in Progress account and itemize the costs comprising the balance.

10B-6 High Standard Manufacturing Corporation produces a single product which it sells for $250 per unit. The production statistics for January are summarized on page 403.

	No. of units	Stage of completion	
		Raw materials, %	Direct labor and factory overhead costs, %
Goods in process inventory, Jan. 1	1,000	25	40
Goods in process inventory, Jan. 31	900	100	80
Units finished during the month	12,000	100	100
Finished goods inventory, Jan. 1	1,500	100	100
Finished goods inventory, Jan. 31	1,100	100	100

The inventories at January 1, manufacturing costs, and operating expenses for January are summarized below:

Raw material inventory, Jan. 1	$ 79,700
Goods in process inventory, Jan. 1.	53,250
Finished goods inventory, Jan. 1	234,000
Raw materials purchased (including transportation-in)	745,800
Direct labor costs	468,160
Factory overhead costs	665,280
Selling, general, and administrative expenses	379,050

The raw materials inventory increased by $12,100 during the month.

Instructions

a Compute the equivalent number of full units produced during the month and the unit cost for (1) raw materials, (2) direct labor, and (3) factory overhead.

b Determine the cost of the goods in process and finished goods inventory at January 31. Inventories are valued on a first-in, first-out basis.

c Prepare a statement of cost of goods manufactured and an income statement for January. Refer to page 70 for an example of a statement of cost of goods manufactured. Assume that federal and state income taxes amount to 50% of income before income taxes.

CHAPTER 11

Plant and equipment: acquisition and retirement

The terms *plant and equipment,* or *property, plant, and equipment,* or *fixed assets* are often used to describe the entire complex of tangible long-lived assets used by a business in its operations. Active use in operations distinguishes these assets from other tangible assets which are reported as investments. Land held as a prospective building site, for example, is an investment; when the building has been constructed and is in service, the same land should be classified as a plant and equipment item. A characteristic common to all plant and equipment items is that they yield services over a period of years. All plant assets except land have a limited useful life; consequently their cost must be allocated to the periods receiving the services.

Classification of assets used in business

Assets used in business operations may be divided into a number of separate classes and subclasses:

I *Tangible assets.* Tangibility is the characteristic of bodily substance, as exemplified by a tract of timber, a bridge, or a piece of machinery.
   A *Plant and equipment.* Included in this category are all long-lived physical properties acquired for use in business operations. Examples are land, buildings and structures of all types, machinery, equipment, furniture, carpeting, tools, orchards, returnable containers, breeding animals, and leasehold improvements. Assets falling in this category have two distinguishing qualities: *(a)* In yielding

services over a number of periods the asset does not change in physical characteristic; that is, it does not become physically incorporated in the finished products. For example, a building or machine wears out and eventually loses the ability to perform its function efficiently, but its physical components remain unchanged. In contrast, raw materials are incorporated into the finished products. **(b)** Plant and equipment items are normally acquired for use rather than resale.

1 Land. In contrast to the other kinds of physical property, land has an indefinite service life. In general it does not deteriorate with the passage of time, and, unlike wasting natural resources, land is not physically exhausted through use. There are, of course, exceptional cases. Agricultural land may suffer a loss of service usefulness through erosion or failure to maintain fertility. Building sites may be damaged or destroyed by slides, floods, or similar natural calamities. In general, however, land is treated for accounting purposes as a nondepreciable asset.

2 Property having a limited service life. With the exception of land, all other items of plant and equipment have limited service lives. The investment in such assets is assigned through the process of **depreciation** to the goods and services produced.

B *Wasting assets.* This term includes all natural resources that are subject to exhaustion through extraction. The principal types of wasting assets are **(a)** mineral deposits, **(b)** oil and gas deposits, and **(c)** standing timber. In essence, wasting assets are large-scale, long-term inventories acquired for piecemeal resale or physical use in production over a number of years. The cost of acquiring and developing wasting assets is transformed into periodic charges **(depletion)** against revenue.

II *Intangible assets.* Intangibility denotes a lack of physical existence or substance. Examples of intangible assets include patents, copyrights, trademarks, franchises, organization costs, and goodwill. The cost of intangible assets should be **amortized** over their estimated service life, but not in excess of 40 years.[1]

Basis of reporting in accounting records

In essence a plant asset is a **bundle of future services.** The cost of acquiring such assets is a measure of the amount invested in future services that will be provided by the asset. At the time of acquisition, cost is also an objective measure of the exchange value of assets. The market price represents the simultaneous resolution of two independent opinions (the buyer's and the seller's) as to the value of the asset changing hands. There are cases where the buyer pays too high a price because of errors

[1] See Chapter 13 for a more complete discussion of intangible assets.

in judgment or excessive construction costs, and it is sometimes possible to acquire assets at bargain prices. These, however, are exceptional cases; the accountant seldom has objective evidence to support either "unfortunate" or "bargain" acquisitions. Accountants use cost as the basis of reporting plant and equipment items because it is objective and because it is a measure of the entity's investment in future services.

The problem of determining carrying value (often referred to as *valuation*) subsequent to acquisition is also important. As a given asset is used in operations, a portion of the original bundle of service potential is used up. This can be illustrated as follows:

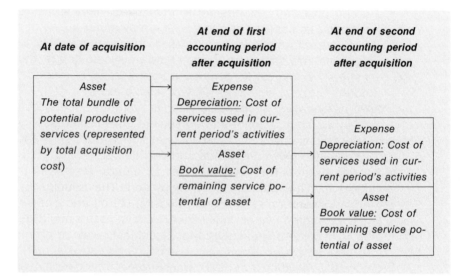

The book value of plant and equipment is thus reduced by depreciation, since a smaller bundle of potential services remains at the end of each period. The problem of measuring depreciation and the book value of assets is discussed in Chapter 12.

Because plant assets have long service lives, it is possible that their fair market value may rise above or fall below book value between the time of initial acquisition and the time the services are used. When such price movements are material, serious questions may be raised about the continuing significance of historical cost. This issue is discussed in Chapter 25.

DETERMINING THE COST OF PLANT ASSETS

The total cost of a plant asset is the cash outlay, or its equivalent, made to acquire the asset and put it in operating condition. This is a clear and simple statement of the principle involved; however, problems arise in applying it to practical situations. In essence these issues may be divided into three categories: (1) What is included in the acquisition cost of an asset? (2) How is acquisition cost measured? and (3) How are costs subsequent to acquisition recorded? Each of these questions will be examined in the following sections.

What is included in the cost of plant assets?

Until a plant asset is ready to perform the services for which it was acquired, it is not complete. Some assets, for example a truck or an adding machine, are complete and ready to function at acquisition. The cost of such assets may be measured by combining the invoice price (including sales tax) and transportation costs. Other assets, for example an automobile assembly line or the machinery for a pulp mill, must be assembled, installed, and tested. All expenditures connected with the assembling, installing, and testing are logically viewed as a part of asset cost.

Capital versus Revenue Expenditures Initial expenditures that are included in the cost of assets are called *capital expenditures,* and such expenditures are commonly said to be *capitalized;* expenditures treated as expenses of the current period are referred to as *revenue expenditures.* This terminology, while not ideal, is satisfactory and is widely used.

The distinction between capital and revenue expenditures is important in arriving at a proper measure of periodic income. If the cost of acquiring assets is treated as a current expense, income of the current period is understated, and income of future periods, when the asset services are used, will be overstated.

The theoretical test to distinguish a capital from a revenue expenditure is simple: Have the services acquired been entirely consumed within the current period, or will there be a carry-over of beneficial services into future periods? As we shall see, this test is not always so simple to apply. At the outset, however, matters of accounting convenience should be distinguished from questions of principle. Many firms follow an arbitrary procedure of charging all asset expenditures of relatively small amounts (for example, those under $100) to expense, in order to avoid excessive accounting effort. Unless these small expenditures are significantly large in the aggregate, such practices, if consistently followed, are reasonable and efficient. They are condoned as a matter of expedience, since they do not materially distort periodic income.

Specific types of capital and revenue expenditures after acquisition, such as additions, betterments, replacements, and repairs, are covered in a subsequent section of this chapter.

Land Special problems arise in determining what to include in the initial cost of land. Normally the acquisition cost of land includes: (1) the purchase price; (2) all costs of closing the transaction and perfecting title, such as commissions, legal fees, title investigations, and title insurance; (3) all costs of surveying, clearing, draining, or filling to make the property suitable for the desired use; and (4) costs of land improvements that have an indefinite life.

It is sometimes necessary to examine the terms of the purchase agreement to determine the price paid for land. Suppose, for example, that a buyer agrees to pay $80,000 for a parcel of land and agrees to pay delinquent property taxes of $5,000 and to make up past-due mortgage payments in the amount of $1,500. The purchase price of the land in this case clearly includes this additional consideration and is $86,500, not $80,000.

When newly acquired land is not in the condition necessary for the contemplated use, the buyer will incur certain costs which should be treated as part of the cost of the land. For example, the cost of clearing trees, or of leveling hills or filling low spots, is properly chargeable to the land. Any salvage realized in the process of clearing land should be treated as a reduction in cost.

Land improvement costs are capitalizable expenditures; they can be treated as a part of land or recorded in a separate Land Improvements account. Such improvements as landscaping and drainage have indefinite service lives and are properly added to land cost. The cost of such improvements as sidewalks, streets, and sewers may or may not have indefinite service lives. In many localities, the cost of streets, sewers, and similar improvements are charged against the owners of the benefited property, but the local governmental unit agrees to maintain and replace them if they are built to standard specifications. In such cases the special assessment expenditure is a part of land cost, since it is permanent in nature. If the property owner is responsible for eventual replacement, however, land improvements have a limited life and should be recorded in a separate account to facilitate depreciation accounting.

Land held as a potential building site or for other speculative or investment purposes is not currently used in operations and should therefore be treated as an investment rather than a part of the plant and equipment category. The carrying charges, such as taxes, interest, and weed control, prior to the time that the land is put to use, should properly be added to the cost of the land. When the site is put to use, the land should be reclassified from the investment category to the plant and equipment category, and future taxes and carrying charges should be treated as operating expenses.

Buildings The distinction between land and building costs may be of considerable importance because of the potential effect on income. For example, suppose that a parcel of land is acquired as the site for a new building. On the land is an old building that must be razed before the new structure can be built. Is the cost of tearing down the old building (net of any salvage recovery) a current expense, a part of the cost of the new building, or an element of land cost? If it is a current expense, it will be charged against revenue immediately; if a part of the cost of the new building, it will be depreciated over the life of the structure; if a part of land cost, it will not be depreciated. What are the guiding standards to be used in resolving these and similar questions?

The primary issue is the nature of the relationship between the expenditure and a particular asset. We must ask: What is the asset that we have acquired, and is the particular cost at issue reasonably related to the acquisition of this particular asset? If a parcel of land is acquired for a building site, the entire cost of putting the land into suitable condition as a building site is allocable to the land; on the other hand, the cost of excavating and surveying in order to construct the foundation for the new building is a part of the cost of the building.

The line of reasoning outlined above can be applied in resolving a number of similar issues that may arise in determining building, construction, or acquisition costs. The examples below are illustrative:

Cost incurred	*Treatment and reason*
1 Cost of temporary buildings used for construction offices or to house tools and materials during construction of a new building.	Charge to new building. This is a necessary cost of constructing the new building.
2 Cost of tearing down a building previously used in operations in order to construct a new building. Building was no longer serviceable.	Recognize as part of loss on retirement of the old building. This cost is related to the services of the **old** building, not the new building.
3 Cost of insurance against risk of claims for accidents or damages while constructing a new building.	Charge to new building. This is an ordinary and necessary cost of constructing the new building.

When a building is constructed, all costs necessary to complete the construction should be included in the cost of the building. This may include architects' fees, building permit, interest on construction loans, and a variety of other overhead costs. When a building is purchased, all charges clearly relating to the building (termite inspection, for example) and considered applicable to future revenue should be capitalized. Separate accounts may be used for the building shell (foundation, walls, and floors), partitions, air-conditioning units, roof, wiring, siding, etc.

The accountant should be careful, however, not to capitalize any costs which will not benefit future periods. For example, suppose that immediately after the purchase of a used building it is found that extensive repairs will be necessary. The proper treatment of such costs must rest on evidence as to the circumstances of the purchase. If the buyer recognized the need for these repairs at the time he negotiated the purchase price, their cost is clearly a part of the cost of placing the building in serviceable condition and should be capitalized. The reasoning is that paying $100,000 for a rundown building and $50,000 for renovation is equivalent to paying $150,000 for a renovated building. If, on the other hand, a building is purchased for $150,000 under the assumption that it is in condition for occupancy and it is later discovered that there are serious defects requiring an expenditure of $50,000 to correct, any portion of the $50,000 expenditure that does not either result in an improved structure or add to the service life of the building should be treated as a loss.

A similar line of reasoning can be used to reject proposals to treat the undepreciated costs of assets replaced because of inadequacy and obsolescence either as costs of new assets acquired or as deferred charges. It is difficult to see how the new asset can have greater value, or how future periods will receive greater service benefit, because of inadequacy and obsolescence of assets no longer in service. Future periods will benefit from the ownership and use of *new* assets and not from the retirement of the old asset or from the failure to depreciate the *old* asset fast enough. To defer losses on asset disposals would amount to charging future revenue with depreciation on both the new asset and on the replaced asset, which, of course, will not contribute in any way to future revenue.

Leaseholds and Leasehold Improvements A *leasehold* is a personal property right granting to the *lessee* the use of real property for a specified length of time. The contract under which this right is granted is called a *lease,* and the owner of the property is known as the *lessor.* A lease contract usually calls for periodic rental payments. On rare occasions, leases provide for a lump-sum payment of the entire rental in advance.[2]

Since the lease contract gives the lessee the right to use the property in exchange for a contractual obligation to make future rental payments, it has been suggested that both this "asset" and the corresponding "liability" should be recorded (capitalized) on the books of the lessee. This topic will be discussed in greater detail in Chapter 19.

Leasehold improvements in the form of buildings or structural alterations are sometimes made on leased property. Accounting for leasehold improvements by the lessee is comparable to accounting for similar owned property, except that service life should be related to the duration of the lease. A building expected to last 20 years which is built on land leased for 15 years with no renewal provision has a 15-year service life insofar as the lessee is concerned, and a salvage value that is determined by the amount, if any, that the lessor agrees to pay upon the termination of the lease. When the lease agreement contains a provision to renew at the option of the lessee, the length of service life becomes uncertain, except in terms of the present intentions of the lessee. In the above example, if the lease contract contained a renewal option for an additional 5-year period, the amortization period for the building should be either 15 or 20 years, depending on the intention of the lessee with respect to renewal.

The lessor generally does not record leasehold improvements made

---

[2] The lump-sum leasehold is almost extinct, largely because of the income tax law, which requires the lessor to include the entire sum received in taxable income in the year of receipt, without regard to the time period covered by the lease.

by the lessee. However, if the lessor pays for any of the improvements, his share of the cost should be recorded in a plant asset account and depreciated over the estimated useful life of the improvements.

Machinery and Equipment   This category may encompass a wide variety of items, including all types of machinery (both stationary and mobile), furniture, fixtures, ships, vehicles of all types, tools, containers, patterns and dies, computers, and office equipment. Cost of machinery and equipment items should be carefully determined and allocated to revenue through the process of depreciation. This is the essence of the ***matching concept*** as used in accounting.

Several topics relating to the acquisition of machinery, equipment, and buildings are discussed below.

Self-constructed Assets   Occasionally a building, a machine, or a piece of equipment may be constructed by the business that intends to use it, either because this is an economical method of acquisition or because the quality and specifications of the asset can be better controlled if the asset is self-constructed. Determining the cost of the completed asset in this situation raises a number of issues.

Accountants generally agree that all direct costs incurred in construction activities should be capitalized. ***Direct costs*** are defined as those that can be specifically identified with the construction project in the sense that they would not have been incurred otherwise. Direct costs include the cost of materials, labor, design, engineering, etc. Whether any manufacturing overhead should be included in the cost of the self-constructed asset is a debatable question.

The basic issue is whether overhead costs that will not change as the result of a self-construction project should be charged to the new asset. Some companies have engineering and construction departments that regularly engage in new construction. The overhead costs assignable to these departments are clearly allocable between ordinary maintenance work and new construction. But what about the overhead costs of a regular producing department that occasionally undertakes the construction of a plant asset? It is difficult to imagine a situation in which any significant self-construction project could be undertaken without increasing overhead to some extent. However, there are a number of fixed costs in manufacturing overhead that will not increase as a result of construction activities. If these fixed costs are allocated between regular production and self-construction projects, the result may be that the average manufacturing cost for units produced will be reduced during periods in which significant self-construction activities are undertaken. Pretax income during the construction period would thus be increased by the amount of the fixed overhead assigned to the self-constructed asset. The three possible approaches to this issue can be summarized as follows:

1 Allocate no overhead to the self-constructed asset. This approach has little to recommend it. At least some overhead is the direct result of new construction, and charging this incremental overhead to current operations is a clear case of distortion of income by failing to recognize a capital expenditure.

2 *Allocate only incremental overhead to self-constructed assets.* This approach may be defended on the ground that incremental overhead represents the relevant cost which management considered in making the decision to construct the asset. Fixed overhead costs, it is argued, are period costs; since they would have been incurred in any case, there is no relationship between the fixed portion of overhead and the self-constructed project. This is probably the method most widely used in practice because, its supporters argue, "it does not distort the cost of normal operations."

3 *Allocate a portion of all overhead to the self-constructed asset.* The argument for this approach is that the proper function of cost allocation is to relate the entire productive costs incurred in a given period to the output of that period. If a company is able to construct an asset and still carry on its regular activities, it has benefited by putting to use some of its *idle capacity,* and this fact should be reflected in higher income. To charge the entire overhead to only a portion of the productive activity is to ignore facts and to understate the cost of the self-constructed asset. The authors feel that this line of reasoning is sound, although at present it is not widely used.

Interest during Construction During the time it takes to complete a self-construction project, money is tied up in materials, labor, and other construction costs. Is the interest cost incurred in borrowing funds for this purpose a part of the cost of the constructed asset? This is a controversial question in accounting theory.

Generally, accountants regard interest as a cost of financing and not as a cost of obtaining asset services. If Firm A pays cash for an asset while Firm B borrows money to buy an identical asset, there is no logical basis for claiming that Firm B has a more valuable asset simply because it has paid interest on borrowed funds. This reasoning, carried over into the self-construction area, leads to the conclusion that interest on funds borrowed and used in construction should not be capitalized.

The opposing view is that interest during construction, including *implicit interest* on capital provided by stockholders, is a cost of acquiring future asset services. Funds are immobilized during the construction period. In deciding to construct the asset, management must have determined that the value created would be sufficient to cover all costs, including interest. Furthermore, interest on investment would be included in the asking price of the asset if it were purchased in finished form. Therefore, it is argued, the accountant should not charge off as expense interest on funds employed in construction of an asset prior to the time that the asset can produce revenue.

In recent years an increasing number of companies have been capitalizing interest paid on debt.[3] Because interest on money borrowed to

---

[3] In the 1972 edition (26th ed.) of *Accounting Trends & Techniques* published by the AICPA, 25 of the 600 companies included in the survey disclosed the practice of capitalizing interest on debt; a few years earlier only 8 companies disclosed such a practice. An example of such disclosure follows: J. C. Penney Company, Inc.,—"Capitalized interest on construction in progress and land held for future use, $6.2 million."

prepare an asset for use is a cost which will benefit revenue during the full productive life of the asset, the authors consider such practice a sound application of the matching concept. A reasonable guideline for capitalizing interest may be stated as follows: Capitalize interest actually paid on loans to finance construction *only during the construction period;* once assets are put to use, interest on the loans should be treated as an expense.

Capitalization of Interest by Regulated Companies Among public utility firms, this line of reasoning is extended even further. The Federal Power Commission authorizes the capitalization, not only of actual interest on funds borrowed from outsiders, but of an *implicit interest* charge for the utilities' own funds used in construction. With utility rates set at levels that limit earnings to a "fair" rate of return on plant, the public utility company has no opportunity to "make up later" for any failure to measure all costs, whereas the unregulated company does.

If $100,000 of interest applies to construction, an asset account would be debited and interest charged to construction would be credited and would be shown on the income statement either as an offset against interest expense or as a revenue item. The effect of this procedure is not only to remove from current expense the interest incurred on borrowed funds used for construction, but to add to income an amount equal to the implicit interest on funds used in construction. In future periods the capitalized interest will be charged to expense as the asset is depreciated.[4]

The capitalization of implicit interest is rarely found outside the public utility field. Capitalizing interest actually incurred and traceable to construction is a common practice. The theoretical case for including interest during construction in asset cost, however, is stronger if interest on *all* funds is capitalized without regard to the method of financing.

Profit on Self-construction Suppose that a company has asked for bids on a piece of equipment and that the lowest bid is $50,000. Management finds that the same equipment can be constructed in the firm's own plant at a total cost, including materials, labor, and incremental overhead, of $40,000. If the company chooses to construct the asset, it might be argued that the asset should be recorded at $50,000 and that the firm should recognize a profit of $10,000. While there may be some support for this view among nonaccountants, the facts do not meet the accounting test of realization. Profits are generated from asset *use and disposal* and not from asset acquisition; the $10,000 is a *saving* which will be realized through lower depreciation charges as the asset is used.

[4]For more extensive discussions of this topic, see: John F. Utley, "Yet Another View of Interest during Construction," *Selected Papers 1970,* Haskins & Sells (New York: 1971), pp. 89–94; Richard Walker, "The Capital Cost of Utility Construction," *Arthur Andersen Chronicle,* vol. 31, no. 4 (September 1971), pp. 30–37.

How is cost of plant assets measured?

We have just reviewed some of the problems that arise in determining what is included in the cost of plant assets. Now let us examine the problems that arise in measuring the cost of plant assets, when the method of acquisition obscures the purchase price. The objective in measuring acquisition cost is to determine the cash outlay or its equivalent necessary to obtain the asset. In general, the problems that arise in this area center around the meaning of the term *cash equivalent.*

Cash Discounts When assets are purchased under terms that allow the deduction of a discount for the payment of cash within a specified period of time, the term "cash equivalent" is logically interpreted to mean the invoice price, net of the discount. For example, if a piece of equipment is purchased for $5,000, terms 2/10, n/30, the buyer has the choice of either paying cash (within a 10-day grace period) of $4,900, or of deferring payment for an additional 20 days, at an added cost of $100. If payment is made within the 10-day period, the cost of the asset is only $4,900; if payment is deferred for 20 days, the additional $100 paid is a penalty for late payment; this should not be viewed as a part of asset cost.

Deferred Payment Contracts In many cases payment for an asset is delayed for longer time periods. For example, suppose that equipment is purchased under an agreement calling for payments of $1,295 at the end of each year for 10 years. To assume that the present value of the liability, and thus the cost of the equipment, is $12,950 (10 × $1,295), is to ignore the fact that there is an interest charge included in the contract. To arrive at a basis for recording this purchase, the accountant should look for evidence of the cash equivalent price of the equipment. He may find that this or similar equipment can be purchased for $10,000 in cash, in which case this amount becomes the measure of cost. If no conclusive evidence of a cash price is available, the rate of interest implicit in the contract price should be estimated. The present value of 10 payments of $1,295 each at 5% interest per year is approximately $10,000,[5] assuming that a 5% rate is reasonable, the purchase and the first two payments should be recorded as illustrated on page 415.

   When payment is deferred for relatively short time periods, the amount of interest implicit in the purchase price may be small and can be ignored. If the length of time and the amount of interest involved are material, however, a reasonable estimate of the cash equivalent purchase price is required.[6]

---

[5] The computation of this amount requires the use of a present value formula. Discussion of this topic is found in Appendix A.
[6] See *APB Opinion No. 21,* "Interest on Receivables and Payables," AICPA (New York: 1971).

At acquisition:

Equipment	10,000	
Equipment Contract Payable		10,000

Purchased equipment under contract requiring payment of $1,295 at the end of each of 10 years. Present value of liability at 5% is $10,000.

Payment on contract at end of first year:

Interest Expense	500	
Equipment Contract Payable	795	
Cash		1,295

Interest on equipment contract for first year, 5% of $10,000.

Payment on contract at end of second year:

Interest Expense	460	
Equipment Contract Payable	835	
Cash		1,295

Interest on equipment contract for second year, 5% of $9,205 ($10,000 − $795).

Property, plant, and equipment items are often acquired by assuming a *purchase-money* obligation. A purchase-money mortgage, for example, is a loan created at the time property is acquired, secured by such property, and having priority over any subsequently created lien on the property.

Lump-sum Acquisitions A single negotiated price may be paid for two or more assets. If the assets in question have different service lives, it is necessary to allocate the total lump-sum cost among them in order to provide a proper basis for computing depreciation. The most common example of this situation is the purchase of real property—land and building—for a flat price. Since the life of land is indefinite and the life of a building is limited, an allocation of cost is necessary. Assume, for example, that a building and the land on which it is located are acquired by Mills Company for $250,000 (see escrow statement on page 417). How is the accountant to determine how much of the $250,000 applies to the land, and how much to the building? An examination of the negotiations that preceded the transaction may show that the price was settled upon under the assumption that $200,000 applied to the building and $50,000 to the land. If such evidence is not available or is considered to be unrealistic, the accountant must look elsewhere for evidence of relative values as a basis for allocation. If, for example, the assessed valuation for property tax purposes (typically set at 20 to 25% of market value) is $38,500 for the building and $16,500 for land, the allocation of the $250,000 total cost can be made as follows:

	Assessed valuation	Relative value	×	Total cost	=	Allocation of cost
Building	$38,500 /55000 = 70%			$250,000		$175,000
Land	16,500 55000 = 30%					75,000
Totals	$55,000	100%				$250,000

The Escrow Statement Buyers and sellers generally engage an agent (a bank or an escrow company) to handle the details of a real estate transaction. When the transaction is closed, each party receives an *escrow statement* which shows the complete details of the transaction. The escrow statement will show (in debit and credit form) such items as the selling price, mortgage assumed by the buyer, tax on the transaction, commission charged to seller, escrow fees, cash received from buyer, final amount paid to buyer or seller to complete the transaction, etc. The allocation of property taxes, interest on mortgage, insurance, rents, and other items is also summarized in the escrow statement. A condensed example of an escrow statement for the Mills Company (the *buyer* of the property discussed in the preceding section) is illustrated on page 417.

The escrow statement for Mills Company (the buyer) shows that the agreed price for the property was $246,700, a debit on the buyer's statement. The Mills Company was also charged $240 for unexpired insurance, and additional costs allocable to the property of $3,300($150 + $1,490 + $140 + $20 + $1,500). Thus the total cost of the property is $250,000 ($246,700 + $3,300). The Mills Company was credited for $104,000 representing the unpaid balance of the mortgage assumed, $2,200 of accrued property taxes, $260 of accrued interest on the mortgage, and $144,080 which was previously deposited in escrow to apply on the purchase price. (The cash deposit was recorded by Mills Company in the Escrow Deposit account.) The "check to balance" of $300 is the amount of cash returned to Mills Company to close the escrow.

The escrow statement provides the information needed to record the purchase of the property on the books of the Mills Company as shown at the bottom of page 417.

WESTERN ESCROW COMPANY
Escrow Statement

Statement of buyer: Mills Company

Date: November 1, 1975
Escrow No.: 01-879

Items	Debits	Credits
Consideration (selling price)	$246,700	
Balance of mortgage payable		$104,000
Interest adjustment @ 6% from Oct. 17, 1975, to Nov. 1, 1975		260
Tax pro rata $6,600 per year, from July 1, 1975 to Nov. 1, 1975		2,200
Fire insurance pro rata $1,440 for three years, Nov. 1, 1975, to May 1, 1976	240	
Deposited in escrow by buyer		144,080
Lender's forwarding fee—Beverly Hills Securities Company	150	
Title policy (buyer agreed to pay full amount)	1,490	
Internal revenue stamps (tax on transaction)	140	
Recording fee	20	
Commission (paid by seller)		
Escrow fee (buyer agreed to pay full amount)	1,500	
Check to balance ~amt. of cash returned to Co.~	300	
Totals . . . . ~to close escrow~	$250,540	$250,540

Journal Entry Based on Escrow Statement

Cash	300	
Building	175,000	
Land	75,000	
Unexpired Insurance	240	
Interest Payable		260
Property Taxes Payable		2,200
Mortgage Payable		104,000
Escrow Deposit		144,080

To record purchase of building and land per Escrow Statement no. 01-879. The total cost of $250,000 ($246,700 + $150 + $1,490 + $140 + $20 + $1,500) is allocated on the basis of property tax valuation of building and land, $38,500 and $16,500, respectively (see allocation schedule on top of page 416).

A similar escrow statement prepared for the seller would provide the required information to record the sale of the property on his records.

Securities Issued in Exchange for Assets When a company issues shares of its own capital stock in payment for assets, the proper basis for recording such a transaction is not always clear. The value of the asset acquired is the cash equivalent received by the company for its shares of stock.[7] On the other hand, the market value of the shares given in exchange is a measure of the consideration given for the asset. The accountant is thus faced with the problem of getting independent evidence of (1) the value of the asset and (2) the value of the shares given in exchange. We should expect that these two values would be roughly equivalent; if they are not, a choice between them must be made based on the factors considered by management in making the purchase and on the validity of each valuation.

Shares of stock represent an interest in the net assets of a business, including the asset being acquired. The market price of the shares issued is thus not an entirely independent variable, since it depends to some extent on the value of the asset received in exchange. This reasoning indicates that our first choice should be independent evidence of the worth of the asset acquired, by appraisal, previous bid prices, or other objective sources. For example, if a machine which was independently appraised at $180,000 is acquired in exchange for 2,000 shares of $50 par value capital stock, the entry would be:

Machinery	180,000	
Capital Stock, $50 par value		100,000
Paid-in Capital in Excess of Par Value		80,000
Exchange of 2,000 shares of $50 par value capital stock for		
machine appraised at $180,000.		

In some cases evidence of the market value of shares of stock is easier to get and more reliable than evidence as to the value of an asset. This is particularly true if the company's shares are listed on a stock exchange and daily quotations of market price are available.

Assets Acquired by Gift Normally there is a presumption against the idea that anyone dealing with a business makes a gift to it. There are occasions, however, where corporations receive property under conditions that are reasonably interpreted as the receipt of a gift. For example,

[7] Procedures for recording assets acquired pursuant to mergers interpreted as **purchases** and as **pooling of interests** are discussed briefly in Chapter 16. A more extensive treatment of this subject is found in the **Advanced Accounting** text of this series.

assume that the City of X is trying to attract industry to its area. In order to induce S Company to locate a manufacturing plant in its city, the City Council agrees to donate a building site and erect a suitable building for the company, in return for which the company promises to maintain an operation employing 200 persons for a period of 10 years. The land is worth $40,000 and the building is worth $200,000.

How is the accountant to record such transactions? If we adopt the view that the accountant's sole responsibility is to keep track of costs incurred, we might argue that no cost is involved in the receipt of the land and building in this instance, and therefore no entry is required. This is, however, too narrow a view of the scope of accounting. A primary justification for recording asset acquisitions at cost is that cost at that time represents more satisfactory evidence of value than any other basis. When cash outlay is no longer a reasonable basis for asset accountability or income measurement, the accountant should be prepared to deal with the problem on its merits rather than bury his head, ostrichlike, in the sands of cost. If a business receives an asset at no cost, the asset should be recorded at its fair market value, determined on the basis of the best evidence obtainable. Referring to the S Company example, the donation of the land and building results in an increase in the stockholders' equity and should be recorded as follows:

Land	40,000	
Building	200,000	
Donated Capital		240,000
To record at fair market value property donated by City of X.		

Conditions are sometimes attached to a gift of property so that title is not transferred until the conditions are met (for example, continuing operations for a specified number of years). So long as indications are that the company intends to comply with the conditions, depreciation should be taken in the regular manner, both before and after title is acquired, in order that the value of the services obtained from the use of the asset (whether purchased or donated to the company) is recognized in the measurement of income.

Investment Tax Credit The Revenue Act of 1971 provided for a reduction of federal income taxes by an amount known as the *investment tax credit.* The investment tax credit is subject to a number of limitations and has been frequently amended and even suspended. The credit may be as high as 7% of the cost of depreciable property other than buildings and their structural components. To illustrate, if a company purchases a machine with a service life of seven years or more for $100,000, it would be entitled to a 7%, or $7,000, reduction in its tax bill. Despite this tax reduction, the full $100,000 cost may be depreciated for tax purposes over the service life of the asset. Two methods have been used to recognize the effect of the investment tax credit in the accounting records.

1 The **flow through** method, which reduces income tax expense by the amount of the investment tax credit in the year the asset is acquired. This method is favored by most businessmen on grounds that immediate tax reduction is the intent of the tax law. Because income tax expense is reduced in the year depreciable assets are acquired, this method allows businessmen to increase earnings per share by simply buying certain types of plant assets.

2 The **deferred** method, which calls for the amortization of the benefit arising from the investment tax credit over the productive life of the depreciable asset acquired. Under this method the investment tax credit is viewed as a reduction in the effective cost of the asset, although it is generally reported as a deferred credit in the balance sheet and is amortized by periodic reduction to Income Taxes Expense. The deferral method is favored by most accountants because it avoids an immediate increase in net income as a result of **buying** an asset and thus provides a more meaningful measurement of net income.[8]

Cost after acquisition

Expenditures relating to plant and equipment will normally be made throughout the service life of such assets. Whether these are expenses to be charged against current revenue or whether they should be capitalized is often a difficult question. The general approach in dealing with these expenditures may be stated as follows: Expenditures that result in additional asset services, more valuable asset services, or extension of service life applicable to future revenue should be capitalized; expenditures to maintain assets in good operating condition are viewed as expenses of the period in which they are incurred. This approach is consistent with the concept of matching costs and revenue and should be applied to any expenditure of significant amount. Future benefit is a characteristic of all capitalized costs relating to plant and equipment; costs which are deemed to be applicable to current or past revenue should be recognized as expenses.

[8] Because this discussion of the investment tax credit is brief, the student should not conclude that the related tax law is not complex or that the accounting issues are not controversial. In 1962, the APB in *Opinion No. 2* took the position that the investment tax credit should be reflected in net income over the productive life of assets on which the credit is allowed and not in the year in which the asset is acquired. Because of strong opposition from the business community and because the SEC permitted either approach, the APB in 1964 issued *Opinion No. 4* in which it stated that even though the deferral method is preferable, the alternative method of treating the credit as a reduction in income tax expense in the year in which the credit arises is also acceptable. Then in 1971, the APB issued an exposure draft of an opinion which would have eliminated this alternative treatment by requiring the deferral method. However, strong pressure on Congress by businessmen resulted in a provision in the Revenue Act of 1971 which **legally** permitted taxpayers to choose the method of accounting for the investment tax credit. The method adopted must be used consistently and must be adequately disclosed.

Although the general approach outlined in the preceding paragraph enables accountants to distinguish between capital and revenue expenditures incurred subsequent to acquisition, a brief discussion relating to different types of these expenditures should be useful.

Additions An *addition* is a new and separate asset or an extension of an old asset. The construction of a new wing on an existing building is an example of an addition to buildings. The installation of two-way communication radios in a fleet of company cars is an example of an addition to equipment. The addition of an entirely new unit is identical in nature to the acquisition of new property and raises no accounting problems not previously discussed. When the addition involves an enlargement or extension of an old property unit, the only problem is to determine whether any portion of the service potential of the old asset has been removed or lost in the process. For example, in connection with construction of a building addition, if it is necessary to remove the old central heating unit and install one with a larger capacity, the old unit should be retired. The recording of the asset addition should be accompanied by an entry removing the cost of the old heating unit and its related accumulated depreciation account from the records and recognizing any resulting loss. The loss *should not* be treated as additional cost of the new unit.

Improvements, Renewals, and Replacements Improvements (or betterments), renewals, and replacements are nonrecurring expenditures that in some way add to the service potential of plant assets. The additional value may be the result of extending the service life, increasing the rate of output, or lowering the cost of operation per unit of output. Such expenditures are, therefore, properly related to these future services and charged against revenue in the period in which the services are used. Improvements and renewals may be accomplished through the substitution of better component parts and hence may be labeled as replacements. The distinction between these different expenditures is obscure and is not germane to the basic accounting issues involved. Costs of this type are often referred to as cost of *plant renovation* or *plant modernization,* particularly when such costs are incurred as a part of a large-scale program of plant rejuvenation.

To the extent that renovation or modernization involves the substitution of new parts for old, the proper accounting is to remove the cost of the old part from the asset account (and the appropriate amount from the related accumulated depreciation account) and to substitute the cost of the new part. If renovation or modernization does not involve a substitution but results only in some modification of the asset, the costs incurred should be added to the book value of the asset by a charge either to the asset account or to the accumulated depreciation account. These three procedures are briefly explained below.

The substitution procedure A considerable improvement in plant accounting is possible if property units are defined in terms of major components
and separate service lives are used in depreciating these components.
To illustrate, suppose that a glass-lined food storage tank is constructed
at a cost of $200,000, of which $40,000 is estimated to be the cost of
the glass lining. The estimated service life of the tank is 20 years; the
lining must be replaced approximately every five years. If a single asset
account, Storage Tanks, is used, there will be a problem of dealing with
the periodic replacement of the lining. A better procedure would be to
use two asset accounts, Storage Tanks and Tank Linings, and to depreciate the former over 20 years and the latter over five. Now assume that
at the beginning of the fifth year the glass lining had to be replaced, at
a cost of $54,000, but a new material was used that is expected to last
six years. The entries to record the lining replacement would be:

Accumulated Depreciation: Tank Linings	32,000	
Loss on Retirement of Tank Linings	8,000	
Tank Linings		40,000
To record removal of old tank linings. Undepreciated cost of tank linings is treated as a loss.		
Tank Linings	54,000	
Cash		54,000
To record replacement of old linings with new materials.		

Depreciation on the new lining will be recorded at $9,000 ($54,000 ÷ 6)
in each of the next six years, and the record of the asset Storage Tanks
is undisturbed by these events. This approach allows the accountant to
shape his records to the facts: to report the change in the estimated life
of the old lining, to report in the asset account the higher cost of the
new lining, and to compute future depreciation on the basis of probable
service life of the new lining material.

A charge to the asset account An expenditure which does not replace an
existing part may enlarge the capacity or improve the efficiency of an
asset without prolonging its service life. Such expenditures should be
recorded in the asset account and depreciated over the remaining service
life of the asset. This treatment is similar to the procedure suggested for
additions.

A charge to the accumulated depreciation account The cost of asset renovation is often charged directly to Accumulated Depreciation. The rationale for this procedure is that such expenditures extend the service life
of the asset and thus restore some of the cost of service previously written
off. Reducing Accumulated Depreciation means that additional time will

be required to depreciate the asset, and it is assumed that this period will correspond to the increased service life of the asset. This procedure is sound in theory and may be used for income tax purposes but it should not be followed blindly, particularly when additions and replacements are involved.

Rearrangements and Moving Costs Costs of rearranging machinery and equipment to secure a more efficient plant layout should be recorded in a separate account and amortized over the period of time expected to benefit from the rearrangement (usually a short period because of the possibility of further rearrangements). Costs of moving the entire plant or office should be similarly treated, unless the moving results from some extraordinary event or catastrophe, in which case the costs of moving would be included as part of the related extraordinary loss.

Ordinary Repairs and Maintenance Minor repair and maintenance expenditures are usually required throughout the life of an asset in order to keep it in efficient operating condition. The distinguishing characteristic of such expenditures is that they neither add to the value of the property nor materially prolong its useful life. The usual procedure is to treat these costs as current expenses since maintenance activities are recurring and the cost is related to current revenue. However, any *unusual* or extraordinary repairs arising from fire or other casualties should be recognized as losses if not covered by insurance.

One solution to the problem of dealing with repair costs which vary widely from period to period and are significant in amount is to anticipate such costs and spread them over the life of the asset. Under this procedure the total expected repair costs are estimated at the time each asset is acquired, and repair expense is charged each period for a portion of the estimated lifetime repair cost. The offsetting credit is to an account titled Allowance for Estimated Repairs. Actual repair expenditures are charged against the allowance, which is carried forward throughout the life of the asset. However, only the actual expenditures are allowed for income tax purposes in the year incurred.

To illustrate, assume that for a particular item of equipment, repair costs are expected to average $250 per year, and that repair costs of $400 are incurred in the second year. The entries to be made during the first two years are given on page 424.

At the end of the second year the allowance account would carry a credit balance of $100 ($500 − $400). Conceivably, a debit balance might appear in the allowance account if major repairs occurred early or if the estimate of repair costs was too low.

A number of criticisms of this method have been raised. Some accountants argue that it is merely an income-smoothing device and that it tends to obscure the fact that repair costs may increase as an asset gets older. Others question whether reliable estimates of repair costs can be made. Finally, the classification of the Allowance for Estimated Repairs

End of Year 1:

Repair Expense	250	
Allowance for Estimated Repairs		250

During Year 2:

Allowance for Estimated Repairs	400	
Cash, Parts, Accrued Payroll, etc.		400

End of Year 2:

Repair Expense	250	
Allowance for Estimated Repairs		250

poses difficulties. A credit balance in the allowance cannot be classified as a part of stockholders' equity since it is clearly illogical to charge an expense and increase stockholders' equity. Classification as a liability may be questioned because no legal obligation exists. Treating the allowance as an asset valuation account (to be deducted from or added to the cost of the related asset) assumes that the "accrued repairs" represent additional depreciation and thus reduce the book value of the asset. This is probably the least objectionable alternative, particularly since treating a debit balance in the allowance as an asset—in the nature of a prepayment of repair expenditures—is consistent.

Anticipation of repair costs does not fit well into the generally accepted measurement concepts of accounting and this practice should be discouraged. Year-to-year accrual of estimated repairs lacks sufficient objectivity and might well encourage the adoption of other artificial income-smoothing techniques by management.

RETIREMENT AND DISPOSAL OF PLANT ASSETS

Whenever a unit of property is retired from use, the proper accounting procedure is to (1) complete the accounting record of depreciation on this asset up to the date of retirement; and (2) remove from the accounts all amounts relating to the retired asset. Assume, for example, that a piece of equipment costing $6,000 has been depreciated at an annual rate of 10% for eight years. In the middle of the ninth year the machine is sold for $1,750 (net of any direct costs incurred on the sale). The entries to record this event are as shown on page 425.

The proper interpretation of any gain or loss that may arise upon disposal of an asset is often uncertain. To the extent that it stems from errors in estimating service life or residual value, the "gain" or "loss" on the disposal is in reality an adjustment of previously reported earnings. To the extent that it is due to changes in the price of the asset, the gain

(1) Depreciation Expense 300
         Accumulated Depreciation: Equipment   300
     To record depreciation at 10% for six months on machine cost-
     ing $6,000.

(2) Cash 1,750
     Accumulated Depreciation: Equipment 5,100
         Gain on Disposal of Equipment.   850
         Equipment   6,000
     To record sale of equipment.

or loss is in the nature of a "windfall" and is an element of income for the current year. In most cases a combination of these factors is present. Material gains and losses (or provisions for losses) from the sale or abandonment of a plant or a significant segment of a business were treated as extraordinary items until **APB Opinion No. 30** was issued in 1973. Current practice requires that all such gains and losses be included in the determination of income before extraordinary items.[9]

Because of inadequate property records, plant assets are sometimes scrapped or abandoned and no record is made of the retirement. Failure to recognize a loss in the period of disposal, and the continuation of depreciation charges on an asset no longer in use, result in a distortion of income in the periods after retirement. On the other hand, assets are sometimes retired from active service and not sold or abandoned but kept on standby status for use in emergency or to meet peak load requirements. When this occurs, an estimate of standby or salvage value should be made and the asset should be written down to this amount. (If salvage value is greater than book value, most accountants would object to a write-up on the grounds that realization of the gain had not taken place.) When the amount of standby equipment is large, it should be separately reported in the balance sheet.

Trade-ins and exchanges of plant assets

When plant assets are retired by exchanging them for new assets, the problem of accounting for the retirement of the old asset becomes intermingled with that of accounting for the acquisition of the new. The basic issue is one of evidence: Is there sufficient evidence to warrant recognition of a gain or loss on the disposal of the old asset? To illustrate, consider the following data:

[9] APB Opinion No. 30, "Reporting the Results of Operations," AICPA (New York: 1973), p. 566. See chap. 3 for a discussion of the nature of extraordinary gains and losses and the problems encountered in reporting such items in the income statement. Chapter 20 includes a discussion of tax allocation problems relating to extraordinary items.

	Case I	Case II
Old asset (evidence of value):		
(1) Book value (cost, $12,000, less accumulated depreciation of $8,000) .	$ 4,000	$ 4,000
(2) Trade-in allowance	6,000	3,800
(3) Estimated fair value at the time of exchange	5,400	3,500
Invoice price of new asset	15,000	15,000
Balance paid in cash	9,000	11,200

In deciding how to record the exchange of the old asset for the new, the accountant is faced with three pieces of evidence as to the value of the old asset at the time of the exchange: (1) its book value, (2) the dealer's trade-in allowance, and (3) an estimate of the fair value. The accounting procedure for the exchange will vary depending on which "value" is accepted.

If the **book value** of the old asset is accepted as the best evidence of its value, no gain or loss is recognized in recording the exchange. The accounting basis of the new asset will be equal to the book value of the old asset plus the balance paid in cash. Thus the basis of the new asset will be $13,000 ($4,000 + $9,000) in Case I and $15,200 ($4,000 + $11,200) in Case II. Book value is not very reliable evidence of consideration given in exchange. Using book value of the old asset as a part of the cost of the new asset results in carrying forward any error in depreciating the old asset as well as any real gain or loss on the disposal of the old asset. However, **this method is required for income tax purposes** and is widely used in current practice. If the resulting errors are relatively small, they may be tolerated by the accountant as a matter of expediency. If the error is material, however, the accountant should recognize that questions of material distortions in current and future income should not be decided on the basis of expediency.

If the dealer's **trade-in allowance** is used as evidence of value of the old asset, a gain or loss equal to the difference between book value and the trade-in allowance will emerge. A gain of $2,000 ($6,000 − $4,000) would be recognized in Case I, and the new asset would be recorded at $15,000 ($6,000 + $9,000); a loss of $200 ($4,000 − $3,800) would be recognized in Case II, and the new asset would also be recorded at $15,000 ($3,800 + $11,200). In using the trade-in allowance as evidence of value, it should be recognized that businessmen often inflate the allowance as a means of cutting price. In fact, invoice prices may be deliberately raised to allow a margin for such marketing strategy without the necessity of lowering the ultimate price below the desired level. Trade-in allowances are thus questionable evidence of the real worth of a used asset.

If the *estimated fair value* is used as evidence of value of the old asset, a gain of $1,400 ($5,400 − $4,000) would be recognized in Case I, and the new asset would be recorded at $14,400 ($5,400 + $9,000); a loss of $500 ($4,000 − $3,500) would be recognized in Case II, and the new asset would be recorded at $14,700 ($3,500 + $11,200). The use of estimated fair value of the old asset at the time of the exchange leads to a cost basis for the new asset in accord with economic reality. The cost of the new asset is then the sum of the cash expended plus the cash equivalent of the old asset given in exchange. The accounting for the old asset is complete since the difference between its book value and salvage value has been reported as a gain or loss at the time of disposal.

In *Opinion No. 29,* the Accounting Principles Board differentiated between *monetary exchanges* involving cash and receivables or payables and *nonmonetary exchanges* involving, for example, inventories, investments in common stocks, and plant assets. An *exchange* is defined as a *reciprocal transfer* between entities that results in one entity receiving assets or services or satisfying obligations by surrendering other assets or services or incurring other obligations. A *nonreciprocal transfer* is defined as a transfer of assets or services in one direction, either (1) from a business enterprise to its owners or another entity or (2) from owners or another entity to the business enterprise.[10] The "basic principle" as presented by the Board follows:

> The Board concludes that in general accounting for nonmonetary transactions should be based on the fair values of the assets (or services) involved which is the same basis as that used in monetary transactions. Thus, the cost of a nonmonetary asset acquired in exchange for another nonmonetary asset is the fair value of the asset surrendered to obtain it, and a gain or loss should be recognized on the exchange. The fair value of the asset received should be used to measure the cost if it is more clearly evident than the fair value of the asset surrendered. Similarly, a nonmonetary asset received in a nonreciprocal transfer should be recorded at the fair value of the asset received. A transfer of a nonmonetary asset to a stockholder or to another entity in a nonreciprocal transfer should be recorded at the fair value of the asset transferred, and a gain or loss should be recognized on the disposition of the asset. The fair value of an entity's own stock reacquired may be a more clearly evident measure of the fair value of the asset distributed in a nonreciprocal transfer if the transaction involves distribution of a nonmonetary asset to eliminate a disproportionate part of owners' interests (that is, to acquire stock for the treasury or for retirement).[11]

The Board modified the basic principle for exchanges which do not essentially complete the earning process. For example, an exchange of a productive asset not held for sale in the ordinary course of business for a similar productive asset would not warrant the recognition of a gain or loss. In other words, the productive asset acquired would be recorded at the book value of the productive asset relinquished.

[10]*APB Opinion No. 29,* "Accounting for Nonmonetary Transactions," AICPA (New York: 1973), p. 541.
[11]*Ibid.,* pp. 547–548.

Involuntary conversions

The services of assets are occasionally lost through condemnation, fire, or other involuntary means. In recording such events, the amount of any loss or gain should be reported, and all amounts relating to such assets should be removed from the accounts. For example, assume that certain land and buildings owned by a business are condemned by the state as the site for an interchange in an arterial highway system, and an agreed price of $140,000 is set as the condemnation award by the state. Accumulated depreciation on the building is $120,000, and its original cost was $160,000. The cost of the land was $40,000. The entry to record this involuntary conversion would be:

Cash	140,000	
Accumulated Depreciation: Building	120,000	
Building		160,000
Land		40,000
Gain on Condemnation of Property		60,000
To record disposal of property condemned by state.		

The income tax rule on involuntary conversion is similar to that for trade-ins. In most cases no gain need be recognized for tax purposes at the time of disposal if the owner of the property uses the funds received to replace the involuntarily converted asset.

When depreciable assets or merchandise are destroyed by fire or other catastrophies, accountants often assist in measuring and recording the losses sustained. Inventories on hand at the time of fire, for example, may have to be estimated through the use of the gross profit method described in Chapter 10.

Insurance on Plant Assets Most companies insure assets for possible losses resulting from fire, theft, explosion, and other insurable events. A *deductible clause* usually limits recovery to losses in excess of a certain amount, such as $100.

Insurance policies provide for recovery of loss based on the fair market value of the asset destroyed. The book value of an asset, while irrelevant in determining the amount of recovery from insurance companies, is used to measure the loss (or gain) as a result of the casualty. For example, if $10,000 is collected from an insurance company upon complete destruction of an asset having a book value of $7,500, a gain of $2,500 would result.

The amount of insurance carried on an asset should never exceed the fair market value of the asset because the amount recovered cannot be greater than the asset is worth. When inadequate insurance is carried on an asset, the insured in effect becomes a "coinsurer" with the insurance company. For example, if an asset worth $5,000 is insured for only $4,000 and is totally destroyed, the insurance company would bear $4,000 of the loss and the owner would absorb the remaining $1,000 of the loss.

Coinsurance Clause in an Insurance Policy   If it were possible to obtain insurance coverage for only a fraction of value of an asset, the owner could benefit by receiving full reimbursement of most losses with a minimum insurance coverage and cost. In practice, however, insurance companies usually employ a **coinsurance clause** to prevent this approach to low-cost insurance protection. A coinsurance clause requires that an asset be insured for a certain minimum amount, usually 80% of fair market value if a loss is to be fully absorbed by the insurance company. If the insurance purchased is below the stipulated percentage, the owner absorbs a portion of the loss even though the loss does not exceed the face amount of the insurance policy.

To illustrate the application of a coinsurance clause in a fire insurance policy, assume the following:

Insurance carried (face amount of policy)	$ 60,000
Coinsurance required by policy	80% of fair market value
Book value of machinery damaged (cost, $140,000)	$ 55,000
Fair value of asset on date of fire	$100,000
Amount of fire loss (based on fair value)	$ 40,000

The recovery of loss from the insurance company is determined by using the **coinsurance formula** as follows:

$$\frac{\$60{,}000 \text{ (amount of insurance)}}{\$80{,}000 \text{ (coinsurance requirement)}} \times \$40{,}000 \text{ (loss)} = \underline{\underline{\$30{,}000}}$$

Several observations may be made at this point. The amount of insurance carried need not be limited to the book value of the asset (which, like cost, is irrelevant for purposes of measuring either the amount of insurance that can be carried or the amount of recoverable loss). Recovery on the loss is dependent on the market value of the asset, on the amount of insurance carried, and on the provisions of the coinsurance clause. If insurance equal to or in excess of the amount required by the coinsurance clause is carried, any loss up to the face of the policies is fully recoverable; if less than the required amount is carried, the loss will be partly absorbed by the **insured.** If the amount of insurance exceeds the coinsurance requirement, there is no need to apply the coinsurance formula. Studying the coinsurance formula indicates that the recoverable portion of the loss is always the lower of (1) the amount of the loss adjusted by the coinsurance formula, or (2) the face amount of the policy.

If an asset were insured under two or more policies, none of which contained a coinsurance clause, any loss would be shared by the several insurance companies in proportion to the amount of insurance written by each company; the same procedure would apply if the policies had the same coinsurance requirement. If two or more policies cover the same asset and the policies stipulate a *different* coinsurance requirement, the coinsurance formula should be applied to each policy. However, the loss absorbed by any insurance company cannot exceed its proportion of the total insurance carried on the asset. For example, assume that a building with a fair value of $40,000 is insured under two policies as follows:

> Policy A: $15,000 with an 80% coinsurance clause
> Policy B: $15,000 with a 70% coinsurance clause

Assuming that a fire causes damage of $24,000 to the building, how much of the loss would be recovered under each policy? If neither policy has a coinsurance clause, each would absorb 50% of the loss ($12,000) because each represents 50% of the total insurance ($30,000). If both policies had a 70% coinsurance requirement, each would again absorb $12,000 of the loss because the total insurance carried ($30,000) exceeds the minimum insurance required by the coinsurance clause ($40,000 $\times$ 70% = $28,000). Because policy A has an 80% coinsurance clause, however, the recovery under each policy is determined as follows:

Policy A:

$$\frac{\$15,000 \text{ (insurance under policy A)}}{\$32,000 \text{ (coinsurance requirement for policy A)}} \times \$24,000 \text{ (loss)} = \underline{\underline{\$11,250}}$$

Policy B:

$$\frac{\$15,000 \text{ (insurance under policy B)}}{\$30,000 \text{ (total insurance on building)}} \times \$24,000 \text{ (loss)} = \underline{\underline{\$12,000}}$$

The recovery under policy A is $\frac{15}{32}$ of the loss, which is less than the pro rata coverage of $\frac{15}{30}$, because the coinsurance requirement under this policy was not met. On the other hand, the recovery under policy B is $\frac{15}{30}$ of the loss because the total insurance on the building ($30,000) exceeds the minimum required under policy B ($28,000) and hence the coinsurance formula is not applicable.

Insurance contracts are complex; the discussion here is brief and oversimplified. Although an accountant need not be an expert in insurance contracts, he should have a basic understanding of various forms of insurance in order to be able to properly account for insurance premiums and proceeds and also to help management formulate a sound insurance program.

REVIEW QUESTIONS

1 Define the following terms: **tangible asset, wasting asset, intangible asset.** Give an example of each.

2 What are the arguments in favor of using original cost as the basis for asset accounting? Can this logically be referred to as an asset valuation procedure?

3 How should the cost of a plant asset be determined for accounting purposes? What three issues are involved in accounting for asset cost?

4 What is meant by the terms **capital expenditure** and **revenue expenditure?** How are they related to the accounting concepts of realization and matching of costs and revenue?

5 Which of the following are capital expenditures? Indicate the proper treatment of items which are not capital expenditures.
a Cost of grading land prior to construction
b Cost of installing equipment, including cost of spoiled material during test runs
c Tax assessment for street paving
d Delinquent property taxes on land just acquired
e Cost of maintaining equipment in good running condition
f Cost of moving and reinstalling equipment to another part of factory
g Cost of repairs to used equipment; need for repair discovered immediately after acquisition
h Cost of tearing down an old building in preparation for new construction (old building used for 24 years and fully depreciated)
i Cost of insurance policy covering claims for damages that may arise during construction of a new building
j Excess of operating expenses over revenue during first year of operations
k Cost of digging to build foundation for new building

6 W Company has constructed a special-purpose machine for its own use. Direct labor and material costs were $10,000. Variable overhead is 10% of direct costs, and fixed overhead allocable to the constructed machine is $2,400. Company engineers estimate that an equivalent machine would cost $15,000 if purchased outside the company. At what figure should the equipment be recorded? Why? Is there a profit on the self-construction? Assuming that the machine could have been acquired for $8,000, how should the machine be recorded?

7 Public utility companies often capitalize interest on funds necessary to finance construction prior to the time that the constructed asset is put into service. Explain the rationale for this procedure and its effect on periodic income measurement.

8 Capitalizing interest during construction is an accepted accounting procedure; adding interest on an installment contract to the cost of the asset acquired is not. Explain the distinction between these two situations.

9 Discuss the accounting problem that arises in dealing with each of the following situations, and explain the proper procedure:
a A group of assets is acquired for a lump-sum price.
b Assets are acquired in exchange for stock or bonds issued by the buyer.
c Assets are acquired in exchange for another asset having limited service life.
d Assets are acquired by gift.

10 What is the *investment tax credit* and how, in your opinion, should it be treated for accounting purposes?

11 Briefly describe the accounting procedures appropriate for the following:
a Additions
b Improvements, renewals, and replacements
c Ordinary repairs and maintenance
d Extraordinary repairs as a result of fire damage

12 The accountant for X Company follows a policy of estimating annual repair costs on equipment and making an entry each year debiting Repair Expense and crediting Allowance for Repairs, which sometimes shows a credit balance and sometimes a debit balance. What is the appropriate classification of this account for statement purposes? Why?

13 Y Company charges the cost of major repairs against Accumulated Depreciation. Evaluate this procedure.

14 How should gains and losses on retirement of assets be reported? Should gains and losses on involuntary conversions be reported even though they have been "forced" on the company?

15 What is meant by *coinsurance?* Describe the coinsurance formula. Can a gain result from the destruction of insured property? Explain.

EXERCISES

Ex. 11-1 A firm replaced an old machine with a new one having a list price of $10,000, subject to a 2% cash discount if paid promptly. Net cost of removing the old machine to make way for the new one amounted to $800. Installation of the new machine cost $400. Costs of testing the new machine were $150 for operator's time and $100 in wasted materials. The discount was lost through late payment of the invoice. What is the cost of the new machine for accounting purposes?

Ex. 11-2 The costs incurred in acquiring land and constructing a building are as follows:

Land (*including miscellaneous acquisition costs*)	$100,000
Construction insurance	1,500
Building contract (*excluding excavation*)	120,000
Architectural fees	2,000
Street and sidewalk (*maintained by the city*)	4,000
Costs of excavation for foundation	3,100
Property taxes on land (*prior to construction*)	1,600
Advertising costs to attract tenants.	1,250
Interest during construction on loan to pay contractor.	2,100

Determine the cost of (*a*) land and (*b*) building for accounting purposes.

Ex. 11-3 Polaski Homes, Inc., acquires land having a fair market value of $600,000 in exchange for $200,000 par value 7% bonds payable and 25,000 shares of its $10 par value common stock. The stock is selling at $17 on the New York Stock Exchange.

Give the entry to record the acquisition of land. (You should record a premium or a discount on bonds payable.)

Ex. 11-4 In 1975, Peter Brown sold a piece of land which cost him $10,000 for $55,000. The contract called for a down payment of $15,000 and a non-interest-bearing note for $40,000 due in four years.

Record the sale of land on Brown's books, assuming that the present value of the note (discounted at compound interest at 6% for four years) was $31,684 and that 6% was a fair rate of interest on this type of note. Record the note receivable at face value and disregard the tax on the gain.

Ex. 11-5 Hans Shield purchased three machines at an auction for a lump-sum price of $14,500 and paid $500 to have the machines delivered to his place of business. His estimate of the resale value of the three machines is shown below:

Machine X	$ 9,000
Machine Y	6,000
Machine Z	5,000
Total	$20,000

Determine the cost that should have been assigned to each machine using the relative value of the machines as a basis of allocating the lump-sum price.

Ex. 11-6 Mr. Seller sold some property to Mr. Buyer. The property had cost Mr. Seller $37,770, including $10,000 allocated to land. Depreciation of $3,500 was recorded on the building by Mr. Seller. At the close of escrow, the following statements were submitted:

	To Mr. Seller		To Mr. Buyer	
	Charges	**Credits**	**Charges**	**Credits**
Sale price		$39,500	$39,500	
Deposit placed in escrow				$ 9,600
Pro rata taxes	$ 120			120
Pro rata interest	70			70
Pro rata insurance		200	200	
Mortgage assumed by buyer	30,160			30,160
Commission	2,370			
Title search fee	150		150	
Escrow fee	110			
Cash to seller	6,720			
Cash to buyer			100	
Totals	$39,700	$39,700	$39,950	$39,950

Instructions

a Prepare a journal entry to record the sale on Mr. Seller's books.

b Prepare a journal entry to record the purchase on Mr. Buyer's books. The value assigned to land is $12,500. Mr. Buyer had recorded the cash placed in escrow, $9,600, in an Escrow Deposit account.

Ex. 11-7 One of the trucks of the Atlantic Trucking Company had just come in for its periodic inspection when it was noticed that the diesel engine, which normally lasts four years, was unexpectedly in need of an overhaul and that the trailer needed replacement. The engine cost $2,000 new and was two and a half years old. However, with a $500 overhaul, it was expected to last two more years. The old trailer cost $5,000 and had a book value of $750. The price of new trailers had increased by $1,000 since the old one was purchased. Atlantic Trucking Company accounts for each truck component separately and records depreciation on a straight-line basis.

Prepare journal entries to record the overhaul of the engine and the replacement of the trailer.

Ex. 11-8 Thomas Kowal, sole proprietor, has been taking care of the books for his business. At the end of 1975, after the accounts were adjusted but before they were closed for the year, you are engaged to review the records. Among the items which require correction are the following:

a Installation costs for fixtures, $1,200, were charged to Maintenance Expense. The fixtures have a five-year life and were installed at the beginning of 1975. Assume straight-line depreciation.

b A machine acquired on January 6, 1973, at a cost of $5,000 has been depreciated on a straight-line basis over a five-year period. This machine was sold on June 20, 1975. Kowal debited Cash and credited Machinery for $2,100, the proceeds on the sale. No depreciation was recorded on this machine in 1975, but you conclude that one-half year's depreciation should be recognized.

Prepare a correcting entry for each of the two items described above.

Ex. 11-9 Simini Corporation acquired a new machine by trading in an old machine and paying $24,000 in cash. The old machine originally cost $40,000 and had accumulated depreciation at the date of exchange of $30,000. The new machine could have been purchased for $50,000 cash.

Instructions

a Record the acquisition of the new machine assuming that (1) a gain on the trade-in is recognized and (2) no gain is recognized.

b Using the theoretically preferable method, give the entry to record the above transaction if the new machine had a list price of $52,000, was commonly selling for $50,000 cash, and Simini Corporation was allowed a trade-in allowance of $28,000 for its old machine.

Ex. 11-10 A building has a book value of $11,000 and a fair market value of $20,000. Determine the amount recoverable from the insurance company in each case below, assuming that the insurance policy in each case contains an 80% coinsurance clause:

Case	Insurance coverage	Loss	Formula
A	$10,000	$12,000	$10,000/$16,000 × $12,000
B	12,000	12,000	$12,000/$16,000 × $12,000
C	14,000	12,000	$14,000/$16,000 × $12,000
D	16,000	12,000	$16,000/$16,000 × $12,000
E	18,000	12,000	$18,000/$16,000 × $12,000

SHORT CASES FOR ANALYSIS AND DECISION

Case 11-1 The Willingham Company has just constructed a new building at a cost of $2 million. After reviewing the contracts and cost data, the controller suggests that the company use the following classifications in future accounting for this building: (1) foundation, framing, and sheathing, (2) outside finish, (3) interior finish, (4) roof, (5) electric wiring and fixtures, (6) partitions, (7) acoustical ceiling, (8) furnace and boiler, and (9) plumbing system.

Instructions Discuss the advantages and the disadvantages of following such a system of accounting for this asset, particularly its effect on accounting for maintenance, depreciation, and retirement.

Case 11-2 Your client found three suitable sites, each having certain unique advantages, for a new plant facility. In order to investigate thoroughly the advantages and disadvantages of each site, one-year options were purchased for an amount equal to 5% of the contract price of each site. The costs of the options cannot be applied against the contracts. Before the options expired, one of the sites was purchased at the contract price of $60,000. The option on this site had cost $3,000. The two options not exercised had cost $3,500 each.

Instructions Present arguments in support of recording the cost of the land at each of the following amounts: (1) $60,000; (2) $63,000; (3) $70,000.

Case 11-3 Arctic Airlines, Inc., is converting from piston-type planes to jets. Delivery time for the jets is three years, during which period substantial progress payments must be made. The multimillion-dollar cost of the planes cannot be financed from working capital: Arctic Airlines, Inc., must borrow funds for the payments.

Because of high interest rates and the large sum to be borrowed, management estimates that interest costs in the second year of the conversion period will be equal to one-third of income before interest and taxes, and one-half or such income in the third year.

After conversion, the passenger-carrying capacity of Arctic Airlines, Inc., will be doubled with no increase in the number of planes, although the investment in planes will be substantially increased. The jet planes have an estimated service life of eight years.

Instructions Make a recommendation concerning the advisability of capitalizing the interest during the conversion period. Support your recommendation with reasons and suggested accounting procedures. (Disregard income tax implications.)

Case 11-4 The Tile Manufacturing Co. has two manufacturing departments, A and B. During the current year Department A secured a bid of $75,000 from an outside company for a piece of equipment needed in the department. The manager of Department B, however, convinced management that he could build the equipment in his department more economically, and the decision was made to allow him to undertake the project. The machine was finished near the end of the year, at a cost of $16,000 for material, $24,000 for direct labor, $10,000 for variable overhead, and $12,000 for fixed overhead allocated on direct labor cost.

The controller entered the equipment on the books at a cost of $50,000 (excluding fixed overhead). The manager of Department B wants to have the equipment recorded at $75,000, stating, "If my men had not been working on this equipment they could have been engaged in profitable production. If you record this at $50,000 my department is going to look bad in the reports at the end of the year. When will I ever get credit for the $25,000 ($75,000 − $50,000) I have earned for the company by manufacturing this equipment?"

Instructions
a What are the basic issues involved in this controversy?
b If the department manager's position were accepted, would the net income

of the company during the current and subsequent periods be changed? Explain.

c Evaluate the two positions and state which you favor and why.

PROBLEMS

Group A

11A-1 Vera Cruz Manufacturing Company purchased land as a factory site for $60,000. Two old buildings were standing on the site. The process of tearing down the old buildings and construction of the factory required six months. Costs incurred in tearing down the old buildings and constructing the factory are listed below:

Tearing down old buildings (*The salvaged lumber and bricks were later sold*	
for $600)	$ 2,950
Legal fees for title investigation and drawing the purchase contract	480
Land survey required before blueprints could be drawn	400
Blueprints for new factory	20,000
Title insurance on land	500
Liability insurance during construction	300
Contract for new construction	800,000

The company paid the contractor in two installments: $400,000 at the end of three months and $400,000 when the contract was completed. The first payment was borrowed from the bank on a three-month, 7% loan. The second payment and the repayment of the bank loan were made at the end of six months, in part from the $600,000 proceeds of a mortgage on the new building. Assume that interest paid during the construction period is capitalized.

Instructions
a Determine the cost of the land and the building as they should be recorded by Vera Cruz Manufacturing Company.
b Discuss the reasoning involved in arriving at your results in (*a*).

11A-2 Celestial Corporation recently purchased new equipment and retired old equipment which cost $15,000 and had a book value of $2,000 at the time of retirement. The company had received two bids on the new equipment, as follows:

(1) M Company offered its machine at $19,000 and agreed to allow $3,000 on the old equipment as a trade-in.
(2) N Company offered an equivalent machine for $20,000, terms 2/10, n/30, but would not accept a trade-in.

Celestial Corporation accepted N's offer and sold its old equipment for $600, after incurring $200 in labor costs to remove it from the building. Additional costs incurred in placing the new equipment in use were:

Freight (*paid in cash*)	$750
Installation:	
Materials.	50
Labor.	240

Travel expenses paid to N Company's engineer who supervised the installation
(There was no charge for the engineer's time.) $210
Costs incurred in testing equipment:
  Operator's wages 60
  Spoiled materials 100

As a result of an error in the treasurer's department, the N Company invoice was not paid until 25 days after invoice date, and therefore the cash discount could not be taken.

In the process of removing the old equipment, a section of the factory floor was damaged, which had to be repaired at a cost of $205 paid to an independent contractor.

Instructions Prepare journal entries, together with supporting computations, to record the retirement of the old equipment and the purchase of the new. Credit Materials Inventory for the cost of materials used and Accrued Payroll for labor costs incurred.

11A-3 Regional Sales Company was incorporated in January of the current year but was unable to begin manufacturing activities until July 1 because plant facilities were not finished until that date.

On December 31, the company's record of the construction and accounting for the plant appears in a New Facility account as follows:

New Facility

Jan. 31	Land and building		$220,000
Feb. 28	Cost of removing old sawmill		7,400
May 1	Partial payment on new construction		100,000
May 1	Legal fees		4,000
June 1	Second payment on new construction		100,000
June 1	Insurance premium paid (effective date of policy is May 1)		3,600
June 1	Special tax assessments		5,000
June 30	General expenses		24,000
July 1	Final payment on new construction		100,000
Dec. 31	Asset write-up		40,000
	Total debits to account		$604,000
Dec. 31	Less: depreciation at 4% for six months		12,080
	Account balance at Dec. 31		$591,920

Additional information

(1) On January 31 the company paid $20,000 in cash and gave 2,000 shares of 6% cumulative preferred stock, par value $100 per share, for land and building. On January 25 a large block of these shares had been sold for $104 per share.

(2) A sawmill and drying kiln were on the land when acquired. The demolition company charged $7,400 for removal and retained all usable materials.

(3) Legal fees covered the organization of the company $1,500; purchase of land, $2,000; construction contract, $500.

(4) Insurance on the new building was taken out on May 1. The three-year premium was paid on June 1, upon receipt of the invoice.
(5) General expenses are for the period from January 2 to June 30 and include president's salary, $12,000; salary of plant superintendent who supervised construction of new building, $10,000; and office salaries, $2,000.
(6) The special tax assessments covered street improvements.
(7) During the six months' construction period, a new union contract for construction workers was negotiated calling for an increase of 15% in wages, and there were increases in construction material prices. On the basis of these facts, the plant superintendent suggested that the building be written up by $40,000 to recognize the increase in the current fair value of the building. The credit was made to Retained Earnings.
(8) The new building is to be depreciated at the rate of 4% per year; depreciation for six months was charged to the Depreciation Expense account.

Instructions
a Prepare a work sheet classifying the transactions of the Regional Sales Company in proper accounts. Allow separate columns for Land and for Building; other accounts should be analyzed in a Miscellaneous column.
b Prepare a single entry which would restate the records on an acceptable accounting basis. The books are still open for the current year.

11A-4 On July 10, 1975, Ivan Pavlov, your client, sold a building to Gregor Gogol. The escrow statements for the seller and the buyer are presented side by side below:

	Ivan Pavlov, Seller		Gregor Gogol, Buyer	
	Charges	*Credits*	*Charges*	*Credits*
Sale price		$300,000	$300,000	
First mortgage assumed by buyer	$110,000			$110,000
Purchase-money mortgage—6% . .	80,000			80,000
Prorations:				
Property taxes from July 1	250			250
Insurance adjustment		200	200	
Interest accrued	350			350
Fees:				
Escrow	100		100	
Title insurance			790	
Recording and legal	40		60	
Revenue stamps (taxes)			550	
Funds deposited in escrow				
account on July 10, 1975				111,100
Items paid from escrow account—				
commission	18,000			
Remit to Ivan Pavlov	91,460			
Totals	$300,200	$300,200	$301,700	$301,700

Pavlov's accounting records are maintained on the accrual basis. When you undertake the September 30, 1975, quarterly audit for your client, the following information is available to you:

(1) A "Suspense" account was opened for cash received in connection with the sale, including monthly receipts on the purchase-money mortgage. The "Suspense" account shows a credit balance of $94,255.

(2) The building and land were purchased on July 1, 1971, for $270,000. The building was depreciated over a 40-year life by the straight-line method. Accumulated depreciation at December 31, 1974, was $17,500. A half-year's depreciation has been consistently recorded for assets purchased or sold during the year. No depreciation has been recorded by Pavlov for 1975.

(3) The purchase-money mortgage payments are $1,000 per month, plus accrued interest on unpaid balance. The first payment was received on August 10 and amounted to $1,400; the second payment was received on September 9 and amounted to $1,395. Both amounts were credited to the "Suspense" account.

Instructions

a Determine the net proceeds to the seller on the land and on the building. The sales price and expenses of sale are allocated by the seller as follows: land, 30%; building, 70%.

b Prepare the adjusting journal entries to record the sale and related transactions on Pavlov's books. Prepare a supporting schedule showing the gain or loss on disposal of land and the gain or loss on disposal of building. Ignore income taxes.

c Prepare the entry to record the purchase of land and building on Gogol's books. The purchase price, including all fees, is allocated 30% to land and 70% to building.

11A-5 The Manrique Corporation manufactures patio furniture. On August 31, 1975, the company had a fire which completely destroyed its building, the goods in process inventory, and machinery. Additional data follow:

(1) The cost of plant assets destroyed and the related accumulated depreciation accounts at August 31, 1975, were:

	Cost	Accumulated depreciation
Building	$40,000	$17,500
Machinery	15,000	4,500

At present prices the cost to replace the destroyed property would be: building, $80,000; machinery, $37,500. At the time of the fire it was estimated that the building was 50% depreciated, and the destroyed machinery was one-third depreciated. Insurance companies agreed that the insurable value of the building and machinery was $65,000 on the date of fire.

(2) After the fire a physical inventory was taken. The raw materials were valued at $26,000 and the finished goods at $52,000.

(3) The inventories on December 31, 1974, were: raw materials, $20,000; goods in process, $48,000; and finished goods, $60,000.

(4) The sales of the first eight months of 1975 were $150,000 and raw material purchases were $55,000. Direct labor for the eight months was $40,000; for the past five years factory overhead has been applied at the rate of 80% of direct labor cost. The gross profit for the last five years has averaged 30% of sales price.

(5) Insurance is carried with two companies, each with an 80% coinsurance clause. The amount of insurance carried with each company is as follows:

	Building and machinery	Inventories
Acme Insurance Company	$42,000	$65,000
Zenith Indemnity Company	20,000	35,000

Instructions

a Compute the estimated cost of the goods in process lost in the fire.

b Compute the expected recovery from each insurance company, assuming that the estimated cost of inventory lost is accepted as a measure of economic value on the date of the fire.

c Assuming that the Manrique Corporation is indemnified as determined in part **(b)**, what is the loss or gain from fire that should be reported on its income statement prepared at the end of 1975? Ignore the tax effect on the loss or gain.

Group B

11B-1 Barna Corporation has negotiated the purchase of a new piece of automatic equipment. The manufacturer's price of the equipment, F.O.B. the factory, was $26,800. Barna Company paid $7,000 cash, gave an installment note calling for payments of $1,400 per month for 10 months plus interest at 8% on the unpaid balance, and traded in used equipment. The used equipment had originally cost $18,000; it had a book value of $5,100 and a secondhand market value of $3,500, as indicated by recent transactions involving similar equipment.

Instructions

Prepare an entry to record this transaction on the books of Barna Corporation under each of the following assumptions:

(1) New equipment is recorded at fair value of consideration paid by Barna Corporation.

(2) Income tax rule (no recognition of gain or loss on trade-in) is used to record the new equipment.

(3) New equipment is recorded at a value equal to cash paid, note issued, and trade-in allowance on used equipment.

Following each entry, write a brief explanation of the reasoning behind that method and indicate the circumstances in which it might be appropriate.

11B-2 In auditing the records of the Harold Larson Company for the fiscal year ended December 31, 1975, you discover the following:

(1) Machine W listed at $9,000 was acquired on April 1, 1975, in exchange for $10,000 par value bonds payable maturing on April 1, 1985. The accountant recorded the acquisition by a debit to Machinery and a credit to Bonds Payable for $10,000. Straight-line depreciation was recorded, based on a five-year life and amounted to $1,200 for nine months. In computing depreciation, salvage value of $2,000 was used.

(2) Machine X listed at $6,400 was purchased on January 2, 1975. The company paid $1,000 down and $500 per month for 12 months. The last payment was made on December 30, 1975. Straight-line depreciation, based on a five-year life and no salvage value, was recorded at $1,400 for the year. Freight of $300 on Machine X was charged to Transportation-in.

(3) Machine Y was recorded at $5,000, which included the book value of $1,000 of a machine accepted as a trade-in. The list price of Machine Y was $4,350 and the trade-in allowance was $250. This transaction took place on December 22, 1975. A loss should be recorded on the trade-in.

(4) Machine Z was acquired on January 10, 1975, in exchange for a past-due account receivable of $14,000 on which an allowance of 20% was established at the end of 1974. The fair value of the machine on January 10 was estimated at $11,000. The machine was recorded by a debit to Machinery and a credit to Accounts Receivable for $14,000. No depreciation was recorded on Machine Z because it was not used in operations. In March it was exchanged for 100 shares of the company's own stock having a market value of $100 per share. The Treasury Stock account was debited for $14,000, the book value of Machine Z.

Instructions Record any correcting entries required as of December 31, 1975, for each transaction (1) through (4) above. Assume that revenue and expense accounts have not been closed for 1975.

11B-3 Ormsby Corporation received a $400,000 low bid from a reputable manufacturer for the construction of special production equipment needed in an expansion program. Because its factory was not operating at capacity, Ormsby Corporation decided to construct the equipment there and recorded the following production costs related to the construction:

Services of consulting engineer	$ 10,000
Work subcontracted	20,000
Materials	200,000
Plant labor normally assigned to production	65,000
Plant labor normally assigned to maintenance	100,000*
Total	$395,000

* Included in factory overhead cost.

Management prefers to record the cost of the equipment under the incremental cost method. Approximately 40% of the corporation's production is devoted to government supply contracts which are all based in some way on cost. The contracts require that any self-constructed equipment be allocated its full share of all costs related to the construction.

The following information is also available:

(1) The above production labor was for partial fabrication of the equipment in the plant. Skilled personnel were required and were assigned from other projects. The maintenance labor would have been idle time of nonproduction plant employees who would have been retained on the payroll whether or not their services were utilized.

(2) Payroll taxes and employee fringe benefits are approximately 30% of labor cost and are included in factory overhead cost. Total factory overhead cost for the year was $5,630,000.

(3) Factory overhead cost is approximately 50% variable and is applied on the basis of production labor cost. Production labor cost for the year for the corporation's normal products totaled $6,810,000.

(4) General and administrative expenses include $22,500 of executive salary cost and $10,500 of postage, telephone, supplies, and miscellaneous costs identifiable with this equipment construction.

Instructions

a Prepare a schedule computing the amount which should be reported as the full cost of the constructed equipment to meet the requirements of the government contracts. Any supporting computations should be in good form.

b Prepare a schedule computing the incremental cost of the constructed equipment.

c What is the largest amount that should be capitalized as the cost of the equipment? Why?

11B-4 Ludwik Kulas keeps his accounting records on a cash basis. On February 28, 1975, he sold property, which he had purchased 17 years earlier for $80,000, to James Blakey for $150,000. The cost allocated to the building was $50,000 and the accumulated depreciation to the date of the sale was $32,500.

The escrow statements as of February 28 for the buyer and the seller are shown below:

Seller's Escrow Statement (Betts Escrow Co., Escrow No. 719)

Sale price		$150,000
Title fee (one-half)	$ 430	
Drawing deed and recording.	5	
Taxes for period Jan. 1 to Feb. 28, 1975, accrued and unpaid. .	200	
Interest accrued on mortgage.	185	
Lease deposits	850	
Pro rata rent.	340	
Mortgage, assumed by buyer	73,460	
Fire insurance, pro rata.		1,430
Revenue stamps (tax on real estate transfers)	150	
Commission	7,500	
Cash to seller, Ludwik Kulas.	68,310	
Total	$151,430	$151,430

Buyer's Escrow Statement (Betts Escrow Co., Escrow No. 719)

Deposit of cash by buyer on Jan. 30 and recorded in Escrow Deposit account.		$ 76,900
Sale price	$150,000	
Title fee (one-half)	430	
Recording deed.	10	
Fire insurance, pro rata.	1,430	
Mortgage, assumed by buyer		73,460
Taxes for period Jan. 1 to Feb. 28, 1975, accrued and unpaid . .		200
Lease deposits		850
Pro rata rent.		340
Interest accrued on mortgage		185
Balance paid to buyer, James Blakey	65	
Total	$151,935	$151,935

Instructions

a Prepare a schedule showing how Kulas should determine his gain or loss on this transaction. Ignore income taxes.

b Prepare a journal entry to record the above transaction on Kulas' books.

c Prepare a journal entry to record the above transaction on Blakey's books, assuming that $50,000 of total cost is allocated to land.

11B-5 On the evening of September 20, 1975, a fire damaged the office and warehouse of the Kimball Corporation, whose fiscal year ends on December 31. The only accounting record saved was the general ledger, from which the following information was obtained as of August 31, 1975.

	Debit	Credit
Accounts receivable	$25,000	
Inventory, Dec. 31, 1974	60,920	
Accounts payable		$ 60,000
Sales		100,000
Merchandise purchases.	80,000	

The following additional data are available:
(1) The September bank statement and canceled checks revealed that checks written during the period September 1 to 20 totaled $15,000: $8,000 paid to accounts payable as of August 31, $2,000 for September merchandise purchases, and $5,000 paid for other expenses. Deposits during the same period amounted to $11,500, which consisted of receipts on account from customers, with the exception of a $1,300 refund from a vendor for merchandise returned in September.
(2) Correspondence with suppliers revealed unrecorded obligations of $7,200 on September 20 for purchases during September.
(3) Customers acknowledged indebtedness of $29,500 as of the close of business on September 20, 1975.
(4) The following insurance was in effect on inventory at the date of the fire:

Insurance company	Amount of coverage	Coinsurance requirement
Allied Mutual	$30,000	80%
Blue Regional	20,000	70%
Claim Free	10,000	None

(5) The insurance companies agreed that the fire loss claim should be based on the assumption that the overall gross profit ratio of 40% for the past two years was in effect during the current year and that the cost so determined is a reasonable estimate of the current value of the inventory.
(6) Inventory with a cost of $44,000 was recovered and is in good condition. The balance of the inventory was a total loss. The office and the warehouse building were not insured. It cost the company $2,100 to repair the damage to the office but the warehouse was a total loss. The warehouse (excluding land) cost $30,000 to construct, was fully depreciated, and had a fair value of $8,000 at the time of the fire.

Instructions
a Prepare a schedule computing the approximate cost of inventory lost in the fire.
b Prepare a schedule computing the pro rata claims to be filed with each insurance company.
c Assuming that the Kimball Corporation is indemnified as determined in part (*b*), what is the loss or gain from fire that should be reported on its income statement for 1975? Ignore income tax effect on the loss or gain.

CHAPTER 12

Plant and equipment: depreciation and depletion

In the previous chapter, we described plant assets as a "bundle of services" and considered the problem of determining the acquisition cost of the future services embodied in such assets. This chapter is concerned with the problem of measuring the cost of asset services as they are "withdrawn from the bundle" and consumed in business operations.

Depreciation is the portion of the cost of plant assets that is deducted from revenue for asset services used in the operations of a business. In practice the term *depreciation* is used to describe the cost of the expired services of tangible plant assets such as buildings and equipment. Recording the expired service cost of such intangible assets as patents, research and development costs, bond issue costs, etc., is called *amortization. Depletion* for accounting purposes refers to the estimated cost of natural resources such as oil, gas, timber, and iron ore that have been removed from their source.

DEPRECIATION

The concept of depreciation is closely linked to the concept of business income. Since part of the service potential of depreciable assets is exhausted in the revenue-generating process each period, the cost of these services must be deducted from revenue in measuring periodic income; the expired cost must be recovered before a business is considered "as well off" as at the beginning of the period. Depreciation is a measure of this cost.

Depreciation is one of the most controversial and troublesome areas in accounting. In the early history of accounting, it was necessary to convince users of accounting information that depreciation was actually a cost of doing business. Businessmen tended to view depreciation as a matter of "setting aside something" during prosperous periods for the replacement of depreciable assets. When earnings were high, large amounts of depreciation might be recorded; when earnings were low or losses were incurred, depreciation was not recorded. Today it is universally agreed that depreciation is an expense that has been incurred whether or not revenue is sufficient to absorb it. Furthermore, it is generally recognized that depreciation relates to the use of assets, not to their replacement.

Accounting for depreciation is a process of cost allocation, not valuation. Acquiring a plant asset means that asset services have been acquired in advance of their use. Between the time of acquisition and the time of use, the value of these services may change materially, because of supply and demand factors or changes in price levels. Therefore, the accountant's measure of the historical cost of the asset services that are used may be materially different from the current cost of acquiring similar services. This difference is germane to a variety of managerial decisions; however, the question of revaluing depreciable assets (in effect, revaluing the remaining unused services) at some time subsequent to acquisition should not be confused with the cost allocation problem. In this chapter we shall deal only with allocating the cost of plant assets; revaluation of assets for accounting purposes in response to increases in replacement costs and the general price level will be considered in Chapter 25.

Factors in estimating periodic depreciation

The estimate of periodic depreciation is dependent on three separate variables:

1 *Estimating service life.* This involves choosing the unit in which service life is to be measured and then estimating how many units of service are embodied in each asset.

2 *Establishing the depreciation base.* An asset may be sold by a business before its service value is completely consumed. The depreciation base is the cost of asset services that will be used by a given firm, and it is usually less than the original investment in the asset.

3 *Choosing the method of cost apportionment.* The problem here is to determine the relative amount of services that has expired in each accounting period. A corollary issue is to decide whether all units of service have an equal cost, or whether some service units have a higher or lower cost than others.

Estimating service life

The service life of an asset is the total units of service expected to be derived from that asset. Businessmen commonly measure service life in terms of time units, for example, months or years. Service life may also be measured in terms of output or activity and expressed in such physical units as tons, miles, board feet, gallons, or machine-hours. We may, for example, describe the estimated service life of an automobile as *four years* or *75,000 miles.* Forces which tend to limit the service life of an asset should be considered in determining the type of *unit of service* to use for a given asset or group of assets. The causes of decrease in asset service life may be divided into two broad classes: (1) *physical causes* (including casualties) and (2) *functional* or *economic causes.*

Physical deterioration results largely from wear and tear due to operating use, and rust, rot, or decay due to the action of the elements. These physical forces terminate the usefulness of plant items by rendering them incapable of performing the services for which they were intended and thus set the maximum limit on service life. Unusual events such as accidents, floods, earthquakes, etc., also serve to terminate or reduce asset usefulness.

Functional or *economic factors* may render an asset in good physical condition no longer useful because it is not economical to keep it in service. Two primary causes of functional depreciation are *obsolescence* and *inadequacy.* Obsolescence refers to the effect of innovations and technical improvements on the economic service life of existing assets. An inevitable result of industrial research and development activities is to make existing plant and equipment obsolete. The jet airliners, for example, made propeller-driven aircraft uneconomical for major airlines to operate. Obsolescence thus terminated the service life of many piston aircraft and sent them to the used plane market even though they had a physical potential of many more miles of service.

Inadequacy refers to the effect of growth and changes in the scale of a firm's operation in terminating the service life of assets. A warehouse may be in sound condition, but if more space is required which cannot economically be provided by adding a separate building, the old warehouse has become inadequate and its economic service life, from the owner's standpoint, is terminated. In a general sense, any asset whose capacity is such that it cannot be operated with optimum results, or which does not fit the requirements of the business, is inadequate.

In a highly developed industrial society, functional causes of depreciation probably have a greater influence on service lives than physical wear and tear, particularly with respect to special-purpose equipment. Estimates of service life are therefore strongly influenced by these factors.

The problem of choosing an appropriate *unit* of service life also calls for search for the causes of depreciation. The objective is to choose the unit most closely related to the cause of service exhaustion. When service life is limited largely by the effect of operating wear and tear, a unit that reflects physical use is appropriate. For example, hours of service might be chosen as the unit of service life for an electric motor, or miles of service for a truck. On the other hand, the physical causes that predominate in limiting the life of buildings are probably related more closely to the passage of time than actual usage; therefore, an estimated service life in terms of years would be more appropriate.

No estimate of service life can be made with high precision. The most fruitful procedure is to start with an estimate of physical service life as a maximum, modify this by considering the probable effects of obsolescence and inadequacy, and then be prepared to adjust these estimates in the light of actual experience.

Establishing the depreciation base

The depreciation base (or "depreciable cost") of an asset is the portion of its cost that should be charged against revenue during its service life. Since the owner of an asset may sell it before its serviceability is ended, the initial cost of a plant asset, as determined using the guidelines established in Chapter 11, is not necessarily its depreciation base. For example, a car rental company may pay $4,000 for a new car and sell it at the end of two years for $1,500, even though its useful life is much longer. The depreciation base is $2,500, the difference between cost and resale value.

Scrapping or removing buildings, structures, and heavy equipment may involve substantial cost in the year of retirement; theoretically, removal costs should be estimated and included in the depreciation base. Including removal cost in the depreciation base means that the entire cost involved in obtaining the services will be charged to the services it yields, without regard to the timing of the expenditure. In practice, however, removal costs may be either ignored or netted against the estimated salvage value of the asset. The formula for arriving at the depreciation base thus becomes:

Depreciation base = acquisition cost − estimated net salvage value

In some instances, net salvage value (gross salvage minus estimated removal costs) is likely to be so small or uncertain that it may be ignored in establishing the depreciation base.

Depreciation methods

When the service life of an asset has been estimated and its depreciation base established, there remains the problem of determining the portion of cost that will expire with each unit of service life.

There are two major variables to be considered in reaching a systematic and rational solution to this problem:

1 The **quantity** of services "withdrawn from the bundle" may be equal or may vary during each period of service life.

2 The **cost** of various units of service may be equal or may differ per unit during each period of service life.

Because of the relatively high degree of uncertainty that surrounds estimates of service life and service use, the distinction between these two variables may become blurred. We may illustrate by reference to a situation that is generally familiar—the depreciation of an automobile used for business purposes. Assume that the auto in question costs $3,300, has an expected net salvage value of $300, and is estimated to have a service life of 100,000 miles. The average depreciation expense per unit of service (1 mile) is 3 cents [($3,300 − $300) ÷ 100,000]. The miles of service used in each accounting period, however, may vary. If 20,000 miles are driven during the first year and 30,000 miles during the second year, there has been a variation in the **quantity** of service used, and depreciation of $600 for the first year and $900 for the second will recognize this fact.

On the other hand, even if the automobile is driven 20,000 miles in each year for five years, there may be a difference in the **cost** of the miles of service in each of these five periods. The miles of service when the auto is new and operating at top efficiency may be more valuable (and thus presumably more costly) than service miles during later years. Therefore, the assumption that each service mile bears the same depreciation expense may not be reasonable, and we might compute depreciation on the assumption that early miles cost more than later miles. For example, depreciation might be computed at 5 cents per mile for the first 20,000 miles; 4 cents for the next 20,000 miles, etc.

There are a number of systematic depreciation methods that attempt to recognize these factors in varying degrees. They may be classified as follows:

1 Straight-line method (based on expiration of time)
2 Accelerated methods (based on expiration of time)
  a Fixed-percentage-of-declining-balance
  b Sum-of-the-years'-digits
3 Units-of-output method (based on physical service or production)
4 Retirement and replacement methods
5 Compound interest methods

Depreciation under the straight-line and accelerated methods is a function of time rather than use. On the other hand, depreciation under the units-of-output method is a function of actual usage rather than the passage of time.

Depreciation may be computed to the nearest month, although other procedures consistently applied may be acceptable. A description of the most widely used depreciation methods follows.

Straight-line Method The distinguishing characteristic of the straight-line method of depreciation is that each year of service absorbs an equal portion of acquisition cost. Depreciation per year is thus computed as follows:

$$\text{Depreciation per year} = \frac{\text{acquisition cost} - \text{estimated net salvage value}}{\text{years of service life}}$$

To illustrate the straight-line method of depreciation, assume that a machine is acquired at the beginning of Year 1 for $7,000 and that the net salvage value of the machine at the end of four years of service life is estimated at $1,000. The depreciation expense, accumulated depreciation, and book value of the machine over its estimated service life are presented below:

	Depreciation expense for year	Accumulated depreciation	Book value of machine
Beginning of Year 1			$7,000
End of Year 1	$1,500	$1,500	5,500
End of Year 2	1,500	3,000	4,000
End of Year 3	1,500	4,500	2,500
End of Year 4	1,500	6,000	1,000

At the end of each year, depreciation expense on this machine would be recorded as follows:

Depreciation Expense   1,500
    Accumulated Depreciation: Machinery.   1,500
To record depreciation for the year.

Accelerated Methods The assumption that plant assets yield either a greater quantity of service or more valuable services in early years of service life has led accountants to devise methods of depreciation that will result in large amounts of depreciation in early years of service life, and smaller amounts in later years. These are known as *accelerated methods* of depreciation, and there are a number of different approaches.

Fixed-percentage-of-declining-balance method Under this method, a percentage depreciation rate is computed which, when applied to the book value of the asset as of the beginning of each period, will result in writing the asset down to estimated net salvage value at the end of its service life. Since the rate computed is applied on a constantly declining asset value, the amount of depreciation decreases each year. The formula for computing the required rate per year (when n = years of service life) is:

$$\text{Depreciation rate} = 1 - \sqrt[n]{\frac{\text{net salvage value}}{\text{acquisition cost}}}$$

Net salvage value greater than zero must be estimated, since it is impossible to reduce any amount to zero by applying a constant percentage to the successively declining remainder. The depreciation rate for an asset costing $10,000, having a net salvage value of $1,296 and a service life of four years, would be computed as follows:

$$\text{Depreciation rate} = 1 - \sqrt[4]{\frac{\$1,296}{\$10,000}} = 1 - \frac{6}{10} = 40\%$$

If the application of this formula yields a rate of, say, 39.6239%, rounding the rate to 40% would not be objectionable, from either a practical or a theoretical point of view, since measurement of depreciation is only a rough estimate.

The following tabulation shows depreciation expense for the four-year period using a fixed percentage of 40% on declining book value:

| Year | Book value at beginning of year | Depreciation expense | | Accumulated depreciation |
		Amount (40% of book value at beginning of year)	Percentage of total	
1	$10,000	$4,000	46.0	$4,000
2	6,000	2,400	27.6	6,400
3	3,600	1,440	16.5	7,840
4	2,160	864	9.9	8,704
Balance	1,296			
		$8,704	100.0	

It should be noted that the book value at the end of the fourth year is equal to the estimated salvage value, $1,296, and that annual depreciation expense decreases rapidly. (In this example, since the depreciation rate is 40%, the depreciation expense in the second and each of the succeeding years is only 60% of the expense reported a year earlier.)

Federal income tax law provides that for certain assets the fixed percentage may be as high as twice the applicable straight-line rate. For example, the straight-line rate for an asset with an estimated service life of four years is 25% and the fixed-percentage rate would be 50% (25% × 2). This approach is referred to as the **double-declining-balance** (or **200%-declining-balance**) method. For some assets the rate may not exceed 150% of the straight-line rate. Current tax regulations require that salvage value be taken into account only as a limiting factor in applying these rates; that is, the asset cannot be depreciated below estimated net salvage value.

Sum-of-the-years'-digits method   Under this method, a decreasing depreciation expense is computed by a simple mathematical procedure relating to arithmetic progressions. The sum of a series of numbers representing the years of service life becomes the denominator of the depreciation fraction in any year.[1] The numerator of the depreciation fraction for each year is the remaining years of service life taken from the beginning of the year. Since the denominator remains constant and the numerator declines each year, the result is a decreasing depreciation charge. Furthermore, since the total of the numerators of the depreciation fractions is equal to the denominator, the sum of all the fractions is 1 and 100% of the depreciation base will ultimately be charged to expense.

The following tabulation illustrates the application of this method to an asset costing $22,000, having a salvage value of $2,000 and a service life of four years:

Year	Depreciation fraction	Depreciation base ($22,000 − $2,000)	Depreciation expense	Accumulated depreciation	Book value
					$22,000
1	$\frac{4}{10}$	$20,000	$8,000	$ 8,000	14,000
2	$\frac{3}{10}$	20,000	6,000	14,000	8,000
3	$\frac{2}{10}$	20,000	4,000	18,000	4,000
4	$\frac{1}{10}$	20,000	2,000	20,000	2,000
Sum 10					

---

[1] The formula for determining the sum of any arithmetic progression of n consecutive numbers is $n\left(\dfrac{n+1}{2}\right)$. Thus the sum of all numbers from 1 to 15 is $15\left(\dfrac{16}{2}\right)$, or 120. Tables are available which provide the decimal equivalent of the depreciation rate for each year of asset life.

Fractional-period depreciation under accelerated methods   Under accelerated methods, depreciation is determined for each full unit of service life. A question of mechanics arises when assets are acquired during the year and less than a full year's depreciation is to be taken during the first and last years of service life. The logical solution to this problem follows:

1 *Double-declining-balance method.* Compute depreciation expense for a fraction of year in the year of acquisition and apply the appropriate percentage to the beginning book value of the asset to compute depreciation for subsequent fiscal years.

2 *Sum-of-the-years'-digits method.* Compute the depreciation for each full year of service life, and then allocate each full year's depreciation charge between two different fiscal years. To illustrate, assume the following data:

Asset cost, Apr. 1, 1975	$8,000
Estimated service life	5 years
Rate using double-declining-balance method	40%
Estimated net salvage value	$500

The computation of depreciation for the first partial year and the next full year under the two accelerated methods is demonstrated in the following tabulation:

Double-declining balance		**Sum-of-the-years' digits**	
Full year of service life	*Deprecia-tion*	*Full year of service life*	*Deprecia-tion*
Year 1 (40% × $8,000)	$3,200	1 ($\frac{5}{15}$ × $7,500)	$2,500
Year 2 [40% × ($8,000 − $3,200)] . .	1,920	2 ($\frac{4}{15}$ × $7,500)	2,000
Depreciation for period from Apr. 1, 1975, to Dec. 31, 1975:			
$\frac{3}{4}$(9 mo) × $3,200	$2,400	$\frac{3}{4}$(9 mo) × $2,500	$1,875
Depreciation for 1976:			
40% × $5,600 ($8,000 −		$\frac{1}{4}$(3 mo) × $2,500	$ 625
$2,400 taken in		$\frac{3}{4}$(9 mo) × $2,000	1,500
1975)	$2,240	Total	$2,125

The depreciation for the remaining $3\frac{1}{4}$ years would be determined in a similar manner.

Units-of-output Method   A more realistic allocation of the cost of some plant assets can be obtained by dividing the cost (minus estimated net salvage value) by the estimated units of output or production (machine-hours, units of product produced, or miles driven) rather than by the estimated years of useful life. A bus company, for example, might compute depreciation on its vehicles by a mileage basis. If a bus costs $30,000 and is estimated to have a useful life of 200,000 miles, the depreciation rate per mile of operation would be 15 cents ($30,000 ÷ 200,000). At the end of each year, the amount of depreciation would be determined by multiplying the 15-cent rate by the number of miles the bus had operated during the year.

The estimated life of an asset using the units-of-output method is measured in terms of potential physical services or units of production and periodic depreciation is based on the actual use of the asset. As a result, *total* depreciation expense for a fiscal period varies if use varies, but the *depreciation per unit of output is constant.* The units-of-output method of depreciation is particularly appropriate when asset use fluctuates widely from period to period and depreciation is deemed to be more closely related to physical usage of the asset rather than to functional obsolescence.

Some accountants and businessmen have suggested that certain assets be depreciated on the basis of appraisal. This method may result in periodic depreciation charges for certain assets which closely parallel the units-of-output method, because the value of an asset depends to a considerable extent on the amount of wear and tear. The *appraisal method* requires a determination of the value of services that *remain in the asset* at the end of each period. Periodic depreciation is estimated by appraising assets on hand at the end of the period, and charging off an amount sufficient to reduce book value to this appraised valuation. The appraisal method of depreciation is particularly appropriate for short-lived assets such as small tools, dies, utensils, and containers.

The most serious objection to the appraisal method is the fact that the going-concern value of specific plant assets can seldom be determined with sufficient precision to make this an objective measure of the cost of asset services consumed.

Retirement and Replacement Methods The accrual methods of depreciation discussed thus far represent an attempt to measure the erosion of asset cost as it occurs. An alternative approach, advocated by some public utilities and railroads, is to recognize depreciation only at the time assets reach the end of their service life.

The *retirement method* is a system whereby the cost of plant units (net of salvage value) is charged to expense in the year in which the asset is retired from service. Under the *replacement method* the original cost of all items of plant is retained in the asset account and the cost of all replacements is charged to expense when they are acquired. The replacement method is somewhat analogous to the use of lifo in pricing inventories, in that the asset account will always show the cost of the first units of each type of property acquired. Under the retirement method, the property accounts will show the full cost of all assets actually in use as of a given date.

There are two objections to these depreciation methods. The first is that no depreciation will be charged against revenues until retirement occurs. Not only is income overstated in the early years of service life, but also the original asset cost appears on the balance sheet, despite the fact that a portion of cost has expired. The second objection is that the charge to operations is determined by the number of assets replaced and the nature of the replacements. The probability that the cost of replacements or retirements in any period will coincide with the cost of asset services used during that period is rather slim. The force of this objection is increased when it is noted that managerial replacement policy is likely to vary in response to the availability of funds for capital expenditures, the stage of the business cycle, and earnings prospects.

Despite these rather obvious flaws, retirement and replacement methods have been used and supported in the public utility industry. This may be explained in part by the fact that utility plants are typically composed of large numbers of interrelated items such as rails, ties, poles, pipe sections, rail cars, transformers, etc., whose individual cost is small. Under these conditions, service life is difficult to estimate, and the distinction between maintenance and replacement is often difficult to draw.

Compound Interest Methods The *annuity* and *sinking fund* methods call for the application of compound interest concepts in measuring periodic depreciation. These methods are discussed in *Advanced Accounting* of this series.

Composite or Group Depreciation Many companies find it expedient to account for depreciation of certain kinds of assets on a composite or group basis. *Revenue Procedure 71-25,* issued by the Internal Revenue Service in 1971, allows useful lives to be applied to broad classes of assets rather than to detailed items of depreciable property. Composite or group depreciation is a process of averaging the service life of a number of property units and taking depreciation on the entire lot as if it were an operating unit. The term *composite* generally refers to a collection of somewhat dissimilar assets; the term *group* usually refers to a collection of similar assets. The procedure for determining the periodic depreciation charge is essentially the same in either case.

Several methods may be used to develop a composite or group depreciation rate to be applied to the total cost of a group of assets. The computation of a straight-line composite depreciation rate for a group of machines is illustrated on page 455.

Once the composite or group depreciation rate is computed, it is continued in use until a material change in the composition of assets or in the estimated service life of assets occurs. The assumptions under-

Computation of Composite Depreciation Rate

Machine	Acquisition cost	Estimated salvage value	Amount to be depreciated	Estimated service life (years)	Annual depreciation expense
W	$ 5,000	$ –0–	$ 5,000	5	$1,000
X	10,000	1,200	8,800	8	1,100
Y	15,000	1,000	14,000	10	1,400
Z	20,000	2,000	18,000	12	1,500
Totals	$50,000	$4,200	$45,800		$5,000

Composite depreciation rate on cost: $5,000 ÷ $50,000 = 10%

Composite life of machines: $45,800 ÷ $5,000 = 9.16 years

lying the use of composite or group depreciation methods are that (1) assets are regularly retired near the end of their estimated service lives, (2) assets are regularly replaced with similar assets, and (3) proceeds on retirement are approximately equal to the estimated salvage value used in computing the composite depreciation rate. If assets are not replaced, for example, the use of the 10% rate computed above would eventually result in excessive depreciation charges.

In determining the yearly depreciation expense, the average rate of 10% is applied to the balance in the asset account at the beginning of the year, which balance excludes the original cost of all units retired prior to the beginning of the year. Thus for each of the first five years, annual depreciation would be $5,000 and in the sixth year (assuming machine W was replaced at the end of the fifth year with another machine costing $8,000), depreciation would be $5,300 ($53,000 × 10%). The group of machines would not, of course, be depreciated below salvage value at any time prior to retirement.

When group or composite procedures are employed, there is no record of accumulated depreciation on individual assets. When an asset is retired from use, an entry is made removing the original cost from the asset account and the difference between original cost and the proceeds received is charged to Accumulated Depreciation. To illustrate, if machine W were sold at the end of the fourth year for $1,230, the entry to record the sale would be:

Cash	1,230	
Accumulated Depreciation	3,770	
Machinery		5,000

The primary disadvantage of group depreciation methods is that the averaging procedure may obscure significant variations from average. The accuracy of the group depreciation rate can only be checked when the last asset in the group is retired. Until this time significant cumulative errors may go undetected.

The advantages claimed for the group method are simplicity, convenience, and a reduction in the amount of detail involved in property records and depreciation computations. The advent of accounting machines and computers has obviously reduced the force of this argument. In many cases unit property records are now feasible, although previously group methods were considered a necessity.

The requisites for the successful operation of group depreciation procedures are that there be a large number of homogeneous assets, of relatively small individual value, with similar life expectancies. Telephone and electric transmission poles, underground cable, railroad track, and hotel furniture are examples of situations in which group depreciation may give satisfactory results.

Depreciation methods and management decisions

In highly industrialized nations, plant and equipment play a large part in the productive process. It is easy to see that the costs of raw materials and direct labor become a part of finished product. It is not always so clearly recognized, however, that a business also sells to its customers the services of the productive assets used in manufacturing and marketing its products.

The primary importance of depreciation stems from the various management decisions that are affected by it. To the extent that depreciation is a relatively significant part of operating costs, and that operating costs are relevant in business decisions, the relative merits of various depreciation methods are a significant issue.

Depreciation is of particular importance in three decision areas:

1 Decisions relating to income measurement
2 Decisions relating to income tax determination
3 Decisions relating to capital investment

The effect of different depreciation methods in relation to each of these decision areas is briefly discussed in the following sections.

Depreciation and income measurement

The purpose of depreciation accounting is to measure the amount that must be recovered from revenue to compensate for the portion of asset cost that has been used up. This idea is embodied in the phrase "maintaining capital intact," which is so often used in relation to income measurement.

The wide use of the straight-line time method of depreciation can be traced to the fact that it is simple and convenient. Three basic objections may be leveled against the straight-line method, each of which becomes a supporting argument for some other method.

1 It tends to report an increasing rate of return on investment.
2 It does not allow for the fact that productivity of assets may decline with age.
3 It does not take into account variations in the rate of asset use.

Let us consider each of these objections to the straight-line method of depreciation.

Increasing Return Argument The point of this objection can best be demonstrated by an example. Assume that Adams acquires a business airplane for $300,000, which he plans to rent on a charter basis. He expects to keep the plane in service for four years and estimates that the salvage value will be $60,000. Anticipated rental revenue is $150,000 per year and operating expenses, exclusive of depreciation, are estimated at $54,000 per year. The effect of the use of straight-line depreciation, assuming that Adams' expectations are fully realized, is shown in the following tabulation:

Year	Revenue	Other operating expenses	Depreciation	Total expenses	Net income	Book value at beginning of year	Rate earned on book value at beginning of year, %
1	$150,000	$54,000	$60,000	$114,000	$36,000	$300,000	12
2	150,000	54,000	60,000	114,000	36,000	240,000	15
3	150,000	54,000	60,000	114,000	36,000	180,000	20
4	150,000	54,000	60,000	114,000	36,000	120,000	30
Salvage value						60,000	

The use of straight-line depreciation results in reporting rates of return on book value that ranges from 12% in the first year to 30% in the last, because income remains constant in the face of a declining book value.[2] The fact that, after distributing income at the end of the first year, Adams has $60,000 in cash and $240,000 invested in his airplane does not alter the situation. The $60,000 may presumably be invested in some other venture and will earn an additional return.

[2] The use of any of the accelerated methods of depreciation would actually exaggerate the apparent increase in the rate of return as long as the earnings before depreciation remain constant. The use of the sum-of-the-years'-digits method, for example, would produce rates of return in the declining book value of the airplane of approximately 0, 12, 36, and 86% over the four-year period.

The idea of an increasing rate of return on investment as an asset approaches retirement does not square with economic reality. Reason suggests that rate of return should remain constant or actually decrease somewhat as an asset ages. The cause of the difficulty in our example is a failure of the straight-line method to take into account the factor of interest that is implicit in a lump-sum investment to be recovered piecemeal over a long period of time. The increasing rate of return argument has particular force in situations where operations focus on a single depreciable asset, for example, a toll bridge, a hydroelectric dam, or an office building.

The assumption that other operating expenses remain constant at $54,000 per year may be questioned on the grounds that repair, maintenance, and fuel costs are likely to increase as the airplane ages. Similarly, the assumption of a constant rental revenue throughout service life may not hold true. Thus the earning power of many assets tends to decline with age because of increasing operating expenses, decreasing revenue, or both. If this decrease in earnings parallels the decline in book value, the straight-line method may tend to produce a constant rate of return on book value.

Declining Productivity Argument   Many businessmen suggest that the decline in productivity of many assets is so pronounced that the value (and thus the cost) of asset services in the early stages of service life is materially greater than in later years. If this is true, accelerated methods of depreciation may relate costs incurred and revenue realized more closely than the straight-line method.

Originally the declining productivity argument centered on a rising curve of repair and maintenance costs as assets aged. In recent years greater weight has been given to the effects of obsolescence. The period of high earnings on new plant is often short because of the inroads of innovation and competition.

Variation in Output Argument   The use of the straight-line time depreciation method makes depreciation a fixed period cost by assumption and thereby fails to allow for the loss of service potential related to wear and tear through usage. If an asset is used twice as heavily in one period as another, it may be unrealistic to assume that the amount and cost of the services consumed is the same in both periods. This objection to straight-line time depreciation becomes a case for using a measure of output or productivity as the unit of service life, which would make depreciation a variable cost.

Depreciation policy and income taxes

Probably the strongest influence on depreciation policy in practice is the income tax law. The direction of the influence is toward accelerated depreciation. Depreciation expense reduces taxable income and income tax expense. Taxpayers cannot deduct more than the actual cost of a depreciable asset over its service life, but income taxes can be postponed by accelerating depreciation deductions, and deferred taxes represent in effect an interest-free loan from the taxing agencies for the period of the postponement. The only possible tax disadvantage to large initial depreciation deductions is that tax rates might increase sufficiently to more than offset the implicit interest savings.

Tax factors encourage the use of minimum estimates of service life and the adoption of accelerated depreciation methods, without regard to issues of accounting theory or economic reality. If such practices applied only to the computation of taxable income, no damage would be done to the validity of financial statements. For many businesses, however, the convenience of keeping only one set of depreciation records is such that the accounting records generally are made to conform to the income tax requirements.

If tax depreciation and accounting depreciation are substantially equivalent, there are practical advantages in keeping the books on a tax basis. Tax deductions, however, are shaped by matters of public policy and the need for revenue by the government and are not necessarily related to the objectives of sound accounting. Material divergence between tax and accounting data is possible. A number of companies, for example, follow a policy of using accelerated depreciation methods for tax purposes but continue to use a straight-line method for financial reporting purposes.

Allowing excessive depreciation deductions for tax purposes is an indirect means of subsidizing business investment. As a result, proposals for extraordinary depreciation allowances as a means of stimulating investment or encouraging certain kinds of investment are constantly being made before Congress. In 1971, for example, a new asset depreciation range (ADR) system was approved by Congress which allows taxpayers to increase the rate of depreciation in computing taxable income. Under the ADR system a taxpayer may select a useful life for assets which is 20% shorter than that previously allowed by the Internal Revenue Service.[3] The pressure to inflate depreciation provisions for maximum tax advantage is not likely to wane. Therefore, the continued usefulness of accounting data for managerial and investment purposes may depend upon maintaining a healthy state of independence between good accounting and income tax rules.

[3] Despite the numerous steps taken by Congress in the last 20 years to liberalize depreciation policies, the United States still lags far behind other industrialized nations in this respect. Business firms in the United States, for example, are permitted to recover on the average less than 70% of the cost of assets over the first seven years of asset life. In contrast, business firms in the United Kingdom, France, Italy, Germany, and Switzerland are allowed to deduct 90% or more of the investment in plant equipment over the first seven years of asset life. (Source: First National City Bank *Monthly Economic Letter,* February 1971, pp. 12–15).

Depreciation and capital investment decisions

The two most important questions relating to the role of depreciation in a capital investment decision are: (1) Is depreciation a relevant cost in making the decision? (2) How does depreciation affect the cash flows from the investment?

Depreciation Expense May Be a Differential Cost or a Sunk Cost In essence, two kinds of costs are relevant to the decision to invest capital in productive assets: (1) *future costs,* that is, costs that will be incurred as the result of this decision; and (2) *differential costs,* that is, costs that will change as the result of the investment decision. The expense represented by depreciation on existing assets is attributable to an expenditure made at some time in the past. Except to the extent that an existing asset can be sold and some portion of the past investment recovered, no present decision can change the amount of cost that has been sunk into that facility. In many instances depreciation is aptly referred to as a *sunk cost.*

A decision to invest in productive facilities should depend on an analysis of future and differential costs and revenue. The book value of existing assets, a sunk cost that cannot be changed in the short run, is an irrelevant factor and should be ignored (except for income tax consideration). Most managerial decisions as to alternative actions such as buying or leasing, buying or making, accepting or not accepting a special order, depend upon an analysis of differential costs and revenue. Depreciation may or may not represent a differential or relevant cost in comparing such alternative courses of action. Depreciation on special equipment which must be purchased specifically for a given activity is always a differential cost to that activity, but depreciation on existing assets would be a differential cost only if the use of the assets for the specific activity clearly reduces their useful life.

We have oversimplified the problem in this discussion, but a valid generalization may be drawn. Whether or not depreciation should be regarded as a differential cost depends on whether the limiting factor in asset life is obsolescence or use, and whether the facility in question is now being used to capacity. For this reason, depreciation expense as computed for purposes of income determination is generally not a relevant figure for management to use in decision making.

Effect of Depreciation on Cash Flows Investment decisions are most frequently made on the basis of the expected rate of return on the investment. In computing the rate of return, *net cash flow* from the investment is generally a more useful concept than net income from the investment. Depreciation expense does not directly generate cash; it is simply an expense which does not currently reduce cash but which may be deducted in arriving at taxable income. Thus depreciation expense indirectly generates greater cash flows from operations by reducing the current income tax expense. For this reason, depreciation is universally viewed as a powerful instrument for speeding up cash flows and improving **payback** calculations on new investments in plant and equipment.

To illustrate the relationships between depreciation and cash flows, assume the following annual results for an asset owned by a leasing company and rented out to customers on a per diem basis:

Amount of cash received from rentals	$5,000
Less: All expenses (except income taxes) paid in cash	1,200
Net cash received	$3,800
Income taxes, 50% of income after depreciation of $2,000 = .5 ×	
($3,800 − $2,000)	900
Net cash flow per year	$2,900

The net cash flow of $2,900 per year may also be determined by adding back the depreciation expense of $2,000 to the accounting net income of $900 earned by the asset ($3,800 − $2,000 − $900). Determining the net cash flow from an investment is an important step in the complex area frequently referred to as **capital budgeting.**

Depreciation procedures and records

Accumulated Depreciation Account In theory depreciation could be recorded as a credit to the asset account, since depreciable assets are basically long-term prepaid costs. The direct write-off procedure is often followed in dealing with large numbers of small-value assets where periodic inventories are taken to determine the portion of asset cost remaining on hand. For larger property units, the almost universal practice is to credit a contra-asset account titled Accumulated Depreciation, Allowance for Depreciation, or Reserve for Depreciation.[4] The primary argument for the use of a separate account is to preserve information about the original cost in plant assets and the proportion of cost that has expired. Also it is convenient when analyzing account balances to be able to distinguish plant additions and retirements from adjustments in accumulated depreciation.

The Accumulated Depreciation account is frequently (but improperly) referred to as a **valuation account.** The Accumulated Depreciation account

[4]The 1972 edition of *Accounting Trends & Techniques,* published by the AICPA, reports that of the 600 companies surveyed, the largest number uses the term **accumulated depreciation** and that the use of the term **reserve for depreciation** is declining. In 1960, 266 companies used the term **accumulated** as compared with 466 companies in 1971. In 1960, the term **allowance** was used by 129 companies as compared with 80 companies in 1971. In 1960, 118 companies used the term **reserve** as compared with only 26 companies in 1971.

Depreciation (Lapsing) Schedule—

Date acquired (or retired)	Type of asset	Machinery account		Accumulated depreciation	
		Debit or (Credit)	Balance	Debit or (Credit)	Balance
Jan. 3, 1976	A	$3,100	$ 3,100		
Jan. 4, 1976	B	6,000	9,100		
July 1, 1976	C	4,800	13,900		
Depreciation for 1976				$(2,740)	$(2,740)
April 1, 1977	D	2,900	16,800		
Aug. 15, 1977	E	4,000	20,800		
Dec. 29, 1977 (retired)	B	(6,000)	14,800	(2 yrs) 3,600	860
Depreciation for 1977				(3,940)	(3,080)
Depreciation for 1978				(2,620)	(5,700)

represents the portion of the acquisition cost of an asset which has been allocated to revenue through the process of depreciation. Its purpose is not to arrive at a valuation of a plant asset in terms of current realizable value but rather to determine the unallocated plant cost (book value) at a given date.

Property Records   The typical business employs many different kinds of property, having varying characteristics and service lives. Precision in accounting for the use of such property is facilitated by detailed and complete property records. Property records may be maintained on ledger cards, tabulating cards, magnetic tapes, or in computer memory systems.

An ideal system is to maintain a record for each asset. The record should show, for each asset, its original cost, capital additions, estimated service life, estimated salvage value, date of installation, location, basis and amount of periodic depreciation, and any other information, such as serial numbers. In addition to providing thorough support for depreciation and retirement entries, such property records are useful in maintaining good internal controls and accountability over plant and equipment items.

Depreciation Schedules   When the number of individual items of property within each class of assets is not large, a depreciation schedule (sometimes known as a *lapsing schedule*) may be used. Lapsing schedules may take many forms and are often prepared by computer if the number of assets is large. A depreciation schedule is a means of keeping unit property records with a minimum of effort. Its purpose is to facilitate the

Finishing Department

Estimated salvage value	Depreciation base	Estimated life, years	Depreciation expense (straight-line)		
			1976	1977	1978 etc.
$400	$2,700	5	$ 540	$ 540	$ 540
600	5,400	3	1,800	1,800	1,800
–0–	4,800	6	$(\frac{1}{2})$ 400	800	800
			$2,740		
500	2,400	3		$(\frac{3}{4})$ 600	800
160	3,840	8		$(\frac{5}{12})$ 200	480
					(1,800) adj.
				$3,940	
					$2,620

computation of periodic depreciation and to provide a continuing record of asset costs and the related accumulated depreciation. An example of a depreciation schedule for a department of a factory appears on pages 462 and 463.

When new property is acquired, the acquisition cost is entered on one line of the schedule and the prospective depreciation charges throughout its life are extended in the annual depreciation columns. If the asset is retired at the end of its estimated service life, the original cost is credited to the asset account, and depreciation to date is debited to Accumulated Depreciation. The gain or loss would be recorded in the general journal or the cash receipts journal. If an asset is retired prematurely, it is not necessary to erase or change the originally scheduled depreciation amounts. It is more convenient simply to cancel the depreciation charges by extending appropriate *deductions* on the line used to record the retirement. This is illustrated in the case of asset B. It was originally estimated that asset B would serve for three years, but it was sold for $2,300 on December 29, 1977, at the end of only two years of service. The removal of $6,000 from the asset account and $3,600 (two years at $1,800 per year) from Accumulated Depreciation is recorded on one line of the schedule. On the same line, in the Depreciation Expense columns, is entered a cancellation of the $1,800 depreciation which was originally scheduled for 1978. Journal entries to record annual depreciation on all machines and the disposal of machine B are shown on page 464.

Disclosure of depreciation in financial statements

Because of the significant effects on financial position and results of operations from depreciation expense and the depreciation methods

1976
Dec. 31 Depreciation Expense.   2,740
                  Accumulated Depreciation.   2,740
              To record depreciation for 1976.

1977
Dec. 29 Cash   2,300
              Accumulated Depreciation   3,600
              Loss on Disposal of Machinery   100
                  Machinery   6,000
              To record disposal of machine B.

1977
Dec. 31 Depreciation Expense.   3,940
                  Accumulated Depreciation.   3,940
              To record depreciation for 1977.

1978
Dec. 31 Depreciation Expense.   2,620
                  Accumulated Depreciation.   2,620
              To record depreciation for 1978.

used, the following disclosures should be made in the financial statements or in the accompanying notes:

1 Depreciation expense for the period
2 Balances of major classes of depreciable assets, by nature or function
3 Accumulated depreciation, either by major classes of depreciable assets or in total
4 A general description of the method or methods used in computing depreciation with respect to major classes of depreciable assets[5]

In the 1972 edition of **Accounting Trends & Techniques,** published by the AICPA, all of the 600 companies surveyed presented the annual charge for depreciation and 583 companies disclosed the method or methods used in determining depreciation. Many of the companies use more than one method. For example, 545 companies used the straight-line method and 202 companies used one of the accelerated depreciation methods; only 36 companies used the unit-of-output method. If a change in the method of computing depreciation is made, the effect of the change on the current year's net income should be disclosed. Similarly, the effect of any extraordinary depreciation charges should be noted. Accounting for changes in depreciation methods, changes in estimated service life

[5]*APB Opinion No. 12,* "Omnibus Opinion—1967," AICPA (New York: 1967), p. 188.

of depreciable assets, and corrections of errors in recording depreciation are discussed in Chapter 22.

DEPLETION

A depreciable asset usually retains its physical characteristics as it performs services. In contrast, a wasting asset is in essence a long-term inventory of raw materials that will be removed physically from the property. In either case—whether the accountant is dealing with a "bundle of services" or a "store of raw materials"—the basic problem is to determine the cost of the units of services or materials that are consumed during each accounting period. The portion of the cost (or other valuation) assigned to property containing natural resources that is applicable to the units removed from the property is known as *depletion.*

The depletion base

The depletion base of any wasting asset is the entire cost of acquiring the property less the estimated residual value of the land after the natural resources have been removed. The estimated cost of restoring mined properties may be taken into account in determining residual value of the land or it may be "accrued ratably as minerals are produced."[6]

Acquisition cost logically includes expenditures for exploring, drilling, excavating, and construction preparatory to the removal of the resources. These are known as *development costs* and should be amortized in proportion to the removal of the natural resource. Structures and equipment used in extracting natural resources may have a service life shorter than the time required to complete the removal, in which case the amortization of these assets should be made over their estimated service life.

What if the expenditures made in acquiring, exploring, and developing natural resources prove unproductive? If each specific property is viewed as a venture, the logical interpretation is that no asset exists and a loss has therefore occurred. On the other hand, from the viewpoint of the company as a whole, particularly if it is seeking constantly to maintain its resource base by exploration and acquisition of new deposits, a certain amount of unproductive effort may be viewed as a normal hazard (expense) of discovering new resources. If, for example, 10 dry holes are drilled on the average for each producing well brought in, the argument that 11 drillings are necessary to bring in a "producer" and that the cost of a producing well includes the cost of 10 unsuccessful efforts has considerable merit. The problem is analogous to that of accounting for

[6] Robert E. Field, *Accounting Research Study No. 11*, "Financial Reporting in the Extractive Industries," AICPA (New York: 1969), p. 74.

spoilage in manufacturing. If a certain amount of spoilage is ordinary and necessary, it is treated as a part of the cost of the good units produced; if the amount of spoilage is abnormal, it is treated as a loss.

In the lumber industry, substantial costs are incurred for fire protection, insect and disease control, property taxes, and other maintenance costs applicable to standing timber that will not be harvested for a considerable length of time. These costs, known as *carrying charges,* should logically be capitalized while the property is being developed. For example, if carrying charges of $40,000 are applicable to a given tract of timber and during the current accounting period 20% of the timber is cut, 80% of the $40,000 in carrying charges is applicable to uncut timber and should be capitalized.

Estimating recoverable units

Forecasting service life for plant and equipment is a relatively simple undertaking when compared with the uncertainties encountered in estimating recoverable units of natural resources. The quantity of ore in a vein or the recoverable deposit in oil- and gas-producing property is often extremely difficult to determine, and revisions are constantly necessary as production takes place and new evidence becomes available. Adding to the problem is the fact that changes in the method of extraction may make it possible to work deposits that were originally deemed uneconomic.

Ideally, the recoverable deposit should be measured in units of *desired* product, such as an ounce of silver or a pound of nickel, rather than in units of *mined* product, such as a ton of ore. If depletion is based on tons of mined ore, the same charge will be applied to a ton of high-grade ore as to a ton of low-grade ore. This treatment is hardly logical in terms of the way mining property is valued and in terms of the accountant's efforts to attain a sound matching of costs and revenue.

Depletion methods based on cost of natural resource

Any of the methods of depreciation previously discussed could be applied in a comparable manner to the computation of depletion. The straight-line method, however, is of doubtful applicability since the exhaustion of natural resources is clearly a matter of physical output rather than the passage of time. Accelerated methods have not been commonly used in measuring depletion, despite the fact that the productivity of wasting assets may decline rapidly when the cost of recovery per unit increases as production moves from richer to poorer veins.

By far the most common method of depletion for accounting purposes is the units-of-output method, which produces a constant depletion charge per unit removed. To illustrate, assume that wasting asset property cost $720,000. It was estimated that there were 1.2 million recoverable units and that the land would have a net residual value (after restoration costs) of $60,000 when the resource was exhausted. The depletion per unit of output would be computed as follows:

$$\text{Depletion} = \frac{\text{cost} - \text{net residual value}}{\text{total recoverable units}}$$

$$= \frac{\$720,000 - \$60,000}{1,200,000 \text{ units}} = \$.55 \text{ per unit} \quad \times \text{ amt. recovered}$$

If 300,000 units were recovered during the current year and 200,000 of these were sold, the cost of goods sold would be determined as follows:

	Total	Unit cost
Cost of goods sold:		
Depletion (300,000 units × $.55)	$165,000	$ .55
Materials, labor, and overhead	237,000	.79
Depreciation of equipment	15,000	.05
Total cost of production (300,000 units)	$417,000	$1.39
Less: Ending inventory (100,000 units @ $1.39)	139,000	
Cost of goods sold (200,000 units @ $1.39)	$278,000	

When additional costs are incurred in developing mining properties or estimates of recoverable units are revised, the depletion rate should be redetermined. Depletion previously recorded, however, should not be revised. The new depletion rate is computed by dividing the unamortized cost of the mining property (including any additional development costs) by the new estimate of recoverable units. The issues relating to changes in accounting estimates are covered in greater detail in Chapter 22.

Percentage depletion for income tax purposes

For income tax purposes, a special depletion method known as *percentage* or *statutory depletion* can be used by producers of oil, gas, and most minerals. Under this procedure the depletion deduction may be computed as a percentage of the gross income received, without regard to the cost of the property or the number of units produced. At one time percentage depletion allowances were granted only for oil and natural gas, but Congress has gradually broadened the coverage until today this provision applies to practically all minerals at rates varying from 5 to 22% of gross income. Some examples of percentage depletion (subject to change at any time) follow:

Oil, natural gas, sulphur, and uranium.	22%
Gold, silver, oil shale, copper, and iron ore	15%
China clay, rock asphalt, borax, and bauxite.	14%
Coal and sodium chloride	10%
Gravel, peat, sand, and magnesium chloride.	5%

Taxpayers may use either cost depletion or percentage depletion, whichever is more advantageous. The only limit on percentage depletion is that it cannot exceed 50% of the taxable income from the property, computed before deducting depletion. To illustrate, assume the following facts for Rich Oil Company for the current year:

Sale of crude oil (500,000 barrels @ $2)	$1,000,000
Expenses (excluding depletion)	$ 550,000
Depletion base (cost) of oil-producing property	$ 750,000
Estimated barrels recoverable from property.	3,000,000
Cost depletion per barrel ($750,000 ÷ 3,000,000).	25 cents
Income tax rate.	40%

Taxable income and net income for financial reporting purposes are determined below:

	Taxable income	Net income for financial reporting purposes
Sale of crude oil	$1,000,000	$1,000,000
Expenses (excluding depletion) . . .	(550,000)	(550,000)
Income before depletion	$ 450,000	
Depletion:		
Percentage basis for income tax		
purposes, $1,000,000 × 22% .	(220,000)	
Cost basis for financial reporting		
purposes, 500,000 barrels @ 25		
cents		(125,000)
Taxable income.	$ 230,000	
Income taxes, $230,000 × 40% . . .		(92,000)
Net income		$ 233,000

The percentage depletion for the current year in computing taxable income is $220,000 (22% of $1,000,000) because this amount exceeds cost depletion ($125,000) and is less than 50% of the $450,000 income before depletion. If expenses excluding depletion amount to $600,000, for example, percentage depletion would be limited to $200,000 (50% of $400,000, the income before depletion). When cost depletion exceeds percentage depletion, taxable income is computed using cost depletion.

The primary advantage of percentage depletion arises not because it may be larger than cost depletion in any given year, but because the cumulative amount of depletion deductions is not limited by the depletion base. There is no cost "base" for percentage depletion other than gross income, and the taxpayer may thus take depletion deductions on his tax return many times over the cost of the property. Percentage depletion is not recorded on the accounting records; it represents a special tax benefit granted to natural resource industries as a matter of public policy.

Although percentage depletion is not used for accounting purposes, income tax rules in this area discourage sound accounting practices in another respect. The tax law allows a considerable freedom of choice between capitalizing development costs and carrying charges or charging them off immediately. Since the amount of cost capitalized will not affect future percentage depletion deductions, the tax pressure to charge development and carrying costs against current revenue is overwhelming; if accounting records are kept on a tax basis, reported net income is inevitably distorted.

Corporation laws provide that companies engaged in extracting natural resources may declare dividends on the basis of earnings computed without regard to depletion. In effect, this means that if a company recovers the cost of its investment as the natural resources are depleted and does not intend to acquire new deposits, it may return the recovered cost to stockholders as a liquidating dividend.

Failure to record depletion

Cost depletion should be recorded as an expense in measuring net income, since it represents the exhaustion of an investment in productive assets. Despite this reasoning, some spokesmen for extractive industries have argued for the omission of depletion in measuring net income on grounds that (1) estimates of recoverable units are uncertain, (2) new discoveries of deposits exceed depletion on existing deposits, and (3) dividends can be declared legally on income excluding depletion. These arguments are weak. Because the amount of depletion is uncertain does not justify the assumption that it is equal to zero. Furthermore, setting legal limits on dividends is not the main purpose of measuring net income. If a venture in wasting assets is so speculative as to make it virtually impossible to estimate recoverable units, it would be more reasonable to assume that no income emerges until the full cost of the property is recovered. Few situations involve such a high degree of uncertainty.

The failure to record depletion may not, in fact, result in an over-statement of income. Because substantial amounts of exploration and development costs *applicable to future production* are commonly charged off in the year they are incurred, the result is similar to using the replacement method of depreciation. In lieu of cost depletion, the cost of exploring for and discovering new deposits is charged to expense. This approach has the weaknesses pointed out in our earlier discussion relating to the retirement and replacement methods of depreciation, and violates the concept of matching costs and revenue.

REVIEW QUESTIONS

1 Some companies, particularly those in the real estate business, report an intermediate figure on their income statement and refer to it as "net income before depreciation." Comment on this practice.

2 Distinguish the terms *depreciation, amortization,* and *depletion.* How is depreciation accounting related to the replacement of an asset at the end of its service life?

3 What are the three variables in estimating periodic depreciation? Is depreciation more properly referred to as a valuation procedure or a cost allocation procedure?

4 The manager of an electric utility states, "Our transmission lines are kept in good operating condition by regular repairs and maintenance, and their efficiency is relatively constant—they just don't depreciate!" Do you agree with this statement? Explain.

5 What is meant by the term *estimated service life* of an asset and how is it measured?

6 What are the main causes of a decrease in asset service life? How reliably can they be estimated?

7 Zurn Company buys delivery trucks for $4,000. These trucks have a useful life of six years and a scrap value of $400. Zurn Company typically sells a truck for $1,600 after running it 50,000 miles. What should be the depreciation base for this delivery truck? What should be its estimated service life?

8 The quantity of asset services used each period and the relative value of the asset services are both factors in choosing a method of depreciation. Explain.

9 List the various methods that may be used to compute depreciation.

10 a State three basic objections against the straight-line (time) method of depreciation.
   b What are the advantages of the straight-line (time) method of depreciation?

11 Many depreciable assets exhibit a declining productivity with advancing age. Explain how this fact may be used both as an argument for and an argument against the straight-line method of depreciation.

12 During 1975 a strike halted manufacturing operations of Carpets, Inc., for four months. Depreciation of its spinning and weaving machines for the full year 1975 using the straight-line method is $216,000. Its operations for 1975 resulted in a loss of $132,000 (after deducting depreciation). The president suggests that the depreciation deduction should be reduced because of the low volume of operations. Do you agree?

13 Describe a situation in which the use of the units-of-output method of depreciation would be appropriate.

14 What is meant by **composite** or **group** depreciation? What are the advantages and limitations of this method?

15 Explain why the use of accelerated depreciation methods is advantageous for income tax purposes, even though depreciation for tax purposes cannot exceed original cost reduced by salvage value.

16 Explain why periodic depreciation on existing equipment is not a relevant factor in arriving at a decision to replace the equipment.

17 What principle should be applied in determining whether depreciation is a fixed or a variable expense for income measurement purposes? Explain the statement: "Depreciation is a non-cash expense."

18 What disclosure relating to depreciation and depreciation methods should
· be made in the financial statements or in the accompanying notes?

19 Mineral Corporation has purchased property for $600,000 from which it expects to extract 1 million tons of 60% concentrate ore and 2 million tons of 30% concentrate ore. Compute the depletion charge per ton of ore extracted. Explain the term **percentage depletion.**

20 Assets donated to corporations are sometimes recorded on the books and depreciation or depletion on them is charged against revenue. Can you justify this practice?

EXERCISES

Ex. 12-1 X Company leased a building and immediately purchased equipment of $400,000 and spent $35,000 to have special platforms and supporting encasements built. The lease agreement provides that when the lease expires X Company must remove the equipment, tear up the platforms and encasements, and restore the property to its original condition, an operation that is expected to cost $20,000. What should be the depreciation base of this equipment?

Ex. 12-2 An asset cost $58,000, has a service life of seven years, and an estimated salvage value of $2,000.
a Compute depreciation for the first year under the sum-of-the-years'-digits method of depreciation.
b Assume that this asset was acquired on April 1, Year 1. Compute depreciation for the full year beginning on January 1, Year 2 under the sum-of-the-years' digits method of depreciation.

Ex. 12-3 A machine with an estimated life of five years, or 100,000 units of output, was acquired on October 4, Year 1. The machine sells for $9,000 and will be paid for as follows:

Old machine accepted as trade-in	$	500
Cash		1,500
Four installments payable at the rate of $2,000 every six months (includes		
$1,000 of interest and financing charges)		8,000
Total		$10,000

Compute depreciation for the three months in Year 1 and for Year 2, assuming that the salvage value of the machine is $1,500, using each of the following methods:

a Straight-line
b Sum-of-the-years'-digits
c Double-declining-balance
d Units-of-output (8,000 units in Year 1 and 30,000 units in Year 2)

Ex. 12-4 The Mason Company purchased an asset at the beginning of Year 1 for a total cost of $16,000. The asset has a useful life of four years and an estimated salvage value of $1,000.

Compute the depreciation on the asset for Year 1, using each of the following methods:

a Straight-line
b Sum-of-the-years'-digits
c Fixed-percentage-of-declining-balance (Compute the theoretically correct rate.)

Ex. 12-5 Y Co. purchased equipment on Jan. 3, 1971. The equipment has an estimated service life of 10 years and a salvage value of $10,000. The depreciation expense for 1975 was $6,000 using the sum-of-the-years'-digits method. What was the original cost of the asset?

Ex. 12-6 The controller of the Sherman Company, an electronics manufacturer, maintains his records of the following small equipment items used in manufacturing on the composite basis. A list of assets acquired at the beginning of Year 1 follows:

Assets	Cost	Estimated salvage value	Estimated service life (years)
A-101	$4,000	$400	3
A-102	1,500	300	4
A-103	7,000	750	5

a Compute the composite depreciation rate.
b If at the end of Year 3, the A-101 assets are sold for $400, what entry would be made to record this sale?

Ex. 12-7 At the beginning of Year 1 a firm acquired for cash 20 similar machines for $4,000 each and developed a composite depreciation rate of 30% based on these expectations:

	Year 2	Year 3	Year 4
Number of machines to be retired	5	10	5
Salvage value of machines to be retired	$6,000	$4,000	–0–

The retirements and proceeds realized were exactly as expected. You may assume that the 30% rate is correct.

Record all transactions for the four-year period in T accounts and explain the balance in the Accumulated Depreciation account at the end of Year 4.

Ex. 12-8 Silver Mining Company acquired mining property for $1.2 million. The mine was expected to yield 600,000 tons of ore, after which the property would have a residual value of $200,000. During the first year, 60,000 tons of ore were mined and sold for $800,000. Operating expenses other than cost depletion amounted to $340,000. The ore mined is eligible for a 15% statutory (percentage) depletion. State and federal income taxes are 45% of taxable income.

Compute the amount of (a) cost depletion on the mining property, (b) income tax expense, and (c) net income for financial reporting purposes.

Ex. 12-9 An analysis of the Machinery account on the books of the Sundown Corporation for the current year appears below:

Jan. 2	Acquired four machines with a useful life of five years	$12,000
Jan. 6	Installation costs	400
	Total debits	$12,400
Dec. 28	Less: Credit representing proceeds on disposal of one machine (debit	
	recorded in Cash)	2,300
	Balance in Machinery account	$10,100

a Prepare a journal entry to record depreciation expense for the current year on the four machines. Useful life is five years and estimated salvage value of each machine is $350. Use the straight-line method of depreciation.

b Prepare an entry to correct the accounts at December 31, including the recognition of the gain or loss (which was not recorded on December 28) on the disposal of one machine.

SHORT CASES FOR ANALYSIS AND DECISION

Case 12-1 Iron Corporation computes depreciation based on the level of the company's operations. In the third quarter of a given fiscal year, the company, according to a financial news story, "returned to profit a sum equal to 25 cents per share that had been written off as depreciation in the previous six months but that it determined had not been needed."

Instructions
a Briefly evaluate the company's depreciation policy.
b Does it seem to you that this company is smoothing its net income through its depreciation policy or simple trying to match the service potential (cost) of its assets with the economic benefits derived (tons of steel produced)?

Case 12-2 Linden Company owned an old factory building carried in its accounts at a book value of $200,000. Machinery and equipment in the building had a book value of $300,000. In 1970 the company built a new building at a cost of $1.2 million and installed new equipment costing $650,000. Some of the equipment in the old building was replaced, and both plants were operated at near capacity from 1970 to 1975. Depreciation was taken on a straight-line basis.

In 1975 the company was forced to shut down the old plant because of a decline in sales. The president proposes to stop taking depreciation on the old building and machinery. He points out that while the old plant is useful, it is not wearing out. Furthermore, he feels that depreciating the old plant increases costs, overstates the inventory, and places the company in a poor position to bid for business since its costs are high.

Instructions Discuss the president's position and evaluate his arguments. What recommendation would you make to the company?

Case 12-3 A news story appeared in a financial periodical which stated that the net income for Prairie Oil Company has decreased from $2 million a year ago to only $500,000 in the current year, largely because of increased charges for depletion and depreciation. These additional charges were necessary because an independent engineering firm prepared new estimates of oil and gas reserves and these turned out to be substantially lower than the company's previous estimates of these reserves. As a result, it was necessary to increase the charges for depletion and depreciation in the current year. The story further stated that these revised estimates do not affect the company's revenue or cash flow, and that revisions in estimates of oil and gas reserves are not unusual in the petroleum industry. The president of the company was quoted as saying, "Because we are a relatively small company, these revisions affect us more seriously than they would larger companies."

Instructions
a How do you suppose the revised depletion and depreciation figure was determined? Should understatements in depletion and depreciation in prior years result in understating income in subsequent years?
b How can the independent auditor confirm the estimates of deposits of natural resources?
c Explain why increased depletion and depreciation charges do not affect revenue or cash flow.
d Why would revisions in estimates of oil and gas reserves affect a small company "more seriously" than they would larger companies? Would such revisions affect the percentage depletion allowed for income tax purposes?

Case 12-4 Res-Con Corporation sells and erects shell houses. These are frame structures that are completely finished on the outside but are unfinished on the inside except for flooring, partition studding, and ceiling joists. Shell houses are sold chiefly to customers who are handy with tools and who have time to do the interior wiring, plumbing, wall completion and finishing, and other work necessary to make the shell houses livable dwellings.

Res-Con buys shell houses from a manufacturer in unassembled packages consisting of all lumber, roofing, doors, windows, and similar materials necessary to complete a shell house. Upon commencing operations in a new area, Res-Con buys or leases land as a site for its local warehouse, field office, and display houses. Sample display houses are erected at a total cost of from $3,000 to $7,000, including the cost of the unassembled packages. The chief element of cost of the display houses is the unassembled packages, since erection is a short low-cost operation. Old sample models are torn down or altered into new models every three to seven years. Sample display houses have little salvage value because dismantling and moving costs amount to nearly as much as the cost of an unassembled package.

Instructions
a A choice must be made between (1) expensing the costs of sample display houses in the period in which the expenditure is made and (2) spreading the costs over more than one period. Discuss the advantages of each method.
b Would it be preferable to amortize the cost of display houses on the basis of (1) the passage of time or (2) the number of shell houses sold? Explain.

PROBLEMS

Group A

12A-1 The following entries are found in an improperly established Property account in the records of the Revsine Company at the end of 1975:

Debit entries:

Feb. 1	Amount paid to acquire building site	$12,500
12	Cost of removing old building from site	1,000
15	Contract price for new building which was completed on Apr. 5	40,000
Apr. 1	Insurance and other cost directly connected with construction of	
	new building	2,000
	Total debits	$55,500

Credit entries:

Feb. 12	Proceeds from sale of material obtained from disman-	
	tling of old building $1,500	
Dec. 31	Depreciation for 1975—5% of balance in account,	
	$54,000 *(Debit was recorded to Depreciation Expense.)* 2,700	
	Total credits	4,200
Balance in Property account on Dec. 31, 1975		$51,300

Instructions

a Prepare a compound correcting entry at December 31, 1975, assuming that the estimated life of the new building is 20 years and that depreciation using the straight-line method is to be recorded for nine months in 1975. The books have not been closed at the end of 1975.

b Compute depreciation on the building for the years 1975, 1976, and 1977 using the following methods: (1) straight-line, (2) double-declining-balance, and (3) sum-of-the-years'-digits.

12A-2 Avery Corporation has made a study of its four-year experience with a group of light trucks. The appraised values of these trucks at the end of each year and average miles driven per year per truck during a typical four-year period are as follows:

Year	Miles driven	Appraised value (% of cost)
1	20,000	65
2	40,000	45
3	30,000	30
4	10,000	24

Instructions On the basis of this information, compute the depreciation each year during the four-year service life of a truck that cost $10,000 and is expected to have a salvage value of $2,400, under each of the following depreciation

methods (round all computations to the nearest dollar):
a Straight-line
b Units-of-output
c Sum-of-the-years'-digits
d Theoretical fixed-percentage-of-declining-balance (The fourth root of $10,000 is 10; the fourth root of $2,400 is approximately 7.)
e Double-declining-balance, allowed for income tax purposes
f Appraisal

12A-3 In auditing the records of the Sterling Corporation, you observe the following entries in the Machinery account:

Debits:	Jan. 3, 1973 Purchased Machine A	$22,000	
	Jan. 10, 1973 Installation of Machine A	2,000	
	Sept. 28, 1973 Purchased Machine B	30,000	
	Mar. 31, 1974 Purchased Machine C	16,000	
	July 1, 1975 Repairs due to flooding	2,500	$72,500
Credits:	Dec. 31, 1973 Depreciation for year	$10,800	
	Dec. 31, 1974 Depreciation for year	11,840	
	Apr. 1, 1975 Proceeds on sale of Machine A	12,560	
	Dec. 31, 1975 Depreciation for year	7,460	42,660
Balance in account, Dec. 31, 1975			$29,840

Depreciation at the end of each year was taken at 20% of the balance in the account. Salvage value is estimated at 10% of invoice cost and useful life is estimated to be five years.

Instructions
a Prepare a depreciation (lapsing) schedule through December 31, 1975, for machinery, using straight-line depreciation.
b Using the information from the lapsing schedule, prepare a single compound entry to restate the accounts of the company in accordance with good accounting practice at December 31, 1975. The income and expense accounts for 1975 are still open.

12A-4 The Flexible Plastics Company acquired 15 used machines on January 2 of Year 1 for $60,000. The machines are not identical but perform similar manufacturing functions. The machines have an average useful life of four years and the salvage value for each machine will approximately equal the removal costs. A group depreciation method (straight-line) is used to allocate the service potential of the machines to revenue. Depreciation on assets retired or sold is computed for the full year.
Machines are retired from service as follows:

End of year	Machines retired or sold	Proceeds on sale
3	3	$ 700
4	10	1,200
5	2	100

New machines of this type are not acquired as replacements.

Instructions

a Prepare a cost allocation schedule using the group depreciation method for the five-year period during which the assets are used. The schedule should have the following headings:

End of year	Depreciation expense	Machinery account		Accumulated depreciation		Book value
		Debit (Credit)	Balance	Debit (Credit)	Balance	

b Prepare a similar schedule but assume that nothing is received on the sale of the machines, that two machines are retired at the end of Year 3, and that 11 machines are retired at the end of Year 4.

c Briefly comment on differences between the results obtained in **(a)** and **(b)**.

12A-5 Big Horn Mining Company paid $1,850,000 for a tract of land containing valuable ore and spent $450,000 in developing the property during Year 1, preparatory to beginning mining activities on January 1, Year 2. Company geologists estimated that the mineral deposit would produce 4 million tons of ore, and it is assumed that the land will have a residual value of $300,000 after the ore deposit is exhausted.

A record of capital investment during the last half of Year 1, exclusive of the development costs previously mentioned, is as follows:

Asset	Estimated service life, years	Cost
Mine buildings	30	$200,000
Railroad and hoisting equipment	20	600,000
Miscellaneous mine equipment	10	250,000

The buildings, railroad, and hoisting equipment cannot be economically removed from the mine location, but the miscellaneous equipment is readily movable and has alternative uses.

Operations during Year 2 are summarized below:

Tons of ore mined	1,000,000
Tons of ore sold at $4.80 per ton, F.O.B. the mine	950,000
Mining labor and other operating costs (exclusive of depreciation and depletion)	$2,400,000
Administrative and selling expenses	$510,000

Income taxes for the year, after deducting percentage depletion, were $380,000.

Instructions

a Prepare an income statement for Big Horn Mining Company for Year 2, showing the computation of depletion and depreciation per ton in supporting schedules.

b Early in Year 3 Big Horn Mining Company received an offer from a foreign firm to buy a single order of 500,000 tons of ore at a price of $4.50 per ton delivered in the foreign country. The company estimates that it will cost $1.40 per ton to ship the ore, and feels that accepting this order will not affect the domestic price. It is estimated that the cost of acquiring and developing additional ore property has not increased. One-fourth of the company's "mining labor and other operating costs" are fixed so long as at least 600,000 tons of ore are produced annually. Would you recommend that the company accept this order? Present data in support of your conclusion.

Group B

12B-1 The cash price of a machine acquired by Larry Phillips Corporation on September 30, 1975, is $60,000, including sales taxes; it was paid for as follows:

In cash—down payment.	$ 4,000
600 shares of company's stock with an agreed value of $42 per share	25,200
Notes payable in 24 equal monthly installments	36,000
Total (paid or payable).	$65,200

The following additional costs were incurred before the machine was ready for use:

Installation costs	$2,400
Direct costs of trial runs	1,200

The machine is expected to produce 100,000 units of output during its service life. It was placed in service on October 4, 1975.

Instructions
a Determine the cost of the machine for accounting purposes. Assume that the discount on the notes is equal to the difference between the total payments to be made and the cash price of the machine.
b Assuming that the estimated salvage value of the machine is $2,400 and that the useful life is estimated to be five years, compute depreciation on the machine for 1975 and 1976 using:
(1) Straight-line method
(2) Sum-of-the-years'-digits method
(3) Rate of 40% applied to declining net book value
(4) Units-of-output method (The machine produced 8,000 units in 1975 and 25,000 units in 1976.)

12B-2 A two-year record of the Equipment account on the books of the Raphael Company is shown below. The company follows a policy of taking one-half year's depreciation in the year of acquisition and one-half year's depreciation in the year of retirement.

Year	Cost of equipment	Estimated		Sales or retirements	
		Service life	Salvage	Year acquired	Cost
1	$220,000	10	20% of cost		
2	84,000	6	20% of cost	1	$27,500

Instructions Prepare a schedule showing beginning balances, additions, reductions, and ending balances for the Equipment account, and for the related

Accumulated Depreciation account, using the following depreciation methods:
a Straight-line
b Sum-of-the-years'-digits
c Percentage-of-declining-balance (double straight-line rate)

12B-3 On July 1, 1970, the Pratt-Houston Die Company established a new manufacturing department which requires a number of different types of machinery. The company uses the sum-of-the-years'-digits method of depreciation and closes its books annually. The transactions involving the machines in this department for a period of three years are described below:

July 5, 1975   Purchased the following machines:

Machine no.	Cost	Estimated salvage	Service life, years
100	$40,000	$8,500	6
101	15,300	1,300	7
102	47,500	2,500	5

Jan. 2, 1976   Purchased machine no. 103 for $60,000. Estimated service life 10 years; estimated salvage value, $5,000.
May 1, 1977   Sold machine no. 100 for $23,000 and replaced it with machine no. 104, which was purchased for $54,000 and has an estimated salvage value of $10,800 at the end of eight years.
Oct. 1, 1978   Traded machine no. 102 for a new machine (no. 105), paying $45,000 in cash and receiving a trade-in allowance (equal to market value) of $16,000. Machine no. 105 has an estimated life of 10 years and estimated salvage value of $6,000.

Instructions
a Prepare a depreciation (lapsing) schedule (illustrated on pages 462 and 463) showing the computation of depreciation for each of the years 1975, 1976, 1977, 1978, and the balances in the Machinery account and Accumulated Depreciation: Machinery account during this period.
b Prepare general journal entries to record the sale of machine no. 100 and the trade-in of machine no. 102. Show computation of the book value of these machines at the time of disposal.

12B-4 Reliable Trucking Co. purchased a fleet of 100 fully equipped trucks on January 1, 1971, for $600,000. The controller of the firm decided to use group depreciation procedures of these trucks, and he estimated the group rate at 21% ($126,000 ÷ $600,000) as follows:

Year	Number of trucks to be retired	Acquisition cost	Estimated salvage value	Amount to be depreciated	Estimated service life, years	Annual depreciation expense
1971	5	$ 30,000	$ 21,000	$ 9,000	1	$ 9,000
1972	20	120,000	72,000	48,000	2	24,000
1973	30	180,000	59,400	120,600	3	40,200
1974	30	180,000	36,000	144,000	4	36,000
1975	15	90,000	6,000	84,000	5	16,800
	100	$600,000	$194,400	$405,600		$126,000

At the end of 1977 when the last truck has been retired, the controller prepared the following summary of the company's actual experience:

Year	Actual number of trucks retired	Actual proceeds received on retirement
1971	4	$ 17,200
1972	11	32,800
1973	28	74,700
1974	42	49,600
1975	8	5,000
1976	5	1,800
1977	2	800
	100	$181,900

The company had followed group depreciation procedures and recorded no gain or loss when the trucks were retired.

Instructions
a Reconstruct the Trucks and Accumulated Depreciation accounts as they would have appeared had the controller's estimates been exactly realized and his computed rate of 21% used as a basis for recording depreciation. Would the controller's rate have produced accurate results if his assumptions had turned out to be correct? Why?
b On the basis of hindsight, that is, the actual record of experience with this fleet, compute the composite depreciation rate that should have been used in depreciating this fleet of trucks. Also determine the composite life of the trucks.
c Using the rate computed in (*b*), reconstruct the Trucks and the Accumulated Depreciation accounts. Explain any balance in the Accumulated Depreciation account at the end of 1977 and state why this balance, if any, differs from the balance in Accumulated Depreciation obtained in (*a*).

12B-5 The following two accounts appear in the records of the Ohio Corporation at December 31, 1975:

Building

Date	Explanation	Debit	Credit	Balance
Dec. 31, 1974	Balance			80,000
Jan. 9, 1975	New boiler, less allowance	14,700		94,700
Feb. 1, 1975	Insurance recovery		1,700	93,000

Accumulated Depreciation: Building

Date	Explanation	Debit	Credit	Balance
Dec. 31, 1974	Balance, 15 years @ 4%			48,000
Dec. 31, 1975	Depreciation for 1975 @ 4%		3,720	51,720

In reviewing the records of the company, you learn that on January 1, 1975, the company's old high-pressure boiler exploded. Damage to the building was negligible but the boiler was replaced by a more efficient oil-burning boiler. The company received $1,700 as an insurance adjustment for damage to the old boiler. A review of the property records discloses that the old boiler was installed at a cost of $10,000 when the building was constructed.

The disbursement voucher charged to the Building account on January 9, 1975, showed the following:

List price, new oil-burning boiler (including fuel tank and 3,000 gallons of fuel oil)	$15,000
Less: Trade-in allowance for old boiler	(1,000)
Sales tax, 5% of $14,000 (net price after trade-in allowance)	700
Total price	$14,700

In verifying expenditures, you note that a voucher for $930 paid to Local Engineering Co. on January 12, 1975, was charged to Repair Expense. The voucher is marked "installation costs for new oil-burning boiler."

The company's fuel oil supplier advised that the price for fuel oil during January was 20 cents per gallon, and on December 31, 22 cents per gallon.

According to its manufacturers, the new boiler should be serviceable for 12 years. The Ohio Corporation consistently treats a fraction of a month as a full month in computing depreciation and plans to depreciate the new boiler over the remaining life of the building (10 years).

Instructions Prepare any correcting journal entries that you would recommend as of December 31, 1975. The books have not been closed. Support your entries with computations in good form.

CHAPTER 13

Intangible assets

know def. of goodwill?
& how to acct.

Nature of intangibles

The basic characteristic that distinguishes intangible from tangible assets is that the former are not physical in nature. In legal terminology this distinction is consistently maintained, the term *intangibles* being applied to all nonphysical properties, including cash, accounts and notes receivable, and investments in corporate securities. The system of asset classification used in accounting, however, places some intangible assets in the "current" and "investment" sections of the balance sheet. Intangible assets for accounting purposes include patents, copyrights, trademarks, trade names, secret formulas, organization costs, franchises, leasehold costs, and goodwill (the excess of cost of an acquired business over the sum of identifiable net assets acquired). Some examples of intangibles included in balance sheets of corporations are presented at the top of page 483.

Some of these companies list other intangibles in their balance sheet. Generally, a note explaining the nature of the intangibles and the amortization policy relating to intangibles accompanies the financial statements.

Intangible and tangible assets have some important similarities since both derive their value from their revenue- and income-generating potential. Mere physical existence (obsolete and inefficient machinery, for example) is no guarantee of economic value, nor does the absence of physical existence (the Listerine formula, for example) preclude economic value. In some businesses the value of intangibles may be greater than the value of the tangible assets.

Consolidated Freightways, Inc.
  Operating rights and goodwill. $11,455,000

General Motors Corporation
  Goodwill—less amortization of $6,344,246 . . . . $57,098,219

National Can Corporation
  Intangibles, excess of cost over net assets of acquired companies $10,698,195

Kinney National Service, Inc.
  Music copyrights, artists' contracts and distribution rights at cost,
  less accumulated amortization of $7,642,000 . . . . $26,892,000

Oxford Industries, Inc.
  Patents and non-compete agreement—at cost, being amortized. . . $ 1,470,933

One reason for distinguishing between tangible and intangible assets is that it is often more difficult to identify intangible property rights. Because you can "stub your toe" on a tangible asset, it is relatively easy to know when you have one. Evidence of the existence of intangible assets is sometimes vague and the relationship between an expenditure and the emergence of an asset is difficult to establish objectively. The economic value of both tangible and intangible assets is dependent on their ability to generate future revenue and earnings, and this is often as difficult to measure for tangible assets as it is for intangibles.

Considerable improvement in the measurement of intangible assets for financial reporting purposes is needed. It is probably safe to say that accounting practices for intangible assets are highly imperfect.

Cost of intangible assets

A business may acquire intangible assets from others or it may develop certain types of intangible assets. The general objectives in accounting for intangible assets are comparable to those for tangible assets; the initial cost should be determined and allocated to the revenue which the intangibles help to generate. A significant and permanent decline in the value of an intangible asset should be charged to expense in the year the decline occurs. Such a write-off should not be shown as an extraordinary item in the income statement.

When an intangible asset is acquired by *purchase,* its cost can be measured with little difficulty. It may be necessary to estimate the value of nonmonetary assets given in exchange for intangibles or to allocate the total cost among various assets acquired as a group. The principles used in dealing with these problems, as previously described in relation to tangible plant assets, are equally applicable to intangibles.

Accounting for intangibles which are *developed* by a company is more difficult. Distinguishing between capital and revenue expenditures (discussed in Chapter 11) applicable to the development of intangible assets is a challenging problem for both management and independent accountants. For example, how much of the total expenditures on research and experimentation should be allocated to a specific patent which results from recurring research and development efforts? Because of the difficulty of this question, there was in the past a tendency to ignore it rather than to grapple with the issue; consequently, expenditures that might have been traced to the development of intangible assets were generally charged to expense. In *Opinion No. 17,* the Accounting Principles Board classified intangibles as *identifiable* and *unidentifiable* and took the following position on the recognition of intangible assets:

> The Board concludes that a company should record as assets the costs of intangible assets acquired from other enterprises or individuals. Costs of developing, maintaining, or restoring intangible assets which are not specifically identifiable, have indeterminate lives, or are inherent in a continuing business and related to an enterprise as a whole—such as goodwill—should be deducted from income when incurred.
>
> Intangible assets acquired singly should be recorded at cost at date of acquisition. Cost is measured by the amount of cash disbursed, the fair value of other assets distributed, the present value of amounts to be paid for liabilities incurred, or the fair value of consideration received for stock issued. . . .
>
> Intangible assets acquired as part of a group of assets or as part of an acquired company should also be recorded at cost at date of acquisition. Cost is measured differently for specifically identifiable intangible assets and those lacking specific identification. The cost of identifiable intangible assets is an assigned part of the total cost of the group of assets or enterprise acquired, normally based on the fair values of the individual assets. The cost of unidentifiable intangible assets is measured by the difference between the cost of the group of assets or enterprise acquired and the sum of the assigned costs of individual tangible and identifiable intangible assets acquired less liabilities assumed. Cost should be assigned to all specifically identifiable intangible assets; cost of identifiable assets should not be included in goodwill.[1]

The Accounting Principles Board thus placed all intangible assets into two categories: (1) those that are specifically *identifiable* and (2) those that are *unidentifiable.* The costs of developing, maintaining, or restoring intangible assets which are not specifically identifiable (such as goodwill) should be deducted from revenue as incurred.

Amortization of intangible assets

The process of systematically writing off the cost of intangible assets is called *amortization.* For many years accountants approached the question of amortization by classifying intangibles into two categories: (1) those having a *limited* term of existence and (2) those with an *indefinite* or *unlimited* term of existence. Those with a limited useful life were amortized; those with an indefinite or unlimited term of existence were maintained intact until they became worthless, at which time they were written off.

[1] *APB Opinion No. 17,* "Intangible Assets," AICPA (New York: 1970), p. 339.

This gave management considerable leeway in accounting for intangibles. In *Opinion No. 17,* however, the Accounting Principles Board established the following rule for intangibles acquired after November 1, 1970:

> The Board believes that the value of intangible assets at any one date eventually disappears and that the recorded costs of intangible assets should be amortized by systematic charges to income over the periods estimated to be benefited.[2]

According to the Accounting Principles Board, then, all intangible assets (identifiable and unidentifiable) must be amortized. The factors which should be considered in estimating the useful lives of intangible assets include:

1 Legal, regulatory, or contractual provisions when they place a limit on the maximum useful life.

2 Provisions for renewal or extension of rights or privileges covered by specific intangible assets.

3 Effects of obsolescence, customer demand, competition, rate of technological change, and other economic factors.

4 Possibility that useful life of intangibles may be related to life expectancies of certain groups of employees.

5 Expected actions of competitors, regulatory bodies, and others.

6 An apparently unlimited useful life may in fact be only *indefinite* and future benefits cannot be reasonably projected.

7 An intangible asset may be a composite of many individual factors with varying estimated useful lives.[3]

The period of amortization for intangible assets should be determined after a careful review of all relevant factors. This should enable management to make a reasonable estimate of useful life of most intangible assets. The cost of intangible assets should not be written off in the period of acquisition unless some extraordinary circumstances caused the intangible to become worthless. According to *Opinion No. 17,* the period of amortization *should not exceed 40 years,* and if a longer useful life is expected, the amortization period should be 40 years rather than an arbitrarily set shorter period.

In the opinion of the authors, the maximum period of amortization of 40 years is much too long. During the current era of major technological innovations and rapid changes in consumer tastes, few intangible assets can be expected to retain their usefulness for 40 years. Many companies probably overstate their net income by choosing a policy of amortizing unidentifiable intangibles over the maximum period allowed.

The accounting procedures for the amortization of intangibles are comparable to those employed for depreciable assets. The cost of intangibles should be amortized in a systematic manner over their estimated service life. A *straight-line* method of amortization is usually employed

[2] *Ibid.,* pp. 339–340.
[3] *Ibid.,* p. 340.

unless management presents a convincing case that some other systematic method is more appropriate. For example, if there is evidence that the value of services expiring in early periods is significantly higher, an accelerated method of amortization may be used.

The amortization of intangibles may be credited directly to the asset account, leaving a balance representing the unamortized cost. This is a matter of custom rather than logic, since an Accumulated Amortization account would be as informative in the case of intangible assets as the Accumulated Depreciation account is in the case of plant assets. The entry to record the amortization of patents, for example, would be:

Amortization Expense: Patents XXX
    Patents (or Accumulated Amortization: Patents)   XXX
To record amortization of patents for current year.

Disclosure of the method of amortization and the estimated useful life of intangibles, as well as the amount of amortization, should be made in the financial statements.

The amortization of intangible assets may be either a factory overhead cost or an operating expense, depending on the nature of the intangible. For example, the expired cost of a patent on a manufacturing process is logically a part of factory overhead, while the amortization of a trademark used to promote the product is a selling expense.

The period used to amortize intangible assets should be continually reviewed to determine whether changing circumstances call for a change in the estimate of useful life. If a change is made in the estimated useful life of intangibles, the unamortized cost should be allocated over the **remaining useful life** of the intangibles. The remaining period of usefulness may be higher or lower than the original estimate. The revised useful life, however, cannot exceed 40 years from the date the intangibles were acquired. A review of the amortization policy may also indicate that a material amount of unamortized cost should be written off as a nonrecurring charge. However, the Accounting Principles Board cautions that "a single loss year or even a few loss years together do not necessarily justify an extraordinary charge to income for all or a large part of the unamortized cost of intangible assets. The reason for an extraordinary deduction should be disclosed." [4]

IDENTIFIABLE INTANGIBLE ASSETS

Certain intangibles, such as patents and copyrights, can be identified as distinct and separable property rights; others, such as goodwill, may be

[4] *Ibid.*, p. 341.

very difficult to identify and thus to account for properly. The more common intangibles which can be identified are discussed in the following sections.

Patents

A patent is a grant by the federal government giving the owner the exclusive right to manufacture and sell a particular invention for a period of 17 years. Patent rights may be assigned in part or in the entirety. Agreements are frequently made under which royalties are paid to the owner of a patent for the right to use or to manufacture a patented product. Legally, patents cannot be renewed, but in practice their effective life is often extended by obtaining patents on slight variations and improvements near the end of the legal life of the original patent.

A patent has economic value only if the protection it affords against competition results in increased earnings through an ability to operate at a lower cost, to manufacture and sell a product, or to charge a higher price for goods and services. The useful life of a patent is generally much shorter than its legal life; therefore amortization over the period of usefulness is usually necessary.

Purchase of Patent If a patent is purchased outright, its cost is measured by the purchase price and related expenditures. The purchase of an existing patent would be recorded as follows:

Patents	*60,000*	
Cash		*60,000*

To record purchase of Patent No. 392468 from Exclusive Designers, Inc.

A patent does not include automatic protection against infringement; the owner must prosecute those who attempt to infringe his patents and defend against infringement suits brought by owners of similar patents. The cost of successfully establishing the legal validity of a patent should be capitalized because it will benefit revenue over the remaining useful life of the patent. If the legal decision is adverse, both the cost of the infringement suit and the unamortized cost of the patent should be written off because no further economic benefits are expected to result from the patent.

The right to use a patent owned by others under a licensing agreement should not be recorded as an intangible asset unless a lump-sum payment is made at the outset of such an agreement. The periodic royalty payments are recorded as factory overhead or as operating expense, depending on the use made of the patent.

Internally Developed Patents: Research and Development Costs When a patent is developed by a company, a careful analysis of costs is required to determine the portion of such costs allocable to the patent. The actual cost of obtaining the patent from the U.S. Patent Office, in terms of drawings, legal fees, and patent fees, is usually small. The research and experimental work that precede the discovery on which a patent is based may be substantial and is often most difficult to measure. The relationship between research and results is often obscure, and it is difficult to determine precisely when the development of any particular discovery began and ended.

Most large companies spend huge sums on research aimed at the discovery and development of improved processes and products. When such research efforts produce an idea that can be patented or copyrighted, an intangible asset can be identified and the related costs should be assigned to it. For example, assume that the sum of $20,000 initially recorded in the Research and Development Costs account is later allocated to a valuable patent. The following entry would be required:

Patents	*20,000*	
Research and Development Costs		*20,000*
To allocate part of research and development costs to Patent		
No. 814231.		

Subsequent accounting procedures for an internally developed patent, such as the one recorded above, would be the same as for a patent purchased from outsiders.

Much research effort results in nonpatentable benefits of a general nature, in the form of better methods and techniques that contribute to future revenue. As these expenditures bulk larger in corporate budgets, their impact on financial statements becomes more significant. An increasing number of firms now recognize the importance of devising cost accounting procedures which will enable them to capitalize research and development costs and to amortize such costs on a reasonable basis. For example, research and development costs may be classified into five categories as follows:[5]

1 *New product development*—experimental effort on new products or product lines

2 *Product improvement*—effort toward improved quality or functional performance of existing products or product lines

3 *Cost and capacity improvement*—effort to develop new and improved processes and equipment, to reduce operating costs, and to improve capacity utilization

[5]Adapted from article by Donald L. Madden, Levis D. McCullers, and Relmond P. Van Daniker, "Classification of Research and Development Expenditures: A Guide to Better Accounting," *The CPA Journal,* (New York: February 1972), pp. 139–142.

4 *Basic research*—experimentation with no specific commercial objective

5 *Safety, health, and convenience*—effort to improve working conditions for employees, reduce pollution, and improve community relations

Classification of research and development costs as suggested above would make it easier to identify the costs that should be deferred and those that should be charged to expense. For example, expenditures in categories 1, 2, and 3 would generally be deferred and amortized; expenditures in categories 4 and 5 would be charged to expense because of the difficulty of identifying the future periods (or revenue) expected to receive benefit.

We should recognize, however, that **APB Opinion No. 17** requires that "a company should record as expenses the costs to develop intangible assets which are not specifically identifiable."[6] To defer costs which cannot be specifically identified with future revenue, or which have questionable service potential, distorts both the income statement and the balance sheet. In recent years many companies accumulated large amounts of deferred research and development costs in their balance sheets. A few years later, some of these same companies wrote off such deferred costs in the year of the "big bath" because of the "deterioration in the demand for the company's products." This, of course, relieved subsequent periods of any amortization charges, and critics were quick to conclude that net income for these companies, both before and after the year of the write-off, was materially overstated. In retrospect, the critics were probably correct.

In **Accounting Research Study No. 14,** research and development costs are classified into categories: (1) continuing research and (2) substantial development projects. The study recommends that costs incurred in continuing research programs should be recognized as expenses immediately; the costs of any substantial development projects, including business-preserving costs which are incurred to preserve the profitability of an enterprise over the long term, should be deferred and amortized over the future periods that they are intended to benefit. The study also calls for more disclosure relating to research and development expenditures and more consistent disclosure practices among companies.[7]

For income tax purposes, all research and development expenditures may be charged to expense as incurred. Congress has thus used the tax law as a means of encouraging research and development activities by reducing the current amount of income taxes payable.

Copyrights

A copyright is a grant by the federal government giving an author, creator, or artist the exclusive right to publish, sell, or otherwise control his literary

---

[6]*APB Opinion No. 17, op. cit.,* p. 334.

[7]Oscar S. Gellein and Maurice S. Newman, *Accounting Research Study No. 14,* "Accounting for Research and Development Expenditures," AICPA (New York: 1973), pp. 6–8.

or artistic products for a period of 28 years, subject to renewal for an additional 28 years. The rights granted under copyrights may be acquired by paying royalties, by outright purchase, or by obtaining a copyright on a product developed within a business. The problems that arise in measuring the cost of copyrights are comparable to those already discussed in connection with patents.

Although a copyright has a potential legal life of 56 years, its economic life is limited to the period of time for which a commercial market exists for the publication. In order to effect a proper matching of costs and revenue, copyright costs should be amortized against the total revenue that is anticipated from the copyright. Because of the difficulty encountered in estimating copyright revenue and because experience indicates that such revenue generally results over only a few years, copyrights are typically amortized over relatively short periods of time. On occasion, copyrights thought to be valueless may bounce back to life with renewed vigor. An outstanding example is old movies: Their production and copyright costs had long since been amortized, but these films suddenly became extremely valuable with the invention of television and the apparent incidence of insomnia among the American people.

Trademarks, trade names, and secret formulas

Trademarks, trade names, secret formulas, and various distinctive labels are important means of building and holding customer acceptance for the products of a company. The value of such product identification and differentiation stems from its contribution to revenue by enabling a firm to sell products in large volume and at prices higher than may be obtained for unbranded items.

Trademarks, trade names, secret formulas, and labels are property rights that can be leased, assigned, or sold. Their service life continues so long as they are used, and their cost should be amortized over their estimated service life or 40 years, whichever is shorter.

The value of a trademark, trade name, or secret formula is often enhanced as the company succeeds in building consumer confidence in the quality of products distributed under a particular brand. Presumably this growth in value is not without cost, since companies typically spend large sums in advertising and otherwise promoting trade names. The relationship between promotional expenditures and the increase in the value of trade names is nebulous; therefore, accountants do not assign a cost to this intangible asset except when it is acquired by purchase.

Organization costs

The organization of a business enterprise usually requires a considerable amount of time, effort, and cost. Compensation must be paid to those who conceive, investigate, and promote the idea; legal fees relating to drafting of corporate charter and bylaws, accounting fees, and incorporation fees will be incurred; and costs may be incurred in conducting initial meetings of stockholders and directors. All these expenditures are made in the expectation that they will contribute to future revenue. It is clear, therefore, that the cost of organizing a business enterprise should logically be treated as an asset and not as a shrinkage in stockholders' equity before activities commence. On the other hand, items such as losses from operations in the early years, bond discount and issue costs, large initial advertising expenditures, or discount on stock issues, should be recorded in separate accounts and not included in organization costs. Expenditures for issuing shares of stock, such as underwriting commissions, professional fees, and printing costs, should be deducted from the proceeds. Similar expenditures relating to issuance of bonds or mortgages should be deferred and amortized over the life of such obligations.

Theoretically the costs of organization have a service life as long as the business remains a going concern and is generating revenue. Since the life of most businesses is not specifically limited, organization costs may be viewed as a permanent asset that will continue in existence until the business is terminated. Despite the logic of this position, organization costs are generally written off over a five-year period, probably because the federal income tax law permits amortization over a period of "not less than five years."

Franchises

A *franchise* is a right received by a business unit for the exclusive right to conduct business in a certain geographic area. The franchise may be granted by a governmental unit or by one business entity to another. For example, public utilities generally receive a franchise from state or federal agencies and are subject to certain regulations; a retailer may obtain an exclusive right from a manufacturer to sell certain products within a specified territory; an operator of a restaurant may obtain the right to utilize certain trade names and recipes developed by another company.

Some franchises granted by manufacturers or retail chains may cost very substantial amounts. The amount paid for such a franchise should be recorded by the *franchisee* as an intangible asset and amortized over its expected useful life. If the right to operate under a franchise is limited to 10 years, for example, the amortization period should not exceed 10 years. While some franchises prove to be worthless within a short period of time, others may increase substantially in value if the location and product prove successful.

The proceeds received by the grantor of the franchise (called the *franchisor*) represent revenue which should be recognized as earned only as contractual commitments to the franchisee are fulfilled.[8]

[8] For a complete discussion on this topic, see *Accounting for Franchise Fee Revenue,* AICPA (New York: 1973).

Leasehold costs

The purchase of an existing lease right and a lump-sum payment to acquire rights to explore for oil and minerals on land are valuable property rights which are frequently included under intangible assets in the balance sheet. Because such assets in effect represent rights in tangible assets, they are occasionally included under plant and equipment.[9]

UNIDENTIFIABLE INTANGIBLE ASSETS: GOODWILL

Thus far we have discussed the major types of identifiable intangibles. The earning power of most prosperous companies, however, is attributable to a variety of factors which cannot be specifically identified either as tangible or intangible assets. Accountants, businessmen, and lawyers often refer to these factors collectively as goodwill.

In ordinary usage the term *goodwill* is associated with a kindly feeling or benevolence. In business and law, however, goodwill has a different connotation. The *most acceptable evidence* of goodwill is the ability of a business enterprise to earn a rate of return on net assets (owners' investment) in excess of a normal rate for the industry in which the business operates. *Goodwill is the difference between the value of a business entity taken as a whole and the sum of the valuations attaching to all its identifiable tangible and intangible assets.* Goodwill is in essence a "master valuation account"—the missing link that reconciles the present value of a business enterprise as a unit with the value of the sum of its parts.

The nature of goodwill

The first obstacle in the path toward an understanding of goodwill is the problem of estimating the value of a business enterprise as a unit. The value of the business may be greater than the amount of identifiable tangible and intangible assets because of the presence of unidentifiable intangible assets. A simple example may help clear this initial obstruction. Assume that Parke Company is to be sold at the end of Year 10 and that the condensed balance sheet on page 493 is presented as a basis for negotiating an exchange price.

Without regard to the question of evidence, we shall assume that Parke Company is expected to earn an average of $60,000 per year indefinitely into the future.

Since the value of net assets depends directly on their earning power,

[9] For example: United Brands Company recently showed the cost of a leasehold acquired for $3,117,000 under an intangible caption "Trademarks and Leaseholds"; Texas Gulf Sulphur Company included contract rights, unproved properties, and exploration projects under "Property, Plant and Equipment"; Union Oil Company capitalizes leasehold costs of exploratory acreage and intangible drilling expenditures and includes them under "Property" labeled "Exploration and Production."

PARKE COMPANY
Balance Sheet
December 31, Year 10

Cash and receivables	$130,000	Liabilities	$100,000
Inventories.	90,000	Capital stock, $1 par	250,000
Plant and equipment (net) .	280,000	Retained earnings	150,000
		Total liabilities & stock-	
Total assets	$500,000	holders' equity.	$500,000

it is clear that under the assumed conditions of certainty we can value the business as a going concern, without reference to its balance sheet, by determining the present value of future earnings of $60,000 per year. A logical way of appraising this is in terms of the rate of return on alternative investment opportunities of comparable risk. We shall assume this rate to be 10%. If it is possible to earn a 10% return on similar investments, the current value of the prospect of receiving $60,000 per year *in perpetuity* may be computed by determining the amount which must be invested at 10% to earn an annual return of $60,000. This procedure is commonly called *capitalizing income,* and the result in this case is a value for the business of $600,000 ($60,000 ÷ .10).

We might inquire why, if the net assets of this company are apparently worth $600,000, they are shown on the balance sheet at only $400,000 (assets, $500,000 less liabilities, $100,000). One possibility is that Parke Company's accounting records do not reflect the current value of net assets. Inventories and plant and equipment, for example, may be worth considerably more than book value and liabilities may be overstated. If these discrepancies are brought to light during the negotiations, appropriate adjustments should be made.

It is entirely possible, however, that the book value of each asset and liability included in the balance sheet closely approximates its current market value, and still the Parke Company is worth $200,000 more than book value of net assets. Is this an accounting exception to the mathematical truism that the whole can be no greater or smaller than the sum of its parts? Or is it simply the case that some of the parts are not included on the balance sheet? The latter is obviously the more likely explanation, and it is apparent that the missing parts are those characteristics of the business that enable it to earn $60,000 per year (10% of $600,000) rather than $40,000 per year (10% of $400,000). The company apparently has intangible assets that are not recorded on the books. Any of the identifiable intangible assets we have previously discussed in this chapter are possible sources of the unexplained $200,000 in the value of the business enterprise.

For purposes of this illustration, we shall assume that Parke Company has a patent worth $30,000 which is not recorded on the books. After all identifiable assets, both tangible and intangible, have been appraised, only $170,000 ($200,000 − $30,000) now remains unexplained and we have isolated the imputed value of all unidentifiable assets, that is, goodwill. Goodwill exists as an asset, therefore, only because it is impossible to trace and identify separately all sources of the prospective earning power of a business entity.

If identifiable intangible assets of $30,000 and goodwill of $170,000 were added to the assets of Parke Company, the book value of its *net assets* then would be $600,000 (assets of $700,000 less liabilities of $100,000). Then if the company earned $60,000, its earnings would no longer be large in relation to the book value of its net assets. Thus the ability to earn a *superior* rate of return on net assets which *do not include* goodwill is evidence that goodwill exists; the ability to earn a normal rate of return on assets which *include* the goodwill and all identifiable intangibles is evidence of the existence of goodwill in the amount computed.

Negative goodwill

Goodwill, as we have defined it, can be either positive or negative in amount. Suppose, for example, that the prospective earnings of Parke Company had been estimated at only $35,000 per year indefinitely into the future and that its identifiable net assets are fairly stated at $400,000. On a 10% basis, the capitalized value of these earnings is $350,000 ($35,000 ÷ .10), and it is evident that the book value of the net assets exceeds the value of the company as a whole by $50,000. This $50,000 may be referred to as *negative goodwill.*

When the earning potential of a business is such that the business as a whole is worth less than its net assets, the owners would be better off to dispose of the assets piecemeal, pay the liabilities, and terminate the business. In reality this may not be done because of concern for the welfare of employees, willingness of the owners to continue operating an unprofitable business, optimism about future prospects, or other considerations. Since the presence of negative goodwill suggests that liquidation is the best course of action, positive goodwill is more likely to be found in going concerns than negative goodwill. Although negative goodwill exists in many unsuccessful businesses, it is not isolated and reported in the balance sheet; the only evidence of its existence is a *low rate of return* on net assets.

If a business with negative goodwill is sold as a going concern, the value assigned to the net assets acquired by the buyer should not exceed the *cost actually paid.* The total market value of identifiable assets acquired less the liabilities assumed may occasionally exceed the price paid for the acquired business. According to *APB Opinion No. 16,* such an excess over cost should be allocated to reduce the values assigned to noncurrent assets in determining their fair values. If this allocation reduces noncurrent assets to zero value, the remaining excess of net assets acquired over cost should be classified as a deferred credit and amortized over a period not exceeding 40 years.[10]

Recognition of goodwill (excess of cost over net assets acquired)

The high degree of certainty about the future assumed in measuring the goodwill of the Parke Company, in the example cited, does not exist in the real world. Assessing the earnings potential of a business is a most uncertain process, and any resulting estimate of enterprise value is a matter of judgment and opinion.

In the face of this uncertainty, accountants have adopted a rule of caution with respect to goodwill. It is generally accepted that goodwill should be recognized in accounting records only when its amount is substantiated by an arm's-length transaction. Since goodwill cannot be either sold or acquired separately, accounting recognition of goodwill is restricted to those occasions in which the entire net assets of a business or a substantial interest in the net assets representing a clearly defined segment of a business are purchased and goodwill can be established with reasonable objectivity.[11] In such cases goodwill is frequently labeled as *Excess of Cost over Net Assets Acquired.*

Limiting recognition to *purchased goodwill* is admittedly not a perfect solution to the problem. *Nonpurchased goodwill* may actually exist in a business and not be recorded; on the other hand, goodwill acquired in the past may appear in the accounting records when there is no current evidence (in terms of earning power) that it actually exists. The financial statements of companies that have changed hands will appear to be inconsistent with those of companies that have had a continuing existence. For example, assume that Parke Company, which was discussed earlier, has identifiable net assets of $430,000 and that a new company is formed to take over its net assets for $600,000 in cash. The opening balance sheet of the new company would show goodwill of $170,000. Is there any justification for a rule that refuses recognition of $170,000 goodwill on the books of Parke Company but permits recording this amount on the balance sheet of the new company?

On balance, an affirmative answer is warranted. Specific assets represent resources in which the capital of a business entity is invested, to the extent that it has been possible to determine them. The periodic adjustment of these asset valuations by a variable amount labeled

[10] *APB Opinion No. 16,* "Business Combinations," AICPA (New York: 1970), p. 321.
[11] Cases in which goodwill is recognized in connection with the transfer of partnership interests and in the preparation of consolidated financial statements are presented in *Advanced Accounting.* Our discussion at this point will be limited to goodwill arising out of the *purchase* of the entire business for cash. When a going business is acquired in exchange for shares of stock, the transaction generally would be treated as a *pooling of interests.* Goodwill may be recognized in a purchase-type transaction but not in a pooling of interests. This subject is briefly discussed in Chapter 16.

"goodwill" to a level consistent with the present value of future earnings would not only be a highly subjective undertaking but would also obscure the significant relationship between actual investment and earning power. If $170,000 of goodwill had been recorded on the books of Parke Company, not only would there be a serious question as to the validity of this amount, but the high level of earnings on investment that Parke Company had been able to attain would be concealed. The investment of the new owners, on the other hand, was not $430,000 but $600,000. The new owners paid $170,000 for anticipated earnings in excess of normal, and if *only* $170,000 of excess earnings should materialize, this amount will not represent income to the new owners but a recovery of their investment. The position that goodwill should be recognized on the books only when it is evidenced by a purchase transaction appears to be consistent with the basic assumptions underlying the determination of accounting income.

Estimating the amount of goodwill

The price to be paid for a business is established as the result of bargaining between independent parties. The bargaining process will take into account the possible existence of goodwill. The amount of goodwill *to be recorded,* however, will be determined after the terms of the contract are set by deducting all identifiable net assets from the total purchase price. Accountants are interested in the process of estimating goodwill because they are often called upon to aid in establishing the value of a business at the time of negotiations for the purchase or sale of a business, in court cases, and in similar circumstances.

Steps generally followed in estimating the value of an enterprise, and thus the amount of goodwill, are as follows:

1 Estimate the current market value of all identifiable tangible and intangible assets, and deduct from this total the amount of all liabilities. This gives the identifiable net asset value of the business.

2 Forecast the average annual earnings that the business expects to earn in future years with present facilities.

3 Choose an appropriate rate of return in order to estimate the normal earnings the business *should earn* on its identifiable net assets.

4 Compute expected annual superior earnings, if any.

5 Capitalize the expected annual superior earnings (if any) at an appropriate rate of return to arrive at an estimate of the present value of such earnings. The present capitalized value of expected annual superior earnings is the estimated value of goodwill.

In the following sections, an estimate of goodwill will be developed for the Reed Company (which is for sale) to serve as a framework for a discussion of the problems that arise in connection with each of the five steps listed above.

Estimating the Current Value of Identifiable Net Assets   Since book values and market values of assets seldom correspond, an appraisal of identifiable assets is necessary in order to establish the value of the business (excluding goodwill) and to identify the assets which generate the earnings of the business.

The book value of current assets, such as cash and receivables, will usually approximate market value. Inventories, if carefully taken and priced on a fifo or average-cost basis, may also be reasonably stated. Lifo inventories, however, are probably stated in terms of costs incurred many years earlier and should be adjusted to current market value. The book values of plant assets are not likely to approximate fair market value. Various methods of indirect valuation may be employed in making an appraisal of such assets on a going-concern basis. The value of any identifiable intangible assets known to exist should be estimated, even if these assets do not appear in the accounting records. The liabilities of the firm should be carefully reviewed, and any unrecorded liabilities should be estimated and recorded. Liabilities which will not be assumed by the new owners should be ignored, unless payment from present assets is contemplated before the business changes hands. Assets at appraised values, less liabilities to be transferred, gives the adjusted amount of net assets for purposes of estimating goodwill.

The following assumed data for the Reed Company illustrate the process of estimating the current market value of identifiable net assets of a business as described above.

REED COMPANY
Book Values and Appraisal of Net Assets—December 31, Year 10

Items	Book value	Adjustments	Estimated current market value
Cash, receivables, marketable securities	$142,000	$ (2,000)	$140,000
Inventories (lifo)	178,000	42,000	220,000
Plant and equipment (net)	480,000	120,000	600,000
Patents and secret formulas	-0-	30,000	30,000
Total assets	$800,000	$190,000	$990,000
Less: Liabilities	160,000	10,000	170,000
Net assets	$640,000	$180,000	$820,000

Forecasting Expected Average Earnings   The aggregate value of any business depends upon its future earnings, not its past earnings. Thus, the key step in any estimate of the value of a going business is a forecast of the future earnings, a process which, unfortunately, can never be more than an intelligent guess. Because the immediate past history of a business ordinarily affords the best available evidence and is most relevant, the usual procedure is to compute the average earnings of the business during the past three to six years and to project them into the future, adjusting for any changing conditions that can be foreseen. The estimate of future conditions and earnings is generally made by the parties to the transaction and not by the accountant. A single year's performance is clearly not a sufficient basis for judgment; on the other hand, little may be gained by reaching too far into the past because both the internal and external conditions influencing business operations may have changed radically.

In attempting to compile a record of past earnings suitable for use in estimating earnings potential, two points should be kept firmly in mind:

1 We are not interested in establishing what past earnings were, but in learning what past experience can tell us about probable future earnings.

2 Our objective is to obtain an estimate of future earnings that is consistent with the adjusted current values of specific identifiable tangible and intangible assets.

It is seldom possible to obtain satisfactory data by simply taking an average of past reported earnings. A more reasonable approach is to work from actual revenue and expense figures, since changes in revenue and expenses are more likely to be related to projected economic and operating conditions. The effect on earnings of a 10% increase in revenue and a 15% increase in operating expenses, for example, may need to be determined. Past data should be adjusted for changes in the value of assets. For example, if inventories and equipment have been understated in terms of current values, adjustments of past cost of goods sold and depreciation expense must be made. Extraordinary items should generally be omitted from past earnings. In view of the subjectivity of estimates and income measurement, minor adjustments can be ignored.

In evaluating an average of past data, particular attention must be given to **significant trends.** Two companies may, for example, have the same five-year average sales, but if the sales of one company have increased in each of the past five years, while the sales of the other have steadily declined, the average sales figure should be interpreted differently.

An important point, often overlooked in adjusting past earnings in the light of future expectations, is that improvements in earnings expected as a result of the efforts of new owners and management should be carefully distinguished from prospective improvements that can be traced to existing conditions. If the buyer of a business expects to make changes in management, production methods, products, and marketing techniques that will increase earnings in the future, he should not include these in valuing the business since they flow from **his** efforts and he should not pay for them.

The schedule shown below is a continuation of the Reed Company example. It represents an assumed computation at December 31, Year 10, of estimated future earnings, based upon an average of the results experienced over the past five years. This estimate might be interpreted by the prospective buyer to indicate a probable range of future annual earnings for the Reed Company of, say, between $90,000 and $120,000 per year. However, for illustrative purposes, we shall use the figure of $106,000.

REED COMPANY

Estimate of Average Future Earnings

Revenue:

  Average annual revenue for past five years, which is expected to be typical of future years (extraordinary gains and losses have been excluded) $920,000

Expenses:

  Average cost of goods sold and operating expenses for past five years, excluding depreciation and income taxes $635,600

  Add: Anticipated annual increase in wages and fringe benefits as the result of a new contract 45,800

  Less: Average of the five-year increase in inventory valuation not included in the lifo basis of pricing inventories ($42,000 ÷ 5) . . . . (8,400)

  Depreciation and amortization:

    Average depreciation on book value 24,000

    Add: Increase in depreciation on the basis of current value (25% increase in value) 6,000

    Amortization of patents and secret formulas, not previously carried on books ($30,000 over useful life of 6 years) 5,000   708,000

Expected average future earnings before income taxes $212,000

Less: Estimated income taxes (50%) 106,000

Estimated average future earnings $106,000

Choosing an Appropriate Normal Rate of Return The rate of return used in capitalizing future earnings and in separating superior from ordinary earnings is determined on the basis of the risks and alternatives involved. The objective is to approximate the rate necessary to attract capital to this particular business under the existing risk conditions. The cost of capital, like other costs, varies in relation to a wide variety of factors. The primary cause of differences in the rate of return necessary to attract capital to different kinds of investment at any given time is the variation in the amount of risk involved.

Data on average earnings rates for companies in particular industries are available in financial services, trade association surveys, and government publications. Care should be exercised in using such figures to be sure that they are being applied to comparable situations, for example, that the earnings rate is consistently assumed to be either before or after income taxes. We shall assume for purposes of illustration that a reasonable normal rate of return for the Reed Company is 10% *after income taxes.*

Computing Estimated Future Superior Earnings The amount of estimated future superior earnings may be defined as the amount of earnings expected in excess of that which constitutes normal earnings on the current value of identifiable tangible and intangible net assets.

All variables necessary to compute the estimated future superior earnings of the Reed Company have been discussed and can now be illustrated. The current estimated value of Reed Company's net assets is $820,000 (see schedule on page 497), and its average future earnings are estimated at $106,000. Since a 10% after-tax rate of return is enough to attract an investment in this company, estimated future superior earnings can be determined as follows:

Estimated average future earnings	$106,000
Less: 10% return on current value of identifiable net assets,	
$820,000 × 10%	82,000
Estimated future superior earnings	$ 24,000

This computation shows that $82,000 ($820,000 × 10%) per year is necessary to support a valuation of $820,000 for the identifiable net assets of the Reed Company. Since the company's prospects are for earnings in excess of $82,000, the source of this excess earning power must be unidentifiable intangibles (goodwill) which enable the company to earn a higher than normal rate of return.

Estimating the Present Value of Superior Earnings—The Final Step A number of different methods can be used in valuing the estimated future superior earnings and thus arriving at an estimate of goodwill. Four methods are illustrated below:

Method 1 *Estimated future superior earnings are capitalized at normal rate of return.* One assumption is that the superior earnings of $24,000 per year, as determined above, will continue unimpaired into the future and that this prospect is entirely attributable to the existing resources of the firm. The annual superior earnings are *capitalized* in answering the following question: How much capital should be invested if the annual return on the investment is $24,000 in perpetuity and the desired rate of return is 10% per year? Under this approach, goodwill would be estimated in one of two ways, as follows:

a *Value of estimated annual average earnings of $106,000 capitalized at 10% in perpetuity, $106,000 ÷ .10* $1,060,000

Less: Estimated current value of identifiable net assets 820,000

Goodwill . . . . $ 240,000

b *Value of estimated future superior earnings capitalized at 10% in perpetuity (goodwill), $24,000 ÷ .10* . . . . $ 240,000

There are serious flaws in the assumptions on which this method rests. It may be reasonable to forecast that a firm will be able to earn a 10% return on its net assets over a very long period of time, but the assumption that superior earning power will persist in perpetuity in the face of competitive pressures and the hazards of free enterprise is optimistic, to say the least. Furthermore, even if superior earnings do continue, it will seldom be possible to trace their lineage to a condition present in the business at the time of acquisition. The frictions that erode superior earnings are such that a persistent ability to earn a higher than normal rate of return will ultimately be due to some additional propellant in the form of research, innovations, efficiency, and business acumen on the part of the new ownership and management.

Method 2 *Estimated future superior earnings are discounted for a limited number of years to determine the present value of such earnings.* The estimate of goodwill may be modified in several ways to allow for the fragile and ephemeral nature of superior earnings. One approach is to assume that any estimated future superior earnings will continue for a *limited period,* say, three, five, or ten years. The *present value* of a given series of superior earnings at a given rate of return can be computed by the use of compound interest principles as described in Appendix A. In the Reed Company example, if estimated future superior earnings of $24,000 will continue for a five-year period, the present value of this prospect on a 10% basis is approximately $91,000, determined as follows:

Estimated future superior earnings $24,000

Present value of ordinary annuity of five payments of $1 each, discounted at 10% . . . . ×3.7908

Present value of estimated future superior earnings (goodwill) $90,979

Method 3 *Estimated future superior earnings are capitalized at a higher-than-normal rate of return.* A variation of method 1 is to use a higher discount rate to capitalize estimated future superior earnings than is used to capitalize normal earnings. For example, if the normal rate of return is considered to be 10%, then a rate of, say, 20, 30, or 40% may be used to capitalize superior earnings. The higher assumed rates of return would allow for greater risk, since the prospect that superior earnings will continue unimpaired into the future is **much more uncertain** than the prospect of continued normal earnings. Referring once more to the Reed Company illustration, if superior earnings of $24,000 per year are capitalized at 30%, for example, goodwill is estimated at $80,000, as follows:

Estimated future superior earnings	$24,000
Discount rate	30%
Capitalized value of estimated future superior earnings discounted at	
30% in perpetuity (goodwill), $24,000 ÷ .30	$80,000

Under this approach, the earnings prospects of the Reed Company have been divided into two layers—$82,000 of normal earnings, and $24,000 of superior earnings—and a different discount rate has been used to value each layer. Any number of different layers and any number of different discount rates might be used in estimating the value of goodwill.

Method 4 *Estimated future superior earnings for a given number of years are purchased.* Another rule-of-thumb approach to the calculation of goodwill is to multiply estimated future superior earnings by a number of years and to refer to the result as a "number of years of estimated future superior earnings purchased." For example, a goodwill estimate of $120,000 is sometimes described as "the purchase of five years of estimated future superior earnings at $24,000 per year." Loose statements of this kind may obscure the real issues involved. As noted previously, the present value of five years of estimated future superior earnings of $24,000 discounted at 10% is not $120,000 but approximately $91,000; therefore, no reason exists for paying $120,000 for five years of estimated future superior earnings totaling $120,000 to be received over a five-year period.

Summary of Methods Uncertainty and subjectivity surround each of the variables involved in estimating goodwill. The probable amount of future earnings, the part that represents superior earnings, the length of time, and the appropriate rate to be used in valuing superior earnings—all are variables not subject to objective verification. They can only be estimated within a reasonable range of probability. The illustrated methods indicate the possible range (from highest to lowest) in the value of goodwill for the Reed Company to be:

> *Estimated future superior earnings of $24,000 are capitalized at 10%*
> *in perpetuity* $240,000
> *Estimated future superior earnings of $24,000 for five years are*
> *purchased* 120,000
> *Estimated future superior earnings of $24,000 for five years are*
> *discounted at 10% (rounded)* 91,000
> *Estimated future superior earnings of $24,000 are capitalized at 30%*
> *(to recognize a much higher risk factor) in perpetuity* 80,000

In a transaction involving the purchase of this business, the value assigned to goodwill would probably be set somewhere between $240,000 and $80,000, depending on the relative bargaining power of the buyer and seller. Inability to agree on a specific value for goodwill frequently results in an agreement to pay a minimum amount for goodwill, to be supplemented by additional payments *contingent* on future superior earnings of the acquired company. Such agreements may raise numerous accounting problems. For example, (1) How should the future payments be recorded? (2) How should the earnings be measured on which the contingent payments are based? (3) How should future contingent payments be disclosed in the balance sheet of the company which may be required to pay them? Answers to these questions are beyond the scope of this chapter.

It is sometimes suggested that the market value of the shares of stock outstanding provides a basis for estimating the value of a corporate enterprise. Thus if the Reed Company, whose net assets have a fair market value of $820,000, has 100,000 shares of stock outstanding, quoted on the market at $12 per share, this suggests that the business is worth $1,200,000 and that goodwill should be estimated at $380,000. This contention would have some merit if the market price per share applied to the entire issue of 100,000 shares or to a block representing a substantial and controlling interest in the company. Only a small fraction of the total shares outstanding, however, are normally offered for sale on the market at any given time. The market prices of this floating supply of stock can fluctuate widely within relatively short periods of time and are strongly influenced by short-run factors that may be unrelated to the long-run prospects of the company. Furthermore, there is no quoted market price for the shares of the vast majority of small businesses. Stock prices may be useful as evidence of *relative* values in negotiating a merger through an exchange of stock, and they may also substantiate or cast doubt upon estimates of goodwill reached independently, but they are seldom useful in arriving at a direct valuation of goodwill.[12]

---

[12]For an extensive coverage of the procedures to be followed in placing a value on a going concern, see *Valuing a Company: Practices and Procedures* by George D. McCarthy and Robert E. Healy, The Ronald Press Company (New York: 1971).

Covenant not to compete or goodwill?

When a going business is purchased, the buyer may pay an amount in excess of the fair market value of the identifiable assets acquired. Typically the excess would be recorded as goodwill. There are situations, however, in which a part of the purchase price may be attributable to a restriction placed on the seller not to engage in a competing business for a specified period of time. The purchaser of a retail store or a restaurant, for example, would not want the former owner to open a competing business in the same vicinity soon after selling his business.

A *covenant not to compete* would be incorporated in the purchase agreement, as for example, "the seller agrees not to engage in the restaurant business in the City of Lee for a period of five years." Such a provision obviously has some value to the buyer, and a portion of the purchase price should be assigned to it. While the value of a covenant not to compete is difficult to determine, the buyer and seller should be able to come up with a reasonable price. The value assigned to goodwill should be reduced by the value assigned to the covenant since it represents an *identifiable* intangible asset. For example, if a business with net assets of $100,000 at current value is purchased for $150,000, it would appear that the buyer is paying $50,000 for goodwill. If, however, the parties agree to place a value of $30,000 on a covenant not to compete for five years, the purchase of the business would be recorded as follows:

Net Assets	100,000	
Covenant Not to Compete	30,000	
Goodwill	20,000	
Cash		150,000
To record the purchase of a going business with covenant not to compete and goodwill valued separately.		

The advantage of reducing the recorded value of goodwill is that the covenant can be amortized at the rate of $6,000 per year, and this amortization is a deductible expense for income tax purposes; amortization of goodwill is not a deductible expense in computing taxable income.

Controversy over amortization of goodwill

Whether goodwill arising out of the purchase of a business entity should be amortized has been a controversial issue for many years. Even after the issuance of *Opinion No. 17,* which required the amortization of goodwill acquired after November 1, 1970, many businessmen and accountants have continued to question the wisdom of charging the cost of purchased goodwill against earnings.

Arguments against Amortization   It has been argued that goodwill has an indefinite life and therefore should not be written off until there is evidence that it no longer exists. Supporters of this view maintain that so long as earnings are sufficiently high to indicate that goodwill is unimpaired, it is a permanent asset. To amortize goodwill in the absence of decline in earnings, it is argued, would obliterate the superior earnings which called for the recording of goodwill in the first place. Those opposing amortization point out that goodwill value is not consumed in the process of producing revenue in the same manner as other property rights and that net income should not be reduced by both amortization of goodwill and current expenditures to maintain superior earnings. Further, it is argued that all methods of amortizing goodwill are highly arbitrary because its useful life is not measurable.

Arguments for Amortization   The opposing view is that the amount paid for goodwill actually represents the purchase of a group of unidentifiable intangible assets and superior earnings for a limited number of years. It is argued that unidentifiable intangibles do not last forever and that the realization of superior earnings is not income to the new owners but merely a recovery of investment. Further, all assets are essentially economic resources and can be classified as those with perpetual existence (like land) or those with limited life (like equipment). Goodwill clearly does not have perpetual existence nor is its period of usefulness clearly determinable. Amortization of purchased goodwill over some reasonable period is thus supported on practical grounds because its value is likely to become zero at some future date.

Evaluation of Arguments   Both sides in this controversy agree that goodwill should be written down in the face of clear evidence that it is overstated. If superior earnings are gradually eroded by competitive pressures and other economic conditions, the consequent disappearance of goodwill should be charged against revenue.

The argument against the amortization of purchased goodwill is particularly strong when earnings continue at a level which indicates that goodwill continues to exist. As previously noted, it is doubtful that continuing goodwill stems from a condition existing at the time of purchase. A more likely situation is that goodwill is maintained through the successful efforts of the new owners and management to keep ahead of competition in production methods, new products, advertising, personnel, and research. It is, of course, unlikely that the exact amount of original goodwill which has dissipated will be supplanted by a new layer of internally developed goodwill. Keeping purchased goodwill on the books would be an attempt to compensate for the accounting inconsistency of recording purchased goodwill and not recording internally developed goodwill. As a practical matter, expenditures on research, development, advertising, etc., necessary to maintain superior earning power are often charged to expense. If purchased goodwill were amortized, there would be a duplication of charges—the write-off of the various costs incurred to build and maintain current goodwill, and the periodic amortization of purchased goodwill.

The argument for amortizing goodwill rests on the idea that an investment in goodwill represents the purchase of certain economic advantages that have a limited term of existence. This investment should be accounted for on the same basis as any other productive asset having a limited life. If expectations were exactly realized, that is, if earnings continued unchanged for the period of years used in estimating and amortizing purchased goodwill, the result of amortization might be the reporting of less than normal earnings on the investment of new owners during the amortization period. This squares with reality since the payment for superior earnings makes their ultimate emergence a return of investment, not income.

Deferred charges and preoperating costs

The term *deferred charges* is frequently used in practice to describe long-term prepayments subject to amortization. For example, the costs of issuing bonds produce benefits by making new funds available for corporate use; however, the funds raised will contribute to revenue over the entire outstanding life of the bonds. Similarly, the cost of machinery rearrangements presumably results in a more efficient and valuable plant and should therefore be allocated to revenue over an appropriate number of years. Other examples of items often classified in the balance sheet as Deferred Charges include the following: prepaid income taxes, research and development costs, start-up costs, and certain pension costs.

The use of the term *deferred charges* may be criticized because all assets other than cash, receivables, securities, and land are forms of deferred charges to revenue. Most deferred charges may be properly classified as either plant and equipment (machinery rearrangement) or as intangible assets (oil exploration costs). If a deferrable cost cannot be classified under plant or intangible assets, it should be included under "other assets" in order to avoid a separate balance sheet category for deferred charges.

Deferring an expenditure can only be justified if a genuine asset with future service potential has resulted. Research and development costs should not be deferred simply because they cannot be readily identified with current revenue; if their potential benefit to future revenue is obscure, they should be written off as expenses.

In recent years, a special category of deferred charges has been receiving increasing attention. Costs incurred by companies in the development stage, particularly costs relating to research and development, exploration, promotion, personnel recruiting and training, market planning, and initial financing are designated as *preoperating* or *start-up costs.* Such costs would be accumulated and amortized over a relatively short period when the company emerges from the development stage.[13] Pre-operating costs applicable to abandoned projects and other costs which probably will not be recovered should be written off as expense (or loss) of the period in which the loss of utility becomes apparent.

Plant and equipment and intangibles in the balance sheet

There is a noticeable trend in corporate financial reporting toward includ-ing all noncurrent assets (other than investments) under a single major heading labeled "plant and equipment," "property, plant and equip-ment," "productive assets," "fixed assets," or simply "property." Tangi-ble and intangible assets should be separately shown. The methods of depreciation and amortization used, as well as the amounts of depre-ciation and amortization for the latest period, should be disclosed.

In a recent survey of 600 industrial companies, 334 reported intangible assets in their balance sheets. The most common types of intangibles reported were goodwill (excess of cost over net assets acquired in a business combination), patents, trademarks, brand names, and copy-rights. The following example illustrates the presentation of plant and equipment and intangible assets in the balance sheet:

Plant and equipment:

Land, at cost	$ 350,000	
Buildings (cost $1,640,000, less accumulated depreciation of $185,000)	1,455,000	
Equipment (cost $870,000, less accumulated depreciation of $150,000)	720,000	
Tools and patterns, at estimated value not in excess of cost	25,000	
Total plant and equipment, net of depreciation		$2,550,000

Intangible assets:

Patents, amortized over 12 years	$ 85,000	
Trademarks and trade names, amortized over 20 years	100,000	
Organization costs, amortized over 5 years	15,000	
Goodwill, amortized over 15 years	180,000	
Total intangible assets, net of amortization to date		380,000

Note: Depreciation and amortization amounted to $310,000 for the latest period. The straight-line method is used to compute depreciation and amortization for both financial reporting and income tax purposes.

---

[13] The balance sheet of Westvaco Corporation a few years ago, for example, included a note which stated that preoperating costs incurred at the new mill site, $12,485,000, have been deferred and will be amortized over a five-year period starting in the following year when the mill was expected to be placed in service.

REVIEW QUESTIONS

1 Accountants use the term **intangible assets** in a more limited sense than the legal meaning of this term. Explain. What are two categories of intangible assets?

2 Why is it more difficult to identify and determine the cost of intangible assets than tangible assets? What are some similarities between tangible and intangible assets?

3 Adams Co. has just been organized. The cost of forming the corporation and selling its shares amounted to $85,000. One officer of the company suggests that this amount be charged immediately against the amount paid in by stockholders in excess of the par value of shares. Another suggests that the amount be amortized over a period of five years against retained earnings. Discuss the logic of these two proposals.

4 In computing the book value of stock, security analysts generally eliminate intangibles. Can you defend this practice?

5 Baker Company applied for and received a patent on a manufacturing process. The cost of drawings, legal fees, and patent application fees totaled $10,000. Research expenditures leading up to the patent have been estimated at $60,000. Shortly after the patent was issued, the company spent $25,000 in legal fees in successfully defending against a suit in which it was claimed that the Baker Company's patent infringed upon the rights of a competitor.
   a At what amount should the patent be carried on Baker Company's books?
   b What is the legal life of this patent?
   c What factors should be considered in determining its economic life?

6 The Cook Corporation carries an asset on its balance sheet labeled Research and Development. The company has not obtained any patents as the result of its research efforts. Is this an acceptable accounting procedure? Explain.

7 Davis Company conducts research on the development of new products, improvement of existing products, and improvement of its manufacturing process. How should these research costs be treated for accounting purposes?

8 What amortization policy should be followed for **copyrights, trademarks, secret formulas,** and **preoperating costs?**

9 It has been argued, on the grounds of conservatism, that all intangible assets should be written off immediately after acquisition. Give the accounting arguments against this treatment.

10 What expenditures are properly included in **organization costs?**

11 What is meant by the term **goodwill?** What is the test of the existence of goodwill? What is meant by the term **negative goodwill?** How is negative goodwill reported on the balance sheet?

12 In negotiations for the sale of a going business, an intangible factor called **goodwill** is sometimes estimated by capitalizing average superior earnings, that is, by dividing average superior earnings by an assumed earnings-rate factor. Explain how the average superior earnings are determined and justify the capitalization of superior earnings in estimating goodwill.

13 What is the distinction between *capitalizing* estimated future earnings and measuring the *present value* of estimated future earnings?

14 If all the individual assets and liabilities of a firm are identified and properly valued, goodwill will not exist. Do you agree?

15 Purchased goodwill is usually recorded and reported on the balance sheet; internally developed goodwill is seldom, if ever, recorded. Explain the basis for this apparent inconsistency.

16 Outline five steps usually followed in estimating the amount of goodwill in an existing business. Can the aggregate market value of shares of stock be used as a basis to estimate goodwill?

17 Endo Company has identifiable net assets having an estimated current fair value of $1 million. The company has an indicated ability to earn $160,000 per year and the normal earning rate in this industry is 10%. Describe three methods that might be used to estimate goodwill for the Endo Company.

18 Briefly state the arguments for and against the amortization of goodwill against revenue.

19 In a news release the Sciences Corporation announced that it will write down and charge against earnings all development and start-up expenses and that its future policy will include charging all such costs as current expenses in the period incurred. The company's former policy was to accumulate development and start-up expenses and to amortize these costs for each program on the basis of its revenue or over its anticipated useful life, whichever provided the earlier amortization. The policy change resulted in a write-down of approximately $59 million and the corporation explained the change in accounting as follows: "This policy change is undertaken in an effort to clarify and reduce to the simplest terms the company's financial status, objectives, and prospects. While we believe our past approach was equally accurate and justifiable, the new policy brings with it greater understandability and certainly greater acceptance."
Briefly evaluate the explanation given for making the accounting change.

EXERCISES

Ex. 13-1 Early in 1972, the Razor Corporation acquired a patent with a remaining life of 15 years and an estimated useful life of 8 years. The cost of the patent was $12,400. Early in 1976, the company paid $4,000 to an inventor who claimed that the patent acquired in 1972 infringed on one of his inventions. Prepare entries to record the acquisition of the patent, the payment on the patent infringement suit, and the amortization for 1976.

Ex. 13-2 From the following list of accounts, prepare the intangible section as it would appear in the balance sheet:

Deposits with advertising agency which will be used to promote goodwill	$ 2,500
Organization costs	6,000
Discount on bonds payable	12,500
Excess of cost over book value of net assets of acquired subsidiary	40,000
Patents	8,400

Franchise to operate in state of Texas. $10,000

Deferred marketing costs of introducing new products 15,000

Ex. 13-3 The Big Corporation purchased the entire business and assumed the liabilities of Sam's Bricks for $400,000 in cash. The balance sheet of Sam's Bricks on the date of purchase is shown below:

Assets	$480,000	Liabilities	$150,000
		Sam Summa, capital	330,000
Total	$480,000	Total.	$480,000

The Big Corporation valued the tangible assets of Sam's Bricks at $525,000 and restated the liabilities at $162,500. Included in the purchase agreement is a restriction that Sam Summa cannot operate a competing business for three years; the purchase price of $400,000 includes $30,000 for this covenant not to compete.

Record the purchase of Sam's Bricks on the books of the Big Corporation.

Ex. 13-4 The earnings (before income taxes) of Stine Company for 1975 were $300,000 and included the following:

Extraordinary gains $80,000

Extraordinary losses 35,000

Profit-sharing payments to employees 25,000

Amortization of goodwill 15,000

Amortization of identifiable intangibles. 17,500

Depreciation on building 44,000

The building is worth three times as much as book value and the remaining life will be increased by 100% by the new owner. The new owner would continue the profit-sharing payments to employees. These payments are based on earnings before depreciation and amortization.

What would be the normal earnings for 1975 for purposes of measuring the possible existence of superior earnings?

Ex. 13-5 Net income and stockholders' equity for a three-year period for the La Fonda Restaurant:

Year	Net income	Stockholders' equity end of year
1973	$62,000	$180,000
1974	75,000	200,000
1975	91,000	250,000

Nati Cano agrees to purchase La Fonda Restaurant on the following basis:
(1) 20% is considered a normal return on restaurant investments.
(2) Payment for goodwill is to be determined by capitalizing at 40% the average annual net income that is in excess of 20% of average stockholders' equity for the past three years.
(3) Net assets, which do not include any goodwill, will be recorded by Nati Cano at carrying value.

Give the entry on Nati Cano's books to record the purchase of the restaurant at the end of 1975.

Ex. 13-6 X Company is planning to purchase Y Company. The past earnings of Y Company have averaged $20,000 per year. It is forecast that Y Company's earnings will be 20% greater in the future. Normal earnings for Y Company are determined to be $16,000 per year.

Compute the amount that X Company should pay for goodwill, assuming that:
a Goodwill is equal to the sum of superior earnings for five years.
b Superior earnings are capitalized at 16%.

Ex. 13-7 Able Company has just acquired Baker Company for $100,000. In acquiring Baker Company, the owners of Able felt that there was unrecorded goodwill associated with Baker's business. They decided to capitalize the estimated superior earnings of Baker Company at 20% to determine the amount of goodwill. The computation to determine goodwill revealed $10,000 worth of this intangible asset. A rate of 10% on net assets before recognition of goodwill was used to determine normal earnings of Baker Company since it is the rate that is earned on net assets in similar industries. All other assets of Baker were properly recorded.

What are the estimated annual earnings of Baker Company?

SHORT CASES FOR ANALYSIS AND DECISION

Case 13-1 The following footnote explaining the composition of "other assets" appeared in the annual report of Software & Research Corporation for Year 2:

Deferred development expenses	$10,860,000
Debt issuance expense, net of amortization	372,000
Other miscellaneous receivables, cash value of life insurance, etc.	783,000
Total other assets	$12,015,000

Deferred development expenses include $8,500,000 relating to a computerized reservations system. Although the computerized reservations system started producing revenue in Year 1, start-up and development operations will continue through Year 3. Costs during this period, net of revenue, are being deferred and will be amortized on a unit-of-revenue basis through Year 6. The deferred computerized reservations system expenses are detailed as follows:

Development expenses (principally software)	$2,591,000
Expenses, net of revenue during start-up and development period	5,505,000
Interest capitalized	404,000
Total	$8,500,000

In addition to the deferred expenses, equipment (principally computer terminals) costing $6,840,000 is included in properties. The company believes that total costs related to the system will be recovered through future operations.

Instructions
a Evaluate the balance sheet presentation of the items included under "other assets."
b Comment on the capitalization and amortization policy for "deferred development expenses." Is the terminology acceptable?

Case 13-2 On June 30, 1975, your client, Vandiver Corporation, was granted two patents covering plastic cartons that it has been producing and marketing profitably for the past three years. One patent covers the manufacturing process and the other covers the related products.

Vandiver executives tell you that these patents represent the most significant breakthrough in the industry in the past 30 years. The products have been marketed under the registered trademarks Safetainer, Duratainer, and Sealrite. Licenses under the patents have already been granted by your client to other manufacturers in the United States and abroad and are producing substantial royalties.

On July 1, Vandiver commenced patent infringement actions against several companies whose names you recognize as those of substantial and prominent competitors. Vandiver's management is optimistic that these suits will result in a permanent injunction against the manufacture and sale of the infringing products and collection of damages for loss of profits caused by the alleged infringement.

The financial vice president has suggested that the patents be recorded at the discounted value of expected net royalty receipts.

Instructions
a Explain the meaning of "intangible assets" and "discounted value of expected net receipts." How would discounted value of royalty receipts be computed?
b What basis of valuation for Vandiver's patents would be generally accepted in accounting? Give supporting reasons for this basis.
c Assuming no practical problems of implementation and ignoring generally accepted accounting principles, what is the preferable basis of valuation and amortization for patents?
d What recognition, if any, should be made of the infringement litigation in the financial statements for the year ending September 30, 1975?

Case 13-3 Wayne Chapin started a business in Year 1 with a capital of $5 million to manufacture a new type of sports car.

In Year 1 and Year 2 he invested $2 million in plant, machinery, and tools, and spent $1 million on materials, labor, advertising, and factory overhead in connection with the first experimental model. There was no revenue from sales or other sources in those years. Chapin charged the $1 million to a Deferred Development Cost account, which was reported as an asset in the balance sheet at the end of Year 2.

In January of Year 3, the model was pronounced a success and the factory was ready to produce at the rate of 150 cars per year, to be sold for $6,000 per car. However, because of manufacturing and other problems, only eight cars were produced in Year 3 and 80 cars in Year 4. Sales were five cars in Year 3 and 30 cars in Year 4. Cars on hand are carried on the balance sheet at a standard cost of $3,500 per car. The income statement for Years 3 and 4 as prepared by Chapin is shown below. (Depreciation on plant, machinery, and tools is included in manufacturing costs.)

	Year 3	Year 4
Revenue ($6,000 per car).	$ 30,000	$180,000
Cost of goods sold, at standard cost.	$ 17,500	$105,000
Manufacturing costs in excess of standard costs	131,000	90,000
Administrative and selling expenses	75,000	100,000
Operating loss charged to Deferred Development Cost	(193,500)	(115,000)
Total costs and expenses	$ 30,000	$180,000
Net income	–0–	–0–

Instructions As a CPA called in to render an opinion on the financial statements for Years 3 and 4, discuss the acceptability of the accounting treatment followed by Wayne Chapin.

Case 13-4 The Octane Corporation, a retail fuel distributor, has increased its annual sales volume to a level three times greater than the annual sales of a dealership it purchased in 1970 in order to begin operations.

In 1975, the board of directors of Octane Corporation received an offer to negotiate the sale of the corporation to a large competitor. The majority of the board wants to increase the recorded value of goodwill on the balance sheet to reflect the larger sales volume developed through intensive promotion and the favorable market price of fuel. However, a few of the board members would prefer to eliminate goodwill altogether from the balance sheet in order to prevent "possible misinterpretations." Goodwill was properly recorded in 1970.

Instructions
a Define goodwill and list the techniques used to calculate its tentative value in negotiations to purchase a going concern. To what extent is goodwill dependent on sales volume?
b Why are the "book" and "market" values for goodwill of the Octane Corporation different?
c Discuss the propriety of increasing or eliminating the recorded value of goodwill prior to negotiations for the sale of a going business.

PROBLEMS

Group A

13A-1 The following information is obtained from the records of Electron Corporation and Laser Products, Inc., at January 2, 1975, in connection with a proposed merger of the two companies:

	Electron Corporation	*Laser Products, Inc.*
Assets other than goodwill	$875,000	$540,000
Liabilities	325,000	240,000
Average income before income taxes for years		
1970–1974	136,000	92,000

The values of assets, including goodwill, will be determined as follows: 20% is considered a reasonable pre-tax return on the net assets, excluding goodwill; average pre-tax income for 1970–1974 in excess of 20% on net assets at January 2, 1975, are to be capitalized at 25% in determining goodwill. The following adjustments to average pre-tax income are required before determining the value of each company:

(1) In 1972, Laser Products, Inc., charged to revenue a perpetual franchise. The cost of the franchise was $18,000.
(2) Equipment of Electron Corporation is estimated to be worth $50,000 more than book value; the equipment has a remaining life of 10 years.
(3) Included in the income of Laser Products, Inc., for 1970–1974 are extraordinary gains of $15,500 and extraordinary losses of $33,000.

Instructions Prepare a schedule showing for each company the valuation of (*a*) net assets other than goodwill and (*b*) goodwill.

13A-2 The Mariachi Manufacturing Co. is being audited at the end of 1975, its first year of operations. The accountant for the company recorded numerous transactions in an account he labeled Intangibles. You have been assigned to audit the Intangibles account, which includes the following entries for 1975:

Debit entries:

Jan. 2	Incorporation fees.		$ 17,500
Jan. 2	Cost of stock certificates (engraving, etc.).		1,500
Jan. 10	Legal fees in connection with organization		5,000
Mar. 1	Large-scale advertising campaign during first year		10,000
July 1	Operating loss for first six months of year		12,200
July 7	Research and development costs on abandoned products.		15,000
Aug. 1	Goodwill set up by credit to Retained Earnings pursuant to estimates of future favorable earnings		50,000
Sept. 25	Cost of EDP program for payroll system to be amortized over four years, starting on Oct. 1, 1975		8,000
Nov. 1	Purchase of patent (remaining useful life of five years from Nov. 1)		12,600
Dec. 30	Bonus to design supervisor for his "creative contribution to the 1975 product lines"		3,000
			$134,800

Credit entries:

Jan. 15	Proceeds on sale of capital stock in excess of par value	$60,500	
Oct. 1	Proceeds from sale of potentially patentable design of new product. The costs of developing this design have been charged to expense during 1975 and probably exceeded $10,000	7,500	68,000
Dec. 31	Balance in Intangibles account.		$ 66,800

Instructions

a Prepare journal entries to correct the accounts, assuming that the books are still open for 1975. Any amount allocated to organization costs should be amortized over five years.

b Prepare the intangible assets section of the balance sheet at December 31, 1975.

13A-3 Zocalo Products, Inc., is considering the acquisition of Aztec Art Company. The data below are available to the management of Zocalo Products, Inc., relating to the Aztec Art Company:

Net assets (stockholders' equity)	$259,600
Total assets on latest balance sheet	400,000
Pre-tax earnings for prior three years ($56,000 + $46,000 + $56,400)	158,400
Dividends paid in cash during last three years.	60,000

Aztec Art Company has a valuable patent which is not recorded on the books and which would be transferred to Zocalo Products, Inc., at $50,400. Other assets have a value equal to book value. The estimated remaining useful life of the patent is no more than five years. The earnings of Aztec Art Company during the next four years are estimated to average 10% more than the average earnings of the past three years (before taking into consideration the amortization of patents).

Instructions Estimate the amount of goodwill under each of the following independent assumptions.

a Average estimated future pre-tax earnings are capitalized at 15% in arriving at the total value of the business.

b Pre-tax earnings at the rate of 14%, based on identifiable net assets at appraised value, are considered minimal for this type of business. Goodwill is estimated to be equal to average superior earnings capitalized at 20%.

c Minimum pre-tax earnings rate on identifiable net assets at appraised value is considered to be 12½% and goodwill is estimated at an amount equal to estimated superior earnings for three years.

d Pre-tax earnings of $38,000 are considered normal. Goodwill is estimated to be equal to the present value of average superior earnings (before income taxes) for four years, discounted at 20%. The present value of an ordinary annuity of four $100 payments, discounted at 20%, is $258.87. (See if you can compute the amount of goodwill without knowing the present value of the four payments of $100 each.)

13A-4 The Plumer Company was organized early in 1971 to manufacture an electronic device patented by Paul J. Plumer. Plumer has been offered $75,000 for his patent, but at about this time he inherited $100,000 and decided to form his own company, issuing himself 20,000 shares of $5 par value capital stock in exchange for $90,000 cash and his patent, which he recorded at $10,000 on the company records. The company's records, kept by Mrs. Plumer, show the following results (before income taxes):

1971—Loss $10,000	*1973—Income $ 5,000*
1972—Loss 20,000	*1974—Income 45,000*

In the middle of 1971, Plumer established a research and development department in his business to improve the original device and to develop new electronic products. Salaries and other operating costs allocated to this department were:

1971—$28,000	*1973—$ 93,000*
1972— 72,000	*1974— 105,000*

At the beginning of 1973, a patent was obtained on an improvement of the original device and in 1974 the company patented a new electronic component. Because Plumer does not have plant capacity to meet the demand for the new component, he has licensed another company to manufacture the component.

At the beginning of 1975, Plumer is trying to interest a friend in investing additional capital in the business to finance expansion. He thinks that the statements prepared by his wife do not fairly reflect the operating results of the company to date, and he has asked you to prepare a revised income statement for the last four years. Plumer feels that the patents developed to date are worth considerably more than the $10,000 now on the books. He has prepared an analysis of research costs and can demonstrate that costs directly related to the development of patents are as follows:

Improvements on original patent:

1972	$40,000
1973	10,400

New component:

1973	$45,000
1974	43,200

In addition, he points out that $25,000 of research costs charged to expense during 1974 relate directly to a new molding process which looks very promising, and which he expects will result in a valuable patent.

Instructions

a On the basis of this information, prepare a schedule showing the revised yearly income or loss (before income taxes) of the Plumer Company for the years 1971 through 1974. Assume that all patents are to be amortized on a straight-line basis over an estimated useful life as follows: 10 years on the original patent, 8 years on the improvement, and 7 years on the new component. A full year's amortization is to be recorded in 1971 on the original patent, a full year on the improvement starting in 1973, and a full year on the new component starting in 1974.

b Prepare a journal entry at January 1, 1975, to reflect the adjustments summarized in (*a*). Ignore income taxes and assume that amortization is recorded as a credit to the Patents account. The net increase in the income for 1971–1974 as a result of the change in the accounting method for patents and research and development costs should be credited to a Cumulative Effect of Change in Accounting Principle account.

13A-5 The founder of Interiors, Inc., Doyle Z. Williams, is about to retire and plans to make a gift of a substantial portion of his stock. In order to establish the value of the stock for gift tax purposes, it is necessary to make a systematic estimate of the current fair value of the stock, which is closely held and has not been previously offered on the market.

The following data summarize the company's operations for the past three years:

Year	Income before income taxes	Stockholders' equity at the end of year
1972	$180,000	$780,000
1973	210,000	850,000
1974	280,000	920,000
1975	250,000	980,000

The company has outstanding 100,000 shares of capital stock. At the end of 1975, a review of the records indicates that a building, purchased near the end of 1955, is undervalued by $160,000. The building has a remaining service life of 15 years. Items of equipment, purchased early in 1973 and having a remaining service life of seven years, are undervalued by $54,000. In both cases the undervaluation is due to excessive amounts of depreciation charged to expense in 1975 and prior years, on a straight-line basis.

Early in 1974, the company obtained a patent on a new wood glue developed during 1973 and 1974. Research costs relating to this product of $67,000 in 1973 were charged to expense, as was the $8,500 cost of securing the patent early in 1974. The patent is estimated to have an economic life of five years from the beginning of 1974.

Included in income before income taxes for 1974 is a $50,000 taxable amount (net of legal fees) collected as damages for an infringement of the wood glue patent. It is agreed that 10% should be considered a normal rate of return in this business, and that average superior earnings should be capitalized at 25%. The earnings performance of the company during the last three years is considered a fair indication of what may be expected in future years without any additional capital investment, other than the normal retention of earnings. The income tax rate, which has averaged 40% of taxable income during the past three years, is not expected to change.

Instructions

a Compute the adjusted average net income (after income taxes) for the three-year period ending in 1975. (Round to the nearest thousand dollars.)

b Compute an adjusted average stockholders' equity figure for the three-year period ending in 1975. (Use adjusted stockholders' equity at the end of the years 1973–1975 to compute the average.) Be sure to adjust the stockholders' equity as of January 1, 1973, for understatement of building value to that date. (Round the final figure to the nearest thousand dollars.)

c Compute an estimate of the current fair value of the capital stock of Interiors, Inc., at the end of 1975.

Group B

13B-1 Wealthy investor Martin Monroe is considering the purchase of three companies. The latest balance sheets and partial income statements of these companies appear below:

	Company A	Company B	Company C
Total assets	$500,000	$500,000	$500,000
Current liabilities	$100,000	$100,000	$100,000
Bonds payable—8%	-0-	100,000	300,000
Stockholders' equity	400,000	300,000	100,000
Total liabilities & stockholders' equity	$500,000	$500,000	$500,000
Income from operations.	$140,000	$140,000	$140,000
Less: Interest expense on bonds	-0-	8,000	24,000
Income before income taxes.	$140,000	$132,000	$116,000
Income taxes—50%	70,000	66,000	58,000
Net income for latest year	$ 70,000	$ 66,000	$ 58,000

The companies are in the same line of business and are offered for sale. Net income in the foreseeable future will be approximately the same as reported for the latest year. The asking price for each company is equal to the total of (1) net assets as reported on the books and (2) goodwill equal to three times annual net income (after interest and income taxes) in excess of 18% of net assets.

Instructions

a What should be the asking price for each company?

b Explain carefully the reasons for any differences in the asking price.

c Why does Company C evidently have the largest goodwill? Is this logical?

d Assuming that the rate of return on net assets for each company is 15, 20, and 30%, respectively, because of the differences in capital structure and the commensurate risks to stockholders inherent in the use of financial leverage, what would be the asking price for each company?

13B-2 Pleasureview, Inc., operates two television stations. On August 1, 1975, the company contracted with a film distributor for a series of films. The contract gave the company an option to run the films as follows:

40 initial weekly telecasts starting on September 1, 1975

12 reruns of the best films during the summer of 1976

50 more reruns during the period from September 1976 to August 1977

The company plans to run the original series during prime viewing hours, the summer reruns as a late show, and second-year reruns as a late-late show. The expected revenue from advertisers on both stations is estimated by the manager as follows:

Revenue from original 40 weeks	$350,000
Revenue from 12 summer reruns	90,000
Revenue from 50 second-year reruns	60,000

The cost of the film rental rights is $200,000, which Pleasureview, Inc., may elect to pay in installments over a two-year period at the rate of $15,000 per month during the first year (starting on September 30) and $3,120 per month during the second year. These payments include interest at approximately 1% per month on the unpaid balance.

Instructions
a Prepare the entry to record the contract, assuming that the company elects to make payments on the installment basis. Record a discount on contract payable.
b Prepare a schedule showing how you would amortize the film rental rights per telecast over the two-year period.
c Prepare entries to record
  (1) The first payment on the contract
  (2) Amortization of the film rental rights for the year ended December 31, 1975 (after 17 telecasts have been run)
d If Pleasureview, Inc., decided in August of 1976 not to rerun the films during the second year, what entry should be made at this time to write off the unamortized film rental rights?

13B-3 You are investigating the possibility of buying Auto Supply Company, a retail tire and auto store owned by Bob Mills. The audited balance sheet of the company at December 31, 1975, is as follows:

Current assets	$161,500	Current liabilities.	$120,000	
Equipment	186,000	6% mortgage payable.	400,000	
Building	640,000	Total liabilities	$520,000	
Accumulated depreciation:				
equipment and building . . .	(92,500)			
Land	5,000	Bob Mills, capital	380,000	
Total assets	$900,000	Total liabilities & capital . . .	$900,000	

You have examined the business thoroughly and have determined that all assets are fairly stated, except that land is worth at least $25,000. An accountant has examined the income statements of the company over the last five years and reports that operating income (before interest on the mortgage) amounted to $80,000 for 1975. The average unpaid balance of the mortgage payable during the next four years will be $376,700. Because of an expected increase in volume, the operating income for each of the next four years is expected to increase by approximately 10% over the preceding year. The company's present facilities are sufficient to handle the expected increase in volume. Mills has listed his business with a broker at an asking price of $500,000 in cash. You consider 16% a normal rate of return (before income taxes) for a business of this type.

Instructions

a Prepare an estimate of the goodwill of Auto Supply Company at December 31, 1975, under each of the following methods. Round estimate of expected average earnings (before income taxes) and goodwill to the nearest hundred dollars.

  (1) Capitalization of the average expected superior earnings (before income taxes) over the next four years at 16%.

  (2) Purchase of expected superior earnings (before income taxes) for the next four years.

  (3) The present value of average superior earnings (before income taxes) expected over the next four years, discounted at 16%. (The present value of $1 per year for four years discounted at 16% is approximately $2.80.)

  (4) Capitalization of the first $5,000 of expected average superior earnings (before income taxes) at 20%, the next $10,000 at 25%, and the balance at 40%.

b Would you pay the price Mills is asking? Explain.

c Suppose that your investigation had indicated that this business could expect to produce average earnings (before income taxes) of $72,000 per year for an indefinite period. What maximum price would you be willing to pay for the business? Prepare the journal entry to record the purchase on your books (assume a single proprietorship), under the assumption that you purchased the business for this price.

13B-4 At the end of the current year, a buyer is negotiating for the purchase of the Imke Company, whose stock is closely held. As a consultant to the buyer, you have examined the records and have compiled the following pertinent data:

	Book value	Estimated current value
Cash, receivables, marketable securities	$ 70,000	$ 68,000
Inventories (lifo)	48,000	92,000
Plant and equipment (net)	370,000	500,000
Deferred research and development costs	–0–	60,000
Total assets	$488,000	$720,000
Liabilities.	122,000	120,000
Net assets.	$366,000	$600,000

Revenue:	
Total revenue reported during last four years	$2,000,000
Budgeted revenue for the next year	600,000
Cost of goods sold and operating expenses (excluding depreciation and income taxes):	
Total for the past four years.	1,200,000
Budgeted for next year (inventories will be valued on fifo basis)	280,000
Estimated portion of the current value of inventories not reflected in lifo valuation over the last four years (it is agreed that net income is to be increased for this item)	40,000
Estimated increase in annual depreciation on the basis of the current value of depreciable assets	15,000

Depreciation has averaged $50,000 per year during the past four years; it is budgeted at $55,000 for next year, computed on the original cost of the assets. The estimated current value of the research and development data is based on a study of the costs incurred in developing a new package for the company's product. These costs were incurred and charged to expense during the current year; the buyer plans to amortize these costs on a straight-line basis over the next five-year period.

As a consultant to the buyer, you have studied the above data and believe they provide a sound basis for arriving at a fair offering price for the shares. The buyer has agreed that the company's average experience over the last four years and the budget for the next year provide the basis for a reasonable estimate of average annual earnings for the next five years. Income taxes may be estimated at 45% of average estimated income before income taxes. The buyer states that he considers an after-tax return of 10% on net assets a normal return in this industry.

Instructions

a On the basis of the information available, compute an estimate of the average annual earnings available to stockholders for the next five-year period.

b Make an estimate of the Imke Company's unrecorded goodwill on the basis of each of the following approaches:
  (1) The sum of estimated superior earnings for the next $3\frac{1}{2}$ years
  (2) Superior earnings capitalized at 20%
  (3) Superior earnings capitalized at 25%
  (4) The first half of superior earnings capitalized at 20%, the second half at 30%

c Assuming that Imke Company has 20,000 shares of capital stock outstanding, recommend to the buyer (based on the estimates of goodwill compiled in b) a range of price per share that he might reasonably be willing to pay for this stock. Explain the reasoning used to arrive at your recommendation.

13B-5 Dr. J. Hyde has been engaged in the manufacture and sale of drug products. On September 1, 1974 he organized Ethical Drug Corporation, which acquired all the assets and goodwill of the proprietorship in exchange for capital stock. The accountant for the corporation made the following entry to record this transaction:

Cash	50,000	
Accounts Receivable	150,000	
Inventory	70,000	
Equipment (less accumulated depreciation of $38,000)	60,000	
Goodwill	260,000	
Accounts Payable		90,000
Capital Stock, $100 par		500,000
To record purchase of business from J. Hyde.		

All the assets are recorded at their tax bases to the proprietorship except for goodwill, which had a zero cost basis. The fair value of all assets was approximately the same as recorded by the corporation.

The corporation's first fiscal period ended June 30, 1975, and as of that date its trial balance was as follows:

	Debit	Credit
Cash	$ 40,000	
Accounts receivable from customers	290,000 (6)	
Receivable from sale of vitamin business ($100,000 due on April 7 of each year for four years)	400,000 (1)	
Inventory	70,000 (2)	
Land and building	420,000 (3)	
Equipment	100,000 (4)	
Deferred patent costs	170,000 (5)	
Goodwill	130,000 (1)	
Bank loans—current		$ 300,000
Accounts payable		230,000
Capital stock, $100 par		500,000
Sales		2,000,000
Gain on sale of vitamin business		370,000 (1)
Purchases	410,000	
Productive labor	360,000	
Other manufacturing costs	100,000	
Other salaries and wages	350,000	
Advertising	375,000	
Other selling and administrative expenses	131,000	
Organization costs	54,000 (6)	
Totals	$3,400,000	$3,400,000

Explanation of the numbered items on the trial balance follows:
(1) On April 7, 1975, the corporation sold all the goodwill, customer lists, patent rights, etc., for its vitamin business. The vitamin business had been originally developed by Dr. Hyde. The gain on the sale was computed as follows:

Selling price, 20% down and 20% annually for four years $500,000

One-half of goodwill transferred to the corporation and allocable to vitamin business 130,000

Gain on sale (Taxable gain is $500,000 since goodwill had no tax basis. The gain is taxable at the rate of 30% as cash is collected.) $370,000

(2) No entries have been made in the Inventory account. The inventory taken on June 30, 1975, amounted to $90,000.
(3) On January 8, 1975, the corporation purchased a 10-year-old building at a total cost of $420,000, of which $120,000 is allocable to land. The building had an estimated remaining life of 25 years from date of purchase. Depreciation on the building is recorded by using the 150% declining-balance method.
(4) The pill crusher is to be depreciated by using the double-declining-balance method, the other two items by using 150% declining-balance method. An analysis of the Equipment account follows:

Date	Description	Estimated remaining life, years	Amount
Sept. 1, 1974	Equipment acquired from proprietorship (original cost $98,000). .	6	$ 60,000
Jan. 1, 1975	Pill crusher (new)	10	10,000
Mar. 1, 1975	Deluxe press (used)	6	30,000
June 30, 1975	Balance in account		$100,000

(5) An analysis of the Deferred Patent Costs account is shown below. Patents should be amortized on a straight-line basis.

Patent No. 400—Purchased Nov. 1, 1974 (patent expires May 1, 1980). .		$ 66,000
Patent No. 401—Granted on Mar. 31, 1975—estimated useful life, 17 years:		
Legal and other fees relating to securing patent	$ 7,000	
Labor and other costs in developing patent	33,800	40,800
Project X—Patent application filed June 1, 1975 (patent granted July 6, 1975, but has not yet been used to produce revenue):		
Legal and other fees relating to securing patent	$ 6,000	
Labor and other costs in developing patent	30,000	36,000
Project Y—In development stage, expected to result in valuable patent:		
Labor and other costs to June 30, 1975.		27,200
Balance in account, June 30, 1975		$170,000

(6) Organization costs are properly recorded and should be amortized over five years as allowed for income tax purposes. Estimated uncollectible accounts amount to 3% of accounts receivable from customers.

Instructions

a Prepare a work sheet for Ethical Drug Corporation at June 30, 1975, using columns for trial balance, adjustments and corrections, income statement, and balance sheet. Income taxes applicable to current income amount to $105,000. The income tax on the portion of the capital gain which is currently taxable is $30,000. You should also set up a deferred income tax liability for capital gain taxes that will be paid when the balance due on the sale of the vitamin business is collected.

b Prepare a balance sheet for Ethical Drug Corporation at June 30, 1975.

CHAPTER 14

Corporations: contributed capital

One of the striking features of our economy is the dominant role played by the business corporation. Corporations are responsible for the great bulk of our national output of goods and services; they are also the principal source of employment, a major medium for the investment of capital, and a leading factor in the research and development activities which are so rapidly altering the shape and character of our economy.

Efficiency of production and distribution in many industries requires more capital than can be obtained by a single proprietor or a partnership. The large amounts of capital needed for successful entry into many fields of business are most easily acquired by selling stock (units of corporate ownership) to the public. The corporation has reached its present dominant role largely because of its efficiency as a device for concentration of capital. Since the typical business corporation has numerous stockholders who do not participate directly in management, an adequate accounting system has become of particular importance as a means of protecting the interests of these many absentee owners.

Several specific advantages of the corporate form of organization help explain why corporations are so successful in attracting capital. Among these advantages are the following:

1 *Limited liability.* A stockholder has no personal liability for the debts of the corporation in which he invests. Creditors can look for payment only to the corporation itself and not to the personal resources of the owners. Freedom from personal liability is an important factor in encouraging both large and small investors to acquire stock in corporations.

2 *Liquidity of investments in corporate securities.* The owner of corporate securities (especially securities listed on a stock exchange) can sell all or part of his investment for cash at any time. The high liquidity of investments in securities is a major reason for their popularity.

3 *Continuity of existence.* The corporation is a separate legal entity with unlimited life, whereas a partnership may be terminated by the death or retirement of any one of the partners.

4 *Separation of the functions of management and ownership.* By attracting capital from a large number of investors and selecting management on a basis of executive ability, the corporation achieves expert direction of large amounts of resources.

Structure of the corporation

To form a corporation, one or more incorporators submit an application to the corporation commissioner or other designated official of a state government. The application identifies the incorporators, states the nature of the business, and describes the capital stock to be issued. After payment of an incorporation fee and approval of the application, articles of incorporation are issued by the state as evidence of the legal existence of the corporation. The incorporators, who must also be subscribers to shares of the corporation's stock, may now elect a board of directors and approve bylaws to serve as general guides to the operation of the enterprise. The board of directors appoints officers to serve as active managers of the business. Corporate officers usually include a president, one or more vice-presidents responsible for such areas as manufacturing, sales, and industrial relations, a treasurer, a controller, and a secretary. The organization process is completed by issuing to the subscribers stock certificates evidencing their ownership of the corporation.

The corporate form of organization is not limited to stock companies organized for profit. The term *public corporation* is applied to government-owned units (such as the Federal Deposit Insurance Corporation), whereas the term *private corporation* includes all companies which are privately owned. Within the meaning of *private corporation* are both the *nonstock* corporations (churches, universities, and hospitals which are not organized for profit) and *stock* companies which operate to earn a profit and which issue shares of stock to the owners. In this book our attention is focused on the profit-oriented stock company. Within this group, one can also recognize subgroups such as *close corporations* with stock held by a small number of owners (perhaps a family), and *open corporations* with stock available for purchase by the public. Open corporations may be *listed* (traded on an organized stock exchange) or *over-the-counter* (a market in which securities dealers buy from and sell to the public). Listed corporations are also often referred to as *publicly held* companies because the number of shareholders often runs into the hundreds of thousands. These very large corporate enterprises with capital gathered from the general public are to a considerable extent responsible for the present-day importance of financial statements and financial reporting.

Although the laws governing the formation and operation of a stock corporation vary among the several states, these state laws all emphasize certain basic concepts. Every state recognizes the corporation as a separate entity and provides for the issuance of shares of capital stock as units of ownership.

Elements of corporate capital

The word *capital* is used in a variety of meanings; consequently, accountants have developed the following more specific terms to describe important elements of corporate capital.

1 Stated capital or legal capital. Stated or legal capital is that portion of the stockholders' equity which the statutes require to be held in the business for the protection of creditors, as opposed to capital which is available for the declaration of dividends to owners.

2 Contributed capital. Contributed capital is that portion of the stockholders' equity which was invested or paid in by the stockholders, as opposed to capital arising from profitable operations. It includes legal capital.

3 Stockholders' equity or proprietary capital. Stockholders' equity represents the combined total of contributed capital and all other increments in capital from profitable operations or other sources. It is the total equity of the owners.

4 Enterprise capital. Enterprise capital represents the combined interests of the stockholders and the creditors. It represents the total resources under the control of corporate management.

Components of stockholders' equity

The balance sheets of corporations show considerable variation in the terms applied to the various elements of stockholders' equity; in fact, it is unusual to find two balance sheets with identical wording. However the following classification illustrates the underlying theme of classification by source.

1 Contributed capital
  a Capital stock, shown at the par or stated value
    (1) Preferred stock
    (2) Common stock
  b Paid-in capital in excess of par or stated value. Includes amounts paid in by owners in excess of the par or stated value of shares issued. (Formerly called *capital surplus,* which is becoming an outmoded term.[1]) In a few cases, includes amounts donated by non-

---

[1] The 1972 edition of *Accounting Trends & Techniques,* published by the American Institute of Certified Public Accountants, indicates a continuing decline in the use of *capital surplus.* The Committee on Terminology of the AICPA had previously recommended: "The use of the term *surplus* (whether standing alone or in such combination as *capital surplus, paid-in surplus, appraisal surplus,* etc.) be discontinued."

owners, such as a donation by a city to induce a corporation to establish a branch in the area.

2 Retained earnings. Represents the accumulated earnings of the corporation since the date of incorporation minus any losses and minus all dividends distributed to stockholders. (The older term *earned surplus* has largely disappeared, in accordance with the recommendation of the AICPA.) A portion of retained earnings may be earmarked or appropriated, thus labeling it as unavailable for declaration of dividends. These appropriations or reserves are becoming much less common than in the past.

In theoretical discussions, another category of stockholders' equity is often considered: the unrealized increment in the owners' equity that arises if assets are written up to a valuation in excess of cost. Such upward revaluations are difficult to support except in unusual circumstances because of the current policy of adhering to historical cost for valuation of assets. Consequently, capital increments from appraisal increases are seldom encountered in published financial statements. The presentation of stockholders' equity in published financial statements is illustrated in Appendix B at the back of this book.

Rights associated with stock ownership

If a corporation has only one class of capital stock, each stockholder usually has certain basic rights to be exercised in proportion to the number of shares he owns. These rights include: (1) a right to vote for directors and thus to be represented in management, (2) a right to share in dividends declared by the board of directors, (3) a preemptive right to purchase additional shares in proportion to one's present holdings in the event that the corporation increases the amount of stock outstanding, and (4) a right to share in the distribution of cash or other assets if the corporation is liquidated. Variations in these rights are of course encountered in individual cases. A preemptive right attached to existing shares may prove inconvenient to a corporation interested in acquiring other companies by issuance of additional stock. Consequently, this preemptive right has been eliminated (with the approval of stockholders) by many corporations.

Common stock and preferred stock

When only one type of capital stock is issued, it has the basic rights described above and is called *common stock*. However, many corporations, in an effort to appeal to all types of investors, offer two or more classes of capital stock with different rights or priorities attached to each class. Stock that carries certain preferences over the basic issue, such as a prior claim on dividends, is called *preferred stock*. Often a preferred stock conveys no voting rights or only limited voting rights to the holders. The characteristics of preferred stocks vary widely among companies; it is unsafe, therefore, to assume that a preferred stock has any particular rights or priorities without positive determination of its status. The special rights of a particular preferred stock are set forth in the articles of incorporation and in the contract between the corporation and the stockholders.

Class A and Class B stock

Companies issuing more than one class of stock may designate the various issues by letter, as Class A stock and Class B stock. In this case one of the issues is common stock and the other issue has some preference or restriction of basic rights. To determine the significant characteristics of stocks identified by letter, it is necessary to examine the stock certificates or other official statements issued by the company.

Typical characteristics of preferred stock   K NOW

The following features are associated with most preferred stock issues:

1 Preference as to dividends at a stated rate or amount
2 Preference as to assets in event of liquidation
3 Callable at the option of the corporation
4 Absence of voting rights

A preference as to dividends does not give positive assurance that dividends will be paid; it signifies merely that the stated dividend rate applicable to the preferred stock must be paid before any dividends can be paid on the common stock. Unlike interest on bonds and notes, dividends do not accrue. A liability to pay a dividend arises only when the board of directors declares a dividend. Any dividend action by the board must take into consideration (1) whether the corporation is in a legal position to pay a dividend, and (2) whether the present cash position and future corporate plans make it expedient to pay a dividend.

Many preferred stocks have a par value, and this feature permits the dividend rate to be stated either as a percentage of par or as a fixed dollar amount. For example, Georgia-Pacific Corporation has issued a $5\frac{1}{2}$%, $100 par, preferred stock. On the other hand, Sperry Rand Corporation has a $4.50 preferred stock with a par value of $25 but with a prior claim of $100 in the event of redemption or liquidation. Preferred stocks of the no-par variety necessarily state the dividend as a fixed dollar amount. An example is National Gypsum Company's "$4.50 Cumulative Preferred Stock (without par value; callable at $103 a share)."

Cumulative and Noncumulative Preferred Stock   Most preferred stocks have a cumulative provision as to dividends. If all or any part of the stated dividend on a cumulative preferred stock is not paid in a given year, the unpaid portion accumulates and must be paid in a subsequent year *before any dividend can be paid on the common stock.*

A dividend is said to have been *passed* if the directors fail to declare a dividend at the established date for dividend action. Any omitted dividends on cumulative preferred stock constitute *dividends in arrears.* The amount in arrears is not a liability of the company because no liability exists until the board of directors declares a dividend. However, no dividends can be declared on common stock until dividends in arrears on preferred stock have been cleared up and the current period's preferred dividend paid. Consequently, the amount of any dividends in arrears on preferred stock is of importance to investors and to other users of the financial statements, and should always be disclosed. The disclosure is usually made by a footnote to the financial statements.

In the case of noncumulative stocks, a dividend omitted or passed in one year is lost forever to the shareholder. Most investors refuse to buy noncumulative preferred stocks; consequently, this type of security is seldom issued.

As an illustration of the significance of dividends in arrears (and the inherent weakness of a noncumulative preference stock), assume that a corporation has three classes of capital stock, each class having a total par value of $1,000,000 as follows:

6% cumulative preferred stock, $100 par value, issued and outstanding 10,000 shares	$1,000,000
5% noncumulative, second preferred stock $100 par value, issued and outstanding 10,000 shares	1,000,000
Common stock, $10 par value, issued and outstanding 100,000 shares	1,000,000

Assume also that operations were unprofitable in 1974, 1975, and 1976, and no dividends were paid during these three years. In 1977, however, large profits were earned and the company decided on December 31, 1977, that the amount of $500,000 should be distributed as dividends. Despite the equal amounts of capital represented by the three stock issues, the dividend payments would heavily favor the cumulative preferred stock and the common stock. The holders of the noncumulative stock would receive relatively little, as shown by the following schedule:

	6% cumulative preferred stock	5% noncumulative preferred stock	Common stock
Dividends in arrears	$180,000		
Preferred dividends, current year	60,000	$50,000	
Remainder, to common stock	-0-	-0-	$210,000
Total dividends paid	$240,000	$50,000	$210,000

Participating and Nonparticipating Preferred Stock A fully participating preferred stock shares equally with the common stock in any dividends paid after the common stock has received a dividend at a rate equal to the preference rate on the preferred stock. Assume, for example, that X Corporation this year has paid the usual 5% dividend on its fully participating $100 par preferred stock and has also paid a dividend of $5 on the common stock. If any additional dividend is paid to the common stockholders, a corresponding additional amount must be paid on the preferred stock. A partially participating preferred stock is one with a ceiling established limiting the extent to which it participates with the common stock.

Actually, participating preferred stocks are extremely rare. The great majority of existing preferred stocks are of the nonparticipating variety. Consequently, even though a company enters a period of great prosperity and pays very large dividends on its common stock, it will typically pay only the stated rate to the preferred shareholders. A preferred stock is nonparticipating unless the stock certificate specifically provides for participation.

Convertible Preferred Stock Many corporations increase the attractiveness of their preferred stock to investors by including a conversion clause which entitles the holder to exchange his shares for common stock in a stipulated ratio. The holder of convertible preferred stock has the advantage of a preferred claim on dividends and also the option of switching into common shares which enjoy unlimited participation in earnings.

Preferred stock will tend to be converted into common if the dividend rate on the common stock is increased. As long as the conversion privilege is open, the preferred stockholder gains the benefit of any rise in market price of the common stock without actually converting because the price of the preferred will rise in proportion to any rise in the price of the common stock. It is sometimes said that the prices of a common stock and the related convertible preferred stock are "in gear." The primary determinant of when to convert may then be the relative yields of the shares on prevailing market value. In addition, consideration may be given to the greater assurance of continued dividend payments on the preferred stock. For some stocks the conversion option expires after a specified number of years; for others the conversion period is unlimited; and in some cases the conversion rate is subject to change at specified future dates.

Callable Preferred Stock Most preferred stocks can be called or redeemed at the option of the corporation. The call price is specified in the stock contract and is usually set a few points above the issuance price. The existence of the call price tends to set a ceiling on the market value of nonconvertible preferred stock. Any dividends in arrears must be paid when a preferred stock is called for redemption.

If a convertible preferred stock is called, the owner has the privilege of converting the shares into common stock rather than surrendering his investment in the company. Consequently, the market price of outstanding convertible preferred stock tends to move with the price of the common stock even though this amount is well above the call price.

Why does a corporation generally make its preferred stock callable? The call feature is advantageous to the company because the capital obtained through issuance of callable preferred stock will be available as long as needed and can be paid off whenever the corporation desires. In some cases the corporation decides to call the preferred stock after retained earnings are sufficient to finance the enterprise adequately; in other cases the decision to call may be made because other sources of capital offering more attractive terms have become available.

Preferences in Event of Liquidation   Most preferred stocks are preferred over common as to assets in the event of liquidation. The claims of creditors of course take preference over both preferred and common stock. The preference of a preferred stock as to assets usually includes any dividends in arrears in addition to the stated liquidation value. It is not safe to assume that every preferred stock has a prior claim on assets; the status of the stock in the event of liquidation depends upon the specific provisions of the stock contract.

The preference which a preferred stock has in the event of liquidation should be disclosed in the financial statements. In *Opinion No. 10,* the Accounting Principles Board stated:

> Companies at times issue preferred (or other senior) stock which has a preference in involuntary liquidation considerably in excess of the par or stated value of the shares. The relationship between this preference in liquidation and the par or stated value of the shares may be of major significance to the users of the financial statements. . . . Accordingly, the Board recommends that, in these cases, the liquidation preference of the stock be disclosed in the equity section of the balance sheet in the aggregate, . . . rather than on a per share basis or by disclosure in notes.[2]

Preferred Stock Regarded as Owners' Equity   The position of the preferred stockholder is in some respects more like that of a creditor than an owner. Typically the preferred shareholder provides capital to the corporation for an agreed rate of return and has no voice in management. If the company prospers it will probably increase the dividend rate on its common stock, but it will not even consider increasing the dividend on preferred stock. Preferred shares have no maturity date, but the preferred stockholder's relationship with the company may be terminated if the company chooses to call in the preferred stock. Despite this lack of some of the traditional aspects of ownership, the preferred stockholder is regarded as an owner, not as a creditor. It is universal practice to include all types of preferred stock in the owners' equity section of the balance sheet. If the corporation encounters financial difficulties, all claims of

[2]*APB Opinion No. 10,* "Omnibus Opinion—1966," AICPA (New York: 1966), p. 148.

creditors take precedence over the equity of both preferred and common stockholders.

Par value and no-par value stock

In the early history of American corporations, all capital stock was required to have a par value, but since 1912 state laws have permitted corporations to choose between par value and no-par value stock. A corporation which chooses to issue par value stock can set the par at any amount desired, such as $1, $5, or $100 a share. If a corporation subsequently splits its par value stock, the par value of each share is reduced accordingly. For example, General Motors common stock, which has been split several times, now has a par value of 1.66\frac{2}{3}$ per share.

The par value of capital stock is the amount per share to be entered in the capital stock account. This portion of the value of assets originally paid in to the corporation must be kept permanently in the business. The par value of the shares issued thus signifies a cushion of equity capital for the protection of creditors.

The par value device was originally introduced for the protection of creditors but proved less effective than anticipated since the intent of the law could easily be circumvented by issuing stock in exchange for property rather than for cash. In the era before rigorous security laws, large amounts of stock were sometimes issued for mining claims, patents, goodwill, and other assets of unproved value. These assets were usually recorded at the par value of the stock issued in payment, with the result of gross overvaluation of assets and overstatement of invested capital on the balance sheet.

To avoid this abuse of the par value concept and to reduce the incentive for corporations to overvalue assets received in exchange for capital stock, most states enacted legislation permitting corporations to issue stock without par value. It was argued that many naïve investors had in the past assumed that any stock was worth as much as its par value, and that the use of no-par stock would force investors to consider more fundamental factors such as earnings, dividends, and fair value of assets.

The trend for corporations to set par values at quite low amounts, such as $1 or $5 per share, has lessened the effectiveness of the arguments for no-par stock and has also destroyed some of the significance attached to the term par value.

Stated capital

From the viewpoint of stockholders, one of the advantages of the corporate form of organization is that of limited liability. Stockholders are not personally liable for the debts of the corporation; creditors of the corporation must look for payment to the corporation alone and not to the stockholders individually, no matter how wealthy they may be.

What would be the effect upon creditors if the stockholders should withdraw virtually all the cash and other liquid assets from the corporation? Such actions would leave the creditors with uncollectible claims against a "hollow corporate shell." To prevent such harsh treatment of creditors, state laws provide that corporations shall not make payments or distribute assets to stockholders which would reduce the stockholders' equity below a designated amount called *stated capital* or *legal capital.*

If a corporation issues par value stock, the stated capital is equal to the total par value of all shares issued or subscribed. Since it is common practice to set the par value as low as $1 or $5 per share and to issue the stock at perhaps $50 or more per share, it is apparent that the stated capital will often be far less than the total capital contributed by stockholders.

If no-par stock is issued, a few states define the stated capital as the total amount received for the no-par shares. In most states, however, the law permits the board of directors to establish an arbitrary stated value for no-par shares; this stated value is often set at an amount far below the issuance price.

The contributed capital of a corporation may be regarded as an accounting concept, whereas stated capital is a legal concept. The contributed capital is often shown in the balance sheet divided into two portions:

1 Stated capital or legal capital, equal to the par or stated value per share times the number of shares issued
2 The excess of contributed capital over and above the stated or legal capital.

In brief, the stated capital concept requires that stockholders keep a permanent stake in the corporation. This cushion of ownership capital not subject to withdrawal stands between the creditors and any losses incurred by a corporation. Of course the stated capital provision does not fully protect the creditors; if losses incurred by a corporation are so large as to wipe out the stockholders' equity, the losses will then fall on the creditors. In other words, stated capital can be impaired by corporate losses but not by dividends or payments to reacquire the corporation's own shares. The reacquisition of shares of stock involves a payment from the corporation to one or more of its stockholders; if not restricted by law, it could be as injurious to creditors as unrestricted payment of dividends.

The corporation laws of the several states also make provision for formal reduction of stated capital through such procedures as a reduction in the number of issued shares, or by lowering the par or stated value per share. These procedures require formal approval by state regulatory authorities; such approval would presumably not be granted if injury to creditors appeared likely to result.

Accounting for capital stock transactions

A clear understanding of the following terms is necessary in accounting for capital stock transactions:

1 *Authorized capital stock* means the number of shares which the state has authorized a corporation to issue. Typically a corporation will obtain authorization for a much larger number of shares than it plans to issue in the foreseeable future. The securing of authority to issue shares of stock does not bring an asset into existence nor does it give the corporation any capital. Authorization merely affords a legal opportunity to obtain assets through the sale of stock. Consequently, authorization of capital stock does not constitute a transaction to be recorded in the debit-credit structure of accounts. A notation of the event in the general journal and in the ledger account for capital stock is appropriate.

2 *Issued capital stock* is the cumulative total number of authorized shares that have been issued to date. The number of issued shares includes treasury stock, as defined below.

3 *Unissued capital stock* describes the authorized shares that have not as yet been issued to investors.

4 *Outstanding capital stock* is the number of authorized shares that have been issued and are presently held by stockholders.

5 *Treasury stock* means the corporation's own shares which have been issued, fully paid, and reacquired by the issuing corporation but not canceled. Treasury stock is included in issued capital stock as defined above, but is not part of outstanding capital stock.

6 *Subscriptions to capital stock* represent an asset, in the form of a receivable from investors who have promised to pay the subscription price at a future date.

7 *Subscribed capital stock* refers to authorized but unissued shares which are earmarked for issuance under existing contracts with subscribers. The subscribed stock is issued when a subscription contract is collected in full. If financial statements are prepared between the date of obtaining stock subscriptions and the date of issuing the stock, the subscribed stock will appear in the stockholders' equity section of the balance sheet.

Ledger accounts for contributed capital

Investments of capital by stockholders usually require the use of two types of stockholders' equity accounts: (1) capital stock accounts, and (2) accounts for paid-in capital in excess of par or stated value.

Capital Stock Accounts A separate ledger account is used for each class of capital stock. The number of shares authorized and the par or stated value may be recorded by a memorandum entry in the general journal and may also be indicated by a memorandum in the ledger accounts as shown below.

6% Preferred Stock
(Authorized 10,000 shares, $100 par value, cumulative)

Common Stock
(Authorized 1,000,000 shares, no par value, stated value $5)

Accounts for Paid-in Capital in Excess of Par or Stated Value Capital stock is often issued at a price well above the par or stated value. This additional paid-in capital is credited to an account with a descriptive title indicating the source of the capital, such as Premium on Preferred Stock or Paid-in Capital in Excess of Par Value: Common Stock. In the preparation of financial statements, it is not necessary to use the exact titles of the ledger accounts as long as the sources of capital are disclosed. For example, the contributed capital indicated by the preceding account titles might appear in the balance sheet as follows:

Stockholders' Equity

Paid-in capital:
6% cumulative preferred stock, $100 par value (callable at $107 per share), authorized 10,000 shares, outstanding 9,000 shares . . .		$ 900,000
Common stock, no-par, stated value $5, authorized 1 million shares, outstanding 600,000 shares		3,000,000
Paid-in capital in excess of par or stated value:		
On preferred stock	$ 45,000	
On common stock	6,000,000	6,045,000
Total paid-in capital		$9,945,000

Some accountants would prefer to list the paid-in capital applicable to the preferred stock immediately following the listing of preferred stock, and to place the paid-in capital applicable to the common stock adjacent to that capital stock item.

Journal Entries for Issuance of Stock for Cash The following journal entries illustrate issuance of the capital stocks summarized in the above balance sheet.

Cash	945,000	
6% Preferred Stock		900,000
Premium on 6% Preferred Stock		45,000
Issued 9,000 shares of $100 par value, 6% cumulative preferred stock for cash at $105 per share.		
Cash	9,000,000	
Common Stock		3,000,000
Paid-in Capital in Excess of Stated Value: Common Stock		6,000,000
Issued 600,000 shares of no-par common stock with a stated value of $5 per share for cash at $15 per share.		

The account title, Premium on Capital Stock, is an alternative to Paid-in Capital in Excess of Par. It may be used for either preferred or common stock but is generally not used in connection with no-par stock. The word *premium* indicates a particular source of paid-in capital in excess of par value and therefore has a narrower scope than the account title *Paid-in Capital in Excess of Par.* Other sources of paid-in capital in excess of par (such as treasury stock transactions) will be discussed later.

Discount on capital stock

Many states now prohibit the issuance of capital stock at less than par value. In planning a stock issue, a corporation is free to set the par value per share as low as it pleases. Since par value is usually set at an amount considerably below the offering price, the question of discount on capital stock is no longer of much practical importance. The topic deserves brief consideration, however, because of its theoretical implications.

In the past some states required a par value of $100 a share, and some corporations were unable to sell shares at such a high price. Consequently, the issuance of stock at a discount was not unusual. Under the laws of some states, if a corporation became unable to pay its debts, the person to whom stock had been issued at less than par might be held personally liable to creditors of the corporation for an amount equal to the discount on the shares purchased.

If capital stock is issued at a price below par, the amount of the discount should be debited to an account entitled Discount on Capital Stock, which will appear as a deduction (or negative element of paid-in capital) in the stockholders' equity section of the balance sheet. In the past, discount on stock was sometimes treated as a deferred charge and written off against current revenue or retained earnings. There is no theoretical basis for such practices because discount on stock has none of the characteristics of an asset. Moreover, it should be carried on the books as long as the related stock issue is outstanding so that an accurate record of the original investment by stockholders is maintained.

Once stock has been issued, it may be sold by one investor to another at more or less than par without any effect on the corporation's accounts. In other words, discount on capital stock refers only to the original issuance of shares by a corporation at a price below par. To avoid any possibility of a contingent liability to the corporation's creditors, a prudent investor may limit his investments to capital stock bearing the inscription "fully paid and nonassessable."

Assessments on capital stock

Although most states require that stock offered to the public be non-assessable, situations are occasionally found in which a corporation may make an assessment against its stockholders. If the stock was originally issued at a discount, the amount received by assessment may properly be credited to the Discount on Capital Stock account. If the debit balance in the discount account is thereby eliminated, any remaining portion of the assessment should be credited to a separate capital account such as Paid-in Capital from Assessment of Stockholders. This account would be credited with the entire amount of the assessment if the shares were originally issued at a price equal to or in excess of par value.

Issuance price and subsequent market price of stock

The preceding discussion of the issuance of stock at prices above and below par raises a question as to how a corporation decides on the issuance price. For a new issue of stock, the corporation usually sets an issuance price based on such factors as (1) expected future earnings and dividends, (2) present financial condition and reputation of the company, and (3) current demand-supply relationships in security markets.

After a stock has been issued, the subsequent market price at which it is traded among investors will tend to reflect the progress and prospects of the company and such external factors as the state of investor confidence and the general trend of the economy. The current market prices of common stocks often bear no discernible relationship to par value or to original issuance price.

Subscriptions to capital stock

The preceding sections have illustrated the issuance of capital stock for cash, but often stock is sold under a subscription contract calling for payment by the subscriber at a later date. Generally the stock certificates are not issued until the subscription price has been collected in full.

From the corporation's viewpoint, a subscription contract in most states is regarded as an asset (a special type of account receivable), and is recorded by debiting Subscriptions Receivable: Common Stock or Subscriptions Receivable: Preferred Stock. When there are a large number of subscribers, the subscriptions receivable accounts may become control accounts supported by subsidiary ledgers containing an individual account with each subscriber. On the balance sheet, stock subscriptions receivable may properly be included among the current assets, provided that early collection is anticipated.

Some accountants argue that stock subscriptions do not represent an asset, and should be shown as a contra item in the stockholders' equity section. Under this view a subscription receivable is contrasted with the ordinary trade receivable; and it is argued that a stock subscription is a dubious claim against the subscriber because the corporation has not delivered merchandise or rendered services to him. As a practical matter, however, stock subscriptions are usually collected promptly and in full. Moreover, they constitute valid legal claims. The market price of newly subscribed shares often changes rapidly; if the subscription agreements were not binding, an unethical investor might benefit by refusing to pay his subscription contract unless market prices were rising.

The increase in assets caused by obtaining a stock subscription receivable is offset by an increase in stockholders' equity. The accounts to be credited (in the case of par value common stock) are Common Stock Subscribed and Paid-in Capital in Excess of Par. At a later date when the stock is issued, the Common Stock Subscribed account will be debited and the Common Stock account will be credited.

If financial statements are prepared between the date of obtaining subscriptions and the date of issuing the stock, the Common Stock Subscribed account will appear in the stockholders' equity section of the balance sheet. In most states a person who signs a subscription contract immediately acquires the legal rights and privileges of a stockholder, even though he does not receive a stock certificate until he makes payment.

Journal Entries for Stock Subscriptions Assume that subscriptions are received for 10,000 shares of $10 par value common stock at a price of $50 per share.

Subscriptions Receivable: Common Stock	500,000	
Common Stock Subscribed		100,000
Paid-in Capital in Excess of Par		400,000
Received subscriptions for 10,000 shares at $50.		

All subscribers paid one-half of the amounts of their subscription contracts. The entry is:

Cash	250,000	
Subscriptions Receivable: Common Stock		250,000
Made partial collection on all subscription contracts.		

Subscribers paid the balance due on their subscription contracts, with the exception of one individual who had subscribed for 100 shares.

Cash	247,500	
Subscriptions Receivable: Common Stock		247,500
Collected balance due on subscriptions for 9,900 shares.		
Common Stock Subscribed	99,000	
Common Stock		99,000
Issued 9,900 shares after collection of subscriptions in full.		

Defaults by subscribers to capital stock

If a subscriber fails to pay all or part of his subscription, the disposition of the contract and of any amounts paid in by the subscriber will depend upon the laws of the state and the policy of the corporation. If no payment has been made by the subscriber and nothing can be collected from him, the corporation may merely reverse the entry used to record the subscription. If the subscriber has made one or more partial payments prior to default, the entire amount paid in prior to default may be refunded. Or, as an alternative, the amount refunded may be the amount paid in minus any expenses or losses in reselling the shares. Another possible alternative calls for amending the subscription contract to permit the issuance of a reduced number of shares corresponding to the cash collected. Still another alternative under some state laws calls for a forfeiture by the subscriber of the amount paid prior to the default.

Default by a subscriber of course requires writing off the uncollectible subscription receivable; the entry will also include a debit to the account for Capital Stock Subscribed and usually a debit to the Paid-in Capital in Excess of Par account. If the corporation retains permanently any amounts paid in on defaulted subscriptions without issuing shares, this increment in capital may be credited to a separate account with a descriptive title such as Capital from Defaulted Stock Subscriptions or may be included in Paid-in Capital in Excess of Par.

Stockholders' ledger and stock certificate book

In addition to maintaining a general ledger account for each class of capital stock, a corporation must maintain detailed supporting records showing the identity of stockholders. A *stockholders' ledger* contains a separate account for each stockholder showing the number of shares owned by him. When a stockholder sells his shares to another investor, an entry must be made in the stockholders' ledger decreasing the number of shares held by the first stockholder and opening an account for the new stockholder. No entry would be necessary in the general ledger since the amount of stock outstanding remains unchanged. The stockholders' ledger is maintained in number of shares rather than in dollars.

A *stock certificate* book is also necessary to control the amount of stock outstanding. When a certificate is issued, the name of the owner and number of shares are listed on the certificate stub. When a stockholder sells his shares to another, he surrenders the original certificate, which is canceled and attached to the stub. A new certificate is issued to the new stockholder. The open stubs in the stock certificate book indicate the number of shares outstanding. Most large corporations retain an independent stock registrar and transfer agent to control stock certificates and ownership records. Such records are maintained by the use of computers when the volume of transactions is large.

Issuance of two types of securities as a unit DELETE

Corporations sometimes offer preferred and common shares as a unit with no indication of the issuance price of either security considered separately. In other cases one or more shares of common stock may be offered as a so-called "bonus" to the purchaser of a bond. Such unit offerings raise a question as to how the proceeds should be divided between the two issues. The same question arises when a company issues two or more kinds of securities to acquire another business entity. The aggregate par value of preferred and common shares issued as a unit will usually be less than the fair value of the consideration received. How should the additional paid-in capital in excess of par be allocated between the two issues? If either security is concurrently being sold on a cash basis, the known market price of that security can be taken as evidence of the value received for that element of the unit sales; the remainder of the issuance price for a unit of preferred and common is applicable to the other class of stock.

It is also possible that units of preferred and common stock might be issued for a consideration less than the aggregate par or stated values of the shares. In such a case, reference to a known market price for either security would permit determination of the discount to be recorded on one or both of the two classes of stock.

Capital stock issued for property or services DELETE

When stock is issued for assets other than cash, the fair value of the property or the market value of the stock, whichever is more definitely determinable, should be used to record the property received and the related amount of contributed capital. In the absence of an arm's-length sale of property for cash, opinions often differ widely as to its fair value, especially in the case of intangible assets. Consequently, it is appropriate to consider how much the stock would have sold for if offered for cash. The underlying reasoning is that the exchange of capital stock for property is essentially the equivalent of selling these shares for cash and using the cash to buy property. The two separate transactions are telescoped into one by the exchange arrangement.

If the company's stock is actively traded, the cash price of the stock prevailing at the date of the exchange constitutes good objective evidence as to the values exchanged. However, if stock sales are infrequent and of small amount, there is no assurance that the company could have issued a large block of stock for cash without forcing the price down. In some cases of management fraud, the purchase or sale of small quantities of stock for cash at an unrealistic price has been specially arranged to set the stage for an exchange of stock for property at an inflated value.

Either treasury stock or previously unissued stock may be given in exchange for property. However, the cost of treasury shares used for this purpose does not constitute a proper basis of valuation for the exchange unless by chance such cost is equal to the present fair market value of the stock.

The establishing of valuations for property acquired in exchange for capital stock is the responsibility of the corporation's board of directors. The decisions of the board and the use made of appraisals or other valuation techniques should be set forth in the corporate minutes. When a certified public accountant performs an independent audit of the company, he will look for such supporting evidence for property values. It is also within his responsibility to challenge any unreasonable valuations even though these carry specific approval by the board of directors. Under no circumstances should the par value of the shares issued in exchange for property be regarded as the decisive factor in establishing the fair value of the assets acquired.

The valuation problem when a corporation issues capital stock for personal services by employees or outsiders, such as attorneys and accountants, parallels that previously described in the exchange of stock for property. The fair value of the services received is an entirely proper basis of valuation, but the market value of the stock is often more readily determinable and is also an acceptable basis for establishing the amounts involved.

Watered stock ~~DELETE~~

A corporation's stock is said to be *watered* if the stockholders' equity is overstated because of a corresponding overvaluation of assets. The expression "watered stock" stems from the era when cattle raisers sometimes gave their herds quantities of salt and then all the water they could drink just before they were delivered to the markets. The "watered stock" weighed more and brought a higher price.

In a corporation, watered stock usually relates to inflated asset values, although capital stock can also be watered through understatement of liabilities. This factor is less common, however, since most liabilities are listed at contractual amounts or at the present value of future payments.

The most direct approach to eliminating water from a corporate capital structure is through writing down the overvalued assets. The reduction in book value of the assets may be accompanied by a reduction in retained earnings, or by reducing the par value per share or number of shares outstanding. Since such a write-down affects each shareholder in proportion to his holdings, no real loss is involved; the proportionate equities in the net assets are unchanged.

Secret reserves ~~DELETE~~

The existence of *secret reserves* in a corporation is merely one way of saying that the stockholders' equity is understated. Such understatement of stockholders' equity may be achieved by using high depreciation rates, by excessive provision for uncollectible accounts, by using lifo inventory procedures in periods of rising price levels, by charging capital expenditures to expense, or by any other step which understates assets or overstates liabilities. The creation of secret reserves is clearly inconsistent with the maintenance of integrity in financial reporting.

INCORPORATION OF A PARTNERSHIP

When a single proprietorship or a partnership grows into a large-scale enterprise, the owner or owners may consider incorporating so that they can enjoy such corporate advantages as limited liability and the availability of outside capital without loss of control. A new set of accounting records may be opened for the new corporate entity, or the books of the old organization may be adjusted to reflect the results of incorporation and continued in use. Since the unincorporated business is selling its assets, including any goodwill which deserves recognition, to the new corporation, the books of the old organization should be adjusted to reflect current values for the assets. A corresponding adjustment is made to increase or decrease the owners' capital accounts by the amount of gain or loss implicit in the adjustment of asset values.

To illustrate the incorporation of a partnership, assume that Blair and Benson, partners who share profits in an 80 to 20% ratio, organize the Blair-Benson Corporation to take over the partnership business. The balance sheet of the partnership on June 30, 19___, the date of incorporation, appears on page 542.

After an appraisal of the equipment and an audit of the accounts, it is agreed that the following adjustments are warranted:

1 Increase the allowance for uncollectible accounts to $1,000.
2 Increase the inventories to current replacement cost of $30,000.
3 Increase the equipment to reproduction cost new of $70,000, less accumulated depreciation on this basis of $30,500.
4 Recognize accrued liabilities of $1,100.
5 Record goodwill of $10,000.

The Blair-Benson Corporation is authorized to issue 10,000 shares of $10 par value capital stock. It issues 5,500 shares to the partnership, in exchange for which the corporation acquires all the assets of the partnership and assumes all the liabilities. (To avoid the need for issuance of fractional shares to a partnership, it is sometimes convenient for the partners to withdraw small amounts of cash so that their capital accounts may be rounded out.) The 5,500 shares received by the partnership are divided between the partners as indicated by their adjusted capital accounts. This step completes the dissolution of the partnership. Blair-Benson Corporation also sells 1,000 shares for cash to outsiders at $15 a share.

BLAIR & BENSON
Balance Sheet
June 30, 19___

Assets

Cash		$12,000
Receivables	$28,100	
Less: Allowance for uncollectible accounts	600	27,500
Inventories		25,500
Equipment	$60,000	
Less: Accumulated depreciation	26,000	34,000
Total assets		$99,000

Liabilities & Capital

Liabilities:		
Notes payable		$20,000
Accounts payable		15,000
Total liabilities		$35,000
Partners' capital:		
Blair, capital	$47,990	
Benson, capital	16,010	64,000
Total liabilities & capital.		$99,000

Establishing accounting records for the new corporate entity

Although the accounting records of the partnership could be modified
to serve as the records of the new corporation, it is customary and more
satisfactory to open a new set of books for the new corporate entity. The
steps to be taken are as follows:

On partnership books

1 Make adjusting entries for revaluation of assets, including recognition of
goodwill if agreed upon.
2 Record any cash withdrawals necessary to adjust partners' capital accounts
to round amounts. (In some instances the agreement may call for transfer to
the corporation of all assets except cash.)
3 Record the transfer of assets and liabilities to the corporation, the receipt of
capital stock by the partnership, and the distribution of this stock to the
partners in settlement of the balances in their capital accounts.

On corporation books

1 Record the acquisition of assets and liabilities from the partnership at the
adjusted valuations.
2 Record the issuance of capital stock in payment of the obligation to the
partnership.

3. Record the issuance of capital stock for cash to other persons acquiring an interest in the business.

The journal entries to illustrate the performance of these steps in the incorporation of the Blair & Benson partnership appear on pages 544 and 545.

The balance sheet of Blair-Benson Corporation after these transactions is shown below. The corporation could as an alternative have chosen not to transfer the Accumulated Depreciation account and to set up the net carrying value of the equipment at its cost to the corporation.

BLAIR-BENSON CORPORATION
Balance Sheet
June 30, 19___

Assets

Cash		$ 27,000
Receivables	$28,100	
Less: Allowance for uncollectible accounts	1,000	27,100
Inventories		30,000
Equipment	$70,000	
Less: Accumulated depreciation	30,500	39,500
Goodwill		10,000
Total assets		$133,600

Liabilities & Stockholders' Equity

Liabilities:		
Notes payable		$ 20,000
Accounts payable		15,000
Accrued liabilities		1,100
Total liabilities		$ 36,100
Stockholders' equity:		
Capital stock, $10 par value, authorized 10,000 shares, issued and outstanding 6,500 shares	$65,000	
Paid-in capital in excess of par	32,500	97,500
Total liabilities & stockholders' equity		$133,600

Tax aspects concerning incorporation of a partnership

For income tax purposes, no gain or loss is recognized on the incorporation of a partnership if the former partners hold control of the corporation immediately after the transfer. As a result of this rule, the basis of

Entries on partnership books:

Inventories	4,500	
Equipment	10,000	
Goodwill	10,000	
Allowance for Uncollectible Accounts		400
Accumulated Depreciation		4,500
Accrued Liabilities		1,100
Blair, Capital		14,800
Benson, Capital		3,700

To adjust assets and liabilities to agreed amounts and to divide net gain between partners in an 80 and 20% ratio.

Receivable from Blair-Benson Corporation, Vendee	82,500	
Notes Payable	20,000	
Accounts Payable	15,000	
Accrued Liabilities	1,100	
Allowance for Uncollectible Accounts	1,000	
Accumulated Depreciation	30,500	
Cash		12,000
Receivables		28,100
Inventories		30,000
Equipment		70,000
Goodwill		10,000

To record the transfer of assets and liabilities to Blair-Benson Corporation.

Stock of Blair-Benson Corporation	82,500	
Receivable from Blair-Benson Corporation, Vendee . . .		82,500

Received 5,500 shares of $10 par value stock valued at $15 a share in payment for net assets transferred to corporation.

Blair, Capital	62,790	
Benson, Capital	19,710	
Stock of Blair-Benson Corporation		82,500

Distributed capital stock to partners; 4,186 shares to Blair and 1,314 shares to Benson.

the property transferred is the same for the corporation as it was for the partnership. Consequently the depreciation program is continued for income tax purposes on the basis of the original cost of the depreciable assets to the partnership. Control of the corporation is defined for income tax purposes as ownership of 80% of the voting stock and also at least 80% of any other classes of stock outstanding.

A conflict evidently exists between the action required for income tax purposes and that indicated by accounting theory. From the viewpoint

Entries on corporation books:

Cash	12,000	
Receivables	28,100	
Inventories	30,000	
Equipment	70,000	
Goodwill	10,000	
Allowance for Uncollectible Accounts		1,000
Accumulated Depreciation		30,500
Notes Payable		20,000
Accounts Payable		15,000
Accrued Liabilities		1,100
Liability to Blair & Benson, Vendor		82,500

To record acquisition of assets and liabilities from Blair & Benson.

Liability to Blair & Benson, Vendor	82,500	
Capital Stock		55,000
Paid-in Capital in Excess of Par		27,500

Issued 5,500 shares of $10 par value stock at price of $15 a share in payment for net assets acquired from Blair & Benson.

Cash	15,000	
Capital Stock		10,000
Paid-in Capital in Excess of Par		5,000

Issued 1,000 shares of $10 par value stock at $15.

of accounting theory, the assets are appropriately recorded on the books of the corporation at the new cost basis established by the transfer of ownership and substantiated by the market value of the stock issued for these assets. This line of reasoning would also indicate the possibility of a gain or loss to the selling entity. As a practical solution to this conflict between income tax requirements and theoretical considerations, the corporation may wish to maintain a separate set of work-sheet records for depreciable assets to facilitate the computation of depreciation expense allowable for income tax purposes.

REVIEW QUESTIONS

1 Why do corporations often issue two or more types of capital stock?

2 What are the basic rights inherent in ownership of capital stock? What modification of these basic rights is usually found in the case of a preferred stock?

3 If a corporation with cumulative preferred stock outstanding fails to pay any dividend during a given year, what disclosure, if any, should be made in the financial statements?

4 Assume that a corporation has 10,000 shares of $5 cumulative convertible preferred stock of $100 par value and 100,000 shares of common stock of $5 par value. Net income amounts to $50,000 in the first year, $160,000 in the second year, and $300,000 in the third year. At the beginning of the third year, 1,000 shares of preferred stock are converted into common stock at the stipulated rate of four shares of common for one share of preferred. Assuming that the company follows a policy of paying dividends each year equal to 70% of net income, what will be the amount of annual dividends to each class of stock?

5 Distinguish between a convertible provision in a preferred stock and a callable provision. May a preferred stock be both convertible and callable? If so, may both provisions be exercised?

6 In what respects does the position of a preferred stockholder resemble that of a bondholder rather than a common stockholder? How does preferred stock differ from bonds?

7 For what purpose was the par value concept originally required for capital stock?

8 What represents stated capital in the case of par value stock and no-par stock?

9 State briefly the accounting principle to be followed in recording the issuance of capital stock in exchange for services or property.

10 What restrictions are commonly placed upon a corporation to guard against impairment of stated capital?

11 From the following list of features which are sometimes found in preferred stock issues, list the three that you believe are most commonly encountered.
  a Voting   *e* Nonvoting
  b Fully participating   *f* Convertible
  c Callable   *g* Noncumulative
  d Cumulative   *h* Partially participating

12 Are most preferred stocks:
  a Voting or nonvoting?
  b Cumulative or noncumulative?
  c Participating or nonparticipating?
  d Callable or noncallable?

13 May a corporation with a deficit also have watered stock? If so, would the elimination of the water from the stock tend to eliminate the deficit? Explain.

14 May a corporation have both watered stock and secret reserves? Explain.

15 A partnership operated by Mann and Field decided to incorporate as the Manfield Corporation. The entire capital stock of the new corporation was divided equally between Mann and Field since they had been equal partners. An appraisal report obtained at the date of incorporation indicated that the land and buildings had increased in value by 50% while owned by the partnership. Should the assets be increased to appraisal value or kept at original cost when transferred to the corporation's books? If the assets are revalued, will the corporation be permitted to take depreciation for income tax purposes on the increased valuations? Explain.

EXERCISES

Ex. 14-1 Identify each of the following statements as True or False.
(1) Retained earnings can never be greater than the accumulated earnings of the company since the date of incorporation minus any losses incurred and dividends declared.
(2) Paid-in capital in excess of par or stated value is often larger than the amount in the capital stock account.
(3) In a company which has always operated at a profit and has distributed approximately half its earnings as dividends, the amount of contributed capital will be less than the stockholders' equity.
(4) The amount of enterprise capital is increased when a corporation obtains a bank loan.
(5) Stated or legal capital cannot be less than net assets minus retained earnings.
(6) Stated or legal capital is usually less than contributed capital, and contributed capital is usually less than stockholders' equity or proprietary capital.
(7) A ledger account entitled Premium on Capital Stock may properly be included under the balance sheet caption of "paid-in capital in excess of par."
(8) A corporation is said to be "listed" if its capital stock has been designated by state officials as an approved investment by savings banks.
(9) A corporation in which stock ownership has always been limited to members of a single family is properly termed a **close corporation.**
(10) General Motors Corporation is a "private corporation," but it is also a "publicly held corporation."

Ex. 14-2 Briarcliff Corporation obtained authorization for 35,000 shares of common stock and promptly sold all the stock at $25 per share. For each of the following independent cases, prepare the stockholders' equity section of the balance sheet, including as complete as possible a description of the stock sold and making any appropriate change in terminology.

Case A:

Common Stock	Paid-in Capital in Excess of Stated Value
105,000	770,000

Case B:

Common Stock	Premium on Common Stock
245,000	630,000

Ex. 14-3 Given the following information, prepare in good form the stockholders' equity section of the balance sheet of Midland Corporation.

Stock subscriptions receivable, common stock	$ 55,000
Premium on preferred stock	50,000
Common stock, $5 par, authorized 40,000 shares, issued 20,000 shares	100,000
Paid-in capital in excess of par, common stock	150,000
Retained earnings, unappropriated	327,000
Reserve for bond sinking fund	125,000
Common stock subscribed	25,000
7% preferred stock, cumulative, $50 par, authorized 20,000 shares, issued 10,000 shares	500,000
Plant site donated	40,000

Ex. 14-4 Bakersfield Corporation, a successful enterprise, received authorization to issue an additional 100,000 shares of no-par common stock with a stated value of $10 per share. The stock was offered to subscribers at a subscription price of $50 per share. Subscriptions were recorded by a debit to Subscriptions Receivable and a credit to Common Stock Subscribed and a paid-in capital account. A short time later, a subscriber who had contracted to purchase 100 shares defaulted on his contract after paying 40% of the subscription price.

The method used by Bakersfield Corporation in recording the default will depend upon the contractual and legal rights of the defaulting subscriber and especially upon the statutes of the state of incorporation. You are to identify four methods of accounting at the time of the default for the amount paid in prior to the default. Prepare a journal entry for each method to show how the default would be recorded.

SHORT CASES FOR ANALYSIS AND DECISION

Case 14-1 After the cancellation of some of its government contracts, Pacific Dynamics Corporation began production under a new long-term government contract. During the period of operating losses the company had suspended dividend payments on all of its four stock issues. These four issues consisted of a $7 cumulative, $100 par, first preferred stock; a $2.50 noncumulative, convertible, $50 par, preferred stock; a 4%, $100 par, noncumulative Class B stock; and a Class A stock without any dividend preference. Of each issue, 10,000 shares were outstanding. All indicated dividends had been paid through the year 1973, but the company had been unable to pay any dividends in 1974 or 1975. During 1976 the company's position improved greatly, and at a directors' meeting near the end of 1976 a proposal was made to pay a dividend of $2.25 a share on the Class A common stock to stockholders of record December 31, 1976.

James Garth, who owned 100 shares of the $2.50 noncumulative, convertible, $50 par, preferred stock, had been considering converting his 100 shares into common stock at the existing conversion rate of four shares of common for each share of preferred. The conversion rate was scheduled to drop to $3\frac{1}{2}$ to one at the end of 1976. Garth had observed that the price of the common stock was rising rapidly. He explained that he was "torn between a desire to retain his preferred stock until the indicated dividend was received and a desire to convert promptly before the common stock went higher and the conversion rate was reduced."

Instructions
a Determine the amount of cash needed for dividend payments if the proposal to pay a $2.25 dividend on the Class A common stock is adopted. (Assume that there is no conversion of preferred stock.)
b Advise Garth on the merits of converting his stock at this time as opposed to converting after the dividends have been paid and the conversion rate decreased. Explain fully the issues involved.

Case 14-2 The Lakeside Turf Club, Inc., was organized to conduct thoroughbred horse racing for profit. Authorization was obtained to issue 60,000 shares of $10 par capital stock, and an issuance price of $25 a share was agreed upon. In order to stimulate the sale of stock in the newly organized corporation, one of the directors, A. B. Peters, suggested that a nontransferable lifetime pass be issued to each person subscribing to 400 shares or more of stock during the original offering. No more passes would be issued after the original issuance of stock was completed.

The company was licensed to operate only 60 days each year, and planned to erect a racetrack capable of accommodating 10,000 persons. The following schedule of daily admission charges was planned: grandstand $2.50 plus $0.30 tax; clubhouse $3.50 plus $0.50 tax; Turf Club $7 plus $1 tax. About 80% of the company's revenue was expected to be derived from a 5% "take" on amounts wagered by patrons in the pari-mutuel system. In addition, significant amounts of revenue were expected from the bar, restaurant, sales of programs, and parking fees.

Another director, Charles Cross, inquired whether the issuance of life passes as proposed by Peters would require placing a liability on the corporation's books, and if so, how the discharge of this liability would be measured and recorded.

A third director, Donald Grant, stated that he had considered and rejected the life pass idea because of the impossibility of accounting for it properly. He explained that if a person paid $10,000 for 400 shares and a life pass, some portion of the $10,000 received by the corporation should be recorded as a liability rather than as contributed capital. This liability would be reduced every day the pass holder attended the track, but the amount of the decrease, Grant explained, was undeterminable because it rested on the life span of the pass holder.

A fourth director, Edward Evans, supported the life pass plan as "an excellent stock-selling gimmick." "Let's ignore the liability if there is one," said Evans. "Anyone who pays $10,000 for stock in this racetrack will make money for us every day he uses his life pass by the amount he bets."

After further discussion, the directors agreed to have the controller, George French, consider the arguments presented and submit a recommendation as to adoption of the life pass plan and the method of accounting, if any, for the use of life passes by stockholders. The directors specifically asked whether a liability for life passes would be necessary in the balance sheet and if so, at what amount.

Instructions Assume the role of George French, the controller, and write the report requested by the board of directors. Your analysis should include but need not be limited to the following issues:

a Whether accounting difficulties are a valid reason for opposing an operating decision considered sound by management
b The materiality of the lifetime passes in relation to total revenue
c The measurement and amortization of the liability, if any, to lifetime pass holders
d The accounting treatment when representatives of the press (sports writers and photographers) are admitted free to racetracks or other places of entertainment
e The amount of contributed capital to be recorded by Lakeside Turf Club, Inc.

Case 14-3 Topper Company was organized on October 1, 1975, with an authorized capital stock of $1 million par value. Shares with a par value totaling $300,000 were issued in equal amounts to A, B, and C in consideration of their transfer to the company of parcels of commercial real estate as of that date. The company planned to operate the properties as rental property. The Property account was debited and the Capital Stock account credited with $300,000 to record the transaction. No other stock was issued.

On December 31, 1975, an entry was recorded, upon the basis of a resolution passed by the board of directors, increasing the Property account by $1.8 million and crediting a Capital Surplus account with a like amount in order to state the property at its fair market value. The adjusted valuation of $2.1 million is equivalent to twice the assessed value for 1975 property tax purposes, which is the average relationship of current quoted prices of similar property to their assessed value. The company has on file a report from a reputable real estate appraisal firm which states that it considers the value at the date the property was deeded to the corporation to be in excess of $2.5 million.

Instructions You are engaged to examine a balance sheet of the company at December 31, 1975.

a In indicating on the balance sheet the valuation of the property, would you recommend stating the valuation to be:

(1) At valuation appraised by the board of directors

(2) At less than appraised valuation

(3) At cost

(4) At book value

(5) At some other amount

State briefly your reasons why your statement of the valuation is correct.

b State the exact description you think should be used on the balance sheet to explain what the "capital surplus" represents.

Case 14-4 The partnership of Bell, Owens, and Weston operated successfully until Owens and Weston reached retirement age. The partners then agreed to incorporate the business as the Bell Corporation with Bell as president. Capital stock of $10 par value was authorized and issued as follows: Bell 12,000 shares, Owens 6,000 shares, and Weston 2,000 shares. Authorized but unissued stock totaling 30,000 shares remained available for future use. At December 31, 1975, the stockholders' equity amounted to a total of $220,000, including $20,000 of retained earnings.

President Bell decided on January 1, 1976, that more working capital was needed. Both the other stockholders were away on extended winter vacations at this time, so Bell decided to supply the needed capital from his own funds. At the time of incorporating the former partnership, Bell had withdrawn $20,000 in cash because his equity was much larger than that of his partners and the business had excess cash on hand. Bell had immediately invested this $20,000 in common stocks of industrial companies and these investments had increased in value to approximately $30,000. On January 2, 1976, Bell sold his investments and deposited the proceeds of $30,000 in the bank account of Bell Corporation. In return for his investment, he arranged for an additional 3,000 shares of stock to be issued in his name.

When Owens learned of this transaction he protested that his basic rights as a stockholder had been violated. Weston also protested on the grounds that Bell should have taken 2,000 shares rather than 3,000, since this smaller amount would have corresponded to the $20,000 originally withdrawn from the business and invested in industrial stocks. Weston explained that if Bell had not made the cash withdrawal of $20,000, he (Bell) would have been entitled to 2,000 additional shares at the date of incorporation.

Bell denied any intent of wrongdoing but offered to reimburse his former partners for any inequity they could substantiate in a logical manner. There had been no trading in the stock of Bell Corporation at any time.

Instructions Evaluate the objections and arguments presented by Owens and Weston. If you think they have been unjustly treated, suggest a basis for remedying the injustice.

Case 14-5 A few months after the organization of the Mack Corporation, one of the largest stockholders, A. J. Hoyt, offered to transfer to the corporation a tract of land and a factory building in exchange for 11,000 shares of Mack Corporation's $10 par value capital stock. Under the terms of the offer, an existing mortgage of $28,000 on the land and buildings was to be assumed by Mack Corporation.

The board of directors of Mack Corporation determined that the property was well suited to the corporation's needs. The board was informed by the secretary of the corporation that 15,000 authorized but unissued shares were available.

One member of the board, A. C. Sparks, opposed the idea of assuming the mortgage, on the grounds that long-term debt could prove burdensome for a new business without established earning power. He suggested making a counteroffer of 13,800 shares with the understanding that Hoyt pay the mortgage in full at date of transferring the property.

A second director, J. B. Brown, argued against further issuance of stock. He pointed out that the company had just obtained $325,000 in cash from issuance of 26,000 shares of stock, and that this cash should be used to the extent necessary to acquire plant and equipment. Brown proposed that the company offer Hoyt $110,000 in cash, assume the mortgage, and pay it in full immediately.

A third director, W. R. Benson, urged prompt acceptance of Hoyt's offer without modification. Benson produced documents showing that the property had been purchased by Hoyt 10 years previously at a total price of $206,000. He stated that Hoyt had also shown him accounting records indicating depreciation to date on the building of $36,000. In conclusion, Benson stated that these facts showed that the company would be saving $32,000 by accepting Hoyt's offer.

Instructions

a Comment on the logic and reasonableness of the views expressed by each of the three directors. Explain how each arrived at the amounts mentioned.

b Indicate which deal you believe would be most advantageous to the company, assuming that it was acceptable to Hoyt.

c Assuming that the company accepted the original offer by Hoyt, draft the journal entry to record the transaction, and explain fully the principles underlying the entry. Assume that the land is worth half as much as the building.

Case 14-6 Subscriptions receivable to capital stock under most circumstances have traditionally been regarded as an asset; however, the theoretical propriety of this treatment has been questioned. An alternative proposal is to treat subscriptions receivable as a contra to stockholders' equity.

Instructions

a Discuss and justify the traditional treatment of subscriptions receivable to capital stock.

b Present arguments which question the theoretical propriety of the traditional treatment and, instead, lend support to the view that subscriptions receivable should be treated as a contra to stockholders' equity.

Case 14-7 In 1960 a new partnership purchased land on the edge of the town of Midvale, erected a building and opened a furniture and appliance merchandising store under the name of Furniture Fair. The partnership agreement specified that profits or losses would be shared equally after the allocation of partners' salary allowances and interest on average capital balances.

Midvale has grown considerably and the store is now the most prominent in a fashionable suburban area. Good management, imaginative merchandising, and the general increase in the economy have made Furniture Fair the leading and most profitable firm of its type in Midvale's trade area.

Now the partners wish to admit an investor and incorporate the business and have obtained a charter for Furniture Fair, Inc. Each partner will purchase at par an amount of preferred stock equal to the book value of his interest in the partnership and common stock equal to that portion of the fair market value which exceeds the book value. The investor will purchase at a 10% premium over par value common and preferred stock equal to one-third the number of shares of each purchased by the partners. The corporation will then purchase the Furniture Fair partnership at its fair market value from the partners. After the consummation of the partners' plan, the corporation will own the partnership's assets, assume its liabilities, and employ the partners as the management of the corporation.

Instructions (Consider only financial reporting. Do not consider income tax reporting.)

a List and explain the differences in items and valuations that you would expect to find between the assets to appear on the balance sheet of the proposed corporation and the assets which appear on the partnership's balance sheet.

b List and explain the differences that would be expected in a comparison of an income statement prepared for the proposed corporation and an income statement prepared for the partnership.

PROBLEMS

Group A

14A-1 The McConnell Corporation was organized April 30, 19___ with authorization to issue capital stock as follows: 60,000 shares of $5 preferred stock, $100 par value; 240,000 shares of no-par common stock, stated value $5 a share.

During the remainder of the year the transactions affecting stockholders' equity were as follows:

May 15 Received subscriptions to 6,000 shares of preferred stock at $110 a share. A down payment of 50% accompanied each subscription; the balance was to be paid on August 15. (Record the full amount subscribed and then in a separate entry, show the cash collection for 50% of this amount.)

May 17 Received subscriptions to 30,000 shares of common stock at $22 a share, payable August 1.

May 30 Issued 300 shares of common stock in payment for legal and accounting services relating to the organization of the corporation and valued at $6,600.

Aug. 1 Received payment in full of the amount due on common stock subscriptions.

Aug. 15 Received payment in full of the balance due on preferred stock subscriptions.

Aug. 30 Issued 1,500 shares of preferred stock for cash of $156,000.

Aug. 30 Issued 2,000 shares of common stock and 750 shares of preferred stock in exchange for property for which the board of directors established the following values:

Land	*$50,500*
Building	*70,000*
Delivery equipment	*1,700*

Aug. 31 Net income earned to August 31 amounted to $21,000. No dividends had been declared.

Instructions
a Prepare journal entries to record these transactions.
b Prepare the stockholders' equity section of the balance sheet at August 31.

14A-2 The Craig Corporation was organized in September with authorization to issue 400,000 shares of $5 par value common stock and 15,000 shares of $50 par value, 8% preferred stock. A going business was acquired in exchange for 8,000 preferred shares plus the assumption of a mortgage liability of $160,000. The assets acquired in this manner were valued by a firm of independent appraisers at $600,000. Subscriptions were obtained for 20,000 common shares at a price of $15 a share.

All subscriptions were collected promptly except for a subscription by William Marshall for 200 shares. Marshall paid $1,000, but defaulted on the balance of the contract. The 200 shares were resold for cash by the corporation at a price of $14 a share. In accordance with statutes of the state, Craig Corporation refunded the amount paid by Marshall after deducting the loss incurred on the resale of the shares.

Operations for the fractional year ended December 31 resulted in net income of $28,000. No dividends were declared on the common stock. A quarterly dividend of $1 a share on the preferred stock was declared on December 1, payable February 1 to stockholders of record on January 10.

Instructions
a Prepare journal entries relating to the capital stock transactions and the dividend declaration. (Debit Retained Earnings.)
b Prepare the stockholders' equity section of the balance sheet at December 31.

14A-3 After several years of successful operation of a partnership business, the two owners, Ripley and Connors, decided to incorporate the business and to sell stock to outsiders.

On January 1, 1975, the Ricon Corporation was organized with authorization to issue 150,000 shares of $10 par value common stock. It issued 20,000 shares for cash to public investors at $16 a share. Ripley and Connors agreed to accept shares at the same price in amounts equal to their respective capital accounts after making the adjustments indicated below and after making cash withdrawals sufficient to avoid the need for issuing fractional shares. In payment for such shares, the partnership's net assets were transferred to the corporation and stock certificates were then issued.

The post-closing trial balance of the partnership of Ripley and Connors appeared as follows on December 31, 1974:

Cash	$ 31,000	
Accounts receivable	30,000	
Inventory	56,000	
Land	28,000	
Buildings	50,000	
Accumulated depreciation		$ 14,000
Accounts payable		10,000
Ripley, capital		60,000
Connors, capital		111,000
Totals	$195,000	$195,000

The partnership agreement provides that Ripley is to receive 40% of the profits and Connors, 60%. It is agreed that the following adjustments should be made to the partnership accounts at December 31, 1974.
(1) Recognize prepayments of $1,500 and accrued liabilities of $1,000.
(2) Provide an allowance for uncollectible accounts of $12,000.
(3) Increase the value of land to $45,000.
(4) Increase the inventory to present replacement cost of $75,000. A new set of accounting records is to be opened for the corporation.

Instructions
a On the partnership books, make the journal entries necessary to adjust the accounts to the agreed values. (One compound journal entry may be used to adjust the accounts to the agreed amounts.) Also make all other entries needed to record the events described.
b On the corporation books, make the journal entries necessary to record the events described.
c Prepare a balance sheet for the corporation after the above transactions have been recorded.

14A-4 The capital structure of Neilson, Incorporated, consists of an authorized issue of 250,000 shares of $60 par value, 5% cumulative preferred stock and an authorized issue of 600,000 shares of no-par common stock with a stated value of $10 a share. For both the preferred and the common stock, the number of shares issued at the time of organization was less than the amount authorized.

Although early operations of the company were profitable, a prolonged strike caused a net loss of $1,300,000 to be shown for the current fiscal year ended June 30. Because of this year's unprofitable operations, the company paid no dividends on its common stock during the current fiscal year. Dividends of $495,000 were paid this year on the preferred stock, but this limited payment left dividends in arrears at June 30 in the amount of $165,000.

A trial balance of the general ledger taken at May 31 (a month before the end of the fiscal year) included the following balances:

Preferred stock, par $60	$13,200,000
Common stock, no-par, stated value $10	3,500,000
Subscriptions receivable: preferred stock	1,550,000
Retained earnings (June 30, prior year)	2,200,000
Premium on preferred stock	490,000
Preferred stock subscribed	1,500,000
Paid-in capital in excess of stated value: common	2,250,000
Subscriptions receivable: common	1,500,000
Common stock subscribed	1,000,000

Cash was received in June representing payment in full for common stock subscriptions covering 30,000 shares. These subscriptions had been received and recorded prior to May 31. All common stock offerings by Neilson, Incorporated, prior to May 31 had been at the same price.

Other transactions during June were the issuance of an additional 5,000 shares of common stock for cash at a price of $18. Another 1,500 shares of common stock were issued in exchange for a patent.

Instructions

a Compute the average price at which the preferred stock was sold by the company.

b Compute the price at which the common stock was offered by the company prior to June.

c Prepare journal entries to record the transactions during June which affected the stockholders' equity accounts.

d Prepare the stockholders' equity section of the balance sheet at June 30, including any notes which should accompany the balance sheet.

14A-5 On December 31, at the end of its first year of operations, Rangeland Corporation presented a balance sheet containing the following items, among others:

Subscriptions receivable: preferred stock		$ 104,000
Subscriptions receivable: common stock		360,000
4% preferred stock, $100 par, cumulative; authorized		
100,000 shares, issued and outstanding, 22,000 shares . . .	$2,200,000	
4% preferred stock subscribed, 2,000 shares	200,000	2,400,000

Common stock, $10 par value, authorized 200,000 shares,
issued and outstanding, 24,000 shares . . . . $ 240,000
Common stock subscribed, 24,000 shares . . . .   240,000 $ 480,000
Paid-in capital in excess of par:
  On preferred stock   16,000
  On common stock   976,000

The corporation had been organized on January 2 and had immediately received subscriptions to 20,000 shares of preferred stock. Subscriptions to common stock were received on the same date. (The number of common shares subscribed and the subscription price can be determined from information given in the problem.) On May 5 subscriptions were received for an additional 4,000 shares of preferred stock at a price of $104 a share.

Cash payments were received from subscribers at frequent intervals for several months after subscription. The company followed a policy of issuing stock certificates only when subscribers had paid in full. On December 22, Rangeland Corporation issued 8,000 shares of its common stock in exchange for a tract of land with a fair market value of $256,000. (Subscriptions were not used in this transaction.)

Instructions

a Prepare journal entries for all the transactions carried out during the year by Rangeland Corporation, as indicated by the December 31 account balances.

b Compute the amount of contributed capital for each class of stock at the year-end. Also determine the amount of stated capital applicable to the common stock.

Group B

14B-1 On March 31, Southwind Corporation was organized and authority received from the state to issue securities as follows:

    $5 preferred stock, $100 par value, 50,000 shares
    Common stock, no-par, stated value $5 a share, 200,000 shares

After this authorization to issue stock, the following transactions affecting stockholders' equity occurred during the remainder of the year.

Apr. 15 Received subscriptions to 5,000 shares of preferred stock at $105 a share. A down payment of 40% accompanied each subscription; the balance was to be paid on July 15.

Apr. 17 Received subscriptions to 25,000 shares of common stock at $20 a share, payable July 1.

Apr. 30 Issued 200 shares of common stock in payment for legal and accounting services relating to the organization of the corporation and valued at $4,000.

July 1 Received payment in full of the amount due on common stock subscriptions.

July 15 Received payment in full of the balance due on preferred stock subscriptions.

July 30 Issued 1,000 shares of preferred stock for cash of $104,000.

July 30 Issued 1,200 shares of common stock and 500 shares of preferred stock in exchange for property for which the board of directors established the following values:

Land	$30,800
Building	41,000
Delivery equipment	4,000

July 31   Net income earned to July 31 amounted to $23,600. No dividends had been declared.

Instructions
a Prepare journal entries to record the preceding information.
b Prepare the stockholders' equity section of the balance sheet at July 31.

14B-2 On October 1 Northwest Corporation was organized with authorization to issue 10,000 shares of $100 par value, 7% preferred stock and 200,000 shares of $10 par value common stock. The first transaction by the new corporation was the acquisition of a going business in exchange for 5,000 shares of the preferred stock plus the assumption of a mortgage payable in the amount of $140,000. A firm of independent appraisers presented a report showing a valuation of $700,000 for the assets acquired in this transaction.

Subscriptions to 10,000 shares of common stock at a price of $30 a share were obtained. All the subscriptions were collected with the exception of a subscription for 100 shares by John Rhine. After paying $1,000, Rhine defaulted on the subscription contract. Northwest Corporation resold the 100 shares for cash at a price of $29 a share. As required by state statutes, Northwest Corporation then refunded to Rhine the amount he had paid minus the loss incurred on the resale of the 100 shares.

For the fractional year from the date of organization, October 1, to December 31, the operations of the corporation produced net income of $35,250. A quarterly dividend of $1.75 a share on the preferred stock was declared on December 31, payable February 1 to stockholders of record on January 15. No dividends were declared on the common stock.

Instructions
a Prepare journal entries for all transactions relating to the stockholders' equity, including declaration of the preferred dividend.
b Prepare the stockholders' equity section of the balance sheet at December 31.

14B-3 Whitney and Ford, after several years of successful operation as a partnership, decided to incorporate and sell stock to outsiders in order to obtain the capital needed for expansion of their growing business.

At December 31, 1975, an after-closing trial balance of the partnership of Whitney and Ford appeared as follows:

Cash	$ 11,000	
Accounts receivable	102,000	
Inventory	153,000	
Land	90,000	
Buildings	244,000	
Accumulated depreciation		$ 45,000
Accounts payable		42,000
Whitney, capital		165,000
Ford, capital		348,000
Totals	$600,000	$600,000

On January 1, 1976, the business was incorporated as Whitford Corporation with authorization to issue 200,000 shares of $10 par value common stock. The corporation issued 10,000 shares for cash to public investors at $54 a share. Whitney and Ford agreed to accept shares at the same price in amounts equal to their respective capital accounts after making the adjustments indicated below and after making cash withdrawals sufficient to avoid the need for issuing fractional shares. In payment for the shares of stock to be issued to Whitney and Ford, the partnership's assets were transferred to the corporation and the partnership's liabilities were assumed by the corporation. Stock certificates were then issued by the corporation in payment for the net assets of the partnership. A new set of accounting records is to be opened for the corporation.

The profit-sharing clause of the partnership agreement provided for Whitney to receive 40% of net income and Ford 60%. The partners agreed that the following adjustments were to be made in the partnership accounts at December 31, 1975, as a preliminary step to incorporation on January 1, 1976.

(1) Recognize accrued liabilities of $2,700 and miscellaneous prepayments of $3,600.
(2) Provide an allowance for uncollectible accounts of $15,000.
(3) Increase the value of land by $30,000.
(4) Increase the inventory to present replacement cost of $180,000.

Instructions

a On the partnership books, make the journal entries necessary to adjust the accounts to the agreed values. Also make all other entries needed to record the events described.

b On the corporation books, make the journal entries necessary to record the events described.

c Prepare a balance sheet for the corporation at January 1, 1976 after the above transactions have been recorded.

14B-4 Seaside Corporation is authorized to issue 300,000 shares of $25 par value, 4% cumulative preferred stock, and 800,000 shares of no-par common stock with stated value of $2.50 a share.

Early operations of the company were profitable but a prolonged strike caused a net loss of $800,000 to be sustained for the current fiscal year ending June 30. Because of the loss, the company paid no dividends on its common stock during the current fiscal year. Dividends on preferred were paid in the amount of $195,000 but dividends were in arrears on the preferred stock at June 30, in the amount of $45,000.

A trial balance of the general ledger at May 31 of the current year included the following:

Preferred stock, par $25	$6,000,000
Common stock, no-par, stated value $2.50	1,000,000
Subscriptions receivable: preferred stock	630,000
Retained earnings (June 30, prior year)	1,200,000
Premium on preferred stock	330,000
Preferred stock subscribed	600,000
Paid-in capital in excess of stated value: common	1,500,000
Subscriptions receivable: common	550,000
Common stock subscribed	250,000

Transactions during June relating to capital stock included the issuance of 2,000 shares of common stock in exchange for a patent. An additional 10,000 shares of common stock were issued for cash during June at a price of $4.50 a share. Cash was also collected during June representing payment in full for common stock subscriptions covering 20,000 shares. These subscriptions had been received and recorded prior to May 31. All common stock offerings by the company prior to May 31 had been at the same price.

Instructions

a Compute the average price at which the preferred stock was sold by the company.

b Compute the price at which the common stock was offered by the company prior to June of the current year.

c Prepare journal entries to record the transactions during June, which affected the stockholders' equity accounts.

d Prepare the stockholders' equity section of the balance sheet at June 30, including any notes which should accompany the balance sheet.

14B-5 Bluestem Company, Inc., was organized on January 10 of the current year and received subscriptions immediately for 10,000 shares of preferred stock at par. Subscriptions to common stock were received on the same date. (The number of common shares subscribed and the subscription price can be determined from information given in the problem.) On May 15 an additional 2,000 shares of preferred stock were subscribed at $52 a share. Cash payments were received from subscribers at frequent intervals for several months after subscription and the company followed the policy of issuing stock certificates only when sub- scribers had paid in full. On December 12, common stock in the amount of 4,000 shares was issued in exchange for land having a fair market value of $64,000. (Subscriptions were not used in this transaction.)

The balance sheet prepared at December 31 contained the following items, among others:

Subscriptions receivable: common stock		$ 90,000
Subscriptions receivable: preferred stock		26,000
Capital stock:		
Preferred, 4% cumulative, $50 par value; authorized 20,000		
shares, issued and outstanding 11,000 shares	$550,000	
Preferred stock subscribed, 1,000 shares	50,000	600,000
Common, $5 par-value, authorized 50,000 shares, issued		
and outstanding 12,000 shares	$ 60,000	
Common stock subscribed, 12,000 shares	60,000	120,000
Paid-in capital in excess of par:		
On preferred stock		4,000
On common stock		244,000

Instructions

a Prepare journal entries showing all the transactions entered into by the Blue- stem Company, Inc., from January 10 to December 31, as suggested by the above account balances.

b What is the dollar amount of contributed capital for each class of stock at December 31? What is the amount of stated capital attributable to the common stock?

CHAPTER 15

Stock rights,
stock options, and
convertible securities

don't worry about detail

WARRANTS AND STOCK RIGHTS *know*

A *stock warrant* is a certificate issued by a corporation conveying to the holder rights to purchase shares of its stock at a specified price. The term *stock right* means the privilege attaching to each outstanding share of stock to buy a fractional share or a specified number of shares of new capital stock. The holder of 100 shares of stock might therefore receive a warrant for 100 rights, which would permit him to purchase a specified number of new shares. For example, American Telephone & Telegraph Company issued rights to its stockholders permitting the purchase of one new share of common stock in exchange for 20 rights and $86 cash. A.T.&T. stock was selling at that time for approximately $125 in open-market transactions. The holder of 100 shares of A.T.&T. stock received 100 rights which entitled him to buy five new shares at the subscription price of $86 a share.

The use of rights is not limited to the acquisition of additional shares of common stock; some companies in recent years have issued rights to their common stockholders entitling them to buy convertible debenture bonds at a stipulated price. The use of rights in buying bonds is considered later in this chapter. For the moment we are concerned only with rights which entitle the holder to purchase common stock at a specified price.

Stock rights are often issued in the following three situations:

1 As a preliminary step to raising more capital through the issuance of additional shares of common stock

2 In combination with an offering of bonds, notes, or preferred stock, thus adding a speculative bonus for investors in these securities

3 As additional compensation to officers, employees, promoters, or underwriters

When stock rights are outstanding, the corporation's balance sheet should disclose the number of shares of stock being held in reserve to meet the demands which may be made by holders of the rights. This disclosure may be made in the stockholders' equity section or in a footnote to the financial statements.

The special characteristics of the three major categories of stock rights listed above are discussed in the following sections along with recommended accounting treatment.

Rights granted to existing stockholders

When rights are granted to existing stockholders as a preliminary step to raising more capital through the issuance of additional shares of common stock, the corporation receives nothing in exchange for the rights when they are issued. Only when they are exercised does the corporation receive funds. This situation is a sharp contrast with the other two situations listed above involving the issuance of stock rights. When rights are issued in combination with an offering of bonds or preferred stock, a portion of the proceeds is in fact attributable to the rights. When rights are issued as additional compensation to corporate officers or key employees, the fact that they constitute a part of a compensation plan and not a gift indicates that the company is receiving services in exchange for them.

Stock rights granted to existing stockholders as a preliminary step to raising more capital through the issuance of additional common stock usually expire within a few weeks or months. Consequently, the corporation can rapidly complete its program of raising capital through sale of additional common stock to present stockholders or other investors. Stock rights of this type are transferable and may be actively traded on the stock exchanges. Consequently, many persons acquire rights by purchase from other investors. When investors who have purchased rights from other investors decide to exercise such rights, the cost they incurred in buying the rights must be combined with their cash payments to the corporation to determine the total cost of their investment in shares of stock.

The purchase price specified in stock rights granted to existing stockholders is usually somewhat less than current market, but above the par or stated value. In the following illustration of a subscription warrant for common stock issued by Pacific Gas and Electric Company, 15 rights are needed for each share of stock to be purchased at the option price (not shown) of $25.65. The market price of the common stock at the time the rights were issued was $27.62. The life of the rights was short—they were issued March 6 and expired on March 27. Through use of these rights the company sold over 4 million shares of stock and raised capital in excess of $102 million within the three-week life span of the rights. The rights were actively traded on the New York Stock Exchange throughout their brief life, with the price per right varying from a low of about one-eighth of a dollar to one-half dollar.

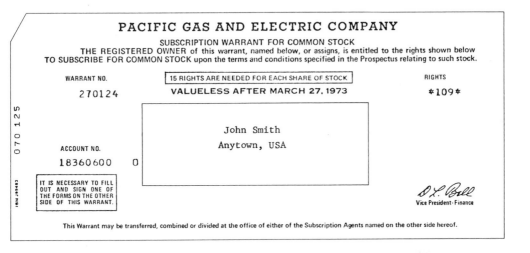

The issuance of rights to stockholders does not require debits or credits to ledger accounts of the issuing corporation, although a memorandum entry stating the number of rights issued may be used. When the rights are exercised by the holders, the corporation issues shares of stock at the price stated in the rights. This issuance of shares requires the usual entry for sale of stock and a memorandum entry to record the decrease in the number of rights outstanding. The maintenance of a memorandum record of the number of rights issued, exercised, and outstanding enables the corporation to hold in reserve a sufficient number of shares to meet the potential demand from outstanding rights.

Rights issued in combination with bonds or preferred stock

A company may add to the attractiveness of its bonds or preferred stock by attaching a right to buy its common stock at a specified price.[1] The longer the life of the right the greater its speculative appeal; rights in this category often run for several years and some have no expiration date.

When bonds are issued with detachable warrants (stock rights), the rate of interest on the bonds is usually less than if the bonds were offered

---

[1] Rights to purchase common stock are also sometimes offered in combination with the sale of common stock. In 1970 Tenneco, Inc., offered 5.5 million shares of common stock with detachable warrants entitling the holder to purchase additional shares of common stock at $24.25 on or before November 1, 1975.

alone. Similarly, preferred stock accompanied by detachable warrants for the purchase of common stock can attract investors even though the dividend rate on the preferred stock is lower than would otherwise be necessary. In other words, a part of the proceeds to the company from issuing bonds or preferred stock with warrants attached represents payment by investors for the warrants. Therefore, proper accounting for these "combination packages" of securities *requires that part of the proceeds be recognized as attributable to the warrants.*

Accounting for bonds payable issued with detachable warrants is illustrated in Chapter 18. At this time our discussion will be focused on the issuance of rights in combination with preferred stock.

The right to purchase common stock at a specified price at any time during a span of future years has an economic value regardless of whether the specified exercise price is higher, lower, or equal to the market price of the stock when the stock right is issued. Since the detachable warrants are often traded separately from the preferred stock or bond with which they were originally issued, objective evidence is available to aid in allocating the proceeds of the offering between the two types of securities.

The method described above of accounting for stock rights attached to preferred stock has not always been followed. In the past it has been common practice to ignore the speculative value of the warrants unless the exercise price specified in the warrant was below the market price of the common stock at the time of issuing warrants. Under this approach, the entire proceeds of the issue were often credited to the preferred stock, even though this resulted in a substantial premium on the preferred stock. It was argued that the value of the stock right could not be objectively determined at the date of issuance unless the exercise price was below the market price. In that case the excess of the market price over the exercise price was allocated to the warrants. For example, assume that Haven Corporation offered 100,000 shares of $100 par value preferred stock at $102, with detachable stock purchase warrants entitling the holder to purchase one share of common stock at $18 at any time during the next ten years. At the date of the offering, the common stock was being actively traded on a stock exchange at $20 a share. According to the usual practice of the past, the sale of the securities would have been recorded as follows:

Cash	10,200,000	
Preferred Stock		10,000,000
Common Stock Warrants		200,000

Issued 100,000 shares of $100 par value preferred stock at par, and detachable stock warrants at $2 each. (Allocation based on excess of market price of common stock over exercise price specified in warrants.)

The preceding entry is unsatisfactory because it limits the value of the warrants to the present excess of the price of the common stock over the exercise price. There is no recognition of the speculative appeal to investors of holding a long-term call on the common stock. The holder of the warrants has the opportunity of unlimited gain from possible increases in price of the common stock over the next ten years. The difficulty of measuring the value of the warrant was used as an excuse for ignoring that value. In this example, the preferred stock in reality sold at a discount; it would surely have sold for less than par had the stock warrants not been included in the offering. One consequence of this inadequate accounting practice was to understate the cost of capital obtained through the issuance of preferred stock.

In *APB Opinion No. 14,* the Accounting Principles Board stated that "the portion of the proceeds of debt securities issued with detachable stock warrants which is allocable to the warrants should be accounted for as paid-in capital. The allocation should be based on the relative fair values of the two securities at time of issuance."[2] Although this discussion related specifically to bonds issued with detachable stock purchase warrants, the reasoning also appears applicable to warrants issued with preferred stock.

Assume, for example, that Gulf, Inc., issues 10,000 shares of $100 par value preferred stock at $110 and gives with each share a right to purchase one share of common stock at $30 at any time during the next 20 years. The common stock has a par value of $5 and a current market price of $25. The right has a speculative value because of the likelihood that the market price of the common stock will rise above $30 during the next 20 years. Assume also that immediately after issuance the rights are traded in the market at a price of $3 each. The following entry should be made to record the proceeds of the stock offering:

Cash	1,100,000	
Preferred Stock		1,000,000
Premium on Preferred Stock		70,000
Common Stock Warrants		30,000
Issued 10,000 shares of $100 par value preferred stock at		
$107 and warrants for 10,000 stock rights at $3 each.		

The account Common Stock Warrants would be classified in the stockholders' equity section of the balance sheet. It is an element of contributed capital. (As previously explained, *stock warrants* are the certificates issued to convey *stock rights;* the terms are often used interchangeably.) If the rights are exercised and the common stock issued at $30 a share, the entry will be:

[2] *APB Opinion No. 14,* "Accounting for Convertible Debt and Debt Issued with Stock Purchase Warrants," AICPA (New York: 1969), p. 209.

Cash	300,000		
Common Stock Warrants	30,000		
Common Stock		50,000	
Paid-in Capital in Excess of Par: Common Stock		280,000	

Issued 10,000 shares of $5 par value common stock in ex-
change for 10,000 rights and cash of $30 a share.

Assume, however, that the market price of the common stock fell below $30 immediately after the issuance of the warrants and remained
below that level. Consequently no warrants were exercised; the following entry would be made upon the expiration date of the warrants:

Common Stock Warrants	30,000	
Paid-in Capital from Expired Warrants		30,000

To record expiration of 10,000 stock rights originally issued at a
valuation of $3 each.

Rights to purchase convertible debentures

The preemptive right of the common stockholder to purchase additional
shares in proportion to his present holdings in the event that the corporation increases the amount of stock outstanding was discussed in
Chapter 14. This preemptive right logically applies also to any new issues
of convertible debentures or convertible preferred stock since these
securities may eventually be converted into common stock.

In recent years convertible debentures have been a popular form of
financing. Rights have been issued to common stockholders entitling
them to buy convertible debentures at a specified price, and usually with
the provision that the rights will expire if not exercised within a month
or two. For example, National Cash Register issued to its common stockholders rights to purchase $4\frac{1}{4}$% convertible debentures maturing in 1992.
Ten rights and $100 cash were required to purchase $100 face value of
debentures. The rights traded for several weeks on the New York Stock
Exchange at prices varying between $1 and $2 per right, while the convertible bonds were concurrently trading on a **when-issued** basis at prices
ranging from about $108 to $116 per $100 face value. (Sales of securities
on a when-issued basis do not require delivery until after the scheduled
date of issuance.)

The accounting procedures for rights to purchase convertible debentures are similar to the procedures described for rights to purchase

common stock. The corporation need make no formal entry in its accounts when the rights are issued but must maintain memorandum records of the number of rights issued, exercised, and outstanding. When the rights are exercised, the entry usually required is to debit cash and credit the liability account for the convertible bonds. Usually the price stipulated by the right is par; hence no discount or premium is involved when the debenture is issued.

STOCK OPTION CONTRACTS

Stock option contracts with officers and key employees represent an important element of executive compensation in many corporations. A stock option plan gives officers and key employees the right to purchase the corporation's stock at a specified price. The option price is usually 100% of the fair market value of the stock at the date of granting the option, and the life of the option is often five years. For example, assume that you, as an executive of X Corporation, receive today a five-year option to buy 1,000 shares of the company's stock at today's price of $20. If, during the next five years, the market price of the stock rises to, say, $70, you will be in the fortunate position of being able to purchase $70,000 worth of stock for $20,000. The option is in reality a call on the stock at a fixed price over a period of years with no risk to the holder. The opportunity for gain is unlimited; the chance of loss is zero. In the event of a stock split or stock dividend, the option price is reduced proportionately and the number of shares under option increased proportionately to avoid injury to the option holder. By means of stock option contracts, corporate officers and other executives are not only rewarded by increases in the price of the company's stock, but the personal income obtained in this manner is usually taxed as a capital gain rather than as ordinary income.

From a theoretical viewpoint, the valuation of stock options is a difficult and challenging problem. In current practice, however, the problem of valuation is generally ignored, and the accounting procedures for stock options are designed merely to comply with income tax rules. The present tax rules state that the option does not constitute income to the recipient, and that no compensation expense may be deducted by the corporation. Thus, the difficult problem of determining the value of a stock option is avoided by assuming that it has no value.

Although this treatment of stock options may be convenient for administration of the tax laws, current practice clearly has little or no theoretical support. Stock options do in fact represent an important part of the total cost to a corporation of compensating its executives. Since we are concerned in this book with accounting principles rather than with current income tax requirements, we need to consider the theoretical issues inherent in a stock option plan. The theoretical accounting problems to be considered are: (1) measuring the amount of compensation (or value to be assigned to the stock issued under an option plan), and (2) determining the accounting period or periods to be charged with this compensation expense.

Impact of tax regulations: Qualified stock options

In adopting stock option plans for executives, corporations have made extensive use of "qualified stock options" as defined in federal income tax legislation. At present, such plans must set the option price at not less than the fair market value of the stock on the date the option is granted. Furthermore, the option must be exercised within five years after it is granted. Among the tax consequences resulting from a qualified stock option plan are the following:

1 No income (for federal income tax purposes) will result to the optionee at the time he receives the option or when he acquires stock by exercising the option.
2 If the stock is held by the optionee for three years after the exercise of the option, he may then sell the stock and treat any gain or loss as a long-term capital gain or loss.
3 The corporation granting a qualified stock option is not permitted to deduct as compensation expense any part of the value of stock delivered under the plan.
4 No amount other than the price paid by the optionee will be considered as received by the corporation for the shares issued under the option plan.

The widespread use of "qualified stock options" reflects the desire of business organizations to attract and retain competent executives by offering them rewards which will not be subject to the higher rates of our graduated personal income tax structure. The opportunity to acquire stock under a stock option plan without recognizing taxable income at the time of acquiring the stock is a strong attraction to most executives. The possibility of selling the stock three years or more after acquisition and treating any gain as a long-term capital gain is also most attractive, since, under existing tax rules, long-term capital gains are taxed at a lower rate than is ordinary income.

The impact of income tax rules upon the development of financial reporting standards is difficult to measure, but it clearly is important. The fact that corporations do not record any compensation expense for the stock issued to executives under qualified stock option plans is at least partially due to the fact that no such compensation expense may be deducted in computing the *taxable income* of the corporation.

Stock options which prove worthless

In a good many cases the qualified stock option is never exercised because the market price of the stock does not rise above the call price during the option period. The following note from the current annual report of Scott Paper Company, a listed corporation on the New York Stock Exchange, vividly illustrates the fact that stock options do not always prove rewarding. *know*

Stock options

Stock options for the purchase of 583,150 common shares were held by officers and other key employees at the end of 1972 under the Company's stock option plans. Option prices of the outstanding grants were at market value of the shares on the dates granted.

Option prices ranged from $15.50 to $37.38 per share with an overall average price of $27.10 per share. The closing market price of Scott shares on the last business day of 1972 was $15.38. Options for 282,355 shares were exercisable at December 31, 1972 (419,066 at December 31, 1971) and additional options for 81,675 shares will become exercisable in 1973.

No options were exercised in 1972 or 1971.

APB Opinion No. 25, Accounting for stock issued to employees

In October 1972, the Accounting Principles Board issued *Opinion No. 25,* which provided a historical résumé of the problems encountered in accounting for stock options, and also set forth current standards.[3] The Opinion deals with both noncompensatory and compensatory plans.

Noncompensatory Plans A *noncompensatory plan* is one not primarily designed as a form of compensation, but rather for such purposes as raising capital or inducing widespread ownership of the corporation's stock among officers and employees. Essential characteristics of a noncompensatory plan are (1) participation of all full-time employees; (2) offering of stock on an equal basis or as a uniform percentage of salary to all employees; (3) a limited time for exercise of the option; and (4) a discount from market price no greater than would be reasonable in an offer to stockholders. In such noncompensatory plans, no compensation is presumed to be involved. Consequently, the corporation records no compensation expense for financial accounting purposes and claims no deduction for tax purposes. The noncompensatory type of stock option plan was apparently summarized in *APB Opinion No. 25* principally to clear the way for consideration of the more controversial issues of accounting for compensatory plans.

Compensatory Plans Any stock option plan not possessing the four specified characteristics of a noncompensatory plan is classified as a *compensatory plan.* The features of a compensatory plan may vary in an almost endless number of respects. For example, the grantee (officer or employee granted the option) may be obligated to continue in the employment of the corporation or of its subsidiaries. The total number of shares specified in the option may be acquired at one time or only in a limited number during each year of the option plan. The consideration

---

[3] *APB Opinion No. 25,* "Accounting for Stock Issued to Employees," AICPA (New York: 1972).

received by a corporation for stock issued through a stock option plan may include cash, notes receivable, or other assets, as well as services from the employee. In all compensatory plans, services from the grantee represent part or all of the consideration for the stock issued.

Measuring Compensation for Services A key provision of *Opinion No. 25* is that compensation for services received as consideration for the stock issued shall be measured by the *quoted market price of the stock at the measurement date less the amount, if any, that the employee is required to pay.*

In applying this policy, determination of the measurement date for determining compensation cost touches the theoretical center of the problem. The measurement date is stated to be the *first date on which are known both the number of shares to be received by each individual and the option price.* In most plans, that early date is the date of granting the option.

APB Opinion No. 25 then concludes that a corporation should recognize compensation cost for stock issued through compensatory plans when the option price is less than the quoted market price of the stock at the measurement date. As previously indicated, qualified stock option plans presently set the option price at the fair market price of the stock at the date of grant. Consequently, no compensation expense will be recognized for most qualified stock option plans.

Illustration of stock option plan KNOW

In this illustration we shall ignore current practice and focus on theoretical issues only. Assume that a corporation adopts a stock option plan with the approval of its stockholders whereby officers and key employees are granted nontransferable options to purchase 100,000 shares of the company's common stock at a price equal to 100% of the market price on the date of grant. The option contracts provide that the selected officers must remain in the employ of the company between the date of grant of the options and the date or dates options are exercised. The options extend over a period of five years. The market price of the stock was as shown below for certain key dates during the option period:

Mar. 1, 1974 Options to purchase a total of 100,000 shares at $30 granted with specific numbers of shares designated to individual officers and key employees. Market price of stock $30.

Mar. 1, 1975 Options become exercisable as grantees have completed the required minimum period of employment. Market price of stock $50.

Feb. 1, 1976 Options exercised and 100,000 shares of stock issued at the option price of $30. Market price of stock $90.

The value of the stock options (and the corresponding amount of non-cash executive compensation) might conceivably be based on the difference between the option price of $30 and any one of the following prices for the stock: (1) the price at the date the options were granted,

(2) the price at the date the options become exercisable, or (3) the price at the date the options were exercised. According to the choice of the most appropriate date, the value of the options covering 100,000 shares varies from zero to $6 million [100,000 × ($90 − $30)].

Some years ago when stock option plans generally set the option price at 95% of current market value in accordance with the provisions then existing in the tax laws, the AICPA Committee on Accounting Procedure argued that the value of the stock option was limited to the 5% spread between the option price and the market price *at date of grant.* That argument was expressed as follows:

> . . . The date as of which measurement is made is of critical importance since the fair value of the shares under option may vary materially in the often extended period during which the option is outstanding. . . . When compensation is paid in a form other than cash, the *amount* of compensation is ordinarily determined by the fair value of the property which was agreed to be given in exchange for the services to be rendered. The time at which such fair value is to be determined may be subject to some difference of opinion but it appears that the date on which an option is granted to a specific individual would be the appropriate point at which to evaluate the cost to the employer, since it was the value at that date which the employer may be presumed to have had in mind . . . . it is the value of the option at that time, rather than the grantee's ultimate gain or loss on the transaction, which for accounting purposes constitutes whatever compensation the grantor intends to pay. . . .
>
> The date of grant also represents the date on which the corporation foregoes the principal alternative use of the shares which it places subject to option, i.e., the sale of such shares at the then prevailing market price. Viewed in this light, the *cost* of utilizing the shares for purposes of the option plan can best be measured in relation to what could then have been obtained through sale of such shares in the open market.[4]

This argument of the committee was never a convincing one, for it is apparent that no reasonable person would have given up the potential gain in a long-term stock option merely for the difference between the option price and the market price at date of grant. Since stock option plans have changed in recent years to the practice of setting the option price at 100% of the market price, the value of an option under the method described above would be zero. Such a conclusion is clearly not in accord with economic reality.

An alternative method of establishing the value of stock options is to use the excess of the market price over the option price at the date the option is first exercisable. In our illustration, this method would assign a value of $20 for each share optioned, that is, $50 market price minus $30 option price. It may be argued that this is the most appropriate date because it is the first date that the employee has control over the option. Only from this date can he be viewed as an investor rather than solely as an employee.

A third alternative method of establishing the value of stock options is to use the excess of the market price over the option price at the date the options are actually exercised. For the options in our illustration, this

[4] *Accounting Research Bulletin No. 43,* (New York: 1961), pp. 121–122.

method would produce a value of $60 for each share optioned—the excess of a $90 market price over a $30 option price. In support of this method, it is argued that only at this date is it certain that exercise of the options will actually occur. Prior to this date, the company has only a contingent obligation to issue shares under the option plan.

Apart from these three methods which assign value to the options based on the difference between market price of the stock and option price at selected dates, we should consider at least two other approaches. The first of these is to estimate the probable value of the option to the recipient at the date of grant. At this date the expected value must be equal to or greater than zero; it can never be less than zero. Any realistic evaluation must indicate a value above zero. To estimate this value it is necessary to project the trend in the future price of the company's stock—obviously a hazardous area of estimating and perhaps involving more uncertainty than other estimates inherent in the accounting process. However, transferable options (calls and warrants) for common stocks are regularly sold in the marketplace; hence such valuations are being made in the normal course of financial affairs. For the nontransferable options with which we are now concerned, however, additional variables exist to make the valuation problem more difficult.

One more method of valuing stock options which deserves consideration is the estimated cash value of the services to be received from the employee for which he is being compensated by the stock option plan. Accounting custom has long dictated that when a non-cash exchange occurs, it should be recorded at the cash value of that which is received. If the value of the asset or services received is difficult to measure and the value of that which is surrendered is more evident, the latter value is used to record the transaction. The grant of a stock option is a non-cash exchange. However, it is difficult to measure either the value of the services received or the value of the nontransferable option granted. In this situation, why not use all available information to estimate the cash value of the executive's services over the option period? For example, in the negotiations leading to employment for an executive, assume that a cash offer of $100,000 a year for five years is rejected as inadequate, but that it is known that the executive will accept and the company is willing to pay either of the following: (1) a cash salary of $125,000 a year for five years or (2) a cash salary of $90,000 a year for five years plus a stock option for 10,000 shares. If the offer including the stock options is agreed upon, a basis is available for measuring the value of the options as the excess of the total bargained value of his services over the cash salary he is to receive.

Estimating the fair value of stock options

Since accountants have not yet found an objective means of measuring the costs presumably envisioned by the parties to a stock option contract, it has been suggested that the options be valued at the amount for which options could be sold to the public at the time similar options are granted to executives.

Let us assume that a leading corporation were to offer to the public stock options permitting purchase of the corporation's shares at any time within the next five years at the market price which prevails today. There seems little doubt that investors and speculators would bid high for a contract offering such potential for capital gain. However, during a hectic market day, the price of a speculative security sometimes goes through such wide swings as to cast doubt on the significance of any of the prices at which trades occurred. The logic of the "market value" approach to the valuing of nontransferable stock options for executives may also be challenged on the historical grounds that many options are in fact never exercised. In addition to the possibility that market conditions may never justify exercising an option, it is also necessary to recognize that pre- requisites such as continued satisfactory employment and other require- ments must be met before the option can be exercised. In other words, the offering of stock options to the public as compared with offering them to executives of the company may differ sufficiently that the values assigned the option contracts would be far from comparable.

The option period

Nearly all qualified stock option plans specify the maximum option period of five years permitted for tax purposes. Some years ago, a 10-year period was acceptable for tax purposes and was used by many corporations. The length of the period during which the option holder may elect to exercise the option is of basic importance in appraising the significance of an option plan. The longer the option period, the greater the opportu- nity for substantial rise in the market value of the stock and a corre- spondingly large gain to the optionee. At present many corporations maintain both a five-year qualified plan and a ten-year nonqualified plan.

The stock option plans of many corporations permit the employee to exercise the option in whole or in part at any date during the five-year life of the plan. Other companies provide that options shall be exercisable in approximately equal annual installments over the option period of five years. From the corporation's viewpoint, it would appear advantageous to "tie" the executive to the company over the entire option period by permitting only partial exercise of the option each year. Such clauses are not common, however, because they would prevent the executive from taking advantage of an early rise in the market price of the stock and thus defeat the basic objective of providing maximum compensation to the executive at minimum cost to the corporation.

A stock option plan should contain a provision permitting the option to be exercised while the optionee is employed either by the granting corporation or by an affiliated corporation. This provision will prevent the loss of option rights if circumstances require that a key employee be transferred between a parent and subsidiary corporation. Stock option contracts are customarily ratified by vote of stockholders.

Does current practice understate compensation expense represented by stock options?

In current practice most corporations do not record any compensation expense from stock option plans, despite universal agreement that stock options are a major element of executive compensation. The comment contained in the annual proxy statement of American Airlines, Inc., is typical of the arguments presented by many corporations seeking shareholder approval of stock option plans: "The Board of Directors has found that the granting of stock options continues to be one of the most effective methods of recruiting and retaining competent managerial personnel."

To emphasize the importance of stock options as compensation to management and concurrently to record no compensation expense from these plans is a striking example of how accounting theory may bow to the pressure of income tax requirements. To be competitive, a corporation *must* adopt a "qualified stock option plan"; and tax requirements specifically prohibit any deduction of compensation expense for shares issued under the option plan. Does it follow that, for general financial reporting, no compensation expense should be recognized? Since stock option plans have become a major element in executive compensation, it is apparent that the corporation has a responsibility to make a meaningful accounting measurement of this form of compensation cost. To ignore the cost of stock options is to understate operating costs and to overstate net income. It has sometimes been suggested that stock options for executives cost the stockholders nothing, but such statements seem unsupportable. In a sense, it is the stockholders who bear the cost of the option plan through dilution of their equity when the optioned shares are issued. This impact on stockholders is part of the reason for requiring adequate disclosure (and objective valuation) of stock options. In the opinion of the authors, the current practice of not recording compensation expense for stock options, although sanctioned by the AICPA, results in substantial understatement of executive compensation and a corresponding understatement of capital contributed for shares of stock issued under an option plan.

The basic accounting principle of matching costs with related revenue suggests that the compensation expense implicit in stock option plans should be accrued throughout the life of the option plan. Such accruals of course would require the use of estimates (perhaps based on the trend of current market prices from year to year). The periodic charges to compensation expense could be offset by credits which would be closed into the stockholder equity accounts when the total amount was determined and the shares were issued to the optionees.

Disclosure of stock options *KNOW DISCLOSURE REQU.*

Although differences of opinion exist as to the best method of measuring the amount of compensation expense implicit in stock options, there is general agreement as to the necessity of disclosing the significant data contained in the option plan. In each set of annual financial statements, information should be given as to the number of shares under option at a given option price and the time periods within which these options may be exercised. Often this disclosure will show that the corporation has options outstanding granted at various dates and at varying option prices.

The following note attached to the financial statements of Diebold, Incorporated, illustrates how detailed the disclosure of stock options may be.

Note 3: Common Stock Options

At a meeting held April 3, 1972, the shareholders adopted a new Stock Option Plan recommended by the Board of Directors, and approved the release of 200,000 shares from preemptive rights thereby making these shares available for purposes of the plan. The reservation of 115,962 common shares previously made for prior plan options was removed and such shares will not be available for future options.

The new plan provides for issuance of qualified stock options, nonqualified stock options, and combination or dual options. The option price will be the fair market value of the common shares on the date of grant in the case of a qualified option and not less than eighty-five per cent of the fair market value of the common shares on the date of grant in the case of a nonqualified option. The qualified option can be granted for a period not in excess of five years from the date of grant and the nonqualified option for a period not in excess of ten years from that date. The term of the plan is limited to ten years from the date of its adoption and no option may be granted after that date.

As of January 9, 1973, combination (parallel) options covering 50,200 shares had been issued at prices of $42.25 to $47.38 per share based upon the fair market value of the common shares of dates of grants.

Options were granted under the prior plan during 1971 for 5,000 shares (before adjustment for the three-for-two stock split and a stock dividend). No options were granted under the prior plan in 1972.

The status of stock options issued under the prior plan that were outstanding as of December 31, 1972, and information with respect to options granted for the two years then ended is shown at the top of page 574.

The number of shares and prices in the following tabulation have been adjusted to reflect subsequent stock dividends paid through April 28, 1972 and the three-for-two stock split paid on May 28, 1971. The company has not made any charge to income in connection with the plan.

All options outstanding are exercisable in cumulative annual installments beginning with the last month of the first year of the option term provided prior qualified options held by an individual are fully exercised or have lapsed.

The Securities and Exchange Commission has specified in some detail in Regulation S-X the information regarded as constituting adequate disclosure of a stock option plan. The SEC requirement includes a statement of the basis of accounting for the options and the charges to expense, if any, during the current period.

	No. of shares	Option price		Market value	
		Per share	**Total**	**Per share**	**Total**
Shares under option	41,413	$16.42 to $50.72	$1,511,351	$16.42 to $50.72 (a)	$1,511,351
Options first exercisable during:					
1971	27,965	$11.37 to $44.27	$ 553,784	$44.23 to $52.04 (b)	$1,324,493
1972	24,893	$13.27 to $50.72	$ 546,028	$36.00 to $50.96 (b)	$1,161,696
Options exercised during:					
1971	35,432	$11.83 to $17.11	$ 487,872	$44.50 to $53.00 (c)	$1,712,291
1972	28,819	$13.27 to $37.50	$ 413,578	$41.00 to $53.75 (c)	$1,446,946

Market value shown above is at
(a) dates options were granted
(b) dates options became exercisable
(c) dates options were exercised

CONVERTIBLE SECURITIES

Characteristics of convertible preferred stock

Many preferred stocks are convertible into common stock at the option of the holders. The appeal of the convertible preferred stock lies in the fact that it combines certain attributes of both common and preferred stock in a single security. Because the convertible preferred stock may be exchanged for common shares in a fixed ratio, convertibles have the same appreciation potential as the related common stock. The status of the convertible preferred stock as a *senior security* with a stated annual dividend gives convertibles the same reduced risk possessed by nonconvertible preferred stock. The extent to which one or the other of these attributes of potential appreciation and reduced risk is more influential varies from one preferred stock issue to another, and even for the same issue over a period of years.

Definitions applicable to convertible preferred stock

The *conversion ratio* indicates the number of common shares for which a convertible preferred stock may be exchanged. The basic ratio is set when the convertible preferred stock is issued, but the ratio is subject to adjustment in the event of a stock split or a stock dividend on the common stock. For example, each share of American Home Products' $2 convertible preferred stock was convertible into 1½ shares of its common stock. When the common stock was split 3 for 1 in 1973, the conversion ratio increased to $4\frac{1}{2}$ shares of common for each share of the convertible preferred.

Conversion value is the value of the preferred stock if exchanged for common; it is calculated by multiplying the market price of the common stock by the conversion ratio.

Conversion premium is the excess, if any, of the market price of the convertible preferred stock over its conversion value. This dollar premium is usually expressed as a percentage, obtained by dividing it by the conversion value. The lower the conversion premium, the more closely the market price of the convertible stock tends to follow market changes in the price of the common stock.

Investment value is an estimated price, influenced by prevailing interest rates, at which the preferred stock would be likely to sell *if it were not convertible.* For example, assume that the prevailing rate of return in the market for securities of a given quality is 6%. It follows that a $4 convertible preferred stock in this particular quality group would have an investment value of $66.67, computed as follows: $4 annual dividend divided by 6% equals $66.67. At a price of $66.67, the $4 convertible preferred stock would provide a dividend yield of 6%. The stock would sell at this price only if its conversion feature were completely ignored. Those convertible preferred stocks which have risen greatly in price by moving "in gear" with a rising price trend in the related common stock often trade at a market price far above the investment value of the preferred stock.

Price risk for a convertible preferred stock is a term used to describe the difference between its current market price and its theoretical investment value as defined above. The dollar excess of market price over investment value is converted to a percentage by dividing the excess amount by the current market price.

To illustrate the application of these terms, we shall extend the previous example of the $2 convertible preferred stock of American Home Products Corporation. Prior to the split of the common stock in 1973, the convertible preferred stock was trading in the market at about $190 per share, while the market price of the common stock was about $127 a share. The *conversion ratio* of the preferred was 1.50 to 1; therefore the *conversion value* of the preferred stock was $1\frac{1}{2}$ times $127, or approximately $190. Consequently, the conversion premium was zero; the market value of the preferred stock did not exceed its conversion value. The yield on the $2 preferred stock was only 1.1% at its $190 price; however, the prevailing rate demanded by investors in stocks of comparable quality without the conversion privilege was about 6.9%. Consequently, we can compute the investment value of this $2 convertible preferred stock by dividing $2 by 6.9%, which gives the amount of $29. The *price risk* was naturally high, since the market value of the convertible was so largely based on its conversion value. To compute the price risk as a percentage, we first deduct the investment value of $29 from the market price of $190. The resulting $161 differential is divided by the market price ($190) to arrive at the price risk of approximately 85%. These relationships are typical of outstanding growth stocks in which current dividend yields are largely ignored because of an excellent record of capital appreciation.

Conversion of preferred stock into common

Many preferred stocks are convertible into common stock at the option of the holder. When such conversions are recorded any premium applicable to the preferred shares should be eliminated by transfer to the accounts representing the common shares being issued.

Assume, for example, a $100 par value preferred stock convertible at the option of the holder into four shares of the company's $10 par value common stock. All the preferred shares were issued at a price of $105 a share, and the account balances relating to the preferred stock are as follows:

Preferred stock	$1,000,000
Premium on preferred stock	50,000

If 100 shares of preferred stock are presented for conversion, the entry will be:

Preferred Stock	10,000	
Premium on Preferred Stock	500	
Common Stock		4,000
Paid-in Capital in Excess of Par: Common Stock		6,500
Issued 400 shares of $10 par common in exchange for 100 shares of		
$100 par convertible preferred stock.		

In the rare situation in which the par or stated values of the shares in a conversion transaction exceeded the par or stated value of the securities being converted, a debit to retained earnings would be necessary. Note, however, that retained earnings is *never* increased by a conversion transaction.

It may be assumed that the original purchaser of a convertible preferred stock was influenced in his investment decision by the possibility that conversion would be advantageous at some future date. The contributed capital received by the issuing corporation for convertible preferred stock may therefore logically be regarded as the appropriate amount of contributed capital applicable to the common shares which the investor receives upon exercise of his conversion option.

Conversion of bonds into common stock

Bond contracts that allow the investor to exchange his bonds for common stock are known as **convertible bonds,** and this feature is called a **conversion option.** Inclusion of the conversion feature makes bonds far more attractive to investors and may enable the issuing corporation to obtain funds at an interest rate well below that which would otherwise have to be paid on long-term borrowings. The conversion feature may also have the effect of providing a relatively automatic retirement of debt as the bondholders over the years elect to exchange their bonds for common stock. Thus by issuing convertible bonds, the corporation in effect sells common stock at a price substantially above the market price prevailing at the time the bonds are issued.

Investors favor the conversion option because they stand to gain if the company is extremely successful; at the same time they limit their risk by retaining preferential status as creditors in case the company suffers reverses. Some indication of the capital gain potential in convertible bonds is available in the current market prices quoted for issues of some highly successful companies. The 8% convertible bonds of Ramada Inns, scheduled to mature in 1995, have traded at prices in excess of $2,700 for each bond of $1,000 denomination. The $4\frac{3}{4}$% convertible bonds of PepsiCo, Inc., maturing in 1996, have increased in value by more than 50%, as have the convertible bonds and convertible preferred stocks of many other companies.

If a convertible bond or convertible preferred stock is called by the issuing company before the scheduled maturity date, the holders are given a limited period, such as 30 or 60 days, within which to exchange their convertible securities for common stock at the predetermined conversion ratio. Consequently, the investor who holds a convertible bond or preferred stock with a market value far above its face amount need not fear a loss caused by the issuing corporation deciding to call the convertible security at or near its par value. When a corporation calls a convertible security which has a market price well above par, the effect is to force investors to convert their holdings into common stock. Convertible securities are seldom called until they are selling well above the call price and probably at little or no premium above the conversion value.

The issuing company sometimes arranges a sliding scale of conversion prices so that the bondholder is encouraged to convert before a date when the conversion ratio is reduced. For example, a 10-year bond may be convertible during the first five years at the rate of 20 shares of stock for one $1,000 bond; during the next three years at 19 shares of stock for one bond; and during the last two years at a ratio of 18 shares of stock for one bond.

Whenever a company has convertible securities outstanding, the balance sheet should disclose the number of common shares held in reserve to meet demands for conversion. This concept was illustrated in detail earlier in this chapter with reference to the balance sheet disclosure required for outstanding stock options. The two situations are alike in that both pose the possibility that the corporation may be called upon to issue additional common shares if stock options are exercised or the holders of convertible securities decide to convert them.

When bonds are converted, the accountant faces the problem of recording the retirement of the debt and the issuance of additional stock. To illustrate, assume that R Corporation has outstanding $100,000 of 5% convertible bonds, carried on its books at $104,000, the $4,000 representing unamortized premium. The bonds at this time are convertible into $75 par value common stock having a market value of $125 per share, at a conversion ratio of 10 shares of common for each $1,000 bond. Assume that the corporation calls the bonds; therefore all bondholders present their bonds for conversion.

The company has exchanged common stock having a market value of $125,000 for bonded debt having a book value of $104,000. However, the market value of the stock and of the bonds can be ignored. The conversion is recorded by assigning the book value of the bonds to paid-in capital, as shown by the following entry:

Bonds Payable	100,000	
Premium on Bonds Payable	4,000	
Common Stock (par of $75)		75,000
Paid-in Capital in Excess of Par		29,000
To record conversion of 100 bonds into 1,000 shares of stock.		

At the original issuance date of the convertible bonds, the price received reflected the prospect that the bonds might be exchanged for stock at some later time under favorable conditions. Thus the original proceeds represented the market value of the debt contract *and* the conversion feature. When the conversion is actually made, the **book value of the debt measures the increase in net assets which resulted from the additional issue of capital stock.**

APB Opinions and convertible bonds

The issuance of convertible bonds raises an interesting question as to whether the amount received by the issuing company should be recorded entirely as debt or should be divided between debt and an element of stockholders' equity representing the portion of the proceeds attributable to the convertible feature of the bonds. Accounting Principles Board *Opinions Nos. 10, 14, and 25* bear on this controversial issue. The rationale underlying these Opinions will be discussed and evaluated in the sections devoted to convertible bonds in Chapter 18.

Protection against dilution of conversion rights

For both convertible preferred stocks and convertible bonds, it is standard practice to include a guarantee against dilution through common stock splits or stock dividends. Any increase in the number of common shares from splits or stock dividends causes a corresponding adjustment in the conversion ratio.

This protection against dilution is most essential in maintaining the relative positions of the holders of stock warrants, stock options, convertible preferred stock, and convertible bonds. For example, assume that you had invested in the $2 convertible preferred stock of American Home Products Corporation at a market price of $190 just prior to the 3-for-1 split of the common stock in 1973. (See page 575.) Each share of the convertible preferred stock you purchased was exchangeable for $1\frac{1}{2}$ shares of common stock which was selling for about $127 per share before the split. After the 3-for-1 split of the common stock, the total number of common shares outstanding was three times as great and the price per share was only one-third of the former price, or about $42 a share. If it had not been for the clause in the preferred stock contract protecting you against dilution, the market price of your convertible preferred stock would probably have declined overnight from $190 per share to about $63, the market value of $1\frac{1}{2}$ new common shares selling at $42. However, because of the guarantee against dilution, your conversion ratio has been increased from $1\frac{1}{2}$ to $4\frac{1}{2}$ as a result of the 3-for-1 split of the common stock. The conversion value of your preferred shares would therefore be little changed and would be computed at $4\frac{1}{2}$ times about $42, or a total of about $190 for each convertible preferred share.

Presentation of stockholders' equity in the balance sheet

An acceptable balance sheet presentation of paid-in capital and retained earnings is shown at the top of page 580.

Note that this illustration discloses the following information:

1 The par value or stated value of each class of stock

2 Dividend preference, conversion privilege, and call price of the preferred stock

3 Number of shares authorized, issued, and outstanding for each class of stock

4 Number of common shares reserved for possible issuance upon conversion of preferred stock and exercise of stock option contracts

5 Additional paid-in capital applicable to each class of stock

6 Total amount of paid-in capital

In published balance sheets of large corporations, the need for concise presentation may cause some of the data concerning contributed capital to be disclosed in the Notes to Financial Statements rather than in the body of the balance sheet. Information concerning stock options, con-

Stockholders' equity:

$4 convertible preferred stock, $100 par value, callable at $106 per share, authorized, issued, and outstanding 100,000 shares	$10,000,000
Common stock, $2.50 par value, authorized 2,000,000 shares, issued and outstanding 1,000,000 shares (Notes 1 and 2)	2,500,000
Additional paid-in capital:	
On preferred stock	400,000
On common stock	5,000,000
Total paid-in capital	$17,900,000
Retained earnings	4,100,000
Total stockholders' equity	$22,000,000

Note 1. *At December 31, 19__, 500,000 shares of common stock were reserved for conversion of the $4 convertible preferred stock on the basis of five shares of common for each share of preferred.*

Note 2. *Stock options. (See pages 573–574 earlier in this chapter for an illustration of footnote disclosure of stock options.)*

version ratios, and subclassifications of additional paid-in capital, for example, may be disclosed by notes referenced to the statements. Examples are shown in Appendix B.

Pro forma financial statements

When significant new financial changes are in prospect, the accountant may be asked to prepare financial statements which will give effect to the planned transactions. These statements reflecting transactions not yet consummated are called **pro forma statements.** For example, when two or more corporations are planning to combine by forming a new corporation, the stockholders and management of each existing corporation will want pro forma financial statements for the planned corporate entity to facilitate study of the relative position of each present organization in the planned new corporation.

Another use for pro forma financial statements arises after a combination of two businesses occurs *during* a fiscal year. A pro forma income statement for a full year may be prepared to show the operating results which *would have* resulted for the entire year *if* the combination of the two companies had taken place at the beginning of the fiscal year. An illustration of such a pro forma income statement appears on page 581.

Pro forma statements are also useful in situations other than business combinations. For example, a corporation might be considering the issuance of preferred stock in order to obtain funds with which to call the bonds outstanding. In weighing the merits of this action, management will need pro forma statements to show the financial position of the company as it will appear if these financial changes are carried out. Since the substitution of preferred stock for bonds will eliminate interest charges and have a bearing on taxable income, it will also be desirable

Unaudited Pro Forma Combined Statement of Earnings

The following pro forma statement of earnings for the twelve-month period ended August 31, 1974, which has not been examined by certified public accountants, includes the operations of King Corporation, combined with Western Land Company, acquired July 1, 1974, as if Western Land Company had been acquired as of the beginning of the fiscal year ended August 31, 1974.

Combined historical:

Sales, less returns and allowances	$50,501,830
Cost of sales	47,712,775
Gross profit on sales	$ 2,789,055
Selling and administrative expenses	1,216,841
Operating profit	$ 1,572,214
Other income (expense):	
Interest expense	$ (207,032)
Miscellaneous income (net)	48,937
	$ (158,095)
Earnings before taxes on income	$ 1,414,119
Taxes on income	729,162
Combined historical net earnings	$ 684,957
Pro forma adjustment:	
Annualized interest expense (net of tax effect) for debt incurred	
in connection with acquisition of Western Land Company.	11,750
Pro forma combined net earnings	$ 673,207
Pro forma combined net earnings per share of common stock (based on	
600,000 shares outstanding)	$1.12

to prepare a pro forma income statement showing how the operating results of the past year would have been modified if the changes in the capital structure had been in effect.

Pro forma financial statements may be prepared on work sheets by using existing account balances as a starting point and making adjustments to reflect the assumed transactions. The headings of financial statements summarizing assumed transactions should indicate clearly their hypothetical nature, and the character or purpose of the assumed transactions to which the statements give effect. The balance sheet heading in the illustration below meets this requirement.

PACIFIC SLOPE CORPORATION
Pro Forma Balance Sheet at September 30, 1975
After Giving Effect to the Proposed Issuance
of 30,000 Additional Shares of Common Stock
in Payment for the Net Assets of the Isle Vista Corporation

REVIEW QUESTIONS

1 What circumstances usually induce a corporation to adopt a qualified stock option plan?

2 What is the theoretical accounting problem relating to qualified stock option plans?

3 Should the financial statements of a corporation include disclosure of outstanding stock options? If so, how should the disclosure be made?

4 Upon the retirement of the vice president in charge of sales after 50 years' service with the company, the board of directors authorized the presentation to him of a certificate for 100 shares of the corporation's $50 par value common stock "in appreciation of loyal services." The shares were part of the company's holding of treasury stock, acquired and carried at cost of $80 a share. Book value per share was $140 and market value $125. How should the presentation to the vice president be recorded in the company's accounts?

5 Wilbur Corporation issued rights to the holders of its 50,000 shares of common stock on November 30, 1975, entitling them to buy one 6%, convertible $100 bond at $100 for each five shares of stock owned. The rights expired on February 28, 1976. At December 31, 1975, bonds in the face amount of $140,000 had been issued through the exercise of rights. What disclosure should be made of these events in the balance sheet at December 31, 1975?

6 Santa Fe Corporation issued five-year options to its key executives on May 21, 1976, at 100% of the market price of the stock on that date. State arguments for and against recording compensation expense corresponding to the estimated market value of these options.

7 Douglas Corporation issued 1,000 shares of $50 preferred stock for $55 a share. Included in this offering at no extra charge were separate stock warrants entitling the holders to purchase one share of common stock for each share of preferred upon presentation of a warrant and $25 cash. At the time of the issue, the common stock was selling on a regional stock exchange at $21 a share. The warrants began trading on the stock exchange prior to their issuance at a price of $2 each. The warrants expire in five years.

Give the necessary journal entry for issuance of the preferred stock with warrants attached. Should the stock warrants be listed in the balance sheet?

8 If common stock warrants are assigned a value at the time of issuance, what action is necessary if the warrants are not exercised and expire?

9 In discussing the establishment of a qualified stock option plan for the Dale Corporation, one director advocated a five-year plan with the grantees permitted to exercise only 20% of the option in any one year. What advantage and/or disadvantage can you see in such a provision?

10 What are the major differences between a compensatory stock option plan and a noncompensatory plan? Does the corporation record compensation expense applicable to either?

11 What date does **APB Opinion No. 25,** "Accounting for Stock Issued to Employees," stipulate for use in measuring compensation for services relating to stock option plans? How is the amount of compensation cost measured, and how does this apply to qualified stock options?

12 Is the preemptive right which is inherent in common stock ownership logically applicable only to additional issues of common stock or should it also apply to preferred stocks and bonds? Explain.

EXERCISES

Ex. 15-1 The $10 par value common stock of Calgary Corporation is listed on a major stock exchange and presently quoted at $30 a share. The company has 10 million authorized shares, of which 4 million are issued and outstanding. Because of a need for additional capital, the company issues to its common stockholders at this time rights permitting the purchase of one new share of common stock in exchange for five rights and $28 cash. The rights expire 21 days after the date of issuance.

a If you are the holder of 100 shares of Calgary Corporation common stock and receive a stock warrant for 100 rights, what alternative courses of action are open to you? Which course of action would be least desirable?

b What journal entry, if any, should be made by the company to record the issuance of the stock rights?

c Assuming that all the rights are exercised, give the journal entry which should be made by the corporation to record the exercising of the stock rights.

d Assuming that only 90% of the rights are exercised before the expiration date, give the journal entry or entries to be made by the company.

Ex. 15-2 Winter Corporation has outstanding three issues of securities: convertible bonds, convertible preferred stock, and common stock. All three securities are actively traded on the New York Stock Exchange. Assume that you bought 10 shares of the 5%, $100 par convertible preferred stock when it was originally issued by the company at a price of $102. The preferred stock is convertible into four shares of $10 par value common stock at any time. When you made your investment in the convertible preferred stock, the common stock had a market value of $22 a share. Now several years later the common stock has risen to a market price of $90 a share and you decide to convert your preferred stock into common shares.

a Prepare the journal entry which should be made by Winter Corporation to record the conversion. Explain why you have or have not utilized the prevailing market prices of the convertible preferred stock and/or the common stock in recording the conversion in the company's accounts.

b As a separate case, assume that while you are still holding your convertible preferred shares and the common stock has reached a market price of $90 a share, you decide that the common stock is grossly overpriced. Under this assumption would you still be inclined to convert your preferred stock into the common stock? Explain.

Ex. 15-3 A corporation granted 10-year stock options to three executives. The options for 30,000 shares of $5 par value common stock stipulated an option price of $25 a share. The current market price of the stock at the option date was $35. The three officers who were each granted 10,000-share options under the plan were given the right to exercise the options at any time within the 10-year period and could sell the shares acquired at any time. The corporation's stock is listed and actively traded every day.

In a discussion of the plan before its adoption, one executive suggested that the difference between the market price and the option price be charged to retained earnings since the cost to the corporation was attributable in large part to the past services of the three executives. Another executive expressed the view that there was no cost to the corporation since no payment of cash or other assets would be required.

a Does the stock option plan described above meet the requirements for a "qualified" stock option plan? Explain.

b In the light of **APB Opinion No. 25,** is there a cost to the corporation which should be recognized? If so, should it be recognized at the time the options are granted, when they are exercised, or at some other time?

c Prepare the journal entry, if any, which you think should be made to record issuance of the stock options, and the entry which should be made to record the exercising of the options for 30,000 shares. The market price at the date the options were exercised was $40. Observe the concepts set forth in **APB Opinion No. 25** in your answer.

Ex. 15-4 The following information applies to the securities of Duke Power Corporation:

	Recent prices	Dividend	Conversion ratio
Convertible preferred stock	$96.50	$6.75	3.25
Common stock	$22.00	$1.40	0

a Compute the following for these securities:
  (1) Yield on the convertible preferred stock
  (2) Yield on the common stock
  (3) Conversion value of the preferred stock
  (4) Conversion premium of the preferred stock (as a percentage)
  (5) Investment value of the preferred stock (assume an interest rate of 7.5% for securities of this quality)
  (6) Price risk of the preferred stock expressed as a percentage of market price

b Would the holder of 100 shares of the convertible preferred stock of Duke Power Corporation increase or decrease his dividend income by converting into common stock at this time? By what amount? Comment on the relationship of your answer to the conversion premium computed in part *(a)*.

Ex. 15-5 The following information applies to the securities of Ralston Purina Company:

	Recent prices	Dividend	Conversion ratio
Convertible preferred stock	$59	$1.20	1.40
Common stock	$42	$0.75	0

a Compute the following for these securities:
  (1) Yield on the convertible preferred stock
  (2) Yield on the common stock
  (3) Conversion value of the preferred stock
  (4) Conversion premium of the preferred stock (as a percentage)
  (5) Investment value of the preferred stock (assume the prevailing rate of return being demanded for investments of this quality is 8%)
  (6) Price risk of the preferred stock expressed as a percentage of market price

b Would the holder of 100 shares of the convertible preferred stock of Ralston Purina Company increase or decrease his dividend income by converting into common stock at this time? By what amount? Comment on the relationship of your answer to the conversion premium computed in part *(a)*.

SHORT CASES FOR ANALYSIS AND DECISION

Case 15-1 James Rogers, assistant to the president of Central Wire Products, Inc., is responsible for answering letters received by the president from the company's stockholders. These letters often contain complaints or suggestions about the company's policies. The instructions Rogers had received from the president required him to draft answering letters (to be signed by the president) which would build favorable relations with stockholders and give them an understanding of the company's policies and actions. One of the letters from a stockholder, Mrs. Anne Cooke, requiring an answer to be drafted by Rogers, read as follows:

> I have learned that officers of Central Wire Products, Inc., exercised stock options last year for 30,000 shares. The average market price of our stock last year was $75 and at December 31 it was $90, but the option price was only $25. According to my calculations that cost the company at least $1,500,000, which is more than the entire salary expense for officers during the last year, according to some statements made in the annual meeting last week. So, I'd like to know where you buried this $1,500,000 expense in the financial statements.
>
> I would also like to know why the stock option plan doesn't prohibit these officers from selling the stock they get through options. I saw an item in the paper that showed the president sold 8,000 shares of his holdings last year. I have never sold any of my shares, and if every one else would follow this policy, the price would really go up. I would appreciate a prompt answer to these questions.

Instructions Draft the letter which Rogers should prepare for the president's signature, answering each of the stockholder's questions as fully as possible. Assume that the stockholder's letter is correct with respect to details such as the number of shares for which options were exercised, the market prices, the sale of shares by the president, and related data.

Case 15-2 John Patino, president of Carton Company, found that an excessive amount of his time was being taken up by correspondence with stockholders. He therefore called a staff assistant, Joe Wilson, to his office and gave him the following assignment:

"Joe, I get quite a few letters from our stockholders offering suggestions and making complaints about various policies of the corporation. I want you to draft appropriate letters to these people for my signature. Be sure to maintain the best possible stockholder relations. Here's one to answer now from a Marvin Jones who says he owns 50 shares of our new convertible preferred stock."

The letter from Jones read as follows:

> After purchasing 50 shares of your $4 convertible preferred stock at $104 a share, I discovered some very unfavorable factors about this stock. As you know, it is convertible into 10 shares of common for each share of preferred and I had hoped the common would go up, and then I could convert my shares at a good profit. Now I have discovered that you have just declared a 10% stock dividend on the common and have said you may continue to do so in future years. This is going to be very hard on me as a preferred stockholder. I can still convert my 50 shares into 500 shares of common but it won't be worth nearly as much, because in five years you will have increased the amount of the common stock by more than 50%. You should only pay cash dividends on the common or you are injuring the convertible preferred shareholder.
>
> Also I find my stock is callable at $110, so it can't go any higher than that because of the danger that you would call it in. In view of these facts I want a refund for my shares or I will be forced to take legal action.

Sincerely,
Marvin Jones

Instructions Put yourself in the position of Joe Wilson and draft a reply to Jones for signature by the president. Indicate clearly in your letter whether the points made by Jones are valid. You should assume that the terms of the company's stock issues and its policies are in accordance with customary business practice.

PROBLEMS

Group A

15A-1 Madison Company, a large listed corporation, showed the following amounts in the stockholders' equity section of its balance sheet at May 31, 1975:

Common stock, $10 par value, authorized 8,000,000 shares, issued and outstanding, 1,000,000 shares	$10,000,000
Paid-in capital in excess of par	5,000,000
Retained earnings	6,310,000
Total stockholders' equity	$21,310,000

The company's operations had been profitable, but management had decided that additional outside capital was needed. Authorization was therefore obtained for 100,000 shares of $4 preferred stock with a par value of $50 a share. To help assure success of this financing, Madison Company offered with each share of preferred stock a detachable stock right which entitled the holder to purchase one share of common stock at $40 a share at any time within the next 10 years. The common stock was selling at a price of $35 at this time. As soon as the terms of the offering were announced, the stock rights began trading on the stock exchange at a price of $6 each.

The sale of 100,000 shares of the preferred stock with rights attached was carried out on June 1 at a price of $60 per share (including the stock right). The price of the common stock rose rapidly during the next several months. On December 1, when the common stock was selling at $65 a share, 10,000 rights were exercised and Madison Company issued the required 10,000 shares of common stock.

Instructions

a Prepare journal entries to record the issuance of the preferred stock and the detachable stock rights on June 1, and the issuance of common stock on December 1 when 10,000 rights were exercised. (Entries are not required for dividends on the preferred stock.)

b Prepare the stockholders' equity section of the balance sheet at December 31, 1975, assuming that net income since May 31 has been $3,000,000 and that dividend action on the preferred stock since that date has been as follows:

Sept. 1 Declared quarterly dividend of $1 per share on preferred stock.
Oct. 1 Paid quarterly dividend on preferred stock.
Dec. 1 Declared quarterly dividend of $1 per share on preferred stock, payable January 10 to stockholders of record December 15.

c Prepare any appropriate note or notes to the financial statements based on the information available in the problem.

15A-2 Field & Stream, Inc., has outstanding two issues of securities: (1) common stock, and (2) a 4.5% convertible bond issue in the face amount of $20,000,000. Interest payment dates of the bond issue are April 1 and October 1. The conversion clause in the bond contract entitles the bondholders to receive 30 shares of $15 par value common stock in exchange for each $1,000 bond.

On March 15, the annual dividend rate on the common stock was raised from

$1.50 to $2. On April 1 the holders of $800,000 face value in bonds exercised the conversion privilege. The market price of the bonds at this date was quoted at $122 per $100 face value; the price per share of common stock was $39. The ledger balances pertaining to the bonds and stock were as follows on April 1 prior to the conversion:

Bonds payable	$20,000,000
Discount on bonds payable	800,000
Common stock, $15 par, authorized 1 million shares, issued and outstanding	
250,000 shares	3,750,000
Paid-in capital in excess of par	2,500,000

Instructions
a Prepare the journal entry to record the conversion of bonds on April 1.
b Evaluate the effects of the conversion upon Field & Stream, Inc., with respect to
  (1) Income before taxes. (Disregard amortization of bond discount.)
  (2) The amount of corporate income taxes. Assume a tax rate of 48%.
  (3) The total annual amount of payments to security holders.
c What effect would the conversion have upon the annual cash income of an individual who converted 15 bonds into stock on April 1?

15A-3 Jones accepted a position as Assistant Vice President—Sales in Cedar Corporation and received a three-year contract at an annual salary of $70,000. Shortly thereafter Jones learned that all vice presidents of the corporation were to be granted five-year qualified stock options for 5,000 shares each. Jones was the only assistant vice president in the company, and he was disappointed to learn that the proposed stock option plan included only executives at the level of vice president and above.

After thinking the matter over, Jones went to the president with the following proposal: "I would like to be included in the stock option plan and receive an option on 5,000 shares of our $5 par common stock at 100% of the present market price of $30. In consideration for my inclusion in the option plan, I am willing for my three-year salary contract to be amended to reduce my annual salary from $70,000 to $55,000."

The president discussed the proposal with the board of directors and received approval to include Jones in the stock option plan. The plan as amended was then approved by vote of the stockholders.

One of the directors, who was also a large stockholder, commented as follows: "We will save $45,000 by the reduction in Jones' salary for the next three years. If the price of the stock does not rise above its present level, the option for the extra 5,000 shares will never be exercised and will cost us nothing. If the stock does go up and Jones exercises the option, we will issue an extra 5,000 shares but we will have no cash payment to make and no expense to recognize. So either way, we will be saving $45,000."

Instructions
a Under current standards of accounting for stock options, what accounting entry, if any, should be made to record the granting of the qualified stock option to Jones? Explain the reasoning involved.
b Without regard to current tax regulations or AICPA pronouncements, what minimum compensation cost, if any, do you think should be assigned to the stock option granted to Jones? Give the journal entry you would use to record issuance of the option.
c Assume that the market price of the stock rose to $50 a share within one year and Jones exercised his option for 5,000 shares. Give the journal entry to record issuance of the 5,000 shares optioned to Jones.
d Discuss the logic of the director's comments on the $45,000 saving by granting the 5,000-share option to Jones in exchange for a reduction in his salary.

15A-4 The following hypothetical example of the issuance to stockholders of rights to purchase a new issue of convertible debentures was included in an examination in financial accounting theory and practice.

Staff Corporation recently announced the issuance to preferred stockholders of two rights for each share of preferred outstanding, and the issuance to common stockholders of one right for each share of common outstanding. The preferred stock is cumulative, but neither convertible nor participating. The announcement stated that 10 rights and $100 cash would be required to purchase $100 principal amount of the 5% convertible debentures and that the rights would expire in 60 days.

Some stockholders sold their rights immediately and active trading in the rights began on a regional stock exchange at prices approximating $3 per right. The convertible debentures, although not yet issued, were also traded on this exchange on a "when issued" basis, meaning that delivery would not be required until after the scheduled issuance date. All the 1 million rights issued were exercised before the stipulated expiration date and the convertible debentures were issued.

Instructions
a Was the distribution of stock rights by Staff Corporation as described in this case typical of current practice? Explain fully.
b What was the approximate trading price of the convertible debentures on a "when issued" basis?
c Would a common stockholder who sold his rights, instead of exercising them, own a smaller share of the net assets of the company than he did before the rights were issued? Explain.
d Give the journal entry Staff Corporation should make when the rights were exercised and the convertible debentures issued.

15A-5 Lee Hawk organized Mohawk Corporation with a modest amount of capital and the business grew steadily during the next 20 years. Hawk served as president of the company and was also the largest single stockholder. His stockholdings included 50,000 shares of preferred stock and 100,000 shares of common stock at the time of his retirement from the presidency in January 1975. Hawk was succeeded as president by Jay Davis, who owned no stock in the company but was proposed for the position by another large stockholder, the Mill Corporation, which owned approximately 80,000 shares of Mohawk common stock.

The capital structure of Mohawk Corporation, consisted of two stock issues, as follows:

5% preferred stock, $100 par, cumulative, callable at 104, authorized, issued, and outstanding 100,000 shares	$10,000,000
Common stock, $1 par, authorized 3 million shares, issued and outstanding 1 million shares	1,000,000

The preferred stock had been issued at par and the common stock at $6 a share. The continued profitable operation of the company had caused retained earnings to grow to $10 million by the time of Hawk's retirement in January 1975. However, start-up expenses associated with bringing new facilities into operation in 1974 had limited earnings in that year to approximately $2 a share. Hawk, who continued as a director after his retirement from the presidency, predicted that earnings would increase very rapidly once the new facilities were operating efficiently.

The change in management in January 1975 was a thoroughgoing one. In addition to the new president, Mill Corporation also arranged for the appointment of two new vice presidents and a new treasurer, all of whom were former executives with Mill Corporation. Four members of the 10-man board of directors of Mohawk Corporation were presently executives of Mill Corporation. The other board members, except Davis and Hawk, were "public members," who had been selected because of their prominence in the community rather than because of any particular interest in the affairs of Mohawk Corporation.

One of the first acts of the new president, Jay Davis, was to propose a stock option plan "to aid the company in attracting and retaining executive personnel of outstanding ability." The stock option plan was designed to meet the requirements of the Internal Revenue Service for a "qualified stock option plan." The plan made available to executives and key employees a total of 100,000 shares. The option price was not to be less than 100% of the fair market value of the stock at the time of granting the option. Options were to run for a period of five years from date of grant but could not be exercised during the first two years from date of grant. The options were not transferable and expired upon termination of employment other than by reason of death. The plan called for options to be granted to key employees by the board of directors upon recommendation of a three-member stock option committee.

The stock option plan was bitterly opposed by Hawk, but was approved by the board of directors and subsequently by stockholders and became effective on May 1, 1975. On May 15, 1975, options to purchase 40,000 shares were granted to 10 officers and employees at a price of $32, the average price of the stock on the Pacific Stock Exchange on the day of grant.

On the day of grant, Hawk, who continued to oppose the stock option plan, made a formal offer to the company to purchase a five-year option on 40,000 shares at the existing price of $32. The price offered by Hawk for this option was $320,000 cash, which he explained was computed as one-fourth of the present market price. Hawk simultaneously resigned from the board and threatened to file suit against the corporation and its directors if they in his words "rejected my cash offer and persisted in robbing the stockholders by giving away stock to a gang of selfish insiders." In a news conference, Hawk predicted that the earnings of the company would triple within the next two years and that "the price of the stock would hit $100 within two years."

Instructions

a If you were a member of the board of directors, would you favor accepting Hawk's offer to purchase an option on 40,000 shares? Explain fully. If his offer were accepted, how should this action be reflected in the accounts and in the financial statements?

b Assume that the company accepted Hawk's offer, that earnings after preferred dividend requirements amounted to $4 million in 1975, and that no dividends were paid on common stock; prepare the stockholders' equity section of the balance sheet at December 31, 1975. No options had been exercised to this date.

c Without regard to current practice or AICPA pronouncements, state what valuation, if any, should be assigned to the 40,000 shares optioned to key employees? Explain fully the reasoning involved and give the journal entry or entries, if any, to be made at the date of grant.

d Assuming that all the options issued to executives were exercised on July 1, 1977, when the market price of the stock reached $100 a share, give the journal entries to record the issuance of these shares. Explain fully the reasoning supporting this entry.

e Assuming that the market price of the stock did not rise above $32 at any time during the option period and that no options were exercised, what recognition, if any, should be given in the accounts for the expiration of the options issued to employees under the qualified stock plan?

Group B

15B-1 On August 31, 1975, the stockholders' equity section of Welborn Corporation appeared as follows:

Common stock, $2.50 par value, authorized 10,000,000 shares, issued and
    outstanding, 2,000,000 shares . . . . $ 5,000,000
Paid-in capital in excess of par 25,000,000
Retained earnings . . *21,050.00* 18,700,000
Total stockholders' equity . . *63,450,000* $48,700,000

At this time Welborn Corporation completed arrangements for public sale of an issue of 200,000 shares of $3 preferred stock with a par value of $50 a share. Accompanying each preferred share was a detachable stock right entitling the holder to purchase one share of common stock at $40 a share at any time within the next 10 years. The common stock was currently being traded on the stock exchange at a price of $36. As soon as the terms of the preferred stock and rights offering were announced, the rights began trading separately on the stock exchange at a price of $3.50 on a when-issued basis.

The entire issue of 200,000 shares of preferred stock with rights attached was sold on September 1 at a price of $57 a share. During the next few months the price of the common stock rose rapidly, and on December 1 it was being traded at $66 a share. On that date, 25,000 rights were exercised and Welborn Corporation issued the required 25,000 shares of common stock.

Instructions
a Prepare journal entries to record the issuance of the preferred stock and detachable stock rights on September 1, and the issuance of common stock on December 1. (Entries are not required for dividend actions.)
b Prepare the stockholders' equity section of the balance sheet at December 31, 1975, assuming that net income since August 31 has been $2,500,000 and that on December 1 a quarterly dividend of 75 cents a share was declared on the preferred stock, payable January 15 to stockholders of record on December 15.
c Prepare any appropriate note or notes to the financial statements based on the information provided.

15B-2 Guard Company has outstanding an issue of $12,000,000 of 6% convertible bonds with interest payment dates of June 1 and December 1. The conversion feature of the bond contract entitles the bondholders to receive 50 shares of $10 par value common stock in exchange for each $1,000 bond.

On May 15, the annual dividend rate on the common stock was increased from $1 to $1.50. On June 1 the holders of $500,000 face value of bonds exercised the conversion privilege. The quoted market price of the bonds at this date was $129½ per $100 face value; the price per share of common stock was $26. The ledger balances pertaining to the bonds and the stock were as follows on June 1 prior to recording the conversion:

Bonds payable $12,000,000
Discount on bonds payable 480,000
Common stock, $10 par value, authorized 1,000,000 shares, issued and out-
    standing 300,000 shares 3,000,000
Paid-in capital in excess of par 2,400,000

Instructions
a Prepare the journal entry to record the conversion of bonds on June 1.
b Evaluate the effects of the conversion upon Guard Company with respect to:

(1) Income before income taxes. (Disregard amortization of bond discount.)
(2) The amount of corporate income taxes. Assume a tax rate of 48%.
(3) The total annual amount of payments to security holders.
c What effect would the conversion have upon the annual cash income of an individual who converted 20 bonds into stock on June 1?

15B-3 John Jensen, president of Pinetree Corporation, commented during the course of a directors' meeting that the corporation had achieved higher sales and higher net income during each of the last seven years. He drew attention to the fact that the market price of both the common stock and the convertible preferred stock had been in a long-term definite uptrend. Jensen also stated:

"We have 10,000 shares of 6%, $100 par, convertible preferred stock outstanding, which was originally issued for cash of $1,040,000. This stock is callable at $106 and convertible at any time into our $5 par common stock in the ratio of three shares of common for each share of preferred. We have been paying $1 a year dividend on our common stock and do not plan any increase in the near future. Although our earnings have been rising, we need to reinvest these earnings to take advantage of our opportunities for growth. Our common stock is now selling for $70 a share, so apparently our stockholders are more interested in our earnings than in dividends."

After these comments, Jensen invited questions or suggestions from the directors. Director D. K. White offered the following suggestion:

"Our convertible preferred stock is too small an issue for a company of our present size. I propose that we call it all in at once and get rid of it. If everyone is forced to convert into common, the additional common dividend will go up by only $30,000 a year and we will be saving $60,000 a year in preferred dividends. Also we can transfer the $40,000 of premium on preferred stock now on the books to our retained earnings or include it as an extraordinary gain on this year's income statement. If any preferred stockholders fail to convert, we will have a larger gain on those shares equal to the excess of the present market price over the call price. And if we want convertible preferred stock in the future we will be able to put out a larger issue at less than the 6% rate we're now paying. Consequently calling this stock will give us several benefits and cost us nothing."

Instructions
a Evaluate point by point the proposal by Director White. For each point indicate (and explain fully) your agreement or disagreement with his statements.
b What is the probable approximate market price of the convertible preferred stock? Explain.
c Prepare the journal entry (or entries) that would be necessary if White's plan to call the preferred stock is carried out.

15B-4 The capital structure of Rayburn Corporation at the time of its organization on January 2, 1971, consisted solely of common stock; 1 million shares with par value of $5 each were authorized and 300,000 shares were issued for cash at a price of $15 each. As the company grew, a need for additional outside capital became apparent. During the course of a directors' meeting in May 1975, two alternative plans were proposed for raising more capital through the issuance of stock rights.

Plan A, proposed by James Avery, required the distribution without charge of 300,000 stock rights to the holders of the 300,000 shares of common stock outstanding. These rights were to be issued on May 15, 1975, and would expire on June 30, 1975. During this brief life span of the rights, the company would be prepared to issue additional common shares upon presentation of five rights and $40 in cash for each share. The market price of the stock had been steady at $48 for some time and it was assumed that a market price of $48 would prevail on May 15.

Plan B was an alternative plan proposed by Robert Bell, which called for selling

300,000 stock rights at $1 each. The rights were to be offered first to present stockholders, but any rights not taken by stockholders were to be sold to the public. In all other respects the two plans were identical; that is, expiration date was June 30 for both and the exercise of the rights under both plans called for the presentation of five rights and $40 cash for each common share.

Director Avery claimed his plan represented more generous treatment of the company's present shareholders, but Director Bell denied that this was the case.

Instructions

a Discuss the merits of the two plans from the viewpoint of the company and also from the viewpoint of the stockholders. Include in your answer a comparison of the amounts which would appear in the capital stock and paid-in capital accounts under both plans, assuming that all the rights were exercised.

b Assume the following additional facts in evaluating Rayburn Corporation's alternative plans for stock rights. On May 30, 1975, the stock began a sharp downward movement and fell in price from $48 on May 30 to $30 on June 30. During the latter part of May, 1,000 stock rights were exercised at the stipulated price of $40 but the declining market for the stock discouraged any further exercise of rights and the remainder of the rights expired on June 30.

(1) Assuming that the stock rights had been distributed free under Plan A, what information, if any, concerning the stock rights should appear in a balance sheet prepared at May 31, 1975? Explain any changes in the stockholders' equity accounts.

(2) Assuming that the stock rights had all been sold at $1 each under Plan B, what information, if any, concerning the stock rights should appear in a balance sheet prepared at May 31, 1975?

(3) Assuming that Plan A had been followed, what information, if any, concerning the stock rights should appear in a balance sheet prepared at June 30, 1975?

(4) Assuming that Plan B had been followed, what information, if any, concerning the rights should appear in a balance sheet prepared at June 30, 1975?

15B-5 Kyle Company uses stock options as a form of compensation for its executives. Since the option provides a call on the stock at a fixed price over a period of years with no risk to the holder, the opportunity for gain is unlimited and the chance of loss is zero. Despite the obvious value of such stock options and their importance in attracting and retaining competent executives, accountants have had great difficulty in agreeing on the most appropriate method of determining a dollar valuation, if any, to be assigned to executive stock options.

Instructions

a Describe very briefly five methods that have been proposed for determining the value of executive stock options. Limit this part of your answer to identifying or distinguishing five methods.

b Discuss the conceptual merits of each of the five methods you identified in part (*a*) above.

CHAPTER **16**

Retained earnings and dividends

RETAINED EARNINGS

Distinguishing between paid-in capital and earned capital

In the balance sheet of a single proprietorship, the owner's equity is customarily shown as a single amount. For a partnership, too, the equity of each owner is presented as a single figure without any distinction between paid-in capital and accumulated earnings. On a corporation balance sheet, however, a basic objective in setting up the stockholders' equity is to distinguish clearly between paid-in capital and earned capital.

Why should the owners' equity be subdivided in the corporate form of organization? One reason is that stockholders and creditors have a right to know whether a corporation in paying dividends is actually distributing earnings or is returning invested capital. In the single proprietorship and partnership, the owners may withdraw capital from the business in any amounts they choose even though such withdrawals may exceed earnings. In a corporation, however, only the accumulated earnings are ordinarily regarded as available for withdrawal. This view reflects corporate policy and desire for continuity of existence as well as legal considerations. Consequently, the accountant tries to keep a clear distinction between paid-in capital and accumulated earnings. The maintenance of these two separate categories of capital is also desirable because stockholders are principally absentee owners not participating in management. They may regard the active management of the corporation as custodians of the paid-in capital and may judge the efficiency of management to some extent by the amount of earnings accumulated by the corporation.

From the standpoint of accounting theory, it is necessary to distinguish total paid-in capital from retained earnings. Any further classification of capital usually rests on legal requirements rather than on accounting concepts. The framers of corporation laws have attempted to protect creditors by creating the concept of *legal capital*—an amount of stockholders' equity not subject to withdrawal. In recognition of these legal requirements, the accountant customarily makes a further classification by subdividing paid-in capital between legal capital (capital stock) and additional paid-in capital (paid-in surplus). Legal capital generally is not subject to withdrawal; in some states, however, additional paid-in capital is legally available for dividends, provided that stockholders are notified of the source of the dividends. In still other states dividends may be paid from net assets in excess of capital stock, which means that dividends could be paid from paid-in capital in excess of par without notice to stockholders. Although dividends can be declared in some states even when a deficit exists, corporate financial policy is usually far more cautious, and dividends from any source other than retained earnings are rare.

In recent years the accounting profession has been quite successful in substituting the term *retained earnings* for the older and somewhat ambiguous term *earned surplus,* but it is interesting to note that many state laws still speak of "surplus" as opposed to "capital." Consequently, corporate announcements, such as merger agreements, which are influenced by state statutes, continue to employ the terms *capital* and *surplus.* Even in financial statements the older terminology still appears occasionally.

The legal and accounting viewpoints as to necessary classification of stockholders' equity are thus somewhat at variance. The accountant, and the businessman as well, tend to view the entire paid-in capital as being permanently committed to the enterprise. But, more strictly speaking, only that portion of paid-in capital which is classified by statute as legal capital (usually capital stock) is definitely unavailable as a source of dividends.

Reasonable compliance with both accounting and legal considerations may be achieved in financial statements by showing the total paid-in capital as a major classification with legal capital as a component thereof. The other major classification should be retained earnings, regardless of whether this amount indicates the total legally available for distribution to stockholders. In fact, the balance sheet of a corporation usually does not purport to show the amount legally available for dividends. Such a determination would be a legal one, guided by the laws of the particular state in which the company was incorporated, and would ordinarily bear little or no relationship to actual dividend policy, since few corporations declare dividends up to the maximum amount legally allowable.

Even though the financial and managerial uses of financial statements outweigh the legal niceties involved, legal considerations have at times had considerable influence on the form and structure of the balance sheet. Much of what the accountant does in this area is purely and simply a matter of legal reporting, as opposed to economic reporting. In the balance sheets of some early-day corporations, the stockholders' equity section showed little more than a division between legal capital (capital stock) and "surplus." Surplus was then regarded merely as the excess of a corporation's total capital over its legal capital. Under such standards the category of surplus was a most confusing catchall, often including premium on capital stock, "gains" from treasury stock transactions, capital donated by outsiders, and retained earnings. Such a balance sheet presentation was quite unsatisfactory from the viewpoint of investors and bankers. A surplus account of $1 million on one balance sheet might represent accumulated earnings of that amount; on another balance sheet a surplus account of $1 million might be the net balance resulting from combining $2 million of paid-in capital with $1 million of an operating deficit. To avoid the confusion caused by this lumping together of unlike elements in the surplus account, accountants began to classify the elements of stockholders' equity according to source, and to show each classification as a separate item in the balance sheet.

Classifying elements of corporate capital by source

The first step toward classifying surplus by source was to use the categories of *capital surplus* and *earned surplus.* The term *capital surplus* soon fell into disrepute, however, because it was used in several different meanings. Some companies limited capital surplus to paid-in capital in excess of par value of shares issued; others included increments in capital arising from arbitrary write-up of asset values; still others added in extraordinary gains and losses, as from the sale of a major segment of the business. The caption of capital surplus is still encountered occasionally on published financial statements, but the term is no longer in good standing. *Paid-in surplus* was another term widely used for a time to distinguish paid-in capital in excess of par from accumulated earnings.

In an effort to develop more uniform and descriptive terminology for the elements of corporate capital, the Committee on Terminology of the AICPA suggested complete discontinuance of the term *surplus.* The committee proposed substituting terms which would distinguish clearly (1) legal capital, (2) capital in excess of legal capital, and (3) undivided profits. Use of the word surplus was also discouraged by the American Accounting Association.

Objections to the terms surplus and capital surplus stressed the prevailing connotations of surplus, such as excess, residue, or "that which remains when use or need is satisfied." No such meaning is intended in accounting. More descriptive terms indicating source such as "retained earnings," "retained income," and "earnings reinvested in the business" were recommended as replacements for "earned surplus."

The recommendations of the AICPA and the American Accounting Association received considerable support. In published financial statements, *earned surplus* is now seldom encountered. However, the word surplus has not been entirely removed from the vocabulary of accountants; it is still frequently used in technical discussions and writings.

Currently accepted terms for the stockholders' equity section

At present the following balance sheet classifications of corporate capital are widely used:

1 Capital stock (legal capital)
2 Paid-in capital in excess of par
3 Retained earnings or deficit

A subtotal entitled "total paid-in capital" should desirably be inserted in the stockholders' equity section of the balance sheet to show the aggregate of the capital stock and paid-in capital in excess of par.

The question of "appraisal capital" has little practical importance, as corporations have generally adhered to the cost principle of asset valuation. If any appreciation is included in the stockholders' equity, it should be shown separately and given a title such as "unrealized appreciation from revaluation of assets" or simply "appraisal capital."

Paid-in Capital in Excess of Par Paid-in capital in excess of par comes principally from the following sources:

1 Premium on par value stock
2 Excess of issuance price over stated value of no-par stock
3 Conversion of convertible bonds or preferred stock
4 Excess of proceeds from reissuance of treasury shares over the cost of these shares
5 Reduction of par or stated value of stock
6 Donations of property to the corporation by stockholders or outsiders

Although capital from all these sources may be combined into the single balance sheet item of Paid-in Capital in Excess of Par, or Additional Paid-in Capital, a separate ledger account is needed for each in order to carry out the principle of classifying by source all elements of the stockholders' equity. If any part of paid-in capital is distributed by a dividend, management has a duty to inform the stockholders that the dividend is a return of capital and not a distribution of earnings.

Neither operating losses nor extraordinary losses of nonrecurring nature should be charged against paid-in capital. Examples of improper charges against paid-in capital in excess of par value to which the SEC has taken exception include the following:

1 Write-offs of purchased goodwill

2 Write-downs of plant and equipment which have lost usefulness because of obsolescence or unexpectedly rapid deterioration

3 Write-off of bond discount at the time of issuing the bonds

4 Losses on sale of investments

In all these situations the SEC has followed the principle set forth in its *Accounting Series Release No. 1* which stated ". . . capital surplus should under no circumstances be used to write off losses which, if currently recognized, would have been chargeable against income." If paid-in capital were to be charged with such losses, it follows that net income and retained earnings would be relieved of the losses and would therefore be overstated.

Although charges against paid-in capital accounts are infrequent, they are warranted in such situations as the following:

1 Payment of a liquidating dividend.

2 Redemption of shares, originally issued at a premium, at a price in excess of par value. For example, X Corporation redeems at the stipulated call price of $106 a portion of its preferred shares originally issued at a price of $110. The $6 per share redemption premium may be charged against the Premium on Preferred Stock account.

3 Absorption of a deficit as part of a quasi-reorganization.

Unrealized Appreciation from Revaluation of Assets Present accounting standards require that assets such as plant and equipment be accounted for on the basis of cost, despite increases or decreases which occur in their fair value. However, in view of the large increases in economic value of certain assets because of their scarcity and also because of the devaluations of the dollar, much attention has been given to the possibility of writing up asset values.

There is general agreement among accountants that if assets are written up to appraisal values, the corresponding unrealized increment in stockholders' equity should be reported as a separate and distinct element of corporate capital. An appropriate title might be Unrealized Appreciation from Revaluation of Assets, or possibly Appraisal Capital. Since such increments in capital are unrealized, they should not be used as a basis for absorbing losses or for the declaration of dividends. If the laws of a given state permit dividends based on appraisal capital accounts, the accountant should insist upon adequate disclosure of the nature of the dividend action.

The retained earnings account   *Know*

Retained earnings represents the accumulated net income of a corporation minus amounts distributed to stockholders and amounts transferred to paid-in capital accounts. Extraordinary gains and losses of a non-recurring nature as well as operating earnings and losses are included in determining the annual net income which is transferred to the Retained Earnings account. A negative amount (debit balance) in the Retained Earnings account is termed a *deficit.*

In many a large corporation, the amount of retained earnings shown on the balance sheet is actually far less than the total income earned and retained, because numerous large transfers have been made from the Retained Earnings account to the Capital Stock and Additional Paid-in Capital accounts. Such transfers are legally permissible because they tend to strengthen the position of corporate creditors by increasing the cushion of capital between creditors and the threat of operating losses. In terms of maintaining a clear distinction between paid-in capital and retained earnings, however, such transfers pose a problem. These transfers will be discussed further in our consideration of stock dividends.

The T account shown below indicates the kinds of debits and credits which may comprise a typical Retained Earnings account.

Retained Earnings

1. Net loss	1. Net income
2. Prior period adjustments to correct overstatement of earnings in previous years	2. Prior period adjustments to correct understatement of earnings in previous years
3. Cash dividends	
4. Stock dividends	

As explained in Chapter 3, current practice requires that extraordinary gains and losses be included in the determination of net income rather than being entered directly in retained earnings. *Prior period adjustments* are entered directly in the Retained Earnings account and not included in the determination of the current year's net income. As defined in *Opinion No. 9* by the Accounting Principles Board, prior period adjustments "are limited to those material adjustments which (a) can be specifically identified with and directly related to the business activities of particular prior periods, and (b) are not attributable to economic events occurring subsequent to the date of the financial statements for the prior period, and (c) depend primarily on determinations by persons other than management and (d) were not susceptible of reasonable estimation prior to such determination."[1] Examples include large amounts from settlements of income taxes, renegotiation proceedings, decisions on public utility rates, and matters under litigation.

Prior period adjustments do not include normal recurring corrections and adjustments arising from the use of estimates in the accounting

[1] *APB Opinion No. 9,* "Reporting the Results of Operations," AICPA (New York: 1966), pp. 115–116.

process. Thus, changes in depreciation because of revised estimates of useful life are not prior period adjustments; they are to be reflected in operations of the current period.

It is a common expression to say that a company pays dividends "out of its retained earnings" or that it "distributes its retained earnings in the form of dividends." These statements are inaccurate because in fact dividends are paid "out of cash" and from no other source. The expressions quoted above tend to create confusion in the minds of persons lacking a knowledge of accounting; such persons may acquire a mental picture of corporate retained earnings in the form of a pile of cash or other property which may be handed out to stockholders. They fail to recognize that retained earnings, like capital stock and additional paid-in capital, are not tangible things but merely an element of the ownership interest in the various assets owned by the corporation. Retained earnings is that portion of the ownership interest which is not paid-in capital. The existence of a retained earnings account with a balance of, say, $100,000 tells us nothing about the amount of cash or any other type of asset held by the company.

After listing the principal sources of retained earnings, it may be useful to mention a few items which do *not* belong in retained earnings but which are sometimes erroneously entered there.

1 Treasury stock transactions which appear to produce a "gain"
2 Donations of property (such as the gift to a corporation or a plant site by a city seeking to attract new industries)
3 Increments in stockholders' equity resulting from writing up plant assets to an appraised value in excess of cost

Let us consider briefly why each of these items does not belong in retained earnings. The issuance of treasury stock at a price in excess of cost merely results in an increase in paid-in capital. The receipt of donated property should be recorded in a separate capital account with a descriptive title, in accordance with the principle of classifying capital by source. Such an account, perhaps entitled Capital from Donation of Plant Site, is one of the several types of paid-in capital. Increases in the carrying value of plant assets, if recorded at all, produce an unrealized increment in the ownership equity and therefore require separate classification.

DIVIDENDS

Cash dividends

The usual meaning of dividend is a distribution of resources to stockholders in proportion to the number of shares owned by each. The term *dividend,* when used by itself, is generally understood to mean a cash dividend; this usage is followed throughout this book. Corporations frequently distribute additional shares of their own stock to stockholders and call such distributions "stock dividends." Strictly speaking, a stock dividend is not a dividend at all because no resources are distributed. However, stock dividends are of considerable practical importance and pose some challenging accounting questions which are discussed later in this chapter.

No obligation to pay a dividend exists until the board of directors has formally declared a dividend. This dividend action by the board consists of a resolution specifying the following points:

1 Date of declaration
2 Date of record
3 Date of payment
4 Rate or amount per share, usually expressed as a dollar amount

On the **date of declaration** of a cash dividend, the newly created liability is usually recorded by debiting Dividends and crediting Dividends Payable. The Dividends account is closed into Retained Earnings at the end of the accounting period. If the corporation has both common and preferred stock, a separate Dividends account should be used for each (Dividends: Common Stock, and Dividends: Preferred Stock).

The **date of record** is specified in the dividend declaration and usually follows the date of declaration by a few weeks. To qualify for the dividend, a person must be listed in the company's stock records on the date of record.

The stocks of companies listed on the stock exchanges sell "ex-dividend" three business days before the date of record, thus facilitating compilation of the list of owners on the record date. An investor who buys shares before the ex-dividend date is entitled to receive the dividend; conversely, a stockholder who sells before the ex-dividend date is selling his right to receive the dividend as well as the shares of stock.

The **date of payment** of a dividend usually is set for a few weeks after the date of record. Payment is recorded by debiting the liability account Dividends Payable and crediting Cash.

After declaration of a dividend by the board of directors and notice of the declaration to stockholders, the dividend action cannot be rescinded by the directors. Of course this generalization as to permissible corporate action is subject to exceptions, as are all such broad statements. For example, Alaska Airlines, Inc. announced in a press release that the directors had declared a 5% stock dividend, but in a later telegram to news media canceled the announcement. The rescission of the original announcement apparently became necessary because the SEC objected to the use of the word dividend under the prevailing circumstances. The SEC requested that the so-called "dividend" be termed a "5% stock distribution," because it represented a distribution of paid-in capital rather than retained earnings.

The declaration of a cash dividend immediately creates a liability, classified in the balance sheet as a current liability, since the date for payment is ordinarily only a few weeks or months away. In the event that a corporation should become insolvent in the interval between the declaration date and payment date, the stockholders are in the same position with respect to their right to receive the dividend as any unsecured creditor.

In an accounting textbook emphasizing principles rather than mechanics, it is convenient to speak of dividends being recorded as a charge against Retained Earnings, rather than indicating that the Dividends account is debited and then later closed into Retained Earnings. Consequently, we shall as a matter of convenience sometimes illustrate the declaration of a dividend by showing a debit to the Retained Earnings account.

As indicated in the preceding discussion, general requirements for payment of a cash dividend include (1) existence of retained earnings, (2) an adequate cash position, and (3) action by the board of directors.

Property dividends

Most dividends are in cash but occasionally a company may choose to pay a dividend in the form of merchandise, or other property such as securities of another company. In most cases of property dividends, the book value of the assets being distributed is the appropriate amount to be recorded as a dividend rather than the current market value of such assets. The retained earnings of a corporation reflects the values at which assets are carried on the books. If some of these assets are distributed to shareholders as a property dividend, retained earnings is reduced by the book value of the assets so distributed. If the dividend were recorded at the current fair market value of the securities or other property being distributed to shareholders, the corporation would show a gain or loss as a consequence of the dividend action. To avoid confusion, the dividend declaration ordinarily refers to the specific securities or other property being distributed rather than establishing a dividend liability based on current fair value. From the viewpoint of the shareholder, however, the dividend received should be recorded at its fair market value. Income tax regulations also require that property received as a dividend by a stockholder be included in his taxable income at its fair market value.

Dividends in scrip (liability dividends)

In theory a corporation which is short of cash might obligate itself by declaring a dividend consisting of promissory notes to its stockholders calling for payment at some future date. In practice, however, such "scrip dividends" almost never occur, because corporations which are short of cash are usually careful not to incur any unnecessary liabilities. The accounting entry for a "scrip dividend" or "liability dividend" would be a debit to the Retained Earnings account and a credit to a liability account with an appropriate title, such as Notes Payable to Stockholders or Scrip Dividends Payable.

Earnings and dividends

The net income earned during an accounting period results in an increase in net assets and an equal increase in the stockholders' equity. The board of directors must decide whether this net income is to be retained for use in the business or is to be distributed to stockholders as dividends. Many "growth companies" pay little or nothing as cash dividends because their rapid expansion creates an urgent need for working capital. In older, more stable companies, cash dividends often range from perhaps 40 to 80% of earnings, with a few industries such as public utilities noted for an even higher percentage distribution of earnings.

Most listed companies follow a policy of regular quarterly dividends with an "extra" being paid at year-end if earnings prove better than expected. Established annual dividend rates such as $4 per share or $1.60 per share thus become associated with certain stocks, and this reputation of stable dividends tends to add to the investment quality of these securities. Once such a rate has become generally known, a company is reluctant to lower the rate unless forced to do so by a sustained decline in earnings or a critical shortage of working capital.

Stock splits

When the market price of a company's stock reaches an inconveniently high trading range such as $100 a share or more, the company may decide to split the shares. A stock split of, say, 3 for 1 of a stock selling for $150 a share will cause the number of shares held by each stockholder to triple and should in theory cause the price to drop to approximately $50 a share. (Since many cross currents are normally present in the stock markets, the actual movement of a security's market price is never precisely predictable.) One result of a stock dividend may be to achieve wider distribution of shares, because many investors (logically or not) are unwilling to purchase stock with a very high price per share. The most popular price range with American investors, according to some students of the securities business, is around $30 to $50 a share. Those companies selling consumer products such as automobiles, gasoline, and household appliances have a particular interest in developing the widest possible distribution of their shares, since each stockholder may be expected to favor his company's products.

A stock split causes no change in the total dollar amount of stockholders' equity and no change in paid-in capital, retained earnings, or other components. The par value or stated value per share is reduced in proportion to the increase in number of shares. For example, in a 4 for 1 split of a stock with par value of $10, the new shares would have a par value of $2.50 each.

When a stock is split, the old shares usually are *not* called in or exchanged for new ones. The company merely issues to each shareholder a sufficient number of new shares to bring his total holdings up to the number indicated by the split. A person holding 100 shares prior to the previously mentioned 4 for 1 split of a $10 par value stock would receive 300 new shares of $2.50 par value. He would continue to hold the original certificate for 100 shares of $10 par value stock. Of course, the par value of all the shares is now $2.50 but it is not necessary for any exchange of certificates to be made. Eventually the old $10 par value certificates will disappear from circulation; whenever such a certificate is sold, the new certificate issued in the name of the new owner will show the reduced par value of $2.50.

Since the only ledger account affected by a stock split is the Capital Stock account, an entry such as the following may be made to record the change in par value and number of outstanding shares.

Capital Stock ($10 par value)	10,000,000	
Capital Stock ($2.50 par value)		10,000,000
To record a 4 for 1 stock split carried out by reducing		
par value from $10 to $2.50 per share and issuing		
3 million additional shares, thus increasing total out-		
standing shares from 1 million to 4 million.		

A *reverse stock split,* as the name suggests, is the opposite of a stock split. The number of outstanding shares is reduced proportionately for all stockholders. For example, the outstanding stock might be reduced from 3 million shares to 1 million shares in a 1 for 3 reverse stock split. All stockholders would surrender their existing shares in exchange for one-third as many new shares. A reverse stock split does not affect the assets or liabilities of the company and therefore does not change the total amount of stockholders' equity. Such transactions are not common; they are usually considered only by companies with stock which has dropped in market price to an extremely low level. The reverse split tends to increase the market price per share in proportion to the reduction in number of outstanding shares.

Stock dividends

In recent years increasing numbers of corporations have chosen to pay stock dividends as well as cash dividends, or in some cases to distribute stock dividends only. A stock dividend is a distribution of additional shares to the stockholders in proportion to their existing holdings. "Common on common" is the usual type of stock dividend; such a distribution is also known as an "ordinary stock dividend."

Distribution of a stock dividend causes no change in the assets or liabilities of a corporation; the only effect is a transfer between accounts in the stockholders' equity group. Since there is no decrease in the net assets of the corporation, a stock dividend does not give the stockholder anything he did not have before. The number of shares held by each stockholder is increased but each share represents a smaller slice of ownership in the corporation. The net assets of the corporation are unchanged by a stock dividend and the proportionate interest of each stockholder in those net assets is unchanged.

Assume, for example, that X Corporation has total stockholders' equity of $12,000, represented by $6,000 of capital stock and $6,000 of retained earnings. There are 100 shares of stock outstanding; therefore, each share represents a 1% interest in the corporation, or $120 of net assets. The X Corporation now distributes a 20% stock dividend, so the total number of shares rises to 120. Since total net assets remain at $12,000, the net assets per share drop to $100. A stockholder who owned 10 shares (a 10% interest) before the stock dividend would now own 12 shares, but this still represents 10% of the shares outstanding. Also the net assets represented by his holdings would be unchanged. Prior to the stock dividend 10 shares represented $1,200 of net assets (10 $\times$ $120); 12 shares after the stock dividend also represent $1,200 of net assets (12 $\times$ $100).

The principal argument for stock dividends is that they enable a "growth company" to retain accumulated earnings in the business yet provide the stockholders with additional shares as tangible evidence of their increasing equity in the corporation. This view was well explained in a recent letter to stockholders by the president of a major corporation which read as follows:

> It is my pleasure to inform you of the action taken by the Board of Directors of our Company today declaring a 5% Common Stock dividend, which is at the rate of one share of Common Stock for each twenty shares of Common Stock you now hold.
>
> The Stockholders' equity in our company has been steadily enhanced in value by continuing large investments in all phases of the business. These large investments are being financed from current operations and cash available from undistributed earnings of prior years. Inasmuch as your equity in the working assets of the business thus has been increased, your Board of Directors now has considered it appropriate to recognize this increase by capitalizing a portion of the reinvestment by means of this stock dividend.

It may be argued that distribution of a stock dividend causes retained earnings to be understated on the corporation's subsequent balance sheets since a portion of the accumulated earnings becomes concealed in the paid-in capital accounts. One answer is that the decision of the board of directors, acting in behalf of the stockholders, to issue a stock dividend constitutes a dedication of earnings to the permanent capital of the corporation. This dedication of earnings for permanent use may be viewed as the equivalent of distributing earnings to stockholders and immediate return by them of such earnings to the corporation, thus increasing the paid-in capital.

What amount of retained earnings should be transferred to the paid-in capital accounts for each share issued in a stock dividend? Although the legal requirement in most states is merely the par or stated value of the dividend shares, current accounting standards call for capitalizing an amount equal to the *fair market value per share* prior to the dividend. Both the SEC and the AICPA support the use of fair market value as a measure of the amount of retained earnings to be capitalized for all stock dividends which increase the number of outstanding shares by less than 20 or 25%. For larger stock dividends, only the par or stated value per share is transferred from retained earnings to permanent capital. The reasons underlying this difference in treatment of small and large stock dividends is explained in a later section of this discussion.

The Committee on Accounting Procedure of the AICPA has stressed that many recipients of stock dividends regard them as distributions of corporate earnings in an amount equal to the market value of the shares received. Such views are strengthened by the fact that small stock dividends often do not cause any apparent decline in the market price of the stock, and the total market value of the original shares held often remains unchanged. The stockholder is thus able, if he wishes, to sell for cash the dividend shares received without any decrease in the market value of his stock investment. If his holdings are small and would entitle him to only a fraction of a dividend share, the company ordinarily will act as his agent in selling the fractional share and will remit to him the cash proceeds.

One explanation for the fact that market prices often do not decline when the outstanding stock is increased by a small stock dividend is that the corporation will presumably continue to pay the established rate of cash dividend per share. The shareholder thus anticipates an increased amount of cash dividends on his investment.

Because of the prevalent belief among some investors that stock dividends constitute a distribution of corporate earnings, the AICPA committee has urged that corporations should in the public interest record stock dividends by transferring from retained earnings to the paid-in capital accounts an amount equal to the fair market value of the dividend shares. If any lesser amount is capitalized, some part of the earnings which stockholders believe to have been distributed to them would remain in retained earnings available for future dividends.

In addition to these views of the AICPA, it should be observed that in many companies with stock selling at prices of $50 to $100 a share or more, the par value is often as low as $1 or less. Consequently, the legal requirement of capitalizing an amount of retained earnings equal to the par value of the additional shares means very little. A company which wished to mislead its stockholders might do so by issuing frequent stock dividends having a fair market value significantly higher than current earnings. Practically no limitation would exist on the extent of such distributions if only a nominal amount of retained earnings were capitalized for each share issued.

Securities which are convertible into common stock (such as convertible preferred stock, warrants, and stock option contracts) contain an antidilution clause which calls for adjusting the conversion ratio to compensate for the "reduced size" of a share of common stock after a stock dividend or a stock split. If, for example, a preferred stock is convertible into three shares of common, the conversion ratio would increase to 3.3 shares after a 10% stock dividend on the common stock.

Large stock dividends and stock splits

A large stock dividend, such as one increasing the number of outstanding shares by 25 or 50%, may be expected to cause a material decrease in the market price per share. Such transactions are in the nature of stock splits, and the arguments outlined in the preceding section as to small stock dividends do not apply. In other words, the amount of retained earnings to be capitalized in the case of large stock dividends is merely an amount equal to the par value of the dividend shares. Let us use a somewhat extreme example to illustrate the probable reaction of the stockholder to a large stock dividend. Assume that Stockholder A owns 10 shares of stock in the Pacific Company and current market price is $150 a share. A 100% stock dividend is distributed and the market price promptly drops to $75 a share. The stockholder will no doubt recognize that the so-called "stock dividend" is not a distribution of earnings but is essentially similar to a splitting of the shares on a 2 for 1 basis.

The Committee on Accounting Procedure recommended that corporations avoid the use of the word "dividend" in corporate notices relating to stock distributions of such magnitude that they will reduce materially the market value per share. If legal requirements demand use of the word "dividend," the transaction might well be described as a "split-up effected in the form of a stock dividend."

Illustrative Entry for a Stock Dividend Assume that a corporation has 100,000 authorized shares of $5 par value capital stock, of which 50,000 shares are outstanding. The fair market value is $80 a share and a cash dividend of 50 cents quarterly has been paid for several years. Current earnings are large and rising but the company wishes to conserve cash to permit expansion of plant. Consequently, the board of directors decides to issue a 2% stock dividend rather than to increase the established cash dividend per share. A condensed entry summarizing both the declaration and distribution of the 2% stock dividend is presented below to emphasize the end results of the transaction.

Retained Earnings	80,000	
Common Stock		5,000
Paid-in Capital from Stock Dividends		75,000

Declared and issued a 2% stock dividend consisting of 1,000 shares of $5 par value stock with a fair market value of $80 each.

The $5,000 credit to Capital Stock of course loses its identity on the balance sheet as part of the total of that account; also the $75,000 credit to Paid-in Capital from Stock Dividends is likely to be merged with other types of additional paid-in capital in the preparation of a condensed balance sheet. Consequently, the reader of a subsequent balance sheet may be unaware that much of the paid-in capital emerged from retained earnings by means of stock dividends.

The preceding illustration of a journal entry for a stock dividend could appear as three separate entries. The first entry would record declaration of the stock dividend by debiting Stock Dividends for the market value of the shares to be issued, crediting Stock Dividends to Be Distributed for the par value of the shares, and crediting Paid-in Capital from Stock Dividends for the excess of the earnings capitalized over the par value of the shares to be issued. The second entry would record issuance of the shares by debiting Stock Dividends to Be Distributed and crediting Common Stock. At the end of the year, the Stock Dividends account would be closed into Retained Earnings. If a balance sheet is prepared between the date of declaring the stock dividend and the date for distributing it, the account Stock Dividends to Be Distributed would be shown as part of the stockholders' equity.

The announcement to stockholders that a stock dividend has been declared should include a statement as to the amount of retained earnings to be capitalized and the date of determining the fair market value. The following language is typical:

> The Company's Board of Directors has declared a 2% stock dividend on the common stock (two common shares for each 100 shares held) to be distributed March 28 to holders of record of common stock at the close of business February 25. Retained earnings is being charged a total of $80,000 to reflect the dividend, computed at $80 per share, the closing price of the stock on January 25, the date of declaration.

Dividing line between "large" and "small" stock dividends

Since current practice calls for quite different accounting treatment of large and small stock dividends, it is appropriate to ask "How large must a stock dividend be to qualify as a large distribution and thereby to avoid the requirement of capitalizing retained earnings in an amount equal to fair market value?''

The AICPA, in **Accounting Research and Terminology Bulletins—Final Edition,** suggested 20 or 25% as a dividing line. Above this amount it may be assumed that the purpose of the distribution is to reduce the unit market price of the stock, as in the case of a stock split. Below this level it may be assumed that the dividend shares will be regarded by most shareholders as a distribution of earnings. (As previously explained, a stock dividend does not really constitute a distribution of earnings, but it is commonly regarded as such by many investors.) The appropriate accounting treatment of the two categories of stock dividends may be restated in concise form as follows: Small stock dividends are recorded by capitalizing retained earnings at the fair market value of the dividend shares; large stock dividends are recorded by capitalizing retained earnings at the par value or stated value of the dividend shares.

Fractional shares

When a small stock dividend is declared, persons owning only a few shares will be entitled to receive only a fraction of a dividend share. For example, in the preceding illustration of a 2% stock dividend, the holder of less than 50 shares would be entitled to only a fraction of a share. To avoid the inconvenience of issuing fractional shares, most companies offer stockholders the alternative of receiving in cash the fair market value of the fraction of a share due, or of paying in sufficient cash to qualify for a full share.

THE STATEMENT OF RETAINED EARNINGS

An income statement is sometimes described as the connecting link between two successive balance sheets. However, an income statement often does not explain fully the change in stockholders' equity from one balance sheet date to the next. Cash dividends, stock dividends, exercise of stock options, and treasury stock transactions are examples of events affecting the stockholders' equity along with the net income or loss for the period.

As explained in Chapters 3 and 4, the balance sheet and income statement may be supplemented by a third statement called the **statement of retained earnings,** which shows the changes in retained earnings during the year, thus reconciling the beginning and ending balances of retained earnings. We shall now review briefly some of the various forms which the statement of retained earnings may take, and then consider the additional problem of reporting changes in paid-in capital.

The content and relative importance of the statement of retained earnings in portraying the year's financial developments have been somewhat reduced by the almost universal adoption of the all-inclusive concept of net income, as opposed to the current operating performance concept.

In **APB Opinion No. 9,** "Reporting the Results of Operations," the APB in essence adopted the all-inclusive concept of net income. The APB concluded that net income should reflect all elements of profit and loss except for **prior period adjustments.** As explained in Chapter 3, very few events will meet the rigorous requirements for classification as **prior period adjustments.** Consequently, there are very few direct charges or credits to the Retained Earnings account and the typical statement of retained earnings is now rather short and simple. It may consist merely of:

1 Beginning balance of retained earnings
2 An addition of the year's net income (or deduction of the year's net loss)
3 A deduction for the dividends declared
4 The ending balance of retained earnings

An illustration of a statement of retained earnings in comparative form for two years appears below.

PACIFIC CORPORATION
Statement of Retained Earnings
For the Years Ended December 31, 1974 and 1975

	1975	1974
Balance at beginning of year	$719,824	$640,000
Add: Net income	230,000	210,000
	$949,824	$850,000
Less: Dividends declared:		
On preferred stock	(30,000)	(30,000)
On common stock:		
In cash ($1 per share)	(41,600)	(40,000)
In common stock (4%)	(72,312)	(60,176)
Balance at end of year	$805,912	$719,824

The widespread adoption of the all-inclusive income concept of net income has tended to reduce the significance of the statement of retained earnings as a reconciling device. The function of the statement has also been narrowed by the trend away from making appropriations of retained earnings. These trends tend to reduce the number of direct charges and credits to Retained Earnings and thus simplify the task of reporting changes in this account. Perhaps these trends are also responsible in part for the fact that many companies now prepare a combined statement of earnings and retained earnings such as the one shown on page 610.

HANDLEY CORPORATION

Combined Statement of Earnings and Retained Earnings

For the Years Ended December 31, 1974 and 1975

(dollars in thousands except per-share figures)

	1975	1974
Revenue		
Sales to customers	$1,317,683	$1,140,485
Other revenue	18,886	15,753
Total revenue	$1,336,569	$1,156,238
Costs and expenses		
Cost of products sold	$ 650,275	$ 567,206
Selling, distribution, and administrative expenses	416,699	362,968
Depreciation and amortization of property, plant, and equipment	41,597	35,862
Federal and foreign taxes on income	103,339	83,747
Other expenses	3,953	4,634
Total costs and expenses	$1,215,863	$1,054,417
Net earnings (per share: 1975, $2.15; 1974, $1.82)	$ 120,706	$ 101,821
Retained earnings at beginning of period	469,647	391,850
Cash dividends paid	(25,136)	(24,024)
Retained earnings at end of period	$ 565,217	$ 469,647

Reporting changes in paid-in capital

Reporting of changes in the accounts for capital stock and paid-in capital in excess of par became a requirement with the issuance of APB *Opinion No. 12* in 1967. The Accounting Principles Board stated:

> When both financial position and results of operations are presented, disclosure of changes in the separate accounts comprising stockholders' equity (in addition to retained earnings) and of the changes in the number of shares of equity securities during at least the most recent annual fiscal period and any subsequent interim period presented is required to make the financial statements sufficiently informative. Disclosure of such changes may take the form of separate statements or may be made in the basic financial statements or notes thereto.[2]

Required disclosure of these changes in capital accounts other than retained earnings may be explained by the practice by many corporations in recent years of issuing frequent small stock dividends. Such dividends cause a transfer from retained earnings to capital stock and also to the account for paid-in capital in excess of par. Another recent trend causing frequent changes in the accounts for capital stock and paid-in capital in excess of par is the continual issuance of shares to executives under

[2]APB Opinion No. 12, "Omnibus Opinion—1967," AICPA (New York: 1967), p. 190.

Statement of Consolidated Shareholders' Equity

	Capital stock	Paid-in capital	Retained earnings
Balance at Dec. 31, 1973.	$ 5,966,000	$21,419,000	$16,161,000
Net income			9,938,000
Cash dividends ($0.10 per common share).			(1,229,000)
Transfer to common stock of amount equal to par value of common stock issued as a result of 2 for 1 stock split	6,266,000	(6,266,000)	
Exercise of common stock options and common stock purchase warrants.	355,000	4,891,000	
Conversion of subordinated indebtedness.	144,000	3,667,000	
Acquisition of Bar, Inc. (preferred stock, $13,527,000; common stock, $1,465,000)	14,992,000	35,723,000	
Balance at Dec. 31, 1974.	$27,723,000	$59,434,000	$24,870,000
Net income			19,518,000
Cash dividends:			
Preferred ($1.50 per share) . . .			(676,000)
Common ($0.12 per share) . . .			(1,741,000)
Exercise of common stock options and common stock purchase warrants.	525,000	5,171,000	
Conversion of subordinated indebtedness and preferred stock	1,260,000	27,558,000	
Balance at Dec. 31, 1975.	$29,508,000	$92,163,000	$41,971,000

Note: Shareholders' Equity: The authorized capital stock of the company consists of 25 million shares of common stock and 2 million shares of preferred stock. The preferred shares outstanding at December 31, 1975, are convertible into 315,561 shares of common stock and have liquidation preference of $13,524,000.

At December 31, 1975, the company had reserved 710,000 shares of its common stock for issuance under outstanding common stock purchase warrants. The warrants are exercisable prior to May 1976 at $12.10 a share. The company has also reserved 525,000 shares of common stock for issuance upon conversion of the 6% subordinated notes and the convertible preferred stock, and 640,000 shares for issuance under stock option plans.

Common shares issued upon exercise of stock options during 1974 and 1975 amounted to 99,939 and 109,846, respectively. There were options outstanding at December 31, 1974 and 1975 for 280,561 and 383,053 common shares, respectively, and the aggregate purchase price of all outstanding stock options was $6,037,000 and $6,067,000, respectively.

Retained earnings of approximately $15,500,000 are available at December 31, 1975, for payment of cash dividends under the most restrictive provisions of the company's indebtedness agreements.

stock option plans. Still another factor affecting paid-in capital is the conversion of bonds or preferred stock. Because of these several factors, an annual financial statement showing changes in paid-in capital may be needed in addition to the statement of retained earnings. One approach to this situation is to prepare a single statement with columns for capital stock, paid-in capital in excess of par, and retained earnings. In the example shown on page 611, the data for preferred stock and common stock are combined into one column headed *"capital stock,"* and an accompanying note explains in more detail the events of the year portrayed in this statement of shareholders' equity.

The financial statements which have been presented to illustrate methods of explaining changes in stockholders' equity show that many alternative forms are in use. Another method favored by many companies for disclosing capital changes is the use of an explanatory note to the financial statements. Typical of footnote disclosure is the following note from a recent annual report by Safeway Stores, Incorporated.

> **Capital stock and additional paid-in capital**   Capital stock as of year-end 1972 and 1971 consisted of 220,372 shares of 4% cumulative preferred, authorized and unissued, and 27,000,000 shares of common stock authorized at a par value of $1.66⅔ per share. Outstanding common stock amounted to 25,720,871 shares at the end of 1972, compared with 25,562,831 shares a year earlier. These are after deducting 45,981 treasury shares at the end of 1972 and 1971. On February 21, 1973, the Board of Directors recommended for stockholder approval an increase in the number of authorized shares of common stock to 75 million.
>
> The increase in Additional Paid-in Capital during 1972 of $3,689,147, and during 1971 of $1,658,832, consists of the excess proceeds over par value of shares issued under options exercised during the year.

Selection of the most appropriate type of disclosure in a particular situation depends upon the number and the character of the changes which have occurred during the year and upon the amount of detailed information desired in the financial statements. In addition, there is the factor of personal judgment as to the most concise, effective, and forceful way of portraying the significant elements of the company's financial progress.

APPROPRIATIONS OF RETAINED EARNINGS

The board of directors of a corporation may restrict or appropriate a portion of the retained earnings by transfer to a separate account. Examples of appropriations of retained earnings are Reserve for Expansion of Plant, Reserve for Retirement of Bonds, Reserve for Redemption of Preferred Stock, and Reserve for Contingencies.

The purpose of appropriating retained earnings for any of the above reserves is to indicate that the appropriated amounts are not available for dividends. It is essential to keep in mind, however, that the appropriation of retained earnings has no effect whatsoever on the kind or composition of the assets. Sometimes, concurrently with the appropriation of retained earnings, a corporation will also segregate assets to be used exclusively for the purpose indicated by the appropriation of retained earnings. Such a segregation of assets earmarked for a particular purpose is called a *fund;* an example is a fund for retirement of bonds.

In a few cases, the appropriation of retained earnings may be required by the terms of a contract with creditors or by statute, but most appropriations represent voluntary actions by the board of directors and usually are not accompanied by related funds.

As a specific example of an appropriation of retained earnings, assume that a corporation during a period of growth and profitable operations decides to enlarge its plant. The new buildings and equipment are to be paid for without resorting to outside financing. In other words, cash accumulated through profitable operation and not distributed to stockholders as dividends is to be invested in new plant and equipment. Because of this decision, there may be relatively little cash available for dividends in the near future. To make this situation clear to stockholders, the board of directors may authorize the establishment of a Reserve for Expansion of Plant by restricting $1,000,000 of retained earnings. The journal entry required by this action of the board follows:

Retained Earnings	*1,000,000*	
Reserve for Expansion of Plant		*1,000,000*
To appropriate a portion of retained earnings per resolution of board of directors.		

The board of directors could, of course, reduce or even eliminate dividends without going through the motions of appropriating retained earnings. The only argument for creating a Reserve for Expansion of Plant is that it may communicate to stockholders the thinking of directors as to the use of profits for expansion and the consequent limitation of dividends.

If a corporation is defendant in a large lawsuit, a reserve could conceivably be established to indicate the possibility of a large loss from an adverse settlement. More realistically, however, the corporation will probably choose not to disclose any estimated dollar outcome of the suit, because such an estimate might influence the course of litigation or the prospects of an out-of-court settlement. A better form of disclosure (not injurious to the defendant) is to attach a note to the financial statements describing the status of any pending litigation.

The amount of stockholders' equity and the amount of retained earnings are not reduced by the establishment of reserves. The reserve is merely an earmarked portion of retained earnings. Once the reserve has been created, what use can be made of it? A Reserve for Expansion of Plant cannot be debited with the cost of plant assets acquired; these costs must be debited to the asset accounts. A Reserve for Retirement of Bonds cannot be debited as an offset to the credit to Cash when the bonds are retired; the debit must be to the Bonds Payable account. The only debit to a reserve is the entry made to return it to the Retained Earnings account when the directors feel the reserve is no longer needed. The creation of reserves and their disposition by transfer back to the Retained Earnings account are not actions initiated by accountants or auditors; entries to create or eliminate reserves are made only upon order of the board of directors.

In the balance sheet, the reserves created by appropriations of retained earnings may be shown as follows:

Retained earnings:		
Appropriated:		
Reserve for redemption of preferred stock	$ 120,000	
Reserve for contingencies	250,000	
Reserve for expansion of plant	1,000,000	
Reserve for bond sinking fund	30,000	$1,400,000
Unappropriated		300,000
Total retained earnings		$1,700,000

Do appropriations of retained earnings serve any useful purpose?

Retained earnings, by definition, are profits which directors have chosen to retain in the business rather than to distribute as dividends. Since such retention of earnings is a normal means of financing expansion and of providing for contingencies, there seems little justification for dividing up the retained earnings into a number of reserves, each bearing a label indicating the reason for its retention in the business. If only a portion of retained earnings is appropriated, the reader of the statement may assume that the unappropriated balance indicates the existence of assets available for distribution as dividends. Such an inference may be entirely erroneous; the company's cash position may not permit any dividends.

It is sometimes said that by transferring retained earnings into reserve accounts directors may reduce pressure by stockholders for dividends. This argument is in essence a plea for misleading statements which will serve to confuse naïve owners; it is incompatible with the objective of building public confidence in financial statements.

Appropriations of retained earnings are no longer commonly required by the terms of bond indentures or bank loan agreements because sophisticated lenders prefer to employ sharper-edged tools, such as outright prohibition of dividend payments which would reduce retained earnings or working capital below specified levels.

The only remaining argument for creating appropriations of retained earnings is that of disclosing information concerning contingencies, loan agreements, expansion plans, or other factors tending to limit dividends. Such disclosure can usually be made more effectively by referencing an explanatory note to the financial statements as follows:

Retained earnings (Note A) *$2,100,000*

Note A:
Under a three-year loan agreement signed with several banks on June 30, 1974, the corporation agreed that, throughout the period of indebtedness incurred under this loan agreement, no dividends shall be paid which would result in reducing retained earnings below the sum of $1,800,000, that amount being the balance of retained earnings as of the date of the loan agreement.

Reserve for self-insurance

Some businesses which have plant and equipment in many scattered locations follow a policy of so-called "self-insurance." A railroad, for example, may self-insure its freight cars; a grocery chain owning thousands of stores may self-insure the store buildings. A self-insurance program means that *no insurance* is carried, in the belief that losses from fire to a large number of scattered units will be less over a period of time than the premiums which would be required to insure the property.

When a company decides not to insure its plant assets, it recognizes of course that fire losses are likely to vary widely from year to year and thus tend to cause net income to fluctuate even though operations are stable. In an effort to avoid wide swings in net income, some companies following self-insurance programs charge operations each year with a hypothetical amount of insurance expense and offset this assumed expense by a credit to Reserve for Self-insurance. The debit to Insurance Expense is for the estimated amount of premiums which would have to be paid if insurance policies were in force. When losses occur, they are charged against the Reserve for Self-insurance. As a result of such accounting policies, net income is reported at more stable amounts from year to year than it would be if the fire losses were treated as deductions from revenue when incurred.

Most accountants believe that there is little theoretical justification for a Reserve for Self-insurance created by charges to expense for hypothetical insurance premiums. A company which carries fire insurance incurs a cost of protection against fire loss; this cost is spread uniformly against the income of successive years by allocating fire insurance premiums paid. In contrast to this situation, consider the case of a company which does not protect itself against fire loss by purchasing fire insurance policies. Such a company pays no insurance premium and incurs no cost of protection. Until and unless property is destroyed, no loss or expense should be recognized. When a fire loss actually occurs, it should be charged against revenue of the current period. According to this dominant view, a reserve for self-insurance created by a charge to expense for hypothetical insurance premiums is no more than a disguised element of retained earnings. Net income has been understated by the assumed amount of insurance expense.

The opposing argument by the supporters of self-insurance emphasizes that a company chooses to be a self-insurer in cases where the risk is spread over a large body of possible loss events and where individual losses are likely to be small in relation to the total potential loss. In effect, the company is subject to the same operating characteristics as an insurance company. The law of large numbers is applicable. By reference to the theory of probability, the company may anticipate with reasonable accuracy that a predictable pattern of losses will emerge. If this predictable pattern of losses is a valid assumption, then a charge to expense each period based on actuarial computations and offset by a credit to a liability representing a measure of the probability that a loss will occur may be little different in principle from established practice in accruing other expenses.

Although recognizing some merit in the argument for a reserve for self-insurance, the authors believe that the traditional view that self-insurance is no insurance is more in keeping with established principles of income determination. A company which chooses not to insure its plant and equipment will usually have some years of heavy property losses and some years with little or no losses of this type. On the other hand, a company which insures its assets actually incurs insurance expense each year and avoids occasional large losses. The financial statements should reveal the actual course of operations in both companies. Good reporting does not permit the concealment of the difference in the annual earnings of the two companies through the use of hypothetical figures for insurance expense.

An alternative method of creating a Reserve for Self-insurance is by charge against retained earnings. A reserve created in this manner should not be debited with any fire losses or related expenses which may occur. To do so would cause an overstatement of net income through the omission of expenses or losses from the income statement. Furthermore, the creation of a Reserve for Self-insurance from retained earnings is subject to the objections previously stated with respect to other types of appropriations of retained earnings. The balance sheet will be more clearly understood if the total of retained earnings appears under that label rather than being split up into various reserve categories.

Reserves as a separate category on the balance sheet

For many years accounting literature has advocated that the term *reserve* be used only to describe appropriations of retained earnings. This viewpoint opposes the presentation of reserves in a separate section between the liabilities and the stockholders' equity section of the balance sheet.

Confusion over the meaning and balance sheet classification of reserves still persists despite efforts to limit this term to appropriations of retained earnings. A number of large corporations continue to publish balance sheets with a "Reserves" section between liabilities and stockholders' equity. Some of these reserves are merely appropriations of retained earnings; others have been created by charges to expense; for still others it is impossible for the reader to determine their origin or nature. Adding together these unlike elements creates further confusion.

For example, a recent balance sheet of International Paper Company shows on the right-hand side of the statement four group headings as follows: Current Liabilities, Long-term Debt, Reserves, and Shareholders' Equity. The Reserves section included the following three items:

Reserves:	
Insurance and deferred liabilities	$ 22,687,000
Anticipated abandonments	39,627,000
Deferred income taxes	66,458,000
	$128,772,000

One might infer from a balance sheet arranged in this format that the fundamental accounting equation should be revised to read: Assets = Liabilities + Reserves + Owners' Equity. Unfortunately no established meaning of the term *reserves* as used in this context is available. A note attached to International Paper Company's financial statements described one of the reserves listed above as having been provided in prior years "for estimated losses to be incurred in connection with the anticipated abandonment of facilities which are obsolete or unusable due to environmental, economic or other reasons . . . ." The note also indicated that during the current year, "$55,246,000 was charged to the reserve principally for the shutdown of three paper mills. . . ."

If losses of the current year are charged against a reserve set up in a prior year, one might assume that the reserve was created by charges to expense in the earlier period, but the explanatory note provides no information on this point.

A similar and equally ambiguous presentation in the balance sheet of American Airlines, Inc., shows on the right-hand side of the statement the major heading Liabilities and Stockholders' Equity, with subordinate group headings of Current Liabilities, Long-term Debt, Deferred Credits, and Stockholders' Equity. The Deferred Credits section contains the following items:

Deferred credits:

Federal income tax (Note 6)	$147,282,000
Self-insurance	20,000,000
Employee stock purchase plan (Note 9)	4,949,000
Other	2,020,000
Total deferred credits	$174,251,000

The referenced notes do not indicate whether these credit balances were created by charges to expense accounts or to retained earnings. In other words, the group heading *Deferred Credits* seems to be used in the same vague manner as *Reserves* on some other financial statements, that is, a category of credit balances which represents neither liabilities nor stockholders' equity.

The balance sheet of General Motors Corporation shows between liabilities and stockholders' equity a section entitled Deferred Credits and Reserves which totals $445 million and includes such items as a "General reserve applicable to foreign operations" of $141,667,396.

Another interesting example of a reserve is found in the published statement of a major food manufacturing corporation, which includes on the balance sheet the following item listed after the current and long-term liabilities but above the stockholders' equity section:

Reserve for renewal of glass tanks	$1,210,620

The position of this item on the statement is clearly apart from the traditional classifications of assets, liabilities, and owners' equity. The unspoken implication is that "reserves" constitute a fourth dimension of the balance sheet, but the reader is given no information as to the origin or nature of the reserve. Only a person familiar with the industry would realize that a food processor uses huge glass tanks which require relining and other costly maintenance every four or five years. In an effort to spread this major maintenance cost uniformly, the company each year debits an expense account and credits Reserve for Renewal of Glass Tanks. In the year in which the renewal work is performed, the reserve account will be charged with the costs.

Is the reserve account a genuine liability? Is the expense recognized when the reserve was created a valid expense? Is the amount set up in the reserve based on past costs of such renewal work or does it represent an estimate of what future costs will be several years hence, after making allowance for the trend of the price level? If the renewal work benefits the operations of several years, why not capitalize it and write off the cost over the several years *subsequent* to the renewal? Is there any reason other than conservatism for charging renewal expense to the years *preceding* the performance of this major maintenance operation?

The food processing industry is by no means alone in this practice of charging expense accounts and crediting a reserve for costly maintenance work to be performed in a future year. Similar practices have been followed by some steel companies in the relining of their furnaces, by some oil companies in the cleaning out of oil tankers every few years, and by a number of other manufacturing industries.

Despite the practice of a number of prominent corporations in presenting reserves as a separate category on the right-hand side of the balance sheet, *there is no fourth dimension in the framework of accounting theory.* Assets are equal to the sum of the liabilities and the stockholders' equity. The uncertainties and complexities which surround certain business events are no justification for the publication of a balance sheet which leaves the reader to guess whether major elements of the statement represent liabilities or are part of the ownership equity.

QUASI-REORGANIZATIONS

A *quasi-reorganization* occurs when a corporation in financial difficulties modifies its capital structure without being forced to do so by creditors and without coming under the supervision of the courts. Typically, a quasi-reorganization involves writing off a deficit against paid-in capital; sometimes there is a reduction in par value of capital stock and a write-down of overvalued assets. Following a quasi-reorganization, the corporation is considered from an accounting standpoint to have a fresh start and the way is cleared for reporting profits and declaring dividends in future years. Although the write-down of asset values and the elimination of a deficit obscure historically significant data, the procedure is generally accepted because it yields more relevant asset figures. Furthermore, a quasi-reorganization may help a corporation to regain its place as a profitable business unit without the stigma that attaches to a large deficit, continuous operating losses, and inability to declare cash dividends. A quasi-reorganization typically involves the following procedures:

1 Assets which are considered to be overstated are written down to current value by charges to retained earnings. If the current value of any asset exceeds book value, increasing the carrying value of such assets is generally discouraged.

2 The deficit in retained earnings following the asset write-downs is eliminated against additional paid-in capital. Gains or losses subsequent to the reorganization which are clearly attributable to the period prior to the reorganization should be recorded as increases or decreases in additional paid-in capital.

3 If additional paid-in capital at the time of the quasi-reorganization is insufficient to absorb the deficit, the par or stated value of capital stock is reduced in order to establish additional paid-in capital which can then be used to absorb the deficit.

4 Retained earnings following a quasi-reorganization must be identified (dated), generally for a period of 10 years, as accruing since the effective date of the quasi-reorganization. In subsequent balance sheets, this disclosure, called "dating the retained earnings," may appear as follows:

Retained earnings, since June 30, 1974, when a deficit of $265,000 was written off against paid-in capital as a result of a quasi-reorganization. $142,600

Illustration of a Quasi-reorganization To illustrate the usefulness of a quasi-reorganization, assume that a business owns two plants, each having a cost of $1 million, as shown by the condensed balance sheet below. (In this illustration, depreciation has been ignored to simplify the issues under consideration.)

INLAND CORPORATION
Balance Sheet
December 31, 1974

Current assets		$ 400,000
Plant and equipment:		
Plant A	$1,000,000	
Plant B	1,000,000	2,000,000
Total assets		$2,400,000
Current liabilities		$ 200,000
Stockholders' equity:		
Capital stock, $10 par	$2,000,000	
Retained earnings	200,000	2,200,000
Total liabilities & stockholders' equity		$2,400,000

Assume that Plant B is completely destroyed by flood and there is no insurance coverage. The removal of $1 million in assets (the carrying value of Plant B) from the balance sheet wipes out the retained earnings of $200,000 and produces a deficit of $800,000, as shown by the following revised balance sheet.

INLAND CORPORATION
Balance Sheet
December 31, 1974 (after flood loss)

Current assets		$ 400,000
Plant and equipment (Plant A).		1,000,000
Total assets		$1,400,000
Current liabilities		$ 200,000
Stockholders' equity:		
Capital stock, $10 par	$2,000,000	
Less: Deficit	(800,000)	1,200,000
Total liabilities & stockholders' equity		$1,400,000

The existence of the $800,000 deficit created by writing off Plant B will make it impossible for the Inland Corporation to pay dividends for many years to come even though the remaining plant operates quite profitably. If we assume that the company does not intend to replace the plant which was destroyed by the flood but merely to operate the remaining plant, why should the deficit be permitted to stand as a barrier preventing the payment of dividends from earnings of future years? Is it not more reasonable to recognize that a portion of the paid-in capital has been lost and to regard the stockholders' equity in the future as consisting of two elements: (1) the paid-in capital remaining after the flood loss and (2) retained earnings produced by profitable operations after the flood loss?

Management may decide, with the approval of stockholders, to effect a quasi-reorganization by reducing the par value of the capital stock from $10 to $5 a share, thus creating paid-in capital in excess of par in the amount of $1,000,000. The deficit of $800,000 could then be written off against the paid-in capital from reduction in par value and the retained

Capital Stock ($10 par)	2,000,000	
Capital Stock ($5 par).		1,000,000
Paid-in Capital from Reduction in Par Value		1,000,000
To reduce the par value of capital stock as part of a		
quasi-reorganization.		
Paid-in Capital from Reduction in Par Value	800,000	
Retained Earnings		800,000
To eliminate a deficit by offsetting it against paid-in		
capital as part of a quasi-reorganization.		

earnings account would have a zero balance. Any future earnings would then be available for dividends. The journal entries for the quasi-reorganization carried out on January 1, 1975, are shown on page 621.

Let us assume that during the first six months following the quasi-reorganization the Inland Corporation had earnings of $100,000; the balance sheet at June 30, 1975, would then appear as follows:

INLAND CORPORATION
Balance Sheet
June 30, 1975

Current assets		$ 500,000
Plant and equipment.		1,000,000
Total assets		$1,500,000
Current liabilities		$ 200,000
Stockholders' equity:		
Capital stock, $5 par	$1,000,000	
Paid-in capital in excess of par.	200,000	
Retained earnings, since Jan. 1, 1975, at which time a deficit of $800,000 was written off against paid-in capital as a result of a quasi-reorganization	100,000	1,300,000
Total liabilities & stockholders' equity		$1,500,000

Business combinations—purchase versus pooling of interests

In recent years many corporations have been brought together or combined to obtain the economies of large-scale operation and the financial strength arising from diversification in various industries. Business combinations are discussed at length in *Advanced Accounting* of this series. Our purpose, at this point, is merely to call attention to the difference in impact upon retained earnings of the *purchase method* and the *pooling-of-interests method* in carrying out business combinations.

When the acquisition of one corporation by another is accounted for as a *purchase,* the acquiring corporation records its investment at the cost established by cash paid or market value of shares issued in exchange for shares of the acquired company. *The retained earnings of the company acquired do not become part of consolidated retained earnings.* Earnings of the two companies are combined only from the date of acquisition.

On the other hand, when a business combination has characteristics that require use of the pooling-of-interests method, the assets of the two corporations are combined at their recorded book values on the premise that no purchase has occurred. The market values of shares issued and of assets acquired are ignored. The pooling-of-interests method rests on an assumption of continuity of common ownership and the *retained earnings accounts of the two corporations are added together to arrive at the amount of retained earnings of the combined entity.* The earnings of the combined entity include the earnings of the constituent companies for the entire year in which the combination occurs.

Prior to issuance of *APB Opinion No. 16,* "Business Combinations," in 1970 many "growth" companies made acquisitions on a pooling-of-interests basis merely to maintain an illusion of ever-increasing earnings per share. The distortion of economic reality by such abuses of accounting concepts was extreme in the 1960s. These abuses have been considerably restricted, although not eliminated, by the stricter requirements imposed by *APB Opinion No. 16* for use of the pooling-of-interests method of accounting for business combinations.

REVIEW QUESTIONS

1 "In the classification of items comprising the stockholders' equity section of the balance sheet, the most important principle followed by accountants is to show clearly the amount which can legally be distributed as dividends." Do you agree? Give reasons for your answer.

2 Distinguish between a *stock dividend* and a *stock split.*

3 Plymouth Corporation follows a practice of distributing a 3% stock dividend each year in addition to paying an annual cash dividend of $2 a share. How should the amount of the charge to retained earnings for the stock dividend be determined?

4 Electronics, Inc., sustained an extraordinary loss of $100,000 from flood damage. Since retained earnings amounted to only $75,000 and paid-in capital in excess of par was $150,000, the company charged one-third of the loss to the former account and two-thirds to the latter. Is this treatment of the loss in accord with generally accepted accounting principles? Explain.

5 Enumerate several types of transactions which would cause an increase in paid-in capital in excess of par or stated value. What types of transactions cause a decrease in paid-in capital in excess of par or stated value?

6 The ledger of Greenback Corporation includes the following accounts, among others:

Land (at appraised value) $100,000
Unrealized appreciation from revaluation of land 60,000

The land originally acquired as a building site is now sold because its value has risen so greatly as to make it unsuitable for the company's use. The sales price is $150,000. Give the journal entry to record the sale.

7 The stock of the San Carlos Corporation is widely distributed among several thousand investors, most of whom own less than 50 shares. The company is planning to distribute a 2% stock dividend. What should be done for those stockholders who own less than 50 shares?

8 Explain briefly the disposition of a Reserve for Expansion of Plant when the planned expansion is carried out. Would your answer be altered if the expansion of the plant was paid for from bank borrowings?

9 To eliminate a deficit of $70,000, the Carroll Corporation obtained approval from its stockholders for a "reverse split." One new share with par value of $5 was issued for each two old shares of $10 par value. The entire issue of 10,000 old shares was retired. Give the journal entries to record the exchange of shares and elimination of the deficit.

10 Under what circumstances should the retained earnings be "dated?" Does dating of the retained earnings refer to an item in the balance sheet or to a ledger account?

11 In what ways might a corporation offer bondholders protection against excessively generous cash dividend payments to stockholders?

12 Would you, as a bondholder of a corporation, be willing to give management a free hand in deciding upon distributions of stock dividends or would you prefer to include in the bond contract some limitation upon the extent of stock dividends?

13 The AB Corporation, a manufacturer of sporting goods, decided to merge with the CD Corporation, a retailer of sporting goods. The National Sports Corporation was formed and received 60% of its total assets from AB Corporation and 40% from CD Corporation. Capital stock was issued by National in these same proportions in payment for its assets. The former officers of the AB Corporation and of the CD Corporation assumed similar positions in the new corporation. Should the National Sports Corporation have a retained earnings account at the beginning of its existence? Could the new corporation have a retained earnings account larger or smaller than the retained earnings accounts of the predecessor corporations? Explain.

14 The right-hand side of the balance sheet of Garth Corporation shows a group heading of Reserves between the sections for liabilities and stockholders' equity. Under the Reserves heading appear the following items:

Reserve for self-insurance $12,800,000
Other 2,500,000

Can you determine from the titles of these reserves and their position on the balance sheet whether they were created by charges to expense or by appropriations of retained earnings? Comment on this method of reporting.

EXERCISES

Ex. 16-1 The Century Corporation has in its ledger a number of accounts established many years ago, but it is considering the adoption of more modern account titles. For each of the following accounts, you are to state (1) the balance sheet classification or account group, and (2) an improved title if you consider the present one unsatisfactory.
a Reserve for depreciation
b Reserve for contingencies
c Reserve for self-insurance
d Earned surplus
e Capital surplus

f Reserve for bad debts
g Reserve for income taxes
h Reserve for depletion
i Reserve for treasury stock purchased
j Reserve for expansion of plant
k Reserve for bond sinking fund
l Reserve for vacation wages

Ex. 16-2 Select information as appropriate from the items listed below and prepare the stockholders' equity section of a balance sheet. Combine items and revise titles if customary.

Unissued capital stock (475,000 shares)	$4,750,000
Bond sinking fund	120,000
Premium on bonds payable	5,000
Reserve for bond sinking fund	120,000
Reserve for contingencies	100,000
Reserve for uncollectible accounts	10,000
Reserve for income taxes	125,000
Reserve for self-insurance	60,000
Paid-in capital from stock dividends	40,000
Premium on capital stock	60,000
Authorized capital stock (500,000 shares)	5,000,000
Earned surplus	350,000
Appraisal capital from revaluation of land (approved by board of directors)	150,000

Ex. 16-3 Select the best answer for each of the following multiple-choice questions.
   a The dating of retained earnings is associated with:
      (1) Earnings accumulated by a subsidiary company subsequent to date of acquisition of controlling interest
      (2) Earnings accumulated subsequent to a quasi-reorganization
      (3) The declaration of a stock dividend in excess of 25%
      (4) Earnings of a foreign subsidiary subsequent to the date of a major currency devaluation
   b A business combination that requires the pooling-of-interests method:
      (1) Involves the acquisition by one company of the assets of another company for cash
      (2) Causes the assets of the acquired company to be restated on the books of the combined entity at fair market value at date of acquisition
      (3) Causes the retained earnings accounts of the two corporations to be added together in arriving at the amount of retained earnings of the combined entity
      (4) Causes the earnings of the combined entity to include the earnings of the constituent companies only after the date of the combination
   c The right-hand side of a corporate balance sheet should show all items clearly identified under group headings of:
      (1) Current liabilities, long-term liabilities, and stockholders' equity
      (2) Current liabilities, long-term liabilities, reserves, and stockholders' equity
      (3) Liabilities, reserves, and stockholders' equity
      (4) Liabilities, reserves and deferred credits, and stockholders' equity

Ex. 16-4 Obsolescence has become a major problem in the inventory of Riverside Corporation. Lack of attention to inventory turnover rates, combined with a change in product design to permit use of lighter-weight materials, has caused much of the existing inventory to become obsolete. A careful analysis of the inventory at December 31 of the current year indicated that inventory value should be reduced by $1,100,000 because of obsolescence.

The net earnings of the current year before considering the obsolescence loss were estimated to be $210,000. The stockholders' equity accounts before year-end entries showed the following balances.

Capital stock	$1,000,000
Paid-in capital in excess of par	600,000
Retained earnings	400,000
Total	$2,000,000

The board of directors informs you that it regards obsolescence as an extraordinary item and that a tentative decision has been made to write down the inventory by the full amount of the obsolescence loss; to charge $400,000 against retained earnings, $600,000 against paid-in capital in excess of par, and $100,000 against operations of the current year.

Evaluate the proposed treatment of the obsolescence loss in the light of generally accepted accounting principles. Disregard income tax considerations. State the amount of income before income taxes for the current year and explain how the obsolescence loss should be reported.

Ex. 16-5 The stockholders' equity section of the balance sheet of Magic Mirror Company at the beginning of the year contained the following items:

Convertible preferred stock, $100 par, authorized, issued, and outstanding 10,000 shares (Note A)	$1,000,000
Common stock, $5 par, authorized 1 million shares, issued and outstanding 400,000 shares	2,000,000
Retained earnings	6,000,000
Total stockholders' equity	$9,000,000

Note A: The preferred shares are convertible at any time into common shares at a conversion ratio of four common shares for each preferred share, with the conversion ratio subject to adjustment for any dilution of the common stock.

On January 10, a 5% common stock dividend was declared, to be distributed January 30 to stockholders of record January 15.

On March 1 all the preferred stock was converted into common shares. Market price per share was as follows: January 10, $40; January 15, $42; January 30, $43; March 1, $45.

Determine the dollar amount of the following accounts after giving consideration to all the listed transactions: **(a)** common stock, **(b)** paid-in capital in excess of par, and **(c)** retained earnings. Also compute the total stockholders' equity after giving effect to these transactions.

SHORT CASES FOR ANALYSIS AND DECISION

Case 16-1 "Since my retirement I have switched my investments into stocks that pay cash dividends, because I need a regular income," said Investor A.

"A regular cash income from stocks is one of my requirements, too," replied Investor B. "However, I find it works better to buy stocks that pay regular stock dividends, and then, in effect, to declare my own cash dividends. I have been getting a reasonable cash flow from my stock investments even though the companies don't pay cash dividends. Furthermore, my investments are retaining their value and some are appreciating."

Instructions How could Investor B obtain a cash flow from investments in stocks that did not pay cash dividends? Evaluate his investment policy.

Case 16-2 After receiving a stock certificate for three shares, Roger Bell, a stockholder in Niagara Corporation, expressed his reaction as follows:

"The Niagara Corporation has just declared another stock dividend despite that letter of protest I wrote to the president last year. I told him I hate to see a company declare a stock dividend because it causes a transfer of retained earnings into legal capital. Such a transfer obviously reduces the amount available for cash dividends."

"You are absolutely right," said Green. "When I bought Niagara stock I was hoping for an increase in cash dividends per share over a period of time, but the declaration of stock dividends certainly reduces my expectations for cash dividends. Let's write him another letter."

Instructions Evaluate the opinions expressed by Bell and Green from the standpoint of accounting principles and also in the light of customary dividend practices. Identify any elements of truth in the statements and any lack of logic in the conclusions reached by Bell and Green.

Case 16-3 James McDermott, CPA, was asked by the president of a client corporation for an explanation of a "quasi-reorganization." The president is unfamiliar with the procedure and is concerned that a competitor might have an advantage since undergoing a quasi-reorganization.

Instructions Prepare the report McDermott should provide to the president explaining a quasi-reorganization. The report should include the following points:
a Definition and accounting features of the procedure.
b The purpose of the procedure. Under what conditions should it be considered?
c Authorization necessary.
d Disclosure required in the financial statements.
e Does the competitor have an advantage? Discuss briefly.

Case 16-4 The stockholders' equity section of Whitney Corporation at the beginning of the current year consisted of the following items:

$4 preferred stock, $50 par value	*$ 6,000,000*
Common stock, $10 par value	*3,000,000*
Paid-in capital in excess of par:	
On preferred stock	*300,000*
On common stock	*3,000,000*
Retained earnings	*1,500,000*
Total stockholders' equity	*$13,800,000*

During the current year Whitney Corporation became aware of major unexpected obsolescence of much of its plant equipment because of the appearance on the market of new types of machinery far less bulky and far more efficient. Some difference of opinion existed among the corporate officials as to how the obsolescence loss, estimated at $2 million, should be reflected in the accounts, if at all.

The corporation had operated successfully during its early years, but it had been incurring losses in recent years and the market prices of its securities were quite depressed, although the company's cash position was still strong. The following suggestions were made by various executives.

(1) Purchase and cancel the company's outstanding preferred stock, which had a current market price of about half the par value. The loss on the obsolete machinery could then be charged against the additional paid-in capital created by purchase of the preferred shares below par.
(2) Write down the machinery by charging the additional paid-in capital accounts applicable to the preferred and common stock.
(3) Write down the machinery by charging retained earnings.
(4) Write down the machinery by a charge against current revenue.
(5) Acquire new machinery but retain the old as standby equipment and continue to depreciate it as in the past.

Instructions Evaluate each of the above five proposals in the light of generally accepted accounting principles.

PROBLEMS

Group A

16A-1 The Asbury Corporation maintains its records on the basis of a fiscal year ending March 31. The stockholders' equity section of the balance sheet at March 31 of the current year appears below.

Stockholders' equity:

Capital stock, par value $10, authorized 200,000 shares, issued and outstanding 75,000 shares	$ 750,000
Paid-in capital in excess of par	675,000
Retained earnings	570,000
Total stockholders' equity	$1,995,000

The board of directors of the Asbury Corporation on April 1 declared a 5% stock dividend payable on May 31 to stockholders of record May 15. The market price of the stock on April 1 was $45 a share. During April the net income amounted to $38,000.

Instructions
a Prepare journal entries for the declaration and the distribution of the stock dividend.
b Prepare the stockholders' equity section of the balance sheet at April 30.

16A-2 The retained earnings of Parker Company at January 1, 1975, amounted to $38 million, and paid-in capital in excess of par was $13 million. Common stock outstanding at this date consisted of 4 million shares with a par value of $10 a share.

On January 30, 1975, a court decision required the company to pay an additional $2 million of income taxes applicable to an unusual transaction which had occurred in 1973.

During 1975 the net income amounted to $9.4 million. A cash dividend of 40 cents a share was paid June 30, 1975, and a 5% stock dividend was declared October 10, 1975, to be distributed December 10, 1975, to stockholders of record November 25, 1975.

The stock of the company was traded on a stock exchange. Market price of the common stock was as follows: October 10, $26; November 25, $32; and December 10, $30.

Instructions

a Prepare a four-column statement of shareholders' equity for the year 1975, with columns showing changes in common stock (number of shares and dollar amounts), paid-in capital in excess of par, and retained earnings.

b Draft a note to the financial statements concerning the retroactive charge for income taxes.

16A-3 The market price of Dunhill Corporation's capital stock at June 30, 1974, was $52 a share. The stockholders' equity at this date included substantial retained earnings in addition to 200,000 shares of $2 par capital stock, which had been issued at a price of $12 a share.

During the fiscal year ended June 30, 1975, net income amounted to $414,000, which represented an earnings rate of 9% on total equity capital at the beginning of the year. A cash dividend of $1.50 a share was declared on June 1, 1975, payable July 20, 1975, to stockholders of record July 1, 1975. A 5% stock dividend was declared at the same time and with the same dates of record and distribution. The cash dividend was not applicable to the dividend shares. The market price of the stock was $55 on June 1, 1975, and $58 on June 30.

Instructions

a Compute the amount of retained earnings at June 30, 1975.

b Prepare the stockholders' equity section of the balance sheet at June 30, 1975.

16A-4 At the beginning of the year, the stockholders' equity of China Company was as follows:

Convertible preferred stock, $100 par (Note 1)	$ 100,000
Common stock, $2 par, authorized 1,000,000 shares, 50,000 shares issued and outstanding (Note 2)	100,000
Common stock subscribed	8,000
Capital in excess of par—common stock	500,000
Retained earnings	1,262,000
Total stockholders' equity	$1,970,000

Note 1: Preferred shares were issued at par, are callable at $105, and are convertible into common shares at a rate of 3 for 1, subject to an antidilution provision.
Note 2: 1,000 shares are reserved for stock options at a price of $33, subject to an antidilution provision.

During the year the following transactions occurred:

Jan. 9 Collected $160,000, representing payment in full for all outstanding common stock subscriptions, and issued the stock.

Feb. 1 Declared a 10% common stock dividend to be distributed March 4 to common stockholders of record February 20.

Mar. 4 Distributed 10% common stock dividend.

Mar. 15 All outstanding stock options were exercised.

Apr. 5 All preferred stock was converted into common.

Market value per share of China Company common stock was as follows: January 9, $50; February 1, $48; February 20, $50; March 4, $52; March 15, $51; April 5, $50.

Instructions

a Prepare journal entries for the transactions described above.

b Compute the dollar balance of each of the following accounts, after giving effect to all the above transactions:

(1) Common stock

(2) Paid-in capital in excess of par
(3) Retained earnings

16A-5 During the initial stages of your audit of Equity Company for the year ended December 31, 1975, you are informed by the president that the company is insolvent and must declare bankruptcy unless a large loan can be obtained immediately. A lender who is willing to advance $450,000 to the company has been located, but he will only make the loan if the company agrees to a quasi-reorganization, as follows:

(1) A $600,000, 6% mortgage payable on the company's land and buildings held by a major stockholder will be canceled along with four months' accrued interest. The mortgage will be replaced by 5,000 shares of $100 par value, 6%, cumulative if earned, nonparticipating, preferred stock.

(2) A $450,000, 8% mortgage payable over 15 years on the land and buildings will be given as security on the new loan.

(3) On May 1, 1974, the company's trade creditors accepted $360,000 in notes payable on demand at 6% interest in settlement of all past-due accounts. No payment has been made to date. The company will offer to settle these liabilities 75 cents per $1 owed or to replace the notes payable on demand with new notes payable for full indebtedness over five years at 6% interest. It is estimated that $200,000 face value of the demand notes will be exchanged for the longer-term notes and that the holders of the remaining notes will accept the offer of a reduced cash settlement.

(4) A new issue of 500 shares of $100 par value, 5%, noncumulative, nonparticipating preferred stock will replace 500 outstanding shares of $100 par value, 7%, cumulative, participating preferred stock. Preferred stockholders will repudiate all claims to $21,000 of dividends in arrears. The company has not formally declared the dividends.

(5) A new issue of 600 shares of $50 par value, Class A common stock will replace 600 outstanding shares of $100 par value, Class A common stock.

(6) A new issue of 650 shares of $40 par value, Class B common stock will replace 650 outstanding shares of $100 par value, Class B common stock.

(7) The deficit is eliminated.

The president of Equity Company asks that you determine the effect of the foregoing on the company and furnishes the following additional condensed account balances at December 31, 1975, which you believe are fairly presented:

Bank overdraft	$ 25,000
Other current assets	420,000
Plant and equipment	840,000
Trade accounts payable	235,000
Other current liabilities	85,000
Paid-in capital in excess of par value	125,000
Retained earnings (deficit)	(345,000)

Instructions

a Prepare pro forma journal entries that you would suggest to give effect to the quasi-reorganization as of January 1, 1976. Entries should be keyed to numbered information in the same sequence as given in the problem.

b Prepare a pro forma balance sheet for the Equity Company at January 1, 1976, as if the quasi-reorganization had been consummated.

Group B

16B-1 The board of directors of Blue Springs, Inc., declared a 6% stock dividend on October 1, payable on November 25 to stockholders of record November 10.

The market price of the company's stock was as follows on these dates: October 1, $63; November 10, $66; and November 25, $70. The accounting records of Blue Springs, Inc., are maintained on the basis of a fiscal year ending September 30.

The stockholders' equity section of the balance sheet at September 30 of the current year is shown below. During October the net income was $32,000.

Stockholders' equity:

Capital stock, par value $15, authorized 100,000 shares, issued and outstanding 40,000 shares	$ 600,000
Paid-in capital in excess of par	450,000
Retained earnings	760,000
Total stockholders' equity	$1,810,000

Instructions

a Prepare journal entries for the declaration and the distribution of the stock dividend.

b Prepare the stockholders' equity section of the balance sheet at October 31.

16B-2 On January 1, 1975, the Dorn Company had a balance in its retained earnings account of $11 million and paid-in capital in excess of par value of $3.5 million. The company has outstanding 1 million shares of common stock with a par value of $5 each.

During 1975 the Dorn Company's net income was $2.4 million. A cash dividend of 20 cents was paid July 31, 1975, and a 10% stock dividend was declared on October 15, 1975, to be distributed November 25, 1975, to stockholders of record November 5, 1975. You are asked to advise on the proper accounting treatment of the stock dividend.

Your inquiries produce the following information. The stock of the company is traded on a national stock exchange. The market price of the stock on October 15 was $16; on November 5 it was $22; and on November 25 it was $20.

Instructions

a Prepare a statement of retained earnings for the year 1975 in a form suitable for inclusion in the annual report.

b Prepare a statement of paid-in capital in excess of par for the year 1975 in a form suitable for inclusion in the annual report.

c Draft a note to the financial statement setting forth the basis of accounting for the stock dividend, and add separately appropriate comments or explanations regarding the basis chosen.

16B-3 The stockholders' equity of Sherwood Company at December 31, 1974, included 100,000 shares of $5 par capital stock which had been issued at a price of $20 per share. The company also had a substantial amount of retained earnings.

Net income for the year 1975 amounted to $350,000, which represented an earnings rate of 8% on total equity capital at the beginning of the year. A cash dividend of $1.40 a share was declared on December 1, 1975, payable January 20, 1976, to stockholders of record on January 2, 1976. A 4% stock dividend was declared at the same time and with the same dates of record and distribution. The cash dividend was not applicable to the dividend shares. The market price of the stock was $45 on December 1, 1975, and $49 on December 31.

Instructions

a Compute the amount of retained earnings at December 31, 1975. Show computations in good form.

b Prepare the stockholders' equity section of the balance sheet at December 31, 1975.

16B-4 Leather Imports, Inc., has only one issue of capital stock consisting of 1,000,000 authorized shares, of which 200,000 shares had been issued several years ago. There were only three items in the stockholders' equity section of the balance sheet at the beginning of the current year: common stock, $1,200,000; paid-in capital in excess of par, $2,800,000, and retained earnings, $3,800,000.

On May 1, the company declared a 2% stock dividend payable June 1 to stockholders of record on May 15. On July 1, a cash dividend of $1 a share was declared payable August 1 to stockholders of record on July 20. On October 1, a 3 for 1 stock split was carried out. (Assume that the stock split was authorized and carried out on the same day.) Net income for the year ended December 31 amounted to $2,100,000. Stock prices at selected dates during the current year were: May 1, $30; May 15, $31; June 1, $35; October 1, $45; December 31, $20.

Instructions
a What was the par value per share and the issuance price per share for the common stock issued in prior years? Show computations.
b What was the dollar increase or decrease in retained earnings as a result of the 2% stock dividend? Explain.
c What was the dollar increase or decrease in total stockholders' equity resulting immediately and directly from (1) the 2% stock dividend and (2) the stock split? Explain.
d Prepare journal entries to record the stock dividend, cash dividend, and stock split. You may debit Retained Earnings directly for dividend declarations rather than using accounts for Dividends and Stock Dividends. Give separate entries for declaration and distribution of dividends.
e Prepare the stockholders' equity section of the balance sheet at December 31.

16B-5 The stockholders of Huron Corporation have voted approval for the corporation to carry out a quasi-reorganization. The balance sheet appeared as follows at September 30, 1975, the effective date of the reorganization:

Assets

Current assets		$ 910,000
Plant and equipment	$800,000	
Less: Accumulated depreciation	395,000	405,000
Excess of cost over book value of acquired companies (goodwill)		1,520,000
Total assets		$2,835,000

Liabilities & Stockholders' Equity

Current liabilities	$ 160,000
Bonds payable, 6%	250,000
Preferred stock, $100 par, 7% (dividends in arrears, $42,000)	200,000
Common stock, $10 par	2,200,000
Retained earnings	25,000
Total liabilities & stockholders' equity	$2,835,000

The company is engaged in the manufacture of space exploration equipment and has acquired numerous small businesses at amounts greatly in excess of the value of their tangible net assets. The purchase price generally included payment for research work and for service of technically trained personnel. The value assigned to acquired assets was based on the par value of stock issued pursuant to the acquisition. The market value of stock was approximately equal to its par value.

In recent months many research projects were abandoned and some key people left the company. As a result, many contracts were lost and the "excess of cost over book value" was deemed to be worthless. In order to get a "fresh start" for financial reporting purposes, the following actions are taken pursuant to a quasi-reorganization approved by stockholders:

(1) Inventories and net receivables are written down by $50,000 and $10,000, respectively.
(2) The net carrying value of plant and equipment is reduced to $300,000 by increasing accumulated depreciation.
(3) The excess of cost over book value of acquired companies is eliminated from the books.
(4) The par value of common stock is reduced to $1.
(5) The dividends in arrears on the preferred stock are paid in cash and 80,000 shares of $1 par value common stock are issued to the preferred stockholders in exchange for their stock.
(6) Following the asset write-offs, the deficit is eliminated against paid-in capital from reduction in par value.
(7) During the last quarter of 1975, the Huron Corporation earned a net income of $45,000, and as a result, current assets increased by $75,000, current liabilities increased by $5,000, and accumulated depreciation increased by $25,000. Current liabilities also increased by $4,000 as a result of additional income tax assessed for 1974.

Instructions

a Prepare journal entries necessary to record the quasi-reorganization and to summarize the activities for the final quarter of 1975.

b What is the balance in retained earnings on December 31, 1975?

CHAPTER 17

Treasury stock; book value and earnings per share

nothing on warrants or options.

Additional topics dealing with stockholders' equity which require special attention are (1) the acquisition and retirement or reissue by a corporation of its capital stock, (2) the computation of book value per share of capital stock, and (3) the computation of earnings per share of common stock. The acquisition of capital stock reduces total stockholders' equity and affects the computation of both book value and earnings per share; book value per share is the net asset value of each share of capital stock outstanding; earnings per share is the amount of net income earned on each share of common stock and is considered by many as the most important financial measurement. These topics present some challenging problems for accountants.

TREASURY STOCK

Treasury stock is usually defined as a corporation's own capital stock which has been legally issued, fully paid for, and subsequently acquired by the corporation but not formally retired. All transactions by a corporation involving its own stock result in a contraction or an expansion of stockholders' equity. When a corporation acquires shares of its own stock, certain stockholders surrender their ownership interest in the corporation. Thus the acquisition of treasury stock by a corporation is logically viewed as a partial liquidation and no gain or loss results from such transactions.

Treasury stock may be acquired by corporations for a variety of reasons, including the following: (1) to buy out a particular stockholder, (2) to use the stock in connection with stock option and bonus plans or for acquiring other companies, (3) to settle claims against debtors who are also stockholders, (4) to increase earnings per share by reducing the number of shares outstanding, and (5) to support the market price of the stock.[1] There is little justification for a corporation to attempt to influence the market price of its stock through the acquisition and reissuance of treasury stock; such efforts necessarily create a conflict of interest between the corporation and its owners and may be illegal in certain circumstances.

Treasury stock and stated (or legal) capital

Stated (or *legal*) capital, as explained in Chapter 14, is a statutory definition of the amount of capital to be held in the business for protection of creditors; it is not available for withdrawal by owners. Legal capital generally consists of the total par or stated value of stock issued. The acquisition of treasury stock is not regarded as a reduction in legal capital; however, such an acquisition usually does involve an outflow of assets to stockholders and therefore certain legal restrictions are necessary to protect the corporation's creditors. Generally, a corporation is not permitted to acquire treasury stock if such acquisitions would cause the stockholders' equity to be reduced below legal capital. Furthermore, the retained earnings become restricted and unavailable for dividends to the extent of the amount paid for treasury stock.

It should be emphasized that the retirement of capital stock reduces legal capital and the acquisition of treasury stock does not. In terms of economic significance, the retirement of capital stock and the acquisition of treasury stock are similar, because both transactions consist of a return of assets (typically cash) to stockholders and a corresponding reduction in the amount of capital being utilized in pursuit of corporate objectives.

Treasury shares not an asset

A corporation cannot own a portion of itself, and for this reason treasury stock is not to be viewed as an asset. The holding of treasury stock does not give the corporation any right to receive dividends, to vote, to exercise

---

[1] In the 26th edition of *Accounting Trends & Techniques* issued by the AICPA in 1972, 443 of the 600 companies included in the survey reported treasury stock, either common or preferred, in their balance sheets. For an additional discussion of the various aspects of treasury stock, see the following: Charles D. Ellis and Allan E. Young, *The Repurchase of Common Stock,* The Ronald Press Company (New York: 1971); Guy J. Agrati, "Practical Considerations in Common Stock Repurchase," *Management Adviser* (May–June 1972), pp. 35–39; W. A. Paton, "Postscript on 'Treasury' Shares," *The Accounting Review* (April 1969), pp. 276–283.

preemptive rights as a stockholder, or to receive assets when the corporation is liquidated. Corporations can and sometimes do formally cancel treasury shares; certainly this action would never be taken if such cancellation actually meant the destruction of genuine assets. If a corporation were to dissolve, any treasury shares owned would contribute nothing in the process of converting assets into cash for distribution to shareholders.

The view that treasury shares are not assets is further strengthened by recognition that treasury shares are essentially much the same as unissued shares and no one advocates that unissued shares be listed as assets.

The policy of carrying treasury shares as assets, if justified at all, must rest on grounds of expediency rather than accounting principles. Treasury shares of a very large publicly owned corporation are sometimes acquired with the intention of reissue in the near future under an employee stock-purchase program.[2] The company may have a liability to employees participating in the stock-purchase program; to meet this liability the company expends cash to acquire treasury shares and soon thereafter discharges the liability by delivery of the treasury shares to employees. If such shares are few in number as compared with outstanding shares, they may conveniently be treated much the same as an investment in securities of any other corporation. The Accounting Principles Board has given recognition to this situation as follows:

> When a corporation's stock is acquired for purposes other than retirement (formal or constructive), or when ultimate disposition has not yet been decided, the cost of acquired stock may be shown separately as a deduction from the total of capital stock, capital surplus, and retained earnings, or may be accorded the accounting treatment appropriate for retired stock, or in some circumstances may be shown as an asset. . . .[3]

The Securities and Exchange Commission stipulates the following reporting requirement for reacquired shares:

> Reacquired shares not retired shall be shown separately as a deduction from capital shares, or from the total of capital shares and other stockholders' equity, or from other stockholders' equity, at either par or stated value, or cost, as circumstances require.[4]

The reasons for refusing to recognize treasury stock as an asset are many and are generally recognized as valid, yet the issue is kept alive by the policy of a few corporations which persist in listing treasury stock among their assets.

---

[2] At the end of 1972, for example, General Motors Corporation reported as an asset 1,693,625 shares, costing $130 million, as "Common Stock Held for Incentive Program."

[3] *APB Opinion No. 6,* "Status of Accounting Research Bulletins," AICPA (New York: 1965), p. 40.

[4] *Accounting Series Release No. 125* (Amendments to Regulations S–X, Rule 3-14), Securities and Exchange Commission (Washington: 1972), p. 10.

Alternative treatments of treasury stock

The two principal alternative treatments of treasury stock are (1) the *cost method* and (2) the *par* or *stated value method.* Although the par or stated value method still receives some theoretical support in accounting literature, practicing accountants have turned increasingly to the cost method in recent years.[5] Both methods come within the range of generally accepted accounting principles.

Under the cost method, the acquisition of treasury shares is regarded as a first step in a financial move which is completed by the reissuance of these shares. Treasury stock is thus viewed as a "suspense" item of stockholders' equity, with the corporation acting as an intermediary between the former and new shareholders. When the cost method is used, the Treasury Stock account is debited for the cost of the stock acquired and this account is shown in the balance sheet as a deduction from the *total* stockholders' equity. With this arrangement of the stockholders' equity section of the balance sheet, there is no reduction in the legal or stated capital. Since the laws of most states indicate that the acquisition of treasury stock does not constitute a reduction in legal capital, this balance sheet presentation may be regarded as reflecting the prevailing legal concept of treasury stock.

Under the par (or stated value) method, the possibility of reissuance of the treasury shares is not given much weight. The relationship between the corporation and the former owners of shares now held in treasury has ended and therefore the account showing paid-in capital in excess of par value relating to the treasury shares is reduced. If the corporation decides to retire the shares, the Capital Stock account also would be reduced; on the other hand, the reissuance of treasury stock would be treated as an original issuance of capital stock.

Illustration of Accounting for Treasury Stock—Cost Method   To illustrate the cost method of accounting for treasury stock transactions, assume that the balance sheet for Rae Corporation includes the following:

Stockholders' equity:

Capital stock, $100 par value, authorized, issued, and outstanding 10,000 shares	$1,000,000
Paid-in capital in excess of par value	200,000
Retained earnings	500,000
Total stockholders' equity	$1,700,000

---

[5] In the 26th edition of *Accounting Trends & Techniques* issued by the AICPA in 1972, common stock held in treasury was carried at cost by 328 companies and at par (or stated) value by only 63 companies.

At this time the Rae Corporation acquires 300 shares of treasury stock at $115 a share. The acquisition of treasury stock is recorded at cost as illustrated below:

Treasury Stock	34,500	
Cash		34,500
Acquired 300 shares of treasury stock at $115 a share.		

The stockholders' equity section of the balance sheet of Rae Corporation appears as follows when treasury stock is carried at cost:

Stockholders' equity:

Capital stock, $100 par value, authorized and issued 10,000 shares of which 300 shares have been purchased and are held in treasury	$1,000,000
Paid-in capital in excess of par value	200,000
Retained earnings (see note)	500,000
Total	$1,700,000
Less: Cost of 300 shares of treasury stock	34,500
Total stockholders' equity	$1,665,500

Note: The declaration of dividends and the acquisition of treasury stock are restricted to the amount of the retained earnings less the cost of treasury stock.

The presentation of stockholders' equity (when treasury stock is carried at cost) has the weakness of failing to show the net amount of capital invested by stockholders; it thus does not achieve one of the more important objectives in the classification of corporate capital. However, the cost approach to treasury stock does have the merit of showing as capital stock an amount equal to the legal capital of the corporation.

Let us assume that Rae Corporation now *cancels* the 300 treasury shares carried at cost. This action causes a reduction in legal capital and in paid-in capital in excess of par value equal to the amount paid for treasury stock. The entry is:

Capital Stock	30,000	
Paid-in Capital in Excess of Par Value	4,500	
Treasury Stock		34,500
To record cancellation of 300 shares of treasury stock carried at cost.		

The 300 shares were originally issued at $120 each ($1,200,000 ÷ 10,000), or for a total of $36,000. The shares were acquired at a cost of $34,500 or $1,500 *less* than the paid-in capital relating to these shares. Therefore, the cancellation of the 300 shares calls for a reduction of only $34,500 in the paid-in capital accounts; the excess of the amount paid in by stockholders over the cost of treasury shares, $1,500 ($36,000 − $34,500), remains in the Paid-in Capital in Excess of Par Value account.

If the Rae Corporation, instead of canceling the 300 shares of treasury stock as previously illustrated, should reissue these shares at a price of $108 per share, or $2,100 *below cost,* the entry would be as follows:

Cash	32,400	
Paid-in Capital in Excess of Par Value	2,100	
Treasury Stock		34,500
Sold 300 shares of treasury stock at $108 a share, or $2,100 below cost.		

Under the cost method, the Treasury Stock account is credited for the cost of the shares being reissued. Cost may be computed on an average basis, on a first-in, first-out basis, or by specific identification. When the reissuance price is less than cost, as in the illustration above, the excess of cost over the proceeds upon reissuance is charged to Paid-in Capital in Excess of Par Value. This account was credited at the time the stock was originally issued; however, if such paid-in capital is insufficient, paid-in capital from previous treasury stock transactions or Retained Earnings can be charged for the excess of cost over the proceeds upon reissuance.

When treasury stock is reissued at a *price above cost,* the excess of the proceeds over cost of the treasury shares is credited to Paid-in Capital in Excess of Par Value as illustrated below:

Cash	37,500	
Treasury Stock		34,500
Paid-in Capital in Excess of Par Value		3,000
Sold 300 shares of treasury stock at $125 a share, or $3,000 above cost.		

Illustration of Accounting for Treasury Stock—Par Value Method To allow a ready comparison between the cost method and par value methods of accounting for treasury stock, we will use the same transactions illustrated above for the Rae Corporation. Using the par value method, the entry to record the acquisition of treasury stock by the Rae Corporation is shown below:

Treasury Stock	30,000	
Paid-in Capital in Excess of Par Value	4,500	
Cash		34,500
Acquired 300 shares of treasury stock at $115 a share.		

In this entry the reduction in the stockholders' equity amounts to $34,500, or $1,500 less than the $36,000 originally invested in the corporation by its stockholders. In other words, $1,500 of the capital originally invested by those stockholders who have relinquished their ownership equity in the corporation remains in the business.[6]

After the acquisition of treasury stock, the stockholders' equity section of Rae Corporation's balance sheet appears as follows:

Stockholders' equity:		
Capital stock, $100 par value, authorized and is-		
sued 10,000 shares	$1,000,000	
Less: Treasury stock, 300 shares at par value	30,000	$ 970,000
Paid-in capital in excess of par value		195,500
Total paid-in capital		$1,165,500
Retained earnings (see note)		500,000
Total stockholders' equity		$1,665,500

Note: Retained earnings is restricted to the extent of $34,500, the amount paid for treasury stock.

[6] If the amount paid for treasury stock is more than the amount originally invested by stockholders, the excess is treated as a reduction in retained earnings. For example, if Rae Corporation paid $40,000 to acquire stock originally issued for $36,000, the transaction would be recorded using the par value method as follows:

Treasury Stock	30,000	
Paid-in Capital in Excess of Par Value	6,000	
Retained Earnings	4,000	
Cash		40,000

If treasury stock is acquired at a price below par value, the excess of par value over cost of treasury stock would be credited to Paid-in Capital in Excess of Par Value. For example, if Rae Corporation paid only $25,000 for the 300 shares of stock, the entry to record the acquisition would be:

Treasury Stock	30,000	
Paid-in Capital in Excess of Par Value		5,000
Cash		25,000

The above form of stockholders' equity section has the merit of showing the net amount for paid-in capital after the treasury stock acquisitions. It may be criticized, however, on the grounds that the net figure shown for capital stock ($970,000) may be erroneously interpreted as the legal capital; the legal capital of $1,000,000 is not reduced by the acquisition of treasury stock.

If the Rae Corporation should *cancel* all 300 of the treasury shares held, the effect in most states would be a reduction of the legal capital, as indicated by the following entry:

Capital Stock	30,000	
Treasury Stock		30,000
To record cancellation of 300 shares of treasury stock.		

After cancellation of the treasury shares, the stockholders' equity section would not include treasury stock and there would be no need to indicate a restriction on retained earnings. The cancellation, in effect, has permanently reduced legal capital to $970,000.

If the Rae Corporation, instead of canceling the 300 shares of treasury stock as previously illustrated, should resell them at a price *above par,* say $108 each, the entry would be:

Cash	32,400	
Treasury Stock		30,000
Paid-in Capital in Excess of Par Value		2,400
Sold 300 shares of treasury stock at $108 a share, or $2,400		
above carrying (par) value.		

Note that the entry for reissuance of treasury shares is similar to an entry for original issuance of stock. The difference between the issuance price of the treasury shares and the par value of the shares, as recorded in the Treasury Stock account, is credited to the Paid-in Capital in Excess of Par Value account. Under the par value approach, the purchase of treasury shares is viewed as a temporary retirement of these shares; the reissuance of treasury shares should then logically be treated in the same manner as an original issuance of stock.

In the event that the shares were reissued at *less than par,* it would not be appropriate to charge a Discount on Capital Stock account because no "discount liability" attaches to treasury shares issued below par. Instead, the deficiency would be recorded by a debit to Paid-in Capital in Excess of Par Value as long as such paid-in capital is available.

In the absence of sufficient paid-in capital in excess of par to absorb the deficiency, it should be charged to Retained Earnings.

Points of emphasis in accounting for treasury stock

Certain key points stand out from the rather involved procedures and alternative methods used in accounting for treasury stock:

1 Treasury stock is not an asset and is not entitled to receive dividends, to vote, or to share in the liquidation of the corporation.

2 No gain or loss is recognized on treasury stock transactions, either for accounting or for income tax purposes.

3 Retained earnings can never be increased through treasury stock transactions; retained earnings may, however, be decreased through such transactions.

4 The total stockholders' equity would be the same regardless of the method chosen for handling treasury stock; however, some variations in the relative amounts of paid-in capital and retained earnings may arise, depending on the method employed.

5 Retained earnings equal to the cost of treasury stock is unavailable as a basis for dividend declaration.

Redemption of preferred stock

Most corporations issuing preferred stock include in the contract a provision that all or any part of the preferred shares may be called for retirement at any time desired by the corporation. The call price is usually above the issuance price; it may be an unchanging amount or it may be a series of amounts on a sliding scale relating to specified time periods and eventually dropping to par value. When preferred shares are called for redemption, they are canceled and hence not available for reissue. Redemption may be effected by calling the stock pursuant to the call provision, by purchase in the open market, or by making a special offer to stockholders to *tender* their shares at a price substantially above the current market value of the stock.

The redemption of preferred stock is not to be confused with the acquisition of treasury stock, because *redemption* signifies both acquisition and cancellation (retirement) of the stock.

Preferred stock can also be acquired for reissue and held as treasury stock. However, acquisitions of preferred stock are generally made for the purpose of retiring the shares.

To illustrate the redemption of preferred stock, assume that D Corporation had issued 10,000 shares of $100 par value preferred stock at $102. The call price is $105 a share. If D Corporation calls the entire issue for redemption at the call price of $105 a share, the entry required is shown at the top of page 643.

This entry eliminates both the Preferred Stock and the Paid-in Capital in Excess of Par Value: Preferred Stock accounts; clearly this action is appropriate since the capital invested by the preferred stockholders has been returned in full and these investors no longer have any ownership

Preferred Stock	1,000,000	
Paid-in Capital in Excess of Par Value: Preferred Stock . .	20,000	
Retained Earnings	30,000	
Cash		1,050,000
Redeemed preferred stock for $30,000 in excess of the original issuance price.		

equity in the company. The $30,000 paid to the preferred stockholders in excess of their original investment, referred to as **premium paid on the retirement of preferred stock,** should be charged against Retained Earnings and not against any paid-in capital accounts applicable to other classes of stock.

When the preferred stock is selling at a price below call price, a company may wish to redeem a portion of the issue by purchase in the open market. Returning to the previous example, assume that D Corporation purchased 1,000 shares at $90. The entry to record the redemption would be:

Preferred Stock	100,000	
Paid-in Capital in Excess of Par Value: Preferred Stock	2,000	
Cash		90,000
Paid-in Capital from Redemption of Preferred Stock . . .		12,000
Redeemed 1,000 shares of preferred stock at a cost $12,000 below the original issuance price.		

By a payment of $90,000, the corporation has eliminated 1,000 shares of preferred stock representing $102,000 of paid-in capital. Recording the $12,000 excess of contributed capital over the amount paid to redeem the 1,000 shares in the manner illustrated above results in an increase in the equity of the common stockholders. However, this increment should not be regarded as a gain to be reported on the income statement; *a corporation cannot realize a gain or loss by dealing with its stockholders in their capacity as owners of the corporation.* It would also be unsound to credit to retained earnings the $12,000 difference between the book value of redeemed stock and the redemption price. The $12,000 was originally recorded as paid-in capital and it continues in that category with a descriptive title indicating the effect of a redemption of preferred shares at less than issuance price.

The two preceding examples illustrate the following general rules for interpreting the redemption of preferred stock:

1 When preferred stock is redeemed at a cost greater than the issuance price, the excess payment is usually treated as a reduction in retained earnings. Such an excess should not be recorded as an extraordinary loss or charged against any paid-in capital relating to outstanding shares of any other class of stock.

2 When preferred stock is redeemed for an amount less than the issuance price, the difference is treated as a paid-in capital item and not as an extraordinary gain or as an increase in retained earnings.

BOOK VALUE PER SHARE OF CAPITAL STOCK

The term *book value* is often used in negotiations for the sale of a going business. In closely held corporations, it is not unusual for an agreement to be signed giving one of the stockholders the right to buy out another stockholder within a specified time period at a price equal to the book value per share of stock.

Book value of stock when only a single issue of stock is outstanding

Book value is based on going-concern values and not on the assumption of a business liquidation. *Book value per share is the amount of net assets represented by each share of outstanding stock.* In a corporation with only one issue of stock outstanding, book value is computed by dividing the total stockholders' equity by the number of shares of stock outstanding. This is illustrated below:

$$\frac{\text{Total stockholders' equity}}{\text{Number of shares outstanding}} = \frac{\$2,500,000}{100,000} = \$25 \text{ book value per share}$$

If the corporation holds treasury stock, the debit balance in the Treasury Stock account would be deducted in determining the total stockholders' equity and the number of shares outstanding would not include treasury shares.

The formula for computing book value is deceptively simple, but the determination of book value under the terms of a contract for sale of stock may be highly controversial for such reasons as the following:

1 Carrying values for assets (especially inventories, depreciable assets, natural resources, and intangible assets) vary greatly according to the accounting methods selected.

2 Changes in accounting method may have been made since the signing of the contract, with significant impact upon the carrying values of assets and liabilities.

3 Accounting errors may have been made in current or past periods, thus providing a basis for arguing that the books must be adjusted to show proper asset valuations.

4 Investments in securities, land, plant and equipment, and intangible assets may have a current cash value far in excess of the cost valuation shown on the books. Some valuable assets may not even be included on the balance sheet.

5 Certain assets may be overstated or contingent liabilities of large amount may exist without being reported on the books. Similarly, large amounts of contingent assets (such as potential tax benefits of operating loss carryforwards) may exist.

When book value per share is used in a contract for the future sale of an interest in a business, the courts may interpret this accounting term in accordance with what is believed to have been the *intent* of the contracting parties.

Since a basic purpose of accounting data is to present *meaningful* information about a business entity, it is the opinion of the authors that the computation of book value requires adjustment of the books to correct many types of errors, including mechanical errors, violations of generally accepted accounting principles, and inconsistencies in the application of the established accounting policies. However, corrective measures of these types may still result in an amount for book value far different from the *fair market value* of the net assets. Substantial differences between book value and fair market value per share are inevitable when accounting records are maintained on a cost basis for an enterprise operating in a dynamic economic environment. The conclusion must be that contracts for the future sale of an interest in a business should be more specific in prescribing how the price per share is to be computed. It is not enough to specify "book value per share."

Book value of common stock when preferred stock is outstanding

Book value is used to some extent as a guide to investors, but usually with recognition that some other concepts, such as earnings per share, may be more closely correlated with changes in market price. Even though common stocks often sell at prices far above and far below the book value per share, some investors feel that the book value figure should be taken into account along with other criteria in reaching investment decisions.[7]

The concept of book value is more meaningful and more widely used for common stock than for preferred stock; however, if a corporation has both types of stock outstanding, the book value of the preferred stock must be determined as a preliminary step to computing book value for the common stock, as shown in the example on page 646.

---

[7] One writer states that any investor who totally ignores book value of stock "can justifiably be accused of having his head in the sand." (Steven C. Leuthold, "Spotting Tops and Bottoms: Multiples of Normalized Earnings, Book Values are Useful Guides," *Barron's,* June 19, 1972, p. 5.)

Book value of common stock—Two classes of stock outstanding:	
Total stockholders' equity (net of treasury stock)	*$9,280,000*
Amount applicable to preferred stock:	
10,000 shares, $100 par value, 5% preferred stock, callable at	
$108	*1,080,000*
Equity applicable to common stock, consisting of 1,000,000 shares	
outstanding (not including treasury stock)	*$8,200,000*
Book value per share of common stock, $8,200,000 ÷ 1,000,000	
shares	*$8.20*

The book value of the preferred stock in this example is $108 per share. In computing the book value of the preferred stock, consideration must be given to any dividend arrearages and other contractual limitations on the equity of preferred stockholders in the net assets of the corporation. On a going-concern basis, is it (1) par or stated value, (2) call price, or (3) liquidation price that is most significant in measuring the book value of the preferred stock? Nearly all preferred stocks issued in recent years contain a call provision; this call price is usually the maximum claim to net assets imposed by the preferred stock contract. Although there may be no immediate prospect that the stock will be called, the call price is nevertheless of more significance from the viewpoint of the going concern than is the liquidation price. The authors therefore favor using the call price of the preferred stock as the most appropriate measure of the stockholders' equity assignable to the preferred stock.

Other factors influencing book value per share of common stock

When significant amounts of convertible securities, warrants to purchase capital stock at specified prices, or stock options are outstanding, the potential effect on book value of common stock may be material. In such cases the computation of book value per share on a *pro forma* basis should accompany the book value figure as determined under the existing capital structure. For example, assume the following capital structure for the Berry Company:

5% convertible bonds payable (each $1,000 bond is convertible into	
40 shares of common stock and is callable at par)	*$1,000,000*
Common stock, $10 par value	*2,000,000*
Retained earnings	*600,000*

What effect would the conversion of the bonds payable have on the book value of common stock? The answer to this question is determined below:

Effect of Conversion of Bonds Payable on Book Value of Common Stock

	Before conversion	To record conversion	Pro forma after conversion
5% convertible bonds payable. . .	$1,000,000	$−1,000,000	$ −0−
Common stock, $10 par value. . .	$2,000,000	+400,000	$2,400,000
Paid in capital—from conversion of bonds payable		+600,000	600,000
Retained earnings	600,000		600,000
Total stockholders' equity	$2,600,000		$3,600,000
Number of shares of common stock outstanding	200,000		240,000
Book value per share of common stock.	$13		$15

Since each additional share of common stock issued pursuant to the conversion of the bonds adds $25 ($1,000,000 ÷ 40,000 shares) to stockholders' equity, the book value of common stock increased from $13 to $15 per share.

Other events which increase or decrease the book value per share of common stock are listed below:

Increases in book value Net income, reverse splits, sale of additional common stock at prices above book value, acquisition of common stock at prices below book value, and retirement of preferred stock at prices below book value of the preferred stock.

Decreases in book value Net loss, cash dividends (including any accumulated dividends on preferred stock), stock dividends, stock splits, sale of additional common stock at prices below book value, acquisition of common stock at prices above book value, and retirement of preferred stock at prices above book value of the preferred stock.

Other more complex situations, such as quasi-reorganizations and business combinations, may materially alter the book value per share of common stock.

EARNINGS PER SHARE

Because of the complexities of business activities and the need for a small number of comparative measurements to highlight financial analysis, earnings per share has become perhaps the most important figure. Probably no financial statistic is cited more widely than earnings per share. In the opinion of many investors, market prices of common stocks are closely related to earnings per share.

Earnings per share is the amount of net income earned on a share of common stock during an accounting period. Earnings per share is meaningful only with respect to common stock; it is not computed for preferred stock because the participation in earnings by preferred stockholders is limited by contract. Assuming that only one class of stock is outstanding and there is no change in the number of shares outstanding during the period, earnings per share would be computed as follows:

$$\frac{\text{Net income}}{\text{Number of shares of stock outstanding}} = \textbf{earnings per share}$$

When preferred stock is also outstanding, the current year's dividend requirement on the preferred stock (whether or not declared by the board of directors) would be deducted from net income to determine the earnings available for the common stock.

Investors use earnings per share to evaluate the profitability of a corporation. By computing the *price-earnings* ratio (price of a share of stock divided by earnings per share), investors attempt to determine whether the market price of the stock is reasonable or whether it might be too high or too low. However, financial statements are only one part of the total information that can be used in evaluating the company's past and predicting its future performance, and the earnings per share figure is only a small piece of the information available in financial statements. Excessive reliance on earnings per share data may result in failure to consider the totality of a company's operations, including nonfinancial data which may be far more important.

Historical perspective

With the increasing importance of the income statement, the process of measuring and reporting net income and earnings per share has attracted greater attention. In 1958, the AICPA issued *Accounting Research Bulletin No. 49,* "Earnings per Share." [8] This bulletin was superseded in 1966 by *APB Opinion No. 9,* which required for the first time that earnings per share be reported in the income statement. [9] Subsequently, the Accounting Principles Board issued *Opinion No. 15* to: (1) recognize the importance

[8] Reproduced in Paul Grady, "Inventory of Generally Accepted Accounting Principles for Business Enterprises," *Accounting Research Study No. 7,* AICPA (New York: 1965), pp. 305–311.

[9] *APB Opinion No. 9,* "Reporting the Results of Operations," AICPA (New York: 1966).

of increasingly complex capital structures in which the distinctions between common stockholders' equity and other forms of capital were not
clearly apparent; (2) provide guidelines and procedures for the computation of earnings per share in a consistent manner which would be meaningful to investors; and (3) specify procedures for reporting the potential
dilution in earnings per share.[10] The Accounting Principles Board recognized that it is difficult to identify all conditions that may be encountered
in computing earnings per share.[11]

Computing weighted-average number of shares outstanding; stock splits and stock dividends

The first step in computing earnings per share is to determine the number
of shares outstanding for each period for which earnings data are to be
presented. Earnings per share should be based on the **weighted-average**
number of common shares outstanding during each period. (At this point
of our discussion we will not be concerned with common stock equivalents or other complexities discussed later in this chapter.)

The weighted-average number of common shares is determined by
relating the portion of time within a period that a given number of common
shares were outstanding to the length of that period. For example, if 1,000
shares were outstanding during the first nine months of a year and 1,400
shares were outstanding during the balance of the year as a result of
the sale of 400 additional shares, the weighted-average number of shares
outstanding during the year would be 1,100, determined as follows:

1,000 shares $\times \frac{3}{4}$ of a year	750
1,400 shares $\times \frac{1}{4}$ of a year	350
Weighted-average number of shares outstanding	1,100

The use of the weighted-average number of shares outstanding is
necessary in order to compute a meaningful earnings per share figure.
Assuming that 400 shares were sold for cash at the end of the ninth month
in the example above, the proceeds on the sale would be available to
generate earnings only during the last three months of the year. These
400 shares would be outstanding for one-fourth of a year, or an equivalent

---

[10] *APB Opinion No. 15,* "Earnings per Share," AICPA (New York: 1969).
[11] Shortly after the issuance of *APB Opinion No. 15,* the AICPA published a 189-page
monograph by J. T. Ball, "Computing Earnings per Share—Unofficial Accounting Interpretations of APB Opinion No. 15" (New York: 1970). *APB Opinion No. 15* has been criticized
on grounds that it deals with financial analysis rather than accounting principles, that it
contains some illogical assumptions, and that it is overly complex. However, the Opinion
has played an important role in standardizing the computation of reported earnings per
share.

of 100 shares for a full year. In other words, the weighted-average number of shares outstanding consists of 1,000 shares during the entire year plus 100 full-year equivalent shares issued during the year.

When the number of shares outstanding changes as a result of a stock split, stock dividend, or reverse split, the computation of the weighted-average shares outstanding should be adjusted retroactively. This is necessary in order to report earnings per share which are fully comparable in terms of the latest capital structure. If a stock split, stock dividend, or reverse split will become effective after the close of the latest period but before financial statements are issued, the per-share computations should be made on the basis of the **new capitalization.** When earnings per share data are computed on this basis, the method of computation should be disclosed in a footnote accompanying the financial statements.

The computation of the weighted-average number of shares of common stock outstanding, showing retroactive adjustment for a stock dividend and a stock split, is illustrated on page 651 for Split Hotel Corporation.

In computing the retroactive weighted-average number of shares outstanding in Year 1, the 20% stock dividend declared in Year 2 is applied to the 650,000 weighted-average number of shares actually outstanding in Year 1; and the 3 for 1 split in Year 3 is applied to the 780,000 weighted-average number of shares after adjustment for the 20% stock dividend.

To continue the example, assume that the net income for Split Hotel Corporation for Year 3 was $5,040,000 and that net income and earnings per share were **originally reported** at the end of each of the preceding two years as follows:

	From income statement for Year 2	From income statement for Year 1
Net income	$3,780,000	$2,574,000
Earnings per share of common stock:		
Year 1: $2,574,000 ÷ 650,000 (weighted-average number of shares outstanding in Year 1, before retroactive adjustment for 20% stock dividend and 3 for 1 stock split)		$3.96
Year 2: $3,780,000 ÷ 840,000 (weighted-average number of shares outstanding in Year 2, before retroactive adjustment for 3 for 1 stock split)	$4.50	

	Year 3	Year 2	Year 1
Analysis of changes in common stock outstanding:			
Number of shares outstanding, beginning of year	840,000	700,000	500,000
Increase as a result of issuance of additional shares for cash on April 1, Year 1			+200,000
Increase as a result of 20% stock dividend in August of Year 2		+140,000	
Increase as a result of 3 for 1 stock split in March of Year 3 (200% increase)	+1,680,000		
Number of shares outstanding, end of year	2,520,000	840,000	700,000
Computation of weighted-average number of shares of common stock outstanding for three-year period (giving retroactive recognition to stock dividend and stock split):			
Year 1: Outstanding, beginning of Year 1			500,000
Add: Full-year equivalent of additional shares issued, 200,000 $\times \frac{3}{4}$ of a year			+150,000
Weighted-average shares outstanding before retroactive adjustment			650,000
Add: Effect of 20% stock dividend in Year 2 [(500,000 + 150,000) $\times$ 20%]			+130,000
Subtotal			780,000
Add: Effect of 3 for 1 stock split in Year 3, or 200% increase			+1,560,000
Year 2: Outstanding, end of Year 2 (see above)		840,000	
Add: Effect of 3 for 1 stock split in Year 3, or 200% increase		+1,680,000	
Year 3: Outstanding at end of Year 3 per analysis above (no adjustments required)	2,520,000		
Weighted-average number of shares outstanding, as adjusted retroactively	2,520,000	2,520,000	2,340,000

A comparative income statement at the end of Year 2 would show earnings per share for Year 1 of $3.30 ($2,574,000 ÷ 780,000 shares outstanding after giving effect to the 20% stock dividend in Year 2). The comparative net income and earnings per share for the Split Hotel Corporation, giving effect to the 20% stock dividend in Year 2 and the 3 for 1 split in Year 3, should be presented *at the end of Year 3* as follows:

	Year 3	Year 2	Year 1
Net income	$5,040,000	$3,780,000	$2,574,000
Earnings per share of common stock:			
Year 1: $2,574,000 ÷ 2,340,000			
shares (adjusted).			$1.10
Year 2: $3,780,000 ÷ 2,520,000			
shares (adjusted).		$1.50	
Year 3: $5,040,000 ÷ 2,520,000			
shares (adjusted).	$2.00		

Earnings per share are thus reported on a fully comparable basis in terms of the capital structure at the end of Year 3. For example, since one share of common stock outstanding in Year 1 is equal to 3.6 shares at the end of Year 3, the earnings for Year 1 are retroactively restated at $1.10 per share ($3.96, as originally reported in Year 1, divided by 3.6).

The difficulties encountered in computing earnings per share do not stop with the computation of the weighted-average number of shares outstanding. For example: How are earnings per share computed for a company which has preferred stock (convertible or nonconvertible) or convertible bonds outstanding? How do outstanding options or warrants to purchase common stock at fixed prices affect the computation of earnings per share? To answer these questions, our discussion will focus on the type of capital structure as follows:

1 For companies that have a *simple capital structure*
2 For companies that have a *complex capital structure*
   a *Primary* earnings per share, which takes into account the potential dilutive effect of common stock equivalents outstanding
   b *Fully diluted* earnings per share, which takes into account the maximum potential dilutive effect of convertible securities, stock options, and warrants outstanding

Simple capital structure

The capital structure of a corporation may consist only of common stock; or the capital structure may include nonconvertible preferred stock, little or no potentially dilutive convertible securities, and small amounts of stock options or warrants. In such cases the corporation is said to have a *simple capital structure*. *Dilution* is the reduction in earnings per share that would occur if convertible securities were converted or if outstanding options and warrants were exercised. If the potential dilution in earnings per share is less than 3% (before taking dilution into account), potentially dilutive securities and options or warrants need not be considered in the computation of earnings per share. In such cases, a *single presentation* of earnings per common share in the income statement is appropriate. This "single" presentation may include an extraordinary item, as illustrated below for the Simplex Corporation:

	Year 2	Year 1
Data required to compute earnings per share of common stock:		
Income before extraordinary item.	$810,000	$750,000
Extraordinary gain, net of taxes	$140,000	
Dividend requirement on nonconvertible preferred stock	$ 50,000	$ 50,000
Shares of common stock outstanding:		
Beginning of year	400,000	300,000
Issued for cash on July 1, Year 1	–0–	100,000
End of year	400,000	400,000
Common shares reserved for employee stock options (1).	10,000	10,000
Weighted-average number of shares outstanding .	400,000	350,000 (2)
Presentation in the income statement:		
Earnings per share of common stock:		
Income before extraordinary item	$1.90 (3)	$2.00 (4)
Extraordinary item	0.35 (5)	–0–
Net income	$2.25	$2.00

(1) *Excluded from weighted-average number of shares because options represent less than 3% of weighted-average number of shares. This is below the limitations established by* **APB Opinion No. 15.**
(2) *300,000 shares for the full year, plus 100,000 shares for one-half year (equivalent to 50,000 for a full year) = 350,000 shares.*
(3) *($810,000 − $50,000) ÷ 400,000 weighted-average number of shares = $1.90.*
(4) *($750,000 − $50,000) ÷ 350,000 weighted-average number of shares = $2.00.*
(5) *$140,000 ÷ 400,000 weighted-average number of shares = $.35.*

The example for the Simplex Corporation shows that the income per share before the extraordinary item decreased in Year 2 despite the fact that the same number of shares were outstanding at the end of each year (400,000 shares) and that *total* income before the extraordinary item actually increased in Year 2. This is attributed to the increase in the *weighted-average* number of shares outstanding; the 100,000 shares issued in Year 1 were outstanding for 6 months in Year 1 and for 12 months in Year 2. In the absence of extraordinary items, only a single earnings per share figure would appear in the income statement for a company with a simple capital structure. When the income statement includes an extraordinary item, three per-share amounts are reported: Income before extraordinary item, extraordinary item, and net income.

Complex capital structure

When a corporation has convertible securities, stock options, warrants, or other potentially dilutive contracts outstanding, its capital structure is viewed as *complex* for purposes of computing earnings per share. The Accounting Principles Board took the position in *Opinion No. 15* that earnings per share should reflect potential dilution when securities which are in substance the equivalent to common stock are outstanding. As a result, companies with a complex capital structure must report with equal prominence in the income statement *primary* earnings per share (which include the dilutive effect of common stock equivalents) and *fully diluted* earnings per share (which include the maximum potential dilutive effect of all convertible securities, stock options, and warrants outstanding); this is referred to as a *dual presentation* of earnings per share. (See page 662 for an example.) These reporting requirements for earnings per share do not change the legal rights of the various security holders or the presentation of other data in the financial statements. The computation of primary earnings per share is explained below; the explanation of fully diluted earnings per share starts on page 660.

Primary Earnings per Share and Common Stock Equivalents *Primary earnings per share* is the amount of earnings applicable to each share of common stock; the number of shares of stock consists of common stock actually outstanding plus any common stock equivalents. A *common stock equivalent* is a security which contains contractual provisions enabling its owner to exchange the security for common stock.[12] Such a security is considered equivalent to common stock because its holders have a right to participate in the appreciation of the value of the common stock. This participation is essentially the same as that of a common stockholder except for the fact that the security generally carries a specified dividend or interest rate. The market value of a security which is a common stock equivalent is dependent to a considerable degree on the market value of the common stock. Neither actual conversion nor the assumption that conversion is likely to take place is necessary before a security can be classified as a common stock equivalent. *Common stock equivalency is*

[12] *APB Opinion No. 15, op. cit.,* p. 225.

determined at the time the security is issued and does not change so long as the security remains outstanding.[13]

In a complex capital structure case, potentially dilutive securities may or may not qualify as common stock equivalents for purposes of computing primary earnings per share. However, common stock equivalents should not be used in computing earnings per share if their use would be *antidilutive,* that is, have the effect of increasing earnings per share or reducing a loss per share. Common stock equivalents generally include convertible bonds, convertible preferred stock, and stock options and warrants.

Convertible Securities A bond or preferred stock which at the time of issuance is substantially equivalent to common stock is treated as a common stock equivalent. Convertible stocks or bonds are considered common stock equivalents if at the time of issuance the cash yield, based on the market price, is less than $66\frac{2}{3}\%$ of the then current bank prime interest rate.[14] The *bank prime interest rate* is the rate banks charge on relatively short-term loans to borrowers with the very best credit standing. If convertible *senior securities* (bonds payable and preferred stock) do not meet the test of a common stock equivalent at the date of issue, they would not be a factor in computing primary earnings per share but would be used in computing fully diluted earnings per share.

A convertible security which qualifies as a common stock equivalent should be assumed to have been converted at the beginning of the earliest period for which earnings per share are being reported or at the time of issuance, whichever is the more recent date. For example, if convertible preferred stock is issued on April 1, the equivalent number of shares of common stock would be considered outstanding for nine months of the year even though some of the preferred stock might have been converted late in the year.

In computing primary earnings per share, net income should be adjusted (increased) by the amount of interest (net of taxes) on convertible bonds which qualify as common stock equivalents. In determining the net income available for common stock, net income would not be reduced by the amount of the dividend requirement on convertible preferred stock which qualifies as a common stock equivalent. These adjustments are necessary because it is assumed that both the convertible bonds and the preferred stock are exchanged for common stock.

Example 1: Convertible preferred stock is a common stock equivalent. On July 1 of Year 1, X Corporation issued at $100 per share, 50,000 shares of $3 convertible preferred stock. At the time the preferred stock was issued, the bank prime interest rate was 6%. Each share of preferred stock is convertible into two shares of common stock; no shares have yet been converted. If the X Corporation has net income of $950,000 in Year 2

13 *Ibid.,* p. 227.
14 *Ibid.,* p. 229.

and 400,000 shares of common stock outstanding, compute the primary earnings per share for Year 2.

Solution: The convertible preferred stock qualifies as a common stock equivalent because its cash yield of 3% ($3 ÷ $100) is less than 4% (66⅔% of the 6% bank prime interest rate at the date the convertible preferred stock was issued). A convertible preferred stock is dilutive any time the dividend per share paid on the stock (calculated on the basis of the number of common shares which would be issued upon conversion) is less than the earnings per share of common stock before considering conversion. In this case the convertible preferred stock is dilutive, since the equivalent converted dividend on the preferred stock is $1.50 ($3 ÷ 2 shares), which is less than the earnings per share of common stock before the conversion is assumed, $2 ($950,000 net income − $150,000 preferred dividend ÷ 400,000 shares of common stock outstanding). Primary earnings per share are computed below:

$$\frac{\text{Net income before preferred dividends}}{\text{Common stock outstanding} + \text{common stock equivalents}}$$

$$= \frac{\$950,000}{400,000 + 100,000} = \underline{\underline{\$1.90}}$$

The conversion of the preferred stock would also be assumed in computing fully diluted earnings per share; this is illustrated in Example 6 on pages 660–662.

Example 2: Common stock equivalent is antidilutive. Assuming the same facts as in Example 1 for X Corporation, except that net income for Year 2 amounts to only $350,000, compute primary earnings per share for Year 2.

Solution: Although the convertible preferred stock is a common stock equivalent, conversion would not be assumed in computing primary earnings per share because such an assumption would be antidilutive. This is illustrated below:

Earnings per share of common stock:

Conversion not assumed: $350,000 net income − $150,000 preferred dividends = $200,000 ÷ 400,000 shares *$0.50*

Conversion assumed: $350,000 net income ÷ 500,000 shares *$0.70*

Since earnings per share would be increased if the common stock equivalent was used in the computation, primary earnings per share would be reported at $0.50 per share, not $0.70 per share. Because the assumed conversion of the preferred stock is antidilutive, conversion would not be assumed in computing fully diluted earnings per share.

Example 3: Convertible bonds are not treated as common stock equivalents. On December 31 of Year 1, Y Corporation issued at par $1 million of 6% convertible bonds when the bank prime rate of interest was $7\frac{1}{2}$%. Each $1,000 bond is convertible into 25 shares of the corporation's common stock. In Year 2, Y Corporation earned $225,000 after interest expense and income taxes. The income tax is assumed to be 40% of taxable income. At December 31, Year 2, no bonds had been converted and 75,000 shares of common stock were outstanding. Compute the primary earnings per share for Year 2.

Solution: The cash yield of 6% ($60 ÷ $1,000) on the convertible bonds was **greater** than 5% ($66\frac{2}{3}$% of $7\frac{1}{2}$% bank prime interest rate at the date the bonds were issued); therefore, the convertible bonds are not considered to be common stock equivalents for purposes of calculating primary earnings per share for Year 2. Primary earnings per share would be $3 ($225,000 ÷ 75,000 shares). However, conversion of the bonds would be assumed in computing fully diluted earnings per share; this is illustrated in Example 4.

Example 4: Convertible bonds are treated as common stock equivalents. Assume the same facts as in Example 3 for Y Corporation, except that the interest rate on the convertible bonds is $4\frac{1}{2}$% rather than 6%. Compute primary earnings per share for Year 2 if net income is $225,000.

Solution: In this case the convertible bonds are common stock equivalents because the cash yield of $4\frac{1}{2}$% ($45 ÷ $1,000) was **less** than 5% ($66\frac{2}{3}$% of $7\frac{1}{2}$% bank prime interest rate at the date the bonds were issued). The computation of primary earnings per share is shown on page 658.

If conversion of the bonds were not assumed, the earnings per share would have been improperly reported at $3 per share ($225,000 ÷ 75,000 shares). Conversion would also be assumed in computing fully diluted earnings per share.

Options or Warrants to Purchase Common Stock A corporation may issue options or warrants which give the holder the contractual right to purchase common stock at a fixed price. Such options or warrants should be regarded as common stock equivalents at all times;[15] however, dilution of less than 3% would be ignored. Therefore, primary earnings per share should reflect the impact from the exercise of options or warrants, including the possible *use of the proceeds* which would be received upon the exercise of the options or warrants. In computing primary earnings

[15] *Ibid.*, p. 230.

Earnings to be used in computing primary earnings per share:		
Net income as reported		$225,000
Add back interest on convertible bonds, net of income taxes:		
Interest, $1,000,000 × 4½%	$45,000	
Less income taxes at 40%	18,000	27,000
Earnings to be used in computing earnings per share		$252,000
Number of shares to be used in computing primary earnings per share:		
Number of shares outstanding at end of Year 2		75,000
Number of shares to be issued, assuming conversion of bonds, 1,000 × 25		25,000
Number of shares to be used in computing primary earnings per share		100,000
Primary earnings per share of common stock, $252,000 ÷ 100,000 shares		$2.52

per share, an assumption should be made that the options or warrants are exercised **only** if such an assumption would result in a dilution of earnings per share.

When the exercise of options or warrants is assumed, any proceeds that would be received are assumed to be used to acquire treasury stock at the average market price during the period. This is known as the **treasury stock method.** For example, if options to purchase 10,000 shares of common stock at $5 per share are outstanding and the average market price during the period was $20 per share, the $50,000 that would be received by the corporation upon exercise of the options and issuance of 10,000 additional shares would be sufficient to acquire only 2,500 shares of common stock ($50,000 ÷ $20 = 2,500). Thus, 7,500 (10,000 − 2,500) shares would be added to the number of shares of common stock already outstanding in computing primary earnings per share. The exercise of the options or warrants is assumed to have taken place at the **beginning of the period** or **at the time of issuance,** whichever is the more recent date.

Opinion No. 15 recommends that the exercise of options or warrants should not be assumed until the common stock sells in excess of the exercise price for "substantially all of three consecutive months ending with the last month of the period to which earnings per share data relate."[16] Under the treasury stock method, options or warrants would have a dilutive effect on earnings per share only when the average market price of the common stock exceeds the exercise price of the options or

[16] *Ibid.,* pp. 230–231.

warrant-option- common st. equity

warrants. The computation of primary earnings per share using the treasury stock method is illustrated in the example below:

Example 5: Options to purchase common stock are outstanding. Z Corporation has 200,000 shares of common stock and options to purchase 30,000 shares of common stock at $10 per share outstanding at the end of Year 2. The options were granted to employees several years ago. The average market price of the common stock during Year 2 was $30 per share. Net income for Year 2 was $550,000. Compute primary earnings per share for Year 2.

Solution:

Computation of number of shares of common stock to be used in determining primary earnings per share:		
Number of shares of common stock outstanding at end of Year 2 . . .		*200,000*
Add: Number of shares of common stock to be issued upon exercise of options		*30,000*
Less: Assumed purchase of common stock using the proceeds received upon exercise of options [(30,000 × $10) ÷ $30]	*10,000*	*20,000*
Number of shares of common stock to be used in determining primary earnings per share		*220,000*
Primary earnings per share of common stock, $550,000 ÷ 220,000 shares		*$2.50*

Opinion No. 15 requires a departure from the procedure illustrated above when the number of additional shares of common stock that may be issued pursuant to outstanding options and warrants exceeds 20% of the number of common shares outstanding at the end of the period. In such cases, it should be assumed that *all* options and warrants were exercised and the total proceeds were used first to purchase 20% of the outstanding stock and the balance was then used to retire outstanding debt. However, if all debt is thus eliminated, it should be assumed that the remaining proceeds are used to purchase short-term investments. Appropriate recognition should be given to the income tax effects of the assumed use of the proceeds from the exercise of the options and warrants.

Computation of fully diluted earnings per share when options to purchase common stock are outstanding is illustrated in Example 6 starting on page 660.

The reader by now should realize that it is virtually impossible to cover all situations which may arise in the computations of common stock equivalents and primary earnings per share; our objective has been to describe the basic issues involved. We now turn our attention to the second part of the *dual presentation* of earnings per share—the computation of fully diluted earnings per share.

Fully Diluted Earnings per Share It is apparent from the foregoing discussion that primary earnings per share may include some potential dilution and that certain potentially dilutive securities are not considered as common stock equivalents. However, in the computation of fully diluted earnings per share, *all* convertible securities, options, and warrants are assumed to have been converted or exercised in order to reflect the maximum potential dilution. As in the computation of primary earnings per share, conversion of securities or the exercise of options or warrants *should not* be assumed when the effect would be antidilutive (would have the effect of increasing earnings per share or reducing a loss per share).

The computation of fully diluted earnings per share differs from the computation of primary earnings per share in two essential respects.

1 All convertible securities, whether or not they qualify as common stock equivalents, which individually would decrease earnings per share if conversion had taken place, are included in the calculation of fully diluted earnings per share. All such conversions are assumed to have taken place at the beginning of the period (or at the time of issuance of the convertible security, if later).

2 In order to recognize the maximum potential dilution, the market price of the common stock at the end of the period, if higher than the average market price during the period, is used to determine the number of shares of common stock which could be acquired using the proceeds received upon the exercise of options or warrants. This procedure reduces the number of shares of common stock which could be purchased with the proceeds and thus has the effect of increasing the number of outstanding shares on a pro forma basis.

The computation of primary and fully diluted earnings per share is illustrated below.

Example 6: Stock options and convertible preferred stock are outstanding. Compute primary and fully diluted earnings per share for Year 10 from the data presented below for the Dual Corporation:

Number of shares of common stock outstanding throughout Year 10 . .	*95,000*
*Number of shares of $4 convertible preferred stock outstanding throughout Year 10; each share of preferred stock is convertible into three shares of common stock; the preferred stock is **not** a common stock equivalent, but is dilutive*	*3,000*
Outstanding options (issued in Year 6) to purchase common stock at $20 per share; average price of common stock during Year 10 was $40 per share and the price at the end of Year 10 was $50 per share	*10,000*
Net income for Year 10	*$330,000*

Solution:

	Primary	Fully diluted
Computation of number of shares of common stock to be used in computing earnings per share for Year 10:		
Number of shares of common stock outstanding at end of Year 10	95,000	95,000
For purposes of computing primary earnings per share:		
Shares of common stock to be issued upon exercise of options at $20 per share 10,000		
Less: Assumed purchase of common stock at average market price during Year 10 using proceeds received upon exercise of options [(10,000 × $20) ÷ $40] 5,000	5,000	
For purposes of computing fully diluted earnings per share:		
Shares of common stock to be issued upon exercise of options at $20 per share 10,000		
Less: Assumed purchase of common stock at market price at end of Year 10 using proceeds received upon exercise of options [(10,000 × $20) ÷ $50] 4,000		6,000
Assume conversion of 3,000 shares of preferred stock into common stock (3 for 1)		9,000
Number of shares of common stock to be used in computing earnings per share for Year 10	100,000	110,000
Earnings per share for Year 10:		
Primary: $318,000* ÷ 100,000 shares	$3.18	
Fully diluted: $330,000 ÷ 110,000 shares		$3.00

* Net income of $330,000 less preferred dividend requirement of $12,000.

In computing fully diluted earnings per share for the Dual Corporation, the $200,000 proceeds from the issuance of 10,000 additional shares upon exercise of options is assumed to be used to acquire common stock at $50 per share, the price at the end of the year. Since only 4,000 ($200,000 ÷ $50) shares can be acquired with the proceeds, the number of shares of common stock to be used in computing fully diluted earnings per share is increased by 6,000 (10,000 − 4,000). In addition, the 3,000 shares of convertible preferred stock which do not qualify as common stock equivalents in computing primary earnings per share are assumed to be converted into 9,000 shares of common stock. These adjustments fully recognize the maximum potential dilution in earnings per share.

It should be pointed out that in computing primary earnings per share, the amount of the dividend requirement on the convertible preferred stock ($12,000) was deducted from net income in arriving at the income available for the common stock; however, when fully diluted earnings per share were computed, net income was *not* reduced by the amount of the preferred dividend requirement because the preferred stock was assumed to have been eliminated through conversion into common stock.

Summary of earnings per share computations

The foregoing discussion relating to the computation of earnings per share is summarized in tabular form on page 663.

Presentation of earnings per share in the income statement

Shown below is an actual presentation of earnings per share (including the accompanying note) by a large manufacturing company with a complex capital structure:

	Year 2	Year 1
Earnings (loss) before extraordinary loss	$5,681,039	$ (8,457,540)
Extraordinary loss:		
Expropriation of foreign operations, less estimated		
income tax credit of $10,000,000	–0–	(12,100,000)
Net earnings (loss) for the year	$5,681,039	$(20,557,540)
Primary:		
Earnings (loss) before extraordinary loss	$0.83	$(1.50)
Extraordinary loss.	–0–	(2.02)
Net earnings (loss) for the year	$0.83	$(3.52)
Fully diluted:		
Earnings (loss) before extraordinary loss	$0.80	$(1.50)
Extraordinary loss.	–0–	(2.02)
Net earnings (loss) for the year	$0.80	$(3.52)

Note 1—Earnings per Share: Primary earnings per common share for Year 2, after preferred dividend requirements, are based on the average number of common shares outstanding during the year plus the common share equivalents applicable to 21,000 shares with respect to employees' stock options and 250,500 shares for the assumed exercise of warrants.

Fully diluted earnings per common share for Year 2 are computed as above with the additional assumption that all of the $5\frac{7}{8}$% subordinated convertible debentures were converted and the related interest expense, net of income taxes, was eliminated.

Computation of primary and fully diluted loss per common share for Year 1 excluded all common share equivalents and the assumed conversion of the $5\frac{7}{8}$% subordinated convertible debentures as the inclusion thereof would have been antidilutive.

Capital structure	Earnings per share in income statement	Explanation
1 Simple	Single presentation	Divide net income by the weighted-average number of shares of common stock outstanding for the period. Dilutive securities are ignored when the potential dilution in the aggregate is less than 3% of earnings.
2 Complex	Dual presentation: **a** Primary	Divide net income (increased by the after-tax effect of assumed conversion of bonds, if any) by the weighted-average number of shares of common stock and common stock equivalents outstanding for the period. Convertible securities may or may not qualify as common stock equivalents at date of issue; options and warrants are always treated as common stock equivalents. In no case should common stock equivalents be used to determine primary earnings per share if inclusion is antidilutive. Potential earnings dilution of less than 3% is ignored
	b Fully diluted	Essentially the same procedure as above, except that all convertible securities are assumed to have been converted (at the beginning of the period or issue date, if later) if the effect of the conversion is dilutive. The proceeds from the assumed exercise of options and warrants are applied to purchase common stock at year-end market price if such price is higher than the average market price during the period covered. Potential earnings dilution of less than 3% is ignored

As stated in Chapter 5, computation of cash flow per share has been discouraged by both the Accounting Principles Board and the Securities and Exchange Commission. Additional examples of presentation of earnings per share appear in Appendix B. See Chapter 22 for the presentation of earnings per share following a change in accounting principle.

REVIEW QUESTIONS

1 Define **treasury stock** and state briefly how it should be shown in the balance sheet.

2 For what reasons do companies acquire their own stock?

3 A spokesman for Tilden Oil Company said, "We seek to purchase 8.4% of our stock in order to secure a ready and safe investment for excess cash." Comment on this quotation.

4 Does the acquisition and resale of its own stock by a corporation result in a profit or loss to the corporation?

5 In reviewing the Miscellaneous Income account of Ranchland Corporation, you find a credit for $200 representing a dividend of $1 per share on 200 shares of treasury stock. You determine that the dividend declaration covered the entire 10,000 shares originally issued, that Retained Earnings was charged for $10,000, and that $9,800 of cash was paid to stockholders. Discuss the propriety of this procedure.

6 a Discuss the propriety of declaring stock dividends on treasury shares.
  b Should treasury shares be split?
  c How would the issuance of treasury stock (recorded at cost) pursuant to a 2% stock dividend be recorded.

7 The Treasury Stock account of a corporation contained a debit balance of $54,000, representing the cost of 6,000 shares reacquired by the corporation. Later the corporation exchanged the 6,000 treasury shares for land which was listed in the balance sheet as "Land, at cost . . . $54,000." Do you approve of this treatment? Explain.

8 Most states place some restriction on the acquisition by a corporation of its own capital stock. What is the usual nature of this restriction? What is the purpose of such restrictions?

9 The majority stockholder in a closely held corporation had an option to buy all the stock of a minority stockholder at book value at any time during the first 10 years of operation. After four years, the method of inventory valuation was changed from fifo to lifo. At the end of the tenth year, the majority stockholder exercised his option. The minority stockholder objected, arguing that the change in inventory valuation method was costing him thousands of dollars. Discuss.

10 What is the appropriate accounting treatment of the difference between original issuance price and the price paid to retire preferred stock?

11 What special steps are required in computing the book value of common stock in each of the following cases:
  a Both preferred and common stock are outstanding.
  b Treasury stock has been acquired.
  c Convertible bonds, stock options, and warrants are outstanding.

12 The book value of 100,000 common shares is $40 per share. Indicate the effect of each of the following four transactions on book value per share:
  a Sale of additional shares at $10 pursuant to stock option agreement
  b Sale of additional shares at $60 through rights offering

    c Purchase of treasury stock at $75 per share
    d Conversion of bonds, 20 shares for every $1,000 bond

13 Define *earnings per share* and indicate how this statistic is used by investors.

14 a How is the weighted-average number of shares outstanding for a given year computed?
    b What effect do stock dividends and stock splits have on the presentation of earnings per share for two or more years?

15 Differentiate between the following:
    a *Simple* and *complex* capital structure
    b *Primary* and *fully diluted* earnings per share
    c *Single* and *dual* presentation of earnings per share

16 Discuss the reasons why securities other than common stock may be considered *common stock equivalents* for the computation of primary earnings per share.

17 Explain how convertible securities are determined to be common stock equivalents and how those convertible senior securities which are not considered to be common stock equivalents enter into the determination of earnings per share data.

18 Explain the *treasury stock method* as it applies to options and warrants in computing primary earnings per share data.

19 For the first six months of the current year, National Corporation reported primary earnings per share of $4.50 and fully diluted earnings per share of only $2. What factors may cause such a large difference between the two earnings per share figures? If the stock of National Corporation sells for $36 per share, what is the price-earnings ratio?

EXERCISES

Ex. 17-1 The stockholders' equity section of Kansas Company's balance sheet at December 31, 1975, was as follows:

Stockholders' equity:

Capital stock—$100 par, authorized 50,000 shares, issued and outstanding 10,000 shares	$1,000,000
Paid-in capital in excess of par value	200,000
Retained earnings	800,000
Total stockholders' equity	$2,000,000

    Early in 1976, the company acquired 400 shares of its stock for $50,000. During the year it sold 100 of the treasury shares at $140 per share, sold 100 shares at $120 per share, and retired the remaining 200 shares of treasury stock. The company records treasury stock at cost.
    Prepare journal entries to record the purchase, the resale, and the retirement of the treasury stock.

Ex. 17-2 Newtech Company has decided that since it has idle cash and since its $100 par value, 5% cumulative preferred stock (which was originally issued at $98) has been selling on the open market at around $85 per share, it should retire as many shares of the stock as possible in an effort to improve the earnings per share on the common stock. On March 2, the company acquired 5,000 shares of the preferred stock from one large shareholder at $84 per share.

What entry would be made to record the retirement of the 5,000 shares of preferred stock?

Ex. 17-3 Abco Corporation has a total stockholders' equity of $35,500,000, including $10,750,000 of paid-in capital in excess of par value and retained earnings. The capital stock included in stockholders' equity follows:

7% preferred stock, $50 par value and callable at $53 per share; 200,000 shares issued and outstanding $10,000,000

Common stock, $10 par value, 5,000,000 shares authorized; 1,550,000 shares were issued and 1,500,000 shares are outstanding (50,000 shares costing $750,000 are held in treasury) 15,500,000

What is the book value per share of common stock?

Ex. 17-4 At the beginning of 1974, the Harned Company had 100,000 shares of common stock and 10,000 shares of $4 preferred stock outstanding. The preferred stock is callable at $55 per share. The Harned Company had not borrowed money since it was incorporated in 1968.

Early in 1975, the company retired the preferred stock at $55. The company used idle cash and the proceeds from the sale of surplus plant at book value to pay for the preferred stock.

At the beginning of 1976, the company borrowed $1 million at 6% and retired 20,000 shares of common stock.

The company reported operating income (before interest expense and income taxes at the rate of 50%) as follows:

1974 . . . . $800,000
1975 750,000
1976 700,000

Compute the earnings per share of common stock for each of the three years 1974–1976. Comment on the trend in earnings per share in the face of the decreasing operating income.

Ex. 17-5 A corporation had 500,000 common shares outstanding on January 1, sold 300,000 shares on April 1, and had net income of $3,625,000 for the year ending December 31. Assuming that the corporation had no preferred stock or potentially dilutive securities outstanding, compute the earnings per share for the year.

Ex. 17-6 A newly organized corporation began business on January 2, 1972, by issuing 2,000 shares of common stock for various assets. On July 1, 1973, an additional 1,000 shares were issued for cash. On April 1, 1974, a 10% stock dividend was issued. On July 1, 1975, the stock was split 3 for 1.

Earnings and dividends per share of common stock for each of the four years of the company's history are to be reported on a comparable basis in the 1975 annual report to stockholders.

Compute the current equivalent number of shares outstanding at the end of each of the four years, to be used in computing the earnings per share of common stock.

Ex. 17-7 The capital structure of Ragan Corporation consists of the following:

$3 preferred stock, no-par, cumulative and nonconvertible, 20,000 shares $1,000,000

$4 convertible preferred stock, no-par, convertible into three shares of com-

mon stock, 10,000 shares 1,000,000

Common stock, no-par, 50,000 shares 500,000

Neither preferred stock issue is a common stock equivalent. Compute primary and fully diluted earnings per share of common stock, assuming that net income for the current year was $220,000.

Ex. 17-8 Warrants exercisable at $20 each to purchase 12,000 shares of common stock were outstanding during a period when the average market price of the common stock was $25 and the ending market price was $30.

Determine the increase in the weighted-average number of outstanding common shares as a result of applying the "treasury stock method" for the assumed exercise of these warrants when computing **(a)** primary earnings per share and **(b)** fully diluted earnings per share.

SHORT CASES FOR ANALYSIS AND DECISION

Case 17-1 The Lunar Development Corporation purchased $180,000 of equipment for $120,000 cash and a promise to deliver an indeterminate number of treasury shares of its $10 par common stock, with a market value of $15,000, on January 1 of each year for the next five years. Hence $75,000 in "market value" of treasury shares will be required to discharge the $60,000 balance due on the equipment.

The corporation immediately acquired 3,000 shares of its own stock for $48,000 in the expectation that the market value of the stock would increase substantially before the delivery dates. A total of 2,500 of these shares were subsequently issued in payment of the balance due on the equipment contract.

Instructions
a Discuss the propriety of recording the equipment at
  (1) $120,000 (the cash payment)
  (2) $180,000 (the cash price of the equipment)
  (3) $195,000 (the $120,000 cash payment plus the $75,000 market value of the treasury stock that must be transferred to the vendor in order to settle the obligation in accordance with the terms of the agreement)
  (4) $160,000 (the $120,000 cash payment plus the $40,000 cost of the 2,500 treasury shares issued in payment for the equipment)
b Discuss the arguments for treating the balance due as
  (1) A liability
  (2) Treasury stock subscribed
c Assuming that legal requirements do not affect the decision, discuss the arguments for treating this corporation's treasury shares as
  (1) An asset awaiting ultimate disposition
  (2) A capital element awaiting ultimate disposition

Case 17-2 The Blue Sky Investment Corporation was at one time quite successful, but in recent years had been operating at a loss. In reaction to these losses, the market price of the stock had dropped to an all-time low of $5 a share. The capital stock had originally been issued at par of $10 a share; present book value was $12 a share.

At this point, the three Candide brothers acquired control of the company by purchasing in small lots a total of 20,000 shares at a total cost of $130,000. Total stock outstanding was 100,000 shares but the remaining 80% of the stock was scattered among many small owners. By an aggressive proxy campaign, the Candide brothers were able to secure enough outside support to elect a full slate of directors.

The Candide brothers had no hopes for profitable operation of the company; sales were in a declining trend and the principal products were gradually becoming obsolete. The attraction of the company to the Candide brothers was its relatively high book value and strong cash position. They planned to recover their investment rapidly through stripping the company of its most salable assets and then selling their shares for whatever they would bring. Retained earnings of the company amounted to only $200,000 but cash, receivables, and marketable securities amounted to $500,000.

At the instruction of the Candide brothers, the new board of directors took the following actions:

(1) Issued optimistic statements to the press concerning planned acquisition of several profitable companies and resumption of cash dividends.
(2) Sold the receivables and securities, thus increasing cash to approximately $500,000.
(3) Borrowed $200,000 secured by pledge of the inventory, thus obtaining additional cash.
(4) Began purchasing the company's own stock at steadily increasing prices. After acquisition of 10,000 shares at an average cost of $9, the company offered to purchase up to 15,000 shares at $15. Stockholders sold 10,000 shares to the company at $15 per share.
(5) Sold the land and building to the Candide brothers for $400,000 more than book value. This gain was included in the quarterly earnings report and was widely publicized. The sale agreement called for payment partially in stock of another company controlled by the Candide brothers and partially in mining lands owned by them. No cash was involved.
(6) Purchased from the Candide brothers their entire holdings of 20,000 shares at a price of $20 a share. This transaction consumed nearly all the available cash. All members of the board then resigned for "personal reasons."

Instructions (Ignore income tax considerations)
a Prepare the stockholders' equity section of the balance sheet after these transactions.
b Did the purchase of treasury stock by the company violate the concept of limiting dividends and purchases of treasury stock to the amount of retained earnings?
c Were any of the actions by the board improper? Explain.

Case 17-3 The owners of the Barajas Company, a closely held corporation, have offered to sell their 100% interest in the company's common stock at an amount equal to the book value of the common stock. They will continue to own the company's preferred stock, which is convertible into common stock at a price substantially below book value.

Your client would like to combine the operations of the Barajas Company with his Ronda Division and he is seriously considering buying the common stock of the Barajas Company. He questions the use of book value as a basis for the sale, however, and has come to you for advice.

Instructions Draft a memorandum to your client covering the following points:
a Definition of book value. Explain its significance in establishing a value for a business that is expected to continue in operation.
b Description of the procedure for computing book value of common stock.
c Your advice to the client regarding this proposed purchase.

Case 17-4 Ocean Properties Corporation, a new audit client of yours, has not reported earnings per share data in its annual reports to stockholders in the past. The president requested that you furnish information about the reporting of earnings per share data in the current year's annual report in accordance with generally accepted accounting principles.

Instructions
a Define the term ***earnings per share*** as it applies to a corporation with a capitalization structure composed of only one class of capital stock. Explain how earnings per share should be computed and how the information should be disclosed in the corporation's financial statements.
b Explain the meanings of the terms (1) ***senior securities*** and (2) ***common stock equivalents,*** which are often used in discussing earnings per share, and give examples of the types of items which each term includes.
c Discuss the treatment, if any, which should be given to each of the following items in computing earnings per share of common stock for financial reporting purposes:
(1) The declaration of current dividends on cumulative preferred stock.
(2) The acquisition of some of the corporation's outstanding common stock during the current fiscal year. The stock was classified as treasury stock.
(3) A 2 for 1 stock split of common stock during the current fiscal year.
(4) A provision created out of retained earnings for a contingent liability from a possible lawsuit.
(5) Outstanding preferred stock issued at a premium with a par value liquidation right.

PROBLEMS

Group A

17A-1 Brian Ida & Company issued 200,000 shares of capital stock at a price of $25 a share. At December 31, 1975, the balance sheet showed the following:

Capital stock, $10 par value, authorized 250,000 shares, issued and out-	
standing 200,000 shares	*$2,000,000*
Paid-in capital in excess of par value	*3,000,000*
Retained earnings	*1,000,000*
Total stockholders' equity	*$6,000,000*

On January 10, 1976, the company acquired 10,000 shares of treasury stock at $49 a share. On December 1, 1976, the company reissued 5,000 shares of treasury stock for $281,500, net of commissions.

Instructions
a Record the foregoing transactions in journal entry form, assuming that treasury stock is recorded at cost.
b Record the foregoing transactions in journal entry form, assuming that treasury stock is recorded at par value.
c Compute the book value per share at December 31, 1975, and after each of the two transactions is completed. Why did book value per share change?

17A-2 Following are the entries recorded in a Stockholders' Equity account of Owner-Accountant, Inc., during 1975, its first year of operations:

Stockholders' Equity

(1) Acquired 1,000 treasury shares	18,000	(5) Sale of 10,000 shares of	
(2) Cash dividends, declared,		capital stock, $10 par;	
payable in 1976	10,000	authorized 25,000	
(3) Discount on bonds payable . .	12,000	shares	162,000
(4) Loss on disposal of		(6) Issuance of 5,000 shares	
equipment	8,800	of capital stock for land	
		worth $80,000. The land	
		was recorded at $50,000 . .	50,000
		(7) Reserve for "contingen-	
		cies" charged to expense. .	1,000
		(8) Proceeds from sale of 500	
		treasury shares	11,500
		(9) Net income for year	58,100

The bonds were sold on June 30, 1975, and mature on June 30, 1995.

Instructions

a Prepare correcting entries for each item (1) through (9). Any corrections to current year's income should be made to Income Summary; the balance in this account is then transferred to Retained Earnings. Record treasury stock at cost.

b Prepare the stockholders' equity section of the balance sheet at December 31, 1975.

c Compute the book value per share of capital stock at December 31, 1975.

17A-3 Gerson Corporation was organized on January 5, 1975, with authority to issue 250,000 shares of $10 par value capital stock. It sold 200,000 shares immediately for cash at a price of $25 a share. Operations were profitable from the beginning; earnings averaged over $30,000 a month, with a total of $361,000 for the first fiscal year ended December 31, 1975. A dividend of 80 cents a share was declared on December 10, 1975, payable January 15, 1976, to stockholders of record December 31, 1975.

Gerson Corporation established a policy of encouraging all its employees to acquire stock in the company. During 1975, the corporation acquired shares from several employee-stockholders who left the company; some of these shares were subsequently reissued to new employees. The following treasury stock transactions occurred during 1975:

May 1   Acquired 200 shares of stock at $30 a share.

July 15   Reissued 100 shares at $36 a share.

Oct. 10   Acquired 500 shares at $28 a share.

Dec. 20   Reissued 100 shares at $26 a share.

The corporation uses the title "additional paid-in capital" on the balance sheet to report various sources of paid-in capital in excess of legal capital.

Instructions

a Assuming the use of the cost method and fifo method of accounting for treasury stock, prepare:
  (1) Journal entries for treasury stock transactions
  (2) Stockholders' equity section of the balance sheet at December 31, 1975

b Assuming the use of the par value method of accounting for treasury stock, prepare:
(1) Journal entries for treasury stock transactions
(2) Stockholders' equity section of the balance sheet at December 31, 1975

17A-4 A comparative summary of the stockholders' equity for the Rizzo Corporation, together with certain additional information, is given below:

	Dec. 31, 1975		Jan. 1, 1975
Stockholders' equity:			
Capital stock, authorized 100,000 shares;			
issued:			
At Dec. 31, 1975, 70,000 shares, $8 par			
value (1,000 held in treasury)	$ 560,000		
At Jan. 1, 1975, 40,000 shares, $10 par			
value			$ 400,000
Stock dividend to be distributed			
(6,900 shares)	55,200	$ 615,200	
Additional paid-in capital:			
From sale of capital stock, including			
$8,000 at Dec. 31, 1975 from treasury			
stock transactions	$ 808,700		200,000
From stock dividends	276,000	1,084,700	
Total paid-in capital		$1,699,900	$ 600,000
Retained earnings:			
Appropriated for purchase of treasury			
stock	$ 37,000		
Unappropriated	1,104,400	1,141,400	1,400,000
Total paid-in capital & retained earnings		$2,841,300	
Less: Cost of 1,000 shares in treasury		37,000	
Total stockholders' equity		$2,804,300	$2,000,000

In February of 1975, the board of directors approved a 5 for 4 stock split which reduced the par value of the capital stock from $10 to $8 per share. The split was approved by stockholders on March 1 and distributed on March 25.

On April 1, 1975, the company acquired 2,000 shares of its stock at $37 a share.

On June 30, 1975, 1,000 shares of treasury stock were reissued at $45 a share.

On July 1, 1975, 20,000 shares of $8 par value capital stock were issued in exchange for the net assets of another company. The total market value of the 20,000 shares issued was $760,700.

A cash dividend of $1 per share was declared on December 2, 1975, payable on December 29, to stockholders of record on December 15; a 10% stock dividend was declared on December 20, to be distributed on January 25, 1976. The market price of the stock on December 20 was $48 a share.

The net income for 1975 was $141,600, which included an extraordinary gain of $35,400 (net of income taxes).

Instructions

a Prepare journal entries to record transactions relating to stockholders' equity that took place during the year ended December 31, 1975.

b Prepare the lower section of the income statement for the year ended December 31, 1975, showing operating income and the extraordinary gain. Also illustrate how the earnings per share should be presented in the income statement, assuming that earnings per share are determined on the basis of the weighted-average number of shares outstanding during the year and that financial statements are issued before the 10% stock dividend is distributed.

c Prepare a statement of retained earnings for the year ended December 31, 1975. Use two columnar headings: "Unappropriated" and "Appropriated for Purchase of Treasury Stock."

d Compute the book value per share of capital stock at December 31, 1975.

17A-5 On February 1, 1976, when your audit and report are nearly complete, the financial vice president of the Steel Plate Company asks you to prepare statistical schedules of comparative financial data for the past two years for inclusion in the company's annual report. Your working papers reveal the following information:

(1) Income statements show net income as follows: 1974, $720,000; 1975, $600,000.

(2) On January 1, 1974, there were outstanding 100,000 shares of common stock, par value $5, and 10,000 shares of 6% convertible preferred stock, par value $100. The preferred stock was issued at par. Each share of preferred stock is initially convertible into 2.5 shares of common stock, to be adjusted for any stock dividends and splits. The market value of common stock has ranged from $45 to $60 per share during the past two years. The prime bank rate of interest was $5\frac{1}{2}\%$ at the time the preferred stock was issued.

(3) On December 31, 1974, a 20% stock dividend was distributed to common stockholders. On this date, the fair market value of the stock was $50 per share.

(4) In June of 1975, common stock was split 2 for 1.

(5) Cash dividends are paid on the preferred stock on June 30 and December 31. Preferred stock dividends were paid in each year; none of the preferred stock has been converted.

Instructions

a In connection with your preparation of the statistical schedule of comparative financial data for the past two years,

(1) Prepare a schedule computing the number of shares of common stock outstanding as of the respective year-end dates.

(2) Prepare a schedule computing the equivalent number of shares of common stock outstanding for each year for purposes of computing primary earnings per share. Equivalent shares means the number of shares outstanding in the respective prior periods in terms of the present capital structure.

(3) Prepare a schedule computing the equivalent number of shares of common stock outstanding for each year for purposes of computing fully diluted earnings per share.

b Prepare the lower section of the income statement, showing primary and fully diluted earnings per share for 1974 and 1975.

17A-6 The stockholders' equity section of Bond Company's balance sheet as of December 31, 1975, appears at the top of page 673.

Included in the liabilities of Bond Company are $5\frac{1}{2}\%$ convertible debentures issued at their face value of $20,000,000 in 1974. The debentures are due in 1994 and until then are convertible into the common stock of Bond Company at the rate of 50 shares of common stock for each $1,000 debenture. To date none of these debentures have been converted.

$1 cumulative convertible preferred stock (par value $25 a share; authorized 1,600,000 shares, issued 1,400,000, converted to common 750,000, and outstanding 650,000 shares; involuntary liquidation value, $30 a share, aggregating $19,500,000)	$16,250,000
Common stock (par value $.25 a share; authorized 15,000,000 shares; issued and outstanding 8,800,000 shares)	2,200,000
Paid-in capital in excess of par value	32,750,000
Retained earnings	40,595,000
Total stockholders' equity	$91,795,000

On April 2, 1975, Bond Company issued 1,400,000 shares of convertible preferred stock at $40 per share. Quarterly dividends to December 31, 1975, have been paid on these shares. The preferred stock is convertible into common stock at the rate of two shares of common for each share of preferred. On October 1, 1975, 150,000 shares and on November 1, 1975, 600,000 shares of the preferred stock were converted into common stock.

During July 1974, Bond Company granted options to its officers and key employees to purchase 500,000 shares of the company's common stock at a price of $20 a share. The options do not become exercisable until 1976.

During 1975 dividend payments and average market prices of Bond Company's common stock were as follows:

	Dividend per share	Average market price per share
First quarter	$0.10	$20
Second quarter	0.15	25
Third quarter	0.10	30
Fourth quarter	0.15	25
Average for the year		25

The December 31, 1975, closing price of the common stock was $25 a share. Assume that the bank prime interest rate was 7% throughout 1974 and 1975. Bond Company's net income for the year ended December 31, 1975, was $19,000,000. Assume that the income tax rate is 50%.

Instructions

a Prepare a schedule which shows the valuation of the common stock equivalency status of the (1) convertible debentures, (2) convertible preferred stock, and (3) employee stock options.

b Prepare a schedule which shows for 1975 the computation of:
  (1) The weighted-average number of shares for computing primary earnings per share
  (2) The weighted-average number of shares for computing fully diluted earnings per share

c Prepare a schedule which shows for 1975 the computation to the nearest cent of:
  (1) Primary earnings per share
  (2) Fully diluted earnings per share

Group B

17B-1 The following data are taken from the balance sheet of the Diverse Corporation at the end of Year 5:

Assets

Current assets	$ 20,000,000
Plant assets (net)	55,000,000
Investment in M Corporation (at cost, market value, $20 million)	10,000,000
Investment in N Corporation (at cost, market value, $10 million)	15,000,000
Total assets	$100,000,000

Equities

Current liabilities	$ 10,000,000
5% bonds payable	40,000,000
Capital stock, 1 million shares	20,000,000
Retained earnings	30,000,000
Total equities	$100,000,000

The securities of the Diverse Corporation are quoted currently on the open market as follows:

5% bonds payable	50% of par value
Capital stock	$20 per share

The investment in M Corporation is exchanged for all bonds payable and the investment in N Corporation is exchanged for 500,000 shares of the company's outstanding capital stock. These treasury shares are recorded at cost of $10 million by the Diverse Corporation.

Instructions

a Prepare separate journal entries to record the two transactions described above. Ignore the income tax effect on the transactions.

b Compute the book value per share of Diverse Corporation's capital stock (1) before the two transactions above and (2) after the two transactions above.

17B-2 The stockholders' equity section of the Rex Crab Corporation's balance sheet at December 31, 1975, is shown below:

Stockholders' equity:

$5 preferred stock $100 par, callable at $105; authorized 20,000 shares, issued and outstanding 10,000 shares	$1,000,000
Common stock, $5 par, authorized 200,000 shares, issued and outstanding 100,000 shares	500,000
Paid-in capital in excess of par value: preferred stock	30,000
Paid-in capital in excess of par value: common stock	1,500,000
Retained earnings	4,200,000
Total stockholders' equity	$7,230,000

Early in 1976, the company redeemed 3,500 shares of its preferred stock at $98 a share. These shares were held by the estate of a deceased stockholder. Shortly thereafter, the remaining 6,500 shares were called for redemption and retired at the established call price. Net income for 1976 was $270,000; dividends of $1 per share were paid on the common stock in 1976.

Instructions
a Prepare journal entries to record the redemption of the preferred stock.
b Prepare the stockholders' equity section of the balance sheet at December 31, 1976.
c Compute the effect of the redemption of preferred stock on the book value per share of the common stock.

17B-3 The balance sheet of Corbett Company at December 31, 1975, shows the following items in the stockholders' equity section:

Stockholders' equity:

6% preferred stock, $100 par, callable at $105 and convertible into four shares of common stock		$ 200,000
Common stock, $10 par, 100,000 shares authorized		400,000
Paid-in capital in excess of par value:		
From sale of preferred	$ 10,000	
From sale of common	100,000	110,000
Total paid-in capital		$ 710,000
Retained earnings		490,000
Total stockholders' equity		$1,200,000

Following is a list of transactions completed by the company during 1976:

Jan. 2   Two hundred shares of preferred stock are acquired and formally retired at a cost of $120 a share.

Mar. 1   A 10% stock dividend on common stock is declared and distributed. At the time of declaration the stock is quoted at $30 a share.

Apr. 1   The remaining preferred stock is called for redemption. Holders of all outstanding shares convert their holdings pursuant to the antidilution provision of the preferred stock contract. Dividends for the first quarter (not previously recorded) amounting to $2,700 are paid at the time of conversion.

Sept. 10   Two hundred shares of common stock are acquired at a cost of $35 a share. The company records treasury stock at cost. Of these, 100 are retired and the other 100 are held in the treasury.

Oct. 3   Fifty shares held in the treasury are sold for $50 a share and on the same date the remaining 50 shares are issued for a patent.

Dec. 31   Net income for the year amounted to $201,930 (debit Other Assets) and cash dividends amounting to $54,520 were paid during the year, including the $2,700 paid on preferred stock during the first quarter of 1976.

Instructions
a Prepare journal entries to record the foregoing transactions.
b Prepare the stockholders' equity section of the balance sheet at December 31, 1976.
c What is the book value per share of common stock on December 31, 1976?

17B-4 The following condensed balance sheet of Sully Corporation was prepared at December 31, 1975:

Assets

Current assets	$ 300,000
Other assets	900,000
Total assets	$1,200,000

Liabilities & Stockholders' Equity

Current liabilities		$ 240,000
Stockholders' equity:		
$5 convertible preferred stock, par and liquidation value, $100		
per share	$200,000	
Common stock, $5 par	100,000	
Paid-in capital in excess of par value: common stock	300,000	
Retained earnings	385,000	
Subtotal	$985,000	
Less: Treasury stock 1,000 shares of common stock at cost .	25,000	960,000
Total liabilities & stockholders' equity		$1,200,000

The preferred stock is convertible into common stock at any time in the ratio of five shares of common for each share of preferred. The bank prime rate of interest was 6% when the preferred stock was issued in 1973.

The following transactions occurred during the fiscal year ended December 31, 1976:

Jan. 2   100 shares of common stock were received in settlement of $4,800 in past-due accounts receivable. The treasury stock is considered to be worth an amount equal to the book value of common stock at this date.

Jan. 3   The 1,100 shares of treasury stock were reissued in exchange for land valued at $45,000.

Feb. 15   Cash dividends were declared and paid as follows: preferred, $2.50 per share; common, $1 per share. (Debit Retained Earnings and credit Cash.)

Aug. 15   Cash dividends were declared and paid as follows: preferred, $2.50 per share; common, $1 per share. (Debit Retained Earnings and credit Cash.)

Dec. 31   Net income for the year was $90,000. (Debit Income Summary and credit Retained Earnings.)

Instructions

a Prepare journal entries to record the above transactions.

b Prepare a condensed balance sheet at December 31, 1976. Assume that the amounts of current assets and current liabilities were unchanged from the balance sheet of the preceding year.

c Compute primary and fully diluted earnings per share on the common stock for 1976. The market value of the common stock at the end of 1976 is $40 per share.

17B-5 Selected data summarizing the earnings performance of the Albers Company for a five-year period are given below (all figures in thousands):

	Year 5	Year 4	Year 3	Year 2	Year 1
Operating income	$64,120	$38,680	$84,480	$69,940	$47,200
Bond interest expense . . .	5,200	5,200	9,100	10,400	10,400
Income before income tax					
expense.	$58,920	$33,480	$75,380	$59,540	$36,800
Income tax expense	24,400	15,000	37,040	28,940	15,140
Net income	$34,520	$18,480	$38,340	$30,600	$21,660
Number of common shares					
outstanding at end of					
year	26,000	36,000	30,000	25,000	12,500
6%, $100 par value					
preferred; number of					
shares at end of					
year	60	70	80	90	100

Late in December of each of the five years, the company called 10,000 shares of its preferred stock, paying the call price of 102 plus the final quarter's dividends. During Year 2, the company split its common stock 2 for 1, and in Year 4 it issued a 20% stock dividend. On October 1, Year 3, 5 million shares of common stock were sold for cash. On July 1, Year 5, the company purchased 10 million shares of common stock from a major stockholder who was unhappy with company profits. The company plans to use the shares for acquisitions. There were no common stock equivalents outstanding during the five-year period.

Instructions Earnings per share of common stock for the five-year period are to be reported on a comparable basis in the company's annual report as of the end of the fifth year. Determine the figures that should be reported for each of the five years.

17B-6 The controller of Cid Company has requested assistance in determining net income, primary earnings per share, and fully diluted earnings per share for presentation in the company's income statement for the year ended September 30, 1975. As currently calculated, the company's net income is $400,000 for the fiscal year ending September 30, 1975. The controller has indicated that the net income figure might be adjusted for the following transactions which were recorded by charges or credits directly to the Retained Earnings account. (The amounts are net of applicable income taxes.)

(1) The sum of $375,000, applicable to a breached 1971 contract, was received as a result of a lawsuit. Prior to the award, legal counsel was uncertain about the outcome of the suit.
(2) A gain of $300,000 was realized on the sale of a subsidiary company.
(3) A special inventory write-off of $150,000 was made, of which $125,000 applied to goods manufactured prior to October 1, 1974.

Your working papers disclose the following analysis for the year ended September 30, 1975:

(1) Common stock (at October 1, 1974, stated value $10, authorized 300,000 shares; effective December 1, 1974, stated value $5, authorized 600,000 shares):

Balance, Oct. 1, 1974—issued and outstanding, 60,000 shares.
Dec. 1, 1974—60,000 shares issued in a 2 for 1 stock split.
Dec. 1, 1974—280,000 shares (stated value $5) issued for cash at $39 per share.

(2) Treasury stock—common:

Mar. 1, 1975—acquired 40,000 shares at $38 per share.
Apr. 1, 1975—sold 40,000 shares at $40 per share.

(3) Series A warrants (each warrant was exchangeable with $60 for one common share; effective December 1, 1974, each warrant became exchangeable for two common shares at $30 per share):

Oct. 1, 1974—25,000 warrants issued at $6 each.

(4) Series B warrants (each warrant is exchangeable with $40 for one common share):

Apr. 1, 1975—20,000 warrants authorized and issued at $10 each.

(5) First mortgage bonds, 5½%, due 1990 (nonconvertible; priced to yield 5% when issued):

Balance Oct. 1, 1974—authorized, issued and outstanding, the face value of $1,400,000.

(6) Convertible debentures, 6.8%, due 1994 (each $1,000 bond was convertible at any time until maturity into 15 common shares; effective December 1, 1974, the conversion rate became 30 shares for each bond as a result of the 2 for 1 stock split).

Oct. 1, 1974—authorized and issued at their face value of $2,400,000.

The following table shows market prices for the company's securities and the bank prime interest rate for selected dates:

	Price (or rate) at			Average for year ended
	Oct. 1, 1974	Apr. 1, 1975	Sept. 30, 1975	Sept. 30, 1975
Common stock . . .	60	40*	36¼*	37½*
First mortgage bonds, 5½%	88½	87	86	87
Convertible debentures, 6.8%	100	120	119	115
Series A warrants .	6	22	19½	15
Series B warrants .	—	10	9	9½
Bank prime interest rate	8%	7¾%	7½%	7¾%

*After 2 for 1 stock split.

Instructions
a Show how net income should be presented in the company's income statement for the year ended September 30, 1975.
b Assuming that net income after income taxes for the year was $540,000 and that that there were no extraordinary items, prepare a schedule computing (1) the **primary earnings per share** and (2) the **fully diluted earnings per share** which should be presented in the company's income statement for the year ended September 30, 1975. A supporting schedule computing the numbers of shares to be used in these computations should also be prepared. (Because of the relative stability of the market price of the common shares, the annual average market price may be used where appropriate in your calculations. Assume an income tax rate of 50%.)

CHAPTER 18

Bonds payable

Bonds payable represent a very common source of long-term financing for large corporations. Those liabilities that do not require the use of funds within one year (or the operating cycle) for their liquidation are designated *long-term liabilities.* Examples of long-term liabilities are: bonds, notes, mortgages, equipment purchase obligations, product warranties extending over a period of years, customer deposits, amounts payable to employees under pension and deferred compensation agreements, certain types of lease obligations, deferred income tax liabilities, and some deferred revenue items.

Long-term debt may be *secured* by liens on business property of various kinds, for example, equipment (equipment notes), real property (mortgages), or other securities (collateral trust bonds). Many of the larger industrial companies issue *debenture bonds* which are backed only by the general credit standing of the issuing company. The title of a long-term debt instrument usually indicates broadly the security upon which it is issued.

As noted in Chapter 7, many current liabilities involve no specific mention of interest payments. Since money has a time value, some amount of interest is probably included in the face amount of such liabilities, but it is often ignored because of the relatively small amounts involved. The interest factor in long-term debt, however, is significant and should be given careful accounting consideration. Accounting for bonds payable is covered in this chapter; other long-term liabilities are discussed in Chapters 19 and 20.

Types of bonds issued by corporations

Bonds are a means of dividing long-term debt into a number of small units. Usually bonds are issued in $1,000 denominations, or in multiples of $1,000. Occasionally additional denominations of $100 or $500 are used. In this way a sum of money larger than could be obtained from a single credit source may be borrowed from a large number of investors. The terms of the borrowing are contained in a contract between the corporation and the bondholders, which is known as the **bond indenture.** This contract is usually held by a **trustee** who acts as an independent third party to protect the interests of both the borrower and the bond-holders.

Bonds may be issued by corporations, by nations, by state and local governments, and by governmental agencies. They may be **registered** or **coupon bonds.** Interest on registered bonds is paid only to the owner of record, while interest on coupon bonds is paid to persons presenting the periodic interest coupon. Some bond issues, known as **serial bonds,** mature in installments, while **term bonds** mature on a single fixed maturity date.

In addition to debenture bonds previously mentioned, bonds may rank behind previously issued **senior bonds** and may be described as **subordinated debentures** or **second mortgage bonds.** Bonds may be **guaranteed** by a second party, may be **callable**[1] at the option of the issuer, or may be **convertible** into common stock of the issuer at the option of the bond-holder. **Income bonds** are occasionally issued which promise to pay interest only if earned, while **revenue bonds** (issued by municipalities, turnpikes, bridge authorities, etc.) pay interest only from specific revenue sources. **Participating bonds** receive interest in excess of a minimum stipulated amount, generally when earnings exceed certain levels.

Bonds may be privately placed with a single institution or sold to investment bankers, who in turn retail the bonds in smaller lots to individual investors. Investment bankers may **underwrite** the bond issue, in which case they guarantee a certain price to the issuer and take the risk in selling the issue to the public. Alternatively, an underwriter may agree to sell the bonds on a commission basis. If a bond issue is underwritten, the entire issue will be recorded at the time of the sale to underwriters. When an entire bond issue is not sold at one time, both the amount of the bonds authorized and the amount issued should be disclosed on the balance sheet, because unissued bonds represent potential indebtedness

---

[1] The call provision protects the issuer who may wish to pay off the debt in advance, particularly when interest rates have fallen and he can secure more favorable financing. The bondholder who is repaid at this time must reinvest his funds at a lower rate of interest, and he therefore insists on a call premium to compensate him, at least in part, for the reduced interest rate. Call premiums are generally established on a decreasing scale as the bonds move closer to maturity. For example, the $10\frac{1}{2}$%, 30-year bonds issued by Youngstown Sheet and Tube Company are callable at $110\frac{1}{2}$ in the first year, at $105\frac{1}{2}$ in the tenth year, and at 100 during the last five years of outstanding life.

which may be incurred without further authorization or additional pledge of properties. Authorized and unissued bonds may be reported on the balance sheet by parenthetical remark or in a footnote.

Financial management considerations

When top-level managers decide to borrow money by issuing bonds, they must resolve a number of questions before they offer the issue on the market. First they must relate the need for funds to the amount of long-term debt which can be safely undertaken, by studying the financial position and earning prospects of the company. They must forecast the ability of the company to meet bond sinking fund requirements or periodic maturities of bonds. A decision must be made regarding the features of the bonds, such as security to be offered, call provisions, convertibility, etc. It is apparent that a great deal of advance preparation and study by the controller and financial officers of the company, in consultation with outside investment advisors, precedes the actual offering of bonds to investors.

Issuance of bonds

In a typical bond contract, the corporation promises two essentially different kinds of future payments: (1) the payment of a fixed sum, called the *face* or *maturity value,* at a specified date; (2) the periodic payment of interest, usually at six-month intervals, in an amount expressed as a percentage of the face value of the bond. In the light of expectations as to what interest rate will be necessary to attract the required funds, a rate of interest is set. It is important to note that the interest expense actually incurred on the bonds is determined by the price at which the bonds are sold; thus the *effective interest rate* (sometimes called the *yield rate*) is set by the money market. Interest on bonds expressed as a percentage of the face value is referred to as the *nominal* or *coupon rate.* If the market is willing to take the bonds at a yield rate identical to the coupon rate, the bonds will sell at face value. If the effective rate is in excess of the coupon rate, the bonds will sell at a *discount,* or less than face value. Conversely, if the effective rate is less than the coupon rate, the bonds will sell at a *premium,* or more than face value. Differences between the coupon rate and the yield rate are thus adjusted by changes in the price at which the bonds are sold, without the necessity of amending the bond contract.[2]

To illustrate this point, assume that $100,000 of five-year, 7% bonds are offered for sale.[3] The bond contract, which promises $100,000 at the

[2] For example, New Jersey Bell Telephone Company's $2\frac{3}{4}$% bonds sold at $102\frac{1}{2}$ in 1950 and below 50 in 1970. These are 40-year bonds with the highest quality rating.

[3] Although bonds issued in amounts as small as $100,000, paying interest annually and maturing in five years, are not found in real life, these amounts are used to facilitate the illustration.

end of five years and $7,000 annual interest, is then offered to investment bankers or investing syndicates. The prices bid by these underwriters will depend on their expectations as to the effective (or yield) rate of interest for this type of bonds. Under two different assumptions as to the effective rate, the price would be determined as follows, using the appropriate present value tables in Appendix A:

Amount bid for 7% bonds, assuming an effective rate of 8%:	
Present value of $100,000	
due in 5 years @ 8%, with	
interest paid annually	
($100,000 × .6806)	$68,060
Present value of $7,000	
every year for 5 years @ 8%	
($7,000 × 3.9927)	27,949
Proceeds of bond issue	$96,009

Amount bid for 7% bonds, assuming an effective rate of 6%:	
Present value of $100,000	
due in 5 years @ 6%, with	
interest paid annually	
($100,000 × .7473)	$ 74,730
Present value of $7,000	
every year for 5 years @	
6% ($7,000 × 4.2124)	29,487
Proceeds of bond issue	$104,217

The underwriters would expect to resell these bonds to the public at a higher price and thus a lower effective rate, to give them a margin to cover their costs and earn a profit. The yield rate to the issuing corporation, however, is determined by the price it receives from the underwriters. The entries to record the sale of bonds at a discount and at a premium are given below:

Issued at effective rate of 8%:	
Cash	96,009
Discount on Bonds	
Payable	3,991
Bonds Pay-	
able	100,000
Issued bonds at	
a discount.	

Issued at effective rate of 6%:	
Cash	104,217
Premium on	
Bonds	
Payable	4,217
Bonds Pay-	
able	100,000
Issued bonds	
at a premium.	

Bonds paying 7% sold to yield 7% would obviously sell at par value, determined as follows:

Present value of $100,000 due in 5 years @ 7%, with interest paid
annually ($100,000 × .71299) . . . . $ 71,299
Present value of $7,000 every year for 5 years @ 7% ($7,000 ×
4.10019) 28,701
Proceeds of bond issue $100,000

Bond interest expense

Since differences between the effective and coupon rate of interest are
reflected in bond prices, the amount of premium or discount will influence
the interest expense to the issuer. This can be demonstrated by comparing the average interest expense per year under each of the two
assumptions as to effective interest rates:

Assuming an effective rate of 8%:		Assuming an effective rate of 6%:	
Coupon interest ($7,000 × 5 annual payments)	$35,000	Coupon interest ($7,000 × 5 payments)	$35,000
Add: Discount ($100,000 − $96,009)	3,991	Less: Premium ($104,217 − $100,000)	4,217
Five-year interest expense . .	$38,991	Five-year interest expense . .	$30,783
Average interest expense per year ($38,991 ÷ 5) . . .	$ 7,798	Average interest expense per year ($30,783 ÷ 5) . . .	$ 6,157

If the bonds are sold to yield 8%, the discount of $3,991 represents
an additional amount of interest which will be paid in a lump sum at
maturity. Similarly, if the bonds are priced to yield 6%, the premium of
$4,217 represents an advance paid by bondholders for the right to receive
larger annual interest checks and should be viewed as a reduction in
the effective interest expense. (The premium is in effect "returned"
to bondholders periodically in the form of more generous interest
payments.)

The additional interest expense (discount) or reduction of interest
expense (premium) may be allocated evenly throughout the life of the
bonds. This method, known as the **straight-line amortization of bond discount
or premium,** results in a uniform periodic interest expense. Entries to
record the annual payment of interest are shown on page 684.

When interest is paid semiannually or when interest payment dates
do not coincide with the end of the fiscal year, a policy of amortizing
the discount or the premium only at the end of the fiscal year can be
adopted in order to minimize the routine work involved.

Bonds sold at a discount:			*Bonds sold at a premium:*		
Bond Interest			Bond Interest		
Expense.	7,798		Expense	6,157	
Discount on			Premium on Bonds		
Bonds Payable		798	Payable	843	
Cash		7,000	Cash		7,000
Payment of annual			Payment of annual		
interest and am-			interest and am-		
ortization of dis-			ortization of pre-		
count.			mium.		

Straight-line versus interest method of amortization

The assumption that an equal interest cost is incurred each period throughout the life of a bond issue is unrealistic. In theory, the recorded interest expense each period should equal the effective interest expense, that is, the effective rate of interest applied to the *carrying value* (book value) of the bond liability at the start of that period. This approach to computing interest expense is known as the *interest method* (or *effective rate method*) of amortization. When bonds are sold at a discount, the carrying value of the debt increases in each period; thus the dollar amount of the effective interest expense increases in each period. When bonds are sold at a premium, the carrying value of the liability declines as the bonds approach maturity; thus the dollar amount of the effective interest expense decreases in each period. The effective interest expense over the life of the bonds is tabulated on page 686.

The Accounting Principles Board has taken the position that "the interest method of amortization is theoretically sound"[4] and that premium or discount on long-term notes should be amortized "in such a way as to result in a constant rate of interest."[5] The position of the APB relating to long-term notes also logically applies to bonds.

Comparing periodic interest expense under the interest method illustrated on page 686 and the straight-line method shown on page 685 reveals the extent of the error involved in using a simple average. For example, if the bonds were issued at a discount, the effective interest expense per year ranges from $7,681 to $7,926; using the straight-line method results in a constant annual interest expense of $7,798. In the first year, for example, interest expense on a $100 million bond issue would be approximately $117,000 more under the straight-line method. In choosing the method to use, the accountant should balance the simplicity

[4]*APB Opinion No. 12,* "Omnibus Opinion—1967," AICPA (New York: 1967), p. 194.
[5]*APB Opinion No. 21,* "Interest on Receivables and Payables," AICPA (New York: 1971), p. 423.

of the straight-line method against the materiality of the error involved. The longer the life of the bond issue and the greater the discount or premium relative to the face value of the bonds, the larger will be the difference between straight-line "average" interest expense and "effective" interest expense.

Bonds Sold at a Discount
Interest Expense Determined Using Straight-line Method of Amortization
($100,000, 5-year bonds, interest at 7%, payable annually,
sold at $96,009, to yield 8% compounded annually)

Year	(A) Interest paid (7% of face value)	(B) Discount amortization ($\frac{1}{5}$ of $3,991)	(C) "Average" interest expense (A + B)	(D) Bond discount balance (D − B)	(E) Carrying value of bonds, end of year ($100,000 − D)
At time of issue				$3,991	$ 96,009
1	$7,000	$798	$7,798	3,193	96,807
2	7,000	798	7,798	2,395	97,605
3	7,000	798	7,798	1,597	98,403
4	7,000	798	7,798	799	99,201
5	7,000	799*	7,799*	−0−	100,000

* $1 adjustment to compensate for rounding average interest expense to the nearest dollar.

Bonds Sold at a Premium
Interest Expense Determined Using Straight-line Method of Amortization
($100,000, 5-year bonds, interest at 7%, payable annually,
sold at $104,217, to yield 6% compounded annually)

Year	(A) Interest paid (7% of face value)	(B) Premium amortization ($\frac{1}{5}$ of $4,217)	(C) "Average" interest expense (A − B)	(D) Bond premium balance (D − B)	(E) Carrying value of bonds, end of year ($100,000 + D)
At time of issue				$4,217	$104,217
1	$7,000	$843	$6,157	3,374	103,374
2	7,000	843	6,157	2,531	102,531
3	7,000	843	6,157	1,688	101,688
4	7,000	843	6,157	845	100,845
5	7,000	845*	6,155*	−0−	100,000

* $2 adjustment to compensate for rounding average interest expense to the nearest dollar.

Bonds Sold at a Discount

Interest Expense Determined Using Effective Rate Method of Amortization

($100,000, 5-year bonds, interest at 7%, payable annually,

sold at $96,009, to yield 8% compounded annually)

Year	(A) Interest paid (7% of face value)	(B) "Effective" interest expense (8% of bond carrying value)	(C) Discount amortization (B − A)	(D) Bond discount balance (D − C)	(E) Carrying value of bonds, end of period ($100,000 − D)
At time of issue				$3,991	$ 96,009
1	$7,000	$7,681	$681	3,310	96,690
2	7,000	7,735	735	2,575	97,425
3	7,000	7,794	794	1,781	98,219
4	7,000	7,858	858	923	99,077
5	7,000	7,926	923*	−0−	100,000

*Adjusted $3 for rounding.

Bonds Sold at a Premium

Interest Expense Determined Using Effective Rate Method of Amortization

($100,000, 5-year bonds, interest at 7%, payable annually,

sold at $104,217, to yield 6% compounded annually)

Year	(A) Interest paid (7% of face value)	(B) "Effective" interest expense (6% of bond carrying value)	(C) Premium amortization (A − B)	(D) Bond premium balance (D − C)	(E) Carrying value of bonds, end of period ($100,000 + D)
At time of issue				$4,217	$104,217
1	$7,000	$6,253	$747	3,470	103,470
2	7,000	6,208	792	2,678	102,678
3	7,000	6,161	839	1,839	101,839
4	7,000	6,110	890	949	100,949
5	7,000	6,057	949*	−0−	100,000

*Adjusted $6 for rounding.

Statement presentation of discount and premium

At the time of issue, the carrying value of the bonds payable is equal to the proceeds of the sale, since these proceeds were computed by determining the present value of all future payments at the yield rate set by the market. Bond discount and bond premium are therefore valuation accounts relating to bonds payable. This is stated by the Accounting Principles Board in relation to notes (but is equally applicable to bonds), as follows:

> . . . the discount or premium should be reported in the balance sheet as a direct addition to or deduction from the face amount of the note. It should not be classified as a deferred charge or deferred credit. The description of the note should disclose the effective interest rate; . . . . Issue costs should be reported in the balance sheet as deferred charges.[6]

Using the figures from the previous illustration, bonds payable on the date of issue would be reported on the balance sheet as follows:

Bonds sold at a discount:		Bonds sold at a premium:	
Long-term debt:		Long-term debt:	
7% bonds payable, due in		7% bonds payable, due in	
5 years, maturity		5 years, maturity	
value	$100,000	value	$100,000
Less: Discount	3,991	Add: Premium	4,217
Net liability (carrying		Net liability (carrying	
value)	$ 96,009	value)	$104,217

At issue date these bonds have a present value smaller or greater than maturity value because the actual interest rate is higher or lower than the periodic interest payments provided in the bond contract. The process of amortizing bond discount or premium is in reality, therefore, a means of recording the increase or decrease *in the value of the debt obligation as it approaches maturity.* In the bond discount case, illustrated above, the issuer incurs an average annual interest expense of $7,798, paying $7,000 in cash and accruing a $798 increase in the carrying value of the bonds payable. The increase in the carrying value of the debt comes about indirectly through the decrease in bond discount. Similarly, in the bond premium case, the company pays $7,000 annually, which represents $6,157 of average interest expense and $843 to reduce the net bond liability. In either case, the carrying value of bonds payable will be $100,000 at maturity.

Some accountants argue that bonds payable should not be reported at less than maturity value because the company would have to pay this amount if the debt were to be settled at the balance sheet date. There are two answers to this argument:

1 Most bond indentures include a call provision, specifying a penalty payment (call premium) over and above maturity value if the bonds are called before maturity date. For example, a bond issue may be callable at 105, which means that $1,050 must be paid to retire any $1,000 bond prior to maturity. The

[6] *Ibid.,* p. 423.

argument that bonds payable should be shown in the balance sheet at the amount necessary to retire the debt at that date would therefore require valuation at call price, not maturity value.

2 Financial statements are prepared on the assumption that the business entity is a going concern. Retirement of long-term debt at balance sheet date is not the normal expectation. There is always the possibility that debt may be retired prior to maturity, and this decision would change the value of the debt, since a liability that is to be paid immediately has a different value than one due a number of years in the future. If a decision to call the bonds has been made, the accountant should disclose this fact in the financial statements. But typically the most probable event is that the entity will meet its debts as they fall due, and the proper accounting valuation of the debt is its present value in terms of the effective rate of interest prevailing when the bonds were sold.

Bond issue costs

A number of costs are incurred in connection with a bond issue: fees paid to accountants, attorneys, underwriters, and other experts in connection with the preparation of the bond contract and prospectus; printing and engraving costs; and costs incurred in advertising the issue. These are costs of securing the use of the funds borrowed and thus of benefits which will accrue to the borrower over the entire period of the loan.

Bond issue costs are classified as an asset and amortized over the life of the bonds because revenue benefits from the use of the bond proceeds over this period. An alternative procedure is to add bond issue costs to the amount of discount or deduct them from bond premium. The latter treatment implies that the amount of funds made available to the borrower is equal to the net proceeds of the bond issue *after* deducting all costs of completing the financing transaction. In this view, bond issue costs simply increase the effective interest expense during the life of the bonds.

Bonds issued between interest dates

Bond interest payments are usually made semiannually on dates specified in the bond contract. Bonds are often sold, however, at a date other than an interest payment date. It would be possible to adjust for this factor by reducing the interest payment for the first "short" period. However, it is much more convenient simply to add to the price of the bond the amount of interest that has accrued since the last interest payment date. The investor, in effect, reimburses the borrowing company for the portion of the full six-month interest payment to which he is not entitled. He will then receive the full six-month interest payment on the next semiannual interest payment date.

Assume that Electronic Devices, Inc., issues $100,000 in 10-year, 6% bonds, with interest payable semiannually on April 1 and October 1 of each year. The bonds are sold on June 1 at $107,080 plus accrued interest for two months. The bonds are dated April 1 and various issue costs amounting to $2,360 are incurred. Note that this borrowing actually runs for 9 years and 10 months, or 118 months, and the accounting for the debt and related issue costs should reflect this fact. The average interest expense per month may be calculated as follows:

Actual interest paid to investors over 10-year period (10 × $6,000) . . .	$60,000
Less:	
Premium received on sale of bonds	(7,080)
Accrued interest received from investors (Apr. 1–June 1)	(1,000)
Total interest expense (9 years and 10 months)	$51,920
Average interest expense per month ($51,920 ÷ 118 months)	$ 440

Since the monthly interest accrual will be $500 ($6,000 ÷ 12 months) and the average interest cost is $440, the monthly premium amortization will be the difference, or $60 ($7,080 ÷ 118 months). Issue costs would be amortized at the rate of $20 per month ($2,360 ÷ 118 months). Assuming that amortization of the issue costs and the premium is recorded at the end of the year, the entries relating to the bond issue during the first calendar year would be as shown on page 690.

It would be possible to credit Bond Interest Expense (rather than Bond Interest Payable) for $1,000 on June 1 for the accrued interest for two months purchased by bondholders. On October 1, then, Bond Interest Expense would be debited for $3,000, thus leaving a balance of $2,000 in Bond Interest Expense representing interest incurred from June 1 to October 1. It would also be possible to amortize the premium and bond issue costs at the time interest is paid and also at the end of the fiscal year.

Acquisition and retirement of bonds payable

Bonds payable may be acquired by the issuing corporation prior to maturity. Such bonds may be held in the treasury or may be formally retired. The acquisition of bonds completes the "transaction cycle" relating to the borrowing and should be viewed as a retirement (temporary or permanent) of a debt instrument. A gain or loss is recognized equal to the difference between the amount paid to retire the bonds and their carrying value less bond issue costs. The amortization of bond discount, bond premium, and bond issue costs should, of course, be adjusted to the date of retirement **before** the entry to record the retirement is made. To illustrate, assume that $20,000 (20%) of the Electronic Devices, Inc., bonds described in the previous example are retired on December 1 of

June 1	Bond Issue Costs	2,360	
	Cash		2,360
	To record various costs of issuing bonds.		

June 1	Cash	108,080	
	Bonds Payable		100,000
	Bond Interest Payable		1,000
	Premium on Bonds Payable		7,080
	To record sale of bonds and accrued interest for two months.		

Oct. 1	Bond Interest Payable	1,000	
	Bond Interest Expense	2,000	
	Cash		3,000
	To record interest payment for first six months.		

Dec. 31	Bond Interest Expense	1,080	
	Premium on Bonds Payable	420	
	Bond Issue Expense	140	
	Bond Issue Costs		140
	Bond Interest Payable		1,500
	To accrue interest expense for three months and record amortization of bond issue costs and premium on bonds payable for seven months. Amounts determined as follows:		

Accrued interest: $100,000 \times 6\% \times \frac{3}{12}$ $1,500

Less: Amortization of premium: $7,080

$\times$ 7/118 420

Bond interest expense (net) $1,080

Amortization of bond issue costs:

$2,360 \times 7/118 . . . . $ 140

the second year, or 18 months after the bonds were issued. If the bonds are retired at $102\frac{1}{2}$, plus accrued interest of $200 for two months, the two entries on page 691 would be required.

The balance of the premium and issue costs applicable to the $20,000 of bonds being retired is eliminated from the records. Gains and losses on bond retirements reflect the changes in interest rates, and perhaps changes in risk factors, since the bonds were issued. The gains and losses (net of income taxes), if unusual and infrequent, should be reported as extraordinary items. On this point *APB Opinion No. 26* states:

A difference between the reacquisition price and the net carrying amount of the extinguished debt should be recognized currently in income of the period

Dec. 1	Premium on Bonds Payable	132	
	Bond Issue Expense	44	
	Bond Interest Expense		132
	Bond Issue Costs		44

To bring amortization up to date on $20,000 (or 20%)
of bonds for period Jan. 1 to Dec. 1.
  Amortization of premium:
    $7,080 × 20% × 11/118 = $132.
  Amortization of bond issue costs:
    $2,360 × 20% × 11/118 = $44.

Dec. 1	Bonds Payable	20,000	
	Premium on Bonds Payable ($1,416 − $216)	1,200	
	Bond Interest Expense	200	
	Cash		20,700
	Bond Issue Costs ($472 − $72)		400
	Gain on Bond Retirement		300

To record retirement of bonds at 102½ plus accrued
interest of $200 for two months. The gain on bond
retirement is determined as follows:

Original proceeds, $107,080 × 20%	$21,416	
Less: Original portion of bond issue		
costs, $2,360 × 20%	472	
Carrying value at issuance date	$20,944	
Amortization for 18 months:		
Premium, $60 × 20% × 18 months . . .	(216)	
Bond issue costs, $20 × 20% × 18		
months	72	
Carrying value of bonds at date of re-		
tirement	$20,800	
Amount paid to retire bonds	20,500	
Gain on bond retirement	$ 300	

of extinguishment as losses or gains and identified as a separate item. The criteria in **APB Opinion No. 9** should be used to determine whether the losses or gains are ordinary or extraordinary items. Gains and losses should not be amortized to future periods.[7]

When bonds are retired at maturity, no gain or loss results since the carrying value of the bonds equals maturity value. Gains on bond retirements represent taxable income; losses on bond retirements are deductible for income tax purposes.

When the entire bond issue is **called** for redemption, the entire un-

[7] *APB Opinion No. 26*, "Early Extinguishment of Debt," AICPA (New York: 1972), pp. 501–502.

amortized premium or discount, along with any bond issue costs, would be written off. A loss will generally result on such a transaction since the sliding call prices would ordinarily be in excess of bond carrying values on corresponding dates.

If bonds are acquired but not formally retired, a Treasury Bonds account may be debited for an amount equal to the par value of the *treasury bonds* held, but a gain or loss should still be recognized as illustrated above. The Treasury Bonds account is not an asset and should be deducted from Bonds Payable on the balance sheet. Interest should not be paid on reacquired bonds unless they are held as an investment by a company-sponsored fund, such as an employee pension fund.

Serial bonds

Thus far we have considered bonds having a single fixed maturity. An alternative type of debt contract, known as a *serial bond*, provides for repayment of the principal in periodic installments.

Serial bonds have the obvious advantage of gearing debt repayment to the periodic cash inflow from operations. Furthermore, when short-term interest rates are lower than long-term rates, the shorter maturities of a serial issue may sell at lower yield rates and reduce the average interest rate for the entire issue.

As in the case of single-maturity bonds, serial bonds may sell at a premium or a discount in response to differences between coupon and effective interest rates. The proceeds of a serial bond issue are somewhat more difficult to compute because of the varying maturities, but the approach is the same: The present value of the series of principal payments plus the present value of the promised interest payments, all at the current rate (effective rate) of interest, equals the total market price of the issue.

At this point the question arises: Is there any *single* interest rate applicable to a serial bond issue? We often refer loosely to the rate of interest, when in fact in the market at any given time there are a number of interest rates, depending on the terms, nature, and length of the contract offered. In a given serial bond issue, the terms of all bonds in the issue are the same except for the differences in maturity. Since short-term interest rates often differ from long-term rates, however, it is likely that each maturity will sell at a different yield rate, so that there will be a different discount or premium relating to each maturity.

In accounting for an issue of serial bonds under these conditions, each maturity should be treated as a separate bond issue. Thus if $100,000 in five-year, 5% serial bonds are issued, to be repaid in the amount of $20,000 each year, and each maturity sells at a price reflecting a different yield rate, the problem would be treated as a summarized accounting for five separate bond issues of $20,000 each, maturing in one, two, three, four, and five years, respectively. Each maturity would have a related discount or premium, and interest expense on each maturity might be computed as previously illustrated for single-maturity bonds.

In many cases, however, this degree of precision in accounting for serial bond issues is not possible because the yield rate for each maturity is not known. Underwriters may bid on an entire serial bond issue on the basis of an average yield rate and may not disclose the particular yield rate for each maturity that was used in arriving at the bid price. In this situation we may have to assume that the same yield rate applies to all maturities in the issue, and proceed accordingly.

If the "interest" method is to be used in accounting for interest expense, the procedure is similar to that illustrated in connection with single-maturity bonds. The interest expense for each period will be an amount equal to the effective rate multiplied by the carrying value of the bonds outstanding during that period, and the difference between interest expense so computed and the actual interest payments will represent the amortization of the bond discount or premium. The result will be a constant rate of interest expense in relation to the carrying value of the bonds outstanding.

A variation of the straight-line method, known as the **bonds outstanding method,** results in a decreasing amount of premium or discount amortization each period proportionate to the decrease in the outstanding debt.

Accounting for Serial Bonds Illustrated   To illustrate the variation in the pattern of interest expense under each of these methods, assume that the James Company issues $100,000 in five-year, 5% serial bonds, to be repaid in the amount of $20,000 each year. To simplify the illustration, assume that interest payments are made annually. If the bonds are sold at an average yield rate of 6% per year, the proceeds will be approximately $97,375. The accounting problem is to determine how the discount of $2,625 should be prorated over the life of the serial bond issue. Schedules determining periodic discount amortization and interest expense using the **bonds outstanding** and **interest** methods are illustrated below:

Amortization of Discount on Serial Bonds—Bonds Outstanding Method

Year	Bonds outstanding (par value)	Fraction of total of bonds outstanding	(A) Amortization of discount ($2,625 x fraction)	(B) Interest payments (5% of bonds outstanding)	Interest expense (A + B)
1	$100,000	10/30	$ 875	$ 5,000	$ 5,875
2	80,000	8/30	700	4,000	4,700
3	60,000	6/30	525	3,000	3,525
4	40,000	4/30	350	2,000	2,350
5	20,000	2/30	175	1,000	1,175
	$300,000	30/30	$2,625	$15,000	$17,625

Amortization of Discount on Serial Bonds—Interest Method

Year	(A) Carrying value of bonds ($100,000 − E − F)	(B) Effective interest expense (6% × A)	(C) Interest payment	(D) Discount amortization (B − C)	(E) Bond discount balance (E − D)	(F) Principal repayment
Issue	$97,375				$2,625	
1	78,217	$ 5,842	$ 5,000	$ 842	1,783	$20,000
2	58,910	4,693	4,000	693	1,090	20,000
3	39,444	3,534	3,000	534	556	20,000
4	19,811	2,367	2,000	367	189	20,000
5	−0−	1,189	1,000	189	−0−	20,000
		$17,625	$15,000	$2,625		

The bonds outstanding method in this case produces results that are a close approximation of the effective interest expense because of the short life of the issue and the relatively small discount. The longer the life of the bonds and the greater the discount or premium, the larger would be the discrepancy between the methods.

Using the straight-line method, amortization would be $525 per year ($2,625 ÷ 5). The bonds outstanding method may also be viewed as a "straight-line" method since it results in a constant amortization of discount or premium *per $1,000 of maturity value of bonds outstanding.* In this example, the amount of discount amortization per $1,000 bond outstanding may be calculated by dividing the total discount by the sum of the bonds outstanding over the life of the issue: ($2,625 ÷ $300,000 = $8.75 per $1,000 bond). If the discount amortization per $1,000 bond is determined at the time of the issuance, it is a simple process to compute the appropriate amount of discount applicable to any amount of bonds in any given year throughout the life of a serial bond issue. Thus in the fourth year, when $40,000 of bonds were outstanding, the discount to be amortized would be computed: $40,000 of bonds times $8.75 per $1,000, or $350.

Retirement of Serial Bonds before Maturity When serial bonds mature and par value is paid to bondholders, Bonds Payable is debited and Cash is credited. Since the carrying value of the bonds in this case is equal to the amount paid, no gain or loss would be recognized. If serial bonds are acquired prior to the regularly scheduled maturity date, a price different from carrying value would generally be paid and a gain or loss would result. The carrying value of serial bonds is equal to the par value plus the related unamortized premium (or less the related unamortized discount and issue costs). All these valuation account balances would have to be canceled at the time of retirement.

In order to illustrate the retirement of serial bonds prior to maturity, assume that $10,000 of James Company bonds described in the preceding example are retired at the end of Year 2, two years ahead of the scheduled retirement date. The bonds are retired at 101 and interest has been paid for Year 2. The discount applicable to the $10,000 of bonds being retired is determined as follows under the bonds outstanding method:

Discount applicable to Year 3: $\frac{10,000}{60,000}$ × $525* . . . . $ 87.50

Discount applicable to Year 4: $\frac{10,000}{40,000}$ × $350* 87.50

Total discount applicable to retired bonds . . . . $175.00†

*From Column A in table on page 693.
†Since the discount amortization amounts to $8.75 per $1,000 per year, this amount can be determined as follows: $8.75 × 10 × 2, or $175. Similar procedures can be used to compute amortization on serial bonds when the "bond year" and the fiscal year of the issuer do not coincide.

The entry to record the retirement, ignoring the income tax effect, is:

Bonds Payable   10,000
Loss on Bond Retirement.   275
    Discount on Bonds Payable   175
    Cash   10,100
To record retirement of serial bonds two years prior to scheduled maturity date.

Bonds with a carrying value of $9,825 have been retired for $10,100, resulting in a loss of $275. The original discount amortization schedule, using the bonds outstanding method, should now be revised as follows:

Year of bond life	Original discount	Discount canceled through retirement	Adjusted discount
Year 3	$ 525.00	$ 87.50	$437.50
Year 4	350.00	87.50	262.50
Year 5	175.00	–0–	175.00
Totals	$1,050.00	$175.00	$875.00

Refunding a bond issue

Refunding is the process of retiring one bond issue with the proceeds of a new bond issue. When refunding occurs at the time the old debt matures, the carrying value of the old debt equals its maturity value; no gain or loss arises from the retirement of the old debt and the new obligation is recorded in the usual manner.

A problem arises when refunding occurs prior to the maturity of the old bonds. This usually happens when interest rates have declined and the borrower sees a chance to reduce his interest expense by canceling the old contract (paying the required penalty in the form of a call premium) and entering into a new one. If the two transactions (canceling old bonds and issuing new) are viewed as separate and unrelated events, no issues are raised that have not already been discussed. Retiring the old bonds results in a realized gain or loss equal to the difference between carrying value and call price; the new bonds are recorded in the usual manner. Some accountants have argued, however, that the recognition of loss on the refunding prior to maturity should be postponed and amortized over part or the entire period of the new bond issue.

For example, assume that the Cleve Corporation has outstanding $1,000,000 in 8% bonds having 10 years to run and a carrying value of $960,000 (maturity $1,000,000 less unamortized discount of $40,000). The company has decided to call the bonds at 105, using for this purpose the proceeds of a new 20-year issue of $6\frac{1}{2}$% bonds (which we will assume can be sold at face value). Debt having a carrying value of $960,000 is thus being refunded at a cost of $1,050,000, and a question arises as to the treatment of the $90,000 difference. Three solutions to this question may be proposed:

1 Write off $90,000 (net of tax effect) immediately as a loss on bond retirement.
2 Record the $90,000 (net of tax effect) as an asset and amortize it over the remaining life of the retired bonds (in this case 10 years).
3 Record the $90,000 (net of tax effect) as an asset and amortize it over the life of the new issue (in this case 20 years).

The first alternative has the clear weight of logic in its favor. The amount of unamortized bond discount at any time measures the liability for additional interest that will accrue during the remaining life of bonds to compensate for the fact that the coupon rate of interest is less than the effective rate of interest. In order to be relieved of the old contract, the company is required to pay this $40,000 of interest now rather than at maturity date, and in addition, to pay a $50,000 call premium. These costs of terminating an unfavorable contract are *related* to past periods but are *caused* by current economic forces (decline in the market rate of interest) and by management action (the decision to refund). To defer these costs would penalize future periods since the new $6\frac{1}{2}$% bonds could be sold even if the 8% bonds had not been outstanding.

The Accounting Principles Board does not make a distinction between refunding and a nonrefunding retirement; it requires that losses or gains on refunding, net of the tax effect "should be recognized currently in income of the period of extinguishment. . . ."[8]

Proponents of deferring gains and losses argue that management may be tempted to issue high-coupon bonds in order to retire low-coupon bonds selling at a deep discount, thus reporting an extraordinary gain on the retirement. Or, management may choose not to replace high-coupon bonds with low-coupon bonds in order to avoid recognition of an extraordinary loss on the refunding. The answer to this point of view is that the purpose of sound accounting is not to formulate business decisions but rather to report the outcome of decisions made by management.

Arguments for the amortization over the life of the retired bonds are based on the accounting doctrine that when a cost is incurred, the benefits of which may reasonably be expected to be realized over a period of years, the cost should be charged against income over those years. It may be argued that the unamortized bond discount and call premium paid to refund an issue are costs incurred to obtain the benefit of lower interest expense during the remaining life of the refunded issue. The payment of a call premium necessary to cancel an unfavorable contract and the write-off of unamortized discount on the contract may be viewed as events relating to the old contract and not as benefits to be derived from the new bonds. Had a larger coupon rate been set on the old bonds, they would have sold originally at face value and there would be no unamortized discount at the refunding date.

The third method rests on the premise that since the new bonds are a continuation of the old, the costs of both the old and new borrowing should be prorated over the life of the new bonds. The life of the new bonds would generally be longer than the unexpired term of the refunded bonds. It was suggested that deferral of the "loss" was appropriate when the refunding takes place because of currently lower interest rates or anticipated higher interest rates in the future. This position assumes that the key reason for the refunding is to obtain a lower interest cost over the term of the new issue.

Deciding When to Refund a Bond Issue A decline in interest rates is not in itself a sufficient basis for a decision to refund an old bond issue. The out-of-pocket costs of refunding must be compared with the present value of future interest savings. In addition, the tax impact of refunding and bond indenture features on both the old and new bonds must be considered. Unamortized discount and bond issue costs applicable to the old debt may be deducted for income tax purposes in the year of refunding. The call premium is immediately deductible for tax purposes, while the issue costs of the new bonds must be amortized over their life. Future

---

[8] *Ibid.*, p. 502.

interest rates should also be considered, since a further decline in rates may mean that refunding can be made under even more favorable conditions at a later date. A more detailed discussion of this topic is found in **Advanced Accounting** of this series.

Convertible bonds

Recording Issuance Current practice for recording the issuance of convertible bonds does not, in the opinion of the authors, portray the real economic substance of such transactions. We shall therefore first present a theoretically desirable treatment, and then explain current practice and the various positions taken by the Accounting Principles Board.

When convertible bonds are issued, a portion of the proceeds is logically attributable to the conversion feature, a factor that is reflected in a lower coupon rate of interest. Since the bondholder receives a "call" on the common stock, a portion of the proceeds attributable to the conversion feature should, in theory, be recorded as paid-in capital and bond discount (or a reduced bond premium should be recorded). The discount (or reduced premium) would be equal to the difference between the price at which the bonds were sold and the estimated price for which they would have been sold in the absence of the conversion feature.

To illustrate, assume that the Brazos Corporation issues, at par, $10 million of 4% convertible debentures due in 10 years when similar non-convertible bonds are yielding 6%. Present value tables indicate that the 4% bonds should sell for $8,512,253 in order to yield 6% compounded every six months. The entry to record the issuance of the bonds **if a value is assigned to the conversion feature** would be:

Cash	10,000,000	
Discount on Bonds Payable	1,487,747	
Bonds Payable		10,000,000
Paid-in Capital—Conversion Option on 4% De-		
bentures		1,487,747

To record issuance of 4% convertible debentures valued at $8,512,253 (exclusive of conversion feature). The bonds mature in 10 years.

The discount could be amortized over the life of the bonds, thus increasing the dollar amount of interest expense. If convertible bonds were issued at an amount below or above par value, a similar procedure should be followed.

Conversion If the bonds are converted prior to maturity, the unamortized discount would be eliminated, thus reducing the credit to paid-in capital upon issuance of shares of stock in exchange for the bonds. For example, if all the bonds issued by the Brazos Corporation are converted into 300,000 shares of $20 par value capital stock eight years after issuance, the following entry would be required:

Bonds Payable 10,000,000
Paid-in Capital—Conversion Option on 4% Debentures . . 1,487,747
  Discount on Bonds Payable 297,549
  Capital stock, $20 par value 6,000,000
  Paid-in Capital in Excess of Par 5,190,198
To record conversion of debentures; unamortized discount: $1,487,747 × $\frac{2}{10}$ = $297,549.

Note that the carrying value of the bonds, $9,702,451 ($10,000,000 − $297,549), and the value assigned to the conversion feature of the bonds, $1,487,747, are assigned to the capital stock. No gain or loss should be recognized on a conversion of bonds; in other words, the market value of the stock is ignored.

In *Opinion No. 10,* the Accounting Principles Board required the assignment of a value to the conversion feature as illustrated above. Shortly after taking this position, the Board "suspended" it in *Opinion No. 12* and a few years later, in *Opinion No. 14,* it took the position that "no portion of the proceeds from the issuance of . . . convertible debt securities . . . should be accounted for as attributable to the conversion feature."[9]

To demonstrate the procedure called for by *APB Opinion No. 14,* the illustrated journal entry on page 698 for issuance of $10 million par value of 4% convertible debentures would be replaced by the following entry:

Cash 10,000,000
  Bonds Payable 10,000,000
To record issuance of 4% convertible debentures at par. The bonds mature in 10 years.

The opposition expressed by corporate managements and investment bankers to the separate accounting for the debt and the conversion feature was a strong reason for the reversal of position by the Accounting Principles Board. In the opinion of the authors, the position finally taken by the Board is difficult to support from a theoretical standpoint. At any rate, the student must be reminded that the earlier illustration on page 698 is not in accord with current practice.

[9]*APB Opinion No. 14,* "Accounting for Convertible Debt and Debt Issued with Stock Purchase Warrants," AICPA (New York: 1969), p. 207.

Early Extinguishment of Convertible Bonds Should a gain or loss be reported on the retirement of convertible bonds before maturity or conversion? A convertible bond is a hybrid security, and a simple answer to this question is not easy to give. When convertible bonds sell at a large premium because of their conversion feature and management wants to retire the entire issue of bonds, it would probably call the bonds to force bondholders to convert. However, if management wishes to retire only a portion of the issue, it could not exercise the call privilege and would have to pay the going market price for the bonds. Because convertible bonds which are selling at a large premium are, in effect, an equity security, sound theory would suggest that the difference between the carrying value of the bonds and the amount paid to retire them should be charged against paid-in capital, not recorded as a loss. Under these circumstances the early retirement of the convertible bonds may be viewed as equivalent to a purchase of common stock for retirement. When convertible bonds sell at a deep discount, not because of higher interest rates but because the common stock is selling at a low price, retirement of such bonds may be viewed as giving rise to paid-in capital. This line of reasoning is based on the fact that the intent of issuing convertible bonds is to raise equity capital, and the low price of the bonds is caused by the fact that the value of the bonds as an equity security has decreased. Despite arguments along these lines, the Accounting Principles Board in *Opinion No. 26* stated:

> The extinguishment of convertible debt before maturity does not change the character of the security as between debt and equity at that time. Therefore, a difference between the cash acquisition price of the debt and its net carrying amount should be recognized currently in income in the period of extinguishment as losses or gains.[10]

This requirement by the Accounting Principles Board may in some cases result in material gains and losses being reported in the income statement which are essentially increases or decreases in paid-in capital. It should be pointed out that if a fair value were assigned to the conversion feature, a retirement of convertible bonds at an amount below carrying value would logically be attributed to an increase in interest rates and the recognition of a gain on the retirement would be appropriate.

Bonds issued with warrants attached

If bonds payable are issued which are not convertible into common stock but, instead, include *detachable warrants* giving the bondholder the right to purchase a certain number of shares of common stock at a fixed price, a separate value should be assigned to the warrants. Thus, if bonds in the amount of $10 million are issued at par with warrants attached which are valued at $500,000, the issuance of the bonds would be recorded as follows:

[10] *APB Opinion No. 26, op. cit.,* p. 502.

Cash	10,000,000	
Discount on Bonds Payable	500,000	
Bonds Payable		10,000,000
Paid-in Capital—Stock Purchase Warrants		500,000
Issuance of bonds with stock purchase warrants attached.		

The APB supported this approach in *Opinion No. 14* as follows:

The Board is of the opinion that the portion of the proceeds of debt securities issued with detachable stock purchase warrants which is allocable to the warrants should be accounted for as paid-in capital. The allocation should be based on the relative fair values of the two securities at the time of issuance. Any resulting discount or premium on the debt securities should be accounted for as such. . . . However, when stock purchase warrants are not detachable from the debt and the debt security must be surrendered in order to exercise the warrant, the two securities taken together are substantially equivalent to convertible debt. . . .[11]

When the warrants are exercised, the value assigned to the stock purchase warrants would be viewed as additional proceeds from the issuance of common stock.

Bond sinking funds

A few bond indentures require that a sinking fund be established for the retirement of bonds. A corporation sometimes establishes a fund voluntarily for the retirement of bonds, either at maturity or at management's discretion. Ordinarily a bond sinking fund would not be created in connection with the issuance of serial bonds; such bonds can be retired periodically in lieu of making sinking fund deposits. A disadvantage inherent in bond sinking funds is that a portion of the money borrowed for use in the business is not being used for this purpose if cash is deposited in a sinking fund. A formal restriction on the payment of dividends, which is common in bond indentures, does not usually require the establishment of an appropriation account; restrictions on retained earnings, however, should be fully disclosed in financial statements or accompanying notes.

Notes and mortgages payable

Other long-term liabilities such as notes payable, equipment contracts payable, purchase-money obligations, and mortgages payable are frequently found on financial statements of business units. The essential

---

[11] *APB Opinion No. 14, op. cit.,* p. 209.

accounting problems relating to these liabilities are similar to those applicable to bonds. The important point to keep in mind is that all long-term liabilities should be initially recorded at the present value of the amounts to be paid. This is particularly important when debts are incurred in connection with acquisition of non-cash assets or are assumed by the acquiring company in a business combination. In the acquisition of a going business, for example, if liabilities are not fairly valued, the amount of unidentifiable intangibles (goodwill) and the periodic amortization of such intangibles will be misstated.

As pointed out in earlier chapters, a variety of other "deferred credit" or "quasi-liability" items are sometimes included under long-term liabilities in condensed balance sheets. These may range from unearned revenue items to items such as "equity in net assets of subsidiary over cost," deferred investment tax credits, and deferred income tax liabilities.

Distinguishing between liabilities and stockholders' equity

Since interest is tax deductible while a payment designated as dividends is not, it is inevitable that creative financial managers will devise liability contracts which bestow on the securities as many of the characteristics of ownership as possible without destroying their income tax status as debt. As a result, the dividing line between debt and stockholders' equity is often blurred. An extreme example on the liability side is the **subordinated income bond.** These bonds are secured only by the general credit standing of the issuer, and the bond contract provides that interest will be paid only when and if earnings are sufficient. Interest payments on such a bond are usually cumulative, but failure to pay interest does not give bondholders the right to interfere in corporate affairs. It is clear that a substantial amount of risk, comparable to that borne by owners of the company, attaches to such securities. The basic characteristic distinguishing subordinated income bonds from preferred stock is that the bonds have a maturity date. The absence of a maturity provision would give the Internal Revenue Service grounds for holding that subordinated income bonds are preferred shares in disguise.

On the stockholders' equity side of the dividing line, some forms of preferred stock are very similar to debt. A preferred stock issue which has no voting rights, carries a stated cumulative dividend, and may be called for redemption at specified times represents only a very limited form of ownership.

The question arises, in dealing with such cases, whether the distinction can be drawn with sufficient clarity to make a clear-cut division in accounting between liabilities and stockholders' equity. Some accountants have argued, for example, that the entire right side of the balance sheet should be labeled "equities" and that the distinction between the two interests is relatively meaningless.

In any system of classification, there are troublesome decisions to be made with respect to borderline items. The issue turns, therefore, not on whether a dividing line is difficult to draw, but on whether the distinction between debt and stockholders' equity is relevant and worth attempting.

Long-term debt in the balance sheet

All long-term debt should be fully described in the balance sheet or accompanying notes. Companies having large amounts of long-term debt in the form of numerous issues often show only one figure in the balance sheet and support this with supplementary schedules showing the details of maturity dates, interest rates, call provisions, conversion privileges, assets pledged to secure payment, dividend, or any other restrictions imposed on the borrower.

Unless an automatic right of offset exists, long-term debt should be reported in full, and any pledged assets intended for use in repayment should be shown in the asset section of the balance sheet. Reacquired debt should not be reported as assets.

Any portion of long-term debt that matures within one year should be shown as a current liability, unless retirement will not require the use of current assets. If, during the ensuing year, debt is likely to be converted into stock, refunded, or repaid from a sinking fund already established, there is no reason to change its classification from long to short term so long as the expected method of retirement is clearly disclosed.

Refer to Appendix B for examples of how bonds payable and other long-term debt are reported in the balance sheets of some leading corporations.

REVIEW QUESTIONS

1 Define the following: **debenture bonds, term bonds, serial bonds, convertible bonds, bond indenture, nominal or coupon rate, effective rate,** and **call premium.**

2 A bond carrying a coupon rate of 5% is sold to yield 5.75%. Will the bond sell at a premium or a discount? Explain.

3 A $1 million bond issue is sold for $960,000. A few months later the bonds are selling at 102. Give possible reasons for the increase in the value of the bonds and explain the significance of the increase to the issuing company.

4 Company A plans to issue $1 million in 6%, 10-year bonds. What will be the average annual interest cost if the bonds are sold at 104? At 97?

5 If bonds are sold at a premium and the **interest method** is used in amortizing the premium, will the annual interest cost increase or decline over the life of the bonds? Explain.

6 Company B has just issued $100 million of 15-year debenture bonds at a discount. At an annual stockholders' meeting, one of the stockholders asks the chairman to explain the nature of bond discount and issue costs included among the company's assets at $4,829,000. The chairman answers, "This represents prepaid interest of $4.7 million and issue costs on our bonds, which are being amortized over the life of the debt." Evaluate this answer.

7 Explain how the interest accrued on bonds can be handled when bonds are sold between interest dates.

8 How should discount and premium on bonds payable be classified in the balance sheet? How should bond issue costs be classified?

9 Describe the preferred treatment of the difference between the carrying value of bonds payable and the amount paid to retire the bonds. How is the difference handled when bonds are refunded?

10 List some factors that management should consider in deciding when to refund a bond issue.

11 What are the advantages to a growing company of issuing convertible bonds?

12 What is the generally accepted practice in regard to the assignment of a value to the conversion feature of convertible bonds? Give an argument in favor of assigning a part of the proceeds received on the sale of convertible bonds to the conversion feature.

13 Briefly describe the accounting for bonds which carry detachable warrants to purchase common stock.

14 A top executive of the Chicago Railroad Company was quoted as saying, "Debt management is a continuous process that is highly essential to good operations. As long as I live, I will never go into debt without a sinking fund." Comment on the executive's position.

15 Corporation C has outstanding an issue of 6% *cumulative preferred stock,* callable at par, and an issue of 6% *subordinated income bonds.* What is the basic distinction between these two securities that determines their balance sheet classification?

EXERCISES

Ex. 18-1 The Jayson Corporation plans to issue $1 million, 6% bonds, due 10 years from date of issue. Interest is payable at the end of each year. Using the present value tables in Appendix A, compute the probable proceeds of the bond issue if the market rate of interest is **(a)** 5% and **(b)** 8%.

Ex. 18-2 On December 1, 1975, the Dean Company issued 10-year bonds of $100,000 at 102. Interest is payable on June 1 and December 1 at the rate of 6% per year. On April 1, 1977, the Dean Company retired 30 of these bonds at 96, plus accrued interest. The accounting period for the Dean Company is the calendar year. Prepare journal entries to record the following:
a The issuance of the bonds on December 1, 1975.
b Interest payments and amortization in 1976. Amortization is recorded only at the end of the year. The company does not follow the policy of preparing reversing entries for the accrual of interest.
c The retirement of $30,000 of bonds on April 1, 1977. (**Hint:** First amortize premium for three months on $30,000 of bonds.)

Ex. 18-3 On October 1, 1975, Company E sold a serial bond issue calling for the payment of $1.2 million in principal per year for each of the next five years.

    a Explain how a $270,000 discount on this bond issue would be amortized if the bonds outstanding method were used.

    b How much of the discount would be amortized in the fiscal year ending November 30, 1977?

Ex. 18-4 Suppose that the bond issue in Ex. 18-3 called for the payment of $1.2 million at the end of each of five years, starting at the end of the third year after issue date. How would this affect the schedule of discount amortization computed by the bonds outstanding method?

Ex. 18-5 On December 31 of the current year, Corporation F has outstanding $10 million of 4%, 20-year bonds due in seven years and nine months. The unamortized discount on these bonds at October 1 of the current year was $840,000. Give the journal entry **(a)** to record the accrual of interest and amortization of the discount for the three months ended December 31 of the current year and **(b)** to record the call of $1 million of these bonds on January 1 of the following year at 102 plus accrued interest for three months, assuming that discount is amortized on a straight-line basis and that reversing entries are not used.

Ex. 18-6 The balance sheet of the Green Corporation includes the following at December 31, 1975:

6% convertible debentures (due Dec. 31, 1991)	*$500,000*
Discount on convertible debentures	*10,000*

No value was assigned to the conversion feature when the bonds were issued. Each $1,000 bond is convertible into 35 shares of $10 par value common stock. Using the theoretically preferable method, record the conversion of all bonds into common stock on January 1, 1976, when the market price of the common stock is $40 per share.

Ex. 18-7 The Resort Company sold a $1 million bond issue with detachable warrants attached. The bonds were sold for $1,015,000. Immediately upon issuance the bonds were quoted at 96 and the warrants had a total market value of $90,000. Prepare an entry to record the sale of the bonds, assuming that no accrued interest was charged to buyers of the bonds.

SHORT CASES FOR ANALYSIS AND DECISION

Case 18-1 Delano Electronics Corporation was organized two years ago by two experienced businessmen and several members of the faculty at a local university. The main product of the company consists of a line of medium-size computers and software for all lines of data-processing and information-gathering systems. The company's total assets amount to $15 million and the liabilities amount to $10.5 million, consisting of $3 million of short-term credit and $7.5 million of notes payable to an insurance company. There are 100,000 shares of common stock outstanding. In order to expand its activities, the company needs $5 million in permanent capital. Members of the board of directors have discussed various ways of raising the capital and have asked for your advice regarding the following alternatives:

    (1) Sell debenture bonds bearing interest at $6\frac{1}{2}$% with a sinking fund provision.

    (2) Sell 5% debentures at par. The debentures would be convertible into 40,000 shares of the company's common stock at $125 per share. The current price of the common stock is $96.

    (3) Sell $4\frac{1}{2}$% preferred stock at a par value of $100. The preferred stock would

be callable at $105 and convertible into three-quarters of one share of common stock.

(4) Sell 60,000 shares of common stock at $85 per share through a rights offering. Stockholders would be given rights to buy one additional share for every 10 shares held.

Instructions Briefly evaluate the advantages and disadvantages of each of the four proposals.

Case 18-2 The directors of Statewide Corporation are contemplating the issuance of $15 million debenture bonds. The corporation does not need the money immediately but Director A, a former banker, has convinced the board that the sale of the bonds should be made "while interest rates are low and credit is readily available."

Robert Tabor, representative of a leading investment banking firm, also recommends that the bonds should be sold now since interest rates are beginning to turn up and he feels that a coupon rate of 6% would probably command a modest premium. He strongly believes, however, that the board is making a mistake in not considering the sale of convertible debentures instead of regular bonds for the following reasons:

(1) It would be cheaper for the company (a rate of about $4\frac{1}{2}$% would probably be suficient).

(2) The company's equity will need "beefing up" as it continues to expand its activities.

(3) It is a means of selling common stock at about 20% above the current market price.

Director B, who is vice president in charge of finance, suggested that a $6\frac{1}{2}$% rate be assigned to nonconvertible bonds stating, "A large premium is a sign of financial strength of our corporation; if interest rates continue to advance, 6% bonds would sell at a discount and I don't want people thinking that our credit is so poor that we have to give a discount in order to sell our bonds."

Director C, a public relations executive, disagrees with Director B. He thinks that investors are bargain hunters who would be more willing to buy bonds of a given company at a discount than at a premium. He would assign a $5\frac{1}{2}$% coupon rate to the bonds, stating "discount on bonds payable is prepaid interest and it won't hurt us to have a jump on our interest payments to bondholders."

Instructions Briefly evaluate each of the four viewpoints mentioned in this case.

Case 18-3 State Food Supply Company recently issued $1 million face value, 5%, 30-year subordinated debentures at 97. The debentures are redeemable at 103 upon demand by the issuer at any date upon 30 days notice 10 years after issue. The debentures are convertible into $10 par value common stock of the company at the conversion price of $12.50 per share for each $500 or multiple thereof of the principal amount of the debentures.

Instructions

a Explain how the conversion feature of convertible debt has a value to the
(1) Issuer
(2) Purchaser

b Management has suggested that in recording the issuance of the debentures a portion of the proceeds should be assigned to the conversion feature.
(1) What are the arguments for according separate accounting recognition to the conversion feature of the debentures?
(2) What are the arguments supporting accounting for the convertible debentures as a single element?

c Assume that no value is assigned to the conversion feature upon issue of the debentures. Assume further that five years after issue, debentures with a face value of $100,000 and carrying (book) value of $97,500 are tendered for

conversion on an interest payment date when the market price of the debentures is 104 and the common stock is selling at $14 per share and that the
company records the conversion as follows:

Bonds Payable	100,000
Discount on Bonds Payable	2,500
Common Stock, $10 par value	80,000
Paid-in Capital in Excess of Par	17,500

Discuss the propriety of the above accounting treatment.

Case 18-4 On January 1, 1976, Gordon Corporation issued for $1,106,775 its 20-year, 8%
bonds which have a maturity value of $1,000,000 and pay interest semiannually
on January 1 and July 1. Bond issue costs were not material in amount. The
following are three presentations of the long-term liability section of the balance
sheet that might be used for these bonds at the issue date:

(1) Bonds payable (maturing Jan. 1, 1996)	$1,000,000
Unamortized premium on bonds payable	106,775
Total bond liability	$1,106,775

(2) Bonds payable—principal (face value $1,000,000, maturing Jan. 1,	
1996)	$ 252,572*
Bonds payable—interest (semiannual payment $40,000).	854,203†
Total bond liability	$1,106,775

(3) Bonds payable—principal (maturing Jan. 1, 1996)	$1,000,000
Bonds payable—interest ($40,000 per period for 40 periods)	1,600,000
Total bond liability	$2,600,000

* The present value of $1,000,000 due at the end of 40 (six-month) periods at the yield rate of $3\frac{1}{2}$% per
period.
† The present value of $40,000 per period for 40 (six-month) periods at the yield rate of $3\frac{1}{2}$% per period.

Instructions
a Discuss the conceptual merit(s) of each of the three balance sheet presentations shown above.
b Explain why investors would pay $1,106,775 for bonds which have a maturity
value of only $1,000,000.
c Assuming that a discount rate is needed to compute the carrying value of the
obligations arising from a bond issue at any date during the life of the bonds,
discuss the conceptual merit(s) of using for this purpose:
(1) The coupon (or nominal) rate
(2) The effective (or yield) rate at date of issue

PROBLEMS

Group A

18A-1 On July 1, 1975, the Swartz Corporation issued $3 million of 5%, 20-year bonds
with interest payable on March 1 and September 1. The company received
proceeds of $3,020,500, *including* the accrued interest from March 1, 1975.

Instructions
Prepare the journal entry required on each of the following dates:
a July 1, 1975 (issuance of bonds)
b September 1, 1975 (payment of interest and amortization of discount for two months)
c December 31, 1975 (accrual of interest and amortization of discount from September 1 to December 31)

18A-2 North Interstate Corporation was authorized to issue $10 million of 10-year, 6% convertible debentures due December 31, 1985. Each $1,000 bond is convertible into 40 shares of $10 par value common stock and the bond indenture contained an antidilution provision. The bonds were issued to underwriters on March 1, 1976, and net proceeds amounted to $9,929,200, plus accrued interest. Interest is payable semiannually on June 30 and December 31 and discount is amortized annually on December 31.

Late in 1976 the company issued a 10% stock dividend on the common stock, and in 1977 the common stock was split 2 for 1. The interest payments and the amortization of discount on a straight-line basis have been recorded to January 1, 1978. On May 1, 1978, $2 million par value bonds were converted and the accrued interest on these bonds was paid in cash.

Instructions
a Prepare the entry to record the issuance of bonds. No value is assigned to the conversion feature.
b Prepare a compound journal entry to record, for the first four months of 1978, the payment of interest and the amortization of discount on the bonds converted.
c Prepare the entry to record the conversion of $2 million of bonds on May 1, 1978.

18A-3 Lancelot Company issued $10 million of 8% serial bonds on January 1, 1976. The bonds mature at the rate of $2 million per year starting on December 31, 1980. The bonds were sold for $10,210,000.

Instructions
a Prepare the journal entry to record the issuance of bonds.
b Prepare a schedule (similar to the one illustrated on page 693) showing the amortization of the premium and the net interest expense for each year over the life of the bonds. The premium is amortized using the bonds outstanding method.
c Assume that on December 31, 1982, the following bonds were retired:
$2,000,000 due on December 31, 1982, at par
$100,000 due on December 31, 1983, at 101
$200,000 due on December 31, 1984, at 102
Prepare a compound entry to record the retirement of bonds. Assume that the interest due on December 31, 1982, has already been recorded.

18A-4 At the beginning of 1975, the Owens Company purchased the going business of Gigi's in exchange for $500,000 in cash and 10-year, 5% bonds payable of $2,000,000. The balance sheet of Gigi's at the date of purchase, stated at the fair market value of all identifiable assets, follows:

Balance Sheet (assets stated at fair market value)
January 1, 1975

Total assets	*$3,000,000*	Total liabilities	*$1,200,000*
		Owner's capital	*1,800,000*
	$3,000,000		*$3,000,000*

The purchase was recorded as follows:

Assets	3,000,000	
Goodwill	700,000	
Liabilities		1,200,000
Cash		500,000
5% Bonds Payable		2,000,000
To record purchase of going business.		

In auditing the records of the Owens Company for the fiscal year 1975, you find that $17,500 was recorded as amortization expense of goodwill (over 40 years) and that the present value of the bonds payable on January 1, 1975, was only $1,600,000, based on the quality of the bonds and the market rate of interest on that date. Closing entries have not been recorded for 1975.

Instructions Prepare a compound entry at December 31, 1975, and a supporting schedule to restate the accounts in accordance with generally accepted accounting principles.

18A-5 The Rustica Company issued, in a private placement with an insurance company, $1 million face value of three-year, 4½% bonds. Interest is payable semiannually on June 30 and December 31 of each year. The bonds were sold on January 1 of the current year at a price yielding the company $959,370, which represents an effective interest cost of 6% per year, or 3% semiannually.

Instructions
a Prepare an amortization table, similar to that illustrated on page 686, showing the interest expense for each six-month period on an effective interest basis. (Round all computations to the nearest dollar.)
b Using the data in the amortization table prepared in (*a*), prepare journal entries to record the issuance of the bonds, the interest payments at the end of the first six months and the last six months of the bond issue, and the retirement of the bonds at maturity.
c What interest expense would have been recorded on the books of the Rustica Company each six months if the straight-line method of discount amortization had been used? Explain why the effective interest method produces a different interest expense per period than the straight-line method.

18A-6 In March of 1975, the California Champagne Corporation was authorized to issue $1 million of 6% convertible debentures due March 31, 1985. Interest is payable on March 31 and September 30 of each year. The bonds are callable at any time prior to maturity at a diminishing call premium. Each $1,000 bond is convertible into eight shares of $10 par value common stock.

The bonds were sold on April 30, 1975, for $965,000, plus accrued interest for one month. Bond issue costs of $24,500 were incurred and combined with the discount for amortization purposes. No value was assigned to the conversion feature.

On May 1, 1976, 100 of the bonds were purchased on the open market for a total consideration of $102,000, including accrued interest for one month. The bonds were retired.

On October 1, 1983, the California Champagne Corporation called the remaining bonds for retirement. All bondholders, except one owning $2,000 par value of bonds, converted their holdings into common stock. The one bondholder was mailed a check for $2,060, the call value of the bonds. The market price of the common stock, which had been split 3 for 1 in 1978, was $70 per share on October 1, 1983.

Instructions

a Prepare journal entries to record the issuance of bonds and the payment of issuance costs on April 30, 1975.

b Prepare a journal entry to record payment of interest on September 30, 1975. Assume that amortization is recorded only at the end of fiscal year, which ends on September 30.

c Prepare a journal entry for the retirement of bonds on May 1, 1976.

d Prepare a journal entry for the conversion and retirement of bonds on October 1, 1983.

Group B

18B-1 The balance sheet of the Colima Coal Company at June 30, 1975, included the following accounts:

6% first mortgage bonds payable, maturing on June 30, 1990	$10,000,000
Discount on bonds payable	300,000
Unamortized bond issue costs.	66,000

Instructions

a Compute the annual interest expense, including amortization of bond issue costs. Straight-line amortization is used.

b Prepare an entry to record the retirement of $2 million of bonds at 104 on July 1, 1980. The company's fiscal year ends on June 30.

c Show how the accounts relating to bonds payable would appear in the balance sheet at June 30, 1985.

18B-2 In July of the current year, the board of directors of the CM Corporation authorized the issuance of $70 million of 6%, 20-year debenture bonds dated September 1. Interest on these bonds is payable semiannually on March 1 and September 1 of each year. The bonds were sold to underwriters on November 1 of the current year. The corporation amortizes discount or premium only at the end of the fiscal year, using the straight-line method.

Instructions Prepare the journal entries necessary to record the issuance of these bonds, the adjusting entry at December 31 (the close of the company's fiscal year), the entries to record the first two semiannual interest payments, and the adjusting entry at the end of the following year, assuming that:

a The bonds were sold to the underwriters at $102\frac{1}{8}$, plus accrued interest which was recorded in Bond Interest Payable.

b The bonds were sold to the underwriters at 96.60, plus accrued interest which was recorded in Bond Interest Payable. (Round any computations to the nearest dollar.)

18B-3 The Western Boots Company issued $2 million of 7% serial bonds for a total price of $1,952,000 on January 1, 1975. The bonds mature at the rate of $400,000 per year starting on December 31, 1975. Interest is payable on June 30 and December 31.

Instructions

a Prepare a schedule showing the amortization of the discount and total interest expense for each year 1975 through 1979. Amortization is computed using the bonds outstanding method.

b Assume that on July 1, 1976, $100,000 of the bonds, which were scheduled to be retired on December 31, 1978, were retired at 101. Prepare the entry to record the retirement, assuming that the amortization of the discount was recorded through June 30, 1976, when the semiannual interest was paid.

18B-4 Computer Industries, Inc., recently established the Elcom Division (not a separate corporation) to manufacture and market a new type computer. The executive committee is considering various financing methods and requests that you make a profit-volume analysis and advise the committee of the probable results of several alternatives available.

Engineering estimates indicate that the variable cost of manufacturing a unit will be $20,000. It is estimated that the variable cost of selling a unit will be $10,000 if the sales price should be set at $50,000 per unit. Thus the contribution margin per unit is estimated at $20,000. State and federal income taxes are estimated at 50% of income before taxes. (Disregard the investment tax credit.)

It is also estimated that Elcom will incur fixed costs totaling $4 million per year, including depreciation. Computer Industries, Inc., must secure an additional $10 million to finance the Elcom Division. Computer Industries, Inc., plans to issue at par either stocks or bonds, and Elcom must bear the financing cost in addition to the other costs listed above.

Instructions Compute the number of units which must be sold annually at $50,000 per unit to cover all costs, meet any dividend requirement, and comply with the stated objective under each of the following alternatives. (Show your computations.)

a 6% nonparticipating, cumulative preferred stock is issued.

b 5% bonds are issued.

c 5% bonds are issued and Computer Industries, Inc., requires that Elcom contribute 5% of its sales to be credited to Computer Industries' retained earnings for internal financing and future expansion.

d 5% bonds are issued and Computer Industries, Inc., requires that Elcom contribute annually both $150,000 to be paid out as dividends on Computer Industries' common stock and 5% of Elcom's sales to be credited to Computer Industries' retained earnings for internal financing and future expansion.

Note: The basic profit-volume formula is:

$$\text{Number of units required to be sold} = \frac{\textbf{total fixed costs} + \textbf{pre-tax income}}{\textbf{contribution margin per unit}}$$

18B-5 Cuco's Department Store needed funds to finance the development of a new product. The company arranged to place privately with a pension fund $5 million face value of five-year, 6% bonds. Interest is payable annually on September 30. The bonds were issued on October 1 of Year 0, and the company received proceeds of $5,445,182. In his annual report, the president wrote, "Although the debt carries a coupon rate of 6%, the financing has been arranged so that the effective interest expense to the company is 4% per annum."

Instructions

a Prepare an amortization table, similar to that illustrated on page 686, showing the interest expense for each year on an effective interest basis. (Round all computations to the nearest dollar, and adjust the interest expense for the last period to compensate for any net rounding error.)

b Using the data in the amortization table in (*a*), prepare journal entries to record the issuance of the bonds, the interest payments at the end of the first and fifth years, and the retirement of the bonds at maturity.

c Prepare the same entries called for in (*b*), assuming that interest is recorded on a straight-line basis.

d Explain the reason for the difference in annual interest cost under the straight-line and effective interest methods.

18B-6 The Cheever Corporation sold $5 million of 10-year, 6% convertible debenture bonds on September 30, Year 1, for $4,532,000, plus interest for three months. Bond issue costs of $11,700 were incurred and recorded in a separate account.

No value was assigned to the conversion feature. Interest is payable semiannually on June 30 and December 31. The bonds are callable after June 30, Year 6, and until June 30, Year 8, at 104; thereafter until maturity, at 102; and convertible into $2.50 par value common stock as follows:

(1) Until June 30, Year 6, at the rate of six shares for each $1,000 bond
(2) From July 1, Year 6, to June 30, Year 9, at the rate of five shares for each $1,000 bond
(3) After June 30, Year 9, at the rate of four shares for each $1,000 bond

The bonds mature on June 30, Year 11. The company adjusts its books monthly and closes yearly on December 31. Any bond premium or discount is to be amortized on a straight-line basis.

The following transactions occurred in connection with the bonds:

July 1, Year 7: $1 million of bonds were converted into common stock.
Jan. 1, Year 9: $500,000 of bonds were purchased on the open market at 98 and were immediately retired.
June 30, Year 9: The remaining $3.5 million of bonds were called for redemption. In order to obtain the necessary funds for redemption and business expansion, a $6 million issue of $5\frac{1}{2}$% bonds was sold at par. These bonds were dated June 30, Year 9, and were due on June 30, Year 29.

Instructions Prepare journal entries necessary to record the above transactions, including monthly adjustments where appropriate, as of each of the following dates. (Do not prepare closing entries, but give supporting computations as part of journal entry explanations.)

a Sept. 30, Year 1. (Record bond issuance costs in a separate entry.)
b Dec. 31, Year 1. (Record one month's interest and amortization in a separate entry before recording the payment of interest.)
c July 1, Year 7.
d Jan. 1, Year 9.
e June 30, Year 9. (Record the accrual of interest and amortization, the payment of interest, the retirement of $3.5 million of bonds, and the issuance of $6 million of bonds in separate entries.)

CHAPTER 19

Pension plans and long-term leases

PENSION PLANS

Most medium and large companies incur continuing obligations under employee pension plans. A *pension plan* is a contract between the company and its employees whereby the company agrees to pay certain benefits to employees upon retirement. In some cases employees contribute to a pension fund; however, in most cases employers bear the full cost of a pension plan. Ordinarily, pension benefits consist of monthly payments to employees upon retirement and additional payments upon death or disability. Pension plans may be formal or may be implied from company policy. A company's practice of paying retirement benefits to selected employees in amounts determined on a case-by-case basis does not constitute a pension plan.[1]

Pension plans are a part of the total employment contract with employees and may be established for one or more of the following reasons:

1 To meet demands from employees and labor unions

2 To increase employee morale and productivity and to reduce employee turnover

3 To fulfill a social responsibility expected of a business enterprise

Assets of corporate (private) pension funds probably exceeded $200 billion at the end of 1973 and are expected to continue growing at a fast rate.[2] Assets of private pension funds have been growing faster than total

[1] *APB Opinion No. 8,* "Accounting for the Cost of Pension Plans," AICPA (New York: 1966), p. 68.

[2] "Pension Funds Pass the Supergrowth Stage," *Business Week,* Dec. 23, 1972, pp. 105–106.

assets of corporations and pension expense has been rising much faster than corporate earnings;[3] an estimated 35 million active workers were covered by private pension plans in 1973. As a result, accounting for pension costs has become one of the more significant topics in corporate financial reporting.

Funded and unfunded pension plans

A company may assume full responsibility for the payment of pension benefits with or without establishing a formal pension fund; or it may limit its legal obligation for the payment of benefits to the amount actually accumulated in the company-administered pension fund. A *funded pension plan* requires the company to make periodic payments to a funding agency (a designated trustee or an outside agency such as an insurance company). The process of making payments to the funding agency is known as *funding.* Funding may be accomplished through an *insured plan* with a life insurance company or through a *trust fund plan.* Under an insured plan, individual policies providing death and retirement benefits may be purchased for each employee; alternatively, a group annuity contract may be purchased by the employer. Under a trust fund plan, the employer makes periodic contributions to a trustee who invests the fund assets and pays benefits to eligible employees according to the terms of the trust agreement. If a pension plan is not administered by a funding agency or if assets are informally set aside for the payment of pensions, the plan is designated as an *unfunded pension plan.* Most corporate pension plans are funded.

To illustrate the basic accounting for a pension plan, assume that the pension expense for the Ross Corporation for the current year amounts to $175,000, and that retired employees are paid $40,000. The journal entries required to record this information follow:

Transactions	Funded plan	Unfunded plan
Recognition of pension expense for the current year.	Pension Expense . . . 175,000 Cash 175,000	Pension Expense . . . 175,000 Liability under Pension Plan . . 175,000
Payment of benefits to retired employees during the current year.	None (Funding agency makes payment directly to retired employees)	Liability under Pension Plan . 40,000 Cash . . 40,000

[3] For example, in 1971 the pension fund assets for American Telephone and Telegraph Company amounted to over $9 billion and its pension cost exceeded $800 million; the unfunded vested benefits for General Motors Corporation were over $700 million and its pension cost increased by 77% over the preceding year.

It should be pointed out that the periodic contributions to the pension fund (or funding agency) may not equal the amount currently recognized as pension expense. If the contribution to the pension fund is less than the amount charged to pension expense, the difference should be recorded in a pension liability account; if the contribution exceeds the amount charged to pension expense, the difference may be charged to a previously recorded pension liability account or to a deferred pension cost account. On this point, *APB Opinion No. 8* states:

> The difference between the amount which has been charged against income and the amount which has been paid [to a fund or funding agency] should be shown in the balance sheet as accrued or prepaid pension cost. If the company has a legal obligation for pension cost in excess of amounts paid or accrued, the excess should be shown in the balance sheet as both a liability and a deferred charge.[4]

Pension plans are generally designed to meet federal income tax requirements of a "qualified" plan. A *qualified* plan has the following tax features: (1) The employer's contributions to the pension fund (within certain limits) are deductible for federal income tax purposes; (2) earnings on pension fund assets are not subject to federal income tax; and (3) generally, only the benefits received by retired employees represent taxable income to them.

General accounting guidelines for pension plans

Accountants are faced with three significant issues relating to pension plans, which are listed below:

1 *Timing* the recognition of pension costs *as expenses* in measuring periodic net income, particularly when pension plans cover employees who have already worked a number of years for the company at the time the plans are adopted

2 *Measuring the amount* of pension expense and any related deferred pension cost or accrued pension liability which should appear in the balance sheet

3 *Presenting* significant information relating to pension plans in the financial statements and the accompanying notes

When the Accounting Principles Board was established in 1959, it quickly recognized the need to clarify the accounting and reporting practices for pension plans, and in 1965 published *Accounting Research Study No. 8,* "Accounting for the Cost of Pension Plans."[5] A year later, *APB Opinion No. 8* was issued which provided guidelines for measuring periodic pension costs and for reporting relevant pension plan data in financial statements and the accompanying notes.[6]

The measurement of pension costs involves numerous complexities, including the application of compound interest concepts, estimates of the average life expectancy of employees, determination of the age of

---

[4] *APB Opinion No. 8,* p. 74.
[5] Ernest L. Hicks, *Accounting Research Study No. 8,* "Accounting for the Cost of Pension Plans," AICPA (New York: 1965).
[6] *APB Opinion No. 8,* "Accounting for the Cost of Pension Plans," AICPA (New York: 1966).

employees at retirement, future level of interest rates, probable employee turnover, gains and losses on pension fund investments, future salary levels of employees, pension benefits to be paid, and vesting provisions under the pension plan. These complexities, combined with the long-range nature of pension plans, cause significant uncertainties as to the amount of pension benefits ultimately to be paid to employees and consequently the amount of periodic pension expense to be reported in the income statement.

Pension costs and the related costs of administering a pension plan should be allocated to revenue on the accrual basis. The amount of periodic expense should not be left to the whims of management. Recognition of pension costs on a pay-as-you-go basis when benefits are paid to retired employees is not an acceptable method of accounting. Ideally, the total pension cost relating to a particular employee should be recognized over the period between the date the employee is hired and the date he retires. All employees who may reasonably be expected to receive benefits under a pension plan should be included in the calculation of the periodic pension expense, with appropriate recognition given to anticipated employee turnover.

APB Opinion No. 8 recognizes that there are differences in viewpoint as to the composition of pension cost, especially the extent to which pension expense should include the cost of employees' services prior to the adoption of the pension plan. The Opinion specifies "that the entire cost of benefit payments ultimately to be made should be charged against income *subsequent* to the adoption or amendment of a plan and that no portion of such cost should be charged directly against retained earnings." [7] The annual provision for pension expense should be determined in a consistent manner and the amount of the provision should be within the following prescribed limits:

a. *Minimum.* The annual provision for pension cost should not be less than the total of (1) normal cost, (2) an amount equivalent to interest on any unfunded prior service cost and (3) if indicated [under circumstances discussed below] . . . a provision for vested benefits. . . .

b. *Maximum.* The annual provision for pension cost should not be greater than the total of (1) normal cost, (2) 10 per cent of the past service cost (until fully amortized), (3) 10 per cent of the amounts of any increases or decreases in prior service cost arising on amendments of the plan (until fully amortized) and (4) interest equivalents . . . on the difference between provisions and amounts funded. The 10 per cent limitation is considered necessary to prevent unreasonably large charges against income during a short period of years.[8]

The Accounting Principles Board expressed a preference for a method of measuring periodic pension expense which would include an appropriate portion of past service cost and prior service cost increments. However, any "rational and systematic" method which is consistently applied and which provides for periodic pension expense between the minimum and maximum range is acceptable.

[7] *Ibid.,* p. 73.
[8] *Ibid.,* pp. 73–74.

The terms used in determining the amount of periodic pension expense within the minimum-maximum range are explained below.

Normal cost   The cost of prospective retirement benefits accrued (on the basis of current service credits) during any year is known as a **normal cost** (or **current service cost**) of the pension plan. Normal cost is generally determined by professional actuaries using an acceptable actuarial cost method (see pages 718–720) for each year subsequent to the inception of a pension plan.

Prior service cost   The cost of prospective retirement benefits considered to have accrued in the years prior to the adoption of a pension plan is referred to as a **past service cost.** The estimated cost of employee services for years prior to the date of a particular actuarial valuation (including the past service cost) is known as a **prior service cost.** Increases or decreases in prior service cost as a result of changes in the contractual provisions of the pension plan are generally known as **prior service cost increments.** Unfunded prior service cost is generally not shown as a liability in the balance sheet.

In the summary of components of the provision for pension expense shown on page 718, we can see that the minimum provision for pension expense includes only the interest charge on any unfunded prior service cost; the maximum provision may include 10% (based on the 10-year minimum amortization period allowed for income tax purposes) of the prior service cost. Once prior service cost is fully amortized, no further consideration would be given to such cost in applying the minimum-maximum guidelines.

Vested benefits   Earned pension benefits that are not contingent on the employee remaining in the service of the employer are known as **vested benefits.** Under some plans the payment of vested benefits will begin only when the employee reaches a stated retirement age; in other cases the payment of vested benefits will begin when the employee actually retires, which may be before or after the normal retirement age. The actuarially computed value of vested benefits at a given date consists of the present value of the **sum** of (1) the expected benefits to be paid to employees who have retired or who were terminated with vested rights, and (2) the benefits already earned and expected to become payable to active employees.

A provision for vested benefits is required only when the pension expense (consisting of normal cost and interest on unfunded prior service cost) does not make a reasonable provision for vested benefits.

Interest equivalents   The purpose of a pension fund is to accumulate amounts needed to pay retirement benefits. The fund is generally accumulated (1) through periodic contributions by the employer and (2) earnings on pension fund assets. If the employer's contributions exceed the actuarially determined pension expense, the earnings on the fund assets will be greater than required and the employer's future contributions should be correspondingly reduced; however, if the contributions by the employer are less than required by actuarial computations, the earnings which would otherwise have been realized on the fund assets must eventually be contributed by the employer.

Under the minimum-maximum guidelines, the annual provision for pension expense should be adjusted by an amount equal to the interest on any difference between pension expense previously recorded and the amounts actually funded. (See amortization and funding tables on pages 722 and 723.)

In arriving at the **minimum** annual pension expense, provision must be made for interest on any unfunded prior service cost (or, in certain cases, on the difference between accounting provisions for normal pension costs and the amounts of normal costs actually funded). In arriving at the **maximum** annual pension expense, provision is made for interest on the unfunded prior service cost under the 10% limitation for such cost; in addition, a provision for interest must be made on the difference, if any, between the cumulative provisions for normal pension costs and the amounts of normal pension costs actually funded.

A summary of the components of the minimum and maximum annual provisions for pension expense is presented below:

Component of annual provision for pension expense	Minimum provision for pension expense	Maximum provision for pension expense
1 Normal cost	Full amount included	Full amount included
2 Prior service cost (which includes past service cost and prior service cost increments)	Only interest provision on unfunded portion is included	Include no more than 10% until fully amortized
3 Vested benefits	May be included in certain cases	Not applicable
4 Interest equivalents on the difference between provisions and amounts funded	Include (or deduct) in certain cases in connection with item (3) above	Include (or deduct)

Actuarial cost methods

The annual provision for pension expense should be based on one of the acceptable *actuarial cost methods.* The factors used in tentatively resolving uncertainties concerning future events affecting pension expense (such as mortality rates, employee turnover, compensation levels, and earnings on pension fund assets) are referred to as *actuarial assumptions.* An *actuarial valuation* of a pension plan is made by actuaries using these assumptions in order to determine the amounts an employer is to contribute to a pension fund. The first step in making an actuarial valuation is to determine the present value on the valuation date of benefits to be paid to employees over varying periods of time in the future. An actuarial cost method is then applied to this present value to determine the current contributions to be made by the employer. The resulting determinations are estimates, since in making an actuarial valuation significant uncertainties concerning future events must be resolved by making actuarial assumptions.

Although actuarial techniques are primarily used to determine the periodic payments to be made to the pension fund (or funding agency), the same techniques are used to measure periodic pension expense because the amount of the pension expense recognized currently is the present value of future pension benefits which are estimated to have accrued during the current accounting period. Acceptable actuarial cost methods include (1) the *accrued-benefit-cost method* and (2) the *projected-benefit-cost methods.*

Accrued-benefit-cost Method Under the accrued-benefit-cost method (sometimes called the *unit-credit method*), the amount of pension expense assigned to the current year usually is equal to the present value of the increase in the employees' retirement benefits resulting from the services performed in the current year. Thus the normal annual pension expense under this method is the present value of the *units* of future benefits credited to employees for current services. For example, if a plan provides benefits of $10 per month for each year of service, the normal pension cost for one employee for the current year would be the present value of an annuity of $10 per month beginning at the employee's expected retirement date and continuing throughout his expected life.

For a given employee, the accrued-benefit-cost method results in an increased pension expense from year to year because the present value of the annual increment in benefits becomes larger as the date of retirement approaches and also because the probability that the employee will reach retirement age increases. In addition, the retirement benefits under most pension plans are related to salary levels, which generally increase during the years. However, the pension expense for an entire work force of a constant size would increase only if the average age or average salary level of the work force increases.

Projected-benefit-cost Methods Under the projected-benefit-cost methods, the amount of pension expense assigned to the current year usually represents a level amount that will provide for the total projected retirement benefits over the service lives of employees. Four projected-benefit-cost methods (entry-age-normal method, individual-level-premium method, aggregate method, and attained-age-normal method) may be used. A description of these methods is beyond the scope of this discussion.[9] The annual pension expense computed using a projected-benefit-cost method tends to be stable or to decline from year to year.

In contrast to the two broad categories of actuarial cost methods mentioned above, the terminal-funding method and the pay-as-you-go method are not considered acceptable. Under the *terminal-funding method,* provision (funding and recognition of pension expense) for future benefit payments is made only at the end of an employee's period of active service; under the *pay-as-you-go method,* pension expense is recognized only when benefits are paid to retired employees. The conclusion in *APB Opinion No. 8* relative to actuarial cost methods is summarized below:

> To be acceptable for determining cost for accounting purposes, an actuarial cost method should be rational and systematic and should be consistently applied so that it results in a reasonable measure of pension cost from year to year. . . . Each of the actuarial cost methods . . . , except terminal funding, is considered acceptable when the actuarial assumptions are reasonable and when the method is applied in conformity with the other conclusions of this Opinion. The terminal funding method is not acceptable because it does not

[9] *Ibid.,* pp. 75–77 and 92–97.

recognize pension cost prior to retirement of employees. For the same reason, the pay-as-you-go method (which is not an actuarial cost method) is not acceptable.[10]

Actuarial gains and losses

We have seen that in measuring periodic pension expense it is necessary to make numerous actuarial assumptions based on estimates of future events. Actual events seldom coincide with previous estimates and the assumptions concerning the future may become invalid. As a result, periodic adjustments may be required to reflect actual experience and to revise the actuarial assumptions to be used in the future. These adjustments are commonly known as *actuarial gains and losses.* Actuaries normally compute the amount of the actuarial gains and losses and management determines the period of time to be used in recognizing such gains and losses in the accounts. Prior to the issuance of *APB Opinion No. 8,* three methods were used: (1) immediate recognition, (2) spreading over the current and future periods, and (3) averaging. *APB Opinion No. 8* considers either the *spreading* or the *averaging* method as acceptable:

> The Board believes that actuarial gains and losses, including realized investment gains and losses, should be given effect in the provision for pension cost in a consistent manner that reflects the long-range nature of pension cost. Accordingly, . . . actuarial gains and losses should be spread over the current year and future years or recognized on the basis of an average. . . . Where spreading is accomplished by separate adjustments, the Board considers a period of from 10 to 20 years to be reasonable.

> Actuarial gains and losses should be recognized immediately if they arise from a single occurrence not directly related to the operation of the pension plan and not in the ordinary course of the employer's business. An example of such occurrences is a plant closing, in which case the actuarial gain or loss should be treated as an adjustment of the net gain or loss from that occurrence and not as an adjustment of pension cost for the year.

> The Board believes unrealized appreciation and depreciation should be recognized in the determination of the provision for pension cost on a rational and systematic basis that avoids giving undue weight to short-term market fluctuations. . . . Ordinarily appreciation and depreciation need not be recognized for debt securities expected to be held to maturity and redeemed at face value.[11]

Accounting for the cost of a pension plan illustrated

Once a pension plan is adopted, actuaries are engaged to determine the present value of past service cost (if any) and to compute the normal pension expense for the current period using an acceptable actuarial cost method. Management then formulates a policy for the amortization and funding of the past service cost. At this point, it is necessary to ascertain

[10] *Ibid.,* p. 77.
[11] *Ibid.,* pp. 79–80.

that the computed amount of normal and past service pension expense falls between the minimum-maximum range outlined earlier in our discussion.

To illustrate the journal entries required to record annual pension expense, we shall assume that the Kim Company adopted a pension plan at the beginning of Year 1. The company plans to fully fund the normal (current) pension cost, which is estimated at $60,000 per year. The company has a number of employees who have been working for the company for many years, and actuaries have determined the present value of the liability for past services applicable to such employees at $210,620. This past service cost was determined using an assumed interest rate of 6% per year.

Assumption 1. Past Service Cost Is Amortized and Funded over 15 Years If management decides to amortize and fund the past service cost of $210,620 over a 15-year period by recognizing the expense and making equal payments to the funding agency *at the end of each year,* the annual amortization of past service cost and the annual payment to the funding agency are determined as follows:

$$\frac{\text{Present value of past service cost}}{\text{Present value of ordinary annuity of 15 payments of \$1 at 6\%}}$$

$$= \frac{\$210,620}{9.7122^*} = \$21,686$$

* See Table 4 in Appendix A.

The entry at the end of each year to record the normal pension cost of $60,000, the amortization of the past service cost of $21,686, and payment to the funding agency follows:

Pension Expense (Normal and Past Service Cost)	81,686	
Cash		81,686

To record annual pension expense (including normal cost of $60,000 and past service cost of $21,686) and payment to the funding agency.

The balance sheet would not include *any* deferred pension cost or accrued pension liability because the entire current provisions for pension expense are fully funded at the end of each year. After the past service cost is fully amortized and funded, only the normal (current) pension expense would be recorded and funded each year.

Assumption 2. Past Service Cost Is Amortized over a Period Longer than Funding Period While management may elect to fund the past service cost over any number of years, the amortization of the past service cost cannot be less than 10 years or longer than 40 years. In order to minimize the computations in the table below, we shall assume that the Kim Company will amortize the past service cost over a period of eight years and will fund this cost by making five equal payments to the funding agency at the end of each of the first five years. The annual amortization and funding payments are computed below:

Amortization: $\dfrac{\text{Present value of past service cost}}{\text{Present value of ordinary annuity of 8 payments of \$1 at 6\%}}$

$$= \frac{\$210,620}{6.2098} = \$33,917$$

Payments: $\dfrac{\text{Present value of past service cost}}{\text{Present value of ordinary annuity of 5 payments of \$1 at 6\%}}$

$$= \frac{\$210,620}{4.2124} = \$50,000$$

A table showing the computation of the annual past service pension expense (column C) and the deferred pension cost balance (column F) is presented below for the Kim Company:

KIM COMPANY
Past Service Pension Cost—Amortization and Funding

Year	Amortization (8 years)			Funding (5 years)	Deferred pension cost	
	(A) Computed annual amount at 6% interest	(B) Less interest (6% of previous balance in F)	(C) Debit to Pension Expense (A − B)	(D) Credit to Cash	(E) Increase or decrease (D − C)	(F) Asset balance (previous balance ± E)
1	$33,917	$ −0−	$33,917	$50,000	$16,083	$16,083
2	33,917	965	32,952	50,000	17,048	33,131
3	33,917	1,988	31,929	50,000	18,071	51,202
4	33,917	3,072	30,845	50,000	19,155	70,357
5	33,917	4,221	29,696	50,000	20,304	90,661
6	33,917	5,440	28,477	−0−	(28,477)	62,184
7	33,917	3,731	30,186	−0−	(30,186)	31,998
8	33,917	1,919*	31,998	−0−	(31,998)	−0−

Adjusted for $1 discrepancy due to rounding of computations.

Because the payments to the funding agency during the first five years exceed the amount charged to expense, an asset (Deferred Pension Cost) is accumulated and reported in the balance sheet. Starting in Year 2, interest earned (column B) on the deferred pension cost balance (column F) *reduces* the annual charge to Pension Expense (column C).

Journal entries to record the amortization and funding of the past service cost for Year 1 and Year 8 are illustrated below for the Kim Company:

Year 1   Pension Expense (Past Service Cost)   33,917
             Deferred Pension Cost   16,083
               Cash   50,000
             To record payment to funding agency; amount paid exceeds amount currently recognized as expense.

Year 8   Pension Expense (Past Service Cost)   31,998
             Deferred Pension Cost   31,998
             To record amortization of deferred pension cost.

An additional entry would be made each year to record the normal cost of the pension plan. Keep in mind that *Opinion No. 8* does not permit the amortization of past service cost over a period less than 10 years; we have used eight years in order to simplify the computations in the example.

KIM COMPANY
Past Service Pension Cost—Amortization and Funding

Year	Amortization (3 years)			Funding (5 years)	Accrued pension liability	
	(A) Computed annual amount at 6% interest	(B) Add interest (6% of previous balance in F)	(C) Debit to Pension Expense (A + B)	(D) Credit to Cash	(E) Increase or decrease (C − D)	(F) Liability balance (previous balance ±E)
1	$78,795*	$ −0−	$78,795	$50,000†	$28,795	$28,795
2	78,795	1,728	80,523	50,000	30,523	59,318
3	78,795	3,559	82,354	50,000	32,354	91,672
4	−0−	5,500	5,500	50,000	(44,500)	47,172
5	−0−	2,828‡	2,828	50,000	(47,172)	−0−

*$210,620 ÷ 2.673 (present value of ordinary annuity of 3 payments of $1 at 6%) = $78,795.
†Same as in example on page 722.
‡Adjusted for $2 discrepancy due to rounding of computations.

Assumption 3. Past Service Cost Is Amortized over a Period Shorter than Funding Period When the past service cost is amortized over a period shorter than the funding period, a pension liability (column F in the table on page 723) is accumulated during the amortization period; this liability is gradually eliminated as payments are made to the funding agency in the years following the amortization period. Because the funding lags behind the recognition of the expense, interest on the fund deficiency (accrued pension liability) is *added* to the annual pension expense. A table illustrating the amortization of the past service cost over a three-year period and the funding of this cost over a five-year period by the Kim Company is shown on page 723.

Journal entries to record the amortization and funding of the past service cost for Year 1 and Year 5 are illustrated below for the Kim Company:

Year 1	Pension Expense (Past Service Cost)	78,795	
	Cash		50,000
	Liability under Pension Plan		28,795
	To record payment to funding agency; amount paid is less than amount currently recognized as expense.		
Year 5	Pension Expense (Past Service Cost)	2,828	
	Liability under Pension Plan	47,172	
	Cash		50,000
	To record payment to funding agency to eliminate balance in Liability under Pension Plan account and to recognize pension expense equal to 6% of liability balance.		

The normal cost of the pension plan also would be recorded each year. Again, we should emphasize that the short amortization period was used only to simplify the computations. Attention should be focused on the principles involved and not on the amortization period used. In practice, the amortization period must exceed 10 years; generally a period of 15 to 30 years is used.

Deferred compensation contracts

The accrual accounting procedures for pension plans also apply to other deferred compensation contracts. Such contracts generally stipulate that the employee to be eligible for benefits must be employed for a specified period and that he should be available for consultation after retirement.

The estimated amounts to be paid under each contract should be accrued in a systematic and rational manner over the period of active employment from the time the contract is entered into, unless it is evident that future services expected to be received by the employer are commensurate with the payments or a portion of the payments to be made. If elements of both current and future services are present, only the portion applicable to the current services should be accrued.[12]

Presentation of pension plans in financial statements

The reporting guidelines for pension plans, as established in *APB Opinion No. 8,* are briefly summarized below:[13]

1 A statement that a pension plan exists and a description of the employee groups covered by the pension plan.

2 A statement of the company's accounting and funding policies.

3 The amount of pension expense for the period.

4 The excess, if any, of the actuarially computed value of vested benefits over the total of the pension fund and any pension accruals in the balance sheet, less any pension prepayments or deferred charges.

5 Nature and effect of significant matters affecting comparability for all periods presented, such as changes in accounting methods, changes in actuarial assumptions, or amendments to the pension plan. The effect on prior year cost of a change in the accounting method for pension cost should be applied prospectively to the current and future years, and should be fully disclosed.

These reporting guidelines are quite limited in scope, which has led some critics to suggest that reporting of pension costs and pension funds in most cases tends to be inadequate, casual, and misleading. At the very least, more information should be reported relative to actuarial assumptions, the composition of pension fund assets, and the earnings performance of the pension fund.

The following note relating to pension plans is taken from an annual report of Fedders Corporation:

Substantially all of the Company's employees are covered under one of the Company's pension plans or under one of the union-sponsored plans to which the Company contributes. The total pension expense connected with the Company's plans was $1,693,000 during 1971 and $921,000 during 1970, including provision for normal cost for all of the plans and provision for either interest on prior service costs or amortization of prior service costs over a period of 30 years. It is the Company's policy to fund pension cost accrued. For those Company pension plans where the actuarially computed value of the vested benefits exceeded the total of the applicable pension fund and any related balance sheet accrual, such aggregate excess value amounted to approximately $1,243,000 at August 31, 1971 and $585,000 at August 31, 1970.

The Company's contributions to the union-sponsored pension plans are based on an hourly rate and amounted to $697,000 in 1971 and $394,000 in 1970.

Additional examples of disclosure of pension plans appear in Appendix B.

[12]*APB Opinion No. 12,* "Omnibus Opinion—1967," AICPA (New York: 1967), p. 189.
[13]*APB Opinion No. 8,* pp. 84–85.

LONG-TERM LEASES

Assets used in business may be acquired by outright purchase or by renting the assets under a lease contract. Lease contracts today are an important means of obtaining the use or financing the acquisition of almost any kind of long-lived asset.

In some cases, a company constructs or buys property, sells it to an investor, and simultaneously leases the property from the investor. These are known as *sale-and-leaseback* transactions. In other cases, a company leases existing property or property constructed to its specifications. A company which leases property for use in its business may agree to pay all the expenses (such as taxes, insurance, maintenance, and repairs) incident to ownership of the property. The recording and reporting of these complex transactions is a controversial issue in accounting. A number of guidelines have been developed to help accountants identify leases of similar economic substance so that leasing transactions may be reported in a consistent and meaningful manner.[14]

A *lease* is a contract in which the owner (*lessor*) of an asset agrees to give another party (*lessee*) the right to use the asset for a specified period of time in return for periodic rental payments. A lease may be essentially a rental arrangement which requires no more than the periodic recognition of rental revenue by the lessor and rental expense by the lessee; or a lease may be a means of obtaining financing for plant assets; other leases may in fact represent an installment purchase of assets, requiring the recognition of both the leased asset and the related obligation in the balance sheet of the lessee. This brief description of different leasing arrangements suggests that lease contracts must be carefully examined to determine the appropriate accounting treatment, both for the lessor and the lessee.

Two types of leases

Two different situations are recognized in connection with leases of real or personal property. When the lessor gives the lessee the use of property in exchange for rental payments and at the same time retains the usual risks (such as early obsolescence) and rewards (such as a gain from appreciation in value at the end of the lease period) of ownership of the leased property, the contract is referred to as an *operating lease;* on the other hand, when the intent is to provide financing to the lessee for the

---

[14] See John H. Myers, *Accounting Research Study No. 4,* "Reporting of Leases in Financial Statements," AICPA (New York: 1962); *APB Opinion No. 5,* "Reporting of Leases in Financial Statements of Lessee," AICPA (New York: 1964); *APB Opinion No. 7,* "Accounting for Leases in Financial Statements of Lessors," AICPA (New York: 1966); *APB Opinion No. 27,* "Accounting for Lease Transactions by Manufacturer or Dealer Lessor," AICPA (New York: 1972); *APB Opinion No. 31,* "Disclosure of Lease Commitments by Lessees," AICPA (New York: 1973).

eventual purchase of property and to transfer the usual risks and rewards of ownership to the lessee, the contract is referred to as a *financing lease.* Some financing leases may be viewed as equivalent to a sale of property by the lessor and a purchase of property by the lessee; other financing leases are viewed as simply giving the lessee a "property right" in the leased asset.

Use of the financing method to record leases on the books of the lessor is considered appropriate when the lease agreements "are designed to pass all or most of the usual ownership risks or rewards to the lessee and to assure the lessor of, and generally limit him to, a full recovery of his investment plus a reasonable return on the use of the funds invested, subject only to the credit risks generally associated with secured loans."[15] On the other hand, *APB Opinion No. 5* stated that the use of the *capitalization method* (lessee records leased asset and related liability in his accounts) is appropriate for the lessee when "the terms of the lease result in the creation of a material equity in the property."[16] Generally speaking, the capitalization of a lease by the lessee would be appropriate only in situations where the financing method is used by the lessor. However, there may be some cases where capitalization by the lessee is not required for a lease accounted for by the financing method on the books of the lessor. This was recognized in *APB Opinion No. 7* as follows:

> . . . the Board considers the principal accounting problem of the lessors to be the allocation of revenue and expense to accounting periods covered by the lease in a manner that meets the objective of fairly stating the lessor's net income; the Board believes that this objective can be met by application of the financing method. . . . As to the lessee, however, capitalization of leases, other than those which are installment purchases of property, may not be necessary in order to state net income fairly since the amount of the lease rentals may represent a proper charge to income.[17]

Accounting for operating and financing leases is illustrated in the following sections.

Accounting for operating leases

The leasing of a copying machine, office space, and furniture are common examples of transactions entered into by many business enterprises. These transactions generally take the form of operating leases and may be contrasted with financing leases as shown on page 728.

This listing of the characteristics of the two types of leases highlights the short-term and conditional nature of operating leases. An operating lease does not give the lessee any property rights in the leased property and is not designed to provide financing for the lessee. In an operating lease, the payments by the lessee are viewed as expenses by the lessee

---

[15]*APB Opinion No. 7,* pp. 55–56.
[16]*APB Opinion No. 5,* p. 30.
[17]*APB Opinion No. 7,* p. 60.

Lease provision	Operating leases	Financing leases
Length of lease period	Short	Long
Option to buy at termination	Not available	Nominal price
Cancelation provisions	Cancelable or non-cancelable	Noncancelable
Rent payment	Covers return on investment **plus** ownership costs	Provides for a fair return on capital invested in property
Property taxes, maintenance, and insurance	Paid by lessor	Paid by lessee

and as revenue by the lessor. Any additional costs connected with an operating lease are recorded as expenses by the party which must absorb such costs as required by the lease agreement.

To illustrate the accounting for an operating lease, assume that Lessor Company agreed to rent office space to Lessee Company and arranged a three-year lease, effective January 1, 1975, which required the Lessee Company to pay $2,400 at the beginning of each month. The lease contract required the Lessor Company to pay utilities, property taxes, insurance, and maintenance. The fiscal year for each company ends on December 31.

The accounting treatment for this operating lease would be similar to any other monthly revenue on the books of the lessor or monthly expense on the books of the lessee. However, if we assume that the lease agreement requires that a payment of $10,692 be made on January 1, 1975, in addition to the first monthly payment of $2,400, the accounting becomes more complex. Two methods may be used to account for the initial payment of $10,692.

Under the *straight-line method* the total of all payments under the lease are recognized evenly as rental revenue by the lessor and as rental expense by the lessee over the life of the lease as follows:

$$\text{Average monthly revenue or expense} = \frac{\$10,692}{36} + \$2,400 = \$2,697$$

Using the straight-line method, the entries for 1975 (the first year of the lease) would be as follows:

Date	Lessor Company		Lessee Company	
Jan. 1	Cash 10,692		Prepaid Lease	
	Unearned Rental		Rental 10,692	
	Revenue	10,692	Cash	10,692
	To record receipt		To record payment	
	from lessee.		to lessor.	
The 1st of each	Cash 2,400		Rent Expense 2,400	
month Jan.1–	Rental		Cash	2,400
Dec. 1	Revenue	2,400	To record monthly	
	To record receipt of		payments to lessor.	
	monthly payments			
	from lessee.			
Dec. 31	Unearned Rental		Rent Expense 3,564	
	Revenue 3,564		Prepaid Lease	
	Rental		Rental	3,564
	Revenue	3,564	To recognize ex-	
	To recognize realized		pired portion of	
	portion of initial		prepaid lease	
	payment: $10,692 ×		rental: $10,692	
	$\frac{12}{36}$ = $3,564.		× $\frac{12}{36}$ = $3,564.	

It should be noted that the Unearned Rental Revenue account on Lessor Company's books and the Prepaid Lease Rental account on Lessee Company's books have a balance of $7,128 ($10,692 − $3,564) at December 31, 1975. The straight-line method is easy to apply and tends to match expenses with the periods benefited. However, it ignores the time value of money concept and for this reason would not be appropriate when the difference between the straight-line method and the present value method is material.

The **present value method** of accounting for the initial payment recognizes the economic consequences in the timing of cash flows. Thus, this method will consider the earnings on cash paid prior to the rendering of services. To illustrate the present value method, we will assume the same three-year lease requiring a $10,692 initial payment and monthly rentals of $2,400, which begins on January 1, 1975. In this case, Lessor Company and Lessee Company agree that a 6% interest rate is to be used. From a present value standpoint, we shall view the initial payment as a deposit on January 1, 1975, which will earn interest at 6% and which will permit the withdrawal of rents by the lessor of equal amounts on December 31, 1975, 1976, and 1977. Thus we can use Table 4 of Appendix A for the "Present Value of an Ordinary Annuity of $1 per Period" to calculate the implied end-of-year "payments" (at an assumed interest rate of 6%) as follows:

Implied end-of-year rent "payments"

$$= \frac{\text{initial payment}}{\text{present value of 3 equal payments of \$1 at 6\%}} = \frac{\$10,692}{2.6730} = \underline{\underline{\$4,000}}$$

A table summarizing the amortization of the initial lease payment using the present value method is presented below:

Amortization of Initial Lease Payment

Date	(A) Lessor's rental revenue (or lessee's rent expense)	(B) Lessor's interest expense (or lessee's interest revenue), 6% of (D)	(C) Reduction in balance (A − B)	(D) Lessor's unearned rental revenue or lessee's prepaid lease rental
Jan. 1, 1975				$10,692
Dec. 31, 1975	$4,000	$642	$3,358	7,334
Dec. 31, 1976	4,000	440	3,560	3,774
Dec. 31, 1977	4,000	226	3,774	−0−

It should be noted that we used a **year-end** "payment" assumption. Alternative assumptions, such as payments at the beginning of the year (or month), may be appropriate. We will not illustrate other assumptions as they are logical extensions of the procedure illustrated above. In accounting for the lease, we shall assume that both the lessor and lessee agree that 6% is an appropriate interest rate and that both use the present value method. The entries necessary to record the lease for the first year (1975) are shown on page 731.

When the operating method is used to account for a lease, the lessor reports the leased property, net of accumulated depreciation, with or near plant and equipment in the balance sheet; the balance sheet of the lessee does not include assets rented through an operating lease.

Accounting for financing leases

Leases which are in essence a form of financing have been widely used in recent years. The financing method of accounting is considered appropriate for measuring periodic income from leasing activities of entities engaged in lending money, including lease-finance companies, banks,

Date	Lessor Company		Lessee Company	
Jan. 1	Cash 10,692		Prepaid Lease	
	Unearned		Rental 10,692	
	Rental		Cash	10,692
	Revenue	10,692	To record pay-	
	To record receipt		ment of rentals	
	of rentals for 3		for 3 years.	
	years.			
The 1st of each	Cash 2,400		Rent Expense 2,400	
month Jan. 1–	Rental		Cash	2,400
Dec. 1	Revenue	2,400	To record monthly	
	To record receipt		payments to lessor.	
	of monthly payments			
	from lessee.			
Dec. 31	Unearned Rental		Rent Expense 4,000	
	Revenue 3,358		Interest	
	Interest Expense . . . 642		Revenue	642
	Rental		Prepaid Lease	
	Revenue	4,000	Rental	3,358
	To recognize		To recognize ex-	
	realized portion		pired portion of pre-	
	of initial payment		paid lease rental	
	(See table on		(See table on	
	p. 730.)		p. 730.)	

insurance companies, and pension funds. These entities generally design lease agreements so that they obtain a fixed rate of return on their investments and the lessee assumes the usual risks and rewards of ownership.

There are two types of financing lease transactions: (1) a lease which is equivalent to an installment sale of property by a manufacturer or a dealer-lessor and (2) a lease which passes all or most of the usual ownership risks and rewards to the lessee but which is not considered equivalent to an installment sale of property. The second type of lease is generally used by lease-finance companies, banks, and other lending institutions.

Lease Which Is Equivalent to a Sale and Purchase of Property In *Opinion No. 5,* the Accounting Principles Board pointed out that some lease agreements should be recorded as a sale by the lessor and as a purchase of an asset by the lessee. The asset and the related liability should be initially recorded by the lessee at an amount equal to the present value of the future

lease rental payments, excluding payments for services such as maintenance, insurance, property taxes, etc. The asset should be depreciated
by the lessee over its estimated *useful life rather than over the initial period
of the lease.*

In order for a noncancelable lease to be treated as a sale and purchase
of property, *either* of the following conditions should be present: (1) The
initial term of the lease is materially less than the estimated useful life
of the property, and the lessee has the option to renew the lease for the
remaining useful life of the property at substantially less than the fair
rental value; or (2) the lessee has the right to acquire the property at
a price which at the inception of the lease appears to be substantially
less than the probable value of the property at the time of permitted
acquisition by the lessee. Other circumstances, such as the acquisition
of the property by the lessor to meet the special needs of the lessee,
may indicate that the lease is equivalent to a sale and purchase of
property on the installment basis.

The Accounting Principles Board approached this problem in *Opinion
No. 27* from the standpoint of manufacturers and dealer-lessors. The
Board took the position that a manufacturer or dealer-lessor should
account for a lease transaction as a sale if (1) collectibility of the payments required from the lessee is reasonably assured, (2) no important
uncertainties exist as to the amount of costs yet to be incurred under
the lease, and (3) the lease transfers title to the property to the lessee
(or gives the lessee the option to obtain title to the property without cost
or at a nominal cost) by the end of its fixed and noncancelable term;
or the leased property is available for sale at a price equal to or below
the present value of the required rental payments.[18] If these conditions
are not met, the lease should be accounted for by the operating method.

When a manufacturer or a dealer-lessor records a lease as a sale,
revenue should be recognized in the period of the sale equal to the
present value of the required rental payments during the fixed and noncancelable term (excluding any renewal option) of the lease. The full cost
of the property and any estimated future costs (other than interest) should
be charged against the revenue of the period of "sale." The difference
between the revenue and the cost thus recognized represents a profit
on the "sale." Thus, if a lease is reported as a sale by the lessor which
is in reality a rental arrangement, income would be prematurely recorded
as realized.

To illustrate the accounting for a lease which is considered to be
equivalent to a sale by the lessor and a purchase by the lessee, assume
that on December 31, 1974, Orr Mfg. Company, a dealer-lessor, leases
a machine (which had a cost of $11,500 and a normal sales price of
$14,250) to LSE, Inc., for four years on the following terms:

1 LSE, Inc., agrees to make four annual rental payments of $4,000 starting on

[18]*APB Opinion No. 27*, pp. 509–510.

December 31, 1974 (representing rent for 1975).[19] The estimated useful life of the machine is seven years with no residual value; LSE, Inc., plans to use the straight-line method of depreciation.

2 LSE, Inc., will absorb all maintenance costs, insurance, and property taxes.

3 LSE, Inc., is given an option to buy the machine for $10 at the termination of the lease, December 31, 1978.

4 The effective rate of interest on December 31, 1974, for this type of transaction is 8% per year.

The present value at December 31, 1974, of the four rental payments consists of the total of (1) $4,000 due on December 31, 1974, and (2) the present value of an ordinary annuity of three additional payments of $4,000 at 8% per year, as computed below:

Payment due on Dec. 31, 1974	*$ 4,000*
Present value of ordinary annuity of 3 payments of $4,000 at 8% per year at Dec. 31, 1975–1977; $4,000 × 2.5771 (see Table 4 in Appendix A)	*10,308*
Present value of 4 payments of $4,000 at 8% per year	*$14,308*

A table summarizing the payments and interest through December 31, 1977, follows:

Summary of Lease Payments and Interest

Date	(A) Lease payments	(B) Lessor's interest revenue (or lessee's interest expense), 8% of (D)	(C) Reduction in balance (A − B)	(D) Balance of lessor's receivable (or lessee's payable)
Dec. 31, 1974	*Balance*			*$14,308*
Dec. 31, 1974	*$4,000*	*$–0–*	*$4,000*	*10,308*
Dec. 31, 1975	*4,000*	*825*	*3,175*	*7,133*
Dec. 31, 1976	*4,000*	*571*	*3,429*	*3,704*
Dec. 31, 1977	*4,000*	*296*	*3,704*	*–0–*

Entries for 1974 and 1975 to record this transaction are illustrated on page 734. We shall assume that lease receivables and payables are recorded net of the discount.

[19] Lease payments are generally made monthly; we have assumed annual payments in order to minimize computations in the table on this page.

Date	Orr Mfg. Company (Lessor)		LSE, Inc. (Lessee)	
1974				
Dec. 31	Cash 4,000		Machinery 14,308	
	Lease Receivables 10,308		Cash	4,000
	Cost of Goods		Lease	
	Sold 11,500		Payables . .	10,308
	Sales	14,308	To record a	
	Inventory . .	11,500	lease which is	
	To record lease		equivalent to a	
	which is equiva-		purchase of	
	lent to a sale		property.	
	of property.			
1975				
Dec. 31	Cash 4,000		Lease Payables . . 3,175	
	Interest		Interest Expense 825	
	Revenue . .	825	Cash	4,000
	Lease		To record second	
	Receivables	3,175	payment to lessor.	
	To record receipt			
	of second payment			
	from lessee.			
			Depreciation	
			Expense 2,044	
			Accumulated	
			Depreci-	
			ation . . .	2,044
			To record depre-	
			ciation over esti-	
			mated life of 7	
			years: $14,308 ÷	
			7 = $2,044.	

It would be possible to record the lease receivables and payables at the gross amount of $12,000 ($4,000 × 3) and a discount of $1,692 ($12,000 — $10,308) representing unearned interest revenue for the lessor and deferred interest expense for the lessee. We should also emphasize that the lessee computes depreciation over the seven-year estimated useful life of the machine and not over the four-year initial period of the lease.

The Orr Mfg. Company (lessor) should report the balance in the Lease Receivables account with or near receivables. The balance expected to be collected within one year should be included under current assets; the balance due beyond one year should be included under a noncurrent classification such as Investments or Other Assets. LSE, Inc., (lessee) should report Machinery and the related Accumulated Depreciation account under plant and equipment, and the balance in the Lease Payables account under liabilities, divided between current and noncurrent maturities.

Lease Which Is Not Equivalent to a Sale and Purchase of Property If a lease contract passes all or most of the usual risks and rewards of ownership to the lessee and essentially meets the requirements of a financing lease (but is not considered equivalent to a sale), the procedures briefly described below should be followed.

The lessor uses the financing method and recognizes the *excess* of the total rentals over the cost (less salvage value at the end of the lease) of the leased property as revenue during the term of the lease. The revenue is recognized in decreasing amounts related to the declining balance of the unrecovered investment. For example, assume that Brown Corporation leases construction equipment to a lessee on April 1 for a total rental of $40,000, payable at the rate of $1,000 at the end of each month. The cost of the construction equipment (which is not expected to have any salvage value at the end of the lease period) is $32,835. The difference of $7,165 between the aggregate rentals and the cost of the equipment is intended to give Brown Corporation a return of 1% per month on the lease investment.[20] The entry for the Brown Corporation (lessor) to record the lease on April 1 is:

Equipment Rentals Receivable	40,000	
Construction Equipment (or Inventory)		32,835
Unearned Lease Revenue		7,165
To record lease on lessor's books using financing method. Lease is not equivalent to a sale.		

Receipt of the first lease rental payment by the Brown Corporation on April 30 is recorded by the following entry:

Cash	1,000	
Unearned Lease Revenue	328	
Equipment Rentals Receivable		1,000
Realized Lease Revenue		328
To record receipt of first lease rental and to recognize realized lease revenue at the rate of 1% per month on unrecovered investment: $32,835 \times 1\% = \$328$ (rounded).		

[20] The present value of an ordinary annuity of 40 payments of $1,000 at 1% interest per period equals $32,835 ($1,000 $\times$ 32.835).

The current portion of equipment contracts receivable, less the applicable amount of unearned lease revenue, should be included among current assets of the lessor; net equipment contracts receivable due beyond one year should be included under Investments.

A lease which is recorded by using the financing method by the lessor generally does not require capitalization (recording the asset and the related obligation) by the lessee. As stated earlier, the "capitalization of leases, other than those which are in substance installment purchases of property, may not be necessary in order to state net income fairly since the amount of the lease rentals may represent a proper charge to income" for the lessee.[21] "The right to use property and a related obligation to pay specific rents over a definite future period are not considered . . . to be assets and liabilities under present accounting concepts."[22]

In *APB Opinion No. 31,* the Board required that separate disclosures be made by the lessee of (1) the total rental expense (reduced by rentals from subleases, with disclosure of such amounts) charged against operations for each period presented; (2) the minimum rental commitments under all noncancelable leases for each of the five succeeding fiscal years, each of the next three five-year periods, and the remainder as a single amount; and (3) the following additional disclosures in general terms:

a The basis for calculating rental payments if dependent upon factors other than the lapse of time

b Existence and terms of renewal or purchase options, escalation clauses, etc.

c The nature and amount of related guarantees made or obligations assumed

d Restrictions on paying dividends, incurring additional debt, further leasing, etc.

e Any other information necessary to assess the effect of lease commitments upon the financial position, results of operations, and changes in financial position of the lessee[23]

The Board also recommended, but did not require, the disclosure of the present value of lease commitments which may be helpful in evaluating the credit capacity of the lessee and in comparing the lessee's financial position with that of other entities. Such disclosure may include, as of the date of the latest balance sheet presented, (1) the present value of the net fixed minimum lease commitments in the aggregate and by major categories of properties; (2) either the weighted-average interest rate and range of rates, or specific interest rates, for all lease commitments; and (3) the present value of rentals to be received from existing noncancelable subleases. Computation of the present value of lease commitments should be based on the interest rates implicit in the terms of the leases at the time the lease contracts were entered into.[24]

---

[21] *APB Opinion No. 7,* p. 60.
[22] *APB Opinion No. 5,* p. 32.
[23] *APB Opinion No. 31,* pp. 576–577.
[24] *Ibid.,* p. 578.

If a lease is capitalized by the lessee, a Rights in Leased Property account would be debited and a Liability under Lease Contract account would be credited for an amount equal to the present value of the lease rentals over the period of the lease. The asset (Rights in Leased Property) would be amortized over the life of the lease using the straight-line, sum-of-the-years'-digits, or some other appropriate depreciation method. Rights in Leased Property, net of accumulated depreciation, would be included under Plant and Equipment in the balance sheet. The Liability under Lease Contract account would be reduced by that portion of periodic rentals in excess of interest paid on the balance of the lease liability. The Liability under Lease Contract account would be reported under current and noncurrent liabilities, depending on the maturity dates.

The capitalization by the lessee of long-term leases which are not equivalent to a purchase of property has been widely debated.[25] Proponents of capitalization point out that the user rights acquired under a lease have all the attributes of an asset and that the lease obligation to make cash outlays at a future time, based on a past transaction, falls within the definition of a liability. They also note that a failure to record leased assets and the related liabilities make the financial statements of companies that lease substantial amounts of property misleading when compared with statements of companies that incur substantial liabilities by purchasing assets.

Those who oppose this approach argue that lease liabilities differ significantly from other forms of debt. Lease arrangements are essentially **executory contracts** which call for **future** performance by both parties. In the event of default on a lease, the lessee may not be liable for the full amount of unpaid rentals but simply for a claim by the lessor for damages suffered by him as a result of the breach of contract. In addition, lease obligations are often uncertain because of such contingent provisions as cancellation clauses, options to renew the lease, and provisions for conditional payments based on sales or net income. For these reasons, many accountants contend that footnote disclosure by the lessee is more appropriate than placing dollar valuations on leased assets and the related obligations. They argue that leases other than those which are equivalent to an installment purchase of assets represent a legitimate form of "off-balance sheet" financing by the lessee.

Sale-and-leaseback transactions

In certain cases an owner of an asset sells it and immediately leases it back from the buyer. Such a transaction gives the lessee the use of the asset in his business operations without a large capital investment and provides the lessor with a profitable investment. In addition, both the

---

[25] See John H. Myers, *op. cit.* This study contains a comprehensive discussion of the lease problem and supports the capitalization of leases in the balance sheet.

lessor and lessee may derive certain income tax advantages from such a transaction.

Because the sale of the asset and the leaseback represents in effect a single transaction, neither the sale price of the asset nor the periodic rental payments can be evaluated separately of the other. For this reason the Accounting Principles Board suggested that a material gain or loss, net of the tax effect, on the disposal of an asset which is immediately leased back from the buyer should be amortized by the lessee over the life of the lease as an adjustment to periodic rental expense (or depreciation expense if the lease is capitalized by the lessee).[26]

Initial direct costs; tax allocation procedures

The initial direct costs of negotiating and closing leases, if material, should be deferred and allocated to the period of the lease. Both the lessor and the lessee may incur such costs, which may include commissions, legal fees, investigation costs, and the costs of processing documents. The amortization policy for initial direct costs of leases should be consistent with the method used to recognize revenue (by the lessor) or rental expense (by the lessee) under the operating or financing methods of accounting for leases.

When lease revenue or expenses are recognized differently for tax purposes and for financial reporting purposes, income tax allocation procedures (as described in Chapter 20) should be used.

Summary of presentation of long-term leases in the balance sheet

The presentation of accounts relating to leases in the balance sheet of lessors and lessees is summarized on page 739.

For an example of lease reporting, see the financial statements of Fruehauf Corporation in Appendix B. Fruehauf Corporation capitalizes certain of its properties leased from others; it also leases certain assets to other parties (treated as operating leases) and its subsidiary, the Fruehauf Finance Company, accounts for leasing of assets to others by the financing method.

REVIEW QUESTIONS

1 Define a ***pension plan*** and explain the difference between a ***funded*** plan and an ***unfunded*** plan.

2 What are the three main accounting issues relating to pension plans?

3 The total cost of contributions that must be paid ultimately to provide pensions for the present participants in a plan cannot be determined precisely in advance; however, reasonably accurate estimates can be made by the use of actuarial techniques. List some of the factors entering into the determination of the ultimate cost of a funded pension plan.

[26] *APB Opinion No. 5*, p. 33.

Type of lease	Lessor	Lessee
1 Operating	Investment in leased property, net of accumulated depreciation, is reported with or near plant and equipment	Leased assets and rental obligations are not reported in the balance sheet. Amount of annual rentals should be disclosed in a footnote
2 Financing:		
a Lease which is equivalent to a sale and purchase of property	Leased asset is not reported in balance sheet; lease receivables (net of financing charges) are reported under current assets or Investments, depending on maturity dates	Leased asset is reported under plant and equipment; lease obligations are reported as current or long-term liabilities, depending on maturity dates
b Lease which is not equivalent to a sale and purchase of property	Leased asset is not reported in the balance sheet; rentals receivable (net of unearned lease revenue) are reported under current assets or under Investments, depending on maturity dates	Leased asset generally is not included in balance sheet; amount of annual rentals and present value of total rentals should be disclosed in a footnote. If lease is capitalized, Rights in Leased Property should be reported under plant and equipment and Liability under Lease Contract should be included under current and long-term liabilities, depending on maturity dates

4 What is the purpose of the **minimum** and **maximum** limits established by the Accounting Principles Board in measuring the annual provision for pension expense?

5 Briefly define each of the following in relation to the measurement of annual pension expense:
a Normal cost
b Past service cost, including amortization policy
c Vested benefits
d Interest equivalents

6 What purpose is served by **actuarial cost methods** in measuring pension expense? List two categories of actuarial cost methods which are considered acceptable for accounting purposes.

7 Define **terminal-funding** and **pay-as-you-go** methods of meeting a company's pension obligations. Why are these methods not considered acceptable?

8 Explain what is meant by **actuarial gains and losses** and describe the treatment of such gains and losses in measuring the annual provision for pension expense.

9 What information should be disclosed about a company's pension plan in financial statements and the accompanying notes?

10 Define the following:
  a Lease
  b Sale-and-leaseback
  c Operating lease
  d Financing lease
  e Lease which is equivalent to a sale and purchase of property

11 Briefly outline the accounting procedures which should be followed by the lessor and by the lessee for **(a)** an operating lease and **(b)** a financing lease.

12 How are the leased assets (or lease receivables) reported in the balance sheet of the lessor when the lease is accounted for by the **(a)** operating method and **(b)** financing method?

13 How are the leased assets and related lease obligations reported in the balance sheet of the lessee when the lease is accounted for by the **(a)** operating method and **(b)** financing method?

14 Burns Company leased a computer for a three-year period at $10,000 a month, with an option to renew the lease for five years at $1,000 per month or to purchase the computer for $20,000 after the initial lease period of three years. How would you report this transaction on the financial statements for Burns Company?

15 Dave James, Inc., has entered into a lease agreement calling for annual lease payments that are substantial in relation to its other operating expenses. Discuss two methods of disclosing this transaction in the company's financial statements.

16 Assets acquired under noncancelable leases that are in substance installment purchases should be capitalized in the accounts of the lessee in order to show the facts properly. List the defects in the lessee's balance sheet and income statement that would result from not recording assets acquired under such contracts.

17 Some noncancelable leases that give the lessee essentially all the rights and obligations of ownership are not installment purchases in substance.
  a Discuss the case against recording assets acquired by such leases.
  b The case for recording assets acquired by such leases rests primarily on the belief that the opportunity to exercise the right of use creates an asset that should be recognized in the accounts with its related liability. Discuss the arguments that support this belief.
18 Shaw Company leases certain property, under a lease calling for the payment of $2,400 per year in rent. At the end of the current year, when the lease has 10 years left to run, Shaw Company subleases the property to a tenant who promises to pay Shaw Company $4,800 per year for 10 years. When will the gain from this transaction be reported by the Shaw Company? Explain.

EXERCISES

Ex. 19-1 Early in 1975, the Esperanza Company adopted a pension plan for its employees which is to be administered by a funding agency. Unfunded past service cost was determined to be $6 million; this amount will be paid to a funding agency in 10 annual payments of $800,000, starting on December 31, 1975. The past service cost will be amortized over a 20-year period; the amortization for 1975 is computed at $530,000. Normal cost of the pension plan for 1975 is $425,000; this amount is remitted to a funding agency at December 31, 1975. Prepare a compound entry to record the foregoing information at the end of 1975.

Ex. 19-2 The information given below relates to the past service pension cost of Abner Company at the beginning of Year 1 when a pension plan was adopted:

Past service cost to be amortized over 10 years and funded over 20 years. $736,010

Annual payments at 6% sufficient to pay off a debt of $736,010 over 10 years. 100,000

Annual payments at 6% sufficient to pay off a debt of $736,010 over 20 years. 64,082

Prepare a partial table (similar to the one illustrated on page 723) summarizing the amortization and funding of the past service pension cost for the first two years of the pension plan.

Ex. 19-3 Using the data in the partial table prepared in Ex. 19-2, prepare the required journal entries for Years 1 and 2 and indicate the information that would appear in the balance sheet at the end of Year 2 relative to the past service pension cost.

Ex. 19-4 On January 1, 1975, the M Company (lessor) received a payment of $5,346 from N Company (lessee) representing an amount equivalent to the present value of three year-end rental payments of $2,000 discounted at 6%.
 a Prepare entries to record the receipt of the $5,346 on the books of M Company and to recognize rental revenue at the end of 1975.
 b Prepare entries to record the payment of the $5,346 on the books of N Company and to recognize rent expense at the end of 1975.

Ex. 19-5 The following information is available for a lease of a machine which is considered equivalent to a sale and purchase:

Cost of machine to lessor $30,000
Initial payment by lessee at inception of lease 1,000
Present value of remaining 47 monthly payments of $1,000 each discounted at 1% per month (discount is not recorded separately in the accounts) 37,354

 a Record the "sale" of the machine (including the initial receipt of $1,000) and the receipt of the second installment of $1,000 on the books of the lessor.
 b Record the "purchase" of the machine (including the initial payment of $1,000) and the payment of the second installment of $1,000 on the books of the lessee.

Ex. 19-6 The Z Corporation leased a heavy crane to Elmo, Inc., on July 1, 1975, on the following terms:
 (1) 48 lease rentals of $1,500 at the end of each month to be paid by Elmo, Inc.
 (2) The cost of the crane to Z Corporation was $63,870.
 (3) Z Corporation will account for this lease using the financing method (not considered equivalent to a sale); the difference between total rental receipts ($1,500 × 48 = $72,000) and the cost of the crane ($63,870) is intended to yield a return of $\frac{1}{2}$ of 1% per month over the life of the lease.
 Prepare entries on the books of the Z Corporation (the lessor) to record the lease agreement and the receipt of the first lease rental on July 31, 1975.

SHORT CASES FOR ANALYSIS AND DECISION

Case 19-1 In examining the costs of pension plans, certain terms are encountered by a CPA. The elements of pension costs which the terms represent must be dealt with appropriately if generally accepted accounting principles are to be reflected in the financial statements of entities with pension plans.

Instructions
a Discuss the theoretical justification for accrual recognition of pension costs.
b Discuss the relative objectivity of the measurement process of accrual versus cash (pay-as-you-go) accounting for annual pension costs.

Case 19-2 On January 2, 1975, the board of directors of the Artukovich Company approved the establishment of a pension plan for all employees. The pension is payable to employees when they reach age sixty-five if they had three or more years of continuous service with the company. All employees currently on the payroll are eligible, thus requiring the recognition of past service cost over an appropriate number of years, starting in 1975. The company was organized early in 1968.

A summary of the active employees as of January 2, 1975, who are eligible for the pension plan is presented below:

Number of employees	Years of service as of Jan. 2, 1975
10	7
18	6
20	5
25	4
40	3
45	2
20	1
178	

A partial list of benefits to be paid to retired employees on the basis of average annual earnings and the number of years of employment appears below:

Average annual earnings	Monthly pension benefits based on years of employment		
	3 years	10 years	25 years
$ 7,500	$30	$120	$360
10,000	40	160	480
12,500	50	200	600
15,000	60	240	720

The company plans to amortize and fund any past service cost over a 10-year period.

Instructions

a List some assumptions that would have to be made in computing the company's liability for past service cost at January 2, 1975.

b List some additional facts that would be required in order to compute the liability for past service cost at January 2, 1975.

c In reference to the work force of 178 employees at January 2, 1975, what factors might cause the normal pension cost for 1980 to increase over the normal pension cost for 1975? What factors might cause the normal pension cost in 1980 to be less than the normal pension cost in 1975?

Case 19-3 Western Airlines recently purchased eight jet liners for a total cost of $180 million. It plans to depreciate the jets using the sum-of-the-years'-digits method over a 12-year period. It is estimated that the jets will have a resale value of $24 million at the end of 12 years. In order to finance the acquisition of the jets, Western Airlines borrowed $180 million, payable at the rate of $20 million per year plus interest at 8% on the unpaid balance. The first payment is due one year after the loan is arranged.

Eastern Airlines leased eight jet liners of the same type purchased by Western Airlines for a 12-year period. Eastern Airlines does not have an option to buy the jets at the end of the lease period and it does not capitalize leases in its balance sheet. Lease rentals are $22 million per year, payable at the end of each year. The lease rentals do not include property taxes, insurance, and maintenance of the jet liners; Eastern Airlines pays all such expenses. The annual rental was computed to give the lessor slightly less than 8% return on his investment, taking into account the $24 million resale value of the jets at the end of the 12-year lease period.

Instructions

a Prepare a schedule of annual expenses (depreciation and interest) for Western Airlines in connection with the ownership of the eight jet liners. How do annual expenses for Western Airlines compare with the annual lease rental incurred by Eastern Airlines? What is the significance of the difference?

b Show the amounts relating to the jets and the related loan that would appear in the balance sheet of Western Airlines at the end of the first year. In what respect is the balance sheet for Eastern Airlines different?

Case 19-4 To meet the need of its expanding operations, Kral Corporation leased a new building for a period of 20 years. During the term of the lease, Kral Corporation has the option of purchasing the building for an amount equal to the present value of the remaining rentals plus $500. Alternatively, at the termination of the lease, the building will be transferred to Kral Corporation for a small consideration.

Instructions

a Under certain conditions, generally accepted accounting principles provide that leased property be included in the balance sheet of a lessee even though legal title remains with the lessor.

(1) Discuss the conditions that would require financial statement recognition of the asset and the related liability by a lessee.

(2) Describe the accounting treatment that should be employed by a lessee under the conditions you described in your answer to part (1) above.

b Unless the conditions referred to in part **(a)** are present, generally accepted accounting principles do not require asset recognition of leases in the financial statements of lessees. However, some accountants do advocate recognition by lessees that have acquired property rights. Explain what is

meant by "property rights" and discuss the conditions under which these rights might be considered to have been acquired by a lessee.
c How should Kral Corporation treat the lease described above?

PROBLEMS

Group A

19A-1 The Evans Company fully funds the current portion of its pension expense. When the company started its pension plan early in Year 1, it adopted a 10-year amortization period and a 12-year funding period for the past service cost of $350,000. The data below relate to the pension plan for Years 1, 2, and 3:

	Year 1	Year 2	Year 3
Normal pension expense	$85,000	$88,900	$95,100
Past service cost:			
Amortization on 10-year basis	43,152	43,152	43,152
Interest at 4% on accrued pension liability	–0–	234	478
Annual payments to funding agency.	37,293	37,293	37,293

Instructions
a Prepare journal entries to record the normal and past pension expenses for the three-year period. Record normal and past service costs in a single Pension Expense account.
b Compute the amount of the accrued pension liability at the end of Year 3.

19A-2 Actuaries have estimated the past service pension liability of Green Awning Corporation at the date it adopted its pension plan at $1,578,846. The actuaries estimate that 6% is a reasonable earnings rate on fund investments. The company plans to recognize the past service cost over 20 years, and to fund it over the next 30 years. The equal annual payment which will amortize $1,578,846 over 20 years at 6% is $137,650 ($1,578,846 ÷ 11.470, present value of $1 per period for 20 years at 6%); over 30 years it is $114,700 ($1,578,846 ÷ 13.765, present value of $1 per year for 30 years at 6%). The following partial table may be prepared:

Year	(A) 20-year amortization at 6%	(B) Add interest (6% of previous balance in E)	(C) Debit to Pension Expense (A + B)	(D) 30-year funding	(E) Accrued Pension Liability account*
1	$137,650	$ –0–	$137,650	$114,700	$ 22,950
2	137,650	1,377	139,027	114,700	47,277
20	137,650	46,461	184,111	114,700	844,203
21	–0–	50,652	50,652	114,700	780,155
29	–0–	12,617	12,617	114,700	108,208
30	–0–	6,492	6,492	114,700	–0–

*The previous year's balance in the accrued pension liability account plus the difference between the pension expense and the payment to the funding agency for the current year.

Instructions

a Prepare journal entries to record the amortization and the funding of past service pension cost for Years 1, 2, 21, and 30.

b Assuming the same liability for past service cost ($1,578,846), amortization over 30 years, and funding over 20 years, the following partial table may be prepared:

Year	(A) 30-year amorti- zation at 6%	(B) Less interest (6% of previous balance in E)	(C) Debit to Pension Expense (A − B)	(D) 20-year funding	(E) Balance in Deferred Pension Cost account*
1	$114,700	$ -0-	$114,700	$137,650	$ 22,950
2	114,700	1,377	113,323	137,650	47,277
20	114,700	46,461	68,239	137,650	844,203
21	114,700	50,652	64,048	-0-	780,155
29	114,700	12,617	102,083	-0-	108,208
30	114,700	6,492	108,208	-0-	-0-

* The previous year's balance in the Deferred Pension Cost account plus the difference between the payment to the funding agency and the pension expense for the current year.

Prepare journal entries to record the amortization and the funding of past service pension cost for Years 1, 2, 21, and 30.

c Explain the balance of $844,203 in the Deferred Pension Cost account at the end of Year 20 as presented in part (*b*) of the problem (*Hint:* The present value of an ordinary annuity of 10 payments of $1 at 6% = 7.3601).

(Adapted from Haskins & Sells CPA Preparation Course)

19A-3 On April 1, 1975, Cardenas of Peru, Inc., signed a five-year, noncancelable lease with Equipment Mfg. Corporation. The leased equipment was designed to meet the unique needs of Cardenas of Peru, Inc. Annual rent of $10,000 is payable in advance, starting on April 1, 1975. The lease agreement gave the lessee an option to purchase the equipment on March 31, 1980, for $1, and is considered to be equivalent to a purchase of equipment.

The estimated useful life of the equipment is 10 years, and management of Cardenas estimates that the salvage value of the equipment at the end of its estimated useful life will approximate the dismantling and removal costs. The straight-line method of depreciation is used by Cardenas, and its fiscal year ends on March 31.

The borrowing rate for Cardenas of Peru, Inc., on April 1, 1975, is 8% per year. The present value of an ordinary annuity of four annual payments of $1 each at 8% is $3.3121. Equipment Mfg. Corporation also considers 8% to be a fair rate of interest.

Instructions

a Prepare a summary of lease payments and lessee's interest expense (similar to the illustration on page 733) for the lease described above.

b Prepare journal entries for Cardenas of Peru, Inc., (lessee) relating to the lease for the fiscal year ended March 31, 1976.

c Assuming that the equipment is carried on the records of the Equipment Mfg. Corporation (lessor) in the Inventory of Equipment account at $38,000, prepare a journal entry to record the lease on the books of Equipment Mfg. Corporation.

19A-4 Hickey Company has decided to acquire a new piece of equipment. It may do so by an outright cash purchase at $25,000 or by a leasing alternative of $6,000 per year (payable at the beginning of each year) for the life of the machine. Other relevant information follows:

Purchase price due at time of purchase $25,000

Estimated useful life . . . . 5 years

Estimated residual value if purchased . . . . $ 3,000

Annual cost of maintenance contract to be acquired with either lease or pur-

chase . . . . $ 500

The full purchase price of $25,000 could be borrowed from a bank at 10% annual interest (payable at the end of each year) and would be repaid in one payment at the end of the fifth year. Additional information is given below:

(1) Assume a 40% income tax rate and use of the straight-line method of depreciation.

(2) The yearly lease rental and maintenance contract fees would be paid at the beginning of each year.

(3) The minimum desired rate of return on investment is 10% before income taxes.

(4) All cash flows, unless otherwise stated, are assumed to occur at the end of the year.

(5) Selected present value factors for a 10% return are given below:

Year	Present value of $1 received at end of year
1	$.9091
2	.8264
3	.7513
4	.6830
5	.6209

Instructions

From the information given, compute the following (carry all computations to nearest dollar):

a Cost of the machine if it is purchased.

b Present value of the five annual rental payments if the machine is leased.

c Present value of the estimated residual value if the machine is purchased.

d Hickey Company's net after-tax cash outflow (or inflow) for each year (1) if machine is purchased and the money is borrowed, and (2) if machine is leased. Assume that the money to purchase the machine is borrowed and that the machine is sold for $3,000 at the end of the fifth year.

19A-5 The Pen Corporation adopted a pension plan early in 1975. The plan was to be administered by an insurance company and stipulated that the payments by Pen Corporation to the insurance company would consist of three parts:

(1) Annual payments of $10,000 beginning on January 2, 1975, and ending on January 2, 1984, covering the past service cost for qualified employees. These payments are to be adjusted periodically by mutual agreement because of changes in pension benefits to be paid to employees or because of separation from service of employees whose rights are forfeited. An interest rate of 6% per year was used in computing the amount of the annual payments.

(2) Payments for current service (normal) costs based on the number of employees, their birth dates, and the earnings rate that the insurance company

is able to earn on the pension fund investments. These payments will be based on payroll data for the latest year and will be paid in two installments as follows: $15,000 on June 30 of each year and the balance (as determined at December 31 of each year) on January 3 of the following year.

(3) Payments for supplemental adjustments agreed upon by the insurance company and the Pen Corporation.

The payments made to the insurance company during the first three years of the pension plan are listed below:

Year	Past service cost	Current service (normal) costs	
	Jan. 2	Jan. 3	June 30
1975	$10,000	$ –0–	$15,000
1976	10,000	16,990	15,000
1977	10,000	18,200	15,000

Payments by the insurance company to retired employees for the first three years were: 1975, $5,500; 1976, $7,500; and 1977, $9,100.

The management of Pen Corporation considers the past service cost to be a legal obligation and wishes to follow the requirement of **APB Opinion No. 8** regarding the accounting for this cost, that is, "If the company has a legal obligation for pension cost in excess of amounts paid or accrued, the excess should be shown in the balance sheet as both a liability and a deferred charge." Current service (normal) costs are accrued only at the end of the fiscal year, which is the calendar year.

Instructions

a Prepare a partial amortization and funding table for the past service cost for 1975 and 1976. Assume that the present value of the 10 annual payments of $10,000 each, beginning on January 2, 1975, and earning interest at 6% per year, is approximately $78,017. The Pen Corporation records $10,000 in Past Service Pension Expense each year.

b Prepare journal entries on the books of the Pen Corporation relating to the pension plan for 1975 and 1976.

c How should the information relating to the pension plan appear in the balance sheet for the Pen Corporation at December 31, 1976?

19A-6 In 1974 the Fuji Freight Company negotiated and closed a long-term lease contract for newly constructed truck terminals and freight storage facilities. The buildings were erected to the company's specifications on land owned by the company. On January 1, 1975, Fuji Freight Company took possession of the leased properties.

Although the terminals have a composite useful life of 40 years, the noncancelable lease runs for 20 years from January 1, 1975, with a favorable purchase option available upon expiration of the lease. You have determined that the leased properties and related obligation should be accounted for as an installment purchase.

The 20-year lease is effective for the period January 1, 1975, through December 31, 1994. Advance rental payments of $1,000,000 are payable to the lessor on January 1 of each of the first 10 years of the lease term. Advance rental payments of $300,000 are due on January 1 for each of the last 10 years of the lease. The company has an option to purchase all these leased facilities for $1 on December 31, 1994. It also must make annual payments to the lessor of $75,000 for property taxes and $125,000 for insurance; these payments also are due on January 1. The lease was negotiated to assure the lessor a 6% rate of return.

Instructions (Round all computations to the nearest dollar.)

a Prepare a schedule to compute for Fuji Freight Company the discounted present value of the terminal facilities and related obligation at January 1, 1975.

b Assuming that the discounted present value of terminal facilities and related obligation at January 1, 1975, was $9,108,620, prepare journal entries for Fuji Freight Company to record the:

(1) Lease transaction and the payment to the lessor on January 1, 1975 (separate entries)

(2) Amortization of the cost of the leased properties for 1975, using the straight-line method and assuming a zero salvage value

(3) Accrual of interest expense at December 31, 1975, using the effective interest method

(4) Payment to the lessor on January 1, 1976

Selected present value factors are as follows:

Periods	For an ordinary annuity of $1 at 6%	For $1 at 6%
1	$ .943396	$.943396
2	1.833393	.889996
8	6.209794	.627412
9	6.801692	.591898
10	7.360087	.558395
19	11.158117	.330513
20	11.469921	.311805

Group B

19B-1 The Rodman Corporation adopted a pension plan early in 1974 and has regularly funded the full amount of its current pension expense. At the time the pension plan was adopted, the past service pension liability amounted to $1,472,020. The Company has been amortizing the past service cost over a 15-year period and depositing $200,000 annually with a funding agency. The annual deposits are intended to provide an amount, plus interest at 6%, at the end of 10 years to enable the funding agency to pay the accrued past service pension liability when employees retire. Pertinent pension plan data for the *third* and *fourth* years of the pension plan are presented below:

	1976	1977
Normal pension expense	$300,000	$340,000
Past service cost:		
Amortization on 15-year basis	151,564	151,564
Interest at 6% on deferred pension cost	5,987	9,252
Annual payments to funding agency	200,000	200,000

Instructions

a Prepare journal entries to record the normal and past pension expense for 1976 and 1977. Record normal and past service costs in a single Pension Expense account.

b Compute the balance in the Deferred Pension Cost account at the end of 1977. (*Hint:* Remember that the plan was adopted in 1974.)

19B-2 Cone-Pine, Inc., adopted a pension plan effective January 1, 1975. Actuaries had determined that the past service pension liability applicable to active employees who were included in the pension plan was approximately $623,110. The company arranged to fund the past service pension cost by making 10 equal payments to a funding agency at the end of each year starting December 31, 1975. The fund earns interest at 5% per year and past service pension cost is being amortized over a 20-year period.

Instructions
a Compute the annual amortization amounts and the annual payments to the funding agency. The present value of an ordinary annuity of 20 annual payments of $1 at 5% is 12.4622 (see Table 4 in Appendix A); the present value of an ordinary annuity of 10 annual payments of $1 at 5% is 7.7217 (see Table 4 in Appendix A). Carry computations to the nearest dollar.
b Prepare a partial amortization and funding table (similar to the table illustrated on page 722) for the first four years of the pension plan.
c Prepare entries for 1975 and 1976 to record the amortization and funding of the past service pension cost.

19B-3 Dolphin Company needs to acquire additional machine capacity to meet the growing demand for its product. The Precise Corporation offers to provide the machines to Dolphin Company using any one of the options listed below. (Each option gives Dolphin Company exactly the same machines and gives Precise Corporation approximately the same net present value cash equivalent at 8%.)

Option A—Purchase for $100,000 in cash.

Option B—Installment purchase requiring 15 equal payments of $10,800 payable at the beginning of each year.

Option C—10-year lease with right to purchase for $1,000, annual lease payments of $13,800 payable at the beginning of each year.

Option D—A 15-year rental contract at $11,500 per year; lessor pays taxes, insurance, etc. The Dolphin Company does not have an option to purchase the machines.

The expected economic life of these machines to Dolphin Company is 15 years; residual value at that time is estimated to be $10,000.

Instructions
a Based upon current generally accepted accounting principles, state how the machines and the obligations will appear, if at all, in the balance sheet (at the beginning of the lease period before the first payment is made) of Dolphin Company for each option. Present your answer in the following format; if it should not appear in the statement, write "not shown" opposite the option:

Option	Asset		Liability	
	Account	Amount	Account	Amount

b Explain the recommended treatment in **(a)**. If you have different treatment for one or more of the options, explain the reason for your differing treatment.

19B-4 The Elia Corporation adopted a qualified profit-sharing plan for its employees on January 1, 1966. The trust agreement contains the following provisions:
(1) For each year in which the amount of eligible net earnings equals or exceeds

the profit-sharing base for that year, the corporation shall remit to the trustee an amount equal to 5% of the profit-sharing base for the year plus 10% of any eligible net earnings for the year in excess of the base.

(2) "Eligible net earnings" with respect to any year shall be net income for the year after deducting the payment to the trustee and the provision for income taxes.

(3) An employee shall be eligible to participate in the plan on January 1 of the year following the completion of one full year of employment.

(4) The annual payment to the trustee shall be allocated to the interests of the participants according to the following unit system:

 a For each full calendar year of employment under the plan, each participant shall be entitled to eight units.

 b For each $10 of average weekly pay earned in the current year, based on a 52-week year, the employee shall be entitled to one unit.

(5) 10% of a participant's total interest is vested for each full year of his participation in the plan.

(6) Forfeitures and investment income will be distributed to the remaining participants at the end of each year in proportion to their interests in the plan at the beginning of the year.

In the course of your audit of Elia Corporation as of December 31, 1975, you find that the trustee has submitted the trial balance below but that the corporation's 1975 contribution to the trust has not been computed and allocated to the participants.

ELIA CORPORATION
Profit-sharing Trust
Trial Balance
December 31, 1975

	Debit	Credit
Cash	$ 500	
Investments, Jan. 1, 1975	26,000	
R. Johnson's interest, Jan. 1, 1975		$ 6,512
K. Kegler's interest, Jan. 1, 1975		5,984
J. Wright's interest, Jan. 1, 1975		7,500
M. Penny's interest, Jan. 1, 1975		5,104
Investment income for 1975		1,400
	$26,500	$26,500

The following information also is available:

Employee	Date employed	Date terminated	1975 salary
R. Johnson	Dec. 8, 1965		$ 8,320
K. Kegler	July 1, 1966		7,280
J. Wright	Nov. 20, 1966	Aug. 1, 1975	6,200
M. Penny	Sept. 15, 1971		5,200
J. Rawlings	Aug. 20, 1974	Dec. 26, 1975	800
A. Morris	May 5, 1974		1,100
			$28,900

The 1975 income for Elia Corporation, before deducting the payment to the trustee and the provision for income taxes, is $88,500.

Instructions
a Assume that the profit-sharing base for 1975 is $30,000 and the income tax rate is 50%. Compute the corporation's 1975 contribution to the trust to the nearest dollar and prepare an entry to record the contribution.
b Assume that the answer to part (*a*) is $4,000. Prepare a schedule allocating the 1975 contribution to the various participants.
c Prepare a schedule allocating the amount of any forfeitures and the investment income to the remaining participants.

19B-5 During the course of your audit of a new client, Warehouse Company, for the year ended December 31, 1975, you learned of the following transactions between Warehouse Company and another client, Investment Company:
(1) Warehouse Company completed construction of a warehouse building on its own land in June 1974 at a cost of $500,000. Construction was financed by a construction loan from the Uptown Savings Bank.
(2) On July 1, 1974, Investment Company bought the building from Warehouse Company for $500,000, which Warehouse Company used to discharge its construction loan.
(3) On July 1, 1974, Investment Company borrowed $500,000 from Uptown Savings Bank, to be repaid quarterly over four years plus interest at 5%. A mortgage was placed on the building to secure the loan and Warehouse Company signed as a guarantor of the loan.
(4) On July 1, 1974, Warehouse Company signed a noncancelable 10-year lease of the warehouse building from Investment Company. The lease specified that Warehouse Company would pay $65,000 per year for 10 years, payable in advance on each July 1, and granted an option, exercisable at the end of the 10-year period, permitting Warehouse Company to either (1) purchase the building for $140,000 or (2) renew the lease for an additional 15 years at $25,000 per year and purchase the building for $20,000 at the end of the renewal period. The lease specified that $10,650 of the annual payment of $65,000 would be for insurance, taxes, and maintenance for the following 12 months; if the lease should be renewed, $11,800 of each annual payment would be for insurance, taxes, and maintenance.
(5) The building has a useful life of 40 years and should be depreciated under the straight-line method. (Assume no salvage value.)
(6) Warehouse Company and Investment Company negotiated the lease for a return of 6%. You determine that the present value of all future lease payments is approximately equal to the sales price and that the sale-and-leaseback transaction is in reality only a financing arrangement.

Instructions For balance sheet presentation by Warehouse Company at December 31, 1975, prepare schedules computing the balances for the following items:
a Prepaid insurance, taxes, and maintenance
b Warehouse building, less accumulated depreciation
c Current liabilities arising from the lease
d Long-term liabilities arising from the lease

19B-6 During 1975, Fina-Leas Associates began leasing equipment; the leases are accounted for by use of the financing method. Information regarding leasing arrangements follows:
(1) Fina-Leas Associates leases equipment with terms from three to five years, depending upon the useful life of the equipment. At the expiration of the lease, the equipment will be sold to the lessee at 10% of the lessor's cost, the expected salvage value of the equipment.

(2) The amount of the lessee's monthly payment is computed by multiplying the lessor's cost of the equipment by the payment factor applicable to the term of the lease.

Term of lease	Payment factor
3 years	3.32%
4 years	2.63%
5 years	2.22%

(3) The excess of the gross contract receivable for equipment rentals over the cost (reduced by the estimated salvage value at the termination of the lease) is recognized as revenue over the term of the lease under the sum-of-the-years'-digits method computed on a monthly basis (for example, the sum-of-the-months' digits for four years $= 48 \left(\dfrac{48 + 1}{2} \right)$, or 1,176).

(4) The following leases were entered into during 1975:

Type of machine	Number of machines	Dates of lease	Period of lease	Cost per machine
Milling	10	July 1, 1975–June 30, 1979	4 years	$50,000
Press	6	Sept. 1, 1975–Aug. 31, 1978	3 years	30,000

Instructions
a Prepare for the lessor a schedule of gross contracts receivable for equipment rentals at the dates of the lease for the milling machines and presses.
b Prepare for the lessor a schedule of unearned lease revenue (rounded to nearest dollar) at December 31, 1975.
c Prepare for the lessor a schedule of present dollar value of total contracts receivable for equipment rentals at December 31, 1975. (The present dollar value of the "contracts receivable for equipment rentals" is the outstanding amount of the gross contracts receivable less the unearned lease revenue included therein.) Without prejudice to your solution to part (b), assume that the total unearned lease revenue at December 31, 1975, was $190,000.

CHAPTER 20

Accounting for income taxes

One of the more interesting and controversial areas of corporate accounting is the reporting problem created when accounting income shown on a corporation's income statement differs materially from taxable income reported on its income tax return. We have seen in previous chapters a number of situations which produce such differences. In preparing an income statement to be issued to the public, the accountant is primarily concerned with measuring business operating results in accordance with generally accepted accounting principles. Taxable income, on the other hand, is a legal concept governed by law. In devising tax statutes, Congress is interested not only in meeting the revenue needs of government but in achieving other economic and social objectives. Since the rules for measuring accounting income and taxable income were developed with different objectives in mind, it is not surprising that the results are sometimes materially different.

The nature of the income tax allocation problem[1]

Why do differences between accounting and taxable income produce a reporting problem? To answer this question, consider the highly condensed income statement for the American Company shown at the top of page 754.

[1] For a more extensive discussion of the income tax allocation problem, see the following: Homer A. Black, "Interperiod Allocation of Corporate Income Taxes," *Accounting Research Study No. 9,* AICPA (New York: 1966); David F. Hawkins, "Deferred Taxes: Source of Non-Operating Funds," *Financial Executive* (February 1969), pp. 35–44; Hugo Nurnberg, *Cash Movements Analysis of the Accounting for Corporate Income Taxes,* MSU Business Studies, Michigan State University (East Lansing: 1971); *APB Opinion No. 11,* AICPA (New York: 1967); *APB Opinion No. 23,* AICPA (New York: 1972); and *APB Opinion No. 24,* AICPA (New York: 1972).

AMERICAN COMPANY
Condensed Comparative Income Statement

	Year 2	Year 1
Sales and other revenue	$ 9,000,000	$ 9,000,000
Less:		
Cost of goods sold	(5,400,000)	(5,400,000)
Operating expenses	(2,600,000)	(2,600,000)
Income before income taxes (operating income)	$ 1,000,000	$ 1,000,000
Income tax expense	600,000	300,000
Net income	$ 400,000	$ 700,000

On examining this two-year income statement, the reader immediately wonders why the same operating income (pre-tax income) resulted in such a large difference in the net income figures. Corporate tax rates are changed by Congress from time to time, but in recent years the rates have been such that companies reporting operating income of $1 million should pay about half of this amount in income taxes. Knowing this, the reader would expect the American Company to pay about $500,000 of income taxes each year, and would want to know why taxes were so much smaller than this in Year 1, and so much larger in Year 2. It is apparent that the company's taxable income in each of the two years differed materially from its operating income. By analyzing the source of the differences between operating income as determined from the accounting records and taxable income as defined by tax statutes, we could determine whether income tax expense was reported in accordance with generally accepted accounting principles.

Another possible distortion between operating income and income tax expense may result when an extraordinary gain or loss is included in the income statement. To illustrate this point, consider the following partial income statement for the General Corporation:

GENERAL CORPORATION
Partial Income Statement for Year 1

Income before income taxes (operating income)	$100,000
Income tax expense (45% of $400,000, including extraordinary gain of $300,000)	180,000
Operating loss before extraordinary gain	$(80,000)
Extraordinary gain (before tax effect)	300,000
Net income	$220,000

The picture presented in this income statement is obviously distorted. The operating income absorbs a charge for income taxes at the rate of 180% while the extraordinary gain is reported at the full pre-tax amount of $300,000. An allocation of income taxes between operating income and the extraordinary gain at the effective tax rate of 45% would be more consistent with the matching concept used in the measurement of income and would remove the distorted relationship between operating income and income tax expense.

Terminology used in accounting for income taxes

A brief definition of terms used in accounting for income taxes is necessary at this point.[2]

1 *Income taxes* Taxes based on income as determined under provisions of federal, state, and, in certain cases, foreign tax laws. This term is also used to describe the amount of income taxes (income tax expense) charged to an accounting period.

2 *Pre-tax accounting income* Income for an accounting period before deducting income taxes. *Accounting income* and *income before income taxes* are alternative terms for pre-tax accounting income.

3 *Taxable income* (or *loss*) The excess of taxable revenue over deductible expenses (or the excess of deductible expenses over taxable revenue) for an accounting period. For purposes of this definition, deductible expenses do not include operating loss carrybacks or carryforwards.

4 *Timing differences* Differences between pre-tax accounting income and taxable income for a fiscal period caused by reporting items of revenue or expense in one period for accounting purposes and in an earlier or later period for income tax purposes. Timing differences thus originate in one accounting period and "reverse" in future periods. Most timing differences reduce income taxes that would otherwise be payable currently; other timing differences increase the amount of income taxes payable currently.

5 *Permanent differences* Differences between pre-tax accounting income and taxable income arising from transactions that, under applicable tax laws and regulations, will not be offset by corresponding differences or reversals in future periods.

6 *Tax effects* Differences between actual income taxes payable currently and income tax expense for a period which are attributable to (**a**) revenue or expense transactions which enter into the determination of pre-tax accounting income in one period and into the determination of taxable income in another period, (**b**) deductions or credits that may be carried backward or forward for income tax purposes, and (**c**) prior period adjustments. A permanent difference between accounting and taxable income does not result in a tax effect.

7 *Deferred taxes* Tax effects which are postponed for allocation (either as increases or decreases) to income tax expense of future periods.

8 *Interperiod tax allocation* The process of apportioning income tax expense among accounting periods.

---

[2] Adapted with some modifications from *APB Opinion No. 11*, "Accounting for Income Taxes," AICPA (New York: 1967), pp. 158–160.

9 *Tax allocation within a period* (or *intraperiod tax allocation*) The process of apportioning income tax expense applicable to a given period among income before extraordinary items, extraordinary items, and prior period adjustments.

Assumptions underlying income tax allocation

Income tax allocation procedures are based on the assumption that income taxes represent an expense of doing business and that income taxes are expected to be assessed by taxing authorities in the future. Income measurement on a going-concern basis requires the application of the accrual concept of accounting. Accrual accounting calls for the matching of realized revenue with expired costs for specific accounting periods. Accordingly, income taxes applicable to income recognized currently in the income statement should be estimated and accrued currently without regard to the time of payment; income taxes required to be paid currently but applicable to income which will be reported in the income statement at some future date should be deferred and recognized as an expense when the related income is included in the income statement. Income taxes (or tax reductions) applicable to an extraordinary gain (or loss) are offset against the pre-tax extraordinary gain (or loss) so that the extraordinary item is reported in the income statement *net of the tax effect.*

Sources of differences between accounting and taxable income

The major sources of differences between corporate accounting income and taxable income fall into three categories:

1 *Timing differences in the recognition of revenue and expense* A number of provisions in the income tax law allow (or sometimes require) the taxpayer to recognize revenue and expense at different times than would be appropriate under generally accepted accounting principles. When the corporation has an option, it is likely to choose accounting methods for tax purposes that delay the recognition of revenue and accelerate the recognition of an expense.

2 *Differences due to carryback and carryforward of losses for income tax purposes* The federal income tax law provides that an operating loss in one year may be offset against taxable income of specified previous and future tax years.[3] As a result, an **operating loss** in a given year may result in either a refund of taxes previously paid or a potential reduction of income taxes in future years. For tax purposes, **capital losses** incurred by corporations may be deducted only against capital gains, and capital losses in excess of capital gains in one year may be carried back and offset against net capital gains of the preceding three years. Any unused net capital loss may be carried over and deducted against net capital gains in the succeeding five years.

3 *Permanent differences caused by legal provisions* Some types of revenue and

[3] The current tax law provides that a *net operating loss* must be carried back to the third year before the loss and applied until exhausted against taxable income in successive years through the fifth year after the loss. As in the case of taxable income, there are certain differences between the definition of net operating loss for tax purposes and the accounting concept of such a loss.

expense are recognized for accounting purposes but not for income tax purposes; some are recognized in computing taxable income but are not included in accounting income.

In the following sections we shall consider the accounting implications of each of these three categories. In all illustrations we shall assume an effective corporate tax rate of 45% on ordinary income and 30% on net capital gains to simplify the computations.

Timing differences

In some cases the period in which an item of revenue is taxable or an expense is deductible for income tax purposes differs from the period in which the revenue or expense is recognized in measuring accounting income. When accounting income in any period differs from taxable income as a result of *timing differences,* the divergence will be counterbalanced in future periods by opposite variations between accounting income and taxable income. When accounting income is *larger* than taxable income, the corporation has a deferred income tax liability; when accounting income is *smaller* than taxable income, the corporation prepays income taxes. The recognition of a "deferred income tax liability" and "prepaid income taxes" is made possible by interperiod tax allocation.

Accounting Income Exceeds Taxable Income: Deferred Income Tax Liability
Most timing differences produce accounting income which is larger than taxable income. The two reasons for such a difference are described below:

Revenue or a gain is recognized in the accounting records in the current period but is not taxed until later periods. An example of this situation occurs when a company sells merchandise on the installment basis and recognizes accounting income on the accrual basis when sales are made, but elects to compute taxable income on the basis of cash collections. Another example involves long-term construction contracts when accounting income is measured on the basis of construction in progress (the percentage-of-completion method described in Chapter 9), but taxable income is reported only when the contracts are completed (the completed-contract method described in Chapter 9). Finally, the use of the equity method of accounting for investments in common stocks generally results in timing differences between taxable income and accounting income.[4]

Expense or a loss is deducted for tax purposes in the current period but is not recognized in the accounting records until later periods. An example of this situation occurs when a business chooses an accelerated method to depreciate plant assets for tax purposes but uses the

[4]See Chapter 21 and *APB Opinions No. 23 and No. 24,* AICPA (New York: 1972).

straight-line method for accounting purposes. Similarly, most research and development costs may be deducted currently in computing taxable income and deferred for accounting purposes.

To illustrate the accounting for a deferred income tax liability, assume that the Slow Company acquired for $1 million an item of equipment with a service life of four years. The company uses the sum-of-the-years'-digits method of depreciation for tax purposes and the straight-line method for accounting purposes. Assuming that the company earns $800,000 each year (before depreciation expense and income taxes), the effect of these procedures on pre-tax accounting income and taxable income is shown below:

Year	Accounting income before depreciation and income taxes	Accounting depreciation	Tax return depreciation	Pre-tax accounting income	Taxable income
1	$ 800,000	$ 250,000	$ 400,000	$ 550,000	$ 400,000
2	800,000	250,000	300,000	550,000	500,000
3	800,000	250,000	200,000	550,000	600,000
4	800,000	250,000	100,000	550,000	700,000
Totals	$3,200,000	$1,000,000	$1,000,000	$2,200,000	$2,200,000

Note that the total pre-tax accounting income and taxable income are identical over the four-year period. The journal entries to record income taxes at the rate of 45% are presented below:

Year 1	Income Tax Expense ($550,000 × 45%)	247,500	
	Current Income Tax Liability		180,000
	Deferred Income Tax Liability		67,500
Year 2	Income Tax Expense	247,500	
	Current Income Tax Liability		225,000
	Deferred Income Tax Liability		22,500
Year 3	Income Tax Expense	247,500	
	Deferred Income Tax Liability	22,500	
	Current Income Tax Liability		270,000
Year 4	Income Tax Expense	247,500	
	Deferred Income Tax Liability	67,500	
	Current Income Tax Liability		315,000

A deferred tax liability of $90,000 ($67,500 + $22,500) arises during the first two years when pre-tax accounting income exceeds taxable income and is extinguished during the last two years when the reverse is true. In the income statement for Year 1, income tax expense should be broken down between the amount currently due and the amount deferred, as follows:

SLOW COMPANY
Partial Income Statement for Year 1

Income before income taxes (operating income)		$550,000
Income tax expense:		
Currently due	$180,000	
Deferred	67,500	247,500
Net income		$302,500

Taxable Income Exceeds Accounting Income: Prepaid Income Taxes   The two reasons why taxable income may exceed the amount of income for financial reporting purposes are described below:

Revenue or a gain is taxed in the current period but is not recognized in the accounting records until later periods. Congress is conscious of the fact that taxpaying ability arises when taxpayers have cash with which to pay the tax. Therefore, the tax law tends to make realization of income in liquid form the general test of tax timing. The accounting test of income recognition depends both on realization and on whether a business has earned the income. Revenue received in advance is not included in accounting income until the earning process is complete, but it must usually be reported for tax purposes in the period it is received. For example, suppose that a corporation leases property for five years at $1,000 per year and receives the first and last year's rental in advance. For tax purposes the entire $2,000 must be included in income in the year of receipt; for accounting purposes the $1,000 rent for the last year is carried as deferred revenue on the balance sheet until the fifth year, when it will be included in accounting revenue but will not be subject to income tax.

Expense or a loss is recognized for accounting purposes in the current period but is not deducted for tax purposes until later periods. In general, the accountant records an expense or a loss when evidence that it has been incurred is reasonably clear. For tax purposes, more definite evidence is sometimes required. For example, businesses often guarantee their products against defect for a number of years. On the basis of experience, a company knows that despite its best efforts a certain portion of the goods sold will prove defective, and it may accrue an estimated liability for performance under the guarantee in order to deduct the estimated cost from revenue in the period of sale. For tax purposes, however, this cost is not deductible until it has actually been incurred. Accounting income will therefore be smaller than taxable income in the year the estimated expense is recorded, and counterbalancing will take place in the year in which customers demand performance on the guarantee.

To illustrate the accounting for prepaid income taxes, assume that Fast Company sells a product that requires frequent servicing. At the time of sale, therefore, the company agrees to furnish service by factory representatives over a five-year period without further charge. The company records estimated servicing expense as a percentage of the sales realized in any period. For tax purposes, however, servicing expenses are deductible as incurred. During a given three-year period the estimated and actual servicing expenses were as follows:

Year	Accounting income before servicing expense	Estimated servicing expense	Pre-tax accounting income	Actual servicing expense	Taxable income
1	$ 600,000	$100,000	$ 500,000	$ 20,000	$ 580,000
2	600,000	100,000	500,000	150,000	450,000
3	600,000	100,000	500,000	70,000	530,000
Totals	$1,800,000	$300,000	$1,500,000	$240,000	$1,560,000

Using tax allocation procedures, the Fast Company would accrue income tax expense each period on the basis of accounting income and would record the difference between the current income tax liability and the income tax expense as prepaid income taxes. Journal entries to record income taxes at the rate of 45% for the three years are shown below:

Year 1   Income Tax Expense ($500,000 × 45%)   225,000
       Prepaid Income Taxes   36,000
         Current Income Tax Liability   261,000

Year 2   Income Tax Expense   225,000
       Prepaid Income Taxes   22,500
         Current Income Tax Liability   202,500

Year 3   Income Tax Expense   225,000
       Prepaid Income Taxes   13,500
         Current Income Tax Liability   238,500

In this illustration, accounting and taxable income are not identical over the three-year period, but there is a presumption that the $60,000 excess of estimated servicing expenses over actual servicing expense will counterbalance in future periods. The debit balance of $27,000 ($36,000 − $22,500 + $13,500) in the Prepaid Income Taxes account at the end of Year 3 represents the future tax benefits that will arise when the cost of product servicing is actually incurred and, although not reported as an expense for accounting purposes, will be deducted in computing taxable income.

In the income statement for Year 1, Fast Company will report a $225,000 income tax expense. To meet the standards of good financial reporting, however, the amount of taxes due currently and prepaid income taxes applicable to future periods should be shown separately as follows:

FAST COMPANY
Partial Income Statement for Year 1

Income before income taxes (operating income)		$500,000
Income tax expense:		
Currently due	$261,000	
Less: Prepaid income taxes	36,000	225,000
Net income		$275,000

Alternative Approaches to Interperiod Tax Allocation Three approaches to the accounting for timing differences have been suggested. These are briefly summarized below:

1 *Deferred method* Under this method, the tax effects of current timing differences are computed using tax rates in effect when the deferral of taxes takes place. No adjustments are made to the Deferred Income Tax Liability account or to the Prepaid Income Taxes account for subsequent changes in tax rates. The deferred taxes are then allocated to income tax expense when the timing differences reverse. "The tax effects of transactions which reduce taxes currently payable are treated as deferred credits; the tax effects of transactions which increase taxes currently payable are treated as deferred charges."[5]

2 *Liability method* This is essentially a balance sheet approach to interperiod tax allocation. Its main objective is the correct measurement of the deferred income tax liability. If the tax rates in the year the deferral takes place are different from the expected tax rates in the year in which the payment of taxes is anticipated, the latter rates are used to measure the deferred income tax liability. Furthermore, subsequent changes in income tax rates would require adjustment of the deferred income tax liability to reflect the new tax rates.

3 *Net-of-tax method* Interperiod tax allocation under the net-of-tax method views the tax effects of timing differences as valuation accounts associated with the related assets and liabilities. The tax effects are applied to reduce

[5] *APB Opinion No. 11*, p. 163.

specific assets or liabilities. For example, the deferred income tax "liability" arising from the use of an accelerated depreciation method for income tax purposes would be deducted from plant assets in the balance sheet; similarly the deferred income tax liability arising from the use of the installment method of accounting for income tax purposes would be deducted from installment receivables.

APB Opinion No. 11 requires the use of the deferred method; the Opinion states:

> The Board has concluded that the deferred method of tax allocation should be followed since it provides the most useful and practical approach to interperiod tax allocation and the presentation of income taxes in financial statements.[6]

A minority view of interperiod tax allocation calls for *partial allocation.* Supporters of partial allocation argue that when recurring differences between pre-tax accounting income and taxable income appear to cause an indefinite postponement of tax payments, tax allocation is not required for such differences. For example, assume that a company with a growing investment in depreciable assets uses straight-line depreciation for accounting purposes but accelerated depreciation for computing taxable income. Under the partial allocation approach, the income tax expense for the company would be the tax actually payable for the period.

Advocates of partial allocation thus make a general presumption that income tax expense for accounting purposes should be the tax payable for the period, except for cases in which nonrecurring differences between taxable income and pre-tax accounting income would cause material misstatement of income tax expense and net income. Such an exception is illustrated by the sale of a plant asset at a gain, which is reported in accounting income of the current period but is not taxable until future periods.

The more widely accepted position is that all timing differences between accounting income and taxable income require the *comprehensive allocation* of income taxes. Under comprehensive allocation, income tax expense for a period includes all accruals, deferrals, and estimates necessary to adjust the income taxes actually payable for the period in order to recognize the tax effects of transactions included in accounting income for that period. The tax effects of initial timing differences should be recognized and allocated to those periods in which the initial differences reverse. Comprehensive allocation thus associates tax effects with related transactions as they are reported in the income statement.

The Accounting Principles Board resolved the issue of partial as opposed to comprehensive tax allocation as follows:

> The Board has considered the various concepts of accounting for income taxes and has concluded that comprehensive interperiod tax allocation is an integral part of the determination of income tax expense. Therefore, income tax expense should include the tax effects of revenue and expense transactions included in the determination of pre-tax accounting income. The tax

---

[6] *Ibid.,* p. 169.

effects of those transactions which enter into the determination of pre-tax accounting income either earlier or later than they become determinants of taxable income should be recognized in the periods in which the differences between pre-tax accounting income and taxable income arise and in the periods in which the differences reverse.

The tax effect of a timing difference should be measured by the differential between income taxes computed with and without inclusion of the transaction creating the difference between taxable income and pre-tax accounting income. The resulting income tax expense for the period includes the tax effects of transactions entering into the determination of results of operations for the period. The resulting deferred tax amounts reflect the tax effects which will reverse in future periods. The measurement of income tax expense becomes thereby a consistent and integral part of the process of matching revenues and expenses in the determination of results of operations.[7]

While the position of the Accounting Principles Board effectively established standards for interperiod tax allocation, it by no means eliminated the conceptual controversies associated with this subject. Many accountants and businessmen continue to argue in favor of the liability method, partial allocation of income taxes, and the net-of-tax method for balance sheet presentation of deferred income tax accounts. Interperiod tax allocation will probably continue to be a controversial topic as long as taxes on business income provide the major source of government revenue.

Carryback and carryforward of operating losses

To help equalize the tax burdens of corporations that have regular earnings and those experiencing alternate periods of income and losses, and to aid corporations that suffer losses during the early years of operations, the federal tax law provides that operating losses may be carried back against the taxable income of several previous years and forward against taxable income earned in the years following the loss. The effect of this provision is to create a receivable for a tax refund or potential future tax savings when an operating loss occurs. When an operating loss is carried back or forward, pre-tax accounting income and taxable income (after the operating loss is deducted) will differ for the fiscal period to which the loss is applied. Thus operating losses create special kinds of tax timing differences.

Operating Loss Carryback When an operating loss occurs following a period of profitable operations, a corporation has a claim for a refund of past income taxes that should be recognized in the accounting records in the year in which the loss occurs. On this point, *APB Opinion No. 11* states:

> The tax effects of any realizable loss *carrybacks* should be recognized in the determination of net income (loss) of the loss periods. The tax loss gives rise to a refund (or claim for refund) of past taxes, which is both measurable

[7] *Ibid.*

and currently realizable; therefore the tax effect of the loss is properly recognizable in the determination of net income (loss) for the loss period.[8]

To illustrate the accounting for an operating loss carryback, assume that X Company reports an operating loss of $100,000 for the current year. Because of certain technical adjustments required by tax laws, the company is able to carryback only $90,000 of this loss and offset it against taxable income of a prior year, thus claiming a tax refund of $40,500 (assuming a 45% corporate tax rate). The following journal entry records the effect of the loss carryback:

Receivable—Refund of Income Taxes Previously Paid	*40,500*	
Refund of Income Taxes due to Operating Loss Carryback		*40,500*
To record claim for income taxes previously paid: $90,000 ×		
45% = $40,500.		

The lower portion of the company's income statement for the year in which the operating loss is incurred is shown below:

X COMPANY

Partial Income Statement for Current Year

Operating loss before income tax effect of operating loss carryback	*$(100,000)*
Less: Estimated refund of prior years' income taxes due to carryback	
of loss for tax purposes	*40,500*
Net loss for year, after income tax effect of operating loss carry-	
back	*$ (59,500)*

Operating Loss Carryforward If a corporation must depend on future earnings to use the operating loss as a tax deduction, the accounting for income taxes presents a more difficult problem. Suppose, for example, that Y Corporation experienced a $200,000 operating loss in the first year of operations. A serious question exists whether the probability of future income tax benefit is sufficiently high to warrant an accounting treatment which *anticipates* the effect of the loss carryforward against future taxable income. On this point, the Accounting Principles Board takes the following position:

> The tax effects of loss *carryforwards* also relate to the determination of net income (loss) of the loss periods. However, a significant question generally exists as to realization of the tax effects of the *carryforwards,* since realization is dependent upon future taxable income. Accordingly, the Board has con-

[8] *Ibid.*, p. 172.

cluded that the tax benefits of loss *carryforwards* should not be recognized until they are actually realized, except in unusual circumstances when realization is *assured beyond any reasonable doubt* at the time the loss *carryforwards* arise. When the tax benefits of loss *carryforwards* are not recognized until realized in full or in part in subsequent periods, the tax benefits should be reported in the results of operations of those periods as extraordinary items.[9]

In its first year of operations, then, the Y Corporation would report the full operating loss of $200,000 in its income statement without adjustment for the possible tax benefits in future years. Assuming that the Y Corporation reports an operating income of $240,000 in the second year, the entry to record income tax expense and the effect of the operating loss carryforward would be:

Income Tax Expense 108,000
    Current Income Tax Liability 18,000
    Extraordinary Item: Tax Benefit of Operating Loss Carry-
    forward 90,000
To record income tax expense and effect of operating loss
carryforward. Amounts are determined below:
  Income tax expense: $240,000 × 45% = $108,000
  Current income tax liability: ($240,000 − $200,000) ×
  45% = $18,000
Tax benefit of operating loss carryforward: $200,000 ×
45% = $90,000

The lower section of the income statement for the second year would be presented as follows:

Y CORPORATION
Partial Income Statement for Second Year

Income before income taxes (operating income)	$240,000
Less: Income tax expense (only $18,000 is actually payable after deducting	
$90,000 effect of operating loss carryforward)	108,000
Income before extraordinary item	$132,000
Extraordinary item: Tax benefit of operating loss carryforward	90,000
Net income	$222,000

If the realization of a potential tax benefit of an operating loss carryforward is "assured beyond any reasonable doubt," the benefit should

[9] *Ibid.*, p. 173.

be recognized in the period of the loss by recording an asset (potential tax benefit) and reducing the operating loss by the same amount. Because the prospect of future income is always uncertain, the recognition of a potential tax benefit of an operating loss carryforward in the year of the loss should be considered an exceptional approach. It might apply, for example, in the case of a well-established company with a history of steadily increasing earnings and good future prospects, which incurs a substantial loss because of an unprofitable venture that is not expected to recur. Under these circumstances the probability that the operating loss will produce a future tax benefit may be sufficiently high to warrant recognizing the carryforward tax benefit as an asset.

The amount of the potential tax benefit recognized in the loss period should be computed using the tax rate expected to be in effect at the time of realization. The asset (potential tax benefit of operating loss carryforward) will be reduced by a charge to income tax expense in determining the results of operations in future profitable periods.

Permanent differences between taxable income and pre-tax accounting income

Accounting income may differ from taxable income because certain revenue is exempt from taxation and because allowable tax deductions differ from expenses recognized for financial reporting purposes. These differences are permanent in the sense that they arise not from differences in the timing of revenue and expense but because Congress has seen fit to use the tax law to accomplish certain public policy objectives. Some possible cases are listed below:

Nontaxable Revenue Examples of accounting revenue which is not subject to federal income taxation are: interest received on state or municipal bonds and life insurance proceeds received by a corporation upon death of its officers.

Nondeductible Expenses Examples of business expenses which are not deductible for tax purposes are: amortization of acquired goodwill, premiums paid on life insurance policies in which the corporation is the beneficiary, certain penalties, and illegal payments made for the purpose of influencing legislation.

Tax Deductions That Are Not Expenses The tax law allows some deductions for tax purposes that do not represent actual business expenses. The special deductions for certain dividends received by corporations and the excess of percentage (statutory) depletion over cost depletion allowed on oil and gas and other minerals are prominent examples.

A corporation that has tax-free revenue, nondeductible expenses, or percentage depletion in excess of cost depletion is taxed at an "average" tax rate that differs from the "normal" tax rate applicable to corporations. This is an economic and political fact which should be reflected in the accountant's measurement of income. Since permanent differences between taxable and pre-tax accounting income do not affect other periods, interperiod tax allocation is not required to account for such differences. Because tax laws are subject to change, a material permanent difference should be explained in notes accompanying the financial statements.

Tax allocation within a period

The need for tax allocation within a period (also known as *intraperiod tax allocation*) may arise when extraordinary items are included in net income or a prior period adjustment is recorded in the current period. If extraordinary items and prior period adjustments are taxable or are deductible for tax purposes, income taxes (or tax refunds) should be apportioned between income before extraordinary items, extraordinary items, and prior period adjustments. Income taxes applicable to income before extraordinary items should be based on the difference between revenue and expenses before giving effect to the tax consequences of extraordinary items. Extraordinary gains and losses and prior period adjustments should be reported *net* of the taxes applicable to these items.

To illustrate, assume that in Year 3 the Z Company reports a pre-tax income of $600,000 and incurs a fully deductible extraordinary loss of $500,000. The tax rate is 45%, and the company's income tax is $45,000 (45% of taxable income of $100,000). The comparative summary below shows how Z Company's income statement would appear using intraperiod tax allocation and without intraperiod tax allocation:

	Using intraperiod tax allocation	Without intraperiod tax allocation
Income before income taxes (operating income)	$600,000	$600,000
Income tax expense	270,000	45,000
Income before extraordinary item	$330,000	$555,000
Extraordinary loss:		
Using intraperiod tax allocation: $500,000 −		
($500,000 × 45%)	275,000	
Without intraperiod tax allocation		500,000
Net income	$ 55,000	$ 55,000

The greater clarity using intraperiod tax allocation in this case is apparent. The tax allocation presentation shows the after-tax effect of the extraordinary loss and the normal impact of taxes on operating income. If tax allocation is not used, the reader of the income statement will question the relationship between the operating income of $600,000 and the disproportionately low income tax expense of $45,000. Without tax allocation, the income before the extraordinary item and the extraordinary item are both overstated by $225,000 ($500,000 × 45%), the tax effect of the extraordinary loss. Using intraperiod tax allocation, income taxes would be recorded as follows:

Income Tax Expense ($600,000 × 45%)...............	270,000	
Extraordinary Loss (Tax Effect)		225,000
Current Income Tax Liability..................		45,000
To record income tax effect on operating income and extraordinary loss.		

Note that the tax effect is recorded as an offset to the Extraordinary Loss account, which was previously recorded at $500,000; it would, of course, be possible to record the tax effect in a separate account. In either case, the extraordinary loss should be reported in the income statement net of taxes, that is, $275,000, with appropriate disclosure of the current income tax liability and the tax effect on the loss.

To illustrate a different situation, involving an extraordinary gain and a prior period adjustment, assume that Z Company reports the following in Year 4:

Income before income taxes (fully taxable at 45%)	$300,000
Extraordinary capital gain (taxable at 30%).................	800,000
Prior period adjustment—settlement of dispute involving contract completed in Year 1 (fully taxable at 45%)	200,000

The presentation of these items in the income statement and the statement of retained earnings using intraperiod tax allocation and without intraperiod tax allocation is shown on page 769.

Failure to apply intraperiod tax allocation procedures in this case not only materially distorts the results from normal operations but also understates net income by $90,000, the tax applicable to the prior period adjustment.

Assuming that the extraordinary gain and the prior period adjustment were previously recorded in the accounts (before recognizing the tax

	Using intraperiod tax allocation	Without intraperiod tax allocation
Income statement:		
Income before income taxes	$300,000	$ 300,000
Income tax expense	135,000	465,000*
Income (loss) before extraordinary item	$165,000	$(165,000)
Extraordinary gain:		
Using intraperiod tax allocation, $800,000 −		
($800,000 × 30%)	560,000	
Without intraperiod tax allocation		800,000
Net income	$725,000	$ 635,000
Statement of retained earnings:		
Prior period adjustment—increase in beginning		
balance in retained earnings	$110,000	$ 200,000

```
* Income tax expense, $300,000 × 45% . . . . . . . . . . . . . . . . . . . .   $135,000
  Tax on capital gain, $800,000 × 30%  . . . . . . . . . . . . . . . . . . .    240,000
  Tax on prior period adjustment, $200,000 × 45% . . . . . . . . . . . . . .     90,000
     Total current income tax liability . . . . . . . . . . . . . . . . . . .   $465,000
```

effects), income taxes at the end of Year 4, using intraperiod tax allocation, should be recorded by the Z Company as follows:

```
Income Tax Expense . . . . . . . . . . . . . . . . . . . . . . . . . .  135,000
Extraordinary Gain (Tax Effect) . . . . . . . . . . . . . . . . . . .  240,000
Prior Period Adjustment (Tax Effect) . . . . . . . . . . . . . . . .   90,000
     Current Income Tax Liability . . . . . . . . . . . . . . . . . .            465,000
To record income tax effect on operating income, extraordi-
nary gain, and prior period adjustment.
```

Since extraordinary items and prior period adjustments create certain tax consequences, tax allocation within a period is simply an effort to match tax expense (or tax credits) with these special items. In this way, extraordinary items and prior period adjustments are reported net of taxes—at amounts representing the net economic impact of such items.

Another intraperiod tax allocation problem arises when a change in an accounting principle calls for the recognition of a *cumulative effect* of the change in the income statement of the current year. Accounting changes are discussed in Chapter 22.

Presentation of tax accounts in financial statements

Thus far we have assumed that tax allocation which stems from differences in the timing of revenue and expense results in either a liability, Deferred Income Tax Liability, or an asset, Prepaid Income Taxes. Whether these accounts meet the definition of liabilities and assets is an issue worth considering.

A deferred income tax liability arises when a corporation recognizes income for financial reporting purposes before it is taxed, either because revenue has been reported as earned before it is subject to tax or because expenses not recognized on the books have been deducted in computing taxable income. There is, of course, no existing debt to the government for taxes on future earnings which may or may not materialize. However, we have previously defined liabilities to include future outlays that result from current or past events that can be measured with reasonable accuracy. Assuming continuing successful operation of a business, it is reasonable to include in this definition the increased taxes that will follow from having recognized income before it is taxed. Even though the deferred income tax liability may not be paid for many years, the Accounting Principles Board has stated that "deferred taxes should not be accounted for on a discounted basis."[10]

The classification of prepaid income taxes as an asset rests on the assumption that there will be a future tax benefit to the corporation. At some later time the corporation will realize revenue which will not be subject to tax, or it will have a tax deduction which will not be reported as an accounting expense.[11] The asset represents the amount of tax that has already been paid on income to be reported in the income statement in future periods.

The Accounting Principles Board emphasized the "deferred" characteristics of the tax accounts resulting from interperiod tax allocation procedures when it established the following guidelines for presenting such accounts in the balance sheet.

> Deferred charges and deferred credits relating to timing differences represent the cumulative recognition given to their tax effects and as such do not represent receivables or payables in the usual sense. They should be classified in two categories—one for the net current amount and the other for the net noncurrent amount. This presentation is consistent with the customary dis-

[10] *APB Opinion No. 10,* "Omnibus Opinion—1966," AICPA (New York: 1966), p. 145.

[11] For example, a few years ago the Sperry and Hutchinson Company reported "future federal tax benefits" of over $25 million as a current asset. This amount was created as a result of the difference between the provision for stamp redemption expense recognized for accounting purposes and the lesser actual amount of stamp redemption expense allowed in computing taxable income.

tinction between current and noncurrent categories and also recognizes the close relationship among the various deferred tax accounts, all of which bear on the determination of income tax expense. The current portions of such deferred charges and credits should be those amounts which relate to assets and liabilities classified as current. Thus, if installment receivables are a current asset, the deferred credits representing the tax effects of uncollected installment sales should be a current item; if an estimated provision for warranties is a current liability, the deferred charge representing the tax effect of such provision should be a current item.[12]

The Board does not permit the use of the net-of-tax method of reporting deferred tax accounts as elements of valuation of assets or liabilities.

Claims for refunds of taxes previously paid or offsets to future taxes arising from the recognition of the tax effects of operating loss carrybacks or carryforwards should be classified either as current or noncurrent, depending on the expected period of realization.

The requirements for reporting income tax accounts in the balance sheet may be summarized as follows:

Current assets:

1 *Prepaid income taxes (related to current liabilities such as estimated warranties outstanding which will be satisfied within one year or the operating cycle of the business)*

2 *Claim for refund of income taxes previously paid*

3 *Potential tax benefit of operating loss (if current benefits are assured beyond any reasonable doubt)*

Noncurrent assets:

1 *Prepaid income taxes (related to noncurrent liabilities such as long-term warranties outstanding)*

2 *Potential tax benefit of operating loss carryforward (if benefits are assured beyond any reasonable doubt)*

Current liabilities:

1 *Current income tax liability (balance of tax due on income taxable currently)*

2 *Deferred income tax liability (related to current assets such as receivables from installment sales or long-term construction in progress)*

Noncurrent liabilities:

1 *Deferred income tax liability (related to timing differences, such as those caused by use of an accelerated depreciation method for income tax purposes)*

In the income statement or in the accompanying notes, the taxes currently payable, the tax effects of timing differences, and the tax effects of operating losses should be disclosed. These amounts should be allocated to income before extraordinary items and to extraordinary items. The tax benefit of an operating loss carryforward not previously recorded

---

[12]*APB Opinion No. 11*, p. 178.

should be reported as an extraordinary item in the period in which it is realized. In addition, notes accompanying the financial statements should include disclosure of unused operating loss carryforwards (along with expiration dates), reasons for significant variations in the customary relationships between income tax expense and pre-tax accounting income, and any other factors relating to income taxes which the reader would find useful in evaluating current earnings and in forecasting future earnings of the company.

The student should refer to Appendix B to see how some corporations report income tax accounts and the related notes in their financial statements.

Evaluation of income tax allocation

We have seen that differences between accounting and taxable income arise from several sources. No allocation problem arises from permanent differences between accounting and taxable income. The allocation of income taxes to extraordinary items and to prior period adjustments, and also the recognition of the income tax benefits of operating loss carrybacks as extraordinary gains, are almost universally accepted. Few people question the desirability of recognizing the income tax effect of operating loss carryforwards when the tax benefits are assured beyond any reasonable doubt. Thus the controversy over income tax allocation centers on interperiod tax allocation when there are differences in the timing of revenue and expenses.

Arguments in Favor of Interperiod Tax Allocation The basic premises on which those who favor income tax allocation rest their case may be summarized as follows:

1 Income taxes are admittedly a period charge since there is no value inherent in their payment that will contribute to future revenue. It is true that a business receives many valuable services from the government, but it receives these services without regard to the size of the tax bill. The issue then is not that of allocating the tax charge into deferred and expired portions, but of determining when the income tax accrues. The income tax liability to the government accrues because a corporation earns income as defined by the tax regulations. Major differences between accounting and taxable income are those of timing in the recognition of revenue and expenses. The earning of income is therefore the basic cause which gives rise to an income tax levy, and the tax charge which should be applied in measuring periodic income is the tax that will have to be paid on each period's earnings, independent of the time of payment. In order to avoid misleading fluctuations in net income, income taxes are matched against income when it is included in the income statement.

2 Differences between taxable and accounting income due to timing of revenue and expenses are temporary. A tax saving due to timing is a postponement of the tax, thus creating a probable future cash outlay based on a current or past event. Similarly, paying taxes on income that will be recognized on the books at some later date makes it probable that the corporation will earn tax-free income in future years. This prospect represents an expected future economic benefit, the right to which results from a current or past transaction. These probable future outlays and expected future benefits qualify as liabilities and assets, respectively, within the accepted meanings of these terms.

3 Future income tax expectations are sufficiently objective to warrant recognition in the accounts whenever the probability is high that: **(a)** tax rates will remain at substantially current levels in the foreseeable future; **(b)** the company will continue in business and continue to earn taxable income in the majority of future years. These conditions simply establish that timing offsets will occur substantially as expected. The assumption that tax rates will seldom fluctuate widely is borne out by past experience. The assumption that the corporation will earn taxable income in most future years is less certain, but continued profitable operation is the expectation for most major corporations. The existence of the operating loss carryback and carryforward provisions in the tax law adds weight to this assumption, since it assures that the timing offsets will occur even though a corporation may not earn taxable income in one particular year.

Arguments against Interperiod Tax Allocation The questions of uncertainty about future tax rates and the existence of future taxable income have not been major issues in the controversy. Opposition to tax allocation is based primarily on two points: (1) the nature of income taxes, and (2) the fact that timing differences may not be temporary.

1 Income taxes have a number of peculiarities. First, they emerge only if income is earned; secondly, they are based on taxable income which diverges from accounting income in a number of respects. This line of reasoning leads to two conclusions: **(a)** Income taxes are not an expense but an involuntary distribution of income since they are determined only after income emerges; and **(b)** the amount of income taxes associated with the operations of any period is the legal tax liability for that period, since income taxes are based on the legal concept of taxable income rather than accounting income.

2 Most cases of tax deferral or prepayment due to timing differences are continuous rather than discrete. When we view the taxable income of a corporation as a whole, the shifting of taxes in time (particularly the postponement of taxes) tends to be a permanent rather than a temporary shift, because as fast as one deferral is reversed another arises to take its place. This argument is raised most frequently with respect to one area of tax timing differences, the case where a corporation adopts accelerated depreciation methods for tax purposes, but not on its books. For example, a stable company purchasing about the same amount of depreciable assets each year will realize a tax postponement in the year that accelerated depreciation is adopted and this postponement is never offset in future years so long as the company continues to replace its depreciable assets at a steady rate. If a company acquires a larger amount of depreciable assets each year, the total difference between tax depreciation and book depreciation will continue to increase so long as depreciable asset acquisitions increase. However, an assumption of unending growth is a dubious one.

If differences between accounting and taxable income produce an indefinite postponement of income taxes, the question naturally arises whether accountants can justify recording deferred taxes as an expense and liability. If it is probable that a corporation will not actually have to pay the deferred taxes, we are faced with a possibility of tax forgiveness, not tax postponement. Some empirical evidence supporting this conclusion is provided in a study involving the tax allocation experience of 100 companies over a period of 12 years.[13] Of the 100 corporations surveyed, 57 followed tax allocation procedures during one or more of the 12 years. During the 12-year period, the amount of charges against income for deferred taxes was almost $1 billion, and the amount of credits to income tax expense for payment of deferred taxes was about $20 million.

The response to this kind of evidence is the "roll-over" argument. Using accelerated depreciation as an example, if we look at a company as a whole and at depreciation in the aggregate, it is likely that the postponement of taxes is indefinite and may have no present value as an obligation. If we look at individual asset acquisitions, however, we see a pattern of deferring taxes in the early life of these assets, the subsequent payment of these deferred taxes in later years, and the simultaneous deferral of taxes relating to new assets acquired in those later years. The situation is somewhat analogous to accounts payable and other interest-free current liabilities. For a company as a whole, current liabilities are permanent in nature and tend to increase in the aggregate as the company grows. When we look at individual accounts, however, we see a continuing turnover of the debt as one series of invoices is paid and another series arises to take its place. However, no one suggests that accounts payable be omitted from the balance sheet merely because the total liability grows larger year by year.

Some accountants contend that the roll-over argument is not valid, since there are vital differences between accounts payable and deferred tax accruals. Accounts payable arise from actual transactions in which goods and services are received. The amount and due date of the obligation are set forth clearly on a source document that serves as evidence of the transaction. The legal necessity of making payment is not conditioned on the profitability of future operations. On the other hand, the deferred tax liability rests on the hypothesis that the consequence of a current tax reduction is the probability that income taxes to be paid will be higher in later years. Therefore, it is argued, tax allocation accounting should occur only when it is demonstrated that current lower tax payments will probably result in higher cash outflows for taxes within a span of time that is relevant to users of financial statements.

The controversy over tax allocation cannot be resolved simply by testing the arguments against the yardstick of logic. The validity of the roll-over analogy, for example, depends to a great extent on how one views the series of events that produces an income tax obligation. In the case of accounts payable, actual cash payments are regularly made to creditors, even though other payables are taking the place of those liquidated. In the income tax case, the obligation for past taxes and the

[13]"Is Generally Accepted Accounting for Income Taxes Possibly Misleading Investors?" Price Waterhouse & Co. (New York: 1967).

deferral of present taxes involve the same creditor—Uncle Sam; therefore, these two events offset without giving rise to invoices and canceled checks. Does this difference make the analogy invalid? There is at least room for an honest difference of opinion.

REVIEW QUESTIONS

1 What are the objectives of generally accepted accounting principles in their application to the income statement? What are the objectives of income tax laws?

2 Differentiate between *interperiod tax allocation* and *tax allocation within a period.*

3 What fundamental assumptions are necessary in the implementation of income tax allocation?

4 What are three basic sources of differences between accounting income and taxable income?

5 Describe two situations which result, under tax allocation procedures, in a Deferred Income Tax Liability account.

6 Describe two situations which result, under tax allocation procedures, in a Prepaid Income Taxes account.

7 Explain the following interperiod tax allocation approaches:
a Deferred method
b Liability method
c Net-of-tax method

8 What is meant by an *operating loss carryback* and an *operating loss carryforward?*

9 Explain the different accounting problems that arise in accounting for an operating loss carryback and an operating loss carryforward.

10 Describe three situations which produce a permanent difference between taxable income and pre-tax accounting income. Give an example of each.

11 Explain how each of the following accounts should be classified (for example, current assets or current liability) in the balance sheet:
a Deferred Income Tax Liability
b Prepaid Income Taxes
c Receivable—Refund of Income Taxes Previously Paid
d Potential Tax Benefit of Operating Loss Carryforward (if recorded)

12 What kind of information regarding income taxes should be included in notes accompanying the financial statements?

13 Some proponents of tax allocation draw an analogy between the Deferred Income Tax Liability account and the Accounts Payable controlling account. Explain how this analogy is used to support the case for tax allocation procedures.

14 Briefly list the arguments for and against interperiod tax allocation.

EXERCISES

Ex. 20-1 In 1975, the Privy Corporation reports $200,000 of income before income taxes in its income statement but only $30,000 on its tax return. In 1976, income before income taxes is $300,000 and taxable income is $400,000.

Prepare the entry to record income tax expense and income taxes payable for 1976, assuming that timing differences were responsible for the disparity between accounting income and taxable income. Assume that the corporate tax rate is 45%.

Ex. 20-2 Company X reports taxable income of $300,000 in Year 1 and $400,000 in Year 2. Income before income taxes was $200,000 in Year 1 and $500,000 in Year 2. The differences between taxable income and the income before income taxes resulted from the inclusion of $100,000 of income on the tax return for Year 1 which was not considered realized for accounting purposes until Year 2.

Assuming that the corporate income tax rate is 45%, prepare the lower section of the income statement for Year 1 and Year 2, (1) using tax allocation and (2) without tax allocation.

Ex. 20-3 The accounting income and taxable income for C. L. Haggard, Inc., for a three-year period were as follows:

Year	Accounting income	Taxable income
1	$ 80,000	$ 40,000
2	110,000	130,000
3	120,000	140,000

Research and development costs in the amount of $60,000 were deducted on the tax return, but only one-third of such costs was deducted as an expense for financial reporting purposes. Tax rates are 22% on the first $25,000 and 48% on income in excess of $25,000.

Prepare the entries required for each year in order to properly allocate income taxes resulting from the timing difference in the accounting for research and development costs.

Ex. 20-4 The accounting and taxable income for the Simms Corporation over a three-year period follows:

Year	Accounting income	Taxable income
1	$100,000	$134,000
2	100,000	98,000
3	100,000	98,000

The differences between accounting income and taxable income are explained as follows:

(1) Taxable income in Year 1 includes $36,000 of rental revenue which for financial reporting purposes was recorded as earned at the rate of $12,000 per year.

(2) Amortization of goodwill at the rate of $10,000 per year is recorded for financial reporting purposes but is not deductible in arriving at taxable income. Amortization of goodwill does not give rise to a timing difference for income tax allocation purposes.

Prepare entries required for each year to properly allocate income taxes. Assume that income taxes are 50% of taxable income.

Ex. 20-5 The income statement for the Rupee Corporation shows the following results for the first three years of its operations:

Year 1: Operating loss (before income taxes) .... $(100,000)

Year 2: Operating income (before income taxes)   240,000

Year 3: Operating loss (before income taxes) ....   (200,000)

The company operates in a cyclical and highly competitive industry.

Prepare entries for each year to recognize the tax effects of net operating loss carryforwards or carrybacks. Assume that net operating losses as reported are fully allowed for income tax purposes and that the income tax rate is 45%.

Ex. 20-6 The Pearl Company reports income before income taxes of $200,000 and a fully deductible extraordinary loss of $150,000 for Year 1. Prepare a journal entry to record the tax effect on the pre-tax income and on the extraordinary loss. Show how the foregoing information should be presented in the income statement. Assume that corporate taxes are levied at the rate of 45% and that the tax effect of the extraordinary loss is credited directly to the loss account.

Ex. 20-7 The Oyster Corporation reports income before income taxes of $300,000 and a capital gain of $1.2 million. Prepare a journal entry to record the tax effect on the pre-tax income and on the extraordinary gain. (Record the tax effect on the extraordinary gain as a debit to the gain account.) Show how the foregoing information should be presented in the income statement. Assume that the tax rate is 45% on income before income taxes and 30% on capital gains.

Ex. 20-8 Prepare a schedule showing the computation of (a) the actual income tax liability and (b) income tax expense for Years 1, 2, and 3. Assume that the accounting income computed after all adjustments and corrections was $180,000 for Year 1, $212,000 for Year 2, and $252,000 for Year 3. The income tax rate was 40% in each of the three years. Assume that depreciation expense, rent revenue, and interest earned have been included in accounting income and taxable income for Year 1 through Year 3, as follows:

	Accounting income	Taxable income
Depreciation expense:		
Year 1	$50,000	$70,000
Year 2	54,000	71,000
Year 3	58,000	68,000
Rent revenue:		
Year 1	9,000	9,500
Year 2	9,000	8,500
Interest earned on municipal bonds:		
Year 1	3,000	–0–
Year 2	4,000	–0–
Year 3	3,800	–0–

SHORT CASES FOR ANALYSIS AND DECISION

Case 20-1 The latest partial income statement and the related note for Rath Packing Company is shown on page 778.

Income before provision in lieu of federal income tax	$7,277,326
Provision in lieu of federal income tax (Note 3)	3,490,000
Income before extraordinary credit........................	$3,787,326
Credit arising from utilization of net operating loss carryforward (Note 3).....................................	3,490,000
Net income	$7,277,326

Note 3—Federal income tax:
No federal income tax is payable with respect to results of operations because of available net operating loss carryforward from prior years. However, in the income statement, a provision in lieu of the federal income tax that would have been required in the absence of the net operating loss carryforward has been charged to income before extraordinary credit, and the credit arising from utilization of the net operating loss carryforward has been reflected as an extraordinary item.

Instructions
a Give a supporting argument in favor of the procedure used to account for the tax effect of the net operating loss carryforward.
b Prepare the journal entry that was required to reflect the tax effect of the net operating loss carryforward. Use the account titles as they appear in the income statement of Rath Packing Company.
c Assuming that Rath Packing Company had recognized the full potential tax benefit of the net operating loss in prior years, how would the income statement differ for the latest period?

Case 20-2 The Raven Construction Company was organized early in Year 1 after Poe Raven was awarded a contract to build a major section of a highway in Alaska. The completion of the contract will take four years, and the company does not plan to bid on additional contracts. All costs incurred by the company will be directly chargeable to the highway contract; in other words, the company will not record any selling and general expenses.
The net profit on the contract is estimated at $100,000. Under the percentage-of-completion method of accounting, $25,000 of the net profit would be recognized in each of the four years. Income taxes of $5,500 ($25,000 × 22%) would be paid on March 15 of each year starting in Year 2 if the percentage-of-completion method were adopted for income tax purposes. If the completed-contract method were adopted for income tax purposes, a tax of $41,500 ($100,000 × 48% − $6,500) would be paid on March 15, Year 5.

Instructions
a Assuming that the company considers 8% a fair rate of return before income taxes, prepare a schedule showing whether the company should use the completed-contract or the percentage-of-completion method of accounting for tax purposes. Compute the net advantage of the method you recommend, in terms of dollar savings, at March 15, Year 5. The amount of an ordinary annuity of four rents of $1 invested at 8% is $4.5061.
b Assuming that the company had a large amount of income each year from other sources and that the profit on the long-term contract is taxed at the marginal rate of 48%, what method of accounting would you recommend? What would be the net advantage at March 15, Year 5, if money is worth 8%?

Case 20-3 Mesa Mining Company received $25,000 in 1974 as a rental advance on one of its mining properties. Under income tax law the advance is subject to federal income tax in 1974, although the company did not report the advance as revenue in its accounting records until 1975.
In 1974, the company reported taxable income of $125,000, paying income taxes of $53,500 (22% on the first $25,000 of taxable income and 48% on the

$100,000 remainder). The controller reported $100,000 as the company's operating income for 1974 and showed the amount of income taxes applicable to
the rental advance (48% of $25,000) as an asset under the heading "prepaid
income taxes."

In 1975, the company suffered a decline in income as a result of severe
declines in world metal prices, and its operations resulted in an operating income
of only $25,000, including revenue from the rental advance received in 1974.
When the controller of the company presented the company's 1975 income
statement to the president, the latter commented, "I thought you said the effect
of income tax allocation was to show in each year a tax expense that bore a
normal relation to reported operating income. You report operating income of
$25,000 and show income taxes at $12,000. If we had taxable income of only
$25,000 we would pay only $5,500 in taxes. I realize we broke even for tax
purposes this year and won't actually pay any tax, but I think your tax allocation
procedures are off someplace."

Instructions
a Prepare a partial comparative income statement for 1974 and 1975, starting
with operating income and following the controller's approach.
b What is the issue implicit in the president's question? How would you reply
if you were the controller?

PROBLEMS

Group A

20A-1 Shown below is the computation of the taxable income and the current income
tax liability for the Taxi Cab Company for the year just ended:

Income before income taxes (per books)	$200,000
Accelerated depreciation per tax return in excess of straight-line depreciation per books	(20,000)
Percentage depletion per tax return in excess of cost depletion per books (this is a permanent difference)	(30,000)
Taxable income	$150,000
Computation of current income tax liability:	
On taxable income ($150,000 × 45%)	$ 67,500
Capital gain tax on disposal of property ($100,000 × 30%)	30,000
Total current income tax liability.	$ 97,500

Instructions
a Prepare a compound journal entry to record income taxes for the year, in
accordance with **APB Opinion No. 11.** The capital gain tax on the disposal
of property not used in the business should be recorded in the Extraordinary
Gain on Disposal of Property account.
b Prepare a partial income statement starting with income before income taxes
and showing the gain on the disposal of property as an extraordinary item.

20A-2 In each of the last three years the taxable income reported by the De Mers
Corporation for income tax purposes has differed from the income before income
taxes reported on its income statement. The record is as follows:

Year	Income statement	Tax return
1	$170,000	$125,000
2	90,000	105,000
3	85,000	100,000

Included in net income as reported on the income statement in Year 1 was $20,000 of income that is not subject to income tax at any time. Also during Year 1, $25,000 of deductions were taken for income tax purposes that will not be reported as expenses on the company's books until later years. In Year 3, the company incurred an accounting loss of $8,000, which is reflected on the income statement; for income tax purposes only $3,000 of this loss was deducti- ble. In all other respects income reported on the income statement is ultimately subject to income taxes. You may assume that the company is subject to a combined state and federal income tax rate of 45% on all taxable income.

Instructions
a Prepare journal entries necessary to record income taxes in each of the three years and to make an interperiod allocation of income taxes on the basis of the information provided. Show supporting computations.
b Assuming that all income taxes due (as reported on the company's tax returns) were paid during the year following their accrual, what are the balances at the end of Year 3 in the company's tax liability accounts (both current and deferred)?

20A-3 The following comparative income statement was presented to Pat Jacobs, president of the Jacobs Corporation, covering operations for a two-year period:

	Year 2	Year 1
Net sales	$990,000	$900,000
Cost of goods sold	590,000	530,000
Gross profit on sales	$400,000	$370,000
Operating expenses	250,000	280,000
Income before income taxes (operating income)	$150,000	$ 90,000
Income tax expense	97,600	17,500
Net income	$ 52,400	$ 72,500

After examining the statement, Pat Jacobs frowned, "When I send this state- ment to my father (who owned 30% of the common stock) he will never understand why net income fell in the face of a substantial increase in operating income."
"There are two reasons," commented the controller. "You will remember that last year (Year 1) we took a $40,000 fully deductible loss on the sale of the North Fork warehouse; and this year (Year 2) we had a capital gain of $107,000 (taxed at 30%) when we sold our Gamin Company stock and used the proceeds to build a new warehouse. Both these transactions were reported in the statement of retained earnings."
"I'll have trouble getting that across to father," Pat Jacobs replied. "He knows we're subject to federal tax of 48% on all income over $25,000 and 22% on the first $25,000. A fivefold increase in income taxes in the income statement is going to be confusing to him. Can't you revise the income statement so that the reasons for these odd tax figures will be apparent?"

Instructions Prepare a revised comparative income statement that will, in your opinion, meet the objections raised by Pat Jacobs.

20A-4 The Aksen Manufacturing Company presents you with the following information for the year ended December 31, 1975:

Sales	$2,000,000
Cost of goods sold	1,100,000*
Operating expenses	400,000
Uninsured loss of machinery due to earthquake, fully deductible for income	
tax purposes	200,000
Taxable prior period adjustment—income applicable to 1973	150,000
Income tax expense for 1975	?

*Includes depreciation of $100,000 on a straight-line basis; however, depreciation for income tax purposes is $140,000.

A corporate income tax rate of 45% is applicable on all items above.

Instructions

a Compute the amount of income taxes currently payable by the Aksen Manufacturing Company as a result of activities in 1975.

b Prepare a compound journal entry to record income taxes for 1975 (including allocation of taxes between operating income, the extraordinary item, and the prior period adjustment). Assume that the Earthquake Loss account shows a pre-tax debit balance of $200,000 and that the Prior Period Adjustment account shows a pre-tax credit balance of $150,000.

c Prepare an income statement and a separate statement of retained earnings for 1975. The balance in retained earnings at the beginning of the year was $675,000. No dividends were declared during the year.

20A-5 Independent Forwarding, Inc., began business on January 1, Year 1. Anticipating a growth in traffic over the next few years, the company has developed plans for the purchase of trucks as shown below:

Date of acquisition (beginning of year)	Cost of new equipment	Salvage value	Estimated service life, years
1	$100,000	$10,000	5
2	220,000	25,000	5
3	300,000	30,000	5
4	50,000	5,000	5
5	10,000	1,000	5
6	25,000	2,500	5

The controller of the company is studying the question of depreciation policies on this equipment. He feels that the company should adopt the sum-of-the-years'-digits method of depreciation for income tax purposes but should use the straight-line method for financial reporting purposes. If this policy were adopted, pre-tax income for accounting purposes would differ from taxable income, and this difference would require, in the controller's opinion, the use of tax allocation procedures in the company's accounting records.

Instructions

a Prepare a schedule showing the difference between taxable income and accounting income that will result in each year of the six-year period if the controller adopts the policy described above.

b Determine the balance that would appear in the Deferred Income Tax Liability account at the close of the sixth year if tax allocation procedures were followed, assuming that an income tax rate of 50% is applicable.

c Assuming that the company's accounting records show pre-tax income of $50,000 in Year 1 and $90,000 in Year 6, prepare partial income statements (starting with income before income taxes) for these two years showing how tax allocation should be disclosed.

Group B

20B-1 Assume the following general fact situation: The Esso Company's ordinary income before income taxes is $200,000 for the current year. The company is subject to a flat-rate income tax of 45% on all income. The company allocates income taxes in its financial statements.

Each of the four independent situations below describes an item of revenue or expense which was included in the computation of $200,000 accounting income stated above, but which is treated differently for income tax purposes:

(1) The company reported on its income statement $40,000 of long-term contract profit, one-fourth of which is reported for tax purposes in the current year.

(2) The company reported on its tax return $58,000 of royalties received in advance; only $8,000 of this royalty was earned during the current year.

(3) The company deducted $52,000 of estimated guarantee and product warranty expenses in computing accounting income; actual costs incurred during the current year, deductible for tax purposes, were $12,000.

(4) The company deducted $75,000 of research and development costs in determining taxable income; these costs are being amortized on its accounting records over a five-year period.

Instructions

a For each of the four independent cases described above, prepare the journal entry that should be made to record income tax expense for the current year, assuming that the company follows interperiod tax allocation procedures.

b What amount of net income will the company report in its income statement in each of the four situations?

20B-2 The Pan-Coat Corporation manufactures bread-wrapping equipment and grants a five-year warranty on its products. The Estimated Liability for Product Warranty account on the company's books shows the following transactions for the first year of operations:

Balance at beginning of current year	$ –0–
Add: Estimated cost of warranty applicable to sales of current year	
(charged to Product Warranty Expense)	150,000
Less: Actual cost of servicing warranty claims during current year	(90,000)
Balance at end of current year	$ 60,000

The financial records of the company were audited for the first time at the close of the current year, in connection with an application for a bank loan. The auditor, after reviewing the company's unsettled warranty claims and claim experience, determined that the balance in the Estimated Liability for Product Warranty account at the end of the year should be $170,000.

The company reported income before income taxes of $500,000. The balance in the Income Tax Expense account at the end of the year is $160,000, representing quarterly payments of estimated income tax expense for the current year. For income tax purposes, only the actual cost of servicing warranty claims may be deducted. Accounting and taxable income are identical except for this difference in the timing of product warranty expense.

Instructions As the auditor, prepare the necessary adjusting journal entries to (1) adjust the Estimated Liability for Product Warranty account and (2) provide for an allocation of income taxes. Assume a 50% tax rate, and support each entry with detailed computations. You may assume that the books have not been closed.

20B-3 In Year 5, Ute Oil Company had sales of $800,000 and income of $300,000 before income taxes. Straight-line depreciation expense of $80,000 was recorded on the books, but accelerated depreciation for tax purposes amounted to $124,000. Cost-based depletion of $100,000 was deducted in arriving at operating income but a deduction for depletion equal to 22% of sales was allowed on the tax return.

Income before income taxes did not include a gain of $40,000 from the sale of land on the installment basis, which was reported as an extraordinary item. Only one-fourth of the sales price was collected during the year, therefore only $10,000 of the gain was taxable at 30%.

Ordinary income was taxed at 22% of the first $25,000 and 48% of the balance. An operating loss of $50,000 and a capital loss of $8,000 were carried forward from Year 4 and are available to reduce the tax liability for Year 5.

Instructions
a Prepare a compound journal entry to record income taxes for Year 5. An asset had not been established for the loss carryforwards. Deferred taxes are recognized for the timing differences between accounting income and taxable income.
b Prepare an income statement for Year 5.

20B-4 The controller of the Merced Company handed his assistant a sheet of paper on which appeared the information shown below. "Here's the story on our accounting and taxable income for the current year," he said, "I'd like you to put these figures together into an income statement and a separate statement of retained earnings."

Computation of Accounting Income for the Current Year

	Debit	Credit
Sales (net).		$750,000
Interest earned on municipal bonds		10,000
Prior period adjustment—refund of income taxes pursuant to audit by Internal Revenue agents		30,000
Gain on sale of property, before tax effect . . . Extra.		90,000
Cost of goods sold.	$400,000	
Operating expenses	158,000	
Casualty loss not covered by insurance, before tax effect. Extra	62,000	
Loss on retirement of bonds, before tax effect. . . Extra. . .	50,000	
	$670,000	$880,000
Income taxes payable for year (see below)	67,000	
Net income and prior period adjustment of $30,000	143,000	
Totals	$880,000	$880,000

total inc. tax expense $ 96,000

NJ → $ 113,000

Computation of Income Tax Liability for the Current Year

Sales		$750,000
Less:		
Cost of goods sold	$400,000	
Operating expenses	158,000	
Casualty loss (fully deductible)	62,000	
Loss on retirement of bonds (fully deductible)	50,000	670,000
Taxable income		$ 80,000
Tax on taxable income, $80,000 × 50%		$ 40,000
Capital gains tax—on gain on sale of property ($90,000 × 30%)		27,000
Total income taxes payable for current year		$ 67,000

Instructions On the basis of this information, and assuming income tax rates of 50% on ordinary income and 30% on capital gains, prepare in suitable form for publication an income statement and a separate statement of retained earnings for the current year. The Merced Company reported a balance in retained earnings at the close of the prior year of $616,800 and declared dividends of $48,000 during the current year. Allocate income taxes where applicable and assume that the gain on sale of property, the casualty loss, and the loss on retirement of bonds all qualify as extraordinary items under the guidelines established in *APB Opinion No. 30*.

20B-5 When Raymond Rae started his own construction business in January, Year 1, he decided to keep his accounting records on the percentage-of-completion basis, but, on the advice of his CPA, he elected to use the completed-contract method for income tax purposes.

Rae determined percentage of completion by taking a ratio of costs incurred to date to total estimated cost at the time the contract was awarded. He had had considerable experience in estimating costs and expected that his total cost estimates would not differ materially from actual total costs.

During the first three years of operations, the Rae Construction Company held four contracts, of which three were completed as follows:

Contract no.	Year completed	Contract price	Total direct costs
39	Year 1	$600,000	$490,000
40	Year 3	750,000	650,000
41	Year 2	900,000	780,000
42	In progress	840,000	710,000 (est.)

The general and administrative expenses incurred during the three-year period, and the completion record on the contracts, are shown on page 785.

	Year 1	Year 2	Year 3
General and administrative expenses	$68,000	$74,500	$70,000
Completion record (% completed):			
Contract 39	100%		
Contract 40	10%	20%	70%
Contract 41	20%	80%	
Contract 42		25%	40%

Instructions

a Prepare a schedule showing the determination of accounting income before income taxes and the net taxable income for each of the three years.

b Assuming a flat 50% income tax rate, prepare the journal entries necessary to record the accrual of income taxes for each of the three years, and determine the balances of current and deferred income taxes payable at the end of Year 3.

CHAPTER 21

Long-term investments in corporate securities

In Chapter 5 we discussed investments in marketable securities, such as an investment in shares of General Motors stock or in American Telephone bonds. Such investments can readily be converted into cash and are classified as current assets. Many companies also make long-term investments in corporate securities in order to create close business ties with another company and thereby improve operating performance. These long-term investments should not be classified as current assets, because they do not represent liquid resources available to meet working capital needs.

The basis of distinction between the asset categories of marketable securities (Chapter 5) and long-term investments lies in the nature and purpose of the investment. Investments which are readily marketable and which can be sold without disrupting corporate policies or impairing the operating efficiency of the business should be classified as current assets. Investments made for the purpose of fostering operational relationships with other entities should be regarded as long-term investments. Also, investments which do not meet the test of ready marketability are usually classified as long-term investments, even if these investments do not promote operational relationships. Long-term investments, as we have defined them, are not current assets. They are usually listed as a separate item below the current asset section. The descriptive title used in the balance sheet is often "Investments" or "Investments and other assets."

Objectives of long-term investments

Companies may make long-term investments in the securities of other corporations for many reasons. For example, these investments may be used to create close ties to major suppliers or to retail outlets. The rights of ownership inherent in common stock investments give a company investing in such securities a degree of influence or control over the management of the owned company. Thus, many companies use investments in common stock as a means of gaining control of a competitor, acquiring ownership of a cash-rich company, or diversifying by acquiring an ownership interest in companies in other industries.

Consolidated financial statements

When one company acquires a controlling interest in the common stock of another, the controlling company is termed the *parent* and the controlled company the *subsidiary.* The investment in the common stock of the subsidiary is shown as a long-term investment on the separate financial statements of the parent. In addition to the financial statements prepared by the parent company and by the subsidiary, *consolidated financial statements* may also be prepared. Consolidated financial statements ignore the legal concept that each corporation is a separate entity and treat the parent and subsidiary companies as a single economic entity.

Viewing both companies as a single economic entity is an alternative to treating the subsidiary as an investment owned by the parent company. The circumstances in which consolidated financial statements are appropriate and the manner in which they are prepared are topics discussed extensively in *Advanced Accounting* of this series.

Cost at acquisition

The cost of an investment in securities includes the purchase price plus brokerage fees, transfer taxes, and any other expenditures necessary to the transaction. If assets other than cash are given in payment for the securities and the fair value of such non-cash assets is unknown, the current market price of the securities may be used to establish the cost of the securities and the value of the non-cash assets given in exchange. When neither a market price for the securities nor the fair value of the assets given in exchange is known, the accountant must rely on independent appraisals to establish dollar values for recording the transaction.

If two or more securities are acquired simultaneously for a lump-sum payment, the total cost should be allocated between the two classes of securities to facilitate the determination of the gain or loss arising from future transactions involving these securities. If the various classes of securities so purchased are traded in the market, the existing market prices serve as the basis for apportioning the total cost into parts. This type of cost apportionment is termed a *relative sales value allocation.*

Assume, for example, that X Company acquires from Y Company 100 units, of five common shares and one preferred share each, at a price of $250 per unit, when the common is selling for $30 and the preferred for $100 per share. The portion of the cost allocated to the common stock is $25,000 × 150/250, or $15,000, and the part allocable to the preferred stock is $25,000 × 100/250, or $10,000. If only one class of the stock is actively traded, that class will usually be recorded at the market price and the remaining portion of the cost will be considered the cost of the other class. When neither class of stock has an established market, the apportionment of the cost may have to be delayed until a fair value of the securities can be established.

ACCOUNTING FOR INVESTMENTS IN STOCKS

Measuring return on investment

What is the "return" on an investment in common stock? One school of thought holds that the stockholder's return consists of the stream of dividends received from the investment. A second point of view is that the stockholder's return consists of his proportionate share of the net income (minus preferred dividends, if any) of the owned company, without regard to whether this income is actually distributed during the period in the form of dividends. Supporting this second viewpoint is the fact that the earnings of the owned company which are not distributed as dividends are retained by the company, causing an increase in stockholders' equity. A third interpretation of the stockholder's return is the dividends received plus (or minus) the change in the market value of the investment.

Three different accounting methods exist, depending upon which return an investor wishes to measure. These methods are:

1 *Cost method.* Investment income consists only of dividends received.
2 *Equity method.* Investment income consists of the stockholder's proportionate share of the owned company's net income.
3 *Market method.* Investment income includes dividends received and changes in the market value of the investment.

The market value method (as a logical alternative to the cost method) was illustrated for use with marketable securities in Chapter 5. However, the market method is much less appropriate with respect to long-term investments. By definition, long-term investments are not held for purposes of realizing changes in market prices. A basic criterion for classifying an investment as long-term is that the investment cannot be sold without impairing the operating efficiency of the investor. When the investor is committed to holding an investment in securities indefinitely, the daily changes in market price lose much of their significance. Therefore, it is the cost and equity methods which are generally used to account for long-term investments in common stock.

Accounting for dividends received

When a company owns only a small portion of the total outstanding common stock of another company, the company owning the investment (termed *investor*) has little or no control over the other company (termed *investee*). In this case, the investor cannot influence the investee's dividend policy, and the only portion of the investee's income which reaches the investor is the dividends paid by the investee. Thus, when the investor has little or no control over the investee, the dividends received represent the only return realized by the investor. Under these circumstances, the cost method of accounting for the investment appears most appropriate.

The payment of dividends on common stock is a discretionary act, requiring that the directors of a corporation first declare the dividend. For this reason, an investor should not accrue dividend revenue, as he does with interest revenue on a bond. There are three acceptable alternatives for timing the recognition of dividend revenue: (1) when the dividend is declared (declaration date), (2) when the dividend will be received by the current stockholder even if the stock is subsequently sold (ex-dividend date), or (3) when the dividend is received (payment date). For the purpose of consistency, all illustrations in this chapter will recognize dividend revenue at the date the dividend is actually received.

Not all dividends received represent revenue to the stockholder. Sometimes corporations may pay dividends in excess of total profits. In such cases the amount by which the cash distribution exceeds total profits to date is considered a return of capital, termed a *liquidating dividend,* rather than dividend revenue.

From the viewpoint of any given stockholder, a liquidating dividend may be deemed to occur whenever dividends exceed total profits *subsequent to the date the investment was acquired.* Liquidating dividends are a return of a portion of the amount invested and logically should be recorded by crediting the investment account rather than by crediting Dividend Revenue.

For income tax purposes, liquidating dividends are defined with respect to the company paying the dividend, rather than with respect to individual investors. Tax laws recognize liquidating dividends only to the extent that total dividends paid exceed total profits earned *over the life of the company* paying the dividend. Under this legal interpretation, a stockholder acquiring his shares in the market from a previous stockholder "steps into his shoes" with respect to the distinction between dividend revenue and return of capital.

Applying the cost method

When the cost method is used, the investment account is kept in terms of the cost of the shares acquired. Revenue is recognized only when dividends are received or distributions of assets are made pro rata to the shareholders. Changes in the assets of the investee are ignored unless a significant and permanent decline occurs in the value of the shares. The two events which may cause a departure from the cost basis are:

1 Dividends representing a distribution of earnings retained in the business prior to the acquisition of the stock by the investor are considered liquidating dividends. The investment account is reduced accordingly.

2 Operating losses of the investee, which reduce the net asset balances substantially and which seriously impair its future prospects, are recognized as losses by the investor. A portion of the investment has been lost and this fact is recorded by reducing the carrying value of the investment account.

The journal entry to record such losses is:

Investment Loss	50,000	
Investment in Partially Owned Company		50,000
To record the effect of losses of a partially owned company		
on the investment in the common shares of that company.		

When the cost method is being followed, ordinary dividends received from an investee are treated the same as dividends on any other investment. Ordinary profits or losses of the investee are recognized by the investor only when and to the extent that dividends are distributed or when reflected in a realized gain or loss at the time the shares are sold.

Applying the equity method

When the investor owns enough stock in the investee to exercise significant control over the investee's management, the dividends paid by the investee may no longer be a good measure of the return on the investment. This is because the investor may control the investee's dividend policy. In such a case, dividends paid by the investee are likely to reflect the *investor's* tax considerations and cash needs, rather than the profitability of the investment.

For example, assume that one company owns all the stock in another company. For two years the subsidiary is very profitable but pays no dividends, because the parent company has no need for additional cash. In the third year, the subsidiary has operating losses but pays a large dividend to the parent company. Clearly, it would be misleading to report no investment income for the parent company while its fully owned subsidiary was operating profitably, and then to show large investment income in a year when the subsidiary operated at a loss.

The investee need not be fully owned for the investor to have a significant degree of control. When an investee is widely held by many stockholders, an investor with much less than 50% of the stock may have effective control, since it is doubtful that the remaining outstanding shares will vote as an organized block.

When the equity method is used, an investment is initially recorded at the cost of the shares acquired but is then adjusted for changes in the net assets of the investee subsequent to acquisition. The investor's proportionate share of the investee's net income is recognized as income, causing an increase in the investment account. If the investee's net income includes extraordinary items, the investor should treat his share of the extraordinary items as an extraordinary item (if material in amount to the investor), rather than as ordinary investment income. Dividends paid by the investee are treated by the investor as a conversion of the investment into cash, causing the investment account to decrease.

For example, assume that Par Company purchases 40% of the common stock of Sub Company for $300,000, which corresponds to the underlying book value. During the subsequent period, Sub Company reports a net income of $70,000 (including a $10,000 extraordinary gain) and pays dividends of $30,000. Par Company would account for its investment as follows:

Investment in Sub Company	300,000	
Cash		300,000
To record acquisition of 40% of the common stock of Sub Company at book value.		
Investment in Sub Company	28,000	
Investment Income (ordinary)		24,000
Investment Income (extraordinary)		4,000
To record 40% of net income of Sub Company (40% × $60,000 = $24,000; 40% × $10,000 = $4,000).		
Cash	12,000	
Investment in Sub Company		12,000
To record dividends received from Sub Company (40% × $30,000 = $12,000).		

Note that the net effect of Par Company's accounting for Sub Company's income and dividends was to increase the investment account by $16,000. This corresponds to 40% of the increase reported in Sub Company's net assets during the period [40% × ($70,000 − $30,000) = $16,000].

Special Problems in Applying the Equity Method Two special problems often arise in applying the equity method. First, intercompany profits and losses resulting from transactions between the investor and investee must be eliminated until realized by a transaction with an unaffiliated entity. This special problem is discussed in *Advanced Accounting* of this series. Second, when the acquisition cost of an investment differs from the book value of the underlying net assets, adjustments may have to be made to the investment income recognized by the investor.

Cost in Excess of Book Value Often an investor will pay more than the underlying book value of an investment because the economic values of the investee's assets may be greater than their book values, or because the investee possesses unrecorded goodwill. In either case, this excess of cost over the underlying book value will benefit the investor only over the useful lives of the undervalued (or unrecorded) assets.

To the extent that the excess of cost over book value was paid to acquire an interest in specific undervalued assets, this amount should be amortized over the useful lives of those assets. The journal entry to reflect the amortization would be:

Investment Income . . . . *XXX*
    Investment in Partially Owned Company . . . .   *XXX*
To adjust investment income for amortization of excess of cost over
book value.

To the extent that the excess cost was incurred because of implied goodwill, the amount should be amortized over the estimated life of the goodwill. The Accounting Principles Board has taken the position in *Opinion No. 17* that amounts paid for goodwill should be amortized over a period of not more than 40 years.[1] As a practical matter, if the excess of the cost over the underlying book value is small, it is usually amortized as goodwill, rather than attempting to associate it with the lives of specific assets.

Cost Less than Book Value In some cases, an investor may acquire an investment in common stock at a cost less than the underlying book value. In this event, it should be assumed that specific assets of the investee are overvalued. If these assets are depreciable, the investor should amortize the excess of book value over cost into investment income over the useful lives of the assets. The journal entry to reflect this amortization would be:

[1]*APB Opinion No. 17*, "Intangible Assets," AICPA (New York: 1970), p. 340.

> *Investment in Partially Owned Company* . . . . *XXX*
>   *Investment Income* . . . . *XXX*
> *To adjust investment income for amortization of excess of book value over cost.*

Note that this adjustment increases investment income. The rationale for this action is that the investee's reported net income is actually understated, since the investee is taking depreciation or amortization based on overstated asset values.

Summary of Procedures under the Equity Method Accounting procedures under the equity method may be summarized as follows:

1 The investment is originally recorded at cost.
2 The investor subsequently records his proportionate share of the investee's reported net income (after elimination of intercompany profits) by debiting the investment account and crediting Investment Income. In event of a loss, Investment Loss would be debited and the investment account credited.
3 The investor views his share of dividends paid by the investee as a conversion of his investment into cash. Thus, the investor debits Cash and credits the investment account.
4 The investor adjusts the income or loss he has recognized by the amortization of any excess of cost over underlying book value associated with depreciable assets. This adjustment consists of debiting Investment Income (or Loss) and crediting the investment account.
5 The investor adjusts the income or loss he has recognized by the amortization of any excess of cost over underlying book value representing goodwill by debiting Investment Income (or Loss) and crediting the investment account.

In the preceding five-step summary, the last two steps apply to the usual situation in which the cost of the investment exceeds the underlying book value. In the less common situation in which the investment is acquired at a cost below book value, the procedure would be similar; however, the adjustment of the investment income or loss recognized would correspond to the journal entry illustrated at the top of this page.

Illustration of the cost and equity methods

To illustrate the differences in the cost and equity methods, assume that on January 1 of the current year P Company buys 4,000 shares (20%) of the common stock of S Company for $1,000,000. At the date of acquisition, the book value of S Company's net assets was $4,550,000. P Company was willing to pay more than book value for the investment because it was estimated that S Company owned land worth $100,000 more than its book value, depreciable assets worth $150,000 more than their book values, and enough goodwill to make a 20% interest in S Company worth the $1,000,000 purchase price.

The excess of the cost of the investment over the underlying book value may be evaluated as follows:

Cost of investment	$1,000,000
Underlying book value (20% × $4,550,000)	910,000
Excess of cost over book value	$ 90,000
Composition of the excess:	
20% interest in undervalued land (20% × $100,000)	$ 20,000
20% interest in undervalued depreciable assets (20% × $150,000)	30,000
Implied purchase of goodwill ($90,000 − $20,000 − $30,000)	40,000
Excess of cost over book value	$ 90,000

The undervalued depreciable assets have an average remaining life of 10 years, and P Company's policy with respect to goodwill is to amortize over 40 years.

During the current year, S Company reported net income of $430,000, including an extraordinary loss of $50,000, and paid dividends at year-end of $200,000. P Company's accounting for its investment in S Company during the year is illustrated below, using both the cost and equity methods:

Step 1 To record acquisition on January 1 of 4,000 shares of S Company stock:

Cost Method

Investment in S Company Stock	1,000,000	
Cash		1,000,000

Equity Method

Investment in S Company Stock	1,000,000	
Cash		1,000,000

Step 2 To record on December 31 P Company's $86,000 share (20% × $430,000) of S Company's reported net income, consisting of a $96,000 share of income before extraordinary items, and a $10,000 share of the extraordinary loss:

Cost Method

No entry.

Equity Method

Investment Loss (extraordinary)	10,000	
Investment in S Company Stock	86,000	
Investment Income (ordinary)		96,000

Step 3 To record on December 31 a $40,000 dividend (20% × $200,000) received from S Company:

Cost Method

Cash	40,000	
Dividend Revenue		40,000

Equity Method

Cash	40,000	
Investment in S Company Stock		40,000

Step 4 To amortize on December 31 a portion of investment cost over book value representing a 20% interest in S Company's undervalued depreciable assets ($30,000 ÷ 10 years = $3,000 per year):

Cost Method

No entry.

Equity Method

Investment Income (ordinary)	3,000	
Investment in S Company Stock		3,000

Step 5 To amortize on December 31 a portion of excess of investment cost over book value representing a 20% interest in S Company's implied goodwill ($40,000 ÷ 40 years = $1,000 per year):

Cost Method

No entry.

Equity Method

Investment Income (ordinary) 1,000
    Investment in S Company Stock 1,000

Note that no adjustment is made under either method for the $20,000 excess of cost over book value representing P Company's 20% interest in S Company's undervalued land. This is because land is a permanent asset, and its cost is not amortized. The results for the current year are illustrated below for both methods.

	Cost method	Equity method
Investment in S Company stock (ending balance)	$1,000,000	$1,042,000
Investment income recognized by P Company:		
Ordinary	$ 40,000	$ 92,000
Extraordinary loss		$ (10,000)

Selecting the appropriate method

When the investor has a significant degree of control over the investee, particularly over the investee's dividend policy, the equity method better describes the benefits accruing to the investor than does the cost method. When the investor has little or no control over the investee, the benefits received by the investor may be limited to the dividends received, indicating the cost method to be more appropriate. The key criterion in selecting between the methods is the *degree of control* the investor is able to exercise over the investee.

The Accounting Principles Board, in studying the problem of accounting for long-term investments in common stock, recognized that the point at which an investor has a significant degree of control may not always be clear. To achieve a degree of uniformity in accounting practice, the APB took the position in *Opinion No. 18* that "an investment (direct or indirect) of 20% or more of the voting stock of an investee should lead to a presumption that in absence of evidence to the contrary an investor has the ability to exercise significant influence over an investee."[2] Thus, investments representing 20% or more of the voting stock are usually accounted for by the equity method, and investments of less than 20% by the cost method. Investments in preferred stock should be accounted for by the cost method, because preferred stockholders usually do not have voting rights and also do not have a residual interest in net income.

[2] *APB Opinion No. 18,* "The Equity Method of Accounting for Investments in Common Stock," AICPA (New York: 1971), p. 355.

ACCOUNTING FOR INVESTMENTS IN BONDS

Bonds as a corporate liability were discussed extensively in Chapter 18. We now focus our attention on the problems of accounting for these same securities from the viewpoint of the investor. A bond contract represents a promise to pay a sum of money at maturity and a series of interest payments during the life of the contract. The investor buys these securities to earn a return on his investment. The effective rate of return (yield) on fixed-income securities to the investor is determined by the price he pays for the securities (since the terms of the contract are fixed); it may differ from the effective interest cost to the borrower since the securities may have been issued at an earlier date at a different price.

Computing the present value of a bond

The cost of an investment in bonds is the present value of the future money receipts promised in the contract, measured in terms of the market rate of interest prevailing at the time of purchase. The stated rate of interest in the bond contract measures the cash to be received semi-annually by the investor. If the rate of return demanded by investors is exactly equal to the coupon rate, the bond can be purchased at the face amount. If the market rate of interest has risen, the bond contract can be purchased at a *discount* because the buyer is demanding a higher return than the contract offers; therefore, to equate the yield on the bond with the market rate of interest, the contract is purchased at an amount below par value. If the market rate of interest is below the rate stated in the bond, the investor will be willing to pay a *premium* for the bond, that is, a price above par value.

This relation of interest rates and bond prices was discussed in Chapter 18; the compound interest techniques necessary to compute bond prices are discussed in Appendix A and in the *Advanced Accounting* text of this series.

Acquisition between interest dates

Interest on bond contracts accrues with the passage of time in accordance with the provisions of the contract. The issuing corporation pays the contractual rate of interest on the stated day to the person holding the bond on that day. If the investor buys a bond between interest dates, he must pay the owner the market price of the bond plus the interest accrued since the last interest payment. The investor is paying the owner of the bond the interest he is entitled to for the first portion of the interest period and will in turn collect that portion plus the additional interest he earns by holding the bond to the next interest date.

Illustration On July 1, the Investment Company wishes to buy 10 bonds of the Key Company which were issued several years ago but which mature on April 1, 10 years from the past April. The bond contract provides for interest at 5% per annum payable semiannually on April 1 and October 1. The market rate of interest is higher than 6% at the present time and the bonds are currently quoted at $92\frac{3}{4}$ plus accrued interest. The entry to record the acquisition is:

Investment in Key Company Bonds.	9,275	
Accrued Interest Receivable	125	
Cash		9,400
To record the purchase of 10 bonds plus accrued interest of $125		
for three months.		

Discount and premium on bond investments

At the date of acquisition, the investment account is usually debited for the cost of acquiring the bonds, including brokerage and other fees but excluding the accrued interest. The use of a separate discount or premium account as a valuation account is acceptable procedure; however, it is seldom used. The subsequent treatment of the investment might conceivably be handled in any one of three ways: (1) The investment might be carried at cost, ignoring the accumulation of discount or amortization of premium; (2) the investment account might be revalued periodically to conform to market conditions; (3) the discount or premium might be systematically accumulated or amortized to reflect the change in the value of the bonds under the conditions prevailing at the time of purchase.

The first alternative (the cost basis) is used primarily in accounting for temporary investments, as discussed in Chapter 5, for convertible bonds, and for other bonds for which the discount or premium is insignificant. The discount or premium on convertible bonds is seldom related to the level of interest rates but rather reflects the effect of the price of the security into which the bond may be converted. These securities are subject to wide price movements related to changes in the market price of common stocks; therefore, the amortization of premium or accumulation of discount does not seem appropriate.

The second alternative (valuation at market) is not in accord with the present interpretation of the realization concept or the doctrine of conservatism, especially during periods of rising bond prices. Changes in market prices of bonds held as long-term investments may be of less significance to the investing firm than changes in prices of short-term investments since the long-term investments are frequently held to maturity, at which time market price and maturity value are equal. When the maturity value of the bond is in jeopardy because of serious cash shortages by the issuing corporation, it is generally acceptable to write the investment down to its expected realizable value and recognize the loss.

The third alternative (the systematic accumulation and amortization) is the preferred treatment for long-term investments in bonds. This approach recognizes the fact that the revenue represented by the discount, or the reduction in revenue represented by the premium, does not come into being instantaneously at maturity but accrues over the life of the bonds. The revenue earned should be consistent with the circumstances surrounding the bonds at the date of purchase. This method is also consistent with the principle that assets should be accounted for on the basis of cost.

Interest revenue

The periodic interest payments provided for in a bond contract will represent the total investment revenue to an investor holding a bond to maturity only if the investor purchased the bond for its face amount. If an investor purchases a bond at a premium, the amount received upon maturity of the bond will be less than the amount of the initial investment, thus reducing the cumulative investment revenue by the amount of the premium. Similarly, if the bond is purchased at a discount, the maturity value will be greater than the initial investment, thereby increasing the cumulative investment revenue by the amount of the discount.

When a bondholder intends to hold an investment in bonds to maturity, there is little logic in treating the discount or premium as a gain or loss occurring instantaneously on the maturity date. Rather, the increase in bond value as a discount disappears should be viewed as part of the compensation accruing to the bondholder over the entire period the bonds are owned. Similarly, the decrease in value when a premium disappears is a cost the investor is willing to incur over the entire holding period to receive periodic interest payments higher than the market rates prevailing when the investment was acquired. Thus, the amount of the discount or premium should be viewed as an integral part of the periodic investment revenue (interest revenue) earned by the investor. The accumulation of a discount increases periodic interest revenue, and amortization of a premium decreases periodic interest revenue.

An extreme illustration of this concept has occurred in certain government savings bonds which provided no periodic interest payments at all. Instead, these bonds sold at a large discount, and the gradual growth of the bonds toward their maturity value (accumulation of the discount) was the bondholder's only return. Although the bondholder received no cash proceeds until the bonds matured, interest revenue was still being earned. To measure the periodic interest revenue, the accumulation of the discount had to be recognized as interest revenue over the life of the bonds.

Methods of discount accumulation or premium amortization

The methods of discount and premium amortization for the issuing corporation were discussed in Chapter 18. They present precisely the same problem for the investor as for the issuer. The purpose of accumulating the discount or amortizing the premium systematically is to reflect accurately the interest revenue derived from the investment.

Straight-line Method   Under the straight-line method, the discount or premium is spread uniformly over the life of the investment. Although the bonds may be sold by the investor or redeemed by the issuer prior to maturity, the accumulation or amortization is always based on the years remaining to maturity. The straight-line method is simple to apply and avoids the necessity for determining the yield rate. The primary objection to the method is that it produces a constant interest revenue each period, which results in a variable rate of return on the investment. However, unless the bond has a number of years to maturity or an exceptionally large premium or discount, the straight-line method produces a close approximation of the true interest revenue.

The accumulation of a discount is added to revenue and the investment account is increased by an equal amount. As an example, assume that 10, $1,000 face value, 6% bonds are purchased on an interest date, four years from maturity, at a price of $9,656.30. At this price, the bonds will yield 7% compounded semiannually. The total discount amounts to $343.70. Spreading this discount equally over the eight remaining semiannual periods, the semiannual interest payments should be increased by $42.96 ($343.70 ÷ 8 periods) to reflect periodic interest revenue. The semiannual journal entry would be:

Cash	*300.00*	
Investment in Bonds	*42.96*	
Interest Revenue		*342.96*

To record interest revenue for the six-month period and to accumulate the discount on a straight-line basis.

Now assume that the same investment had initially been purchased for $10,358.51, to yield 5% compounded semiannually. In this case, there is a $358.51 premium to be allocated to the eight six-month periods, which will reduce semiannual interest revenue by $44.81 ($358.51 ÷ 8 periods). The appropriate semiannual journal entry would be:

Cash	*300.00*	
Investment in Bonds		*44.81*
Interest Revenue		*255.19*

To record interest revenue for the six-month period and to amortize the premium on a straight-line basis.

Effective Interest Method The effective interest method produces a constant rate of return on the investment. That is, the periodic interest revenue will always represent the same percentage return on the carrying value of the investment. Thus, when a discount is being accumulated and the investment account is increasing, the interest revenue recognized each period will also have to increase. This is accomplished by accumulating an ever-increasing portion of the discount each period. To apply the method, the interest revenue is computed every period by multiplying the balance of the investment account by the effective interest rate. The accumulation of the discount (or amortization of the premium) will then be the difference between the periodic cash receipt and the computed interest revenue.

To illustrate, refer to the example used for the straight-line method, in which bonds were purchased for $9,656.30 to yield 7% compounded semiannually. The interest revenue for the first six-month period should be $337.97 ($3\frac{1}{2}$% of $9,656.30). Since the periodic interest payment is only $300, the discount accumulation must be $37.97. The appropriate journal entry is:

Cash	300.00	
Investment in Bonds	37.97	
Interest Revenue		337.97
To record interest revenue for the six-month period and to		
accumulate discount on an effective interest basis.		

The balance in the investment account has now been increased to $9,694.27 ($9,656.30 + $37.97). The interest revenue for the second six-month period should therefore be $339.30 ($3\frac{1}{2}$% of $9,694.27), which requires discount accumulation of $39.30.

The same principle can be applied to the amortization of a premium. A decreasing interest revenue will result, since the carrying value of the investment account is periodically being reduced. The interest revenue, however, will remain a constant percentage return on the investment. Using the example from the straight-line method, in which bonds were purchased for $10,358.51 to yield 5% semiannually, interest revenue for the first semiannual period would be $258.96 ($2\frac{1}{2}$ percent of $10,358.51) and would be recognized as follows:

First semiannual period:		
Cash	300.00	
Investment in Bonds		41.04
Interest Revenue		258.96
To record interest revenue for the six-month period and to		
amortize the premium on an effective interest basis.		

The balance in the investment account now has been decreased to $10,317.47 ($10,358.51 − $41.04). The interest revenue for the second six-month period should therefore be $257.94 ($2\frac{1}{2}$% of $10,317.47) which requires premium amortization of $42.06.

Accumulation and amortization tables can be prepared for the investor in the same manner as they are prepared for the issuer. The preparation of these tables can be reviewed on page 686.

Accounting for investments between interest dates

The interest earned on bond investments, like interest earned on any other investment, is accrued only at significant dates. The significant dates are: (1) interest payment dates, (2) the end of the investor's accounting period, and (3) the time of any transaction involving the particular investment, which does not coincide with a regular interest payment date.

The interest on bond investments must be accrued, therefore, at the end of the accounting period and before the bonds are sold. The discount should be accumulated or the premium amortized in accordance with whatever method is being used. Regardless of whether the straight-line method or the effective interest method is used, amortization between interest dates may be allocated on the straight-line basis for the fractional period as a matter of convenience.

Illustration Assume that 10, $1,000 face value, 6% bonds are purchased for $9,656.30 on April 2, four years from maturity. Interest is payable on April 1 and October 1. If the bondholder closes his books on December 31, it will be necessary to make an adjusting entry to accrue interest and accumulate the discount from October 1 through December 31. The year-end adjustment, accumulating the discount on a straight-line basis, would be:

Accrued Interest Receivable	150.00	
Investment in Bonds	21.48	
Interest Revenue		171.48

To accrue interest and accumulate discount for three months.
Accumulation: $343.70 × $\frac{3}{48}$ = $21.48.

In the event that any of the bonds are sold, a similar entry should be made to accrue interest and to accumulate the discount to the date of sale.

SPECIAL PROBLEMS IN ACCOUNTING FOR SECURITIES

Cost identification

Securities, like inventories, may pose a problem as to which costs should be offset against revenue in the period of sale. Assume, for instance, that A Company buys 1,000 shares of B Company common stock at a price of $80 per share, and that later it acquires another 1,000 shares at $90 per share. Several years later, A Company sells 1,000 shares of B Company common stock for $84 per share. Should A Company recognize a $4,000 gain or a $6,000 loss?

The solution to this problem requires making a *cost flow assumption,* as with inventories. Since securities are usually identified by a certificate number, it would be possible to use specific identification of stock certificates in establishing the cost of the 1,000 shares sold. However, some alternative cost flow assumption might be adopted. These alternative methods of cost flow include: (1) fifo—the first shares acquired are assumed to be the first ones sold; (2) lifo—the last shares acquired are assumed to be the first ones sold; and (3) weighted-average cost—each share of a given security investment is assigned the same cost basis.

Income tax rules require the use of either the specific identification method or the first-in, first-out method in measuring the *taxable gain or loss.* Neither lifo nor weighted-average cost is an acceptable method for income tax purposes. The specific identification method is usually more advantageous to the taxpayer, because it allows him to select for sale those particular certificates which will lead to the most desirable tax consequences. For accounting purposes, most firms use the same method of cost selection used for income tax purposes in order to simplify record keeping. From a theoretical viewpoint, however, weighted average is the only cost flow assumption that recognizes the economic equivalence of identical securities. In our above illustration of successive purchases of the stock of B Company at different prices, it is undeniable that each share of B Company stock owned has exactly the same economic value regardless of the price paid to acquire it. The weighted-average flow assumption recognizes the economic reality that, except for tax purposes, it really makes no difference which 1,000-share certificate is sold and which is retained.

Accounting for stock dividends and stock splits

The nature of stock dividends and stock splits was discussed in Chapter 16. Emphasis was placed on the fact that these corporate actions do not result in income to investors. The income tax regulations are in agreement with financial accounting standards on this point.

Since a shareholder's interest in the corporation remains unchanged by a stock dividend or split-up except as to the number of share units constituting such interest, the cost of the shares previously held should be allocated equitably to the total shares held after receipt of the stock dividend or split-up. When any shares are later disposed of, a gain or loss should be determined on the basis of the adjusted cost per share.[3]

The accounting procedure by the investor to record receipt of additional shares from a stock dividend or stock split is usually confined to a memorandum entry which indicates the number of shares received and the new cost per share.

Stock purchase warrants and stock rights

As explained in Chapter 15, a *stock warrant* is a certificate issued by a corporation conveying to the holder *rights* to purchase shares of its stock at a specified price within a specified time period. A single right attaches to each share of outstanding stock and several rights are usually required to purchase one new share at the stipulated price. For example, when rights are issued, the owner of 100 shares of common stock will receive a warrant representing 100 rights and specifying the number of rights required to purchase one new share of stock. The life of these rights is usually limited to a few weeks. They must be exercised or sold before the expiration date or they become worthless.

Accounting for Stock Warrants Acquired by Purchase The accounting problems involved when a corporation buys warrants are similar to those relating to the acquisition of any security. The purchase price, plus brokerage fees and other acquisition costs, is debited to Investment in Warrants and the credit is to Cash. When warrants are acquired as a part of a package, the total cost must be allocated to the various securities included in the package.

When the warrants are used to acquire stock, the initial cost of the warrants used plus the cash required to complete the purchase is the cost of the stock. The Investment in Stock is debited; Cash and the Investment in Warrants are credited. If the market price of the stock is greater or less than this combined cost, this fact is ignored until the stock is sold, at which time a gain or loss is recognized.

Accounting for Stock Rights Stock rights are distributed to the stockholders of a corporation in proportion to their holdings. The receipt of a stock right can be compared to the receipt of a stock dividend. The corporation has not distributed any assets; instead, the way has been opened for an additional investment by the stockholders. Until the stockholder elects to exercise or sell his right, his investment in the corporation is represented by (1) shares which have been purchased and (2) the right to acquire other shares at a specified price, usually below the market price.

[3] *Accounting Research and Terminology Bulletins—Final Edition,* AICPA (New York: 1961), chap. 7b, p. 51.

The cost of the original investment is therefore the cost of the share and the right. The cost of the original investment should be apportioned between these two parts of the investment on the basis of relative market prices. The stock will trade in the market on a "rights on" basis until the ex-rights date, at which time the stock sells "ex rights" and the rights have a market of their own. Relative sales value allocation may be used to apportion the cost between the original shares and the rights as follows:

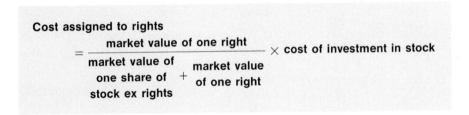

Cost assigned to rights

$$= \frac{\text{market value of one right}}{\text{market value of one share of stock ex rights} + \text{market value of one right}} \times \text{cost of investment in stock}$$

Illustration The Black Co. owns 100 shares of Warner Corporation common stock, acquired at a cost of $10,000. Now Warner Corporation declares that additional shares will be sold to present stockholders at $104 per share, at the rate of one new share for each 15 shares now held. On the date that the stock sells ex rights, the market price of the right is $2 and of the stock $123. The cost of the investment in Warner Corporation stock should be allocated between the rights and the stock as follows:

Cost of 100 shares owned $10,000
Market values at date of issue of rights:
  One share of stock . . . . $ 123
  One right 2
Allocation of cost of $10,000:
  $10,000 × 2/125 = $160 cost of 100 rights

The journal entry required to record the cost allocation is:

Investment in Warner Corporation Rights 160
    Investment in Warner Corporation Stock 160
To allocate portion of investment cost to rights.

Subsequently, Black Co. decides to exercise 90 of the rights and to sell the remaining 10 rights at the market price of $2.25. Assuming that

Black Co. uses a first-in, first-out cost flow assumption and therefore must keep track of the basis of each lot of Warner Corporation stock, the entries to record the transaction are:

Investment in Warner Corporation Stock—Batch no. 2	768	
Investment in Warner Corporation Rights		144
Cash		624
To record acquisition of six additional shares of Warner Corporation through exercise of 90 rights.		
Cash	22.50	
Investment in Warner Corporation Rights		16.00
Gain on Sale of Rights		6.50
To record sale of 10 rights.		

The original 100 shares of stock now have a cost of $9,840, or $98.40 per share, and the six shares purchased with the rights have a cost of $128 per share.

In the case of Black Co., all rights were exercised or sold; however, in the event that the rights were allowed to lapse, the investor should recognize a loss to the extent of the cost applicable to the rights. If the rights are not sold or exercised, a portion of the interest in the corporation has been lost; therefore, the cost of that part of the investment is a loss.

Tax Rules If the market value of the rights is less than 15% of the market value of the securities, the taxpayer is not required to apportion the cost of the investment. The taxpayer may, however, allocate the cost if he desires, in which case the cost of the stock so acquired is the subscription price plus the cost of the old shares apportioned to the rights. The new shares acquired are considered to have been purchased on the date the rights are exercised.

Convertible securities

A corporation may invest in bonds or preferred stocks that are convertible into the common stock of the issuing company at the option of the holder. The characteristics of convertible securities were discussed in Chapters 15 and 18. At this point we shall consider the action to be taken by an investor who exercises the conversion privilege and receives common stock in exchange for convertible bonds or convertible preferred stock.

The *market value* of the common stock received may differ materially from the *cost* of the converted securities. However, it is virtually universal practice to use the cost of the convertible security as the carrying value of the common stock acquired. Thus, *no gain or loss is recognized at the time of conversion.* This treatment is required for tax purposes and is also supported by the theoretical argument that the investor contemplates the conversion transaction when he purchases a convertible security and thus no gain or loss should be recognized until the stock acquired by conversion is sold.

The following journal entry illustrates the entry by an investor to record the conversion of bonds which cost $96,720.

Investment in ABC Company Common Stock	96,720	
Investment in ABC Company Convertible Bonds.		96,720
To record conversion of bonds into common stock.		

Valuation of investments at lower of cost or market

In Chapter 5, the valuation of marketable securities at lower of cost or market was discussed. This valuation method is less appropriate for most long-term investments. Long-term investments in stock are usually valued at cost, or at cost plus the changes in the net assets of the investee (equity method). Long-term investments in bonds are usually valued at cost, or cost plus accumulation of a discount or minus amortization of a premium.

A few companies, however, apply the lower-of-cost-or-market rule to the valuation of long-term investments. This practice appears overly conservative, if we assume that long-term investments are held primarily for purposes of promoting operational relationships rather than for generating current investment revenue or realizing market price gains. When the current market value of an investment can be objectively determined, the principle of full disclosure of all material facts points to the desirability of disclosing the market value, but this is usually best accomplished by parenthetical note.

OTHER LONG-TERM INVESTMENTS

Investments in special-purpose funds

Occasionally a corporation will accumulate a fund of cash, usually invested temporarily in securities, for a special purpose. The creation of the fund may be by voluntary action on the part of the management or it may be required by contract. Funds are generally created to pay off a liability or to acquire specific assets. In general, funds are treated as long-term investments only when they are created as a part of a contractual arrangement and the use of the money so invested is not available to management for general operating needs. A fund may be classified as a current asset if it is created voluntarily and the management may liquidate it for operating purposes.

Accounting for funds

The transactions which must be accounted for in connection with fund accumulation and administration are: (1) the transfer of assets to the fund, (2) the investment of the assets in corporation-managed funds, (3) the collection of revenue and payment of expenses if managed by the corporation, and (4) the use of fund resources for the intended purpose.

There are two methods of handling funds: (1) The fund may be created and managed by the corporate personnel; or (2) the assets may be deposited with a trustee who is charged with receiving the deposit, investing the assets, collecting the revenue, paying the expenses, and accounting to the responsible officials for the receipts and disbursements.

Typically, the funds which are created voluntarily are administered by the corporate personnel, whereas those created by contract are handled by a trustee. The periodic deposit to the fund is generally set in advance. It may be related to the level of operations; it may be set as a stated amount each period, or as a stated amount less earnings of the fund for the period. The method of determining the amount and time for the deposit can generally be found by referring to the document authorizing the creation of the fund. In cases when the fund is irrevocably committed for the purpose designated and the cash is actually deposited with a trustee, the fund itself may not appear among the assets of the corporation and the liability which is to be paid from fund assets may be excluded from the liabilities. This procedure is used most often when the liability does not exceed the fund balance, which means that the corporation has no liability other than that for the periodic deposits as stipulated in the contract. Most employee benefit plans, such as pension plans and supplemental unemployment benefit plans, are of this type.

Bond sinking funds are usually included among the assets and bonds outstanding are shown as a corporate liability. The sinking fund should not be offset against the bond liability. This particular fund and other similar funds are usually included on the balance sheet as an asset even though they are irrevocable and are held by trustees. To omit the fund balance from the balance sheet and include the net liability could conceal a significant amount of the company's liabilities, thus understating the extent to which the company was using borrowed capital.

One of the most common methods of accumulating a fund, particularly for purposes of retiring a bond liability, is to deposit a given sum each period. The periodic deposit is computed, using a compound interest formula for determining the periodic deposits required to total a certain sum in a definite period at an assumed rate of interest. The details of this calculation are covered in Appendix A and in the ***Advanced Accounting*** text of this series. The assumption of this calculation is that the funds deposited each period will be invested to yield the assumed rate of interest. Subsequent deposits and interest earned are both invested accordingly. The success or failure of the investment policy will be considered in the final accounting for the fund. As a matter of portfolio management, assets in special-purpose funds are usually invested in fixed-income securities rather than in variable-income securities, in an effort to assure the assumed balance in the fund at the proper time.

A schedule for the accumulation of a fund balance is illustrated below. These three assumptions have been made: An equal sum will be deposited annually at the end of the year; the deposit will be invested the next day; and the income earned will be reinvested in income-producing assets. In addition, assume that a corporation wants to accumulate a fund of $100,000 in 10 years and that investments are available which yield 5% interest annually. The annual deposit in the fund is $7,950.46 ($100,000 ÷ 12.5779, the amount of an ordinary annuity of $1 at 5%). The fund is administered by the corporation and no expenses are charged to the fund. The same schedule might be used if the cash is deposited with a trustee, provided that the expenses of the trustee are paid by the corporation in addition to the annual deposit and the fund is considered an asset of the corporation.

Fund Accumulation Schedule

End of year	Debit to fund	Credit to cash	Credit to interest revenue	Total fund
1	$ 7,950.46	$ 7,950.46		$ 7,950.46
2	8,347.98	7,950.46	$ 397.52	16,298.44
3	8,765.38	7,950.46	814.92	25,063.82
4	9,203.65	7,950.46	1,253.19	34,267.47
5	9,663.83	7,950.46	1,713.37	43,931.30
6	10,147.03	7,950.46	2,196.57	54,078.33
7	10,654.38	7,950.46	2,703.92	64,732.71
8	11,187.10	7,950.46	3,236.64	75,919.81
9	11,746.45	7,950.46	3,795.99	87,666.26
10	12,333.74	7,950.46	4,383.28	100,000.00
	$100,000.00	$79,504.60	$20,495.40	

The transactions relating to the purchase and sale of securities, and the accrual and collection of income for the fund, are accounted for in the same manner in which transactions in the general investments account are recorded.

Cash surrender value of life insurance

In cases where a business is particularly dependent on certain officers for direction and management, life insurance policies may be purchased on the lives of these officers with the business as the beneficiary. Certain types of insurance policies combine a savings program and an insurance plan. When these are purchased, the savings portion of the premium should be reflected on the balance sheet as an investment.

The savings part of the plan is generally referred to as the **cash surrender value** of the policy. This is the amount of money which the business would receive in the event that the policy were canceled; this same amount frequently serves as collateral for a loan by a bank or the insurance company.

The following data represent the first four years' experience of White Co. with a $100,000 life insurance policy carried on one of its officers.

Year	Gross premium	Less dividend	Premium paid	Cash value increase	Insurance expense
1	$2,959	–0–	$2,959	–0–	$2,959
2	2,959	$424	2,535	$ 264	2,271
3	2,959	490	2,469	2,279	190
4	2,959	558	2,401	2,292	109

From this limited data, we can readily see the increase in the asset and the decreasing annual cost of insurance. The journal entries for the first two years are as follows:

Year 1	Insurance Expense	2,959	
	Cash		2,959
	To record the payment of life insurance premium.		
Year 2	Insurance Expense	2,271	
	Cash Surrender Value of Life Insurance	264	
	Cash		2,535
	To record the payment of life insurance premium.		

In the event of death of the insured officer, White Co. would collect the face amount of the insurance policy. The entry to record this event, assuming death occurs at the end of the fourth year, would be as follows:

Cash	100,000	
Gain on Settlement of Life Insurance Policy		95,165
Cash Surrender Value of Life Insurance		4,835
To record collection of insurance on life of officer.		

For income tax purposes, the premiums paid on life insurance policies in which the company is the beneficiary are not deductible. Similarly, the gain on the settlement pursuant to the death of the insured is not taxable income.

The procedures adopted in accounting for life insurance often sacrifice theory for expediency. For example, the dividends on life insurance actually accrue at the end of the policy year, so that in effect they are reductions of premiums already paid instead of those being paid. Prepaid insurance might be debited when the premium is paid, with subsequent entries to write off the prepaid amount as time passes. These are refinements that can be considered when the materiality of the expense justifies a more theoretical treatment.

Presentation in financial statements

Long-term investments which cannot readily be sold without impairing corporate relationships are classified as noncurrent assets. The classification of the investment on the balance sheet varies in practice. The materiality of the item appears to be of prime importance in the choice between placing it immediately following or preceding plant assets. If investments are a large amount relative to other asset groups, the item, Investments, is generally found immediately following the current assets; however, if the amount involved is relatively insignificant, this item may follow the plant asset group, or it may be combined with other assets that are not included in the major classifications, under a heading such as Other Assets.

Dividends and interest earned are normally listed under the caption Other Income and are included in the determination of income before extraordinary items. When the equity method is used, ordinary investment income (or loss) should also be included in Other Income, but the investor's share of any extraordinary item should retain its character and be classified as an extraordinary item by the investor.

Because of the nature of long-term investments, gains and losses from sales occur relatively infrequently. Until 1973, such gains and losses were often treated as extraordinary items. A trend then developed to avoid this classification for events which, although infrequent, may be expected to recur. A company with numerous long-term investments can expect occasional gains and losses from sales of these investments and should generally include such gains and losses in income before extraordinary items, under the caption of Other Income. On the other hand, if a company with very few long-term investments disposes of a major investment at a material gain or loss, classification as an extraordinary item might still be appropriate. The difference in views is significant because investment decisions often hinge upon reported earnings per share, which may be quoted either before or after extraordinary items.

REVIEW QUESTIONS

1 Distinguish between the asset categories of marketable securities and long-term investments. Could the same securities constitute marketable securities to one firm and long-term investments to another? Explain.

2 What is the cost of a security purchased for cash? Acquired in exchange for assets for which market value is not readily determinable? Acquired as part of a group purchase?

3 Explain three concepts of the "return on investment" to a common stockholder, and identify the appropriate accounting method for each concept of return on investment.

4 Why should dividend revenue not be accrued by an investor as is interest revenue? What are the alternatives for the timing of dividend revenue?

5 XYZ Corporation acquires 1,000 shares of ABC Company on May 15 for $75 per share when the book value of the ABC Company stock is composed of the following:

Capital stock, par value	$1,000,000
Capital paid-in in excess of par	2,000,000
Retained earnings	4,500,000
Total stockholders' equity	$7,500,000

There were 100,000 shares outstanding at the time. On May 16 ABC Company declares a dividend of $3 per share. What is the nature of this distribution from the point of view of XYZ Corporation? Of ABC Company? What is the legal interpretation of this distribution to XYZ Corporation?

6 Distinguish between the **cost** and **equity** methods of accounting for a long-term investment in common stock. When is each appropriate?

7 Identify two events which will cause a write-down of the investment account under the cost method.

8 How can the acquisition price of an investment affect subsequent investment income under the equity method?

9 Why does the effective yield of an investment in bonds often differ from the interest rate stated in the bond contract? Explain the effect of interest rate fluctuations on bond prices.

10 Why is the discount or premium on bond investments treated as an adjustment of the interest revenue rather than as a gain or loss upon sale, redemption, or retirement?

11 Distinguish between the **straight-line** and **effective interest** methods of accumulating a discount and amortizing a premium.

12 What is the theoretical support for using weighted average as a basis for determining cost when units of the same security are acquired at different dates and prices? What methods are allowed for income tax purposes?

13 From the investor's point of view, is there any significant difference between a stock dividend and a stock split? Does either represent income?

14 What are **stock rights?** How should they be accounted for by an investor?

15 When a convertible bond is converted into common stock, what entry should the investor make? Would your answer be different if the market price of the common stock were known? If the market price were not known? Explain.

16 If you were the accountant for Loo Co., which is required to make periodic deposits in a bond sinking fund held by a trustee, what entry would you make when the trustee notified you that the investments in the sinking fund earned $1,500, net of trustee's expenses of $300?

17 Why is the **cash surrender value** of an insurance policy on the life of a company official carried as an asset on the corporate balance sheet?

EXERCISES

Ex. 21-1 The following events relate to Seaboard Corporation's long-term investment in Century Development Co.:

Apr. 10   Purchased 500 shares of common stock at $22 per share, plus brokerage commission and transfer costs of $400.

June 15   Purchased 1,000 shares of common stock at $29 per share, plus brokerage commission and transfer costs of $712.

Aug. 31   Century Development Co. distributed a 20% stock dividend.

Instructions
a Prepare entries on Seaboard's books to record the events.
b Compute the basis per share of the investment in Century assuming (1) the two purchases are treated as separate lots (to permit the use of fifo), and (2) a weighted average is computed for the investment as a whole.
c Prepare a journal entry to record the sale of 800 shares at $21 per share, assuming the cost of the shares sold is determined by (1) fifo, and (2) weighted average.

Ex. 21-2 At the beginning of the current year, Riley Corporation acquired 20% of the 100,000 outstanding shares of Stroud Company capital stock. During the year, Stroud Company reported net income of $140,000.
    Compute the book value per share of Stroud Company stock and the basis per share of Riley Corporation's investment at the end of the current year under each of the following independent assumptions:
a Riley Corporation acquired the shares at their book value of $12 per share, and accounts for the investment by the cost method. Stroud Company paid dividends during the year of $80,000.
b Same facts as case (a), except that Stroud Company paid dividends during the year of $160,000.
c Same facts as case (a), except that Riley Corporation uses the equity method to account for the investment.
d Same facts as case (c), except that Riley Corporation acquired the shares at

a price of $15 per share, although their book value was only $12 per share. The excess of cost over book value was paid because a certain patent with a remaining life of 12 years was undervalued on Stroud's books.

Ex. 21-3 Using the information in Exercise 21-2, make all journal entries on Riley Corporation's books relating to the investment in Stroud Company during the current year, under each of the four assumptions. (Omit closing entries.)

Ex. 21-4 Prepare journal entries on the books of Southland Company to record the following events:

Feb. 10   Southland Company purchased 1,000 shares of Commuter Airlines common stock at $88 per share.

Mar. 31   Commuter Airlines issued a 10% stock dividend to common stockholders.

June 30   Commuter Airlines issued rights to common stockholders, enabling the purchase of one additional share at $90 for every five shares held. The stock was trading ex-rights at $114 per share and the rights had a market value of $6 each.

July 18   Southland Company exercised 1,000 rights to acquire new shares.

July 20   The remaining rights were sold for $5.50 each.

Oct. 12   Southland Company sold 400 shares of Commuter Airlines stock for $44,000. The shares sold were specifically identified as being from those acquired on February 10.

Ex. 21-5 The following data are the beginning of an amortization table prepared by Moscowitz Company to account for its investment in $80,000 face value Sable Co. bonds, maturing in 17 years, which pay interest annually:

Year	Payment received	Interest revenue	Accumulation of discount	Carrying value of investment
				$61,132.08
1	$4,000.00	$4,584.91	$584.91	61,716.99
2	4,000.00	4,628.77	628.77	62,345.76
3				

a Is the discount being accumulated by the straight-line or the effective interest method?

b What is the contract rate of interest paid on the bonds?

c What is the effective yield on the investment?

d Prepare a journal entry to reflect Moscowitz Company's interest revenue in Year 2.

e Compute the amounts to be entered in each column of the table for Year 3.

f What would be the interest revenue recognized per year if the discount were accumulated by the straight-line method?

g Compute the percentage return on the carrying value of the investment in Years 1 and 3, assuming that the discount was accumulated by the straight-line method.

Ex. 21-6 Prepare journal entries to record the following events relating to long-term investments:

Apr. 30   Purchased $60,000 face value, 8% bonds issued by Disc Company at a cost of $61,880 plus accrued interest. Bonds pay interest semiannually on March 1 and September 1, and mature 94 months from the date of acquisition.

July   10   Purchased for the lump sum of $155,000 a package of 500 shares of 6%, $100 par, preferred stock and 1,000 shares of common stock in Pyramid Corporation. The preferred and common stock were trading at $80 per share and $120 per share, respectively.

Sept. 1   Received semiannual interest payment on the Disc Company bonds. (Premium is amortized only at year-end.)

Oct. 15   Received the quarterly dividend on the Pyramid Corporation preferred stock.

Oct. 25   Received new shares from a 2 for 1 stock split of the Pyramid Corporation common stock.

Dec. 31   Adjusting entries are made for the end of the fiscal year. Premium is amortized by the straight-line method.

SHORT CASES FOR ANALYSIS AND DECISION

Case 21-1 Westech purchased 2,000 of the 50,000 outstanding shares of Universal Products capital stock on March 15 at $40 per share.

On April 1 Universal Products declared a cash dividend of 75 cents per share payable April 20 to stockholders of record April 12. The operations of Universal Products had been extremely unsuccessful during the first three quarters of the year and operating losses exceeded the accumulated retained earnings. On November 20 Universal Products declared a liquidating dividend of 50 cents per share payable December 20 to stockholders of record December 10.

Instructions
a Record these two dividend distributions by Universal Products on the books of Westech following the legal assumption.
b From the viewpoint of Westech, do you favor the legal or economic treatment of these dividends? Give your reasons.

Case 21-2 Bordeaux Instrument Co. acquired 45,000 of 150,000 outstanding shares of Miles Company on January 2 at $30 per share. The book value of Miles Company stock as of December 31, three days earlier, was $22.75 per share. During the year following the acquisition of the stock by Bordeaux Instrument, Miles earned $325,000 and paid dividends of $1.10 per share. The management of Bordeaux Instrument is concerned about the appropriate method of presenting the investment in Miles Company in the financial statements. The controller argues that Bordeaux has earned 30% of Miles's profit by virtue of the fact that it holds 30% of Miles's common stock. The vice president of finance argues that the investment must be carried at cost as are all other assets and that the earnings of Bordeaux should include only the dividends received from Miles.

Instructions
a Attempt to resolve this debate by pointing out the relevant issues on both sides of the argument.
b The vice president counters your points in favor of the controller's position with the statement that, "What you say makes sense until you try to explain what the dollar amount of the investment represents. It is not market value of the stock, since the current market value is $29 per share, and it most certainly is not cost." Present your answer to the vice president.

Case 21-3 On December 1 Blue Company acquired 4% convertible debenture bonds with par value of $1.5 million for $1,620,000 plus accrued interest. The debentures pay interest semiannually on February 1 and August 1 and mature in 14 years and 2 months from date of acquisition. Each bond is convertible on any interest date into six shares of common stock at the option of the holder.

On August 1, 500 bonds were converted into common stock. At the date of conversion the common stock was selling for $200 per share. On September 1 a 10% stock dividend was declared on the common stock to be distributed on October 10 to stockholders of record on September 20. On December 1, 1,100 common shares are sold for $205 per share.

Instructions

a Record the above transactions, including receipt of interest, in journal entries, assuming that the conversion of the bonds is recorded at cost.

b Justify your reason for amortizing or not amortizing the premium on the investment in convertible bonds.

Case 21-4 Imperial Motor Co. holds 1,000 shares of Yellow Bus common stock, par value $10, acquired at a price of $50 a share. On March 15 Yellow Bus declares that stock rights will be issued to shareholders of record on April 1. The rights will permit the purchase of one share of common at $62 for every eight shares held. The rights expire on April 25. On April 1 the stock is selling for $78 and the rights for $2. Imperial Motor Co. exercises 800 rights on April 20 and sells the remaining 200 at $2.25 per right.

Subsequently on September 30 Yellow Bus announces that the stock will be split five shares for four on November 1 and that a cash dividend of 20 cents per share will be paid on the new shares on December 15 to shareholders of record on November 30.

Instructions

a Record the above transactions in the accounts of Imperial Motor Co.

b If Yellow Bus had chosen to make the November 1 distribution a stock dividend instead of a stock split, how would it have been announced? What changes would have been required in the journal entries of Imperial Motor Co. recorded in part (*a*)? If changes are needed, show what they are and explain why they are necessary. If no changes are indicated, explain why there is no need for changes.

PROBLEMS

Group A

21A-1 On June 30, 1975, Amalgamated Retailing bought 20% of the 20,000 outstanding shares of Desert Hotel, Inc. The net assets of Desert Hotel, Inc., on the date of acquisition were as follows:

Common stock ($10 par value)	$ 200,000
Paid-in capital in excess of par	350,000
Retained earnings	470,000
Total stockholders' equity	$1,020,000

Amalgamated Retailing paid $280,000 cash for the Desert Hotel shares. The excess of the cost over the underlying book value was paid because (1) the land owned by the Desert Hotel had a fair market value $100,000 greater than its value on Desert Hotel's books, (2) the depreciable assets of the Desert Hotel (remaining life 12 years) were worth $90,000 more than their undepreciated cost, and (3) the Desert Hotel possessed at least the amount of goodwill imputed by the price Amalgamated paid for the 20% interest. Amalgamated's accounting policy with respect to goodwill is to amortize over 40 years.

During the last six months of 1975, Desert Hotel, Inc., earned a net income of $54,000, including an extraordinary loss of $9,000, and paid dividends of $1 per share. In 1976, the Desert Hotel reported a net loss of $18,000 but paid dividends of $2 per share. Both companies end their fiscal years on December 31.

Instructions

a Compute the total amount of goodwill imputed by the price paid by Amalgamated for a 20% interest in Desert Hotel, Inc.

b Prepare all journal entries relating to the investment on Amalgamated's books for the years 1975 and 1976, using the cost method. Assume that all adjustments are made and dividends received only at year-end.

c Prepare all journal entries relating to the investment for 1975 and 1976 on Amalgamated's books, using the equity method.

d On January 1, 1977, Amalgamated decided that Desert Hotel no longer possessed any of the goodwill imputed by the original acquisition price of the investment and that the investment account should be reduced to the fair market value of the underlying tangible net assets. Prepare a journal entry to reflect this revaluation, assuming that the equity method has been in use.

21A-2 Grace Company acquired 200, $1,000 bonds of Carr, Inc., for $191,469.80 on October 1. The bonds carry a 5% coupon with interest payable semiannually on April 1 and October 1. The remaining life of the bonds is five years with an effective yield to maturity of 6% per annum (compounded semiannually).

Instructions

a Prepare tables for the first two years to show the accumulation of the discount and interest revenue, using both the straight-line method and the effective interest method.

b Make the journal entries required to record the first year's transactions, excluding closing entries, using both the straight-line method and the effective interest method.

21A-3 Hargrave Company had just acquired 10,000 of the 100,000 outstanding shares in Miracle Corporation when Miracle Corporation issued nontransferable rights to all stockholders to buy an additional share of stock at $30 for every two shares owned. If not exercised, the rights will lapse in 90 days. At the time of the rights offering, the market price of Miracle Corporation stock was equal to its book value of $35 per share. Hargrave's cost per share was also $35.

The vice president of finance at Hargrave is concerned about whether to exercise the Miracle rights or let them lapse. He is reluctant to immediately increase Hargrave's cash investment in Miracle, but he is worried that if other stockholders exercise their rights, Hargrave's 10% equity in Miracle Corporation will be substantially diluted.

Instructions

a Compute the percentage of Miracle Corporation stock that will be owned by Hargrave after the rights expire, if (1) all stockholders, including Hargrave, exercise their rights; (2) all stockholders except Hargrave exercise their rights; and (3) 60% of all rights are exercised and 40% lapse, but all of Hargrave's rights are exercised. (Round to the nearest tenth of a per cent.)

b Compute the total cost and total market value of Hargrave's investment in Miracle for each of the three situations described in **(a)** above, assuming that the market price of Miracle stock is equal to its book value *after* the exercise date.

c Assuming that Hargrave Company intends to acquire additional shares of Miracle later and that it has enough cash available to exercise the rights if such action appears advantageous, draft a summary of your findings and your recommendations to the vice president of finance.

21A-4 The Dodds Corporation is required, in accordance with the terms of a long-term debt contract, to create a sinking fund with a trustee to pay off $100,000 of the obligation at the end of five years. The trustee offers Dodds two plans: (1) Pay $18,098 at the end of each year for five years to the trustee, plus expenses of administering the trust; (2) pay $18,463 at the end of each year for five years to the trustee, with the expenses of the trust being paid out of the resources of the trust fund. The trustee expects to earn 5% before expenses on the funds on deposit. The expenses of administration, payable at the end of each year, are estimated as follows:

Year 1	$–0–
Year 2	200
Year 3	365
Year 4	570
Year 5	780

The trustee does not guarantee the accumulation of $100,000. Dodds will be expected to make up any deficit or have refunded to it any excess accumulated in the fund at the end of the fifth year.

Instructions
a Prepare a fund accumulation schedule for each of the two alternatives, based on the stated assumptions.
b Prepare journal entries to record the transactions of the fifth year, including repayment of the obligation, assuming that the estimates are correct.
c Which alternative is Dodds likely to prefer? Why?

21A-5 The following transactions relate to the long-term investments of Hewitt Enterprises:

Jan. 1   Purchased 15,000 of 50,000 outstanding shares of Davis Company common stock for $14 per share. Book value was $12 per share; Hewitt attributed the excess of cost over book value to goodwill, to be amortized over 40 years. The acquisition gave Hewitt a significant degree of control over Davis.

Jan. 5   Purchased $100,000 of Baker Company first mortgage 5% bonds at face value plus accrued interest. Interest is payable semiannually on December 1 and June 1 with maturity 10 years from this past December 1. The bonds are callable at 105.

Feb. 15   Purchased 1,000 shares of Callison Company, $10 par value, common stock at $65 per share.

May 5   Received cash dividend on Callison Company common of 50 cents per share.

June 1   Received semiannual interest on Baker Company bonds.

Aug. 5   Received cash dividend on Callison Company common of 50 cents per share and a 2% stock dividend.

Sept. 15 Sold the shares of Callison Company common received as a stock dividend for $72 per share and purchased 50, $1,000, 5% subordinated debenture bonds of Donald's, Inc., at 94 (94% of par value) with interest payable semiannually on September 15 and March 15, with maturity 16 years from date of purchase. The bonds are callable at 102. (Round cost per share of Callison Company stock to the nearest $.05.)

Sept. 30 Received a cash dividend of 75 cents per share from Davis Company. (Dividend paid from earnings.)

Nov. 5   Received cash dividend on Callison Company common of 50 cents per share.

Dec. 1   Received semiannual interest on Baker Company bonds and surrendered to Baker Company 60 of the $1,000 bonds at the call price in accordance with the provisions of the bond indenture.

Dec. 31 Davis Company reported net income for the year of $82,000, including a $12,000 extraordinary gain.

Instructions
a Record the above transactions in journal form and record any adjustments required at December 31. Amortize all premiums and accumulate all discounts to the nearest half-month, using the straight-line method.
b Prepare a schedule of investments as they would appear on the balance sheet at the end of the year.

Group B

21B-1 On July 1 of the current year Skyline Realty acquired 25% of the outstanding shares of Rural Development Company at a total cost of $240,000. The book value of the stock purchased by Skyline was only $200,000, according to Rural's books. Skyline had been willing to pay more than book value for the shares for the following reasons:
(1) Rural owned depreciable assets (10-year remaining life) with a fair market value $20,000 greater than their book value.
(2) Rural owned land with a fair market value $100,000 greater than its carrying value on Rural's books.
(3) Skyline believed that Rural possessed enough goodwill to justify the remainder of the purchase price. Skyline's accounting policy with respect to goodwill is to amortize it over 20 years.
Rural Development Company earned a net income of $180,000 uniformly over the current calendar year ended December 31. On December 31, Rural paid a cash dividend of $120,000. Both companies close their books on December 31.

Instructions
a Compute the total amount of goodwill Skyline believes Rural to possess, based on the price paid by Skyline for the Rural stock.
b Prepare all journal entries on Skyline's books relating to the investment for the year ended December 31, using the cost method.
c Prepare all journal entries on Skyline's books relating to the investment for the year ended December 31, using the equity method.

21B-2 Stem Company purchased 150, $1,000 face value, 8% bonds maturing in four years, of Reynolds, Inc., on December 1 for $155,155.47. The bonds pay interest on June 1 and December 1, and the investment shows an effective yield of 7% per annum, compounded semiannually.

Instructions
a Prepare tables for the first two years to show the amortization of the premium and the interest revenue, using the straight-line method and the effective interest method.
b Prepare the journal entries necessary to record the first year's transactions, excluding closing entries, using each method of amortization. Assume that Stem Company closes its books on January 31 of each year.

21B-3 Austin Corporation purchased three blocks of Houston Company common stock as follows:

Lot	Number of shares	Price per share	Brokerage and other costs
1	1,000	$28	$280
2	800	36	288
3	1,200	30	360

Houston Company issued a 10% stock dividend on May 10 and stock rights on August 15 entitling common stockholders to purchase at $40 one new share for every 10 shares held. Shortly after the rights were issued, the common stock was trading ex rights at $49 and the rights at $1 per right. Austin sold 300 rights at $1.05 with brokerage and other costs of $10. The remaining rights were exercised.

Instructions

a Compute the gain or loss on the sale of rights using (1) fifo, (2) lifo, and (3) average cost to determine the cost of the rights sold. Round off cost per right to the nearest cent.

b Prepare a schedule showing the number of shares in each lot, the total cost of each lot, and the unit cost of each lot, assuming the use of fifo in part (a) and considering the shares bought through the exercise of rights as Lot 4.

21B-4 The Porter Company is considering issuing $100,000 of 6%, 10-year bonds, interest to be payable annually. A sinking fund will be established to accumulate the $100,000 at the end of 10 years. Porter Company will make payments of $7,950.45 to the fund at the end of each year. The fund balance will be invested to earn 5% per annum.

In addition to the sinking fund, Porter Company will take out a $100,000 life insurance policy on Elvin Porter, the company's president. The terms of the insurance policy are as follows:

Year	Gross premium	Dividend	Guaranteed cash value
1	$2,123		
2	2,123	$277	
3	2,123	313	$ 1,689
4	2,123	350	3,462
5	2,123	387	5,255
6	2,123	426	7,066
7	2,123	465	9,440
8	2,123	503	11,291
9	2,123	542	13,164
10	2,123	581	15,059

Instructions

a Prepare a fund accumulation schedule for the sinking fund for the first three years.

b Prepare a schedule determining the net cash outlay, and the effect upon net income, of the insurance contract for each of the first three years.

c Prepare journal entries for all transactions involving the bonds, the sinking fund, and the insurance contract for each of the first three years.

d Compute (1) the net cash outlay, and (2) the cumulative effect on net income of all the transactions in (c) above over the entire three-year period.

21B-5 Miller Company has two investments acquired prior to the current year. Three years ago, Miller acquired 60% of the 15,000 shares of Mendicino Co., at a total cost of $720,000. This cost exceeded the underlying book value by $80,000, which Miller considered to be a purchase of unrecorded goodwill. Miller has adjusted the income it recognizes from Mendicino for the amortization of this amount over a 40-year period. During the last three years, Mendicino has reported earnings of $1,030,000 and has paid dividends of $975,000. Miller accounts for the investment in Mendicino by the equity method.

Two years ago, Miller acquired 5% of the 1,000,000 shares of Phillips, Inc., at a cost of $1,200,000. During those two years, Phillips has reported profits of $2,400,000 and has paid dividends of $2,000,000. Miller accounts for the investment by the cost method.

The following events relate to Miller's long-term investments during the current fiscal year ending June 30:

July	30	Purchased $70,000 face value of Montgomery Co. 7% bonds at 102.9, plus accrued interest. The bonds pay interest on December 1 and June 1 and mature 58 months from the date of purchase. Round all amounts.
Sept.	30	Mendicino paid a $1 per share dividend; Phillips paid a 25 cents per share dividend.
Dec.	1	Received the interest payment on the Montgomery Co. bonds.
Dec.	31	Mendicino paid a $1 per share dividend; Phillips paid a 25 cents per share dividend.
Mar.	31	Mendicino paid a $1 per share dividend; Phillips paid a 25 cents per share dividend.
June	1	Received the interest payment on the Montgomery Co. bonds.
June	30	Mendicino reported a net loss of $20,000, consisting of an income of $90,000 before extraordinary items and an extraordinary loss of $110,000; it paid a $1 per share dividend. Phillips reported a net income of $120,000 and paid a 25 cents per share dividend.

Instructions

a Illustrate the balance sheet presentation of all items relating to Miller's long-term investments at the beginning of the current year. (Round to the nearest dollar throughout the problem.)

b Compute the total earnings reported and dividends paid by Mendicino Co. and by Phillips, Inc., from the date Miller acquired an interest in each to the end of the current year.

c Prepare journal entries on Miller's books for all the transactions and adjustments relating to long-term investments during the current year. All amortization is done by the straight-line method.

d Illustrate the balance sheet presentation of all items relating to Miller's long-term investments at the end of the current year.

CHAPTER 22

Accounting changes; statements from incomplete records

As accounting principles change in response to changes in the economic and social environment, accountants must find ways to implement the new principles into financial reporting. Putting new principles and new accounting estimates into the stream of annual reports may make current financial statements inconsistent with those of prior years. However, we cannot ignore new improved principles and estimates merely to maintain continuity with the financial reporting of the past. In this chapter we shall explore some approaches to the adoption of new principles and estimates with the goal of maintaining the maximum degree of comparability and, at the same time, gaining the advantages inherent in a change to new and improved accounting concepts.

Also in this chapter we shall discuss methods of correcting and reporting errors which are discovered to exist in financial statements issued in prior years. Finally, we shall consider ways in which the accountant may develop financial statements from incomplete accounting records.

ACCOUNTING CHANGES

Prior to the issuance of *APB Opinion No. 20,* "Accounting Changes," few explicit guidelines existed for reporting the effects of accounting changes on financial statements. Disclosures were often incomplete and obscure, resulting in suggestions by some critics that accounting changes were used as "tools of management" to manipulate earnings. Numerous users of financial data not only misunderstood the reasons for accounting changes but also failed to grasp their impact on financial statements. *Opinion No. 20* was the result of an extensive effort to define the types of accounting changes and to establish workable guidelines for reporting such changes.

Major types of accounting changes

Accounting changes may be classified into two categories as follows:

Change in accounting principle   This type of change occurs when a company adopts an accounting principle which is different from the generally accepted accounting principle used previously for financial reporting purposes. The term *accounting principle* includes the various *methods* which may be used in applying accounting principles. A change in the method of computing depreciation on previously recorded plant assets (for example, a change from an accelerated to a straight-line method) and a change in the reporting entity are examples of changes in accounting principle.

Change in accounting estimate   This type of change may be required as new events occur and as better information becomes available about the probable outcome of future events. Examples of changes in accounting estimates include: Decrease in percentage used to estimate uncollectible accounts expense from 2 to 1% of sales, a major write-down of inventory because of obsolescence, an increase (or decrease) in the estimated service life of tangible or intangible assets, a change in the estimated recoverable units of natural resources, and a revision in the amount of estimated liability for outstanding product warranties.

Introducing accounting changes into financial statements

Financial statements for a given entity are most useful when they are prepared on a *consistent* basis, thus making comparisons between periods meaningful. For this reason, many accountants argue that financial statements for prior periods should be *retroactively restated* following an accounting change. Others would not restate previously issued financial statements, on grounds that such restatements would confuse users and reduce the credibility of financial statements.

Three approaches will be described for reporting the effect of accounting changes. These approaches are not alternatives for a given type of accounting change; instead, they represent methods of reporting different types of accounting changes. The three approaches are summarized below:

1 *Cumulative effect of the change is reported in the income statement of the current year.* The cumulative effect on the net income of prior periods of a change in an accounting principle is *reported in the income statement* of the year in which the change is made.

2 *Prior years' statements are retroactively restated.* The financial statements for prior periods presented are **restated** to conform to the new basis of accounting. The retained earnings at the beginning of the earliest period presented is adjusted for the cumulative effect of the change on net income for the periods prior to those being presented.

3 *The accounting change is viewed as affecting the computation of operating income for the current and future periods.* The effect of the change in accounting principle or estimate **is not carried back** to prior periods and no recognition is given to the cumulative effect of the change in the current period. Thus, the financial statements presented for earlier periods would not be retroactively restated and all accounting changes are viewed as **prospective** for financial reporting purposes.

The application of these possible interpretations to the two types of accounting changes (a change in principle and a change in estimate) is described in the following sections.

Change in accounting principle

At first glance, a change in accounting principle would seem to violate the assumption that financial statements are prepared "in conformity with generally accepted accounting principles applied on a basis consistent with that of the preceding year." In the preparation of financial statements there is a presumption that accounting principles once adopted should not be changed, so that meaningful comparisons of successive financial statements for a company are possible.

A change in an accounting principle would be appropriate only if the reporting entity adopts an alternative accounting principle which is clearly preferable. For example, the issuance of a new accounting standard by the Financial Accounting Standards Board would be sufficient support for a change in accounting principle. However, the initial adoption of an accounting principle to report transactions occurring for the first time, or to report transactions that are substantially different from those previously occurring, is not a change in accounting principle. Replacing an accounting principle that is **not** generally accepted with one that **is** generally accepted is viewed as a correction of an error and not as a change in accounting principle.[1] A change to a preferable accounting principle in the current year would render successive financial statements not comparable and thus raises the following question: How should a change in accounting principle be reported so that comparability of successive financial statements can be preserved?

The answer to this question depends on the type of change in accounting principle and on the magnitude of its effect. A change which **does not materially affect net income** need not be reported as completely as a change which **has a material effect on net income.** Material changes in accounting principle are classified into two categories as follows: (1) Those for which the cumulative effect is included in the income statement

[1] *APB Opinion No. 20,* "Accounting Changes," AICPA (New York: 1971), p. 389.

of the period in which the change is made, and (2) those requiring the restatement of prior years' financial statements.

Cumulative Effect of Change Reported in Current Period The Accounting Principles Board concluded that "most changes in accounting should be recognized by including the cumulative effect, based on a retroactive computation, of changing to a new accounting principle in net income of the period of the change. . . ." [2] The possibility that public confidence in financial statements would be reduced if financial statements of prior periods were retroactively restated was a major factor in reaching this conclusion. Examples of changes in accounting principle in this category are: A change in the method of computing depreciation expense for a previously recorded asset (for example, a change from the sum-of-the-years'-digits method to the straight-line method); a change from expensing research and development costs to a policy of deferring and amortizing such costs; and a change from the fifo to the lifo method of pricing inventory. The following guidelines should be followed for those changes in accounting principle which require recognition of the cumulative effect of the change:

1 Financial statements for prior periods included for comparative purposes should be presented as previously reported.

2 The **cumulative effect** of the change on the retained earnings balance at the beginning of the period in which the change is made should be included in the net income of the period of the change. The amount of the cumulative effect is the difference between **(a)** the **actual** amount of retained earnings at the beginning of the period of a change and **(b)** the amount of retained earnings that **would have been reported** at that date if the new accounting principle had been applied retroactively for **all** prior periods. In computing the cumulative effect, appropriate consideration should be given to income taxes. The total and per-share amount of the cumulative effect should be shown in the income statement immediately below extraordinary items.

3 The total and per-share effect of the change on the income before extraordinary items and on the net income of the period of the change should be disclosed.

4 Income before extraordinary items and net income computed on a **pro forma basis** [3] should be shown on the face of the income statement for all prior periods presented as if the newly adopted accounting principle had been used in the prior periods. If an income statement is presented for the current period only, the actual and pro forma amounts (including earnings per share) for the immediately preceding period should be disclosed.

Computation of the cumulative effect of a change in accounting principle will not be illustrated since this is essentially a mechanical procedure. The **format for reporting the cumulative effect** of a change in accounting principle in the income statement, along with the related footnote disclosure, is illustrated on page 826 for the Shift Corporation.

[2] *Ibid.,* pp. 391–392.
[3] *Pro forma* means "on the assumption that certain transactions are completed or that different principles are used." In connection with our discussion of accounting changes, pro forma means that net income and earnings per share of earlier periods are retroactively restated to conform to the newly adopted accounting principle.

SHIFT CORPORATION
Partial Income Statement
Year Ended December 31

	Year 5	Year 4
Income before extraordinary item and cumulative effect on prior years of change in accounting principle ...	$3,000,000	$2,300,000
Add: Extraordinary item—tax benefit of operating loss carryforward	–0–	60,000
Add: Cumulative effect on prior years (to end of Year 4) of change in accounting principle (see note)	340,000	
Net income	$3,340,000	$2,360,000
Earnings per share of common stock (1 million shares):		
Income before extraordinary item and cumulative effect of change in accounting principle	$3.00	$2.30
Add: Extraordinary item—tax benefit of operating loss carryforward		0.06
Add: Cumulative effect on prior years (to end of Year 4) of change in accounting principle (see note below)....................	0.34	
Net income per share of common stock	$3.34	$2.36
Pro forma amounts, assuming the change in accounting principle is applied retroactively (see note below):		
Income before extraordinary item	$3,000,000	$2,460,000
Earnings per share of common stock (1 million shares)	$3.00	$2.46
Net income, including extraordinary item	$3,000,000	$2,520,000
Earnings per share of common stock	$3.00	$2.52

Note—Change in accounting principle: *During the year ended December 31, Year 5, the company changed its method of accounting for interest and property taxes during construction from expensing such items to capitalizing them as building costs. The new method is a generally accepted method used in the industry, and it is believed such method will cause the company's results to be more comparable to others in the industry. The new method has been applied retroactively to construction in prior years. The effect of the change for the year ended December 31, Year 5, was to increase income before the extraordinary item by $200,000 (or $.20 per share). The adjustment of $340,000 (after reduction of $280,000 for deferred income taxes) to apply retroactively the new method is included in net income of Year 5. The pro forma amounts for Year 4 have been adjusted for the effect of retroactive application of the change on building costs, depreciation expense, and related income taxes.*

The change in accounting principle was recorded as follows by the Shift Corporation:

Buildings	620,000	
Cumulative Effect on Prior Years of Change in Account-		
ing Principle		340,000
Deferred Income Tax Liability		280,000

To record effect of change in accounting principle. Interest
and property taxes of $620,000 incurred prior to Jan. 1,
Year 5, are retroactively capitalized in the Buildings
account (net of accumulated depreciation).

The credit to the Deferred Income Tax Liability account represents the tax effect of that portion of depreciation expense on the building which will be reported for accounting purposes but which will not be allowed in computing future taxable income. The increase of $620,000 in the Buildings account cannot be depreciated for income tax purposes because this amount was previously deducted as interest and property tax expense in computing taxable income. (See Chapter 20 for a more complete coverage of income tax allocation among accounting periods.)

In the income statement for the Shift Corporation the pro forma income before the extraordinary item for Year 4 was increased by $160,000 ($2,460,000 − $2,300,000), or $0.16 per share. The pro forma amounts for Years 4 and 5 are thus fully comparable because they are stated in terms of the newly adopted accounting principle.

In some situations, the determination of the cumulative effect of a change in accounting principle may be impossible. An example of this type of change is a change in inventory pricing method from the fifo to the lifo method. In such situations, the disclosure would be limited to showing the effect of the change on the net income and earnings per share of the period of change. The reason for not showing the cumulative effect of the change in accounting principle also should be clearly stated.

Change Requiring Restatement of Prior Years' Financial Statements In *Opinion No. 20,* the Accounting Principles Board took the position "that a few specific changes in accounting principles should be reported by restating the financial statements of prior periods."[4] Examples of changes that require the restatement of financial statements of prior periods include the following:

1 A change from the lifo method of inventory pricing to another method of inventory pricing such as the fifo method
2 A change in the method of accounting for long-term construction contracts
3 A change in the accounting for development costs in the extractive industries
4 A change in the reporting entity
5 A change from an acceptable accounting principle to another acceptable accounting principle for a closely held company issuing financial statements to the public for the first time

[4] *APB Opinion No. 20,* p. 392.

The consensus of opinion among accountants is that the advantages of restating the financial statements of prior periods in the situations listed above outweigh the disadvantages. The nature of the change in accounting principle, as well as the justification for the change, should be fully disclosed in the financial statements for the period in which the change is made. Disclosure of the effect of the change on income before extraordinary items, net income, and the related per-share amounts should be made for all periods presented. This disclosure may be in the income statement or in the accompanying notes and need not be repeated in the financial statements for the periods following the change.[5]

To illustrate the restatement of an income statement for a prior period as a result of a change in accounting principle, assume the following: The Retro Company adopted the completed-contract method of accounting for long-term construction contracts when it was incorporated in Year 1. The company had reported net income of $137,500 in Year 1 and $330,000 in Year 2. In Year 3, the company decides to change to the percentage-of-completion method. The effect of this change in accounting principle, assuming an average income tax rate of 45%, is summarized below:

| | Operating income using | | Differences | | |
Year	Completed-contract method	Percentage-of-completion method	Before tax effect	Tax effect, 45%	Increase in net income
1	$250,000	$550,000	$300,000	$135,000	$165,000
2	600,000	700,000	100,000	45,000	55,000
3	700,000	850,000	150,000	67,500	82,500

The partial comparative income statement at the end of Year 3, giving retroactive effect to the change in accounting principles, appears at the top of page 829.

To illustrate the effect of the change in the presentation of retained earnings, the comparative statement of retained earnings for the Retro Company is illustrated at the bottom of page 829. In this illustration we have assumed that the company has not declared any dividends since it was organized in Year 1.

In some situations the pro forma effect on the net income of individual prior periods cannot be computed or reasonably estimated, although the cumulative effect on retained earnings at the beginning of the period of change can be determined. The cumulative effect in such cases should be reported in the income statement of the period of change and the reason for not restating prior years' results should be given.[6]

[5] Ibid., p. 396.
[6] Ibid., p. 395.

RETRO COMPANY
Partial Income Statement

	Year 3	Year 2 (restated—see Note 1)
Operating income	$850,000	$700,000
Income tax expense	382,500	315,000
Net income	$467,500	$385,000
Earnings per share (100,000 shares outstanding) . .	$4.68	$3.85

Note 1—Change in method of accounting for long-term construction contracts: *The company has accounted for long-term construction contracts by the percentage-of-completion method in Year 3, whereas in all prior years the completed-contract method was used. The new method of accounting was adopted to report the results of operations in a manner which more closely portrays the economic activity of the company. Financial statements of prior years have been restated to apply the new method of accounting retroactively. For income tax purposes, the completed-contract method will be continued. The effect of the accounting change on net income and earnings per share of Year 3, and on net income and earnings per share previously reported for Year 2, follows:*

	Year 3	Year 2
Increase in:		
Net income	$82,500	$55,000
Earnings per share	$0.83	$0.55

The balances of retained earnings for Year 2 and Year 3 have been adjusted for the effect (net of income taxes) of applying retroactively the new method of accounting.

Certain events, such as a merger of two or more entities through a pooling of interests, result in financial statements that are in effect the statements for a *different reporting entity.* A change in the reporting entity is viewed as a special type of change in accounting principle which should be reported by restating the financial statements of all prior periods as though the new entity had existed all along.

RETRO COMPANY
Statement of Retained Earnings

	Year 3	Year 2
Balance at beginning of year, as previously reported . . .	$ 467,500	$137,500
Add: Cumulative effect on prior years of applying retroactively the new method of accounting for long-term construction contracts	220,000	165,000
Balance at beginning of year, as restated	$ 687,500	$302,500
Net income	467,500	385,000
Balance at end of year, as restated	$1,155,000	$687,500

As pointed out earlier, certain changes from one acceptable accounting principle to another acceptable principle do not require the restatement of financial statements of prior periods. An exception is made for a closely held company *issuing securities publicly for the first time.* Potential investors in the securities of a company "going public" are better served by earnings summaries for a period of years prepared on the basis of the newly adopted accounting principle. Comparisons of operating results will be more meaningful because the newly adopted accounting principle will also be used in future periods. Therefore, the financial statements issued in connection with the initial public offering of securities should be retroactively restated for all periods for which financial statements are presented.

Change in accounting estimate

A change in accounting estimate would also appear to violate the assumption of *consistency.* As previously stated, a change in accounting estimate may be made as a result of new events and as better information becomes available about the probable outcome of future events. A change in accounting estimate affects the computation of operating income of the period in which the change is made and if the change has a continuing effect, it should be consistently applied to the periods following the change. A change in accounting estimate *does not* require the recognition of a cumulative effect in the current period or the retroactive restatement of financial statements for prior periods. A change in estimate which has a significant effect on current income and earnings per share should be disclosed in the notes accompanying the financial statements.

The use of estimates is unavoidable in the preparation of financial statements. Estimates require the exercise of judgment because the future outcome of events cannot be fully anticipated. It is inevitable, then, that changes must be made in earlier estimates on the basis of more reliable and timely information. For example, assume that management had established a useful service life of a plant asset at 10 years with no salvage value at the end of that period. The cost of the asset, $20,000, has been depreciated at the rate of $2,000 per year for 7 years. At the beginning of the eighth year, management determines that the asset has a remaining service life of 5 years and that it will have a salvage value of $500 at the end of 12 years of service life. The revised annual depreciation expense over the newly estimated remaining service life of the asset is determined as follows:

Cost of asset	$20,000
Less: Depreciation for Years 1–7 @ $2,000 per year	14,000
Unrecovered cost at beginning of Year 8	$ 6,000
Less: Estimated salvage value at end of Year 12	500
Amount to be depreciated in Years 8–12	$ 5,500
Revised annual depreciation for Years 8–12, $5,500 ÷ 5 years of remaining life	$ 1,100

The change in estimated service life and salvage value affects only the remaining years of service life (Years 8 through 12); no correction to the previously reported net income for Years 1 through 7 is required. Since the accounting process is imperfect and some disparity between past and subsequent estimates cannot be avoided, retroactive restatements of previously reported earnings as a result of changes in accounting estimates may cast suspicion on both the original and the revised earnings figures. The information used to revise the service potential of the asset could not have been fully anticipated at the time the asset was acquired. Revised estimates are based on present economic facts and management decisions and for this reason, it seems logical to assign the unexpired cost of an asset over the remaining estimated service life based on the latest evidence and conditions.

A revision in the service life or salvage value of an asset, as described above, is a *change in accounting estimate.* A change in the *method* of computing depreciation on a *previously recorded asset* would be a *change in accounting principle.* If a new method of depreciation is adopted for newly acquired assets, no cumulative adjustment in the income statement would be required as long as the company continues to depreciate previously recorded assets using the same method as before. However, the effect of the new method of depreciation for newly acquired assets on the net income of the period of change should be disclosed.

A change in accounting estimate that is effected by a change in accounting principle should be reported as a change in estimate. On this point, *APB Opinion No. 20* stated:

> Distinguishing between a change in an accounting principle and a change in an accounting estimate is sometimes difficult. For example, a company may change from deferring and amortizing a cost to recording it as an expense when incurred because future benefits of the cost have become doubtful. The new accounting method is adopted, therefore, in partial or complete recognition of the change in estimated future benefits. The effect of the change in accounting principle is inseparable from the effect of the change in accounting estimate. Changes of this type are often related to the continuing process of obtaining additional information and revising estimates and are therefore considered as changes in estimates for purposes of applying this Opinion.[7]

[7] *Ibid.,* p. 388.

CORRECTION OF ERRORS

In previous chapters we have noted the difficulties inherent in any attempt to determine the periodic income of a business. At best accountants can only measure the impact of past transactions and events and make informed estimates of the present effect of probable future events. In addition, *errors* in financial statements may result from mathematical mistakes, mistakes in the application of accounting principles, or the oversight or misuse of facts that existed at the time statements were prepared.[8] An example of a correction of an error is a change from an accounting principle that is not generally accepted to one that is generally accepted. On the other hand, a *change in accounting estimate* results from new information or events which enable the accountant to improve accounting measurements. Examples of changes in accounting estimates were given earlier on page 823.

Correction of an error in previously issued financial statements

When a material error is discovered in previously issued financial statements, the correction of the error should be reported as a *prior period adjustment.* The nature of the error and the effect of its correction on net income and earnings per share should be disclosed in the period in which the error is corrected. An example of such disclosure, generally presented in a note accompanying the financial statements, is illustrated below:

> **Note 1—Correction of error:** *A major revision of labor standards in February 1976 resulted in a charge to 1975 earnings of $2,500,000 because of reduced labor and factory overhead costs included in the inventories at December 31, 1975. In connection with the pricing of the December 31, 1975, inventory in February 1976, it was determined that **an error** had been made in applying factory overhead to the December 31, 1974, inventory. The correction resulted in a reduction of the December 31, 1974, inventory by $450,000. Earnings before income taxes for 1974 were reduced from $1,500,000 to $1,050,000; net income was reduced from $816,000 to $600,000 and earnings per share were reduced from $0.41 to $0.30.*

If the error has a material effect on previously issued financial statements, retroactive revision of the statements for prior periods may be warranted. Whenever a reader of financial statements makes a serious analysis of the affairs of a company, he will, for example, want to see comparative income statement data for a series of years. When such comparative statements are prepared, it is always desirable to revise prior years' income statements to reflect material errors discovered after the original statements were issued. The Committee on Auditing Procedure of the AICPA recently made the following recommendation:

---

[8] *Ibid.,* p. 389.

If the effect on the financial statements or auditor's report of the subsequently discovered information can promptly be determined, disclosure should consist of issuing, as soon as practicable, revised financial statements and auditor's report. . . . Generally, only the most recently issued audited financial statements would need to be revised, even though the revision resulted from events that had occurred in prior years.[9]

Anyone who attempts to assess probable future earnings and financial position relies heavily on information about the recent past. An error which causes a material misstatement of income in any of the recent years results in a misleading picture of the earnings pattern of a business. This kind of distortion can affect the decisions of those who rely on financial statements for investment information.

Correction of error and corrected financial statements illustrated

To illustrate the correction of a material error, assume that the Errata Corporation purchased a machine early in Year 1 for $100,000. The machine had an estimated useful life of 10 years and was being depreciated on a straight-line basis. The accountant incorrectly recorded annual depreciation expense for Year 1 through Year 4 at $1,000 per year rather than at the correct amount of $10,000 per year because of a clerical error in computing annual depreciation. Thus depreciation expense was understated by $9,000 per year, or $36,000 for the four years ending with Year 4. The error is discovered early in Year 5, after the condensed financial statements shown at top of page 834 were prepared.

Ignoring the income tax effect of the error, the following correcting entry would be required in Year 5:

Prior Period Adjustment: Error in Computing Depreciation . . .	*36,000*	
Accumulated Depreciation		*36,000*
To correct mechanical error in computing depreciation in		
Years 1 to 4.		

If corrected financial statements for prior periods were not issued in Year 5, the account Prior Period Adjustment: Error in Computing Depreciation would be closed directly to the Retained Earnings account; in the retained earnings statement for Year 5, the prior period adjustment of $36,000 would be shown as a correction to retained earnings at the beginning of Year 5. When corrected financial statements are prepared in Year 5, the "Prior Period Adjustment" account would also be closed to the Retained Earnings account but the ending balances for retained earnings would be retroactively corrected (both in the balance sheet and

[9] *Statement on Auditing Standards No. 41*, "Codification of Auditing Standards and Procedures," AICPA (New York: 1973), p. 129.

ERRATA CORPORATION
Comparative Income Statement (Before Correction)
For Years 3 and 4

	Year 4	Year 3
Sales	$300,000	$280,000
Cost of goods sold and expenses	270,000	260,000
Net income	$ 30,000	$ 20,000
Earnings per share	$3.00	$2.00

ERRATA CORPORATION
Comparative Balance Sheet (Before Correction)
End of Years 3 and 4

	Year 4	Year 3
Assets, excluding machinery	$260,000	$225,000
Machinery	320,000	290,000
Less: Accumulated depreciation	(80,000)	(65,000)
Total assets	$500,000	$450,000
Liabilities	$170,000	$150,000
Capital stock, $10 par value	100,000	100,000
Retained earnings	230,000	200,000
Total liabilities & stockholders' equity	$500,000	$450,000

in the retained earnings statement) for each prior year for which corrected statements are presented.

As an example, the corrected comparative financial statements for Year 3 and Year 4 are presented below:

ERRATA CORPORATION
Comparative Income Statement (After Correction)
For Years 3 and 4

	Year 4	Year 3
Sales	$300,000	$280,000
Cost of goods sold and expenses	279,000	269,000
Net income	$ 21,000	$ 11,000
Earnings per share	$2.10	$1.10

ERRATA CORPORATION
Comparative Balance Sheet (After Correction)

	Year 4	Year 3
Assets, excluding machinery	$260,000	$225,000
Machinery	320,000	290,000
Less: Accumulated depreciation	(116,000)	(92,000)
Total assets	$464,000	$423,000
Liabilities	$170,000	$150,000
Capital stock, $10 par value	100,000	100,000
Retained earnings	194,000	173,000
Total liabilities & stockholders' equity	$464,000	$423,000

In the corrected income statement, "cost of goods sold and expenses" are retroactively increased by the $9,000 understatement in annual depreciation expense, thus reducing net income for each year by $9,000.

The two balance sheet accounts requiring correction at the end of Year 4 and Year 3 are Accumulated Depreciation and Retained Earnings. Since depreciation was understated by $9,000 per year, the cumulative effect is $36,000 at the end of Year 4 and $27,000 at the end of Year 3. The corrected balance in Accumulated Depreciation at the end of Year 4 is $116,000 ($80,000 as originally reported plus $36,000 correction) and at the end of Year 3 it is $92,000 ($65,000 as originally reported plus $27,000 correction). Retained Earnings is restated at $194,000 ($230,000 − $36,000) at the end of Year 4 and at $173,000 ($200,000 − $27,000) at the end of Year 3.

Types of errors

Many potential accounting errors are automatically brought to light by the controls in the double-entry system. Outside auditors and Internal Revenue agents may uncover errors during an examination of the accounting records. The installation of an improved accounting system may bring to light material errors resulting from the inadequacies of the previous system. Thus the necessity of correcting accidental errors is more likely to occur in a small business than in a large publicly held corporation.

The problem of dealing with errors of the same type can be generalized to some extent. Once the student understands the nature of the distortion created by a given class of error, he should be able to determine the effect of any errors in this particular class.

Errors Affecting only Balance Sheet Accounts   An error that affects only balance sheet accounts may arise because entries were made to the wrong account, because transactions were omitted, or because the amounts of certain entries were too large or too small. For example, if Accounts Payable is debited instead of Accounts Receivable, assets are understated and liabilities are understated by the same amount. When the error is discovered, only balance sheet accounts are affected.

Errors Affecting only Income Statement Accounts An error that is confined to income statement accounts will have no effect on the amount of periodic income. Such errors may arise through misclassification; for example, an expense or revenue may be debited or credited to the wrong account.

Errors Affecting both Balance Sheet and Income Statement Accounts Errors that affect both the balance sheet and the income statement fall into two subclasses:

Counterbalancing errors Some errors, if not discovered, will be counterbalanced in the regular course of the next period's accounting. The typical counterbalancing error causes a misstatement of the income of one period and the balance sheet at the end of that period, which is offset by a misstatement of income in the opposite direction in the following period. The balance sheet at the end of the second period and the income of subsequent periods are not affected by the error, which has in a sense "corrected itself" over two accounting periods.

An example of a counterbalancing error is the failure to record accrued wages at the end of a given year. The liability, accrued wages, is understated at the end of the year, and because wage expense is understated, income is overstated in the year the error is made. In the following period the payment of the unrecorded accrued wages will be charged to wage expense, thus overstating the expenses for the second period. As a result, income in the second year is understated by an amount exactly equal to the overstatement of the previous year. If proper wage accruals are made at the end of the second year, the liability account on the balance sheet at that date will be correct. Retained earnings will also be properly stated at the end of the second year, since the errors in income in the two periods will have counterbalanced.

Noncounterbalancing errors Some errors affect both the balance sheet and the income statement accounts but are not automatically counterbalanced in the next accounting period. For example, suppose a purchase of equipment is charged to expense by mistake. Since expenses are overstated in the year of the error, net income for that year will be understated. Net income will also be overstated in subsequent years by the amount of unrecorded depreciation on the equipment while it is in service. Plant assets on the balance sheet will be understated throughout the life of the equipment.

Analyzing the effect of errors

When an error is discovered, the accountant must make a careful analysis of the effect of the error on financial data for previous, current, and subsequent accounting periods. Because it is not feasible to discuss every possible error that might occur, we shall illustrate the reasoning used in determining the effect of errors. The illustrations are designed to show corrections made in order to produce revised income statements of prior years, and do not purport to illustrate the application of **APB Opinion No. 9** or **APB Opinion No. 20.** In other words, we are primarily concerned with major omissions and other accidental errors which may occur in a *small business which does not issue financial statements to the public.*

As an example, let us trace through the effect of an error in determining the amount of inventory on hand at the end of a given period. Assume that we discover that the ending inventory at December 31, 1974, was overstated by $3,400. We can analyze the effect of this error (ignoring income taxes) as follows:

1974	*1975*	*1976*
	Income Statement	
Income overstated by $3,400. *(Cost of goods sold was understated, since ending inventory was too high.)*	Income understated by $3,400. *(Cost of goods sold was overstated, since beginning inventory was too high.)*	Error has fully counterbalanced; no correction is required.
	Balance Sheet	
Assets overstated by $3,400. *(Ending inventory was too high.)* Retained earnings overstated by $3,400. *(Income was overstated.)*	Balance sheet items are properly stated since Dec. 31, 1975, inventory is correct and overstatement of retained earnings in 1974 has been offset by understatement of income in 1975.	No correction required.

The action to be taken upon discovery of this error depends on when the error is discovered and the extent of the revision of financial statements that is desired.

Discovery in 1974 If the error were discovered in 1974 before the books were closed, a separate correcting entry would not be necessary. The ending inventory is typically recorded on the books at the time closing entries are made, and it would be a simple matter to use the revised inventory figure in making the closing entries. The ending inventory in the income statement for 1974 would be decreased by $3,400 and reported income would be smaller by this amount.

Discovery in 1975 If the error were discovered at any time up to the closing of the books in 1975, the correcting entry would be

> *Prior Period Adjustment: Correction to Net Income for 1974* . . .   *3,400*
>   *Inventory, Dec. 31, 1974* *3,400*
> *To correct overstatement in beginning inventory.*

The purpose of this entry is to correct the financial statements for 1975; both the income for 1975 and the balance sheet at the end of 1975 will be properly stated after the prior period adjustment is closed to the Retained Earnings account. In the retained earnings statement for 1975, the "prior period adjustment" would be reported as a correction to the balance in retained earnings at the beginning of 1975.

Discovery in 1976 If the error in the 1974 ending inventory were not discovered until 1976, no entry would be required, since the error has been fully counterbalanced. If the 1974 and 1975 financial statements are to be corrected retroactively, this could be accomplished by simply changing the inventory and retained earnings figures on these statements or by the use of a separate working paper to accomplish the same results in a systematic manner. As of the beginning of 1976, however, all account balances are free of this particular error.

Working-paper analysis of errors

The first step in correcting discovered errors is to analyze the effect of the errors on financial data. The next is to prepare the necessary correcting entries. In the course of an audit or when an accountant is called in to straighten out records that have been improperly kept, a substantial number of errors, affecting several accounting periods, may be discovered. In such cases it may be helpful to use a working paper as an orderly means of analyzing the extent to which errors have counterbalanced and their effect on current financial statements and the statements of previous periods. The working paper will also serve as the underlying support for a single or small number of combined correcting entries. There is no standard form of working-paper analysis; one form that has proved useful for this purpose is illustrated in the following example:

Illustration An audit of the records of Small Company early in 1978 has revealed a number of errors affecting the financial statements for 1976 and 1977, as follows:

1 Unexpired insurance was omitted from the records; insurance premiums were charged to expense as paid. The proper amount of prepayment at the end of 1976 was $550; at the end of 1977, $980.

2 No entry had been made to accrue interest on notes payable at the end of the year. Interest was charged to expense at the time of payment. Accrued interest payable at the end of 1976 was $1,700; at the end of 1977, $480.

3 Interest on notes receivable was credited to Interest Revenue as received. At the end of 1976 accrued interest receivable amounted to $450; at the end of 1977, $840.

4 The company rented certain land, receiving rent in advance; receipts were credited to Rental Revenue. Unearned rental revenue at the end of 1976 was $1,800; at the end of 1977, $740.

5 The company is subject to state and federal income taxes at a rate of 30% of taxable income. There are no differences between taxable income and accounting income. It is assumed that 1976 tax returns will be revised to reflect the foregoing errors, and that the company will claim a refund for excess taxes paid in 1976 or will pay any tax deficiency.

Small Company reported net income of $10,000 in 1976, and net income of $6,000 in 1977. We wish to determine the extent of the errors in the net income for 1976 and 1977 and to correct the accounting records at December 31, 1977. The working paper on page 840 illustrates the procedure.

Let us assume that the books *have been closed* at the end of 1977. On the basis of our working-paper analysis, the following entry will correct the accounting records at December 31, 1977.

Unexpired Insurance	*980*	
Interest Receivable	*840*	
Tax Refund Receivable, 1976	*750*	
Prior Period Adjustment: Correction to Net Income for 1976	*1,750*	
Prior Period Adjustment: Correction to Net Income for 1977		*2,170*
Interest Payable		*480*
Unearned Rental Revenue		*740*
Income Taxes Payable		*930*
To correct errors revealed by audit in 1978 after books have been closed for 1977.		

Trace the figures in this entry to the working paper and you will see that all the data necessary for the correcting entry were developed in the working-paper analysis. In order to prepare a corrected 1977 income statement, it would be necessary to revise the individual expense and

SMALL COMPANY
Working Paper Analysis of Errors
December 31, 1977

Explanation	Net income for 1976 (Dr) Cr*	Net income for 1977 (Dr) Cr*	Balance sheet accounts requiring correction at Dec. 31, 1977 (Dr) Cr*	Account title
(1) Unexpired insurance omitted:				
Dec. 31, 1976	$ 550	$ (550)		
Dec. 31, 1977		980	$(980)	Unexpired Insurance
(2) Accrued interest on notes payable omitted:				
Dec. 31, 1976	(1,700)	1,700		
Dec. 31, 1977		(480)	480	Interest Payable
(3) Accrued interest on notes receivable omitted:				
Dec. 31, 1976	450	(450)		
Dec. 31, 1977		840	(840)	Interest Receivable
(4) Unearned rental revenue omitted:				
Dec. 31, 1976	(1,800)	1,800		
Dec. 31, 1977		(740)	740	Unearned Rental Revenue
Change in income before income taxes:				
1976 income decreased	$ (2,500)			
1977 income increased		$3,100		
(5) Revision of income taxes (30%):				
1976 income taxes overstated	750		(750)	Tax Refund Receivable, 1976
1977 income taxes understated		(930)	930	Income Taxes Payable
Total corrections to net income	$ (1,750)	$2,170	420	Prior Period Adjustment
Net income as originally reported	10,000	6,000		
Corrected net income	$ 8,250	$8,170		

*Separate columns for debit and credit amounts may be used.

revenue accounts to reflect the total increase of $2,170 in 1977 net income. If the books **had not been closed** at the time the correcting entry was made, it would be necessary to expand the above entry to include the correction of expense and revenue accounts for 1977 as follows:

Unexpired Insurance	980		
Interest Receivable	840		
Tax Refund Receivable, 1976	750		
Prior Period Adjustment: Correction to Net Income for 1976	1,750		*Correction of*
Income Tax Expense, 1977	930		*revenue and*
Insurance Expense ($980 − $550)		430	*expense accounts*
Interest Expense ($1,700 − $480)		1,220	*to reflect*
Interest Revenue ($840 − $450)		390	*$2,170*
Rental Revenue ($1,800 − $740)		1,060	*increase in net*
Interest Payable		480	*income for 1977*
Unearned Rental Revenue		740	
Income Taxes Payable		930	

To correct errors revealed by audit in 1978.
Books not yet closed at Dec. 31, 1977.

The analysis of errors in the working paper indicates that net income for 1977 was understated by $2,170. If 1977 revenue and expense accounts are to be corrected, it is necessary to look at the details in the column headed "Net income for 1977" and determine the individual revenue and expense accounts that require adjustment. All the necessary amounts appear in this column, but the working paper does not show the accounts involved. It would be possible to add a column or two to the working paper and enter the account titles at the time the working paper is prepared. It is usually easier, however, to determine the appropriate revenue or expense account by noting the description of the error in the explanation column. For example, when we see that unexpired insurance was omitted at the end of both 1976 and 1977, it is apparent that the adjustment involves insurance expense. Since unexpired insurance increased from $550 to $980 during 1977, it is clear that insurance expense was overstated by the $430, since an increase in assets in this amount was charged to expense in error. This reasoning determines the credit of $430 to Insurance Expense in the correcting entry.

The working-paper analysis of errors illustrated above is very helpful in tracing through the effect of errors on net income for several years, and in providing the basis for the necessary journal entry or entries to correct general ledger account balances at the end of the current year. Once the necessary entries have been recorded, the balance sheet and income statement for the current year can be prepared in the normal way.

If comparative statements are to be prepared, there remains the problem of revising the income statements and balance sheets of prior years to reflect the correction of errors. A correcting journal entry will always revise a company's balance sheet accounts to their corrected balances as of the end of the current year, but it will not correct account balances as of any prior date. Similarly, once the revenue and expense accounts for any given year are closed, an entry to correct errors will have no effect on the particular revenue and expense items for that year.

If the number of errors affecting data for prior years is small, it is usually a simple matter to make the necessary changes in amounts appearing on financial statements for prior years. When there are a large number of errors or when the correcting entries are complex, however, it may be desirable to use a working paper to correct the financial statements for prior years. A working paper which provides two columns for the original balances, two columns for the correcting entries, and two columns each for the income statement and balance sheet amounts will serve the purpose, and will also constitute a record of the revision for the accounting files.

STATEMENTS FROM INCOMPLETE RECORDS

The heart of the double-entry accounting system is the process of analyzing the effect of each transaction on the basic accounting equation: Assets = liabilities + owners' equity. Many small organizations operate with varying degrees of success with only minimal records and without the benefit of a complete accounting system. A system (or lack of system) of record keeping in which transactions are not analyzed and recorded in the double-entry framework is sometimes called a *single-entry* system. The records of clubs, civic organizations, and small business units are often maintained on a single-entry basis.

At some time after the data have been well muddled, an accountant is likely to be called on to sift through such records and gather enough information to complete an income tax return and to prepare a balance sheet and an income statement. The process of recasting single-entry information into the double-entry framework is thus a very practical analytical exercise.

Balance sheet from incomplete records

A business having no formal accounting system would still find it necessary to record certain basic information to stay in operation. For example, a record of cash received and checks written and a record of amounts due from customers and amounts owed to creditors would be essential. It would be possible to prepare a balance sheet at any given date for such a business from various sources of information. Cash on hand could be determined by count and by examining bank statements. Amounts due from customers could be summarized from unpaid sales invoices. Inventory on hand could be counted and its cost determined from purchase invoices. The cost of land, buildings, and equipment owned could be similarly established. The amount owing to creditors could be determined from purchase invoices and monthly statements. Ownership equity would be the difference between the valuations assigned to assets and liabilities.

Determining income from single-entry records

One way to determine net income from single-entry records is to analyze the change in owners' equity during any given period. We know that owners' equity is the residual interest in the net assets of a business and that it is increased by net income and additional investment, and decreased by losses and distributions of assets to the owners. By the process of elimination, if we know the beginning and ending balance of owners' equity and the amount of any additional investments or withdrawals by owners, we can arrive at the change in owners' equity attributable to the income or loss from operations during the period under consideration. For example:

	Case I (net income)	Case II (net loss)
Owners' equity at end of period	$22,000	$20,000
Owners' equity at beginning of period	18,500	25,000
Total increase or (decrease) in owners' equity	$ 3,500	$(5,000)
Add: Amounts withdrawn by owners	4,800	2,600
Less: Additional investment by owners	(1,000)	(500)
Net income or (loss) for the period	$ 7,300	$(2,900)

For many purposes a more complete picture of operations is needed than that conveyed by a single net income figure. The Internal Revenue Service insists on some details of revenue and expenses. For even the most elementary budgeting and managerial control purposes, information is required as to how net income was determined. The problem then is how to develop these operating details from single-entry records.

Since money transactions are of major importance in any business, a detailed record of cash receipts and payments is a valuable source of information. This is demonstrated in the tabulation on page 844.

If, in addition to cash receipts and payments data, we have (1) a list of assets at the beginning and end of the period and (2) a list of liabilities at the beginning and end of the period, we can determine the owners' equity at the beginning and end of the period, and prepare comparative balance sheets.

From a detailed list of cash receipts we can determine:	From a detailed list of cash payments we can determine:
Cash receipts from sales and other revenue	Cash paid for purchases of merchandise and operating expenses
Collections on customers' accounts	Payments to creditors
Proceeds from sale of plant assets	Cash paid to acquire plant assets
Amounts borrowed	Payments on loans
Investments by owners	Cash withdrawals by owners

From this basic information, plus some help from miscellaneous sources, we can reconstruct the major components (sales, other revenue, cost of goods sold, and operating expenses) of the income statement. In the sections that follow are some examples to illustrate how these various revenue and expense items can be derived, using the information available in single-entry records.

Preparation of Income Statement from Incomplete Records Illustrated To illustrate the preparation of an income statement, we shall assume a relatively simple situation. The following balance sheet at the end of Year 1, summary of operations for Year 2, and other information for Joe's Place, a single proprietorship, will serve as a basis for our illustration:

JOE'S PLACE

Balance Sheet—End of Year 1

(Prepared from Incomplete Records)

Assets		Liabilities & Capital	
Cash	$ 4,680	Accounts payable	$ 9,400
Notes receivable from suppliers	12,000	Accrued salaries	1,100
Accounts receivable	4,000	Unearned rental revenue	600
Interest receivable	320	Total liabilities	$11,100
Inventory	18,000	Joe Palermo, capital	55,900
Unexpired insurance	500		
Building and equipment	40,000		
Less: Accumulated depreciation	(12,500)		
Total assets	$67,000	Total liabilities & capital	$67,000

Summary of operations for Year 2 (from cash and supplementary records)

Cash receipts:

Collections on accounts receivable	$35,000	
Sales on cash basis	42,000	
Interest revenue	540	
Rental revenue	3,600	$81,140
Cash payments:		
For merchandise (including freight)	$53,400	
Insurance premiums	940	
Salaries	10,700	
Other operating expenses	3,000	
Withdrawals by owner	6,000	74,040
Sales returns and allowances		1,800
Cash discounts taken by customers (sales discounts)		600
Accounts written off as uncollectible during the year		300
Cash discounts taken on purchases (purchases discounts)		1,100
Purchases returns and allowances		970

Account balances at end of Year 2 (from supplementary analyses)

Cash (verified through count and bank reconciliations)	$?
Notes receivable (no change during the year)	12,000
Accounts receivable	7,600
Interest receivable	530
Inventory	25,000
Unexpired insurance	700
Accounts payable	8,500
Accrued salaries payable	1,900
Unearned rental revenue	450

Additional data and assumptions

(1) No acquisitions or disposals of buildings or equipment took place during Year 2.
(2) Depreciation is computed by the accountant at $2,800 for Year 2.
(3) Payroll taxes and income tax withholdings are ignored in order not to complicate the example.
(4) The direct write-off method is used to recognize uncollectible accounts expense.

Reconstructing Gross Sales Sales arise from two sources, cash receipts from customers and gross increases in accounts receivable. Since beginning receivables reflect revenue realized in prior periods, cash collections of these receivables during the current period have no connection with the revenue of the current period. Therefore, the beginning balance of accounts receivable must be deducted from the total cash collections to arrive at sales of the current period that were realized in cash. On the other hand, receivables at the end of the current period represent sales which are not reflected in cash receipts and which must be added in to convert a cash receipts figure into the sales figure. Receivables included in this computation should include only accounts and notes arising from merchandise transactions.

Sales returns and allowances, sales discounts, and receivables written off as uncollectible during the period represent sales during the period that were never realized in cash and are not included in the accounts receivable balance at the end of the year. These amounts, however, should be included in the computation of gross sales. Applying this reasoning, we can reconstruct gross sales for Joe's Place as follows:

JOE'S PLACE
Gross Sales for Year 2

Sales on account for Year 2:

Collections on accounts receivable	$35,000	
Receivables written off as uncollectible	300	
Sales returns and allowances	1,800	
Cash discounts taken by customers	600	
Accounts receivable at the end of Year 2	7,600	
Less: Accounts receivable at the beginning of Year 2	(4,000)	$41,300
Cash sales		42,000
Gross sales for Year 2		$83,300

Reconstructing Other Revenue The amount of such other revenue items as rental revenue, sales of scrap, and interest earned may be determined from comparative balance sheet and cash data as illustrated on page 847 for Joe's Place.

Reconstructing Cost of Goods Sold The cost of goods sold is derived from information about purchases and inventories. Inventories at the end of a period can be determined by a physical count. Hopefully, beginning inventories were also determined by count at the end of the previous period; if not, an estimated amount must be used.

The purchases figure may be reconstructed from cash payments records and schedules of accounts payable at the start and end of the

JOE'S PLACE
Other Revenue for Year 2

	Interest revenue	Rental revenue
Amount of revenue received in cash in Year 2	$540	$3,600
Less: Amounts included in cash receipts but not earned in Year 2:		
Advance payments by tenants at end of Year 2		450
Interest receivable at beginning of Year 2	320	
Cash receipts representing revenue for Year 2	$220	$3,150
Add: Amounts earned in Year 2 but not included in cash receipts:		
Advance payments by tenants at beginning of Year 2 . . .		600
Interest receivable at end of Year 2	530	
Revenue for Year 2	$750	$3,750

period. Once more we must call upon our understanding of the relation between cash flows and expenses. The balance of accounts payable at the beginning of the period reflects purchases during prior periods that are not germane to the operating results of the current year. Therefore, from total cash payments to merchandise creditors we must deduct the beginning balance of accounts payable to arrive at the cash outlays for merchandise purchases applicable to this period. Unpaid accounts payable at the end of the period represent credit purchases during the current year, which must be added in to arrive at an estimate of the total amount of purchases for the period. An analysis of invoices will supply information as to the cash discounts taken during the period and the credits received for purchases returns and allowances.

The following illustration for Joe's Place demonstrates how reasoning and a systematic organization of the available data enable the accountant to arrive at a cost of goods sold figure. The first step is to compute the amount of gross purchases for Year 2 as shown below:

JOE'S PLACE
Gross Purchases for Year 2

Payments on accounts payable during Year 2	$53,400
Cash discounts taken on purchases	1,100
Purchases returns and allowances	970
Accounts payable balance at end of Year 2	8,500
Less: Accounts payable balance at beginning of Year 2	(9,400)
Gross purchases for Year 2	$54,570

In deriving gross purchases, the accountant must be careful to include in accounts payable only accounts relating to merchandise purchases. This analysis, together with the inventory figures taken from comparative balance sheets, provides all the information necessary to compute cost of goods sold as shown below:

JOE'S PLACE
Cost of Goods Sold for Year 2

Beginning inventory		$18,000
Gross purchases (see above)	$54,570	
Less:		
Cash discounts taken on purchases	$1,100	
Purchases returns and allowances	970	(2,070)
Net purchases		52,500
Cost of goods available for sale		$70,500
Less: Ending inventory		25,000
Cost of goods sold for Year 2		$45,500

Reconstructing Operating Expenses Expenses arise from cash payments, from purchases of goods and services on credit, and from the consumption of assets on hand. Since cash payments during any given period may involve the acquisition of assets or the payment of debts that relate to expenses of prior periods, reconstructing the expenses of the current period requires an analysis of both asset and liability accounts as well as cash payments.

The balance of any asset that is subject to amortization increases as a result of the acquisition of additional assets, and decreases as the asset is used up. The normal process of determining the ending balance of the asset is: Beginning asset balance, plus acquisitions, less assets consumed, equals the ending balance. In reconstructing expenses we usually are able to determine the beginning and ending balance of the related asset and the cost of new acquisitions during the period (through an analysis of cash payments and credit transactions). We can convert this information into the amount of expense for the period as follows:

Assets acquired during the period	XX
Less: Asset balance at the end of the period	(XX)
Add: Asset balance at the beginning of the period	XX
Equals expense for the period	XXX

The determination of expenses by analyzing accrued liability balances and related cash payments is a similar process. The beginning balance of the accrued liability is deducted from the total cash payments during the current period to arrive at the cash payments relating to current period's expense. Adding to this figure the accrued liability at the end of the period produces the expense for the current period. Reconstruction of operating expenses for Joe's Place is illustrated below:

JOE'S PLACE
Operating Expenses for Year 2

	Insurance expense	Salary expense	Other operating expenses	Depreciation expense
Cash payments during Year 2	$ 940	$10,700	$3,000	
Less amounts included in payments but not expenses of Year 2:				
Prepayments at end of Year 2	(700)			
Accrued liability at beginning of Year 2 . . .		(1,100)		
Add amounts not included in cash payments, but chargeable to the operations of Year 2:				
Prepayments at beginning of Year 2	500			
Accrued liability at end of Year 2		1,900		
Depreciation expense as computed by accountant				$2,800
Operating expenses for Year 2	$ 740	$11,500	$3,000	$2,800

Working Paper for Preparation of Financial Statements from Incomplete Records The foregoing computations and other information derived from incomplete records can now be used to prepare a complete set of financial statements. Most accountants, however, prefer to summarize the information in working-paper form, as illustrated on page 850 for Joe's Place. Formal financial statements may be prepared from the information in the last four columns of the working paper.

JOE'S PLACE
Working Paper for Preparation of Financial Statements from Incomplete Records
For Year 2

Accounts	Balances, beg. of Year 2		Transactions for Year 2		Income statement for Year 2		Balance sheet, end of Year 2	
	Debit	Credit	Debit	Credit	Debit	Credit	Debit	Credit
Cash	4,680		(1) 42,000 (2) 35,000 (3) 4,140	(5) 53,400 (6) 14,640 (8) 6,000			11,780	
Notes receivable	12,000						12,000	
Accounts receivable	4,000		(1) 41,300	(2) 37,700			7,600	
Interest receivable	320		(3) 210				530	
Beginning Inv.	18,000				18,000			
Unexpired insurance	500			(6) 200			700	
Bldg. & equipment	40,000						40,000	
Accum. deptn.		12,500		(7) 2,800				15,300
Accounts payable		9,400	(5) 55,470	(4) 54,570				8,500
Accrued sal. pay.		1,100		(6) 800				1,900
Unearned rent rev.		600	(3) 150					450
J. Palermo, capital		55,900						55,900
J. Palermo, drawing			(8) 6,000				6,000	
Sales				(1) 83,300		83,300		
Sales ret. & all.			(2) 1,800		1,800			
Sales discounts			(2) 600		600			
Uncoll. accts. exp.			(2) 300		300			
Interest revenue				(3) 750		750		
Rental revenue				(3) 3,750		3,750		
Purchases			(4) 54,570		54,570			
Purchases ret. & all.				(5) 970		970		
Purchase discounts				(5) 1,100		1,100		
Insurance expense			(6) 740		740			
Salary expense			(6) 11,500		11,500			
Other operating exp.			(6) 3,000		3,000			
Depreciation exp.			(7) 2,800		2,800			
Ending inventory						25,000	25,000	
					93,310	114,870	103,610	82,050
Net income					21,560			21,560
	79,500	79,500	259,780	259,780	114,870	114,870	103,610	103,610

Explanation of transactions:
(1) Gross sales, $42,000 in cash and $41,300 on account.
(2) Collection on account, sales returns and allowances, sales discounts, and uncollectible accounts expense.
(3) Collection of interest and rental revenue; adjust interest receivable and unearned rental revenue.
(4) Gross purchases.
(5) Payment on accounts payable; also to record purchases returns and allowances and purchase discounts.
(6) Payments for expenses; adjust unexpired insurance and acquired salaries payable.
(7) Depreciation expense (given).
(8) Owner's drawings.

REVIEW QUESTIONS

1 Briefly describe the purpose of **Opinion No. 20** issued by the Accounting Principles Board.

2 What are two types of **accounting changes?** Briefly describe each type.

3 List the three possible approaches that may be applicable to reporting the effect of an accounting change.

4 Describe a situation in which a **change in accounting principle** would be considered appropriate.

5 How is the **cumulative effect** of a change in accounting principle determined and reported in the income statement for the period in which the change is made?

6 List five examples of changes in accounting principle which would require the retroactive restatement of financial statements for prior periods.

7 The Optical Radiation Corporation has been capitalizing research and development costs for many years and amortizing such costs over a four-year period. At the end of Year 5, the Deferred Research and Development Cost account shows a balance of $115,000, including $40,000 incurred in Year 5. Because the future benefits of the deferred costs are uncertain, the company decides to write off the entire amount of deferred research and development costs and recognize such costs as expenses in the future. How should the write-off be reported in the financial statements?

8 The Ould Sulphur Company wrote down its plant and equipment by $15 million in 1975. The reasons given were:
a To reduce excess capacity by closing inefficient plants
b To recognize obsolescence attributed to new technological developments and a shift in the demand for the company's products
How should the write-off be reported in the financial statements?

9 Occidental Petroleum Corp. charged $87.9 million against operating income as a result of a write-down of its seagoing tanker fleet. Included in this amount was $65 million "for possible losses in the future." Evaluate the accounting treatment of this write-down.

10 How should an error in previously issued financial statements be reported in the year the error is discovered?

11 What is the basis for distinguishing between an error in measuring the net income of a prior period that should be treated as a prior period adjustment, and an error whose correction should be considered a part of the determination of net income in the period in which it is discovered?

12 Which of the following errors should be treated as a prior period adjustment?
a A depreciable asset which was estimated to have a service life of four years is used for six years.
b A substantial deficiency in income taxes relating to the income of two years ago is assessed by the Internal Revenue Service.
c An analysis of credit experience indicates that losses from uncollectible accounts over the past three years have exceeded the provision for such losses made at the rate of 1% of sales.
d Merchandise in transit at the close of the previous year was included in purchases but not included in the ending inventory.

e An audit reveals that the purchase of a depreciable asset was inadvertently charged to expense last year.

13 Errors affecting both the balance sheet and the income statement may be classified into two major types. State and define each type.

14 Why is it important to correct material errors even after they have counter-balanced?

15 Explain what is meant by the term *single-entry accounting system.*

16 Briefly describe two general approaches that may be followed in arriving at the amounts required to prepare financial statements from incomplete records.

EXERCISES

Ex. 22-1 During the year ended December 31, Year 3, the Jackson Motels Company changed its method of accounting for interest and property taxes during construction from expensing such items to capitalizing them as building costs. The company was organized in Year 1. The data below have been accumulated from the accounting records.

	Year 3	Year 2	Year 1
Income before cumulative effect of accounting change in Year 3.	$400,000	$270,000	$150,000
Interest and property taxes during construction	125,000	75,000	25,000
Depreciation on buildings—based on accounting principle formerly followed	50,000	35,000	30,000
Depreciation on buildings—based on newly adopted accounting principle	59,000	39,000	31,000
Earnings per share as reported, before cumulative effect of accounting change in Year 3	$2.00	$1.35	$0.75

The income for Year 3 was determined using the newly adopted accounting principle. The number of shares of common stock outstanding during the three-year period has not changed.

a Compute the cumulative effect of the change in accounting principle which should appear in the income statement for Year 3. Assume a 40% income tax rate.

b What was the effect of the change in accounting principle on the per-share earnings for each of the three years?

Ex. 22-2 From the data in Ex. 22-1, prepare a partial comparative income statement for Years 2 and 3. The income statement should include the cumulative effect on prior years of the change in accounting principle, the earnings per share of common stock, and pro forma amounts for Year 2, as illustrated on page 826.

Ex. 22-3 Ox Bow Incinerator, Inc., included the following items on its balance sheet at the end of 1975:

Equipment	$3,780,000	
Less: Accumulated depreciation	1,260,000	$2,520,000
Goodwill (excess of cost over book value of acquired		
companies)		1,225,000

Both assets were acquired early in 1971. The equipment has been depreciated over an estimated useful life of 15 years and the goodwill has been amortized over a period of 20 years. Late in 1976 the company decided that the total useful life of the equipment should be reduced to 12 years and that goodwill should be amortized over a period of 40 years from the date of acquisition. Compute the depreciation on the equipment and the amortization of goodwill for 1976, assuming that the residual value of the equipment is estimated at $140,000.

Ex. 22-4 At the end of Year 1, York Company's accountant capitalized costs incurred in developing a patent, intending to amortize these costs over the next five years. At the end of Year 3 it was discovered that the sales manager's Year 1 salary of $25,000 had inadvertently been included in the patent cost at the end of Year 1. The company is subject to a 50% income tax rate and intends to file amended tax returns for Years 1 and 2. Give the journal entry to correct this error at the end of Year 3, after normal adjusting entries have been made but before the books have been closed.

Ex. 22-5 The following errors in the records of the Sims & Tims partnership are discovered in Year 4:

	Inventory overstated	Depreciation understated	Accrued revenue not recorded	Accrued expenses not recorded
Year 1	$10,000	$ -0-	$3,000	$ -0-
Year 2	-0-	2,500	1,000	-0-
Year 3	4,000	-0-	-0-	500

The partners share profits and losses equally.
a Prepare a correcting entry in Year 4, assuming that the books are closed for Year 3.
b Prepare a correcting entry in Year 4, assuming that the books are still open for Year 3.

Ex. 22-6 During the current month the cash records of Retail Auto Parts show that $15,200 was collected from credit customers and $12,400 was received from cash sales. The amount due from credit customers increased from $7,300 at the beginning of the month to $8,150 at the end of the month. During the month the credit manager had written off $790 of accounts receivable as uncollectible. From this information, determine the gross sales for the month.

Ex. 22-7 CATV, Inc., sells TV cable services to customers, who may choose to pay $4 per month for the service or may pay in advance a yearly charge of $42 for 12 months of service. During the current year the company collected $45,700 from customers. Additional information for the current year follows:

	Beginning of year	End of year
Advance payments by customers	$3,500	$5,700
Accounts receivable from customers	6,820	6,930

From the information given, compute the total cable revenue earned during the year.

Ex. 22-8 The inventory of Hockett Company increased by $21,000 during the year, and its accounts payable to merchandise suppliers increased by $9,500. During the year the company paid $30,200 to suppliers and $7,200 in transportation charges on merchandise. The company also bought $4,100 of merchandise for cash. Determine the cost of goods sold for the year.

Ex. 22-9 The following information is taken from the records of the Spiers Company for Year 1:

	Jan. 1	Dec. 31
Stockholders' equity (no stock issued or retired)	$98,000	$107,000
Cash	6,000	12,400
Inventory	20,000	14,000
Payable to merchandise creditors	8,000	8,500
Receivable from customers	14,200	18,200
Cash paid to merchandise creditors		60,000
Operating expenses and income taxes paid in cash (including $800 prepaid at end of year)		22,000
Current year's sales written off as uncollectible (an additional allowance of $250 is required at Dec. 31)		500
Dividends declared and paid		15,000
Depreciation expense		4,200
Other assets	77,800	82,350
Other liabilities	12,000	12,000

Prepare an income statement on the accrual basis for Year 1 in good form. Show supporting schedules for sales, cost of goods sold, and total operating expenses and income taxes. (**Hint:** First compute net income and work back to sales).

SHORT CASES FOR ANALYSIS AND DECISION

Case 22-1 Given below is an abstract from a news item which appeared in the **Wall Street Journal:**

Libby McNeill & Libby said a change in its method of inventory valuation will contribute an extraordinary gain of about $15 million to results for the fiscal year ending July 3. The food company said it's changing to first-in, first-out from last-in, first-out inventories.

The company said it incurred losses in prior years and reported that it has about $18.8 million of these losses available to offset taxable income earned in the future.

While Libby didn't detail reasons for the change, industry sources said the switch to FIFO can be advantageous under certain circumstances. In the case of companies having large tax-loss carryforwards that may be due to expire, for example, the switch to FIFO permits the taxable gain realized to be offset by the tax-loss carryforward. This lessens at least in part the tax impact and, at the same time, permits utilization of the loss carryforward that otherwise might expire unused.

The industry source also stated that a change to FIFO from LIFO tends to improve earnings during periods of inflation. That situation arises because under the FIFO method, inventories are valued on a current cost basis while under LIFO they are valued as of an earlier date and presumably at a lower cost basis.

Instructions

a The news item uses the term **extraordinary gain** in reference to the change in inventory pricing method. Describe how the effect of this change should be reported in the financial statements and indicate whether an extraordinary gain results from a change from lifo to the fifo method of inventory pricing.
b Why would a company change from lifo to fifo if such a change results in a significant amount of back taxes which may have to be paid to the government?

Case 22-2 The 1970 annual report for Hilton Hotels Corporation contained the following paragraph in a note titled, "Commitments and contingent liabilities:"

The Company is defendant in various litigation but legal counsel are of the opinion that it has meritorious defenses and do not anticipate that it will be liable for any material amounts.

The 1971 annual report for Hilton Hotels Corporation included the following note:

Restatement of Prior Years:
The 1970 financial statements have been restated to reflect the provision for disposition of claims arising from a settlement in 1971 of allegedly illegal message service charges relating to years prior to 1971 as summarized below:

	Reported	*Restated*
Net income	$15,162,000	$14,628,000
Income per common and common equivalent share	1.94	1.88

Such estimated claims, credits, costs and expenses total $4,203,000, the income tax reduction applicable thereto is $2,102,000 (which reduced the tax liability at December 31, 1971) and the reduction in earnings of unconsolidated affiliates is $178,000. The settlement is subject to numerous conditions and final approval by the Court.

In addition, certain amounts for 1970 have been restated to conform with classifications adopted in 1971.

A comparison of the balance sheet at December 31, 1970, included in the 1970 annual report, with the retroactively restated balance sheet at December 31, 1970, which was included in the 1971 annual report, disclosed that the unfavorable outcome of the litigation was recorded as follows:

Income Tax Reduction from Settlement of Litigation	2,102,000	
Retained Earnings—Jan. 1, 1970	1,745,000	
Net Income for 1970 (various revenue and expense accounts)	534,000	
Accrued Expenses		4,203,000
Investment in Unconsolidated Affiliates		178,000

To record effect of settlement of litigation relating to illegal message service charges to customers.

The income tax reduction from settlement of litigation, $2,102,000, was included among current assets in the restated balance sheet for 1970. Total assets reported by Hilton Hotels Corporation at December 31, 1970, were $381,299,000 before the restatement and $383,224,000 after the restatement. The earnings per share for 1971 were $1.77.

Instructions

a With the benefit of hindsight, do you think that the note in the 1970 annual report presented a fair assessment of the litigation resolved in 1971?

b Briefly explain the entry which was made to record the outcome of the litigation. Why is the income tax reduction of $2,102,000 shown as a current asset?

c Was this an accounting change, a correction of an error in previously issued financial statements, or a prior period adjustment? Do you think it was proper to restate the financial statements retroactively? Was the effect of the outcome of the litigation material in amount?

Case 22-3 The Lisa Company, which is closely held, plans to sell additional shares of stock to the public to finance an expansion program. The company has been in operation for five years and has never had an audit. To meet the requirements of the Securities and Exchange Commission in connection with its registration, the company has hired a firm of CPA's to audit its records for the first time, as of the end of 1975.

In its financial statements for the past five years the company has reported the following earnings and stockholders' equity:

	Net income	Earned per share of common stock	Stockholders' equity
1971	$368,000	$1.84	$4,945,000
1972	390,000	1.95	5,195,000
1973	435,000	2.18	5,350,000
1974	470,000	2.35	5,620,000
1975	510,000	2.55	5,870,000

The auditor discovered in the course of his examination that the company had consistently omitted from its ending inventory in each of the five years an inventory of goods in a warehouse in Ohio. This warehouse operation had not proved successful and had been discontinued in 1975; therefore the inventory at the end of 1975 was not affected by the error. Warehouse records show that the inventory of goods in the warehouse at the end of each year, stated at average cost, was as follows: 1971, $180,000; 1972, $90,000; 1973, $210,000; 1974, $115,000. The auditor also discovered that because the sales report from the warehouse was late in arriving at the end of 1972, $80,000 of sales applicable to 1972 operations were not recorded as revenue until 1973.

When the auditor insisted that these errors be corrected retroactively in presenting income data for the five-year period in the registration statement, the company treasurer objected. "The warehouse has been discontinued. There is no inventory there now. All these errors you have dug up have washed themselves out in the records and there is no point in going back and raking over the dead coals of past history. There's nothing wrong with our balance sheet at the end of 1975, or our income statement for 1975, and that's what the people who buy our stock are interested in."

Instructions Determine the effect of the errors discovered by the auditor on the financial statements of the Lisa Company. You may ignore income taxes. What position would you take with respect to the treasurer's objection?

PROBLEMS

Group A

22A-1 The following fragmentary information relates to the affairs of Sonja's Place during the current year:

	Beginning of year	End of year
Owner's equity	$75,900	$89,000
Merchandise inventory	15,800	27,320
Payables to merchandise creditors	40,000	25,000
Short-term prepayments	1,800	2,400

A summary of checks written shows that $200,000 was paid to merchandise suppliers during the year, $66,000 was paid for operating expenses, and $15,000 was withdrawn in cash by the owner. Estimated depreciation on buildings and equipment for the year is $8,400, and a reasonable provision for uncollectible accounts is 2% of gross sales.

Instructions   On the basis of the above information, prepare an income statement for Sonja's Place for the current year. Show all supporting computations. (Deduct the provision for uncollectible accounts from gross sales in the income statement.)

22A-2 The accountant for the Taj Mahal Corporation has just completed the comparative income statement for Years 1 and 2. The statement appears below:

	Year 2	Year 1
Sales	$ 605,000	$ 580,000
Cost of goods sold (lifo basis)	(365,000)	(350,000)
Gross profit on sales	$ 240,000	$ 230,000
Operating expenses	(125,000)	(130,000)
Operating income	$ 115,000	$ 100,000
Income tax expense, 40%	(46,000)	(40,000)
Income before extraordinary item	$ 69,000	$ 60,000
Extraordinary loss	(30,000)	(10,000)
Net income	$ 39,000	$ 50,000
Earnings per share of capital stock:		
Income before extraordinary loss	$ 6.90	$ 6.00
Extraordinary loss	(3.00)	(1.00)
Net income	$(3.90)	$(5.00)

When the president saw the comparative statement he said: "This is the year we should do what we have been talking about for years. Take this thing back downstairs and revise it using the fifo method of inventory pricing. We have kept careful records of our inventories so that restating the financial statements from the lifo basis to the fifo basis will not be difficult. The change would give us a more realistic working capital position and would make our statements more comparable with those of our competitors; all of them use fifo."

Within a few hours, the accountant was able to come up with the required data and recomputed the cost of goods sold for each year follows:

	Year 2	Year 1
Cost of goods sold (first-in, first-out basis)	$345,000	$340,000

The company had 10,000 shares of capital stock outstanding throughout the two-year period.

Instructions Restate the comparative income statement giving retroactive recognition to the change in accounting principle. Prepare a note which should accompany the financial statements issued at the end of Year 2, including the effect of the change in accounting principle on net income and earnings per share. (See page 829 for illustrative note describing this type of an accounting change.)

22A-3 Amber Company started in business in Year 1 and adopted a policy of writing off research and development costs as incurred. At the end of Year 4, after the net income was computed, the company decided to implement a change in accounting principle by adopting a policy of capitalizing research and development costs and amortizing such costs over a five-year period. The following information is available:

	Year 4	Year 3	Year 2	Year 1
Net income (after income tax expenses)	$100,000	$80,000	$120,000	$50,000
Research and development costs incurred	40,000	35,000	25,000	30,000
Amount of amortization that would have been recorded had a policy of amortization for research and development costs been followed . .	26,000	18,000	11,000	6,000

Research and development costs incurred each year were deducted in computing net income. Assume that the company has 100,000 shares of a single class of capital stock outstanding and that the effective income tax rate is 45%.

Instructions
a Compute the cumulative effect (after income taxes) of the change in accounting principle to be reported in the income statement for Year 4 and prepare the journal entry to record the change. Assume that the books are still open for Year 4.
b What was the effect of the change in accounting principle on the earnings per share for Year 4?
c Prepare a partial income statement in comparative form for Years 3 and 4, including earnings per share and pro forma amounts for Year 3, as illustrated on page 826.

22A-4 The office manager of the Mautz Sales Company has prepared the balance sheet on page 859 for the company at the end of Year 3:

The company began business early in Year 1, and income statements prepared by the office manager have shown the following net income (after income taxes) for the three-year period: Year 1, $16,000; Year 2, $9,200; Year 3, $6,300.

MAUTZ SALES COMPANY
Balance Sheet
End of Year 3

Cash	$ 9,800	Accounts payable	$15,600
Accounts receivable (net) . . .	27,000	Income taxes payable	2,700
Inventory	25,000	Capital stock	30,000
Furniture & fixtures (net)	18,000	Retained earnings	31,500
	$79,800		$79,800

Mautz, the president, is concerned about this income trend, and asked an accounting firm to review his records. This review revealed that the following errors and omissions had not been corrected during the applicable years:

End of	Inventory overstated	Inventory understated	Prepaid expense omitted	Unearned revenue omitted	Accrued expense (misc. payables) omitted	Accrued revenue (misc. receivables) omitted
Year 1	$8,700		$ 950		$1,400	
Year 2	6,500		1,100	$ 800	1,200	$400
Year 3		$4,900	1,300	1,250	900	700

Combined federal and state income taxes are 30% of pre-tax income. The company will file amended tax returns for Years 1 and 2; the tax return for Year 3 had not yet been filed at the time the above errors were discovered. No dividends have been declared by the company.

Instructions
a Prepare a working-paper analysis of errors to correct income for Years 1 to 3.
b Assuming that the books have been closed at the end of Year 3, prepare a journal entry to correct the records of this company as of the end of Year 3.
c Prepare a corrected balance sheet as of the end of Year 3.
d If you were presented with revised income statements for the Mautz Sales Company for the past three years, would your impression of its operating performance be substantially changed? Comment.

22A-5 Edward Skiles organized the Skiles Corporation to manufacture an improved riveting gun he had invented. At the close of his third year of operations, Skiles found it necessary to apply for a bank loan. He showed his comparative three-year income statement to the bank loan officer and pointed out with some pride that net income had grown by about 25% in each year; his statement showed net income as follows: Year 1, $9,900; Year 2, $12,500; Year 3, $15,600. The bank officer suggested that Skiles have his records audited and present comparative statements backed by the opinion of a CPA. The audit revealed a number of errors, summarized in the schedule on page 860. The auditor determined that all errors relating to Years 1 and 2 qualify as prior period adjustments.

The auditor recommends that amended income tax returns be filed for Years 1 and 2. Tax returns for Year 3 have not yet been filed. Assume that the corporation is subject to an income tax rate of 30%.

	Year 1	Year 2	Year 3
Ending finished goods inventory understated.		$4,600	
Ending finished goods inventory overstated			$2,280
Customers' deposits on future sales recorded as			
revenue	$850	1,300	1,920
Accrued interest receivable omitted	480		150
Expenditures capitalized as deferred charges and			
amortized at 10% per year which should have been			
charged to selling expense in year costs were in-			
curred		5,000	4,000

Instructions

a Prepare a working-paper analysis of errors showing the corrected net income (after income taxes) for each of the three years.

b Prepare a correcting entry at the end of Year 3, assuming that the books have been closed.

c Prepare a correcting entry at the end of Year 3, assuming that the books are still open for that year.

22A-6 Grosch Corporation was organized on July 1, 1975, with authorized stock of 200,000 shares of $5 par value common and 10,000 shares of $100 par value, 6% preferred stock. Paul Grosch was given 200 shares of preferred and 2,000 shares of common for his work and expenses in organizing and promoting the corporation. Attorneys' fees of $1,800, incurred in connection with the formation of the corporation, have not been paid as of September 30, 1975.

Additional information

(1) On July 15, 1975, Grosch transferred assets from his single proprietorship in exchange for 6,000 shares of preferred stock. The current fair values of these assets were as follows: notes receivable, $360,000; inventories $60,000; equipment, $180,000. The business did not begin operation until August 1, but interest of $900 accrued on the notes receivable between the time they were turned over to the corporation and July 31. This amount was recorded as Interest Receivable on July 31.

(2) On July 31, 1975, 160,000 shares of common were sold at par for cash, $120,000 of which was used to buy land and $600,000 applied to the price of a building. The building cost $1,340,000; the balance was represented by a $7\frac{1}{2}$% mortgage due in 10 years. Interest on the mortgage payable did not begin until August 1 and is payable monthly.

(3) On September 30, 1975, the accountant for the corporation prepared a summary of all transactions completed by the corporation during August and September in the form of "net" debit and credit **changes in ledger accounts.** This information, which includes all adjusting entries, except for ending inventory and income taxes, is shown on page 861.

The organization costs are being amortized over 60 months starting August 1, 1975. The inventory on September 30, 1975, amounts to $68,200.

Instructions

a Prepare the balance sheet of the Grosch Corporation at July 31, 1975. Income taxes should be accrued at the rate of 40% on the interest earned in July. This was the only item of revenue or expense through July 31, 1975.

b Prepare an income statement for the Grosch Corporation, summarizing its activities for the two months ending September 30, 1975. Assume that income taxes are 40% of income before income taxes.

	Net changes in ledger accounts	
	Debits	**Credits**
Accounts showing changes during two months ended Sept. 30, 1975:		
Cash		$ 20,350
Accounts receivable	$ 64,285	
Allowance for uncollectible accounts		1,250
Interest receivable	3,600	
Accumulated depreciation—building		8,375
Accumulated depreciation—equipment		6,500
Organization costs		1,060
Accounts payable		18,500
Retained earnings (first quarterly dividend on preferred stock) . .	9,300	
Sales		154,800
Purchases	104,000	
Operating expenses (includes depreciation, amortization of		
organization costs, and uncollectible accounts expense)	24,000	
Interest expense	9,250	
Interest revenue (does not include $900 earned in July)		3,600
	$214,435	$214,435

c Prepare a balance sheet for the Grosch Corporation at September 30, 1975.
d Prepare a schedule for cash receipts and cash payments reconciling the decrease of $20,350 in the Cash account during the two-month period ended September 30.

Group B

22B-1 Pablo Ruiz purchased a stock of merchandise in a bankruptcy sale for $9,200 and with $2,000 of his own cash opened a pipe shop near a college campus. During his first year of operations he paid $35,000 to merchandise suppliers and spent $9,800 for clerks' salaries and operating expenses. He withdrew $7,200 in cash from the business and $200 of pipes and tobacco for his personal use, including gifts to nonbusiness friends.

On New Year's Eve at the end of his first year of operations, while en route from his store to his apartment, Ruiz lost a briefcase containing the firm's accounting records. From bank records he was able to determine that he had $2,500 in cash at year-end. The accounts receivable ledger at the store showed total accounts receivable of $5,900, of which he considers $150 to be probably uncollectible. Ruiz had to retake the inventory of merchandise in the store, which he found totaled $8,300 at cost. Statements from suppliers showed that he owed $6,300 at the close of the year.

Instructions On the basis of the above information, prepare an income statement for the Ruiz Pipe Shop for the first year of operations. Include supporting schedules which show how you determined sales and the cost of goods sold for the year.

22B-2 Pyramid Builders, Inc., has used the completed-contract method of accounting for long-term construction contracts for over 20 years. In 1975, the company decided to change to the percentage-of-completion method in order to achieve a better matching of construction effort and realized construction profits reported in its income statement. The company recently added an expert in cost estimation, and management feels that it is now able to make reasonably accurate estimates of costs to be used in determining the percentage of completion on each contract. In addition, management thinks that it would be unfair to stockholders to report a decrease in earnings for 1975, which can be attributed to two significant factors as follows:

(1) Several major contracts were completed in 1974 which resulted in unusually high net income.
(2) Few contracts were completed in 1975, although the company has 40% more work under construction in 1975 than it did in 1974 and has 30% more employees on the payroll.

A summary of results for the last two years using the completed-contract method follows:

	1975	1974
Contract revenue realized	$2,000,000	$6,200,000
Construction costs applicable to contract revenue realized	1,500,000	4,900,000
Operating expenses	350,000	300,000
Income tax expense, 45%	67,500	450,000
Net income	82,500	550,000

Application of the percentage-of-completion method to the operations of the last two years would have given the following results:

	1975	1974
Contract revenue realized	$5,800,000	$3,100,000
Construction costs applicable to contract revenue realized	4,700,000	2,500,000

Operating expense using the percentage-of-completion method would be the same as was reported under the completed-contract method. The completed-contract method will continue to be used for income tax purposes. Income tax allocation procedures for timing differences will be used in preparing revised financial statements giving retroactive effect to the change in accounting principle. Assume that income taxes are 45% of operating income.

Instructions Restate the comparative income statement for 1974 and 1975, giving retroactive recognition to the change in accounting principle. Assume that the company had 165,000 shares of capital stock outstanding during the two-year period. Prepare a note suitable for inclusion in the annual report which explains the reason for the change in accounting principle and the effect of the change on net income and earnings per share. (See illustrative note on page 829 describing this type of accounting change.)

22B-3 Bridge-Hall & Company acquired the following assets in January of Year 1:

Equipment, estimated service life 10 years, residual value $30,000	$800,000
Building, estimated service life 30 years, no residual value	465,000

The assets have been depreciated using the sum-of-the-years'-digits method for the first three years, both for financial reporting and income tax purposes. In Year 4, the company decided to change the method of computing depreciation to the straight-line method. No change was made in estimated service life or residual value of assets.

The company has 100,000 shares of capital stock outstanding. Results of operations for the latest two years are shown below:

	Year 4	Year 3
Net income, before cumulative effect of change in computing depreciation for Year 4: depreciation for Year 4 has been determined using the straight-line method	$406,000	$400,000
Net income per share, before cumulative effect of change in computing depreciation for Year 4	$4.06	$4.00

For purposes of this problem, assume that the income tax rate is 50%.

Instructions
a Compute the cumulative effect of the change in accounting principle to be reported in the income statement for Year 4, and prepare the journal entry required to record the change.
b Compute the effect of the change in accounting principle on the earnings per share for Year 4.
c Prepare a partial income statement in comparative form for Years 3 and 4, including earnings per share and pro forma amounts for Year 3, as illustrated on page 826.

22B-4 Alan Blair started a business on July 10, 1974, by investing $50,000 in cash and merchandise. His net income for the calendar year 1974 was $20,000 and for 1975 it was $37,500. Blair has made no additional investments and has not made any withdrawals since July 10, 1974. A comparative balance sheet prepared by Blair's wife, who once took a short correspondence course in introductory accounting while she was in the Peace Corps in Ghana, is shown below:

ALAN BLAIR
Balance Sheet
December 31

	1975	1974
Cash	$ 15,100	$ 11,100
Accounts receivable	45,000	32,500
Inventory	40,000	28,400
Equipment (at cost)	30,000	30,000
Total assets	$130,100	$102,000
Accounts payable	$ 22,600	$ 22,000
Note payable to bank	–0–	10,000
Alan Blair, capital	107,500	70,000
Total liabilities & capital	$130,100	$102,000

The following errors are discovered by the auditor who was engaged in January 1976 to review the records of the business:
(1) Inventory was overstated by $3,000 at the end of 1974.
(2) Accrued expense of $1,200 was not recorded at the end of 1974.
(3) A prepaid expense of $700 was not recorded as an asset at the end of 1974; a prepaid expense of $300 at the end of 1975 was charged to expense.
(4) Accrued revenue of $800 at the end of 1975 was not recorded as a receivable.
(5) An allowance for uncollectible accounts equal to 4% of accounts receivable should be established at the end of each year. No accounts receivable were written off during the last two years.
(6) Depreciation of $1,000 was not recorded in 1974; depreciation of $2,000 was not recorded in 1975.

Instructions
a Prepare a working-paper analysis of errors to correct the net income for 1974 and for 1975.
b Prepare a correcting entry early in 1976, assuming that the books are closed for 1975.
c Prepare a corrected comparative balance sheet for 1974 and 1975. (**Note to student:** Be sure that capital for Blair at the end of 1974 is equal to his original investment plus the corrected net income for 1974. Similarly, the capital for Blair at the end of 1975 should equal his original investment plus the total corrected net income for 1974 and 1975.)

22B-5 Lee Fitzgerald organized the Fitz Bakery in Year 1. A friend set up an accounting system for Fitzgerald, which showed that at the end of Year 1, Fitzgerald's capital had grown from $40,000 to $45,000. A summary of his capital account for Years 2 and 3 is shown below:

Lee Fitzgerald, Capital

	Debit	Credit	Balance
Balance, Jan. 1, Year 2			$45,000
Net income, Year 2		$6,400	51,400
Drawings, Year 2	$6,000		45,400
Net loss, Year 3	800		44,600
Drawings, Year 3	7,200		37,400

Discouraged by this record, Fitzgerald is considering admitting a partner who can provide his business with more management talent. Early in Year 4, he engaged a CPA to audit the books of his company and prepare comparative financial statements for Years 2 and 3. The auditor discovered the following in the course of his examination:
(1) Accrued commissions payable to route salesmen at the end of the year were not recorded. These amounted to $1,150 at the end of Year 1; $1,400 at the end of Year 2, and $960 at the end of Year 3.
(2) Delivery and installation costs of $1,200 on new baking equipment were charged to expense when they were incurred on September 30, Year 2. The machinery has a service life of 10 years and negligible salvage value.
(3) Personal drawings of Fitzgerald in the amount of $750 were charged to Purchases in Year 3.
(4) Raw materials costing $3,800, which were received near the end of Year 2, were included in the ending inventory but were recorded as purchases early in Year 3.
(5) A three-year insurance premium of $570 paid in advance at the end of Year 3 was charged to Year 3 expense.

(6) An analysis of accounts receivable indicates that accounts originating in the following years should be written off: Year 1, $180; Year 2, $890; Year 3, $80. The auditor estimates that a provision for uncollectible accounts of $500 at the end of Year 3 would be adequate to cover uncollectible accounts originating in Year 3.

Instructions

a Prepare a working-paper analysis of errors to determine the corrected net income for Years 2 and 3.

b Assuming that the books had been closed at the end of Year 3, prepare the necessary correcting journal entry at the beginning of Year 4.

c Prepare a corrected statement of Fitzgerald's capital account from the beginning of Year 2 to the end of Year 3.

d On the basis of the audited data, is the company significantly better or worse off than the accounting records indicated?

22B-6 Malcolm Soliman started the Solid State Products Company several years ago. For a number of years his wife kept the accounting records, but early in the current year she became seriously ill. Soliman got in touch with a bookkeeping service whose manager told him, "You keep a record of your cash receipts and payments, and a list of your assets and liabilities at the beginning and end of the year, and I'll prepare financial statements for you at the end of the year."

At the close of the current year Soliman presented the following data to the manager of the bookkeeping service:

Analysis of Cash Receipts and Payments

Cash receipts:		Cash payments:	
Jan. 1, balance	$ 18,460	Paid on accounts payable (net	
Proceeds of bank loan	40,000	of $6,480 cash discounts	$225,650
Cash sales	87,300	Paid for equipment	25,000
Interest received	1,590	Operating expenses	47,610
Collected on notes receivable	13,000	Insurance policy premium	980
Received from equipment		Freight-in on purchases	12,400
rental	7,000	Payment on bank notes (in-	
Received from customers (net		cluding interest of $600)	15,600
of $4,130 in cash discounts)	173,290	Dec. 31, balance	13,400
Total cash receipts	$340,640	Total cash payments	$340,640

List of Assets and Liabilities

	Jan. 1	Dec. 31
Cash	$ 18,460	$ 13,400
Notes receivable	15,000	2,000
Accrued interest on notes receivable	900	500
Accounts receivable	43,560	64,320
Inventory	38,900	43,400
Unexpired insurance	1,900	1,500
Equipment (net of depreciation)	124,000	136,000
Total	$242,720	$261,120

Notes payable	$ 10,000	$ 35,000
Accrued interest on notes payable	500	1,750
Accounts payable	47,500	52,300
Accrued liabilities (expenses)	3,400	6,300
Unearned rental revenue	1,200	1,800
Total	$ 62,600	$ 97,150

Soliman reported that all accounts and notes receivable arose from merchandise sales. When questioned about the state of his receivables, he noted that he had written off $1,400 of accounts receivable during the period, of which $850 were on the books before January 1. Soliman estimates that $1,320 of the December 31 receivables will prove uncollectible.

Instructions
a On the basis of the above information, prepare an income statement for the Solid State Products Company for the current year. Show supporting schedules. It is the company's policy to deduct uncollectible accounts expense and cash discounts allowed from gross sales in the income statement.
b Prepare a statement of the changes in Soliman's capital account during the year.

CHAPTER 23

Statement of changes in financial position

For many years the basic financial statements of a business were three in number: the balance sheet, the income statement, and a statement of retained earnings. Many companies also prepared a fourth financial statement, called a statement of source and application of funds. This fourth statement was originally developed as a means of explaining to creditors why net income was often not accompanied by a corresponding increase in cash or working capital. The inclusion of such a financial statement in annual reports was an optional matter for many years, and even among those companies which prepared funds statements, the content and terminology varied greatly.

In 1963, *APB Opinion No. 3*, "The Statement of Source and Application of Funds," encouraged but *did not require* the presentation of a funds statement as supplementary information in financial reports.[1] That APB Opinion recognized that the term *funds* was sometimes used to mean cash or cash equivalents. A funds statement based on this narrow definition of funds was really a statement of cash receipts and disbursements. Most companies, however, defined funds more broadly as *working capital* (current assets less current liabilities). A funds statement prepared on the working capital concept of funds usually included only those transactions which directly affected current assets and/or current liabilities.

After considering the different prevailing concepts of funds and the varying forms of funds statements, the Accounting Principles Board in

---

[1] *APB Opinion No. 3*, "The Statement of Source and Application of Funds," AICPA (New York: 1963), p. 16.

Opinion No. 3 recommended that the concept of funds be broadened to include "all financial resources." Under this broad all financial resources concept, a funds statement would not be limited to transactions affecting cash or working capital but would include the financial aspects of such significant transactions as the issuance of capital stock in exchange for property.

In 1971, *APB Opinion No. 19* recommended that the funds statement be given the new title of Statement of Changes in Financial Position. The Statement of Changes in Financial Position is a descendant of the former Statement of Sources and Applications of Funds. The new title, however, better describes the broader concept of "all financial resources" made mandatory by *APB Opinion No. 19.* The new requirements called for a business to "disclose all important aspects of its financing and investing activities regardless of whether cash or other elements of working capital are directly affected."[2]

APB Opinion No. 19 also made mandatory the inclusion in annual reports of a statement of changes in financial position, as follows:

> When financial statements purporting to present both financial position (balance sheet) and results of operations (statement of income and retained earnings) are issued, a statement summarizing changes in financial position should also be presented as a basic financial statement for each period for which an income statement is presented.[3]

Two important consequences of *APB Opinion No. 19* deserve emphasis. First, the newly named Statement of Changes in Financial Position became a *basic financial statement,* mandatory in financial reports. Second, the statement requires use of the all financial resources concept rather than being limited to a cash or working capital concept. Disclosure must be made of all important aspects of financing and investing activities regardless of whether working capital is directly affected. Illustrative of the broader scope of the statement is the requirement for including such transactions as the conversion of bonds or preferred stock into common stock, and also transactions involving the acquisition of property in exchange for other property or by the issuance of securities.

Objectives of statement of changes in financial position

To summarize the impact of the developments described above, we can identify the objectives of a statement of changes in financial position. The objectives are:

1 To provide information on all financing and investing activities of a business
2 To show the funds generated from operations and other sources
3 To show the uses or applications of funds

---

[2] *APB Opinion No. 19,* "Reporting Changes in Financial Position," AICPA (New York: 1971), p. 374.
[3] *Ibid.,* p. 373.

4 To disclose the amounts and causes of all other changes in financial position during the period

In preparing a statement of changes in financial position, attention will usually be focused first on working capital and then on those financing and investing activities not affecting working capital. It is therefore appropriate that we now turn to careful consideration of working capital.

Working capital

One of the primary financial responsibilities of management is seeing that a business has sufficient liquid resources to meet obligations as they fall due and to take advantage of favorable investment opportunities as they arise. Managers and also those outsiders who evaluate managerial performance keep a sharp eye on the inflow and outflow of liquid resources (funds) and the prospective balance between funds available and funds required.

The *working capital* of a business is the amount by which current assets exceed current liabilities. The amount of working capital is a measure of the safety factor that exists for the protection of short-term creditors. Working capital may also be viewed as funds available for investment in noncurrent assets or to liquidate noncurrent liabilities. Increases in working capital occur when noncurrent assets are decreased (sold) and also when noncurrent liabilities and stockholders' equity are increased (as by additional investment in the business). Decreases in working capital occur when noncurrent assets are increased (purchased) and also when noncurrent liabilities and stockholders' equity are decreased (as by retirement of long-term debt and by dividends to stockholders). The major sources and uses of working capital are summarized below:

Sources	Uses
1 Revenue from operations	*1 Operating expenses*
2 Disposal of noncurrent assets	*2 Acquisition of noncurrent assets*
3 Long-term borrowing	*3 Retirement of long-term debt, or reclassification of it as current*
4 Issuance of equity securities	*4 Distributions to stockholders, including cash dividends, purchase of treasury stock, and redemption of preferred stock*

Both managers and outsiders are vitally concerned with the flows of working capital because an adequate supply of working capital is essential to the health of any business. The ability of a business entity to generate working capital internally is also an important factor in forecasting possible cash flows and in estimating ability to pay liabilities at maturity. In the typical operating cycle of a business, the first step is the purchase of inventory (usually on short-term credit); the inventory is then converted into a larger amount of accounts receivable; these receivables are in turn collected and the inflow of cash is used to retire current payables. The operating cycle then begins anew. The statement of changes in financial position depicts these dynamics of the operating cycle as well as the inflow and outflow of other economic resources employed in the business.

The revenue and expenses shown in the income statement do not run parallel to the inflow of working capital. Consequently, the income statement alone does not call attention to the development of a shortage or an oversupply of liquid assets. In order to prepare budgets and to plan for future growth, management must coordinate the expected flow of internally generated liquid assets with the inflow of funds obtained from external sources, as through borrowing or by the issuance of capital stock. Statements showing past and projected flows of working capital thus become basic tools of financial planning and analysis. The statement of changes in financial position does not supplant either the income statement or the balance sheet; it is intended to provide information that the other statements either do not provide or provide only indirectly about the flow of financial resources for a business entity. The information included in a statement of changes in financial position is useful to a variety of users of financial statements in making business decisions; consequently this statement has achieved the stature of a basic financial statement.[4]

Analysis of changes in financial position: a simple illustration

The income statement, the statement of retained earnings, and the comparative balance sheet provide the basic information for preparing a statement of changes in financial position. Using this basic information, the major movements of working capital can be identified for the period under study.

In the analysis of working capital flows, the noncurrent assets of a business represent the resources in which working capital has been invested; the long-term liabilities and the stockholders' equity represent the sources from which working capital was obtained. The first clue to a source or use of working capital, therefore, is a change in any of these noncurrent items during the period. The income statement and the statement of retained earnings help to explain the change in financial position that resulted from operations and from distributions to stockholders. The difference between the inflow and outflow of working capital during any

---

[4]The 1972 edition of *Accounting Trends & Techniques,* 26th ed., published by the AICPA indicated that 597 of the 600 companies surveyed included a statement of changes in financial position in their annual reports.

period must equal the change in the amount of working capital between the beginning and end of the period.

The data below for the Port Supply Company will be used to illustrate the preparation of a relatively simple statement of changes in financial position. These are the same data used in Chapter 5 to illustrate the preparation of a cash flow statement. This will facilitate a comparison between the cash flow statement on page 174 and the statement of changes in financial position on page 876.

PORT SUPPLY COMPANY
Income Statement
For Year Ended December 31, Year 2

Sales (net)		$107,000
Cost of goods sold:		
Beginning inventory	$40,000	
Purchases (net)	50,000	
Cost of goods available for sale	$90,000	
Less: Ending inventory	30,000	
Cost of goods sold		60,000
Gross profit on sales		$ 47,000
Expenses:		
Operating expenses (excluding depreciation)	$10,000	
Depreciation expense	7,500	
Interest expense	1,500	19,000
Income before incomes taxes		$ 28,000
Income tax expense		7,000
Net income		$ 21,000
Earnings per share		$2.10

PORT SUPPLY COMPANY
Statement of Retained Earnings
For Year Ended December 31, Year 2

Balance, Jan. 1, Year 2	$40,000
Net income	21,000
Subtotal	$61,000
Dividends	5,000
Balance, Dec. 31, Year 2	$56,000

PORT SUPPLY COMPANY
Comparative Balance Sheet
December 31

	Year 2	Year 1	Net change Debit (Credit)
Assets			
Cash	$ 24,900	$ 14,000	$ 10,900
Accounts receivable (net)	33,000	27,000	6,000
Inventory	30,000	40,000	(10,000)
Short-term prepayments	1,600	1,000	600
Equipment	130,000	100,000	30,000
Less: Accumulated depreciation . .	(19,500)	(12,000)	(7,500)
Total assets	$200,000	$170,000	$ 30,000
Liabilities & Stockholders' Equity			
Accounts payable	$ 15,500	$ 23,400	$ 7,900
Interest payable.	1,500	–0–	(1,500)
Current income tax liability.	7,000	6,600	(400)
Long-term notes payable	20,000	–0–	(20,000)
Capital stock, $10 par	100,000	100,000	–0–
Retained earnings	56,000	40,000	(16,000)
Total liabilities & stockholders' equity	$200,000	$170,000	$(30,000)

Additional information for Year 2

(1) Equipment costing $30,000 was acquired for $18,000 cash and a long-term note for $12,000.

(2) The company borrowed $8,000 from a private investor, signing a note due in Year 5.

As stated earlier, the statement of changes in financial position is generally prepared as a summary of working capital flows. Thus the statement will explain the reasons for an increase or decrease in working capital for a specific period of time, such as a year or a quarter of a year. Referring to the comparative balance sheet for the Port Supply Company, we can determine the change in working capital during Year 2 as shown on page 873.

The increase in working capital can now be viewed as a *result* which is to be explained by analyzing the changes in non-working capital accounts. In other words, the *causes* of the increase in working capital can only be found in the changes that have occurred in the noncurrent accounts. As you will see later in our discussion, however, not all changes

PORT SUPPLY COMPANY

Change in Working Capital during Year 2

	End of Year 2	End of Year 1	Increase or (decrease) in working capital
Current assets:			
Cash	$24,900	$14,000	$10,900
Accounts receivable (net)	33,000	27,000	6,000
Inventory	30,000	40,000	(10,000)
Short-term prepayments	1,600	1,000	600
Total current assets	$89,500	$82,000	
Current liabilities:			
Accounts payable	$15,500	$23,400	7,900
Interest payable	1,500	–0–	(1,500)
Current income tax liability	7,000	6,600	(400)
Total current liabilities	$24,000	$30,000	
Working capital	$65,500	$52,000	
Increase in working capital			$13,500

in noncurrent accounts result in increases or decreases in working capital.

Working Paper for Statement of Changes in Financial Position The primary factors responsible for the increase of $13,500 in working capital during Year 2 will be revealed by a statement of changes in financial position. In the working paper on page 874, only the non-working capital accounts are shown, and working capital amounts at the beginning of the year ($52,000) and at the end of the year ($65,500) appear in the first line. The analysis of working capital flows can also be accomplished by using T accounts or a series of separate schedules.

The similarity of the working paper for the statement of changes in financial position to that used for the cash flow statement in Chapter 5 should be noted. In both cases the account balances at the end of Year 1 are shown in the first column. Working capital at the end of Year 1, $52,000, appears as a single figure. Transactions for Year 2 which affected noncurrent accounts are analyzed in the next pair of columns in order to arrive at the account balances at the end of Year 2. Explanations of transactions for Year 2, as listed on the working paper for statement of changes in financial position, are presented below.

(1) Net income of $21,000 is recorded (a debit to Operations and a credit to Retained Earnings) as the first step in determining the working

PORT SUPPLY COMPANY
Working Paper for Statement of Changes in Financial Position
For Year Ended December 31, Year 2

	Account balances, end of Year 1	Analysis of transactions for Year 2 Debit	Analysis of transactions for Year 2 Credit	Account balances, end of Year 2
Debits				
Working capital	52,000	(X) 13,500		65,500
Equipment	100,000	(5) 30,000		130,000
Totals	152,000			195,500
Credits				
Accumulated depreciation	12,000		(2) 7,500	19,500
Long-term notes payable	–0–		(3) 12,000	20,000
			(4) 8,000	
Capital stock, $10 par value	100,000			100,000
Retained earnings	40,000	(6) 5,000	(1) 21,000	56,000
Totals	152,000	48,500	48,500	195,500
Sources of working capital:				
Operations, net income		(1) 21,000		From operations, $28,500
Add: Depreciation (an expense which				
did not reduce working capital) . . .		(2) 7,500		
Long-term borrowing to purchase				
equipment		(3) 12,000		
Long-term borrowing, loan from				
private investor		(4) 8,000		
Uses of working capital:				
Purchase of equipment			(5) 30,000	
Cash dividends			(6) 5,000	
Total sources and uses of working				
capital		48,500	35,000	
Increase in working capital in Year 2 .			(X) 13,500	
		48,500	48,500	

Explanation of transactions for Year 2:
(1) *Net income, $21,000, is recorded as an increase in Retained Earnings. This is a tentative source of working capital to be adjusted in (2) below.*
(2) *Depreciation for the year, $7,500, is added to net income in arriving at the working capital provided by operations because it did not reduce working capital (reduce a current asset or increase a current liability).*
(3) *To record source of working capital as a result of long-term borrowing to purchase equipment.*
(4) *To record source of working capital as a result of long-term borrowing from private investor.*
(5) *Purchase of equipment for $30,000. Under the all resources concept of funds, the entire purchase price of $30,000 is a use of working capital even though a long-term note for $12,000 was issued in partial payment.*
(6) *To record declaration of cash dividends as a use of working capital.*
(X) *Balancing figure—increase in working capital during Year 2.*

capital provided by operations. Individual revenue and expense account balances could be shown if more detailed analysis of working capital flows from operations were required.

(2) Depreciation of $7,500 is debited to Operations and credited to the Accumulated Depreciation account. Since net income was determined after deducting depreciation and since depreciation does not involve the use of working capital, this working-paper entry eliminates depreciation and shows that working capital provided by operations is larger than net income by the amount of depreciation.

(3) A long-term note payable of $12,000 issued for the purchase of equipment represents a source of working capital under the all financial resources concept of funds recommended by the Accounting Principles Board in *Opinion No. 19;* the offsetting credit is to the Long-term Notes Payable account.

(4) The $8,000 borrowed from a private investor on a long-term note is recorded as a source of working capital (a debit) and as a credit to the Long-term Notes Payable account.

(5) The purchase of equipment, $30,000, is recorded as an increase in the Equipment account and as a use of working capital. Although a long-term note payable was issued in partial payment for the equipment, the entire purchase price is considered a use of working capital under the all financial resources concept of funds.

(6) The cash dividends declared, $5,000, reduced retained earnings and working capital and is thus recorded as a use of working capital.

(X) The increase in working capital of $13,500 is entered in the first line to determine the amount of working capital at the end of Year 2 ($52,000 + $13,500 = $65,500); the increase is also entered at the bottom of the working paper as a reconciling figure between total sources of working capital, $48,500, and total uses of working capital, $35,000.

Statement of Changes in Financial Position A formal statement of changes in financial position for the Port Supply Company is on page 876.

This form highlights the increase in working capital; some companies prepare the statement in "balancing form," showing an increase in working capital as a use of funds or a decrease in working capital as a source of funds. The statement generally consists of two parts, the sources and uses of working capital and the composition of working capital. The Accounting Principles Board stated that "the objectives of the Statement usually require that the net change in working capital be analyzed in appropriate detail in a tabulation accompanying the Statement, and accordingly this detail should be furnished."[5] In addition, the Accounting Principles Board offered the following guideline in reporting the effects of financing and investing activities:

---

[5] *APB Opinion No. 19*, p. 376.

PORT SUPPLY COMPANY
Statement of Changes in Financial Position
For Year Ended December 31, Year 2

Sources of working capital:
Operations:

Net income	$21,000	
Add: Expense not requiring use of working capital—		
depreciation	7,500	
Working capital provided by operations		$28,500
Borrowing on long-term notes		20,000
Total sources of working capital		$48,500
Uses of working capital:		
Purchase of equipment	$30,000	
Declaration of cash dividends	5,000	
Total uses of working capital		35,000
Increase in working capital		$13,500

	End of Year 2	End of Year 1	Increase or (decrease) in working capital
Composition of working capital:			
Current assets:			
Cash	$24,900	$14,000	$ 10,900
Accounts receivable (net)	33,000	27,000	6,000
Inventory	30,000	40,000	(10,000)
Short-term prepayments	1,600	1,000	600
Total current assets	$89,500	$82,000	
Current liabilities:			
Accounts payable	$15,500	$23,400	7,900
Interest payable	1,500	-0-	(1,500)
Current income tax liability	7,000	6,600	(400)
Total current liabilities	$24,000	$30,000	
Working capital	$65,500	$52,000	
Increase in working capital			$13,500

For example, both outlays for acquisitions and proceeds from retirements of property should be reported; both long-term borrowings and repayments of long-term debt should be reported; and outlays for purchases of consolidated subsidiaries should be summarized in the consolidated Statement by major categories of assets obtained and obligations assumed. Related items should be shown in proximity when the result contributes to the clarity of the Statement. Individual immaterial items may be combined.[6]

[6] *Ibid.*

Summary of Procedures The procedures illustrated to develop the information needed for a statement of changes in financial position may be summarized as follows:

1 Determine the amount of working capital at the beginning and end of the period under consideration. Use a working paper to analyze all changes in noncurrent accounts.

2 Enter the amount of working capital and the amount of all noncurrent accounts at the beginning of the period in the first column of the working paper.

3 Enter in summary form all transactions which caused increases and decreases in working capital, listing the specific sources and uses of working capital in the lower part of the working paper. Certain transactions which involved only noncurrent accounts (stock dividends, for example) will simply be recorded in the accounts affected since they are neither sources nor uses of working capital. Exchange transactions (issuance of stock in exchange for plant assets, for example) will represent both sources and uses of working capital.

4 Determine that the difference between the sum of the sources and the uses of working capital is equal to the increase or decrease in the working capital during the period. The fact that the difference between the sources and the uses of working capital is equal to the change in working capital does not necessarily prove that the working-paper analysis is correct, but it does indicate that all account changes have been analyzed and that no purely arithmetic errors have been made. An error in classifying a current asset as noncurrent, for example, will not be disclosed at this point.

5 Prepare a formal statement of changes in financial position, showing the sources and uses of working capital during the period as well as the composition of working capital at the beginning and at the end of the period.

SPECIAL PROBLEMS

When a statement of changes in financial position is prepared by an accountant who has access to the detailed accounting records, all the necessary information may be obtained from the general ledger accounts or computer printouts. The task is more difficult when the statement must be prepared only from comparative balance sheets, the income statement, the statement of retained earnings, and other miscellaneous information. Some special problems involved in this process are described in the following sections.

Measuring working capital provided by operations

Special problems arise in determining the working capital provided by operations. Deductions from revenue which did not require the use of working capital must be added to net income; revenue items and offsets to expenses which did not provide working capital must be subtracted from net income. This procedure is summarized in *APB Opinion No. 19* as follows:

> The Statement for the period should begin with income or loss before extraordinary items, if any, and add back (or deduct) items recognized in determining that income or loss which did not use (or provide) working capital or cash during the period. Items added and deducted in accordance with this

procedure are not sources or uses of working capital or cash, and the related captions should make this clear, e.g., "Add—Expenses not requiring outlay of working capital in the current period."[7]

Examples of items which should be added and deducted from net income (after extraordinary items) in arriving at the amount of working capital provided by operations are listed below:

Computation of Working Capital Provided by Operations

	Additions	Deductions	
Net income +	Depreciation expense Increase in deferred income tax liability Amortization of intangibles and deferred charges Amortization of bond discount and issue costs Amortization of premium on investment in bonds Loss accrued on investment in stock using the equity method Extraordinary and other losses (net of tax)	Decrease in deferred income tax liability Amortization of investment tax credit and deferred revenue Amortization of premium on bonds payable Accumulation of discount on investment in bonds Income accrued on investment in stock using the equity method Extraordinary and other gains (net of tax)	Working capital = provided by operations

Depreciation expense, an increase in the deferred income tax liability, the amortization of intangibles and deferred charges, and the amortization of bond discount and issue costs all reduce net income without reducing working capital and are therefore added back to net income. Similarly, the amortization of a premium on investment in bonds and a loss accrued on investment in stock using the equity method reduce long-term investments and net income but have no effect on working capital; therefore, these items also are added to net income in order to measure the working capital provided by operations.

A decrease in the deferred income tax liability, the amortization of investment tax credit and of deferred revenue, and the amortization of premium on bonds payable all represent increases in net income and decreases in long-term liability accounts. Since these items increase net income but are not sources of working capital, they are deducted from net income. The accumulation of discount on investment in bonds and

---

[7] *Ibid.*, pp. 374–375.

the income accrued on investment in stock using the equity method represent increases in long-term investments and net income but do not affect working capital; therefore, these items also are deducted from net income in order to measure the working capital provided by operations.

Extraordinary and other gains and losses are reported in the income statement; therefore, some companies report these items as part of working capital provided by operations. However, it is preferable to eliminate extraordinary and other gains and losses from net income and report separately the full amount of sources and uses of working capital from nonoperating transactions. The Accounting Principles Board essentially supported this position but permitted the reporting of the effect of extraordinary items *separately* below working capital provided by operations:

> The ability of an enterprise to provide working capital or cash from operations is an important factor in considering its financing and investing activities. Accordingly, the Statement should prominently disclose working capital or cash provided from or used in operations for the period, and the Board believes that the disclosure is most informative if the effects of extraordinary items . . . are reported separately from the effects of normal items. . . . the resulting amount of working capital or cash should be appropriately described, e.g., "Working capital provided from [used in] operations for the period, exclusive of extraordinary items." This total should be immediately followed by working capital or cash provided or used by income or loss from extraordinary items, if any; extraordinary income or loss should be . . . adjusted for items recognized that did not provide or use working capital or cash during the period.[8]

Gain or loss on sale of securities

When securities are sold at a gain or loss, we must first determine whether the securities are current assets or long-term investments. If, for example, securities which are classified as current are sold at cost, there is no effect on working capital; if the securities are sold at a gain, working capital would be increased by the amount of the after-tax gain; if the securities are sold at a loss, working capital would be reduced by the amount of the after-tax loss. If the gain or loss is not material, it may be reported as an element of working capital provided by operations; material, unusual, and infrequent gains and losses on the sale of short-term investments should be reported separately as sources and uses of working capital.

On the other hand, the sale of securities classified as long-term investments generates working capital equal to the *net proceeds* (sales price less the income tax effect of any gain or loss). If gains and losses on the sale of long-term investments were included in computing the working capital provided by operations, the proceeds from the sale of securities would be shown in two places in the statement of changes in financial position. A better approach is to present the net proceeds as a source of working capital and to exclude the gains and losses from net income in computing the working capital provided by operations.

[8] *Ibid.*

Uncollectible accounts

Neither the recognition of the uncollectible accounts expense (by a debit to Uncollectible Accounts Expense and a credit to Allowance for Uncollectible Accounts) nor the actual write-off of uncollectible accounts requires any action in preparing a statement of changes in financial position. The recognition of uncollectible accounts expense reduces net accounts receivable and is properly reflected as a deduction from revenue in measuring working capital provided by operations; a write-off against the allowance account does not change the balance of net accounts receivable, hence it has no effect on working capital.

Analysis of changes in plant and equipment accounts

When a number of changes have occurred in plant and equipment accounts, it is helpful to prepare an analysis of such accounts preliminary to isolating the effect on working capital. For example, assume that we have the following information:

	End of current year	End of previous year	Change Debit (Credit)
Equipment	$540,000	$620,000	$(80,000)
Accumulated depreciation .	230,000	195,000	(35,000)
Depreciation expense	60,000		60,000
Gain on disposal of equipment	10,000		(10,000)

In order to isolate the effect on working capital, it will be helpful to develop the following analysis:

	Equipment	Accumulated depreciation
Balance at beginning of current year	$ 620,000	$(195,000)
Purchase of equipment (gave five-year note for $40,000)	50,000	
Disposal of equipment	(130,000)	25,000
Depreciation expense for current year		(60,000)
Balance at end of current year	$ 540,000	$(230,000)

From this information we can identify the transactions that caused the changes in the two accounts and affected working capital. The entries made at the time of each transaction and the entries required in the working paper are summarized below:

Entries made at time of transaction:			Entries in the working paper:		
Equipment	50,000		Equipment	50,000	
Cash		10,000	Sources of Working		
Long-term			Capital: Issuance		
Notes Pay-			of Long-term		
able		40,000	Notes Payable . .	40,000	
To record purchase			Long-term		
of equipment.			Notes Pay-		
			able		40,000
			Uses of Work-		
			ing Capital:		
			Purchase of		
			Equipment		50,000
Cash	115,000		Sources of Working		
Accumulated De-			Capital: Disposal		
preciation	25,000		of Equipment. . . .	115,000	
Equipment .		130,000	Accumulated De-		
Gain on Dis-			preciation	25,000	
posal of			Equipment .		130,000
Equipment		10,000	Operations:		
To record disposal			Deduct Gain		
of equipment.			on Disposal		
			of Equipment		10,000
Depreciation			Operations: Add		
Expense	60,000		Depreciation Ex-		
Accumulated			pense	60,000	
Depreciation		60,000	Accumulated		
To record depre-			Depreciation		60,000
ciation expense.					

In the working paper, the titles "Sources of Working Capital: Issuance of Long-term Notes Payable," and "Uses of Working Capital: Purchase of Equipment," are entered below the list of noncurrent accounts. This procedure is illustrated in the working paper on page 874.

The acquisition of equipment in exchange for $40,000 in long-term notes is reported as both a source and a use of working capital under the all financial resources concept of funds, even though this part of the transaction did not affect any current asset or current liability accounts.

Exchange transactions: the all financial resources concept of funds

For many years accountants generally excluded from the funds statement certain exchange transactions, because they did not directly affect the flow of current assets or current liabilities during the fiscal period. However, as explained earlier in this chapter, the Accounting Principles Board caused the scope of the statement of changes in financial position to be enlarged to include all financial resources:

> To meet all its objectives, a funds statement should disclose separately the financing and investing aspects of all significant transactions that affect financial position during a period. These transactions include acquisition or disposal of property in exchange for debt or equity securities and conversion of long-term debt or preferred stock to common stock.[9]

For example, an issuance of 10,000 shares of capital stock having a market value of $48 per share in *exchange* for patents would be reported in the statement of changes in financial position as follows:

Sources of working capital:	
Issuance of capital stock	$480,000
Uses of working capital:	
Acquisition of patents	$480,000

A *conversion* of $1 million of bonds payable into capital stock would be reported as:

Sources of working capital:	
Issuance of capital stock pursuant to conversion of bonds payable	$1,000,000
Uses of working capital:	
Retirement of bonds payable through conversion into capital stock	$1,000,000

Other examples of exchange transactions are: refunding of bonds payable, exchanges of property, capitalization of long-term leases, and donation of property to the corporation. Stock dividends, write-offs of noncurrent assets, and appropriations of retained earnings, on the other hand, are not considered to be exchange transactions and their effect on account balances would not be listed in a statement of changes in financial position.

Purchase of a going business

If a going business is acquired either for cash or in exchange for securities, the effect of the acquisition on working capital requires careful analysis. For example, assume the following transaction:

[9] *Ibid.*, p. 373.

Current Assets	100,000	
Noncurrent Assets	150,000	
Current Liabilities		40,000
Cash		210,000
To record purchase of a going business.		

The purchase of noncurrent assets represents a use of working capital of $150,000; the purchase of the current assets and the assumption of the current liabilities, however, does not affect working capital flows since another current asset (cash of $60,000) was given in exchange.

Assume now that capital stock was issued in exchange for the business; working capital of $60,000 ($100,000 − $40,000) would be increased as a result of the issuance of stock, and the *exchange* of an additional $150,000 capital stock for noncurrent assets would be reported both as a source and a use of working capital. Thus, $210,000 would be shown as "Working Capital Provided by Issuance of Capital Stock" and $150,000 would be shown as "Working Capital Used to Acquire Noncurrent Assets."

Reclassification of noncurrent items into current category

When some part of a long-term obligation will fall due within a year, that part should be reclassified as a current liability in the balance sheet. For example, serial bonds and mortgage notes due for payment within one year from current assets are generally moved from long-term debt to the current liability category. This reclassification decreases the amount of working capital and thus constitutes a use of funds during the period. Similarly, a long-term receivable which will mature within a year should be placed among current assets, thus representing a source of working capital.

COMPREHENSIVE ILLUSTRATION OF STATEMENT OF CHANGES IN FINANCIAL POSITION

The following illustration is designed to show how the reasoning discussed thus far can be applied to an analysis of working capital flows in a more complex situation. The data on which the analysis is based are contained in the comparative after-closing trial balances, an income statement for the current year, a statement of retained earnings for the current year, and the additional information for the Kane Corporation listed on the following pages.

KANE CORPORATION
Comparative After-closing Trial Balances
At End of Current and Previous Year

	Current year		Previous year	
	Debit	**Credit**	**Debit**	**Credit**
Cash	$ 21,600		$ 52,800	
Notes receivable	50,000		30,000	
Accounts receivable (net)	38,400		52,300	
Allowance for uncollectible				
accounts		$ 1,500		$ 1,900
Inventory	96,050		57,300	
Short-term prepayments . .	12,600		9,600	
Building and equipment. . .	506,000		426,000	
Accumulated depreciation .		172,200		155,000
Investment in stock of Z				
Company (equity method).	53,250		40,000	
Accounts payable		52,150		31,300
Accrued liabilities		17,600		16,300
Current income tax liability.		15,300		17,000
Dividends payable		14,000		
Bonds payable, 8%.		150,000		200,000
Premium on bonds payable		6,750		10,000
Deferred income tax liability		30,000		20,000
Capital stock, $10 par. . . .		150,000		100,000
Paid-in capital in excess				
of par		106,200		58,000
Retained earnings		79,700		58,500
Treasury stock (cost: 1,000				
shares)	17,500			
Totals	$795,400	$795,400	$668,000	$668,000

KANE CORPORATION
Income Statement
For Current Year

Sales		$313,600
Cost of goods sold		158,000
Gross profit on sales		$155,600
Operating expenses:		
Depreciation expense	$30,000	
Other	28,000	58,000
Income from operations		$ 97,600
Nonoperating income and expense:		
Investment income from Z Company	$13,250	
Less: Interest expense	11,250	2,000
Income before income taxes		$ 99,600
Income tax expense (including $10,000 deferred)		48,300
Income before other gains and losses		$ 51,300
Other gains and losses:		
Loss on disposal of equipment	$15,200	
Less: Gain on retirement of bonds payable	4,500	10,700
Net income		$ 40,600

(**Note:** Earnings per share data are not given in order to avoid unnecessary detail.)

KANE CORPORATION
Statement of Retained Earnings
For Current Year

Retained earnings, beginning of year		$58,500
Less: Stock dividend (360 shares @ $15 per share)	$ 5,400	
Cash dividends	14,000	19,400
Subtotal		$39,100
Add: Net income		40,600
Retained earnings, end of year		$79,700

Additional information for current year

(1) An analysis of the changes in the Building and Equipment account during the current year follows:

	Building and equipment	Accumulated depreciation
Balance, beginning of current year	$426,000	$(155,000)
Disposal of equipment	(48,000)*	12,800
Purchase of equipment	128,000†	
Depreciation expense for current year		(30,000)
Balance, end of current year	$506,000	$(172,200)

*This equipment was sold for $20,000, resulting in a loss of $15,200 (ignoring the income tax effect).

†Acquired through issuance of 4,640 shares of capital stock at an agreed value of $92,800 and $35,200 in cash, a total of $128,000.

(2) During the year, the Kane Corporation accrued its share, $13,250, of net income earned by Z Company. The Kane Corporation owns 25% of the common stock of Z Company.

(3) At the beginning of the current year, the bonds payable of $200,000 had a remaining life of 10 years. At the beginning of the current year, $50,000 of the bonds were retired at 96 and $2,500 ($10,000 × ¼) of the premium on bonds payable at the beginning of the current year was written off, resulting in a gain of $4,500 (ignoring the income tax effect). The balance in the Premium on Bonds Payable account, $7,500, is being amortized over a 10-year period, or $750 per year.

(4) During the current year the Kane Corporation acquired 1,000 shares of its own capital stock at a cost of $17,500. At a time when 9,000 shares of capital were outstanding and the market price was $15 per share, the company declared a 4% stock dividend. The board of directors of Kane Corporation authorized a transfer of $5,400 (360 shares × $15) from retained earnings to paid-in capital accounts to record the stock dividend. Later in the year, 4,640 shares of capital stock, valued at $20 per share, were issued in exchange for equipment. A cash dividend of $1 per share was declared on the 14,000 (9,000 + 360 + 4,640) shares outstanding at the end of the year, payable in January of the following year.

Schedule of changes in working capital

The first step in preparing a statement of changes in financial position for Kane Corporation is to determine its working capital at the beginning and at the end of the current year, and the increase or decrease in working capital during the year. The composition of working capital is shown in the lower section of the statement of changes in financial position which appears on page 893.

Working paper for statement of changes in financial position

After the schedule of changes in working capital is prepared, the beginning balance of working capital, $135,500, is entered in the first column of the working paper. Similarly, the beginning balances in all other noncurrent accounts are recorded in the first column of the working paper. Transactions for the current year are then analyzed and the sources and uses of working capital are determined as described earlier in this chapter. The working paper for the statement of changes in financial position for the Kane Corporation is shown on page 888.

Analysis of Transactions in the Working Paper By studying the changes in the noncurrent accounts, we are able to find the specific reasons for the $17,400 decrease in working capital during the current year. As previously stated, only changes in the noncurrent accounts represent sources and uses of working capital. The analysis of the transactions completed by the Kane Corporation during the current year are explained below (the numbers correspond to the numbers used in the working paper):

(1) The net income of $40,600 is closed to the Retained Earnings account and is shown under "Sources of Working Capital: Operations." Net income represents an increase in stockholders' equity and is one of the major sources of working capital for most business units. Net income, however, is only a tentative measure of the increase in working capital from operations because not all revenue and expense items represent sources and uses of working capital. Furthermore, any nonoperating gains and losses are eliminated from net income because the transactions giving rise to such gains and losses should be *reported separately* if they generate or use working capital and if they are material in amount.

(2) Since depreciation expense does not reduce a current asset or increase a current liability, it has no effect on working capital. Therefore, the depreciation expense of $30,000 for the current year is shown as an increase to net income and is credited to Accumulated Depreciation. In other words, since depreciation is a nonfund expense, the increase in working capital as a result of operations was more than the amount of net income.

(3) Depreciation, however was not the only expense which did not reduce working capital. The income tax expense of $48,300 includes $10,000 payable in future years and appears as an increase in the Deferred Income Tax Liability account. This portion of income tax expense is added to net income because it did not reduce working capital.

(4) The disposal of the equipment was recorded by the Kane Corporation as follows (see page 886 for details):

	Account balances at beginning of current year	Analysis of transactions for current year		Account balances at end of current year
		Debit	Credit	
Working capital	135,500		(X) 17,400	118,100
Building and equipment	426,000	(8) 128,000	(4) 48,000	506,000
Investment in stock of Z				
Company (equity method) .	40,000	(7) 13,250		53,250
Treasury stock (cost:				
1,000 shares)	–0–	(9) 17,500		17,500
Totals	601,500			694,850
Accumulated depreciation	155,000	(4) 12,800	(2) 30,000	172,200
Bonds payable, 8%	200,000	(5) 50,000		150,000
Premium on bonds payable	10,000	(5) 2,500 (6) 750		6,750
Deferred income tax liability	20,000		(3) 10,000	30,000
Capital stock, $10 par	100,000		(8) 46,400 (11) 3,600	150,000
Paid-in capital in excess				
of par	58,000		(8) 46,400 (11) 1,800	106,200
Retained earnings	58,500	(10) 14,000 (11) 5,400	(1) 40,600	79,700
Totals	601,500	244,200	244,200	694,850
Sources of working capital:				
Operations—net income,				
including other gains				
and losses		(1) 40,600		
Add: Depreciation expense		(2) 30,000		
Increase in deferred				
income tax liability		(3) 10,000		
Loss on disposal of				From
equipment		(4) 15,200		operations,
Less: Gain on retirement				$77,300
of bonds payable			(5) 4,500	
Amortization of pre-				
mium on bonds payable . .			(6) 750	
Investment income from				
Z Company			(7) 13,250	
Disposal of equipment		(4) 20,000		
Issuance of capital stock in				
exchange for equipment		(8) 92,800		
Uses of working capital:				
Retirement of bonds			(5) 48,000	
Purchase of equipment			(8) 128,000	
Acquisition of treasury stock . . .			(9) 17,500	
Declaration of cash dividends . . .			(10) 14,000	
Total sources and uses				
of working capital		208,600	226,000	
Decrease in working capital		(X) 17,400		
		226,000	226,000	

Explanations of transactions for current year start on page 887.

Cash	20,000	
Accumulated Depreciation	12,800	
Loss on Disposal of Equipment	15,200	
Building and Equipment		48,000

In the working paper, the disposal of equipment is recorded as a source of working capital of $20,000 because cash was increased, and cash is one of the accounts making up working capital. The accumulated depreciation applicable to the equipment disposed ($12,800) is debited to the Accumulated Depreciation account and the loss on the disposal of equipment ($15,200) is shown as an increase in net income in order that the net proceeds on the disposal ($20,000) can be listed in full as a source of working capital. The original cost of the equipment ($48,000) is credited to the Building and Equipment account as it was in the original entry to record the disposal. Note that when the increase of $30,000 as a result of current year's depreciation and the decrease of $12,800 in the Accumulated Depreciation account is combined with the beginning balance of $155,000, we come up with the ending balance of $172,200.

(5) At the beginning of the current year bonds payable were retired at 96 as follows:

Bonds Payable	50,000	
Premium on Bonds Payable	2,500	
Cash		48,000
Gain on Retirement of Bonds Payable		4,500

This entry is recognized in the working paper by debits to Bonds Payable and to Premium on Bonds Payable (same as in the original entry); however, the reduction in cash is recognized as a use of working capital and the gain is deducted from net income because it is not a source of working capital provided by operations. At this point we have accounted for the decrease in the Bonds Payable account during the current year from $200,000 to $150,000.

(6) The amortization of the premium on bonds payable was recorded as an adjusting entry in the accounting records as follows:

Premium on Bonds Payable	750	
Interest Expense		750

The working-paper treatment of this adjusting entry is to debit the Premium on Bonds Payable account and to record the reduction in working capital provided by operations because the credit to Interest Expense increased net income without increasing working capital. The amount actually paid for interest on bonds payable during the current year was $12,000 ($150,000 × 8%) and not $11,250 reported as interest expense in the income statement. The debit of $750 to the Premium on Bonds Payable account, combined with the debit of $2,500 in entry (5), explains the reduction of this account from a balance of $10,000 at the beginning of the year to a balance of $6,750 at the end of the year.

(7) The net income for the current year includes an accrual of $13,250 of income on the investment in the stock of Z Company. The investment income was recorded in the accounts of Kane Corporation as follows:

Investment in Stock of Z Company (equity method)	13,250	
Investment Income from Z Company		13,250

In the working paper, the increase in the investment acount is recorded as a debit and as a reduction (a credit) to working capital provided by operations because the investment income did not generate working capital. After this entry is entered in the working paper, the ending balance of $53,250 in the Investment in Stock of Z Company account may be determined by adding $13,250 to the balance of $40,000 at the beginning of the current year.

(8) The purchase of equipment for cash and the issuance of 4,640 shares of capital stock was recorded as follows:

Building and Equipment	128,000	
Cash		35,200
Capital Stock, $10 par		46,400
Paid-in Capital in Excess of Par		46,400

Although this transaction actually reduced working capital by only $35,200, the full purchase price of the equipment should be shown as a use of working capital. The reason for this is that the issuance of capital stock valued at $92,800 is viewed as both a source and a use of working capital. The working-paper analysis of this transaction follows:

Building and Equipment *128,000*	
Sources of Working Capital: Issuance of Capital Stock	
in Exchange for Equipment *92,800*	
Uses of Working Capital: Purchase of Equipment . .	*128,000*
Capital Stock, $10 par	*46,400*
Paid-in Capital in Excess of Par	*46,400*

This analysis records the changes in the non-working capital accounts in the upper part of the working paper and also recognizes in the lower part of the working paper the source and use of financial resources as a result of the purchase of equipment and the issuance of capital stock. The debit of $128,000 in the Building and Equipment account, less the credit of $48,000 in entry (4) above, explains the net increase in this account during the current year from $426,000 to $506,000.

(9) The acquisition of treasury stock for $17,500 is recorded in the working paper as a debit to the Treasury Stock account, thus establishing the ending balance in this account, and as a credit to Uses of Working Capital: Acquisition of Treasury Stock.

(10) The declaration of cash dividends, $14,000, is entered in the working paper as a debit to Retained Earnings and a credit to Uses of Working Capital: Declaration of Cash Dividends. A cash dividend need not be paid in order to represent a reduction in working capital; the declaration of the cash dividend creates a current liability and thus reduces working capital. The payment of the cash dividend has no effect on working capital because the payment reduces a current liability (Dividends Payable) and a current asset (Cash) by the same amount; *a transaction which changes only current accounts cannot be a source or a use of working capital.*

(11) The declaration of a stock dividend required a transfer from Retained Earnings to paid-in capital accounts; a stock dividend has no effect on working capital and is not considered as a financing and investing transaction under the all resources concept of funds. The working-paper entry for the 4% stock dividend (360 shares valued at $15 per share) requires a debit to Retained Earnings for $5,400, a credit to Capital Stock for $3,600, and a credit of $1,800 to Paid-in Capital in Excess of Par. After this transaction is recognized in the working paper, we are able to determine the ending balances in the Capital Stock, Paid-in Capital in Excess of Par, and Retained Earnings accounts.

(X) After all changes in noncurrent accounts are analyzed in the working paper, the sources ($208,600) and the uses ($226,000) of working capital are totaled. At this point, the decrease in working capital during the year, $17,400, should be entered as a credit to "Working Capital" in the first line of the third column in the working paper and also as a balancing figure on the next to the last line of the second column in the working paper. The account balances at the end of the current year can now be determined in the last column of the working paper (including the ending working capital of $118,100) and the subtotals obtained for the "Debits" and "Credits" columns. If the totals ($694,850) for account balances at the end of the current year agree, we can be reasonably certain that all relevant transactions have been analyzed and that the decrease in working capital has been satisfactorily explained.

Statement of changes in financial position

The statement of changes in financial position for the Kane Corporation prepared from the working paper is presented on page 893.

It would be possible to list individual nonfund adjustments to net income but generally this is not necessary unless the amounts have some special significance.

Alternative Form of Statement Showing Revenue and Expense Detail An acceptable procedure, which gives the same result, is to begin with total revenue that provided working capital during the period and deduct operating costs and expenses that required the outlay of working capital during the period.[10] This form is illustrated on page 894 for the Kane Corporation.

The impact of income taxes on working capital is equal to the income tax expense of $48,300 as reported in the income statement, less $10,000 deferred income taxes; the impact of interest expense on working capital is equal to the interest expense of $11,250 as reported in the income statement, plus $750 amortization of the premium on bonds payable, or $12,000 which is the amount of interest paid in cash during the year.

Reporting practices by corporations

The statement of changes in financial position appears in a variety of forms in the annual reports of publicly owned corporations. In a recent survey of 600 annual reports, 346 used one of the forms on page 893 in which the increase or decrease in working capital is determined; 117 companies "balanced" the statement by reporting the increase in working capital as a use of funds (or a decrease in working capital as a source of funds); 95 companies arrived at the ending balance in working capital;

---

[10] *Ibid.*, p. 375.

KANE CORPORATION
Statement of Changes in Financial Position
For Current Year

Sources of working capital:
  Operations:
    Net income, including other gains and losses . . . . $ 40,600
    Add: Charges not requiring use of working capital, net of
        credits (see working paper on page 888 for detail) 36,700
    Working capital provided by operations . . . . $ 77,300
  Disposal of equipment 20,000
  Issuance of capital stock in exchange for equipment 92,800
    Total sources of working capital $190,100

Uses of working capital:
  Purchase of equipment (including $92,800 acquired in
    exchange for capital stock) $128,000
  Acquisition of treasury stock 17,500
  Retirement of bonds payable 48,000
  Declaration of cash dividends 14,000
    Total uses of working capital 207,500
  Decrease in working capital . . . . $(17,400)

	End of current year	End of previous year	Increase or (decrease) in working capital
Composition of working capital:			
Current assets:			
Cash	$ 21,600	$ 52,800	$(31,200)
Notes receivable	50,000	30,000	20,000
Accounts receivable (net)	36,900	50,400	(13,500)
Inventory	96,050	57,300	38,750
Short-term prepayments	12,600	9,600	3,000
Total current assets	$217,150	$200,100	
Current liabilities:			
Accounts payable	$ 52,150	$ 31,300	(20,850)
Accrued liabilities	17,600	16,300	(1,300)
Current income tax liability	15,300	17,000	1,700
Dividends payable	14,000	-0-	(14,000)
Total current liabilities	$ 99,050	$ 64,600	
Working capital	$118,100	$135,500	
Decrease in working capital			$(17,400)

KANE CORPORATION
Statement of Changes in Financial Position
For Current Year

Sources of working capital:		
Sales		$313,600
Less: Cost of goods sold	$158,000	
Operating expenses (other than depreciation)	28,000	
Income tax expense	38,300	
Interest expense	12,000	236,300
Working capital provided by operations		$ 77,300
Disposal of equipment		20,000
Issuance of capital stock in exchange for equipment		92,800
Total sources of working capital		$190,100
Uses of working capital:		
Purchase of equipment (including $92,800 acquired in exchange for capital stock)	$128,000	
Acquisition of treasury stock	17,500	
Retirement of bonds payable	48,000	
Declaration of cash dividends	14,000	
Total uses of working capital		207,500
Decrease in working capital		$(17,400)
Composition of working capital: (same as on page 893)		

and 39 companies used "cash and cash equivalents" as the definition of funds.[11] An example of the "balancing" form of the statement of changes in financial position appears in Appendix B for Cities Service Company; an example in which funds are viewed as cash and marketable securities appears in Appendix B for Eastman Kodak Company.

Working-paper format using only changes in account balances

The working paper for the statement of changes in financial position may be adapted to meet varying needs when the information for solving problems is given in somewhat different form. For example, assuming that only *changes* in account balances for Chang Corporation during Year 10 are given and that beginning and ending account balances are not available, the working paper for the statement of changes in financial position may take the following form:

---

[11] *Accounting Trends & Techniques,* 26th ed., AICPA (New York: 1972), p. 301.

CHANG CORPORATION
Working Paper for Statement of Changes in Financial Position
Year 10

	Changes in account balances during Year 10		Analysis of transactions for Year 10	
	Debit	**Credit**	**Debit**	**Credit**
Increase in working capital.	80,000		(X) 80,000	
Noncurrent assets (net)		10,000		(2) 10,000
Noncurrent liabilities	5,000		(4) 5,000	
Capital stock		25,000		(3) 25,000
Retained earnings		50,000	(5) 15,000	(1) 65,000
Totals	85,000	85,000	100,000	100,000
Sources of working capital:				
Operations—net income			(1) 65,000	
Add: Depreciation expense			(2) 10,000	
Issuance of capital stock.			(3) 25,000	
Uses of working capital:				
Retirement of noncurrent liabilities				(4) 5,000
Cash dividends declared				(5) 15,000
Total sources and uses of				
working capital			100,000	20,000
Increase in working capital.				(X) 80,000
Totals			100,000	100,000

Explanation of transactions for Year 10:
(1) Net income for the year, a tentative measure of working capital provided by operations
(2) Depreciation expense added to net income to obtain working capital provided by operations, $75,000
(3) Issuance of capital stock for cash, a source of working capital
(4) Retirement of noncurrent liabilities, a use of working capital
(5) Declaration of cash dividends, a use of working capital
(X) Balancing entry—increase in working capital during Year 10

In the analysis of transactions for Year 10, the objective is to **summarize the changes in noncurrent accounts** and to identify the sources and uses of working capital in the process. The credit changes in noncurrent assets ($10,000) and capital stock ($25,000) are explained by entries to record depreciation and the issuance of capital stock. Similarly, the net credit change of $50,000 in retained earnings consists of net income of $65,000 less cash dividends declared of $15,000; and the debit change of $5,000 in noncurrent liabilities represents retirement of debt.

REVIEW QUESTIONS

1 What are some meanings that may be attached to the term **funds** in preparing a statement of changes in financial position?

2 Briefly describe the "all financial resources" concept of funds flows.

3 Briefly discuss the uses to which a statement of changes in financial position may be put by readers of financial statements.

4 "Last year, Company B earned $8 per share on sales of $250 million. Its cash flow for the year, a generous $60 million, represented a fabulous return on equity capital." Comment on the implications of this quotation.

5 What basic data are necessary in order to prepare a statement of changes in financial position?

6 In analyzing working capital flows, business transactions may be classified into three categories: Transactions which affect only current asset or current liability accounts, transactions which affect both current and noncurrent accounts, and transactions which affect only noncurrent accounts. Indicate the effect of each category on working capital.

7 Give an example of each of the following situations, assuming that a statement of changes in financial position is being prepared:
   a A decrease in a noncurrent asset that **is not** a source of working capital
   b A decrease in a noncurrent asset that **is** a source of working capital
   c An increase in a noncurrent liability that **is not** a source of working capital
   d A decrease in stockholders' equity that **is** a use of working capital
   e An increase in stockholders' equity that **is not** a source of working capital
   f An increase in a noncurrent asset that **is not** a use of working capital
   g A decrease in a noncurrent liability that **is not** a use of working capital

8 The following transaction was recorded during the current year:

Land	35,000
Building	450,000
Mortgage Payable	380,000
Marketable Securities	50,000
Cash	55,000

Describe two ways this transaction can be reported in a statement of changes in financial position. Which do you prefer?

9 Shirley Company has outstanding a $5 million issue of serial bonds. The first series of bonds, in the amount of $500,000, mature in July of 1976. In preparing a statement of changes in financial position for the calendar year 1975, the accountant shows a use of working capital of $500,000 relating to these bonds. Is this correct? Explain.

10 Explain why the accumulation of a discount on bonds held as investments and the amortization of deferred revenue items would be deducted from net income in arriving at working capital provided by operations.

11 How would the retirement of bonds be reported in a statement of changes in financial position, assuming that sinking fund securities are liquidated and the proceeds used to retire the bonds?

12 What are the two approaches that may be followed in arriving at working capital provided by operations in the statement of changes in financial position?

EXERCISES

Ex. 23-1 Account balances relating to equipment during Year 1 follow:

	End of year	Beginning of year
Equipment	$210,000	$96,000
Less: Accumulated depreciation	38,000	30,000

Equipment with a book value of $10,000 and original cost of $22,000 was sold at a gain (net of income taxes) of $8,000. Compute the following for Year 1:
a Working capital provided by sale of equipment
b Working capital used to acquire equipment
c Depreciation expense on equipment which should be added to net income in computing working capital provided by operations.

Ex. 23-2 Explain how each of the following transactions would be shown on a statement of changes in financial position for Year 10.
a Cash dividends of $200,000 were declared on December 11, payable on January 14 of Year 11.
b A 5% stock dividend was distributed; the market value of the dividend shares, $1,020,000, was transferred from retained earnings to paid-in capital accounts.
c Mining properties valued at $380,000 were acquired on January 3, Year 10, in exchange for bonds payable with a par value of $400,000. The bonds mature on December 31, Year 19.
d An additional income tax assessment of $100,000 was charged to the Retained Earnings account as a prior period adjustment.
e Research and development costs of $150,000 were deferred in Year 8 for accounting purposes but were deducted in computing taxable income. As a result, the Deferred Income Tax Liability account was credited for $72,000. In Year 10, the research and development costs were written off as follows:

Research and Development Costs Written Off	78,000	
Deferred Income Tax Liability	72,000	
Deferred Research and Development Costs		150,000

Ex. 23-3 The Exposition Co. reported a net loss of $30,000 for the fiscal year just ended. In arriving at the net loss, the following items were included:

Amortization of research and development costs	$10,000
Amortization of premium on bonds payable	5,000
Gain on disposal of land (net of taxes)	20,000
Depreciation expense	15,000
Uncollectible accounts expense	2,500
Uninsured fire loss (net of taxes)	35,000
Amortization of organization costs	3,000
Write-down of obsolete inventory	8,000
Income taxes, of which $14,000 is payable two or more years hence.	20,000

Compute the increase or decrease in working capital as a result of recurring operations.

Ex. 23-4 The following data are taken from the latest financial statements of the Cash
Register Corporation:

	End of year	Beginning of year
Cash	$ 20,000	$ 15,000
Marketable securities	40,000	55,000
Accounts receivable	50,000	30,000
Inventories	70,000	60,000
Short-term prepayments	5,000	3,000
Noncurrent assets (net)	242,500	209,000
Accounts payable	60,000	30,000
Notes payable (short-term)	25,000	50,000
Accrued liabilities	2,500	2,000
Long-term debt & stockholders' equity	340,000	290,000

Determine the increase or decrease in working capital during the year.

Ex. 23-5 A summary of the financial position for the Kimball Company at the beginning
and ending of the current year follows:

	End of year	Beginning of year
Working capital	$ 87,500	$ 91,000
Noncurrent assets:		
Investment in stock of R Corporation (equity method)	82,500	75,000
Land	60,000	50,000
Buildings	120,000	100,000
Less: Accumulated depreciation	(50,000)	(46,000)
	$300,000	$270,000
Long-term debt & stockholders' equity:		
Notes payable, due in 5 years	$ 20,000	$ -0-
Capital stock, no par	200,000	200,000
Retained earnings	80,000	70,000
	$300,000	$270,000

The net income of $25,000 (after depreciation of $4,000) included unrealized
investment income of $7,500 from R Corporation. A cash dividend was de-
clared during the year.
Prepare a statement of changes in financial position for the year.

Ex. 23-6 The following data for Year 1 were obtained from the records of the Mary Lees
Company:

	Net changes during Year 1	
	Debits	Credits
Current assets	$ 98,100	
Plant and equipment (net)	30,000	
Goodwill (amortized over 25 years).		$ 1,500
Current liabilities		68,500
Bonds payable, 7%.		100,000
Discount on bonds payable	1,900	
Preferred stock, $10 par	100,000	
Common stock, no par		50,000
Retained earnings		10,000
	$230,000	$230,000

Retained Earnings

Premium on retirement of preferred stock . .	5,000	Balance, Jan. 1	60,000
Stock dividend on common stock	50,000	Net income	80,000
Cash dividends	15,000		

Ten-year bonds of $100,000 were issued on July 1 at 98, proceeds being used for the retirement of preferred stock. Land with a cost of $55,000 was exchanged at an agreed value of $70,000 for a new building costing $95,000; the balance of $25,000 was paid in cash. Depreciation for the year amounted to $10,000.

Prepare a statement of changes in financial position. A working paper is not required.

SHORT CASES FOR ANALYSIS AND DECISION

Case 23-1 The following statement of changes in financial position was improperly prepared by the accountant for the Jeffrey Company:

JEFFREY COMPANY
Statement of Changes in Financial Position
December 31, Year 1

Funds provided:

Acquisition of land	$105,000
Cash dividends declared (to be paid on Jan. 21, Year 2)	30,000
Stock dividend distributed	50,000
Acquisition of equipment.	15,000
Purchase of marketable securities as short-term investment	150,000
Total funds provided	$350,000

Funds applied:

Net income, including gain of $20,000 net of taxes	$120,000
Issuance of note payable—due Year 4	85,000
Depreciation and amortization expense	60,000
Sale of equipment—book value (sold at gain of $20,000 net of taxes)	10,000
Issuance of capital stock pursuant to stock dividend	50,000
Decrease in working capital	25,000
Total funds applied	$350,000

The president of the company is upset because he had hoped to increase the working capital during Year 1 by at least $100,000. Furthermore, he is somewhat confused with the arrangement of the statement and wonders if he should plan to issue additional shares of capital stock early in Year 2 in order to "bolster working capital."

Instructions
a Identify and discuss the weaknesses in the presentation of the statement of changes in financial position for Jeffrey Company as prepared by the accountant. Your discussion should explain why you consider them to be weaknesses and suggest the proper treatment of any item improperly presented.
b Prepare a revised statement of changes in financial position and advise the president whether or not the Jeffrey Company should issue additional shares of capital stock in order to improve its working capital position.

Case 23-2 The consolidated statement of source and disposition of working capital for Pacific Airlines, Inc., is shown below:

	Year 10 **(in thousands)**	
Sources of working capital:		
Operations:		
Income before gain on sale of aircraft	$ 3,770	(1)
Add: Charges against income not involving working capital:		
Depreciation	11,380	(2)
Deferred federal income tax, amortization of investment tax		
credit, and deferred debt expense	1,400	(3)
Net loss of unconsolidated subsidiaries	450	(4)
Total operations	$17,000	(5)
Gain on sale of aircraft, including $1 million of deferred federal		
income tax	2,100	(6)
Addition to long-term debt	40,000	(7)
Sale of common stock, less expense of issue	5,800	(8)
Disposal of flight and other property—book value	1,800	(9)
Increase in current portion of contracts receivable on aircraft		
leases	1,200	(10)
Total sources of working capital	$67,900	

Dispositions of working capital:

Dividends on common stock . . . . $	610 (11)
Addition to long-term contract receivable, excluding	
aircraft reclassifications	3,205 (12)
Investment of funds held for purchase of aircraft	4,785 (13)
Additions to flight, other property and equipment,	
and deposits on purchase contracts	62,100 (14)
Long-term debt refinanced	12,000 (15)
Provision for current portion of long-term debt	8,500 (16)
Investment in and advances to unconsolidated	
subsidiaries	2,250 (17)
Total dispositions of working capital	93,450
Increase (decrease) in working capital	$(25,550) (18)
Working capital at end of year	$ 12,600 (19)

Instructions Briefly explain each item numbered (1) through (19) and comment on the propriety of the format of the statement and the terminology used by Pacific Airlines, Inc.

Case 23-3 Ecology Design Corporation began business in the current year, and reported a net income of $300,000 for the first year. At the end of the year, the inventory of goods in process amounted to $100,000 and the inventory of finished goods amounted to $400,000. Depreciation of $350,000 on factory building and equipment had been recorded, of which $120,000 was included as a part of the factory overhead allocated to the ending inventories.

In preparing a statement of changes in financial position at the end of the year, the assistant controller added back to net income the entire depreciation of $350,000, to arrive at a figure of $650,000 as the working capital provided by operations. After reviewing the statement, the controller raised the question whether the $120,000 depreciation allocated to ending inventories was actually a nonfund expense. He suggested that $120,000 of the depreciation charge for the year be eliminated from inventories at the end of the year in preparing a statement of changes in financial position.

Instructions
a State what position you would take in this controversy and defend your position. Explain clearly the basis for your conclusion.
b Would your position be the same in preparing a statement of cash flows?

Case 23-4 The Union Country Club constructed a clubhouse at a cost of $500,000. It was financed by a $500,000 bond issue, the bonds being purchased by the members. The bonds are due in 25 years, but present plans are to call the bonds at the rate of $20,000 per year. A 4% straight-line depreciation rate on the clubhouse is considered to be proper. You are asked by the directors of the club to advise them as to whether the provision for the $20,000 annual reduction of the bond issue, the annual depreciation of $20,000, or both, should be included in the budget to be covered by club dues and fees.

Instructions Write a report, explaining the effect of including the following in the club dues and fees:
(1) Only out-of-pocket expenses
(2) Out-of-pocket expenses and bond retirements
(3) Out-of-pocket expenses, bond retirements, and depreciation expense

PROBLEMS

Group A

23A-1 The income statement of the Moxie Trading Company for 1975 includes the following items:

Net income, including miscellaneous gains and losses	$210,000
Deferred income tax expense	20,000
Depreciation expense	160,000
Accumulation of discount on investment in bonds	1,000
Amortization of discount on bonds payable	1,500
Uncollectible accounts expense	7,600
Realized gross profit on installment sales made in 1973 and 1974	62,000
Gain on sale of factory site, net of income taxes	102,000
Interest revenue accrued	4,800
Expenses which will be paid in 1976	12,000
Amortization of deferred "investment tax credit"	4,000
Loss on sale of marketable securities (current assets), net of income taxes .	1,200
Investment income accrued on investment in Q Co. stock (equity method) . .	5,000

Instructions

a Determine the amount of working capital provided by operations, assuming that the effects of nonoperating transactions on working capital are separately reported.

b Briefly explain the effect on working capital of each item above.

23A-2 A comparative balance sheet at December 31, for the Robinson Corporation follows:

	Year 2	Year 1
Cash	$ 52,500	$ 60,000
Accounts receivable (net)	100,000	90,000
Inventory	97,500	40,000
Plant and equipment	260,000	160,000
Less: Accumulated depreciation	(85,000)	(50,000)
Total assets	$425,000	$300,000
Accounts payable	$ 70,000	$ 60,000
Capital stock, $10 par	280,000	200,000
Paid-in capital in excess of par	20,000	–0–
Retained earnings	55,000	40,000
Total liabilities & stockholders' equity	$425,000	$300,000

On June 15, Year 2, the company issued 8,000 shares of capital stock in exchange for equipment. There were no retirements of plant and equipment items in Year 2. Dividends of $25,000 were paid to stockholders during Year 2. The allowance for uncollectible accounts was reduced by $3,000 during Year 2 as a result of writing off accounts known to be uncollectible, and increased by $5,000 at the end of the year.

Instructions
Prepare a statement of changes in financial position without using a working paper. Include a summary of changes in working capital accounts in the statement. The net income can be derived from the data given.

23A-3 The following information is obtained from the records of Ray Powell, Inc., for the year 1975:

Net Changes in Account Balances

	Debit	Credit
Cash	$ 29,950	
Accounts receivable	45,000	
Allowance for uncollectible accounts		$ 2,500
Inventories	35,050	
Equipment	150,000	
Accumulated depreciation		65,000
Goodwill		10,000
Income taxes payable		15,000
Accounts payable		5,000
Bonds payable—7% due Jan. 2, 1995		250,000
Premium on bonds payable		9,500
Preferred stock, $100 par	240,000	
Common stock, no par		105,000
Retained earnings		38,000
	$500,000	$500,000

A summary of the activity in the Retained Earnings account follows:

Balance, Jan. 1, 1975		$3,300,000
Add:		
Net income for year, after amortization of goodwill	$352,500	
Refund received on 1973 income taxes	12,500	365,000
		$3,665,000
Less:		
Cash dividends	$210,000	
Stock dividends on common stock	105,000	
Retirement premium on preferred stock	12,000	327,000
Balance, Dec. 31, 1975		$3,338,000

Accounts receivable of $20,000 were written off during the year. Equipment costing $200,000 which was 80% depreciated was sold at book value and new equipment with larger capacity was acquired. The bonds were issued on January 2, 1975, at 104. The bond interest checks were mailed on December 31, 1975.

Instructions Prepare a statement of changes in financial position (working capital concept) for 1975. A working paper is not required. If you use a working paper, the form illustrated on page 895 would be appropriate for this problem. A summary of changes in working capital accounts should be prepared as a part of the statement of changes in financial position.

23A-4 The operating data for Boise Dry Goods, Inc., for the current year include the following:

Sales (net of returns and allowances)	$420,000
Purchases (including $6,000 acquired by issuance of stock)	240,000
Operating expenses, including $22,000 depreciation expense	100,000
Interest expense	4,100
Income tax expense	25,200
Cash dividends paid	21,050

The following information is taken from year-end statements of financial position:

	End of year	Beginning of year
Cash	$?	$ 9,800
Accounts receivable (net)	42,250	46,000
Merchandise inventory	61,000	70,000
Miscellaneous short-term prepayments	3,000	2,200
Furniture and equipment	178,000	165,000
Less: Accumulated depreciation	(135,000)	(113,000)
Land for future expansion	40,000	–0–
Totals	$?	$ 180,000
Accounts payable	$ 14,150	$ 25,000
Income taxes payable	25,200	10,000
Interest payable	300	350
Equipment notes payable ($11,000 was current at beginning of year and $12,100 was current at end of year)	47,400	58,400
Capital stock, $10 par	70,000	55,000
Paid-in capital in excess of par	12,000	2,000
Undistributed earnings	?	?
Totals	$?	$ 180,000

Late in the current year, 1,500 shares of capital stock were issued in exchange for assets with fair values as follows: land, $15,000; merchandise, $6,000; furniture, $4,000.

Instructions
a Prepare a reconciliation of the Undistributed Earnings account for the current year.
b Prepare a statement of changes in financial position, showing the flow of all financial resources and supported by a schedule of changes in working capital accounts. The use of a working paper is not necessary.

23A-5 The comparative balance sheets for the Planek Corporation are as follows:

PLANEK CORPORATION
Comparative Balance Sheets
For Years Ended December 31, Year 1 and Year 2

	Year 2	Year 1	Increase (Decrease)
Assets			
Cash	$ 142,100	$ 165,300	$ (23,200)
Marketable securities (at cost)	122,800	129,200	(6,400)
Accounts receivable (net)	312,000	371,200	(59,200)
Inventories	255,200	124,100	131,100
Short-term prepayments	23,400	22,000	1,400
Bond sinking fund		63,000	(63,000)
Investment in subsidiary (equity method) .	134,080	152,000	(17,920)
Plant and equipment (net)	1,443,700	1,534,600	(90,900)
Totals	$2,433,280	$2,561,400	$(128,120)
Equities			
Accounts payable	$ 238,100	$ 213,300	$ 24,800
Notes payable—current		145,000	(145,000)
Accrued payables	16,500	18,000	(1,500)
Current income tax liability.	97,500	31,000	66,500
Deferred income tax liability	53,900	43,400	10,500
6% mortgage bonds (due in Year 14) . . .		300,000	(300,000)
Premium on mortgage bonds		10,000	(10,000)
8% debentures (due in Year 22)	125,000		125,000
Capital stock, $10 par value	1,033,500	950,000	83,500
Paid-in capital in excess of par	67,700	51,000	16,700
Reserve for casualty losses	74,000	85,000	(11,000)
Retained earnings	761,580	758,200	3,380
Treasury stock—at cost of $15 per share .	(34,500)	(43,500)	9,000
Totals	$2,433,280	$2,561,400	$(128,120)

Other sources disclose the following additional information relating to the activities of Year 2:
(1) The Retained Earnings account was analyzed as follows:

Retained earnings, Dec. 31, Year 1		$758,200
Add: Net income, including nonoperating items		236,580
Subtotal		$994,780
Less:		
Cash dividends declared	$130,000	
Reissue of treasury stock at a price below cost	3,000	
Stock dividend (8,350 shares)	100,200	233,200
Retained earnings, Dec. 31, Year 2		$761,580

The determination of net income complied with **Opinion No. 30** of the Accounting Principles Board.

(2) On January 2, Year 2, marketable securities were sold for $127,000. The proceeds from this sale, the cash and securities in the bond sinking fund, and the amount received from the issuance of the 8% debentures were used to retire the 6% mortgage bonds at a price of 105.

(3) The treasury stock (600 shares) was reissued at $10 per share on March 1, Year 2.

(4) The stock dividend was declared on November 1, Year 2, when the market price of Planek Corporation's stock was $12 per share.

(5) On April 30, Year 2, a fire destroyed a warehouse which cost $100,000 and upon which depreciation of $65,000 had accumulated. The deferred income tax liability relating to the difference between tax and book depreciation on the warehouse was $12,700. The loss of $22,300 was charged to the Reserve for Casualty Losses account. An additional provision for possible casualty losses was charged against net income. (The student should recognize that this is not a generally accepted accounting procedure.)

(6) Plant and equipment transactions consisted of the sale of a building at its book value of $4,000 and the purchase of machinery for $28,000.

(7) In Year 2, a $30,000 charge was made to Accumulated Depreciation and credited to net income for excessive depreciation taken in prior years but disallowed by the Internal Revenue Service. A tax deficiency of $16,000 was paid and charged against the Deferred Income Tax Liability account.

(8) The subsidiary, which is 80% owned, reported a net loss of $22,400 for Year 2.

Instructions Prepare a working paper for a statement of changes in financial position (all financial resources concept) for the year ended December 31, Year 2. The working capital at the end of Year 1 was $404,500, and at the end of Year 2 it was $503,400. Key the analyses of transactions for Year 2 in the working paper and give a brief explanation for each transaction.

23A-6 Comparative balance sheet data for the Starr Corporation follow:

	Dec. 31	
	Year 2	Year 1
Cash on hand and in banks	$ 6,000	$ 175,000
Marketable securities (at cost)	–0–	30,000
Accounts receivable, less allowances of $20,000 and $8,000		
for Year 2 and Year 1, respectively	435,000	260,000
Inventories	475,000	400,000
Investments (at cost)	520,000	610,000
Equipment (net of accumulated depreciation)	1,953,000	1,700,000
Discount on mortgage bonds payable	16,000	25,000
Totals	$3,405,000	$3,200,000

Bank overdraft	$ 5,000	$ -0-
Notes payable to banks (current)	350,000	40,000
Accounts payable	315,000	290,000
6% mortgage bonds payable	800,000	1,000,000
Preferred stock ($100 par, each share convertible into three		
shares of common)	250,000	300,000
Common stock ($5 par)	532,500	500,000
Paid-in capital in excess of par	577,500	340,000
Retained earnings	575,000	730,000
Totals	$3,405,000	$3,200,000

An analysis of account changes disclosed the following:
(1) Uncollectible accounts amounting to $10,250 were written off in Year 2.
(2) Some investments were sold at a gain of $80,000. Marketable securities, however, were sold at a loss of $3,500. (Show the loss on sale of marketable securities separately as a use of working capital.)
(3) Mortgage bonds mature on December 31, Year 6. On July 1, Year 2, bonds of $200,000 were retired at 102.
(4) Additional shares of common stock were issued during the year at $44 per share, and 1,500 shares were issued as a result of conversion of preferred stock.
(5) Equipment, cost $60,000, was sold at its book value of $30,000. Depreciation of $120,000 was taken during the year. Additional equipment was purchased for cash.
(6) Net loss for Year 2, including nonoperating gains and losses, amounted to $135,000.
(7) Cash dividends paid during the year amounted to $20,000.

Instructions
a Prepare a schedule determining the change in working capital during Year 2.
b Prepare a statement of changes in financial position which explains the reasons for the change in working capital. (Use of a working paper is recommended; if a working paper is not used, supporting schedules and computations should be presented.)

Group B

23B-1 The following statements were prepared for Sawmill Road, Incorporated:

SAWMILL ROAD, INCORPORATED
Balance Sheet
January 1, Year 1

Assets

Current assets	$ 37,000
Equipment	48,000
Less: Accumulated depreciation	(15,000)
Patents	5,000
Total assets	$ 75,000

Liabilities & Stockholders' Equity

Current liabilities	$ 12,000
Capital stock, no par	27,000
Retained earnings	36,000
Total liabilities & stockholders' equity	$ 75,000

SAWMILL ROAD, INCORPORATED
Statement of Changes in Financial Position
For Year 1

Working capital, Jan. 1		$25,000
Working capital provided:		
Operations:		
Net income	$24,000	
Add: Depreciation expense	10,000	
Amortization of patents	1,000	
Less: Gain on disposal of equipment	(4,000)	31,000
Issue of capital stock		13,000
Disposal of equipment		7,000
Total working capital provided		$76,000
Working capital applied:		
Dividends paid	$ 12,000	
Purchase of land	14,000	
Purchase of equipment	30,000	56,000
Working capital, Dec. 31		$20,000

Total assets on the balance sheet at December 31, Year 1, are $110,000. Accumulated depreciation on the equipment sold was $6,000.

Instructions Based on the information available from the balance sheet at January 1, Year 1, and the statement of changes in financial position for Year 1, prepare a balance sheet for Sawmill Road, Incorporated, at December 31, Year 1.

23B-2 Given below are the **changes** in account balances of Robert Maust's retail business for the fiscal year ended July 31, 1975:

Cash	$ 30,500
Accounts receivable	(8,000)
Allowance for uncollectible accounts	(200)
Merchandise inventory	(15,000)
Equipment	25,000
Accumulated depreciation	10,000
Accounts payable	(5,000)
Accrued miscellaneous liabilities	400
Robert Maust, capital	27,300

The parentheses denote a decrease in the debit or credit balance normal to a given account.

Accounts receivable of $1,000 were written off as uncollectible. Equipment costing $7,500 was sold for $3,000, resulting in a loss of $600. Net income, including the loss on sale of equipment, amounted to $47,300. The balance of the change in the owner's capital account represents drawings.

Instructions Prepare a statement of changes in financial position without using a working paper. The statement should include a schedule of the changes in working capital accounts.

23B-3 The *net changes* in the balance sheet accounts of the Ernst Company for the year 1975 are shown below:

	Debit	Credit
Working capital	$ 53,200	
Investments, at cost		$ 42,800
Land	3,200	
Buildings	95,000	
Machinery	6,000	
Office equipment		1,500
Accumulated depreciation:		
Buildings		2,000
Machinery		900
Office equipment	600	
Bonds payable (issued at 97¾ during 1975)		100,000
Discount on bonds payable	2,000	
Capital stock—preferred ($100 par)	10,000	
Capital stock—common ($10 par)		12,400
Paid-in capital in excess of par—common		5,600
Retained earnings		4,800
Total changes	$170,000	$170,000

Additional information

(1) Net income for the year amounted to $26,300, including nonoperating gains and losses.

(2) Cash dividends of $18,000 were declared December 15, 1975, payable January 15, 1976. A 2% stock dividend was issued March 31, 1975, when the market value was $12.50 per share. See item (8) below in order to determine the number of shares of common stock outstanding.

(3) The investments were sold at a gain of $2,500 (after taxes).

(4) A building which cost $45,000 and had a carrying value of $40,500 was sold for $50,500. Capital gain tax of $3,000 was accrued at the time of sale. A new building was purchased during the year.

(5) The following entry was made to record an exchange of an old machine for a new one:

Machinery	13,000	
Accumulated Depreciation: Machinery	5,000	
Machinery		7,000
Cash		11,000

(6) Fully depreciated office equipment which cost $1,500 was written off.

(7) Preferred stock was redeemed at a premium of $500, which was charged to retained earnings.

(8) The company issued 1,000 shares of its common stock on June 15, 1975, for $15 a share. There were 13,240 shares outstanding on December 31, 1975.

Instructions

a Prepare a working paper for a statement of changes in financial position. Use the form illustrated on page 895, and exclude nonoperating gains and losses from the section for working capital provided by operations.

b Prepare a formal statement of changes in financial position, showing a single figure for working capital provided by operations as summarized in the working paper.

23B-4 The following balances are provided by Touche-Ross Manufacturing Company to assist you in explaining the decrease in working capital for 1975:

	Dec. 31		Increase or (decrease)
	1975	*1974*	
Current assets	$ 491,900	$ 525,000	$ (33,100)
Cash surrender value of life insurance . .	21,200	17,500	3,700
Unamortized debt discount.	12,800	14,600	(1,800)
Securities held for plant			
expansion purposes.	98,000	-0-	98,000
Stock of associated companies (at cost,			
less than 20% ownership)	124,500	100,000	24,500
Machinery and equipment	823,200	743,800	79,400
Accumulated depreciation	(378,700)	(310,400)	(68,300)
Leasehold improvements (net).	96,500	104,600	(8,100)
Totals	$1,289,400	$1,195,100	$94,300
Current liabilities	$ 266,700	$ 234,200	$ 32,500
Deferred profit on installment sales	12,200	14,300	(2,100)
5% serial bonds payable	250,000	310,000	(60,000)
Capital stock, $5 par	500,000	250,000	250,000
Retained earnings, Jan. 1	386,600	208,400	178,200
Net income	213,900	228,200	(14,300)
Dividends—stock	(250,000)	-0-	(250,000)
Dividends—cash	(40,000)	(50,000)	10,000
Settlement of lawsuit—prior period			
adjustment	(50,000)	-0-	(50,000)
Totals	$1,289,400	$1,195,100	$ 94,300

On June 10, 1975, the company's directors declared a cash dividend of $0.80 per share payable on July 1, 1975, to stockholders of record June 20, 1975, and also declared a 100% stock dividend payable at the same time. An analysis of the plant asset accounts shows that machinery was purchased in 1975 at a cost of $197,900 and certain obsolete equipment having a net book value of $36,200 was sold for $28,000. No other entries were recorded in plant asset and related accounts other than charges for depreciation. During the year the company wrote off accounts receivable aggregating $4,000.

Instructions
a Prepare a working paper for a statement of changes in financial position which will explain the causes of the $65,600 decrease in working capital.
b Prepare a formal statement of changes in financial position. Show only the net working capital provided by operations as determined in the working paper. Show uses of working capital first, followed by sources of working capital.

23B-5 Comparative financial data for the Arthur-Young Corporation, in millions of dollars, as of December 31, appear below:

	Year 2	Year 1
Cash	$ 21.0	$ 24.4
Marketable securities (lower of cost or market)	8.7	–0–
Trade receivables (net)	36.4	29.5
Income tax refund receivable	3.8	–0–
Inventories	17.5	11.3
Short-term prepayments	2.5	1.9
Investment in other companies, at cost	28.0	18.0
Land	16.0	15.2
Buildings	52.0	49.5
Accumulated depreciation: buildings	(25.0)	(24.0)
Equipment	82.5	76.8
Accumulated depreciation: equipment	(44.4)	(32.6)
Totals	$199.0	$170.0
Accounts payable	$ 33.6	$ 20.9
Notes payable (current)	28.0	20.0
Current income tax liability	–0–	9.7
Mortgage payable (noncurrent)	14.0	14.0
Preferred stock ($100 par)	45.0	30.0
Common stock ($5 stated value)	58.0	50.0
Capital in excess of stated value	16.1	14.1
Retained earnings	4.3	11.3
Totals	$199.0	$170.0
Sales	$245.0	$230.0
Cost of goods sold	188.3	148.2
Selling and administrative expenses	64.0	47.9
Interest expense	1.0	1.2
Income tax expense (credit)	(3.8)	15.8
Cash dividends paid	2.5	10.8

Short-term prepayments relate entirely to administrative costs. Depreciation on building is 80% applicable to manufacturing activities, and depreciation on equipment is entirely applicable to manufacturing. During Year 2, the company issued common stock in exchange for 18% of the common stock of a major supplier. Additional preferred stock was issued at par value.

Instructions

a Prepare a schedule of changes in working capital during Year 2. Assume that the income tax refund receivable is a current asset.

b Prepare a working paper for working capital flows for Year 2.

c Prepare a statement of changes in financial position in which the amount of working capital provided by operations is taken as a single figure from the working paper in (*b*). Do not include a summary of changes in working capital accounts in the statement of changes in financial position.

d Prepare a statement of changes in financial position showing the revenue and expense items which provided or used working capital as a result of recurring operations.

23B-6 The financial statements of Miller Corporation for Year 10 and Year 9 appear on pages 913 and 914. The company was formed on January 1, Year 7.

The following information was given effect in the preparation of these financial statements:

(1) The 10% stock dividend was distributed on August 1, Year 10. The investment in land for a future plant site was obtained by the issuance of 10,000 shares of the corporation's capital stock on October 1, Year 10. On December 1, 20,000 shares of capital stock were sold to obtain additional working capital. There were no other transactions in Year 10 affecting paid-in capital.

(2) During Year 10 depreciable assets with a total cost of $17,500 were retired and sold as scrap for a nominal amount. These assets were fully depreciated at December 31, Year 9. The only depreciable asset acquired in Year 10 was a new building.

(3) When new equipment, with an estimated life of 10 years, was purchased on January 2, Year 9 for $300,000, the decision was made to defer the resulting investment tax credit, with the benefit of the credit being allocated over the useful life of the equipment by a reduction in income tax expense. The income tax rate is 50%.

(4) In Year 10, $10,000 was paid in advance on long-term notes payable. The balance of the long-term notes is due in Year 11.

(5) An appropriation of retained earnings for possible contingencies of $25,000 was established in Year 10.

Instructions

a Prepare a working paper for a statement of changes in financial position for the year ended December 31, Year 10.

b Prepare a formal statement of changes in financial position for Year 10. You need not show a summary of the composition of working capital, which is generally included in the lower section of the statement.

MILLER CORPORATION
Comparative Balance Sheets
December 31, Year 10 and Year 9

	Year 10	Year 9	Increase (decrease)
Current assets:			
Cash	$ 33,500	$ 27,000	$ 6,500
Accounts receivable (net of allowance for un-			
collectible accounts of $2,900 and $2,000) . .	89,900	79,700	10,200
Inventories (fifo, lower of cost or market) . . .	136,300	133,200	3,100
Short-term prepayments	4,600	12,900	(8,300)
Total current assets	$264,300	$252,800	$ 11,500
Investments: Land held for future plant site . . .	$ 35,000	$ -0-	$ 35,000
Plant and equipment:			
Land	$ 47,000	$ 47,000	$ -0-
Buildings and equipment (net of accumulated			
depreciation of $155,600 and $117,000). . . .	551,900	425,000	126,900
Total plant and equipment	$598,900	$472,000	$126,900
Other assets: Organization costs	$ 1,500	$ 3,000	$ (1,500)
Total assets	$899,700	$727,800	$171,900
Current liabilities:			
Accounts payable	$ 3,000	$ 7,800	$ (4,800)
Notes payable	8,000	5,000	3,000
Mortgage payable	3,600	3,600	-0-
Accrued liabilities	6,200	4,800	1,400
Current income tax liability	87,500	77,900	9,600
Total current liabilities	$108,300	$ 99,100	$ 9,200
Long-term liabilities:			
Notes payable	$ -0-	$ 18,000	$(18,000)
Mortgage payable	70,200	73,800	(3,600)
Total long-term liabilities	$ 70,200	$ 91,800	$(21,600)
Deferred investment tax credit	$ 16,800	$ 18,900	$ (2,100)
Stockholders' equity:			
Capital stock; $1 par value; shares authorized,			
300,000 in Year 10 and 200,000 in Year 9;			
shares issued and outstanding, 162,000 in			
Year 10 and 120,000 in Year 9.	$162,000	$120,000	$ 42,000
Paid-in capital in excess of par.	306,900	197,900	109,000
Retained earnings appropriated for contin-			
gencies	25,000	-0-	25,000
Retained earnings—unappropriated	210,500	200,100	10,400
Total stockholders' equity	$704,400	$518,000	$186,400
Total liabilities & stockholders' equity	$899,700	$727,800	$171,900

MILLER CORPORATION
Statement of Income and Retained Earnings
For the Years Ended December 31, Year 10 and Year 9

	Year 10	Year 9	Increase (decrease)
Sales	$980,000	$900,000	$ 80,000
Cost of goods sold.	540,000	490,000	50,000
Gross profit on sales	$440,000	$410,000	$ 30,000
Selling and administrative expenses	262,000	248,500	13,500
Operating income	$178,000	$161,500	$ 16,500
Other expenses.	(3,000)	(1,500)	1,500
Income before income taxes.	$175,000	$160,000	$ 15,000
Income tax expense	85,400	77,900	7,500
Net income	$ 89,600	$ 82,100	$ 7,500
Retained earnings, Jan. 1	200,100	118,000	82,100
Stock dividend distributed, 10%	(36,000)	–0–	(36,000)
Cash dividends paid	(18,200)	–0–	(18,200)
Appropriation for contingencies	(25,000)	–0–	(25,000)
Retained earnings, Dec. 31	$210,500	$200,100	$ 10,400

CHAPTER 24

Analysis of financial statements

Many groups outside the business enterprise—creditors, investors, regulatory agencies, financial analysts, labor union leaders—are interested in its financial affairs. Management is also interested in the results and relationships reported in financial statements. Outsiders do not have access to the detailed data that are available to management and must therefore rely on published information in making decisions that relate to a business firm. In this chapter we shall consider the analysis of financial statements as a basis for decision making by outsiders.

Management makes operating and financial decisions based on a wide variety of reports which are generated by the company's own information system or which are available from other sources. Management's use of financial information for certain decision-making purposes has been mentioned in preceding chapters. More sophisticated analyses of profit-volume relationships, make or buy decisions, differential costs, budgets, product line profitability, gross profits, distribution costs, internal rates of return, etc., are usually covered in cost or management accounting courses and for that reason are not discussed in this book.

Sources of financial information available to outsiders

The first step in financial analysis is to obtain as much factual information as possible. The major sources of corporate financial information are as follows:

Published Reports   Corporations whose stock is publicly owned issue annual and quarterly reports. Annual reports generally contain comparative financial statements and the accompanying notes, supplementary financial information, and comments by management on the year's operations and prospects for the future. They are made available to the public as well as to stockholders.

Securities and Exchange Commission (SEC)   Publicly owned corporations are required to file periodic statements with the SEC, copies of which may be acquired at nominal cost. These statements are particularly valuable sources of financial information because the SEC prescribes a standard format and terminology and because they typically contain more detailed information than reports to stockholders.

Credit and Investment Advisory Services   Organizations such as Moody's Investors Service and Standard & Poor's Corporation compile financial information for investors in annual volumes and periodic supplements. A wide variety of data on companies, particularly small and medium-sized businesses, is published by such organizations as Dun & Bradstreet, Inc., and Robert Morris Associates. Many trade associations collect and publish average ratios for companies in an industry. Major brokerage firms and investment advisory services compile financial information about publicly owned companies from all sources and make it available to their customers. In addition, such firms maintain a staff of analysts who study business conditions and review published financial statements; make plant visitations and talk with executives to get information on new products, industry trends, and management changes; and interpret all this information for investors.

Audit Reports   When a CPA performs an audit, his report is addressed to the board of directors, and frequently to the stockholders, of the audited company. The CPA's opinion on financial statements is included in annual reports. Frequently his report consists only of the opinion; however, when dealing with smaller businesses, the CPA generally prepares a "long-form report" which contains rather detailed financial information and comments. Banks and other lending institutions rely heavily on this type of audit report for financial information about firms applying for loans.

What is financial analysis?

Knowing what to look for and how to interpret it is the essence of the art of analysis. Financial analysis is a process of *selection, relation, and evaluation.* The first step is to select from the total information available about a business the information relevant to the decision under consideration. The second is to arrange the information in a way that will bring out significant relationships. The final step is to study these relationships and interpret the results.

Financial statements themselves are organized summaries of detailed information, and are thus a form of analysis. The type of statements the accountant prepares, the way he arranges items on these statements, and his standards of disclosure are all influenced by a desire to provide information in convenient form. In using these statements, the analyst focuses his attention on key figures and relationships. He may then extend his investigation to find out why the conditions revealed by the financial statements exist.

Procedures of analysis

Financial analysis is not primarily a matter of making computations. The important part of the analytical process begins when the computational task is finished. There are, however, some analytical procedures that are useful in highlighting important relationships and reducing masses of detail into brief, convenient numerical form so that the essential facts can be readily grasped.

Ratios   Ratios may be expressed as percentages, as fractions, or as a stated comparison between simple numbers. For example, we might describe the relationship between $120 million of sales and $24 million of operating income as: (1) operating income is 20% of sales; (2) operating income is $\frac{1}{5}$ of sales; (3) the ratio of sales to operating income is 5 to 1; (4) for every dollar of sales the company earned 20 cents in operating income. Each of these ratios describes concisely the relationship between sales and operating income. Computing a ratio does not add any information not already inherent in the figures under study. A useful ratio can be computed only when a significant relationship exists; a ratio of two unrelated figures is meaningless.

Component Percentages   The ratio of one item on a financial statement to the total that includes that item is called a *component percentage.* Reducing data to component percentages helps the analyst visualize quickly the relative importance of any item on financial statements and of significant changes from period to period.

Statements expressed in component percentages are sometimes called "common size" statements. Two examples, one for Company A and one for Companies A and B, are presented on page 918.

In the first example for Company A, reducing the operating data to component percentages helps the reader to see the major factors that brought about an increase in the rate of earnings per dollar of sales. In the second example, component percentages highlight the difference in the asset and capital structure of Companies A and B. Company A has a larger proportion of debt and a relatively larger amount of current

COMPANY A
Common Size Income Statements

	Year 2	Year 1
Net sales.	100.0%	100.0%
Cost of goods sold.	63.2	66.4
Gross profit on sales	36.8%	33.6%
Operating expenses	23.2	24.2
Operating income	13.6%	9.4%
Income tax expense	5.0	3.2
Net income	8.6%	6.2%

COMPANIES A AND B
Common Size Balance Sheets
December 31, Year 1

	Company A	Company B
Assets:		
Current assets	56.4%	43.2%
Plant and equipment (net)	38.7	50.1
Other assets	4.9	6.7
Total assets	100.0%	100.0%
Liabilities & stockholders' equity:		
Current liabilities.	36.2%	20.5%
Long-term liabilities	24.0	12.6
Total liabilities	60.2%	33.1%
Stockholders' equity	39.8	66.9
Total liabilities & stockholders' equity	100.0%	100.0%

assets; Company B is financed more heavily by use of owners' capital and has a relatively larger investment in plant and equipment.

When information is reduced to simple terms, there may be some loss of clarity or completeness, but there may be some gains. Component percentages emphasize relative size; they obscure differences in absolute amounts. For example, if Company A has managed to increase its net income from 6.2 to 8.6% of sales only by cutting sales volume in half, there is no hint of this in the common size income statements. Similarly, the common size balance sheets will not reveal, for example, the fact that Company A is four times the size of Company B.

Changes Over Time The analytical information that can be gleaned from the financial statements of only one year is limited. We have seen in previous chapters the difficulty of measuring income and financial position accurately. Furthermore, the company's experience in any given year may not be typical. Investigating performance during several periods is therefore a useful form of analysis.

Most corporate annual reports now include a 5-, 10-, or 15-year summary of important financial data. The selected figures below, for example, are taken from the annual report of the International Corporation.[1] We can see at a glance that the sales, net income, and cash dividends of the International Corporation are growing steadily.

INTERNATIONAL CORPORATION
Sales, Net Income, and Dividends

	Year 5	Year 4	Year 3	Year 2	Year 1
Sales (millions)	$4,248	$3,573	$3,239	$2,863	$2,591
Net income (millions) . .	526	477	431	364	305
Net income per share (dollars)	9.66	9.03	8.20	6.96	5.84
Cash dividends per share	4.30	4.00	3.17	2.27	1.60

There are a number of ways to reduce this five-year record of items to be analyzed to a form that aids analysis. In the schedule below relating to sales and net income, the dollar increase each year over the previous year, the percentage increase over the previous year, and the **trend percentage** in relation to the first year in the series are shown for the International Corporation:

INTERNATIONAL CORPORATION
Analysis of Changes over Five-year Period

Year	Dollar increase over previous year (in millions of dollars)		Percentage increase over previous year		Trend percentage in relation to Year 1	
	Sales	Net income	Sales	Net income	Sales	Net income
1					100.0%	100.0%
2	$272	$59	10.5%	19.3%	110.5	119.3
3	376	67	13.1	18.4	125.0	141.3
4	334	46	10.3	10.7	137.9	156.4
5	675	49	18.9	10.3	163.9	172.5

[1] When financial data for a number of years are reported, common practice is to report the *most recent* data in the first column and the older data in succeeding columns to the right. We shall follow this practice in this chapter.

Each of these computations points up the change in sales and net income over the five-year period in a slightly different way. If the analyst is primarily interested in absolute change, the dollar changes tell the story. The percentage of increase or decrease year by year expresses growth in relation to the prior year's performance. Trend percentages (computed by dividing the figure for each year by the figure for the base year) reveal a total growth of 63.9% in sales volume and an increase of 72.5% in net income over a period of four years.

A great deal of importance has been placed in recent years on the **compound growth** rates in earnings. Those companies whose earnings increase at a rate substantially above the average rate for other companies are referred to as **growth companies.** The compound growth rate in net income for the International Corporation during the Years 2 through 5, for example, is the simple average of the percentage increases in net income over the previous year. Thus 19.3 + 18.4 + 10.7 + 10.3, or 58.7 ÷ 4 years gives a compound growth rate in net income of approximately 14.7%. This figure can also be estimated from compound interest tables by first determining the increase in net income for a period of years (72.5% in four years for the International Corporation) and then determining the compound rate that would result in a cumulative increase of 72.5% over the four-year period.[2]

Analytical objectives

The outcome of business decisions (to buy or sell a company's securities or to extend or refuse to extend credit, for example) naturally depends on future events. Financial statements are essentially a record of the past. Outsiders, therefore, study accounting data as evidence of past performance which may be useful in making predictions of future performances. The management of an enterprise is responsible for earning as large a return as possible on the resources invested in the business, consistent with the objectives of maintaining a sound financial condition, meeting social responsibilities, and conducting the business in accordance with high ethical standards. Insofar as the attainment of these objectives can be measured quantitatively—and quantitative information is usually only a part of the basis for any decision—financial statements provide pertinent information.

In looking at past performance and present position, the financial analyst seeks answers to two primary questions: (1) What is the company's earnings performance? and (2) Is the company in sound financial condition? We can therefore examine the process of analysis within the framework of these two questions.

[2] Net income for Year 5 is approximately 173% of Year 1 net income or 1.73 in terms of a decimal value. Compound interest tables show that $1 would accumulate to $1.69 in four years at 14%, or to $1.81 in four years at 16%. Since $1.73 is $\frac{4}{12}$ between $1.69 and $1.81, the interpolated compound growth rate would be 14% + $\frac{4}{12}$ of 2%, or approximately 14.7%.

ANALYSIS OF EARNINGS PERFORMANCE

Unfortunately an outsider does not usually have access to many of the important details that lie behind reported net income. Most published income statements are highly condensed. The outsider must usually content himself with a general review of the relation between revenue, total operating expenses, and net income. This usually requires a careful analysis of gross profit percentages and *operating expense ratios* (total operating expenses divided by net sales) over a period of years. He will also look carefully at any items of nonoperating revenue and expense, and extraordinary items in order to forecast the likely earning power of a company.

Net income and accounting practices

The point has been made throughout this text that the amount of net income reported in a given period can be materially affected by the accounting practices followed. These practices are selected by management; the independent auditor simply informs readers that the accounting practices used are "in conformity with generally accepted accounting principles (standards) applied on a basis consistent with that of the preceding year." Unfortunately, a wide variety of principles or standards is considered "generally accepted" and the analyst must first determine the accounting practices used and then evaluate the effect of such practices on reported net income. In other words, the analyst is concerned with the *quality of reported earnings.*

In recent years significant progress has been made in reducing areas of differences in financial reporting and additional steps are contemplated by authoritative bodies. An encouraging sign is the inclusion in annual reports of a description of the accounting policies used in the preparation of financial statements.[3] The accounting for depreciation, inventories, leases, pension plans, research and development costs, unconsolidated subsidiaries, mergers and acquisitions, and income taxes, for example, are especially significant to the analyst. In addition, the notes accompanying financial statements often provide useful information on these and other matters.

Trend in earnings

The analysis of income performance should always cover several periods not only because of the difficulty of measuring income year by year, but also because it is important to know how a company performs in periods of both prosperity and adversity. Net income may be satisfactory in one year and shrink to nothing in the next because of unfavorable business conditions.

[3] *APB Opinion No. 22,* "Disclosure of Accounting Policies," AICPA (New York: 1972).

One of the first things an analyst looks for is the trend of revenue over a period of years. A rising trend of sales is usually a sign of an expanding company. Obviously the revenue trend is not the whole story, since a growth in sales volume is not always accompanied by a corresponding increase in net income. The ideal situation is to find a company maintaining a constant or increasing *rate* of net income on a rapidly growing sales volume.

The pattern of revenue and operating earnings throughout the business cycle is also an important factor. There is obviously greater risk in investing in or lending to a firm whose income varies widely with changes in business conditions, than in a company able to show stability of earnings throughout all phases of the business cycle. A firm that must cut back its operations severely during recessions inevitably suffers in terms of such factors as effective product planning and employee morale and may find it difficult to meet fixed expenses. Furthermore, earnings tend to sag faster than revenue because of the presence of fixed expenses. An investor is interested in identifying a *cyclical* company not only because the risk of investment is higher, but because the timing of his investment will depend on the company's performance in relation to cyclical trends. The shifts to *defensive stocks* (stocks of companies that perform well in all phases of the business cycle) when a recession is in the offing and to cyclical shares at the first sign of an upturn is a well-known investment strategy.

Return on investment

Businessmen invest capital with the objective of earning a satisfactory return. The rate that is earned depends on numerous factors, including the nature of competition and the risks inherent in the venture. Management is often evaluated in terms of the rate it is able to earn on invested capital. While outsiders cannot determine return on the investment for particular divisions or segments of a business, they can make some overall estimates of rate of return. This rate can serve as a valuable index in evaluating the relative standing of a particular company and the quality of its management.

The return on investment for any period is determined by dividing net income by average investment. The appropriate income figure to be used depends on the related concept of investment. This is illustrated on page 923.

In all cases net income should exclude any extraordinary items, and the investment would be computed as an average for the period. Computations 1 and 2 provide related measurements. Ratio 1 is a measure of the earnings (after income taxes and interest) that relate to the total resources under the control of the firm. It would be possible to add interest expense back to net income in order to arrive at an approximation of earnings before payment of interest to creditors but after income taxes. Some analysts prefer to compute return on total assets *before income taxes,* in which case a ratio of operating income to total assets is used.

Appropriate income figure		Meaning of investment (in all cases an average for the period covered by the income figure)
1 Return on total assets: Net income	÷	total assets
2 Return on long-term capital: Net income + interest on long-term debt	÷	total assets less current liabilities
3 Return on stockholders' equity: **a** Net income	÷	total stockholders' equity
b Net income applicable to common stock	÷	common stockholders' equity

If total assets include some unproductive assets, bond sinking funds, or long-term investments, these assets and the related earnings generated by these assets may be excluded from rate of return computations.

Ratio 2 is a measure of return (after taxes) on long-term capital, reflecting the view that the portion of total assets financed by current liabilities should not be included in the investment base, since most of the cost of short-term financing is included in operating expenses (as a part of prices paid for goods and services) and is not stated as a separate item.

Ratio 3 is computed from the viewpoint of stockholders, and the alternatives (3*a* or 3*b*) depend on whether the analyst is interested in the rate of return on total stockholders' equity or on common stockholders' equity.

The following data for the Barker Company (given in millions of dollars) will be used to compute these returns on investment ratios:

Income statement data			Balance sheet data			
	Year 2	**Year 1**		**Year 2**	**Year 1**	**Year 0**
Sales	$130	$ 95	Current assets	$19	$20	$18
Other revenue	10	5				
Total revenue	$140	$100	Less: Current liabilities	6	10	9
Cost of goods sold . .	$ 95	$ 65	Working capital	$13	$10	$ 9
Operating expenses .	26	20	Noncurrent assets . . .	61	60	56
Interest expense . . .	1	1	Total	$74	$70	$65
Income tax expense .	9	7	Long-term debt	$19	$20	$21
Total expenses . . .	$131	$ 93	Preferred stock	16	16	16
Net income	$ 9	$ 7	Common stockholders'			
Preferred dividends .	1	1	equity	39	34	28
Available for common	$ 8	$ 6	Total long-term capital	$74	$70	$65

The return on investment ratios described in the outline on page 923 are computed below (all dollar figures are stated in millions):

Return on investment	Computation			
	Year 2		**Year 1**	
1 Return on total assets	$\dfrac{\$9}{\frac{1}{2}(\$80 + \$80)}$	$= \dfrac{\$9}{\$80} = 11.2\%$	$\dfrac{\$7}{\frac{1}{2}(\$80 + \$74)}$	$= \dfrac{\$7}{\$77} = 9.1\%$
2 Return on long-term capital . . .	$\dfrac{\$9 + \$1}{\frac{1}{2}(\$74 + \$70)}$	$= \dfrac{\$10}{\$72} = 13.9\%$	$\dfrac{\$7 + \$1}{\frac{1}{2}(\$70 + \$65)}$	$= \dfrac{\$8}{\$67.5} = 11.9\%$
3 a Return on total stock-holders' equity	$\dfrac{\$9}{\frac{1}{2}(\$55 + \$50)}$	$= \dfrac{\$9}{\$52.5} = 17.1\%$	$\dfrac{\$7}{\frac{1}{2}(\$50 + \$44)}$	$= \dfrac{\$7}{\$47} = 14.9\%$
b Return on common stockholders' equity	$\dfrac{\$8}{\frac{1}{2}(\$39 + \$34)}$	$= \dfrac{\$8}{\$36.5} = 21.9\%$	$\dfrac{\$6}{\frac{1}{2}(\$34 + \$28)}$	$= \dfrac{\$6}{\$31} = 19.4\%$

Interpreting Return on Investment All four measures of return on investment for the Barker Company show an improved performance in the second year. If we look at the underlying factors—the revenue generated per dollar of investment (or asset turnover rate) and the net income per dollar of revenue—we can obtain some additional insight:

	Year 2	Year 1
Revenue generated per dollar of assets:		
$\dfrac{\text{Total revenue}}{\text{Average investment (total assets)}}$	$\dfrac{\$140}{\$80} = \$1.75$	$\dfrac{\$100}{\$77} = \$1.30$
Net income per dollar of revenue:		
$\dfrac{\text{Net income}}{\text{Total revenue}}$	$\dfrac{\$9}{\$140} = 6.4\%$	$\dfrac{\$7}{\$100} = 7.0\%$

Although the firm earned a smaller margin of income per dollar of total revenue in the second year, it was able to improve its volume of revenue per dollar of investment from $1.30 to $1.75. This ratio may be referred to as the *asset turnover* rate and can be used to verify the rates of return on total assets as follows:

> Year 2: $1.75 × 6.4% = 11.2 cents per dollar of assets, or 11.2%
> Year 1: $1.30 × 7.0% = 9.1 cents per dollar of assets, or 9.1%

What we have done here is simply multiply the rate earned on revenue by the asset turnover rate in order to measure the earnings rate on assets. This concept is really a truism: If a profit of 3%, for example, can be earned on sales and $10 of sales is generated by each $1 of assets, then the rate earned on assets would be 10 × 3%, or 30%.

Trading on the Equity When a business unit borrows money for long-term purposes, it is said to be *trading on the equity.* The results from trading on the equity can be favorable or unfavorable to common stockholders. If the rate earned before interest and income taxes on total assets is greater than the interest rate paid for the use of money, the common stockholders will gain; if the interest rate is higher than the earnings rate on assets, then a loss arises from trading on the equity. Issuance of preferred stock produces similar results but is more "expensive" to the common stockholders since dividends on preferred stock are not deductible in computing taxable income.

The fact that return on stockholders' equity for the Barker Company is higher than the return on total assets is significant. The firm is successfully trading on the equity, that is, the total of interest on bonds and dividends on preferred stock is less than the earnings on capital raised through these *senior securities* (bonds payable and preferred stock). The company has about $20 million in long-term debt at an interest cost of about 5% before taxes and $2\frac{1}{2}$% after taxes, and it has $16 million in preferred stock paying dividends of about 6.3% ($1 ÷ $16). The company earned 11.2% after taxes on its total assets during Year 2. Therefore, an average dollar furnished by issuance of senior securities earns considerably more than the fixed interest and dividends. This excess accrues to the common stockholders, resulting in a 21.9% rate earned on common stockholders' equity in Year 2 and 19.4% in Year 1.

Earnings and dividends per share

Since a stockholder thinks in terms of the number of shares he owns or plans to buy or sell, reducing corporate financial information to per-share terms puts it in a useful perspective for stockholders. Perhaps the most commonly used statistics relating to common stock are *earnings (or loss) per share* and dividends per share. These appear widely in financial press releases, prospectuses, proxy material, and reports to stockholders.

Comparative earnings per share data, supported by complete financial statements, can be useful in evaluating the performance of a company from the common stockholders' point of view. There is no doubt that earnings (or loss) per share is a highly significant summary figure, but it has some serious limitations and there are some dangers in focusing too much attention on this single index of performance.

The manner of computing and reporting of earnings per share has been a major concern not only of the accounting profession but also of the SEC and the major stock exchanges. The technical aspects of computing and reporting **primary** and **fully diluted** earnings per share are illustrated in Chapter 17.

Dividends on capital stock represent historical facts and should be reported at amounts actually paid, except in cases following stock splits or large stock dividends. In such cases, "the presentation of dividends per share should be in terms of the current equivalent of the number of shares outstanding at the time of the dividend, so that the earnings and dividends per share will be reported on a comparable basis. When dividends per share are presented on other than an historical basis, the basis of presentation should be disclosed." [4]

Price-Earnings Ratio and Dividend Yield An investor in corporate securities is more interested in earnings and dividends in relation to the **market value** of his shares than in relation to the **book value** (see Chapter 17) of his stock interest, because market value measures the amount of money he foregoes at any given time by his decision to continue to hold his stock. To illustrate, suppose that Adams owns one share of common stock in a company that currently earns $5 per share and pays a dividend of $2 per share. The book value of the stock is $40 per share and the current market price is $50. The fact that the company is earning a return of $12\frac{1}{2}\%$ on stockholders' equity ($5 \div $40) is of secondary interest to Adams, since he gives up the use of $50 by his decision to own this share. Thus Adams views his investment as one producing an **earnings yield** of 10% ($5 \div $50) and a **dividend yield** of only 4% ($2 \div $50). In investment circles the earnings yield is usually expressed in reverse as a **price-earnings ratio** [5] of 10 to 1 ($50 \div $5).

An intelligent investor watches carefully the relation between earnings, dividends, and the market prices of stock and seeks to evaluate these relationships by analyzing the financial data available to him. The data on page 927 show these relationships for three companies.

This divergence in price-earnings and yield ratios (an even wider spread often exists among listed stocks) suggests that investors assess the risk and future prospects of these three investments in quite different

---

[4] *APB Opinion No. 9*, "Reporting the Results of Operations," AICPA (New York: 1966), p. 126.
[5] The price-earnings ratios are generally determined using the primary earnings per share for the latest 12 months, excluding extraordinary items. Starting in October 1972, the price-earnings ratios for stocks traded on the New York and American Stock Exchanges have been reported in most daily newspapers, along with the annual price range, the daily high and low prices, the closing price, and the net price change from the previous day's closing price.

	Company C	Company D	Company E
Earnings per share	$1.00	$2.50	$5.00
Dividends per share	$0.80	$1.50	$1.20
Market price per share during the year:			
High	$ 20	$ 52	$ 162
Low	$ 8	$ 36	$ 105
End	$ 12	$ 50	$ 150
Price-earnings ratio (year-end)	12–1	20–1	30–1
Dividend yield on market price at the end of			
the year	6.7%	3.0%	0.8%

terms. Company C, for example, may be a marginal producer in its industry with highly volatile earnings performance and low growth prospects. As a result, its stock sells at a low price-earning ratio and yields a fairly generous 6.7%. The stock of Company D sells at a much higher multiple of earnings and yields only 3% since a small proportion of current earnings is distributed to stockholders. Company E, on the other hand, appears to be a "growth company"; the price-earnings ratio for its stock is 30 to 1, yield is below 1%, and less than 25% of the current income is distributed to stockholders.

An investor who tries to determine whether the market price of a share of stock is reasonable must consider a variety of factors. All, however, relate to an estimate of the ultimate return on his investment; this return will depend on the dividends received during the time he holds the shares and the price he obtains when he sells the stock, both of which are difficult to project with any degree of precision.

Earnings and Fixed Charges   A company that finances its operations through long-term debt or preferred stock is committed to pay a fixed return to the holders of these securities. The commitment on long-term debt is clearly stronger than on preferred stock, since in the latter case the obligation is only that preferred dividends will be paid before any dividends on common are declared. A firm that *passes* a preferred dividend has impaired its financial reputation to some degree, but a firm that passes a bond interest payment is in serious financial trouble.

Bondholders and preferred stockholders have learned from experience that the relation between earnings and dividend and fixed interest commitments is a good measure of the safety of their investment. The following information is used to illustrate two ratios commonly calculated to measure these relationships:

	Company F	Company G
Operating income	$600,000	$900,000
Less: Interest on long-term debt	200,000	100,000
Income before income tax expense	$400,000	$800,000
Less: Income tax expense	200,000	400,000
Net income	$200,000	$400,000
Less: Preferred dividends	50,000	200,000
Net income available to common stockholders	$150,000	$200,000

Times interest earned The times interest earned ratio may be computed in two ways as shown below:

	Company F	Company G
Method 1: Times interest earned before taxes:		
(a) Operating income	$600,000	$900,000
(b) Interest charges	200,000	100,000
Times interest earned (a ÷ b)	3 times	9 times
Method 2: Times interest earned after taxes:		
Net income	$200,000	$400,000
(a) Add back interest charges	200,000	100,000
(b) Income before interest charges	$400,000	$500,000
Times interest earned (b ÷ a)	2 times	5 times

Since interest expense is deductible in arriving at taxable income, logic would seem to be on the side of method 1. Businessmen and investors are strongly conditioned to an after-tax view of corporate affairs, however, which may explain why method 2 is usually found in practice. The after-tax computation will always result in a more conservative figure for coverage of interest charges.

Times preferred dividends earned The computation of the number of times preferred dividends are earned may also be made in two ways, as illustrated below:

	Company F	Company G
Method 1: Net income to preferred dividends:		
(a) Net income	$200,000	$400,000
(b) Preferred dividend requirement	50,000	200,000
Times preferred dividends earned (a ÷ b)	4 times	2 times

These ratios make it appear that F Company's preferred dividends are better protected by earnings than its bond interest; yet bond interest obviously has a prior claim. To overcome this objection, the test of preferred dividend safety most often encountered is the number of times that *the combined interest charges and preferred dividends* are earned. The computation for these two companies would be as follows:

	Company F	Company G
Method 2: Times interest charges and preferred dividends are earned:		
Interest charges	$200,000	$100,000
Preferred dividend requirement	50,000	200,000
(a) Total interest and dividend requirements	$250,000	$300,000
(b) Net income (after taxes) plus interest charges	400,000	500,000
Number of times interest charges and preferred dividends are earned (b ÷ a)	1.6 times	1.7 times

"Times-earned" ratios are of interest not only to creditors and preferred stockholders but also to common stockholders. Holders of common stock know that a company that has to omit either interest or preferred dividends will suffer financial embarrassment at the very least; furthermore, they are concerned about a sufficiency of earnings to allow for common dividends. There is no equivocation in interpreting times-earned ratios—the higher the ratio the more favorable for bondholders and preferred stockholders. The more difficult question is how high the ratios should be to satisfy these two groups without being detrimental to the common stockholders. In general this will depend on the stability of past and potential earnings over the business cycle; if earnings are stable, lower times-earned ratios can be viewed as satisfactory.

In analyzing financial statements, the coverage of fixed charges should logically be expanded to include *all* fixed obligations of the reporting entity. A company must, for example, make regular payments on long-term leases, property taxes, and other relatively fixed commitments in addition to interest on long-term debt before dividends can be declared.[6]

[6] In computing the ratio of earnings to fixed charges, some companies have in the past deducted earnings on investments (interest and dividends earned) and gains on retirement of debt from the fixed charges. In *Accounting Series Release No. 119* (June 15, 1971), the Securities and Exchange Commission stated:

> The propriety of reducing fixed charges by amounts representing interest or investment income or gains on retirement of debt has been considered in the light of the purposes for which ratios of earnings to fixed charges are used and the Commission has determined that the reduction of fixed charges by the amount of either actual or imputed interest or investment income or debt retirement gains for the purpose of computing fixed charge ratios results in incorrect ratios and is therefore inappropriate. Accordingly, such reductions will no longer be deemed acceptable in registration statements or reports filed with the Commission.

The ability of a business unit to generate sufficient revenue over variable expenses to cover fixed charges is one of the most important considerations to the analyst.

ANALYSIS OF FINANCIAL STRENGTH

A strong earnings record usually accompanies a strong financial condition. Furthermore, an unsatisfactory financial position looks much less unfavorable in the face of a good earnings record; a company with proved earning power can usually work out its financial problems. Good earnings, however, is not the whole story. A company's ability to meet its obligations, to weather adversity, to shift resources to meet changing conditions—in short, its financial strength, is an important factor to continuing survival and growth.

In seeking evidence of financial soundness, the analyst looks first at the relation between resources and obligations. He asks himself: Will the company be able to meet its debts as they fall due? Has it the resources to meet current commitments and future demands for funds necessary to carry on the business successfully?

Ability to meet short-term obligations

A company's short-term financial strength is dependent on two primary factors: its working capital position and the speed with which it generates liquid assets.

The financial information for Company H shown on page 931 will be used as a basis for discussion of these factors.

Working Capital Position The amount by which current assets exceed current liabilities is known as the *working capital* of a business. Changes in the amount of working capital from period to period are significant because working capital represents the margin of short-term debt-paying ability over short-term debt.

In addition to the dollar amount of working capital, two analytical indices of current position are often computed. The *current ratio* (current assets divided by current liabilities) helps put the amount of working capital in perspective by showing the relationship between current resources and short-term debt. The *quick ratio* (sometimes called the *acid-test ratio*) focuses on immediate liquidity. Inventories and short-term prepayments, the least liquid assets in the current asset category, are excluded from consideration in computing the quick ratio. Quick assets are defined as cash, marketable securities, and receivables, and the quick ratio is computed by dividing quick assets by current liabilities.

In terms of these three analytical measures, the current position of Company H is summarized at the bottom of page 931.

COMPANY H
Selected Financial Data
(in thousands of dollars)

	Year 3	Year 2	Year 1
Current assets:			
Cash	$ 50	$ 80	$ 60
Marketable securities	-0-	50	150
Receivables (net)	500	400	300
Inventory (fifo, cost).	1,100	700	500
Short-term prepayments	70	60	50
Total current assets	$1,720	$1,290	$1,060
Current liabilities:			
Notes payable	$ 120	$ 100	$ -0-
Accounts payable	680	330	170
Accrued liabilities	220	170	140
Current portion of long-term debt	180	200	200
Total current liabilities	$1,200	$ 800	$ 510
Net sales.	$3,500	$3,000	$2,600
Cost of goods sold.	(2,600)	(2,000)	(1,900)
Operating expenses	(600)	(500)	(400)
Interest on long-term debt	(48)	(49)	(50)
Income before income tax expense	$ 252	$ 451	$ 250
Income tax expense	122	231	125
Net income	$ 130	$ 220	$ 125

COMPANY H
Analysis of Current Position
(in thousands of dollars)

	Year 3	Year 2	Year 1
(a) Current assets	$1,720	$1,290	$1,060
(b) Current liabilities.	1,200	800	510
Working capital (a − b)	$ 520	$ 490	$ 550
Current ratio (a ÷ b)	1.4	1.6	2.1
(c) Total quick assets (cash, marketable			
securities, and receivables)	$ 550	$ 530	$ 510
Quick ratio (c ÷ b)	.5	.7	1.0

Each of these three analytical measures contributes something to the whole picture. The company has maintained its working capital at about $500,000 during the three-year period. However, its relative short-term liquidity has worsened, as indicated by the steady decline in the current ratio from 2.1 to 1.4 and in the quick ratio from 1.0 to .5 during the three-year period. This is a picture of a company that may be heading into financial difficulty, unless these trends can be reversed. The growth of accounts payable from $170,000 to $680,000 during the last two years suggests that payments to creditors may be falling behind schedule. The analysis has thus brought to light a potential trouble spot in the firm's financial position. On the other hand, if the large increase in accounts payable is the result of large current expenditures for research and product development, or for inventories in anticipation of a sharp increase in sales, then the trend can be evaluated in a different light.

Need for Working Capital A business generates working capital through a series of events called the *operating cycle.* The operating cycle refers to the process of investing in inventories, converting these through sale into receivables, and transforming receivables by collection into cash, which is in turn used to pay current debts incurred for operating costs and to replace inventories. The average length of time necessary to complete this cycle is an important factor in determining a firm's working capital needs. A company with a very short operating cycle can manage comfortably on a relatively small amount of working capital and with relatively low quick and current ratios. A long operating cycle requires a larger margin of current assets and higher quick and current ratios unless the credit terms of suppliers can be extended accordingly. The average length of the operating cycle can be roughly estimated by adding the number of days' sales in average inventory to the average age of receivables.

Inventory turnover The total cost of all goods that have been moved out of inventories during the year is represented by the cost of goods sold figure on the income statement. Therefore the ratio of cost of goods sold to the average inventory during any period is a measure of the number of times that inventories turn over on the average and must be replaced. The higher this turnover ratio, the shorter the average time between investment in inventories and the sale transaction.

Average inventory should be determined by averaging monthly or quarterly inventory figures, as illustrated in Chapter 8. This information is not usually available to external analysts, however, and therefore only an average of the inventory at the beginning and end of the year is ordinarily feasible. Because many companies adopt an accounting year that ends when inventories are at a minimum, inventory turnover computed in this manner may appear larger than it really is.

Dividing the annual cost of goods sold by average inventory produces a "times per year" turnover figure. Turnover may be expressed in days by dividing 365 by the number of turnovers per year. An additional useful measure is the **number of days' sales in ending inventory,** computed by multiplying 365 days by the fraction of which the ending inventory is the numerator and cost of goods sold is the denominator. The three-year inventory analyses for Company H are as follows (dollar figures are in thousands):

	Year 3	Year 2	Year 1
(a) Cost of goods sold	$2,600	$2,000	$1,900
Inventory at beginning of year	$ 700	$ 500	$ 540*
Inventory at end of year	1,100	700	500
(b) Average inventory	$ 900	$ 600	$ 520
(c) Turnover per year (a ÷ b) . . .	2.9 times	3.3 times	3.7 times
Number of days' sales in			
average inventory (365 ÷ c) .	126 days	111 days	99 days
Number of days' sales in			
ending inventory	154 days	128 days	96 days

*Assumed

This computation shows that inventory turnover has slowed during the three-year period from a little over three months to about four months, and that there is enough inventory on hand at the end of Year 3 to meet sales requirements at current levels for approximately five months (154 days).

For a manufacturing company, the overall inventory turnover can be estimated by dividing the cost of goods sold by the sum of the three inventories: raw material, goods in process, and finished goods. A more precise computation would involve three separate turnover figures: (1) cost of goods sold divided by average finished goods inventory; (2) cost of goods manufactured divided by average goods in process inventory; and (3) raw materials used divided by average raw materials inventory.

It should be pointed out that the foregoing computations would be misleading if the replacement value of inventories is substantially higher than cost. In such cases, alternative measurements should be used to analyze the inventory position of the firm.

Receivables turnover The turnover of accounts receivable may be computed in a manner comparable to that just described for inventories. Unless a firm has a significant amount of cash sales, the total sales for any period represents the flow of claims into the receivable category. When the sales total is divided by the average balance of receivables during the period, the result is a rough indication of the average length of time necessary to convert receivables into cash. Ideally, only credit sales should be included in the sales figure, and an average monthly balance of *gross* receivables should be used. These refinements may not be possible in external analysis, however, and a less exact computation may serve the purpose of indicating favorable or unfavorable trends. The reasonableness of the ending balance in receivables may be evaluated by computing the **number of days' sales in receivables** at the end of the year. The receivables for Company H may be analyzed as follows (dollar figures are in thousands):

	Year 3	Year 2	Year 1
(a) Net sales	$3,500	$3,000	$2,600
Receivables at beginning of year	$ 400	$ 300	$ 280*
Receivables at end of year . . .	500	400	300
(b) Average receivables.	$ 450	$ 350	$ 290
(c) Receivables turnover (a ÷ b) . .	7.8 times	8.6 times	9.0 times
Number of days' sales in average receivables (365 ÷ c)	47 days	42 days	41 days
Number of days' sales in ending receivables	52 days	49 days	42 days

* Assumed

It is evident that, barring a change in credit terms, collections have slowed down over the three-year period. The trend is obviously unfavorable; interpretation of the absolute figures depends on the credit terms and policies of the company.

Length of operating cycle By putting together the average days' sales in inventories and in receivables, we can obtain a rough estimate of the average length of the operating cycle for Company H as follows:

	Year 3	Year 2	Year 1
Average days to dispose of inventory . . . . *. .	126	111	99
Average days to collect receivables	47	42	41
Average days in operating cycle	173	153	140

The operating cycle of this company has increased by more than a full month (33 days) from Year 1 to Year 3. If this has happened inadvertently, it may explain the unfavorable trend in the current and quick ratios. If the change is the result of deliberate company policy, it indicates the need for a greater amount of working capital, particularly cash, to finance current operations.

Number of days' operations to cover working capital deficit When current liabilities exceed current assets, management may wish to estimate the length of time it would take to eliminate the working capital deficit from regular operations. For example, assume that the working capital for the Ross Company on March 31 shows a $20,000 deficit as shown below:

Current assets	$ 60,000
Less: Current liabilities	(80,000)
Working capital deficit	$(20,000)

Assume further that the company's operations are relatively stable over a fiscal year and normally generate working capital as follows:

Net income for year	$ 75,000
Add: Depreciation and other expenses recognized during the year which do not require the use of working capital	45,000
Working capital normally provided by operations over 12-month period	$120,000

From the foregoing information management can determine that the working capital deficit will be covered in approximately two months, determined as follows:

$$\frac{\$20,000 \text{ (working capital deficit)}}{\$120,000 \text{ (annual working capital provided by operations)}} \times 365 \text{ days}$$

$$= 61 \text{ days}$$

Interpreting the analysis of current position

The following factors should be taken into account in interpreting the short-term position of a company as shown by the analytical procedures just described:

1 Creditors tend to adopt the view that the higher the current and quick ratios and the shorter the operating cycle, the better. From the viewpoint of company performance, there are upper limits. It is possible for a company to accumulate working capital in excess of the amount that can be profitably employed. Thus, excessive current and quick ratios are unfavorable indicators. Similarly, an unusually high rate of inventory turnover may indicate that a company is losing business by failing to maintain a stock adequate to serve customers' needs. A rapid turnover of receivables may indicate overly severe credit policies that hold revenue below levels that could profitably be obtained by granting more favorable credit terms.

2 Because creditors and other outsiders place considerable emphasis on current position as evidence of short-run solvency, there is a temptation for managers to take steps just before statements are prepared to make current position appear better than it is. This process is called **window dressing.** By postponing purchases, allowing inventories to fall below normal levels, using all available cash to pay current creditors, and pressing collections on accounts receivable, the current and quick ratios and inventory and receivable turnover ratios may be artificially improved. Decreases in receivable and inventory balances will raise turnover ratios. Any equal decrease in both current assets and current liabilities will improve a current ratio that is already greater than 1 to 1.

3 Even when no deliberate attempt has been made to present an artificially good picture, the current position shown on year-end statements is probably more favorable than at any other time of the year. This is particularly true when a firm has adopted a natural business year that ends during an ebb in the seasonal swing of business activity. At times of peak activity receivables, inventories, and current liabilities tend to be at higher levels. There are, of course, many reasons why a **natural business year** is desirable, and accountants generally encourage firms to adopt such an accounting period. An analysis of current position based solely on year-end data will tend to overstate a firm's average current position.

Analysis of capital structure

The way in which a firm has met its long-run financing needs is an important factor in assessing its financial strength. The important relationships in this area may be expressed, for analytical purposes, in several ways. One is to reduce the major elements of the equity side of the balance sheet to component percentages of total assets. Alternatively, we may concentrate on only the long-term sources of financing, known as the **capital structure** of a firm. The first approach is more widely used and is illustrated below:

Component percentages		Debt and equity ratios	
Total assets	100%	Debt ratio	28%
Sources of financing:		Equity ratio	72%
Current liabilities	10%	Debt to equity ratio (.28 ÷ .72) .	39%
Long-term debt	18%		
Total debt	28%		
Preferred stock 9%			
Common stockholders'			
equity 63%	72%		
Total liabilities & stockholders' equity	100%		

Debt and Equity Ratios Analysts often condense the essence of the capital structure of a company into any one of three ratios. The *debt ratio* is the ratio of total debt to total assets; the *equity ratio* is the ratio of stockholders' equity to total assets; the *debt to equity ratio* is the ratio of total liabilities to stockholders' equity. Any one of these three ratios tells the essential story about the debt-equity relationship for any firm; the choice among them is a matter of personal preference.

Financial analysts compute other ratios to aid them in evaluating capital structure. For example, the ratio of tangible plant and equipment to stockholders' equity is sometimes used as a test of the adequacy of equity capital. If the investment in plant and equipment is high relative to stockholders' equity, this indicates that a firm has borrowed heavily to invest in nonliquid assets, which may lead to difficulties should earnings not prove satisfactory.

Book value per share of stock, which was discussed in detail in Chapter 17, is a significant indicator of stockholders' investment in company assets. It should be recognized, however, that book value may have very little relationship either to the *intrinsic value* or to the current market value of stock.

Evaluating capital structure

Whatever ratios are used to establish capital structure relationships, the important question is the significance of the findings. What factors should be considered in evaluating the capital structure of a firm?

Creditors' View Creditors are primarily concerned with the safety of their capital. They view a relatively low debt ratio as a favorable factor because it indicates a substantial cushion of protection against a shrinkage in asset values. Since ultimate repayment of debt will come from either new borrowing or internal cash flow, all creditors are interested in long-run financial strength and a healthy earnings picture. The debt ratio and the times interest earned ratio are the prime indices of financial strength from the creditors' viewpoint.

As was pointed out in Chapter 19, the use of long-term leases as a method of financing has increased substantially in recent years. Frequently such leases are a substitute for other forms of long-term borrowing, and their existence should be carefully considered in evaluating capital structure. Most firms having long-term operating leases do not reflect the related property rights and obligations on their balance sheets; information concerning operating lease commitments is simply set forth in footnotes to financial statements. The analyst should watch for evidence of these leases and recognize that the debt position of companies having substantial lease commitments is understated.

Stockholders' View Present or prospective stockholders are concerned with the firm's ability to meet its long-term obligations, because failure to pay interest charges or meet maturities of debt is a serious matter affecting adversely both the credit standing of the company and the stockholders' interest. A very low debt ratio, or the absence of long-term debt, however, is not necessarily to the stockholders' advantage. To the extent that a company can earn a return in excess of the interest rate paid on long-term obligations, the stockholder gains from the leverage factor inherent in a fixed commitment. However, this gain may be offset by the increased risk of bankruptcy and the subjective costs of the various protective covenants put into the debt contract by the lender, which may limit management's freedom of action.

It has been argued that the existence of long-term debt or other senior securities increases the risk borne by owners of the common stock and causes the stock to sell at a lower price-earnings ratio. In a well-managed and profitable firm, it is doubtful whether a reasonable amount of debt increases the common shareholders' risk sufficiently to be reflected in the price-earnings ratio. If the amount of long-term debt is excessive and earnings are not growing at a fast pace, it is likely that the advantage of increased trading on the equity will be offset by the dampening effect of the larger debt on the price of common stock.

Capacity for additional investment and growth in earnings

A business firm is seldom able to maintain a stable position over a long period of time; it either changes and grows, or stagnates and dies. A healthy firm must be able to finance the development of new products and customers as the old ones lose their profit potential, and to move in new directions as demand and technology change. An important element of financial strength is the ability to generate additional funds when they are needed.

In part this means the ability to borrow or to issue additional stock. The primary source of industrial growth in recent years, however, has been through the retention of earnings. Furthermore, because of the existence of expenses that are not a current drain on working capital, most businesses generate substantially more working capital each period than the amount of net income (see Chapter 23). The amount of working capital provided by operations, less dividend and sinking fund requirements, offers a rough indicator of the internally generated funds available to expand the level of operations (build plant capacity, develop new products or markets, etc.) or to retire debt.

Standards for comparison in analysis

When the analyst has computed the significant dollar and percentage changes and ratios and has otherwise reduced the mass of financial data to digestible form, he needs some criteria as a guide in evaluating his findings and in making decisions. Three possibilities are discussed below.

Past Record of the Company A comparison of analytical data over time (sometimes called *horizontal analysis* in contrast to *vertical analysis* which deals with single-year financial statements) may reveal trends in performance and position that will aid in determining progress or lack of progress and may help in assessing future prospects. Many companies present trends in sales, earnings, and other data in graphic form. As a basis for forecasting, the projecting of past trends into the future has serious limitations, since changes may reverse direction at any time. However, knowing that the trend is favorable or unfavorable leads to further inquiry as to the underlying reasons.

Another limitation of horizontal analysis is that the past does not afford a basis for comparison with similarly situated companies. For example, if the sales of a company have increased 10% but industry sales have increased 50%, the trend looks favorable but the company's sales performance in its industry is relatively poor.

Comparison with Competitors or Industry as a Whole Perhaps the best way to put a company's performance in perspective is to compare its position and operating results with those of similar firms. For example, a study by Dun & Bradstreet, Inc., of the financial statements of 52 drug manufacturers for a recent year showed the following:

	Current ratio	Net profits on net sales	Return on owners' investment	Total debt to owners' equity	Net sales to inventory (times)
Upper quartile	3.5	11.3%	20.4%	35.8%	9.1
Median	2.6	6.8	15.4	43.5	6.3
Lower quartile	1.8	2.9	5.5	63.6	4.6

On the basis of this kind of information, an analyst examining the financial statements of a drug manufacturing firm could get some idea of the position of the firm in relation to others in the industry. Note that Dun & Bradstreet, Inc., computes the inventory activity by dividing net sales by the inventory figure. Although this is often done by financial analysts as a matter of convenience, this procedure does not give a turnover figure but simply relates the average level of inventory (at cost) to the sales volume for the year (at sales price), a measurement which defies logical interpretation.

One of the difficulties in interfirm comparisons is that some companies that appear to be in the same industry are not in fact comparable. Industries are often difficult to define. Many companies have diversified their activities by moving into new fields or acquiring other companies whose business is not closely related, with the result that firms falling roughly within the same industry are no longer comparable in many respects. When such *diversified companies* report product line sales and net income figures, it is much easier to analyze their results in the major areas in which they operate.[7]

Even when firms are reasonably comparable in terms of industry classification, they may choose different methods of operation that destroy comparability. One firm may own its plants, another may lease; one firm may be vertically integrated, another may concentrate heavily on production or marketing. And finally, differences in accounting policies may affect the comparability of firms for analytical purposes.

Comparison and Independent Statistical Measures   It is often useful to relate certain financial indices for a firm to statistical measures. For example, comparing the trend of sales or net income with an *index of industrial production* may show whether a firm is growing more slowly or faster than the economy. Similarly, indices may be developed for sales and net income, for example, comparing the performance of a single company to the industry performance index during the same period. Price indices may be used to deflate sales figures to determine whether the growth in sales is a growth in physical volume or the result of price increases. It may also be possible to relate financial data to physical measures of production or output. For example, in analyzing railroads, such statistics as the average freight haul in miles per ton, or the average revenue per ton-mile, give a useful basis for comparing the operating performance of different railroads.

Inflation and analysis of financial statements

Financial statements prepared in terms of historical costs do not fully reflect the economic resources or the *real* income (in terms of purchasing power) of a business enterprise. The analyst should therefore attempt to evaluate the impact of inflation on the financial position and results of operations of the business he is evaluating. He should raise questions such as: How much of the income can be attributed to price increases? Are expenses (such as depreciation) understated in terms of current price levels? Is the company gaining or losing from inflation because of the composition of its assets and the amount of its liabilities? Financial statements adjusted for price-level changes are illustrated in Chapter 25.

---

[7]The Securities and Exchange Commission now requires diversified companies to report product-line information. In 1967, the Accounting Principles Board issued "Disclosure of Supplemental Financial Information by Diversified Companies" in which it recommended that the following types of data be disclosed: (*a*) Revenues by industry activity, or type of customer; (*b*) revenues and profits by separable industry segments; (*c*) separate financial statements of segments of the business which operate autonomously and employ distinctly different types of capital structure; (*d*) earnings from major segments or product lines; and (*e*) information that the operations of a segment of the enterprise are resulting in a loss, with or without disclosure of the amount of such loss.

Summary of ratios and other analytical measurements

The more widely used ratios and other measurements discussed in this chapter and their significance are summarized below:

Ratio or other measurement	Method of computation	Significance
1 Return on total assets	$$\frac{\text{Net income} + \text{interest expense}}{\text{Average investment in assets}}$$	Measures the productivity of assets.
2 Return on common stockholders' equity	$$\frac{\text{Net income} - \text{preferred dividends}}{\text{Average common stockholders' equity}}$$	Indicates the earning power on common stockholders' equity.
3 Earnings per share of common stock	$$\frac{\text{Net income} - \text{preferred dividends}}{\text{Shares of common outstanding}}$$	Gives the amount of earnings applicable to a share of common stock.
4 Price-earnings ratio on common stock	$$\frac{\text{Market price per share}}{\text{Earnings per share}}$$	Indicates whether price of stock is in line with earnings.
5 Dividend yield	$$\frac{\text{Dividend per share}}{\text{Market price per share}}$$	Shows the rate earned by stockholders based on current price of stock.
6 Book value per share of common stock	$$\frac{\text{Common stockholders' equity}}{\text{Shares of common outstanding}}$$	Measures net assets as reported on books applicable to each share of common stock.
7 Number of times interest earned (before income taxes)	$$\frac{\text{Operating income}}{\text{Annual interest expense}}$$	Measures the coverage of interest charges (particularly on long-term debt) before income taxes.
8 Times preferred dividends earned	$$\frac{\text{Net income}}{\text{Annual preferred dividends}}$$	Shows the adequacy of current earnings to pay preferred dividends.
9 Current ratio	$$\frac{\text{Current assets}}{\text{Current liabilities}}$$	Measures short-run debt-paying ability.

Ratio or other measurement	Method of computation	Significance
10 Quick (acid-test) ratio	$\dfrac{\text{Quick assets}}{\text{Current liabilities}}$	Measures the short-term liquidity.
11 Inventory turnover	$\dfrac{\text{Cost of goods sold}}{\text{Average inventory}}$	Indicates management's ability to control the investment in inventory.
12 Receivables turn-over	$\dfrac{\text{Net sales on credit}}{\text{Average receivables}}$	Indicates reasonableness of accounts receivable balance and effectiveness of collections.
13 Debt ratio	$\dfrac{\text{Total liabilities}}{\text{Total assets}}$	Shows the percentage of assets financed through borrowing and the extent of trading on the equity.
14 Equity ratio	$\dfrac{\text{Total stockholders' equity}}{\text{Total assets}}$	Shows the protection to creditors and the extent of trading on the equity.
15 Debt to equity ratio	$\dfrac{\text{Total debt}}{\text{Total stockholders' equity}}$	Indicates relationship between borrowed capital and invested capital.

The relevance of any of the foregoing measurements depends on the direction of its trend and on its relationship to some predetermined standard. The information available in financial statements can be of great value in appraising the financial position, in forecasting the earning power, and in making other predictive judgments about a business entity. Relationships among reported data can be extremely informative. However, we must remember that financial statements have limitations and that intangible and qualitative factors may be far more important. For example, factors such as the following cannot be ignored by the analyst in forecasting the likely earnings performance of a company: (1) Source of markets for the company's products or services; (2) growth potential for the company's products or services; (3) company's market share in its industry; (4) patent protection, if any, for major products; (5) sensitivity to economic fluctuations; and (6) effect of technological and environmental changes on the company's business.

The analyst should keep in mind that while the balance sheet is a statement of assets and claims against these assets, many assets are stated at historical cost and not all valuable assets are included in the balance sheet (for example, good management, good credit standing, potential new products, internally developed goodwill, appreciation in the value of natural resources). Furthermore, the *quality of the reported assets* must be carefully evaluated. The income statement, on the other hand, is a product of matching historical costs with realized revenue and covers ‚only a brief period of a company's life. In short, the income statement does not necessarily measure the *improvement in the company's economic wealth.* The dangers of attaching too much significance either to the balance sheet or to the income statement should be clearly recognized by the analyst.

REVIEW QUESTIONS

1 Describe four sources from which an outsider might obtain financial information about a business in which he is interested.

2 Explain what is meant by the following terms:
a Trend percentage *d* Capital structure
b Common size statements *e* Growth companies
c Trading on the equity *f* Price-earnings ratio

3 a Discuss some inherent limitations of single-year financial statements for purposes of analysis and interpretation.
b To what extent are these limitations overcome by the use of comparative statements?
c In what possible ways can a 10-year summary of financial data be misleading?

4 Describe the effect of each of the transactions listed below on the indicated ratios. Will the ratio increase, decrease, or remain unchanged?

Transactions	Ratio
a Purchase of merchandise for cash	*a* Current ratio of 2 to 1
b Payment of accounts payable	*b* Quick ratio of .6 to 1
c Accounts receivable written off against Allowance for Uncollectible Accounts	*c* Average age of accounts receivable of 60 days
d Declaration of cash dividend on preferred stock	*d* Equity ratio of .60
e Distribution of a 10% stock dividend	*e* Loss per share of common stock, $1.20
f Conversion of long-term debt into common stock	*f* Return on total long-term capital
g Change from fifo to lifo during period of rising prices	*g* Inventory turnover

5 The following ratios have been suggested at one time or another by financial analysts. Briefly explain what the ratio indicates about a business and why you think it has or lacks significance.
a Ratio of plant to long-term debt
b Ratio of sales to working capital (working capital turnover)

c Ratio of current liabilities to inventory

d Ratio of total operating expenses to current liabilities

e Ratio of plant and equipment to stockholders' equity

f Ratio of long-term debt to working capital

g Ratio of net sales to stockholders' equity

h Ratio of net income to current assets

6 In analyzing the position and performance of a firm, it is necessary to have some standards or criteria for comparison. Suggest several standards which may be usefully employed.

7 An estimate of inventory turnover is sometimes made by dividing net sales by average inventory. What is wrong with this method of computing turnover?

8 Two companies have the same amount of working capital. The current debt-paying ability of one firm is much weaker than the other. Explain how this could occur.

9 Explain how you would determine the ability of a given company to meet payments on long-term debt or to finance replacements of plant and equipment, assuming that you had available financial statements for the last five years.

10 If you were asked to choose three analytical computations (ratios, percentages, etc.) that would be of greatest use in appraising the financial statements of a company from the viewpoint of the following parties, which computations would you make, and why do you feel these are of prime importance?

a Short-term creditor

b Long-term creditor

c Prospective purchaser of preferred stock

d Prospective purchaser of common stock

11 In response to a request that its profit margins on different products be disclosed, the Duncan Electric Company claims, "Public disclosure would cause us to suffer at the hands of our principal competitors, particularly in regard to the watt-hour meter which accounts for 90% of our sales." In what ways could the disclosure of product line information possibly be detrimental to Duncan Electric Company?

EXERCISES

Ex. 24-1 Ruiz Company has the following capital structure (in millions): 5% bonds, $12.5; 6% preferred stock, $30.0; common stock (paid-in capital and retained earnings), $50.0. The average rate of return on long-term capital (after taxes but before interest expense) is 8%. Compute the amount of earnings available for common stockholders.

Ex. 24-2 Sully Corporation reported earnings per share last year at $4.50 on 100,000 shares of stock outstanding. On April 1 of the current year, the company declared a 50% stock dividend and on October 1 issued 60,000 shares of stock for cash. Net income for the current year was $353,000. What is the amount of increase or decrease in earnings per share over last year?

Ex. 24-3 A partial list of trend and common size percentages for the Space Travel Company for Years 1 and 2 is shown below:

	Year 2	Year 1
Trend percentages:		
Sales (net)	120%	100%
Cost of goods sold	?	100
Gross profit on sales	?	100
Operating expenses and income tax expense	?	100
Net income	?	100
Common size percentages:		
Sales (net)	100%	100%
Cost of goods sold	?	?
Gross profit on sales	45%	? %
Operating expenses and income tax expense	27.5	30
Net income	?%	10%

a Compute the missing trend and common size percentages.
b If the net income in Year 1 amounted to $10,000, compute the net income for Year 2.

Ex. 24-4 Information for the Ravioli Company is presented below:

	Year 2	Year 1
Cash	$ 20,000	$ 30,000
Accounts receivable (net)	60,000	40,000
Inventories	45,000	35,000
Plant and equipment (net)	235,000	185,000
Total	$360,000	$290,000
Accounts payable	$ 50,000	$ 40,000
6% bonds payable	100,000	100,000
Capital stock, $5 par value	130,000	100,000
Retained earnings	80,000	50,000
Total	$360,000	$290,000
Sales (all on account)	$180,000	$120,000
Cost of goods sold	100,000	70,000
Gross profit on sales	$ 80,000	$ 50,000
Operating expenses and income tax expense	50,000	30,000
Net income	$ 30,000	$ 20,000

Compute each of the following for Year 2:
a Quick (acid-test) ratio.
b Number of days' sales in accounts receivable at year-end. Assume a 365-day year.
c Inventory turnover.

d Book value per share of capital stock at year-end.
e Number of days' sales in inventories at year-end. Assume a 365-day year.

Ex. 24-5 The following information (in thousands of dollars) for three companies is presented to you at the end of Year 10:

	M Company	N Company	O Company
Total assets	$140,000	$140,000	$140,000
Current liabilities	$ 20,000	$ 50,000	$ 20,000
8% bonds payable, due in Year 15	40,000		
6% bonds payable, due in Year 20		10,000	
8% bonds payable, due in Year 22			80,000
Stockholders' equity	80,000	80,000	40,000
Total liabilities & stockholders' equity .	$140,000	$140,000	$140,000
Net income	$ 14,000	$ 12,600	$ 9,800

Compute the following for each company:
a Number of times interest was earned (before income taxes). Assume income tax rate is 50%.
b Rate earned on ending stockholders' equity.
c Rate earned on total assets at end of year (before interest expense and income taxes of 50%).

Ex. 24-6 Following are financial statements of Brumel Company, a retail firm. Dollar amounts are given in thousands of dollars:

Comparative Balance Sheets
December 31

	Year 2	Year 1
Cash	$ 7,000	$ 4,000
Marketable securities	2,000	4,000
Accounts receivable (net)	13,000	9,000
Inventory	9,000	7,000
Land		
Buildings and equipment (net)	69,000	66,000
Total assets	$100,000	$90,000
Current liabilities	$ 14,000	$16,000
Bonds payable, due in Year 15	24,000	20,000
Common stock—$10 par value	30,000	30,000
Retained earnings	32,000	24,000
Total liabilities & stockholders' equity	$100,000	$90,000

Sales for Year 2 were $100 million and cost of goods sold amounted to $58 million. Other items from the income statement for Year 2 are: Interest expense, $2 million; income taxes, $10 million; and net income, $12 million.

Show how you would compute the following ratios (or measurements) for Year 2 by determining the appropriate dollar amounts (or other figures) to be used in computing each item. (You need not perform the division.)

Example: Debt ratio . . . . $38,000 ÷ $100,000

a Current ratio
b Quick (acid-test) ratio
c Times interest earned (before income taxes)
d Rate of gross profit on sales
e Earnings per share

SHORT CASES FOR ANALYSIS AND DECISION

Case 24-1 Sudan Corporation needs additional capital for plant expansion. The board of directors is considering obtaining the funds by issuing additional short-term notes, long-term bonds, preferred stock, or common stock.

Instructions
a What primary factors should the board of directors consider in selecting the best method of financing plant expansion?
b One member of the board of directors suggests that the corporation should maximize trading on the equity, that is, using stockholders' equity as a basis for borrowing additional funds at a lower rate of interest than the expected earnings from the use of the borrowed funds.
  (1) Explain how trading on the equity affects earnings per share of common stock.
  (2) Explain how a change in income tax rates affects trading on the equity.
  (3) Under what circumstances should a corporation seek to trade on the equity to a substantial degree?
c Two specific proposals under consideration by the board of directors are the issue of 7% subordinated income bonds or 7% cumulative, nonparticipating, nonvoting preferred stock, callable at par. In discussing the impact of the two alternatives on the debt to equity ratio, one member of the board of directors stated that he felt the resulting debt to equity ratio would be the same under either alternative because the income bonds and preferred stock should be reported in the same balance sheet classification. What are the arguments (1) for and (2) against using the same balance sheet classification in reporting the income bonds and preferred stock?

Case 24-2 The information below is extracted from reports to stockholders of three major corporations:
1 Revenues have increased steadily for the past few years and in 19____ rose 10% over those for the previous year to a record $1.6 billion. Earnings from operations rose 19% to $134.2 million, or $3.95 per common share after preferred dividends. Union's profits have grown steadily for the last five years. They have also exceeded industry growth. Our 19% increase compares with 12% for the oil industry and 9% for all industry. (Union Petrol Company)
2 Income reinvested in the business, which also is to the benefit of stockholders, was $130.1 million, or $2.40 per common share. (Steel Corporation)
3 The information at the top of page 948 relates to the Gulf Company.

Instructions
a Do you think that the information regarding the company's growth compared to industry growth as presented by Union Petrol Company is useful to stock-

	Year 3	Year 2	Year 1
Gross revenue (millions)	$133	$ 99	$70
Net income (millions)	$ 28	$ 18	$12
Working capital (millions).	$ 34	$ 52	$87
Current ratio.	2 to 1	5 to 1	10 to 1
Property, plant, and equipment, net (millions)	$275	$145	$92

holders? Are there any possibilities that such information can be misleading?
b Comment on the information taken from the annual report of Steel Corporation
in view of the following additional facts for the latest year:
(1) Earnings amounted to $4.60 per share compared to an average of $6.59
per share 8 to 10 years ago.
(2) The rate earned on stockholders' equity amounted to less than 8%.
(3) The balance sheet included over $1.28 billion of marketable securities and
over $268 million in cash.
c As a stockholder, would you be concerned over the decrease in the current
ratio for the Gulf Company? Explain carefully.

Case 24-3 Natex Products, Inc., one of your audit clients, requested that you review the
proposed presentation of selected financial data to be included in its 1975 annual
report in graphic form. The company has three divisions: a Natural Gas Division
formed in 1957, a Chemical Division formed in 1964, and a Textile Division formed
in 1972. Management compiled the following data and graphs from the company's financial statements:

	1975	1974	1973
Sales (in thousands):			
Natural gas	$1,100	$1,100	$1,000
Chemicals	1,000	900	800
Textiles	900	400	200
Total sales	$3,000	$2,400	$2,000
Sources of working capital (in thousands):			
Net income (after extraordinary items)	$ 400	$ 290	$ 200
Add: Depreciation, depletion, and amortization	80	55	40
Total	$ 480	$ 345	$ 240
Issuance of bonds payable	100	50	60
Total sources of working capital	$ 580	$ 395	$ 300
Uses of working capital (in thousands):			
Dividends	$ 330	$ 160	$ 100
Acquisition of plant and equipment	180	170	135
Increase in working capital	60	35	45
Other	10	30	20
Total uses of working capital	$ 580	$ 395	$ 300

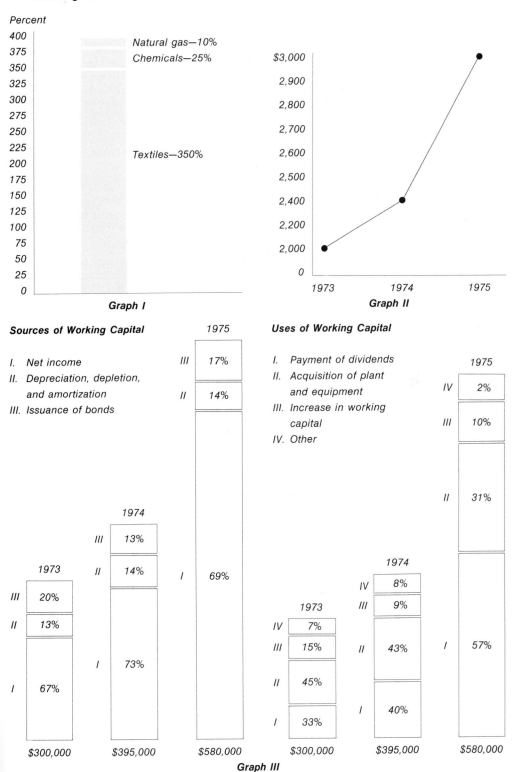

Percentage Growth in Sales 1973–1975

Growth in Sales 1973–1975 (thousands)

Percent

Natural gas—10%
Chemicals—25%

Textiles—350%

Graph I

Graph II

Sources of Working Capital

I.   Net income
II. Depreciation, depletion,
     and amortization
III. Issuance of bonds

1975
III | 17%
II | 14%

1974
III | 13%
II | 14%
I | 69%

1973
III | 20%
II | 13%
I | 73%
I | 67%

$300,000 $395,000 $580,000

Uses of Working Capital

I.   Payment of dividends
II. Acquisition of plant
     and equipment
III. Increase in working
     capital
IV. Other

1975
IV | 2%
III | 10%
II | 31%

1974
IV | 8%
III | 9%
II | 43%
I | 57%

1973
IV | 7%
III | 15%
II | 45%
I | 40%
I | 33%

$300,000 $395,000 $580,000

Graph III

949

Instructions

a Why is it desirable to present comparative financial statements and other historical, statistical-type summaries of financial data, including graphs and charts, for a number of periods in annual and other financial reports?

b Evaluate each of the three graphs prepared by Natex Products, Inc., for possible inclusion in its 1975 annual report. Recommend changes, if any, which should be made in the graphs. Consider each graph separately. (Do not draw new graphs.)

Case 24-4 The executive vice president of Gromoor Corporation is having lunch with three students from three different universities who are being considered for a position as his assistant. The vice president points out that quite a few of his clients are active in acquiring other companies and that "the young man who will be hired should be able to make effective overall analyses of the financial strength and operating results of companies that are for sale." In order to get a better line on the business and financial acumen of the three students, he poses the following question to them:

> Suppose that I called one of you at 10 P.M. one evening and asked you to fly to San Francisco the next morning in order to look over the operation and financial position of Digico Corporation, which is for sale at a price of $5 million. I would like to have a preliminary report by phone before 5 P.M. on that same day and a final report within a week. Arrangements have been made for you to visit the corporate offices of Digico Corporation. What approach would you take in preparing these reports?

> The three students then proceeded to summarize their approach to this hypothetical assignment.

Instructions Assuming that you are one of the three students being considered for the position as assistant to the vice president, write a brief report summarizing the broad areas you would evaluate and the approach you would take in preparing the preliminary and the final reports.

PROBLEMS

Group A

24A-1 Goldman Corporation's management is concerned over the corporation's current financial position and return on investment. They request your assistance in analyzing their financial statements and furnish the following statements:

GOLDMAN CORPORATION
Statement of Working Capital Deficit
December 31, 1975

Current liabilities		$223,050
Less current assets:		
Cash	$ 5,973	
Accounts receivable, net	70,952	
Inventory	113,125	190,050
Working capital deficit		$ 33,000

GOLDMAN CORPORATION
Income Statement
For the Year Ended December 31, 1975

Sales	$760,200
Cost of goods sold	452,500
Gross profit on sales	$307,700
Selling and general expenses, including $22,980 depreciation expense	155,660
Income before income tax expense	$152,040
Income tax expense	76,020
Net income	$ 76,020

Assets other than current assets consisted of land, building, and equipment with a book value of $352,950 on December 31, 1975.

Instructions Assuming that Goldman Corporation operates 300 days per year, compute the following (show your computations):
a Number of days' sales uncollected at December 31, 1975.
b Inventory turnover. Assume that average inventory approximates the year-end balance.
c Number of days' operations to cover the working capital deficit.
d Return on total assets as a product of asset turnover and the net income ratio (sometimes called profit margin).

24A-2 The balance sheet, income statement, and related information for the Weatherby Company are shown below:

WEATHERBY COMPANY
Balance Sheet
December 31, 1975

Assets

Cash	$ 106,000
Accounts receivable	566,000
Inventories	320,000
Plant and equipment, net of accumulated depreciation	740,000
Patents	26,000
Other intangible assets	14,000
Total	$1,772,000

Liabilities & Stockholders' Equity

Accounts payable	$ 170,000
Federal income tax payable	32,000
Miscellaneous accrued payables	38,000
4% bonds payable, due 1992	300,000

Preferred stock, $100 par value, 7% cumulative, nonparticipating, and
callable at $110 . . . . $ 200,000
Common stock, no par, 20,000 shares authorized, issued, and outstanding   400,000
Retained earnings   720,000
Treasury stock, 800 shares of preferred stock . . . .   (88,000)
Total $1,772,000

WEATHERBY COMPANY
Income Statement
For Year Ended December 31, 1975

Net sales	$1,500,000
Cost of goods sold	900,000
Gross profit on sales	$ 600,000
Expenses (including bond interest expense)	498,000
Income before income tax expense	$ 102,000
Income tax expense	37,000
Net income	$ 65,000

Additional information There are no preferred dividends in arrears and the balances in the Accounts Receivable and Inventories accounts are unchanged from January 1, 1975. There were no changes in the Bonds Payable, Preferred Stock, or Common Stock accounts during 1975. All sales are made on credit.

Instructions From the information presented above, compute the following to the nearest decimal:
a Current ratio at December 31, 1975.
b The number of times bond interest was earned during 1975, using the theoretically preferable method.
c The number of times bond interest and preferred dividends were earned during 1975.
d The number of days' sales in inventories at the end of 1975. Use calendar days rather than working days.
e The approximate average number of days in the operating cycle during 1975.
f The book value per share of common stock at December 31, 1975.
g The rate of return for 1975, based on the year-end common stockholders' equity.
h The debt to equity ratio, with debt defined as total liabilities, at December 31, 1975.

24A-3 The following statistics are available for the General Wholesale Company for the most recent three years:

	Year 3	Year 2	Year 1
Gross profit percentage	36%	33⅓%	30%
Inventory turnover	20 times	25 times	14 times
Average inventory	$ 9,600	$ 9,000	$17,500
Average accounts receivable	$100,000	$84,375	$43,750
Income tax rate	40%	30%	20%
Net income as percentage of sales	12%	7%	6%
Maximum credit period allowed to customers . .	90 days	60 days	30 days

Instructions

a Prepare income statements in comparative form for the three years.

b Comment on the trend in sales volume, the gross profit percentage, and the net income percentage.

c Compute the accounts receivable turnover rates and briefly comment on the trend in view of the changing credit terms. All sales are made on credit.

24A-4 The capital structure of Bismark Corporation at the end of the current year is as follows:

Long-term debt, 8%	$6,000,000
Capital stock, $50 par value	4,000,000
Retained earnings	5,000,000

The Bismark Corporation reported earnings of $4 per share for the year, after income taxes of approximately 50% of before-tax net income. The common stock currently sells on the market at $160 per share.

The company is considering the need to raise $1.6 million of additional capital to finance a proposed plant expansion. Capital budgeting studies show that the additional plant should produce a return of 15%, or $240,000 per year before income taxes. Two proposals are being considered: (1) Sell additional 8% bonds at par value; (2) sell shares of capital stock at the current market price of $160 per share.

At a board of directors meeting one of the directors commented: "The choice is obvious to me. With our stock selling at 40 times earnings, now is the time to take advantage of the stock market and issue additional shares." To this the controller replied, "You're wrong, Fred. You've forgotten that Uncle Sam foots the bill for 50% of our bond interest, so bonds will cost us only 4% while we are earning a return of 15%. You can't beat that kind of margin."

Instructions

a Prepare an analysis which will demonstrate whether the director or the controller is correct, and state your own recommendations as to the choice of financing methods. (Ignore bond issue costs.)

b Would your answer in (**a**) be different if the issuance of additional bonds were expected to cause the price of the shares to fall to 30 times earnings after giving effect to the increase in earnings as a result of the plant expansion?

24A-5 Ratio analysis is often applied to test the reasonableness of the relationships among current financial data against those of prior financial data. Given prior financial relationships and a few key amounts, a CPA could prepare estimates of current financial data to test the reasonableness of data furnished by his client.

Agricultural Sales Corporation has in recent prior years maintained the following relationships among the data on its financial statements:

(1) Gross profit rate on net sales	40%
(2) Net income rate on net sales	10%
(3) Rate of selling expenses to net sales	15%
(4) Accounts receivable turnover	8 per year
(5) Inventory turnover	6 per year
(6) Quick (acid-test) ratio	2 to 1
(7) Current ratio	3 to 1
(8) Quick-asset composition—8% cash, 32% marketable securities, 60% accounts receivable	
(9) Asset turnover	2 per year
(10) Ratio of total assets to intangible assets	20 to 1
(11) Ratio of accumulated depreciation to cost of plant assets	1 to 3
(12) Ratio of accounts receivable to accounts payable	1.5 to 1
(13) Ratio of working capital to stockholders' equity	1 to 1.6
(14) Ratio of total debt to stockholders' equity	1 to 2

The corporation had a net income of $120,000 for 1975, after income taxes at the rate of 50%, which resulted in earnings of $5.20 per share of common stock. Additional information includes the following:

(1) Capital stock authorized, issued (all in 1967), and outstanding:
   Common, $10 per share par value, issued at 10% above par value
   Preferred, 6% nonparticipating, $100 per share par value, issued at 10% above par value
(2) Market value per share of common stock at Dec. 31, 1975: $78.
(3) Preferred dividends paid in 1975: $3,000.
(4) Times interest earned in 1975: 33 times (after income taxes).
(5) The amounts of the following were the same at Dec. 31, 1975, as at Jan. 1, 1975: inventory, accounts receivable, 5% bonds payable—due 1987, and total stockholders' equity.
(6) All purchases and sales were on account.

Instructions

a Prepare in good form the condensed (1) income statement and (2) balance sheet for the year ending December 31, 1975, presenting the amounts you would expect to appear on Agricultural Sales Corporation's financial statements. Major captions appearing on the balance sheet are: Current Assets, Plant Assets, Intangible Assets, Current Liabilities, Long-term Liabilities, and Stockholders' Equity. In addition to the accounts divulged in the problem, you should include accounts for Prepaid Expenses, Accrued Liabilities, and Administrative Expenses. Supporting computations should be in good form.

b Compute the following for 1975 (show your computations): (1) Rate of return on stockholders' equity, (2) price-earnings ratio for common stock, (3) dividends paid per share of common stock, and (4) dividends paid per share of preferred stock.

Group B

24B-1 The comparative balance sheet for Moro Bay Corporation follows:

MORO BAY CORPORATION
Comparative Balance Sheets
December 31

	1975	1974
Cash	$ 6,000	$ 4,000
Marketable securities	2,000	4,000
Accounts receivable (net)	14,000	10,000
Allowance for uncollectible accounts	(4,000)	(2,000)
Inventory	9,000	7,000
Plant and equipment	90,000	87,000
Accumulated depreciation	(23,000)	(20,000)
Total	$ 94,000	$ 90,000
Accounts payable	$ 4,000	$ 5,000
Miscellaneous liabilities	3,000	1,000
7% long-term note payable, due 1985	20,000	20,000
Preferred stock	5,000	10,000

Common stock, $2 par value	$10,000	$10,000
Paid in capital in excess of par value	30,000	30,000
Retained earnings	22,000	14,000
Total	$94,000	$90,000

All sales are made on account and amounted to $150,000 in 1975. Gross profit on sales is 42% of sales and net income is 10% of sales. Income taxes are 40% of income before income taxes.

Instructions Compute the following for 1975:
a Return (before income taxes and interest) on total assets
b Receivables turnover
c Inventory turnover
d Current ratio
e Quick ratio
f Times interest earned (before income taxes)

24B-2 Selected information taken from the financial statements for Mayhugh Corporation for the past four years is shown below:

	1975	1974	1973	1972
Net sales	$800,000	$642,000	$624,000	$600,000
Cost of goods sold	560,000	417,300	411,840	408,000
Gross profit on sales	240,000	224,700	212,160	192,000
Net income (after income taxes)	56,000	25,680	30,000	34,500
Merchandise inventory (fifo), year-end . .	80,000	125,000	82,400	102,000
Accounts receivable, end of year	88,000	45,000	50,000	40,000
Industry sales index (1972 = 100)	110	112	108	100

All sales are made on credit terms of 2/10, n/30. Assume there are 300 business days in a year.

Instructions
a For each of the four years, compute the following and present in tabular form:
    (1) Gross profit as percentage of sales
    (2) Net income as percentage of sales
    (3) Operating expenses (including income taxes) as percentage of sales
    (4) Number of days' sales in ending inventory (nearest day)
    (5) Number of days' sales in ending accounts receivable (nearest day)
    (6) Index of company's sales to industry sales
b Briefly comment on the trend in each item (1) through (6) in part *(a)*.

24B-3 The analytical information on page 956 has been prepared from the financial statements of the Cobb Corporation as of December 31 for four years (designated Year 0, Year 1, Year 2, and Year 3).
    The first column shows the increase or decrease in Year 3 amounts as compared to Year 2 amounts expressed as a percentage. The second column represents Year 2 amounts expressed as component percentages of total assets of $1,800,000. The third column shows Year 1 amounts expressed as a trend percentage, using Year 0 as a base year. The fourth column represents the dollar amounts for Year 0.

	Percentage increase (decrease), Year 3 over Year 2	Component percentage, Year 2	Trend percentage, Year 1 (Year 0 = 100%)	Dollar amount, Year 0
Current liabilities	25.0%	12.6%	65.0%	$ 270,000
Long-term debt	(100.0)	17.0	92.5	360,000
Capital stock, $5 par value . .	50.0	35.0	140.0	450,000
Paid-in capital in excess				
of par value	101.0	15.0	900.0	30,000
Retained earnings	50.0	20.4	103.0	450,000
Total liabilities & stock-				
holders' equity	29.0%	100.0%	120.0%	$1,560,000

Instructions

a Prepare a comparative statement of liabilities and stockholders' equity at the end of Year 1, Year 2, and Year 3.

b At what dollar amount per share was the common stock sold in Year 1 and Year 3? How many shares were sold in each year? (Show computations.)

24B-4 The Cumberland Corporation is applying for a short-term bank loan. The following information (in thousands of dollars) has been extracted from comparative financial statements submitted by the company as of December 31.

	Year 2	Year 1
Cash and marketable securities	$ 20	$ 50
Receivables (net)	80	100
Inventories (fifo)	90	120
Miscellaneous current prepayments	20	30
Current liabilities	80	160
Sales	315	290
Cost of goods sold	240	220

The loan officer of the bank has asked for certain quarterly information during Year 2, which appears below:

	Apr. 1	July 1	Oct. 1
Current assets	$390	$450	$410
Quick assets	160	185	180
Receivables (net)	80	175	165
Inventories	200	190	170
Current liabilities	240	335	275

Instructions

a Assuming that only the information at the end of Year 1 and Year 2 was available, compute the following for Year 2:

(1) Average current ratio
(2) Average quick ratio
(3) Inventory turnover (times per year)
(4) Receivables turnover (times per year)
(5) Length of operating cycle (assume 365 days in a year)
b Recompute the ratios listed in (*a*), using annual averages based on the quarterly information submitted to the loan officer.
c Comment on the difference in the company's current position as revealed by your comparative analysis in (*a*) and (*b*).

24B-5 Comparative balance sheet and income statement data for the Nils Company for a two-year period are presented below and on page 958 (all figures are rounded to the nearest thousand dollar):

NILS COMPANY

Comparative Balance Sheet

as of December 31

(in thousands of dollars)

	Year 2	Year 1	Increase or (decrease)
Assets:			
Current assets	$2,340	$1,890	$450
Plant and equipment (net)	1,025	840	185
Total assets	$3,365	$2,730	$635
Liabilities & stockholders' equity:			
Current liabilities	$ 970	$ 900	$ 70
Long-term liabilities	400	500	(100)
Total liabilities	$1,370	$1,400	$(30)
Capital stock, $20 par value	$1,100	$ 800	$300
Paid-in capital in excess of par value	342	100	242
Retained earnings	553	430	123
Total stockholders' equity	$1,995	$1,330	$665
Total liabilities & stockholders' equity	$3,365	$2,730	$635

Additional information
(1) Additional shares of capital stock were issued on January 2, Year 2.
(2) At the beginning of Year 1, inventories were $440,000 and net receivables were $620,000. Terms of sale are net 90 days.
(3) The market value of the capital stock was $20 per share at the end of Year 1 and $40 per share at the end of Year 2.
(4) Dividends paid on capital stock amounted to $40,000 in Year 1 and $77,000 in Year 2.

NILS COMPANY
Details of Current Assets and Liabilities
as of December 31
(in thousands of dollars)

	Year 2	Year 1	Increase or (decrease)
Current assets:			
Cash	$ 550	$ 440	$ 110
Receivables (net)	830	700	130
Inventories	750	500	250
Prepaid expenses	210	250	(40)
Total	$2,340	$1,890	$ 450
Current liabilities:			
Accounts payable	$ 590	$ 690	$(100)
Accrued expenses	380	210	170
Total	$ 970	$ 900	$ 70

NILS COMPANY
Comparative Income Statements
For Years Ended December 31
(in thousands of dollars)

	Year 2	Year 1	Percentage of net sales Year 2	Year 1
Net sales	$2,600	$2,300	100.0	100.0
Cost of goods sold	1,600	1,500	61.5	65.2
Gross profit on sales	$1,000	$ 800	38.5	34.8
Operating expenses	600	580	23.1	25.2
Operating income	$ 400	$ 220	15.4	9.6
Interest expense	20	25	.8	1.1
Income before income tax expense . . .	$ 380	$ 195	14.6	8.5
Income tax expense	180	90	6.9	3.9
Net income	$ 200	$ 105	7.7	4.6

Instructions

a Make a comparative analysis of the working capital position of the Nils Company for the two years. Compute whatever ratios you feel are useful and write a brief statement of your conclusions as to favorable and unfavorable trends, from the viewpoint of a prospective short-term creditor. Assume there are 365 days in a year.

b Prepare an analysis of the Nils Company from the viewpoint of a prospective long-term investor in its capital stock. Compute any ratios you feel would be useful, and write a brief statement of your conclusions.

CHAPTER 25

Price-level and fair-value accounting

One of the primary purposes of financial statements is to provide information for decision making. Decision makers such as investors, creditors, and management realize that financial statements prepared using "generally accepted accounting principles" may not reflect current economic realities. As a result, it has been suggested that financial statements would be more useful if historical costs were adjusted for the changing value of the dollar, or if historical costs were abandoned entirely and replaced with current economic values.

In this chapter we shall deal with some conceptual issues which would be faced by accountants and users of financial statements if changes in the general price level or changes in the fair value of assets were incorporated into the accounting model.

FINANCIAL STATEMENTS RESTATED FOR CHANGES IN THE GENERAL PRICE LEVEL

Needed: A stable unit of value

We have seen in preceding chapters that money is the common denominator used in the preparation of financial statements. The dollar, or any other monetary unit, represents a unit of value; that is, it measures the amount of purchasing power available to obtain goods and services through exchange transactions. Implicit in the use of money as a measuring unit is the assumption that the dollar is a stable unit of value, just as the mile is a stable unit of distance, and an acre is a stable unit of area. But unlike the mile and the acre, the dollar is not a stable measuring unit.

For many reasons, the prices of goods and services in our economy change over time. When the general price level increases, for example, the value of money decreases. The **general price level** is the weighted average of the prices of goods and services within the economy and is measured by an **index** with a base year assigned a value of 100. The reciprocal of the general price-level index represents the **purchasing power** of the dollar. Thus, if Year 1 = 100 and Year 5 = 125, the current purchasing power of the dollar amounts to only 80% (100 ÷ 125) of the base-year dollar; in other words, prices have risen 25% and purchasing power has decreased by 20%. The most common measures of the general price level are: **Consumer Price Index, Wholesale Price Index,** and **Gross National Product Implicit Price Deflator.** The GNP Implicit Price Deflator is the most comprehensive index and is widely recognized as the best measure of the general price level in the United States economy. Prices as measured by the GNP Deflator increased by almost 50% during the period 1958–1973, and by nearly 250% during the 35 years between 1938 and 1973.

Despite the steady erosion in the purchasing power of the dollar in the United States for over 35 years, accountants generally continue to assume that the value of the dollar is stable. Income tax laws also ignore changes in the purchasing power of the dollar and thus to some extent deter businesses from adopting price-level accounting. This unrealistic assumption is one of the reasons why traditional financial statements are sometimes viewed by creditors, investors, and other users as potentially misleading. As a result, proposals have been made to restate historical-cost financial statements to current dollars by using an appropriate general price-level index.

Historical costs versus current fair value

Even if historical-dollar financial statements were restated to reflect the changing value of the dollar, the resulting statements would still be presented in terms of historical costs and would not reflect current fair value of assets. For example, a tract of land which cost $1 million would be restated at $1.5 million if the general price level had risen by 50%. However, the current fair value of the land might be $5 million because the price of land had risen more than the general price level. Historical cost reflects the current fair value of an asset at the date of acquisition; but a significant change in the fair value of the asset after acquisition tends to make historical cost irrelevant for decision-making purposes. Consequently, many users of financial statements and accounting educators have argued that current fair value of assets should replace historical costs as a valuation basis used in the preparation of financial statements.

Effects of inflation on financial statements

As stated earlier, the United States economy has experienced persistent inflation (increase in the general level of prices) for many years. Stated another way, the value of the dollar has been decreasing. How does creeping inflation affect the measurement of net income and the presentation of financial position for a business enterprise? Suppose that a company acquired a building for $1 million early in Year 1 when the general price-level index was 100. The building has an estimated useful life of 20 years and has been depreciated at the rate of $50,000 per year. At the end of Year 5, assume that the general price-level index is 200, and a comparable building acquired new would cost $2 million. The higher current cost of the building is attributed entirely to the decrease in the purchasing power of the dollar; a doubling in the general price-level index means that a dollar at the end of Year 5 is worth only half as much as a dollar was worth in Year 1. Financial statements prepared in conformity with generally accepted accounting principles at the end of Year 5 would show the following information relating to the building:

Using historical cost:

	Balance sheet		Income statement	
Building		$1,000,000	Depreciation expense	$ 50,000
Less: Accumulated				
depreciation	250,000			
Book value of building		$ 750,000		

Is this a meaningful portrayal of economic facts? Clearly it is not. Giving effect to the 50% reduction in the purchasing power of the dollar (100% increase in the general price-level index), the information would be presented more meaningfully as follows:

Using historical cost restated to reflect 100% increase in the general price-level index:

	Balance sheet		Income statement	
Building		$2,000,000	Depreciation expense	$100,000
Less: Accumulated				
depreciation	500,000			
Book value of building		$1,500,000		

Both presentations are stated in terms of historical costs; however, in the latter the historical costs were adjusted to reflect the current general price-level index. When financial statements are not adjusted for changes in the general price-level index, carrying values of depreciable assets and depreciation expense may be significantly misstated; similarly, inventories, cost of goods sold, other assets, and various other expenses also may be misstated. When the effects of changes in the general price-level index are ignored, net income is measured by matching costs and revenue expressed in dollars having *different* purchasing power.

Income or Recovery of Capital?   Suppose you buy 1,000 pounds of sugar for $100 when the general price level is 100 and sell the sugar for $103 when the general price level reaches 105. How much profit did you make on the transaction? By comparing your cost of $100 with the proceeds of $103, you conclude that you earned a profit of $3. However, in arriving at this result, you are using different types of dollars. It would be more logical to say that your investment of $100 is now equivalent to $105 in terms of current purchasing power and that you actually lost $2 on the transaction because you cannot buy for $103 now what you could have bought for $100 when you made the investment. In other words, you failed to recover your full capital investment and thus suffered an economic loss of $2.

To illustrate this point with another example, suppose that a company acquired land in Year 1 for $100,000 and sold it for $200,000 in Year 11. If the general price-level index doubled during that 10-year period, thus cutting the value of money in half, we might say that the company is not better off from an economic standpoint as a result of these two transactions; the $200,000 received for the land in Year 11 is equal to the $100,000 invested in Year 1. In terms of the dollar as a measuring unit, however, accountants would record a gain of $100,000 ($200,000 − $100,000) in Year 11. Thus, by combining the Year 1 and Year 11 transactions in dollar terms, accountants conclude that the company is better off economically if it recovers more than the original *number of dollars* invested in the land.

Failure to consider the changing value of money in the preparation of financial statements in a period of inflation means that what is reported as income may be, in part, a recovery of capital. Taxable income, income tax expense, and net income may be overstated. Taxable income may be overstated because depreciation charges are not large enough to offset the inflation in the prices of plant and equipment items. This characteristic of conventional financial statements is perhaps the major argument in favor of price-level accounting. However, failure to recognize the effect of price-level changes during a period of inflation does not necessarily result in an overstatement of net income, because there may be offsetting general price-level gains from borrowing. This point is expanded in the following section.

Monetary Items and General Price-level Gains and Losses In discussing the changing value of the dollar, balance sheet accounts are classified either as monetary or as nonmonetary items. Cash, certificates of deposit, notes receivable, accounts receivable, investment in bonds which will be held to maturity, and all liabilities are generally considered to be *monetary items* because they represent current buying power or legal obligations to pay out a fixed number of dollars. All other balance sheet accounts (inventories, investments in stock of other companies, plant and equipment, intangibles, and stockholders' equity accounts) are generally considered to be *nonmonetary items.*

Changes in the general price level give rise to gains and losses (known as *general price-level* or *purchasing-power gains and losses*) as a result of holding monetary items. The ownership of cash or claims to cash in the form of notes and accounts receivable results in a loss of purchasing power when the general price-level index is rising; a policy of borrowing during a period when the general price-level index is rising, on the other hand, results in a gain of purchasing power because fixed-dollar liabilities can be paid off with cheaper dollars. We can summarize this point as follows: When the general price-level index is rising, it is advantageous to be in a *negative monetary position,* that is, to hold an excess of liabilities over monetary assets; a *positive monetary position* (excess of monetary assets over liabilities) results in a loss of purchasing power when prices are rising. To illustrate, assume the following balance sheets (in millions of dollars) for two companies:

	X Company	Y Company
Cash, notes, and accounts receivable	$600	$100
Inventories and plant and equipment (net)	300	800
Total assets	$900	$900
Liabilities (current and long-term)	$200	$650
Stockholders' equity	700	250
Total liabilities & stockholders' equity	$900	$900

If the general price-level index increased by 10% (from 120 to 132, for example) since the two companies acquired the nonmonetary assets (inventories and plant and equipment) and incurred the liabilities, the balance sheets restated to current dollars would be as follows:

	X Company	Y Company
Cash, notes, and accounts receivable .	$600	$100
Inventories and plant and equipment (net)	330 ($300 × 1.1)	880 ($800 × 1.1)
Total assets	$930	$980
Liabilities (current and long-term) . . .	$200	$650
Stockholders' equity	770 ($700 × 1.1)	275 ($250 × 1.1)
Net general price-level (loss) or gain .	(40)*	55†
Total liabilities & stockholders' equity	$930	$980

* Loss from holding cash and receivables, $60 ($600 × .10), reduced by the gain from borrowing, $20 ($200 × .10) = $40. X Company has a <u>positive monetary position.</u>
† Gain from borrowing, $65 ($650 × .10), reduced by the loss from holding cash and receivables, $10 ($100 × .10) = $55. Y Company has a <u>negative monetary position.</u>

The nonmonetary items (inventories and plant and equipment, and stockholders' equity) are restated to current dollars by using a **conversion factor** of 1.1 (132 ÷ 120).[1] Stated another way, the current general price-level index is equal to 110% of the index at the date when inventories and plant and equipment were acquired. Monetary items are not restated because these items are already stated in terms of current dollars. The ownership of monetary assets during a period of rising prices results in a general price-level loss because the value of money is falling; being in debt during a period of rising prices results in a general price-level gain because the debtor company can pay its liabilities in a fixed number of dollars which are worth less than the amount borrowed. If prices were falling, the opposite would be true.

In order to illustrate the fundamental effects of inflation on the two companies, we used a somewhat static and oversimplified example; we assumed that all assets and liabilities remained unchanged while the general price-level index was rising by 10%. The effects of general price-level changes on revenue and expenses are illustrated in a subsequent section of this chapter.

Emergence of price-level accounting—summary of APB Statement No. 3

The restatement of financial statements to reflect the effects of changes in the general price level is known as **price-level accounting.** Price-level accounting is not new. Most nations around the world have experienced

[1] The adjustment of financial statements for changes in the general price-level index is generally facilitated by computing the relationship between the current index and the base-year index as a *conversion factor* in decimal form. For example, a current index of 126.9 and a base-year (or date-of-transaction) index of 90 gives a conversion factor of 1.41 (126.9 ÷ 90).

severe inflation in the twentieth century and have used various approaches to restate financial statements for the changing value of their currencies. Although the inflationary trend in the United States has been persistent, it generally has not been considered severe enough to warrant a departure from the basic assumption that the monetary unit is stable. As prices continue to rise, however, a change in this assumption may have to be made; some accountants and businessmen think that already we have waited too long.

The first significant work on price-level accounting in the United States was published by Henry W. Sweeney in 1936. His book, **Stabilized Accounting,** established the framework for later studies and official pronouncements.[2] In 1961, the Accounting Principles Board authorized a study of the price-level problem which resulted in the publication of **Accounting Research Study No. 6.**[3] **ARS No. 6** recommended that the effects of price-level changes should be disclosed as a supplement to the conventional financial statements. Six years later, the Board issued **Statement of the Accounting Principles Board No. 3,** which outlined detailed procedures for the restatement of financial statements to recognize changes in the general price level.[4] A condensed summary of the key recommendations of **APB Statement No. 3** is presented below:

1 General price-level statements or information may be presented in addition to the basic historical-dollar financial statements, but general price-level statements should not be presented as the basic statements. Price-level financial statements are **supplementary** in nature and are **not required** for fair presentation.

2 The same accounting principles used in preparing historical-dollar financial statements should be used in preparing general price-level financial statements, except that changes in the general purchasing power of the dollar are recognized in general price-level financial statements. Price-level financial statements represent an **extension of** (not a departure from) **the historical-cost basis of accounting.**

3 An **index of the general price level,** not an index of the price of a specific type of goods or services, should be used to prepare general price-level financial statements. The GNP Implicit Price Deflator is the most comprehensive indicator of the general price level in the United States and should normally be used for this purpose.

4 General price-level financial statements should be prepared in terms of the general purchasing power of the dollar at the **latest balance sheet date.** Current economic actions take place in terms of current dollars, and translating items to current dollars expresses them in the context of current actions.

5 **Monetary** and **nonmonetary** items should be distinguished for the purpose of preparing general price-level statements. Monetary assets and liabilities (including income taxes payable) in historical-cost balance sheets are stated

[2] Henry W. Sweeney, *Stabilized Accounting,* Harper & Brothers (New York: 1936). Reprinted in 1964 by Holt, Rinehart and Winston, Inc., New York.
[3] *Accounting Research Study No. 6,* "Reporting the Financial Effects of Price-level Changes," authored by the staff of the Research Division, AICPA (New York: 1963).
[4] *Statement of the Accounting Principles Board No. 3,* "Financial Statements Restated for General Price-level Changes," AICPA (New York: 1969).

in terms of dollars of current general purchasing power and appear in current general price-level statements at the same amounts. The amounts of non-monetary items should be restated to dollars of current general purchasing power at the end of the period. Restatement of nonmonetary items does not introduce current values or replacement costs in price-level financial statements.

6 The amounts of *income statement items* (revenue and expenses) should be restated to dollars of current general purchasing power at the end of the period. Income tax expense in the general price-level income statements is based on the income tax expense as reported in the historical-dollar income statement and is *not* computed in direct relationship to the income before income taxes reported in the general price-level income statement.

7 *General price-level gains and losses* should be calculated by means of the general price-level index and included in current net income. The gain from holding liabilities during a period of inflation should be recognized as part of net income of the period in which the general price-level rises. Recognition of such gains should not be deferred until the related assets (if any) are consumed or sold. General price-level gains and losses should be netted and reported as a separate item in the general price-level income statement.

8 General price-level statements of *earlier periods should be updated* to the dollars of the general purchasing power at the end of each of the subsequent periods for which they are presented as comparative information. Statements of earlier periods are "rolled forward" (updated) by multiplying each item by the ratio of the current general price-level index to the general price-level index of the earlier period. All general price-level information presented should be based on complete general price-level calculations. Partial restatement (of depreciation, for example) is not acceptable.

9 General price-level information as a supplement to the basic historical-dollar statements should be designed to promote *clarity and minimize possible confusion.* Presentation in separate schedules, not in parallel columns, should be encouraged. Ratio and trend analyses based on price-level data are appropriate.

10 The basis of preparation of general price-level information and what it purports to show should be clearly explained in the notes to the general price-level financial statements or other appropriate places. The explanation should include the following points:

a The general price-level statements and related information are supplementary to the basic historical-dollar financial statements.

b All amounts shown in general price-level statements are stated in terms of units of the same general purchasing power.

c The net general price-level gain or loss in the general price-level statements indicates the effects of inflation (or deflation) on the company's net holdings of monetary items.

d The same generally accepted accounting principles used in preparing historical-dollar statements are used in preparing general price-level statements.

e The general price-level statements do not purport to represent appraised value, replacement cost, or other measures of the current value of assets or the prices at which transactions would take place currently.

f The general price-level statements of prior years have been rolled forward (updated) to current dollars. This rolling forward is required to make prior years' statements comparable with current information; it does not change the statements of the prior years in any way except to update the amounts to dollars of current general purchasing power.

g Income taxes are based on income (or gains and losses) before restatement for general price-level changes because inflation and deflation are not recognized by tax laws.

Illustration of price-level accounting

Data for Illustration A relatively simple set of financial statements for the Baker Company will be used to illustrate the application of **APB Statement No. 3**. The Baker Company was organized on December 31, Year 4, as a result of a merger of several separate businesses which were previously operated as partnerships or single proprietorships. All assets were recorded by Baker Company at fair market values. Movements in the Gross National Product Implicit Price Deflator during Year 5 are presented below:

	GNP Implicit Price Deflator (general price-level index)	Conversion factor to restate to end-of-Year 5 dollars
End of Year 4 (and beginning of Year 5) . . .	150.0	1.092*
Average for Year 5 (also at July 1)	157.5	1.040†
End of Year 5	163.8	1.000

* 163.8 ÷ 150.0 = 1.092.
† 163.8 ÷ 157.5 = 1.040.

The comparative balance sheet (before price-level adjustments) at the end of Year 5 for the Baker Company is shown below:

BAKER COMPANY
Comparative Balance Sheet
End of Year 4 and Year 5

	End of Year 4	End of Year 5
Assets		
Monetary assets (cash and receivables)	$200,000	$260,000
Inventories (first-in, first-out method)	150,000	130,000
Land	40,000	40,000
Equipment	210,000	270,000
Less: Accumulated depreciation	–0–	(24,000)
Total assets	$600,000	$676,000
Liabilities & Stockholders' Equity		
Current liabilities	$ 80,000	$ 90,000
Long-term liabilities	100,000	116,000
Capital stock, $10 par value	140,000	140,000
Paid-in capital in excess of par	280,000	280,000
Retained earnings	–0–	50,000
Total liabilities & stockholders' equity	$600,000	$676,000

Shown below is the statement of income and retained earnings for the Baker Company, before price-level adjustments, for Year 5 (the first year of operations):

BAKER COMPANY
Statement of Income and Retained Earnings
For Year 5 (the first year of operations)

Sales (net)		$800,000
Cost of goods sold:		
Beginning inventories (first-in, first-out method)	$150,000	
Purchases (net)	500,000	
Cost of goods available for sale	$650,000	
Less: Ending inventories (first-in, first-out method)	130,000	
Cost of goods sold		520,000
Gross profit on sales		$280,000
Operating expenses (excluding depreciation)	$ 96,000	
Depreciation expense	24,000	120,000
Income before income taxes		$160,000
Income tax expense		70,000
Net income		$ 90,000
Less: Dividends paid		40,000
Retained earnings, end of Year 5		$ 50,000

Equipment costing $60,000 was acquired on July 1 when the GNP Implicit Price Deflator stood at 157.5. Depreciation expense was computed as follows:

$210,000 × 10%	$21,000	
$60,000 × 5% (one-half of year)	3,000	$24,000

Net sales, net purchases, and operating expenses (excluding depreciation) took place evenly throughout the year. Inventories are priced on a first-in, first-out basis; goods in ending inventories were acquired evenly during the year. The dividend of $40,000 was declared and paid near the end of Year 5.

Exhibit 1—Statement of Income and Retained Earnings A working paper to restate the statement of income and retained earnings for Year 5, in terms of end-of-Year 5 dollars, is presented in Exhibit 1 on page 969.

Exhibit 1

BAKER COMPANY

Statement of Income and Retained Earnings Restated for
General Price-level Changes

For Year 5 (the first year of operations)

	Per accounting records	Conversion factor	Restated to end-of-Year 5 dollars
Sales (net)	$800,000	1.040 (A)	$832,000
Cost of goods sold:			
Beginning inventories (fifo method)	$150,000	1.092 (B)	$163,800
Purchases (net)	500,000	1.040 (A)	520,000
Cost of goods available for sale	$650,000		$683,800
Less: Ending inventories			
(fifo method)	130,000	1.040 (A)	135,200
Cost of goods sold	$520,000		$548,600
Gross profit on sales	$280,000		$283,400
Less: Operating expenses (ex-			
cluding depreciation) . . .	(96,000)	1.040 (A)	(99,840)
Depreciation expense	(24,000)	(C)	(26,052)
Income before general price-level			
gain or loss	$160,000		$157,508
General price-level loss		(Exhibit 2)	4,800
Income after general price-level			
loss			$152,708
Income tax expense	70,000	1.040 (A)	72,800
Net income	$ 90,000		$ 79,908
Less: Dividends paid.	40,000	1.000 (D)	40,000
Retained earnings, end of Year 5 .	$ 50,000		$ 39,908

(A) The general price-level index at the end of Year 5 (163.8), divided by the average general price-level index during Year 5 (157.5) = 1.040.

(B) The general price-level index at the end of Year 5 (163.8), divided by the general price-level index at the end of Year 4 (150.0) when inventories were acquired = 1.092.

(C) Depreciation expense is restated for the increase in the general price-level index as follows:

On equipment acquired at end of Year 4: $21,000 × 1.092 . . . . . $22,932
On equipment acquired on July 1, Year 5: $3,000 × 1.040 . . . . . 3,120 $26,052

(D) Dividends were declared and paid near the end of Year 5, and are therefore stated in terms of current dollars at the end of Year 5.

A brief explanation of the procedures followed to restate the statement of income and retained earnings follows:

Sales Sales were made at a fairly uniform rate during Year 5; therefore, the amount of sales reported in the accounting records ($800,000) is stated in terms of the average general price-level index for the year. In order to restate sales in terms of end-of-Year 5 dollars, a conversion factor of 1.040 is used. This factor is computed by dividing the end-of-Year 5 index of 163.8 by 157.5, the average index for Year 5.

Beginning inventories The goods comprising the beginning inventories were acquired when the general price-level index was 150.0. The beginning inventories is restated by using a conversion factor of 1.092, the end-of-Year 5 general price-level index of 163.8 divided by 150.0, the index at the time the inventories were acquired.

Purchases Since purchases took place at a fairly uniform rate, the restatement is accomplished by multiplying by a conversion factor of 1.040, the end-of-Year 5 general price-level index of 163.8 divided by 157.5, the average index during Year 5.

Ending inventories Because inventories are priced on a first-in, first-out basis, it is assumed that the goods in the ending inventories were acquired at the average general price level for Year 5. Thus ending inventories are restated to current dollars by using the average general price-level index conversion factor of 1.040 (the same conversion factor used to restate purchases).

Operating expenses (other than depreciation) Because we have assumed that operating expenses were incurred evenly throughout the year, this amount is restated to current dollars by applying the average general price-level index conversion factor of 1.040.

Depreciation expense Depreciation expense on the accounting records consists of two amounts: (1) depreciation of $21,000 on equipment acquired on December 31, Year 4, when the general price-level index was 150.0 and (2) depreciation of $3,000 on equipment acquired on July 1, Year 5, when the general price-level index was 157.5. Depreciation expense is therefore restated as follows:

$21,000 × 1.092 (163.8 ÷ 150.0)	$22,932
$3,000 × 1.04 (163.8 ÷ 157.5)	3,120
Total depreciation expense, as restated	$26,052

General price-level loss Any gain or loss resulting from the ownership of monetary assets or from borrowing activities is computed in a separate schedule and is added to or subtracted from income before general price-level gain or loss. The determination of the general price-level loss of $4,800 for the Baker Company appears in Exhibit 2 on page 972.

Income tax expense Income taxes accrue throughout the year as revenue and expenses are recorded. Since sales and expenses accrued evenly throughout the year, income tax expense is adjusted to end-of-Year 5 dollars by multiplying the actual income tax expense of $70,000 by the average general price-level conversion factor of 1.040. As stated on page 966, income tax expense in the general price-level income statement is based on the income tax expense as reported in the historical-dollar income statement and is not computed in direct relationship to the income before income taxes reported in the general price-level income statement.

Dividends paid Since dividends were declared and paid near the end of Year 5, the amount of dividends paid is stated in terms of current dollars and requires no restatement.

Exhibit 1 shows that Baker Company earned a net income of $79,908 rather than $90,000 as shown in the conventional income statement. The difference of $10,092 is caused by three major factors: (1) an increase in the cost of goods acquired at the end of Year 4 and sold in Year 5; (2) an increase in depreciation expense because of an increase in the general price level since the equipment was acquired; and (3) a general price-level loss as a result of holding an excess of monetary assets over liabilities during a period when the general price level was going up. As a result of the difference in net income, the retained earnings will appear in the price-level balance sheet (see Exhibit 3 on page 974) at $39,908 ($50,000 − $10,092).

Exhibit 2—Computation of General Price-level Gain or Loss The general price-level loss of $4,800 which appears in the statement of income and retained earnings restated for general price-level changes is presented in Exhibit 2 on page 972.

In preparing Exhibit 2, transactions (such as net sales) which caused an increase in monetary assets during Year 5 are added to the amount of net monetary items at the beginning of the year; those transactions which caused an increase in liabilities or a decrease in monetary assets are deducted. Included under deductions are net purchases, operating expenses other than depreciation, income tax expense for the year, dividends declared and paid, and the purchase of equipment. You will note that depreciation expense is not included in Exhibit 2 because depreciation is a nonmonetary expense. The amount of net monetary items at the beginning of Year 5 (restated to end-of-Year 5 dollars), plus sources and less uses of net monetary assets (restated to end-of-Year 5 dollars) gives $58,800 as the amount of net monetary items that *should be* on hand if there were no general price-level gain or loss. Since net monetary items at the end of Year 5 amount to only $54,000, the general price-level loss is $4,800 ($58,800 − $54,000).

Exhibit 2

BAKER COMPANY
Computation of General Price-level Gain or Loss
For Year 5 (the first year of operations)

	Amounts per accounting records		Conversion factor	Restated to end-of-Year 5 dollars
Net monetary items at beginning of Year 5:				
Monetary assets (cash and receivables)	$200,000			
Current liabilities	(80,000)			
Long-term liabilities	(100,000)	$ 20,000	1.092 (A)	$ 21,840
Add: Sources of net monetary items during Year 5:				
Sales (net)		800,000	1.040 (B)	832,000
Subtotal		$820,000		$853,840
Less: Uses of net monetary items during Year 5:				
Purchases (net)	$500,000		1.040 (B)	$520,000
Operating expenses (excluding depreciation) . . .	96,000		1.040 (B)	99,840
Income tax expense	70,000		1.040 (B)	72,800
Dividends paid	40,000		1.000 (C)	40,000
Purchase of equipment . . .	60,000		1.040 (D)	62,400
Total uses		766,000		$795,040
Net monetary items as restated at the end of Year 5 if there were no general price-level gain or loss ($853,840 − $795,040)				$ 58,800
Net monetary items actually on hand at the end of Year 5:				
Monetary assets (cash and receivables)	$260,000			
Current liabilities	(90,000)			
Long-term liabilities	(116,000)	$ 54,000		54,000
General price-level loss during Year 5				$ 4,800

(A) The amount of net monetary items at the beginning of Year 5 is rolled forward by multiplying $20,000 by the conversion factor of 1.092, which is the ratio of end-of-Year 5 general price-level index to the index at the beginning of Year 5.

(B) Sales, purchases, operating expenses, and income tax expense are restated in the same manner as in Exhibit 1, that is, by using a conversion factor for the average general price-level index for Year 5.

(C) Dividends were declared and paid near the end of Year 5 and therefore are already stated in terms of current dollars.

(D) Equipment was purchased on July 1, Year 5, when the general price-level index was 157.5; this amount is restated by multiplying the cost of $60,000 by 1.040 (163.8 ÷ 157.5).

Exhibit 3—Comparative Balance Sheet A working paper to restate the comparative balance sheet, in terms of end-of-Year 5 dollars, is presented on page 974. Note that the balance sheet amounts (as taken from the accounting records) at the end of Year 4 are rolled forward, in order to reflect end-of-Year 5 dollars, by multiplying each amount by 1.092 (163.8 ÷ 150.0). This rolling forward of the balance sheet amounts is necessary so that the balance sheet at the end of Year 4 can be meaningfully compared with the restated balance sheet at the end of Year 5. Thus, balance sheet amounts at both dates are stated in terms of current dollars having uniform purchasing power.

The restatement of the balance sheet accounts at the end of Year 5 is explained below:

Monetary items Monetary assets (cash and receivables) and liabilities are already reported in terms of end-of-Year 5 dollars and require no restatement.

Inventories Inventories at the end of Year 5 are priced using the first-in, first-out method. Goods comprising the ending inventories were acquired evenly throughout the year and therefore are restated by using a conversion factor of 1.040, the general price-level index at the end of Year 5, 163.8, divided by the average index during Year 5, 157.5. This is consistent with the restatement of ending inventories in Exhibit 1 on page 969.

If inventories were priced on a last-in, first-out basis, the ending inventories would consist entirely of the cost layer on hand at the beginning of Year 5 and would be restated by applying a conversion factor of 1.092 (163.8 ÷ 150.0).

Land Because land was acquired at the end of Year 4 when the general price-level index was 150.0, it is restated to $43,680 by multiplying the cost of $40,000 by 1.092 (163.8 ÷ 150.0).

Equipment and accumulated depreciation Equipment costing $210,000 was acquired at the end of Year 4 when the general price-level index was 150.0 and equipment costing $60,000 was acquired on July 1, Year 5, when the index was 157.5. One possible approach to the restatement of equipment and accumulated depreciation accounts at the end of Year 5 is presented below:

	Equipment			*Accumulated depreciation*		
Per books ×	*Conversion factor*	*= Adjusted*		*Per books* ×	*Conversion factor*	*= Adjusted*
$210,000	×1.092 (163.8 ÷ 150.0) =	$229,320		$21,000 ×	1.092	= $22,932
60,000	×1.040 (163.8 ÷ 157.5) =	62,400		3,000 ×	1.040	= 3,120
$270,000		$291,720		$24,000		$26,052

Exhibit 3

BAKER COMPANY

Comparative Balance Sheet Restated for

General Price-level Changes

End of Year 4 and Year 5

	End of Year 4			End of Year 5		
	Per accounting records	Conversion factor	Rolled forward to end-of-Year 5 dollars	Per accounting records	Conversion factor	Restated to end-of-Year 5 dollars
Assets						
Monetary assets (cash and receivables)	$200,000	1.092 (A)	$218,400	$260,000	(B)	$260,000
Inventories (fifo method)	150,000	1.092	163,800	130,000	1.040 (E)	135,200
Land	40,000	1.092	43,680	40,000	1.092 (A)	43,680
Equipment	210,000	1.092	229,320	270,000	(C)	291,720
Less: Accumulated depreciation	–0–		–0–	(24,000)	(D)	(26,052)
Total assets	$600,000		$655,200	$676,000		$704,548
Liabilities & Stockholders' Equity						
Current liabilities	$ 80,000	1.092	$ 87,360	$ 90,000	(B)	$ 90,000
Long-term liabilities	100,000	1.092	109,200	116,000	(B)	116,000
Capital stock, $10 par value	140,000	1.092	152,880	140,000	1.092 (A)	152,880
Paid-in capital in excess of par	280,000	1.092	305,760	280,000	1.092 (A)	305,760
Retained earnings	–0–		–0–	50,000	(Exhibit 1)	39,908
Total liabilities & stockholders' equity	$600,000		$655,200	$676,000		$704,548

(A) General price-level index at end of Year 5 (163.8) divided by the general price-level index at the end of Year 4 (150.0) = 1.092.

(B) Monetary items at the end of Year 5 are not adjusted because these are already stated in terms of end-of-Year 5 dollars.

(C) Equipment is adjusted for the increase in the general price-level index as follows:

Acquired at the end of Year 4: $210,000 × 1.092	$229,320
Acquired on July 1, Year 5: $60,000 × 1.04 (163.8 ÷ 157.5)	62,400
Total as restated	$291,720

(D) Accumulated depreciation is adjusted for the increase in the general price-level index as follows:

On equipment acquired at the end of Year 4: $21,000 × 1.092	$ 22,932
On equipment acquired on July 1, Year 5: $3,000 × 1.04	3,120
Total accumulated depreciation as restated	$ 26,052

(E) General price-level index at end of Year 5 (163.8), divided by the average general price-level index during Year 5 (157.5) = 1.040.

The book value of the equipment at the end of Year 5 is $246,000 ($270,000 − $24,000) in terms of actual cost and $265,668 ($291,720 − $26,052) when actual cost is adjusted for general price-level changes. Thus if the equipment were sold for $250,000 at the beginning of Year 6, a gain of $4,000 would result in terms of historical cost and a loss of $15,668 would result when general price-level accounting is applied.

Capital stock and paid-in capital in excess of par Paid-in capital accounts are carried in the accounting records at amounts invested by stockholders. These amounts should be restated to current dollars by multiplying each amount by a fraction (conversion factor) in which the current general price-level index is the numerator and the index at the time the paid-in capital was invested by stockholders is the denominator. The conversion factor used to restate the paid-in capital accounts for Baker Company is 1.092 (163.8 ÷ 150.0).

Retained earnings The balance in retained earnings was previously determined in Exhibit 1 on page 969.

If the foregoing steps have been correctly applied, the total of assets, as restated, should equal the restated total of liabilities and stockholders' equity.

Similar procedures would be followed in subsequent years to adjust financial statements for changes in the general price-level index. If comparative financial statements are presented at the end of Year 6, the amounts appearing in the statements for Year 5, as restated in terms of end-of-Year 5 dollars, would have to be rolled forward so that they are stated in end-of-Year 6 dollars. For example, if the general price-level index during Year 6 increased by 6%, the financial statements for Year 5 would be rolled forward by applying a conversion factor of 1.06 to all balance sheet and income statement items.

Price-level information in practice

Financial statements adjusted for changes in the general price level are not generally accepted as primary reports to stockholders. The 1972 edition of *Accounting Trends & Techniques* discloses that none of the 600 companies included in the survey presented financial statements adjusted for price-level changes; however, reference to the effects of inflation or price-level changes was made by 68 companies.[5] A few companies not included in the survey above publish price-level financial statements. The financial statements of Indiana Telephone Corporation included in Appendix B are an example of such reporting. The reader should note, however, that the Indiana Telephone Corporation does not completely follow the recommendations of *APB Statement No. 3.*

The practice of presenting supplementary price-level statements has not been widely followed in the United States, perhaps because the business community considers the cost of providing such statements to be greater than the value to users. With modern computer technology, it is probably safe to conclude that the additional cost and effort required to prepare price-level statements would not be excessive. Should the high rate of inflation continue, we are likely to see an increasing number of companies present price-level statements in their annual reports.

[5] *Accounting Trends & Techniques,* 26th ed., AICPA (New York: 1972), p. 66.

FAIR-VALUE ACCOUNTING

Significance of changes in value

The restatement of historical-cost financial statements for price-level changes is an effort to recognize the fact that the value of the dollar is not stable. Such statements require no other departures from generally accepted accounting principles. Some accountants feel that an additional departure is needed in order to add greater relevance and usefulness to financial statements. In their view, historical costs and completed transactions should be replaced by *fair-value accounting.* They argue that fair-value financial statements showing current fair values (or current replacement costs) of assets and the changes in such values would convey a more meaningful picture of a company's financial position and economic earning power.

To illustrate, suppose that a company purchased land for $30,000 and erected a plant for $600,000, which is being depreciated over a 30-year life, or $20,000 per year. During the first 10 years of operation, the area grew in population, and new industries were attracted to the location. The market for the company's products increased, building costs in the area rose, and land values increased. At the end of the 10-year period, it was apparent that the land and building were worth considerably more than their book values. The financial statements for the company in the eleventh year show: (1) Assets are substantially below current value; (2) net income is overstated because the full economic cost of using the building is not reflected in the annual depreciation charge; and (3) the rate of return on assets and stockholders' equity is overstated, since what really amounts to capital recovery in terms of current prices is being reported as income.

Assuming that a reasonable estimate of fair value of land and building could be obtained, the land and building would be restated to fair values, and depreciation on the building would be revised accordingly to reflect the current cost of building services being consumed. The balance sheet would now show land and building at a figure approximating current worth, and reported net income would represent the amount by which the company was better off after recovering the current value of the remaining building services over the next 20 years (assuming that no further value changes occurred during that period).

Relationship between price-level and fair-value accounting

The use of fair-value accounting does not mean that changes in the general price level would be ignored. Price-level accounting and fair-value accounting are complementary responses to different measurement problems. The two approaches are not mutually exclusive alternatives. Dealing with one is not a substitute for dealing with the other and either or both approaches may be adopted in a single set of financial statements. Restatement of financial statements for general price-level changes does not attempt to deal with specific-price changes while fair-value accounting does not deal with inflation as such. The different alternatives that may be followed in preparing financial statements are:[6]

1 Historical cost

2 Historical cost restated for general price-level changes

3 Fair value, without separate identification of the effects of general price-level changes

4 Fair value, with the effects of general price-level changes being shown separately

Financial statements adjusted for changes in the general price level continue to be based on historical cost; however, the unit of measurement (the dollar) is adjusted to reflect changes in its general purchasing power. In contrast, fair-value accounting is a departure from historical cost because the fair values for assets are derived from appraisals which reflect both changes in the general price level and changes in the relative price levels of specific goods. Thus fair-value accounting represents a clear break from historical cost for a particular company. For example, if M Company and N Company bought identical assets at different dates and price levels, price-level accounting would give different adjusted values for the assets of each company. However, fair-value accounting would give the *same value* for the assets of both companies, since fair-value accounting is not concerned with historical costs.

When changes in the general price level *are not* incorporated in fair-value financial statements, the difference between historical costs and appraised values of assets is referred to as an unrealized *holding gain or loss;* the unrealized holding gain or loss, net of the tax effect, would be reported as a separate item in the income statement. When changes in the general price level *are* incorporated in fair-value financial statements, the unrealized holding gain or loss (difference between historical costs and appraised values of assets) would consist of a net general price-level gain or loss and the net gain or loss resulting from changes in the relative values of specific assets; these two distinct types of net gains or losses would be reported separately in the income statement.

Use of fair values in preparation of financial statements

Proposals to incorporate fair values in accounting measurements are not entirely of recent origin. For example, fair values are used in applying the lower-of-cost-or-market rule to the valuation of inventories and marketable securities, and assets may be written down to fair value pursuant to a quasi-reorganization. In such cases the use of fair values results in a reduction in the carrying value of assets *below* cost (or book value).

[6]*APB Statement No. 3*, pp. 69–70.

However, fair values also are used when such values exceed historical cost. For example, marketable securities held by mutual funds and inventories of certain metals and agricultural products are frequently reported at fair (market) value. A significant number of companies increased the carrying value of plant assets during the inflation of the 1920s, only to write the same assets down during the Depression of the 1930s. In response to a recommendation by the authors of *Accounting Research Study No. 3* for the use of current replacement costs for plant and equipment, Carman G. Blough made the following observation: "Shades of the 1920s! Those of us who remember how impossible it was to determine the fairness or reasonableness of the results of an appraisal shudder at the idea of going through it all over again." [7] Past experience indicates that valuations not subject to independent verification can be manipulated to the possible disadvantage of users of financial statements.

Nevertheless, the idea persists. In *A Statement of Basic Accounting Theory,* issued in 1966 by the American Accounting Association, a recommendation was made that financial statements should be presented in two-column form; one column would present data in terms of historical costs and the other in terms of current costs.[8] This recommendation has been widely supported; some writers even have suggested that historical-cost financial statements should be supplanted by fair-value financial statements. The American Institute of Certified Public Accountants has not sanctioned the issuance of financial statements in which all assets are stated at fair value. For example, in *APB Opinion No. 6,* the Accounting Principles Board stated that it was "of the opinion that property, plant and equipment should not be written up by an entity to reflect appraisal, market or current values which are above cost to the entity." [9]

The meaning of *value*

The term *value* has many meanings and connotations, and its use in the business world often conveys a deceptively reassuring message. Value is closely related to the economic concept of *utility.* Goods and services have utility because they are scarce and because they are demanded by users in a certain *form,* at a certain *time,* and at a certain *place.* In short, goods and services have economic utility because they are capable of satisfying human wants. In our economy, goods and services are valued and exchanged through the price mechanism. Some goods and services

---

[7] Robert T. Sprouse and Maurice Moonitz, *Accounting Research Study No. 3,* "A Tentative Set of Broad Accounting Principles for Business Enterprises," AICPA (New York: 1962), p. 62.
[8] *A Statement of Basic Accounting Theory,* American Accounting Association (Sarasota, Fla.: 1966), pp. 30–32.
[9] *APB Opinion No. 6,* "Status of Accounting Research Bulletins," AICPA (New York: 1965), p. 42.

which are widely used or regulated by governmental agencies have a readily ascertainable price tag (value); on the other hand, the price or fair value of a large number of other goods and services is more difficult to pinpoint.

The basic purpose of a manufacturing or merchandising business is to create economic utility through the process of production and/or distribution. For example, raw materials are acquired by a manufacturer, the raw materials are converted into a finished product, and then the finished product is sold. The cost of a finished product may be $10 to the manufacturer; the wholesaler may purchase the finished product from the manufacturer for $15 and sell it to a retailer for $20; the retailer in turn may sell it to the ultimate consumer for $28. What is the fair value of this product? Obviously the question cannot be answered without asking: To whom? At what location? At what point in time? The same questions apply in determining the fair value of any asset. The value of almost any business asset depends on the use that is being made (or will be made) of the asset, the place where the asset is located, and the business and economic conditions at the time the valuation is made.

But the difficulties do not end here. For a long time courts of law have recognized that the fair value of some assets (such as a patent, shares of a closely held company, or a going concern) depends on the *purpose* for which the valuation is made. In addition, several different approaches may be used in arriving at fair value. As a basic proposition, we can say that the economic worth of any asset is equal to the present value of the future earnings it can produce when it is put to its most efficient use. This is a somewhat idealistic definition of value, but it stems from the fact that the "fair value" of an asset is directly dependent upon its expected earning power. However, earnings generated by specific assets are difficult to identify because they are dependent on a multitude of economic factors. Similar difficulties are encountered in arriving at an appropriate interest rate to be used in computing the present value of estimated future earnings, and in identifying the "most efficient use" for the asset.

It may be useful to recall at this point that changes in value are caused by two major factors: (1) change in general price levels, and (2) changes in relative value of goods and services. As was pointed out earlier in this chapter, the market price (value) of assets may rise or fall, not because of any increase or decrease in their economic utility, but simply because the value of money—the unit in which values are measured—has changed. A characteristic of inflationary or deflationary periods is that most prices move upward or downward in some discernible pattern. The cost of constructing all reproducible assets goes up or down; revenue from the sale of goods and services—the products of asset use—increase or decrease; and the *monetary* value of assets rises or falls in response to these conditions.

The *relative* or *comparative* value of an asset changes when an asset becomes more or less valuable *in relation to other goods and services in the economy.* For example, if prices in general are holding steady and an asset rises in value from $10,000 to $15,000, the asset has become more valuable in relation to other goods and services.

In a competitive economy, the value of reproducible assets is closely tied in to the cost of manufacture or construction. Any evidence of higher value will presumably encourage the production of more assets of this type and thus bring their value down to levels consistent with cost of production. The primary cause of a change in the relative or comparative value of a reproducible asset, therefore, is a change in the expected earning power of the asset not counterbalanced by the forces of competition. This may occur if the cost of producing a particular asset (as distinguished from costs in general) has risen or if production is limited for any reason, such as a patent restriction or a general shortage of investment capital in the economy.

The possibility of wide and permanent change in the value of nonreproducible assets (such as land or natural resources) is much greater, because they cannot be duplicated and thus their earning power is strongly influenced by scarcity. The effect of the discovery of oil or other minerals on the value of land is usually spectacular. Similarly, land located in a growing metropolitan area may increase greatly in value, just as land in an area that has deteriorated may lose value rapidly.

Arriving at fair (current) value

Thus far, we have mentioned the possibility of replacing historical costs of assets with more current values without specifying how these values might be determined. The concept of value most widely referred to in legal proceedings is *fair value,* defined as "an exchange price that a willing and well-informed buyer and an equally willing and well-informed seller would reach through negotiation." This should not be confused with *market value,* which is the price obtainable currently for any security, commodity, or other property. Market value is subject to independent determination; fair value is a synthesis rather than an independent approach to valuation. Fair value may be determined by reference to a number of different methods of valuation, taking into account a variety of factors. No single method of estimating fair value is entirely satisfactory; therefore, in order to be able to evaluate intelligently the arguments for and against fair-value accounting, it may be helpful to identify some of the methods used in estimating fair value.

Capitalization of Net Cash Inflows In theory, the ideal way to estimate the fair or *economic value* of any asset would be to compute the present discounted amount of the probable future net cash inflows expected to result from the use of the asset. This is known as *direct valuation.* A limitation of the direct valuation approach is that estimates of future net cash inflows are likely to be highly subjective and inaccurate. More importantly, the earnings of a business, entity, and thus the net cash inflows, are a joint product of all its resources, and it is virtually impossible to identify clearly the contribution to earnings and net cash inflows of any particular asset. The concept of direct valuation, although somewhat impractical for valuing specific assets, is useful in appraising the merits of other *indirect valuation* methods discussed below.

Liquidation Value   The liquidation of an asset is the amount that could be realized from its current sale. Liquidation value may be viewed as fair value only for assets that are in fact offered for sale, and as a minimum value for assets that are continued in use. However, in many cases the fair value of an asset may be materially above liquidation value. Liquidation value is related but not identical to market value; it is a narrower concept since it implies an urgent need to sell. Although a reasonable estimate of liquidation can be made for certain assets such as stocks and bonds and some items of inventory, estimates of such value for many types of special-purpose equipment and intangible assets may be quite difficult to obtain.

Replacement Cost   Replacement cost is the estimated cost of acquiring *new* and substantially *equivalent* property, at current prices, adjusted for observed depreciation due to the loss of service life that has already occurred. Replacement cost should be distinguished from *reproduction cost,* which is the estimated cost of producing *new* substantially *identical* assets, at current prices, adjusted for estimated physical and functional depreciation to date.

Specific-price Index Replacement Cost   Replacement cost may be approximated by applying an appropriate *specific-price index* to the historical cost or book value of assets, particularly plant and equipment items. Specific-price indices are readily available for broad classifications of equipment, buildings, and land. The application of specific-price indices to plant assets is illustrated below:

Assets	Historical cost	Specific-price index at date of acquisition	Current specific-price index	Conversion factor	Current specific-price index replacement cost
Building	$200,000	100	125	125/100	$250,000
Less: Accumulated					
depreciation	60,000	100	125	125/100	75,000
Book value	$140,000				$175,000
Land	240,000	120	130	130/120	260,000

The building was acquired for $200,000 when the specific-price index for building construction in this industry was 100. Since the index is now 125, the historical cost of the building is restated to a current specific-price index replacement cost of $250,000 ($200,000 × 125/100); accumulated depreciation is similarly adjusted. The specific-price index of land costs in the geographic area where the land is located increased from 120 to 130 since the land was acquired; therefore, the historical cost of the land, $240,000, is multiplied by 130/120 to arrive at the current specific-price index replacement cost of $260,000.

This brief discussion should serve to point out that much sharper asset valuation techniques must be developed before fair-value accounting becomes a practical alternative for the preparation of financial statements.

Implementing fair-value accounting

Proposals for the implementation of fair-value accounting may be placed into four categories as follows:[10]

1 Abandon traditional historical-cost accounting and adopt fair-value accounting, both for income measurement purposes and for balance sheet presentation.

2 Issue fair-value statements as supplements to historical-cost statements, or issue historical-cost statements as supplements to fair-value statements.

3 Adopt fair values for assets as rapidly as reasonably objective measures for fair values can be developed; ultimately, all or at least most items in the financial statements would be stated on a fair-value basis.

4 Continue the traditional emphasis on historical costs and *disclose* fair values of assets in supplementary form when fair values can be determined with a reasonable degree of objectivity and when disclosure would be useful.

Implicit in each of these proposals is the assumption that the fair value of most assets is determinable, that the value of a company is equal to the sum of the value of its assets less its liabilities, and that fair-value financial statements are more useful than historical-cost statements. While the fair value of some assets may be readily determined, the fair value of many other assets cannot be ascertained with any reasonable degree of precision. But even if the fair values of all identifiable assets could be readily determined with a reasonable degree of precision, the problems of valuing unidentifiable assets (goodwill) would still remain. It may also be argued that fair-value financial statements may be misleading to users because such statements might convey the impression that assets were stated at "true value" when in fact no such true value exists; besides being subjectively determined in most cases, values based on future expectations change constantly. Finally, serious doubt has been expressed by some accountants and financial analysts that users of

---

[10]*Additional Views on Accounting Objectives* (pamphlet), Ernst & Ernst (Cleveland: 1972), p. 8.

financial statements really want subjectively determined fair values incorporated into the accounting model.

A switch to fair-value accounting would probably weaken the accounting model as a device for holding management responsible for the custody of economic resources entrusted to it by stockholders. Also, in an era of unprecedented litigation involving auditors, a change to fair-value accounting might so enlarge the opportunities for charging that financial statements were misleading as to reduce the entire financial reporting process to a state of chaos.

It seems doubtful, then, that proposals (1) and (2) listed above are feasible in the near future or that proposal (3) is desirable. As stated earlier, certain assets, such as cash, receivables, and inventories valued on a lower-of-cost-or-market basis, have been reported at fair value for many years. Extension of this practice to inventories when market exceeds cost, investments in listed securities, and plant assets may be possible in some situations. For example, since it is customary to make parenthetical disclosure of the market value of marketable securities, a switch from the cost basis of accounting to fair value of accounting for marketable securities may be less difficult than for most other assets.

Thus the last proposal, that is, "continue the traditional emphasis on historical costs and disclose fair values of assets in supplementary form when fair values can be determined with a reasonable degree of objectivity and when disclosure would be useful," may well represent the most logical course of action in the short run. Many accountants even question the usefulness of this proposal because estimates of fair value lack objectivity. However, when assets increase significantly in value, it may be useful to provide fair-value information in supplementary form despite the absence of precision and objectivity inherent in such information. It is probably safe to conclude that financial reporting would be improved if more relevant information were made available to users even by sacrificing some precision and objectivity. In 1973, the Study Group on Objectives of Financial Statements headed by Robert M. Trueblood recommended that "current values should also be reported when they differ significantly from historical cost."[11] This issue will probably continue to receive considerable attention in the years ahead.[12]

---

[11] *Objectives of Financial Statements,* AICPA (New York: 1973), p. 64.

[12] Additional references on the general topic of fair-value accounting are: Lawrence Revsine, *Replacement Cost Accounting,* Prentice-Hall, Inc. (Englewood Cliffs, N.J.: 1973); Robert R. Sterling (ed.), *Asset Valuation and Income Determination,* Scholars Book Co. (Lawrence: 1971); Edgar O. Edwards and Philip W. Bell, *The Theory and Measurement of Business Income,* University of California Press (Berkeley: 1961); Raymond J. Chambers, *Accounting, Evaluation and Economic Behavior,* Prentice-Hall, Inc. (Englewood Cliffs, N.J.: 1966); George J. Staubus, *A Theory of Accounting to Investors,* University of California Press (Berkeley: 1961); Howard J. Trienens and Daniel U. Smith, "Legal Implications of Current Value Accounting," *Financial Executive* (September 1972), pp. 44–47.

REVIEW QUESTIONS

1 What evidence can you offer in support of the assertion that "the dollar is not a stable unit of value?"

2 List three indices of the general price level in the United States. Which index is considered to be best measure of the general movement in prices?

3 Evaluate the following quotation: "If historical-dollar financial statements were restated to reflect the changing value of the dollar, assets would be stated at market value and net income would not be determined by matching realized revenue with expired costs."

4 Explain how the use of generally accepted accounting principles may result in reporting as income what is in reality a recovery of capital.

5 Explain each of the following:
 a Monetary items
 b Positive monetary position
 c Negative monetary position
 d General price-level gains and losses (or purchasing-power gains and losses)

6 What is meant by the expression **conversion factor?** Compute the conversion factor for land if the general price-level index was 80 on the date the land was acquired and is 144 today.

7 What is meant by **price-level accounting?**

8 a What suggestion is made in **APB Statement No. 3** for reporting price-level information as a supplement to the basic historical-dollar statements?
 b What points should be explained in the notes relating to the price-level information accompanying the basic historical-dollar statements?

9 To what extent have fair values been used by accountants in preparing financial statements?

10 What is the position of the Accounting Principles Board in **Opinion No. 6** regarding the reporting of plant assets at current fair value?

11 What are the causes of changes in the **relative** or **comparative value** of reproducible assets?

12 Distinguish between **relative** or **comparative value changes** for assets and **price-level changes.**

13 The basic method of valuation used in accounting for assets is actual costs less depreciation. At various times during their service life it is possible to estimate the current fair value of such assets by using one of the following methods:
 a Capitalization of net cash inflows (or direct valuation)
 b Liquidation value
 c Replacement cost
 d Specific-price index replacement cost
 Explain the meaning of the term **fair value** and briefly define each of the four methods of arriving at fair value listed above.

14 Evaluate the following quotation: "Accounting is no more than the recording and reporting of transactions. Recognition of current values of assets in the financial statements is neither feasible nor useful; besides, it lacks objectivity."

15 Proposals for the implementation of fair-value accounting may be placed into four categories. List the categories and indicate which one seems to be most feasible at the present time.

EXERCISES

Ex. 25-1 A building was acquired for $400,000 at the beginning of Year 1 when the general price-level index was 60 and has been depreciated at a straight-line rate of $2\frac{1}{2}\%$ per year. At the end of Year 30 the general price-level index is 150. Show how the building and the related accumulated depreciation would be shown at the end of Year 30 in a balance sheet restated for changes in the general price-level index.

Ex. 25-2 For each independent situation below, compute the general price-level gain or loss, assuming that assets and liabilities remained unchanged during the entire period. The general price level rose by 4% during the period:

a Monetary assets	$100,000
Current liabilities	40,000
b Monetary assets	$150,000
Current liabilities	100,000
Long-term liabilities	250,000
c Cash	$ 50,000
Accounts receivable	60,000
Notes receivable	90,000
Inventories	100,000
Investment in common stocks	200,000
Plant and equipment (net of accumulated depreciation)	600,000
Liabilities	575,000
Stockholders' equity	525,000

Ex. 25-3 From the following year-end general price-level indices, compute the conversion factors to restate the financial statements for Year 1, Year 2, and Year 3 in terms of end-of-Year 4 dollars:

Year 1	90
Year 2	100
Year 3	120
Year 4	126

Ex. 25-4 At the beginning of Year 1, when the general price level was 100, John Rover had total assets of $100,000 consisting of $25,000 in cash and $75,000 in copper. At the end of Year 1, when the general price level was 140, the copper was sold for $100,000. Compute the general price-level gain or loss for Year 1. What was the "real" (economic) gain or loss on the sale of the copper?

Ex. 25-5 The Cox Supply Company was formed and began business operations in Year 1. The company adopted the lifo method of inventory pricing and has consistently used this method. At the end of Year 15, the composition of the inventory and the average general price-level index in the year of acquisition were as follows:

Acquired in Year 1 (index = 90) $380,000

Year 3 layer (index = 100) 20,000

Year 10 layer (index = 120) 5,000

Year 15 layer (index = 135) 15,000

   Total inventory at lifo cost, as shown on financial statements at Dec. 31,
   Year 15 .... $420,000

Prepare a schedule restating the inventory at December 31, Year 15, to reflect changes in the general price level.

Ex. 25-6 Western Baking Company bought 10,000 bushels of wheat at $2 per bushel and later another 10,000 bushels of the same grade at $2.50 per bushel. The general price level has risen 10% since the first purchase and 5% since the second purchase, but because of bad weather the market price of wheat is now $4 per bushel. Both lots of wheat are included in the ending inventory. What is the value of each lot of wheat under **(a)** price-level accounting and **(b)** fair-value accounting?

Ex. 25-7 Given below is a balance sheet for Admiralty Consultants at the beginning and end of Year 1, the first year of business:

	Beginning of Year 1	*End of Year 1*
Monetary assets	$60,000	$ 82,000
Office equipment (net)	20,000	18,000
Total	$80,000	$100,000
Liabilities...................................	$10,000	$ 17,000
John Admiralty, capital	70,000	83,000
Total	$80,000	$100,000

The income statement for Year 1 is presented below:

Fees earned		$40,000
Less:		
Operating expenses (excluding depreciation)	$15,000	
Depreciation expense......................................	2,000	17,000
Net income		$23,000

Fees were earned and expenses were incurred evenly through the year. The owner withdrew $10,000 from the business at the end of Year 1. The general price-level index at the beginning of Year 1 was 100; at the end of Year 1 it was 120; and the average for the year was 109. Compute the general price-level gain or loss for Year 1. (Carry the computation of conversion factors to two decimal places.)

Ex. 25-8 a From the information given in Exercise 25-7, prepare a balance sheet for Admiralty Consultants at the end of Year 1, restated for the change in the general price level.
  b Prepare an income statement for Year 1 restated for the change in the general price level. Assume that the general price-level loss (computed in Exercise 25-7) is $12,500.
  c Prepare a statement of owner's capital restated for the change in the general price level.

SHORT CASES FOR ANALYSIS AND DECISION

Case 25-1 A common objective of accountants is to prepare meaningful financial statements. To attain this objective many accountants maintain that the financial statements must be adjusted for changes in the general price level. Other accountants believe that financial statements should continue to be prepared on the basis of unadjusted historical cost.

Instructions
  a List arguments for adjusting financial statements for changes in the general price level.
  b List the arguments for preparing financial statements only on the basis of unadjusted historical cost.
  c In their discussions about accounting for changes in the general price level and the methods of measuring them, uninformed individuals have frequently failed to distinguish between adjustments for changes in the price levels of specific goods and services and adjustments for changes in the general purchasing power of the dollar. What is the distinction? Which are "price-level adjustments"? Discuss.

Case 25-2 Joan Roberts, the controller of the Roberts Company, is discussing a comment you made in the course of presenting your audit report.
  ". . . and frankly," Miss Roberts continued, "I agree that we, too, are responsible for finding ways to produce more relevant financial statements which are as reliable as the ones we now produce.
  "For example, suppose we acquired a finished item for inventory for $40 when the general price-level index was 110. And, later, the item was sold for $75 when the general price-level index was 121 and the current replacement cost was $54. We could calculate and report a 'holding gain' of $10."

Instructions
  a Explain to what extent and how current replacement costs already are used ***within*** the generally accepted accounting principles to value inventories.
  b Show how Miss Roberts computed the holding gain of $10.
  c Why is the use of current replacement cost for ***both*** inventories and cost of goods sold preferred by some accounting authorities to the generally accepted use of fifo or lifo?

Case 25-3 Financial statements are tools for the communication of quantifiable economic information to readers who use them as one of the factors in making a variety of management and investment decisions and judgments. To fulfill this function accounting data should be quantifiable and should also be relevant to the kinds of judgments and decisions made. They should be verifiable and free from personal bias. There are many who believe that for some purposes current cost is a more useful measure than historical cost and recommend that dual statements be prepared showing both historical costs and fair values.

Instructions
  a Discuss the ways in which historical costs and fair values conform to the standards of verifiability and freedom from bias.

b Describe briefly how the fair values of the following assets might be determined.
(1) Inventory
(2) Investments in marketable securities
(3) Equipment and machinery
(4) Natural resources
(5) Goodwill

c While historical cost might be described as being objectively measurable, there is still an element of uncertainty in determining at any point in time the portion that has expired and should be expensed and the unexpired portion that should be carried as an asset. Explain how probability analysis might be employed in estimating the unexpired portion of research and development costs.

Case 25-4 Ray Chen, a small but growing road-building contractor, would like to bid on a contract to rebuild and surface 8 miles of road. The job is considerably larger than any he has attempted in the past and, if he wins the contract, he estimates that he will need a $200,000 line of credit for working capital.

Chen's most recent balance sheet shows that he has a capital of $180,000, of which $150,000 represents the book value of road-building equipment. Most of the equipment was acquired a few years ago at a bankruptcy sale. The equipment has a fair value several times as great as book value. He knows that his bank will not give him a $200,000 line of credit on the basis of a balance sheet which shows his capital at only $180,000. He wants to adjust his accounting records to show the fair value of the equipment and to prepare a revised balance sheet.

Instructions
a List the factors that, alone or in combination, may have caused the difference between the book value and the fair value of the equipment.
b Discuss the propriety of adjusting the accounting records to show the current fair value of the equipment and preparing a revised balance sheet. Suggest a possible alternative approach. Your answer should take into consideration the factors that may have caused the difference between the book value and the current fair value of the equipment.
c Do bankers tend to place as much emphasis on the balance sheet prepared in conventional form as Chen apparently thinks they do?

PROBLEMS

Group A

25A-1 Select the best answer for each of the following items relating to price-level accounting. Choose only one answer for each item.

1 The valuation basis used in conventional (historical-dollar) financial statements is
a Fair value
b Historical cost
c Replacement cost
d A mixture of historical costs and fair values
e None of the above

2 An unacceptable practice for presenting general price-level information in annual reports of corporations is
a The inclusion of general price-level gains and losses on monetary items in the general price-level income statement

b The inclusion of extraordinary items in the general price-level income statement

c The use of charts, ratios, and narrative information

d The use of specific-price indices to restate inventories and plant assets

e None of the above

3 When a general price-level balance sheet is prepared, it should be presented in terms of

a The general purchasing power of the dollar at the end of the latest period presented

b The general purchasing power of the dollar in the base period

c The average general purchasing power of the dollar for the latest period

d The general purchasing power of the dollar at the time the financial statements are issued

e None of the above

4 The restatement of historical-dollar financial statements to reflect general price-level changes results in presenting assets at

a Lower-of-cost-or-market values

b Current appraisal values

c Historical costs adjusted for purchasing-power changes

d Current replacement costs

e None of the above

The following information is applicable to items 5 through 8:

Equipment purchased for $120,000 on January 1, Year 1, when the general price-level index was 100, was sold on December 31, Year 3, at a price of $85,000. The equipment originally was expected to last six years with no salvage value and was depreciated on a straight-line basis. The general price-level index at the end of Year 1 was 125, at Year 2 was 150, and at Year 3 was 175.

5 The general price-level financial statements prepared at the end of Year 1 would include

a Equipment of $150,000, accumulated depreciation of $25,000, and a gain of $30,000

b Equipment of $150,000, accumulated depreciation of $25,000, and no gain or loss

c Equipment of $150,000, accumulated depreciation of $20,000, and a gain of $30,000

d Equipment of $120,000, accumulated depreciation of $20,000, and a gain of $30,000

e None of the above

6 In general price-level comparative financial statements prepared at the end of Year 2, the Year 1 financial statements should show equipment (net of accumulated depreciation) at

a $150,000   **b** $125,000   **c** $100,000   **d** $80,000   **e** None of the above

7 The general price-level financial statements prepared at the end of Year 2 should include depreciation expense of

a $35,000   **b** $30,000   **c** $25,000   **d** $20,000   **e** None of the above

8 The general price-level income statement prepared at the end of Year 3 should include

a A gain of $35,000

b A gain of $25,000

c No gain or loss

d A loss of $20,000

e None of the above

25A-2 The latest income statement for the Sequoia Pacific Corporation is given below (in historical dollars):

SEQUOIA PACIFIC CORPORATION
Income Statement
For Current Year

Sales (net)		$620,000
Cost of goods sold:		
Inventory, Jan. 1 (lifo method)	$ 80,000	
Purchases (net)	450,000	
Cost of goods available for sale	$530,000	
Less: Inventory, Dec. 31 (lifo method)	95,000	435,000
Gross profit on sales		$185,000
Operating expenses:		
Selling (reducing net monetary assets)	$ 30,000	
General (reducing net monetary assets)	25,000	
Depreciation	15,000	70,000
Income before income taxes		$115,000
Income tax expense		50,000
Net income		$ 65,000

All items in the income statement were recorded at a fairly uniform rate throughout the year. The beginning inventory and depreciable assets were acquired when the general price-level index was 125. The lifo layer of $15,000 added to the inventory during the current year consists of goods acquired throughout the year. Changes in the general price-level index during the current year are summarized below:

Beginning of year (conversion factor = 1.200)	150
Average for the year (conversion factor = 1.078)	167
End of year (conversion factor = 1.000)	180

Instructions Prepare a working paper to restate the income statement in terms of the general price-level index at the end of the current year. Assume that the general price-level loss as a result of holding net monetary assets during the year was $5,000.

25A-3 The Sweeney Trading Corporation was organized on December 30, Year 4, by issuing 100,000 shares of $1 par value capital stock for $500,000 in cash, and it started doing business early in Year 5. On January 2, Year 5, it completed the following transaction:

Land	80,000
Buildings	200,000
Equipment	150,000
Cash	300,000
Long-term Notes Payable	130,000
Acquired assets in exchange for cash and notes.	

The changes in the general price-level index during Year 5 are summarized on page 991.

	General price-level index	Conversion factor to restate to end-of-Year 5 dollars
Dec. 31, Year 4 (also for beginning of Year 5) . .	100	1.232
July 1, Year 5 (also the average for Year 5) . . .	110	1.120
Sept. 30, Year 5	115.5	1.067
Dec. 31, Year 5	123.2	1.000

On September 30, Year 5, the corporation declared and paid a dividend of 40 cents per share and issued 10,000 additional shares of capital stock at $8 per share.

The balance sheet at December 31, Year 5 and the income statement for Year 5 (in historical dollars) are summarized below:

Balance Sheet
End of Year 5

Assets		Liabilities & Stockholders' Equity	
Monetary assets	$370,000	Current liabilities	$110,000
Inventory	100,000	Long-term notes payable	130,000
Land	80,000	Capital stock, $1 par value . . .	110,000
Buildings (net)	192,000	Additional paid-in capital	470,000
Equipment (net)	138,000	Retained earnings	60,000
	$880,000		$880,000

Income Statement
for Year 5

Sales (net)		$1,200,000
Cost of goods sold		920,000
Gross profit on sales		$ 280,000
Expenses:		
Depreciation	$ 20,000	
Other (including interest expense and income taxes)	160,000	180,000
Net income		$ 100,000

Sales amounted to approximately $100,000 per month, and expenses accrued at the rate of $15,000 per month. Both cost of goods sold and the ending inventory consist of a representative cross section of merchandise acquired throughout the year.

Instructions
a Prepare a working paper to restate the statement of income and retained earnings for Year 5 for general price-level changes. Compute any general price-level gain or loss in a supporting schedule.

b Prepare a working paper to restate the balance sheet at December 31, Year 5, for general price-level changes.

25A-4 Irell Merchandising Company was organized at the end of Year 9. Irell's management has decided to supplement its Year 12 historical-dollar financial statements with general price-level financial statements. The following general ledger trial balance (historical-dollar basis) and additional information are available:

IRELL MERCHANDISING COMPANY
Trial Balance
December 31, Year 12

	Debit	Credit
Cash and receivables (net)	$ 540,000	
Marketable securities (common stocks)	400,000	
Inventory	440,000	
Equipment	650,000	
Accumulated depreciation		$ 164,000
Accounts payable		300,000
6% first mortgage bonds payable, due in Year 30		500,000
Common stock, $10 par		1,000,000
Retained earnings, Dec. 31, Year 11	46,000	
Sales		1,900,000
Cost of goods sold	1,508,000	
Depreciation expense	65,000	
Other operating expenses and interest expense	215,000	
Totals	$3,864,000	$3,864,000

Additional information
(1) Monetary assets (cash and receivables) exceeded monetary liabilities (accounts payable and bonds payable) by $445,000 at December 31, Year 11. The amounts of monetary items are fixed in terms of numbers of dollars regardless of changes in specific prices or in the general price level.
(2) Net purchases ($1,840,000 in Year 12) and sales were made uniformly throughout Year 12.
(3) Depreciation expense was computed on a straight-line basis, with a full year's depreciation being taken in the year of acquisition and none in the year of retirement. The depreciation rate is 10% and no salvage value is anticipated. Acquisitions and retirements have been made fairly evenly over each year, and the retirements in Year 12 consisted of assets purchased during Year 10 which were scrapped. An analysis of the Equipment account reveals the following:

Year	Beginning balance	Additions	Retirements	Ending balance
10	$ -0-	$550,000	$ -0-	$550,000
11	550,000	10,000	-0-	560,000
12	560,000	150,000	60,000	650,000

(4) The mortgage bonds payable were issued in Year 10 and the marketable securities were purchased at regular intervals during Year 12. Other operating

expenses and interest expense are assumed to be incurred evenly throughout the year.

(5) Assume that Gross National Product Implicit Price Deflators (Year 1 = 100) were as follows:

Annual averages	Index	Conversion factors* (Year 12, 4th quarter = 1.000)
Year 9	113.9	1.128
Year 10	116.8	1.100
Year 11	121.8	1.055
Year 12	126.7	1.014

Quarterly averages		
Year 11 4th	123.5	1.040
Year 12 1st	124.9	1.029
2nd	126.1	1.019
3rd	127.3	1.009
4th	128.5	1.000

*Average index for 4th quarter of Year 12 (128.5) divided by the index for any preceding period. For example, the conversion factor for Year 9 = 128.5 ÷ 113.9 = 1.128.

Instructions

a Prepare a schedule to restate the Equipment account balance at December 31, Year 12, from historical cost to general price-level adjusted dollars.

b Prepare a schedule to analyze in historical dollars the Accumulated Depreciation account for the Year 12.

c Prepare a schedule to analyze in general price-level dollars the Accumulated Depreciation account for Year 12.

d Prepare a schedule to compute Irell Merchandising Company's general price-level gain or loss on its net holdings of monetary items for Year 12 (ignore income tax implications). The schedule should give consideration to appropriate items on or related to the balance sheet and the income statement.

Group B

25B-1 Select the best answer for each of the following items relating to price-level accounting. Choose only one answer for each item:

1 When preparing general price-level financial statements, it would not be appropriate to use

a The lower-of-cost-or-market rule in the valuation of inventories

b Replacement costs in the valuation of plant assets

c The historical-cost basis in reporting income tax expense

d The actual amounts payable in reporting liabilities in the balance sheet

e Any of the above

2 For comparison purposes, general price-level financial statements of earlier periods should be restated to the general purchasing-power dollars

a At the beginning of the base period

b Representing an average for the current (latest) period

c At the beginning of the current (latest) period

d At the end of the current (latest) period
e None of the above

3 In preparing price-level financial statements, monetary items consist of
a Cash items plus all receivables with a fixed maturity date
b Cash, other assets expected to be converted into cash, and current liabilities
c Assets and liabilities whose amounts are fixed by contract or otherwise in terms of dollars, regardless of price-level changes
d Assets and liabilities which are classified as current in the balance sheet
e None of the above

4 In preparing price-level financial statements, a nonmonetary item would be
a Accounts payable
b Long-term bonds payable
c Accounts receivable
d Allowance for uncollectible accounts
e None of the above

5 If land were purchased in Year 10 for $100,000 when the general price-level index was 100 and sold at the end of Year 19 for $160,000 when the index was 170, the general price-level income statement for Year 19 would show
a A general price-level gain of $70,000 and a loss on sale of land of $10,000
b A gain on sale of land of $60,000
c A general price-level loss of $10,000
d A loss on sale of land of $10,000
e None of the above

6 If land were purchased at a cost of $20,000 in January of Year 13 when the general price-level index was 120 and sold in December of Year 19 when the index was 150, the selling price that would result in no gain or loss would be
a $30,000   *b* $24,000   *c* $20,000   *d* $25,000   *e* None of the above

7 If the base year is Year 1 (when the general price-level index = 100) and land is purchased for $50,000 in Year 5 when the general price-level index is 108.5, the cost of the land restated to Year 1 general purchasing power (rounded to the nearest whole dollar) would be
a $54,250   *b* $50,000   *c* $46,083   *d* $45,750   *e* None of the above

8 Assume the same facts as in item (7). The cost of the land restated to December 31, Year 10, general purchasing power when the general price-level index was 119.2 (rounded to the nearest whole dollar) would be
a $59,600   *b* $54,931   *c* $46,083   *d* $45,512   *e* None of the above

25B-2 The income statement for the Sutton-Barna Company for Year 1, in historical dollars, follows:

Sales (net)	$900,000
Cost of goods sold	690,000
	$210,000

Expenses:		
Depreciation	$ 15,000	
Other (including interest expense and income taxes)	120,000	135,000
Net income		$ 75,000

Sales per month generally averaged $75,000 and expenses (including income taxes) were incurred at a relatively even rate throughout the year. Both cost of goods sold and the ending inventory consist of a representative sample of goods purchased during the year.

A comparative balance sheet (in historical dollars) at January 1 and December 31, Year 1, follows:

	Jan. 1, Year 1	Dec. 31, Year 1
Assets		
Monetary assets	$127,500	$ 92,500
Investment in common stock of Y Company	–0–	40,000
Inventory (*fifo method*)	–0–	160,000
Land	60,000	60,000
Building (*net*)	150,000	144,000
Equipment (*net*)	112,500	103,500
Total assets	$450,000	$600,000
Liabilities & Stockholders' Equity		
Current liabilities	$ 25,000	$135,000
Long-term notes payable	175,000	150,000
Capital stock, $5 par value	200,000	200,000
Paid-in capital in excess of par	50,000	50,000
Retained earnings	–0–	65,000
Total liabilities & stockholders' equity	$450,000	$600,000

On April 30 of Year 1, the company invested $40,000 in the common stock of Y Company. Also on April 30, the Sutton-Barna Company declared a dividend of $10,000.

The changes in the general price-level index during Year 1 are summarized below:

	General price-level index	Conversion factor to restate to end-of-Year 1 dollars
January 1	110	1.100
April 30	112	1.080
July 1 (also the average for the year)	115	1.052
December 31	121	1.000

Instructions

a Prepare a working paper to restate the income statement for Year 1 for changes in the general price level. Compute any general price-level gain or loss in a supporting schedule (Schedule A).

b Prepare a working paper to restate the balance sheets at January 1, Year 1, and at December 31, Year 1, for changes in the general price-level index. (Use the form illustrated on page 974.)

c "Prove" the amount of retained earnings needed in part **(b)** to balance total assets (as restated) with total liabilities and stockholders' equity (as restated) by preparing a separate statement of retained earnings (adjusted for changes in the general price-level index).

25B-3 Minahan Corporation purchased a tract of land as an investment in Year 11 for $100,000; late in that year the company decided to construct a shopping center on the site. Construction began in Year 12 and was completed in Year 14; one-third of the construction was completed each year. Minahan originally estimated the costs of the project would be $1,200,000 for materials, $750,000 for labor, $150,000 for variable overhead, and $600,000 for depreciation of plant assets used on this construction project.

Actual costs (excluding depreciation) incurred for construction were:

	Year 12	Year 13	Year 14
Materials	$418,950	$434,560	$462,000
Labor	236,250	274,400	282,000
Variable overhead	47,250	54,208	61,200

Shortly after construction began, Minahan sold the shopping center for $3,000,000 with payment to be made in full on completion in December, Year 14. Of the total sales price, $150,000 was allocated for the land.

The transaction was completed as scheduled and now a controversy has developed between the two major stockholders of the company. One feels the company should have invested in land because a high rate of return was earned on the land. The other feels the original decision was sound and that changes in the general price level which were not anticipated affected the original cost estimates.

You were engaged to furnish guidance to these stockholders in resolving their controversy. As an aid, you obtained the following information:

(1) Using Year 11 as the base year, the general price-level indices for relevant years are: Year 8 = 90, Year 9 = 93, Year 10 = 96, Year 11 = 100, Year 12 = 105, Year 13 = 112, and Year 14 = 120.
(2) The company allocated $200,000 per year for depreciation of plant assets used on this construction project; of that amount $25,000 was for a building purchased in Year 8 and $175,000 was for equipment purchased in Year 10.

Instructions

a Prepare a schedule to restate in base-year (Year 11) dollars the actual construction costs, including depreciation, incurred each year. Disregard income taxes and assume that each year's price-level index was valid for the entire year. Use a fraction for the conversion factor, for example, 100/105, 100/112, etc.

b Prepare a schedule comparing the originally estimated costs of the project with the total actual costs for each element of cost (materials, labor, variable overhead, and depreciation) adjusted to the Year 11 general price level.

c Prepare a schedule to determine the gain or loss on the sale of the shopping center in terms of base-year (Year 11) purchasing power. The gain or loss should be determined separately for the land and the building. Briefly evaluate the results.

25B-4 Beke-Quinn & Company was organized on July 1, 1970. Under the partnership agreement, $900,000 was provided by Beke and $600,000 by Quinn as initial capital; income and losses were to be shared in the same ratio as the initial capital contributions. No additional capital contributions have been made.

The December 31, 1975, balance sheet appears at the top of page 997.

Assets

Cash	$ 500,500
Accounts receivable, net of allowance for uncollectible accounts	950,000
Inventory (lifo method)	1,500,000
Unexpired insurance	18,000
Land	58,000
Machinery, net of accumulated depreciation	1,473,500
Total assets	$4,500,000

Liabilities & Capital

Current liabilities	$1,475,000
Beke, capital	1,815,000
Quinn, capital	1,210,000
Total liabilities & capital	$4,500,000

Beke and Quinn are considering selling their business but are concerned that the financial statements do not reveal its current worth. You have been requested to assist in determining the current fair value of the assets.

You compile the following information in addition to the asset section of the balance sheet:

(1) An aging of accounts receivable disclosed the following:

Year accounts originated	Gross amount	Allowance for uncollectible accounts	Net valuation
1972	$ 40,000	$ 35,000	$ 5,000
1973	125,000	105,000	20,000
1974	160,000	67,500	92,500
1975	925,000	92,500	832,500
Totals	$1,250,000	$300,000	$950,000

A review of past experience shows that all receivables over two years old have been uncollectible; those over one year old have been 50% collectible; and those less than one year old have been 90% collectible.

(2) The inventory level has been increasing and its cost has been determined using the last-in, first-out cost flow assumption. The cost of the last-in, first-out layers at the average price for the indicated year of acquisition and the inventory specific-price increases have been as follows:

Last-in, first-out layers		Specific-price increases	
Year acquired	Cost	Period	Increase
1971	$ 60,000	1971–1975	20%
1972	150,000	1972–1975	18%
1973	240,000	1973–1975	15%
1974	350,000	1974–1975	11%
1975	700,000	1975	5%
	$1,500,000		

(3) Machinery was purchased in 1971, 1973, and 1974 for $500,000, $850,000, and $660,000, respectively. The straight-line depreciation method and a 10-year estimated life have been used for all machinery, with a half-year of depreciation taken in the year of acquisition. The experience of other companies over the last several years indicates that the machinery can be sold at 125% of its book value.

(4) An independent appraisal made in December, 1975, placed a current fair value of $70,000 on the land.

Instructions Prepare a comparative statement of assets showing historical costs and current fair values at December 31, 1975. Supporting schedules should be in good form.

Present and future value of cash flows

The principles of accumulating and discounting cash flows due at varying points in time through the use of compound interest concepts are summarized in this appendix. Compound interest concepts have a wide application in business and economic analysis. Such concepts are fundamental in evaluating many types of business decisions and in preparing financial statements.

All business organizations are at some time faced with two basic types of decisions: (1) committing present funds in the expectation of realizing periodic benefits in future periods; (2) receiving present funds in return for a promise to pay or deliver resources at some future time. These "investment-and-return" and "borrowing-and-repayment" situations have an important common characteristic: The difference in the *timing* of the receipts and payments has an important effect on the worth of the various commitments and thus on the value of the resulting assets and liabilities. Consequently investment and borrowing decisions should be made only after a careful analysis of the relative values of the prospective cash outlays and inflows. Measuring these values involves the use of compound interest formulas and tables.

In the financial accounting area, the accountant encounters a number of situations where an objective measure of what has happened is dependent on a present evaluation of future prospects. An installment note receivable, for example, represents a series of future cash inflows. The proceeds of a bond issue reflect the present value of the promise to make a series of future payments of principal and interest. Leases and pension plans are arranged on compound interest principles. To deal effectively with financial reporting problems, the accountant should understand and be able to measure the present value of prospective cash inflows and outflows. This measurement also requires an understanding of compound interest concepts.

The significance of simple and compound interest

Interest is fundamentally the growth in a principal sum representing the fee charged for the use of money for a given time period. Our concept of economic earnings (whether in the form of interest or some other kind of return on investment) is periodic. Economic activity is carried on during specifiable time periods and we typically think of return on investment in terms of return per year.

Simple interest is the return on (or growth of) a principal sum for one time period. We may also think of simple interest as a return for more than one time period if we assume that the interest (growth) itself does not earn a return, but this kind of situation occurs rarely in the real world. Simple interest is usually applicable only to short-term investment and borrowing transactions involving a time span of one year or less.

Compound interest is the return on (or growth of) a principal sum for two or more time periods, assuming that the growth in each time period is added to the principal sum at the end of the period and earns a return in all subsequent periods. Many important investment and borrowing transactions involve more than one time period. Businessmen evaluate investment opportunities in terms of a series of periodic returns, each of which may be reinvested in turn to yield additional returns.

Simple interest formula[1]

The basic components of the computation of simple interest I_s are the principal amount p_s, the rate of interest r, and the time t. The basic formula is:

$$I_s = p_s \times r \times t \quad \text{or} \quad I_s = p_s rt$$

Formula for simple interest

It is assumed that the interest rate and time are expressed in common units; that is, if r is an annual rate then t is expressed in years. Interest rates are expressed in terms of annual rates unless otherwise stated.

Example 1 Find the interest on a loan of $1,000 for two months at 6%.

Solution $I_s = p_s rt = \$1{,}000 \times .06 \times \frac{1}{6} = \underline{\underline{\$10}}$

---

[1] The subscript s is used to distinguish symbols for simple interest from symbols relating to compound interest used in later sections of this appendix.

The *amount* to which a principal sum will accumulate at interest during a given time period, designated by the symbol a_s, is the principal sum plus the interest; this may be expressed:

Amount = principal + interest
$$a_s = p_s + (p_s rt)$$

or

$$a_s = p_s(1 + rt)$$

Formula for amount at simple interest

Example 2 To what amount would $1,000 accumulate in three months if invested at 6% annual interest?

Solution $a_s = p_s(1 + rt) = \$1,000[1 + (.06 \times \frac{1}{4})]$

$$= \$1,000(1.015) = \underline{\underline{\$1,015}}$$

If we wish to know the present value p_s of a future sum that includes simple interest, the formula for determining the amount of the future sum a_s may be adapted by solving for the principal amount p_s, as follows:

We know that $a_s = p_s(1 + rt)$

Formula for present value at simple interest

Solve for p_s $p_s = \dfrac{a_s}{1 + rt}$

Example 3 Able has the prospect of receiving $1,030 at the end of six months. What is the present value of this prospect if money is worth 6% per year?

Solution $p_s = \dfrac{a_s}{(1 + rt)} = \dfrac{\$1,030}{(1 + .06 \times \frac{1}{2})} = \dfrac{\$1,030}{1.03} = \underline{\underline{\$1,000}}$

We can diagram the simple interest relationships just described as illustrated on page 1002.

COMPOUND INTEREST

Future value of a single sum at compound interest

Suppose that, knowing only simple interest formulas, we wished to determine the amount to which $100,000 would accumulate at 6% annual interest for three years, assuming that the interest at the end of each

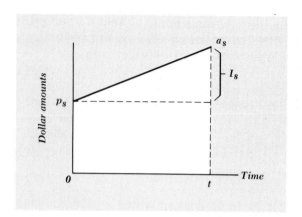

year is added to the principal and in turn earns interest. We might compute this amount (which we shall designate a), as follows:

$$p \qquad\quad r \quad t = \qquad a$$

Amount at end of 1st year: $\$100,000(1 + .06 \times 1) = \$106,000.00$
Amount at end of 2d year: $\$106,000(1 + .06 \times 1) = \$112,360.00$
Amount at end of 3d year: $\$112,360(1 + .06 \times 1) = \$119,101.60$

On the basis of the formulas previously developed, we can designate each of the above three amounts as follows:

Amount at end of 1st year: $p(1 + rt)$
Amount at end of 2d year: $p(1 + rt)(1 + rt)$, or $p(1 + rt)^2$
Amount at end of 3d year: $p(1 + rt)(1 + rt)(1 + rt)$, or $p(1 + rt)^3$

The answer obtained above could therefore have been obtained directly as follows:

$$a = p(1 + rt)^3 = \$100,000(1 + .06 \times 1)^3 = \$100,000(1.06)^3$$
$$= \$100,000(1.191016) = \underline{\underline{\$119,101.60}}$$

Simplifying the Formula The general situation in which a sum of money is accumulated at compound interest is shown in the diagram below:

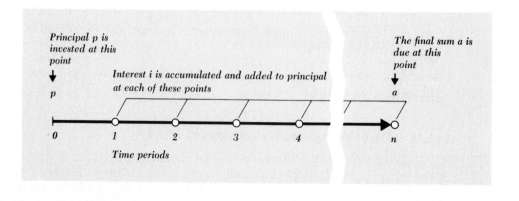

To develop a general formula that will enable us to deal with the entire class of fact situations which fit the above picture, it is useful to define the following symbols:

i = the rate of interest *per time period.* (Note that this is merely the substitution of the single term i for the multiplied term rt used in simple interest formulas. For example, if i is the interest rate per year, $i = r \times 1$; if i is the interest rate per quarter, then $i = r \times \frac{1}{4}$, etc.)

p = the principal sum which accumulates at i interest per period, compounded once each period.

n = the number of periods during which the principal sum accumulates at compound interest.

a = the amount to which a principal sum accumulates at compound interest.

Using these symbols, the formula for determining the amount a of a principal sum p at compound interest of i rate per period for n periods becomes:

$$a = p(1 + i)^n$$

Formula for the amount of a single sum p for n periods at i interest per period

Example 4 If $10,000 is invested for three years at 5% interest per year, compounded annually, how much will be accumulated by the end of the third year?

Solution $a = p(1 + i)^n = \$10,000(1.05)^3 = \$10,000(1.157625) = \underline{\$11,576.25}$

Amount of $1 It will also be useful to define the following symbol:

$a_{\overline{n}|i}$ = the amount to which $1 will accumulate at i rate of interest per period for n periods, assuming that i is compounded (that is, added to the principal) once each period. This symbol is read "small a angle n at i." The amount to which $1 will accumulate at 3% interest compounded annually for 12 years would be stated "small a angle 12 at 3%" and would be written $a_{\overline{12}|3\%}$.

The advantage of defining an amount at compound interest in terms of $1 is that the result may then be multiplied by **any** principal sum to obtain a desired accumulation. The formula for $a_{\overline{n}|i}$ is $1 (1 + i)^n$; since the principal of $1 is always understood and multiplication by 1 has no effect on the result, the $1 may be omitted and the formula written simply as follows:

$$a_{\overline{n}|i} = (1 + i)^n$$

Formula for amount of $1 at i compound interest for n periods

Note in particular that the symbols a and $a_{\overline{n}|i}$ are two distinct terms. The symbol a represents **any** dollar amount due or payable at some future date. The symbol $a_{\overline{n}|i}$ is the **specific** amount to which $1 will accumulate in n periods at i rate of interest per period.

Table for amount of $1   The amount of $1 can be computed for any given values of n and i by the process of repeated multiplication. However, tables have been constructed which make it possible to evaluate $a_{\overline{n}|i}$ by simply referring to the appropriate line and column in the table. Table 1, showing the amount of $1 for various periods at selected interest rates, appears on page 1005.

The amount of $1 for any number of periods n and varying rates of interest i may be determined by finding the appropriate line and column in Table 1. For example: $a_{\overline{6}|8\%} = 1.5869$. The value given in the table may be multiplied by any principal sum to obtain the amount to which that sum will accumulate at compound interest. For example, $10,000 will accumulate in six years at 8% interest per year to $15,869 ($10,000 \times 1.5869$).

Note that i and n are related, since i is defined as the interest rate **per time period,** and there are n specified time periods. When interest is expressed in terms of an annual rate but the compounding period is less than one year, it is necessary to convert the annual rate r into the rate i per compounding period by dividing the annual rate by the number of interest periods per year, and to adjust n by multiplying the number of years by the number of compounding periods per year. To illustrate, if we want to know the amount to which $1 will accumulate in five years at 8% annual interest compounded **quarterly,** we have $i = .08 \div 4 = .02$; and $n = 4 \times 5 = 20$. We would thus read the result from a table: $a_{\overline{20}|2\%}$.

Example 5   Mock invested $10,000 five years ago. During the first two years his investment earned 6% compounded semiannually. During the last three years it earned 8% compounded quarterly. How much does Mock have at the end of the fifth year?

Solution   At the end of the second year Mock had

$10,000 \times a_{\overline{4}|3\%} = \$10,000(1.1255) = \underline{\underline{\$11,255}}$

During the last three years this amount ($11,255) grew at the rate of 8% compounded quarterly and became

$11,255 \times a_{\overline{12}|2\%} = \$11,255(1.2682) = \underline{\underline{\$14,274.}}$

Present value of a future single sum at compound discount

Because many business decisions are based on the present worth of a prospective inflow or outflow of cash, the concept of present value is more widely applicable in accounting than the concept of accumulation.

Table 1   Future Amount of \$1 at Compound Interest Due in n Periods: $a_{\overline{n}|i} = (1+i)^n$

					i = interest rate per period					
n = number of periods	1.0%	1.5%	2.0%	2.5%	3.0%	4.0%	5.0%	6.0%	8.0%	10.0%
1	1.0100	1.0150	1.0200	1.0250	1.0300	1.0400	1.0500	1.0600	1.0800	1.1000
2	1.0201	1.0302	1.0404	1.0506	1.0609	1.0816	1.1025	1.1236	1.1664	1.2100
3	1.0303	1.0457	1.0612	1.0769	1.0927	1.1249	1.1576	1.1910	1.2597	1.3310
4	1.0406	1.0614	1.0824	1.1038	1.1255	1.1699	1.2155	1.2625	1.3605	1.4641
5	1.0510	1.0773	1.1041	1.1314	1.1593	1.2167	1.2163	1.3382	1.4693	1.6105
6	1.0615	1.0934	1.1262	1.1597	1.1941	1.2653	1.3401	1.4185	1.5869	1.7716
7	1.0721	1.1098	1.1487	1.1887	1.2299	1.3159	1.4071	1.5036	1.7138	1.9487
8	1.0829	1.1265	1.1717	1.2184	1.2668	1.3686	1.4775	1.5938	1.8509	2.1436
9	1.0937	1.1434	1.1951	1.2489	1.3048	1.4233	1.5513	1.6895	1.9990	2.3579
10	1.1046	1.1605	1.2190	1.2801	1.3439	1.4802	1.6289	1.7908	2.1589	2.5937
11	1.1157	1.1779	1.2434	1.3121	1.3842	1.5395	1.7103	1.8983	2.3316	2.8531
12	1.1268	1.1956	1.2682	1.3449	1.4258	1.6010	1.7959	2.0122	2.5182	3.1384
13	1.1381	1.2136	1.2936	1.3785	1.4685	1.6651	1.8856	2.1329	2.7196	3.4523
14	1.1495	1.2318	1.3195	1.4130	1.5126	1.7317	1.9799	2.2609	2.9372	3.7975
15	1.1610	1.2502	1.3459	1.4483	1.5580	1.8009	2.0789	2.3966	3.1722	4.1772
16	1.1726	1.2690	1.3728	1.4845	1.6047	1.8730	2.1829	2.5404	3.4259	4.5950
17	1.1843	1.2880	1.4002	1.5216	1.6528	1.9479	2.2920	2.6928	3.7000	5.0545
18	1.1961	1.3073	1.4282	1.5597	1.7024	2.0258	2.4066	2.8543	3.9960	5.5599
19	1.2081	1.3270	1.4568	1.5987	1.7535	2.1068	2.5270	3.0256	4.3157	6.1159
20	1.2202	1.3469	1.4859	1.6386	1.8061	2.1911	2.6533	3.2071	4.6610	6.7275
21	1.2324	1.3671	1.5157	1.6796	1.8603	2.2788	2.7860	3.3996	5.0338	7.4002
22	1.2447	1.3876	1.5460	1.7216	1.9161	2.3699	2.9253	3.6035	5.4365	8.1403
23	1.2572	1.4084	1.5769	1.7646	1.9736	2.4647	3.0715	3.8197	5.8715	8.9543
24	1.2697	1.4295	1.6084	1.8087	2.0328	2.5633	3.2251	4.0489	6.3412	9.8497
25	1.2824	1.4509	1.6406	1.8539	2.0938	2.6658	3.3864	4.2919	6.8485	10.8347
26	1.2953	1.4727	1.6734	1.9003	2.1566	2.7725	3.5557	4.5494	7.3964	11.9182
27	1.3082	1.4948	1.7069	1.9478	2.2213	2.8834	3.7335	4.8223	7.9881	13.1100
28	1.3213	1.5172	1.7410	1.9965	2.2879	2.9987	3.9201	5.1117	8.6271	14.4210
29	1.3345	1.5400	1.7758	2.0464	2.3566	3.1187	4.1161	5.4184	9.3173	15.8631
30	1.3478	1.5631	1.8114	2.0976	2.4273	3.2434	4.3219	5.7435	10.0627	17.4494
35	1.4166	1.6839	1.9999	2.3732	2.8139	3.9461	5.5160	7.6861	14.7853	28.1024
40	1.4889	1.8140	2.2080	2.6851	3.2620	4.8010	7.0400	10.2857	21.7245	45.2593
45	1.5648	1.9542	2.4379	3.0379	3.7816	5.8412	8.9850	13.7646	31.9204	72.8905
50	1.6446	2.1052	2.6916	3.4371	4.3839	7.1067	11.4674	18.4202	46.9016	117.3909

The general situation involving the determination of the present value of a future single sum is shown on the following time diagram:

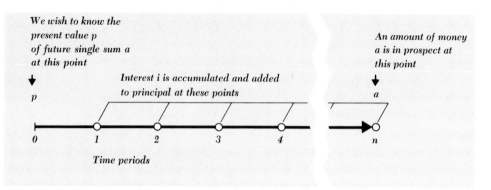

We wish to know the present value p of future single sum a at this point

An amount of money a is in prospect at this point

p

Interest i is accumulated and added to principal at these points

a

0   1   2   3   4   n

Time periods

From this diagram we see that finding the present value of a single future sum is a reversal of the process of finding the amount to which a present sum will accumulate. As in the case of simple interest, the formula for present value may be derived from the formula we have already developed for the amount of *any* principal sum:

We know that $a = p(1 + i)^n$

If we solve for p by dividing both sides of the equation by $(1 + i)^n$, we get

$$p = \frac{a}{(1 + i)^n} \quad \text{or} \quad p = \frac{1}{(1 + i)^n} \times a$$

Formula for present value of any future amount a

Present value of $1   It is clear that we can determine the present value p of any future amount a by dividing the amount by $(1 + i)^n$. However, since multiplication is usually an easier arithmetic process than division, it will be useful for computational purposes to define the following symbol:

$p_{\overline{n}|i}$ = the present value of $1 due in n periods at i rate of interest per period, assuming that i is compounded at the end of each period. This symbol is read "small p angle n at i." The present value of $1 due in 18 years at 4% annual interest would be stated "small p angle 18 at 4%" and would be written $p_{\overline{18}|4\%}$.

The formula for the present value of $1 is:

$$p_{\overline{n}|i} = \frac{1}{(1 + i)^n}$$

Formula for present value of $1 due in n periods at i rate of interest per period

Table for present value of $1 It is apparent that a table evaluating $1/(1 + i)^n$ at varying rates of interest and for different n's would be useful. Such a table (Table 2) appears on page 1008.

The present value of $1 for a given value of n and i may be read directly from the appropriate line and column of Table 2. For example, $p_{\overline{18}|4\%} = .4936$. This value may be multiplied by any future amount due in 18 periods to determine its present value at 4%.

Example 6 Find the present value of $20,000 due in 18 periods at 4%.

Solution $20,000 \times p_{\overline{18}|4\%} = \$20,000(.4936) = \underline{\underline{\$9,872}}$

Relation of Amounts and Present Values to n and i In dealing with computations of accumulations and present values, it is useful to have some general idea of relationships as a basis for verifying the reasonableness of results. We can reason, for example, that $a_{\overline{n}|i}$ should grow *larger* for increasing rates of interest i and for an increasing number of periods n, since the longer a principal sum accumulates the larger it grows, and the higher the rate of interest the larger the future amount. The reverse situation is true of present values. The longer the time period n or the higher the rate of interest i, the *smaller* will be the present value of any future sum. This squares with our intuition that a far-distant prospect is worth less than one in the near future, and that the higher the rate of interest that can be earned on a present-dollar amount, the less valuable is the prospect of receiving an amount of money in the future.

Compound Interest and Compound Discount The terms *compound interest* or *compound discount* are sometimes used to describe the excess of the amount to which an investment will grow at compound interest over the original investment (principal sum). Compound interest or discount may thus be defined in general as $a - p$.

If we express the concepts of compound interest I and compound discount D in terms of $1, then we may define the following terms:

$$I_{\overline{n}|i} = (1 + i)^n - 1 = a_{\overline{n}|i} - 1$$

$$D_{\overline{n}|i} = 1 - \frac{1}{(1 + i)^n} = 1 - p_{\overline{n}|i}$$

Tables are not normally constructed for values of I and D at $1, since these quantities can always be obtained from tables for a and p by a simple process of subtraction.

ANNUITIES

Cases involving the accumulation of a single principal sum or the present value of a single future amount do not occur as frequently in business as do situations in which a series of equal dollar amounts are to be paid

Table 2 Present Value of $1 at Compound Interest Due in n Periods: $p_{\overline{n}|i} = \dfrac{1}{(1+i)^n}$

i = interest rate per period

n = number of periods	2.0%	2.5%	3.0%	4.0%	5.0%	6.0%	8.0%	10.0%	15.0%	20.0%
1	.9804	.9756	.9709	.9615	.9524	.9434	.9259	.9091	.8696	.8333
2	.9612	.9518	.9426	.9246	.9070	.8900	.8573	.8264	.7561	.6944
3	.9423	.9286	.9151	.8890	.8638	.8396	.7938	.7513	.6575	.5787
4	.9238	.9060	.8885	.8548	.8227	.7921	.7350	.6830	.5718	.4823
5	.9057	.8839	.8626	.8219	.7835	.7473	.6806	.6209	.4972	.4019
6	.8880	.8623	.8375	.7903	.7462	.7050	.6302	.5645	.4323	.3349
7	.8706	.8413	.8131	.7599	.7107	.6651	.5835	.5132	.3759	.2791
8	.8535	.8207	.7894	.7307	.6768	.6274	.5403	.4665	.3269	.2326
9	.8368	.8007	.7664	.7026	.6446	.5919	.5002	.4241	.2843	.1938
10	.8203	.7812	.7441	.6756	.6139	.5584	.4632	.3855	.2472	.1615
11	.8043	.7621	.7224	.6496	.5847	.5268	.4289	.3505	.2149	.1346
12	.7885	.7436	.7014	.6246	.5568	.4970	.3971	.3186	.1869	.1122
13	.7730	.7254	.6810	.6006	.5303	.4688	.3677	.2897	.1625	.0935
14	.7579	.7077	.6611	.5775	.5051	.4423	.3405	.2633	.1413	.0779
15	.7430	.6905	.6419	.5553	.4810	.4173	.3152	.2394	.1229	.0649
16	.7284	.6736	.6232	.5339	.4581	.3936	.2919	.2176	.1069	.0541
17	.7142	.6572	.6050	.5134	.4363	.3714	.2703	.1978	.0929	.0451
18	.7002	.6412	.5874	.4936	.4155	.3503	.2502	.1799	.0808	.0376
19	.6864	.6255	.5703	.4746	.3957	.3305	.2317	.1635	.0703	.0313
20	.6730	.6103	.5537	.4564	.3769	.3118	.2145	.1486	.0611	.0261
21	.6598	.5954	.5375	.4388	.3589	.2942	.1987	.1351	.0531	.0217
22	.6468	.5809	.5219	.4220	.3418	.2775	.1839	.1228	.0462	.0181
23	.6342	.5667	.5067	.4057	.3256	.2618	.1703	.1117	.0402	.0151
24	.6217	.5529	.4919	.3901	.3101	.2470	.1577	.1015	.0349	.0126
25	.6095	.5394	.4776	.3751	.2953	.2330	.1460	.0923	.0304	.0105
26	.5976	.5262	.4637	.3607	.2812	.2198	.1352	.0839	.0264	.0087
27	.5859	.5134	.4502	.3468	.2678	.2074	.1252	.0763	.0230	.0073
28	.5744	.5009	.4371	.3335	.2551	.1956	.1159	.0693	.0200	.0061
29	.5631	.4887	.4243	.3207	.2429	.1846	.1073	.0630	.0174	.0051
30	.5521	.4767	.4120	.3083	.2314	.1741	.0994	.0573	.0151	.0042
35	.5000	.4214	.3554	.2534	.1813	.1301	.0676	.0356	.0075	.0017
40	.4529	.3724	.3066	.2083	.1420	.0972	.0460	.0221	.0037	.0007
45	.4102	.3292	.2644	.1712	.1113	.0727	.0313	.0137	.0019	.0003
50	.3715	.2909	.2281	.1407	.0872	.0543	.0213	.0085	.0009	.0001

or received periodically. Borrowings to be repaid in installments, investments that will be partially recovered at regular intervals, cost savings that occur repeatedly—all are common business events.

It is possible to deal with cases involving periodic receipts or payments by repeating the process of computing the amount or present value of each individual sum and adding to obtain the desired result for the whole series. Fortunately, in certain standard cases, we can greatly simplify the arithmetic by using *annuity formulas and tables.*

An investment situation which involves a series of equal payments or receipts (usually called *rents*) at regular time intervals is called an *annuity.* The regular time intervals between rents are assumed to be equal in length, but they may be any period, such as a month, a half-year, a year, etc. It is also assumed in an annuity that *interest is compounded once each time period.*[2]

Computing amount of an ordinary annuity

An *ordinary annuity* is one in which equal periodic rents occur at the end of each period. The amount of an ordinary annuity is the sum of the periodic rents and the compound interest that accumulates on these rents. If we designate the amount of an ordinary annuity as A, the equal periodic rents as R, and the number of time periods as n, an ordinary annuity situation might be diagrammed as follows:

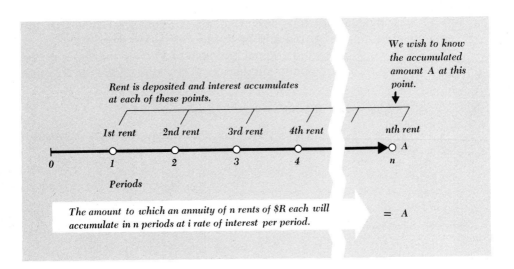

We wish to know the accumulated amount A at this point.

Rent is deposited and interest accumulates at each of these points.

1st rent   2nd rent   3rd rent   4th rent   nth rent

0   1   2   3   4   n   = A

Periods

The amount to which an annuity of n rents of $R each will accumulate in n periods at i rate of interest per period.

---

[2] It is possible to compute amounts and present values when interest is compounded more frequently than rents are received by determining the effective rate of interest for each rental period. Similarly, we can handle cases in which rents are received more frequently than compounding periods by computing an effective rent per compounding period. These situations occur rarely, however, and are not discussed here.

Formula for the future amount of an ordinary annuity We might compute the future amount of an ordinary annuity by summing the accumulated amounts of the individual rents. For example, the amount of an annuity of $1 per period for four periods at 6% interest might be determined as follows:

The first rent accumulates at 6% for three periods and grows to

$1(a_{\overline{3}|6\%}) = \$1(1.1910)$ $1.191

The second rent accumulates at 6% for two periods and grows to

$1(a_{\overline{2}|6\%}) = \$1(1.1236)$ 1.124

The third rent accumulates at 6% for one period and grows to

$1(a_{\overline{1}|6\%}) = \$1(1.06)$ 1.060

The fourth rent is due at the end of the annuity period 1.000

Amount of ordinary annuity of $1 for four periods at 6% $4.375

For future reference, let us define the following symbol:

$A_{\overline{n}|i}$ = the amount to which an ordinary annuity of $1 per period will accumulate in n periods at i rate of interest per period. This symbol is read "capital A angle n at i"; for example, the amount to which an annuity of $1 will accumulate in four periods at 6% is stated "capital A angle 4 at 6%" and is written $A_{\overline{4}|6\%}$.

We can derive a formula for arriving at the future amount of an annuity of $1 (A_{\overline{n}|i})$ by examining the relationship between compound interest and an annuity of the amounts of the interest. To illustrate, assume the sum of $1 was invested for four periods of 6% interest. We know that the accumulated amount at the end of the fourth period would be: $a_{\overline{4}|6\%} = 1.2625. If we subtract the original principal of $1 from this amount, we get the amount of compound interest on $1 for four periods at 6%; that is,

$$I_{\overline{4}|6\%} = (a_{\overline{4}|6\%} - 1) = (\$1.06)^4 - \$1 = \$1.2625 - \$1 = \$.2625$$

Now examine the diagram below of just ***the annuity of the 6% interest*** on $1:

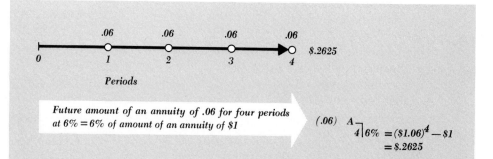

Future amount of an annuity of .06 for four periods at 6% = 6% of amount of an annuity of $1

$(.06) \ A_{\overline{4}|6\%} = (\$1.06)^4 - \$1$
$= \$.2625$

Observe that the amount of compound interest on $1 is nothing more than the future amount of an annuity of 6 cents per period for four periods at 6%. Furthermore, note that if we divide both sides of the above equation by the interest rate (6% in this case), we can convert the equation to one that will give us the *future amount of an ordinary annuity of $1* per period for four periods at 6%: (We know from our previous computation that this amount should be $4.375.)

Divide by 6%: $\dfrac{.06\ A_{\overline{4}|6\%}}{.06} = \dfrac{(\$1.06)^4 - \$1}{.06}$

Therefore $A_{\overline{4}|6\%} = \dfrac{(\$1.06)^4 - \$1}{.06} = \dfrac{\$.2625}{.06} = \$4.375$

The reasoning we have applied to the specific case of an annuity of $1 for four periods at 6% can now be generalized for any n and any i as follows:

$$A_{\overline{n}|i} = \frac{(1 + i)^n - 1}{i}$$

Formula for future amount of annuity of $1 for n periods at i interest per period

The formula for the future amount of *any* annuity for R dollars per period may be stated:

$$A = R(A_{\overline{n}|i}) = R\left(\frac{(1 + i)^n - 1}{i}\right)$$

Formula for amount of annuity of R for n periods at i interest per period

Table for the future amount of an ordinary annuity of $1 A table for the future amount of an ordinary annuity of $1 for varying periods and interest rates appear on page 1012 (Table 3).

By multiplying the values found in the appropriate line and column of Table 3 by the dollar amount of any rents involved in an ordinary annuity, the accumulated sum of the rents and compound interest to the date of the last rent may be readily obtained.

Example 7. Given periodic rents, compute future amount of ordinary annuity Jones plans to deposit $1,000 at the end of each quarter for six years in a savings account that will earn interest at the rate of 4% compounded quarterly. How much will he have in the fund at the end of the sixth year?

Table 3 Future Amount of an Ordinary Annuity of $1 per Period: $A_{\overline{n}|i} = \dfrac{(1+i)^n - 1}{i}$

n = number of periods	1.0%	1.5%	2.0%	2.5%	3.0%	4.0%	5.0%	6.0%	8.0%	10.0%
						i = interest rate per period				
1	1.0000	1.0000	1.0000	1.0000	1.0000	1.0000	1.0000	1.0000	1.0000	1.0000
2	2.0100	2.0150	2.0200	2.0250	2.0300	2.0400	2.0500	2.0600	2.0800	2.1000
3	3.0301	3.0452	3.0604	3.0756	3.0909	3.1216	3.1525	3.1836	3.2464	3.3100
4	4.0604	4.0909	4.1216	4.1525	4.1836	4.2465	4.3101	4.3746	4.5061	4.6410
5	5.1010	5.1523	5.2040	5.2563	5.3091	5.4163	5.5256	5.6371	5.8666	6.1051
6	6.1520	6.2296	6.3081	6.3877	6.4684	6.6330	6.8019	6.9753	7.3359	7.7156
7	7.2135	7.3230	7.4343	7.5474	7.6625	7.8983	8.1420	8.3938	8.9228	9.4872
8	8.2857	8.4328	8.5830	8.7361	8.8923	9.2142	9.5491	9.8975	10.6366	11.4359
9	9.3685	9.5593	9.7546	9.9545	10.1591	10.5828	11.0266	11.4913	12.4876	13.5795
10	10.4622	10.7027	10.9497	11.2034	11.4639	12.0061	12.5779	13.1808	14.4866	15.9374
11	11.5668	11.8633	12.1687	12.4835	12.8078	13.4864	14.2068	14.9716	16.6455	18.5312
12	12.6825	13.0412	13.4121	13.7956	14.1920	15.0258	15.9171	16.8699	18.9771	21.3843
13	13.8093	14.2368	14.6803	15.1404	15.6178	16.6268	17.7130	18.8821	21.4953	24.5227
14	14.9474	15.4504	15.9739	16.5190	17.0863	18.2919	19.5986	21.0151	24.2149	27.9750
15	16.0969	16.6821	17.2934	17.9319	18.5989	20.0236	21.5786	23.2760	27.1521	31.7725
16	17.2579	17.9324	18.6393	19.3802	20.1569	21.8245	23.6575	25.6725	30.3243	35.9497
17	18.4304	19.2014	20.0121	20.8647	21.7616	23.6975	25.8404	28.2129	33.7502	40.5447
18	19.6147	20.4894	21.4123	22.3863	23.4144	25.6454	28.1324	30.9057	37.4502	45.5992
19	20.8109	21.7967	22.8406	23.9460	25.1169	27.6712	30.5390	33.7600	41.4463	51.1591
20	22.0190	23.1237	24.2974	25.5447	26.8704	29.7781	33.0660	36.7856	45.7620	57.2750
21	23.2392	24.4705	25.7833	27.1833	28.6765	31.9692	35.7193	39.9927	50.4229	64.0025
22	24.4716	25.8376	27.2990	28.8629	30.5368	34.2480	38.5052	43.3923	55.4568	71.4027
23	25.7163	27.2251	28.8450	30.5844	32.4529	36.6179	41.4305	46.9958	60.8933	79.5430
24	26.9735	28.6335	30.4219	32.3490	34.4265	39.0826	44.5020	50.8156	66.7648	88.4973
25	28.2432	30.0630	32.0303	34.1578	36.4593	41.6459	47.7271	54.8645	73.1059	98.3471
26	29.5256	31.5140	33.6709	36.0117	38.5530	44.3117	51.1135	59.1564	79.9544	109.1818
27	30.8209	32.9867	35.3443	37.9120	40.7096	47.0842	54.6691	63.7058	87.3508	121.0999
28	32.1291	34.4815	37.0512	39.8598	42.9309	49.9676	58.4026	68.5281	95.3388	134.2099
29	33.4504	35.9987	38.7922	41.8563	45.2189	52.9663	62.3227	73.6398	103.9659	148.6309
30	34.7849	37.5387	40.5681	43.9027	47.5754	56.0849	66.4388	79.0582	113.2832	164.4940
35	41.6603	45.5921	49.9945	54.9282	60.4621	73.6522	90.3203	111.4348	172.3168	271.0244
40	48.8864	54.2679	60.4020	67.4026	75.4013	95.0255	120.7998	154.7620	259.0565	442.5926
45	56.4811	63.6142	71.8927	81.5161	92.7199	121.0294	159.7002	212.7435	386.5056	718.9048
50	64.4632	73.6828	84.5794	97.4843	112.7969	152.6671	209.3480	290.3359	573.7702	1163.9085

Solution

Future amount $= R(A_{\overline{n}|i}) = \$1,000(A_{\overline{24}|1\%}) = \$1,000(26.9735) = \underline{\underline{\$26,973.50}}$

Example 8. Given desired future amount of ordinary annuity, compute periodic rents Smith can invest money to earn an annual return of 8% compounded semiannually. How much should he deposit (to the nearest dollar) at the end of each six-month period if he wishes to accumulate a fund of $12,000 by the end of four years?

Solution First convert the formula for the future amount of an ordinary annuity into a formula for the semiannual rent:

$$A(\text{amount}) = R(\text{rent})(A_{\overline{n}|i})$$

Solve for rent by dividing both sides of the equation by $A_{\overline{n}|i}$: $R = \dfrac{A}{A_{\overline{n}|i}}$

Using the data from the example,

$$n = 4 \times 2 = 8 \qquad i = .08 \div 2 = .04$$

$$R = \frac{\$12,000}{A_{\overline{8}|4\%}} = \frac{\$12,000}{9.2142} = \underline{\underline{\$1,302}}$$

The accuracy of the computation in Example 8 is demonstrated in the following tabulation. (All amounts are rounded to the nearest dollar.)

Years	Periods	Interest on balance in fund (4%)	Deposit at end of period	Total increase in fund during period	Balance in fund at end of period
1	1	–0–	$1,302	$1,302	$ 1,302
	2	$ 52	1,302	1,354	2,656
2	3	106	1,302	1,408	4,064
	4	163	1,302	1,465	5,529
3	5	221	1,302	1,523	7,052
	6	282	1,302	1,584	8,636
4	7	345	1,302	1,647	10,283
	8	411	1,306*	1,717	12,000

*Because the annual deposit was rounded to the nearest dollar and because interest computations were similarly rounded, it is necessary to assume the addition of $4 to the final deposit to compensate for these cumulative errors. Computations to the nearest dollar are sufficiently accurate for most accounting purposes; the slight rounding error causes no difficulty and is a cheap price to pay for the saving in computational time. Accuracy to the penny may be obtained, when necessary, by using annuity tables which carry results to more places to the right of the decimal point.

Computing the present value of an ordinary annuity

The present value of an ordinary annuity P is the amount which, if invested now to earn compound interest at a rate i per period, would be sufficient to allow for the withdrawal of equal rents R at the end of each of n periods.

The concept of the present value of an annuity is applicable to a wide variety of business decisions in which a present investment is to be made in contemplation of a series of future returns.

Formula for the present value of an ordinary annuity It is apparent that the present value of an ordinary annuity is the sum of the present values of each of the individual rents. For example, the present value of an ordinary annuity of $1 per period for four periods at 6% might be computed as follows:

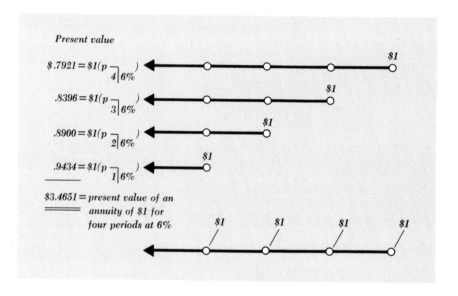

This computation tells us that if $3.47 were invested at 6% interest for four periods, it would be possible to withdraw $1 at the end of each period.

We can develop a formula for the present value of an ordinary annuity in a manner comparable to that used in deriving a formula for the amount of an ordinary annuity. First it is useful to define the following symbol:

$P_{\overline{n}|i}$ = the present value of an ordinary annuity of n rents of $1 at the end of each of n periods at i rate of interest per period. This symbol may be read "capital P angle n at i."

It has previously been shown (see page 1007) that the compound discount on $1 is computed as

$$D_{\overline{n}|i} = \$1 - P_{\overline{n}|i} \quad \text{or} \quad \$1 - \frac{\$1}{(1 + i)^n}$$

Thus the compound discount on $1 due in four periods at 6% in our present example is:

$$D_{\overline{4}|6\%} = \$1 - \frac{\$1}{(1.06)^4} = \$1 - \$.7921 = \underline{\underline{\$.2079}}$$

Now we observe that the compound discount on $1 for n periods at i rate of interest is equivalent to the present value of an ordinary annuity whose rents are the amounts of periodic interest on $1 ($1 $\times$ i) each period discounted at the same i interest rate. We can diagram the compound discount on the $1 annuity in our example as follows:

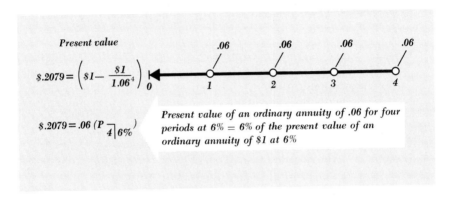

If the compound discount on $1 at 6% ($.06) is 6% of the present value of an ordinary annuity of $1, we can arrive at the formula for the present value of an annuity of $1 per period by dividing the formula for compound discount by the rate of interest (6% in this case):

$$\text{Divide by 6\%:} \quad \frac{\$.06(P_{\overline{4}|6\%})}{.06} = \frac{\left(\$1 - \dfrac{\$1}{(1.06)^4}\right)}{.06}$$

$$\text{Therefore:} \quad P_{\overline{4}|6\%} = \frac{\left(\$1 - \dfrac{\$1}{(1.06)^4}\right)}{.06} = \frac{\$.2079}{.06} = \underline{\underline{\$3.47}}$$

The reasoning we have applied to the specific case of an annuity of $1 for four periods at 6% may now be generalized into a formula for the present value of an ordinary annuity of $1 per period for **any** n and **any** i, as follows:

$$P_{\overline{n}|i} = \frac{\left(1 - \dfrac{1}{(1 + i)^n}\right)}{i} = \frac{(1 - p_{\overline{n}|i})}{i} = \frac{D_{\overline{n}|i}}{i}$$

Formula for present value of an ordinary annuity of $1 for n periods at i rate of interest per period

The formula for the present value of *any* ordinary annuity of R dollars per period may be stated:

$$P = R(P_{\overline{n}|i}) = R \left[\frac{1 - \dfrac{1}{(1 + i)^n}}{i} \right]$$

Formula for present value of an ordinary annuity of $R for n periods at i rate of interest per period

Table for the present value of an ordinary annuity   A table showing the present values of ordinary annuities of $1 per period for various numbers of periods and varying rates of interest *i* is shown on page 1017 (Table 4).

By multiplying the value in the appropriate line and column of the above table by the dollar amount of the equal periodic rents R involved in any ordinary annuity, the present value of the rents can be computed.

Example 9. Given periodic rents, determine present value of ordinary annuity. Jose Luis has arranged to buy a certain property by paying $1,000 at the end of each six-month period for the next four years. What present cash payment would be equivalent to these future installments if money is worth 6% compounded semiannually?

Solution $n = 4 \times 2 = 8$ $i = .06 \div 2 = 3\%$ **per period**
$P = R(P_{\overline{n}|i}) = \$1,000(P_{\overline{8}|3\%}) = \$1,000(7.0197) = \underline{\$7,019.70}$

Example 10. Given present value of an ordinary annuity, find periodic rent. Pepe Cohen has $10,000 saved to finance his son's education. If this money can be invested to earn 4% annually, what equal amounts (to the nearest dollar) can his son withdraw at the end of each of the next five years if he plans to exhaust the fund at the end of the fifth year?

Solution   We must first solve the general equation for the rent R:
$$P = R(P_{\overline{n}|i})$$

Solve for R: $R = \dfrac{P}{P_{\overline{n}|i}}$

Now substituting the data given in the example,

$$R = \frac{\$10,000}{P_{\overline{5}|4\%}} = \frac{\$10,000}{4.4518} = \underline{\underline{\$2,246}}$$

The schedule on page 1018 demonstrates the accuracy of the computation in Example 10:

Table 4 Present Value of an Ordinary Annuity of $1 per Period: $P_{\overline{n}|i} = \dfrac{1 - \dfrac{1}{(1+i)^n}}{i}$

n = number of periods	2.0%	2.5%	3.0%	4.0%	5.0%	6.0%	8.0%	10.0%	15.0%	20.0%
					i = interest rate per period					
1	.9804	.9756	.9709	.9615	.9524	.9434	.9259	.9091	.8696	.8333
2	1.9416	1.9274	1.9135	1.8861	1.8594	1.8334	1.7833	1.7355	1.6257	1.5278
3	2.8839	2.8560	2.8286	2.7751	2.7232	2.6730	2.5771	2.4869	2.2832	2.1065
4	3.8077	3.7620	3.7171	3.6299	3.5460	3.4651	3.3121	3.1699	2.8550	2.5887
5	4.7135	4.6458	4.5797	4.4518	4.3295	4.2124	3.9927	3.7908	3.3522	2.9906
6	5.6014	5.5081	5.4172	5.2421	5.0757	4.9173	4.6229	4.3553	3.7845	3.3255
7	6.4720	6.3494	6.2303	6.0021	5.7864	5.5824	5.2064	4.8684	4.1604	3.6046
8	7.3255	7.1701	7.0197	6.7327	6.4632	6.2098	5.7466	5.3349	4.4873	3.8372
9	8.1622	7.9709	7.7861	7.4353	7.1078	6.8017	6.2469	5.7590	4.7716	4.0310
10	8.9826	8.7521	8.5302	8.1109	7.7217	7.3601	6.7101	6.1446	5.0188	4.1925
11	9.7868	9.5142	9.2526	8.7605	8.3064	7.8869	7.1390	6.4951	5.2337	4.3271
12	10.5753	10.2578	9.9540	9.3851	8.8633	8.3838	7.5361	6.8137	5.4206	4.4392
13	11.3484	10.9832	10.6350	9.9856	9.3936	8.8527	7.9038	7.1034	5.5831	4.5327
14	12.1062	11.6909	11.2961	10.5631	9.8986	9.2950	8.2442	7.3667	5.7245	4.6106
15	12.8493	12.3814	11.9379	11.1184	10.3797	9.7122	8.5595	7.6061	5.8474	4.6755
16	13.5777	13.0550	12.5611	11.6523	10.8378	10.1059	8.8514	7.8237	5.9542	4.7296
17	14.2919	13.7122	13.1661	12.1657	11.2741	10.4773	9.1216	8.0216	6.0472	4.7746
18	14.9920	14.3534	13.7535	12.6593	11.6896	10.8276	9.3719	8.2014	6.1280	4.8122
19	15.6785	14.9789	14.3238	13.1339	12.0853	11.1581	9.6036	8.3649	6.1982	4.8435
20	16.3514	15.5892	14.8775	13.5903	12.4622	11.4699	9.8181	8.5136	6.2593	4.8696
21	17.0112	16.1845	15.4150	14.0292	12.8212	11.7641	10.0168	8.6487	6.3125	4.8913
22	17.6580	16.7654	15.9369	14.4511	13.1630	12.0416	10.2007	8.7715	6.3587	4.9094
23	18.2922	17.3321	16.4436	14.8568	13.4886	12.3034	10.3711	8.8832	6.3988	4.9245
24	18.9139	17.8850	16.9355	15.2470	13.7986	12.5504	10.5288	8.9847	6.4338	4.9371
25	19.5235	18.4244	17.4131	15.6221	14.0939	12.7834	10.6748	9.0770	6.4641	4.9476
26	20.1210	18.9506	17.8768	15.9828	14.3752	13.0032	10.8100	9.1609	6.4906	4.9563
27	20.7069	19.4640	18.3270	16.3296	14.6430	13.2105	10.9352	9.2372	6.5135	4.9636
28	21.2813	19.9649	18.7641	16.6631	14.8981	13.4062	11.0511	9.3066	6.5335	4.9697
29	21.8444	20.4535	19.1885	16.9837	15.1411	13.5907	11.1584	9.3696	6.5509	4.9747
30	22.3965	20.9303	19.6004	17.2920	15.3725	13.7648	11.2578	9.4269	6.5660	4.9789
35	24.9986	23.1452	21.4872	18.6646	16.3742	14.4982	11.6546	9.6442	6.6166	4.9915
40	27.3555	25.1028	23.1148	19.7928	17.1591	15.0463	11.9246	9.7791	6.6418	4.9966
45	29.4902	26.8330	24.5187	20.7200	17.7741	15.4558	12.1084	9.8628	6.6543	4.9986
50	31.4236	28.3623	25.7298	21.4822	18.2559	15.7619	12.2335	9.9148	6.6605	4.9995

Period	Interest on fund balance during period (4%)	Withdrawal from fund at end of period	Net decrease in fund during period	Fund balance at end of period
0				$10,000
1	$400	$2,246	$1,846	8,154
2	326	2,246	1,920	6,234
3	249	2,246	1,997	4,237
4	169	2,246	2,077	2,160
5	86	2,246	2,160	–0–

Comparing values over time

Since money can be readily invested to earn a return, there is a universal service charge (interest) for its use and any given amount of money available on a stated date has a different value at all other points in time. In essence the compound interest procedures discussed here are nothing more than a means of moving money inflows and outflows forward and backward in time on a basis that enables us to compare values in equivalent terms.

For example, if we are given a choice between $10,000 in two years or $15,000 in eight years, the optimal decision is not obvious. These two sums of money can no more be subtracted in a meaningful sense than we could subtract n apples from m automobiles and obtain a meaningful result. Assuming that money is worth 8% per annum, we can compare these sums at any point in time only by measuring their value at that point. If we choose *now* (time point zero), the appropriate analysis would show that the $10,000 in two years is preferable to receiving $15,000 in eight years.

$$\$10,000(p_{\overline{n}|i}) = \$10,000(p_{\overline{2}|8\%}) = \$10,000(.8573) = \underline{\$8,573}$$

$$\$15,000(p_{\overline{8}|8\%}) = \$15,000(.5403) = \underline{\$8,105}$$

We can reach the same decision by comparing values at the end of eight years:

$$\$10,000a_{\overline{6}|8\%} = \$10,000(1.5869) = \underline{\$15,869}$$

$15,000 at the end of eight years is equivalent to $\underline{\$15,000}$

The $10,000 in two years is still shown to be preferable to $15,000 in eight years since, if invested at 8%, $10,000 would grow to $15,869 by the end of eight years. We could choose any other point in time and make a similar comparison without changing the validity of the decision in favor of the $10,000 option.

Sample financial statements

Financial statements are presented in this appendix for the following companies:

Cities Service Company

Fruehauf Corporation (and unconsolidated subsidiary, Fruehauf Finance Company)

Indiana Telephone Corporation

Eastman Kodak Company

These financial statements have been audited by well-known firms of certified public accountants. The report of the independent auditors accompanies each set of financial statements. These particular companies were chosen because they provided realistic illustrations of many of the issues discussed in this book as, for example, the adjustment of historical cost for changes in price levels (Indiana Telephone Corporation), and the capitalization of lease obligations (Fruehauf Corporation).

CITIES SERVICE COMPANY AND SUBSIDIARIES

Consolidated Balance Sheet

ASSETS	December 31 1972	December 31 1971
Current Assets		
Cash	$ 21,500,000	25,500,000
Short-term cash investments (approximate market value)	89,600,000	72,100,000
Accounts and notes receivable, less allowance for doubtful accounts	269,600,000	259,800,000
Inventories of petroleum and other products	172,900,000	169,700,000
Materials and supplies	28,900,000	30,000,000
Prepaid expenses (includes deferred Federal income taxes of $21,500,000 in 1972 and $13,600,000 in 1971)	30,800,000	26,400,000
Total current assets	613,300,000	583,500,000
Investments and Sundry Assets		
Securities of and advances to unconsolidated foreign subsidiaries	14,400,000	10,800,000
Atlantic Richfield Company Common Stock—at cost	—	17,800,000
Other securities and advances	27,700,000	33,800,000
Accounts and notes receivable—not current	36,100,000	24,300,000
	78,200,000	86,700,000
Property, Plant and Equipment—at cost	3,051,500,000	3,031,900,000
Less accumulated depreciation, depletion and amortization	1,356,400,000	1,389,600,000
	1,695,100,000	1,642,300,000
Deferred Charges	19,200,000	12,800,000
	$2,405,800,000	2,325,300,000

Cities Service Company and Subsidiaries

LIABILITIES AND STOCKHOLDERS' EQUITY	December 31 1972	December 31 1971
Current Liabilities		
Notes payable and long-term debt maturing within one year	$ 28,900,000	101,700,000
Accounts payable and accrued liabilities	269,800,000	215,100,000
Federal and foreign income taxes	46,900,000	21,700,000
Total current liabilities	345,600,000	338,500,000
Long-Term Debt (see schedule)		
Principal amount	577,000,000	576,300,000
Less unamortized discount	13,000,000	13,500,000
	564,000,000	562,800,000
Other Credits		
Deferred Federal income taxes	50,000,000	51,200,000
Advances to be repaid from future production	5,400,000	—
	55,400,000	51,200,000
Minority Interests in Subsidiaries	7,000,000	7,300,000
Stockholders' Equity		
Common Stock, $5.00 par value		
Authorized 40,000,000 shares		
Issued: 1972—26,465,728 shares; 1971—26,232,537 shares	132,300,000	131,200,000
Capital surplus	92,100,000	81,200,000
Retained earnings	1,230,500,000	1,177,900,000
	1,454,900,000	1,390,300,000
Less treasury stock—at cost		
(1972—527,187 shares; 1971—619,126 shares)	21,100,000	24,800,000
Total stockholders' equity	1,433,800,000	1,365,500,000
	$2,405,800,000	2,325,300,000

Cities Service Company and Subsidiaries

Consolidated Income

	Year ended December 31 1972	Year ended December 31 1971
Gross Income		
Sales and operating income (including sales of purchased crude oil $379,500,000 in 1972 and $384,200,000 in 1971)	$1,862,100,000	1,809,900,000
Investment and other non-operating income, net	8,300,000	16,400,000
	1,870,400,000	1,826,300,000
Costs and Expenses		
Costs and operating expenses	1,309,100,000	1,275,000,000
Exploration expenses including dry hole costs and lease amortization	64,500,000	60,100,000
Selling, general and administrative expenses	157,000,000	162,300,000
Taxes, other than Federal and foreign income taxes	60,100,000	54,500,000
Depreciation and depletion	114,800,000	110,100,000
Interest expense	42,700,000	41,000,000
Federal and foreign income taxes	21,600,000	17,500,000
Income applicable to minority interests	1,500,000	1,300,000
	1,771,300,000	1,721,800,000
Income Before Extraordinary Credit	99,100,000	104,500,000
Extraordinary Credit (net)—(note 3)	13,000,000	—
Net Income	$ 112,100,000	104,500,000
Per Share of Common Stock		
Income before extraordinary credit	$3.84	3.78
Extraordinary credit (net)	.50	—
Net income	$4.34	3.78

Consolidated Retained Earnings

	Year ended December 31 1972	Year ended December 31 1971
Amount at beginning of year	$1,177,900,000	1,135,000,000
Net income	112,100,000	104,500,000
Cost of treasury stock (less related par value and capital surplus) issued under Employees Thrift Plan	(2,800,000)	—
Dividends paid—$2.20 per share	(56,700,000)	(61,600,000)
Amount at end of year	$1,230,500,000	1,177,900,000

Consolidated Capital Surplus

	Year ended December 31 1972	Year ended December 31 1971
Amount at beginning of year	$81,200,000	76,200,000
Credit resulting from retirement of Common Stock received in exchange for Atlantic Richfield Company Common Stock	—	4,900,000
Credit (net) arising from issuance of Common Stock at market value to Employees Thrift Plan	10,600,000	—
Excess of proceeds over par value of stock (or cost of treasury stock) issued on exercise of options	260,000	70,000
Excess of market value over cost of treasury stock issued under incentive compensation plan	40,000	30,000
Amount at end of year	$92,100,000	81,200,000

See accompanying notes to financial statements.

Long-Term Debt (Excluding current maturities)

	December 31 1972	December 31 1971
Cities Service Company		
7.65% Debentures due 1982 to 2001	$100,000,000	100,000,000
6⅝% Debentures due 1980 to 1999; unamortized discount 1972—$12,500,000 and 1971—$13,000,000 (discount is based on imputed interest of 7.9%)	100,000,000	100,000,000
6⅛% Debentures due 1978 to 1997; unamortized discount 1972 and 1971—$600,000	100,000,000	100,000,000
3% Sinking Fund Debentures due 1977; excludes debentures in treasury 1972—$8,700,000 and 1971—$10,200,000	39,300,000	39,300,000
Notes payable 4½% to 7% due 1974 to 1978; unamortized premium 1972 and 1971—$100,000	50,600,000	51,700,000
	389,900,000	391,000,000
Subsidiaries—other than natural gas transmission company		
Bonds and Debentures, 3.35% to 5½% due 1974 to 1983	11,100,000	13,600,000
Purchase obligations, 3% to 7% due 1974 to 1986	200,000	400,000
Notes payable, 3⅝% to 8% due 1974 to 1982	88,700,000	96,600,000
Non-interest bearing debt due 1974 to 1996	18,100,000	1,700,000
	118,100,000	112,300,000
Subsidiary—natural gas transmission company		
First mortgage bonds, 4½% due 1974 to 1977	16,000,000	20,000,000
8¼% Debentures due 1978 to 1991	53,000,000	53,000,000
	69,000,000	73,000,000
Total	$577,000,000	576,300,000

The maturities of the foregoing long-term debt at 12/31/72 are as follows: 1974, $17,200,000; 1975, $34,600,000; 1976, $40,200,000; 1977, $52,900,000; 1978 to 2001, $432,100,000.

Cities Service Company and Subsidiaries

Changes in Consolidated Financial Position

	Year ended December 31 1972	Year ended December 31 1971
Source		
Income before extraordinary credit	$ 99,100,000	104,500,000
Depreciation and depletion	114,800,000	110,100,000
Dry holes and lease amortization	31,600,000	28,400,000
Deferred Federal income taxes	7,300,000	4,400,000
Funds from operations before extraordinary credit	252,800,000	247,400,000
Extraordinary credit (net)	13,000,000	—
Charges included in extraordinary credit (net) which did not affect working capital	34,500,000	—
Total funds from operations	300,300,000	247,400,000
Long-term debt issued	22,300,000	222,000,000
Property sales and retirements	18,300,000	6,100,000
Sales and repayments of investments and advances	20,700,000	4,800,000
Advances to be repaid from future production	5,400,000	—
Exchange of Atlantic Richfield Company shares for Cities Service Common Stock	—	5,800,000
Issuance of Common Stock under employee plans		
Original issue	9,100,000	100,000
Treasury	3,800,000	300,000
Other transactions (net)	300,000	5,700,000
Total	$380,200,000	492,200,000
Application		
Capital expenditures		
Plant additions	$260,400,000	293,900,000
Investments and advances	1,300,000	2,600,000
	261,700,000	296,500,000
Reduction of long-term debt	27,300,000	71,300,000
Cash dividends paid	56,700,000	61,600,000
Acquisition of Cities Service Common Stock (subsequently retired) in exchange for Atlantic Richfield Company shares plus related expenses	—	7,100,000
Increase in non-current advances for services/products (net)	11,800,000	(300,000)
Accumulation of working capital	22,700,000	56,000,000
Total	$380,200,000	492,200,000
Changes in working capital		
Cash and short-term cash investments	$ 13,500,000	9,300,000
Accounts and notes receivable	9,800,000	(5,100,000)
Inventories	2,100,000	14,000,000
Prepaid expenses	4,400,000	10,600,000
Short-term notes payable	75,600,000	(2,400,000)
Current maturities of long-term debt	(2,800,000)	27,800,000
Accounts payable and accrued liabilities	(54,700,000)	(5,900,000)
Federal and foreign income taxes	(25,200,000)	7,700,000
Accumulation of working capital	$ 22,700,000	56,000,000

Notes to Consolidated Financial Statements

1. ACCOUNTING POLICIES—The following is a summary of significant accounting policies.

Principles of Consolidation—The consolidated financial statements include the accounts of Cities Service Company, all domestic and certain foreign subsidiaries. Foreign currency items, which are not material, have been converted into United States dollars at appropriate rates of exchange.

Investments in unconsolidated foreign subsidiaries, 50 percent owned companies and certain companies in which the ownership is less than 50 percent are accounted for under the equity method, with appropriate provision for the possibility of less than full realization of such equity. Such companies when considered in the aggregate would not constitute a significant subsidiary.

Inventories—Inventories of petroleum and other products are valued at the lower of cost or market. Cost has been determined under the last-in first-out method for approximately 55 percent of the inventories, which amount is substantially lower than current replacement cost. For the remaining inventories cost has been determined under the first-in first-out or average methods. Materials and supplies are valued at average cost.

Exploration Expenses—Petroleum and mineral exploration expenses including geological and geophysical costs, prospecting costs, annual delay rentals and all dry hole costs are charged to income as incurred. Nonproducing lease costs are capitalized and are amortized to income based on the Company's discovery experience.

Depreciation and Depletion—The costs of producing properties, including leaseholds, drilling, development and equipment costs, are capitalized for accounting purposes. Depreciation and depletion are provided on a field basis, generally on the unit-of-production method based upon estimates of recoverable reserves.

Depreciation of other than producing properties is provided by the straight-line method over the estimated lives of the properties with due allowance for salvage.

Property Retirement—Upon sale or retirement of major items of property, the cost and related accumulated depreciation, depletion, and amortization are eliminated from the accounts and the gain or loss is reflected in income. The cost, less salvage value, of other items of depreciable property disposed of is charged to accumulated depreciation.

Research and Development Costs—Generally all expenditures for research, except buildings and equipment with extended useful lives, are expensed when incurred.

Interest—Interest on general corporate indebtedness is normally expensed. Interest expense is capitalized only on construction projects for regulated pipeline operations and on major construction projects for which specific borrowings are made.

Income Taxes—Certain income and expense items are recorded on one basis for financial accounting purposes and on another basis for income tax purposes. Deferred taxes are provided in the financial statements to compensate for significant timing differences, principally depreciation, lease amortization, geological and geophysical petroleum exploration costs and equity income. Tax reductions arising from percentage depletion and intangible development costs are included in current income. Investment tax credits are accounted for under the flow-through method.

Excise Taxes—The taxes collected for government agencies on the sale of products are not included in the income statement as revenue or expense.

2. FINANCIAL REVIEW—Certain information relative to sale of the Company's investment in Atlantic Richfield Company Common Stock, 1972 financing and employee termination expense is presented in the Financial Review.

3. EXTRAORDINARY CREDIT—The net extraordinary credit of $13 million for the year 1972 consisted of the following items ($ millions):

a) Gain on the sale of 1.4 million shares of Atlantic Richfield Company Common Stock of $48 million (net of income taxes of $22.1 million). The divestiture of this investment was made pursuant to a court order $48.0

b) Provision for loss on disposition of certain marginal oil and gas leases amounting to $16.3 million (net of deferred income tax credit of $5.6 million). The Company accepted bids for the major portion of these leases in January 1973. . . . .   (16.3)

c) Provision for loss on the disposition of the agricultural chemicals business amounting to $18.7 million (net of deferred income tax credit of $13.6 million). This provision is subject to possible future adjustment when the disposition is completed. In January 1973, the Company made arrangements for the sale of the agricultural chemicals manufacturing facilities and the associated phosphate mining operations located in Florida. Consummation of the sale is scheduled to occur before May 1. Negotiations for the divestiture of the retail fertilizer marketing operations are currently underway. . . . .   (18.7)

Net extraordinary credit. $13.0

Cities Service Company and Subsidiaries

NOTES TO CONSOLIDATED FINANCIAL STATEMENTS (continued)

The assets to be disposed of had an aggregate book value at December 31, 1972 of $106 million, after provision for estimated loss.

The agricultural chemicals operations to be disposed of had sales of $123.4 million in 1972 and $124.9 million in 1971, and net income of $2 million in 1972 and a net loss of $300,000 in 1971.

4. ACCOUNTING CHANGES—Commencing in 1971, the Company retroactively adopted the more common industry practices of (a) amortizing the cost of nonproducing petroleum leases (with provision for deferred income taxes) based upon the Company's discovery experience and (b) providing deferred tax accounting with respect to timing differences arising from the expensing of geological and geophysical petroleum exploration expenditures for financial statement purposes in advance of the deduction for income tax purposes. The Company also extended the equity method of accounting for investments to include certain less-than-50 percent-owned companies.

The effect of these changes, considered separately and collectively, on the earnings of each of the prior periods was not material. The cumulative effect on earnings at January 1, 1971 (a net credit of $700,000), which was credited to other income in 1971, was as follows ($ millions):

Amortization of the cost of nonproducing petroleum leases (net of deferred taxes of $15.3 million)	$(15.2)
Deferred taxes on geological and geophysical petroleum exploration expenditures	14.4
Equity accounting for certain investments (net of deferred taxes of $0.3 million)	1.5
Net cumulative credit	$ .7

Net income for 1971 was increased by $1.2 million (including the net cumulative credit at January 1, 1971) as a result of these changes.

5. EARNINGS PER SHARE—Earnings per share are based upon the average number of shares outstanding during each year.

In 1971, the Company acquired and retired 2.4 million shares of its Common Stock through an exchange offer for Atlantic Richfield Common Stock. If this transaction had been effected as of the beginning of 1971, earnings per share for the year 1971 would have been $3.96.

6. STOCK OPTION PLANS—Under the Company's qualified stock option plan, options may be granted to pur-

chase shares of its Common Stock at prices not less than fair market value at date of grant. The options are exercisable over varying periods commencing twelve to eighteen months after grant. Options issued prior to 1964 expire ten years after grant and those issued subsequently expire five years after grant.

	1972		1971	
During 1972 and 1971 options:	Shares	Price per share	Shares	Price per share
Were granted to purchase	51,500	$37.25	—	—
Became exercisable	2,818	31.00	182,077	$31.00-$48.38
Were exercised	3,092	31.00	2,717	27.81- 31.00
Were terminated	7,834		230,718	

At year-end there were 265,565 shares under option (211,811 of which were exercisable) at prices from $31.00 to $48.38 per share and there were 141,250 unoptioned shares.

Options which had been granted under various stock plans of acquired companies were all exercised by December 31, 1972.

7. PENSION PLANS—The Company and its subsidiaries have non-contributory pension plans covering substantially all employees. Benefits under the principal plan were liberalized in 1971. Pension expense for 1972 of $23.2 million and for 1971 of $20.5 million includes prior service costs. The unfunded past service cost at December 31, 1972 approximates $35.7 million most of which is being amortized over a period of years ending in 1996. Pension cost is funded as accrued. At year-end pension fund assets were in excess of the actuarially computed value of vested benefits for all plans.

8. RETAINED EARNINGS—Approximately $697 million of consolidated retained earnings at December 31, 1972 were restricted as to the payment of cash dividends under trust indentures and other agreements of subsidiaries.

9. FEDERAL INCOME TAX—Federal and foreign income taxes includes provisions for deferred taxes of $7.3 million in 1972 and $4.4 million in 1971. Tax expense was reduced by investment credit of $9.2 million in 1972 ($2.9 million applied against deferred) and $5.8 million in 1971.

10. CAPITAL STOCK—Changes in shares of Common Stock were as follows:

	1972		1971	
	Issued*	Treasury	Issued*	Treasury
Balance at 1/1 . .	26,232,537	619,126	28,619,106	626,209
Retirements re exchange offer .	—	—	(2,390,348)	—
Issued:				
Thrift plan . .	226,865	(85,500)	—	—
Stock options .	6,326	(957)	3,779	(1,300)
Incentive compensation plan .	—	(5,482)	—	(3,594)
Other transactions	—	—	—	(2,189)
Balance at 12/31 .	26,465,728	527,187	26,232,537	619,126

*Includes treasury shares

At December 31, 1972 there were 979,950 shares of unissued Common Stock reserved for sale under the Company's thrift plan and for issuance under the stock option plan.

In April 1972 the Stockholders approved the authorization of 2.5 million shares of a new class of Preferred Stock, none of which has been issued.

11. COMMITMENTS AND CONTINGENT LIABILITIES:

(a) Minimum annual rentals under noncancelable long-term leases approximate $16.5 million (without regard to reduction for related rental income), of which $2.2 million pertain to leases which contain options to purchase the underlying properties. A substantial portion of the leases, which relate principally to marketing properties and office buildings, expires within eleven years.

(b) The Company and certain subsidiaries have guaranteed debt obligations of approximately $16.9 million of companies in which substantial stock investments are held. Also, under long-term agreements with certain pipeline companies in which stock interests are held, the Company and its subsidiaries have agreed to provide minimum revenue for product shipments or purchases. It is not anticipated that any loss will result from such agreements.

(c) Deferred charges include a payment made in 1972 by a gas transmission subsidiary of $6.8 million including interest (before taxes) in satisfaction of a judgment arising from a 1966 civil action. It is anticipated that the payment will be recovered in increased rates to the subsidiary's customers. The deferral will be amortized as increased rates are realized or, if the increase is denied, the deferral will be charged to income.

(d) During 1971, a U. S. Appeals Court determined that the Company and others may be liable for additional payments, in an amount to be determined by further court action, for gas used in the helium extraction process. The Company has provided a reserve for its potential liability in this action which, in the opinion of counsel for the Company, is adequate.

(e) Various suits and claims arising in the ordinary course of business, some of which involve substantial amounts, are pending against the Company and its subsidiaries. While the ultimate effect of such litigation cannot be ascertained at this time, in the opinion of counsel for the Company the liabilities which may arise from such actions would not result in losses which would materially affect the financial position of the Company and its subsidiaries or the results of their operations.

PEAT, MARWICK, MITCHELL & CO.
CERTIFIED PUBLIC ACCOUNTANTS
345 PARK AVENUE
NEW YORK, NEW YORK 10022

The Board of Directors and Stockholders
Cities Service Company:

We have examined the consolidated balance sheets of Cities Service Company and subsidiaries as of December 31, 1972 and 1971 and the related statements of income, retained earnings, capital surplus and changes in financial position for the respective years then ended. Our examination was made in accordance with generally accepted auditing standards, and accordingly included such tests of the accounting records and such other auditing procedures as we considered necessary in the circumstances.

In our opinion, the accompanying consolidated financial statements present fairly the financial position of Cities Service Company and subsidiaries at December 31, 1972 and 1971 and, subject to the effect of any future adjustment of the 1972 extraordinary provision for loss upon disposition of the agricultural chemicals business described in note 3 of notes to consolidated financial statements, the results of their operations and changes in their financial position for the respective years then ended, in conformity with generally accepted accounting principles consistently applied during the period subsequent to the changes (with which we concur) made as of January 1, 1971, as described in note 4 of notes to consolidated financial statements.

Peat, Marwick, Mitchell & Co.

February 22, 1973

FRUEHAUF CORPORATION AND CONSOLIDATED SUBSIDIARIES

Consolidated Balance Sheet
FRUEHAUF CORPORATION AND CONSOLIDATED SUBSIDIARIES

ASSETS	December 31, 1972	December 31, 1971
CURRENT ASSETS:		
Cash	$ 22,703,177	$ 33,096,427
Trade receivables (Note A):		
Accounts receivable	$ 87,775,946	$ 90,484,873
Installment contracts	21,098,570	24,044,888
From Fruehauf Finance Company	790,904	
	$109,665,420	$114,529,761
Less allowance for doubtful receivables	1,750,000	1,750,000
	$107,915,420	$112,779,761
Inventories (Note B)	105,805,368	97,355,505
Prepaid expenses	3,180,613	3,553,819
TOTAL CURRENT ASSETS	$239,604,578	$246,785,512
EQUIPMENT LEASED TO CUSTOMERS—at cost, less accumulated depreciation of $61,025,922 and $68,176,169 at December 31, 1972 and 1971, respectively	118,241,397	87,882,132
INVESTMENTS AND OTHER ASSETS:		
Investment in and amount due from Fruehauf Finance Company (Note C)	$ 20,539,067	$ 42,344,822
Investments in and amounts due from other affiliated companies not consolidated	19,643,811	16,813,269
Transport Investment Division loans—secured (Note A)	19,139,592	21,300,769
Other accounts and investments	11,548,185	13,694,097
TOTAL INVESTMENTS AND OTHER ASSETS	$ 70,870,655	$ 94,152,957
PROPERTY, PLANT AND EQUIPMENT (Note E):		
Land	$ 13,510,915	$ 13,451,951
Buildings and building equipment	71,732,881	65,284,986
Machinery and other equipment	108,026,377	91,868,636
	$193,270,173	$170,605,573
Less accumulated depreciation	66,860,828	61,165,832
TOTAL PROPERTY, PLANT AND EQUIPMENT	$126,409,345	$109,439,741
UNAMORTIZED DEBT ISSUANCE EXPENSE	1,499,796	1,610,245
	$556,625,771	$539,870,587

FRUEHAUF CORPORATION AND CONSOLIDATED SUBSIDIARIES

LIABILITIES AND SHAREHOLDERS' INVESTMENT	December 31, 1972	December 31, 1971
CURRENT LIABILITIES:		
Notes payable to banks and commercial paper............................	$ 48,775,562	$ 42,131,578
Accounts payable and accrued expenses:		
Trade accounts...	$ 52,078,043	$ 45,174,880
To Fruehauf Finance Company...............................		2,988,409
Salaries, wages, and employee benefits............................	11,051,822	10,158,500
Taxes—other than income...................................	7,819,325	7,419,935
Interest...	1,626,631	1,711,648
	$ 72,575,821	$ 67,453,372
Dividends payable..	3,718,971	3,713,552
Taxes on income (Note D).....................................	10,025,530	17,211,039
TOTAL CURRENT LIABILITIES	$135,095,884	$130,509,541
OTHER LIABILITIES:		
Deferred compensation......................................	$ 1,830,969	$ 1,388,612
Deferred taxes on income (Note D)...............................	36,480,000	33,095,000
Capitalized lease obligations—production facilities (Note E).............	23,206,509	23,781,186
Debentures (Note F)..	114,961,000	117,053,000
TOTAL OTHER LIABILITIES	$176,478,478	$175,317,798
DEFERRED CREDIT AND MINORITY INTEREST................	2,881,322	3,760,719
SHAREHOLDERS' INVESTMENT:		
4% Preferred Stock, cumulative, par value $100.00 a share; redemption price $104.50 a share (no sinking fund payments required until 1981): Authorized and outstanding 20,103 and 21,995 shares at December 31, 1972 and 1971, respectively.......................	$ 2,010,300	$ 2,199,500
Common Stock, par value $1.00 a share (Note G): Authorized 15,000,000 shares Issued 8,831,963 and 8,819,094 shares at December 31, 1972 and 1971, respectively...	8,831,963	8,819,094
Additional paid-in capital......................................	132,713,701	132,324,087
Earnings retained for use in the business (Note F)......................	100,556,342	88,882,067
Cost of Common Stock held in treasury—81,443 shares (deduction*).......	1,942,219*	1,942,219*
TOTAL SHAREHOLDERS' INVESTMENT	$242,170,087	$230,282,529
COMMITMENTS AND CONTINGENT LIABILITIES (Notes D, E, and H)		
	$556,625,771	$539,870,587

Consolidated Statement of Net Earnings
Years ended December 31, 1972, and December 31, 1971
FRUEHAUF CORPORATION AND CONSOLIDATED SUBSIDIARIES

	1972	1971
REVENUES:		
Commercial sales	$484,198,416	$422,951,162
Leased equipment rentals	41,029,307	35,060,013
Defense sales	25,178,329	24,952,391
SALES AND RENTALS	$550,406,052	$482,963,566
Earnings before taxes on income of Fruehauf Finance Company (Note D)	11,928,844	11,851,156
Finance revenue	4,968,196	6,834,281
Revenue from international affiliates	3,184,561	2,734,320
Miscellaneous	1,893,236	2,261,026
	$572,380,889	$506,644,349
COSTS AND EXPENSES:		
Cost of products and service sold, other than items below	$422,917,148	$374,816,478
Selling and administrative expenses	40,378,491	36,059,096
Depreciation	30,992,585	30,914,341
Taxes—other than income	13,015,871	11,488,895
Interest, including $6,245,874 in 1972 and $5,458,461 in 1971 to Fruehauf Finance Company	17,716,811	16,507,114
	$525,020,906	$469,785,924
EARNINGS BEFORE TAXES ON INCOME	$ 47,359,983	$ 36,858,425
TAXES ON INCOME (Note D):		
Current	$ 18,660,000	$ 17,600,000
Deferred (credit*)	1,940,000	100,000*
	$ 20,600,000	$ 17,500,000
NET EARNINGS	$ 26,759,983	$ 19,358,425
NET EARNINGS PER SHARE OF COMMON STOCK—		
after deducting dividends on Preferred Stock—based on average number of shares outstanding:		
Primary	$3.05	$2.21
Fully diluted—reflects conversion of debentures	$2.81	$2.08

Consolidated Statement of Earnings Retained for Use in the Business
Years ended December 31, 1972, and December 31, 1971
FRUEHAUF CORPORATION AND CONSOLIDATED SUBSIDIARIES

	1972	1971
Balance at beginning of the year.	$ 88,882,067	$ 84,530,879
Net earnings for the year.	26,759,983	19,358,425
	$115,642,050	$103,889,304
Less cash dividends declared:		
4% Preferred Stock.	$ 87,154	$ 89,741
Common Stock ($1.70 a share).	14,998,554	14,917,496
TOTAL DIVIDENDS	$ 15,085,708	$ 15,007,237
Balance at end of the year.	$100,556,342	$ 88,882,067

Consolidated Statement of Additional Paid-In Capital
Years ended December 31, 1972, and December 31, 1971
FRUEHAUF CORPORATION AND CONSOLIDATED SUBSIDIARIES

	1972	1971
Balance at beginning of the year.	$132,324,087	$131,955,298
Excess of principal amount of Convertible Subordinated Debentures over the par value of Common Stock issued upon conversion (1972—12,869 shares; 1971—13,209 shares).	324,917	333,614
Excess of par value over cost of 4% Preferred Stock purchased (1972—1,892 shares; 1971—777 shares).	64,697	35,175
Balance at end of the year.	$132,713,701	$132,324,087

Consolidated Statement of Changes in Financial Position
Years ended December 31, 1972, and December 31, 1971
FRUEHAUF CORPORATION AND CONSOLIDATED SUBSIDIARIES

	1972	1971
SOURCES OF WORKING CAPITAL:		
Operations:		
Net earnings	$ 26,759,983	$ 19,358,425
Depreciation of equipment leased to customers	20,682,233	20,872,022
Depreciation of plant and equipment	10,310,352	10,042,319
Increase in deferred taxes on income	3,385,000	1,636,129
	$ 61,137,568	$ 51,908,895
Increase (decrease*) in net amount received from Fruehauf		
Finance Company to finance equipment leased to customers	27,994,599	3,239,380*
	$ 89,132,167	$ 48,669,515
APPLICATION OF WORKING CAPITAL:		
Cash dividends	$ 15,085,708	$ 15,007,237
Additions to equipment leased to customers, less disposals	51,041,498	15,004,215
Additions to property, plant and equipment, less disposals	27,279,956	13,287,288
Increase in investments and other assets		
(excluding net amount received from Fruehauf Finance Company)	4,712,297	13,713,868
Purchase of debentures and Preferred Stock to		
satisfy future sinking fund requirements	1,878,717	2,997,525
Decrease in capitalized lease obligations	574,677	2,078,284
Miscellaneous	326,591	746,018
	$100,899,444	$ 62,834,435
NET DECREASE* IN WORKING CAPITAL FOR THE YEAR	$ 11,767,277*	$ 14,164,920*
Working capital at beginning of the year	116,275,971	130,440,891
WORKING CAPITAL AT END OF THE YEAR	$104,508,694	$116,275,971
INCREASE (DECREASE*) IN COMPONENTS OF WORKING CAPITAL:		
Cash	$ 10,393,250*	$ 834,126*
Trade receivables—net	4,864,341*	19,624,366*
Inventories	8,449,863	7,599,171
Prepaid expenses	373,206*	1,086,071
Notes payable and commercial paper	6,643,984*	8,214,743
Accounts payable and accrued expenses	5,122,449*	7,911,393*
Dividends payable	5,419*	5,663*
Taxes on income	7,185,509	2,689,357*
DECREASE* IN WORKING CAPITAL	$ 11,767,277*	$ 14,164,920*

Summary of Accounting Principles
Years ended December 31, 1972, and December 31, 1971
FRUEHAUF CORPORATION AND CONSOLIDATED SUBSIDIARIES

The significant accounting principles used by the Corporation are described below.
These accounting principles have been applied consistently during the two years ended December 31, 1972.

Principles of Consolidation	The consolidated financial statements include the accounts of the Corporation and its domestic and Canadian subsidiaries other than Fruehauf Finance Company. The investments in Fruehauf Finance Company and foreign affiliates in which the Corporation has an ownership interest in excess of 20% are carried at equity in net assets in the consolidated balance sheet, and their earnings for the year are included in net earnings.
Inventories	Inventory amounts are based upon physical determinations during the year and have been stated at the lower of cost or market prices. Cost prices are determined by the first-in, first-out method, and market prices represent the lower of replacement cost or estimated net realizable amount.
International Earnings	Operating revenues and expenses of foreign affiliates are translated at the average rate of exchange during the period. Current assets and liabilities are translated at the current rate of exchange, and noncurrent assets and liabilities generally are translated at the rate of exchange at dates of acquisition. Exchange gain or loss on conversions between currencies is included in net earnings.
Property, Plant and Equipment	The Corporation records property, plant and equipment at cost and uses straight-line depreciation methods in its financial statements while employing accelerated depreciation for income tax purposes. Maintenance and repairs are charged to earnings as incurred.
Capitalized Lease Obligations	The Corporation has capitalized certain leasehold interests and recorded the related long-term lease obligations. The assets are included in property, plant and equipment and are being amortized over their estimated useful lives. The lease obligations generally are payable over 20 years and give the Corporation the right to acquire the property for the unpaid principal balance.
Taxes on Income	The financial statements include appropriate provision for taxes on income for all items included in net earnings regardless of the period when such taxes are payable. No provision has been made for United States taxes on the undistributed portion of the Corporation's equity in earnings of its international affiliates since it is anticipated that foreign tax credits would substantially extinguish such domestic liabilities. The Corporation files a consolidated tax return. Profit from sales financed by installment contracts (most contracts are held by Fruehauf Finance Company) is recognized for financial reporting purposes in the year of sale; such profit is recognized for tax purposes ratably over the terms of the contracts.
Investment Tax Credit	The reduction in federal income taxes resulting from the investment tax credit on certain additions to equipment leased to customers and plant and equipment is reflected in net earnings currently.
Research and Development	Current operations are charged with all research, engineering, testing, and product development costs as incurred.
Pensions	The Corporation has noncontributory pension plans covering substantially all employees. The Corporation's policy is to fund pension costs in the year accrued. Past service costs are being amortized over 30-year periods.

Notes to Financial Statements
Years ended December 31, 1972, and December 31, 1971
FRUEHAUF CORPORATION AND CONSOLIDATED SUBSIDIARIES

NOTE A—TRADE RECEIVABLES AND TRANSPORT INVESTMENT DIVISION LOANS

Installment contracts at December 31, 1972, and December 31, 1971, are stated after deduction of deferred finance charges of $2,531,000 and $2,995,000, respectively, and include installments of approximately $10,157,000 and $14,550,000, respectively, which are due after one year.

The Transport Investment Division loans at December 31, 1972, and December 31, 1971, are stated after deduction of deferred finance charges of $4,084,760 and $7,167,161, respectively, and exclude payments due within one year of $2,392,690 and $2,952,468, respectively, which are included in accounts receivable. The Company has perfected liens on various customer assets as security for these loans.

NOTE B—INVENTORIES

A summary of inventories follows:

	December 31	
	1972	1971
New trailers	$ 15,457,743	$ 17,147,079
Production parts, work in process, and raw materials	56,462,977	48,759,050
Service parts and orders in process	24,875,038	21,253,641
Used trailers	9,009,610	10,195,735
TOTAL	$105,805,368	$ 97,355,505

NOTE C—INVESTMENT IN AND AMOUNT DUE FROM FRUEHAUF FINANCE COMPANY

A summary of the carrying value of Fruehauf Finance Company (100% owned) follows:

	December 31	
	1972	1971
Investment—at equity in net assets	$106,082,585	$99,893,741
Note receivable, due October 12, 1992	775,000	775,000
Other noncurrent amounts due	96,200	96,200
Amount payable, less deferred finance revenue—secured by pledge of rentals on equipment leased to customers (deduction*)	86,414,718*	58,420,119*
TOTAL	$ 20,539,067	$42,344,822

NOTE D—UNITED STATES AND CANADIAN TAXES

The Internal Revenue Service is in substantial disagreement with the Corporation's method of computing excise taxes. In the opinion of management, based upon advice of special tax counsel, any liability that may result from such disagreement will not have a material effect on the financial statements.

On November 9, 1970, the Corporation and two of its officers were indicted for allegedly conspiring to evade payment of $12,344,587 in excise taxes during the period from October 1, 1956, to December 31, 1965. Fruehauf and the two officers have denied the allegations and, in the opinion of special counsel, the charges in the indictment cannot be sustained.

The provision for taxes on income includes taxes ($5,740,000 in 1972 and $5,705,000 in 1971) on income of the finance subsidiary. The provision for taxes on income is stated after investment tax credit of $1,800,000 in 1972 and $250,000 in 1971. Deferred taxes of $4,200,000 at December 31, 1972, and $5,950,000 at December 31, 1971, applicable to current assets, are included in current liabilities.

NOTE E—LEASES

The Corporation leases certain production facilities and most of its sales and service branches under agreements expiring from 1973 to 1996. Annual rentals in 1973 will be $4,400,000, exclusive of taxes, insurance, maintenance, and repairs. Certain agreements include options to purchase the properties. The rental payments and purchase prices in most cases decline gradually over the lease terms. If all the rights to purchase were exercised at December 31, 1972, the aggregate purchase price would amount to approximately $15,000,000.

The Corporation has capitalized other lease obligations; the current portion ($1,600,000 at December 31, 1972, and $2,200,000 at December 31, 1971) of such obligations has been included in trade accounts payable.

NOTE F—DEBENTURES

Debentures outstanding are described below:

	December 31	
	1972	1971
Sinking Fund Debentures:		
3¾%, due June 1, 1974	$ 4,778,000	$ 5,967,000
4%, due March 1, 1976	2,717,000	2,777,000
5¼%, Series "A", of Fruehauf Trailer Company of Canada Limited, due November 1, 1976	1,100,000	1,250,000
6%, due April 1, 1987	44,947,000	45,302,000
Convertible Subordinated Debentures:		
4%, due March 1, 1976, presently convertible into Common Stock at $26.24 a share	1,419,000	1,757,000
5½%, due April 15, 1994, presently convertible into Common Stock at $46.25 a share	60,000,000	60,000,000
TOTAL	$114,961,000	$117,053,000

The indentures relating to Sinking Fund Debentures contain provisions for sinking fund payments. Sinking fund payments of $145,000 are required in 1973. The indentures impose certain restrictions on the declaration of cash dividends on Common Stock and purchase of shares of such stock. Retained earnings of approximately $45,000,000 were free from such restrictions at December 31, 1972.

NOTE G—RESERVATION OF COMMON STOCK

At December 31, 1972, 54,078 and 1,297,297 shares of Common Stock were reserved for conversion of the 4% and 5½% Convertible Subordinated Debentures, respectively, and 350,000 shares for stock option plans, a total of 1,701,375 shares.

At the beginning of 1971 and 1972, options to purchase 135,000 shares were outstanding. No options were granted or canceled in 1971; options to purchase 12,000 shares were granted and options to purchase 16,000 shares were canceled in 1972. As of December 31, 1972, options for 147,000 shares had been granted under this plan and options for 131,000 shares were outstanding (of which 119,000 were exercisable), at prices ranging from $34.75 to $36.63 per share.

NOTE H—PENSIONS

Total pension expense was $4,820,000 in 1972 and $4,130,000 in 1971. The actuarially computed value of unfunded vested benefits of all plans was $8,760,000 at December 31, 1972, and $6,460,000 at December 31, 1971. These increases were due to an increase in benefits effective January 1, 1972.

Accountants' Report

TOUCHE ROSS & CO.

1300 First National Building, Detroit, Michigan 48226
21 East Long Lake Road, Bloomfield Hills, Michigan 48013

Board of Directors and Shareholders   February 9, 1973
Fruehauf Corporation, Detroit, Michigan

We have examined the accompanying consolidated balance sheet of Fruehauf Corporation and consolidated subsidiaries as of December 31, 1972, and December 31, 1971, and the related statements of net earnings, earnings retained for use in the business, additional paid-in capital, and changes in financial position for the years then ended. We have also examined the accompanying balance sheet of Fruehauf Finance Company as of December 31, 1972, and December 31, 1971, and the related statements of net earnings and earnings retained for use in the business and changes in financial position for the years then ended. Our examinations were made in accordance with generally accepted auditing standards, and accordingly included such tests of the accounting records and such other auditing procedures as we considered necessary in the circumstances.

In our opinion, the aforementioned financial statements present fairly the consolidated financial position of Fruehauf Corporation and consolidated subsidiaries and the financial position of Fruehauf Finance Company at December 31, 1972, and December 31, 1971, and the respective results of their operations and changes in their financial position for the years then ended, in conformity with generally accepted accounting principles applied on a consistent basis.

Touche Ross + Co.

Certified Public Accountants

Statement of Net Earnings and Earnings Retained for Use in the Business
Years ended December 31, 1972, and December 31, 1971
FRUEHAUF FINANCE COMPANY

	1972	1971
FINANCE REVENUE:		
From installment equipment contracts..............................	$ 22,654,955	$ 22,556,381
From Fruehauf Corporation with respect to loans		
secured by pledge of leased equipment rentals.......................	6,245,874	5,458,461
	$ 28,900,829	$ 28,014,842
EXPENSES:		
Operating expenses....................................	$ 1,905,674	$ 1,835,778
Provision for losses on installment equipment contracts.................	890,451	375,268
Interest...	14,175,860	13,952,640
	$ 16,971,985	$ 16,163,686
EARNINGS BEFORE TAXES ON INCOME	$ 11,928,844	$ 11,851,156
TAXES ON INCOME:		
Current..	$ 5,435,000	$ 4,890,000
Deferred..	305,000	815,000
	$ 5,740,000	$ 5,705,000
NET EARNINGS	$ 6,188,844	$ 6,146,156
Earnings retained for use in the business—at beginning of the year...........	50,893,741	44,747,585
Earnings retained for use in the business—at end of the year...............	$ 57,082,585	$ 50,893,741

Balance Sheet
FRUEHAUF FINANCE COMPANY

ASSETS	December 31, 1972	December 31, 1971
Cash...	$ 7,791,394	$ 9,682,043
Account receivable from Fruehauf Corporation...........................		2,892,209
Installment receivables (including installments of approximately $305,300,000 at December 31, 1972, and $260,600,000 at December 31, 1971, maturing after one year):		
Installment equipment contracts purchased from Fruehauf Corporation without recourse..........................	$284,483,666	$285,561,473
Amount receivable from Fruehauf Corporation, secured by pledge of leased equipment rentals.....................	126,035,949	77,508,730
	$410,519,615	$363,070,203
Less:		
Deferred finance revenue......................................	$ 83,469,790	$ 64,881,908
Allowance for losses...	3,008,025	2,997,198
	$ 86,477,815	$ 67,879,106
INSTALLMENT RECEIVABLES—NET	$324,041,800	$295,191,097
Repossessed trailers—at appraised values, less estimated disposal costs.......	1,218,598	1,063,378
Unamortized debt issuance expense and other assets......................	1,489,233	1,241,954
	$334,541,025	$310,070,681

Fruehauf Finance Company

LIABILITIES AND SHAREHOLDER'S INVESTMENT	December 31, 1972	December 31, 1971
Notes payable to banks and commercial paper (Note C)................	$ 61,740,000	$ 95,600,000
Account payable to Fruehauf Corporation.............................	887,104	
Account payable to subsidiary not consolidated........................	1,379,991	1,388,259
Accrued interest...	4,436,345	3,478,681
Deferred taxes on income..	9,240,000	8,935,000
Senior long-term debt (Note C).....................................	150,000,000	100,000,000
Subordinated note payable to Fruehauf Corporation, due October 12, 1992 (Note B).....................................	775,000	775,000
CAPITAL NOTE payable to Fruehauf Corporation, due October 12, 1992; not subject to prepayment while other indebtedness is outstanding (Note B)..	$ 48,000,000	$ 48,000,000
SHAREHOLDER'S INVESTMENT:		
Common Stock, par value $100.00 a share—authorized and outstanding 10,000 shares.................................	$ 1,000,000	$ 1,000,000
Earnings retained for use in the business...........................	57,082,585	50,893,741
SHAREHOLDER'S INVESTMENT	$ 58,082,585	$ 51,893,741
SHAREHOLDER'S INVESTMENT AND CAPITAL NOTE	$106,082,585	$ 99,893,741
	$334,541,025	$310,070,681

Statement of Changes in Financial Position
Years ended December 31, 1972, and December 31, 1971
FRUEHAUF FINANCE COMPANY

	1972	1971
SOURCES OF FUNDS:		
Net earnings..........	$ 6,188,844	$ 6,146,156
Liquidations of installment receivables...........	144,380,416	157,904,615
Issuance of long-term notes and debentures to public..........	50,000,000	50,000,000
Increase (decrease*) in deferred finance revenue..........	18,587,882	8,056,411*
Decrease (increase*) in cash..........	1,890,649	656,457*
Increase in account payable, accrued interest,		
and taxes on income..........	5,033,709	506,613
	$226,081,500	$205,844,516
APPLICATION OF FUNDS:		
Acquisitions of installment receivables..........	$191,829,828	$136,481,526
Decrease in notes payable to banks and commercial paper..........	33,860,000	43,467,000
Repayment of term notes to banks..........		25,000,000
Other applications—net..........	391,672	895,990
	$226,081,500	$205,844,516

See notes to financial statements.

Notes to Financial Statements
Years ended December 31, 1972, and December 31, 1971
FRUEHAUF FINANCE COMPANY

NOTE A—SUMMARY OF ACCOUNTING PRINCIPLES

The significant accounting principles used by the Company are described below. These accounting principles have been applied consistently during the two years ended December 31, 1972.

Finance Revenue

A portion of finance revenue on installment equipment contracts (approximately 10%), equal to estimated allowance for losses and acquisition expenses, is taken into earnings at the time the contracts are purchased; the remaining amount of finance revenue on these contracts and all finance revenue earned through lease financing transactions with Fruehauf Corporation is taken into earnings on a "money-in-use" basis as collections are received.

Allowance for Losses

The allowance for losses is based on historical bad debt experience and a current evaluation of the aging and collectibility of the installment receivables outstanding.

Taxes on Income

Deferred taxes on income are applicable principally to the difference in method of recognizing finance revenue for tax and financial reporting purposes.

Unamortized Debt Issuance Expense

Costs incurred in connection with public debt financing are amortized over the terms of the debt.

NOTE B—TRANSACTIONS WITH FRUEHAUF CORPORATION (PARENT COMPANY)

Fruehauf Finance Company purchases installment equipment contracts, without recourse, from Fruehauf Corporation, paying as consideration the contract balance less a finance charge, and finances long-term leases held by Fruehauf Corporation, generally advancing an amount which is equal to the sum of the rentals receivable under the lease less a finance charge.

The Company pays Fruehauf Corporation a fee, based upon finance charges collected and number of contracts serviced, as compensation for services by Fruehauf Corporation. Fruehauf Corporation reconditions repossessed trailers and is reimbursed by the Company for all reconditioning costs plus a commission of 5% from the disposition of all repossessed trailers sold.

The Capital Note and Subordinated Note are due October 12, 1992, and bear interest at the prime rate. Fruehauf Corporation has waived interest on the Notes from April 1, 1969, through December 31, 1973. By their terms, no interest can be accrued for any year on these Notes to the extent that such accrual would reduce the ratio of net earnings to fixed charges below 1.5 to 1. The Capital Note is convertible into Common Stock at $100 per share.

NOTE C—NOTES PAYABLE AND DEBENTURES

At December 31, 1972, notes payable totaling $40,000,000 were outstanding under a credit agreement with a group of banks which provides a $100,000,000 revolving line of credit which expires on April 30, 1973. The Company intends to convert the revolving line of credit to open credit lines available either to the Company or Fruehauf Corporation. Senior long-term debt is described below:

	December 31	
	1972	1971
Notes payable, 8.70%, due February 15, 1975.........	$ 50,000,000	$ 50,000,000
Notes payable, 7.50%, due January 1, 1978.........	50,000,000	50,000,000
Notes payable, 7.00%, due November 15, 1979.........	25,000,000	
Debentures, 7.60%, due May 15, 1984..........	25,000,000	
TOTAL	$150,000,000	$100,000,000

Indentures related to the indebtedness provide, among other covenants, that the Company maintain a ratio of assets to liabilities, as defined, of at least 120%.

INDIANA TELEPHONE CORPORATION

Statement of Income

	Column A Historical Cost		Column B Historical Cost Restated for Changes in Purchasing Power of Dollar	
	1972	1971	1972	1971
OPERATING REVENUES:				
Local service	$ 6,187,012	$ 5,744,356	$ 6,242,998	$ 5,964,020
Toll service	5,208,814	4,852,156	5,255,949	5,037,703
Miscellaneous	337,136	304,522	340,187	316,167
Total operating revenues	11,732,962	10,901,034	11,839,134	11,317,890
OPERATING EXPENSES:				
Depreciation provision, Note 1 (b)	2,053,700	1,943,551	2,620,440	2,572,577
Maintenance	1,548,758	1,486,495	1,562,773	1,550,974
Total depreciation and maintenance	3,602,458	3,430,046	4,183,213	4,123,551
Traffic	1,101,833	1,226,906	1,111,803	1,274,544
Commercial	581,311	511,661	586,571	531,227
General and administrative	1,003,875	1,055,318	1,015,121	1,100,994
State, local and miscellaneous Federal taxes.......	967,974	912,601	976,733	947,499
Federal income taxes, Note 1 (b)				
Currently payable	1,363,382	1,132,500	1,375,719	1,175,807
Deferred until future years	264,200	315,800	266,591	327,876
Deferred investment tax credit (net)	152,618	9,708	145,524	3,361
Total operating expenses	9,037,651	8,594,540	9,661,275	9,484,859
OPERATING INCOME	2,695,311	2,306,494	2,177,859	1,833,031
INCOME DEDUCTIONS:				
Interest on funded debt..........................	789,579	651,195	796,724	676,097
Other deductions	41,540	36,828	53,285	41,445
Allowance for funds used during construction (credit), Note 1 (d)	(141,241)	(63,905)	(142,519)	(66,349)
Other income (credit)	(196,647)	(177,974)	(198,426)	(184,780)
Nonoperating Federal income taxes	92,500	82,000	93,337	85,136
Gain from retirement of long-term debt through operation of sinking fund (credit)	(11,985)	(15,192)	(12,093)	(15,773)
Price-level gain from retirement of long-term debt (credit), Note 1 (a)	—	—	(36,528)	(62,985)
Gain from retirement of preferred stock through operation of sinking fund (credit)	(4,709)	(5,055)	(4,752)	(5,248)
Price-level gain from retirement of preferred stock (credit), Note 1 (a)	—	—	(14,034)	(13,298)
Price-level loss from other monetary items	—	—	84,646	90,154
Total income deductions	569,037	507,897	619,640	544,399
NET INCOME, Note 1 (a)	2,126,274	1,798,597	1,558,219	1,288,632
Preferred stock dividends applicable to the period ..	94,890	96,209	95,749	99,888
EARNINGS APPLICABLE TO COMMON STOCK.......$	$ 2,031,384	$ 1,702,388	$ 1,462,470	$ 1,188,744
EARNINGS PER COMMON SHARE ....$	4.16	$ 3.49	$ 3.00	$ 2.44
BOOK VALUE PER SHARE ....$	24.82	$ 21.45	$ 23.01	$ 20.81
Stations in service at end of year...................	80,439	75,016	80,439	75,016

Statement of Assets—December 31, 1972

	Column A Historical Cost	Column B Historical Cost Restated for Changes in Purchasing Power of Dollar
TELEPHONE PLANT, at original cost, Note 1 (a):		
In service	$37,084,382	$47,050,796
Less—Accumulated depreciation	11,842,883	16,041,306
	25,241,499	31,009,490
Plant under construction	968,792	977,559
	26,210,291	31,987,049
WORKING CAPITAL:		
Current assets—		
Cash	795,971	795,971
Temporary cash investments accumulated for construction—at cost, which approximates market	4,482,550	4,482,550
Accounts receivable, less reserve	1,498,689	1,498,689
Materials and supplies	602,669	612,751
Prepayments	144,090	145,394
	7,523,969	7,535,355
Current liabilities—		
Sinking fund obligations, Note 2	121,000	121,000
Accounts payable	819,978	819,978
Advance billings	338,760	338,760
Dividends payable	168,904	168,904
Federal income taxes, Note 1 (b)	494,297	494,297
Other accrued taxes	677,736	677,736
Other current liabilities	986,941	986,941
	3,607,616	3,607,616
Net working capital	3,916,353	3,927,739
OTHER:		
Debt expense being amortized, Note 1 (c)	208,617	264,648
Other deferred charges	18,553	19,070
Other deferred credits	(40,818)	(41,187)
Deferred Federal income taxes, Note 1 (b)	(1,599,454)	(1,765,204)
Unamortized investment tax credit, Note 1 (e)	(544,396)	(632,744)
	(1,957,498)	(2,155,417)
TOTAL INVESTMENT IN TELEPHONE BUSINESS	$28,169,146	$33,759,371

INDIANA TELEPHONE CORPORATION

Statement of Capital—December 31, 1972

	Column A Historical Cost		Column B Historical Cost Restated for Changes in Purchasing Power of Dollar	
	Amount	Ratio	Amount	Ratio
FIRST MORTGAGE SINKING FUND BONDS:				
Series 6, 5⅜% due September 1, 1991	$ 1,820,000		$ 1,820,000	
Series 7, 4¾% due May 1, 1994	1,974,000		1,974,000	
Series 8, 4¾% due July 1, 2005	2,869,000		2,869,000	
Series 9, 6½% due October 1, 2007	2,910,000		2,910,000	
Series 10, 7¾% due June 1, 2008	4,875,000		4,875,000	
Less—Current sinking funds, Note 2	(101,000)		(101,000)	
Total first mortgage sinking fund bonds	14,347,000	51%	14,347,000	43%
PREFERRED STOCK (no maturity):				
Cumulative, sinking fund, par value $100 per share, 30,000 shares authorized of which 10,000 are unissued—				
1950 Series 4.80%	235,000		235,000	
1951 Series 4.80%	239,800		239,800	
1954 Series 5¼%	327,800		327,800	
1956 Series 5%	252,900		252,900	
1967 Series 6⅛%	679,000		679,000	
Less—Current sinking funds, Note 2	(20,000)		(20,000)	
Total preferred stock	1,714,500	6	1,714,500	5
COMMON SHAREHOLDERS' INTEREST:				
Common stock, no par value, authorized 500,000 shares, issued 492,086 shares	4,251,785		6,678,779	
Retained earnings ($3,147,223 restricted as to the payment of cash dividends on common stock, Note 4)	7,937,320		4,675,412	
	12,189,105		11,354,191	
Less—Treasury stock, 4,336 shares, at cost	(5,192)		(8,130)	
Stock discount and expense	(76,267)		(123,194)	
Total common shareholders' interest	12,107,646	43	11,222,867	33
UNREALIZED EFFECTS OF PRICE-LEVEL CHANGES, Note 1 (a)	—	—	6,475,004	19
TOTAL INVESTMENT IN TELEPHONE BUSINESS..........	$28,169,146	100%	$33,759,371	100%

Statement of Changes in Financial Position

	1972	1971
FUNDS WERE PROVIDED BY:		
Operations per Column A—		
Net income	$2,126,274	$1,798,597
Items which did not require current expenditure of funds—		
Depreciation—		
Charged to income	2,053,700	1,943,551
Charged to clearing accounts	43,897	41,558
Deferred Federal income taxes	326,200	315,800
Investment tax credit (net)	152,618	9,708
Allowance for funds used during construction	(141,241)	(63,905)
Series 10 First Mortgage Sinking Fund Bonds	4,875,000	—
Net salvage on plant retirements	87,853	56,514
Miscellaneous, net	90,136	9,162
	9,614,437	4,110,985
FUNDS WERE EXPENDED FOR:		
Gross additions to telephone plant	4,586,237	3,411,941
Cash dividends declared—Common stock	365,812	182,906
—Preferred stock	118,507	72,001
Redemption of bonds and preferred stock	136,700	182,000
Refinancing First Mortgage Sinking Fund Bonds, Series 1-5	3,375,000	—
	8,582,256	3,848,848
INCREASE IN WORKING CAPITAL	$1,032,181	$ 262,137
INCREASE IN WORKING CAPITAL REPRESENTED BY CHANGES IN:		
Cash	$ 116,496	$ (22,555)
Temporary cash investments	1,408,199	960,698
Accounts receivable, less reserve	278,134	(47,043)
Materials and supplies and prepayments	143,845	43,695
Sinking fund obligations	41,000	—
Accounts payable and advance billings	(207,539)	(326,056)
Dividends payable	(145,018)	85,510
Accrued taxes	(329,450)	(87,290)
Other current liabilities	(273,486)	(344,822)
INCREASE IN WORKING CAPITAL	$1,032,181	$ 262,137

INDIANA TELEPHONE CORPORATION

Statement of Retained Earnings for the Year 1972

	Column A Historical Cost	Column B Historical Cost Restated for Changes in Purchasing Power of Dollar
BALANCE, December 31, 1971	$6,295,365	$3,605,894
NET INCOME	2,126,274	1,558,219
	8,421,639	5,164,113
DEDUCT:		
Cash dividends declared—		
Common stock, annual rate—$.50 per share	365,812	369,122
Preferred stock	118,507	119,579
	484,319	488,701
BALANCE, December 31, 1972, Note 4	$7,937,320	$4,675,412

AUDITORS' REPORT

To the Shareholders of Indiana Telephone Corporation:

We have examined the statements of assets and capital of INDIANA TELEPHONE CORPORATION (an Indiana corporation) as of December 31, 1972, and the related statements of income, retained earnings, and changes in financial position for the year then ended. Our examination was made in accordance with generally accepted auditing standards and accordingly included such tests of the accounting records and such other auditing procedures as we considered necessary in the circumstances. We have previously examined and reported on the financial statements for the preceding year.

In our opinion, the accompanying financial statements shown under Column A present fairly the financial position of the Corporation as of December 31, 1972, and the results of its operations and the changes in its financial position for the year then ended, in conformity with generally accepted accounting principles applied on a basis consistent with that of the preceding year.

In our opinion, however, the accompanying financial statements shown under Column B more fairly present the financial position of the Corporation as of December 31, 1972, and the results of its operations for the year then ended, as recognition has been given to changes in the purchasing power of the dollar, as explained in Note 1(a).

ARTHUR ANDERSEN & CO.

Indianapolis, Indiana,
March 2, 1973.

Notes to Financial Statements

1. SUMMARY OF SIGNIFICANT ACCOUNTING POLICIES

(a) EXPLANATION OF FINANCIAL STATEMENTS

In the accompanying financial statements, costs measured by the dollars disbursed at the time of the expenditure are shown in "Column A—Historical Cost." In "Column B—Historical Cost Restated For Changes in Purchasing Power of Dollar" (where the amounts in A and B differ), these dollars of cost have been restated in terms of the price level at December 31, 1972, as measured by the Gross National Product Implicit Price Deflator. Since 1954, the Corporation has presented supplemental financial information recognizing the effect of the change in the purchasing power of the dollar relating to telephone plant and depreciation expense in the annual report to shareholders.

In computing the amounts set forth in Column B of the accompanying financial statements, the Corporation has followed the methods set forth in Statement No. 3 released in June, 1969, by the Accounting Principles Board of the American Institute of Certified Public Accountants, **except that**, contrary to Statement No. 3, the effects of price-level changes on long-term debt and preferred stock have been reflected **as income in the year in which the debt and preferred stock are retired** (as required by the specific instruments under which they were issued) **and not refinanced.** The Accounting Principles Board has tentatively taken the position that all such amounts should be taken into income in the year of price-level change. **In the opinion of the Corporation's management and of its independent public accountants, such tentative viewpoint of the Accounting Principles Board does not result in a proper determination of income for the period.** "Unrealized Effects of Price-Level Changes" recognizes the excess of adjustments on the Statement of Assets over the adjustments of Common Shareholders' Interest.

Dollars are a means of expressing purchasing power at the time of their use. **Conversion or restatement of dollars of differing purchasing power to the purchasing power of the dollar at the date of conversion results in all the dollars being treated as mathematical likes for the purpose of significant data.** The resulting financial statements recognize the change in price levels between the periods of expenditure of funds and the periods of use of property. **Accordingly, the earnings, results of operations, assets and other data available for use by management and other readers of financial statements provide important information and comparisons not otherwise available.**

No one would attempt to add, subtract, multiply, or divide marks, dollars and pounds. The failure to change the title of the monetary unit may be partially responsible for this violation of mathematical principle. This conceals the fact that mathematical unlikes are being used and therefore unfortunate results have been produced by generally accepted accounting methods.

(b) RECOVERY OF CAPITAL AND RETURN ON CAPITAL

Under the law of Indiana, the Corporation is entitled to recover the fair value of its property used and useful in public service by accruing depreciation based on the "fair value" thereof and is entitled to earn a fair return on such "fair value." The amount shown in Column B for telephone plant approximates the fair value of the property as determined based on the principles followed by the Public Service Commission of Indiana in an order dated September 1, 1967, authorizing the Corporation to increase its subscriber rates.

In the accompanying financial statements, Column A includes depreciation expense based on historical cost and Column B includes depreciation expense, as well as other expenses, on the basis of historical cost repriced in current dollars to reflect the changes in the purchasing power of the dollar. Also, the annual reports to the Indiana Commission are in the same basic form shown herein.

It must be kept in mind that this determination of depreciation expense is a year-to-year estimate and there are involved the questions of obsolescence, foresight, and judgment giving due consideration to maintenance, but the regulatory process does not adjust even to this accurately. In 1971 the Corporation petitioned the Indiana Commission for approval to increase its depreciation rates to a level to reflect properly these factors, but certain of these rates were not approved. If all of the requested rates were applied to the average cost of depreciable property accounts in 1972 and 1971, depreciation expense, operating income and net income (net of applicable income tax effects), as shown in the accompanying financial statements, would have been as follows:

	Column A Historical Cost	
	1972	1971
Depreciation provision	$2,109,258	$1,997,871
Operating income	2,666,421	2,278,248
Net income	2,097,384	1,770,351

	Column B Historical Cost Restated for Changes in Purchasing Power of Dollar	
	1972	1971
Depreciation provision	$2,690,932	$2,644,049
Operating income	2,134,276	1,788,662
Net income	1,514,636	1,244,263

INDIANA TELEPHONE CORPORATION

If use of property, obsolescence and current denominators (in the case of monetary inflation) are used accurately by way of keeping the allowable expense of depreciation current and rates sufficient to return it along with a fair return, and the proceeds are immediately invested in property used and useful in the public service, there more likely will be a real return of capital and a fair return thereon. However, if monetary inflation continues, as it usually does, purchasing power of capital is unlikely ever to be truly returned. It must be observed there is a substantial lag in the regulatory process. In rate making there is no guarantee of recovery of capital or of an adequate rate of return to the Corporation. This is an added risk which should be considered in estimating a fair return.

Since the present Internal Revenue Code does not recognize the costs measured in current dollars, they are not deductible for computing Federal income tax payments, and the Corporation in fact pays taxes on alleged earnings which do not exist in true purchasing power. If they were deductible, as they should be, reductions in Federal income taxes as shown in Column B of $312,000 in 1972 and $274,000 in 1971 would result. By requiring the use of the Uniform System of Accounts for utility accounting and by virtue of the Internal Revenue Code, the Government has condemned and confiscated during the last 8 years over $1.3 million (in terms of the dollars of the years in which they were paid) of the assets of this Corporation through taxation of overstated earnings. This is true to a greater or lesser extent in each case where we have been able to ascertain the facts. We do not understand why this is currently concealed by management and accountants—to their detriment.

For book and financial reporting purposes, the Corporation provides for depreciation on a straight-line basis over the average service lives of the various classes of depreciable plant. In 1972, the overall rate was 6.1%. For Federal income tax purposes, beginning in 1967, an accelerated depreciation method is used and a provision is made in the Statement of Income for the taxes deferred as a result thereof.

(c) DEFERRED CHARGES

Debt expense is being amortized over the lives of the related issues. Gains realized from reacquisition of bonds and preferred stock for sinking fund purposes are recognized in the year of retirement.

(d) ALLOWANCE FOR FUNDS USED DURING CONSTRUCTION

The Corporation capitalizes the cost of capital employed during the period of construction on major projects. Amounts so capitalized are determined by applying a rate of 7% to the average dollar balance of these projects under construction.

(e) UNAMORTIZED INVESTMENT TAX CREDIT

The Corporation is deferring investment tax credits and amortizing the balance over the useful lives of the related property.

2. SINKING FUNDS

The aggregate annual sinking fund requirement on First Mortgage Sinking Fund Bonds for 1973 and 1974 is $101,000. The required annual sinking fund payment on the Series 10 Bonds begins in 1975 and is $48,750 (1%). The indenture for Series 10 Bonds also allows for an additional 1% ($48,750) or 2% ($97,500) or a total of $146,250 in sinking fund payments, beginning in 1978, at the option of the Corporation.

As shown in the accompanying Statement of Changes in Financial Position, the level of funds provided for 1972 (which includes the $1,500,000 additional long-term funds from the issuance of the Series 10 Bonds) would have been adequate to have allowed the Corporation to make the required and optional sinking fund payments on Series 10 Bonds with sufficient remaining funds to meet construction expenditures and it would have left an increase in working capital of $885,931. The ability of the Corporation in the future to meet sinking fund payments and projected construction expenditures (to provide customer service) depends, in a large part, upon the level of earnings allowed by the Indiana Commission, with due regard to regulatory lag and monetary inflation.

At respective maturity dates, after all required sinking fund payments, the remaining balances to be paid will be as follows:

Series	Maturity Date	Call Price = 100	Balance to be Paid at Maturity
6	Sept. 1, 1991	1988	$1,440,000
7	May 1, 1994	1990	1,533,000
8	July 1, 2005	1985	1,909,000
9	Oct. 1, 2007	1997	1,890,000
10	June 1, 2008	2003	3,266,250

If the maximum optional sinking fund payments on Series 10 Bonds are made by the Corporation, the balance to be paid at maturity on this issue will be $341,250.

To the annual bond sinking funds aggregating $101,000 should be added the annual sinking fund requirement on preferred stock of $20,000. For the years 1973 and 1974, the total annual sinking fund requirement on both preferred stock and bonds is $121,000.

3. RETIREMENT PLAN

The Corporation would prefer to pay the employees all that they earn in any year and to have no pension plan. However, the employees can have a greater amount after taxes if a qualified retirement plan is used and, accordingly, the plan exists.

Since 1966, the Corporation has maintained a money-purchase retirement plan. The plan covers all full-time employees with more than three years of service. All contributions to the plan are made by the Corporation.

In a money-purchase plan, an amount equal to a fixed percentage of the employee's earnings is paid into the plan each year, and there it is managed to produce as large a payment as possible for the employee during retirement. This is in contrast to the "fixed-benefit" plan where retirement benefits are determined by a formula. Any accumulated payments in a fixed-benefit plan not needed for benefits are returned to the employer by decreasing his payments, and any deficit in accumulated payments must be made up by the employer or his employees.

Before 1966 the Corporation had a fixed-benefit plan which required both the employer and employee to make contributions sufficient to support a pension based upon the last five years' compensation before retirement. In a fixed-benefit plan, the Internal Revenue Service does not permit an assumption of continuing monetary inflation. As a result, the amounts required to be paid in under such a plan are based upon the then existing compensation levels without recognition of the monetary inflation which will occur before retirement. As monetary inflation does occur, the actuaries require and the Internal Revenue Service permits pension contributions to make up for the failure in the past to anticipate monetary inflation. In a period of rapid monetary inflation, the contributors to the plan cannot be expected to pay the pension requirements which will be increased by the rate of monetary inflation compounded.

To avoid a pension contract which neither the employees nor the Corporation could expect to fulfill, the Corporation adopted a five percent, money-purchase plan. The annual contribution is related to the payroll of the employee and is not based upon an estimate of unknown mortality, unknown future investment return, unknown future retention of personnel, and most of all, does not depend on estimates of future salaries without adjustment for monetary inflation.

The pension payment made to the retired employee is completely divorced from social security or any other governmental program. It is hoped that the government will allow corporate management to continue to use its own best judgment in setting up private pension plans such as ours which it is believed have a more hopeful chance of surviving a period of monetary inflation.

In order to help the employees realize as much as possible from the plan—and particularly to attempt to protect the pension plan against monetary inflation, the Corporation made an extensive search for competent investment people, and finally caused the United States Trust Company of New York to be employed as the trustee to operate the fund. It is hoped that their investment skills will protect the pension fund against the continuing monetary inflation. To further help the employee in his contest with monetary inflation, the retiring employee is given **as much time to leave his funds in the care of the United States Trust Company as the Internal Revenue Service will permit.** The government has said that this is limited to the employee's life expectancy at retirement—about fifteen years. After that time, or sooner, if the employee elects a retirement annuity or obtains a lump sum, the employee himself will have to defend his property against both taxation and monetary inflation.

Historically, monetary inflation has accelerated from creeping to galloping. The end result sought is that these funds will be invested in a store of value of which some portion of value will exist after monetary inflation has run its course. That date is, of course, unknown and it is a difficult task to have both current purchasing power and a maximum remainder of stored value.

Unlike many other retirement plans, the money-purchase plan of Indiana Telephone Corporation has no unfunded liability. The Corporation considers this an important factor in its ability to survive in a society dominated by governmental regulation and monetary inflation.

The Corporation's contributions under the plan, which is fully funded each year, and other data relating to the trust fund are summarized as follows:

	1972	1971
Corporation contributions ...	$103,000	$ 87,000
Cost of assets in fund at December 31	627,244	450,624
Market value of fund at December 31	836,990	572,205

4. DIVIDEND RESTRICTION

The supplemental indenture of the Series 10 First Mortgage Sinking Fund Bonds provides that cash dividends on common stock and purchases of common stock are limited to net earnings, as defined, after December 31, 1971, plus $600,000.

5. CONSTRUCTION COMMITMENTS

Construction expenditures for the year 1973 are estimated at $7,379,000. Substantial commitments have been made in connection therewith.

EASTMAN KODAK COMPANY AND SUBSIDIARY COMPANIES

Consolidated Balance Sheet

Assets	Dec. 31, 1972	Dec. 26, 1971
Current Assets	(in thousands)	
Cash	$ 209,169	$ 88,994
Marketable securities at cost (approximates market value)	653,210	560,439
Receivables	552,256	460,086
Inventories	648,972	572,268
Prepaid charges applicable to future operations	57,687	37,085
Total current assets	2,121,294	1,718,872
Properties		
Land, buildings, machinery, and equipment at cost	3,007,020	2,812,241
Less: Accumulated depreciation	1,447,845	1,302,044
Net properties	1,559,175	1,510,197
Other Assets		
Unamortized excess cost of investments in consolidated subsidiaries over net assets acquired	16,926	11,343
Long-term receivables and other noncurrent assets	60,059	57,620
TOTAL ASSETS	$3,757,454	$3,298,032

Liabilities and Shareowners' Equity

	Dec. 31, 1972	Dec. 26, 1971
Current Liabilities		
Payables	$ 465,882	$ 388,286
Taxes—income and other	237,001	202,332
Dividends payable	98,390	95,134
Total current liabilities	801,273	685,752
Other Liabilities and Deferred Credits		
4½% convertible debentures—due 1988	66,559	70,000
Other long-term liabilities	59,221	46,196
Deferred income taxes	75,224	66,411
Total liabilities and deferred credits	1,002,277	868,359
Shareowners' Equity		
Common stock ($2.50 par value, 360,000,000 shares authorized) Issued 161,581,258 shares (161,545,436 shares in 1971) Par value—paid in or transferred from retained earnings	403,953	403,864
Additional capital paid in or transferred from retained earnings	265,557	262,208
Retained earnings	2,085,667	1,763,601
Total shareowners' equity	2,755,177	2,429,673
TOTAL LIABILITIES AND SHAREOWNERS' EQUITY	$3,757,454	$3,298,032

Eastman Kodak Company and
Subsidiary Companies

Consolidated Statement of Earnings

	1972 (53 weeks)	1971 (52 weeks)
Sales	(in thousands, except earnings per share)	
Sales to: Customers in the United States	$2,236,625	$1,947,206
Customers outside the United States	1,241,139	1,028,722
TOTAL SALES	3,477,764	2,975,928
Costs		
Cost of goods sold	1,856,080	1,623,181
Sales, advertising, distribution, and administrative expenses	646,451	564,538
Total costs and expenses	2,502,531	2,187,719
Earnings		
EARNINGS FROM OPERATIONS	975,233	788,209
Interest income	32,133	28,216
Other income	36,004	18,405
Less: Other charges	13,120	18,025
EARNINGS BEFORE INCOME TAXES	1,030,250	816,805
Provision for United States, foreign, and other income taxes	484,000	397,500
NET EARNINGS	$ 546,250	$ 419,305
Average number of shares of common stock outstanding	161,274	161,243
Net earnings per share	$3.39	$2.60

Consolidated Statement of Retained Earnings

Retained Earnings		
Retained earnings at beginning of year	$1,763,601	$1,560,364
Net earnings	546,250	419,305
TOTAL	2,309,851	1,979,669
Cash dividends declared at $1.39 per share ($1.34 in 1971)	224,184	216,068
RETAINED EARNINGS at end of year	$2,085,667	$1,763,601

*Eastman Kodak Company and
Subsidiary Companies*

Consolidated Statement of Changes in Financial Position

Funds Provided by:	1972 (53 weeks)	1971 (52 weeks)
	(in thousands)	
Net earnings	**$546,250**	$419,305
Charges to earnings not requiring cash outlay:		
Depreciation	**178,968**	161,257
Plant and equipment retired, less accumulated depreciation	**24,442**	8,360
Provision for deferred income taxes, net	**(7,050)**	11,500
Amortization of excess cost of investments in subsidiaries over net assets acquired	**1,291**	1,150
Total from earnings	**743,901**	601,572
Decrease in inventories	**–**	5,246
Increase in current liabilities:		
Payables	**77,596**	–
Taxes payable	**34,669**	34,325
Dividends payable	**3,256**	3,232
Increase in other long-term liabilities	**13,025**	4,687
Issuance of common stock in exchange for convertible debentures	**3,438**	–
Other items, net	**–**	1,212
TOTAL FUNDS PROVIDED	**875,885**	650,274

Funds Used for:		
Dividends to shareowners	**224,184**	216,068
Additions to properties	**252,388**	294,732
Increase in receivables	**92,170**	44,177
Increase in inventories	**76,704**	–
Increase in long-term receivables and other noncurrent assets	**2,439**	2,072
Decrease in current liabilities—payables	**–**	3,473
Excess cost of investment in subsidiary over net assets acquired	**6,874**	–
Conversion of convertible debentures	**3,441**	–
Other items, net	**4,739**	–
TOTAL FUNDS USED	**662,939**	560,522
Increase in cash and securities	**212,946**	89,752
Cash and securities at beginning of the year	**649,433**	559,681
Cash and securities at end of the year	**$862,379**	$649,433

Eastman Kodak Company and
Subsidiary Companies

Financial Data of Subsidiary Companies Outside the United States

	Canada and Latin America	British Isles and Continental Europe	Africa, Asia, Australasia, and the Far East	Total	
Balance Sheet	1972	1972	1972	1972	1971
Assets			(in thousands)		
Current assets	$106,953	$491,209	$ 67,818	$ 665,980	$536,510
Properties and other assets, net	111,315	244,351	43,406	399,072	368,146
Total assets	$218,268	$735,560	$111,224	$1,065,052	$904,656
Liabilities and Equity					
Current liabilities	$ 58,158	$236,173	$ 39,894	$ 334,225	$253,492
Other liabilities and deferred credits	12,893	114,246	756	127,895	117,146
Interest of minority shareowners	—	4,667	27	4,694	4,033
Total liabilities and deferred credits	71,051	355,086	40,677	466,814	374,671
Eastman Kodak Company equity	147,217	380,474	70,547	598,238	529,985
Total liabilities and equity	$218,268	$735,560	$111,224	$1,065,052	$904,656
Summary of Sales and Earnings					
Sales	$221,202	$824,252	$132,093	$1,177,547	$970,875
Earnings from operations	37,127	149,251	19,310	205,688	164,658
Net earnings (Eastman Kodak Company equity)	$ 16,914	$103,232	$ 10,797	$ 130,943*	$ 88,027

Includes a fourth quarter gain of $14.8 million, after applicable foreign taxes, arising from the sale of certain real estate properties in England and Belgium.

Report of Independent Accountants

To the Board of Directors and Shareowners of Eastman Kodak Company:

In our opinion, the accompanying consolidated financial statements appearing on pages 36 through 43 of this report present fairly the financial position of Eastman Kodak Company and its subsidiaries at December 31, 1972 and December 26, 1971 and the results of their operations and the changes in financial position for the years then ended, in conformity with generally accepted accounting principles consistently applied. Our examinations of these statements were made in accordance with generally accepted auditing standards and accordingly included such tests of the accounting records and such other auditing procedures as we considered necessary in the circumstances.

Price Waterhouse + Co.

60 Broad Street, New York, N.Y. 10004
February 21, 1973

*Eastman Kodak Company and
Subsidiary Companies*

**NOTES
TO
FINANCIAL
STATEMENTS**

Accounting Policies

A summary of the major accounting policies followed by the company in preparation of the accompanying consolidated financial statements is set forth below:

Basis of Consolidation. The consolidated financial statements include the accounts of all subsidiary companies. Intercompany transactions are eliminated and net earnings are reduced by the portion of the earnings of subsidiaries applicable to minority shareowners. The excess of the cost of investments in subsidiaries acquired since 1965, over the value ascribed to the company's equity in such subsidiaries at the time of acquisition, is amortized over the succeeding 15-year period.

Fiscal Year. The fiscal year of the parent company and several major subsidiary companies customarily consists of 13 four-week periods for a total of 52 weeks. Once every five or six years an extra week is included in the fiscal year in order to keep the fiscal year in near alignment with the calendar year. In 1972 the parent company's fiscal year covered the 53 weeks ended December 31, 1972.

Translation of Foreign Currencies. The financial statements of subsidiaries operating outside the United States are translated into U.S. dollar equivalents at appropriate exchange rates applied as follows: (1) net current assets, except inventories, and long-term debt at fiscal year-end rates; (2) inventories, properties and accumulated depreciation and deferred income taxes at rates applicable to the time of acquisition or deferment; (3) income and expense at average rates with dollar equivalents adjusted for exchange differences resulting from the foregoing procedures.

Inventories. Inventories are valued generally at cost or market, whichever is lower. The last-in, first-out method is used to determine the cost of certain inventories in the United States.

Sales. The amount reported as sales represents revenue from sales of products and services, equipment rentals and other operating fees.

Depreciation. Depreciation is calculated on the basis of the cost of the assets and generally on their estimated useful lives. The provision for depreciation of assets in the United States is calculated by the straight-line method for assets acquired prior to 1954 and generally by the sum-of-the-years-digits method for assets acquired after December 31, 1953. The provision for depreciation of assets outside the United States is calculated generally by the straight-line method.

Property Retirements. When assets are retired or otherwise disposed of, the cost of the assets and the related accumulated depreciation are removed from the accounts. Any profit or loss on retirements is reflected in the earnings for the period.

Maintenance and Repairs. Costs of maintenance and repairs are charged to expense. Costs of renewals and betterments, where significant in amount, are capitalized, and deduction is made for retirements resulting from the renewals or betterments.

Research and Development Costs. Research and development costs are charged to expense as incurred.

Income Taxes. The company defers the income tax effects of differences in the time of recording material items of income and expense on the books and the inclusion of such items in taxable income. The tax amounts deferred are reflected in earnings when the reverse situation occurs.

U.S. investment tax credits are applied to reduce the provision for income taxes for the year in which the related properties are acquired.

In 1972 the company changed its policy with respect to the additional income tax, if any, payable when earnings of subsidiaries are distributed. In accordance with Opinion 23 of the Accounting Principles Board, issued in April, 1972, the amount of such taxes estimated to be payable on the portion of current earnings that is not expected to be reinvested indefinitely is being charged to current earnings. In prior years the additional income taxes payable were charged to earnings in the year of distribution. This accounting change has no material effect on the financial statements of the current year, nor would the effect on the statements of any prior year have been material had the change been applied retroactively.

Vacations. The company's liability for vacations earned in the current year and to be taken in the following year is accrued.

Receivables

Current receivables are shown after deducting reserves of $22,900,000 (1971—$20,265,000).

Inventories

Inventories valued at cost based on the last-in, first-out method are about 12 percent of total inventories (1971—9 percent). The current cost for these inventories exceeds their valuation determined on a LIFO basis by $30,750,000 (1971—$25,000,000).

*Eastman Kodak Company and
Subsidiary Companies*

Properties and Accumulated Depreciation

Properties	United States	Other Countries	Total 1972	Total 1971
		(in thousands)		
Balance at beginning of year	$2,221,191	$591,050	$2,812,241	$2,559,414
Additions	178,322	74,066	252,388	294,732
Deductions	(41,980)	(15,629)	(57,609)	(41,905)
Balance at end of year	$2,357,533	$649,487	$3,007,020	$2,812,241
Made up of:				
Land	$ 43,517	$ 26,554	$ 70,071	$ 66,506
Buildings and building equipment	673,426	254,329	927,755	868,651
Machinery and equipment	1,581,085	344,825	1,925,910	1,757,190
Construction in progress	59,505	23,779	83,284	119,894
Totals as above	$2,357,533	$649,487	$3,007,020	$2,812,241
Accumulated Depreciation				
Balance at beginning of year	$1,068,717	$233,327	$1,302,044	$1,174,332
Provision for depreciation	139,432	39,536	178,968	161,257
Deductions	(22,815)	(10,352)	(33,167)	(33,545)
Balance at end of year	$1,185,334	$262,511	$1,447,845	$1,302,044

Long-Term Receivables & Other Noncurrent Assets

The total of $60,059,000 includes $8,462,000 representing
the cost of 281,885 shares of Eastman Kodak Company
common stock purchased and held by the company (1971—
$8,599,000 and 301,661 shares). These shares are approxi-
mately equal to the shares contingently allotted to participants under the Deferred Compensation Plan. The total
is shown after deducting reserves of $7,157,000 (1971—
$2,164,000).

Payables

Current payables include $115,967,000 (1971—
$109,948,000) accrued for the wage dividend and company
payments under the Eastman Kodak Employees' Savings
and Investment Plan, and $13,100,000 (1971—$11,573,000)
of bank loans of subsidiary companies outside the United
States which are payable within a year.

*Eastman Kodak Company and
Subsidiary Companies*

Other Long-Term Liabilities

The totals include:

	1972	1971
	(in thousands)	
Loans of subsidiaries outside the U.S.	$27,314	$19,218
Other liabilities	17,899	14,355
Contingent allotments under Deferred Compensation Plan	8,973	8,590
Equity of minority interests in subsidiaries	5,035	4,033
Total	$59,221	$46,196

Debentures

The $66,559,000 (1971—$70,000,000) of 4½% debentures due in 1988, issued by the Eastman Kodak International Capital Company, Inc., a wholly-owned subsidiary, are fully guaranteed by the Eastman Kodak Company and are convertible into Eastman Kodak Company common stock at $96 per share. In 1972, $3,441,000 of debentures were converted into common stock.

Income Taxes

The provision for United States, foreign and other income taxes appearing in the Consolidated Statement of Earnings is made up as follows:

	1972	1971
	(in thousands)	
United States income taxes		
Current provision	$342,500	$275,250
Deferred provision, net	(3,100)	9,900
Foreign income taxes		
Current provision	100,950	74,500
Deferred provision, net	(3,950)	1,600
State and other income taxes	47,600	36,250
Total	$484,000	$397,500

The provision for United States income taxes was reduced by U.S. investment credits of approximately $8.3 million (1971—$2.1 million).

Retained Earnings

The totals include:

	1972	1971
	(in thousands)	
Parent company and subsidiaries in the U.S.	$1,609,743	$1,349,726
Subsidiaries outside the U.S.		
Capitalized or transferred to statutory reserves	129,341	125,093
Remainder	346,583	288,782
Total	$2,085,667	$1,763,601

The retained earnings shown above include approximately $193,800,000 (1971—$143,100,000) of subsidiary earnings which would be subject to additional income taxes if distributed. No provision for such taxes has been made since these earnings are considered to have been reinvested in the subsidiaries for an indefinite period of time.

Retirement Plan

The parent company and many of its subsidiary companies have retirement plans covering substantially all of their employees, including those in many overseas countries. Retirement plan benefits are financed generally by company payments made either directly to insurance companies from which annuities are purchased for eligible employees, or to trust funds for investment until such time as the funds are used for the purchase of annuities. Employees covered have a vested right in annuities generally after 15 years of service and all such rights have been funded.

The total cost of the pension plans for the parent company and its subsidiaries was $74.5 million (1971—$56.5 million). Included are amortization of prior service costs over periods of up to 30 years and certain supplemental payments. The company's policy in the U.S. and in most other countries is to fund the pension cost accrued.

Subsidiary companies in certain foreign countries pay severance benefits in accordance with the laws of the various countries in which the operations are conducted. The cost of these benefits, which is not material in amount, is generally charged to operations when paid.

Common Stock

There are 693,322 (1971—729,166) authorized, but unissued, shares of common stock reserved for the conversion of the debentures issued by the Eastman Kodak International Capital Company, Inc. In 1972, 35,822 shares of common stock were issued under the conversion privilege of the debentures. These transactions increased common stock outstanding and additional capital paid in by $89,000 and $3,349,000, respectively.

A summary of objectives of financial statements*

In the development of objectives of financial statements, the Study Group has attempted to identify and evaluate the desirable goals of the financial accounting process.

Accounting is not an end in itself. As an information system, the justification for accounting can be found only in how well accounting information serves those who use it. Thus, the Study Group agrees with the conclusion drawn by many others that

The basic objective of financial statements is to provide information useful for making economic decisions.

In satisfying this objective, accounting should serve the goals of both the private and public sectors of the economy. By fulfilling the information needs of those in the private sector who make economic decisions, accounting assists in a more efficient allocation of resources, thus contributing to the attainment of broad social goals.

Users' needs for information are not known with any degree of certainty. The specific role financial statements play in the economic decision-making process has not been identified. This Study is therefore dependent upon certain assumptions which are supported by its research:

- Users of financial statements seek to predict, compare, and evaluate the cash consequences of their economic decisions.

*The material in this appendix is from *Objectives of Financial Statements,* AICPA (New York: 1973), pp. 61–66.

● Information about the cash consequences of decisions made by the enterprise is useful for predicting, comparing, and evaluating cash flows to users. (If the value of the unit of measure is unstable, that is, if inflation or deflation is so great that direct cash consequences are no longer comparable, such circumstances should be recognized in the financial statements.)

● Financial statements are more useful if they include, but distinguish, information that is primarily factual, and therefore can be measured objectively, from information that is primarily interpretive.

The objectives of financial statements developed in this Study are intended to follow logically from these assumptions.

Some users of financial information often have access to much more information than is available to users of general purpose financial statements. Therefore, users who ordinarily rely on financial statements alone may be served most by developing accounting objectives. Financial statements should meet the needs of those with the least ability to obtain information and the needs of others as well. Consequently,

An objective of financial statements is to serve primarily those users who have limited authority, ability, or resources to obtain information and who rely on financial statements as their principal source of information about an enterprise's economic activities.

Most economic decisions involve a sacrifice (something given or used up) and a benefit (something received). Creditors and investors are concerned with the ability of the enterprise to generate cash flows to them and with their ability to predict, compare, and evaluate the amount, timing, and related uncertainty of these future cash flows. Therefore,

An objective of financial statements is to provide information useful to investors and creditors for predicting, comparing, and evaluating potential cash flows to them in terms of amount, timing, and related uncertainty.

The primary goal of every commercial enterprise is to increase its monetary wealth so that over time it can return the maximum amount of cash to its owners. Economic decision-makers need information about the enterprise's degree of success periodically before dissolution, because they make decisions every day. A fundamental purpose of accounting is to provide interim measures of enterprise progress. Accounting earnings should measure such progress. They should recognize the notion of economic better-offness, but should be directed specifically to the enterprise's success in using cash to generate maximum cash.

Given appropriate financial information, the decision-maker uses his judgment to evaluate the enterprise's potential. This judgment aims at estimating the enterprise's ability to be better off, to generate more cash, and to have earnings convertible into cash at some future date. This ability is the enterprise's earning power. Therefore,

> An objective of financial statements is to provide users with information for predicting, comparing, and evaluating enterprise earning power.

An enterprise is accountable for its actions, or inactions, in discharging a wide range of responsibilities. Accountability involves the reporting of periodic measures of progress toward enterprise goals. Thus, measures useful for assessing earning power are also useful for accountability. Accordingly,

> An objective of financial statements is to supply information useful in judging management's ability to utilize enterprise resources effectively in achieving the primary enterprise goal.

The earning process consists of effort and performance directed at reaching the primary enterprise goal of returning over time the maximum amount of cash to its owners. The activities that are part of the earning process of the enterprise can be related to earnings cycles. An earnings cycle can be classified as completed, incomplete, or prospective. A completed earnings cycle involves a series of events whose entire impact on enterprise earnings and earning power is considered to have occurred. An incomplete earnings cycle involves a series of events underway whose full impact on enterprise earnings and earning power has not yet occurred. A prospective earnings cycle involves a series of planned events or unilateral actions. The earnings cycle concept is believed to be useful because the classifications assist users in evaluating uncertainties and the earning power of the enterprise.

Earnings as reported in financial statements have come to be, and in all probability will continue to be, the single most important criterion for assessing the enterprise's accomplishments and earning power. In the final analysis, ideal determination of earnings—the change during a period in the present values of future cash flows—can be approached no faster than the increase in user confidence in accounting measures permits. However, it seems reasonable to assume that, even in the long run, a distinction will have to be made between that portion of earnings resulting from completed cycles and estimates of recognizable progress toward the completion of incomplete cycles, and that portion of earnings arising from changes in value.

Economic decision-makers need both factual and interpretive information—identified separately to the extent possible—about transactions and other events in order to assess uncertainty. In all reporting, the assumptions, interpretations, predictions, and estimations that underlie the preparer's conclusions should be set forth. Thus,

> An objective of financial statements is to provide factual and interpretive information about transactions and other events which is useful for predicting, comparing, and evaluating enterprise earning power. Basic underlying assumptions with respect to matters subject to interpretation, evaluation, prediction, or estimation should be disclosed.

Based on an analysis of users' needs, it can be concluded that

- Financial statements should emphasize information about transactions and other events that significantly affect enterprise earning power or changes in it. Such information should be stated in terms of actual or prospective cash impact and should facilitate comparisons.

- Financial statements should report both facts and interpretations about transactions and other events.

- Financial statements should assist in the assessment of the uncertainties with respect to the amount and timing of prospective cash receipts and disbursements.

- Financial statements should report on series of transactions and other events, including value changes, in terms of earnings cycles.

The Group concludes that these goals can be attained through financial statements consisting of a statement of financial position, a statement of earnings, and a statement of financial activities. Thus,

> An objective is to provide a statement of financial position useful for predicting, comparing, and evaluating enterprise earning power. This statement should provide information concerning enterprise transactions and other events that are part of incomplete earnings cycles. Current values should also be reported when they differ significantly from historical cost. Assets and liabilities should be grouped or segregated by the relative uncertainty of the amount and timing of prospective realization or liquidation.

> An objective is to provide a statement of periodic earnings useful for predicting, comparing, and evaluating enterprise earning power. The net result of completed earnings cycles and enterprise activities resulting in recognizable progress toward completion of incomplete cycles should be reported. Changes in the values reflected in successive statements of financial position should also be reported, but separately, since they differ in terms of their certainty of realization.

(For some time there has been consistent demand for a single earnings figure. Members of the Study Group disagree on whether value changes that meet the qualitative criteria discussed in this report should be included in earnings. Some believe the objective should be to reflect current value changes in earnings. Others believe that inclusion of unrealized value changes in earnings may be desirable but is not now practicable. Still others believe that their inclusion is neither desirable nor practicable.)

> An objective is to provide a statement of financial activities useful for predicting, comparing, and evaluating enterprise earning power. This statement should report mainly on factual aspects of enterprise transactions having or expected to have

significant cash consequences. This statement should report data that require minimal judgment and interpretation by the preparer.

Each of the financial statements should be structured to enhance the user's ability to assess the following.

- The extent to which sacrifices and benefits vary over time and among themselves, such as differentiation between fixed and variable expenses.

- The extent to which sacrifices and benefits vary in relation to changes in the industry and the economy.

- The extent to which the occurrence of sacrifices and benefits, or their allocation to time periods, is discretionary or arbitrary. Examples are contributions, unusual research expenditures, or the recognition of gains or losses whose timing can be controlled.

- The extent to which sacrifices and benefits are unusual or infrequent and, therefore, require special consideration for predicting, comparing, and evaluating.

- The extent to which sacrifices and benefits pertain to various lines of activity of the enterprise.

Financial statement objectives are based on the user's need for information useful for predicting, comparing, and evaluating earning power. The Study Group concludes that, to satisfy these information requirements, different valuation bases are preferable for different assets and liabilities. The objectives of financial statements cannot be best served by the exclusive use of a single valuation basis. Each of the valuation bases should be analyzed in terms of the stated objectives. Selection of the specific basis or combination of bases to be used is an implementation issue.

All economic decisions look to the future. Since economic decision-makers cannot know the future, they look to the past and the present. Financial statements that provide information about the past and the present are useful for making predictions on which to base economic decisions. In many instances, however, the past may not be a good indicator of the future. Publication of explicit forecasts of enterprise activities may well fit the objectives of financial statements. The important consideration is not the accuracy of management forecasts themselves, but rather the relative accuracy of users' predictions with and without forecasts in financial statements. Thus,

An objective of financial statements is to provide information useful for the predictive process. Financial forecasts should be provided when they will enhance the reliability of users' predictions.

Many of the aspects of economic decisions concerned with governmental and not-for-profit organizations are similar to those of decisions concerning commercial enterprises. As with commercial enterprises, decision-makers are interested in predicting, comparing, and evaluating benefits and sacrifices in terms of amount, timing, and related uncertainty, even though they seek nonmonetary benefits. For governmental and not-for-profit organizations, assessments of performance should relate to the goals of the enterprise, even though these goals are essentially nonmonetary.

Managers of governmental and not-for-profit organizations are also accountable for their performance and goal attainment. Thus, reporting on such accountability is as important for not-for-profit organizations as it is for commercial enterprises. Consequently,

> **An objective of financial statements for governmental and not-for-profit organizations is to provide information useful for evaluating the effectiveness of the management of resources in achieving the organization's goals. Performance measures should be quantified in terms of identified goals.**

The objectives structure of this report, while primarily directed toward private goals, applies at least indirectly to social goals as well. The accounting objectives in this report are intended to produce financial information that will facilitate decisions that advance the common good. Thus,

> **An objective of financial statements is to report on those activities of the enterprise affecting society which can be determined and described or measured and which are important to the role of the enterprise in its social environment.**

Information contained in financial statements to satisfy users' needs should possess the qualitative characteristics of relevance and materiality, reliability, freedom from bias, comparability, consistency, understandability, and the recognition of substance over form. Information is not useful unless it is relevant and material to the user's decision. In making decisions, users should be able not only to understand the information presented, but to assess differences in its reliability, to rely on its fairness, to compare it with information about alternative opportunities, and to assess its consistency with previous presentations.

The Study Group concludes that the objectives developed in this report can be looked upon as attainable in stages within a reasonable time. Selecting the appropriate course of action for gaining acceptance of these objectives is not within the purview of the Study Group. However, the Study Group urges that its conclusions be considered as an initial step in developing objectives important for the ongoing refinement and improvement of accounting standards and practices.

Index